COLORADO REVISED STATUTES
Vehicles and Traffic

Complete through the
2011 Legislation Session

This portion of the Colorado Revised Statutes is an officially sanctioned publication using the official text of the Colorado Revised Statutes.

Published by Bradford Publishing Company

Citations:
Canon = Code of judicial conduct
Contingent for rule = Rules governing contingent fees for attorneys
Crim. P. = Rules of criminal procedure
C.A.R. = Appellate rules
C.M.C.R. = Municipal court rules of procedure
C.R.C.P. = Rules of civil procedure
C.R.E. = Rules of evidence
C.R.J.D. = Rules of judicial discipline
C.R.J.S.S. = Rules of jury selection and service
C.R.P.P. = Rules of probate procedure
C.R.M. = Rules for magistrates
C.R.T.I. = Rules for traffic infractions
DR = Disciplinary rules of the code of professional responsibility for attorneys
EC = Ethical considerations of the disciplinary rules of the code of professional responsibility for attorneys
Juvenile procedure rules = Rules of juvenile procedure
R.T.V.B. = Rules for country court traffic violations bureaus

ISBN: 978-1-932779-58-5

All rights reserved.
No part of this book may be reproduced
in any form or by any means
without permission in writing
from the publisher.

© 2011 Published by Bradford Publishing Company
1743 Wazee Street, Denver, CO 80202

Contents

Quick Guide to Traffic Penalties	v
Vehicle and Traffic Violations Listed by Statute	vi

Colorado Revised Statutes

	Page
Title 42, Vehicles and Traffic	
Article 1, General and Administrative	3
Article 2, Drivers' Licenses	21
Article 3, Registration, Taxation, and License Plates	80
Article 4, Regulation of Vehicles and Traffic	141
Article 5, Automobile Theft Law - Inspection of Motor Vehicle Identification Numbers	293
Article 6, Certificates of Title - Used Motor Vehicle Sales	301
Article 7, Motor Vehicle Financial Responsibility Law	316
Article 8, Port of Entry Weigh Stations	331
Article 9, Motor Vehicle Repair Act	334
Article 9.5, Vehicle Protection Products	339
Article 10, Motor Vehicle Warranties	340
Article 11, Motor Vehicle Service Contract Insurance	342
Article 12, Motor Vehicles as Collector's Items	343
Article 13, Disposition of Personal Property	347
Article 14, State Idling Standard	349
Article 20, Transportation of Hazardous and Nuclear Materials	350
Title 43, Article 5, Highway Safety	365
Title 12, Article 6, Automobiles	371
Title 12, Article 15, Commercial Driving Schools	398
Title 24, Article 60, Interstate Compacts and Agreements	403
General Index	415

CSP Common Codes
Title 42 and Related Laws

	Page
Legend of Abbreviations	iii
Title 42 Index	iv
Title 42 Related Laws and Common Codes	1
Alcohol / Drugs / Under the Influence	1
Auto Theft – Abandoned Vehicles	1
Bicycles	3
Bicycle Equipment	3
Commercial Vehicle (D.P.S. & P.U.C. Rules & Regulations)	4
Crimes Involving Assault	5
Crimes Involving Child Abuse	5
Crimes Involving Death	5

Driver's License	6
Drugs / Marijuana	7
Emissions	9
Equipment	9
Financial Responsibility / Insurance	11
Firearms / Weapons	11
Hazardous Materials Violations	11
Hit and Run / Failure to Report	12
Identification Cards	12
Improper / Reckless / Careless Driving and Actions	12
Interference	13
Lane Usage	14
Lights / Reflectors	14
Low-Power Scooters	16
Motorcycles	16
Obscured Vision / Interference With Driver	16
Oversize / Overwidth / Overlength / Overweight / Projecting Load	17
Parking Violations	18
Passing	19
Pedestrian / Animal Rider Violations	19
Recreational Vehicles / Areas / Services	20
Registration / Title	21
Right-of-Way (Vehicle / Pedestrian)	22
Safety Belts / Restraints	23
School Bus	23
Signaling	23
Speed	23
Spilling Loads / Damaging Highway / Littering	25
Theft	25
Towing	26
Traffic Controls	26
Turns	27
Wrong Way / Wrong Side	27
Presumptive Penalty and Enforcement Guide	29
Registration Violations Fine Schedule	29
Penalty Chart for Weight in Excess of Weight Authorized by Special Permit	29
PCC Codes (CSP Use Only)	29
Patrol Codes (CSP Use Only)	29
Felony Offenses	30
Misdemeanor Offenses	31
Misdemeanor Traffic Offenses	31
Traffic Infractions	31
Safety Zone Definitions	32
Drug Schedule Reference Guide	33
NIBRS System Guide	37

Quick Guide to Traffic Penalties

Points Assessed for Each Violation or Conviction   **Points**

Violation	Points
Leaving scene of accident	12
Driving while intoxicated or under the influence of drugs	12
Driving while ability is impaired by alcohol	8
Speed contests	12
Eluding or attempting to a police officer	12
Reckless driving	8
Careless driving	4
Failure to yield right-of-way	3
Speeding over the posted limit	
5-9 m.p.h.	1
10-19 m.p.h.	4
20-39 m.p.h.	6
40-or more m.p.h.	12
Failure to stop for a school bus	6
Driving on wrong side of road	4
Failure to maintain or show proof of insurance	4
Improper passing	4
Failure to observe traffic sign or signal	4
Improper turn	3
Driving through safety zone	3
Driving in wrong lane or direction on one-way street	3
Failure to signal or improper signal	2
Failure to yield to emergency vehicle	4
Improper backing	2
Failure to dim or turn on lights	2
Operating an unsafe vehicle	2
Operated vehicle with defective/missing headlights	1

Speeding Violations for Low Power Scooters

1-4 m.p.h. over 40	0
5-9 m.p.h. over 40	2
More than 9 m.p.h. over 40	4

Cylinder capacity for low-power scooters may not exceed fifty cubic centimeters Or 4476 watts if powered by electricity.

Minimum Points to Cause Suspension

Age Group	12 month	24 month	Per. of Lic.
Minor driver (16–17)	6 points		7 points
Minor driver (18–20)	9 points	12 points	14 points
Adult Driver	12 points	18 points	

Vehicle and Traffic Violations Listed by Statute

STATUTE	CHARGE	FINE+ S.C.	PT
12-28-102 (5)	Unlawful (Possession/Use/Sale) of Fireworks	SUM	0
12-47-901 (1)(a.5)	Attempted to provide an alcoholic beverage to a person under 21 years of age	SUM	RA
12-47-901 (1)(c)	Unlawful Possession of Alcohol Beverage by Person Under 21 Years of Age (Juvenile Court)	SUM	RA
12-47-901 (1)(k)	Allowed the Use of Personal Identification by a Person Under 21 Years of Age	SUM	RA
12-47-902.5 (3)	Unlawful (Possession/Purchase/Sale/Use) of an AWOL Device	SUM	RA
18-3-206	Menacing: Placed Another Person in Fear of Imminent Serious Bodily Injury	HB	RA
18-3-206	Menacing: Placed Another Person in Fear of Imminent Serious Bodily Injury by Use of a Deadly Weapon	NIBR	RA
18-3-208	Reckless Endangerment	SUM	0
18-3-501 (1)(a)	(Sold/Bartered/Leased) an Adult Person in a Human Trafficking Transaction	SUM	0
18-3-501 (1)(b)	Received an Adult Person in a Human Trafficking Transaction	SUM	0
18-3-501 (3)	Participated in Human Trafficking Involving an Adult Illegally in the U.S.	SUM	0
18-4-509 (2)	Defaced (Public/Private) Property	HB	RA
18-4-511 (1)	(Left/Deposited/Threw) Litter On (Public/Private/Water)	HB	0
18-4-511 (4)	Littering	HB	0
18-4-511 (6)	Littering from Motor Vehicle	HB	0
18-5-102 (3)	Presented Forged Document to Police Officer	NIBR	RA
18-5-113	Criminal Impersonation	NIBR	RA
18-5-902	Identity Theft	NIBR	RA
18-5-903	Criminal Possession of a Financial Device	NIBR	RA
18-5-905	Possession of Identity Theft Tools	NIBR	RA
18-6-402 (1)(a)	(Sold/Bartered/Leased) a Child in a Human Trafficking Transaction	SUM	0
18-6-402 (1)(b)	Received a Child in a Human Trafficking Transaction	SUM	0
18-7-301	Public Indecency	NIBR	RA
18-7-302	Indecent Exposure	NIBR	RA
18-8-110	Made False Report of (Explosives/Bomb/Weapons/Biological or Chemical Agent/Poison/Radioactive Substance)	NIBR	0
18-8-111 (1)	Made False Report to Authorities	HB	RA
18-8-112 (1)	Impersonating a Peace Officer	SUM	RA
18-9-107	Obstructed (Highway/Street/Sidewalk)	HB	0
18-9-107 (1)(a)	Obstructed (Highway/Street/Sidewalk)	HB	RA

STATUTE	CHARGE	FINE+ S.C.	PT
18-9-114	Hindering Transportation	HB	RA
18-9-116	Throwing Missiles at Vehicles	HB	0
18-9-116 (2)	Throwing Missiles at Bicycles	SUM	0
18-9-116.5	Vehicular Eluding Created a Substantial Risk of Bodily Injury by Operating a Vehicle in a Reckless Manner	NIBR	12
18-9-116.5	Vehicular Eluding Resulted in Bodily Injury to Another Person	NIBR	RA
18-9-116.5	Vehicular Eluding Resulted in Death to Another Person	NIBR	RA
18-9-117	Unlawful Conduct on Public Property (Fires/Prohibited Activities by Lawful Order)	HB	0
18-13-107 (1)	Non-disabled Person Used (White Cane/Blazed Orange Leash for Dog)	HB	RA
18-13-112 (1)	Intentionally (Spilled/Abandoned Vehicle Containing) Hazardous Waste	NIBR	0
18-13-122 (2)(a)	Illegal (Possession/Consumption) of Ethyl Alcohol by an Underage Person (Applicable Anywhere)	HB	RA
18-13-128 (1)	Illegally Assisted a Person to (Enter/Remain in/Travel Through) the (U.S./ Colorado)	SUM	0
25-14-204	Violated Restrictions on Tobacco Use	SUM	0
25-17-204 (1)	Illegal (Transportation/Storage) of Waste Tires	SUM	0
29-22-108 (1)	(Intentionally Caused/Substantially Contributed to) a Hazardous Substance Incident	NIBR	0
29-22-108 (2)	(Willfully/Recklessly/with Criminal Negligence) (Caused/Substantially Contributed to the Occurrence of) a Hazardous Materials Incident	NIBR	0
33-14-102 (1)(a)	Failed to (Register/Comply With Registration Requirements Relating to) Snowmobile	SUM	0
33-14-104 (5)	Failed to Display Valid Registration (Decal/Number) on Snowmobile	SUM	0
33-14-104 (6)	Displayed Unauthorized Number on Snowmobile/Failed to (Carry/ Provide) Registration Certificate	SUM	0
33-14-105	Failed to (Surrender Registration for/Re-register) Snowmobile as Required	SUM	0
33-14-105 (3)	Failed to Notify Division of Wildlife of (Theft/Destruction/Removal From State) of Snowmobile	SUM	0
33-14-109 (1)	Minor Under Age 10 Operated Snowmobile (unless supervised or on family land)	SUM	0
33-14-109 (2)	Minor Under Age 16 Operated Snowmobile Without (Supervision/ Safety Certificate) Note: Does not apply on family land	SUM	0
33-14-110	Snowmobile Operation on Roadway	SUM	0
33-14-111 (1)	Operated Snowmobile on Right-of-Way of Interstate Highway	SUM	0
33-14-111 (2)	Operated Snowmobile on Highway in an Unlawful Manner	SUM	0

STATUTE	CHARGE	FINE+ S.C.	PT
33-14-112	Operated Snowmobile on Railroad Right-of-Way (Except when crossing at intersection)	SUM	0
33-14-113	Operated Snowmobile on Private Property Without Permission	SUM	0
33-14-114	Snowmobile Operated on Highway Did Not Have Required Equipment	SUM	0
33-14-115 (1)	Failed to Notify Police of Snowmobile Accident	SUM	0
33-14-115 (3)	Failed to Report Accident to Division of Wildlife	SUM	0
33-14-116 (1)	Careless Operation of a Snowmobile	SUM	0
33-14-116 (2)	Reckless Operation of a Snowmobile	SUM	0
33-14-116 (3)	Operated Snowmobile Under the Influence of (Alcohol/Controlled Substance)	SUM	RA
33-14-116 (4)	Permitted Unlawful Operation of Snowmobile	SUM	0
33-14-117 (1)(a)	Hunted Wildlife From Snowmobile	SUM	0
33-14-117 (1)(b)	Unlawfully Carried Weapon on Snowmobile	SUM	0
33-14-117 (1)(c)	(Harassed/Drove) Wildlife With Snowmobile (Except to protect crops or property)	SUM	0
33-14.5-102	Failed to (Register/Comply With Registration Requirements Relating to Off-Highway Vehicle)	SUM	0
33-14.5-108	Operated Off-Highway Vehicle on Roadway of Streets and Highways Where Prohibited	SUM	0
33-15-106	Built Fire Where Prohibited (Only Use if Fire is on Division of Parks Land)	SUM	0
35-46-105	Knowingly Permitted Livestock on Public Highway	SUM	0
40-10-108	Operated as Motor Vehicle Carrier Without PUC Permit		0
40-10-113	Motor Vehicle Carrier Failed to Comply With PUC Rules and Regulations		0
40-11-107	Operated as Contract Carrier Without PUC Permit		0
40-11-111	Contract Carrier Failed to Comply With PUC Rules and Regulations		0
42-2-101 (1)	Drove Vehicle Without Valid Driver's License	35+11	3
42-2-101 (1)	Drove Vehicle Without Valid Driver's License (2nd/Subsequent Offense)	35+11	6
42-2-101 (1)	Drove Vehicle Without Valid Driver's License (Resident more than 30 days)	35+11	3
42-2-101 (2)	Drove Vehicle When Driver's License Expired One Year or Less	15+7	0
42-2-101 (4)	Drove Vehicle Without Proper Class of Driver's License	35+11	3
42-2-101 (4)	Provisional Driver (18 to 20 Years Old) (Not Qualified/No CDL)	35+11	3
42-2-101 (5)	Drove Vehicle Without Valid Driver's License on Person	15+7	0
42-2-105 (1)	Person Under 18 Not Qualified to Operate Commercial Vehicle	70+11	3

STATUTE	CHARGE	FINE+ S.C.	PT
42-2-105 (1)	Person Under 18 Transported (Explosives/ Inflammable Material)	70+11	3
42-2-105 (1)	Person Under 18 Transported Children in School Bus	70+11	3
42-2-105.5 (3)	Operator Under 18 (Not Wearing Seat Belt /Allowed Occupants Without Seat Belts/ Child Restraint Systems) *THIS CHARGE IS NON-ARRESTABLE*	SUM	2
42-2-105.5 (4)	Operator Under Age 18 Driving With More Passengers Than Seat Belts	65+11	2
42-2-106	Violated Restrictions on Temporary Instruction Permit	70+11	3
42-2-116 (6)(b)	Drove Vehicle Other Than Vehicle Equipped With Approved Ignition Interlock Device	SUM	RA
42-2-116 (6)(b)	Violated Restrictions on Driver's License Regarding Interlock Device	SUM	RA
42-2-116 (a)	Violated Restrictions on Driver's License	30+7	3
42-2-119 (1)	Failed to Notify Authorities of Change of (Name/Address) Within 30 Days	15+7	0
42-2-126.3 (1)	Tampered With Ignition Interlock Device	SUM	RA
42-2-126.3 (2)	Drove Vehicle Knowingly With Ignition Interlock Device (Intercepted/ Bypassed/Interfered With)	SUM	RA
42-2-134	Used Foreign License During Suspension or Revocation of Colorado Driving Privileges	35+11	0
42-2-136 (1)	Possessed Altered (Driver's License/Instruction Permit)	35+11	RA
42-2-136 (2)	Possessed (Fictitious/Fraudulent) (Driver's License/Instruction Permit)	35+11	RA
42-2-136 (3)	Displayed Driver's License that was Issued to Another Person	35+11	RA
42-2-136 (5)	Permitted Unlawful Use of Driver's License	35+11	RA
42-2-136 (5.5)	Reproduced Driver's License Without Authorization	SUM	RA
42-2-137	Made False Affidavit Concerning Driver's License	SUM	RA
42-2-138 (1)(a)	Drove (Motor/Off highway) Vehicle When License Under Restraint (Denied)	SUM	RA
42-2-138 (1)(a)	Drove (Motor/Off highway) Vehicle When License Under Restraint (Revoked)	SUM	RA
42-2-138 (1)(a)	Drove (Motor/Off highway) Vehicle When License Under Restraint (Suspended)	SUM	RA
42-2-138 (1)(d)(I)	Drove (Motor/Off highway) Vehicle upon Highway When (License/ Privilege to Drive) was Restrained for Express Consent or Alcohol/ Drug Related Offense	SUM	RA
42-2-139	Permitted Unlicensed Minor to Drive Vehicle	35+11	0
42-2-140	Permitted Unlicensed Person to Drive Vehicle	35+11	0
42-2-141 (1)	(Rented/Loaned) Vehicle to Unlicensed Person	35+11	0
42-2-141 (2)	Failed to Inspect License of Renter	35+11	0
42-2-141 (3)	Failed to Keep Rental Records	35+11	0
42-2-206 (1)(a)	Drove Vehicle When License Revoked As an Habitual Offender	SUM	RA

STATUTE	CHARGE	FINE+ S.C.	PT
42-2-206 (1)(b)	Drove Vehicle When License Revoked as an Habitual Offender (Aggravated)	NIBR	RA
42-2-307	Failed to Notify Authorities of change of (Name/Address) Within 30 Days	SUM	0
42-2-309	Improper Use/Reproduction of Identification Card (Refer to Statute for Charging)	SUM	0
42-2-404 (1)	Drove Commercial Vehicle (When Not Qualified or Without CDL)	SUM	3
42-2-404 (2)	Driver of Commercial Vehicle had More Than One License	SUM	3
42-2-409 (1)(a)	Knowingly Possessed an Unlawfully Altered Commercial Driver's License	SUM	RA
42-2-409 (1)(b)	Fraudulently Obtained a Commercial Driver's License	SUM	RA
42-2-409 (1)(c)	Knowingly Possessed a (Document/Instrument) Pertaining to a Commercial Driver's License	SUM	RA
42-2-409 (1)(d)	Displayed a Commercial Driver's License Issued to Another Person	SUM	RA
42-2-409 (1)(e)	(Failed/Refused) to Surrender a Commercial Driver's License Issued to Another Person	SUM	RA
42-2-409 (1)(f)	Permitted the Unlawful Use of a Commercial Driver's License	SUM	RA
42-2-409 (1)(g)	Unlawfully Reproduced a Commercial Driver's License	SUM	RA
42-3-103 (1)	Failed to Obtain Registration Within 60 Days of Purchase of Vehicle	50+17	0
42-3-103 (1)	Failed to Obtain Registration Within 60 Days of Purchase of Vehicle	50+17	0
42-3-103 (4)(a)	Failed to Obtain Valid Colorado Registration Within 30 Days After Becoming a Resident	SUM	0
42-3-103 (4)(a)	Failed to Obtain Valid Colorado Registration Within 30 Days After Becoming a Resident	SUM	0
42-3-113 (6)	No Registration Card in Vehicle	15+7	0
42-3-113 (7)	Failed to Notify Authorities within 30 Days of Change of Name or Address	15+7	0
42-3-114	Displayed Expired Number Plates	List	0
42-3-116 (2)	(Manufacturer/Transporter/Dealer) Failed to Display Number Plate as Required	50+17	0
42-3-116 (4)(a)	(Failed to Display/Misused) Depot Tag	50+17	0
42-3-116 (7)(c)	Misuse of Demonstration Plates on Special Mobile Machinery	50+17	0
42-3-121 (1)(a)	(Operated/Permitted Use of) Unregistered Vehicle	75+25	0
42-3-121 (1)(a)	Failed to Display Valid Registration	75+25	0
42-3-121 (1)(b)	(Displayed/Possessed/Offered For Sale) (Fictitious/ Cancelled/Revoked/Suspended/Altered/Stolen) (Title/Number Plate/Validation Tab or Sticker)	SUM	0

STATUTE	CHARGE	FINE+ S.C.	PT
42-3-121 (1)(c)	(Lent/Permitted Unauthorized Use of) (Title/Registration Card/Number Plate)	35+11	0
42-3-121 (1)(d)	Failed to Surrender (Title/ Registration Card/Number Plate) as Required	SUM	0
42-3-121 (1)(e)	(Made False Statement/Gave Fictitious Name or Address) on Registration Application	SUM	0
42-3-121 (1)(f)	Permitted/Used(Noncommercial/ Recreational) Vehicle to Transport (Cargo/Passengers) for (Hire/Commercial Purposes)	75+25	0
42-3-121 (1)(g)	Operated Commercial Vehicle While Registered as Collector Vehicle		0
42-3-122 (1)	Committed Perjury on a Motor Vehicle Registration Application	SUM	0
42-3-126 (1)	Failed to Notify Authorities Within 30 Days of Change of Vehicle Primary Color	15+7	0
42-3-202 (1)	Vehicle Had No Number Plates Attached	15+7	0
42-3-202 (1)	Vehicle Had Only One Number Plate Attached	15+7	0
42-3-202 (1)(b)	Vehicle Validation Tab/Sticker Improperly Attached	15+7	0
42-3-202 (2)(a)	Number Plate(s) Improperly Attached	15+7	0
42-3-202 (2)(a)	Vehicle Number Plates Not Clearly (Legible/Visible)	15+7	0
42-3-202 (2)(b)	Number Plate Obstructed by (Distorted/Colored/ Smoked/Tinted/Scratched/Dirty) Device	100+33	3
42-3-203 (3)(a)	Displayed Expired Temporary Permit	List	0
42-3-233(4)	Improper Display of Livery License Plates	75+25	0
42-3-304 (2)	Operated Vehicle in Excess of Declared Vehicle Weight	50+17	0
42-3-304 (7)(b)	Transporter Failed to Keep Written Record of Vehicles Transported	50+17	0
42-3-304 (8)(a)	Transporter Misused In-transit Plate	50+17	0
42-3-304 (8)(b)	Improper Use of Manufacturer Plate	50+17	0
42-3-305 (4)(a)	Used Farm Truck in Commercial Operation	50+17	0
42-3-311 (1)	Low-Power Scooter(Not Registered/ Registration Decal Not Affixed)	15+7	0
42-4-106	Drove (truck/Commercial Vehicle) Where Prohibited		0
42-4-106	Vehicle Exceeded Posted Weight Limitation (Specify Posted and Actual Weights)		0
42-4-106 (3)	Vehicle Exceeded Posted Weight Limitation (Specify Posted and Actual Weights)	35+11	0
42-4-106 (5)(a)(I)	Failed to Comply With (Tire/Chain) Restrictions	100+33	0
42-4-106 (5)(a)(II)	Failed to Comply With (Tire/Chain) Restrictions That Resulted in Road Closure of a Travel Lane in One or More Directions	500+157	0
42-4-106 (5)(a)(III)	Commercial Vehicle Failed to Comply With (Tire/Chain) Restrictions (Safety Zone)		0

STATUTE	CHARGE	FINE+ S.C.	PT
42-4-106 (5)(a)(IV)	Commercial Vehicle Failed to Comply with Tire Chain Restrictions Resulting in Road Closure of Travel Lane in one or More Direction (Safety Zone)		0
42-4-106 (6)	Disobeyed Sign Closing Highway for (Construction/Event)	35+11	0
42-4-107	Disregarded (Lawful Order/ Direction) of Police Officer Directing Traffic	SUM	3
42-4-109 (1)	Low-Power Scooter Rider Failed to Obey Provisions of Article 4 (State Violation, i.e., Failed to Signal, or Speeding)	15+12	0
42-4-109 (11)	Failed to Use Bicycle Path When Directed by Official Signs	15+12	0
42-4-109 (11)	Low-Power Scooter Failed to Use Bicycle Path When Directed By Official Signs	15+12	0
42-4-109 (12)	(Parent/Guardian) Knowingly permitted Child to Violate Section 42-4-109	15+12	0
42-4-109 (2) thru (6)	Rode Low-Power Scooter in an Improper Manner (Specify the Violation)	15+12	0
42-4-109 (6.5)	Low-Power Scooter(Operator/Passenger) Under 18 Not Wearing an Approved Protective Helmet on Highway (Primary)	100+31	3
42-4-109 (8)	(Rode/Lead) Animal on Wrong Side of Highway	15+12	0
42-4-109 (9)	Used (Skis/Sled/Skates/Coaster/ Toy Vehicle/ etc.) on Highway	15+12	0
42-4-109.5	Operated Low-Speed Electric Vehicle Where Prohibited	SUM	0
42-4-109.5 (1)	Operated Low Speed Electric Vehicle Where Prohibited	15+7	0
42-4-109.5 (2)	Operated Low Speed Electric Vehicle on Limited Access Highway	15+7	0
42-4-109.6 (1)	Operated Low Speed Electric Vehicle (Class B) Where Prohibited	15+7	0
42-4-109.6 (2)	Operated Low Speed Electric Vehicle (Class B) on Limited Access Highway	15+7	0
42-4-116 (1)(a)	Minor Driver Operated a Motor Vehicle with an Unauthorized Passenger (secondary violation)	50+17	2
42-4-116 (2)(a)	Minor Driver Operated Motor Vehicle Between 12 Midnight and 5 AM (secondary violation)	50+17	2
42-4-201 (1)	Number of Persons in Front Seat of Vehicle Interfered With Driver	35+11	0
42-4-201 (1)	Number of Persons in Front Seat of Vehicle Obstructed Vision	35+11	0
42-4-201 (2)	Driver of Vehicle Allowed Passenger to Ride in an Unsafe Manner	35+11	0
42-4-201 (3)	Television Visible to Vehicle Operator	35+11	0
42-4-201 (4)	Driver's Vision Obstructed Through Required Glass	35+11	0
42-4-201 (5)	Driver of Vehicle Allowed Passenger to Interfere With Driving	35+11	0
42-4-201 (5)	Passenger in Vehicle (Interfered With/Obstructed	35+11	0

STATUTE	CHARGE	FINE+ S.C.	PT
	Vision of) Driver		
42-4-201 (6)	Driver Permitted Person to (Hang On/Attach Himself) to the Outside of Vehicle	35+11	0
42-4-201 (6)	Person (Hung On/Attached Himself) to the Outside of Vehicle	35+11	0
42-4-202	Operated Vehicle With Defective/Missing Headlamps	35+11	1
42-4-202 (1)	Drove a (Defective/Unsafe) Vehicle	35+11	2
42-4-202 (4)(c)	Moved Exempt Construction Equipment on Highway When Vision Less Than 500 Feet	35+11	0
42-4-202 (4)(e)	Owner of Identification Plate Failed to Remove Plate and Forward It to the Dept. of Revenue	35+11	0
42-4-202 (4)(f)	Failed to Report Lost/Damaged/Stolen Identification Plate to the Dept. of Revenue	35+11	0
42-4-203	Drove a Defective or Unsafe Vehicle (Notice Must Accompany Citation)	SUM	2
42-4-204 (1)	Failed to Display Lamps When Required	15+7	2
42-4-205 (1)	Motor Vehicle Not Equipped With Head Lamps as Required	15+7	0
42-4-205 (2)	Motorcycle Not Equipped With Head Lamp as Required	15+7	0
42-4-205 (3)	Height of Headlamp Failed to Meet Requirements	15+7	0
42-4-206 (1)	Vehicle Not Equipped With Tail Lamps as Required	15+7	0
42-4-206 (2)	Height of Tail Lamp Failed to Meet Requirements	15+7	0
42-4-206 (3)	Vehicle Had (No/Defective) License Plate Lamps	15+7	0
42-4-206 (4)	Vehicle Failed to Have Reflector as Required	15+7	0
42-4-206 (5)	1958 or Newer Vehicle Failed to Have Two Reflectors as Required	15+7	0
42-4-206 (6)	Height of Reflector Failed to Meet Requirements	15+7	0
42-4-207	Vehicle Not Equipped With (Clearance/Side Marker) (Lamps/Reflectors) as Required	15+7	0
42-4-208	Vehicle Had (Defective/No) Stop Light(s)	15+7	0
42-4-208	Vehicle Not Equipped With Turn Signals as Required	15+7	0
42-4-209	(Improper/No) Red (Flag/Light) on Projecting Load	15+7	0
42-4-210	Failed to Display Required Lights When Parked	15+7	0
42-4-211	(Farm Tractor/Farm Equipment/ Implement of Husbandry/Animal-Drawn Vehicle) Not Equipped With (Lamps/Reflectors) as Required	15+7	0
42-4-212	(Spot Lamps/Fog Lamps/Auxiliary Passing Lamps/Auxiliary Driving Lamps) Failed to Meet Requirements	15+7	0
42-4-212	Improper Use of (Spot Lamps/Fog Lamps/Auxiliary Passing Lamps/Driving Lamps)	15+7	0
42-4-213 (1)	Defective (Audible/Visual Signal) on Emergency Vehicle	15+7	0
42-4-213 (4)	(Unauthorized/Improper) Use of Green Light on (Motor/Emergency) Vehicle	15+7	0
42-4-214	Failed to Display Lamps on Service Vehicle as	15+7	0

STATUTE	CHARGE	FINE+ S.C.	PT
	Required		
42-4-214	Lamps on Service Vehicle (Failed to Meet Requirements/Not Yellow)	15+7	0
42-4-215	Signal (Lamps/Devices) Failed to Meet Requirements	15+7	0
42-4-215	Vehicle Did Not Have Turn Signals as Required	15+7	0
42-4-216	Vehicle Had No Upper-Lower Beam (Switch/Indicator)	15+7	0
42-4-217 (1)	Improper Headlight Distribution	15+7	0
42-4-217 (1)(a)	Failed to Dim Lights When Approaching an Oncoming Vehicle	15+7	2
42-4-217 (1)(b)	Failed to Dim Lights When Following Another Vehicle	15+7	2
42-4-218	Single-Beam Head Lamps Failed to Meet Requirements	15+7	0
42-4-219	Displayed More Than Four Lamps When Prohibited	15+7	0
42-4-220	Motor-Driven Cycle Not Equipped With Head Lamp as Required	15+7	0
42-4-220	Low-Power Scooter Did Not Have (Lamp/Reflector/Audible Signal/Brake) as Required	15+7	0
42-4-220 (3)(a)	Motor Vehicle had High Intensity Light Improperly Directed	15+7	0
42-4-220 (4)	(Had for Sale/Sold/Offered for Sale) Lighting Equipment (Altered from Original Design/Not Approved by the Dept of Revenue)	15+7	0
42-4-220 (5)	(Had for Sale/Sold/Offered for Sale) Lamp or Device Without Name Under Which Approval was Granted by Dept of Revenue	15+7	0
42-4-220 (6)	(Used/Attached/Operated) an Unapproved Lamp or Lighting Device Upon a Motor Vehicle	15+7	0
42-4-221 (2)	Bicycle Not Equipped With Front Lamp Visible 500 Feet to Front	15+7	0
42-4-221 (3)	Bicycle Not Equipped With Red Reflector Visible 600 Feet to Rear	15+7	0
42-4-221 (4)	Bicycle Not Equipped With Side Reflective Material or Lamps	15+7	0
42-4-222 (1)	Improper Auxiliary (Signal Lamps/Audible Signal) on (Volunteer Firefighter Vehicle/Volunteer Ambulance Attendant)	15+7	0
42-4-222 (1)	Misuse of Auxiliary (Signal Lamps/Audible Signal) by (Volunteer Firefighter/ Volunteer Ambulance Attendant)	15+7	0
42-4-223 (1)(b)	(Motorcycle/Motorized Bicycle/ Bicycle with Motor) Not Equipped With One Brake	15+7	2
42-4-223 (1)(c)	(Trailer/Semi-trailer) Did Not Have Breakaway Brakes as Required	15+7	2
42-4-223 (1)(d)	(Motor Vehicle/Trailer/Semi-Trailer) Did Not Have Service Brake as Required	15+7	2
42-4-223 (2)	Performance of (Service/Hand) Brake Did Not Meet Requirements	15+7	2

STATUTE	CHARGE	FINE+ S.C.	PT
42-4-224	Operated Vehicle With Unauthorized Audible Signal	15+7	0
42-4-224	Unlawful Use of (Siren/Whistle) upon a Motorized Bicycle	15+7	0
42-4-224	Vehicle Had (No/Defective) Horn	15+7	0
42-4-225	Vehicle Had (Defective/Improper/No) Mufflers	15+7	0
42-4-225 (1.5)	(No/Inadequate) Muffler on Vehicle Equipped With an Engine Compression Brake (Jake Brake)		0
42-4-226	Rearview Mirror Did Not Permit Minimum 200 Ft. Vision	15+7	0
42-4-226	Vehicle Did Not Have Rearview Mirror(s)	15+7	0
42-4-226 (2)	Load Obstructed View to Rear – No Mirrors	15+7	0
42-4-227 (1)	Material on (Windshield/Front Side Windows) Presented (Nontransparent/Metallic/Mirrored) Appearance (Note: Metallic/ Mirrored Applies to Any Window)	50+17	0
42-4-227 (2)	Vehicle Had (No/Defective) Windshield Wipers	15+7	0
42-4-227 (3)(b)	Person (Installed/Covered/Treated) (Windows/ Windshield) with Material that Does Not Meet Requirements	SUM	0
42-4-228 (1)	Solid Rubber Tire Failed to be at Least One Inch Thick	15+7	0
42-4-228 (3)	Tire had (Block/Flange/Cleat/Spike) Protruding From Rubber	15+7	0
42-4-228 (5)	Operated a Vehicle With (Improper/Unsafe) Tires	15+7	0
42-4-228 (6)	Operated Vehicle on Highway with Tires Designed for Non-Highway Use	15+7	0
42-4-228 (7)	Sold a Vehicle With (Improper/Unsafe) Tires	SUM	0
42-4-229 (4)	Vehicle Not Equipped With (Front Windshield/Safety Glass in Front Windshield)	15+7	0
42-4-230	Failed to Use (Warning Signal Flashers/Emergency Reflective Triangles) as Required	15+7	0
42-4-230	Vehicle Did Not Have Emergency Reflective Triangles as Required	15+7	0
42-4-231	Drove on Highway With Park Lights When Headlights Required	15+7	0
42-4-232 (1)	Motorcycle (Operator/Passenger) Had No Protective Eye Wear as Required	15+7	0
42-4-232 (1)	Low-Power Scooter(Operator/ Passenger) Had No Protective Eye Wear as Required	15+7	0
42-4-232 (3)	Motorcycle Not Equipped With Passenger Footrests	15+7	0
42-4-232 (3)	Low-Power Scooter Not Equipped With Passenger Footrests	15+7	0
42-4-234 (1)	Failed to Display Slow-Moving Vehicle Emblem	15+7	0
42-4-234 (3)	Misused Slow-Moving Vehicle Emblem	15+7	0
42-4-235 (2)(a)	Commercial Vehicle Failed to Comply With D.P.S. Rules and Regulations Governing Safety Standards and Specifications		0
42-4-236 (2)(a)(I)	Failed to (Provide/Properly Use) Rear Facing Child	65+17	0

STATUTE	CHARGE	FINE+ S.C.	PT
	Restraint System (Less Than 1 Year Old and Less Than 20 lbs) (Primary)		
42-4-236 (2)(a)(II)	Failed to (Provide/Properly Use) Forward Facing Child Restraint System (1 - 3 Years of Age/ More Than 20 lbs but Less Than 40 lbs) (Primary)	65+17	0
42-4-236 (2)(b)(I)	Failed to (Provide/Properly Use) An Approved Child Restraint System (4 - 5 Years of Age/Less Than Fifty-Five Inches Tall) (Secondary Offense)	65+17	0
42-4-236 (2)(b)(II)	Failed to (Provide/Properly Use) Seatbelt (6-17 Years of Age or More than 55" Tall) (Primary)	65+17	0
42-4-237 (2)	Drove Vehicle When Front Seat Passenger Not Secured By Safety Belt	65+7	0
42-4-237 (2)	Drove Vehicle When Safety Belt Not in Use	65+7	0
42-4-238 (1)	Knowingly Possessed Vehicle Equipped With a Red or Blue Light	SUM	0
42-4-239 (2)	Misuse of a Mobile Communication Device While Operating a Motor Vehicle	15+7	1
42-4-239 (5)(a)	Person <18 Used Telephone While Operating a M.V.	50+7	1
42-4-239 (5)(a)	Person 18 and Over Engaged in Text Messaging While Operating a Motor Vehicle	50+7	1
42-4-239 (5)(b)	Person <18 Used Telephone While Operating a M.V. (Subsequent Violation)	100+7	1
42-4-239 (5)(b)	Person 18 and Over Engaged in Text Messaging While Operating a Motor Vehicle (Subsequent Viol.)	100+7	1
42-4-240	Low Speed Electric Vehicle Failed to Conform to Equipment Requirements	15+7	0
42-4-313 (1)	Displayed (Certification of Emissions Control/ Verification of Emission Test) that was Counterfeit	SUM	0
42-4-313 (2)	Issued a Certificate of Emissions Control to a Vehicle That Did Not Qualify	SUM	0
42-4-313 (3)(a)	Owner Failed to Provide Valid Verification of Emissions Test	50+17	0
42-4-313 (3)(d)	Non-owner Driver Failed to Provide Valid Verification of Emissions Test	15+7	0
42-4-314 (1)	(Deactivated/Disconnected) a Pollution Control Device	35+11	0
42-4-314 (2)	Operated a Vehicle With a (Deactivated/ Disconnected) Pollution Control System	35+11	0
42-4-405.5 (1)	Commercial Vehicle Operator Carrying (Hazardous Material/Passengers) Violated Out-of Service Order		RA
42-4-405.5 (1)	Commercial Vehicle Operator Violated Out-of Service Order		RA
42-4-412 (1)(a)(I)	Vehicle Not Powered by Diesel Emitted Visible Air Pollutants	SUM	0
42-4-412 (1)(a)(II)	Visible Diesel Exhaust Emission Exceeded Maximum Lawful Limit (Use outside air program area and include percentage)	SUM	0
42-4-413 (1)	(Owner/Operator) Operated Diesel When Visible Diesel Exhaust Emissions Exceeded Maximum	SUM	0

STATUTE	CHARGE	FINE+ S.C.	PT
	Lawful Limit in AIR Program Area (Notice must accompany citation)		
42-4-502 (3)	Vehicle Had (Chains/Rope/Wire) (Swinging/ Dragging/Projecting)	75+25	0
42-4-504 (2)	Single Vehicle Exceeded 45 Feet in Length	75+25	0
42-4-504 (3)	Bus Exceeded 60 Feet in Length	75+25	0
42-4-504 (4)	Combination of Vehicles Exceeded (Four Units/70 Feet in Length)	75+25	0
42-4-504 (4.5)	(Saddle Mount Combination/Laden Truck Tractor Semitrailer Combination /Auto or Boat Transporter) Exceeded (Four Units/75 Feet)	75+25	0
42-4-504 (5)	Projecting Load on Vehicle Obstructed Driver's Vision	75+26	0
42-4-505	Operated Longer Vehicle Combination Where Prohibited	75+25	0
42-4-506 (1)	Unlawful Drawbar	15+7	0
42-4-506 (2)	Failed to Use White Flag on Tow (Chain/ Cable/Rope)	15+7	0
42-4-506 (3)	Failed to Use Safety Chain or Cable on Towed Vehicle	15+7	0
42-4-507	(Wheel/Axle) Loads Exceeded Maximum Lawful Limit (Specify)	List	0
42-4-508	Gross Weight of Vehicle Exceeded Maximum Lawful Limit (Specify)	List	0
42-4-509 (3)	(Refused/Failed) to Stop for Weighing (Load/Vehicle)	50+17	0
42-4-509 (3)	(Failed/Refused) to Stop for Weighing (Load/Vehicle)		0
42-4-510	Exceeded Maximum Permitted Weight on (Axle/Gross) Weight Authorized by Transport Permit	List	0
42-4-510	Failed Have Escort Vehicle When Required by Oversize/Overweight Permit		0
42-4-510	Failed to Have Escort Vehicle When Required By Oversize/Overweight Permit	250+93.5	0
42-4-510	Failed to Have Proof of Insurance in Cab of Commercial Vehicle		0
42-4-510	Failed to Reduce Speed When Required by Oversize/Overweight Weight Permit	250+93.5	0
42-4-510	Failed to Reduce Speed When Required by Oversized/Overweight Permit		0
42-4-510 (12)(a)	Operated Vehicle in Violation of Overwidth/Over-length Permit	35+11	0
42-4-510 (12)(a)	Operated Vehicle in Violation of Overwidth/ Overlength Permit For weight violations		0
42-4-510 (12)(b)	Owner Moved Manufactured Home Without a Paid Ad Valorem Tax Certificate and a Transportable Manufactured Home Permit		0
42-4-510 (12)(b)	Owner Moved Manufactured Home Without a Paid Ad Valorem Tax Certificate and a Transportable Manufactured Home Permit	SUM	0
42-4-510 (12)(b)	Owner Moved Manufactured Home Without a Paid Ad	SUM	0

STATUTE	CHARGE	FINE+ S.C.	PT
	Valorem Tax Certificate and a Transportable Manufactured Home Permit 2 or More Times		
42-4-510 (12)(b)	Owner Moved Manufactured Home Without a Paid Ad Valorem Tax Certificate and a Transportable Manufactured Home Permit 2 or More Times		0
42-4-512	Damaged (Highway/Highway Structure)	75+25	0
42-4-603	(Failed to Observe/Disregarded) Traffic Control Device	100+11	4
42-4-603	Made Turn Where Prohibited by Traffic Control Device	100+11	4
42-4-604	Failed to Obey Lane-Use Control Signal	100+11	4
42-4-604	Failed to Obey Traffic Control Signal	100+11	4
42-4-604	Failed to Stop for Traffic Control Signal at Place Required	100+11	4
42-4-604	Made (Right/Left) Turn on Red Light Where Prohibited by Sign	100+11	4
42-4-604	Pedestrian (Disregarded/Failed to Obey) Traffic Control Signal	100+11	0
42-4-605	Failed to Obey Flashing (Red/ Yellow) Signal Light as Required	70+11	4
42-4-606	Displayed Unauthorized (Sign/Signal/Marking/Device)	15+7	0
42-4-607 (1)(a)	(Attempted to/Removed/I/Altered/Defaced/Knocked Down/Injured) Traffic Control (Sign/Device)	50+17	0
42-4-607 (1)(b)	Unlawfully (Possessed/Sold) Electronic Device Designed to Affect a Traffic Control Device	50+17	0
42-4-607 (2)(a)	Interfered With Traffic Control Device By Using Electronic Device	100+33	3
42-4-607 (2)(b)	Use of Device to Change Traffic Signal Caused Bodily Injury	SUM	3
42-4-608 (1)	Failed to Use Turn Signals	70+7	2
42-4-608 (2)	Vehicle Not Equipped With Turn Signals as Required	15+7	0
42-4-609	Gave Improper Hand Signal	15+7	2
42-4-610	Displayed Unauthorized Insignia	15+7	0
42-4-611	Misuse of Authorized Distress Flag	SUM	0
42-4-612	Failed to Proceed (With Caution/as Required) at Inoperative or Malfunctioning Control Signal	70+11	4
42-4-613	Failed to Pay (Toll/Fee/Rate) Established by Regional Transportation Authority	35+11	3
42-4-702	Failed to Yield Right-of-Way When Turning Left in Front of Approaching Traffic	70+11	3
42-4-703 (3)	(Disregarded/Failed to Stop as Required at) Stop Sign at Through Highway	70+11	4
42-4-706	Disregarded (Railroad Signal/ Crossing Gate/Barricade/Flagman)	70+11	4
42-4-706 (1)	Disregarded Stop Sign at Railroad Crossing	70+11	4
42-4-707	(School Bus/Commercial Vehicle) Failed to Stop at Railroad Crossing When Required	70+11	4

STATUTE	CHARGE	FINE+ S.C.	PT
42-4-707	Vehicle Carrying Placarded Load of Hazardous Material Failed to Stop at Railroad Crossing	70+11	4
42-4-707 (1)	(School Bus/Commercial) Driver (Failed to Stop/Used Improper Gear) at Railroad Crossing When Required	70+11	4
42-4-708	Unlawful Moving of Heavy Equipment Across Railroad Grade Crossing	35+11	0
42-4-709	Driver Stopped Vehicle in (Intersection/Marked Crosswalk/ Railroad Grade Crossing) When Prohibited	70+11	3
42-4-710 (3)	Drove Vehicle Upon Sidewalk	70+11	3
42-4-711 (1)	Drove Vehicle Improperly on Mountain Highway	100+11	3
42-4-712 (3)	Disregarded (Instructions/Signals) of Authorized Flag-Person in Highway Work Area	70+11	3
42-4-801	Pedestrian Disregarded Traffic Control Device	15+7	0
42-4-802 (3)	Pedestrian Suddenly (Walked/Ran/Rode Bicycle) Into Path of Vehicle	15+7	0
42-4-802 (4)	Passed Vehicle Stopped for Pedestrian in (Marked/Unmarked) Crosswalk	30+7	3
42-4-803	Pedestrian Failed to Cross Roadway as Required	15+7	0
42-4-803	Pedestrian Failed to Yield Right-of-Way to Vehicle	15+7	0
42-4-805 (1)	(Pedestrian/Animal Rider) Failed to (Walk/ Ride) (Along/Upon) Roadway as Required	15+7	0
42-4-805 (2)	Pedestrian Solicited Rides in Roadway	15+7	0
42-4-805 (3)	Pedestrian on Highway Under the Influence of (Alcohol/Controlled Substance)	15+7	0
42-4-805 (4)	Animal Rider on Highway Under the Influence of (Alcohol/Controlled Substance)	15+7	0
42-4-805 (7)	Vehicle (Endangered/Impeded) Traffic to Pick Up Pedestrian	15+7	0
42-4-805 (8)	(Pedestrian/Animal Rider) Failed to Yield to Emergency Vehicle	15+7	0
42-4-806	Drove Vehicle Through or Within Pedestrian Safety Zone	70+11	3
42-4-806	Drove Vehicle Through Safety Zone	70+11	3
42-4-808	Pedestrian Failed to Yield Right-of-Way to Disabled Person	70+11	0
42-4-901 (1)(a)	Made Right Turn From Wrong (Position/Lane)	70+11	3
42-4-901 (1)(b)	Made Left Turn From Wrong (Position/Lane)	70+11	3
42-4-901 (1)(c)	Made Improper Left Turn at Multi turn Intersection	70+11	3
42-4-901 (2)	Failed to Turn as Required by Traffic Control Device	70+11	3
42-4-901 (2)	Failed to Turn From Turn-Only Lane	70+11	3
42-4-902 (1)	Made U-Turn on Hill or Curve	70+11	3
42-4-902 (2)	Made Unsafe U-Turn at Intersection	70+11	3
42-4-902 (3)	Made U-Turn Where Prohibited	70+11	3
42-4-903	(Failed to Signal as Required/Gave Improper Signal) for (Turn/Stop/ Sudden Decrease in Speed)	70+11	2

STATUTE	CHARGE	FINE+ S.C.	PT
42-4-903	Improper Use of Flashing Turn Signal	70+11	2
42-4-1001	Failed to Drive Vehicle (on Right Side of Road/in Right-Hand Lane) as Required	70+11	4
42-4-1001 (1)(b)	Failed to Yield Right-of-Way When Forced to Drive on Left Side of Road	70+11	4
42-4-1002	Failed to Yield One-Half of the Roadway to Oncoming Vehicle	100+11	4
42-4-1003 (1)(a)	Passed on Left in Unsafe Manner	100+11	4
42-4-1003 (1)(b)	Driver Failed to Give Way When Overtaken	100+11	3
42-4-1004	Passed on Right When (Not Permitted/Not Safe)	100+11	4
42-4-1005 (1)	Passed on Left When Not Clear to Traffic	100+11	4
42-4-1005 (1)	Passed Without Giving Oncoming Traffic Sufficient Clearance	100+11	4
42-4-1005 (2)(a)	Passed on (Hill/Curve) When View Obstructed	100+11	4
42-4-1005 (2)(b)	Passed When (Crossing/Within 100 Ft. of) (Intersection/Railroad Crossing)	100+11	4
42-4-1005 (2)(c)	Passed Within 100 Ft. of (Bridge/ Tunnel/ Viaduct) When View Obstructed	100+11	4
42-4-1005 (3)	Passed on Left When Prohibited By (Signs/ Markings)	100+11	4
42-4-1006 (1)	Drove Vehicle Wrong Way on One-Way Roadway	70+11	3
42-4-1006 (2)	Drove Vehicle Wrong Way Around Rotary Island	70+11	3
42-4-1007 (1)(a)	Changed Lanes When Unsafe	100+11	3
42-4-1007 (1)(a)	Failed to Drive in Single Lane (Weaving)	100+11	3
42-4-1007 (1)(b)	(Attempted to Pass/Passed) on Shoulder of Right Hand Traffic Lane	100+11	4
42-4-1007 (1)(b)	Drove Vehicle in Center Lane When (Unnecessary/Prohibited)	100+11	3
42-4-1007 (1)(c)	Failed to Drive in Designated Lane	100+11	3
42-4-1007 (1)(d)	Changed Lanes Where Prohibited by Official Traffic Control Device	100+11	4
42-4-1008 (1)	Following Too Closely	100+11	4
42-4-1008 (2)	Unlawful Following By Vehicle Drawing Another Vehicle	100+11	4
42-4-1008 (2)	Unlawful Following by Vehicle Drawing Another Vehicle (Following too Closely)	100+11	4
42-4-1008 (3)	Following Too Closely in Motorcade	100+11	4
42-4-1009 (1)	Coasted Vehicle Down Grade With Gears in Neutral	70+11	3
42-4-1010	Failed to Drive as Required on (Divided/ Controlled-Access) Highway	70+11	3
42-4-1010	Vehicle Crossed Roadway Dividing (Space/ Median/Barrier) in an Unlawful Manner	70+11	3
42-4-1010 (1)	(Improper Turn/Turned Where Prohibited) Across Median of Divided Highway	70+11	3
42-4-1010 (1)	Drove Vehicle on Wrong Side of Divided Highway	70+11	4
42-4-1011	(Illegal Use Of/Obstructed) a Runaway Vehicle Ramp	200+33	3

STATUTE	CHARGE	FINE+ S.C.	PT
42-4-1012 (3)(a)	Drove Unauthorized Vehicle In High Occupancy Lane	65+1	0
42-4-1012 (3)(b)	Drove Unauthorized Vehicle in High Occupancy Lane Three or More Times	125+1	0
42-4-1013 (1)	Drove Vehicle in Passing Lane When Prohibited (Posted 65 MPH or more roadway)	100+1	3
42-4-1101 (1)	Speeding (1-4 MPH Over Prima Facie Limit)	30+22	0
42-4-1101 (1)	Speeding (5-9 MPH Over Prima Facie Limit)	70+26	1
42-4-1101 (1)	Speeding (10-19 MPH Over Prima Facie Limit)	135+32	4
42-4-1101 (1)	Speeding (20-24 MPH Over Prima Facie Limit)	200+48	6
42-4-1101 (1)	Speeding (25-39 MPH Over Prima Facie Limit)	SUM	6
42-4-1101 (1)	Speeding (40 MPH Over Prima Facie Limit)	SUM	12
42-4-1101 (1)	Speeding (1-4 MPH Over Posted Limit in Construction/School Zone)		0
42-4-1101 (1)	Speeding (5-9 MPH Over Posted Limit in Construction/School Zone)		1
42-4-1101 (1)	Speeding (10-19 MPH Over Posted Limit in Construction/School Zone)		4
42-4-1101 (1)	Speeding (20-24 MPH Over Posted Limit in *Construction Zone* Only)		6
42-4-1101 (1)	Speeding (20-24 MPH Over Posted Limit in *School Zone* Only)		6
42-4-1101 (1)	Speeding (25-39 MPH Over Posted Limit in Construction/School Zone)		6
42-4-1101 (1)	Speeding (40 MPH or more Over Posted Limit in Construction/School Zone)		12
42-4-1101 (1)	Speeding (10-14 MPH Over Prima Facie Limit) [Commercial Vehicle Only]		4
42-4-1101 (1)	Speeding (15-19 MPH Over Prima Facie Limit) [Commercial Vehicle Only]		4
42-4-1101 (3)	Exceeded Safe Speed for Conditions (Indicate actual speed/safe speed)	100+26	3
42-4-1101 (8)(b)	Speeding (1-4 MPH Over the Maximum 75 MPH Limit)	30+17	0
42-4-1101 (8)(b)	Speeding (5-9 MPH Over the Maximum 75 MPH Limit)	70+21	1
42-4-1101 (8)(b)	Speeding (10-19 MPH Over the Maximum 75 MPH Limit)	135+32	4
42-4-1101 (8)(b)	Speeding (20-24 MPH Over the Maximum 75 MPH Limit)	200+48	6
42-4-1101 (8)(b)	Speeding (25-39 MPH Over the Maximum 75 MPH Limit)	SUM	6
42-4-1101 (8)(b)	Speeding (10-14 MPH Over the Maximum 75 MPH Limit) [Commercial Vehicle Only]		4
42-4-1101 (8)(b)	Speeding (15-19 MPH Over the Maximum 75 MPH Limit) [Commercial Vehicle Only]		4
42-4-1101 (8)(g)	Low Powered Scooter Exceeded Max. Speed of 40 MPH (1-4 MPH Over)	50+22	0
42-4-1101 (8)(g)	Low Powered Scooter Exceeded Max. Speed of 40 MPH (5-9 MPH Over)	75+26	2

STATUTE	CHARGE	FINE+ S.C.	PT
42-4-1101 (8)(g)	Low Powered Scooter Exceeded Max. Speed of 40 MPH (10-19 MPH Over)	100+32	4
42-4-1103 (1)	Impeded Normal Flow of Traffic	50+22	3
42-4-1104 (1)	Exceeded Posted Safe Speed on Elevated Structure	30+22	3
42-4-1105 (1)(a)	Engaged in Speed Contest	SUM	12
42-4-1105 (2)(a)	Engaged in Exhibition of Speed	SUM	5
42-4-1105 (3)	Obstructed Highway Incident to a Speed Contest	SUM	12
42-4-1105 (3)(a)	(Aided in/Facilitated) a Speed Contest	SUM	12
42-4-1105 (3)(a)	(Aided in/Facilitated) an Exhibition of Speed	SUM	5
42-4-1105 (8)(a)	Removed Immobilization Device Prior to End of Order	SUM	5
42-4-1105 (8)(b)	Removed Immobilization Device Prior to Payment of Fees	SUM	5
42-4-1106	Violated Left Lane Minimum Speed on 1-70 Corridor (Posted 6% Grade)	100+32	3
42-4-1201	Improper Starting From (Parked/Stopped) Position	30+7	3
42-4-1201	Improper Starting From Parked Position	30+7	3
42-4-1202	(Stopped/Parked/Left Standing) Vehicle on Paved Portion of Highway	30+7	0
42-4-1204	Improper (Stopping/Standing/ Parking) Specify the Violation	15+7	0
42-4-1204	Improper Moving of Parked Vehicle	15+7	0
42-4-1205 (1)	Failed to Park as Close as Practical to Edge of Shoulder	15+7	0
42-4-1205 (1)	Parked Vehicle More Than 12 Inches From Curb	15+7	0
42-4-1205 (2)	Parked Vehicle (on Wrong Side of/in Wrong Direction on) Roadway	15+7	0
42-4-1206	Failed to (Lock Ignition of/Remove Key From) Parked Vehicle	15+7	0
42-4-1206	Parked Vehicle on Grade Without Turning Wheels to Side of Curb	15+7	0
42-4-1206	Parked Vehicle Without Setting Brakes	15+7	0
42-4-1207	(Opened Door/Left Door Open) Into Lane of Traffic (When Not Safe/and Interfered With Traffic)	15+7	0
42-4-1208 (5)	Improper Use of Designated Disabled Parking When Not Disabled (1st Offense)	350+33	0
42-4-1208 (5)	Improper Use of Designated Disabled Parking When Not Disabled (2nd Offense)	600+33	0
42-4-1208 (5)	Improper Use of Designated Disabled Parking When Not Disabled (3rd/Subsequent Offense)	SUM	0
42-4-1208 (7)	Improper Use of Disability (License Plate/Placard) To Receive Disability Privileges (1st Offense)	SUM	0
42-4-1208 (7)	Improper Use of Disability (License Plate/Placard) To Receive Disability Privileges (2nd Offense)	SUM	0
42-4-1208 (7)	Improper Use of Disability (License Plate/Placard) To Receive Disability Privileges (3rd/Subsequent Offense)	SUM	0

STATUTE	CHARGE	FINE+ S.C.	PT
42-4-1208 (11)(a)	Illegal (Use/Creation) of Disabled (License Plate/Placard)	SUM	0
42-4-1208 (11)(b)	Illegal (Use/Creation) of Disabled (License Plate/Placard) for Remuneration	SUM	0
42-4-1208 (15)(a)	Misuse of Time Limited Disabled Parking	150+33	0
42-4-1208 (16)(a)	Improper Commercial Use of Disability (License Plate/Placard)	150+33	0
42-4-1211 (1)(a)	Backed Vehicle in Parking Area (When Not Safe/and Interfered With Traffic)	30+7	2
42-4-1211 (1)(b)	Backed Vehicle on (Shoulder/Roadway) of Controlled-Access Highway	30+7	2
42-4-1301 (1)(a)	Drove Vehicle While Under the Influence of Alcohol or Drugs or Both	SUM	12
42-4-1301 (1)(a)	Drove Vehicle While Under the Influence of Drugs	SUM	12
42-4-1301 (1)(b)	Drove Vehicle While Ability Impaired by Alcohol or Drugs or Both	SUM	8
42-4-1301 (1)(b)	Drove Vehicle While Ability Impaired by Drugs	SUM	8
42-4-1301 (1)(c)	Habitual User of Controlled Substance Drove (Motor Vehicle/Low-Power Scooter)	SUM	RA
42-4-1301 (2)(a)	Drove Vehicle With Blood Alcohol Content of 0.08 or More	SUM	12
42-4-1301 (2)(a.5)	Person or CMV Driver Under 21 Drove Vehicle with BAC of 0.02 but Less Than 0.05 (First Offense)	100+32	4
42-4-1301 (2)(a.5)(I)	Person or CMV driver Under 21 Drove Vehicle With BAC of 0.02 but Less Than 0.05 (Second Offense)	SUM	4
42-4-1305 (2)(a)	(Drank From/Possessed) an Open Alcoholic Beverage Container in a Motor Vehicle	50+17	3
42-4-1401 (1)	Reckless Driving	SUM	8
42-4-1402 (1)	Rode Bicycle in Careless Manner	150+17	0
42-4-1402 (2)(a)	Careless Driving	150+17	4
42-4-1402 (2)(b)	Careless Driving Caused Bodily Injury	SUM	4
42-4-1402 (2)(c)	Careless Driving Caused Death	SUM	12
42-4-1403	Following Too Closely Behind Fire Apparatus	30+7	3
42-4-1404	Drove Vehicle Over Fire Hose	15+7	0
42-4-1405	Person Rode in Trailer	15+7	0
42-4-1406 (1)(a)	(Left/Deposited/Threw) Foreign Matter on Highway	35+11	0
42-4-1406 (1)(b)	(Left/Deposited/Threw) Burning Material from a Motor Vehicle	SUM	0
42-4-1406 (2)	Failed to Remove (Lighted/Burning) Matter (Left/Deposited/Thrown) on Highway	35+11	0
42-4-1406 (3)	Removed Wrecked or Damaged Vehicle From Highway Without Removing Injurious Substance From Highway	35+11	0
42-4-1406 (4)	Constructed on Highway Without Authorization	35+11	0
42-4-1406 (4)	Excavated on Highway Without Authorization	35+11	0
42-4-1406 (5)(b)(II)	(Left/Deposited/Threw) Human Waste Container on Highway	SUM	0

STATUTE	CHARGE	FINE+ S.C.	PT
42-4-1407 (2.4)(a)	Vehicle Transporting Trash or Recyclables Failed to (Cover/ Properly Secure) Load on Highway	35+11	0
42-4-1407 (3)(b)	Spilled Load From Car/Pick-Up Truck on Highway	100+33	3
42-4-1407 (3)(c)	Spilled Load from Car/Pick-Up Truck on Highway Causing Bodily Injury	SUM	3
42-4-1407 (l)	Spilled Load on Highway/Failed to Cover Load/No Flaps When Required	35+11	0
42-4-1407.5	Splash Guards Required	35+11	0
42-4-1408	Operated Motor Vehicle in Recreation Area or District Where Prohibited	15+7	0
42-4-1409 (1)	Owner Operated an Uninsured Motor Vehicle on a Public Roadway	SUM	4
42-4-1409 (2)	Operated an Uninsured Motor Vehicle on a Public Roadway	SUM	4
42-4-1409 (3)	Failed to Present Evidence of Insurance Upon Request	SUM	4
42-4-1409 (7)	Failed to Sign Affirmation of Insurance	15+7	0
42-4-1411	Drove Vehicle While Wearing Earphones	15+7	0
42-4-1412 (10)(a)	Bicycle Rider on (Sidewalk/ Roadway/Crosswalk/Pathway) Failed to Yield Right of Way to Pedestrian	15+7	0
42-4-1412 (10)(b)	Rode Bicycle on (Sidewalk/ Roadway/Pathway) When Prohibited by (Sign/Device)	15+7	0
42-4-1412 (11)	Improper Parking of a Bicycle	15+7	0
42-4-1412 (3)	Unlawful Number of Persons on Bicycle	15+7	0
42-4-1412 (4)	Bicycle Rider Attached Himself to Motor Vehicle	15+7	0
42-4-1412 (5)	Bicycle Rider Failed to Ride in Right-hand Lane as Required	15+7	0
42-4-1412 (5)	Bicycle Rider Failed to Ride on Right Side of Lane When Being Overtaken	15+7	0
42-4-1412 (5)	Bicycle Rider Failed to Ride on Suitable Paved Shoulder	15+7	0
42-4-1412 (6)(a)	Bicycle Rider Failed to Ride Single File When Required	15+7	0
42-4-1412 (6)(b)	Bicycle Rider Failed to Ride in Single Lane When Riding Two Abreast	15+7	0
42-4-1412 (7)	Bicycle Rider Failed to Keep at Least One Hand on Handlebars	15+7	0
42-4-1412 (8)(a)	Bicycle Rider Made Improper Left Turn	15+7	0
42-4-1412 (8)(b)	Bicycle Rider Intending to Turn Left Disregarded Official Traffic Control Device	15+7	0
42-4-1412 (9)	Bicycle Rider Failed to Signal Intention to (Turn/Stop)	15+7	0
42-4-1413	(Eluded/Attempted to Elude) a Police Officer	SUM	12
42-4-1414 (2)(a)	Unlawful Use of Dyed Diesel Fuel (First Offense)	500+157	0
42-4-1414 (2)(b)	Unlawful Use of Dyed Diesel Fuel (Second Offense)	1000+313	0
42-4-1414 (2)(c)	Unlawful Use of Dyed Diesel Fuel (Third or Subsequent Offense)	5000+1561	0

STATUTE	CHARGE	FINE+ S.C.	PT
42-4-1415 (1)(a)	(Offered for Sale/Possessed) Radar Jamming Device	150+17	0
42-4-1415 (1)(b)	Operated a Vehicle with a Radar Jamming Device	150+17	0
42-4-1502	Improper Riding on Motorcycle: (State Violation)	35+7	3
42-4-1502 (4.5)(a)	Motorcycle (Operator/Passenger) Under 18 Not Wearing an Approved Protective Helmet (Primary)	100+31	3
42-4-1503	Illegal Operation of Motorcycle on Lane Roads	35+7	3
42-4-1504	Person on Motorcycle Clung to Another Vehicle	35+7	3
42-4-1601 (2)(a)	Failed to (Remain at the Scene/Give Information and/or Aid) After Accident Involving Injury	SUM	RA
42-4-1601 (2)(b)	Failed to (Remain at the Scene/Give Information and/or Aid) After Accident Involving Serious Bodily Injury	SUM	RA
42-4-1601 (2)(c)	Failed to (Remain at the Scene/Give Information and/or Aid) After Accident Involving Death	NIBR	RA
42-4-1602 (1)	Failed to Give Information and/or Aid After Damaging Another Vehicle	SUM	12
42-4-1603 (1)	Driver Failed to Provide Information After Accident Involving (Injury/Serious Injury/death)	SUM	12
42-4-1604	Left Scene Without Providing Required Information After Striking Unattended (Vehicle/Property)	SUM	12
42-4-1605	Failed to Report Accident Involving Highway Fixture	SUM	12
42-4-1606 (1)	Failed to (Remain at/Return to) Accident Scene as Directed by Police	SUM	12
42-4-1606 (1)	Failed to Notify Police of Accident	SUM	12
42-4-1607 (1)	Passenger Failed to Provide Information After Accident Involving (Injury/Serious Injury/Death)	SUM	0
42-4-1703	Aiding and Abetting - To Wit: (Specify the Offense or Infraction)	SUM	0
42-4-1704	Directed Operator of Vehicle Contrary to Law	15+7	0
42-4-1716 (2)	Failed to Obey Summons to Appear in Court	SUM	0
42-4-1901	Operated School Bus on Mountainous Terrain With Passengers in (Front Row Seats/Seats Next to Emergency Exit) When School Bus Not Equipped With Supplementary Brake Retarders	35+11	0
42-4-1903 (1)	Failed to Stop for Stopped School Bus Displaying Flashing Red Lights	SUM	6
42-4-1903 (2)	School Bus Driver Failed to Actuate Visual Signals as Required	SUM	2
42-4-1903 (5)	School Bus Driver Failed to Stop as Required	SUM	3
42-4-1903 (6)(b)	Failed to Stop for Stopped School Bus Displaying Flashing Red Lights Two or More Times Within Five Years	SUM	6
42-6-139 (2)	(Registered/Titled) Vehicle in County Other than County of Residence	SUM	0
42-6-140	Failed to Obtain Colorado Title Within 30 Days after Becoming Resident	SUM	0
42-7-422	Drove Vehicle While Under FRA Suspension	SUM	RA
42-8-105	Failed to Obtain Port of Entry Clearance		0

STATUTE	CHARGE	FINE+ S.C.	PT
42-13-105	Released Vehicle Held by Colorado State Patrol Officer Without Authorization	SUM	0
42-20-109 (1)	Violation of CSP Rules & Regulations Concerning the (Transporting/Shipping) of Hazardous Materials. (Specify HMS Rule)	SUM	0
42-20-109 (2)	Violation of CSP (Permitting/Routing) Rules & Regulations Concerning Hazardous Materials. (Specify HMR or HMP Rule)	250+67	0
42-20-111	Knowingly/Intentionally) (Conspired/Aiding & Abetting) in Violations of the Provisions of Title 42, Article 20, CRS	SUM	0
42-20-204 (1)	Intentionally Transported Hazardous Materials Without a Permit as Required in 42-20-201	SUM	0
42-20-204 (1)	Transported Hazardous Materials Without a Permit as Required in 42-20-201	250+1	0
42-20-204 (2)	No (Annual/Single Trip) Hazardous Materials Transportation Permit in Vehicle	25+0	0
42-20-204 (3)	Knowingly Violated Hazardous Materials Transportation Permit Terms & Conditions	SUM	0
42-20-305 (2)	Unauthorized Deviation From Designated Route While Transporting Hazardous Materials	250+1	0
42-20-305 (2)	Unauthorized Deviation From Designated Route While Transporting Hazardous Materials. (2nd or Subsequent Offense Within a Twelve-Month Period)	SUM	0
43-1-417	(Erected/Used/Maintained) Unlawful Highway Advertising Device	SUM	0
43-4-1407.5	Splash Guards Required	35+11	0
43-5-301	Obstructed Highway	SUM	0
43-5-303	Allowed Water to (Flow/Fall/ Sprinkle) on Highway to Cause a Hazard to Vehicular Traffic	SUM	0

TITLE 42
VEHICLES AND TRAFFIC

TITLE 42

VEHICLES AND TRAFFIC

GENERAL AND ADMINISTRATIVE

Art. 1. General and Administrative, 42-1-101 to 42-1-407.

DRIVERS' LICENSES

Art. 2. Drivers' Licenses, 42-2-101 to 42-2-409.

TAXATION

Art. 3. Registration, Taxation, and License Plates, 42-3-101 to 42-3-312.

REGULATION OF VEHICLES AND TRAFFIC

Art. 4. Regulation of Vehicles and Traffic, 42-4-101 to 42-4-2301.

AUTOMOBILE THEFT LAW

Art. 5. Automobile Theft Law - Inspection of Motor Vehicle Identification Numbers, 42-5-101 to 42-5-207.

CERTIFICATES OF TITLE

Art. 6. Certificates of Title - Used Motor Vehicle Sales, 42-6-101 to 42-6-206.

MOTOR VEHICLE FINANCIAL RESPONSIBILITY LAW

Art. 7. Motor Vehicle Financial Responsibility Law, 42-7-101 to 42-7-609.

PORT OF ENTRY WEIGH STATIONS

Art. 8. Port of Entry Weigh Stations, 42-8-101 to 42-8-111.

MOTOR VEHICLE REPAIRS

Art. 9. Motor Vehicle Repair Act, 42-9-101 to 42-9-113.
Art. 9.5. Vehicle Protection Products, 42-9.5-101 to 42-9.5-106.
Art. 10. Motor Vehicle Warranties, 42-10-101 to 42-10-107.
Art. 11. Motor Vehicle Service Contract Insurance, 42-11-101 to 42-11-108.

COLLECTOR'S ITEMS

Art. 12. Motor Vehicles as Collector's Items, 42-12-101 to 42-12-405.

DISPOSITION OF PERSONAL PROPERTY

Art. 13. Disposition of Personal Property, 42-13-101 to 42-13-109.

IDLING STANDARD

Art. 14. State Idling Standard, 42-14-101 to 42-14-106.

HIGHWAY SAFETY

Art. 20. Transportation of Hazardous and Nuclear Materials, 42-20-101 to 42-20-511.

GENERAL AND ADMINISTRATIVE

ARTICLE 1
General and Administrative

PART 1
DEFINITIONS AND CITATION

42-1-101. Short title.
42-1-102. Definitions.

PART 2
ADMINISTRATION

42-1-201. Administration - supervisor.
42-1-202. Have charge of all divisions.
42-1-203. Executive director to cooperate with others - local compliance required.
42-1-204. Uniform rules and regulations.
42-1-205. Record of official acts - seal.
42-1-206. Records open to inspection - furnishing of copies.
42-1-207. No supplies for private purposes - penalty.
42-1-208. Information on accidents - published.
42-1-209. Copies of law published. (Repealed)
42-1-210. County clerk and recorders and manager of revenue or other appointed official as agents - legislative declaration - fee.
42-1-211. Colorado state titling and registration system.
42-1-212. Consolidated data processing system - voter registration. (Repealed)
42-1-213. Commission of county clerk and recorders and manager of revenue or other appointed official.
42-1-214. Duties of county clerk and recorders.
42-1-215. Oaths.
42-1-216. Destruction of obsolete records.
42-1-217. Disposition of fines and surcharges.
42-1-218. Revocations and suspensions of licenses published. (Repealed)
42-1-218.5. Electronic hearings.
42-1-219. Appropriations for administration of title.

42-1-220.	Identification security fund - repeal.
42-1-221.	Fuel piracy computer reprogramming cash fund - repeal. (Repealed)
42-1-222.	Motor vehicle investigations unit.
42-1-223.	Monitoring driving improvement schools - fund - rules.
42-1-224.	Criminal history check.
42-1-225.	Commercial vehicle enterprise tax fund - creation.
42-1-226.	Disabled parking education and enforcement fund - created.
42-1-227.	Disabled parking education program.

PART 3
GREEN TRUCK GRANT PROGRAM

42-1-301.	Short title.
42-1-302.	Legislative declaration.
42-1-303.	Definitions.
42-1-304.	Green truck grant program - created.
42-1-305.	Green truck grant program fund - created.

PART 4
LICENSE PLATE AUCTIONS

42-1-401.	Definitions.
42-1-402.	License to buy and sell selected registration numbers for license plates.
42-1-403.	License plate auction group.
42-1-404.	Sale of registration numbers by group.
42-1-405.	Creation of a private market for registration numbers - fee.
42-1-406.	Administration.
42-1-407.	Registration number fund.

PART 1
DEFINITIONS AND CITATION

42-1-101. Short title. Articles 1 to 4 of this title shall be known and may be cited as the "Uniform Motor Vehicle Law".

42-1-102. Definitions. As used in articles 1 to 4 of this title, unless the context otherwise requires:

(1) "Acceleration lane" means a speed-change lane, including tapered areas, for the purpose of enabling a vehicle entering a roadway to increase its speed to a rate at which it can more safely merge with through traffic.

(2) "Administrator" means the property tax administrator.

(3) "Alley" means a street or highway intended to provide access to the rear or side of lots or buildings in urban areas and not intended for the purpose of through vehicular traffic.

(4) "Apportioned registration" means registration of a vehicle pursuant to a reciprocal agreement under which the fees paid for registration of such vehicle are ultimately divided among the several jurisdictions in which the vehicle travels, based upon the number of miles traveled by the vehicle in each jurisdiction or upon some other agreed criterion.

(4.5) "Appurtenance" means a piece of equipment that is affixed or attached to a motor vehicle or trailer and is used for a specific purpose or task, including awnings, support hardware, and extractable equipment. "Appurtenance" does not include any item or equipment that is temporarily affixed or attached to the exterior of a motor vehicle for the purpose of transporting such vehicle.

(5) "Authorized agent" means the officer of a county or city and county designated by law to issue annual registrations of vehicles and to collect any registration or license fee imposed thereon by law.

(6) "Authorized emergency vehicle" means such vehicles of the fire department, police vehicles, ambulances, and other special-purpose vehicles as are publicly owned and operated by or for a governmental agency to protect and preserve life and property in accordance with state laws regulating emergency vehicles; said term also means the following if equipped and operated as emergency vehicles in the manner prescribed by state law:

(a) Privately owned vehicles as are designated by the state motor vehicle licensing agency necessary to the preservation of life and property; or

(b) Privately owned tow trucks approved by the public utilities commission to respond to vehicle emergencies.

(7) "Authorized service vehicle" means such highway or traffic maintenance vehicles as are publicly owned and operated on a highway by or for a governmental agency the function of which requires the use of service vehicle warning lights as prescribed by state law and such other vehicles having a public service function, including, but not limited to, public utility vehicles and tow trucks, as determined by the department of transportation under section 42-4-214 (5). Some vehicles may be designated as both an authorized emergency vehicle and an authorized service vehicle.

(8) "Automobile" means any motor vehicle.

(8.5) "BAC" means either:

(a) A person's blood alcohol content, expressed in grams of alcohol per one hundred milliliters of blood as shown by analysis of the person's blood; or

(b) A person's breath alcohol content, expressed in grams of alcohol per two hundred ten liters of breath as shown by analysis of the person's breath.

(9) "Base jurisdiction" means the state, province, or other jurisdiction which receives, apportions, and remits to other jurisdictions moneys paid for registration of a vehicle pursuant to a reciprocal agreement governing registration of vehicles.

(10) "Bicycle" means a vehicle propelled by human power applied to pedals upon which a person may ride having two tandem wheels or two parallel wheels and one forward wheel, all of which are more than fourteen inches in diameter.

(10.5) "Bulk electronic transfer" means the mass electronic transfer of files, updated files, or portions thereof, in the same form as those files exist within the department.

(11) "Business district" means the territory contiguous to and including a highway when within any six hundred feet along such highway there are buildings in use for business or industrial purposes, including but not limited to motels, banks, office buildings, railroad stations, and public buildings which occupy at least three hundred feet of frontage on one side or three hundred feet collectively on both sides of the highway.

(12) "Calendar year" means the twelve calendar months beginning January 1 and ending December 31 of any year.

(13) "Camper coach" means an item of mounted equipment, weighing more than five hundred pounds, which when temporarily or permanently mounted on a motor vehicle adapts such vehicle for use as temporary living or sleeping accommodations.

(14) "Camper trailer" means a wheeled vehicle having an overall length of less than twenty-six feet, without motive power, which is designed to be drawn by a motor vehicle over the public highways and which is generally and commonly used for temporary living or sleeping accommodations.

(15) "Chauffeur" means every person who is employed for the principal purpose of operating a motor vehicle and every person who drives a motor vehicle while in use as a public or common carrier of persons or property.

(16) "Classified personal property" means any personal property which has been classified for the purpose of imposing thereon a graduated annual specific ownership tax.

(17) "Commercial carrier" means any owner of a motor vehicle, truck, laden or unladen truck tractor, trailer, or semitrailer used in the business of transporting persons or property over the public highways for profit, hire, or otherwise in any business or commercial enterprise.

(17.5) "Commercial vehicle" means a vehicle used to transport cargo or passengers for profit, hire, or otherwise to further the purposes of a business or commercial enterprise. This subsection (17.5) shall not apply for purposes of sections 42-4-235 and 42-4-707 (1).

(18) "Controlled-access highway" means every highway, street, or roadway in respect to which owners or occupants of abutting lands and other persons have no legal right of access to or from the same except at such points only and in such manner as may be determined by the public authority having jurisdiction over such highway, street, or roadway.

(19) "Convicted" or "conviction" means:
(a) A plea of guilty or nolo contendere;
(b) A verdict of guilty;
(c) An adjudication of delinquency under title 19, C.R.S.;
(d) The payment of a penalty assessment under section 42-4-1701 if the summons states clearly the points to be assessed for the offense; and
(e) As to a holder of a commercial driver's license as defined in section 42-2-402 or the operator of a commercial motor vehicle as defined in section 42-2-402:
(I) An unvacated adjudication of guilt or a determination by an authorized administrative hearing that a person has violated or failed to comply with the law;
(II) An unvacated forfeiture of bail or collateral deposited to secure the person's appearance in court;
(III) The payment of a fine or court cost or violation of a condition of release without bail, regardless of whether or not the penalty is rebated, suspended, or probated; or
(IV) A deferred sentence.

(20) "Court" means any municipal court, county court, district court, or any court having jurisdiction over offenses against traffic regulations and laws.

(21) "Crosswalk" means that portion of a roadway ordinarily included within the prolongation or connection of the lateral lines of sidewalks at intersections or any portion of a roadway distinctly indicated for pedestrian crossing by lines or other marking on the surface.

(22) "Dealer" means every person engaged in the business of buying, selling, or exchanging vehicles of a type required to be registered under articles 1 to 4 of this title and who has an established place of business for such purpose in this state.

(23) "Deceleration lane" means a speed-change lane, including tapered areas, for the purpose of enabling a vehicle that is to make an exit to turn from a roadway to slow to the safe speed on the ramp ahead after it has left the mainstream of faster-moving traffic.

(23.5) "Declared gross vehicle weight" means the combined weight of the vehicle or combination vehicle and its cargo when operated on the public highways of this state. Such weight shall be declared by the vehicle owner at the time the vehicle is registered. Accurate records shall be kept of all miles operated by each vehicle over the public highways of this state by the owner of each vehicle.

(24) "Department" means the department of revenue of this state acting directly or through its duly authorized officers and agents.

(24.5) "Distinctive special license plate" means a special license plate that is issued to a person because such person has an immutable characteristic or special achievement honor. Such special achievement honor shall not include a common achievement such as graduating from an institution of higher education. Such special achievement shall include honorable service in the armed forces of the United States. "Distinctive special license plate" shall include a license plate that is issued to a person or the person's family to honor such person's service in the armed forces.

(25) "Divided highway" means a highway with separated roadways usually for traffic moving in opposite directions, such separation being indicated by depressed dividing strips, raised curbings, traffic islands, or other physical barriers so constructed as to impede vehicular traffic or otherwise indicated by standard pavement markings or other official traffic control devices as prescribed in the state traffic control manual.

(26) "Drive-away transporter" or "tow-away transporter" means every person engaged in the transporting of vehicles which are sold or to be sold and not owned by such transporter, by the drive-away or tow-away methods, where such vehicles are driven, towed, or transported singly, or by saddlemount, towbar, or fullmount methods, or by any lawful combination thereof.

(27) "Driver" means every person, including a minor driver under the age of twenty-one years, who drives or is in actual physical control of a vehicle.

(27.3) "DUI" means driving under the influence, as defined in section 42-4-1301 (1) (f), and use of the term shall incorporate by reference the offense described in section 42-4-1301 (1) (a).

(27.5) "DUI per se" means driving with a BAC of 0.08 or more, and use of the term shall incorporate by reference the offense described in section 42-4-1301 (2) (a).

(27.7) "DWAI" means driving while ability impaired, as defined in section 42-4-1301 (1) (g), and use of the term shall incorporate by reference the offense described in section 42-4-1301 (1) (b).

(28) "Effective date of registration period certificate" means the month in which a fleet owner must register all fleet vehicles.

(28.5) "Electrical assisted bicycle" means a vehicle having two tandem wheels or two parallel wheels and one forward wheel, fully operable pedals, an electric motor not exceeding seven hundred fifty watts of power, and a top motor-powered speed of twenty miles per hour.

(28.7) "Electric personal assistive mobility device" or "EPAMD" means a self-balancing, nontandem two-wheeled device, designed to transport only one person, that is powered solely by an electric propulsion system producing an average power output of no more than seven hundred fifty watts.

(29) "Empty weight" means the weight of any motor vehicle or trailer or any combination thereof, including the operating body and accessories, as determined by weighing on a scale approved by the department.

(30) "Essential parts" means all integral parts and body parts, the removal, alteration, or substitution of which will tend to conceal the identity or substantially alter the appearance of the vehicle.

(31) "Established place of business" means the place actually occupied either continuously or at regular periods by a dealer or manufacturer where such dealer's or manufacturer's books and records are kept and a large share of his or her business transacted.

(32) "Explosives and hazardous materials" means any substance so defined by the code of federal regulations, title 49, chapter 1, parts 173.50 through 173.389.

(33) "Farm tractor" means every implement of husbandry designed and used primarily as a farm implement for drawing plows and mowing machines and other implements of husbandry.

(34) "Flammable liquid" means any liquid which has a flash point of seventy degrees Fahrenheit or less, as determined by a Tagliabue or equivalent closed-cup test device.

(35) "Fleet operator" means any resident who owns or leases ten or more motor vehicles, trailers, or pole trailers and who receives from the department a registration period certificate in accordance with article 3 of this title.

(36) "Fleet vehicle" means any motor vehicle, trailer, or pole trailer owned or leased by a fleet operator and registered pursuant to section 42-3-125.

(37) "Foreign vehicle" means every motor vehicle, trailer, or semitrailer which is brought into this state otherwise than in the ordinary course of business by or through a manufacturer or dealer and which has not been registered in this state.

(38) "Fullmount" means a vehicle which is mounted completely on the frame of the first vehicle or last vehicle in a saddlemount combination.

(39) "Garage" means any public building or place of business for the storage or repair of automobiles.

(39.5) "Golf car" means a self-propelled vehicle not designed primarily for operation on roadways and that has:

(a) A design speed of less than twenty miles per hour;

(b) At least three wheels in contact with the ground;

(c) An empty weight of not more than one thousand three hundred pounds; and

(d) A carrying capacity of not more than four persons.

(40) "Graduated annual specific ownership tax" means an annual tax imposed in lieu of an ad valorem tax upon the personal property required to be classified by the general assembly pursuant to the provisions of section 6 of article X of the state constitution.

(41) "Gross dollar volume" means the total contracted cost of work performed or put in place in a given county by the owner or operator of special mobile machinery.

(41.5) "Group special license plate" means a special license plate that is not a distinctive plate and is issued to a group of people because such people have a common interest or affinity.

(41.7) "Habitual user" shall incorporate by reference the offense described in section 42-4-1301 (1) (c).

(42) "High occupancy vehicle lane" means a lane designated pursuant to the provisions of section 42-4-1012 (1).

(43) "Highway" means the entire width between the boundary lines of every way publicly maintained when any part thereof is open to the use of the public for purposes of vehicular travel or the entire width of every way declared to be a public highway by any law of this state.

(43.5) "Immediate family" means a person who is related by blood, marriage, or adoption.

(44) (a) On and after July 1, 2000, "implement of husbandry" means every vehicle that is designed, adapted, or used for agricultural purposes. It also includes equipment used solely for the application of liquid, gaseous, and dry fertilizers. Transportation of fertilizer, in or on the equipment used for its application, shall be deemed a part of application if it is incidental to such application. It also includes hay balers, hay stacking equipment, combines, tillage and harvesting equipment, agricultural commodity handling equipment, and other heavy movable farm equipment primarily used on farms or in a livestock production facility and not on the highways. Trailers specially designed to move such equipment on highways shall, for the purposes of part 5 of article 4 of this title, be considered as component parts of such implements of husbandry.

(b) Effective July 1, 2013, for purposes of this section, "implements of husbandry" includes personal property valued by the county assessor as silvicultural.

(45) "Intersection" means the area embraced within the prolongation of the lateral curb lines or, if none, then the lateral boundary lines of the roadways of two highways which join one another at, or approximately at, right angles, or the area within which vehicles traveling upon different highways joining at any other angle may come in conflict. Where a highway includes two roadways thirty feet or more apart, every crossing of each roadway of such divided highway by an intersecting highway shall be regarded as a separate intersection. In the event such intersecting highway also includes two roadways thirty feet or more apart, every crossing of two roadways of such highways shall be regarded as a separate intersection. The junction of an alley with a street or highway does not constitute an intersection.

(45.5) "Kit vehicle" means a passenger-type motor vehicle assembled, by other than a licensed manufacturer, from a manufactured kit that includes a prefabricated body and chassis and is accompanied by a manufacturer's statement of origin.

(46) "Lane" means the portion of a roadway for the movement of a single line of vehicles.

(47) "Laned highway" means a highway the roadway of which is divided into two or more clearly marked lanes for vehicular traffic.

(48) "Local authorities" means every county, municipal, and other local board or body having authority to adopt local police regulations under the constitution and laws of this state.

(48.5) (a) "Low-power scooter" means a self-propelled vehicle designed primarily for use on the roadways with not more than three wheels in contact with the ground, no manual clutch, and either of the following:

(I) A cylinder capacity not exceeding fifty cubic centimeters if powered by internal combustion; or

(II) A wattage not exceeding four thousand four hundred seventy-six if powered by electricity.

(b) "Low-power scooter" shall not include a toy vehicle, bicycle, electrical assisted bicycle, wheelchair, or any device designed to assist mobility-impaired people who use pedestrian rights-of-way.

(48.6) "Low-speed electric vehicle" means a vehicle that:

(a) Is self-propelled utilizing electricity as its primary propulsion method;

(b) Has at least three wheels in contact with the ground;

(c) Does not use handlebars to steer; and

(d) Exhibits the manufacturer's compliance with 49 CFR 565 or displays a seventeen-character vehicle identification number as provided in 49 CFR 565.

(49) "Manufacturer" means any person, firm, association, corporation, or trust, whether resident or nonresident, who manufactures or assembles new and unused motor vehicles of a type required to be registered under articles 1 to 4 of this title.

(50) "Manufacturer's suggested retail price" means the retail price of such motor vehicle suggested by the manufacturer plus the retail price suggested by the manufacturer for each accessory or item of optional equipment physically attached to such vehicle prior to the sale to the retail purchaser.

(51) "Markings" means all lines, patterns, words, colors, or other devices, except signs, set into the surface of, applied upon, or attached to the pavement or curbing or to objects within or adjacent to the roadway, conforming to the state traffic control manual and officially placed for the purpose of regulating, warning, or guiding traffic.

(52) "Metal tires" means all tires the surface of which in contact with the highway is wholly or partly of metal or other hard, nonresilient material.

(52.5) "Military vehicle" means a vehicle of any size or weight that is valued for historical purposes, that was manufactured for use by any nation's armed forces, and that is maintained in a condition that represents its military design and markings.

(53) "Minor driver's license" means the license issued to a person who is at least sixteen years of age but who has not yet attained the age of twenty-one years.

(54) (Deleted by amendment, L. 2010, (HB 10-1172), ch. 320, p. 1486, § 1, effective October 1, 2010.)

(55) "Motorcycle" means a motor vehicle that uses handlebars or any other device connected to the front wheel to steer and that is designed to travel on not more than three wheels in contact with the ground; except that the term does not include a farm tractor, low-speed electric vehicle, or low-power scooter.

(56) (Deleted by amendment, L. 2009, (HB 09-1026), ch. 281, p. 1260, § 22, effective October 1, 2009.)

(57) "Motor home" means a vehicle designed to provide temporary living quarters and which is built into, as an integral part of or a permanent attachment to, a motor vehicle chassis or van.

(58) "Motor vehicle" means any self-propelled vehicle that is designed primarily for travel on the public highways and that is generally and commonly used to transport persons and property over the public highways or a low-speed electric vehicle; except that the term does not include low-power scooters, wheelchairs, or vehicles moved solely by human power. For the purposes of the offenses described in sections 42-2-128, 42-4-1301, 42-4-1301.1, and 42-4-1401 for farm tractors and off-highway vehicles, as defined in section 33-14.5-101 (3), C.R.S., operated on streets and highways, "motor vehicle" includes a farm tractor or an off-highway vehicle that is not otherwise classified as a motor vehicle. For the purposes of sections 42-2-127, 42-2-127.7, 42-2-128, 42-2-138, 42-2-206, 42-4-1301, and 42-4-1301.1, "motor vehicle" includes a low-power scooter.

(59) (Deleted by amendment, L. 2009, (HB 09-1026), ch. 281, p. 1260, § 22, effective October 1, 2009.)

(60) "Mounted equipment" means any item weighing more than five hundred pounds that is permanently mounted on a vehicle, including mounting by means such as welding or bolting the equipment to a vehicle.

(60.3) "Multipurpose trailer" means a wheeled vehicle, without motive power, that is designed to be drawn by a motor vehicle over the public highways. A "multipurpose trailer" is generally and commonly used for temporary living or sleeping accommodation and transporting property wholly upon its own structure and is registered as a vehicle.

(60.5) (Deleted by amendment, L. 2009, (SB 09-075), ch. 418, p. 2320, § 4, effective August 5, 2009.)

(61) "Noncommercial or recreational vehicle" means a truck, or unladen truck tractor, operated singly or in combination with a trailer or utility trailer or a motor home, which truck, or unladen truck tractor, or motor home is used exclusively for personal pleasure, enjoyment, other recreational purposes, or personal or family transportation of the owner, lessee, or occupant and is not used to transport cargo or passengers for profit, hire, or otherwise to further the purposes of a business or commercial enterprise.

(62) "Nonresident" means every person who is not a resident of this state.

(63) "Off-highway vehicle" shall have the same meaning as set forth in section 33-14.5-101 (3), C.R.S.

(64) "Official traffic control devices" means all signs, signals, markings, and devices, not inconsistent with this title, placed or displayed by authority of a public body or official having jurisdiction, for the purpose of regulating, warning, or guiding traffic.

(65) "Official traffic control signal" means any device, whether manually, electrically, or mechanically operated, by which traffic is alternately directed to stop and to proceed.

(66) "Owner" means a person who holds the legal title of a vehicle; or, if a vehicle is the subject of an agreement for the conditional sale or lease thereof with the right of purchase upon performance of the conditions stated in the agreement and with an immediate right of possession vested in the conditional vendee or lessee or if a mortgagor of a vehicle is entitled to possession, then such conditional vendee or lessee or mortgagor shall be deemed the owner for the purpose of articles 1 to 4 of this title. The term also includes parties otherwise having lawful use or control or the right to use or control a vehicle for a period of thirty days or more.

(67) "Park" or "parking" means the standing of a vehicle, whether occupied or not, other than very briefly for the purpose of and while actually engaged in loading or unloading property or passengers.

(68) "Pedestrian" means any person afoot or any person using a wheelchair.

(68.5) "Persistent drunk driver" means any person who has been convicted of or had his or her driver's license revoked for two or more alcohol-related driving violations; who continues to drive after a driver's license or driving privilege restraint has been imposed for one or more alcohol-related driving offenses; or who drives a motor vehicle while the amount of alcohol in such person's blood, as shown by analysis of the person's blood or breath, was 0.17 or more grams of alcohol per one hundred milliliters of blood or 0.17 or more grams of alcohol per two hundred ten liters of breath at the time of driving or within two hours after driving. Nothing in this subsection (68.5) shall be interpreted to affect the penalties imposed under this title for multiple alcohol- or drug-related driving offenses, including, but not limited to, penalties imposed for violations under sections 42-2-125 (1) (g) and (1) (i) and 42-2-202 (2).

(69) "Person" means a natural person, estate, trust, firm, copartnership, association, corporation, or business entity.

(70) "Pneumatic tires" means all tires inflated with compressed air.

(71) "Pole", "pipe trailer", or "dolly" means every vehicle of the trailer type having one or more axles not more than forty-eight inches

apart and two or more wheels used in connection with a motor vehicle solely for the purpose of transporting poles or pipes and connected with the towing vehicle both by chain, rope, or cable and by the load without any part of the weight of said dolly resting upon the towing vehicle. All the registration provisions of articles 1 to 4 of this title shall apply to every pole, pipe trailer, or dolly.

(72) "Police officer" means every officer authorized to direct or regulate traffic or to make arrests for violations of traffic regulations.

(72.2) "Power takeoff equipment" means equipment that is attached to a motor vehicle and is powered by the motor that powers the locomotion of the motor vehicle.

(72.5) "Primary user" means an organization that collects bulk data for the purpose of in-house business use.

(72.7) "Principal office" means the office in this state designated by a fleet owner as its principal place of business.

(73) "Private road" or "driveway" means every road or driveway not open to the use of the public for purposes of vehicular travel.

(74) Repealed.

(75) "Railroad sign or signal" means any sign, signal, or device erected by authority of a public body or official or by a railroad and intended to give notice of the presence of railroad tracks or the approach of a railroad train.

(76) "Reciprocal agreement" or "reciprocity" means an agreement among two or more states, provinces, or other jurisdictions for coordinated, shared, or mutual enforcement or administration of laws relating to the registration, operation, or taxation of vehicles and other personal property in interstate commerce. The term includes without limitation the "international registration plan" and any successor agreement providing for the apportionment, among participating jurisdictions, of vehicle registration fees or taxes.

(77) "Reconstructed vehicle" means any vehicle which has been assembled or constructed largely by means of essential parts, new or used, derived from other vehicles or makes of vehicles of various names, models, and types or which, if originally otherwise constructed, has been materially altered by the removal of essential parts or by the addition or substitution of essential parts, new or used, derived from other vehicles or makes of vehicles.

(78) "Registration period" or "registration year" means any consecutive twelve-month period.

(79) "Registration period certificate" means the document issued by the department to a fleet owner, upon application of a fleet owner, which states the month in which registration is required for all motor vehicles owned by the fleet owner.

(80) "Residence district" means the territory contiguous to and including a highway not comprising a business district when the frontage on such highway for a distance of three hundred feet or more is mainly occupied by dwellings or by dwellings and buildings in use for business.

(81) "Resident" means any person who owns or operates any business in this state or any person who has resided within this state continuously for a period of ninety days or has obtained gainful employment within this state, whichever shall occur first.

(82) "Right-of-way" means the right of one vehicle operator or pedestrian to proceed in a lawful manner in preference to another vehicle operator or pedestrian approaching under such circumstances of direction, speed, and proximity as to give rise to danger of collision unless one grants precedence to the other.

(83) "Road" means any highway.

(84) "Road tractor" means every motor vehicle designed and used for drawing other vehicles and not so constructed as to carry any load thereon independently or any part of the weight of a vehicle or load so drawn.

(85) "Roadway" means that portion of a highway improved, designed, or ordinarily used for vehicular travel, exclusive of the sidewalk, berm, or shoulder even though such sidewalk, berm, or shoulder is used by persons riding bicycles or other human-powered vehicles and exclusive of that portion of a highway designated for exclusive use as a bicycle path or reserved for the exclusive use of bicycles, human-powered vehicles, or pedestrians. In the event that a highway includes two or more separate roadways, "roadway" refers to any such roadway separately but not to all such roadways collectively.

(86) "Saddlemount combination" means a combination of vehicles in which a truck or laden or unladen truck tractor tows one or more additional trucks or laden or unladen truck tractors and in which each such towed truck or laden or unladen truck tractor is connected by a saddle to the frame or fifth wheel of the vehicle immediately in front of such truck or laden or unladen truck tractor. For the purposes of this subsection (86), "saddle" means a mechanism which connects the front axle of a towed vehicle to the frame or fifth wheel of a vehicle immediately in front of such towed vehicle and which functions like a fifth wheel kingpin connection. A saddlemount combination may include one fullmount.

(87) "Safety zone" means the area or space officially set aside within a highway for the exclusive use of pedestrians and which is so plainly marked or indicated by proper signs as to be plainly visible at all times while set apart as a safety zone.

(88) "School bus" means a motor vehicle that is designed and used specifically for the transportation of school children to or from a public or private school or a school-related activity, whether the activity occurs within or without the territorial limits of any district and whether or not the activity occurs during school hours. "School bus" does not include informal or intermittent arrangements, such as sharing of actual gasoline expense or participation in a car pool, for the transportation of school children to or

from a public or private school or a school-related activity.

(88.5) (a) "School vehicle" means a motor vehicle, including but not limited to a school bus, that is owned by or under contract to a public or private school and operated for the transportation of school children to or from school or a school-related activity.

(b) "School vehicle" does not include:

(I) Informal or intermittent arrangements, such as sharing of actual gasoline expense or participation in a car pool, for the transportation of school children to or from a public or private school or a school-related activity; or

(II) A motor vehicle that is owned by or under contract to a child care center, as defined in section 26-6-102 (1.5), C.R.S., and that is used for the transportation of children who are served by the child care center.

(89) "Semitrailer" means any wheeled vehicle, without motor power, designed to be used in conjunction with a laden or unladen truck tractor so that some part of its own weight and that of its cargo load rests upon or is carried by such laden or unladen truck tractor and that is generally and commonly used to carry and transport property over the public highways.

(90) "Sidewalk" means that portion of a street between the curb lines or the lateral lines of a roadway and the adjacent property lines intended for the use of pedestrians.

(91) "Snowplow" means any vehicle originally designed for highway snow and ice removal or control or subsequently adapted for such purposes which is operated by or for the state of Colorado or any political subdivision thereof.

(92) "Solid rubber tires" means every tire made of rubber other than a pneumatic tire.

(93) "Specially constructed vehicle" means any vehicle which has not been originally constructed under a distinctive name, make, model, or type by a generally recognized manufacturer of vehicles.

(93.5) (a) "Special mobile machinery" means machinery that is pulled, hauled, or driven over a highway and is either:

(I) A vehicle or equipment that is not designed primarily for the transportation of persons or cargo over the public highways; or

(II) A motor vehicle that may have been originally designed for the transportation of persons or cargo over the public highways, and has been redesigned or modified by the addition of mounted equipment or machinery, and is only incidentally operated or moved over the public highways.

(b) "Special mobile machinery" includes vehicles commonly used in the construction, maintenance, and repair of roadways, the drilling of wells, and the digging of ditches.

(94) "Stand" or "standing" means the halting of a vehicle, whether occupied or not, other than momentarily for the purpose of and while actually engaged in receiving or discharging passengers.

(95) "State" means a state, territory, organized or unorganized, or district of the United States.

(96) "State motor vehicle licensing agency" means the department of revenue.

(97) "State traffic control manual" means the most recent edition of the "Manual on Uniform Traffic Control Devices for Streets and Highways", including any supplement thereto, as adopted by the transportation commission.

(98) "Steam and electric trains" includes:

(a) "Railroad", which means a carrier of persons or property upon cars, other than street cars, operated upon stationary rails;

(b) "Railroad train", which means a steam engine, electric, or other motor, with or without cars coupled thereto, operated upon rails, except streetcars;

(c) "Streetcar", which means a car other than a railroad train for transporting persons or property upon rails principally within a municipality.

(99) "Stinger-steered" means a semitrailer combination configuration wherein the fifth wheel is located on a drop frame located behind and below the rearmost axle of the power unit.

(100) "Stop" or "stopping" means, when prohibited, any halting, even momentarily, of a vehicle, whether occupied or not, except when necessary to avoid conflict with other traffic or in compliance with the directions of a police officer or official traffic control device.

(101) "Stop line" or "limit line" means a line which indicates where drivers shall stop when directed by an official traffic control device or a police officer.

(101.5) "Street rod vehicle" means a vehicle manufactured in 1948 or earlier with a body design that has been modified for safe road use.

(102) "Supervisor" means the executive director of the department of revenue or head of a group, division, or subordinate department appointed by the executive director in accordance with article 35 of title 24, C.R.S.

(102.5) "Surge brakes" means a system whereby the brakes of a trailer are actuated as a result of the forward pressure of the trailer against the tow vehicle during deceleration.

(102.7) "Temporary special event license plate" means a special license plate valid for a limited time period that is issued to a person or group of people in connection with a special event. "Temporary special event license plate" does not mean a special plate for the purposes of section 42-3-207.

(103) "Through highway" means every highway or portion thereof on which vehicular traffic is given preferential right-of-way and at the entrances to which other vehicular traffic from intersecting highways is required by law to yield the right-of-way to vehicles on such through highway in obedience to a stop sign, yield sign, or other official traffic control device when such signs or devices are erected as provided by law.

(103.5) (a) "Toy vehicle" means any vehicle that has wheels and is not designed for use on public highways or for off-road use.

(b) "Toy vehicle" includes, but is not limited to, gas-powered or electric-powered vehicles commonly known as mini bikes, "pocket" bikes, kamikaze boards, go-peds, and stand-up scooters.

(c) "Toy vehicle" does not include off-highway vehicles or snowmobiles.

(104) "Traffic" means pedestrians, ridden or herded animals, and vehicles, streetcars, and other conveyances either singly or together while using any highway for the purposes of travel.

(105) "Trailer" means any wheeled vehicle, without motive power, which is designed to be drawn by a motor vehicle and to carry its cargo load wholly upon its own structure and that is generally and commonly used to carry and transport property over the public highways. The term includes, but is not limited to, multi-purpose trailers as defined in subsection (60.3) of this section.

(106) (a) "Trailer coach" means a wheeled vehicle having an overall length, excluding towing gear and bumpers, of not less than twenty-six feet, without motive power, that is designed and generally and commonly used for occupancy by persons for residential purposes, in temporary locations, and that may occasionally be drawn over the public highways by a motor vehicle and is licensed as a vehicle.

(b) "Manufactured home" means any preconstructed building unit or combination of preconstructed building units, without motive power, where such unit or units are manufactured in a factory or at a location other than the residential site of the completed home, which is designed and commonly used for occupancy by persons for residential purposes, in either temporary or permanent locations, and which unit or units are not licensed as a vehicle.

(107) "Transporter" means every person engaged in the business of delivering vehicles of a type required to be registered under articles 1 to 4 of this title from a manufacturing, assembling, or distributing plant to dealers or sales agents of a manufacturer.

(108) "Truck" means any motor vehicle equipped with a body designed to carry property and which is generally and commonly used to carry and transport property over the public highways.

(109) "Truck tractor - laden" or "laden truck tractor" means any motor vehicle carrying cargo that is generally and commonly designed and used to draw, and is drawing, a semitrailer or trailer and its cargo load over the public highways.

(109.5) "Truck tractor - unladen" or "unladen truck tractor" means any motor vehicle not carrying cargo that is generally used to draw a semitrailer or trailer and its cargo load over the public highways.

(109.7) "UDD" means underage drinking and driving, and use of the term shall incorporate by reference the offense described in section 42-4-1301 (2) (a.5).

(110) "Used vehicle" means every motor vehicle which has been sold, bargained for, exchanged, or given away, or has had the title transferred from the person who first acquired it from the manufacturer or importer, and has been so used as to have become what is commonly known as "secondhand" within the ordinary meaning thereof.

(111) "Utility trailer" means any wheeled vehicle weighing two thousand pounds or less, without motive power, which is designed to be drawn by a motor vehicle and which is generally and commonly used to carry and transport personal effects, articles of household furniture, loads of trash and rubbish, or not to exceed two horses over the public highways.

(112) "Vehicle" means a device that is capable of moving itself, or of being moved, from place to place upon wheels or endless tracks. "Vehicle" includes, without limitation, a bicycle, electrical assisted bicycle, or EPAMD, but does not include a wheelchair, off-highway vehicle, snowmobile, farm tractor, or implement of husbandry designed primarily or exclusively for use and used in agricultural operations or any device moved exclusively over stationary rails or tracks or designed to move primarily through the air.

(112.5) "Vendor" means an organization that collects bulk data for the purpose of reselling the data.

(113) "Wheelchair" means a motorized or nonmotorized wheeled device designed for use by a person with a physical disability.

PART 2

ADMINISTRATION

42-1-201. Administration - supervisor. The executive director of the department is empowered to administer and enforce the provisions of articles 1 to 4 of this title. There shall be at least one supervisor who shall be employed under section 13 of article XII of the state constitution.

42-1-202. Have charge of all divisions. The supervisor shall have charge of all divisions as provided in articles 1 to 4 of this title to carry out the purposes of said articles.

42-1-203. Executive director to cooperate with others - local compliance required. (1) The executive director of the department shall coordinate motor vehicle enforcement throughout the state by cooperating with other officials connected with traffic enforcement, as may appear to the executive director as advantageous. The executive director shall bring to the attention of proper officials information and statistics in connection with enforcement and shall urge the desirability and necessity of uniformity. It is the executive director's duty to cooperate and confer with officials of other states charged with like duties, and the executive director is authorized to attend conferences called among said officials, and the executive director's necessary traveling expenses in attending said meetings shall be paid as are other traveling expenses of said department.

(2) In the coordination of motor vehicle law enforcement reporting throughout the state, the executive director, upon the failure of any local jurisdiction to take the necessary steps to achieve uniformity, may order such local jurisdiction to come into conformity with state coordination plans, including all information and statistics relating thereto.

42-1-204. Uniform rules and regulations. The executive director of the department has the power to make uniform rules and regulations not inconsistent with articles 1 to 4 of this title and to enforce the same.

42-1-205. Record of official acts - seal. The executive director of the department shall keep a record of all the executive director's official acts and shall preserve a copy of all decisions, rules, and orders made by the executive director, and the executive director shall adopt an official seal for the department. Copies of any act, rule, order, or decision made by the executive director or of any paper or papers filed in the executive director's office may be authenticated by the executive director or the executive director's deputy under said seal at a cost not exceeding one dollar for each authentication and when so authenticated shall be evidence equally with and in like manner as the originals and may be received by the courts of this state as evidence of the contents.

42-1-206. Records open to inspection - furnishing of copies. (1) (a) Except as provided in part 2 of article 72 of title 24, C.R.S., and subsection (6) of this section, all records made public records by any provision of this title and kept in the office of the department shall be open to inspection by the public during business hours under such reasonable rules relating thereto as the executive director of the department may prescribe.

(b) (I) For purposes of subsections (1) to (3) and (5) of this section, "law" shall mean the federal "Driver's Privacy Protection Act of 1994", 18 U.S.C. sec. 2721 et seq., the federal "Fair Credit Reporting Act", 15 U.S.C. sec. 1681 et seq., part 2 of article 72 of title 24, C.R.S., and this section. The department shall prepare a requestor release form and make such form available to the department's authorized agents. The form shall include the following:

(A) A statement indicating whether the requestor will use the motor vehicle or driver records or transfer or resell such records to another person for any purpose prohibited by law;

(B) A warning that any person using motor vehicle or driver records, or obtaining, reselling, or transferring the same, for purposes prohibited by law may be subject to civil penalties under federal and state law; and

(C) An affidavit of intended use that states that such requestor shall not obtain, use, resell, or transfer the information for any purpose prohibited by law.

(II) The department or an authorized agent shall require any person, other than a person in interest as defined in section 24-72-202 (4), C.R.S., or a federal, state, or local government agency carrying out its official functions, requesting inspection of a motor vehicle or driver record from the department or agent individually or in bulk, to sign a requestor release form and, under penalty of perjury, an affidavit of intended use prior to providing the record to such person. The department or authorized agent may allow inspection of motor vehicle and driver records only as authorized under section 24-72-204 (7), C.R.S.

(2) (a) Except as provided in subsection (6) of this section, upon written application and the payment of a fee of two dollars and twenty cents per copy, or a record search for each copy requested, the department shall furnish to any person a photostatic copy of any specified record or accident report specifically made a public record by any provision of this title and shall, for the additional fee of fifty cents per certification, if requested, certify the same. Fees collected under this subsection (2) shall be used to defray the expenses of providing such copies; except that ten cents of each fee collected by the authorized agent shall be credited to the special purpose account established under section 42-1-211 and the entire fee for vehicle and manufactured home records, if collected directly by the department, shall be credited to the special purpose account established under section 42-1-211.

(b) An authorized agent of the department shall not provide the service of furnishing copies of certain records to members of the public if copies of such records are available to the public directly from the department.

(3) Repealed. / (Deleted by amendment, L. 99, p. 345, § 3, effective April 16, 1999.)

(3.5) (a) The department shall not sell, permit the sale of, or otherwise release to anyone other than the person in interest any photograph, electronically stored photograph, digitized image, fingerprint, or social security number filed with, maintained by, or prepared by the department of revenue pursuant to section 42-2-121 (2) (c) (I) (F) or (2) (c) (I) (H).

(b) Nothing in this subsection (3.5) shall prevent the department from sharing any information with a criminal justice agency as defined in section 24-72-302 (3), C.R.S.

(c) (Deleted by amendment, L. 2000, p. 1340, § 2, effective May 30, 2000.)

(d) The department of revenue shall make every effort to retrieve all copies of photographs, electronically stored photographs, or digitized images that may have been sold by the department under subsection (3), as said subsection existed prior to its repeal in 1999, of this section.

(3.7) (a) The department shall establish a system to allow bulk electronic transfer of information to primary users and vendors who are permitted to receive such information pursuant to section 24-72-204 (7), C.R.S. Bulk transfers to vendors shall be limited strictly to vendors who transfer or resell such information for purposes permitted by law. Such information shall consist of the information contained in a driver's license application under section 42-2-107, a driver's license renewal application under section 42-2-118, a duplicate driver's license application under section 42-2-117, a commercial driver's license application under section 42-2-403, an identification card application under section 42-2-302, a motor vehicle title application under section 42-6-116, a motor vehicle registration application under section 42-3-113, or other official record or document maintained by the department under section 42-2-121.

(b) The department shall promulgate rules governing annual contracts with primary users and vendors for the purpose of establishing bulk electronic transfer of information to primary users and vendors pursuant to an annual affidavit and release form and shall require that the contracts include, at a minimum:

(I) A provision for a reasonable fee that encompasses all direct costs of the department related to the bulk electronic transfer of information to that primary user or vendor;

(II) A provision that prohibits any use not otherwise authorized by law;

(III) A provision that requires the primary user or vendor to specify the designated use and recipients of the information; and

(IV) A provision that prohibits any resale or transfer of the information other than as specified in the contract or in a manner that is prohibited by law.

(c) Repealed.

(d) The department shall provide bulk electronic transfer in accordance with the limitations and restrictions regarding release of information in this section as well as section 24-72-204, C.R.S. The department shall not release photographs, electronically stored photographs, digitized images, or fingerprints filed with, maintained by, or prepared by the department through bulk electronic transfer.

(e) The department shall forward all fees collected pursuant to contracts entered into with primary users or vendors pursuant to this subsection (3.7) to the state treasurer, who shall credit the same to the highway users tax fund. The general assembly shall make annual appropriations from the general fund for the costs associated with the administration of this subsection (3.7).

(f) The executive director of the department shall promulgate rules as are consistent with current law and necessary to carry out the provisions of this subsection (3.7).

(4) Notwithstanding the amount specified for any fee in this section, the executive director of the department by rule or as otherwise provided by law may reduce the amount of one or more of the fees if necessary pursuant to section 24-75-402 (3), C.R.S., to reduce the uncommitted reserves of the fund to which all or any portion of one or more of the fees is credited. After the uncommitted reserves of the fund are sufficiently reduced, the executive director of the department by rule or as otherwise provided by law may increase the amount of one or more of the fees as provided in section 24-75-402 (4), C.R.S.

(5) Any person who willfully and knowingly obtains, resells, transfers, or uses information in violation of law shall be liable to any injured party for treble damages, reasonable attorney fees, and costs.

(6) The record of conviction and actions taken by the department for violating section 18-13-122 or 12-47-901 (1) (c), C.R.S., held by the department of revenue, shall not be a public record after the period of revocation imposed under such sections has been concluded; except that this subsection (6) shall not prevent the department from sharing such information with a criminal justice agency as defined in section 24-72-302 (3), C.R.S.

42-1-207. No supplies for private purposes - penalty. No officer or employee at any time shall use for private or pleasure purposes any of the equipment or supplies furnished for the discharge of such officer or employee's duties. The use of such equipment for private or personal use is declared to be a misdemeanor, and, upon conviction thereof, the violator shall be punished by a fine of not more than three hundred dollars, or by imprisonment in the county jail for not more than six months, or by both such fine and imprisonment and by dismissal from office.

42-1-208. Information on accidents - published. The department shall receive accident reports required to be made by law and shall tabulate and analyze such reports and publish annually, or at more frequent intervals, statistical information based thereon as to the number, cause, and location of highway accidents. The statistical information shall be issued in accordance with the provisions of section 24-1-136, C.R.S.

42-1-209. Copies of law published. (Repealed)

42-1-210. County clerk and recorders and manager of revenue or other appointed official as agents - legislative declaration - fee. (1) (a) The county clerk and recorder in each county in the state of Colorado, the clerk and recorder in the city and county of Broomfield, and, in the city and county of Denver, the manager of revenue or such other official of the city and county of Denver as may be appointed by the mayor to perform functions related to the registration of motor vehicles are hereby designated as the authorized agents of the department for the administration of the provisions of articles 3 and 6 of this title relating to registrations of motor vehicles in such counties; and for the enforcement of the provisions of section 42-6-139 relating to the registering and titling of motor vehicles in such counties; and for the enforcement of the provisions of section 38-29-120, C.R.S., relating to the titling of manufactured homes; but any such authorized agent in a county has the power to appoint and employ such motor vehicle registration and license clerks as are actually necessary in the issuance of motor vehicle licenses and shall retain for the purpose of defraying such expenses, including mailing, a sum equal to four dollars per paid motor vehicle registration and registration requiring a metallic plate, plates, individual temporary registration number plates, or validation tab or sticker as provided in section 42-3-201. This fee of four dollars shall apply to every registration of a motor vehicle that is designed primarily to be operated or drawn on any highway of this state, except such vehicles as are specifically exempted from payment of any registration fee by the provisions of article 3 of this title, and shall be in addition to the annual registration fee prescribed by law for such vehicle. The fee of four dollars, when collected by the department, shall be credited to the same fund as registration fees collected by the department. The county clerk and recorders, the clerk and recorder in the city and county of Broomfield, and the manager of revenue or such other official of the city and county of Denver as may be appointed by the mayor to perform functions related to the registration of motor vehicles in the city and county of Denver so designated as the authorized agents of the department, as provided in this section, shall serve as such authorized agents under the provisions of this part 2 without additional remuneration or fees, except as otherwise provided in articles 1 to 6 of this title.

(b) The fee established by paragraph (a) of this subsection (1) does not apply to a shipping and handling fee for the mailing of a license plate pursuant to section 42-3-105 (1) (a).

(2) The general assembly hereby finds that, since it is the government that requires citizens to register, license, and undertake other actions concerning their motor vehicles, it is thus the duty of government to provide convenient and easily accessible motor vehicle services to the public.

42-1-211. Colorado state titling and registration system. (1) The department is hereby authorized to coordinate the management of a statewide distributive data processing system, which shall be known as the Colorado state titling and registration system. This system is to provide the necessary data processing equipment, software, and support and training to:

(a) Aid the authorized agents of the department in processing motor vehicle registration and title documents; and

(b) Establish, operate, and maintain a telecommunications network that provides access from the offices of county clerk and recorders and the clerk and recorder in the city and county of Broomfield to the master list of registered electors maintained pursuant to sections 1-2-301 and 1-2-302, C.R.S., for those county clerks and recorders that do not yet have access to the master list on the internet pursuant to section 1-2-301 (4) (b), C.R.S. Subject to annual appropriation, the department of state shall reimburse the department of revenue for the reasonable direct and indirect costs of providing such service. The department of revenue and the department of state shall enter into a memorandum of understanding that establishes the method of calculating and verifying such costs and that provides for a proportionate reduction in charges as counties terminate their use of the distributive data processing system and begin accessing the master list on the internet pursuant to section 1-2-301 (4) (b), C.R.S. The memorandum of understanding may also allow the department of revenue to access the master list on the internet subject to reimbursement as may be agreed by the two departments.

(1.5) (a) In accordance with the requirements of section 1-2-302 (6), C.R.S., the department of revenue and the department of state shall allow for the exchange of information on residence addresses, signatures, and party affiliation between the systems used by the department of revenue, the master list of registered electors maintained by the department of state, and, no later than January 1, 2006, the computerized statewide voter registration list created in section 1-2-301 (1), C.R.S., for the purpose of updating information in these systems.

(b) For purposes of this section, the systems used by the department of revenue shall include, but not be limited to, the Colorado state titling and registration system, the driver's license database, the motor vehicle registration database, the motorist insurance database, and the state income tax information systems.

(c) The executive director of the department of revenue, as the official responsible for the division of motor vehicles, shall enter into an agreement with the federal commissioner of social security for the purpose of verifying applicable information in accordance with the requirements of section 303 (a) (5) (B) (ii) of the federal "Help America Vote Act of 2002", Pub.L. 107-252.

(1.7) No later than July 1, 2011, the department of revenue shall make available on the department's official web site a link to the secretary of state's official web site, whereby a person may change his or her address information on file with the secretary of state for voter registration purposes.

(2) There is hereby created a special purpose account in the highway users tax fund, which shall be known as the Colorado state titling and registration account, for the purpose of providing funds for the development and operation of the Colorado state titling and registration system, including operations performed under article 6 of this title. Moneys received from the fees imposed by section 38-29-138 (1), (2), (4), and (5), C.R.S., and sections 42-1-206 (2) (a), 42-3-107 (22), 42-3-213 (1) (b), and 42-6-137 (1), (2), (4), (5), and (6), as well as any moneys received through gifts, grants, and donations to the account from private or public sources for the purposes of this section shall be credited to the special purpose account in accordance with the provisions of section 38-29-139, C.R.S., and sections 42-1-206 (2) (a), 42-3-107 (22), 42-3-213 (1) (b), and 42-6-138. Any interest earned on moneys credited to the special purpose account shall be credited to and used for the same purpose as other moneys in said account. The general assembly shall appropriate annually the moneys in the special purpose account for the purposes of this subsection (2). Any unexpended and unencumbered moneys remaining in the account at the end of any fiscal year shall remain in the account and shall not be transferred to the general fund or any other fund.

(3) The department is hereby authorized to transfer moneys not otherwise expended from funds appropriated to the department for the fiscal year commencing July 1, 1983, to the special purpose account. Any moneys transferred shall be remitted back to the department after sufficient moneys have accrued in the special purpose account. The sum transferred shall not exceed the amount authorized to be appropriated from such special purpose account for the fiscal year commencing July 1, 1983.

(4) (a) There is hereby created the Colorado state titling and registration system advisory committee comprised of seven authorized agents who must be county clerk and recorders, the clerk and recorder in the city and county of Broomfield, or the manager of revenue for the city and county of Denver or such other official of the city and county of Denver as may be appointed by the mayor to perform functions related to the registration of motor vehicles, and shall be appointed by the executive director of the department. The committee shall:

(I) Assist in the development of annual operational plans and budget proposals regarding the Colorado state titling and registration system and the special purpose account;

(II) Give final approval of all plans for the development and operation of the Colorado state titling and registration system and the annual budget and any supplemental budget requests funded by the special purpose account; and

(III) Make presentations with the department to the appropriate legislative committees regarding the use of funds in the special purpose account.

(b) Repealed.

(5) The department and the authorized agents' advisory committee shall develop procedures and provide a formula for the reimbursement of expenditures made by any county that has a data processing system for the registration and titling of motor vehicles. Such reimbursement shall not commence until July 1, 1984, and shall not exceed an amount that would be required to establish and maintain such system as if it were a component of the Colorado state titling and registration system established pursuant to this section.

(6) After July 1, 1983, all counties, except those operating data processing systems for motor vehicle registration and titling on such date or having a data processing system on such date which will be operational for such registration and titling purposes by January 1, 1984, shall utilize the data processing system established pursuant to this section.

(7) (Deleted by amendment, L. 2001, p. 815, § 3, effective July 1, 2001.)

(8) Repealed.

42-1-212. Consolidated data processing system - voter registration. (Repealed)

42-1-213. Commission of county clerk and recorders and manager of revenue or other appointed official. County clerk and recorders, and the manager of revenue in the city and county of Denver or such other official of the city and county of Denver as may be appointed by the mayor to perform functions related to the registration of motor vehicles, are authorized to retain fifty cents out of the moneys collected by them on each specific ownership tax, which fifty cents shall be the only fee allowed county clerk and recorders, and the manager of revenue in the city and county of Denver or such other official of the city and county of Denver as may be appointed by the mayor to perform functions related to the registration of motor vehicles, for collecting specific ownership taxes and issuing receipts therefor. In counties of the fifth class the sums so retained by the county clerk and recorder shall be used in defraying the necessary expenses in connection with the collection and administration of specific ownership taxes as directed by articles 1 to 4 of this title, but the manager of revenue in the city and county of Denver or such other official of the city and county of Denver as may be appointed by the mayor to perform functions related to the registration of motor vehicles and the county clerk and recorders in all other counties above the fifth class shall deposit in the general fund of said city and county, or of said county, all such sums so retained under this section, and the necessary costs of said collection and administration shall be paid by regular warrant of said city and county, or county, upon voucher duly submitted and approved.

42-1-214. Duties of county clerk and recorders. Every county clerk and recorder or other person designated as an authorized agent of the department for the administration of the provisions of articles 1 to 4 (except part 3 of article 2) of this title, on or before the fifteenth day of each calendar month, shall transmit to the department all fees and moneys collected by such agent under the provisions of said articles during the preceding calendar month, except such sums as are by said articles specifically authorized to be retained by said county clerk and recorder, together with a complete report of all vehicles registered and all licenses issued in said county during said previous month, such reports to be made on blank report sheets to be furnished free by the department. The county clerk and recorders or other authorized agents shall deposit weekly all moneys received in the administration of any motor vehicle license law with the county treasurers of their respective counties and take a receipt therefor, said moneys to be kept in a separate fund by said county treasurers, and the county clerk and recorders or other authorized agents shall not be held liable for the safekeeping of such funds after so depositing them. Said county treasurers shall accept all moneys tendered to them by the county clerk and recorders or authorized agents for deposit as provided in this section. On or before the fifteenth day of each calendar month, the county clerk and recorders or other authorized agents of the department shall send, together with their monthly report to the department, a warrant drawn on the county treasurer of their county, payable to the department on demand, covering the amount of such funds that may have been deposited with the county treasurer the previous month, and the county treasurer shall pay such warrant on demand and presentation of same by the legal holders thereof.

42-1-215. Oaths. The executive director of the department, the deputy director of the department, the supervisor, and the authorized agents of the department are empowered to administer oaths or affirmations as provided in articles 1 to 4 of this title.

42-1-216. Destruction of obsolete records. The department is empowered to destroy or otherwise dispose of all obsolete motor and other vehicle records, number plates, and badges after the same have been in its possession for twelve calendar months; but all records of accidents must be preserved by the department for a period of six years.

42-1-217. Disposition of fines and surcharges. (1) All judges, clerks of a court of record, or other officers imposing or receiving fines, penalties, or forfeitures, except those moneys received pursuant to sections 42-4-313 (3), 42-4-413, 42-4-1409, 42-4-1701 (5) (a), 42-8-105, and 42-8-106, collected pursuant to or as a result of a conviction of any persons for a violation of articles 1 to 4 (except part 3 of article 2) of this title, shall transmit, within ten days after the date of receipt of any such fine, penalty, or forfeiture, all such moneys so collected in the following manner:

(a) The aggregate amount of such fines, penalties, or forfeitures, except for a violation of section 42-4-1301 or 42-4-237, shall be transmitted to the state treasurer, credited to the highway users tax fund, and allocated and expended as specified in section 43-4-205 (5.5) (a), C.R.S.

(b) Fifty percent of any fine, penalty, or forfeiture for a violation of section 42-4-1301 occurring within the corporate limits of a city or town shall be transmitted to the treasurer or chief financial officer of said city or town, and the remaining fifty percent shall be transmitted to the state treasurer, credited to the highway users tax fund, and allocated and expended as specified in section 43-4-205 (5.5) (a), C.R.S.; except that twenty-five percent of any fine, penalty, or forfeiture for a violation of section 42-4-1301 occurring on a state or federal highway shall be transmitted to the treasurer or chief financial officer of said city or town, and the remaining seventy-five percent shall be transmitted to the state treasurer, credited to the highway users tax fund, and allocated and expended as specified in section 43-4-205 (5.5) (a), C.R.S.

(c) Any other provision of law notwithstanding, all moneys collected pursuant to section 42-4-1301.3 shall be transmitted to the state treasurer to be credited to the account of the alcohol and drug driving safety program fund.

(d) Fifty percent of any fine, penalty, or forfeiture for a violation of section 42-4-1301 occurring outside the corporate limits of a city or town shall be transmitted to the treasurer of the county in which the city or town is located, and the remaining fifty percent shall be transmitted to the state treasurer, credited to the highway users tax fund, and allocated and expended as specified in section 43-4-205 (5.5) (a), C.R.S.; except that twenty-five percent of any fine, penalty, or forfeiture for a violation of section 42-4-1301 occurring on a state or federal highway shall be transmitted to the treasurer of the county in which the city or town is located, and the remaining seventy-five percent shall be transmitted to the state treasurer, credited to the highway users tax fund, and allocated and expended as specified in section 43-4-205 (5.5) (a), C.R.S.

(e) Any fine, penalty, or forfeiture collected for a violation of section 42-4-237 shall be transmitted to the treasurer of the local jurisdiction in which the violation occurred; except that:

(I) If the citing officer was an officer of the Colorado state patrol, the fine, penalty, or forfeiture shall be transmitted to the state treasurer, credited to the highway users tax fund, and allocated and expended as specified in section 43-4-205 (5.5) (a), C.R.S.; or

(II) If the violation occurred on a state or federal highway, fifty percent of the fine, penalty, or forfeiture shall be transmitted to the treasurer of the local jurisdiction in which the violation occurred and the remaining fifty percent shall be transmitted to the state treasurer, credited to the highway users tax fund, and allocated and expended as specified in section 43-4-205 (5.5) (a), C.R.S.

(2) Except for the first fifty cents of any penalty for a traffic infraction, which shall be retained by the department and used for administrative purposes, moneys collected by the department pursuant to section 42-4-1701 (5) (a) shall be transmitted to the state treasurer, who shall credit the same to the highway users tax fund for allocation and expenditure as specified in section 43-4-205 (5.5) (a), C.R.S.; except that moneys collected pursuant to section 42-4-1701 (5) (a) for a violation of section 42-4-237 shall be allocated pursuant to paragraph (e) of subsection (1) of this section.

(3) Failure, refusal, or neglect on the part of any judicial or other officer or employee to comply with the provisions of this section shall constitute misconduct in office and shall be grounds for removal therefrom.

(4) (a) All moneys collected by the department as surcharges on penalty assessments issued for violations of a class A or a class B traffic infraction or a class 1 or a class 2 misdemeanor traffic offense, pursuant to section 42-4-1701, shall be transmitted to the court administrator of the judicial district in which the offense or infraction was committed and credited fifty percent to the victims and witnesses assistance and law enforcement fund established in that judicial district and fifty percent to the crime victim compensation fund established in that judicial district.

(b) Repealed.

42-1-218. Revocations and suspensions of licenses published. (Repealed)

42-1-218.5. Electronic hearings. (1) Notwithstanding any other provision of this title to the contrary, at the discretion of the department, any hearing held by the department pursuant to this title may be conducted in whole or in part, in real time, by telephone or other electronic means.

(2) The general assembly recognizes that there is an increase in the number of hearings conducted by the department; that a licensee has the right to appear in person at a hearing; and that a licensee or a law enforcement officer may not be able to appear in person at a hearing. The general assembly therefore directs the department to consider the circumstances of the licensee when a licensee requests to appear in person, and grant the request whenever possible. The general assembly further directs the department to consider the circumstances of the licensee and the law enforcement officer when either may not be able to appear in person, and allow the appearance by electronic means whenever possible.

(3) and (4) Repealed.

42-1-219. Appropriations for administration of title. The general assembly shall make appropriations for the expenses of administration of this title.

42-1-220. Identification security fund - repeal. (1) There is hereby created a special purpose account in the highway users tax fund for the purpose of enhancing the security of drivers' licenses and identification cards. Moneys received from the fees imposed in sections 42-2-114 (2) (a) (I) (F) and 42-2-306 (1) (a) (V) shall be transmitted to the state treasurer, who shall credit the same to such special account within the highway users tax fund, to be known as the identification security fund. All interest derived from the deposit and investment of moneys in the identification security fund shall be credited to the fund. Moneys in the identification security fund shall be used, subject to appropriation by the general assembly, to cover the costs of driver's license and identification card security enhancements required by sections 42-2-106 (2) (b), 42-2-107 (1) (a) (II), 42-2-114 (1) (a), 42-2-302 (5), and 42-2-303 (3). At the end of any fiscal year, all unexpended and unencumbered moneys in the identification security fund shall remain in the fund and shall not revert to the general fund or any other fund.

(2) On or before July 1, 2008, the state auditor shall submit a report to the transportation legislation review committee, created in section 43-2-145, C.R.S., concerning the effectiveness of the security features that are part of the driver's license system in reducing the incidence of issuance of fraudulent drivers' licenses and identification cards.

(3) This section is repealed, effective July 1, 2014.

42-1-221. Fuel piracy computer reprogramming cash fund - repeal. (Repealed)

42-1-222. Motor vehicle investigations unit. The department shall establish a motor vehicle investigations unit to investigate and prevent fraud concerning the use of driver's licenses, identification cards, motor vehicle titles and registrations, and other motor vehicle documents issued by the department. Such unit shall also assist victims of identity theft by means of such documents.

42-1-223. Monitoring driving improvement schools - fund - rules. (1) The defensive driving school fund, referred to in this section as the "fund", is hereby created in the state treasury. The fund shall consist of penalty surcharges collected pursuant to section 42-4-1717 (3). The moneys in the fund shall be used to implement a program to monitor and evaluate driver improvement schools pursuant to this section.

The moneys in the fund at the end of each fiscal year shall not revert to the general fund.

(2) The department shall, in accordance with article 103 of title 24, C.R.S., contract with a private entity by July 1, 2010, to monitor and evaluate the curriculum and effectiveness of driver improvement classes required by section 42-4-1717. The private entity shall submit a report to the referring court within three months after a school has been evaluated summarizing the curriculum, location, security, quality, and effectiveness of the classes. The private entity shall also submit an abstract of such reports to the department annually.

(3) The department may promulgate rules setting standards for frequency and types of evaluations based upon the revenue received pursuant to section 42-4-1717 and the expected effectiveness of frequencies and types of evaluations.

42-1-224. Criminal history check. The department may submit fingerprints of an employee or prospective employee to the Colorado bureau of investigation to obtain a fingerprint-based criminal history record check if the employee's duties do or will provide them with access to Colorado driver's licenses and identification cards issued pursuant to article 2 of this title or personal identifying information collected or stored by the department in order to issue driver's licenses or identification cards. The department of revenue shall require all such employees hired on or after April 15, 2010, to obtain a fingerprint-based criminal history record check prior to performing their official duties, and shall require all such employees hired before April 15, 2010, to obtain a fingerprint-based criminal history record check by July 1, 2011. The department may use this information to make employment decisions concerning such employees. Upon receipt of fingerprints and payment for the costs, the Colorado bureau of investigation shall conduct a state and national fingerprint-based criminal history record check utilizing records of the Colorado bureau of investigation and the federal bureau of investigation. The department shall be the authorized agency to receive information regarding the result of the national criminal history record check. The Colorado bureau of investigation shall charge the department a fee for record checks conducted pursuant to this section. The Colorado bureau of investigation shall set such fee at a level sufficient to cover the direct and indirect costs of processing requests made pursuant to this section. Moneys collected by the bureau pursuant to this section shall be subject to annual appropriation by the general assembly for the administration of this section.

42-1-225. Commercial vehicle enterprise tax fund - creation. (1) The commercial vehicle enterprise tax fund is hereby created in the state treasury. The fund consists of moneys collected and transmitted to the fund pursuant to section 42-4-1701 (4) (a) (II). The general assembly shall annually appropriate the moneys in the fund to cover the cost of the sales tax refund created by section 39-26-113.5, C.R.S., and the actual cost of administering sections 39-26-113.5 and 39-30-104 (1) (b), C.R.S. After receiving the statement pursuant to section 39-30-104 (1) (b) (VI), C.R.S., the state treasurer shall credit the total cost of the amount of the tax credits stated therein to the general fund. Any moneys remaining in the commercial vehicle enterprise tax fund at the end of the fiscal year shall not revert to the general fund.

(2) (a) On July 1, 2011, and each July 1 thereafter, the department shall allocate one-third of the fund balance, not including the amount appropriated to cover the actual cost of administering sections 39-26-113.5 and 39-30-104 (1) (b), C.R.S., to make the sales tax refunds granted in section 39-26-113.5, C.R.S.

(b) On July 1, 2011, and each July 1 thereafter, the department shall allocate two-thirds of the fund balance, not including the amount appropriated to cover the actual cost of administering sections 39-26-113.5 and 39-30-104 (1) (b), C.R.S., to offset the income tax credit granted in section 39-30-104 (1) (b), C.R.S. By January 1, 2012, the department shall notify the Colorado economic development commission created in section 24-46-102, C.R.S., of the amount allocated for such purposes.

42-1-226. Disabled parking education and enforcement fund - created. There is hereby created in the state treasury the disabled parking education and enforcement fund, which consists of moneys collected pursuant to this section and section 42-4-1208 (6) and (7). The general assembly shall appropriate the moneys in the fund for the purposes specified in sections 42-1-227, 42-3-204, and 42-4-1208. Unexpended and unencumbered moneys in the fund at the end of a fiscal year shall remain in the fund and shall not be credited or transferred to the general fund or another fund. The department may accept gifts, grants, or donations from private or public sources for the purposes of this section. All private and public funds received through gifts, grants, or donations shall be transmitted to the state treasurer, who shall credit the moneys to the fund.

42-1-227. Disabled parking education program. (1) Subject to the availability of funds appropriated under section 42-1-226, the Colorado advisory council for persons with disabilities, created in section 24-45.5-103, C.R.S.:

(a) May make grants or develop or deliver education programs for the purpose of providing peace officers, local governments, medical providers, drivers, and persons with disabilities with education concerning eligibility standards for parking privileges available to a person with a disability affecting mobility, appropriate use of the parking privileges, the legal standards and violations contained in sections 42-3-204 and 42-4-1208, and the advantages of creating a volunteer enforcement program; and

(b) Shall create or make available a training program to assist professionals in understanding the standards that need to be met to obtain an identifying license plate or placard.

PART 3

GREEN TRUCK GRANT PROGRAM

42-1-301. Short title. This part 3 shall be known and may be cited as the "Green Truck Grant Program Act".

42-1-302. Legislative declaration. (1) The general assembly hereby finds and declares that:

(a) It is common for truck drivers to run their engines to stay warm or cool in their vehicles while resting after long hauls. The general assembly finds that driver comfort is essential to the job.

(b) Long-duration idling is costly to the driver, the fleet owner, and the environment. Some surveys say that trucks idle anywhere from six to eight hours a day for as many as three hundred days each year. Depending on fuel prices, this can cost six thousand dollars or more per year in fuel costs per truck.

(c) Long-duration idling of truck engines annually consumes over one billion gallons of diesel fuel and annually emits eleven million tons of carbon dioxide, two hundred thousand tons of oxides of nitrogen, and five thousand tons of particulate matter into the air. Idling can increase engine maintenance costs, shorten engine life, adversely affect driver well-being, and create elevated noise levels.

(d) Alternatives to long-duration idling exist and a grant program to help truck owners install such alternatives on their trucks is in the interest of the state's environment; and

(e) Better fuel economy and a cleaner ride will give all carriers a significant return on their investment.

(2) The general assembly further finds and declares that:

(a) Trucks that are twenty years old or older emit some of the highest levels of pollutants into the air and consume more diesel fuel; and

(b) A grant program to encourage the retirement and scrapping of older trucks is in the interest of the state's environment.

42-1-303. Definitions. As used in this part 3, unless the context otherwise requires:

(1) "Governor's energy office" or "office" means the governor's energy office created in section 24-38.5-101, C.R.S.

(2) "Green truck grant program" or "grant program" means the green truck grant program created in section 42-1-304 (1).

(3) "Qualified recipient" means an owner of a commercial truck registered in the state for purposes of interstate or intrastate commerce.

(4) "Truck" means a truck, truck tractor, trailer, or semitrailer registered in the state for purposes of interstate or intrastate commerce.

42-1-304. Green truck grant program - created. (1) There is hereby created in the governor's energy office the green truck grant program to provide grants to qualified recipients for reductions in truck emissions and energy usage by:

(a) (I) Reimbursements of twenty-five percent, not to exceed fifty thousand dollars to a qualified recipient, of the overall cost incurred by a qualified recipient in purchasing or installing fuel-efficient technologies and emission-control devices approved by the United States environmental protection agency's smartway transport partnership program, or any successor program, to reduce fuel consumption and emissions of greenhouse gases and other harmful air pollutants from trucks.

(II) The total of all reimbursements issued by the office to qualified recipients pursuant to subparagraph (I) of this paragraph (a) shall not exceed five hundred thousand dollars in a fiscal year.

(b) (I) Providing grants of up to five thousand dollars per qualified recipient for the retirement and scrapping of a 1989 or older model year truck that is:

(A) Documented to have been in use for at least ten thousand miles during the calendar year preceding the qualified recipient's application for the grant; and

(B) Donated to an established auto parts recycler, as defined in section 42-4-2201 (1), or a scrap metal recycler, that operates pursuant to all laws, rules, and regulations of the state and the United States environmental protection agency regarding recycling.

(II) The total of all grants issued by the office to qualified recipients pursuant to subparagraph (I) of this paragraph (b) shall not exceed two hundred fifty thousand dollars in a fiscal year.

(2) (a) The office shall administer the grant program and shall award reimbursements and grants as provided in this part 3. Reimbursements and grants shall be paid out of the green truck grant program fund created in section 42-1-305.

(b) The office shall adopt policies for the implementation of the green truck grant program. At a minimum, the policies shall specify the procedures for applying for a reimbursement or grant, the form of the reimbursement or grant application, and the information to be provided by the applicant.

(c) The office shall review each reimbursement or grant application received from a qualified recipient and shall make a determination as to whether the reimbursement or grant should be awarded and, subject to the limitations in paragraphs (a) and (b) of subsection (1) of this section, the amount of the reimbursement or grant. If the office determines an application is missing any information required to be included with the application, the office may contact the applicant to obtain the missing information.

(3) Nothing in this section shall be construed to prohibit or restrict the ability of an auto parts recycler, as defined in section 42-4-2201 (1), from recycling any part of a scrapped vehicle for use as a replacement part.

42-1-305. Green truck grant program fund - created. (1) There is hereby created in the state treasury the green truck grant program fund, referred to in this section as the "fund". The fund shall be administered by the office and shall consist of:

(a) Any gifts, grants, or donations from private or public sources that the office is hereby authorized to seek and accept; and

(b) Any moneys appropriated to the fund by the general assembly.

(2) All moneys in the fund shall be continuously appropriated by the general assembly to the office to be used for the purposes set forth in this part 3. All moneys not expended or encumbered, and all interest earned on the investment or deposit of moneys in the fund, shall remain in the fund and shall not revert to the general fund or any other fund at the end of any fiscal year.

PART 4

LICENSE PLATE AUCTIONS

42-1-401. Definitions. As used in this part 4, unless the context otherwise requires:

(1) "Group" means the license plate auction group created in section 42-1-403.

(2) "Registration number" means the unique combination of letters and numbers assigned to a vehicle by the department under section 42-3-201 and required to be displayed on the license plate by section 42-3-202.

(3) "Vehicle" means a vehicle required to be registered pursuant to part 1 of article 3 of this title.

42-1-402. License to buy and sell selected registration numbers for license plates. (1) The state or a person may sell, and the state or a person may purchase, the exclusive right to use a registration number selected by the group under section 42-1-404 for the purpose of registering a vehicle under article 3 of this title.

(2) The right to use a registration number is a perpetual license, the use of which is subject to compliance with this part 4.

42-1-403. License plate auction group. (1) The license plate auction group is hereby created within the office of the governor.

(2) The group consists of seven members, appointed as follows:

(a) One member who is appointed by the executive director of the department of revenue and who is not a member of the Colorado advisory council for persons with disabilities created in section 24-45.5-103, C.R.S.;

(b) One member who is appointed by the governor to represent persons with disabilities and who is not a member of the Colorado advisory council for persons with disabilities;

(c) One member appointed by the president of the senate to represent persons with disabilities;

(d) One member appointed by the Colorado advisory council for persons with disabilities;

(e) One member appointed by the director of the Colorado office of economic development;

(f) One member appointed by the chief of the Colorado state patrol; and

(g) One member appointed by the chief information officer appointed under section 24-37.5-103, C.R.S.

(3) An act of the group is void unless a majority of the governing body votes for the act.

(4) The members of the group serve at the pleasure of the appointing entity.

(5) The group has the following duties and powers:

(a) To adopt and use a seal and to alter the same at its pleasure;

(b) To sue and be sued and otherwise assert or defend the group's legal interests;

(c) To acquire office space, equipment, services, supplies, and insurance necessary to carry out the purposes of this part 4;

(d) To accept any gifts, grants, and loans of money, property, or other aid from the federal government, the state, any state agency, or any other source if the group complies with this part 4 and part 13 of article 75 of this title;

(e) To have and exercise all rights and powers necessary or incidental to, or implied from, the specific powers granted in this part 4;

(f) To fix the time and place at which meetings may be held;

(g) To elect a member as executive director of the group and other officers; and

(h) To hire employees and professional advisers as needed.

(6) The attorney general is the legal counsel for the group.

42-1-404. Sale of registration numbers by group. (1) The group shall raise money by auctioning to a buyer the right to use valuable letter and number combinations for a registration number.

(2) (a) The group shall study the market and determine which registration numbers are the most valuable, including both the types of plates currently issued and any type of plate that has been historically issued. Based on the study, the group shall select the most valuable registration numbers and request the department to verify

whether plates with the registration numbers are currently issued. The group shall not send the request to the department more than once every six months.

(b) Upon receiving the group's request, the department shall verify whether the plates are currently issued. If the plate is not currently issued, the department shall reserve the registration number until the group notifies the department to release the registration number.

(c) If a registration number is not currently issued, the group may auction the right to use the registration number in a manner calculated to bring the highest price; except that the department may deny the sale or use of a registration number that is offensive or inappropriate.

42-1-405. Creation of a private market for registration numbers - fee. (1) The group shall raise money by creating a market, which may include an on-line auction site, for registration numbers using methods that are commercially reasonable, account for expenditures, and ensure the collection of the state's approval and transfer royalty.

(2) The royalty for the state's approval and transfer of the right to use a registration number is twenty-five percent of the sale price of the transfer. At the time of sale, the purchaser shall pay the royalty to the group. This payment is not in lieu of the normal registration fees or specific ownership tax.

(3) A person shall not sell a registration number and the department shall not assign a registration number as a result of the right to use the number being sold to a vehicle unless the registration number was sold using the market created by the group.

42-1-406. Administration. (1) The group shall notify the department when the right to use a registration number has been sold and the group has collected the state's sale proceeds or approval and transfer royalty. Upon receiving the notice, the department shall create a record in the Colorado state titling and registration system, created in section 42-1-211, containing the name of the buyer, the vehicle identification number, if applicable, and the corresponding registration number.

(2) If the registration number consists of a combination of letters and numbers that is not within the normal format of license plate currently produced for the department, the department shall issue the plates as personalized plates under section 42-3-211.

(3) The group shall transfer the moneys collected under this part 4 to the state treasurer, who shall credit them to the registration number fund created in section 42-1-407.

(4) The group may contract with one or more public or private entities to implement this part 4.

(5) Any moneys received by the group shall be deposited in the registration number fund.

42-1-407. Registration number fund. (1) The registration number fund is hereby created in the state treasury. The moneys in the fund consist of the proceeds from the sale of registration numbers under section 42-1-404 and the royalty from private sales of registration numbers under section 42-1-405.

(2) The general assembly shall appropriate the amounts necessary, not to exceed five percent of the fund, to implement this part 4 from the registration number fund to the department, the governor's office, and the group.

(3) (a) (I) Except as specified in paragraph (b) of this subsection (3), at the end of each fiscal year, the state treasurer shall transfer one million five hundred thousand dollars, or the balance of the registration number fund if the balance is a lesser amount, from the registration number fund to the disability-benefit support fund created in section 24-30-2205, C.R.S.

(II) If any moneys remain in the registration number fund after the transfer required by subparagraph (I) of this paragraph (a), the state treasurer shall transfer two million five hundred thousand dollars, or the balance of the fund if the balance is a lesser amount, from the registration number fund to the general fund.

(III) If any moneys remain in the registration number fund after the transfers required by subparagraphs (I) and (II) of this paragraph (a), the state treasurer shall transfer the balance from the registration number fund to the disability-benefit support fund created by section 24-30-2205, C.R.S.

(b) The treasurer shall adjust the transfers required by paragraph (a) of this subsection (3) on July 1 of each year in proportion to the aggregate change in the United States department of labor bureau of labor statistics consumer price index for all urban consumers for the Denver-Boulder-Greeley consolidated metropolitan statistical area. The treasurer may round the dollar amount of the adjustment to the nearest ten dollars.

DRIVERS' LICENSES

ARTICLE 2

Drivers' Licenses

PART 1
DRIVERS' LICENSES

42-2-101.	Licenses for drivers required.
42-2-102.	Persons exempt from license.
42-2-103.	Motorcycles - low-power scooters - driver's license required.
42-2-104.	Licenses issued - denied.
42-2-105.	Special restrictions on certain drivers.
42-2-105.5.	Restrictions on minor drivers under eighteen years of age - penalties - legislative declaration.
42-2-106.	Instruction permits and temporary licenses.

Vehicles and Traffic

42-2-107.	Application for license or instruction permit - anatomical gifts - donations to Emily Maureen Ellen Keyes organ and tissue donation awareness fund - legislative declaration - repeal.
42-2-108.	Application of minors.
42-2-109.	Release from liability.
42-2-110.	Revocation upon death of signer for minor.
42-2-111.	Examination of applicants and drivers - when required.
42-2-112.	Medical advice - use by department - physician immunity.
42-2-113.	License examiners appointed.
42-2-114.	License issued - fees - repeal.
42-2-114.5.	Licensing services cash fund.
42-2-115.	License, permit, or identification card to be exhibited on demand.
42-2-116.	Restricted license.
42-2-117.	Duplicate permits and minor licenses - replacement licenses.
42-2-118.	Renewal of license in person or by mail - donations to Emily Maureen Ellen Keyes organ and tissue donation awareness fund - repeal.
42-2-119.	Notices - change of address or name.
42-2-120.	Methods of service.
42-2-121.	Records to be kept by department - admission of records in court.
42-2-121.5.	Emergency contact information - web site form - license application - driver's license database.
42-2-122.	Department may cancel license - limited license for physical or mental limitations.
42-2-123.	Suspending privileges of nonresidents and reporting convictions.
42-2-124.	When court to report convictions.
42-2-125.	Mandatory revocation of license and permit.
42-2-126.	Revocation of license based on administrative determination.
42-2-126.1.	Probationary licenses for persons convicted of alcohol-related driving offenses - ignition interlock devices - fees - interlock fund created - violations of probationary license - repeal. (Repealed)
42-2-126.3.	Tampering with an ignition interlock device.
42-2-126.5.	Revocation of license based on administrative actions taken under tribal law - repeal.
42-2-127.	Authority to suspend license - to deny license - type of conviction - points.
42-2-127.3.	Authority to suspend license - controlled substance violations. (Repealed)
42-2-127.4.	Authority to suspend license - forgery of a penalty assessment notice issued to minor under the age of eighteen years. (Repealed)
42-2-127.5.	Authority to suspend license - violation of child support order.
42-2-127.6.	Authority to suspend license - providing alcohol to an underage person.
42-2-127.7.	Authority to suspend driver's license - uninsured motorists - legislative declaration.
42-2-128.	Vehicular homicide - revocation of license.
42-2-129.	Mandatory surrender of license or permit for driving under the influence or with excessive alcoholic content.
42-2-130.	Mandatory surrender of license or permit for drug convictions. (Repealed)
42-2-131.	Revocation of license or permit for failing to comply with a court order relating to nondriving alcohol convictions.
42-2-131.5.	Revocation of license or permit for convictions involving defacing property. (Repealed)
42-2-132.	Period of suspension or revocation.
42-2-132.5.	Mandatory and voluntary restricted licenses following alcohol convictions - rules.
42-2-133.	Surrender and return of license.
42-2-134.	Foreign license invalid during suspension.
42-2-135.	Right to appeal.
42-2-136.	Unlawful possession or use of license.
42-2-137.	False affidavit - penalty.
42-2-138.	Driving under restraint - penalty.
42-2-139.	Permitting unauthorized minor to drive.
42-2-140.	Permitting unauthorized person to drive.
42-2-141.	Renting or loaning a motor vehicle to another.
42-2-142.	Violation - penalty.
42-2-143.	Legislative declaration.
42-2-144.	Reporting by certified level II alcohol and drug education and treatment providers - notice of administrative remedies against a driver's license - rules.

PART 2
HABITUAL OFFENDERS

42-2-201.	Legislative declaration concerning habitual offenders of motor vehicle laws.
42-2-202.	Habitual offenders - frequency and type of violations.
42-2-203.	Authority to revoke license of habitual offender.
42-2-204.	Appeals.
42-2-205.	Prohibition.
42-2-206.	Driving after revocation prohibited.
42-2-207.	No existing law modified.
42-2-208.	Computation of number of convictions.

PART 3
IDENTIFICATION CARDS

42-2-301. Definitions.
42-2-302. Department may issue - limitations.
42-2-303. Contents of identification card - repeal.
42-2-304. Validity of identification card - rules.
42-2-304.5. Cancellation or denial of identification card - failure to register vehicles in Colorado.
42-2-305. Lost, stolen, or destroyed cards.
42-2-306. Fees - disposition - repeal.
42-2-307. Change of address.
42-2-308. No liability on public entity.
42-2-309. Unlawful acts.
42-2-310. Violation.
42-2-311. County jail identification processing unit - report - repeal.
42-2-312. County jail identification processing unit fund.
42-2-313. Department consult with counties on county jail identification processing unit.

PART 4
COMMERCIAL DRIVERS' LICENSES

42-2-401. Short title.
42-2-402. Definitions.
42-2-403. Department authority - rules - federal requirements.
42-2-404. License for drivers - limitations.
42-2-405. Driver's license disciplinary actions - grounds for denial - suspension - revocation - disqualification.
42-2-405.5. Violations of out-of-service order.
42-2-406. Fees.
42-2-407. Licensing of testing units and driving testers - hearings - regulations.
42-2-408. Unlawful acts - penalty.
42-2-409. Unlawful possession or use of a commercial driver's license.

PART 1

DRIVERS' LICENSES

42-2-101. Licenses for drivers required. (1) Except as otherwise provided in part 4 of this article for commercial drivers, no person shall drive any motor vehicle upon a highway in this state unless such person has been issued a currently valid driver's or minor driver's license or an instruction permit by the department under this article.

(2) No person shall drive any motor vehicle upon a highway in this state if such person's driver's or minor driver's license has been expired for one year or less and such person has not been issued another such license by the department or by another state or country subsequent to such expiration.

(3) No person shall drive any motor vehicle upon a highway in this state unless such person has in his or her immediate possession a current driver's or minor driver's license or an instruction permit issued by the department under this article.

(4) No person who has been issued a currently valid driver's or minor driver's license or an instruction permit shall drive a type or general class of motor vehicle upon a highway in this state for which such person has not been issued the correct type or general class of license or permit.

(5) No person who has been issued a currently valid driver's or minor driver's license or an instruction permit shall operate a motor vehicle upon a highway in this state without having such license or permit in such person's immediate possession.

(6) A charge of a violation of subsection (2) of this section shall be dismissed by the court if the defendant elects not to pay the penalty assessment and, at or before the defendant's scheduled court appearance, exhibits to the court a currently valid driver's or minor driver's license.

(7) A charge of a violation of subsection (5) of this section shall be dismissed by the court if the defendant elects not to pay the penalty assessment and, at or before the defendant's scheduled court appearance, exhibits to the court a currently valid license or permit issued to such person or an officially issued duplicate thereof if the original is lost, stolen, or destroyed.

(8) The conduct of a driver of a motor vehicle which would otherwise constitute a violation of this section is justifiable and not unlawful when:

(a) It is necessary as an emergency measure to avoid an imminent public or private injury which is about to occur by reason of a situation occasioned or developed through no conduct of said driver and which is of sufficient gravity that, according to ordinary standards of intelligence and morality, the desirability and urgency of avoiding the injury clearly outweigh the desirability of avoiding the injury sought to be prevented by this section; or

(b) The applicable conditions for exemption, as set forth in section 42-2-102, exist.

(9) The issue of justification or exemption is an affirmative defense. As used in this subsection (9), "affirmative defense" means that, unless the state's evidence raises the issue involving the particular defense, the defendant, to raise the issue, shall present some credible evidence on that issue. If the issue involved in an affirmative defense is raised, then the liability of the defendant must be established beyond a reasonable doubt as to that issue as well as all other elements of the traffic infraction.

(10) Any person who violates any provision of subsection (1) or (4) of this section is guilty of a class 2 misdemeanor traffic offense. Any per-

son who violates any provision of subsection (2), (3), or (5) of this section commits a class B traffic infraction.

(11) Notwithstanding any law to the contrary, a second or subsequent conviction under subsection (1) or (4) of this section, when a person receiving such conviction has not subsequently obtained a valid Colorado driver's license or the correct type or general class of license, shall result in the assessment by the department of six points against the driving privilege of the person receiving such second or subsequent conviction.

42-2-102. Persons exempt from license. (1) The following persons need not obtain a Colorado driver's license:

(a) Any person who operates a federally owned military motor vehicle while serving in the armed forces of the United States;

(b) Any person who temporarily drives or operates any road machine, farm tractor, or other implement of husbandry on a highway;

(c) Any nonresident who is at least sixteen years of age and who has in his or her immediate possession a valid driver's license issued to such nonresident by his or her state or country of residence. A nonresident who is at least sixteen years of age and whose state or country of residence does not require the licensing of drivers may operate a motor vehicle as a driver for not more than ninety days in any calendar year, if said nonresident is the owner of the vehicle driven and if the motor vehicle so operated is duly registered in such nonresident's state or country of residence and such nonresident has in his or her immediate possession a registration card evidencing such ownership and registration in his or her own state or country.

(d) A nonresident on active duty in the armed forces of the United States if that person has in his or her possession a valid driver's license issued by such nonresident's state of domicile or, if returning from duty outside the United States, has a valid driver's license in his or her possession issued by the armed forces of the United States in foreign countries, but such armed forces license shall be valid only for a period of forty-five days after the licensee has returned to the United States;

(e) The spouse of a member of the armed forces of the United States who is accompanying such member on military or naval assignment to this state, who has a valid driver's license issued by another state, and whose right to drive has not been suspended or revoked in this state;

(f) Any nonresident who is temporarily residing in Colorado for the principal purpose of furthering such nonresident's education, is at least sixteen years of age, has a valid driver's license from his or her state of residence, and is considered a nonresident for tuition purposes by the educational institution at which such nonresident is furthering his or her education.

(2) Any person who has in his or her possession a valid driver's license issued by such person's previous state of residence shall be exempt, for thirty days after becoming a resident of the state of Colorado, from obtaining a license, as provided in section 42-2-101.

42-2-103. Motorcycles - low-power scooters - driver's license required. (1) (a) The department shall establish a motorcycle endorsement program for driver's licenses, minor driver's licenses, and instruction permits issued pursuant to this article.

(b) The department shall require an applicant for a general motorcycle endorsement to demonstrate the applicant's ability to exercise ordinary and reasonable care and control in the operation of a motorcycle. The department shall also require an applicant for a limited three-wheel motorcycle endorsement to demonstrate the applicant's ability to exercise ordinary and reasonable care and control in the operation of a three-wheel motorcycle.

(c) A person shall not operate a two-wheel motorcycle on a roadway without a general motorcycle endorsement, but a person who possesses a general motorcycle endorsement may operate any motorcycle on the roadway.

(d) A person with only a limited three-wheel motorcycle endorsement may operate a three-wheel motorcycle but shall not operate a two-wheel motorcycle on a roadway.

(2) (a) An operator of a low-power scooter shall possess a valid driver's license or minor driver's license.

(b) No low-power scooter shall be operated on any interstate system as described in section 43-2-101 (2), C.R.S., except where a bicycle may be operated on such interstate system, on any limited-access road of the state highway system as described in section 43-2-101 (1), C.R.S., or on any sidewalk, unless such operation is specifically designated. Low-power scooters may be operated upon roadways, except as provided in this section, and in bicycle lanes included within such roadways.

(3) A person who operates a motorcycle in violation of subsection (1) of this section commits the offense of driving a motor vehicle without the correct class of license in violation of section 42-2-101 (4) and shall be punished as provided in section 42-2-101 (10).

42-2-104. Licenses issued - denied. (1) Except as otherwise provided in this article, the department may license the following persons in the manner prescribed in this article:

(a) Any person twenty-one years of age or older, as a driver;

(b) (Deleted by amendment, L. 2000, p. 1348, § 11, effective July 1, 2001.)

(c) Any person sixteen years of age or older who has not reached his or her twenty-first birthday, as a minor driver;

(1.5) Repealed.

(2) Except as otherwise provided in this article, a person shall not be licensed by the department to operate any motor vehicle in this state:

(a) and (b) (Deleted by amendment, L. 2007, p. 504, § 2, effective July 1, 2007.)

(b.5) While the person's privilege to drive is under restraint;

(c) Who has been adjudged or determined by a court of competent jurisdiction to be an habitual drunkard or addicted to the use of a controlled substance, as defined in section 12-22-303 (7), C.R.S.;

(d) Who has been adjudged or determined by a court of competent jurisdiction to be afflicted with or suffering from any mental disability or disease and who has not at the time of application been restored to competency in the manner prescribed by law.

(3) The department shall not issue any license to:

(a) Any person required by this article to take an examination until such person has successfully passed the examination;

(b) Any person required under the provisions of any motor vehicle financial safety or responsibility law to deposit or furnish proof of financial responsibility until such person has deposited or furnished such proof;

(c) Any person whose license is subject to suspension or revocation or who does not have a license but would be subject to suspension or revocation pursuant to section 42-2-125, 42-2-126, or 42-2-127;

(d) Any person not submitting proof of age or proof of identity, or both, as required by the department;

(e) Any person whose presence in the United States is in violation of federal immigration laws;

(f) A person who, while under the age of sixteen, was convicted of any offense that would have subjected the person to a revocation of driving privileges under section 42-2-125 for the period of such revocation if such person had possessed a driver's license.

(4) (a) The department shall not issue a driver's license, including, without limitation, a temporary driver's license pursuant to section 42-2-106 (2), to a person under eighteen years of age, unless the person has:

(I) Applied for, been issued, and possessed an appropriate instruction permit for at least twelve months;

(II) Submitted a log or other written evidence on a standardized form approved by the department that is signed by his or her parent or guardian or other responsible adult who signed the affidavit of liability or the instructor of a driver's education course approved by the department, certifying that the person has completed not less than fifty hours of actual driving experience, of which not less than ten hours shall have been completed while driving at night.

(b) In no event shall the department issue a minor driver's license to anyone under sixteen years of age.

(5) The department shall not issue a driver's license to a person under sixteen years and six months of age unless the person has either:

(a) Received a minimum of twelve hours of driving-behind-the-wheel training directed by a parent, a legal guardian, or an alternate permit supervisor, which training shall be in addition to the driving experience required by subsection (4) of this section, if no entity offers approved behind-the-wheel driver training at least twenty hours a week from a permanent location with an address that is within thirty miles of the permit holder's residence; or

(b) Received a minimum of six hours of driving-behind-the-wheel training with a driving instructor employed or associated with an approved driver education course.

42-2-105. Special restrictions on certain drivers. (1) A person under the age of eighteen years shall not drive any motor vehicle used to transport explosives or inflammable material or any motor vehicle used as a school vehicle for the transportation of pupils to or from school. A person under the age of eighteen years shall not drive a motor vehicle used as a commercial, private, or common carrier of persons or property unless such person has experience in operating motor vehicles and has been examined on such person's qualifications in operating such vehicles. The examination shall include safety regulations of commodity hauling, and the driver shall be licensed as a driver or a minor driver who is eighteen years of age or older.

(2) Notwithstanding the provisions of subsection (1) of this section, no person under the age of twenty-one years shall drive a commercial motor vehicle as defined in section 42-2-402 (4) except as provided in section 42-2-404 (4).

(3) Any person who violates any provision of this section commits a class A traffic infraction.

42-2-105.5. Restrictions on minor drivers under eighteen years of age - penalties - legislative declaration. (1) The general assembly finds, determines, and declares that:

(a) Teenage drivers, in order to become safe and responsible drivers, need behind-the-wheel driving experience before they can begin to drive without restrictions;

(b) Providing additional behind-the-wheel training with a parent, guardian, or other responsible adult before obtaining a minor driver's license is the beginning of the young driver's accumulation of experience;

(c) Once a teenage driver begins to drive without a parent, guardian, or other responsible adult in the vehicle, it is necessary to place restrictions on a teenage driver who holds a minor driver's license until such driver turns eighteen years of age in order to give that driver time to exercise good judgment in the operation of a vehicle while keeping that driver, his or her passengers, and the public safe;

(d) Penalties for the violation of these restrictions on minor drivers under eighteen years of age, including the assessment of points where they may not otherwise be assessed, should be sufficient to ensure that chronic violations would result in swift and severe repercussions to reinforce the importance of obeying the driving laws in order to keep the minor driver, his or her passengers, and the public safe.

(2) Repealed.

(3) Occupants in motor vehicles driven by persons under eighteen years of age shall be properly restrained or wear seat belts as required in sections 42-4-236 and 42-4-237.

(4) No more than one passenger shall occupy the front seat of the motor vehicle driven by a person under eighteen years of age, and the number of passengers in the back seat of such vehicle shall not exceed the number of seat belts.

(5) (a) Except as otherwise provided in paragraph (b) of this subsection (5), any person who violates this section commits a class A traffic infraction.

(b) A violation of subsection (3) of this section is a traffic infraction, and, notwithstanding the provisions of section 42-4-1701 (4) (a) (I) (D), a person convicted of violating subsection (3) of this section shall be punished as follows:

(I) By the imposition of not less than eight hours nor more than twenty-four hours of community service for a first offense and not less than sixteen hours nor more than forty hours of community service for a subsequent offense;

(II) By the levying of a fine of not more than sixty-five dollars for a first offense, a fine of not more than one hundred thirty dollars for a second offense, and a fine of one hundred ninety-five dollars for a subsequent offense; and

(III) By an assessment of two license suspension points pursuant to section 42-2-127 (5) (hh).

42-2-106. Instruction permits and temporary licenses. (1) (a) (I) A person who is sixteen years of age or older and who, except for the person's lack of instruction in operating a motor vehicle or motorcycle, would otherwise be qualified to obtain a license under this article may apply for a temporary instruction permit in accordance with sections 42-2-107 and 42-2-108. The department shall issue a permit entitling an applicant, who is sixteen years of age or older but under eighteen years of age, while having the permit in the applicant's immediate possession, to drive a motor vehicle or motorcycle upon the highways when accompanied by the parent, stepparent, grandparent with power of attorney, or guardian or foster parent, who signed the affidavit of liability pursuant to section 42-2-108 (1) (a), who holds a valid Colorado driver's license, and who occupies the front seat in close proximity to the driver or, in the case of a motorcycle, under the immediate proximate supervision of a licensed driver, who holds a valid Colorado driver's license and is twenty-one years of age or older, authorized under this article to drive a motorcycle. In addition, the parent, stepparent, grandparent with power of attorney, or guardian or foster parent, who is authorized pursuant to this section to supervise the minor driver while the minor is driving, may allow the minor, while having the permit in the applicant's immediate possession, to drive with an individual who holds a valid driver's license and is twenty-one years of age or older for additional driving experience, but such additional driving experience shall not count toward the requirement established in section 42-2-104. The permit shall expire three years after issuance. The department shall issue a permit entitling the applicant, who is eighteen years of age or older, while having the permit in the applicant's immediate possession, to drive a motor vehicle or motorcycle upon the highways when accompanied by a driver, who holds a valid Colorado driver's license and is twenty-one years of age or older, who occupies the front seat of the motor vehicle, or if the vehicle is a motorcycle under the immediate proximate supervision of a driver, who is authorized under this article to drive a motorcycle. The permit shall expire three years after issuance.

(II) If the parent, stepparent, grandparent with power of attorney, or guardian or foster parent, who signed the affidavit of liability pursuant to section 42-2-108 (1) (a), does not hold a valid Colorado driver's license, the parent, stepparent, grandparent with power of attorney, or guardian or foster parent may appoint an alternate permit supervisor. An alternate permit supervisor shall hold a valid Colorado driver's license and be twenty-one years of age or older or, if the vehicle is a motorcycle, is authorized under this article to drive a motorcycle. A minor who is issued a permit under this paragraph (a) may drive a motor vehicle, including a motorcycle, under the supervision of the alternate permit supervisor if the minor has the permit in the minor's immediate possession and the alternate permit supervisor occupies the front seat of the motor vehicle or, if the vehicle is a motorcycle, is in close proximity to the driver.

(III) If the parent, stepparent, grandparent with power of attorney, or guardian or foster parent, who signed the affidavit of liability pursuant to section 42-2-108 (1) (a), does not hold a valid Colorado driver's license but holds a valid driver's license from another state and is authorized to drive a motor vehicle or motorcycle and has proper military identification, then the applicant, while having the permit in the applicant's immediate possession, shall be authorized to drive a motor vehicle, including a motorcycle, under the supervision of the parent, stepparent, grandparent with power of attorney, or guardian or foster parent, who cosigned the application for the minor's instruction permit, if the parent, stepparent, grandparent with power of attorney, or guardian or foster parent occupies the front seat of the motor vehicle or, if the vehicle is a motorcycle, is in close proximity to the driver while the minor is driving.

(b) (I) A minor who is fifteen years of age or older and has completed a department-approved driver education course within the last six months may apply for a minor's instruction permit, pursuant to sections 42-2-107 and 42-2-108. Nothing in this subparagraph (I) shall require a minor who is fifteen years of age or older and in the foster care system to complete and present an affidavit of liability to register for a department-approved driver education course prior to applying for a minor's instruction permit. Upon presentation of a written or printed statement signed by the parent, stepparent, grandparent with power of attorney, or guardian or foster parent and the instructor of the driver education course that the minor has passed an approved driver education course, and a signed affidavit of liability pursuant to section 42-2-108, the department shall issue the permit entitling the applicant, while having the permit in the applicant's immediate possession, to drive a motor vehicle, including a motorcycle, under the supervision of the parent, stepparent, grandparent with power of attorney, or guardian or foster parent, who cosigned the application for the minor's instruction permit, if the parent, stepparent, grandparent with power of attorney, or guardian or foster parent holds a valid Colorado driver's license and occupies the front seat of the motor vehicle or, if the vehicle is a motorcycle, is authorized under this article to drive a motorcycle and is in close proximity to the driver while the minor is driving. In addition, the parent, stepparent, grandparent with power of attorney, or guardian or foster parent, who is authorized pursuant to this section to supervise the minor driver while the minor is driving, may allow the minor, while having the permit in the applicant's immediate possession, to drive with an individual who holds a valid driver's license and is twenty-one years of age or older for additional driving experience, but such additional driving experience shall not count toward the requirement established in section 42-2-104. The permit shall also entitle the applicant to drive a motor vehicle, including a motorcycle, that is marked to indicate that it is a motor vehicle used for instruction and that is properly equipped for instruction, upon the highways when accompanied by or under the supervision of an approved driver education instructor who holds a valid Colorado driver's license. Driver education instructors giving instruction in motorcycle safety shall have a valid motorcycle driver's license from Colorado and shall have successfully completed an instruction program in motorcycle safety approved by the department. The permit shall expire three years after issuance.

(II) If the parent, stepparent, grandparent with power of attorney, or guardian or foster parent, who signed the affidavit of liability pursuant to section 42-2-108 (1) (a), does not hold a valid Colorado driver's license, the parent, stepparent, grandparent with power of attorney, or guardian or foster parent may appoint an alternate permit supervisor. An alternate permit supervisor shall hold a valid Colorado driver's license and be twenty-one years of age or older or, if the vehicle is a motorcycle, is authorized under this article to drive a motorcycle. A minor who is issued a permit under this paragraph (b) may drive a motor vehicle, including a motorcycle, under the supervision of the alternate permit supervisor if the minor has the permit in the minor's immediate possession and the alternate permit supervisor occupies the front seat of the motor vehicle or, if the vehicle is a motorcycle, is in close proximity to the driver.

(III) If the parent, stepparent, grandparent with power of attorney, or guardian or foster parent, who signed the affidavit of liability pursuant to section 42-2-108 (1) (a), does not hold a valid Colorado driver's license but holds a valid driver's license from another state and is authorized to drive a motor vehicle or motorcycle and has proper military identification, then the applicant, while having the permit in the applicant's immediate possession, shall be authorized to drive a motor vehicle, including a motorcycle, under the supervision of the parent, stepparent, grandparent with power of attorney, or guardian or foster parent, who cosigned the application for the minor's instruction permit, if the parent, stepparent, grandparent with power of attorney, or guardian or foster parent occupies the front seat of the motor vehicle or, if the vehicle is a motorcycle, is in close proximity to the driver while the minor is driving.

(c) A person sixteen years of age or older who, except for his or her lack of instruction in operating a motorcycle would otherwise be qualified to obtain a driver's license under this article to drive a motorcycle may apply for a temporary instruction permit, pursuant to sections 42-2-107 and 42-2-108. The department shall issue the permit entitling the applicant, while having the permit in the applicant's immediate possession, to drive a motorcycle upon the highways while under the immediate supervision of a licensed driver, who holds a valid Colorado driver's license and is twenty-one years of age or older, authorized under this article to drive a motorcycle. The permit shall expire three years after issuance.

(d) (I) A minor fifteen and one-half years of age but less than sixteen years of age who has completed a four-hour prequalification driver awareness program approved by the department may apply for a minor's instruction permit pursuant to sections 42-2-107 and 42-2-108. Upon presenting a written or printed statement signed by the parent, stepparent, grandparent with power of attorney, or guardian or foster parent of the applicant and documentation that the minor completed the driver awareness program, the department shall issue a permit entitling the applicant, while having the permit in the applicant's immediate possession, to drive a motor vehicle, including a motorcycle, under the supervision of the parent, stepparent, grandparent with power of attorney, or guardian or foster parent, who cosigned the application for the minor's instruction permit, if the parent, stepparent, grandparent with power of attorney, or guardian or foster parent holds a valid Colorado driver's license and occupies the front seat of the motor vehicle or, if the vehicle is a motorcycle, is authorized under this article to drive a motorcycle and is in close proximity to the driver while he or she is driving. In addition, the parent, stepparent, grandparent with power of attorney, or guardian or foster parent, who is authorized pursuant to this section to supervise the minor driver while the minor is driving, may allow the minor, while having the permit in the applicant's immediate possession, to drive with an individual who holds a valid driver's license and is twenty-one years of age or older for additional driving experience, but such additional driving experience shall not count toward the requirement established in section 42-2-104. The permit shall expire three years after issuance.

(II) If the parent, stepparent, grandparent with power of attorney, or guardian or foster parent, who signed the affidavit of liability pursuant to section 42-2-108 (1) (a), does not hold a valid Colorado driver's license, the parent, stepparent, grandparent with power of attorney, or guardian or foster parent may appoint an alternate permit supervisor. An alternate permit supervisor shall hold a valid Colorado driver's license and be twenty-one years of age or older or, if the vehicle is a motorcycle, is authorized under this article to drive a motorcycle. A minor who is issued a permit under this paragraph (d) may drive a motor vehicle, including a motorcycle, under the supervision of the alternate permit supervisor if the minor has the permit in the minor's immediate possession and the alternate permit supervisor occupies the front seat of the motor vehicle or, if the vehicle is a motorcycle, is in close proximity to the driver.

(III) If the parent, stepparent, grandparent with power of attorney, or guardian or foster parent, who signed the affidavit of liability pursuant to section 42-2-108 (1) (a), does not hold a valid Colorado driver's license but holds a valid driver's license from another state and is authorized to drive a motor vehicle or motorcycle and has proper military identification, then the applicant, while having the permit in the applicant's immediate possession, shall be authorized to drive a motor vehicle, including a motorcycle, under the supervision of the parent, stepparent, grandparent with power of attorney, or guardian or foster parent, who cosigned the application for the minor's instruction permit, if the parent, stepparent, grandparent with power of attorney, or guardian or foster parent occupies the front seat of the motor vehicle or, if the vehicle is a motorcycle, is in close proximity to the driver while the minor is driving.

(e) Repealed.

(f) Notwithstanding paragraphs (a) to (d) of this subsection (1), a temporary instruction permit to operate a commercial motor vehicle as defined in section 42-2-402 shall expire one year after issuance.

(2) (a) The department, in its discretion, may issue a temporary driver's license to an applicant, who is not a first time applicant in Colorado or who is under eighteen years of age and is accompanied by a responsible party meeting the requirements of section 42-2-108 (1), for a minor driver's or driver's license which will permit such applicant to operate a motor vehicle while the department completes its verification of all facts relative to such applicant's right to receive a minor driver's or driver's license.

(b) The department shall issue a temporary driver's license to a first time applicant in Colorado for a minor driver's or driver's license that will permit such applicant to operate a motor vehicle while the department completes its verification of all facts relative to such applicant's right to receive a minor driver's or driver's license including the age, identity, and residency of the applicant, unless such applicant is under eighteen years of age and is accompanied by a responsible adult meeting the requirements of section 42-2-108 (1). Such verification shall include a comparison of existing driver's license and identification card images in department files with the applicant's images to ensure such applicant has only one identity.

(c) A temporary license is valid for up to one year as determined by the department, unless extended by the department, and must be in such applicant's immediate possession while operating a motor vehicle. It shall be invalid when the permanent license has been issued or has been refused for good cause.

(3) Any person who violates any provision of this section commits a class A traffic infraction.

42-2-107. Application for license or instruction permit - anatomical gifts - donations to Emily Maureen Ellen Keyes organ and tissue donation awareness fund - legislative declaration - repeal. (1) (a) (I) Every application for an instruction permit or for a driver's or minor driver's license shall be made upon forms furnished by the department. Every application shall be accompanied by the required fee. The fee for an application for any instruction permit is thirteen dollars and forty cents, which shall be transferred to the state treasurer, who shall credit ten dollars to the highway users tax fund and three dollars and forty cents to the licensing services cash fund created in section 42-2-114.5; except that, for fiscal years 2010-11 and 2011-12, the state treasurer shall credit the fees to the licensing services cash fund created in section 42-2-114.5. Every applicant shall submit, with the application, proof of age or proof of identity, or both, as the department may require.

(II) If an applicant is applying for an instruction permit or driver's or minor driver's license for the first time in Colorado and the applicant otherwise meets the requirements for such license or permit, the applicant shall receive a temporary license or instruction permit pursuant to section 42-2-106 (2) until the department verifies all facts relative to such applicant's right to receive an instruction permit or minor driver's or driver's license including the age, identity, and residency of the applicant.

(b) (I) An applicant who submits proof of age or proof of identity issued by an entity other than a state or the United States shall also submit such proof as the department may require that the applicant is lawfully present in the United States.

(II) An applicant who submits, as proof of age or proof of identity, a driver's license or identification card issued by a state that issues drivers' licenses or identification cards to persons who are not lawfully present in the United States shall also submit such proof as the department may require that the applicant is lawfully present in the United States.

(c) The department may not issue a driver's or minor driver's license to any person who is not lawfully present in the United States.

(d) The department may not issue a driver's or minor driver's license to any person who is not a resident of the state of Colorado. The department shall issue such a license only upon the furnishing of such evidence of residency as the department may require.

(2) (a) Every application shall state the full name, date of birth, sex, and residence address of the applicant; briefly describe the applicant; be signed by the applicant with such applicant's usual signature; have affixed thereon the applicant's fingerprint; and state whether the licensee has ever been licensed as a minor driver or driver and, if so, when and by what state or country and whether any such license has ever been denied, suspended, or revoked, the reasons therefor, and the date thereof. These statements shall be verified by the applicant's signature thereon.

(b) (I) In addition to the requirements of paragraph (a) of this subsection (2), an application shall state that:

(A) The applicant understands that, as a resident of the state of Colorado, any motor vehicle owned by the applicant must be registered in Colorado pursuant to the laws of the state and the applicant may be subject to criminal penalties, civil penalties, cancellation or denial of the applicant's driver's license, and liability for any unpaid registration fees and specific ownership taxes if the applicant fails to comply with such registration requirements; and

(B) The applicant agrees, within thirty days after the date the applicant became a resident, to register in Colorado any vehicle owned by the applicant.

(II) The applicant shall verify the statements required by this paragraph (b) by the applicant's signature on the application.

(2.5) (a) Any male United States citizen or immigrant who applies for an instruction permit or a driver's license or a renewal of any such permit or license and who is at least eighteen years of age but less than twenty-six years of age shall be registered in compliance with the requirements of section 3 of the "Military Selective Service Act", 50 U.S.C. App. sec. 453, as amended.

(b) The department shall forward in an electronic format the necessary personal information of the applicants identified in paragraph (a) of this subsection (2.5) to the selective service system. The applicant's submission of an application shall serve as an indication that the applicant either has already registered with the selective service system or that he is authorizing the department to forward to the selective service system the necessary information for such registration. The department shall notify the applicant that his submission of an application constitutes consent to registration with the selective service system, if so required by federal law.

(3) (a) Except as otherwise provided in paragraph (b) of this subsection (3), an application for a driver's or minor driver's license shall include the applicant's social security number, which shall remain confidential and shall not be placed on the applicant's driver's or minor driver's license; except that such confidentiality shall not extend to the state child support enforcement agency, the department, or a court of competent jurisdiction when requesting information in the course of activities authorized under article 13 of title 26, C.R.S., or article 14 of title 14, C.R.S. If the applicant does not have a social security number, the applicant shall submit a sworn statement made under penalty of law, together with the application, stating that the applicant does not have a social security number.

(b) If federal law is changed to prohibit the collection of social security numbers on driver's license applications, the department shall automatically stop its practice of including applicants' social security numbers on applications for driver's and minor driver's licenses as specified in paragraph (a) of this subsection (3).

(c) A sworn statement that is made under penalty of perjury shall be sufficient evidence of the applicant's social security number required by this subsection (3) and shall authorize the department to issue a driver's or minor driver's license to the applicant. Nothing in this paragraph (c) shall be construed to prevent the department from cancelling, denying, recalling, or updating a driver's or minor driver's license if the department learns that the applicant has provided a false social security number.

(4) (a) (Deleted by amendment, L. 2004, p. 1891, § 4, effective August 4, 2004.)

(b) (I) (A) The general assembly hereby finds, determines, and declares that the availability of human organs and tissue by voluntary designation of donors under the provisions of the "Revised Uniform Anatomical Gift Act", part 1 of article 34 of title 12, C.R.S., is critical for advancements in medical science to occur and for the successful use of various medical treatments to save and prolong lives.

(B) The general assembly further finds, determines, and declares that state government should play a role in increasing the availability of human organs and tissue to procurement organizations, as defined in section 12-34-102, C.R.S., by acting as a conduit to make moneys available for promoting organ and tissue donation and that this role constitutes a public purpose.

(II) There is hereby created in the state treasury the Emily Maureen Ellen Keyes organ and tissue donation awareness fund, which shall consist of all moneys credited thereto from all sources including but not limited to moneys collected from voluntary contributions for organ and tissue donation pursuant to subparagraph (V) of this paragraph (b) and section 42-2-118 (1) (a) (II). All moneys in the fund are hereby continuously appropriated to the department of the treasury and shall remain in the fund to be used for the purposes set forth in subparagraph (III) of this paragraph (b) and shall not revert to the general fund or any other fund. All interest derived from the deposit and investment of this fund shall be credited to the fund. At least quarterly, the state treasurer shall transfer all available moneys in the Emily Maureen Ellen Keyes organ and tissue donation awareness fund to donor alliance, inc., or its successor organization, as directed by sub-subparagraph (A) of subparagraph (III) of this paragraph (b).

(III) At least quarterly, the state treasurer shall transfer all available moneys from the Emily Maureen Ellen Keyes organ and tissue donation awareness fund:

(A) To donor alliance, inc., or its successor organization, to provide funding for activities to promote organ and tissue donation through the creation and dissemination, by means of electronic media and otherwise, of educational information including public service announcements and information to increase awareness in the medical professions and related fields. Donor alliance, inc., or its successor organization, shall create, by amendment to its articles of incorporation or bylaws or otherwise, as appropriate, an advisory group to allocate moneys received pursuant to this sub-subparagraph (A). Such advisory body shall include a representative of any qualified transplant organization. Such organizations shall include those for organs, tissue, bone marrow, and blood. The advisory body created under this sub-subparagraph (A) shall report in writing in a form and manner determined by the department and at such intervals as required by the department on the use of moneys received under this sub-subparagraph (A). No moneys made available pursuant to this paragraph (b) shall be used to encourage fetal tissue donation.

(B) (Deleted by amendment, L. 98, p. 1172, 9, effective June 1, 1998.)

(C) Before any payment to donor alliance, inc., or its successor organization, from the Emily Maureen Ellen Keyes organ and tissue donation awareness fund may be made for any purpose, to the department for the reasonable costs associated with the initial installation of the organ and tissue donor registry, the setup for electronic transfer of the donor information for the organ and tissue donor registry to the federally designated organ procurement organization, computer programming and form changes necessary as a result of the creation of the organ and tissue donor registry.

(D) To donor alliance, inc., or its successor organization, for the costs associated with educating the public about the organ and tissue donor registry pursuant to section 12-34-120, C.R.S.

(IV) Appropriations made by the general assembly pursuant to subparagraph (III) of this paragraph (b) shall not exceed moneys in the Emily Maureen Ellen Keyes organ and tissue donation awareness fund that are available for appropriation.

(V) An applicant may make a donation of one dollar or more to the Emily Maureen Ellen Keyes organ and tissue donation awareness fund, created in subparagraph (II) of this paragraph (b), to promote the donation of organs and tissues under the provisions of the "Revised Uniform Anatomical Gift Act", part 1 of article 34 of title 12, C.R.S. The department shall collect such donations and transmit them to the state treasurer, who shall credit the same to the Emily Maureen Ellen Keyes organ and tissue donation awareness fund. The donation prescribed in this subparagraph (V) is voluntary and may be refused by the applicant. The department shall make available informational booklets or other informational sources on the importance of organ and tissue donations to applicants as designed and approved by the advisory body created under sub-subparagraph (A) of subparagraph (III) of this paragraph (b). The department shall inquire of each applicant at the time the completed application is presented whether the applicant is interested in making a donation of one dollar or more and shall also specifically inform the applicant of the option for organ and tissue donations. The department shall also provide written information designed and approved by the advisory body created under sub-subparagraph (A) of subparagraph (III) of this paragraph (b) to each applicant volunteering to become an organ and tissue donor. The written information shall disclose that the applicant's name shall be transmitted to the organ and tissue donor registry authorized in section 12-34-120, C.R.S., and that the applicant shall notify the federally designated organ procurement organization of any changes to the applicant's donor status.

(V.5) Designation on a donor's driver's license or permit shall fulfill the release requirements set forth in section 24-72-204 (7) (b), C.R.S.

(VI) The provisions of article 16 of title 6, C.R.S., shall not apply to the activities of the department under this paragraph (b).

(VII) This paragraph (b) is repealed, effective July 1, 2018.

(5) (a) (I) Prior to the issuance of a driver's or minor driver's license, the department shall determine if there are any outstanding judgments or warrants entered or issued against the applicant pursuant to section 42-4-1709 (7).

(II) For the purposes of this subsection (5), "outstanding judgments or warrants" does not include any judgment or warrant reported to the department in violation of the provisions of section 42-4-110.5 (2) (c).

(b) If the department determines that there are no outstanding judgments or warrants entered or issued against the applicant and if all other conditions for issuance required by articles 1 to 4 of this title are met, the department shall issue the license.

(c) If the department determines that there are outstanding judgments or warrants entered or issued against the applicant and the applicant is subject to the provisions of section 42-4-1709 (7), the license shall not be issued until the applicant has complied with the requirements of that section. Any person who satisfies an outstanding judgment or warrant entered pursuant to section 42-4-1709 (7) shall pay to the court a thirty-dollar administrative processing fee for each such judgment or warrant in addition to all other penalties, costs, or forfeitures. The court shall remit fifty percent of the administrative processing fee to the department of revenue, and the other fifty percent shall be retained by the issuing court.

(6) Notwithstanding the amount specified for any fee in this section, the executive director of the department by rule or as otherwise provided by law may reduce the amount of one or more of the fees if necessary pursuant to section 24-75-402 (3), C.R.S., to reduce the uncommitted reserves of the fund to which all or any portion of one or more of the fees is credited. After the uncommitted reserves of the fund are sufficiently reduced, the executive director of the department by rule or as otherwise provided by law may increase the amount of one or more of the fees as provided in section 24-75-402 (4), C.R.S.

42-2-108. Application of minors. (1) (a) The application of any person under eighteen years of age for an instruction permit or minor driver's license shall be accompanied by an affidavit of liability signed and verified by the parent, stepparent, grandparent with power of attorney, guardian, spouse of the applicant if the spouse is eighteen years of age or older, or, in the event there is no such person, guardian, or spouse, any other responsible adult who is willing to assume the obligation imposed under this article upon an adult signing the affidavit of liability for a minor. When an applicant has been made a ward of any court in the state for any reason and has been placed in a foster home, the foster parents or parent may sign the affidavit of liability for the minor. If the parent or foster parent is unwilling or unable to sign the affidavit of liability, a guardian ad litem, a designated official of the county department of social services having custody of the applicant, or a designated official of the division of youth corrections in the department of human services having custody of the applicant may sign the application for an instruction permit without signing the affidavit of liability for the minor if the requirements of paragraph (b) of this subsection (1) are met; except that, prior to signing the application for an instruction permit, the guardian ad litem or other designated official shall notify the court of his or her intent to sign the application, and except that, the guardian ad litem or designated official shall not sign the application for an instruction permit for a minor who is placed in a foster care home and is under seventeen and one-half years of age without first obtaining the consent of the foster parent. If the minor is seventeen and one-half years of age or older and is in the care of a foster parent, in order to prepare the minor for emancipation from foster care and to assist the minor in obtaining important life skills, the guardian ad litem or designated official shall consult with the foster parent of the minor about the opportunity for the minor to learn driving skills under the restrictions provided in paragraph (b) of this subsection (1) prior to signing an application for an instruction permit. The guardian ad litem or designated official shall solicit the opinion of the minor's foster parent concerning the minor's ability to exercise good judgment and make decisions as well as the minor's overall capacity to drive. When a minor to whom an instruction permit or minor driver's license has been issued is required to appear before the department for a hearing pursuant to any provision of this article, the minor shall be accompanied by the person who signed the affidavit of liability for the minor or by the guardian ad litem or designated official who signed the application for an instruction permit for the minor. If the person who signed the minor's affidavit of liability or application for an instruction permit is unable to attend the hearing, he or she shall submit to the department a verified signed statement certifying under oath that he or she is aware of the purpose of the hearing but cannot attend.

(b) The department shall issue an instruction permit to an applicant under the age of eighteen years who is otherwise eligible to obtain an instruction permit and who has been made a ward of the court and who is in out-of-home placement without the requirement of a parent, guardian, stepparent, or foster parent signing an affidavit of liability if the following requirements are met:

(I) The guardian ad litem, a designated official of the county department of social services having custody of such applicant, or a designated official of the division of youth corrections in the department of human services having custody of such applicant signs the application for an instruction permit;

(II) (A) If the minor is in the care of a foster parent and is under seventeen and one-half years of age, the foster parent consents to the minor learning driving skills under the restrictions provided in this subsection (1); or

(B) If the minor is in the care of a foster parent and is at least seventeen and one-half years of age, the guardian ad litem or the designated official has consulted with the foster parent prior to signing the application for an instruction permit;

(III) The applicant is enrolled in or will be enrolled in a commercial driving course that insures the motor vehicles in which the applicant will be driving as a student for property damage and personal injury; and

(IV) The commercial driving course maintains possession of the applicant's instruction permit at all times.

(1.5) (a) The application of any person under the age of eighteen years for an instruction permit or minor driver's license shall include the option for a minor to be an organ or tissue donor.

(b) Repealed.

(c) Any person under the age of eighteen years who volunteers to donate anatomical gifts by designation on an instructional permit or minor driver's license shall include a notice of consent signed and verified by the father or the mother of the applicant, or, in the event neither parent is living, by the person or guardian having proof of legal custody of such minor, or by the spouse of the applicant if the spouse of the applicant is eighteen years of age or older.

(d) If the person under the age of eighteen years who volunteers to donate anatomical gifts by designation on an instructional permit or minor driver's license is an emancipated minor, a notice of consent is not necessary for an anatomical gift to be valid.

(2) Any negligence or willful misconduct of a minor under the age of eighteen years who drives a motor vehicle upon a highway is imputed to the person who signed the affidavit of liability which accompanied the application of such minor for a permit or license. Such person is jointly and severally liable with such minor for any damages caused by such negligence or willful misconduct, except as otherwise provided in subsection (3) of this section.

(3) In the event this state requires a minor under the age of eighteen years to deposit, or there is deposited upon such minor's behalf, proof of financial responsibility with respect to the operation of a motor vehicle owned by such minor or, if such minor is not the owner of a motor vehicle, with respect to the operating of any motor vehicle, in form and in amounts as required under the motor vehicle financial responsibility laws of this state, then the department may accept the application of such minor when accompanied by an affidavit of liability signed by one parent or the guardian of such minor, except as otherwise provided in subsection (1) of this section. While such proof is maintained, such parent or guardian is not subject to the liability imposed under subsection (2) of this section. Nothing in this section requires a foster parent to sign an affidavit of liability for a foster child and nothing in this section precludes a foster parent from obtaining a named driver's exclusion on the foster parent's insurance policy.

(4) Repealed.

42-2-109. Release from liability. (1) Any person who has signed the affidavit of liability which accompanied the application of a minor for a minor driver's license or permit may thereafter file with the department a verified written request that the license of said minor be cancelled. Upon receipt of such request, the department shall cancel the license of said minor, unless the minor has already reached the age of eighteen years, and the person who signed the affidavit of liability for such minor shall be relieved from all liability imposed by section 42-2-108 (2).

(2) When such minor reaches the age of eighteen years, the person who signed the minor's affidavit of liability is relieved of all liability imposed by section 42-2-108 (2).

42-2-110. Revocation upon death of signer for minor. (1) The department, upon receipt of satisfactory evidence of the death of the person who signed the affidavit of liability which accompanied the application for a license of such minor, shall cancel such license, unless the minor has already reached the age of eighteen years, and shall not issue a new license until such time as a new application is made pursuant to the provisions of this article.

(2) In the event of the death of the signer, a licensee under the age of eighteen years shall notify the department and secure the necessary new signer.

42-2-111. Examination of applicants and drivers - when required. (1) (a) The department shall examine every applicant for a driver's or minor driver's license. The executive director of the department, in the director's discretion, may conduct the examination in any county convenient for the applicant. The examination shall include a test of the applicant's eyesight, his or her ability to read and understand highway signs that regulate, warn, and direct traffic, and his or her knowledge of the traffic laws of this state, an actual demonstration of the applicant's ability to exercise ordinary and reasonable care and control in the operation of a motor vehicle, and such further physical and mental examination as the department finds necessary to determine the applicant's fitness to operate a motor vehicle safely upon the highways; except that an applicant seeking renewal of a driver's license by mail under section 42-2-118 need only submit the information required by that section.

(b) The department, in issuing the drivers' licenses for certain types or general classes of vehicles, may waive any examination required by paragraph (a) of this subsection (1) for applicants and may certify certain employers, governmental agencies, or other appropriate organizations to train and examine all applicants for such certain types or general classes of licenses, if such training and examination is equal to the training and examination of the department.

(2) Repealed.

(3) (a) If the department has evidence that indicates that a licensed driver or minor driver is incompetent or otherwise not qualified to be licensed, it may, upon written notice of at least ten days to the licensee, require such driver to submit to an examination.

(b) If a fatal motor vehicle accident involving one or more licensed drivers or minor drivers occurs, the department, if deemed appropriate, shall mail a written notice to all such drivers involved in the accident requiring such drivers to submit to examination. If the department has not mailed a written notice to any driver involved in a fatal accident within ninety days after the department receives notice regarding such accident, the department shall not require an examination of such driver based upon such accident.

(c) Upon the conclusion of an examination required under this subsection (3), the department shall take such action as it deems appropriate and may deny, cancel, suspend, or revoke the license of such person or permit that person to retain such license subject to the restrictions under section 42-2-116. Refusal or failure of the licensee to submit to such examination shall be grounds for suspension or revocation of such person's license. Such decision of the department shall be reviewed by a court of record upon appeal to that court by the party aggrieved.

(4) The department shall prepare and print rules, requirements, and regulations for the mandatory use of license examiners, and the same shall be strictly adhered to in the examination of all drivers.

42-2-112. Medical advice - use by department - physician immunity. (1) In order to determine whether any licensed driver or any applicant for a driver's license is physically or mentally able to operate a motor vehicle safely upon the highways of this state, the department is authorized, pursuant to this section and upon the adoption of rules concerning medical criteria for driver licensing, to seek and receive a written medical opinion from any physician, physician's assistant, or optometrist licensed in this state. Such written medical opinion may also be used by the department in regard to the renewal, suspension, revocation, or cancellation of drivers' licenses pursuant to this article. No written medical opinion shall be sought pursuant to this section unless the department has reason to believe that the driver or applicant is physically or mentally unable to operate a motor vehicle safely upon the highways of this state.

(2) In addition to the written medical opinion sought and received pursuant to subsection (1) of this section, the department may consider a written medical opinion received from the personal physician, physician's assistant, or optometrist of an individual driver or applicant. Any written medical opinion requested by the applicant or driver from a personal physician or optometrist shall be provided to the department at the expense of the applicant or driver. Any written medical opinion required by the department shall also be at the expense of the applicant or driver.

(3) No civil or criminal action shall be brought against any physician, physician's assistant, or optometrist licensed to practice in this state for providing a written medical or optometric opinion pursuant to subsection (1) or (2) of this section if such physician or optometrist acts in good faith and without malice.

(4) A written medical opinion received by the department which relates to an individual applicant or driver is for the confidential use of the department in making decisions on the individual's qualifications as a driver, and the written medical opinion shall not be divulged to any person, except to the applicant or driver, or used in evidence in any trial or proceeding except in matters concerning the individual's qualifications to receive or retain a driver's license.

(5) Written medical opinions received by the department pursuant to this section, in addition to other sources of information, may be used by the department in the adoption of administrative rules concerning medical criteria for driver licensing.

42-2-113. License examiners appointed. The department may appoint license examiners for any county in this state to conduct local examinations for all types of drivers' licenses. The officers of the department shall conduct the examination as prescribed by law for all drivers in the county and collect the fees as provided in section 42-2-114 and remit the same to the department, which shall deposit the same in the state treasury to the credit of the highway users tax fund; except that, for fiscal years 2010-11 and 2011-12, the state treasurer shall credit the fees to the licensing services cash fund created in section 42-2-114.5.

42-2-114. License issued - fees - repeal. (1) (a) (I) The department, upon payment of the required fee and the surrender or cancellation of any previously issued Colorado identification card, shall issue to every applicant, who is not a first time applicant in Colorado or who is under eighteen years of age and is accompanied by a responsible adult meeting the requirements of section 42-2-108 (1), qualifying therefor either a driver's or minor driver's license according to the qualification for either license.

(II) The department, after payment of the required fee and the surrender or cancellation of any previously issued Colorado identification card, shall issue an instruction permit or minor driver's or driver's license to a first time applicant in Colorado only after the department completes its verification of all facts relative to such applicant's right to receive an instruction permit or minor driver's or driver's license including the age, identity, and residency of the applicant, unless such applicant is under eighteen years of age and is accompanied by a responsible adult meeting the requirements of section 42-2-108 (1). By July 1, 2002, such verification shall utilize appropriate and accurate technology and techniques. Such verification shall include a comparison of existing driver's license and identification card images in department files with the applicant's images to ensure such applicant has only one identity. Only one fee shall be assessed for the issuance of a temporary license and a subsequent minor driver's or driver's license issued as a result of the same application.

(III) Such license shall bear thereon the following:

(A) The photograph of the licensee, which shall be taken and processed with equipment leased or owned by the department;

(B) A distinguishing number assigned to the licensee;

(C) The full name, date of birth, and residence address and a brief description of the licensee;

(D) The type or general class of vehicles the licensee may drive;

(E) Any restrictions applicable to the licensee;

(F) The expiration date of the license;

(G) The official seal of the department;

(H) A reference to the previous license issued to the licensee;

(I) The usual signature of the licensee;

(J) Repealed.

(K) One or more security features that are not visible and are capable of authenticating such license and any information contained therein.

(IV) The department shall promulgate rules that shall not allow the access and use of images, unless such images are used for the following:

(A) To aid a federal, state, or local government agency in carrying out such agency's official functions pursuant to section 24-72-204 (7), C.R.S.;

(B) To aid the department to ascertain a person's correct identity; or

(C) To aid the department to prevent the issuance of multiple driver's licenses or identification cards to the same person.

(V) The department shall promulgate rules that shall not allow the access and use of image comparison technology, unless such technology is used for the following:

(A) To aid a federal, state, or local government agency in carrying out such agency's official functions pursuant to section 24-72-204 (7), C.R.S., so long as such federal, state, or local government agency has a reasonable suspicion that a crime has been committed or will be committed and a reasonable suspicion that the image requested is either the perpetrator of such crime or a victim of such crime;

(B) To aid the department to ascertain a person's correct identity when there is reasonable suspicion that the person has used a driver's license or identification card to create a false identity. Nothing in this sub-subparagraph (B) shall be construed to prohibit the department from ascertaining an applicant's correct identity upon application for a driver's license or identification card.

(C) To aid the department to prevent the issuance of multiple driver's licenses or identification cards to the same person.

(VI) Nothing in subparagraph (IV) or (V) of this paragraph (a) shall be construed to require the department to purchase or implement a system that can be used by a person who is not an employee, officer, or agent of the department to access image comparison technology.

(b) (I) In the event the department issues a driver's license that contains stored information, such license may include only the information that is specifically referenced in paragraph (a) of this subsection (1) and that appears in printed form on the face of the license issued by the department to the licensee; except that such stored information shall not include the licensee's social security number.

(II) As used in this paragraph (b), "stored information" includes information that is stored on the driver's license by means of magnetic or electronic encoding, or by any other technology designed to store retrievable information.

(2) (a) (I) Except as provided in subsection (3) of this section:

(A) The fee for the issuance of a driver's license to a person twenty-one years of age or older and sixty years of age or younger is twenty dollars and forty cents, which license shall expire on the birthday of the applicant in the fifth year after the issuance thereof. The fee shall be transferred to the state treasurer, who shall credit fifteen dollars to the highway users tax fund and five dollars and forty cents to the licensing services cash fund created in section 42-2-114.5; except that, for fiscal years 2010-11 and 2011-12, the state treasurer shall credit the fees to the licensing services cash fund created in section 42-2-114.5. In the case of such a driver's license issued by the office of the county clerk and recorder in each county, the office of the county clerk and recorder shall retain the sum of eight dollars, and twelve dollars and forty cents shall be forwarded to the department for transmission to the state treasurer, who shall credit three dollars and forty cents to the licensing services cash fund and nine dollars to the highway users tax fund; except that, for fiscal years 2010-11 and 2011-12, the state treasurer shall credit such amount to the licensing services cash fund. The general assembly shall make appropriations therefrom for the expenses of the administration of this part 1 and part 2 of this article; except that eight dollars and fifty cents of each fee shall be allocated pursuant to section 43-4-205 (6) (b), C.R.S., other than during fiscal years 2010-11 and 2011-12.

(B) (Deleted by amendment, L. 2005, p. 644, § 8, effective May 27, 2005.)

(C) (Deleted by amendment, L. 2007, p. 1571, § 3, effective July 1, 2007.)

(D) The fee for the issuance of a driver's license to a person sixty-one years of age or older is twenty dollars and forty cents, which license shall expire on the birthday of the applicant in the fifth year after the issuance thereof. The fee shall be transferred to the state treasurer, who shall credit fifteen dollars to the highway users tax fund and five dollars and forty cents to the licensing services cash fund created in section 42-2-114.5; except that, for fiscal years 2010-11 and 2011-12, the state treasurer shall credit the fees to the licensing services cash fund created in section 42-2-114.5. In the case of a driver's license issued by the office of the county clerk and recorder in each county, the office of the county clerk and recorder shall retain the sum of eight dollars, and twelve dollars and forty cents shall be forwarded to the department for transmission to the state treasurer, who shall credit three dollars and forty cents to the licensing services cash fund and nine dollars to the highway users tax fund; except that, for the fiscal years 2010-11 and 2011-12, the state treasurer shall credit such amount to the licensing services cash fund. The general assembly shall make appropriations therefrom for the expenses of the administration of this part 1 and part 2 of this article; except that eight dollars and fifty cents of each fee shall be allocated pursuant to section 43-4-205 (6) (b), C.R.S., other than during fiscal years 2010-11 and 2011-12.

(E) Repealed.

(F) In addition to the fees imposed in sub-subparagraphs (A) to (D) of this subparagraph (I), the fee for the issuance of a minor driver's or driver's license shall include a sixty-cent surcharge. The moneys collected pursuant to the surcharge shall be forwarded to the department for transmission to the state treasurer, who shall credit the same to the identification security fund created in section 42-1-220. This sub-subparagraph (F) is repealed, effective July 1, 2014.

(II) Repealed.

(b) (I) Prior to July 1, 2006, there shall be a surcharge of one dollar added for issuance of a driver's or provisional driver's license for which a motorcycle endorsement is requested which shall be credited to the motorcycle operator safety training fund created in section 43-5-504, C.R.S.

(II) On and after July 1, 2006, there shall be a surcharge of two dollars added for issuance of a driver's or provisional driver's license for which a motorcycle endorsement is requested which shall be credited to the motorcycle operator safety training fund created in section 43-5-504, C.R.S.

(2.5) The department shall charge a fee for issuing any probationary license. Such fee shall be set by rule by the department.

(3) Driver's licenses required by the "Commercial Motor Vehicle Safety Act of 1986", Public Law 99-570, shall expire on the birthday of the applicant in the fourth year after the issuance thereof.

(4) (a) The fee for the issuance of a minor driver's license is twenty dollars and forty cents, which license shall expire twenty days after the twenty-first birthday of the licensee. The fee shall be transferred to the state treasurer, who shall credit fifteen dollars to the highway users tax fund and five dollars and forty cents to the licensing services cash fund created in section 42-2-114.5; except that, for fiscal years 2010-11 and 2011-12, the state treasurer shall credit the fees to the licensing services cash fund created in section 42-2-114.5. In the case of the issuance of any minor driver's license by the office of the county clerk and recorder, the fee therefor shall be apportioned in the same manner as for the issuance of a driver's license pursuant to paragraph (a) of subsection (2) of this section.

(b) (I) Prior to July 1, 2006, a surcharge of one dollar shall be added for issuance of a minor driver's license for which a motorcycle endorsement is requested which shall be credited to the motorcycle operator safety training fund created in section 43-5-504, C.R.S.

(II) On and after July 1, 2006, a surcharge of two dollars shall be added for issuance of a minor driver's license for which a motorcycle endorsement is requested which shall be credited to the motorcycle operator safety training fund created in section 43-5-504, C.R.S.

(5) (Deleted by amendment, L. 2007, p. 1571, § 3, effective July 1, 2007.)

(6) (a) A photograph showing the full face of the licensee shall be affixed to every driver's license and minor driver's license issued under this section.

(b) Every minor driver's license issued shall graphically emphasize the age group of the licensee on the face of such license, as prescribed by the department.

(7) Any other provision of law to the contrary notwithstanding, no liability or other sanctions shall be imparted to any person who relies upon the date of birth or identification as set out on any license issued pursuant to this article if such date of birth or identification should be later proved incorrect or fraudulently entered upon said license.

(8) Repealed.

(9) Notwithstanding the amount specified for any fee in this section, the executive director of the department by rule or as otherwise provided by law may reduce the amount of one or more of the fees if necessary pursuant to section 24-75-402 (3), C.R.S., to reduce the uncommitted reserves of the fund to which all or any portion of one or more of the fees is credited. After the uncommitted reserves of the fund are sufficiently reduced, the executive director of the department by rule or as otherwise provided by law may increase the amount of one or more of the fees as provided in section 24-75-402 (4), C.R.S.

(10) (a) At the applicant's voluntary request, the department shall issue a driver's license bearing an identifier of a branch of the United States armed forces, such as "Marine Corps", "Navy", "Army", "Air Force", or "Coast Guard", if the applicant possesses a currently valid military identification document, a DD214 form issued by the United States government, or any other document accepted by the department that demonstrates that the applicant is an active member or a veteran of the branch of service that the applicant has requested be placed on the driver's license. The applicant shall not be required to provide documentation that the applicant is an active member or a veteran of a branch of the United States armed forces to renew or be reissued a driver's license bearing an identifier issued pursuant to this subsection (10). The department shall not place more than one branch of the Unit-

ed States armed forces identifier on an applicant's driver's license.

(b) (I) To be issued a driver's license bearing a branch of service identifier, or to have such license renewed, the applicant shall pay a fee of fifteen dollars to the department, which shall be in addition to any other fee for a driver's license. The department shall transfer the fee to the state treasurer, who shall credit the fee to the highway users tax fund, except as provided in subparagraph (II) of this paragraph (b).

(II) (A) The department may retain up to ninety-eight thousand five hundred thirty-eight dollars of the fees collected pursuant to subparagraph (I) of this paragraph (b) as necessary to offset the direct and indirect cost of implementing this subsection (10).

(B) This subparagraph (II) is repealed, effective July 1, 2012.

(c) Repealed.

42-2-114.5. Licensing services cash fund. (1) The licensing services cash fund is hereby created in the state treasury. Moneys in the fund shall be appropriated by the general assembly to the department for the cost of personal services and operating expenses incurred in the operation of driver's license offices. At the end of each fiscal year, the state treasurer shall credit the money in the fund, less sixteen and one-half percent of the amount appropriated from the fund for such operation in the fiscal year, to the highway users tax fund.

(2) Notwithstanding any provision of subsection (1) of this section to the contrary, on June 15, 2010, the state treasurer shall deduct two million five hundred eighty-nine thousand eight hundred ninety-four dollars from the licensing services cash fund and transfer such sum to the general fund.

42-2-115. License, permit, or identification card to be exhibited on demand. (1) No person who has been issued a driver's or minor driver's license or an instruction permit or an identification card as defined in section 42-2-301 (2), who operates a motor vehicle in this state, and who has such license, permit, or identification card in such person's immediate possession shall refuse to remove such license, permit, or identification card from any billfold, purse, cover, or other container and to hand the same to any peace officer who has requested such person to do so if such peace officer reasonably suspects that such person is committing, has committed, or is about to commit a violation of article 2, 3, 4, 5, 6, 7, or 8 of this title.

(2) Any person who violates any provision of this section commits a class 2 misdemeanor traffic offense.

42-2-116. Restricted license. (1) The department, upon issuing a driver's or minor driver's license or an instruction permit, has authority, whenever good cause appears, to impose restrictions, limitations, or conditions which are suitable to the licensee's driving ability with respect to the type of special mechanical control device required on a motor vehicle which the licensee may operate or which limit the right of the licensee to drive a motor vehicle except when such licensee is required to drive to and from the licensee's place of employment or to perform duties within the course of employment or to impose such other restrictions applicable to the licensee as the department may determine to be appropriate to assure the safe operation of a motor vehicle by the licensee.

(2) The department either may issue a special restricted license or must set forth such restrictions, limitations, or conditions upon the usual license form issued to the applicant.

(3) The department, upon receiving satisfactory evidence of any violation of the restrictions, limitations, or conditions of such license, may cancel or suspend such restricted license, but the licensee shall be entitled to a hearing as upon a suspension or revocation under this article.

(4) No person shall operate a motor vehicle upon a highway or elsewhere within this state in any manner in violation of the restrictions, limitations, or conditions imposed in a special restricted license, in a driver's or minor driver's license, or in an instruction permit issued to such person by the department or by another state or country.

(5) The department is authorized after examination to issue a restricted license to a person with a mental illness or a developmental disability, containing such restrictions as may be imposed upon said person by a court pursuant to part 3 or part 4 of article 14 of title 15, C.R.S., or section 27-65-109 (4) or 27-65-127, C.R.S.

(6) (a) Except as otherwise provided in paragraph (b) of this subsection (6), any person who violates any provision of this section commits a class A traffic infraction.

(b) Any person whose privilege to drive is restricted to the operation of a motor vehicle equipped with an approved ignition interlock device as defined in section 42-2-132.5 (7) (a), who operates a motor vehicle other than a motor vehicle equipped with an approved ignition interlock device or who circumvents or attempts to circumvent the proper use of an approved ignition interlock device commits a class 1 traffic misdemeanor.

(7) Whenever a peace officer issues a citation pursuant to paragraph (b) of subsection (6) of this section, the peace officer shall immediately confiscate the license, shall file an incident report on a form provided by the department, and shall not permit the driver to continue to operate the motor vehicle.

(8) No court shall accept a plea of guilty to another offense from a person charged with a violation of subsection (6) (b) of this section; except that the court may accept a plea of guilty to another offense upon a good faith representation by the prosecuting attorney that the attorney could not establish a prima facie case if the defendant were brought to trial on the offense.

42-2-117. Duplicate permits and minor licenses - replacement licenses. (1) If an instruction permit or a minor driver's license issued under this article is lost, stolen, or destroyed, the person to whom the same was issued, upon request and the payment of a fee of six dollars and ninety cents for the first duplicate and thirteen dollars and forty cents for any subsequent duplicate to the department, may obtain a duplicate or substitute therefor upon furnishing satisfactory proof to the department that the permit or minor license had been lost, stolen, or destroyed and that the applicant is qualified to have a permit or license. The fee for the first duplicate license shall be transferred to the state treasurer, who shall credit five dollars to the highway users tax fund and one dollar and ninety cents to the licensing services cash fund created in section 42-2-114.5; except that, for fiscal years 2010-11 and 2011-12, the state treasurer shall credit the fees to the licensing services cash fund created in section 42-2-114.5. The fee for a subsequent duplicate license shall be transferred to the state treasurer, who shall credit ten dollars to the highway users tax fund and three dollars and forty cents to the licensing services cash fund; except that, for fiscal years 2010-11 and 2011-12, the state treasurer shall credit the fees to the licensing services cash fund.

(1.5) Upon furnishing satisfactory proof to the department that a driver's license issued under the provisions of this article has been lost, stolen, or destroyed, the person to whom the same was issued shall apply for renewal of the license pursuant to section 42-2-118. The new driver's license shall expire as provided in section 42-2-114.

(2) Notwithstanding the amount specified for the fee in this section, the executive director of the department by rule or as otherwise provided by law may reduce the amount of the fee if necessary pursuant to section 24-75-402 (3), C.R.S., to reduce the uncommitted reserves of the fund to which all or any portion of the fee is credited. After the uncommitted reserves of the fund are sufficiently reduced, the executive director of the department by rule or as otherwise provided by law may increase the amount of the fee as provided in section 24-75-402 (4), C.R.S.

42-2-118. Renewal of license in person or by mail - donations to Emily Maureen Ellen Keyes organ and tissue donation awareness fund - repeal. (1) (a) (I) Every license issued under section 42-2-114 shall be renewable prior to its expiration, upon application in person, by mail as provided in subsection (1.3) of this section, or by electronic means as provided in subsection (1.5) of this section, payment of the required fee, passing of an eye test, passing of such other examinations as the applicant's physical limitations or driver's record indicates to be desirable, and payment of any penalty assessment, fine, cost, or forfeiture as prescribed by subsection (3) of this section. If a person renews his or her license pursuant to this subparagraph (I) by electronic means, the person shall attest under penalty of perjury that he or she has had an eye examination by any optometrist or an ophthalmologist within three years before the date of application.

(II) (A) An applicant may make a donation of one dollar or more to the Emily Maureen Ellen Keyes organ and tissue donation awareness fund, created in section 42-2-107 (4) (b) (II), to promote the donation of organs and tissues under the provisions of the "Revised Uniform Anatomical Gift Act", part 1 of article 34 of title 12, C.R.S. The department shall collect such donations and transmit them to the state treasurer, who shall credit the same to the Emily Maureen Ellen Keyes organ and tissue donation awareness fund. The donation prescribed in this sub-subparagraph (A) is voluntary and may be refused by the applicant. The department shall make available informational booklets or other informational sources on the importance of organ and tissue donations to applicants as designed and approved by the advisory body created under section 42-2-107 (4) (b) (III) (A). The department shall inquire of each applicant at the time the completed application is presented whether the applicant is interested in making a donation of one dollar or more and shall also specifically inform the applicant of the option for organ and tissue donations by having a "Y" placed in the donor field on the front of the document. The department shall also advise each applicant volunteering to become an organ and tissue donor that the applicant's name shall be transmitted to the organ and tissue donor registry authorized in section 12-34-120, C.R.S., and that the applicant shall notify the federally designated organ procurement organization of any changes to the applicant's donation.

(B) This subparagraph (II) is repealed, effective July 1, 2018.

(b) (I) Any license referred to in section 42-2-114 which at the time of its expiration is held by a resident of this state who is temporarily outside of this state or is prevented by disability from complying with paragraph (a) of this subsection (1) may be extended for a period of one year if the licensee applies to the department for an extension of the expiration date prior to the date the license expires and pays a fee of three dollars. This extension will become null and void ninety days after the licensee renews his or her residency in the state or otherwise becomes able to comply with the provisions of paragraph (a) of this subsection (1). No more than one extension shall be granted under the provisions of this paragraph (b); except that, when a resident of this state is temporarily residing in a foreign country, no more than two extensions shall be granted.

(II) A surcharge of one dollar shall be added to any extension sought for a license for which a motorcycle endorsement is requested which shall be credited to the motorcycle operator safety training fund created in section 43-5-504, C.R.S.

(1.3) (a) The department may, in its discretion, allow renewal of a driver's license issued under section 42-2-114 by mail subject to the following requirements:

(I) Renewal by mail shall be available only to drivers twenty-one years of age or older;

(II) Renewal by mail shall only be available every other driver's license renewal period as provided in section 42-2-114 (2) (a) and (3);

(III) A person who is less than sixty-six years of age renewing by mail shall attest under penalty of law that he or she has had an eye examination by an optometrist or ophthalmologist within three years before the renewal. A person who is sixty-six years of age or older renewing by mail shall obtain, on a form as required by the department, a signed statement from an optometrist or ophthalmologist attesting that he or she has had an eye examination within the last six months and attesting to the results of the applicant's eye examination; and

(IV) A person renewing by mail who requires vision correction shall attest under penalty of law to his or her prescription for vision correction.

(b) Every applicant for renewal of a driver's license by mail shall submit the following to the department:

(I) Payment of the required fee;
(II) Repealed.
(III) Payment of any penalty assessment, fine, cost, or forfeiture as prescribed by subsection (3) of this section.

(c) The department may promulgate rules necessary for the implementation of this subsection (1.3).

(1.5) (a) The department may, in its discretion, allow renewal of a driver's license issued under section 42-2-114 by electronic means subject to the following requirements:

(I) Electronic renewal shall be available only to drivers twenty-one years of age or older and less than sixty-six years of age;

(II) Electronic renewal shall be available only every other driver's license renewal period as provided in section 42-2-114 (2) (a) and (3);

(III) A person renewing electronically shall attest under penalty of law that he or she has had an eye examination by an optometrist or ophthalmologist within three years before the renewal; and

(IV) A person renewing electronically who requires vision correction shall attest under penalty of law to his or her prescription for vision correction.

(b) Pursuant to sections 24-19.5-103 (3) and 29-11.5-103 (3), C.R.S., the department shall not allow any third-party charges that may be assessed to complete the electronic transaction to reduce the amount of revenue that would otherwise be required to be distributed to the highway users tax fund or the licensing services cash fund.

(c) Every applicant for renewal of a driver's license by electronic means shall submit the following to the department:

(I) Payment of the required fee; and
(II) Payment of any penalty assessment, fine, cost, or forfeiture as prescribed by subsection (3) of this section.

(d) To implement electronic renewal of a driver's license pursuant to this section, the department shall:

(I) Submit to the office of information technology created in the office of the governor for review and approval the department's plan for the renewal of a driver's license by electronic means;

(II) Develop and implement electronic renewal of a driver's license in a manner that is consistent with the nation's policy on national security and in conformance with federal and state law for homeland security;

(III) Develop and implement an information security program and utilize a layered security approach, which shall consist of the following:

(A) A business impact analysis that assesses the criticality of services;
(B) A risk or security assessment that identifies vulnerabilities of the system;
(C) A risk management process;
(D) A contingency plan for disaster recovery of information and services and business continuity;
(E) Procedures that identify security safeguards for asset protection;
(F) A secure architectural design;
(G) Security awareness and training programs; and
(H) Monitoring and audit systems for back-end reviews to evaluate efficiency and efficacy;

(IV) Develop security policies that address, at a minimum, the following:

(A) System protection from viruses and system virus detection;
(B) Firewall security;
(C) Logging capability;
(D) Server security;
(E) Intrusion detection;
(F) Encryption;
(G) Physical security; and
(H) Secure remote access communication, if applicable; and

(V) Develop a migration plan that sets out the department's goals and objectives and establishes priorities and the department's time line for achieving such requirements.

(e) Failure to comply with the requirements of paragraph (d) of this subsection (1.5) may result in the department being removed from or denied access to the state network or mainframe computer until all of the provisions of paragraph (d) of this subsection (1.5) are demonstrated by the department.

(f) Repealed.

(g) The department may promulgate any necessary rules for the implementation of this subsection (1.5).

(2) Every license referred to in this section which is at the time of its expiration, as provided in subsection (1) of this section, held by a member of the armed forces of the United States,

then serving on active duty outside of this state, shall not expire as provided in subsection (1) of this section, but such expiration date shall be extended for a period of three years or until ninety days after such licensee returns to this state, whichever occurs first.

(3) (a) (I) Prior to the renewal of a permanent driver's license or the issuance or renewal of a probationary license, the department shall determine if the applicant has any outstanding judgments or warrants entered or issued against the applicant or if the applicant has issued a check or order to the department for the payment of a penalty assessment and such check or order was returned for insufficient funds or a closed account and remains unpaid as set forth in section 42-4-1709 (7).

(II) For the purposes of this subsection (3), "outstanding judgments or warrants" does not include any judgment or warrant reported to the department in violation of the provisions of section 42-4-110.5 (2) (c).

(b) (I) If there are no outstanding judgments or warrants entered or issued against the applicant and the applicant has not issued a check or order to the department that was returned for insufficient funds or a closed account and that remains unpaid as set forth in section 42-4-1709 (7) and if all other conditions for renewal pursuant to articles 1 to 4 of this title are met, the department shall renew the applicant's permanent driver's license.

(II) If there are no outstanding judgments or warrants entered or issued against the applicant and the defendant has not issued a check or order to the department that was returned for insufficient funds or a closed account and that remains unpaid as set forth in section 42-4-1709 (7) and if all other conditions for renewal pursuant to articles 1 to 4 of this title are met, the department may issue or renew the applicant's probationary license.

(c) If the department determines that the applicant is subject to the requirements of section 42-4-1709 (7), the permanent driver's license shall not be renewed or the probationary license may not be issued or renewed until such applicant has complied with said section. Any person who pays any outstanding judgments, who has any warrants entered, or who makes payment for a check or order to the department that had been returned for insufficient funds or a closed account pursuant to section 42-4-1709 (7) shall pay to the court or to the department a thirty-dollar administrative processing cost for each such judgment, warrant, check, or order in addition to all other penalties, costs, or forfeitures. If the court collects an administrative processing fee, the court shall remit fifty percent of the administrative processing fee to the department of revenue, and the other fifty percent of that fee is to be retained by the issuing court. If the department collects an administrative processing fee, the department shall retain the fee.

(d) Beginning January 1, 1986, the executive director shall ascertain whether the administrative fee established in paragraph (c) of this subsection (3) adequately compensates the department for administration of this subsection (3).

(e) The department of revenue shall coordinate the design and implementation of the necessary delinquency notification forms, satisfaction forms, and time requirements for utilization of such forms by the courts.

(f) There shall be a twenty-day period to appeal any penalty under this section when it can be shown by the applicant or defendant that sufficient funds were in the financial institution and the error was that of the financial institution. In this event the department shall review the documentation and, if it was the fault of the financial institution that the check or order was returned, no penalty or fee shall be imposed.

(4) Notwithstanding the amount specified for any fee in this section, the executive director of the department by rule or as otherwise provided by law may reduce the amount of one or more of the fees if necessary pursuant to section 24-75-402 (3), C.R.S., to reduce the uncommitted reserves of the fund to which all or any portion of one or more of the fees is credited. After the uncommitted reserves of the fund are sufficiently reduced, the executive director of the department by rule or as otherwise provided by law may increase the amount of one or more of the fees as provided in section 24-75-402 (4), C.R.S.

42-2-119. Notices - change of address or name. (1) (a) Whenever any person, after applying for or receiving a driver's license or identification card, moves from the address named in such application or in the license or identification card issued to such person or when the name of the licensee is changed, such person shall, within thirty days, provide notice to the department of such person's old and new address and the number of any license or identification card held by such person. Such notice shall be provided to the department in writing or in electronic form on the department's official web site. A licensee who changes his or her name shall, within thirty days, apply in person to renew such license pursuant to section 42-2-118 and in compliance with sections 42-2-107 and 42-2-305.

(b) Repealed. / (Deleted by amendment, L. 2005, p. 645, § 11, effective May 27, 2005.)

(2) All notices and orders required to be given to any licensee or registered owner under the provisions of the motor vehicle laws shall be in writing; and, if mailed, postpaid by first-class mail, to him or her at the last-known address shown by the records kept by the department pursuant to this article. Such mailing shall be sufficient notice in accord with the motor vehicle laws. Any notice or order of the department mailed first-class under the provisions of this title creates a presumption for administrative purposes that such notice or order was received if the department maintains a copy of the notice or order and maintains a certification that the notice or order was deposited in the United States mail by an employee of the department.

Evidence of a copy of the notice mailed to the last-known address of the licensee as shown by the records kept by the department pursuant to this article and a certification of mailing by a department employee, or evidence of delivery of notice in person to the last-known address of the licensee as shown by the records kept by the department pursuant to this article, or evidence of personal service upon the licensee or upon any attorney appearing on the licensee's behalf of the order of denial, cancellation, suspension, or revocation of the license by the executive director of the department, or by the executive director's duly authorized representative, is prima facie proof that the licensee received personal notice of said denial, cancellation, suspension, or revocation.

(2.5) For purposes of subsection (2) of this section, "last-known address" means:

(a) For notifications regarding motor vehicles, the most recent address provided on a vehicle registration or vehicle registration address change notification provided pursuant to section 42-3-113;

(b) For notifications regarding driving privileges, driver's licenses, or identification cards when there is a driver's license or identification card on file with the department, the most recent of either:

(I) The mailing address provided by an applicant for a driver's license or identification card;

(II) The mailing address stated on an address change notification provided to the department pursuant to subsection (1) of this section; or

(III) The corrected address as reported by an address correction service licensed by the United States postal service;

(c) For notifications regarding driving privileges or identification cards when there is no driver's license or identification card on file with the department, the most recent address shown on any other record on file with the department pursuant to this article and as may be corrected by an address correction service licensed by the United States postal service.

(3) Any person who violates subsection (1) of this section commits a class B traffic infraction.

42-2-120. Methods of service. (1) Any notice or order required to be served under the provisions of the motor vehicle laws may be served in any manner reasonably designed to notify the person to be served of the material provisions of such notice or order. A person has been served with a notice or order when such person has knowledge of the material provisions of such notice or order, regardless of the manner in which such knowledge was acquired. Any irregularity in the form or manner of service or documentation of the proof of service or the means by which knowledge of the material provisions of a notice or order is acquired shall not affect the validity of such notice or order.

(2) For purposes of notices or orders relating to driving restraints only, "material provisions" means those provisions which identify the affected person, and those provisions which state that a restraint against the person's license or privilege to drive in this state has been, or will be, entered on the records of the department, or those provisions which advise the person that he or she has a right to request a hearing regarding the imposition of a restraint against such person's license or privilege to drive.

(3) The department shall develop proof of service forms which may be used to document proof of service under this subsection (3). Such forms shall include but need not be limited to the following:

(a) The name and date of birth of the person served;

(b) The date and time of service;

(c) The identification number of the notice or order served, if any, or, in the event the notice or order is not available, a description of the information relayed to the person served;

(d) The name, title, signature, and employing agency of the person making service;

(e) The signature of the person served; and

(f) The right index fingerprint of the person served.

(4) In addition to service by mail or any other means, service of notices or orders may be personally made by any employee of the department, any peace officer, any municipal, county, or state prosecutor, or any municipal, county or district court judge, magistrate, or judicial officer. If service is personally made under this subsection (4), proof of such service of any notice or order may be made by sending a written notification of service in any form to the department. Such notification shall be an official record of the department under section 42-2-121. It shall not be necessary that the written notification is on a form supplied by the department, but the department may refuse to accept as an official record a written notification which does not provide substantially the same information as specified in subsection (3) of this section.

(5) Peace officers and employees of the department shall serve notices and orders relating to driving restraints upon the affected person anytime the affected person is contacted by a peace officer or employee of the department, when such peace officer or employee believes that the affected person may not have been previously personally served with any notice or order affecting such person's license or privilege to drive a motor vehicle in this state.

42-2-121. Records to be kept by department - admission of records in court. (1) The department shall file every completed application for a license received by it and shall maintain suitable indexes containing in alphabetical order:

(a) All applications denied and on each thereof note the reasons for such denial;

(b) All applications granted; and

(c) The name of every licensee whose license has been suspended or revoked by the department and after each such name note the reasons for such action in each case.

(2) (a) The department shall also file all accident reports, abstracts of court records of convictions received by it under the laws of this state, departmental actions, suspensions, restrictions, revocations, denials, cancellations, reinstatements, and other permanent records and, in connection therewith, maintain a driver's history by making suitable notations in order that an individual record of each licensee showing the convictions of such licensee, the departmental actions, and the traffic accidents in which the licensee has been involved, except those accidents not resulting in a conviction and those traffic violations which occur outside of the boundaries of this state, shall be readily ascertainable and available for the consideration of the department upon any application for renewal of license and at other suitable times.

(b) The department shall also keep a separate file of all abstracts of court records of dismissals of DUI, DUI per se, DWAI, habitual user, and UDD charges and all abstracts of records in cases where the original charges were for DUI, DUI per se, DWAI, habitual user, and UDD and the convictions were for nonalcohol- or nondrug-related traffic offenses. This file shall be made available only to criminal justice agencies, as defined in section 24-72-302 (3), C.R.S.

(c) (I) The following records and documents filed with, maintained by, or prepared by the department are official records and documents of the state of Colorado:

(A) Accident reports;

(B) Abstracts of court records of convictions received by the department under the laws of the state of Colorado;

(C) Records of and documents relating to departmental actions pertaining to the driving privileges of any person concerning licensing, restrictions, probationary conditions, suspensions, revocations, denials, cancellations, or reinstatements of such driving privileges;

(D) Records of and documents relating to the status of any person's privilege to drive a vehicle in the state of Colorado on a specific date or dates;

(E) Drivers' histories;

(F) Records of and documents relating to the identification of persons, including, but not limited to, photographs, fingerprints, handwriting, physical features, physical characteristics, dates of birth, and addresses;

(G) Records of and documents relating to the ownership, registration, transfer, and licensing of vehicles;

(H) All other records and documents required by law or rule and regulation to be kept by the department;

(I) Written summaries and data compilations, if prepared by the department from records and documents filed with, maintained by, or prepared by the department, as defined in sub-subparagraphs (A) to (H) of this subparagraph (I);

(J) Written guidelines, procedures, policies, and rules and regulations of the department.

(II) In any trial or hearing, all official records and documents of the state of Colorado, as defined in subparagraph (I) of this paragraph (c), shall be admissible in all municipal, county, and district courts within the state of Colorado without further foundation, shall be statutory exceptions to rule 802 of the Colorado rules of evidence, and shall constitute prima facie proof of the information contained therein, if such record or document is accompanied by a certificate stating that the executive director of the department or the executive director's appointee has custody of such record or document and is accompanied by and attached to a cover page which:

(A) Specifies the number of pages, exclusive of such cover page, which constitutes the record or document being submitted; and

(B) Bears the signature of the executive director of the department or the executive director's appointee attesting to the genuineness of such record or document; and

(C) Bears the official seal of the department or a stamped or printed facsimile of such seal.

(III) For purposes of subparagraph (II) of this paragraph (c), "official records and documents" shall include any mechanically or electronically reproduced copy, photograph, or printout of any record or document or any portion of any record or document filed with, maintained by, or prepared by the department pursuant to this paragraph (c). The department may also permit the electronic transmission of information for direct recording in the department's records and systems. Information transmitted by an electronic means that is approved by the department constitutes an official record for the purposes of this section whether or not an original source document for such information exists or ever existed.

(III.5) The certificate and cover page and its contents required by subparagraph (II) of this paragraph (c) may be electronically produced and transmitted. An electronic reproduction of the certificate and cover page, including an electronic signature of the executive director of the department or of the executive director's appointee and an electronic reproduction of the official seal of the department, shall be admissible in court as provided in subparagraph (II) of this paragraph (c).

(IV) For purposes of subparagraph (II) of this paragraph (c), a record or document shall not be required to include every page of a record or document filed with, maintained by, or prepared by the department pursuant to this paragraph (c) to be an official record or document, if such official record or document includes all of those portions of such record or document relevant to the trial or hearing for which it is prepared. There shall be a presumption that such official record or document contains all that is relevant to such trial or hearing.

(d) Notwithstanding the provisions of paragraph (a) of this subsection (2), the department shall not maintain records of convictions of traffic offenses defined in this title for which no points are assessed pursuant to section 42-2-127 (5) other than convictions pursuant to sections 42-2-134, 42-2-138, 42-2-206, and 42-7-422.

(e) Records or documents filed with, maintained by, or prepared by another state that are equivalent to the records maintained in Colorado under paragraph (a) of this subsection (2) shall be admissible in a trial or hearing in accordance with this section.

(3) The department seal required under subsection (2) of this section and under section 42-1-205 may also consist of a rubber stamp producing a facsimile of the seal stamped upon the document.

(4) (a) The department shall place a confidentiality notice on any driver's license application form under section 42-2-107, driver's license renewal application under section 42-2-118, duplicate driver's license application under section 42-2-117, commercial driver's license application under section 42-2-404, identification card application form under section 42-2-302, motor vehicle title application form under section 42-6-116, or motor vehicle registration application form under section 42-3-113. The department shall indicate in such notice that, unless the person waives his or her confidentiality, the information contained in the person's motor vehicle or driver record shall not be used for any purpose other than a purpose authorized by law.

(b) The department shall prepare a confidentiality waiver form and shall provide the form to the designated agents of the department. The department and the designated agents shall make such form available to any person on request. The department and the designated agents shall be the sole distributors of such form. The form shall contain instructions for filing the form with the department.

(I) to (IV) (Deleted by amendment, L. 2000, p. 1341, § 3, effective May 30, 2000.)

(c) Any person executing a waiver under this subsection (4) that information in motor vehicle or driver records may be used for any purpose shall provide the information requested by the department in the confidentiality waiver form and file the form directly with the department. The department shall process such forms and shall notify the designated agents regarding which motor vehicle and driver records are subject to confidentiality waivers.

(d) A confidentiality waiver expires upon a request by the person to rescind the confidentiality waiver or upon the renewal of the motor vehicle or driver record; except that a confidentiality waiver form filed in connection with a motor vehicle registration application shall remain in force until the motor vehicle is transferred or the person requests that the confidentiality waiver be rescinded.

(5) (a) Upon application by a person, the department shall expunge all records concerning a conviction of a person for UDD with a BAC of at least 0.02 but not more than 0.05 and any records concerning an administrative determination resulting in a revocation under section 42-2-126 (3) (b) or (3) (e) if:

(I) Such person presents a request for expungement to the department and provides all information required by the department to process such request;

(II) Such person is over twenty-one years of age and any department action regarding the offense or administrative determination has been concluded;

(III) The person has not been convicted for any other DUI, DUI per se, DWAI, habitual user, or UDD offense that was committed while such person was under twenty-one years of age and is not subject to any other administrative determination resulting in a revocation under section 42-2-126 for any other occurrence while such person was under twenty-one years of age;

(IV) Such person pays the fine and surcharge for such conviction and completes any other requirements of the court with regard to such conviction, including, but not limited to, any order to pay restitution to any party;

(V) Such person has never held a commercial driver's license as defined in section 42-2-402; and

(VI) Such person was not operating a commercial motor vehicle as defined in section 42-2-402.

(b) Upon receiving a request for expungement, the department may delay consideration of the request until sufficient time has elapsed to ensure that the person is not convicted for any additional offense under section 42-4-1301 committed while the person was under twenty-one years of age and that there is no additional administrative determination resulting in a revocation under section 42-2-126 (3) (b) or (3) (e) for actions taken while the person was under twenty-one years of age.

(6) The department shall electronically transmit the name, address, telephone number, date of birth, and gender of each individual who has volunteered to donate organs or tissue upon death on an instructional permit, a minor driver's license, a driver's license, an identification card, or any other license application received by it to the organ and tissue donor registry authorized in section 12-34-120, C.R.S.

42-2-121.5. Emergency contact information - web site form - license application - driver's license database. (1) (a) No later than January 1, 2009, the department shall create and make available on its official web site an electronic form that allows a person with a driver's license, minor driver's license, instruction permit, or temporary driver's license issued pursuant to this part 1 or an identification card issued pursuant to part 3 of this article to input the names, addresses, and telephone numbers of up to two persons to be contacted in an emergency pursuant to subsection (3) of this section. The form shall include a statement that the information may be disclosed only to authorized law enforcement or public safety personnel for the purpose of notifying the persons listed in an emergency and a place for the person entering the information to assent to the use of the information for this purpose.

(b) The department shall add the emergency contact information received from a person in accordance with paragraph (a) of this subsection (1) to the person's record in the driver's license database.

(2) (a) On and after January 1, 2009, the department shall include on the application form for a driver's license, minor driver's license, or instruction permit used pursuant to section 42-2-107, the driver's license renewal application used pursuant to section 42-2-118, the duplicate driver's license application used pursuant to section 42-2-117, and the identification card application form used pursuant to section 42-2-302 a place for the applicant to specify the names, addresses, and telephone numbers of up to two persons to be contacted in an emergency pursuant to subsection (3) of this section. The application shall include a statement that the information will be disclosed only to authorized law enforcement or public safety personnel for the purpose of notifying the persons listed in an emergency and a place for the person providing the information to assent to the use of the information for this purpose.

(b) The department shall add the emergency contact information specified on an application in accordance with paragraph (a) of this subsection (2) to the person's record in the driver's license database.

(3) An officer of a law enforcement or public safety agency who is authorized to access the driver's license database may obtain a person's emergency contact information from the database if the person is injured or killed as a result of an accident, criminal act, or other emergency situation. The officer may contact the persons listed in the emergency contact information and notify them of the emergency situation and the condition and location of the person who has been injured or killed.

(4) The department shall not disclose the information received in accordance with this section to any person except as authorized by subsection (3) of this section and section 24-72-204 (7) (d), C.R.S.

42-2-122. Department may cancel license - limited license for physical or mental limitations. (1) The department has the authority to cancel, deny, or deny the reissuance of any driver's or minor driver's license upon determining that the licensee was not entitled to the issuance thereof for any of the following reasons:

(a) Failure to give the required or correct information in an application, or commission of any fraud in making such application or in submitting any proof allowed under this section;

(b) Inability to operate a motor vehicle because of physical or mental incompetence;

(c) Permission of an unlawful or fraudulent use or conviction of misuse of license, titles, permits, or license plates;

(d) That such license would have been subject to denial under the provisions of section 42-2-104;

(e) Failure of the licensee to register in Colorado all vehicles owned by the licensee under the requirements of section 42-3-103;

(f) The person is not lawfully present in the United States;

(g) The person is not a resident of the state of Colorado;

(h) (I) The person has an outstanding judgment or warrant referred to in section 42-4-1709 (7) issued against such person; except that, as used in this paragraph (h), "judgment or warrant" shall not include any judgment or warrant reported to the department in violation of section 42-4-110.5 (2) (c).

(II) Upon receipt of a judgment or warrant from a court clerk on or after September 1, 2000, the department shall send written notice to the person identified in the court order that such person is required to provide the department with proof that the judgment or warrant is no longer outstanding within thirty days after the date such notice is sent or such person's driver's license shall be canceled or any application for a new license shall be denied. Proof that the judgment or warrant is no longer outstanding shall be in the form of a certificate issued by the clerk of the court entering the judgment or issuing the warrant in a form approved by the executive director.

(III) If acceptable proof is not received by the department within thirty days after notice was sent, the department shall cancel the driver's license or deny any application for a license of the person against whom the judgment was entered or the warrant was issued.

(IV) The general assembly finds that the department currently has record of a large number of outstanding judgments and warrants and that it does not know whether such judgments and warrants are still outstanding. All outstanding judgments and warrants that are in the department's records as of August 31, 2000, shall be deemed void for purposes of this section effective September 1, 2005.

(i) Failure of the person to complete a level II alcohol and drug education and treatment program certified by the unit in the department of human services that administers behavioral health programs and services, including those related to mental health and substance abuse, pursuant to section 42-4-1301.3, as required by section 42-2-126 (4) (d) (II) (A) or 42-2-132 (2) (a) (II). The failure shall be documented pursuant to section 42-2-144.

(2) The department has the authority to cancel any driver's or minor driver's license if, subsequent to the issuance of such license, the depart-

ment has authentic information that a condition developed or an act was committed which places such licensee in one of the categories for which cancellation is authorized.

(2.5) (a) Any person who has had a driver's or minor driver's license or driving privilege cancelled pursuant to paragraph (b) of subsection (1) of this section who is receiving or has received therapy treatment for physical or mental incompetence or an evaluation for such incompetence through a rehabilitation provider or licensed physician certified by the department to provide rehabilitative driving instruction may receive a limited license with such limitations as the department deems necessary after consultation with and upon the recommendation of the rehabilitation provider or licensed physician.

(b) (I) Any person licensed pursuant to this subsection (2.5) shall be subject to the examination requirements set forth in section 42-2-111.

(II) Rehabilitation providers and licensed physicians shall be subject to the provisions governing medical advice in section 42-2-112.

(c) The department shall adopt rules as necessary to carry out this subsection (2.5).

(3) Upon such cancellation, the licensee must surrender the license so cancelled to the department, and thereafter such licensee shall be entitled to a hearing by the department if such license is returned and if such request is made within thirty days from the date of such cancellation; except that a denial or cancellation under paragraph (h) or (i) of subsection (1) of this section shall be deemed to be final agency action for judicial review purposes under section 24-4-104, C.R.S. Such hearing, if requested, shall be held no later than thirty days from the date of such cancellation. Notification of such cancellation shall be given as provided in section 42-2-119.

(4) (a) Upon the holding of a hearing as provided in subsection (3) of this section or upon determination by the department, the license shall be returned if the licensee is able to prove that cancellation should not have been made. When the original cancellation is sustained by the department, such licensee may apply for and receive a new license whenever the licensee can show that the reason for the original cancellation no longer applies. The licensee may also appeal the decision of the department after the hearing to the district court as provided in section 42-2-135.

(b) A licensee who has proved that cancellation should not have been made shall not be required to give proof of financial responsibility pursuant to article 7 of this title.

42-2-123. Suspending privileges of nonresidents and reporting convictions. (1) The privilege of driving a motor vehicle on the highways of this state given to a nonresident is subject to suspension or revocation by the department in like manner and for like cause as a driver's license may be suspended or revoked.

(2) The department is further authorized, upon receiving a record of the conviction in this state of a nonresident driver of a motor vehicle of any offense under the motor vehicle laws of this state, to forward a certified copy of such record to the motor vehicle administrator in the state wherein the person so convicted is a resident.

42-2-124. When court to report convictions. (1) (a) Except as otherwise provided, whenever any person is convicted of any offense for which this article makes mandatory the revocation or suspension of the driver's or minor driver's license of such person by the department, the court in which such conviction is had shall require the offender to immediately surrender such driver's or minor driver's license or any instruction permit to the court at the time of conviction, and the court shall, not later than ten days after such conviction, forward the license to the department, together with a record of such conviction on the form prescribed by the department. Any person who does not immediately surrender such person's license or permit to the court commits a class 2 misdemeanor traffic offense, unless such person swears or affirms under oath administered by the court and subject to the penalties of perjury that the license or permit has been lost, destroyed, or is not in said person's immediate possession. Any person who swears or affirms that the license or permit is not in the immediate possession of said person shall surrender said license or permit to the court within five days of the sworn or affirmed statement, and if not surrendered within such time, said person commits a class 2 misdemeanor traffic offense.

(b) Whenever the driver's history of any person shows that such driver is required to maintain financial responsibility for the future and is unable to show to the court that the driver is maintaining the required financial responsibility for the future, the court shall require the immediate surrender to it of the driver's, minor driver's, or temporary driver's license or any instruction permit held by such person, and the court, within forty-eight hours after receiving the license, shall forward the license to the department with the form prescribed by the department.

(2) Every court having jurisdiction over offenses committed under this article or any other law of this state regulating the operation of motor vehicles on highways and every military authority having jurisdiction over offenses substantially the same as those set forth in section 42-2-127 (5) which occur on a federal military installation in this state shall forward to the department a record of the conviction of any person in said court or by said authority for a violation of any said laws not later than ten days after the day of sentencing for such conviction and may recommend the suspension or retention of the driver's, minor driver's, or temporary driver's license or any instruction permit of the person so convicted.

(3) For the purposes of this section, the term "convicted" or "conviction" means a sentence

imposed following a plea of guilty or nolo contendere, a verdict of guilty by the court or a jury, or an adjudication of a delinquency under title 19, C.R.S. The payment of a penalty assessment under the provisions of section 42-4-1701 shall also be considered a conviction if the summons states clearly the points to be assessed for that offense. Whenever suspension or revocation of a license is authorized or required for conviction of any offense under state law, a final finding of guilty of a violation of a municipal ordinance governing a substantially equivalent offense in a city, town, or city and county shall, for purposes of such suspension or revocation, be deemed and treated as a conviction of the corresponding offense under state law. A stay of sentence, pending appeal, shall not deprive the department of the authority to suspend, revoke, or deny a driver's or minor driver's license pending any final determination of a conviction on appeal.

(4) An expungement of an adjudication of delinquency shall not result in a rescission of the revocation or suspension of the driving privilege unless said expungement is a result of a reversal of the adjudication on appeal.

42-2-125. Mandatory revocation of license and permit. (1) The department shall immediately revoke the license or permit of any driver or minor driver upon receiving a record showing that such driver has:

(a) Been convicted of vehicular homicide or vehicular assault as described in sections 18-3-106 and 18-3-205, C.R.S., or of criminally negligent homicide as described in section 18-3-105, C.R.S., while driving a motor vehicle;

(b) Been convicted of driving a motor vehicle while under the influence of a controlled substance, as defined in section 12-22-303 (7), C.R.S., or while an habitual user of such a controlled substance;

(b.5) In the case of a driver twenty-one years of age or older, been convicted of an offense described in section 42-4-1301 (1) (a) or (2) (a). Except as provided in section 42-2-132.5, the period of revocation based upon this paragraph (b.5) shall be nine months. The provisions of this paragraph (b.5) shall not apply to a person whose driving privilege was revoked pursuant to section 42-2-126 (3) (a) (I) for a first offense based on the same driving incident.

(c) Been convicted of any felony in the commission of which a motor vehicle was used;

(d) Been convicted of failing to stop and render aid as required by section 42-4-1601;

(e) Been convicted of perjury in the first or second degree or the making of a false affidavit or statement under oath to the department under any law relating to the ownership or operation of a motor vehicle;

(f) Been three times convicted of reckless driving of a motor vehicle for acts committed within a period of two years;

(g) (I) Been twice convicted of any combination of DUI, DUI per se, DWAI, or habitual user for acts committed within a period of five years;

(II) In the case of a minor driver, been convicted of DUI, DUI per se, DWAI, or habitual user committed while such driver was under twenty-one years of age;

(g.5) In the case of a minor driver, been convicted of UDD committed when such driver was under twenty-one years of age;

(h) Been determined to be mentally incompetent by a court of competent jurisdiction and for whom a court has entered, pursuant to part 3 or part 4 of article 14 of title 15, C.R.S., or section 27-65-109 (4) or 27-65-127, C.R.S., an order specifically finding that the mental incompetency is of such a degree that the person is incapable of safely operating a motor vehicle;

(i) Been convicted of DUI, DUI per se, DWAI, or habitual user and has two previous convictions of any of such offenses. The license of any driver shall be revoked for an indefinite period and shall only be reissued upon proof to the department that said driver has completed a level II alcohol and drug education and treatment program certified by the unit in the department of human services that administers behavioral health programs and services, including those related to mental health and substance abuse, pursuant to section 42-4-1301.3 and that said driver has demonstrated knowledge of the laws and driving ability through the regular motor vehicle testing process. In no event shall such license be reissued in less than two years.

(j) Been required to file and maintain proof of financial responsibility for the future as provided by section 42-4-1410 or article 7 of this title and who, at the time of a violation of any provision of this title, had not filed or was not maintaining such proof;

(k) Repealed.

(l) Been found to have knowingly and willfully left the scene of an accident involving a commercial motor vehicle driven by the person;

(m) (I) Been convicted of violating section 12-47-901 (1) (b) or (1) (c) or 18-13-122 (2), C.R.S., or any counterpart municipal charter or ordinance offense to such sections and having failed to complete an alcohol evaluation or assessment, an alcohol education program, or an alcohol treatment program ordered by the court in connection with such conviction; or

(II) Been convicted of violating section 12-47-901 (1) (b) or (1) (c) or 18-13-122 (2), C.R.S., or any counterpart municipal charter or ordinance offense to such sections and has a previous conviction for such offenses;

(n) (Deleted by amendment, L. 2009, (HB 09-1266), ch. 347, p. 1816, § 8, effective August 5, 2009.)

(o) Been:

(I) (Deleted by amendment, L. 2009, (HB 09-1266), ch. 347, p. 1816, § 8, effective August 5, 2009.)

(II) Convicted of, or has received a deferred judgment for, an offense described in section 18-4-409 or 18-4-503 (1) (c), C.R.S., or a comparable municipal charter or ordinance offense.

(III) (Deleted by amendment, L. 2007, p. 504, § 3, effective July 1, 2007.)

(2) Unless otherwise provided in this section, the period of revocation shall be not less than one year; except that the period of revocation based on paragraphs (b) and (c) of subsection (1) of this section involving a commercial motor vehicle transporting hazardous materials as defined under section 42-2-402 (7) shall result in a revocation period of three years.

(2.3) (Deleted by amendment, L. 2007, p. 504, § 3, effective July 1, 2007.)

(2.4) After the expiration of the period of revocation pursuant to this section and any subsequently imposed periods of revocation, any person whose license is revoked under subparagraph (I) of paragraph (g) or paragraph (i) of subsection (1) of this section shall be required to have a restricted license pursuant to the provisions of section 42-2-132.5.

(2.5) The period of revocation under paragraph (g.5) of subsection (1) of this section for a person who is less than twenty-one years of age at the time of the offense and who is convicted of driving with an alcohol content of at least 0.02 but not more than 0.05 under section 42-4-1301 (2) (a.5) is as follows:

(a) Except as provided in subsection (2.7) of this section, three months for a first offense;

(b) Six months for a second offense;

(c) One year for a third or subsequent offense.

(2.7) (a) A person whose license is revoked for a first offense under paragraph (g.5) of subsection (1) of this section may request that, in lieu of the three-month revocation, the person's license be revoked for a period of not less than thirty days, to be followed by a suspension period of such length that the total period of revocation and suspension equals three months. If the hearing officer approves such request, the hearing officer may grant such person a probationary license that may be used only for the reasons provided in section 42-2-127 (14) (a).

(b) The hearing to consider a request under paragraph (a) of this subsection (2.7) may be held at the same time as the hearing held under subsection (4) of this section; except that a probationary license may not become effective until at least thirty days have elapsed since the beginning of the revocation period.

(2.8) A person whose license has been revoked pursuant to paragraph (o) of subsection (1) of this section shall not be eligible for reinstatement of his or her license until the department receives proof that the person has satisfied any order for restitution entered in connection with the conviction.

(3) Upon revoking the license of any person as required by this section, the department shall immediately notify the licensee as provided in section 42-2-119 (2). Where a minor driver's license is revoked under paragraph (m) of subsection (1) of this section, such revocation shall not run concurrently with any previous or subsequent suspension, revocation, cancellation, or denial that is provided for by law.

(4) Upon receipt of the notice of revocation, the licensee or the licensee's attorney may request a hearing in writing, if the licensee has returned said license to the department in accordance with the provisions of section 42-2-133. The department, upon notice to the licensee, shall hold a hearing at the district office of the department closest to the residence of the licensee; except that, at the discretion of the department, all or part of the hearing may be conducted in real time, by telephone or other electronic means in accordance with section 42-1-218.5. The department shall hold the hearing not less than thirty days after receiving such license and request through a hearing commissioner appointed by the executive director of the department, which hearing shall be conducted in accordance with the provisions of section 24-4-105, C.R.S. After such hearing, the licensee may appeal the decision of the department to the district court as provided in section 42-2-135. Should a driver who has had his or her license revoked under this section be subsequently acquitted of such charge by a court of record, the department shall immediately, in any event not later than ten days after the receipt of such notice of acquittal, reinstate said license to the driver affected.

(5) Except where more than one revocation occurs as a result of the same episode of driving, license revocations made pursuant to this section shall not run concurrently with any previous or subsequent revocation or denial in lieu of revocation which is provided for by law. Any revocation unused pursuant to this section shall not preclude other actions which the department is required to take pursuant to the provisions of this title, and unless otherwise provided by law, this subsection (5) shall not prohibit revocations from being served concurrently with any suspension or denial in lieu of suspension of driving privileges.

(6) (a) Any person who has a license revoked pursuant to paragraph (m) of subsection (1) of this section shall be subject to the following revocation periods:

(I) After a first conviction and failure to complete an ordered evaluation, assessment, or program, three months;

(II) After a second conviction, six months;

(III) After any third or subsequent conviction, one year.

(b) (Deleted by amendment, L. 2007, p. 504, § 3, effective July 1, 2007.)

(c) Repealed.

(7) (Deleted by amendment, L. 2009, (HB 09-1266), ch. 347, p. 1816, § 8, effective August 5, 2009.)

(8) If a suspension or revocation of a license is authorized or required for conviction of an offense under state law, a final finding of guilt for a violation of a municipal ordinance governing a substantially equivalent offense in a municipality,

county, or another state for purposes of a suspension or revocation shall be deemed as a conviction of the corresponding offense under state law. A stay of sentence or a pending appeal shall not deprive the department of the authority to suspend, revoke, or deny a driver's license or minor driver's license pending a final determination of a conviction on appeal.

42-2-126. Revocation of license based on administrative determination. (1) **Legislative declaration.** The purposes of this section are:

(a) To provide safety for all persons using the highways of this state by quickly revoking the driver's license of any person who has shown himself or herself to be a safety hazard by driving with an excessive amount of alcohol in his or her body and any person who has refused to submit to an analysis as required by section 42-4-1301.1;

(b) To guard against the potential for any erroneous deprivation of the driving privilege by providing an opportunity for a full hearing; and

(c) Following the revocation period, to prevent the relicensing of a person until the department is satisfied that the person's alcohol problem is under control and that the person no longer constitutes a safety hazard to other highway users.

(2) **Definitions.** As used in this section, unless the context otherwise requires:

(a) "Excess BAC" means that a person had a BAC level sufficient to subject the person to a license revocation for excess BAC 0.08, excess BAC underage, excess BAC CDL, or excess BAC underage CDL.

(b) "Excess BAC 0.08" means that a person drove a vehicle in this state when the person's BAC was 0.08 or more at the time of driving or within two hours after driving.

(c) "Excess BAC CDL" means that a person drove a commercial motor vehicle in this state when the person's BAC was 0.04 or more at the time of driving or at any time thereafter.

(d) "Excess BAC underage" means that a person was under the age of twenty-one years and the person drove a vehicle in this state when the person's BAC was in excess of 0.02 but less than 0.08 at the time of driving or within two hours after driving.

(e) "Excess BAC underage CDL" means that a person was under the age of twenty-one years and the person drove a commercial motor vehicle in this state when the person's BAC was in excess of 0.02 but less than 0.04 at the time of driving or at any time thereafter.

(f) "Hearing officer" means the executive director of the department or an authorized representative designated by the executive director.

(g) "License" includes driving privilege.

(h) "Refusal" means refusing to take or complete, or to cooperate in the completing of, a test of the person's blood, breath, saliva, or urine as required by section 18-3-106 (4) or 18-3-205 (4), C.R.S., or section 42-4-1301.1 (2).

(i) "Respondent" means a person who is the subject of a hearing under this section.

(3) **Revocation of license.** (a) **Excess BAC 0.08.** (I) The department shall revoke the license of a person for excess BAC 0.08 for:

(A) Nine months for a first violation committed on or after January 1, 2009; except that such a person may apply for a restricted license pursuant to the provisions of section 42-2-132.5;

(B) One year for a second violation; and

(C) Two years for a third or subsequent violation occurring on or after January 1, 2009, regardless of when the prior violations occurred; except that such a person may apply for a restricted license pursuant to the provisions of section 42-2-132.5.

(II) (Deleted by amendment, L. 2008, p. 833, § 3, effective January 1, 2009.)

(b) **Excess BAC underage.** (I) The department shall revoke the license of a person for excess BAC underage for three months for a first violation, for six months for a second violation, and for one year for a third or subsequent violation.

(II) (A) Notwithstanding the provisions of subparagraph (I) of this paragraph (b), a person whose license is revoked for a first offense under subparagraph (I) of this paragraph (b) and whose BAC was not more than 0.05 may request that, in lieu of the three-month revocation, the person's license be revoked for a period of not less than thirty days, to be followed by a suspension period of such length that the total period of revocation and suspension equals three months. If the hearing officer approves the request, the hearing officer may grant the person a probationary license that may be used only for the reasons provided in section 42-2-127 (14) (a).

(B) The hearing to consider a request under this subparagraph (II) may be held at the same time as the hearing held under subsection (8) of this section; except that a probationary license may not become effective until at least thirty days have elapsed since the beginning of the revocation period.

(c) **Refusal.** (I) The department shall revoke the license of a person for refusal for one year for a first violation, two years for a second violation, and three years for a third or subsequent violation; except that the period of revocation shall be at least three years if the person was driving a commercial motor vehicle that was transporting hazardous materials as defined in section 42-2-402 (7).

(II) Notwithstanding the provisions of subparagraph (I) of this paragraph (c), such a person whose license has been revoked for two years for a second violation or for three years for a third or subsequent violation may apply for a restricted license pursuant to the provisions of section 42-2-132.5.

(d) **Excess BAC CDL.** The department shall revoke for the disqualification period provided in 49 CFR 383.51 the commercial driving privilege of a person who was the holder of a commercial driver's license or was driving a commercial motor vehicle for a violation of excess BAC 0.08, excess BAC CDL, or refusal.

(e) **Excess BAC underage CDL.** The department shall revoke the commercial driving privilege of a person for excess BAC underage CDL for three months for a first violation, six months for a second violation, and one year for a third or subsequent violation.

(4) **Multiple restraints and conditions on driving privileges.** (a) (I) Except as otherwise provided in this paragraph (a), a revocation imposed pursuant to this section shall run consecutively and not concurrently with any other revocation imposed pursuant to this section.

(II) If a license is revoked for excess BAC and the person is also convicted on criminal charges arising out of the same occurrence for DUI, DUI per se, DWAI, or UDD, both the revocation under this section and any suspension, revocation, cancellation, or denial that results from the conviction shall be imposed, but the periods shall run concurrently, and the total period of revocation, suspension, cancellation, or denial shall not exceed the longer of the two periods.

(III) If a license is revoked for refusal, the revocation shall not run concurrently, in whole or in part, with any previous or subsequent suspensions, revocations, or denials that may be provided for by law, including but not limited to any suspension, revocation, or denial that results from a conviction of criminal charges arising out of the same occurrence for a violation of section 42-4-1301. Any revocation for refusal shall not preclude other action that the department is required to take in the administration of this title.

(IV) The revocation of the commercial driving privilege under excess BAC CDL may run concurrently with another revocation pursuant to this section arising out of the same incident.

(b) (I) The periods of revocation specified in subsection (3) of this section are intended to be minimum periods of revocation for the described conduct. A license shall not be restored under any circumstances, and a probationary license shall not be issued, during the revocation period.

(II) Notwithstanding the provisions of subparagraph (I) of this paragraph (b), a person whose privilege to drive a commercial motor vehicle has been revoked because of excess BAC CDL and who was twenty-one years of age or older at the time of the offense may apply for a driver's license of another class or type as long as there is no other statutory reason to deny the person a license. The department may not issue the person a probationary license that would authorize the person to operate a commercial motor vehicle.

(c) Upon the expiration of the period of revocation under this section, if a person's license is still suspended on other grounds, the person may seek a probationary license as authorized by section 42-2-127 (14) subject to the requirements of paragraph (d) of this subsection (4).

(d) (I) Following a license revocation, the department shall not issue a new license or otherwise restore the driving privilege unless the department is satisfied, after an investigation of the character, habits, and driving ability of the person, that it will be safe to grant the privilege of driving a motor vehicle on the highways to the person; except that the department may not require a person to undergo skills or knowledge testing prior to issuance of a new license or restoration of the person's driving privilege if the person's license was revoked for a first violation of excess BAC 0.08 or excess BAC underage.

(II) (A) If a person was determined to be driving with excess BAC and the person had a BAC that was 0.17 or more or if the person's driving record otherwise indicates a designation as a persistent drunk driver as defined in section 42-1-102 (68.5), the department shall require the person to complete a level II alcohol and drug education and treatment program certified by the unit in the department of human services that administers behavioral health programs and services, including those related to mental health and substance abuse, pursuant to section 42-4-1301.3 as a condition to restoring driving privileges to the person and, upon the restoration of driving privileges, shall require the person to hold a restricted license requiring the use of an ignition interlock device pursuant to section 42-2-132.5 (1) (b.5).

(B) If a person seeking reinstatement is required to complete, but has not yet completed, a level II alcohol and drug education and treatment program, the person shall file with the department proof of current enrollment in a level II alcohol and drug education and treatment program certified by the unit in the department of human services that administers behavioral health programs and services, including those related to mental health and substance abuse, pursuant to section 42-4-1301.3, on a form approved by the department.

(5) **Actions of law enforcement officer.** (a) If a law enforcement officer has probable cause to believe that a person should be subject to license revocation for excess BAC or refusal, the law enforcement officer shall forward to the department an affidavit containing information relevant to the legal issues and facts that shall be considered by the department to determine whether the person's license should be revoked as provided in subsection (3) of this section. The executive director of the department shall specify to law enforcement agencies the form of the affidavit to be used under this paragraph (a) and the types of information needed in the affidavit and may specify any additional documents or copies of documents needed by the department to make its determination in addition to the affidavit. The affidavit shall be dated, signed, and sworn to by the law enforcement officer under penalty of perjury, but need not be notarized or sworn to before any other person.

(b) (I) A law enforcement officer, on behalf of the department, shall personally serve a notice of revocation on a person who is still available to the law enforcement officer if the law enforcement officer determines that, based on a refusal or on test results available to the law enforcement officer, the person's license is subject to revocation for excess BAC or refusal.

(II) When a law enforcement officer serves a notice of revocation, the law enforcement officer shall take possession of any driver's license issued by this state or any other state that the person holds. When the law enforcement officer takes possession of a valid driver's license issued by this state or any other state, the law enforcement officer, acting on behalf of the department, shall issue a temporary permit that is valid for seven days after the date of issuance.

(III) A copy of the completed notice of revocation form, a copy of any completed temporary permit form, and any driver's, minor driver's, or temporary driver's license or any instruction permit taken into possession under this section shall be forwarded to the department by the law enforcement officer along with an affidavit as described in paragraph (a) of this subsection (5) and any additional documents or copies of documents as described in said paragraph (a).

(IV) The department shall provide to law enforcement agencies forms for notice of revocation and for temporary permits. The law enforcement agencies shall use the forms for the notice of revocation and for temporary permits and shall follow the form and provide the information for affidavits as provided by the department pursuant to paragraph (a) of this subsection (5).

(V) A law enforcement officer shall not issue a temporary permit to a person who is already driving with a temporary permit issued pursuant to subparagraph (II) of this paragraph (b).

(6) **Initial determination and notice of revocation.** (a) Upon receipt of an affidavit of a law enforcement officer and the relevant documents required by paragraph (a) of subsection (5) of this section, the department shall determine whether the person's license should be revoked under subsection (3) of this section. The determination shall be based upon the information contained in the affidavit and the relevant documents submitted to the department, and the determination shall be final unless a hearing is requested and held as provided in subsection (8) of this section. The determination of these facts by the department is independent of the determination of a court of the same or similar facts in the adjudication of any criminal charges arising out of the same occurrence. The disposition of the criminal charges shall not affect any revocation under this section.

(b) (I) If the department determines that the person is subject to license revocation, the department shall issue a notice of revocation if a notice has not already been served upon the person by the law enforcement officer as provided in paragraph (b) of subsection (5) of this section. A notice of revocation shall clearly specify the reason and statutory grounds for the revocation, the effective date of the revocation, the right of the person to request a hearing, the procedure for requesting a hearing, and the date by which a request for a hearing must be made.

(II) In sending a notice of revocation, the department shall mail the notice in accordance with the provisions of section 42-2-119 (2) to the person at the last-known address shown on the department's records, if any, and to any address provided in the law enforcement officer's affidavit if that address differs from the address of record. The notice shall be deemed received three days after mailing.

(c) If the department determines that the person is not subject to license revocation, the department shall notify the person of its determination and shall rescind any order of revocation served upon the person by the law enforcement officer.

(d) A license revocation shall become effective seven days after the person has received the notice of revocation as provided in subsection (5) of this section or is deemed to have received the notice of revocation by mail as provided in paragraph (b) of this subsection (6). If the department receives a written request for a hearing pursuant to subsection (7) of this section within that same seven-day period and the department issues a temporary permit pursuant to paragraph (d) of subsection (7) of this section, the effective date of the revocation shall be stayed until a final order is issued following the hearing; except that any delay in the hearing that is caused or requested by the person or counsel representing the person shall not result in a stay of the revocation during the period of delay.

(7) **Request for hearing.** (a) A person who has received a notice of revocation may make a written request for a review of the department's determination at a hearing. The request may be made on a form available at each office of the department.

(b) A person must request a hearing in writing within seven days after the day the person receives the notice of revocation as provided in subsection (5) of this section or is deemed to have received the notice by mail as provided in paragraph (b) of subsection (6) of this section. If the department does not receive the written request for a hearing within the seven-day period, the right to a hearing is waived, and the determination of the department that is based on the documents and affidavit required by subsection (5) of this section becomes final.

(c) If a person submits a written request for a hearing after expiration of the seven-day period and if the request is accompanied by the person's verified statement explaining the failure to make a timely request for a hearing, the department shall receive and consider the request. If the department finds that the person was unable to make a timely request due to lack of actual notice of the revocation or due to factors of physical incapacity such as hospitalization or incarceration, the department shall waive the period of limitation, reopen the matter, and grant the hearing request. In such a case, the department shall not grant a stay of the revocation pending issuance of the final order following the hearing.

(d) At the time a person requests a hearing pursuant to this subsection (7), if it appears from the record that the person is the holder of a valid driver's or minor driver's license or of an instruction permit or of a temporary permit issued pursuant to paragraph (b) of subsection (5) of this section and that the license or permit has been surrendered, the department shall stay the effective date of the revocation and issue a temporary permit that shall be valid until the scheduled date for the hearing. If necessary, the department may later extend the temporary permit or issue an additional temporary permit in order to stay the effective date of the revocation until the final order is issued following the hearing, as required by subsection (8) of this section. If the person notifies the department in writing at the time that the hearing is requested that the person desires the law enforcement officer's presence at the hearing, the department shall issue a written notice for the law enforcement officer to appear at the hearing. A law enforcement officer who is required to appear at a hearing may, at the discretion of the hearing officer, appear in real time by telephone or other electronic means in accordance with section 42-1-218.5.

(e) At the time that a person requests a hearing, the department shall provide to the person written notice advising the person:

(I) Of the right to subpoena the law enforcement officer for the hearing and that the subpoena must be served upon the law enforcement officer at least five calendar days prior to the hearing;

(II) Of the person's right at that time to notify the department in writing that the person desires the law enforcement officer's presence at the hearing and that, upon receiving the notification, the department shall issue a written notice for the law enforcement officer to appear at the hearing;

(III) That, if the law enforcement officer is not required to appear at the hearing, documents and an affidavit prepared and submitted by the law enforcement officer will be used at the hearing; and

(IV) That the affidavit and documents submitted by the law enforcement officer may be reviewed by the person prior to the hearing.

(f) Any subpoena served upon a law enforcement officer for attendance at a hearing conducted pursuant to this section shall be served at least five calendar days before the day of the hearing.

(8) **Hearing.** (a) (I) The hearing shall be scheduled to be held as quickly as practicable but not more than sixty days after the date the department receives the request for a hearing; except that, if a hearing is rescheduled because of the unavailability of a law enforcement officer or the hearing officer in accordance with subparagraph (III) or (IV) of this paragraph (a), the hearing may be rescheduled more than sixty days after the date the department receives the request for the hearing, and the department shall continue any temporary driving privileges held by the person until the date to which the hearing is rescheduled. At least ten days prior to the scheduled or rescheduled hearing, the department shall provide in the manner specified in section 42-2-119 (2) a written notice of the time and place of the hearing to the respondent unless the parties agree to waive this requirement. Notwithstanding the provisions of section 42-2-119, the last-known address of the respondent for purposes of notice for any hearing pursuant to this section shall be the address stated on the hearing request form.

(II) A law enforcement officer who submits the documents and affidavit required by subsection (5) of this section need not be present at the hearing unless the hearing officer requires that the law enforcement officer be present and the hearing officer issues a written notice for the law enforcement officer's appearance or unless the respondent or the respondent's attorney determines that the law enforcement officer should be present and serves a timely subpoena upon the law enforcement officer in accordance with paragraph (f) of subsection (7) of this section.

(III) If a law enforcement officer, after receiving a notice or subpoena to appear from either the department or the respondent, is unable to appear at the original or rescheduled hearing date due to a reasonable conflict, including but not limited to training, vacation, or personal leave time, the law enforcement officer or the law enforcement officer's supervisor shall contact the department not less than forty-eight hours prior to the hearing and reschedule the hearing to a time when the law enforcement officer will be available. If the law enforcement officer cannot appear at the original or rescheduled hearing because of medical reasons, a law enforcement emergency, another court or administrative hearing, or any other legitimate, just cause as determined by the department, and the law enforcement officer or the law enforcement officer's supervisor gives notice of the law enforcement officer's inability to appear to the department prior to the dismissal of the revocation proceeding, the department shall reschedule the hearing following consultation with the law enforcement officer or the law enforcement officer's supervisor at the earliest possible time when the law enforcement officer and the hearing officer will be available.

(IV) If a hearing officer cannot appear at an original or rescheduled hearing because of medical reasons, a law enforcement emergency, another court or administrative hearing, or any other legitimate, just cause, the hearing officer or the department may reschedule the hearing at the earliest possible time when the law enforcement officer and the hearing officer will be available.

(b) The hearing shall be held in the district office nearest to where the violation occurred, unless the parties agree to a different location; except that, at the discretion of the department, all or part of the hearing may be conducted in real time, by telephone or other electronic means in accordance with section 42-1-218.5.

(c) The department shall consider all relevant evidence at the hearing, including the testimony of any law enforcement officer and the reports of any law enforcement officer that are submitted to the department. The report of a law enforcement officer shall not be required to be made under oath, but the report shall identify the law enforcement officer making the report. The department may consider evidence contained in affidavits from persons other than the respondent, so long as the affidavits include the affiant's home or work address and phone number and are dated, signed, and sworn to by the affiant under penalty of perjury. The affidavit need not be notarized or sworn to before any other person.

(d) The hearing officer shall have authority to:

(I) Administer oaths and affirmations;

(II) Compel witnesses to testify or produce books, records, or other evidence;

(III) Examine witnesses and take testimony;

(IV) Receive and consider any relevant evidence necessary to properly perform the hearing officer's duties as required by this section;

(V) Take judicial notice as defined by rule 201 of article II of the Colorado rules of evidence, subject to the provisions of section 24-4-105 (8), C.R.S., which shall include:

(A) Judicial notice of general, technical, or scientific facts within the hearing officer's knowledge;

(B) Judicial notice of appropriate and reliable scientific and medical information contained in studies, articles, books, and treatises; and

(C) Judicial notice of charts prepared by the department of public health and environment pertaining to the maximum BAC levels that people can obtain through the consumption of alcohol when the charts are based upon the maximum absorption levels possible of determined amounts of alcohol consumed in relationship to the weight and gender of the person consuming the alcohol;

(VI) Issue subpoenas duces tecum to produce books, documents, records, or other evidence;

(VII) Issue subpoenas for the attendance of witnesses;

(VIII) Take depositions or cause depositions or interrogatories to be taken;

(IX) Regulate the course and conduct of the hearing; and

(X) Make a final ruling on the issues.

(e) When an analysis of the respondent's BAC is considered at a hearing:

(I) If the respondent establishes, by a preponderance of the evidence, that the respondent consumed alcohol between the time that the respondent stopped driving and the time of testing, the preponderance of the evidence must also establish that the minimum required BAC was reached as a result of alcohol consumed before the respondent stopped driving; and

(II) If the evidence offered by the respondent shows a disparity between the results of the analysis done on behalf of the law enforcement agency and the results of an analysis done on behalf of the respondent, and a preponderance of the evidence establishes that the blood analysis conducted on behalf of the law enforcement agency was properly conducted by a qualified person associated with a laboratory certified by the department of public health and environment using properly working testing devices, there shall be a presumption favoring the accuracy of the analysis done on behalf of the law enforcement agency if the analysis showed the BAC to be 0.096 or more. If the respondent offers evidence of blood analysis, the respondent shall be required to state under oath the number of analyses done in addition to the one offered as evidence and the names of the laboratories that performed the analyses and the results of all analyses.

(f) The hearing shall be recorded. The hearing officer shall render a decision in writing, and the department shall provide a copy of the decision to the respondent.

(g) If the respondent fails to appear without just cause, the right to a hearing shall be waived, and the determination of the department which is based upon the documents and affidavit required in subsection (5) of this section shall become final.

(9) **Appeal.** (a) Within thirty days after the department issues its final determination under this section, a person aggrieved by the determination shall have the right to file a petition for judicial review in the district court in the county of the person's residence.

(b) Judicial review of the department's determination shall be on the record without taking additional testimony. If the court finds that the department exceeded its constitutional or statutory authority, made an erroneous interpretation of the law, acted in an arbitrary and capricious manner, or made a determination that is unsupported by the evidence in the record, the court may reverse the department's determination.

(c) A filing of a petition for judicial review shall not result in an automatic stay of the revocation order. The court may grant a stay of the order only upon a motion and hearing and upon a finding that there is a reasonable probability that the person will prevail upon the merits and that the person will suffer irreparable harm if the order is not stayed.

(10) **Notice to vehicle owner.** If the department revokes a person's license pursuant to paragraph (a), (c), or (d) of subsection (3) of this section, the department shall mail a notice to the owner of the motor vehicle used in the violation informing the owner that:

(a) The motor vehicle was driven in an alcohol-related driving violation; and

(b) Additional alcohol-related violations involving the motor vehicle by the same driver may result in a requirement that the owner file proof of financial responsibility under the provisions of section 42-7-406 (1.5).

(11) **Applicability of "State Administrative Procedure Act".** The "State Administrative Procedure Act", article 4 of title 24, C.R.S., shall apply to this section to the extent it is consistent with subsections (7), (8), and (9) of this section relating to administrative hearings and judicial review.

42-2-126.1. Probationary licenses for persons convicted of alcohol-related driving offenses - ignition interlock devices - fees - interlock fund created - violations of probationary license - repeal. (Repealed)

42-2-126.3. Tampering with an ignition interlock device. (1) No person may intercept, bypass, or interfere with or aid any other person in intercepting, bypassing, or interfering with an ignition interlock device for the purpose of preventing or hindering the lawful operation or purpose of the ignition interlock device required under section 42-2-132.5.

(2) No person may drive a motor vehicle in which an ignition interlock device is installed pursuant to section 42-2-132.5 if the person has knowledge that any person has intercepted, bypassed, or interfered with the ignition interlock device.

(3) Any person violating any provision of this section commits a class 1 misdemeanor and shall be punished as provided in section 18-1.3-501, C.R.S.

42-2-126.5. Revocation of license based on administrative actions taken under tribal law - repeal. (1) As used in this section:

(a) "Indian" means a person who is a member of a federally recognized Indian tribe.

(b) "Reservation" means the Southern Ute Indian reservation, the exterior boundaries of which were confirmed in the Act of May 21, 1984, Pub.L. 98-290, 98 Stat. 201, 202 (found at "Other Provisions" note to 25 U.S.C. sec. 668).

(c) "Reservation driving privilege" means the driving privilege of an Indian that arises under and is governed by the tribal code when the Indian is operating a motor vehicle within the boundaries of the reservation.

(d) "Tribal code" means the laws adopted by the tribe pursuant to the tribe's constitution.

(e) "Tribe" means the Southern Ute Indian tribe.

(2) **Legislative declaration.** (a) The general assembly finds that:

(I) The tribal code, including traffic provisions, governs the conduct of Indians within the reservation;

(II) The tribal code grants reservation driving privileges to Indians based on possession of a state-issued driver's license but does not authorize application of state driver's license revocation laws based on the conduct of Indians within the reservation; and

(III) When Indians drive outside of the reservation, state and municipal traffic laws apply to their state driving privileges.

(b) In enacting this section, the general assembly intends to provide safety for all persons using the highways of the state by authorizing a process whereby the state shall revoke the Colorado driving privileges of a person after the tribe has entered a final order under the tribal code revoking the reservation driving privileges of that person, in a manner similar to how the state revokes the state driving privileges of a Colorado licensee whose driving privileges are revoked for an action occurring and adjudicated in a foreign jurisdiction.

(3) When the tribe initially revokes the reservation driving privilege of an Indian pursuant to the tribal code pending a tribal hearing, the tribe shall take possession of the person's Colorado driver's license. The tribe is authorized to issue a temporary permit which shall provide temporary Colorado driving privileges to the person until the tribe enters a final order of revocation of the person's reservation driving privileges.

(4) If the tribe enters a final order of revocation of the person's reservation driving privileges, the tribe shall send notice of such revocation to the department via fax, mail, or electronic means.

(5) The state shall give full faith and credit to a tribal administrative or judicial determination related to the tribe's revocation of the reservation driving privileges of an Indian.

(6) Upon receiving notice of revocation from the tribe pertaining to any Indian, the department shall immediately revoke the Colorado driving privileges of that person. The period of the state revocation shall run concurrently with the revocation action taken by the tribe. The state's driver record for the revoked individual shall indicate concurrent dates for the revocation period. The department shall send notice of revocation by first-class mail to the person at the address last shown on the department's records.

(7) The department's revocation of the person's Colorado driving privileges shall be a final agency action of the department. Any appeal of the state's final revocation action may be taken in accordance with section 42-2-135 and section 24-4-106, C.R.S. Because the state is giving full faith and credit to the tribal determination, the department's revocation action shall be affirmed if, upon review, the reviewing court determines that the tribe's revocation of tribal driving privileges met both of the following conditions:

(a) The revocation occurred after providing the person whose driving privilege was revoked reasonable notice and an opportunity to be heard sufficient to protect due process rights; and

(b) The tribal administrative or judicial tribunal that made the determination had jurisdiction over the parties and over the subject matter.

(8) When a person whose license is revoked under this section has completed the terms and conditions of the tribal revocation order, the tribe shall provide the person with written notification of the completion and shall also send written notice to the department. When the department receives the tribe's written notification of the completion, the person may seek reinstatement of his or her Colorado driving privileges. The person must comply with sections 42-2-126 (4) (d), 42-2-132, and 42-7-406 to obtain a new license or otherwise restore his or her Colorado driving privileges.

(9) The provisions of this section do not apply to the department's revocation, suspension, cancellation, or denial of a Colorado driver's license of an Indian for any driving offense that occurs while operating a motor vehicle outside the boundaries of the reservation.

(10) This section shall automatically repeal on the occurrence of any one or more of the following events:

(a) The tribe repeals the express consent law of the tribal code;

(b) Either the tribe or the state terminates any intergovernmental agreement between the parties pertaining to driver's license revocations of Indians; or

(c) A repeal of this section by the general assembly acting by separate bill.

42-2-127. Authority to suspend license - to deny license - type of conviction - points. (1) (a) Except as provided in paragraph (b) of subsection (8) of this section, the department has the authority to suspend the license of any driver who, in accordance with the schedule of points set forth in this section, has been convicted of traffic violations resulting in the accumulation of twelve points or more within any twelve consecutive months or eighteen points or more within any twenty-four consecutive months, or, in the case of a minor driver eighteen years of age or older, who has accumulated nine points or more within any twelve consecutive months, or twelve points or more within any twenty-four consecutive months, or fourteen points or more for violations occurring after reaching the age of eighteen years, or, in the case of a minor driver under the age of eighteen years, who has accumulated more than five points within any twelve consecutive months or more than six points for violations occurring prior to reaching the age of eighteen years; except that the accumulation of points causing the subjection to suspension of the license of a chauffeur who, in the course of employment, has as a principal duty the operation of a motor vehicle shall be sixteen points in one year, twenty-four points in two years, or twenty-eight points in four years, if all the points are accumulated while said chauffeur is in the course of employment. Any provision of this section to the contrary notwithstanding, the license of a chauffeur who is convicted of DUI, DUI per se, DWAI, habitual user, UDD, or leaving the scene of an accident shall be suspended in the same manner as if the offense occurred outside the course of employment. Whenever a minor driver under the age of eighteen years receives a summons for a traffic violation, the minor's parent or legal guardian or, if the minor is without parents or guardian, the person who signed the minor driver's application for a license shall immediately be notified by the court from which the summons was issued.

(b) If any applicant for a license to operate a motor vehicle has illegally operated a motor vehicle in this state prior to the issuance of a valid driver's or minor driver's license or instruction permit or in violation of the terms of any instruction permit within thirty-six months prior to said application, the department has the authority to deny the issuance of said license for not more than twelve months.

(c) For the purpose of this section, any points accumulated by a minor under an instruction permit shall apply to the minor driver's license subsequently issued to or applied for by such minor.

(d) No suspension or denial shall be made until a hearing has been held or the driver has failed to appear for a hearing scheduled in accordance with this section. This section shall not be construed to prevent the issuance of a restricted license pursuant to section 42-2-116.

(2) (a) The time periods provided in subsection (1) of this section for the accumulation of points shall be based on the date of violation, but points shall not be assessed until after conviction for any such traffic violation.

(b) The accumulation of points within the time periods provided in subsection (1) of this section shall not be affected by the issuance or renewal of any driver's or minor driver's license issued under the provisions of this article or the anniversary date thereof.

(3) Nothing in subsections (1) and (2) of this section shall affect or prevent any proceedings to suspend any license under the provisions of law existing prior to July 1, 1974.

(4) Statutory provisions for cancellation and mandatory revocation of drivers' licenses shall take precedence over this section.

(5) Point system schedule:

Type of conviction..Points

(a) Leaving scene of accident 12
(b) (I) DUI or DUI per se 12
(II) Habitual user...12
(III) DWAI..8
(IV) UDD..4
(c) (I) Engaging in a speed contest in violation of section 42-4-1105 (1) 12
(II) Aiding or facilitating engaging in a speed contest in violation of section 42-4-1105 (3)..12
(III) Engaging in a speed exhibition in violation of section 42-4-1105 (2) 5

(IV) Aiding or facilitating engaging in a speed exhibition in violation of section 42-4-1105 (3) 5
(d) Reckless driving..8
(e) Careless driving 4
(e.5) Careless driving resulting in death....12
(f) Speeding:
(I) One to four miles per hour over the reasonable and prudent speed or one to four miles per hour over the maximum lawful speed limit of seventy-five miles per hour......................................0
(II) Five to nine miles per hour over the reasonable and prudent speed or five to nine miles per hour over the maximum lawful speed limit of seventy-five miles per hour......................................1
(III) Ten to nineteen miles per hour over the reasonable and prudent speed or ten to nineteen miles per hour over the maximum lawful speed limit of seventy-five miles per hour..4
(IV) Twenty to thirty-nine miles per hour over the reasonable and prudent speed or twenty to thirty-nine miles per hour over the maximum lawful speed limit of seventy-five miles per hour..6
(IV.5) Forty or more miles per hour over the reasonable and prudent speed or forty or more miles per hour over the maximum lawful speed limit of seventy-five miles per hour..12
(V) Failure to reduce speed below an otherwise lawful speed when a special hazard exists..3
(VI) One to four miles per hour over the maximum lawful speed limit of forty miles per hour driving a low-power scooter........................0
(VII) Five to nine miles per hour over the maximum lawful speed limit of forty miles per hour driving a low-power scooter........................2
(VIII) Greater than nine miles per hour over the maximum lawful speed limit of forty miles per hour driving a low-power scooter..................4
(g) Failure to stop for school signals............6
(h) Driving on wrong side of road or driving on wrong side of divided or controlled-access highway in violation of section 42-4-1010..4
(i) Improper passing......................................4
(j) Failure to stop for school bus 6
(k) Following too closely 4
(l) Failure to observe traffic sign or signal, except as provided in paragraph (ff) of this subsection (5)..4
(m) Failure to yield to emergency vehicle ..4
(n) Failure to yield right-of-way, except as provided in paragraphs (y) to (bb) of this subsection (5)..3
(o) Improper turn 3
(p) Driving in wrong lane or direction on one-way street...3
(q) Driving through safety zone 3
(r) Conviction of violations not listed in this subsection (5) while driving a moving vehicle, which are violations of a state law or municipal ordinance other than violations classified as class B traffic infractions under section 42-4-1701 or having an equivalent classification under any municipal ordinance 3
(s) Failure to signal or improper signal 2
(t) Improper backing.....................................2
(u) Failure to dim or turn on lights...............2
(v) (I) Except as provided in subparagraph (II) of this paragraph (v), operating an unsafe vehicle..2
(II) Operating a vehicle with defective head lamps..1
(w) Eluding or attempting to elude a police officer..12
(x) Alteration of suspension system 3
(y) Failure to yield right-of-way to pedestrian...4
(z) Failure to yield right-of-way to pedestrian at walk signal..4
(aa) Failure to yield right-of-way to pedestrian upon emerging from alley, driveway, or building in a commercial or residential area...............4
(bb) Failure to yield right-of-way to person with a disability pursuant to section 42-4-808....6
(cc) Failure to exercise due care for pedestrian pursuant to section 42-4-807 4
(dd) A second or subsequent violation of section 42-2-101 (1) and (4)....................................6
(ee) Failure to maintain or show proof of insurance pursuant to section 42-4-1409............4
(ff) Failure to observe high occupancy vehicle lane restrictions pursuant to section 42-4-1012..0
(gg) (Deleted by amendment, L. 2005, p. 334, § 2, effective July 1, 2005.)
(hh) Driving a motor vehicle while not wearing a seat belt in violation of section 42-2-105.5 (3) 2
(ii) Driving with more passengers than seat belts in violation of section 42-2-105.5 (4) 2
(jj) A violation of section 42-4-239 1
(kk) Driving with a passenger who is under twenty-one years of age or driving between 12 midnight and 5 a.m. in violation of section 42-4-116 2
(5.5) If a person receives a penalty assessment notice for a violation under section 42-4-1701 (5) and such person pays the fine and surcharge for the violation on or before the date the payment is due, the points assessed for the violation are reduced as follows:
(a) For a violation having an assessment of three or more points under subsection (5) of this section, the points are reduced by two points;
(b) For a violation having an assessment of two points under subsection (5) of this section, the points are reduced by one point.
(5.6) (a) Any municipality may elect to have the provisions of subsection (5.5) of this section apply to penalty assessment notices issued by the municipality pursuant to counterpart municipal ordinances. Whenever a municipality reduces a traffic offense, the reduced offense and the points assessed for such reduced offense shall conform to the point assessment schedule under subsection (5) of this section.
(b) Any county may elect to have the provisions of subsection (5.5) of this section apply to

penalty assessment notices issued by the county pursuant to counterpart county ordinances. Whenever a county reduces a traffic offense, the reduced offense and the points assessed for such reduced offense shall conform to the point assessment schedule under subsection (5) of this section.

(5.7) Notwithstanding any other provision of the statutes to the contrary, if a penalty assessment for a traffic infraction is not personally served on the defendant or the defendant has not accepted the jurisdiction of the court for such penalty assessment, then the traffic infraction is a class B traffic infraction and the department has no authority to assess any points under this section upon entry of judgment for such traffic infraction.

(5.8) Notwithstanding any other provision of this section, the department may not assess any points for a violation if such assessment of points is prohibited under section 42-4-110.5 (3).

(6) (a) "Convicted" and "conviction", as used in this section, include conviction in any court of record or municipal court, or by the Southern Ute Indian tribal court, or by any military authority for offenses substantially the same as those set forth in subsection (5) of this section which occur on a military installation in this state and also include the acceptance and payment of a penalty assessment under the provisions of section 42-4-1701 or under the similar provisions of any town or city ordinance and the entry of a judgment or default judgment for a traffic infraction under the provisions of section 42-4-1701 or 42-4-1710 or under the similar provisions of any municipal ordinance.

(b) For the purposes of this article, a plea of no contest accepted by the court or the forfeiture of any bail or collateral deposited to secure a defendant's appearance in court or the failure to appear in court by a defendant charged with DUI, DUI per se, habitual user, or UDD who has been issued a summons and notice to appear pursuant to section 42-4-1707 as evidenced by records forwarded to the department in accordance with the provisions of section 42-2-124 shall be considered as a conviction.

(c) The provisions of paragraph (r) of subsection (5) of this section shall not be applicable to violations of sections 42-2-115, 42-3-121, and 42-4-314.

(7) Upon the accumulation by a licensee of half as many points as are required for suspension, the department may send such licensee a warning letter in accordance with section 42-2-119 (2) or order a preliminary hearing, but the failure of the department to send such warning letter or hold such preliminary hearing shall not be grounds for invalidating the licensee's subsequent suspension as a result of accumulating additional points as long as the suspension is carried out under the provisions of this section. Should a preliminary hearing be ordered by the department and should the licensee fail to attend or show good cause for failure to attend, the department may suspend such license in the same way as if the licensee had accumulated sufficient points for suspension and had failed to attend such suspension hearing.

(8) (a) Whenever the department's records show that a licensee has accumulated a sufficient number of points to be subject to license suspension, the department shall notify the licensee that a hearing will be held not less than twenty days after the date of the notice to determine whether the licensee's driver's license should be suspended. The notification shall be given to the licensee in writing by regular mail, addressed to the address of the licensee as shown by the records of the department.

(b) (I) If the department's records indicate that a driver has accumulated a sufficient number of points to cause a suspension under subsection (1) of this section and the driver is subject to a current or previous license restraint with a determined reinstatement date for the same offense or conviction that caused the driver to accumulate sufficient points to warrant suspension, the department may not order a point suspension of the license of the driver unless the license or driving privilege of the driver was revoked pursuant to section 42-2-126 (3) (c).

(II) If the department does not order a point suspension against the license of a driver because of the existence of a current or previous license restraint with a determined reinstatement date under the provisions of subparagraph (I) of this paragraph (b), the department shall utilize the points that were assessed against the driver in determining whether to impose any future license suspension if the driver accumulates any more points against the driver's license.

(9) Repealed.

(10) Suspension hearings when ordered by the department shall be held at the district office of the department closest to the residence of the licensee; except that all or part of the hearing may, at the discretion of the department, be conducted in real time, by telephone or other electronic means in accordance with section 42-1-218.5. A hearing delay shall be granted by the department only if the licensee presents the department with good cause for such delay. Good cause shall include absence from the state or county of residence, personal illness, or any other circumstance which, in the department's discretion, constitutes sufficient reason for delay. In the event that a suspension hearing is delayed, the department shall set a new date for such hearing no later than sixty days after the date of the original hearing.

(11) Upon such hearing, the department or its authorized agent may administer oaths, issue subpoenas for the attendance of witnesses and the production of books and papers, apply to the district court for the enforcement thereof by contempt proceedings, and require a reexamination of the licensee.

(12) If at the hearing held pursuant to subsection (8) of this section it appears that the record of the driver sustains suspension as provided in this section, the department shall imme-

diately suspend such driver's license, and such license shall then be surrendered to the department. If at such hearing it appears that the record of the driver does not sustain suspension, the department shall not suspend such license and shall adjust the accumulated-point total accordingly. In the event that the driver's license is suspended, the department may issue a probationary license for a period not to exceed the period of suspension, which license may contain such restrictions as the department deems reasonable and necessary and which may thereafter be subject to cancellation as a result of any violation of the restrictions imposed therein. The department may also order any driver whose license is suspended to take a complete driving reexamination. After such hearing, the licensee may appeal the decision to the district court as provided in section 42-2-135.

(13) If the driver fails to appear at such hearing after proper notification as provided in subsections (7) and (8) of this section and a delay or continuance has not been requested and granted as provided in subsection (10) of this section, the department shall immediately suspend the license of the driver. A driver who failed to appear may request a subsequent hearing, but the request shall not postpone the effectiveness of the restraint.

(14) (a) (I) If there is no other statutory reason for denial of a probationary license, any individual who has had a license suspended by the department because of, at least in part, a conviction of an offense specified in paragraph (b) of subsection (5) of this section may be entitled to a probationary license pursuant to subsection (12) of this section for the purpose of driving for reasons of employment, education, health, or alcohol and drug education or treatment, but:

(A) If ordered by the court that convicted the individual, the individual shall be enrolled in a program of driving education or alcohol and drug education and treatment certified by the unit in the department of human services that administers behavioral health programs and services, including those related to mental health and substance abuse; and

(B) If the individual is a persistent drunk driver, as defined in section 42-1-102 (68.5), any probationary license shall require the use of an approved ignition interlock device, as defined in section 42-2-132.5 (7) (a), and the time that the individual holds a probationary license under this section shall not be credited against the time that the individual may be required to hold a restricted license pursuant to section 42-2-132.5.

(II) A probationary license issued pursuant to this subsection (14) shall contain any other restrictions as the department deems reasonable and necessary, shall be subject to cancellation for violation of any such restrictions, including but not limited to absences from alcohol and drug education or treatment sessions or failure to complete alcohol and drug education or treatment programs, and shall be issued for the entire period of suspension.

(b) The department may refuse to issue a probationary license if the department finds that the driving record of the individual is such that the individual has sufficient points, in addition to those resulting from the conviction referred to in this subsection (14), to require the suspension or revocation of a license to drive on the highways of this state, or if the department finds from the record after a hearing conducted in accordance with subsection (12) of this section that aggravating circumstances exist to indicate the individual is unsafe for driving for any purpose. In refusing to issue a probationary license, the department shall make specific findings of fact to support such refusal.

(c) No district attorney shall enter into, nor shall any judge approve, a plea bargaining agreement entered into solely for the purpose of permitting the defendant to qualify for a probationary license under this subsection (14).

(15) (a) (I) Whenever the department receives notice that a person has twice been convicted of, adjudicated for, or entered a plea of guilty or nolo contendere to a violation of section 18-4-418, C.R.S., the department shall suspend the license of the person for a period of six months.

(II) Whenever the department receives notice that a person has three or more times been convicted of, adjudicated for, or entered a plea of guilty or nolo contendere to a violation of section 18-4-418, C.R.S., the department shall suspend the license of the person for a period of one year.

(b) Upon suspending the license of any person as required by this subsection (15), the department shall immediately notify the licensee as provided in section 42-2-119 (2).

(c) Upon a licensee's receipt of the notice of suspension, the licensee or the licensee's attorney may submit a written request to the department for a hearing. The department shall hold a hearing not less than thirty days after receiving such request. The hearing shall be conducted by a hearing commissioner appointed by the executive director of the department, and shall be conducted in accordance with the provisions of section 24-4-105, C.R.S.

(d) If a driver who has had a license suspended under this subsection (15) is subsequently acquitted of such charge by a court of record, the department shall immediately, or in any event no later than ten days after the receipt of notice of such acquittal, reinstate said license.

42-2-127.3. Authority to suspend license - controlled substance violations. (Repealed)

42-2-127.4. Authority to suspend license - forgery of a penalty assessment notice issued to minor under the age of eighteen years. (Repealed)

42-2-127.5. Authority to suspend license - violation of child support order. (1) The department shall suspend the license of any driver who is not in compliance with a child support order pursuant to the provisions of this section.

(2) Upon receipt of a notice of failure to comply from the state child support enforcement agency pursuant to section 26-13-123 (4), C.R.S., the department shall send written notice to the person identified in the court order that such person shall be required to provide the department with proof of compliance with the child support order. Such proof shall be in the form of a notice of compliance as defined in section 26-13-123 (1) (c), C.R.S.

(3) (a) If a notice of compliance is not received by the department within thirty days after the date written notice is sent pursuant to subsection (2) of this section, the department shall suspend the driver's license of the person from whom proof is required and may not reinstate such license until proof in the form of a notice of compliance is provided.

(b) The driver shall not have a right to a hearing before license suspension pursuant to this subsection (3), and the driver's right to any hearing shall be limited to the rights set forth in section 26-13-123, C.R.S.

(4) In the event that a driver's license is suspended pursuant to subsection (3) of this section, the department may issue a probationary license for a period not to exceed ninety days from the date of issuance, which probationary license shall restrict the driver to driving to and from the place of employment or to performing duties within the course of the driver's employment. The department is authorized to charge a fee for such probationary license that covers the direct and indirect costs of issuing the license. The department may not issue a probationary license to an individual unless at the time of license restraint such individual has a valid driver's privilege and has no outstanding judgments or warrants issued against such individual pursuant to the requirements of section 42-2-118 (3).

(5) Repealed.

42-2-127.6. Authority to suspend license - providing alcohol to an underage person. (1) (a) Whenever the department receives notice that a person, other than a business licensed pursuant to article 46, 47, or 48 of title 12, C.R.S., or an employee or agent of the business acting in the scope of his or her employment, has been convicted of an offense pursuant to section 12-47-901 (1) (a.5) or (1) (k), C.R.S., the department shall immediately suspend the license of the person for a period of not less than six months.

(b) For purposes of this subsection (1), a person has been convicted when the person has been found guilty by a court or a jury, entered a plea of guilty or nolo contendere, or received a deferred sentence for an offense.

(2) (a) Upon suspension of a person's license as required by this section, the department shall immediately notify the person as provided in section 42-2-119 (2).

(b) Upon receipt of the notice of suspension, the person or the person's attorney may request a hearing in writing. The department shall hold a hearing not less than thirty days after receiving the request through a hearing commissioner appointed by the executive director of the department, which hearing shall be conducted in accordance with the provisions of section 24-4-105, C.R.S. The hearing shall be held at the district office of the department closest to the residence of the person; except that all or part of the hearing may, at the discretion of the department, be conducted in real time by telephone or other electronic means in accordance with section 42-1-218.5, unless the person requests to appear in person at the hearing. After the hearing, the person may appeal the decision of the department to the district court as provided in section 42-2-135. If a person who has had a license suspended under this section is subsequently acquitted of the conviction that required the suspension by a court of record, the department shall immediately, in any event not later than ten days after the receipt of the notice of acquittal, reinstate said license to the person affected, unless the license is under other restraint.

(3) (a) If there is no other statutory reason for denial of a probationary license, a person who has had a license suspended by the department because of, in whole or in part, a conviction of an offense specified in subsection (1) of this section shall be entitled to a probationary license for the purpose of driving for reasons of employment, education, health, or compliance with the requirements of probation. Such a probationary license shall:

(I) Contain any other restrictions the department deems reasonable and necessary;

(II) Be subject to cancellation for violation of any such restrictions; and

(III) Be issued for the entire period of suspension.

(b) The department may refuse to issue a probationary license if the department finds that the driving record of the person is such that the person has sufficient points to require the suspension or revocation of a license to drive on the highways of this state pursuant to section 42-2-127 or if the department finds from the record after a hearing conducted in accordance with this section that aggravating circumstances exist to indicate the person is unsafe for driving for any purpose. In refusing to issue a probationary license, the department shall make specific findings of fact to support the refusal.

42-2-127.7. Authority to suspend driver's license - uninsured motorists - legislative declaration. (1) The general assembly hereby finds, determines, and declares that the purpose of this section is to induce and encourage all motorists to provide for their financial responsibility for the protection of others and to assure the widespread availability to the insuring public of insurance protection against financial loss caused by negligent, financially irresponsible, motorists.

(2) (a) The department may suspend the driver's license of any person upon its determination that the person drove a vehicle in this state without having in full force and effect a complying policy or certificate of self-insurance as required by sections 10-4-619 and 10-4-624, C.R.S., as follows:

(I) Upon the first determination that a person operated a motor vehicle in this state without having in full force and effect a complying policy or certificate of self-insurance as required pursuant to section 10-4-619 or 10-4-624, C.R.S., the department shall suspend the driver's license of a person until the person furnishes proof of financial responsibility, as defined in section 42-7-103 (14), in the manner contemplated by section 42-7-301 (1), in the amount specified in section 10-4-620, C.R.S.

(II) Upon the second determination that the person operated a motor vehicle in this state without having in full force and effect a complying policy or certificate of self-insurance as required by sections 10-4-619 and 10-4-624, C.R.S., within five years, the department shall suspend the person's driver's license for a period of four months.

(III) Upon the third or subsequent determination that the person operated a motor vehicle in this state without having in full force and effect a complying policy or certificate of self-insurance as required by sections 10-4-619 and 10-4-624, C.R.S., the department shall suspend the person's driver's license for a period of eight months.

(b) The department shall make a determination of such facts on the basis of the documents and affidavit of a law enforcement officer as specified in subsection (3) of this section, and this determination shall be final unless a hearing is requested and held as provided in subsection (7) of this section.

(c) The determination of the facts specified in this subsection (2) by the department is independent of the suspension taken under article 7 of this title.

(d) For purposes of this section, "license" includes any driving privilege.

(3) Whenever a law enforcement officer determines, by checking the motorist insurance identification database created in section 42-7-604, and by any other means authorized by law, that a driver violates section 42-4-1409 by not having a complying policy or certificate of self-insurance in full force and effect as required by sections 10-4-619 and 10-4-624, C.R.S., the law enforcement officer making such determination shall forward to the department an affidavit that includes a statement of the officer's probable cause that the person committed such violation, and a copy of the citation and complaint, if any, filed with the court. The affidavit shall be dated, signed, and sworn to by the law enforcement officer under penalty of perjury, but need not be notarized or sworn to before any other person.

(4) (a) Upon receipt by the department of the affidavit of the law enforcement officer and the relevant documents required by subsection (3) of this section, the department shall make the determination described in subsection (2) of this section. The determination shall be based upon the information contained in the affidavit and the relevant documents. If the department determines that the person is subject to license suspension, the department may issue a notice of suspension if such notice has not already been served upon the person by the law enforcement officer as required in subsection (5) of this section.

(b) The notice of suspension sent by the department shall be mailed in accordance with the provisions of section 42-2-119 (2) to the person at the last-known address shown on the department's records, if any, and to any address provided in the law enforcement officer's affidavit if that address differs from the address of record. The notice shall be deemed received three days after mailing.

(c) The notice of suspension shall clearly specify the reason and statutory grounds for the suspension, the effective date of the suspension, the right of the person to request a hearing, the procedure for requesting a hearing, and the date by which that request for a hearing must be made. The notice shall also state that the person may avoid suspension by filing with the department proof of financial responsibility for the future, or by compliance with section 42-7-302 on the first determination. For subsequent offenses, a person's driver's license shall be suspended in accordance with the provisions of subsection (2) of this section. If the person files proof of financial responsibility for the future, such proof of financial responsibility for the future shall be maintained for three years from the date such proof of financial responsibility for the future is received by the department and after any applicable suspension period.

(d) If the department determines that the person is not subject to license suspension:

(I) The department shall notify the person of its determination and shall rescind any order of suspension served upon the person by the law enforcement officer;

(II) (A) The person whose driver's license was taken possession of by a law enforcement officer pursuant to this section may obtain such license by the payment of a fee of five dollars to the department.

(B) Notwithstanding the amount specified for the fee in sub-subparagraph (A) of this subparagraph (II), the executive director of the department by rule or as otherwise provided by law may reduce the amount of the fee if necessary pursuant to section 24-75-402 (3), C.R.S., to reduce the uncommitted reserves of the fund to which all or any portion of the fee is credited. After the uncommitted reserves of the fund are sufficiently reduced, the executive director of the department by rule or as otherwise provided by law may increase the amount of the fee as provided in section 24-75-402 (4), C.R.S.

(5) (a) Whenever a law enforcement officer determines, by checking the motorist insurance identification database created in section 42-7-604, and by any other means authorized by law, that a driver violates section 42-4-1409 by not having a complying policy or certificate of self-insurance as required by sections 10-4-619 and 10-4-624, C.R.S., the officer, acting on behalf of the department, may serve the notice of suspension personally on such driver. If the law enforcement officer serves the notice of suspension, the officer shall take possession of any driver's license issued by this state or any other state that is held by the person. When the officer takes possession of a valid license, the officer, acting on behalf of the department, shall issue a temporary permit that is valid for seven days after its date of issuance.

(b) A copy of the completed notice of suspension form, a copy of any completed temporary permit form, and any driver's, minor driver's, or temporary driver's license or any instruction permit taken into possession under this section shall be forwarded to the department by the law enforcement officer along with the affidavit and documents required in subsections (2) and (3) of this section.

(c) The department shall provide forms for notice of suspension and for temporary permits to law enforcement agencies. The department shall establish a format for the affidavits required by this section and shall give notice of such format to all law enforcement agencies which submit affidavits to the department. Such law enforcement agencies shall follow the format determined by the department.

(d) A temporary permit may not be issued to any person who is already driving with a temporary permit issued pursuant to paragraph (a) of this subsection (5).

(6) (a) The license suspension shall become effective seven days after the subject person has received the notice of suspension as provided in subsection (5) of this section or is deemed to have received the notice of suspension by mail as provided in subsection (4) of this section unless the person files with the department proof of financial responsibility for the future or complies with section 42-7-302 prior to the effective date of the suspension. If the person files proof of financial responsibility for the future, such proof of financial responsibility for the future must be maintained for three years from the date such proof of financial responsibility for the future is received by the department. If a written request for a hearing and evidence of current liability insurance in the respondent's name is received by the department within that same seven-day period, the effective date of the suspension shall be stayed until a final order is issued following the hearing; except that any delay in the hearing that is caused or requested by the subject person or counsel representing that person shall not result in a stay of the suspension during the period of delay.

(b) The period of license suspension under paragraph (a) of subsection (2) of this section shall be for an indefinite period. The person may reinstate at any time by complying with section 42-7-302 or by filing with the department proof of financial responsibility for the future and paying the required reinstatement fee pursuant to section 42-2-132. If the person files proof of financial responsibility for the future, such proof of financial responsibility for the future must be maintained for three years from the date such proof of financial responsibility for the future is received by the department.

(7) (a) Any person who has received a notice of suspension may make a written request for a review of the department's determination at a hearing. The request may be made on a form available at each office of the department. Evidence of current liability insurance in the respondent's name and the person's driver's license, if the license has not been previously surrendered, shall be submitted at the time the request for a hearing is made.

(b) The request for a hearing shall be made in writing within seven days after the day the person received the notice of suspension as provided in subsection (5) of this section or is deemed to have received the notice by mail as provided in subsection (4) of this section. If written request for a hearing and evidence of current liability insurance in the respondent's name is not received within the seven-day period, the right to a hearing is waived, and the determination of the department that is based upon the documents and affidavit required by subsections (2) and (3) of this section becomes final.

(c) If a written request for a hearing is made after expiration of the seven-day period and if it is accompanied by the applicant's verified statement explaining the failure to make a timely request for a hearing, the department shall receive and consider the request. If the department finds that the person was unable to make a timely request due to lack of actual notice of the suspension or due to factors of physical incapacity such as hospitalization or incarceration, the department shall waive the period of limitation, reopen the matter, and grant the hearing request upon receipt of evidence of current liability insurance in the respondent's name. In such a case, a stay of the suspension pending issuance of the final order following the hearing shall not be granted.

(d) At the time the request for a hearing is made, if it appears from the record that the person is the holder of a valid driver's or minor driver's license or any instruction permit issued by this state or temporary permit issued pursuant to subsection (5) of this section and that the license has been surrendered as required pursuant to subsection (5) of this section, the department shall issue a temporary permit upon the receipt of evidence of current liability insurance in the respondent's name. The temporary permit will be valid until the scheduled date for the hearing. If necessary, the department may later issue an additional temporary permit or permits in order to stay the effective date of the suspension until the final order is issued following the hearing, as required by subsection (6) of this section.

(e) (I) The hearing shall be scheduled to be held as quickly as practicable but not more than sixty days after the day that the request for a hearing is received by the department; except that, if a hearing is rescheduled because of the unavailability of the hearing officer in accordance with subparagraph (II) of this paragraph (e), the hearing may be rescheduled more than sixty days after the day that the request for the hearing is received by the department, and the department shall continue any temporary driving privileges held by the respondent until the date that such hearing is rescheduled. The department shall provide a written notice of the time and place of the hearing to the respondent in the manner provided in section 42-2-119 (2) at least ten days prior to the scheduled or rescheduled hearing, unless the parties agree to waive this requirement. Notwithstanding the provisions of section 42-2-119, the last-known address of the respondent for purposes of notice for any hearing pursuant to this section shall be the address stated on the hearing request form.

(II) If a hearing officer cannot appear at any original or rescheduled hearing because of medical reasons, another administrative hearing, or any other legitimate just cause, such hearing officer or the department may reschedule the hearing at the earliest possible time when the hearing officer will be available.

(f) If a hearing is held pursuant to this subsection (7), the department shall review the matter and make a final determination on the basis of the documents and affidavit submitted to the department pursuant to subsections (2) and (3) of this section. The law enforcement officer who submitted the affidavit need not be present at the hearing. The department shall consider all other relevant evidence at the hearing, including the reports of law enforcement officers that are submitted to the department. The reports of law enforcement officers shall not be required to be made under oath, but such reports shall identify the officers making the reports. The department may consider evidence contained in affidavits from persons other than the respondent, so long as such affidavits include the affiant's home or work address and telephone number and are dated, signed, and sworn to by the affiant under penalty of perjury. The affidavit need not be notarized or sworn to before any other person. The respondent must present evidence in person.

(8) (a) The hearing shall be held in the district office of the department closest to the residence of the driver; except that all or part of the hearing may, at the discretion of the department, be conducted in real time, by telephone or other electronic means in accordance with section 42-1-218.5. The person requesting the hearing may be referred to as the respondent.

(b) The presiding hearing officer shall be the executive director of the department or an authorized representative designated by the executive director. The presiding hearing officer shall have authority to administer oaths and affirmations; to consider the affidavit of the law enforcement officer filing such affidavit as specified in subsection (3) of this section; to consider other law enforcement officers' reports that are submitted to the department, which reports need not be under oath but shall identify the officers making the reports; to examine and consider documents and copies of documents containing relevant evidence; to consider other affidavits that are dated, signed, and sworn to by the affiant under penalty of perjury, which affidavits need not be notarized or sworn to before any other person but shall contain the affiant's home or work address and telephone number; to take judicial notice as defined by rule 201 of article II of the Colorado rules of evidence, subject to the provisions of section 24-4-105 (8), C.R.S., which shall include judicial notice of general, technical, or scientific facts within the hearing officer's knowledge; to compel witnesses to testify or produce books, records, or other evidence; to examine witnesses and take testimony; to receive and consider any relevant evidence necessary to properly perform the hearing officer's duties as required by this section; to issue subpoenas duces tecum to produce books, documents, records, or other evidence; to issue subpoenas for the attendance of witnesses; to take depositions, or cause depositions or interrogatories to be taken; to regulate the course and conduct of the hearing; and to make a final ruling on the issues.

(c) (I) When a license is suspended under paragraph (a) of subsection (2) of this section, the sole issue at the hearing shall be whether by a preponderance of the evidence the person drove a vehicle in this state without having in force a complying policy or certificate of self-insurance as required by sections 10-4-619 and 10-4-624, C.R.S. If the presiding hearing officer finds the affirmative of the issue, the suspension order shall be sustained. If the presiding hearing officer finds the negative of the issue, the suspension order shall be rescinded.

(II) Under no circumstances shall the presiding hearing officer consider any issue not specified in this paragraph (c).

(d) The hearing shall be recorded. The decision of the presiding hearing officer shall be rendered in writing, and a copy shall be provided to the person who requested the hearing.

(e) If the person who requested the hearing fails to appear without just cause, the right to a hearing shall be waived, and the determination of the department which is based upon the documents and affidavit required in subsections (2) and (3) of this section shall become final.

(9) (a) Within thirty days of the issuance of the final determination of the department under this section, a person aggrieved by the determi-

nation shall have the right to file a petition for judicial review in the district court in the county of the person's residence.

(b) The review shall be on the record without taking additional testimony. If the court finds that the department exceeded its constitutional or statutory authority, made an erroneous interpretation of the law, acted in an arbitrary and capricious manner, or made a determination which is unsupported by the evidence in the record, the court may reverse the department's determination.

(c) The filing of a petition for judicial review shall not result in an automatic stay of the suspension order. The court may grant a stay of the order only upon motion and hearing and upon a finding that there is a reasonable probability that the petitioner will prevail upon the merits and that the petitioner will suffer irreparable harm if the order is not stayed.

(10) The "State Administrative Procedure Act", article 4 of title 24, C.R.S., shall apply to this section to the extent it is consistent with subsections (7), (8), and (9) of this section relating to administrative hearings and judicial review.

(11) This section shall take effect when the motorist insurance identification database, created in section 42-7-604, has been developed and is operational, but not later than January 1, 1999.

42-2-128. Vehicular homicide - revocation of license. The department shall revoke the driver's license of any person convicted of vehicular homicide, including the driver's license of any juvenile who has been adjudicated a delinquent upon conduct which would establish the crime of vehicular homicide if committed by an adult.

42-2-129. Mandatory surrender of license or permit for driving under the influence or with excessive alcoholic content. Upon a plea of guilty or nolo contendere, or a verdict of guilty by the court or a jury, to DUI, DUI per se, or habitual user, or, for a person under twenty-one years of age, to DUI, DUI per se, DWAI, habitual user, or UDD, the court shall require the offender to immediately surrender the offender's driver's, minor driver's, or temporary driver's license or instruction permit to the court. The court shall forward to the department a notice of plea or verdict, on the form prescribed by the department, together with the offender's license or permit, not later than ten days after the surrender of the license or permit. Any person who does not immediately surrender the license or permit to the court, except for good cause shown, commits a class 2 misdemeanor traffic offense.

42-2-130. Mandatory surrender of license or permit for drug convictions. (Repealed.)

42-2-131. Revocation of license or permit for failing to comply with a court order relating to nondriving alcohol convictions. Upon a plea of guilty or nolo contendere or a verdict of guilty by the court or a jury to an offense under section 12-47-901 (1) (b) or (1) (c) or 18-13-122 (2), C.R.S., or any counterpart municipal charter or ordinance offense to such section and upon a failure to complete an alcohol evaluation or assessment, an alcohol education program, or an alcohol treatment program ordered by the court in connection with such plea or verdict, the court shall forward to the department a notice of plea or verdict or such failure to complete on the form prescribed by the department. Any revocation pursuant to section 42-2-125 (1) (m) shall begin when the department gives notice of the revocation to the person in accordance with section 42-2-119 (2).

42-2-131.5. Revocation of license or permit for convictions involving defacing property. (Repealed)

42-2-132. Period of suspension or revocation. (1) The department shall not suspend a driver's or minor driver's license to drive a motor vehicle on the public highways for a period of more than one year, except as permitted under section 42-2-138 and except for noncompliance with the provisions of subsection (4) of this section or section 42-7-406, or both.

(2) (a) (I) Any person whose license or privilege to drive a motor vehicle on the public highways has been revoked is not entitled to apply for a probationary license, and, except as provided in sections 42-2-125, 42-2-126, 42-2-132.5, 42-2-138, 42-2-205, and 42-7-406, the person is not entitled to make application for a new license until the expiration of one year from the effective date of the revocation; then the person may make application for a new license as provided by law.

(II) (A) Following the period of revocation set forth in this subsection (2), the department shall not issue a new license unless and until it is satisfied that the person has demonstrated knowledge of the laws and driving ability through the appropriate motor vehicle testing process and that the person whose license was revoked pursuant to section 42-2-125 for a second or subsequent alcohol- or drug-related driving offense has completed not less than a level II alcohol and drug education and treatment program certified by the unit in the department of human services that administers behavioral health programs and services, including those related to mental health and substance abuse, pursuant to section 42-4-1301.3.

(B) If the person was determined to be in violation of section 42-2-126 (3) (a) and the person had a BAC that was 0.17 or more at the time of driving or within two hours after driving, or if the person's driving record otherwise indicates a designation as a persistent drunk driver as defined in section 42-1-102 (68.5), the department shall require the person to complete a level II alcohol and drug education and treatment program certified by the unit in the department of human services that administers behavioral health programs and services, including those related to mental health and substance abuse, pursuant to section 42-4-1301.3.

(C) If a person seeking reinstatement has not completed required level II alcohol and drug education and treatment, the person shall file with the department proof of current enrollment in a level II alcohol and drug education and treatment program certified by the unit in the department of human services that administers behavioral health programs and services, including those related to mental health and substance abuse, pursuant to section 42-4-1301.3, on a form approved by the department.

(III) In the case of a minor driver whose license has been revoked as a result of one conviction for DUI, DUI per se, DWAI, habitual user, or UDD, the minor driver, unless otherwise required after an evaluation made pursuant to section 42-4-1301.3, must complete a level I alcohol and drug education program certified by the unit in the department of human services that administers behavioral health programs and services, including those related to mental health and substance abuse.

(IV) Any person whose license or privilege to drive a motor vehicle on the public highways has been revoked under section 42-2-125 (1) (g) (I) or (1) (i) or 42-2-203 where the revocation was due in part to a DUI, DUI per se, DWAI, or habitual user conviction shall be required to present an affidavit stating that the person has obtained at the person's own expense a signed lease agreement for the installation and use of an approved ignition interlock device, as defined in section 42-2-132.5 (7), in each motor vehicle on which the person's name appears on the registration and any other vehicle that the person may drive during the period of the restricted license and a copy of each signed lease agreement.

(V) The department shall take into consideration any probationary terms imposed on such person by any court in determining whether any revocation shall be continued.

(b) Repealed.

(c) A person whose driving privilege is restored prior to a hearing on the merits of any driving restraint waives the person's right to a hearing on the merits of the driving restraint.

(3) Any person making false application for a new license before the expiration of the period of suspension or revocation commits a class 2 misdemeanor traffic offense. The department shall notify the district attorney's office in the county where such violation occurred, in writing, of all violations of this section.

(4) (a) (I) Any person whose license or other privilege to operate a motor vehicle in this state has been suspended, cancelled, or revoked, pursuant to either this article or article 4 or 7 of this title, shall pay a restoration fee of ninety-five dollars to the executive director of the department prior to the issuance to the person of a new license or the restoration of the license or privilege.

(II) Notwithstanding the amount specified for the fee in subparagraph (I) of this paragraph (a), the executive director of the department by rule or as otherwise provided by law may reduce the amount of the fee if necessary pursuant to section 24-75-402 (3), C.R.S., to reduce the uncommitted reserves of the fund to which all or any portion of the fee is credited. After the uncommitted reserves of the fund are sufficiently reduced, the executive director of the department by rule or as otherwise provided by law may increase the amount of the fee as provided in section 24-75-402 (4), C.R.S.

(b) All restoration fees collected pursuant to this subsection (4) shall be transmitted to the state treasurer, who shall credit:

(I) (A) Sixty dollars to the driver's license administrative revocation account in the highway users tax fund, which account is hereby created and referred to in this subparagraph (I) as the "account".

(B) The moneys in the account shall be subject to annual appropriation by the general assembly for the direct and indirect costs incurred by the department in the administration of driver's license restraints pursuant to either this article or article 4 or article 7 of this title, including, but not limited to, the direct and indirect costs of providing administrative hearings under this title, without the use of moneys from the general fund. At the end of each fiscal year, any unexpended and unencumbered moneys remaining in the account shall be transferred out of the account, credited to the highway users tax fund, and allocated and expended as specified in section 43-4-205 (5.5) (c), C.R.S.; and

(II) (A) Thirty-five dollars to the first time drunk driving offender account in the highway users tax fund, which account is hereby created and referred to in this subparagraph (II) as the "account".

(B) The moneys in the account shall be subject to annual appropriation by the general assembly on and after January 1, 2009, first to the department of revenue to pay its costs associated with the implementation of House Bill 08-1194, as enacted at the second regular session of the sixty-sixth general assembly; second, to the department of revenue to pay a portion of the costs for an ignition interlock device as required by section 42-2-132.5 (1.5) (a) (II) for a first time drunk driving offender who is unable to pay the costs of the device; and then to provide two million dollars to the department of transportation for high visibility drunk driving enforcement pursuant to section 43-4-901, C.R.S. Any moneys in the account not expended for these purposes may be invested by the state treasurer as provided by law. All interest and income derived from the investment and deposit of moneys in the account shall be credited to the account. At the end of each fiscal year, any unexpended and unencumbered moneys remaining in the account shall remain in the account and shall not be credited or transferred to the general fund, the highway users tax fund, or another fund.

42-2-132.5. Mandatory and voluntary restricted licenses following alcohol convictions - rules. (1) The following persons shall be required to hold a restricted license pursuant to this section for at least one year prior to being eligible to obtain any other driver's license issued under this article:

(a) Any person who has been convicted on two or more occasions of DUI or DUI per se, which offenses were committed within a period of five years and one of the offenses occurred on or after July 1, 1999, and on or before June 30, 2000;

(b) Any person whose privilege to drive was revoked pursuant to section 42-2-125 (1) (g) (I) or (1) (i) and one of the offenses giving rise to the revocation occurred on or after July 1, 2000;

(b.5) Any person whose license has been revoked pursuant to the provisions of section 42-2-126 when the person's BAC was 0.17 or more at the time of driving or within two hours after driving;

(c) Any person whose privilege to drive was revoked under section 42-2-203 where the revocation was due in part to a DUI, DUI per se, DWAI, or habitual user conviction and one of the offenses giving rise to the revocation occurred on or after July 1, 2000; or

(d) Any person whose privilege to drive was revoked pursuant to subsection (5) of this section.

(1.5) (a) (I) A person whose privilege to drive has been revoked for more than one year because of a DUI, DUI per se, or DWAI conviction or has been revoked for more than one year under any provision of section 42-2-126 may voluntarily apply for an early reinstatement with a restricted license under the provisions of this section after the person's privilege to drive has been revoked for one year. Except as provided in subparagraph (II) of this paragraph (a) or subsection (1.7) of this section, the restrictions imposed pursuant to this section shall remain in effect for the longer of one year or the total time period remaining on the license restraint prior to early reinstatement.

(II) (A) For revocations under section 42-2-125 (1) (b.5) or 42-2-126 (3) (a) (I) for a first violation that requires only a nine-month revocation, a person twenty-one years of age or older at the time of the offense may voluntarily apply for an early reinstatement with a restricted license under the provisions of this section after the person's privilege to drive has been revoked for at least one month. Except as provided in paragraph (b.5) of subsection (1) of this section, subsection (1.7) of this section, and sub-subparagraph (B) of this subparagraph (II), the restrictions imposed pursuant to this subparagraph (II) shall remain in effect for eight months.

(B) For a person with a restricted license issued pursuant to sub-subparagraph (A) of this subparagraph (II), if the department's monthly monitoring reports required by paragraph (c) of subsection (4) of this section show that, for four consecutive monthly reporting periods, the approved ignition interlock device did not prevent the operation of the motor vehicle due to an excessive blood alcohol content or did not detect that there has been tampering with the device, there have been no other reports of circumvention or tampering, and there are no grounds to extend the restriction pursuant to paragraph (a) of subsection (5) of this section, then the person shall be eligible for a license without the restriction required by this section. If the department determines that a person is eligible for a license without the restriction required by this section pursuant to this sub-subparagraph (B), the department shall serve upon the person a notice of such eligibility. A person eligible for a license without the restriction required by this section pursuant to this sub-subparagraph (B) may request a hearing on the person's eligibility. The provisions of this sub-subparagraph (B) shall not apply to a person covered by subsection (1.7) of this section.

(C) The department shall establish a program to assist persons who apply for a restricted license under this subparagraph (II) who are unable to pay the full cost of an ignition interlock device. The program shall be funded from the first time drunk driving offender account in the highway users tax fund established pursuant to section 42-2-132 (4) (b) (II). The executive director of the department may promulgate rules governing the program.

(b) (I) To be eligible for early reinstatement with a restricted license pursuant to this subsection (1.5), a person must have satisfied all conditions for reinstatement imposed by law including time periods for non-alcohol-related restraints; except that a person whose license was restrained pursuant to section 42-2-138 may be eligible for early reinstatement under this section so long as the restraint was caused in part by driving activity occurring after an alcohol-related offense and the length of any license restriction under this section includes the period of restraint under section 42-2-138.

(II) Before being eligible for early reinstatement with a restricted license under this section, a person must provide proof of financial responsibility to the department pursuant to the requirements of the "Motor Vehicle Financial Responsibility Act", article 7 of this title. Such person must maintain such proof of financial responsibility with the department for the longer of three years or the period that the person's license is restricted under this section.

(c) No person who has been designated an habitual offender under the provisions of section 42-2-202 for any offense other than a violation of section 42-4-1301, 42-2-138, or 42-4-1401 shall be eligible for a restricted license pursuant to this subsection (1.5).

(d) Repealed.

(1.7) A person required to hold a restricted license pursuant to this section who is a persistent drunk driver as defined in section 42-1-102 (68.5), based on an offense that occurred on or after July 1, 2004, shall be required to hold the restricted license for at least two years prior to being eligible to obtain any other driver's license issued under this article.

(1.8) As soon as a person meets the conditions of subsection (1) of this section, the department shall note on the driving record of any person required to hold a restricted license under this section that the person is required to have an ignition interlock device. A person whose driving record contains the notation required by this subsection (1.8) shall not operate a motor vehicle without an approved ignition interlock device until the restriction is removed pursuant to this section.

(2) (Deleted by amendment, L. 2000, p. 1076, § 4, effective July 1, 2000.)

(3) (a) (I) The department shall issue a restricted license under this section if the department receives from a person described in subsection (1), (1.5), or (1.7) of this section an affidavit stating that the person has obtained:

(A) A signed lease agreement for the installation and use of an approved ignition interlock device in each motor vehicle on which the person's name appears on the registration and any other vehicle that the person may drive during the period of the restricted license; and

(B) The written consent of all other owners, if any, of each motor vehicle in which the approved ignition interlock device is installed.

(II) A copy of each signed lease agreement shall be attached to the affidavit.

(a.5) (I) Notwithstanding the requirements of paragraph (a) of this subsection (3), the department shall issue a restricted license to any person who is required to hold a restricted license pursuant to subsection (1) of this section who is not the registered owner or co-owner of a motor vehicle if the person submits an affidavit stating that the person is not the owner or co-owner of any motor vehicle and has no access to a motor vehicle in which to install an approved ignition interlock device.

(II) Any restricted license issued pursuant to this paragraph (a.5) shall require that if the license holder becomes an owner or co-owner of a motor vehicle or otherwise has access to a motor vehicle in which an approved ignition interlock device may be installed, he or she shall submit to the department a signed lease agreement for the installation and use of an approved ignition interlock device on such vehicle for a period equal to the remaining period of the restricted license.

(b) The terms of the restricted license shall include that the person shall not drive a motor vehicle other than a vehicle in which an approved ignition interlock device is installed.

(c) The department shall not issue a license under this section that would authorize operation of a commercial motor vehicle as defined in section 42-2-402 (4) until the restriction created by this section has expired.

(4) (a) and (b) Repealed.

(c) The leasing agency for any approved ignition interlock device shall provide monthly monitoring reports for the device to the department to monitor compliance with the provisions of this section. The leasing agency shall check the device at least once every sixty days to ensure that the device is operating and that there has been no tampering with the device. If the leasing agency detects that there has been tampering with the device, the leasing agency shall notify the department of that fact within five days of the detection.

(5) (a) Upon receipt of a conviction under section 42-2-116 (6) (b), the department shall revoke any license of such person issued under this section and shall not reinstate the license for a period of the longer of one year or the remaining period of license restraint imposed prior to the issuance of a license pursuant to this section. A person shall be entitled to a hearing on the question of whether the revocation is sustained and the length of the ineligibility.

(b) Upon receipt of a record other than a conviction described in paragraph (a) of this subsection (5) indicating that any person who is subject to the restrictions of this section has operated a motor vehicle other than a vehicle in which an approved ignition interlock device is installed or has circumvented or attempted to circumvent the proper use of an approved ignition interlock device, the department may revoke any license of such person issued under this section and not reinstate the license for a period of one year or the remaining period of license restraint imposed prior to the issuance of a license pursuant to this section, whichever is longer. A person shall be entitled to a hearing on the question of whether the license should be revoked and the length of the ineligibility.

(c) If a lease for an approved ignition interlock device is terminated for any reason prior to the expiration of the period of the restriction and no other such lease has been provided by the licensee, the department shall notify the licensee that the license shall be suspended unless and until a new signed lease agreement for the remaining period of the restriction is filed with the department.

(d) If the monthly monitoring reports required by paragraph (c) of subsection (4) of this section show that the approved ignition interlock device prevented the operation of the vehicle due to excessive blood alcohol content in three of any twelve consecutive reporting periods, the restriction on the person's license shall be extended for an additional twelve months after the expiration of the existing restriction. The department shall notify the person that the ignition interlock restriction provision is being extended and that any license shall be suspended unless the person provides a new signed lease agreement for the use of an approved ignition interlock device for the extended period. The person shall be entitled to a hearing on the extension of the restriction. Based upon findings at the hearing, including aggravating and mitigating factors, the hearing office may sustain the extension, rescind the extension, or reduce the period of extension.

(6) The department may promulgate rules to implement the provisions of this section.

(7) (a) For the purposes of this section, "approved ignition interlock device" means a device approved by the department of public health and environment that is installed in a motor vehicle and that measures the breath alcohol content of the driver before a vehicle is started and that periodically requires additional breath samples during vehicle operation. The device may not allow a motor vehicle to be started or to continue normal operation if the device measures an alcohol level above the level established by the department of public health and environment.

(b) The state board of health may promulgate rules to implement the provisions of this subsection (7) concerning approved ignition interlock devices.

42-2-133. Surrender and return of license. (1) The department, upon suspending or revoking a license, shall require that such license be surrendered to the department.

(2) At the end of the period of suspension, the licensee may apply for and receive a replacement license upon payment of a fee of five dollars.

42-2-134. Foreign license invalid during suspension. No resident or nonresident whose driver's license or right or privilege to operate a motor vehicle in this state has been suspended or revoked as provided in this article shall operate a motor vehicle in this state under a license, permit, or registration certificate issued by any other jurisdiction or otherwise during such suspension or after such revocation until a new license is obtained when and as permitted under this article.

42-2-135. Right to appeal. (1) Every person finally denied a license or identification card, whose identification card has been finally cancelled, or whose license has been finally cancelled, suspended, or revoked by or under the authority of the department may, within thirty days thereafter, obtain judicial review in accordance with section 24-4-106, C.R.S.; except that the venue for such judicial review shall be in the county of residence of the person seeking judicial review.

(2) The district attorney of the judicial district in which review is applied for pursuant to this section, upon request of the attorney general, shall represent the department.

42-2-136. Unlawful possession or use of license. (1) (a) No person shall have in such person's possession a lawfully issued driver's, minor driver's, or temporary driver's license or instruction permit, knowing that such license or permit has been falsely altered by means of erasure, obliteration, deletion, insertion of new matter, transposition of matter, or any other means so that such license or permit in its thus altered form falsely appears or purports to be in all respects an authentic and lawfully issued license or permit.

(b) No person shall fraudulently obtain a driver's, minor driver's, or temporary driver's license or an instruction permit.

(2) No person shall have in such person's possession a paper, document, or other instrument which falsely appears or purports to be in all respects a lawfully issued and authentic driver's, minor driver's, or temporary driver's license or instruction permit, knowing that such instrument was falsely made and was not lawfully issued.

(3) No person shall display or represent as being such person's own any driver's, minor driver's, or temporary driver's license or any instruction permit which was lawfully issued to another person.

(4) No person shall fail or refuse to surrender to the department upon its lawful demand any driver's, minor driver's, or temporary driver's license or any instruction or temporary permit issued to such person which has been suspended, revoked, or cancelled by the department. The department shall notify the district attorney's office in the county where such violation occurred, in writing, of all violations of this subsection (4).

(5) No person shall permit any unlawful use of a driver's license issued to such person.

(5.5) No person shall photograph, photostat, duplicate, or in any way reproduce any driver's license or facsimile thereof for the purpose of distribution, resale, reuse, or manipulation of the data or images contained in such driver's license unless authorized by the department or otherwise authorized by law.

(6) (a) Any person who violates any provision of subsections (1) to (5) of this section commits a class 2 misdemeanor traffic offense.

(b) Any person who violates any provision of subsection (5.5) of this section commits a class 3 misdemeanor and, upon conviction thereof, shall be punished as provided in section 18-1.3-501, C.R.S.

42-2-137. False affidavit - penalty. Any person who makes any false affidavit or knowingly swears or affirms falsely to any matter or thing required by the terms of this part 1 to be sworn to or affirmed commits a class 2 misdemeanor traffic offense. The department shall notify the district attorney's office in the county where such violations occurred, in writing, of all violations of this section.

42-2-138. Driving under restraint - penalty. (1) (a) Any person who drives a motor vehicle or off-highway vehicle upon any highway of this state with knowledge that the person's license or privilege to drive, either as a resident or a nonresident, is under restraint for any reason other than conviction of DUI, DUI per se, DWAI, habitual user, or UDD is guilty of a misdemeanor. A court may sentence a person convicted of this misdemeanor to imprisonment in the county jail for a period of not more than six months and may impose a fine of not more than five hundred dollars.

(b) Upon a second or subsequent conviction under paragraph (a) of this subsection (1) within five years after the first conviction thereunder, in addition to any penalty imposed pursuant to said paragraph (a) of this subsection (1), except as may be permitted by section 42-2-132.5, the defendant shall not be eligible to be issued a driver's or minor driver's license or extended any driving privilege in this state for a period of three years after such second or subsequent conviction.

(c) This subsection (1) shall apply only to violations committed on or after July 1, 1974.

(d) (I) A person who drives a motor vehicle or off-highway vehicle upon any highway of this state with knowledge that the person's license or privilege to drive, either as a resident or nonresident, is restrained under section 42-2-126 (3), is restrained solely or partially because of a conviction of DUI, DUI per se, DWAI, habitual user, or UDD, or is restrained in another state solely or partially because of an alcohol-related driving offense is guilty of a misdemeanor and, upon conviction thereof, shall be punished by imprisonment in the county jail for not less than thirty days nor more than one year and, in the discretion of the court, by a fine of not less than five hundred dollars nor more than one thousand dollars. Upon a second or subsequent conviction, the person shall be punished by imprisonment in the county jail for not less than ninety days nor more than two years and, in the discretion of the court, by a fine of not less than five hundred dollars nor more than three thousand dollars. The minimum county jail sentence imposed by this subparagraph (I) shall be mandatory, and the court shall not grant probation or a suspended sentence thereof; but, in a case where the defendant is convicted although the defendant established that he or she had to drive the motor vehicle in violation of this subparagraph (I) because of an emergency, the mandatory jail sentence, if any, shall not apply, and, for a first conviction, the court may impose a sentence of imprisonment in the county jail for a period of not more than one year and, in the discretion of the court, a fine of not more than one thousand dollars, and, for a second or subsequent conviction, the court may impose a sentence of imprisonment in the county jail for a period of not more than two years and, in the discretion of the court, a fine of not more than three thousand dollars.

(II) In any trial for a violation of subparagraph (I) of this paragraph (d), a duly authenticated copy of the record of the defendant's former convictions and judgments for DUI, DUI per se, DWAI, habitual user, or UDD or an alcohol-related offense committed in another state from any court of record or a certified copy of the record of any denial or revocation of the defendant's driving privilege under section 42-2-126 (3) from the department shall be prima facie evidence of the convictions, judgments, denials, or revocations and may be used in evidence against the defendant. Identification photographs and fingerprints that are part of the record of the former convictions, judgments, denials, or revocations and the defendant's incarceration after sentencing for any of the former convictions, judgments, denials, or revocations shall be prima facie evidence of the identity of the defendant and may be used in evidence against the defendant.

(e) Upon a second or subsequent conviction under subparagraph (I) of paragraph (d) of this subsection (1) within five years after the first conviction thereunder, in addition to the penalty prescribed in said subparagraph (I), except as may be permitted by section 42-2-132.5, the defendant shall not be eligible to be issued a driver's or minor driver's license or extended any driving privilege in this state for a period of four years after such second or subsequent conviction.

(f) Upon a verdict or judgment of guilt for a violation of paragraph (a) or (d) of this subsection (1), the court shall require the offender to immediately surrender his or her driver's license, minor driver's license, provisional driver's license, temporary driver's license, or instruction permit issued by this state, another state, or a foreign country. The court shall forward to the department a notice of the verdict or judgment of guilt on the form prescribed by the department, together with the offender's surrendered license or permit. Any person who violates the provisions of this paragraph (f) by failing to surrender his or her license or permit to the court commits a class 2 misdemeanor traffic offense.

(2) (a) In a prosecution for a violation of this section, the fact of the restraint may be established by certification that a notice was mailed by first-class mail pursuant to section 42-2-119 (2) to the last-known address of the defendant, or by the delivery of such notice to the last-known address of the defendant, or by personal service of such notice upon the defendant.

(b) In a prosecution for a violation of this section, the fact of restraint in another state may be established by certification that notice was given in compliance with such state's law.

(3) The department, upon receiving a record of conviction or accident report of any person for an offense committed while operating a motor vehicle, shall immediately examine its files to determine if the license or operating privilege of such person has been restrained. If it appears that said offense was committed while the license or operating privilege of such person was restrained, except as permitted by section 42-2-132.5, the department shall not issue a new license or grant any driving privileges for an additional period of one year after the date such person would otherwise have been entitled to

apply for a new license or for reinstatement of a suspended license and shall notify the district attorney in the county where such violation occurred and request prosecution of such person under subsection (1) of this section.

(4) For purposes of this section, the following definitions shall apply:

(a) "Knowledge" means actual knowledge of any restraint from whatever source or knowledge of circumstances sufficient to cause a reasonable person to be aware that such person's license or privilege to drive was under restraint. "Knowledge" does not mean knowledge of a particular restraint or knowledge of the duration of restraint.

(b) "Restraint" or "restrained" means any denial, revocation, or suspension of a person's license or privilege to drive a motor vehicle in this state or another state.

(5) It shall be an affirmative defense to a violation of this section, based upon a restraint in another state, that the driver possessed a valid driver's license issued subsequent to the restraint that is the basis of the violation.

42-2-139. Permitting unauthorized minor to drive. (1) No parent or guardian shall cause or knowingly permit his or her child or ward under the age of eighteen years to drive a motor vehicle upon any highway when such minor has not been issued a currently valid minor driver's license or instruction permit or shall cause or knowingly permit such child or ward to drive a motor vehicle upon any highway in violation of the conditions, limitations, or restrictions contained in a license or permit which has been issued to such child or ward.

(2) Any person who violates any provision of this section commits a class B traffic infraction.

42-2-140. Permitting unauthorized person to drive. (1) No person shall authorize or knowingly permit a motor vehicle owned by such person or under such person's hire or control to be driven upon any highway by any person who has not been issued a currently valid driver's or minor driver's license or an instruction permit or shall cause or knowingly permit such person to drive a motor vehicle upon any highway in violation of the conditions, limitations, or restrictions contained in a license or permit which has been issued to such other person.

(2) Any person who violates any provision of this section commits a class B traffic infraction.

42-2-141. Renting or loaning a motor vehicle to another. (1) Except as provided in subsection (4) of this section, no person shall rent or loan a motor vehicle to any other person unless the latter person is then duly licensed under this article or, in the case of a nonresident, duly licensed under the laws of the state or country of that person's residence except a nonresident whose home state or country does not require that an operator be licensed.

(2) Except as provided in subsection (4) of this section, no person shall rent a motor vehicle to another until that person has inspected the driver's license of the person to whom the vehicle is to be rented and compared and verified the signature thereon with the signature of such person written in his or her presence.

(3) Every person renting a motor vehicle to another shall keep a record of the registration number of the motor vehicle so rented, the name and address of the person to whom the vehicle is rented, the number of the license of said latter person or any authorized driver under subsection (4) of this section, and the date and place when and where said license was issued. Such record shall be open to inspection by any police officer or officer or employee of the department.

(4) A person may rent a motor vehicle to a person who is blind, as defined in section 26-2-103 (3), C.R.S., subject to all of the following conditions:

(a) The blind person is accompanied by at least one person with a valid license issued under this article or, in the case of a nonresident, a valid license issued under the laws of the state or country of such person's residence.

(b) The person renting the motor vehicle to a blind person:

(I) Inspects the license of each person who accompanies the blind person and wishes to be authorized to drive the motor vehicle; and

(II) Compares and verifies the signatures thereon with the signatures of such persons written in his or her presence.

(c) Only persons whose licenses and signatures have been compared and verified by the person renting the motor vehicle to the blind person are authorized to drive the motor vehicle, and the names of such persons are listed in the rental agreement.

(d) The renter and the driver of the motor vehicle pursuant to this subsection (4) shall have the same financial or insurance responsibilities under Colorado law as other renters of motor vehicles.

42-2-142. Violation - penalty. Any person who violates any provision of this part 1 for which no other penalty is provided in this part 1 commits a class B traffic infraction and shall be punished as provided in section 42-4-1701 (3) (a).

42-2-143. Legislative declaration. The general assembly declares that the provisions of this article as enacted in Senate Bill No. 318 by the forty-ninth general assembly in its first regular session shall not supersede, unless in direct conflict, and shall be harmonized with, the provisions of any other act enacted in the same session which also amends, in any way, this article.

42-2-144. Reporting by certified level II alcohol and drug education and treatment providers - notice of administrative remedies against a driver's license - rules. (1) The department shall require all providers of level II alcohol and drug education and treatment programs certified by the unit in the department of human services that administers behavioral health programs and services, including those related to mental health and substance abuse, pursuant to section 42-4-1301.3 to provide quarterly reports to the department about each person who is enrolled and who has filed proof of such enrollment with the department as required by section 42-2-126 (4) (d) (II).

(2) A person determined not to be in compliance with level II alcohol and drug education and treatment pursuant to subsection (1) of this section shall be sent a letter from the department notifying the person of such noncompliance, any administrative remedies that may be taken against the person's privilege to drive, and the time period the person has to comply with the requirements for level II alcohol and drug education and treatment before administrative remedies will be exercised against the person's driving privilege.

(3) The department may promulgate rules necessary for the implementation of this section.

PART 2

HABITUAL OFFENDERS

42-2-201. Legislative declaration concerning habitual offenders of motor vehicle laws. (1) It is declared to be the policy of this state:

(a) To provide maximum safety for all persons who travel or otherwise use the public highways of this state;

(b) To deny the privilege of operating motor vehicles on such highways to persons who by their conduct and record have demonstrated their indifference to the safety and welfare of others and their disrespect for the laws of this state, the orders of its courts, and the statutorily required acts of its administrative agencies; and

(c) To discourage repetition of criminal acts by individuals against the peace and dignity of this state and its political subdivisions and to impose increased and added deprivation of the privilege to operate motor vehicles upon habitual offenders who have been convicted repeatedly of violations of the traffic laws.

42-2-202. Habitual offenders - frequency and type of violations. (1) An habitual offender is any person, resident or nonresident, who has accumulated convictions for separate and distinct offenses described in subsection (2) of this section committed during a seven-year period or committed during a five-year period for separate and distinct offenses described in subsection (3) of this section; except that, where more than one included offense is committed within a one-day period, such multiple offenses shall be treated for the purposes of this part 2 as one offense. The record as maintained in the office of the department shall be considered prima facie evidence of the said convictions.

(2) (a) An habitual offender is a person having three or more convictions of any of the following separate and distinct offenses arising out of separate acts committed within a period of seven years:

(I) DUI, DUI per se, DWAI, or habitual user;

(II) Driving a motor vehicle in a reckless manner, in violation of section 42-4-1401;

(III) Driving a motor vehicle upon a highway while such person's license or privilege to drive a motor vehicle has been denied, suspended, or revoked, in violation of section 42-2-138;

(IV) Knowingly making any false affidavit or swearing or affirming falsely to any matter or thing required by the motor vehicle laws or as to information required in the administration of such laws;

(V) Vehicular assault or vehicular homicide, or manslaughter or criminally negligent homicide which results from the operation of a motor vehicle, or aggravated motor vehicle theft, as such offenses are described in title 18, C.R.S.;

(VI) Conviction of the driver of a motor vehicle involved in any accident involving death or personal injuries for failure to perform the duties required of such person under section 42-4-1601.

(b) The offenses included in subparagraphs (I), (II), (III), and (V) of paragraph (a) of this subsection (2) shall be deemed to include convictions under any federal law, any law of another state, or any ordinance of a municipality that substantially conforms to the statutory provisions of this state regulating the operation of motor vehicles. For purposes of this paragraph (b), the term "municipality" means any home rule or statutory city or town, a territorial charter city, or a city and county.

(3) A person is also an habitual offender if such person has ten or more convictions of separate and distinct offenses arising out of separate acts committed within a period of five years involving moving violations which provide for an assessment of four or more points each or eighteen or more convictions of separate and distinct offenses arising out of separate acts committed within a period of five years involving moving violations which provide for an assessment of three or less points each in the operation of a motor vehicle, which convictions are required to be reported to the department and result in the assessment of points under section 42-2-127, including any violations specified in subsection (2) of this section.

(4) For the purpose of this section, the term "conviction" has the meaning specified in section 42-2-127 (6) and includes entry of judgment for commission of a traffic infraction as set forth in section 42-4-1701.

42-2-203. Authority to revoke license of habitual offender. The department shall immediately revoke the license of any person whose record brings such person within the definition of an habitual offender in section 42-2-202. The procedure specified in section 42-2-125 (3) and (4) shall be employed for the revocation.

42-2-204. Appeals. An appeal may be taken from any action entered under the provisions of this part 2 as provided in section 42-2-135.

42-2-205. Prohibition. (1) No license to operate motor vehicles in this state shall be issued to an habitual offender, nor shall an habitual offender operate a motor vehicle in this state:

(a) For a period of five years from the date of the order of the department finding such person to be an habitual offender except as may be permitted by section 42-2-132.5; and

(b) Until such time as financial responsibility requirements are met.

42-2-206. Driving after revocation prohibited. (1) (a) (I) It is unlawful for any person to operate any motor vehicle in this state while the revocation of the department prohibiting the operation remains in effect. Any person found to be an habitual offender, who operates a motor vehicle in this state while the revocation of the department prohibiting such operation is in effect, commits a class 1 misdemeanor.

(II) Notwithstanding the provisions of section 18-1.3-501, C.R.S., any person convicted of violating subparagraph (I) of this paragraph (a) shall be sentenced to a mandatory minimum term of imprisonment in the county jail for thirty days, or a mandatory minimum fine of three thousand dollars, or both. The minimum jail sentence and fine required by this subparagraph (II) shall be in addition to any other penalty provided in section 18-1.3-501, C.R.S. The court may suspend all or a portion of the mandatory jail sentence or fine if the defendant successfully completes no less than forty hours, and no greater than three hundred hours, of useful public service. In no event shall the court sentence the convicted person to probation. Upon the defendant's successful completion of the useful public service, the court shall vacate the suspended sentence. In the event the defendant fails or refuses to complete the useful public service ordered, the court shall impose the jail sentence, fine, or both, as required under this subparagraph (II).

(b) (I) A person commits the crime of aggravated driving with a revoked license if he or she is found to be an habitual offender and thereafter operates a motor vehicle in this state while the revocation of the department prohibiting such operation is in effect and, as a part of the same criminal episode, also commits any of the following offenses:

(A) DUI or DUI per se;
(B) DWAI;
(C) Reckless driving, as described in section 42-4-1401;
(D) Eluding or attempting to elude a police officer, as described in section 42-4-1413;
(E) Violation of any of the requirements specified for accidents and accident reports in sections 42-4-1601 to 42-4-1606; or
(F) Vehicular eluding, as described in section 18-9-116.5, C.R.S.

(II) Aggravated driving with a revoked license is a class 6 felony, punishable as provided in section 18-1.3-401, C.R.S.

(III) If a defendant is convicted of aggravated driving with a revoked license based upon the commission of DUI, DUI per se, or DWAI pursuant to sub-subparagraph (A) or (B) of subparagraph (I) of this paragraph (b):

(A) The court shall convict and sentence the offender for each offense separately;
(B) The court shall impose all of the penalties for the alcohol-related driving offense, as such penalties are described in section 42-4-1307;
(C) The provisions of section 18-1-408, C.R.S, shall not apply to the sentences imposed for either conviction;
(D) Any probation imposed for a conviction under this section may run concurrently with any probation required by section 42-4-1307; and
(E) The department shall reflect both convictions on the defendant's driving record.

(2) For the purpose of enforcing this section in any case in which the accused is charged with driving a motor vehicle while such person's license, permit, or privilege to drive is revoked or is charged with driving without a license, the court, before hearing such charges, shall require the district attorney to determine whether such person has been determined to be an habitual offender and by reason of such determination is barred from operating a motor vehicle on the highways of this state. If the district attorney determines that the accused has been so held, the district attorney shall cause the appropriate criminal charges to be lodged against the accused.

42-2-207. No existing law modified. Nothing in this part 2 shall be construed as amending, modifying, or repealing any existing law of this state or any existing ordinance of any political subdivision relating to the operation of motor vehicles or the providing of penalties for the violation thereof; nor shall anything in this part 2 be construed as precluding the exercise of the regulatory powers of any division, agency, department, or political subdivision of this state having the statutory authority to regulate such operation or licensing.

42-2-208. Computation of number of convictions. With respect to persons charged as habitual offenders, in computing the number of convictions, all convictions must result from offenses occurring on or after July 1, 1973.

PART 3

IDENTIFICATION CARDS

42-2-301. Definitions. As used in this part 3, unless the context otherwise requires:

(1) "Department" means the department of revenue.

(2) "Identification card" means the identification card issued under this article.

(3) "Registrant" means a person who acquires an identification card under the provisions of this part 3.

42-2-302. Department may issue - limitations. (1) (a) (I) A person who is a resident of Colorado may be issued an identification card by the department, attested by the applicant and department as to true name, date of birth, current address, and other identifying data the department may require.

(II) An application for an identification card shall contain the applicant's fingerprint.

(III) An application for an identification card shall include the applicant's social security number or a sworn statement made under penalty of law that the applicant does not have a social security number.

(IV) An identification card shall not be issued until any previously issued instruction permit or minor driver's or driver's license is surrendered or cancelled.

(V) The applicant's social security number shall remain confidential and shall not be placed on the applicant's identification card. Such confidentiality shall not extend to the state child support enforcement agency, the department, or a court of competent jurisdiction when requesting information in the course of activities authorized under article 13 of title 26, C.R.S., or article 14 of title 14, C.R.S.

(b) (I) In addition to the requirements of paragraph (a) of this subsection (1), an application for an identification card shall state that:

(A) The applicant understands that, as a resident of the state of Colorado, any motor vehicle owned by the applicant must be registered in Colorado pursuant to the laws of the state and the applicant may be subject to criminal penalties, civil penalties, cancellation or denial of the applicant's identification card, and liability for any unpaid registration fees and specific ownership taxes if the applicant fails to comply with such registration requirements; and

(B) The applicant agrees, within thirty days after the date the applicant became a resident, to register in Colorado any vehicle owned by the applicant.

(II) The applicant shall verify the statements required by this paragraph (b) by the applicant's signature on the application.

(c) A sworn statement that is made under penalty of perjury shall be sufficient evidence of the applicant's social security number required by this subsection (1) and shall authorize the department to issue an identification card to the applicant. Nothing in this paragraph (c) shall be construed to prevent the department from cancelling, denying, recalling, or updating an identification card if the department learns that the applicant has provided a false social security number.

(2) (a) The department shall issue an identification card only upon the furnishing of a birth certificate or other documentary evidence of identity that the department may require. An applicant who submits a birth certificate or other documentary evidence issued by an entity other than a state or the United States shall also submit such proof as the department may require that the applicant is lawfully present in the United States. An applicant who submits as proof of identity a driver's license or identification card issued by a state that issues drivers' licenses or identification cards to persons who are not lawfully present in the United States shall also submit such proof as the department may require that the applicant is lawfully present in the United States. The department may assess a fee under section 42-2-306 (1) (b) if the department is required to undertake additional efforts to verify the identity of the applicant.

(b) The department may not issue an identification card to any person who is not lawfully present in the United States.

(c) The department may not issue an identification card to any person who is not a resident of the state of Colorado. The department shall issue an identification card only upon the furnishing of such evidence of residency that the department may require.

(3) (a) The department has the authority to cancel, deny, or deny the reissuance of the identification card of a person upon determining that the person is not entitled to issuance of the identification card for the following reasons:

(I) Failure to give the required or correct information in an application or commission of any fraud in making such application;

(II) Permission of an unlawful or fraudulent use or conviction of misuse of an identification card;

(III) The person is not lawfully present in the United States; or

(IV) The person is not a resident of the state of Colorado.

(b) If the department cancels, denies, or denies the reissuance of the identification card of a person, such person may request a hearing pursuant to section 24-4-105, C.R.S.

(4) (a) Any male United States citizen or immigrant who applies for an identification card or a renewal or duplicate of any such card and who is at least eighteen years of age but less than twenty-six years of age shall be registered in compliance with the requirements of section 3 of the "Military Selective Service Act", 50 U.S.C. App. sec. 453, as amended.

(b) The department shall forward in an electronic format the necessary personal information of the applicants identified in paragraph (a) of this subsection (4) to the selective service system. The applicant's submission of an application shall serve as an indication that the applicant either has already registered with the selective service system or that he is authorizing the department to forward to the selective service system the necessary information for such registration. The department shall notify the applicant that his submission of an application constitutes consent to registration with the selective service system, if so required by federal law.

(5) The department shall not issue an identification card to a first time applicant in Colorado until the department completes its verification of all facts relative to such applicant's right to receive an identification card including the residency, identity, age, and current licensing status of the applicant. Such verification shall utilize appropriate and accurate technology and techniques. Such verification shall include a comparison of existing driver's license and identification card images in department files with the applicant's images to ensure such applicant has only one identity.

(6) The department shall not issue an identification card to a person who holds a valid minor driver's or driver's license.

42-2-303. Contents of identification card. (1) (a) The identification card shall be the same size as a driver's license issued pursuant to parts 1 and 2 of this article. The card shall adequately describe the registrant, bear the registrant's picture, and bear the following: "State of Colorado", "Identification Card No. .....", and "This is not a driver's license." Each identification card issued to an individual under this section shall show a photograph of the registrant's full face.

(b) (I) In the event the department issues an identification card that contains stored information, such card may include only the information that is specifically referenced in paragraph (a) of this subsection (1) and that appears in printed form on the face of the card issued by the department to the registrant; except that such stored information shall not include the registrant's social security number.

(II) As used in this paragraph (b), "stored information" includes information that is stored on the identification card by means of magnetic or electronic encoding, or by any other technology designed to store retrievable information.

(2) Repealed.

(3) An identification card shall contain one or more security features that are not visible and are capable of authenticating such card and any information contained therein.

(4) (a) At the applicant's voluntary request, the department shall issue an identification card bearing an identifier of a branch of the United States armed forces, such as "Marine Corps", "Navy", "Army", "Air Force", or "Coast Guard", if the applicant possesses a currently valid military identification document, a DD214 form issued by the United States government, or any other document accepted by the department that demonstrates that the applicant is an active member or a veteran of the branch of service that the applicant has requested be placed on the identification card. The applicant shall not be required to provide documentation that the applicant is an active member or a veteran of a branch of the United States armed forces to renew or be reissued an identification card bearing an identifier issued pursuant to this subsection (4). The department shall not place more than one branch of the United States armed forces identifier on an applicant's identification card.

(b) To be issued an identification card bearing a branch of service identifier, or to have such license renewed, the applicant shall pay a fee of fifteen dollars to the department, which shall be in addition to any other fee for an identification card. The department shall transfer the fee to the state treasurer, who shall credit the fee to the highway users tax fund.

(c) Repealed.

42-2-304. Validity of identification card - rules. (1) Except as provided in subsection (2) of this section, an identification card issued pursuant to this part 3 expires on the birthday of the registrant in the fifth year after issuance of the identification card. The department may purge its records of such cards twelve years after issuance; except that any records concerning identification cards issued prior to April 16, 1996, may not be purged until October 1, 2003.

(1.5) (a) Any individual who has been issued an identification card pursuant to this section may renew the card prior to the expiration of the card upon application in person and payment of the required fee.

(b) The department may not renew an identification card for a person if the person would not be eligible for an identification card pursuant to section 42-2-302 (2) (b) or (2) (c).

(1.7) (a) If allowed under federal law, the department shall allow renewal of an identification card issued under section 42-2-302 by mail subject to the following requirements:

(I) Renewal by mail shall be available to qualifying individuals as determined by the department of revenue including but not limited to persons with disabilities and individuals who are sixty-five years of age or older.

(II) Renewal by mail shall only be available every other renewal period.

(III) A person renewing by mail shall attest under penalty of perjury that he or she is lawfully present in the United States.

(IV) A person renewing by mail shall attest under penalty of perjury that he or she is a resident of the state of Colorado.

(b) Every applicant for renewal of an identification card by mail shall submit the required fee or surcharge, if any.

(c) The department may promulgate rules necessary for the implementation of this subsection (1.7).

(2) (a) An identification card issued on or before June 30, 2001, to a person less than eighteen years of age shall expire on the registrant's eighteenth birthday. Such person may renew the card prior to its expiration upon application in person and by paying the required fee. The renewed card for such person shall expire on the registrant's twenty-first birthday.

(b) An identification card issued to an individual prior to April 16, 1996, does not expire unless the true name or social security number, if any, of the individual changes. An individual who has been issued a card prior to April 16, 1996, may voluntarily surrender such card to the department and, upon payment of the fee required for an identification card application, may request issuance of a new identification card containing an expiration date pursuant to the provisions of subsection (1) of this section.

(b.5) An identification card issued on or after July 1, 2001, to a person less than twenty-one years of age shall expire on the registrant's twenty-first birthday.

(c) An identification card issued to an individual sixty-five years of age or older expires on the birthday of the registrant in the fifth year after issuance of the identification card.

42-2-304.5. Cancellation or denial of identification card - failure to register vehicles in Colorado. The department may cancel, deny, or deny reissuance of an identification card upon determining that the registrant has failed to register in Colorado all vehicles owned by the registrant under the requirements of section 42-3-103. Upon such cancellation, the registrant shall surrender the identification card to the department. The registrant is entitled to a hearing under the procedures provided in section 42-2-122.

42-2-305. Lost, stolen, or destroyed cards. If an identification card is lost, destroyed, or mutilated or a new name is acquired, the registrant may obtain a new identification card upon furnishing satisfactory proof of such fact to the department. Any registrant who loses an identification card and who, after obtaining a new identification card, finds the original card shall immediately surrender the original card to the department. The same documentary evidence shall be furnished for a new identification card as for an original identification card. A new identification card issued pursuant to this section shall expire on the birthday of the registrant in the fifth year after the issuance of the new identification card; except that, if the registrant is under the age of twenty-one years at the time the application for the new identification card is made, the new identification card shall expire on the registrant's twenty-first birthday.

42-2-306. Fees - disposition - repeal. (1) The department shall charge and collect the following fees:

(a) (I) (Deleted by amendment, L. 2007, p. 1572, § 5, effective July 1, 2007.)

(II) Except as provided in subparagraphs (III) and (III.5) of this paragraph (a), a fee of nine dollars and ninety cents at the time of application for an identification card or renewal of an identification card.

(III) The fee for the renewal of an identification card pursuant to section 42-2-304 (2) (a) for a person under eighteen years of age who received an identification card on or before June 30, 2001, shall be three dollars and fifty cents payable at the time of the application for renewal of the identification card.

(III.5) The department shall not charge a fee to an applicant who is:

(A) Sixty years of age or older;

(B) Referred by a county department of social services pursuant to section 25.5-4-205 (3), 26-2-106 (3), or 26-5-101 (3) (o), C.R.S.; or

(C) Referred by the department of corrections, the division of youth corrections, or a county jail.

(IV) On or before July 1, 2005, the department shall submit a report to the transportation legislation review committee, created in section 43-2-145, C.R.S., concerning the effect of extending the expiration of identification cards on the fee revenue of the department, and the advisability of continuing the fees imposed in subparagraph (V) of this paragraph (a) and the identification security fund created in section 42-1-220 that is funded through such fees.

(V) (A) In addition to the fees imposed in subparagraphs (II) and (III) of this paragraph (a), the fee for the issuance of an identification card shall include a sixty-cent surcharge. Such surcharge shall be forwarded to the department for transmission to the state treasurer, who shall credit the same to the identification security fund created in section 42-1-220.

(B) This subparagraph (V) is repealed, effective July 1, 2014.

(b) A fee of twenty dollars to cover the costs incurred by the department for the reissuance of an identification card that has been cancelled or denied pursuant to section 42-2-302 (3), or to verify the identity of the applicant.

(2) Fees collected under this section shall be remitted monthly to the state treasurer, who shall deposit the fee in the licensing services cash fund created in section 42-2-114.5.

42-2-307. Change of address. Any registrant who acquires an address different from the address shown on the identification card issued to the registrant shall, within thirty days thereafter, notify the department of such change as specified in section 42-2-119 (1) (a). The department may thereupon take any action deemed necessary to ensure that the identification card reflects the proper address of the registrant.

42-2-308. No liability on public entity. No public entity shall be liable for any loss or injury directly or indirectly resulting from false or inaccurate information contained in identification cards provided for in this part 3.

42-2-309. Unlawful acts. (1) It is unlawful for any person:

(a) To display, cause or permit to be displayed, or have in that person's possession any surrendered, fictitious, fraudulently altered, or fraudulently obtained identification card;

(b) To lend that person's identification card to any other person or knowingly permit the use thereof by another;

(c) To display or represent any identification card not issued to that person as being that person's card;

(d) To permit any unlawful use of an identification card issued to that person;

(e) To do any act forbidden or fail to perform any act required by this part 3, which would not include use of such card after the expiration date;

(f) To photograph, photostat, duplicate, or in any way reproduce any identification card or facsimile thereof in such a manner that it could be mistaken for a valid license, or to display or have in that person's possession any such photograph, photostat, duplicate, reproduction, or facsimile unless authorized by law;

(g) To photograph, photostat, duplicate, or in any way produce any identification card as defined in section 42-2-301 (2), or facsimile thereof, unless authorized by law, in such a manner that it could be mistaken for a valid identification card or to display or possess any such photograph, photostat, duplicate, production, or facsimile;

(h) To photograph, photostat, duplicate, or in any way reproduce any identification card or facsimile thereof for the purpose of distribution, resale, reuse, or manipulation of the data or images contained in such identification card unless authorized by the department or otherwise authorized by law.

42-2-310. Violation. Any person who violates any of the provisions of this part 3 commits a class 3 misdemeanor, as provided in section 18-1.3-501, C.R.S.

42-2-311. County jail identification processing unit - report - repeal. (1) (a) There is hereby created the county jail identification processing unit, referred to in this section as the "unit", in the division that issues drivers' licenses within the department.

(b) The unit shall consist of a mobile identification processing vehicle staffed by the department. The unit shall travel to the county jails in Adams, Arapahoe, Boulder, Douglas, and Jefferson counties, the city and county of Denver, and the city and county of Broomfield on a regular basis to process identification cards for each prisoner who is a legal resident of this state and who does not possess an identification card issued pursuant to this part 3 or a driver's license issued pursuant to part 1 of this article. Each prisoner shall bear the cost of the identification card; except that a county or jail may choose to bear the cost of the identification card. The unit shall, upon the prisoner meeting all of the requirements for obtaining an identification card, process an identification card for each prisoner who is scheduled to be released prior to the unit's scheduled return date to that county jail. The unit shall give priority to a prisoner who has a medically documented mental illness.

(c) The department personnel are authorized to work with county jail personnel and volunteers to assist prisoners in the process of obtaining the identification cards. County jail personnel may assist a prisoner with obtaining the necessary documentation for the identification card.

(d) The department shall develop a schedule with the sheriff of each of the counties pursuant to which the unit will visit each of the participating county jails. The unit shall visit the participating county jails specified in paragraph (b) of this subsection (1). After establishing the schedule for visiting the counties specified in paragraph (b) of this subsection (1), the department shall determine whether it has the resources to expand the number of county jails or other facilities that the unit may serve, which facilities may include, but need not be limited to, correctional facilities, youth detention facilities, and mental health institutions.

(2) Beginning July 1, 2011, and by July 1 each year thereafter, the department shall submit a report regarding the unit to the judiciary committees of the house of representatives and the senate, or any successor committees. The report shall include, but need not be limited to:

(a) The number of identification cards issued by the unit;

(b) The number of identification card requests denied by the unit and the reasons for the denials;

(c) The level of in-kind contributions made by the participating counties;

(d) The successes the unit achieved and the challenges faced by the unit; and

(e) An account of the costs and employee time associated with the operation of the unit for:

(I) The unit;

(II) The participating counties specified in paragraph (b) of subsection (1) of this section; and

(III) The respective sheriff's departments.

(3) (a) The provisions of this section shall only take effect if by June 15, 2012, the department of revenue receives an amount through gifts, grants, and donations that is equal to or greater than the final fiscal estimate for Senate Bill 09-006, as enacted at the first regular session

of the sixty-seventh general assembly, to cover the estimated costs of implementing this section. Any gifts, grants, or donations received by the state department pursuant to this subsection (3) shall be deposited into the county jail identification processing unit fund created pursuant to section 42-2-312.

(b) On or before June 30, 2012, the executive director shall file a written notice with the revisor of statutes indicating that the estimated amount of moneys was received pursuant to paragraph (a) of this subsection (3). If the notice is not received by the revisor of statutes by June 30, 2012, this section is repealed, effective July 1, 2012. If the notice is received by the revisor of statutes by June 30, 2012, this paragraph (b) is repealed, effective July 1, 2012.

42-2-312. County jail identification processing unit fund. The department of revenue is authorized to accept gifts, grants, or donations from private or public sources for the purposes of implementing section 42-2-311; except that no gift, grant, or donation may be accepted by the state treasurer if it is subject to conditions that are inconsistent with this article or any other law of the state. All moneys collected pursuant to this section shall be transmitted to the state treasurer, who shall credit the same to the county jail identification processing unit fund, which fund is hereby created and referred to in this section as the "fund". The moneys in the fund shall be subject to annual appropriation by the general assembly for the direct and indirect costs associated with the implementation of section 42-2-311. Any moneys in the fund not expended for the purpose of this section may be invested by the state treasurer as provided by law. All interest and income derived from the investment and deposit of moneys in the fund shall be credited to the fund. Any unexpended and unencumbered moneys remaining in the fund at the end of a fiscal year shall remain in the fund and shall not be credited or transferred to the general fund or another fund.

42-2-313. Department consult with counties on county jail identification processing unit. The department shall meet with representatives of Adams, Arapahoe, Boulder, Douglas, and Jefferson counties, the city and county of Denver, and the city and county of Broomfield on a regular basis to discuss future implementation of a county jail identification processing unit that would travel to county jails to process identification cards for prisoners, as well as to discuss intergovernmental agreements for cost-sharing solutions to fund the unit, solutions to technical and equipment issues that the department has identified, and implementation of program timelines.

PART 4

COMMERCIAL DRIVERS' LICENSES

42-2-401. Short title. This part 4 shall be known and may be cited as the "Commercial Driver's License Act".

42-2-402. Definitions. As used in this part 4, unless the context otherwise requires:

(1) "Commercial driver's license" means a license issued to an individual in accordance with the requirements of the federal "Commercial Motor Vehicle Safety Act of 1986", 49 App. U.S.C. sec. 2701 et seq., and any rules or regulations promulgated thereunder, that authorizes such individual to drive a commercial motor vehicle.

(2) "Commercial driver's license driving tester" or "driving tester" means an individual licensed by the department under the provisions of section 42-2-407 to perform commercial driver's license driving tests.

(3) "Commercial driver's license testing unit" or "testing unit" means a business, association, or governmental entity licensed by the department under the provisions of section 42-2-407 to administer the performance of commercial driver's license driving tests.

(4) (a) "Commercial motor vehicle" means a motor vehicle designed or used to transport passengers or property, if the vehicle:

(I) Has a gross vehicle weight rating of 26,001 or more pounds or such lesser rating determined by federal regulation; or

(II) Is designed to transport sixteen or more passengers, including the driver; or

(III) Is transporting hazardous materials and is required to be placarded in accordance with 49 CFR part 172, subpart F.

(b) "Commercial motor vehicle" does not include:

(I) Recreational vehicles;

(II) Military vehicles that are driven by military personnel;

(III) Any farm vehicles:

(A) Controlled and operated by a farmer;

(B) Used to transport agriculture products, farm machinery, or farm supplies to or from a farm;

(C) Not used in the operations of a common or contract motor carrier; or

(D) Used within one hundred fifty miles of the person's farm;

(IV) Firefighting equipment.

(5) "Department" means the department of revenue.

(6) "Gross vehicle weight rating" or "GVWR" means the value specified by the manufacturer as the maximum loaded weight of a single or a combination (articulated) vehicle, or registered gross weight, whichever is greater. The GVWR of a combination (articulated) vehicle, commonly referred to as the "gross combination

weight rating" or "GCWR" is the GVWR of the power unit plus the GVWR of any towed unit.

(7) "Hazardous materials" means materials as defined under section 103 of the federal "Hazardous Materials Transportation Act of 1987", 49 App. U.S.C. sec. 1801, as may be amended from time to time.

(8) "Out-of-service order" means an "out-of-service order" as defined by 49 CFR 383.5.

42-2-403. Department authority - rules - federal requirements. (1) The department shall develop, adopt, and administer a procedure for licensing drivers of commercial motor vehicles in accordance with applicable federal law governing commercial motor vehicle safety and any rules promulgated thereunder. The department is hereby specifically authorized to adopt and effectuate, whether by rule, policy, or administrative custom or practice, any licensing sanction imposed by federal statutes or rules governing commercial motor vehicle safety.

(2) (a) The department shall promulgate such rules and regulations as are necessary for the implementation of this part 4. Such rules and regulations shall govern all aspects of licensing commercial drivers, including, but not limited to, testing procedures, license issuance procedures, out-of-service regulations, denial procedures, including suspensions, revocations, cancellations and denials, records maintenance, reporting requirements, and cooperation with the commercial driver's license information system.

(b) The department, with the advice of the commissioner of education, shall develop testing and license issuance procedures for school bus drivers who are employed by any Colorado school district.

(c) (I) In addition to any other requirements, an application for a commercial driver's license shall state that:

(A) The applicant understands that, as a resident of the state of Colorado, any motor vehicle owned by the applicant must be registered in Colorado pursuant to the laws of the state and the applicant may be subject to criminal penalties, civil penalties, cancellation or denial of the applicant's driver's license, and liability for any unpaid registration fees and specific ownership taxes if the applicant fails to comply with such registration requirements; and

(B) The applicant agrees, within thirty days after the date the applicant became a resident, to register in Colorado any vehicle owned by the applicant.

(II) The applicant shall verify the statements required by this paragraph (c) by the applicant's signature on the application.

(d) The department may not consider the following with regard to an application from a person for a commercial driver's license:

(I) A conviction for UDD;

(II) A license revocation imposed under section 42-2-126 (3) (b) if the person was under twenty-one years of age at the time of the offense and such person drove a motor vehicle while such person's BAC was at least 0.02 but not more than 0.05; or

(III) A license revocation imposed under section 42-2-126 (3) (e) if the person was under twenty-one years of age at the time of the offense and such person drove a commercial motor vehicle while such person's BAC was at least 0.02 but less than 0.04.

(e) With regard to every person who holds or applies for a commercial driver's license in this state, the department shall maintain, for at least three years, records of such person's application and of any convictions, disqualifications, and licensing actions for violation of state or local laws relating to motor vehicle traffic control, other than parking violations, committed while the person was operating a commercial motor vehicle or that would affect the person's commercial driving privilege, and shall make such records available to the specified persons and entities as follows:

(I) To law enforcement officers, courts, prosecutors, administrative adjudicators, and motor vehicle licensing authorities in Colorado or any other state, all information on all such persons;

(II) To the federal secretary of transportation, all information on all such persons;

(III) To the individual to whom such information pertains, all such information pertaining to that individual;

(IV) To the motor carrier employer or prospective motor carrier employer of the individual to whom such information pertains, all such information pertaining to that individual.

(2.5) Any application for the issuance or renewal of a license pursuant to this section shall include the applicant's social security number as required in section 14-14-113, C.R.S.

(3) Nothing in this part 4 shall be construed to prevent the state of Colorado from complying with federal requirements in order to qualify for funds under the federal "Commercial Motor Vehicle Safety Act of 1986" or other applicable federal law.

(4) (a) Any male United States citizen or immigrant who applies for a commercial driver's license, or a renewal of any such license, and who is at least eighteen years of age but less than twenty-six years of age shall be registered in compliance with the requirements of section 3 of the "Military Selective Service Act", 50 U.S.C. App. sec. 453, as amended.

(b) The department shall forward in an electronic format the necessary personal information of the applicants identified in paragraph (a) of this subsection (4) to the selective service system. The applicant's submission of an application shall serve as an indication that the applicant either has already registered with the selective service system or that he is authorizing the department to forward to the selective service system the necessary information for such registration. The department shall notify the applicant that his signature serves as consent to registration with the selective service system, if so required by federal law.

42-2-404. License for drivers - limitations. (1) Except as provided in subsection (4) of this section, no person shall operate a commercial motor vehicle upon the highways in this state on or after April 1, 1992, unless such person has attained the age of twenty-one years and has been issued and is in immediate possession of a commercial driver's license.

(1.5) (a) The department shall not issue a commercial driver's license to, and shall immediately cancel the commercial driver's license of, any person subject to a federal disqualification order on the basis of imminent hazard to public safety pursuant to 49 CFR 383.52.

(b) A person who is subject to a federal disqualification order on the basis of imminent hazard, or whose commercial or noncommercial driver's privilege is under restraint, shall not be eligible for a restricted, probationary, or hardship license that would permit the person to operate a commercial motor vehicle during the period of such disqualification or restraint.

(c) (I) The department shall not issue, renew, upgrade, or transfer a hazardous materials endorsement for a commercial driver's license that would have the effect of authorizing a person to operate a commercial motor vehicle transporting hazardous material in commerce unless the federal transportation security administration has determined that the person does not pose a security risk warranting a denial of the endorsement.

(II) Fingerprinting for the purpose of a criminal history record check for a hazardous materials endorsement on a commercial driver's license may be conducted by a state or local law enforcement agent or any other person who has the authorization or approval of a federal agency including, without limitation, the transportation safety administration or the federal bureau of investigation.

(III) A person enrolled in a commercial driver training school or holding a commercial driving learner's permit shall not be eligible to apply for or receive a hazardous materials endorsement and is prohibited from operating a commercial motor vehicle transporting hazardous material at any time.

(2) No person who drives a commercial motor vehicle may have more than one driver's license.

(3) In addition to any applicable federal penalty concerning commercial motor vehicle operators, any person who violates subsection (1) or (2) of this section, or any rule or regulation promulgated by the department pursuant to this part 4, is guilty of a misdemeanor and, upon conviction thereof, shall be punished by a fine of not less than twenty-five dollars nor more than one thousand dollars, or by imprisonment in the county jail for not more than one year, or by both such fine and imprisonment.

(4) The provisions of this part 4 shall not apply to any person who is at least eighteen years of age but less than twenty-one years of age and who operates a commercial motor vehicle upon the highways of this state solely in intrastate operations. Pursuant to the provisions of section 42-2-101 (4), no such person of such age shall operate any commercial motor vehicle upon the highways of this state unless such person has been issued and is in immediate possession of a minor driver's license of the correct type of general class for the type or general class of motor vehicle which is issued.

42-2-405. Driver's license disciplinary actions - grounds for denial - suspension - revocation - disqualification. (1) A person who holds a commercial driver's license or who drives a commercial motor vehicle, as defined under this part 4, shall be subject, in addition to this part 4, to disciplinary actions, penalties, and the general provisions under parts 1, 2, and 3 of this article and article 7 of this title.

(2) In addition to applicable penalties imposed under the sections listed in subsection (1) of this section:

(a) A person who drives, operates, or is in physical control of a commercial motor vehicle while having any alcohol in his or her system, or who refuses to submit to a test to determine the alcoholic content of the driver's blood or breath while driving a commercial motor vehicle, shall be placed out of service as defined in section 42-2-402 (8).

(b) (I) If any person possesses or knowingly transports a schedule I drug or other substance identified in 49 CFR chapter III, subchapter B, appendix D, an amphetamine, a narcotic drug, a formulation of an amphetamine, or a derivative of a narcotic drug while operating a commercial vehicle during on-duty time, the department shall cancel such person's commercial driver's license for a period of six months or, if such person does not have a commercial driver's license, the department shall not issue a commercial driver's license to such person until at least six months have elapsed since the date of the latest such occurrence.

(II) If any person makes unlawful use of a schedule I drug or other substance identified in 49 CFR chapter III, subchapter B, appendix D, an amphetamine, a narcotic drug, a formulation of an amphetamine, or a derivative of a narcotic drug while operating a commercial vehicle during on-duty time, the department shall cancel such person's commercial driver's license for a period of one year or, if such person does not have a commercial driver's license, the department shall not issue a commercial driver's license to such person until at least one year has elapsed since the date of the latest such occurrence.

(3) For purposes of the imposition of restraints and sanctions against commercial driving privileges:

(a) A conviction for DUI, DUI per se, DWAI, or habitual user, or a substantially similar law of any other state pertaining to drinking and driving, or an administrative determination of a violation of section 42-2-126 (3) (a) or (3) (b) shall be deemed driving under the influence; and

(b) A conviction for violating section 42-4-706, 42-4-707, 42-4-708, or a substantially similar law of any other state pertaining to conduct at or near railroad crossings, shall be deemed a railroad crossing offense.

(4) A commercial driver whose privilege to drive a commercial motor vehicle has been cancelled or denied pursuant to this section may, following any applicable revocation period, apply for another type or class of driver's license in accordance with section 42-2-104, as long as there is no other statutory reason to deny such person such a license.

42-2-405.5. Violations of out-of-service order. (1) A person who operates a commercial motor vehicle in violation of an out-of-service order commits a class 1 traffic misdemeanor.

(2) No court shall accept a plea of guilty to another offense from a person charged with a violation of subsection (1) of this section; except that the court may accept such a plea upon a good faith representation by the prosecuting attorney that there is not a prima facie case for the original offense.

(3) Upon receipt of notice of a conviction or deferred sentence under subsection (1) of this section, the department shall immediately suspend the commercial driver's license for the maximum period set forth in the United States federal regulations governing violations of out-of-service orders for commercial drivers and section 42-2-403 (1).

(4) Notice of suspension under subsection (3) of this section shall be mailed to the person by the department in compliance with section 42-2-119 (2).

(5) (a) Upon receipt of the notice of suspension, the person may request a hearing in writing if the person has surrendered to the department a commercial driver's license issued by any state. The department, upon notice to the person, shall hold a hearing as soon as practicable at the district office of the department closest to the residence of the person; except that, at the discretion of the department, all or part of the hearing may be conducted in real time by telephone or other electronic means in accordance with section 42-1-218.5.

(b) The only issues at such hearing are whether the driver was convicted of or received a deferred sentence for a violation of subsection (1) of this section and the appropriate length of suspension. If the driver was convicted, the license shall be suspended. The hearing officer may reduce the period of suspension based on findings at the hearing, including without limitation the circumstances of the violation, the prior driving record, and aggravating and mitigating factors. A hearing officer shall not reduce the suspension period below the minimum disqualification period imposed by 49 CFR 383.51.

(c) (I) The order of the hearing officer is the final agency action and may be appealed under section 42-2-135. A petition for judicial review shall be filed within thirty days after the date of the order.

(II) Judicial review shall be on the record of the hearing without taking additional testimony. If the court finds that the department exceeded its constitutional or statutory authority, made an erroneous interpretation of the law, acted in an arbitrary and capricious manner, or made a determination that is unsupported by the evidence in the record, the court may reverse the department's determination.

(III) The court may grant a stay of the order only upon motion, after a hearing, and upon a finding that there is a reasonable probability that the petitioner will prevail upon the merits and that the petitioner will suffer irreparable harm if the order is not stayed.

42-2-406. Fees. (1) The fee for the issuance of a commercial driver's license is thirty-four dollars and forty cents, which shall be transferred to the state treasurer, who shall credit twenty-five dollars to the highway users tax fund and nine dollars and forty cents to the licensing services cash fund created in section 42-2-114.5; except that, for fiscal years 2010-11 and 2011-12, the state treasurer shall credit the fees to the licensing services cash fund created in section 42-2-114.5. Such license shall expire on the birthday of the applicant in the fourth year after its issuance. When issuing a commercial driver's license, the office of the county clerk and recorder shall retain eight dollars, and twenty-six dollars and forty cents shall be forwarded to the department for transmission to the state treasurer, who shall credit nineteen dollars to the highway users tax fund and seven dollars and forty cents to the licensing services cash fund; except that, for fiscal years 2010-11 and 2011-12, the state treasurer shall credit the fees to the licensing services cash fund. The general assembly shall make annual appropriations therefrom for the expenses of the administration of parts 1 and 2 of this article and this part 4; except that eight dollars and fifty cents of each commercial driver's license fee shall be allocated pursuant to section 43-4-205 (6) (b), C.R.S., other than during fiscal years 2010-11 and 2011-12.

(2) Notwithstanding any other provision of law, the fee for a person eighteen years of age or older for issuance of a minor driver's license that authorizes operation of a commercial motor vehicle upon the highways of this state is thirty-four dollars and forty cents, which shall be transferred to the state treasurer, who shall credit twenty-five dollars to the highway users tax fund and nine dollars and forty cents to the licensing services cash fund created in section 42-2-114.5; except that, for fiscal years 2010-11 and 2011-12,

the state treasurer shall credit the fees to the licensing services cash fund created in section 42-2-114.5. When issuing a minor driver's license, the office of the county clerk and recorder shall retain eight dollars, and twenty-six dollars and forty cents shall be forwarded to the department for transmission to the state treasurer, who shall credit nineteen dollars to the highway users tax fund and seven dollars and forty cents to the licensing services cash fund; except that, for fiscal years 2010-11 and 2011-12, the state treasurer shall credit such amount to the licensing services cash fund created in section 42-2-114.5. The general assembly shall make annual appropriations therefrom for the expenses of the administration of parts 1 and 2 of this article and this part 4; except that eight dollars and fifty cents of each such minor driver's license fee shall be allocated pursuant to section 43-4-205 (6) (b), C.R.S., other than during fiscal years 2010-11 and 2011-12.

(3) (a) (I) The fee for the administration by commercial driver's license testing units of the driving test for licensing commercial drivers shall not exceed the fee set by rule.

(II) The department shall promulgate rules setting a limit on the amount that may be charged for the administration of the driving test by commercial driver's license testing units for licensing commercial drivers. The rules shall also provide for a lower fee limit for the administration of the driving test to an employee or volunteer of a nonprofit organization that provides specialized transportation services for the elderly and for persons with disabilities, to any individual employed by a school district, or to any individual employed by a board of cooperative services. The department shall promulgate such rules by December 1, 2008, and every three years thereafter.

(b) The fee for the administration of driving tests by the department shall be one hundred dollars; except that the fee for the administration of such driving test to any employee or volunteer of a nonprofit organization that provides specialized transportation services for the elderly and for persons with disabilities, to any individual employed by a school district, or to any individual employed by a board of cooperative services shall not exceed forty dollars.

(c) The department may provide by rule for reduced fees for applicants who are retested after failing all or any part of the driving test.

(d) All fees collected by the department for the administration of driving tests shall be forwarded to the state treasurer, who shall credit the same to the licensing services cash fund. The general assembly shall make annual appropriations therefrom for the expenses of the administration of parts 1 and 2 of this article and this part 4, and any fees credited to the fund pursuant to this subsection (3) in excess of the amount of the appropriations shall be allocated and expended as specified in section 43-4-205 (5.5) (f), C.R.S., other than during fiscal years 2010-11 and 2011-12.

(4) The annual license fee for a commercial driver's license testing unit shall be three hundred dollars for the initial license issuance and one hundred dollars for each succeeding annual license renewal. The department may provide by regulation for reduced license fees for testing units operated by nonprofit organizations which provide specialized transportation services for the elderly and for persons with disabilities, by school districts, or by boards of cooperative services. The provisions of this subsection (4) shall not apply to any public transportation system.

(5) The annual license fee for a commercial driver's license driving tester shall be one hundred dollars for the initial license issuance and fifty dollars for each succeeding annual license renewal. The department may provide by regulation for reduced license fees for employees or volunteers of nonprofit organizations which provide specialized transportation services for the elderly and for persons with disabilities, for individuals employed by school districts, or for individuals employed by boards of cooperative services. The provisions of this subsection (5) shall not apply to any public transportation system.

(6) All fees collected by the department for the issuance of testing unit licenses and driving test licenses pursuant to subsections (4) and (5) of this section shall be forwarded to the state treasurer, who shall credit the same to the highway users tax fund; except that, for fiscal years 2010-11 and 2011-12, the state treasurer shall credit the fees to the licensing services cash fund. The general assembly shall make annual appropriations therefrom for the expenses of the administration of parts 1 and 2 of this article and this part 4, and any fees credited to the fund pursuant to this subsection (6) in excess of the amount of the appropriations shall be allocated and expended as specified in section 43-4-205 (5.5) (f), C.R.S., other than during fiscal years 2010-11 and 2011-12.

(7) Notwithstanding the amount specified for any fee in this section, the executive director of the department by rule or as otherwise provided by law may reduce the amount of one or more of the fees if necessary pursuant to section 24-75-402 (3), C.R.S., to reduce the uncommitted reserves of the fund to which all or any portion of one or more of the fees is credited. After the uncommitted reserves of the fund are sufficiently reduced, the executive director of the department by rule or as otherwise provided by law may increase the amount of one or more of the fees as provided in section 24-75-402 (4), C.R.S.

42-2-407. Licensing of testing units and driving testers - hearings - regulations. (1) Commercial driver's license driving tests may be performed only by employees of the department or by commercial driver's license driving testers employed by commercial driver's license testing units.

(2) The department is hereby authorized to issue, deny, suspend, or revoke licenses for the operation of commercial driver's license testing units. The department shall furnish all necessary instructions and forms to such testing units.

(3) The department is hereby authorized to issue, deny, suspend, or revoke licenses for commercial driver's license driving testers. The department shall furnish all necessary instructions and forms to such driving testers.

(4) The department shall supervise the activities of testing units and driving testers. The department shall provide for the inspection of testing units. Testing units shall be open for business at reasonable hours to allow inspection of the operations of such testing units.

(5) Testing units shall keep records as required by the department and shall make such records available to the department for inspection.

(6) The department shall require the surrender of the license of any commercial driver's license testing unit or commercial driver's license driving tester upon the suspension or revocation of such license.

(7) Any person aggrieved by the denial of issuance, denial of renewal, suspension, or revocation of a testing unit license or driving tester license shall be entitled to a hearing. Hearings held under this subsection (7) shall be conducted by a hearing officer before the department. Such hearing shall be held within thirty days after a written request for a hearing is received by the department. Such hearing shall be held before a hearing officer of the department and shall be held at the district office of the department which is nearest to the residence of the licensee, unless the hearing officer and the licensee agree that such hearing may be held at some other district office. Such hearing officer may administer oaths and may issue subpoenas for the attendance of witnesses and the production of relevant books, records, and papers at such hearing. The aggrieved person shall not perform any act under the license pending the outcome of such hearing.

(8) The department shall adopt regulations for the administration and operation of commercial driver's license testing units and the conduct of commercial driver's license driving testers.

42-2-408. Unlawful acts - penalty. (1) It is unlawful for any person other than an employee of the department to perform commercial driver's license driving tests, to act as a commercial driver's license testing unit, or to act as a commercial driver's license driving tester unless such person has been duly licensed by the department under the provisions of section 42-2-407.

(2) Any person who violates the provisions of this section is guilty of a misdemeanor and, upon conviction thereof, shall be punished by a fine of not less than twenty-five dollars nor more than one thousand dollars, or by imprisonment in the county jail for not more than one year, or by both such fine and imprisonment.

42-2-409. Unlawful possession or use of a commercial driver's license. (1) (a) A person shall not have in his or her possession a lawfully issued commercial driver's license knowing that the license has been falsely altered by means of erasure, obliteration, deletion, insertion of new information, transposition of information, or any other means so that the license in its altered form falsely appears or purports to be in all respects an authentic and lawfully issued license.

(b) A person shall not fraudulently obtain a commercial driver's license.

(c) A person shall not have in his or her possession a paper, document, or other instrument that falsely appears or purports to be in all respects a lawfully issued and authentic commercial driver's license knowing that the instrument was falsely made and was not lawfully issued.

(d) A person shall not display, or represent as being his or her own, a commercial driver's license that was lawfully issued to another person.

(e) A person shall not fail or refuse to surrender to the department upon its lawful demand a commercial driver's license issued to the person that has been suspended, revoked, or cancelled by the department. The department shall notify in writing the district attorney's office in the county where the violation occurred of all violations of this paragraph (e).

(f) A person shall not permit the unlawful use of a commercial driver's license issued to the person.

(g) A person shall not photograph, photostat, duplicate, or in any way reproduce a commercial driver's license or facsimile thereof for the purpose of distribution, resale, reuse, or manipulation of the data or images contained in the commercial driver's license unless authorized by the department or otherwise authorized by law.

(2) A person who violates a provision of subsection (1) of this section commits a misdemeanor and shall be punished as follows:

(a) Imposition of a fine of not less than five hundred dollars and not more than one thousand dollars for a first offense; or

(b) Imposition of a fine of not less than one thousand dollars and not more than two thousand dollars for a second or subsequent offense within five years after the first offense.

(3) (a) Upon receipt of a notice of conviction under this section, the department shall permanently revoke the person's right to receive a commercial driver's license.

(b) A notice of revocation under this section shall be mailed to the person by the department in compliance with section 42-2-119 (2).

(c) Upon receipt of the notice of revocation, the person or the person's attorney may request a hearing in writing. The department, upon notice to the person as provided in section 42-2-119 (2), shall hold a hearing as soon as practicable at the district office of the department closest to the residence of the person; except that, at the discretion of the department, all or part of the hearing may be conducted in real time by telephone or other electronic means in accordance with section 42-1-218.5.

(d) The order of the hearing officer is the final agency action and may be appealed under section 42-2-135. A petition for judicial review shall be filed within thirty days after the date of the order.

(4) A court shall not accept a plea of guilty to another offense from a person charged with a violation of this section; except that the court may accept a plea of guilty to another offense upon a good faith representation by the prosecuting attorney that the attorney cannot establish a prima facie case if the defendant is brought to trial on the original offense.

TAXATION

ARTICLE 3

Registration, Taxation, and License Plates

PART 1
REGISTRATION AND TAXATION

42-3-101.	Legislative declaration.
42-3-102.	Periodic registration - rules.
42-3-103.	Registration required - exemptions.
42-3-104.	Exemptions - specific ownership tax - registration - domicile and residency - rules - definitions.
42-3-105.	Application for registration - tax.
42-3-106.	Tax imposed - classification - taxable value.
42-3-107.	Taxable value of classes of property - rate of tax - when and where payable - department duties - apportionment of tax collections - definitions.
42-3-108.	Determination of year model - tax lists.
42-3-109.	Tax for registration period.
42-3-110.	Payment of motor vehicle registration fees and specific ownership taxes in installments.
42-3-111.	Tax year - disposition.
42-3-112.	Failure to pay tax - penalty - rules.
42-3-113.	Records of application and registration.
42-3-114.	Expiration.
42-3-115.	Registration upon transfer.
42-3-116.	Manufacturers or dealers.
42-3-117.	Nonresidents.
42-3-118.	Registration suspended upon theft - recovery - rules.
42-3-119.	No application for registration granted - when.
42-3-120.	Department may cancel or deny registration.
42-3-121.	Violation of registration provisions - penalty.
42-3-122.	Perjury on a motor vehicle registration application.
42-3-123.	Payment by bad check - recovery of plates.
42-3-124.	Violation - penalty.
42-3-125.	Fleet operators - registration period certificates - multi-year registrations.
42-3-126.	Notice - primary body color.
42-3-127.	Sale of special mobile machinery.

PART 2
LICENSE PLATES

42-3-201.	Number plates furnished - style - periodic reissuance - tabs - rules.
42-3-202.	Number plates to be attached.
42-3-203.	Standardized plates - rules.
42-3-204.	Parking privileges for persons with disabilities - applicability - rules.
42-3-205.	Substitute plates - waiting period for reissuance of identical combination of numbers and letters.
42-3-206.	Remanufacture of certain license plates.
42-3-207.	Special plates - rules - new plates - retirement.
42-3-208.	Special plates - qualifications for issuance of special license plates.
42-3-209.	Legislative license plates.
42-3-210.	Radio and television license plates.
42-3-211.	Issuance of personalized plates authorized.
42-3-212.	Issuance of optional plates authorized - retirement.
42-3-213.	Special plates - military veterans - rules - retirement.
42-3-214.	Special plates - alumni associations - retirement.
42-3-215.	Special plates - United States olympic committee - retirement.
42-3-216.	Special plates - Colorado foundation for agriculture and natural resources - definitions - retirement.
42-3-217.	Special plates - Colorado commission of Indian affairs.
42-3-217.5.	Special plates - breast cancer awareness - retirement.
42-3-218.	Special plates - active and retired members of the Colorado National Guard - retirement.
42-3-219.	Special registration of collector's items. (Repealed)
42-3-220.	Temporary special event license plates.
42-3-221.	Special plates - Denver Broncos.
42-3-222.	Special plates - support public education.
42-3-223.	Special plates - support the troops - retirement.
42-3-224.	Special plates - Colorado "Kids First".

42-3-225.	Special plates - Italian-American heritage.
42-3-226.	Special plates - share the road.
42-3-227.	Special plates - Colorado horse development authority.
42-3-228.	Special plates - Colorado carbon fund.
42-3-229.	Special plates - boy scouts.
42-3-230.	Special plates - "Alive at Twenty-five".
42-3-231.	Special plates - Colorado ski country.
42-3-232.	Special plates - donate life.
42-3-233.	Special plates - Colorado state parks.
42-3-234.	Special plates - adopt a shelter pet.
42-3-235.	Livery license plates - luxury limousines - repeal.
42-3-236.	Taxicab license plates - taxicabs - repeal.
42-3-237.	Special plates - girl scouts.
42-3-238.	Special plates - type 1 diabetes.
42-3-239.	Special plates - Colorado Avalanche or Denver Nuggets.
42-3-240.	Special plates - Craig hospital.

PART 3
FEES AND CASH FUNDS

42-3-301.	License plate cash fund - license plate fees.
42-3-302.	Special plate fees.
42-3-303.	Persistent drunk driver cash fund - programs to deter persistent drunk drivers.
42-3-304.	Registration fees - passenger and passenger-mile taxes - clean screen fund - repeal.
42-3-305.	Registration fees - passenger and passenger-mile taxes - fee schedule for years of TABOR surplus revenue - applicability. (Repealed)
42-3-306.	Registration fees - passenger and passenger-mile taxes - fee schedule.
42-3-307.	Enforcement powers of department.
42-3-308.	Taxpayer statements - payment of tax - estimates - penalties - deposits - delinquency proceedings.
42-3-309.	Permit to be secured - records kept - penalties.
42-3-310.	Additional registration fees - apportionment of fees.
42-3-311.	Low-power scooter registration - fee.
42-3-312.	Special license plate surcharge.

PART 1
REGISTRATION AND TAXATION

42-3-101. Legislative declaration. (1) The general assembly declares that its purpose in enacting this article is to implement by law the purpose and intent of section 6 of article X of the state constitution, wherein it is provided that "The general assembly shall enact laws classifying motor vehicles and also wheeled trailers, semitrailers, trailer coaches, and mobile and self-propelled construction equipment, prescribing methods of determining the taxable value of such property, and requiring payment of a graduated annual specific ownership tax thereon, which tax shall be in lieu of all ad valorem taxes upon such property; ...".

(2) The general assembly further declares that it intends to classify in this article the personal property so specified, to prescribe methods by which the taxable value of such classified property shall be determined, to require payment of a graduated annual specific ownership tax upon each item of such classified personal property, and to provide for the administration and collection of such tax, and for the apportionment and distribution of the revenue derived therefrom.

42-3-102. Periodic registration - rules. (1) The department may establish by rule a periodic vehicle registration program whereby certain vehicles shall be registered at:

(a) Subject to the provisions of subsection (3) of this section, twelve-month intervals, in which case the registration of such vehicles shall expire on the last day of the month of each twelve-month registration period;

(b) Five-year intervals upon payment of a five-year registration fee and any five-year specific ownership tax that may be due. An owner of any of the following motor vehicles may elect a five-year registration pursuant to this paragraph (b), which registration shall expire on the last day of the last month of each five-year registration period:

(I) A utility trailer; or

(II) Special mobile machinery.

(2) (a) Except for motor vehicles of model year 1981 or older and except for motorcycles of any model year, the department may register motor vehicles at two-year intervals upon payment of a two-year registration fee and a two-year specific ownership tax. The owner of a motor vehicle that is eligible as determined by the department for two-year registration may elect a two-year registration pursuant to this subsection (2), which registration shall expire on the last day of the last month of each two-year registration period.

(b) This subsection (2) shall not apply to class A property that is registered through the international registration plan. Such vehicles shall continue to be registered every twelve months.

(3) (a) The department may register vehicles at intervals of less than one year upon payment of the appropriate registration fee and specific ownership tax in order to allow the owner of more than one vehicle to provide for the owner's vehicle registrations to expire simulta-

neously. The owner of a vehicle that is eligible as determined by the authorized agent may elect a registration pursuant to this subsection (3). The department may adopt such rules as deemed necessary for the administration of this subsection (3).

(b) This subsection (3) shall not apply to class A property that is registered through the international registration plan. Such vehicles shall continue to be registered every twelve months.

42-3-103. Registration required - exemptions. (1) (a) Within sixty days after purchase, every owner of a motor vehicle, trailer, semitrailer, or vehicle that is primarily designed to be operated or drawn upon any highway of this state or any owner of a trailer coach or of special mobile machinery whether or not it is operated on the highways, shall register such vehicle with the department. A person who violates this subsection (1) commits a class B traffic infraction.

(b) This subsection (1) shall not apply to the following:

(I) A bicycle, electric assisted bicycle, or other human-powered vehicle;

(II) Vehicles specifically exempted by section 42-3-104; and

(III) Any vehicle whose owner is permitted to operate it under provisions of this article concerning lienholders, manufacturers, dealers, nonresidents, and fleet owners.

(c) A person who violates this subsection (1) two or more times in five years commits a class 1 misdemeanor and shall be punished as provided in section 18-1.3-501, C.R.S.

(2) An owner of a foreign vehicle operated within this state for the transportation of persons or property for compensation or for the transportation of merchandise shall register such vehicle and pay the same fees and tax required by this article with reference to like vehicles. This provision shall not be construed to require registration or reregistration in this state of any motor vehicle, truck, bus, trailer, semitrailer, or trailer coach that is used in interstate commerce, but registration or reregistration shall be required in accordance with or to the extent that reciprocity exists between the state of Colorado and a foreign country or another state, territory, or possession of the United States.

(3) Every nonresident person who operates a business within this state and owns and operates in such business any motor vehicle, trailer, semitrailer, or trailer coach within this state shall be required to register each such vehicle and pay the same fees and tax therefor as are required with reference to like vehicles owned by residents of this state. This provision shall not be construed to require registration or reregistration in this state of any motor vehicle, trailer, or trailer coach that is used in interstate commerce, but registration or reregistration shall be required in accordance with or to the extent that reciprocity exists between the state of Colorado and a foreign country or another state, territory, or possession of the United States.

(4) (a) Within ninety days after becoming a resident of Colorado, an owner of a motor vehicle required to be registered by subsection (1) of this section shall register such vehicle with the department, irrespective of such vehicle being registered within another state or country. A person who violates this paragraph (a) is subject to the penalties provided in sections 42-6-139 and 43-4-804 (1) (d), C.R.S.

(b) Within forty-five days after the owner has returned to the United States, the provisions of this title relative to the registration of motor vehicles and the display of number plates shall not apply to motor vehicles registered with and displaying plates issued by the armed forces of the United States in foreign countries for vehicles owned by military personnel.

(c) (I) Notwithstanding paragraph (a) of this subsection (4) and section 42-1-102 (62) and (81), a nonresident shall be exempt from registering a motor vehicle owned by such person if the motor vehicle is a private passenger vehicle weighing less than sixty-five hundred pounds and the person is:

(A) A nonresident, gainfully employed within the boundaries of this state, who uses a motor vehicle in commuting daily from such person's home in another state to and from such person's place of employment within this state; or

(B) A nonresident student who is enrolled in a full-time course of study at an institution of higher education located within this state, if the motor vehicle owned by such person displays a valid nonresident student identification tag issued by the institution where the student is enrolled.

(II) Any person who is exempt from the provisions of this title concerning the registration of a motor vehicle pursuant to this paragraph (c) shall comply with the applicable provisions of the motor vehicle registration laws of such person's state of residence.

(III) This paragraph (c) shall apply only if the state in which the owner resides extends the same privileges to Colorado residents gainfully employed or enrolled in an institution of higher education within the boundaries of that state.

(5) The provisions of this title concerning the registration of motor vehicles and the display of number plates or of other identification shall not apply to manufactured homes.

42-3-104. Exemptions - specific ownership tax - registration - domicile and residency - rules - definitions. (1) Only those items of classified personal property that are owned by the United States government or an agency or instrumentality thereof, by the state of Colorado or a political subdivision thereof, or by a service member either individually or jointly with a dependent shall be exempt from payment of the annual specific ownership tax imposed in this article.

(2) An item of classified personal property that is leased by the state of Colorado or a political subdivision thereof may be exempted by the department from payment of the annual specific ownership tax imposed in this article if the agreement under which such item is leased is first submitted to the department and approved by it. Such item shall remain exempt only if used and operated in strict conformance with the terms of such approved agreement.

(3) Registration shall not be required for the following:

(a) Vehicles owned by the United States government or by an agency thereof;

(b) Fire-fighting vehicles;

(c) Police ambulances and patrol wagons;

(d) Farm tractors and implements of husbandry designed primarily for use and used in agricultural operations;

(e) Special mobile machinery used solely on property owned or leased by the owner of such machinery and equipment and not operated on the public highways of the state, if the owner lists all of the machinery or equipment for assessment and taxation under part 1 of article 5 of title 39, C.R.S.;

(f) Special mobile machinery not operated on the highways of this state owned by a public utility and taxed under article 4 of title 39, C.R.S.

(4) At the request of the appropriate authority, motor vehicles owned and operated by the state of Colorado or any agency or institution thereof or by a town, city, county, or city and county may be assigned, in lieu of the distinct registration number specified in this article, a special registration number indicating that such vehicle is owned and operated by the state of Colorado or any agency or institution thereof or by a town, city, county, or city and county, but only one such special registration number shall be assigned to each vehicle. An application for the special registration provided in this section that is made by the state of Colorado or any agency or institution thereof shall be made to the department only. An application for the special registration provided in this section that is made by any town, city, county, or city and county shall be made only to the authorized agent in the county wherein the applicant local government entity is located, and any such special registration shall be obtained directly from such authorized agent. Special registrations obtained under this subsection (4) shall be renewed annually pursuant to the requirements prescribed by the department.

(5) One Class B or Class C motor vehicle weighing less than sixteen thousand pounds empty weight owned by a person who is a veteran and has established rights to benefits under the provisions of Public Law 663, 79th Congress, as amended, and Public Law 187, 82nd Congress, as amended, or is a veteran of the armed forces of the United States who incurred a disability and is receiving compensation from the veterans administration or any branch of the armed forces of the United States for a fifty percent or more, service-connected, permanent disability, or for loss of use of one or both feet or one or both hands, or for permanent impairment or loss of vision in both eyes that constitutes virtual blindness shall be exempt from the imposition of the annual specific ownership tax imposed by this article. Only one such Class B or Class C motor vehicle per veteran shall be exempted.

(6) One Class B or Class C motor vehicle weighing less than sixteen thousand pounds empty weight owned by a natural person who, while serving in the armed forces of the United States, was incarcerated by an enemy of the United States during armed conflict with the United States or who survived the attack on Pearl Harbor shall be exempt from the imposition of the annual specific ownership tax imposed by this article. Only one such Class B or Class C motor vehicle per former prisoner of war shall be exempted. A person who survived the attack on Pearl Harbor shall be exempt from the imposition of specific ownership tax under this subsection (6) only if the person qualifies for a survivor's of the attack on Pearl Harbor license plate issued pursuant to section 42-3-213 (6).

(7) Those items of classified personal property that are owned or leased by an individual or organization that is exempt from payment of Colorado ad valorem taxes shall be exempt from imposition of the annual specific ownership tax imposed by this article.

(8) Either one Class B or one Class C motor vehicle weighing less than sixteen thousand pounds empty weight owned by a natural person who received a purple heart or medal of valor and who is authorized to use the purple heart or military valor special license plate pursuant to section 42-3-213 shall be exempt from the imposition of the annual specific ownership tax imposed by this article. Only one such Class B or Class C motor vehicle per purple heart or medal of valor recipient shall be exempted.

(9) (a) Notwithstanding that a service member has registered to vote in Colorado or paid or not paid taxes in the service member's state of residence, personal property owned by the service member, either individually or jointly with a dependent, while the service member is a resident of another state but domiciled in Colorado in compliance with military orders, shall be exempt from the imposition of the annual specific ownership tax imposed by this article.

(b) The personal property of a service member who is a resident of another state but domiciled in Colorado in compliance with military orders shall be not be deemed to be located in, be present in, or have a situs in the local jurisdiction of Colorado.

(c) A service member shall neither lose nor acquire residency or domicile in Colorado for the purpose of taxation, with regard to personal property of the service member in any tax jurisdiction of Colorado, if the domicile is in compliance with military orders.

(d) The residency of a service member shall not be established solely for the purpose of taxation. A service member shall be deemed to be a resident of Colorado when the service member is not domiciled in Colorado if the domicile is in compliance with military orders and the service member is a resident as defined by section 42-1-102 (81).

(e) For the purpose of voting in a federal, state, or local election, a service member who is in Colorado in compliance with military orders shall not:

(I) Be deemed to have lost residence or domicile in another state regardless of whether the person intends to return to the other state;

(II) Be deemed to have acquired residence or domicile in another state; or

(III) Be deemed to become a resident of another state.

(f) The executive director of the department may issue forms and promulgate rules necessary to implement this subsection (9).

(10) For the purposes of this section:

(a) "Dependent" means a service member's spouse, child, or an individual for whom the service member has provided more than one-half of the individual's support for at least one hundred eighty days immediately preceding an application for specific ownership tax exemption.

(b) "Service member" means a member of the United States armed forces.

(11) A Class A commercial vehicle that was registered in Colorado under the international registration plan, subsequently registered in another state, and then reregistered in Colorado is not subject to the specific ownership tax or registration fees during the period of time that the motor vehicle was registered in another state; except that the owner of a motor vehicle with an apportioned registration may be liable for the portion of the miles traveled in Colorado.

42-3-105. Application for registration - tax. (1) (a) Application for the registration of a vehicle required to be registered under this article shall be made by the owner or the owner's agent and, if applicable, simultaneously with the application for certificate of title, as required by this section. The application for registration, which shall be in writing and signed by the owner of the vehicle or the owner's duly authorized agent, shall include:

(I) The name of the applicant;

(II) The name and correct address of the owner determined pursuant to section 42-6-139, designating the county, school district, and city or town within the limits of which the owner resides;

(III) A description of the motor vehicle in a form required by the department;

(IV) The purpose for which the vehicle is used;

(V) Whether the vehicle is a commercial vehicle;

(VI) The notice described in subsection (2) of this section;

(VII) Whether the applicant requests that the department should, if it approves the application, mail to the owner the license plate required under this article; and

(VIII) Any other pertinent information as required by the department, including but not limited to a class B, class C, class D, or class F vehicle owner's or registrant's personal identification number as provided on a state-issued driver's license or assigned by the department.

(b) An application for new registration of a vehicle shall include the primary body color of the motor vehicle. A motor vehicle registration application submitted in person to an authorized agent or department office for a previously registered motor vehicle shall include the primary body color of the motor vehicle.

(c) (I) The department may require those vehicle-related entities specified by rule to verify information concerning any vehicle through the physical inspection of such vehicle. The information required to be verified by such a physical inspection shall include:

(A) The vehicle identification number or numbers;

(B) The make of vehicle;

(C) The vehicle model;

(D) The type of vehicle;

(E) The year of manufacture of such vehicle;

(F) The primary body color of such vehicle;

(G) The type of fuel used by such vehicle;

(H) The odometer reading of such vehicle; and

(I) Such other information as required by the department.

(II) For the purposes of this paragraph (c), "vehicle-related entity" means any county clerk and recorder or designated employee of such county clerk and recorder, any Colorado law enforcement officer, any licensed Colorado dealer, any licensed inspection and readjustment station, or any licensed diesel inspection station.

(d) (I) The department or its authorized agents shall not register a motor vehicle or low-power scooter unless the applicant has a complying motor vehicle insurance policy pursuant to part 6 of article 4 of title 10, C.R.S., or a certificate of self-insurance in full force and effect as required by sections 10-4-619 and 10-4-624, C.R.S. The requirements of this paragraph (d) apply only to motor vehicles classified as Class C personal property under section 42-3-106 (2) (c), to light trucks that do not exceed sixteen thousand pounds empty weight, to sports utility vehicles that are classified as Class B personal property under section 42-3-106 (2) (b), or to low-power scooters. The applicant shall provide the department or its authorized agents with the proof of insurance certificate or insurance identification card provided to the applicant by the applicant's insurer pursuant to section 10-4-604.5, C.R.S., or provide proof of insurance in such other media as is authorized by the department. Nothing in this paragraph (d) shall be interpreted to preclude the department from electronically transmitting insurance information to designated agents pursuant to section 42-7-604 for the purpose of ensuring compliance with mandatory insurance requirements.

(II) Any person who knowingly provides fraudulent information or documents under subparagraph (I) of this paragraph (d) to obtain registration of a motor vehicle or low-power scooter is guilty of a misdemeanor and is subject to the criminal and civil penalties provided under section 42-6-139 (3) and (4).

(e) The department shall establish a set of standard color descriptions for use in identifying the primary body color of a motor vehicle. An application that specifies the primary body color shall use the standard color descriptions of the department to identify the primary body color of the motor vehicle.

(f) The owner of a motor vehicle that is required to be registered under this article need not comply with subparagraph (I) of paragraph (d) of this subsection (1) if such owner signs and submits to the department in compliance with this paragraph (f) a written statement of nonuse. Such written statement of nonuse shall include:

(I) The name, date of birth, driver's license number, and address of the motor vehicle's owner;

(II) The make, year, and vehicle identification number of the motor vehicle;

(III) The time period during which such vehicle will not be operated and a statement that the owner is neither operating such vehicle nor permitting any other person to operate such vehicle during the time period stated; and

(IV) Proof that the owner currently has insurance coverage under subparagraph (I) of paragraph (d) of this subsection (1).

(2) Upon applying for registration, the owner of a motor vehicle or low-power scooter shall receive a written notice printed on the application for registration in type that is larger than the other information contained on the application for registration. Such notice shall state that motor vehicle insurance or operator's coverage is compulsory in Colorado, that noncompliance is a misdemeanor traffic offense, that the minimum penalty for such offense is a five-hundred-dollar fine, and that the maximum penalty for such offense is one year's imprisonment and a one-thousand-dollar fine, and that such owner shall be required as a condition of obtaining a registration card to sign an affirmation clause that appears on the registration. The clause shall state, "I swear or affirm in accordance with section 24-12-102, C.R.S., under penalty of perjury that I now have in effect a complying policy of motor vehicle insurance including an operator's policy pursuant to part 6 of article 4 of title 10, C.R.S., or a certificate of self-insurance to cover the vehicle or operator of the vehicle for which this registration is issued, and I understand that such insurance must be renewed so that coverage is continuous.

Signature _____, Date _____."

(3) The owner of such vehicle or the owner's agent shall, upon filing the application for registration, pay such fees as are prescribed by sections 42-3-304 to 42-3-306, together with the annual specific ownership tax on the motor vehicle, trailer, semitrailer, or trailer coach for which the license is to be issued.

(4) (a) A motor vehicle dealer or used motor vehicle dealer licensed under article 6 of this title may act as an authorized agent of the department for the purposes of compliance with this section and collection of fees required for the registration of low-power scooters required by this article. When the owner of the low-power scooter complies with this section, the dealer shall forward to the department an affidavit swearing that the owner has insurance, the statement required by subsection (2) of this section, and the fees required by part 3 of this article for the registration of a low-power scooter.

(b) Notwithstanding any provision of law to the contrary, in a civil action for damages or indemnification resulting from the operation of a motor vehicle, a motor vehicle dealer, used motor vehicle dealer, or employee thereof shall not be liable for an act or omission arising as a result of the dealer or employee performing the functions of an agent pursuant to this subsection (4).

(c) Upon finding a pattern of failure to comply with the requirements of paragraph (a) of this subsection (4), the department may withdraw a motor vehicle dealer's or used motor vehicle dealer's authorization to act as an agent of the department.

42-3-106. Tax imposed - classification - taxable value. (1) The owner of each item of classified personal property shall pay an annual specific ownership tax unless exempted by this article. Such specific ownership tax shall be annually computed in accordance with section 42-3-107 in lieu of all annual ad valorem taxes.

(2) For the purpose of imposing graduated annual specific ownership taxes, the personal property specified in section 6 of article X of the state constitution is classified as follows:

(a) Every motor vehicle, truck, laden or unladen truck tractor, trailer, and semitrailer used in the business of transporting persons or property over any public highway in this state as an interstate commercial carrier for which an application is made for apportioned registration, regardless of base jurisdiction, shall be Class A personal property.

(b) Every truck, laden or unladen truck tractor, trailer, and semitrailer used for the purpose of transporting property over any public highway in this state and not included in Class A shall be Class B personal property; except that multipurpose trailers shall be Class D personal property.

(c) Every motor vehicle not included in Class A or Class B shall be Class C personal property.

(d) Every utility trailer, camper trailer, multipurpose trailer, and trailer coach shall be Class D personal property.

(e) Every item of special mobile machinery, except power takeoff equipment, that is required to be registered under this article is Class F personal property. If a farm tractor, meeting the definition of special mobile machinery, is used for any purpose other than agricultural production for more than a seventy-two-hour period at the site where it is used for nonagricultural purposes, it is Class F personal property, but it is granted a prorated registration under section 42-3-107 to cover the use. The authorized agent shall notify the owner of the farm tractor of the prorated registration. Storing a farm tractor at a site does not give rise to a presumption that the tractor was used for the same purposes that other equipment is used for at the site.

(3) (a) An owner of a vehicle shall not permanently attach to the vehicle mounted equipment unless:

(I) The owner applies for registration of the mounted equipment to the authorized agent in the county where the equipment is required to be registered within twenty days after the equipment is mounted to the vehicle; or

(II) The mounted equipment is power take-off equipment.

(b) The application shall be on forms prescribed by the department and shall describe the equipment to be mounted, including serial number, make, model, year of manufacture, weight, and cost.

(4) The taxable value of every item of classified personal property shall be the value determined for the year of its manufacture or the year it is designated by the manufacturer as a current model, and such determined taxable value shall not change. Regardless of the date of acquisition by an owner, the year of manufacture or the year for which designated by the manufacturer as a current model shall be considered as the first year of service. The maximum rate of specific ownership taxation shall apply to the taxable value in the first year of service, and annual downward graduations from such maximum rate shall apply to such taxable value for the number of later years of service specified for each class of personal property.

(5) Manufactured homes shall not be classified for purposes of imposing specific ownership taxes but shall be subject to the imposition of ad valorem taxes in the manner provided in part 2 of article 5 of title 39, C.R.S.

(6) (a) If a vehicle and the equipment mounted on the vehicle are the same model year:

(I) The owner of the vehicle and the mounted equipment may register both as Class F personal property; or

(II) The owner of the vehicle may register the vehicle as Class A, Class B, Class C, or Class D personal property and the mounted equipment may be registered as Class F personal property.

(b) If a vehicle and the equipment mounted on the vehicle are different model years:

(I) The owner of the vehicle shall register the vehicle as Class A, Class B, Class C, or Class D personal property; and

(II) The owner of the vehicle shall register the mounted equipment as Class F personal property.

42-3-107. Taxable value of classes of property - rate of tax - when and where payable - department duties - apportionment of tax collections - definitions. (1) (a) (I) The taxable value of every item of Class A or Class B personal property greater than sixteen thousand pounds declared empty vehicle weight shall be the actual purchase price of such property. Such price shall not include any applicable federal excise tax, including the excise tax on the first retail sale of a heavy truck, trailer, or tractor for which the seller is liable, transportation or shipping costs, or preparation and delivery costs. The taxable value of every item of Class A or Class B personal property less than or equal to sixteen thousand pounds declared empty vehicle weight shall be seventy-five percent of the manufacturer's suggested retail price.

(II) For the purposes of this section, the actual purchase price used to set taxable value shall be the price of the vehicle when the vehicle is initially purchased at the retail level by a person who intends to put the vehicle into initial use. The taxable value shall not change for the life of the vehicle.

(III) For the purposes of this section, "actual purchase price" means the gross selling price, including all property traded to the seller in exchange for credit toward the purchase of a vehicle.

(b) Every licensed motor vehicle dealer in Colorado shall furnish on the application for title the manufacturer's suggested retail price and the actual purchase price on each new motor vehicle sold and delivered in Colorado.

(c) If a motor vehicle purchased outside Colorado is registered for the first time in Colorado and neither the manufacturer's suggested retail price nor the actual purchase price is available, the agent of the department shall establish the taxable value of such vehicle through the use of a compilation of values furnished by the department.

(2) The annual specific ownership tax payable on every item of Class A personal property shall be computed in accordance with the following schedule:

Year of service	Rate of tax
First year	2.10% of taxable value
Second year	1.50% of taxable value
Third year	1.20% of taxable value
Fourth year	.90% of taxable value
Fifth, sixth, seventh, eighth, and ninth years	.45% of taxable value or $10, whichever is greater
Tenth and each later year	$ 3

(3) The owner of any Class A personal property shall file a list with the department describing each item owned, reciting the year of manufacture or model designation, and stating the original sale price of any mounted equipment mounted on or attached to such item after its manufacture or first retail sale. As soon thereafter as practicable, the department shall compute the annual specific ownership tax payable on each item shown on such list and shall send to the owner a statement showing the aggregate amount of specific ownership tax payable by such owner.

(4) In computing the amount of annual specific ownership tax payable on an item of Class A or Class B personal property, the department may take into account the length of time such item may be operated in intrastate or interstate commerce within Colorado, giving due consideration to any reciprocal agreements concerning general property taxation of such item as may exist between Colorado and other states, and also to the number of miles traveled by such item in each state.

(5) The annual specific ownership tax on Class A personal property shall become due and payable to the department on the last day of the month at the end of each twelve-month registration period and shall be renewed, upon application by the owner and payment of required fees, no later than one month after the date of expiration.

(6) The aggregate amount of specific ownership taxes to be collected by the department on Class A personal property during a registration period shall be apportioned to each county of the state in the proportion that the mileage of the state highway system located within the boundaries of each county bears to the total mileage of the state highway system.

(7) The department shall transmit all specific ownership taxes collected on items of Class A and Class F personal property to the state treasurer and shall advise the treasurer on the last day of each month of the amounts apportioned to each county from the preceding month's collections. The state treasurer shall pay such amounts to the respective treasurers of each county.

(8) The annual specific ownership tax payable on every item of Class B personal property shall be computed in accordance with the following schedule:

Year of service	Rate of tax
First year	2.10% of taxable value
Second year	1.50% of taxable value
Third year	1.20% of taxable value
Fourth year	.90% of taxable value
Fifth, sixth, seventh, eighth, and ninth years	.45% of taxable value or $10, whichever is greater
Tenth and each later year	$ 3

(9) (a) The taxable value of every item of Class C or Class D personal property shall be eighty-five percent of the manufacturer's suggested retail price, not including applicable federal excise tax, transportation or shipping costs, or preparation and delivery costs.

(b) Every licensed motor vehicle dealer in Colorado shall furnish on the application for title the manufacturer's suggested retail price of each new motor vehicle sold and delivered in Colorado.

(c) If a motor vehicle purchased outside of Colorado is registered for the first time in Colorado and the manufacturer's suggested retail price is not available, the agent of the department shall establish the taxable value of such vehicle through the use of a compilation of values furnished by the department.

(d) The computation of taxable values as set forth in this subsection (9) shall apply to each motor vehicle sold on or after September 1, 1981, and shall not apply to a motor vehicle sold or registered prior to that date.

(10) The annual specific ownership tax payable on every item of Class C personal property shall be computed in accordance with the following schedule:

Year of service	Rate of tax
First year	2.10% of taxable value
Second year	1.50% of taxable value
Third year	1.20% of taxable value
Fourth year	.90% of taxable value
Fifth, sixth, seventh, eighth, and ninth years	.45% of taxable value
Tenth and each later year	$ 3

(11) (a) In lieu of payment of the annual specific ownership tax in the manner specified in subsections (2), (8), and (10) of this section, a person who owns vehicles that are based in Colorado for rental purposes and whose primary business is the rental of such vehicles for periods of less than forty-five days, including renewals, to another person may elect to pay specific ownership tax as authorized in this subsection (11).

(b) To obtain authorization to pay specific ownership tax pursuant to this subsection (11), an owner shall apply to the authorized agent in the county in which the principal place of business of the owner of such rental vehicles in Colorado is located. Such authorization shall apply to all rental vehicles of the owner that satisfy the requirements set forth in this section.

(c) Upon receiving authorization as provided in paragraph (b) of this subsection (11), the owner shall collect from the user of a rental vehicle the specific ownership tax in an amount equivalent to two percent of the amount of the rental payment, or portion thereof, that is subject to the imposition of sales tax pursuant to part 1 of article 26 of title 39, C.R.S. Such specific ownership tax shall be collected on vehicles that are based in Colorado for rental purposes and rented from a place of business in Colorado. No later than the twentieth day of each month, the owner shall submit a report, using forms furnished by the department, to the authorized agent in the county where the vehicles are rented and the remittance for all specific ownership taxes collected for the preceding month. A copy of the report shall be submitted simultaneously by the owner to the department. The department may also require, by rule, the owner to submit a copy of the owner's monthly sales tax collection form to the authorized agent when the owner's monthly report is submitted.

(d) Failure to submit the report or to remit the specific ownership tax collected for the preceding month by the last day of each month shall be grounds for the termination of the right of an owner to pay specific ownership tax under this subsection (11). If an owner fails to remit specific ownership tax received pursuant to this subsection (11), the authorized agent may collect such delinquent taxes in the manner authorized in subsection (21) of this section.

(e) A person who owns vehicles and whose primary business is the rental of such vehicles as specified in paragraph (a) of this subsection (11) shall be exempt from payment of the specific ownership tax at the time of registration if such tax is collected and remitted pursuant to this subsection (11). Such owner shall pay a fee of one dollar per rental vehicle registered at the time of registration. Such fee shall be in addition to other registration fees and shall be distributed pursuant to subsection (22) of this section.

(f) Every person who owns vehicles and whose primary business is the rental of such vehicles as specified in paragraph (a) of this subsection (11) shall register and pay all applicable taxes and fees for all vehicles rented from a place of business located in Colorado. If the owner of such vehicles fails to register or to pay such taxes and fees, the owner shall, upon conviction, be punished by a fine equal to two percent of the annual gross dollar volume of the primary business of such person that is attributable to the rental of vehicles from a place of business in Colorado.

(12) (a) In lieu of payment of the annual specific ownership tax in the manner specified in subsections (2), (8), and (10) of this section, any person who owns vehicles that are based in a state other than Colorado for rental purposes and whose primary business is the rental of such vehicles for periods of less than forty-five days, including renewals, to another person shall pay specific ownership tax as prescribed in this subsection (12).

(b) The owner shall collect from the user of a rental vehicle the specific ownership tax in an amount equivalent to two percent of the amount of the rental payment, or portion thereof, that is subject to the imposition of sales tax pursuant to part 1 of article 26 of title 39, C.R.S. Such specific ownership tax shall be collected on all vehicles based in a state other than Colorado for rental purposes that are rented from a place of business in Colorado. By the twentieth day of each month, the owner shall submit a report, using forms furnished by the department, to the authorized agent in the county where the vehicles are rented, together with the remittance for all specific ownership taxes collected for the preceding month. A copy of the report shall be submitted simultaneously by the owner to the department. The department may also require, by rule, the owner to submit a copy of the owner's monthly sales tax collection form to the authorized agent when the owner's monthly report is submitted.

(c) If any owner fails to remit specific ownership tax received pursuant to this subsection (12), the authorized agent may proceed to collect such delinquent taxes in the manner authorized in subsection (21) of this section.

(d) Every person who owns vehicles and whose primary business is the rental of such vehicles as specified in paragraph (a) of this subsection (12) shall pay all applicable taxes for all vehicles based in a state other than Colorado and rented from a place of business located in Colorado. If the owner of such vehicles fails to pay such taxes, the owner shall, upon conviction, be punished by a fine in an amount equal to two percent of the annual gross dollar volume of the primary business of such person that is attributable to the rental of vehicles from a place of business in Colorado.

(13) The annual specific ownership tax payable on every item of Class D personal property shall be computed in accordance with the following schedule:

Year of service	Rate of tax
First year	2.10% of taxable value
Second year	1.50% of taxable value
Third year	1.20% of taxable value
Fourth year	.90% of taxable value
Fifth, sixth, seventh, eighth, and ninth years	.45% of taxable value
Tenth and each later year	.45% of taxable value or $ 3, whichever is greater

(14) The department shall designate suitable compilations of the manufacturer's suggested retail price or actual purchase price of all items of Class A, Class B, Class C, and Class D personal property and shall provide each authorized agent with copies. Unless the actual purchase price is used as the taxable value, such compilation shall be uniformly used to compute the annual specific ownership tax payable on any item of such classified personal property purchased outside Colorado and registered for the first time in Colorado. Such actual purchase price shall not be used unless the department receives or has received a manufacturer's statement or

certificate of origin for such vehicle. The department shall provide continuing supplements of such compilation to each authorized agent in order that the agent may have available current information relative to the manufacturer's suggested retail price of newly manufactured items.

(15) (a) The property tax administrator shall compile and have printed a comprehensive schedule of all vehicles defined and designated as Class F personal property, wherein all such vehicles shall be listed according to make, model, year of manufacture, capacity, weight, and any other terms that serve to describe such vehicles.

(b) Except as provided in paragraph (c) of this subsection (15) for property acquired prior to January 1, 1997, the taxable value of Class F personal property shall be determined by the property tax administrator and shall be either:

(I) The factory list price and, in case any equipment has been mounted on or attached to such vehicle subsequent to its manufacture, the factory list price plus seventy-five percent of the original price of such mounted equipment, exclusive of any state and local sales taxes; or

(II) When the factory list price of such vehicle is not available, then seventy-five percent of its original retail delivered price, exclusive of any state and local taxes, and, in case any equipment has been mounted on or attached to such vehicle subsequent to its first retail sale, then seventy-five percent of such original retail delivered price plus seventy-five percent of the original retail delivered price of such mounted equipment, exclusive of any state and local sales taxes; or

(III) When neither the factory list price of such vehicle nor the original retail delivered price of the vehicle or any equipment subsequently mounted thereon is ascertainable, then such value as the property tax administrator shall establish based on the best information available to the property tax administrator.

(c) The taxable value of Class F personal property acquired on or after January 1, 1997, shall be determined by the property tax administrator and shall be either:

(I) Eighty-five percent of the manufacturer's suggested retail price and, in case any equipment has been mounted on or attached to such vehicle subsequent to its manufacture, eighty-five percent of the manufacturer's suggested retail price plus eighty-five percent of the manufacturer's suggested retail price of such mounted equipment, exclusive of any state and local sales taxes; or

(II) When the manufacturer's suggested retail price of such vehicle is not available, then one hundred percent of its original retail delivered price to the customer, exclusive of any state and local taxes, and, in case any equipment has been mounted on or attached to such vehicle subsequent to its first retail sale, then one hundred percent of such original retail delivered price to the customer plus one hundred percent of the original retail delivered price to the customer of such mounted equipment, exclusive of any state and local taxes; or

(III) When neither the manufacturer's suggested retail price of such vehicle nor the original retail delivered price of either the vehicle or any equipment subsequently mounted thereon is ascertainable, then such value as the property tax administrator shall establish based on eighty-five percent of the value set forth in a nationally recognized standard or reference for such figures or, if such a standard or reference for the figures is not available, then on the best information available to the property tax administrator.

(d) By whichever of the above three methods determined, the taxable value of each item of Class F personal property shall be listed opposite its description in the schedule required by this subsection (15) to be compiled by the property tax administrator.

(e) The annual specific ownership tax payable on each item of Class F personal property shall be computed in accordance with the following schedule:

Year of service	Rate of tax
First year	2.10% of taxable value
Second year	1.50% of taxable value
Third year	1.25% of taxable value
Fourth year	1.00% of taxable value
Fifth year	.75% of taxable value
Sixth and each later year	.50% of taxable value, but not less than $5

(f) The county clerk and recorder shall include the value of all equipment that has been mounted on or attached to Class F personal property in the calculation of the annual specific ownership tax. The registrations for such personal property and equipment shall be made available to the county assessor.

(16) (a) In lieu of payment of the annual specific ownership tax in the manner provided in subsection (15) of this section, the owner of special mobile machinery who is an equipment dealer regularly engaged in the sale or rental of special mobile machinery and who rents or leases such equipment to another person in which the owner has not held an interest for at least thirty days may elect to pay specific ownership tax as prescribed in this subsection (16).

(b) Authorization for payment of specific ownership tax under this subsection (16) shall be obtained from the authorized agent in the county in which the owner's principal place of business is located. The owner shall also apply for an identifying decal for each item of equipment to be rented or leased that shall be affixed to the item when it is rented or leased. The owner shall keep records of each identifying decal issued and a description of the item of equipment to which it is affixed. The fee for each identifying decal shall be five dollars, paid upon application to the authorized agent. An identifying decal shall expire when the registration of the special mobile machinery to which it is affixed expires pursuant to section 42-3-114. An identifying decal shall not be issued to special mobile machinery unless the machinery is registered, but a decal may be issued concurrently with the registration and shall expire pursuant to section 42-3-114. The owner shall be required to remove an identifying decal upon the sale or change of ownership of such item of equipment. The fee of five dollars for each identifying decal as required by this section shall be distributed as follows:

(I) Two dollars shall be retained by the authorized agent issuing such decal; and

(II) Three dollars shall be available upon appropriation by the general assembly to fund the administration and enforcement of this section.

(c) Upon receiving authorization under paragraph (b) of this subsection (16), the owner shall collect from the user the specific ownership tax in the amount equivalent to two percent of the amount of the rental or lease payment. No later than the twentieth day of each month, the owner shall submit a report, using forms furnished by the department, to the authorized agent in each county where the equipment is used, together with the remittance of the taxes collected for the use in the county for the preceding month. A copy of each report shall be submitted simultaneously by the owner to the department.

(d) Such reports shall be made monthly to the department and to the authorized agent in the county where the equipment is located with a user, even if no specific ownership taxes were collected by the owner in the previous month. Failure to make such reports in a period of sixty days shall be grounds for the termination of such owner's right to pay the specific ownership taxes on the owner's Class F personal property in the manner provided under this subsection (16). If the owner fails to remit specific ownership taxes received from a renter or lessee during such sixty-day period, the authorized agent may proceed to collect such delinquent taxes in the manner authorized in subsection (21) of this section.

(e) The owner of an item of special mobile machinery that is required to be registered for highway use under section 42-3-304 (14) shall be exempt from payment of the specific ownership tax at the time of registration if such tax is collected and remitted under this subsection (16).

(17) (a) For purposes of this subsection (17), unless the context otherwise requires:

(I) "Owner" means an owner, as defined in section 42-1-102 (66), that owns an item of special mobile machinery. The term includes any person authorized to act on the owner's behalf.

(II) "Prorated specific ownership tax" means the prorated special mobile machinery specific ownership tax assessed pursuant to this subsection (17).

(III) "Special mobile machinery" means every item of Class F personal property described in section 42-3-106 (2) (e) that is required to be registered under section 42-3-103.

(b) In lieu of payment of the annual specific ownership tax in the manner provided in subsection (15) of this section, an owner may apply for and pay prorated specific ownership tax in accordance with this subsection (17).

(c) To be eligible for prorated specific ownership tax, an owner shall have entered into a written contract to perform a service requiring use of the special mobile machinery for which specific ownership tax under this section is required.

(d) (I) An owner who desires prorated specific ownership tax shall submit an application to the department. The application shall include the terms of the owner's service, which shall be evidenced by a copy of the written contract specified in paragraph (c) of this subsection (17) and signed by the owner. The validity of the contract shall be evidenced either by sufficient documentation to substantiate its validity or by the fact that such owner is an established business in Colorado, as shown by registration with the Colorado secretary of state or department of revenue as required by law.

(II) An owner of special mobile machinery that is not registered in Colorado shall submit the application upon the arrival in Colorado of the special mobile machinery for which specific ownership tax under this section is required.

(III) An owner of special mobile machinery that is registered in Colorado shall submit the application when the owner renews the registration of the special mobile machinery for which specific ownership tax under this section is required.

(IV) When satisfied as to the genuineness and regularity of the application submitted, the department shall assess, and the owner shall pay, the prorated specific ownership tax in an amount equal to the annual specific ownership tax that would otherwise be imposed pursuant to subsection (15) of this section, prorated by the number of months during which the owner is expected to use the special mobile machinery in Colorado.

(V) (A) Prorated specific ownership taxes shall be assessed for a period of not less than two months nor more than eleven months in a twelve-month period.

(B) After a prorated specific ownership tax has been assessed and paid, an owner may have the prorated specific ownership tax assessment period adjusted for between two and eleven months upon the owner's request to the department that the owner requires additional time to complete the contract referred to in paragraph (c) of this subsection (17) and upon payment of any additional prorated specific ownership tax pursuant to this subsection (17).

(e) (I) A person who, in an application made under this subsection (17), uses a false or fictitious name or address, knowingly makes a false statement, knowingly conceals a material fact, or otherwise perpetrates a fraud commits a class 2 misdemeanor traffic offense. Such person continues to be liable for any unpaid specific ownership taxes.

(II) A person shall not operate special mobile machinery in Colorado unless the owner has paid the specific ownership tax assessed pursuant to this article, and a person shall not operate special mobile machinery in Colorado after the expiration of the period for which the specific ownership tax was paid. A person who violates this subparagraph (II) is subject to, in addition to any other penalty, an administrative penalty of the lesser of five hundred dollars or double the amount of the specific ownership tax. The penalty may be levied by an authorized agent or a peace officer under the authority granted by section 42-8-104 (2). The violation is to be determined by, paid to, and retained by the municipality or county where the motor vehicle is or should have been registered, subject to judicial review pursuant to rule 106 (a) (4) of the Colorado rules of civil procedure.

(18) (a) The annual specific ownership tax provided in subsection (15) of this section for Class F personal property registered in Colorado shall be determined and collected by the authorized agent in the county in which the owner of such Class F personal property resides.

(b) (I) The owner of any Class F personal property shall, within sixty days after the purchase of new or used Class F personal property, apply for registration with the authorized agent.

(II) No person shall operate Class F personal property unless the property is registered with the authorized agent or exempt from registration pursuant to section 42-3-104 (3).

(c) The property tax administrator shall furnish each authorized agent with a printed copy of the schedule of taxable values of Class F personal property compiled as provided in subsection (15) of this section, and such schedule shall be uniformly used by every authorized agent in computing the amount of annual specific ownership tax payable on any Class F personal property. The property tax administrator shall also furnish continuing supplements of such schedule to each authorized agent in order that the agent may have available current information relative to the taxable value of newly manufactured Class F personal property.

(19) The annual specific ownership tax on each item of Class B, Class C, Class D, and Class F personal property shall become due and payable to the authorized agent in the county where such item is to be registered, shall be paid at the time of registration of such item, and if not paid within one month after the date a registration expires, shall become delinquent.

(20) Except as provided in subsection (27) of this section, it is the duty of each authorized agent to collect the registration fee on every item of classified personal property located in the agent's county when registered and to collect the specific ownership taxes payable on each such item registered, except those items classified as Class A upon which the specific ownership tax is collected by the department and except those items classified as Class F when such tax is collected under subsection (16) of this section, at the time of registration. The failure of any authorized agent to collect the registration fee and specific ownership tax on any item of classified personal property shall not release the owner thereof from liability for the registration of such vehicle.

(21) Each authorized agent shall advise the owner of any item of Class F personal property upon which the annual specific ownership tax is due, by notice mailed to such owner indicating the amount of tax due. If payment is not made, the authorized agent shall report such fact to the county treasurer, who shall thereupon proceed to collect the amount of delinquent tax by distraint, seizure, and sale of the item upon which the tax is payable, in the same manner as is provided in section 39-10-113, C.R.S., for the collection of ad valorem taxes on personal property.

(22) Each authorized agent shall retain, out of the amount of annual specific ownership tax collected on each item of classified personal property, the sum of fifty cents, which sum shall constitute remuneration for the collection of such tax. The sums so retained shall be transmitted to the county treasurer and credited in the manner provided by law. In addition, each authorized agent shall retain, out of the amount of annual specific ownership tax collected on each item of classified personal property, the sum of fifty cents, which sum shall be transmitted to the state treasurer, who shall credit the same to the special purpose account established under section 42-1-211.

(23) Each authorized agent shall transmit to the county treasurer, at least once each week, all specific ownership taxes collected on items of classified personal property, reporting the aggregate amount collected for each class.

(24) (a) Each January, the treasurer of each county shall calculate the percentages that the dollar amount of ad valorem taxes levied in the treasurer's county during the preceding calendar year for county purposes and for the purposes of each political and governmental subdivision located within the boundaries of the treasurer's county were of the aggregate dollar amount of ad valorem taxes levied in such county during the preceding calendar year for said purposes. The percentages so calculated shall be used for the apportionment between the county itself and each political and governmental subdivision located within its boundaries of the aggregate amount of specific ownership tax revenue to be paid over to the treasurer during the current calendar year.

(b) On the tenth day of each month, the aggregate amount of specific ownership taxes on Class A, B, C, D, and F personal property received or collected by the county treasurer during the preceding calendar month shall be apportioned between the county and each political and governmental subdivision located within the boundaries of the county according to the percentages calculated in the manner prescribed in paragraph (a) of this subsection (24), and the respective amounts so determined shall be credited or paid over to the county and each such subdivision.

(c) The fee for the collection of specific ownership taxes having been charged when collected by the authorized agent, the treasurer shall make no further charge against the amount of specific ownership taxes credited or paid over to any political or governmental subdivision located in the treasurer's county.

(d) An insolvent taxing district, as defined in section 32-1-1402 (2), C.R.S., that has increased its mill levy for the purpose of paying for maturing bonds of the district, interest on bonds of the district, or prior deficiencies of the district shall not be entitled to receive any larger proportion of the specific ownership taxes collected in the county in which such district is located as the result of such increase in the district's mill levy. For the purpose of apportioning specific ownership tax revenues in a county, dollar amounts from the levying of ad valorem taxes by an insolvent taxing district located in the county for the purpose of paying for maturing bonds of the district, interest on bonds of the district, or prior deficiencies of the district shall be excluded from the calculation of the percentages required by paragraph (a) of this subsection (24).

(25) A credit shall be allowed for taxes paid on any item of Class A, Class B, Class C, Class D, or Class F personal property if the owner disposes of the vehicle during the registration period or if the owner converts the vehicle from any class of personal property to Class F property. The credit may apply to payments of taxes on a subsequent application by the owner for registration of an item of Class A, Class B, Class C, Class D, or Class F personal property made during the registration period or may be assigned by the owner to the transferee of the property for which taxes were paid; except that, when the transferee is a dealer in new or used vehicles, the transferee shall account to the owner for any assignment of the credit. The credit shall be prorated based on the number of months remaining in the registration period after the transfer and disposal of the vehicle. The calculation for the credit shall be determined by using the period beginning with the first day of the month following the date of transfer through the last day of the month for the period for which the vehicle was registered. Specific ownership tax credit will be allowed only if the total ownership tax credit due exceeds ten dollars.

(26) Notwithstanding the amount specified for the fees in paragraph (e) of subsection (11) and paragraph (b) of subsection (16) of this section, the executive director of the department by rule or as otherwise provided by law may reduce the amount of one or more of the fees if necessary pursuant to section 24-75-402 (3), C.R.S., to reduce the uncommitted reserves of the fund to which all or any portion of one or more of the fees is credited. After the uncommitted reserves of the fund are sufficiently reduced, the executive director of the department by rule or as otherwise provided by law may increase the amount of one or more of the fees as provided in section 24-75-402 (4), C.R.S.

(27) (a) Notwithstanding any provision in this article to the contrary, a fleet owner may process the registration renewal for any fleet vehicle, with the exception of Class A personal property, in the county in which the fleet owner's principal office or principal fleet management facility is located instead of in the county in which the fleet vehicle is located at the time of registration. A fleet vehicle for which the registration renewal is processed pursuant to this subsection (27) shall continue to be registered in the county in which it is located at the time of registration. This subsection (27) shall not apply to a fleet vehicle that was not previously registered in Colorado at the time of registration.

(b) If a fleet owner chooses to process the registration renewal of a fleet vehicle in the county in which the owner's principal office or principal fleet management facility is located instead of in the county in which the vehicle is located, the authorized agent in the county where the owner's principal office or principal fleet management facility is located shall collect the registration fee and specific ownership tax payable on each fleet vehicle for which the registration renewal is processed by the fleet owner in such county.

(c) The authorized agent in a county in which a fleet vehicle registration renewal is processed pursuant to this section shall retain and not disburse the sum authorized pursuant to section 42-1-210 (1) (a) to defray the costs associated with vehicle registration. The authorized agent in the county in which a fleet vehicle registration renewal is processed pursuant to this section shall transmit to the department all fees and moneys collected by the agent pursuant to section 42-1-214.

(d) The authorized agent in the county in which a fleet vehicle registration renewal is processed pursuant to this section shall transmit the registration fees collected pursuant to section 42-3-310 to the department. The department shall then transmit such fees to the authorized agent in the county in which the fleet vehicle is located at the time of registration, and the authorized agent shall transmit such fees to the county treasurer pursuant to section 42-3-310.

(e) The annual specific ownership tax on each fleet vehicle for which the registration renewal is processed in the county in which the fleet owner's principal office or principal fleet management facility is located shall become due and payable to the authorized agent in such county pursuant to this article. The authorized agent in such county shall apportion the specific ownership taxes collected for all fleet vehicles for which the registration renewal is processed in such county pursuant to this subsection (27) to the counties in which the fleet vehicles are located at the time of registration in proportion to the number of fleet vehicles located in each county.

(f) (I) This subsection (27) shall apply to registration renewal for fleet vehicles upon implementation of the Colorado state titling and registration system, established in section 42-1-211, by the department.

(II) Repealed.

(g) Nothing in this section shall be construed to affect the allocation of highway users tax fund moneys to counties or municipalities pursuant to sections 43-4-207 and 43-4-208, C.R.S.

42-3-108. Determination of year model - tax lists. All vehicles of the current year model, as designated by the manufacturer, shall, for the payment of the specific ownership tax, be considered in the first year of service regardless of the date of purchase, and those charged with the collection of annual specific ownership taxes on vehicles subject to specific ownership taxation shall use the year that the model was manufactured or constructed as the basis of computation of the annual specific ownership tax.

42-3-109. Tax for registration period. Except as provided in sections 42-3-110, 42-3-304 (10), and 42-4-305 (5), the owner shall pay upon a purchased vehicle subject to registration under this article the prescribed fee for a twelve-month registration. In no event shall the specific ownership tax collected on any classified personal property be less than one dollar and fifty cents.

42-3-110. Payment of motor vehicle registration fees and specific ownership taxes in installments. (1) An owner of a motor vehicle, other than a trailer or semitrailer, classified as Class A or Class B personal property under section 42-3-106 (2) (b) may apply to the department to pay the twelve-month registration fee and specific ownership tax for the owner's fleet of such vehicles in installments. The department shall approve an application from a fleet owner to make payments for a fleet in installments if all the following requirements are met:

(a) The total of the twelve-month registration fee and the twelve-month specific ownership tax for the fleet equals one thousand dollars or more;

(b) The applicant pays one-third of the total amount due for registration and specific ownership tax with the application;

(c) The fleet owner does not owe past due motor vehicle registration fees or specific ownership taxes or outstanding penalties imposed for nonpayment of such fees or taxes;

(d) The owner is not denied the privilege of paying in installments pursuant to paragraph (b) of subsection (3) of this section; and

(e) The fleet owner has a performance bond issued by a surety company authorized to do business in Colorado, a bank letter of credit, or a certificate of deposit in an amount equal to no less than the remaining amount of the annual registration fee and specific ownership tax that will be paid in installments. The performance bond, letter of credit, or certificate of deposit shall be payable to the department if the owner fails to pay the required installments.

(2) If an application to pay in installments is approved pursuant to subsection (1) of this section, the applicant shall pay the remainder of the registration fee and specific ownership tax in two equal installments as follows:

(a) The first installment on or before the first day of the fifth month of the registration period; and

(b) The second installment on or before the first day of the ninth month of the registration period.

(3) (a) If a fleet owner fails to pay an installment under this section on or before the date the installment was due, the remaining amount of the unpaid registration fee and specific ownership tax for the fleet is due in full immediately. Such owner shall not operate the vehicles in such fleet on the highways of the state until the owner has paid such amount.

(b) If a fleet owner fails to pay an installment for a motor vehicle under this section within thirty days after the installment was due, the department may deny such owner the privilege of paying registration fees and specific ownership taxes in installments under this section.

(4) The provisions of this section do not modify the amount of the registration fee or specific ownership tax owed by an owner for a motor vehicle during a registration period.

(5) The department may promulgate rules to implement the installment payment process established by this section.

42-3-111. Tax year - disposition. (1) The annual specific ownership tax shall attach and apply to motor vehicles, trailers, semitrailers, or trailer coaches operated upon the highways of this state for the registration period within which it is levied and collected.

(2) Payment of an annual specific ownership tax on a trailer coach to the authorized agent of a county of this state in which the situs of the trailer coach is established at the time of registration for all of a registration period shall constitute the entire tax payable on such vehicle.

42-3-112. Failure to pay tax - penalty - rules. (1) If a vehicle subject to taxation under this article is not registered when required by law, the vehicle owner shall pay a late fee of twenty-five dollars for each month or portion of a month following the expiration of the registration period, or, if applicable, the expiration of the grace period described in section 42-3-114 for which the vehicle is unregistered; except that the amount of the late fee shall not exceed one hundred dollars. The late fee shall be due when the vehicle is registered.

(1.5) (a) Notwithstanding the provisions of subsection (1) of this section, the executive director of the department shall promulgate rules in accordance with article 4 of title 24, C.R.S., that establish circumstances in addition to the circumstances described in subsection (3) of this section in which a vehicle owner shall be exempted from paying the late fee described in said subsection (1). The rules shall apply uniformly throughout the state and shall include, but shall not be limited to, exemptions for:

(I) Acts of God and weather-related delays;
(II) Office closures and furloughs;
(III) Temporary registration number plates, tags, or certificates that have expired;
(IV) Medical hardships; and
(V) Information technology failures.

(b) The executive director of the department shall also promulgate rules in accordance with article 4 of title 24, C.R.S., that allow the department or an authorized agent to reduce or waive the late fee that would otherwise be due upon the registration of a trailer that is a commercial or farm vehicle, as part of the normal operation, if the owner can establish, in accordance with criteria specified in the rules, that the trailer was idled so that it was not operated on any public highway in this state for at least a full registration period. Nothing in this paragraph (b) shall be construed to exempt the owner of an idled trailer from paying any fees imposed pursuant to this article other than the late fee before again operating the trailer on a public highway in this state or from paying any taxes imposed pursuant to this article. The owner shall provide to the department or authorized agent a sworn affidavit that states that the trailer has not been operated on the public highways during the period for which it was not registered as required and describes the nature of the business conditions that resulted in the removal of the trailer from service.

(c) The executive director of the department shall consult with the county clerk and recorders in promulgating the rules required by paragraph (a) of this subsection (1.5).

(1.7) Notwithstanding the provisions of subsection (1) of this section, on and after July 1, 2010, the amount of the late fee payable by the owner of a vehicle without motive power that weighs sixteen thousand pounds or less or a camper trailer or a multipurpose trailer regardless of its weight, that is subject to taxation under this article, and that is not registered when required by law shall be ten dollars. For purposes of this subsection (1.7), the weight of a trailer of any kind is the empty weight.

(2) Ten dollars of the late registration fee shall be retained by the department or the authorized agent who registers the motor vehicle. Each authorized agent shall remit to the department no less frequently than once a month, but otherwise at the time and in the manner required by the executive director of the department, the remainder of the late registration fees collected by the authorized agent. The executive director shall forward all late registration fees remitted by authorized agents plus the remainder of the late registration fees collected directly by the department to the state treasurer, who shall credit the fees to the highway users tax fund in accordance with section 43-4-804 (1) (e), C.R.S.

(3) The late fee described in subsection (1) of this section shall not be imposed on a vehicle subject to taxation under this article if:

(a) The person who owns the vehicle uses the vehicle in operating a commercial business and, as part of the normal operation of the business, idles the vehicle so that it is not operated on any public highway in this state for at least one full registration period. Nothing in this paragraph (a) shall be construed to exempt the owner of an idled vehicle from paying any fees imposed pursuant to this article other than the late fee before again operating the vehicle on a public highway in this state or from paying any taxes imposed pursuant to this article.

(b) The person who owns the vehicle is in the active military service of the United States and is serving outside the state when a registration period and grace period for renewal of registration for the vehicle end and the vehicle is not operated on any public highway of the state between the time the registration period and grace period end and the time the vehicle is reregistered. Nothing in this paragraph (b) shall be construed to exempt the owner of such a vehicle from paying any fees imposed pursuant to this article other than the late fee before again operating the vehicle on a public highway in this state or from paying any taxes imposed pursuant to this article.

(c) The vehicle registration expired during the period the vehicle was reported stolen.

42-3-113. Records of application and registration. (1) The department shall file each application received and, when satisfied that the applicant is entitled to register the vehicle, shall register the vehicle and the owner of such vehicle as follows:

(a) The owner and vehicle shall be assigned a distinct registration number, referred to in this article as the "registration number". Each registration number assigned to a vehicle and its owner shall be designated "urban" if the owner resides within the limits of a city or incorporated town. Each registration number assigned to a vehicle and its owner shall be designated "rural" if the owner resides outside the limits of a city or incorporated town. The county clerk and recorder of each county shall certify to the department as soon as possible after the end of the calendar year, but not later than May 1 of the following year, the total number of vehicles classified as "urban" and the total number of vehicles classified as "rural".

(b) The registration shall be filed alphabetically under the name of the owner.

(c) The registration shall be filed numerically and alphabetically under the identification number and name of the vehicle.

(2) The department, upon registering a vehicle, shall issue to the owner a registration card, which shall contain upon its face the following:

(a) The date issued;
(b) The registration number assigned to the owner and vehicle;
(c) The name and address of the owner;
(d) A notice, in type that is larger than the other information contained on the registration card:
(I) That motor vehicle insurance coverage is compulsory in Colorado;
(II) That noncompliance is a misdemeanor traffic offense;
(III) That the minimum penalty for such offense is a one-hundred-dollar fine;
(IV) That the maximum penalty for such offense is one year's imprisonment and a one-thousand-dollar fine;
(V) That such owner shall be required upon receipt of the registration card to sign the affirmation clause on such card that states:

I swear or affirm under penalty of perjury that I now have in effect a complying policy of motor vehicle insurance pursuant to part 6 of article 4 of title 10, C.R.S., or a certificate of self-insurance to cover the vehicle for which this registration is issued, and I understand that such insurance must be renewed so that coverage is continuous.

Signature _____, Date _____.

(e) A notice that Colorado law provides for a thirty-day grace period after a registration is due for renewal;
(f) A description of the registered vehicle, including the identification number;
(g) If it was a new vehicle sold in this state after January 1, 1932, the date of sale by the manufacturer or dealer to the person first operating such vehicle; and
(h) Such other statements of fact as may be determined by the department.
(3) A notice for renewal of registration shall include a notice, in type that is larger than the other information contained in the notice, that specifies that motor vehicle insurance coverage is compulsory in Colorado, that noncompliance is a misdemeanor traffic offense, that the minimum penalty for such offense is a one-hundred-dollar fine, and that the maximum penalty for such offense is one year's imprisonment and a one-thousand-dollar fine.
(4) The department shall notify all registered owners of the provisions and requirements of subsection (2) and (3) of this section.
(5) The owner, upon receiving the registration card, shall sign the usual signature or name of such owner with pen and ink in the space provided upon the face of such card.
(6) The registration card issued for a vehicle required to be registered under this article shall, at all times while the vehicle is being operated upon a highway, be in the possession of the driver or carried in the vehicle and subject to inspection by any peace officer.

(7) Within thirty days after moving from an address or changing the name of the owner listed upon a vehicle registration, a person shall notify the county of residence in which the vehicle is to be registered in writing of the person's old and new address, including county, or old and new name, the registration numbers assigned to the vehicles for which the address is being changed, and the registration numbers for all registrations then held by such person.
(8) (a) As used in this subsection (8):
(I) "Eligible vehicle" means a motor vehicle that has a valid certificate of registration issued by the department of revenue to a person whose address of record on such certificate is within the boundaries of the program area, as defined in section 42-4-304 (20). The term "eligible vehicle" shall not include motor vehicles held for lease or rental to the general public, motor vehicles held for sale by motor vehicle dealers, including demonstration vehicles, motor vehicles used for motor vehicle manufacturer product evaluations or tests, law enforcement and other emergency vehicles, or nonroad vehicles, including farm and construction vehicles.
(II) "Program area fleet" means a person who owns ten or more eligible vehicles. In determining the number of vehicles owned or operated by a person for purposes of this subsection (8), all motor vehicles owned, operated, leased, or otherwise controlled by such person shall be treated as owned by such person.
(b) (I) Upon the registration of an eligible vehicle, the owner shall report on forms provided by the department:
(A) The types of fuel used by such vehicle; and
(B) Whether such vehicle is dual-fueled or dedicated to one fuel.
(II) The forms provided by the department shall include spaces for the following fuels: Gasoline, diesel, propane, electricity, natural gas, methanol or M85, ethanol or E85, biodiesel, and other.
(c) Upon registration of a vehicle that is a part of a program area fleet, the owner shall report on forms provided by the department that such vehicle is owned by a program area fleet and shall list the owner's tax identification number.
(d) Within a reasonable period of time and upon the request of a political subdivision or the state of Colorado or any institution of the state or the state's political subdivisions, the department shall provide a report listing the owners of eligible vehicles that use fuels other than gasoline or diesel, listing the fuel type of each such eligible vehicle, and identifying whether or not such eligible vehicles are part of a program area fleet.
(9) Except for vehicles owned by a trust created for the benefit of a person with a disability, for purposes of enforcing disabled parking privileges granted pursuant to section 42-4-1208, the department, when issuing a registration card under this section, shall clearly indicate on the

card if an owner of a vehicle is a person with a disability as defined in section 42-3-204. If the vehicle is owned by more than one person and the registration reflects that joint ownership, the department shall clearly indicate on the registration card which of the owners are persons with disabilities and which of the owners are not.

(10) (a) Whenever a person asks the department or any other state department or agency for the name or address of the owner of a motor vehicle registered under this section, the department or agency shall require the person to disclose if the purpose of the request is to determine the name or address of a person suspected of a violation of a state or municipal law detected through the use of an automated vehicle identification system as described in section 42-4-110.5. If the purpose of the request is to determine the name or address of such a suspect, the department or agency shall release such information only if the county or municipality for which the request is made complies with section 42-4-110.5.

(b) No person who receives the name or address of the registered owner of a motor vehicle from the department or from a person who receives the information from the department shall release such information to a county or a municipality unless the county or municipality complies with state laws concerning the use of automated identification devices.

42-3-114. Expiration. Every vehicle registration under this article shall expire on the last day of the month at the end of each twelve-month registration period and shall be renewed, upon application by the owner, the payment of the fees required by law, and in accordance with section 42-3-113 (3), not later than the last day of the month following the date of expiration. No license plates other than those of the registration period to which they pertain shall be displayed on a motor vehicle operated on the highways of Colorado. A person who violates any provision of this section commits a class B traffic infraction.

42-3-115. Registration upon transfer. (1) Whenever the owner of a motor vehicle registered under this article transfers or assigns the owner's title or interest, the registration of such vehicle shall expire, and such owner shall remove the number plates. The owner, upon applying for registration in such owner's name during the same registration period of another motor vehicle, may receive credit upon the fees due for such new registration for such portion of the fees paid for the cancelled registration as the department may determine to be proper and proportionate to the unexpired part of the original term of registration. A transfer fee of one dollar shall be paid in all cases.

(2) (a) Except as provided in paragraph (b) of this subsection (2), the transferee, before operating or permitting the operation of a motor vehicle upon a highway, shall register the vehicle.

(b) A transferee may operate a motor vehicle on the highway before registering it if:

(I) The vehicle is exempt from registration pursuant to section 42-3-103 or 42-3-104; or

(II) The vehicle has been temporarily registered pursuant to section 42-3-203 (3); or

(III) (A) The transferee has purchased the motor vehicle within the last thirty-six hours from a person who is not a motor vehicle dealer under article 6 of title 12, C.R.S.;

(B) The vehicle was purchased either on a Saturday, on a Sunday, on a legal holiday, or between 5 p.m. and 8 a.m.;

(C) The vehicle is being driven from the place where the transferor stored the vehicle to the place where the transferee intends to store the vehicle;

(D) The owner possesses, in the vehicle, a bill of sale that shows the time and date of sale and that is signed by both the buyer and seller; and

(E) The owner possesses, in the vehicle, proof of insurance as required by section 42-4-1409.

(3) If a title to or interest in a motor vehicle is transferred by operation of law, as upon inheritance, devise, or bequest, order in bankruptcy of insolvency, execution, sale, repossession upon default in performing the terms of a lease or executory sales contract, chattel mortgage, secured transaction, or otherwise, the registration thereof shall expire, and the vehicle shall not be operated upon the highways unless the vehicle is registered; except that a person repossessing the vehicle pursuant to rights granted by a mortgage or applicable law may operate the vehicle upon the highways from the place of repossession to the vehicle's new place of storage, either upon displaying upon such vehicle the number plates issued to the former owner or without displaying number plates but under a written permit obtained from the department or the police authorities with jurisdiction over such highways and upon displaying upon such vehicle a placard bearing the name and address of the person authorizing and directing such movement, plainly readable from a distance of one hundred feet during daylight.

(4) The owner of a motor vehicle who has made a bona fide sale or transfer of such owner's title or interest and who has delivered possession of such vehicle and the certificate of title, properly endorsed, to the purchaser or transferee shall not be liable for any damages thereafter resulting from negligent operation of such vehicle by another.

42-3-116. Manufacturers or dealers. (1) Upon application using the proper form and payment of the fees required by law, a manufacturer of, drive-away or tow-away transporter of, or dealer in, motor vehicles, trailers, special mobile machinery, or semitrailers operating such vehicle upon any highway, in lieu of registering each vehicle, may obtain from the department and attach to each such vehicle one number plate, as required in this article for different classes of vehicles. Such plate shall bear a distinctive number; the name of this state, which may be abbreviated; the year issued; and a distinguishing word or symbol indicating that such plate was issued to a manufacturer, drive-away or tow-away transporter, or dealer. Such plates may, during the registration period for which they were issued, be transferred from one such vehicle to another when owned and operated by or with the authority of such manufacturer or representative of such manufacturer or operated by such drive-away or tow-away transporter or dealer.

(2) No manufacturer of or dealer in motor vehicles, trailers, or semitrailers shall cause or permit a vehicle owned by such person to be operated or moved upon a public highway without displaying upon such vehicle a number plate, except as otherwise authorized in this article.

(3) A manufacturer of motor vehicles, trailers, or semitrailers may operate or move upon the highways any such vehicle from the factory where manufactured to a railway depot, vessel, or place of shipment or delivery, without registering the same and without an attached number plate, under a written permit first obtained from the police authorities with jurisdiction over such highways and upon displaying upon each such vehicle a placard bearing the name and address of the manufacturer authorizing or directing such movement, plainly readable from one hundred feet away during daylight.

(4) (a) Any dealer in motor vehicles, trailers, or semitrailers may operate, move, or transport a vehicle owned by such dealer on the streets and highways of this state without registering such vehicle and without an attached numbered plate if there is displayed on such vehicle a depot tag issued by the department. Such tag may be purchased from the department for a fee of five dollars. Such tags shall only be used for moving authorized vehicles for purposes of testing, repairs, or transporting them from the point of delivery to the dealer's place of business and for similar legitimate business purposes; but nothing in this section shall be construed to allow the use of such tag for private purposes.

(b) The executive director of the department shall promulgate rules for the use of depot tags and dealer plates, and a violation of such rules shall subject the violator to a suspension or revocation of the violator's depot tag and dealer plates after a hearing pursuant to article 4 of title 24, C.R.S.

(5) A manufacturer or dealer, upon transferring a motor vehicle, trailer, or semitrailer, whether by sale, lease, or otherwise, to any person other than a manufacturer or dealer shall immediately give written notice of such transfer to the department upon the form provided by the department. Such notice shall contain the date of such transfer, the names and addresses of the transferor and transferee, and such description of the vehicle as may be required by the department.

(6) (a) (I) An application for a full-use dealer plate may be submitted by a motor vehicle dealer or wholesaler who:

(A) Has sold more than twenty-five motor vehicles in the twelve-month period preceding application;

(B) Purchases an existing motor vehicle dealership or wholesale business that has sold more than twenty-five vehicles during the twelve-month period preceding application; or

(C) Obtains a license to operate a new or used motor vehicle dealership or wholesale business with an inventory of fifty or more motor vehicles.

(II) Full-use dealer plates may be used in lieu of, in the same manner as, and to the same extent as number plates issued pursuant to section 42-3-201.

(b) (I) The department shall issue full-use dealer plates upon payment of the fee specified in subparagraph (II) of this paragraph (b) and upon application of a motor vehicle dealer or wholesaler accompanied by satisfactory evidence that the applicant is entitled to the plate in accordance with the criteria established in subparagraph (I) of paragraph (a) of this subsection (6).

(II) The annual fee for full-use dealer plates shall be established and adjusted annually by the department based on the average of specific ownership taxes and registration fees paid for passenger vehicles and light duty trucks that are seven model years old or newer and that were registered during the one-year period preceding January 1 of each year. Such annual fee shall be prorated on a monthly basis. The annual fee for full-use dealer plates for motorcycles shall be established and adjusted annually by the department based on the average of specific ownership taxes and registration fees paid for motorcycles that are seven model years old or newer and that were registered during the one-year period preceding January 1 of each year. Such annual fee for motorcycles shall be prorated on a monthly basis.

(III) Full-use dealer plates shall be valid for a period not to exceed one year.

(IV) Each full-use dealer plate shall be returned to the department within ten days after the sale or closure of a motor vehicle dealership or wholesale business listed in an application submitted pursuant to subparagraph (I) of this paragraph (b).

(c) Full-use dealer plates may be used only for vehicles owned and offered for sale by the dealer or wholesaler. Full-use dealer plates shall not be used on vehicles owned by dealerships or wholesalers that are commonly used by that dealer as tow trucks or vehicles commonly used by that dealer to pick up or deliver parts. At the dealer's or wholesaler's discretion, the full-use plate may be transferred from one motor vehicle to another motor vehicle. The dealer or wholesaler shall not be required to report any such transfer to the department.

(d) A motor vehicle dealer or wholesaler may assign a full-use dealer plate only to the following persons:

(I) Owners or co-owners of the licensed dealership or wholesale motor vehicle business;

(II) An employee of the motor vehicle dealer or wholesaler;

(III) To any person, including former, current, and prospective customers, in order to serve the legitimate business interest of the motor vehicle dealership or motor vehicle wholesale business; and

(IV) A spouse or dependent child living in the same household as the licensed dealer or wholesaler.

(e) As used in this subsection (6), "motor vehicle dealer or wholesaler" includes motor vehicle dealers, used motor vehicle dealers, and wholesalers as those terms are defined in section 12-6-102 (13), (17), and (18), C.R.S.

(7) (a) A person who sells special mobile machinery in the ordinary course of business may submit an application for a demonstration plate.

(b) (I) The department shall issue a demonstration plate upon payment of the fee specified in subparagraph (II) of this paragraph (b) and upon application of a motor vehicle dealer or wholesaler accompanied by satisfactory evidence that the applicant is entitled to the plate in accordance with this subsection (7).

(II) The department shall establish and adjust the annual fee for a demonstration plate based on the average of specific ownership taxes and registration fees paid for items of special mobile machinery that are seven model years old or newer during the previous year.

(III) A demonstration plate shall be valid for one year.

(IV) The owner of a demonstration plate shall return the plate to the department within ten days after the sale or closure of the business that sells special mobile machinery in the ordinary course of business.

(c) No person shall operate special mobile machinery with a demonstration plate unless the machinery is offered for sale and being demonstrated for the purposes of a sale. The owner may transfer the plate from one item of special mobile machinery to another and without reporting the transfer to the department.

(d) A person who violates this subsection (7) commits a class 2 misdemeanor, and shall be punished as provided in section 18-1.3-501, C.R.S.

42-3-117. Nonresidents. (1) A nonresident owner, except as otherwise provided in this section, owning a foreign motor vehicle may operate or permit such vehicle to operate within this state without registering such vehicle or paying fees so long as the vehicle is currently registered in the state, country, or other place of which the owner is a resident, and the motor vehicle displays the number plate or plates issued for such vehicle in the place of residence of such owner.

(2) An owner or operator of a foreign vehicle operated within this state for the transportation of persons or property for compensation or for the transportation of merchandise shall register such vehicle and pay the same fees as required for similar vehicles owned by residents of this state; except that a motor vehicle, truck, semitractor, truck tractor, bus, trailer, or semitrailer registered in a foreign state or country that has a registration reciprocity agreement with Colorado shall be registered in accordance with such agreement.

42-3-118. Registration suspended upon theft - recovery - rules.
(1) Repealed.

(2) (a) After receiving an application for a motor vehicle registration, the department or its authorized agent shall electronically verify with the department of public safety that the motor vehicle has not been reported stolen. The department or its authorized agent shall not register a motor vehicle reported stolen in the system until the vehicle is recovered by the owner. The department shall promulgate rules setting forth procedures to notify the local law enforcement agency upon discovery that a person is attempting to register a stolen motor vehicle.

(b) This subsection (2) is effective July 1, 2009.

42-3-119. No application for registration granted - when. (1) The department shall not grant an application for the registration of a vehicle in any of the following events:

(a) When the applicant for registration is not entitled thereto under this article;

(b) When the applicant has neglected or refused to furnish the department with the information required on the appropriate official form or reasonable additional information required by the department;

(c) When the registration fees required by law have not been paid;

(d) When a certification of emissions control is required pursuant to part 4 of article 4 of this title, and such certification has not been obtained.

42-3-120. Department may cancel or deny registration. (1) The department shall cancel the registration of any vehicle that the department determines is unsafe or unfit to be operated or is not equipped as required by law.

(2) The department shall cancel the registration of a vehicle whenever the person to whom registration number plates have been issued unlawfully uses or permits the unlawful use of the same.

(3) (a) Upon receiving written notice from the Colorado state patrol that a motor carrier has failed to timely pay civil penalties imposed in accordance with section 42-4-235 (2), the department shall cancel the registration of any vehicle that is owned by the carrier and shall deny the registration of any vehicle that is owned by the carrier until the department receives notice from

the Colorado state patrol that the penalty has been paid in full.

(b) Repealed.

(4) (a) Upon receiving written notice from the public utilities commission that a person has failed to timely pay civil penalties imposed in accordance with section 40-7-113, the department shall cancel the registration of any vehicle that is owned by the person for which the penalty was assessed and shall deny the registration of any such vehicle until the department receives written notice from the public utilities commission that the penalty has been paid in full.

(b) On or after August 10, 2011, this subsection (4) applies to all vehicles regardless of when the vehicles were purchased.

42-3-121. Violation of registration provisions - penalty. (1) It is unlawful to commit any of the following acts:

(a) To operate or permit the operation, upon a highway, of a motor vehicle subject to registration under this article or to possess or control a trailer coach or trailer that is not registered and does not display the number plates issued for such vehicle or trailer coach for the current year, except for trailer coaches or trailers owned by a licensed dealer or licensed manufacturer while being held for sale or resale or while operated on the streets or highways with dealer plates or depot tags authorized pursuant to section 42-3-116;

(b) To display or permit to be displayed, to have in possession, or to offer for sale a certificate of title, validation tab or sticker, or registration number plate knowing the same to be fictitious or to have been stolen, cancelled, revoked, suspended, or altered;

(c) To lend to or knowingly permit the use by one not entitled thereto a certificate of title, registration card, or registration number plate issued to the lending or permitting person;

(d) To fail or refuse to surrender to the department, upon demand, a certificate of title, registration card, or registration number plate that has been suspended, cancelled, or revoked;

(e) To use a false name or address, to knowingly make a false statement, or to knowingly conceal a material fact in an application for the registration, renewal registration, or duplicate registration of a motor vehicle;

(f) To use or permit the use of a noncommercial or recreational vehicle to transport cargo or passengers for profit or hire or in a business or commercial enterprise;

(g) To use or permit the use of a truck or truck tractor registered as a collector's item pursuant to section 42-12-401 (1) (c) to transport cargo or passengers for profit or hire or in a business or commercial enterprise;

(h) To drive or permit to be driven a truck or truck tractor registered as a collector's item pursuant to section 42-12-401 (1) (c) for any purpose other than those purposes allowed in section 42-12-401 (1) (c).

(2) (a) A person who violates paragraph (a) or (c) of subsection (1) of this section commits a class B traffic infraction.

(b) A person who violates paragraph (b), (d), or (e) of subsection (1) of this section commits a class 2 misdemeanor traffic offense.

(c) A person who violates paragraph (f) or (g) of subsection (1) of this section commits a class B traffic infraction.

42-3-122. Perjury on a motor vehicle registration application. (1) A person commits perjury on a motor vehicle registration application if such person knowingly makes a materially false statement, other than those prohibited by sections 18-8-502 and 18-8-503, C.R.S., on a motor vehicle registration application that such person does not believe to be true, under an oath required or authorized by law.

(2) Perjury on a motor vehicle registration application is a class 1 petty offense.

42-3-123. Payment by bad check - recovery of plates. (1) If the registration of a vehicle required to be registered under this article is procured or perfected by the owner, or by a person or agent in the owner's behalf, and the registration fee and specific ownership tax are paid by check, money order, draft, bill of exchange, or other negotiable instrument that is dishonored and not paid by the person upon whom drawn, the registration shall be revoked as soon as the dishonored or unpaid instrument is returned to the authorized agent. Upon the return of such check, money order, draft, bill of exchange, or other negotiable instrument to the authorized agent, evidencing nonpayment or dishonor of same, the authorized agent shall notify the owner in writing, at the address appearing on the person's ownership tax receipt, by registered or certified mail, of the revoked registration resulting from such nonpayment or dishonor. The notice shall request the return to the authorized agent of the tax receipt, license fee receipt, and registration number plates issued under such revoked registration within ten days after the date of mailing of the notice.

(2) If the owner fails to return the tax receipt, license fee receipt, and registration number plates to the authorized agent within ten days after the date of mailing of said notice, the authorized agent shall immediately repossess such tax receipt, license fee receipt, and registration number plates as may have been issued under such revoked registration, and the county sheriff or the Denver manager of safety, or an equivalent person in the city and county of Broomfield, upon request by an authorized agent, shall sequester or recover possession of such receipts and registration number plates within his or her jurisdiction. All receipts and registration number plates repossessed under this section shall be returned to the issuing authorized agent. An owner attaching and using registration number plates acquired under a revoked registration

shall be subject to the penalties provided in section 42-3-121.

(3) The authorized agent, upon accounting for repossessed plates, shall receive a refund of any sum paid over to the county treasurer, or such equivalent position in the city and county of Broomfield, or to the department, as provided by sections 42-3-304 to 42-3-306, in each case where an owner or the owner's agent has issued a check, money order, draft, bill of exchange, or other negotiable instrument that has been dishonored and not paid by the person upon whom drawn; and, likewise, the county treasurer, or such equivalent position in the city and county of Broomfield, and the department making such refund shall further effect appropriate refunds and deductions as may be necessary to adjust and balance the books and records of the county treasurer and the department after making the initial refund to the authorized agent.

42-3-124. Violation - penalty. A person who violates a provision of this article for which no other penalty is provided in this article commits a class B traffic infraction and shall be punished as provided in section 42-4-1701 (3) (a).

42-3-125. Fleet operators - registration period certificates - multi-year registrations. (1) (a) The department may issue to a fleet operator, upon application of the fleet operator, a registration period certificate. Such registration period certificate shall be presented to the appropriate authorized agent no later than the tenth day of the month in which registration of any motor vehicle is required by this article. When so presented, the twelve-month period stated in the registration period certificate shall govern the date on which registration is required for all fleet vehicles owned or leased by the fleet operator.

(b) Notwithstanding section 42-3-207 (1) (b), the department may promulgate rules to establish requirements for a fleet operator to register the operator's fleet vehicles and have them identified by special license plates that do not require an annual validating tab or sticker. Registration fees payable on fleet vehicles under a multi-year agreement shall not be discounted below the otherwise applicable annual registration fees.

(2) (a) Vehicles registered by a fleet operator after the issuance of a registration period certificate or the execution of a multi-year agreement shall be subject to section 42-3-109.

(b) The annual registration fees prescribed in sections 42-3-304 to 42-3-306 for fleet vehicles shall be reduced by twenty-five percent at the end of each successive quarter of the registration period that has elapsed prior to making application for the balance of the registration period.

(3) The fees and taxes for vehicles registered prior to the effective date of the registration period certificate or multi-year agreement shall be apportioned in the manner prescribed in subsection (2) of this section.

(4) This section shall not apply to vehicles registered under reciprocal agreements between the state of Colorado and any foreign country or another state or territory or a possession of the United States.

42-3-126. Notice - primary body color. (1) If the primary body color of a motor vehicle is subsequently changed from the primary body color that is identified in the application for registration for the motor vehicle, the owner of the motor vehicle shall notify the department in writing, within thirty days after the color of such motor vehicle is changed, of the new primary body color of the motor vehicle. The primary body color of a motor vehicle shall be identified using the standard color descriptions of the department that are established pursuant to section 42-3-105 (1) (e).

(2) Any person who violates subsection (1) of this section commits a class B traffic infraction.

42-3-127. Sale of special mobile machinery. A person who sells special mobile machinery in the ordinary course of business shall notify in writing the buyer of the machinery that the machinery is required to be registered under this article. A person who violates this section commits a class B traffic infraction for each item of special mobile machinery sold without such a notice.

PART 2

LICENSE PLATES

42-3-201. Number plates furnished - style - periodic reissuance - tabs - rules. (1) (a) (I) The department shall issue to every owner whose vehicle is registered two number plates; except that the department shall issue one number plate for the following:

(A) A motorcycle;
(B) A street rod vehicle;
(C) A trailer or semitrailer;
(D) A vehicle drawn by a motor vehicle; or
(E) An item of special mobile machinery.

(II) At the discretion of the executive director of the department, the department may issue one number plate for any vehicle not listed in subparagraph (I) of this paragraph (a).

(III) The department may require the return to the department of all number plates upon termination of the lawful use of such plates by the owner.

(b) (I) The department may issue the number plates required in this section for one or more registration periods. If the number plates are issued for multi-year use, the department may issue a validating tab or sticker to indicate the year of registration of the vehicle.

(II) Any validating tab or sticker that evidences the receipt of taxes under this article may be obtained by the department through normal purchasing procedures and may be produced and issued by the department through its authorized agents. Such validation tab or sticker shall be produced in accordance with the minimum specifications of the department, and such specifications shall reflect, at a minimum, the same quality control standards employed by the department of corrections in the production of such validation tab or sticker as those standards existed on January 1, 1999.

(2) Every number plate shall have displayed upon it the registration number assigned to the vehicle and owner, the year number for which it is issued, the month in which it expires, and any other appropriate symbol, word, or words designated by the department. The department may adopt rules for the issuance of permanent number plates that do not display the year number for which it is issued or the month in which it expires. Such plate and the required letters and numerals, except the year number for which issued, shall be of sufficient size to be plainly readable from a distance of one hundred feet during daylight.

(3) The department shall issue for every passenger motor vehicle, rented without a driver, the same type of number plates as the type of plates issued for private passenger vehicles.

(4) The department shall issue, for every noncommercial or recreational vehicle registered as such pursuant to this article, numbered plates or other insignia of a color or design different from any other Colorado plates, to be determined by the department, in order that such numbered plates or other insignia may be plainly recognized at a distance of at least one hundred feet during daylight.

(5) (a) A new or replacement license plate issued by the department shall, to the extent that it is practical, have standardized coloring and identifying characters limited to no more than a total of six numbers and letters; except that such character limitation does not apply to personalized license plates issued under section 42-3-211.

(b) The department of revenue may require the replacement of any license plate as necessary to ensure that license plates are legible as required by section 42-3-202 (2).

(6) (a) The department shall promulgate rules that require the destruction, recycling, or other permanent disposal of license plates that are no longer used to evidence registration of a motor vehicle and are voluntarily given to the department, an authorized agent, or a person who receives license plates in the ordinary course of business.

(b) The department, an authorized agent, or a person who receives license plates in the ordinary course of business shall destroy, recycle, or dispose of a license plate in accordance with rules promulgated by the department under this subsection (6).

42-3-202. Number plates to be attached. (1) (a) Number plates assigned to a self-propelled vehicle other than a motorcycle or street rod vehicle shall be attached thereto, one in the front and the other in the rear. The number plate assigned to a motorcycle, street rod vehicle, trailer, semitrailer, other vehicle drawn by a motor vehicle, or special mobile machinery shall be attached to the rear thereof. Number plates shall be so displayed during the current registration year, except as otherwise provided in this article.

(b) If the department issues a validating tab or sticker to a motor vehicle pursuant to section 42-3-201, the current month validating tab or sticker shall be displayed in the bottom left corner of the rear license plate. The current year validating tab or sticker shall be displayed in the bottom right corner of the rear license plate. The tabs or stickers shall be visible at all times.

(2) (a) Every number plate shall at all times be securely fastened to the vehicle to which it is assigned, so as to prevent the plate from swinging, and shall be horizontal at a height not less than twelve inches from the ground, measuring from the bottom of such plate, in a place and position to be clearly visible, and shall be maintained free from foreign materials and in a condition to be clearly legible.

(b) A person shall not operate a motor vehicle with an affixed device or a substance that causes all or a portion of a license plate to be unreadable by a system used to automatically identify a motor vehicle. Such a device includes, without limitation, a cover that distorts angular visibility; alters the color of the plate; or is smoked, tinted, scratched, or dirty so as to impair the legibility of the license plate.

(3) (a) A person who violates any provision of this section commits a class B traffic infraction.

(b) A person who violates paragraph (b) of subsection (2) of this section commits a class A traffic infraction and shall be punished by a fine of one hundred dollars.

(4) Notwithstanding subsections (1) to (3) of this section, the owner of a military vehicle may elect to not display the vehicle's assigned license plate if the license plate is physically in the military vehicle and is available for inspection to any peace officer who requests the plate.

42-3-203. Standardized plates - rules. (1) Unless otherwise authorized by statute, all Class C vehicles shall be issued a single type of standardized license plate. Unless otherwise authorized by statute, all Class B vehicles, except recreational trucks, shall be issued a single type of standardized license plate.

(2) An owner who has applied for renewal of registration of a vehicle but who has not received the number plates or plate for the ensuing registration period may operate or permit the operation of such vehicle upon the highways, upon displaying the number plates or plate issued for the preceding registration period, for such time as determined by the department as it may find necessary for issuance of such new plates.

(3) (a) (I) The department may issue individual temporary registration number plates, tags, or certificates good for a period not to exceed sixty days upon application by an owner of a motor vehicle or the owner's agent and the payment of a registration fee of two dollars, one dollar and sixty cents to be retained by the authorized agent or department issuing the plates, tags, or certificates and the remainder to be remitted monthly to the department to be transmitted to the state treasurer for credit to the highway users tax fund.

(II) The authorized agent may issue individual temporary registration number plates, tags, or certificates good for a period not to exceed sixty days upon application by an owner of special mobile machinery or the owner's agent and the payment of a registration fee of two dollars, one dollar and sixty cents to be retained by the authorized agent or department issuing the plates, tags, or certificates and the remainder to be remitted monthly to the department to be transmitted to the state treasurer for credit to the highway users tax fund.

(III) It is unlawful for a person to use such number plate, tag, or certificate after it expires. A person who violates any provision of this paragraph (a) commits a class B traffic infraction.

(b) The department may issue to licensed motor vehicle dealers temporary registration number plates, tags, or certificates in blocks of twenty-five upon payment of a fee of twelve dollars and fifty cents for each block of twenty-five, fifty percent thereof to be retained by the county clerk and recorder and the remainder to be remitted monthly to the department to be transmitted to the state treasurer for credit to the highway users tax fund and allocation and expenditure as specified in section 43-4-205 (5.5) (b), C.R.S.

(c) (I) Subject to subparagraph (III) of this paragraph (c), the department shall not issue more than two temporary registration number plates, tags, or certificates per year to a Class A or Class B motor vehicle.

(II) Beginning July 1, 2008, the department shall track by vehicle identification number the number of temporary registration number plates, tags, or certificates issued to a motor vehicle.

(III) The department may promulgate rules authorizing the issuance of more than two temporary registration number plates, tags, or certificates per year if the motor vehicle title work or lien perfection has caused the need for such issuance.

(4) All or part of the face of the license plates furnished pursuant to this section shall be coated with a reflective material.

42-3-204. Parking privileges for persons with disabilities - applicability - rules. (1) As used in this section:

(a) "Disability" or "disabled" means a physical impairment that meets the standards of 23 CFR 1235, which impairment is verified, in writing, by a professional. To be valid, the verifying professional shall certify to the department that the person meets the standards on forms published by the department.

(b) "Extended" means a condition that is not expected to change within thirty months after the issuance of an identifying figure, given the current state of medical or adaptive technology.

(c) "Identifying figure" means a figure that provides notice that a person is authorized to use a reserved parking space.

(d) "Identifying license plate" means a license plate bearing an identifying figure.

(e) "Identifying placard" means a placard bearing an identifying figure.

(f) "Permanent" means a condition that is not expected to change within a person's lifetime, given the current state of medical or adaptive technology.

(g) "Professional" means a physician licensed to practice medicine or practicing medicine pursuant to section 12-36-106 (3) (i), C.R.S., a physician assistant licensed pursuant to section 12-36-107.4, C.R.S., a podiatrist licensed under article 32 of title 12, C.R.S., an advanced practice nurse registered pursuant to section 12-38-111.5, C.R.S., or a physician, physician assistant, podiatrist, or advanced practice nurse authorized to practice professionally by another state that shares a common border with Colorado.

(h) "Reserved parking space" means a parking space reserved for a person with a disability.

(2) (a) A person with a disability may apply to the department for:

(I) An identifying license plate to be supplied at the same cost as a standard plate and to be displayed as provided in section 42-3-202 on a motor vehicle owned by such person or that is owned by a trust created for the benefit of and the name of which includes the name of such person, subject to the following:

(A) An identifying license plate shall be renewed once each year in a manner to be determined by the department.

(B) The issuance of an identifying license plate to a person with a disability shall not preclude such person from obtaining an identifying placard.

(C) The verification requirements of paragraph (a) of subsection (1) of this section shall be met once every three years.

(II) An identifying placard to be prominently displayed on a motor vehicle used to transport such person, subject to the following:

(A) The department shall not issue a permanent or extended identifying placard unless the applicant provides a driver's license or identification card issued pursuant to article 2 of this title, or a federally issued identification card; except that a parent or guardian of a person with a disability under sixteen years of age may provide the parent's or guardian's driver's license or identification card in lieu of the minor with a disability, and a business entity that transports people with disabilities for hire may provide an employee identification number and such other information as required by the department.

(B) An identifying placard valid for more than ninety days shall have the last four digits of the holder's identification number printed on its face; except that a placard issued for a person under sixteen years of age may bear the parent's or guardian's identification number if the parent or guardian provided the identification required by sub-subparagraph (A) of this subparagraph (II), and, if an entity that transports people with disabilities for hire obtains a placard, the placard shall bear the true name of the entity providing such service. If the placard bears the last four digits of the parent's or guardian's identification number, the placard shall also bear the letter "C" as a designator.

(C) Identifying information about the person with the disability shall be strictly confidential and only available to law enforcement or to personnel within the department for official business related to the identifying placard.

(D) When in use, the identifying placard's face shall be legible and visible to any law enforcement officer or authorized parking enforcement official when viewed from outside the vehicle.

(E) A holder of an identifying placard shall renew the placard every three years in a manner to be determined by the department, including renewal by mail.

(F) The holder of an identifying placard shall meet the verification requirements of paragraph (a) of subsection (1) of this section each time the placard is renewed.

(G) The department shall place an expiration date on an identifying placard using a date system that removes a portion of the placard to indicate the expiration date. The department shall affix a validating sticker indicating the expiration date to the placard.

(H) Repealed.

(III) Disabled veteran special license plates with the identifying figure for a person with a physical impairment affecting mobility, so long as the person with a disability meets the eligibility criteria specified in section 42-3-213 (5).

(b) (Deleted by amendment, L. 2010, (HB 10-1019), ch. 400, p. 1918, § 2, effective January 1, 2011.)

(c) An identifying license plate or placard shall be issued to a person upon presentation to the department of a written statement, verified by a professional, that such person has a disability. The application for an identifying license plate or placard shall be sent to the department every three years; except that a person who has been issued a disabled veteran special license plate shall not send an application to the department every year.

(d) (I) An identifying license plate or placard may be revoked by the department upon receipt of a sworn statement from a peace officer or an authorized parking enforcement official that the person with a disability has improperly used the privilege defined in section 42-4-1208. The peace officer or authorized parking enforcement official shall include with the statement the name of the person who misused the license plate or placard and either the license plate or placard number, the last four digits of the driver's license or identification card number printed on the placard, or the true name of the owner printed on the placard. Upon a first violation of section 42-4-1208, the department shall deny reissuance of such license plate or placard for a period of one year following the date of revocation. Upon a second or subsequent violation of section 42-4-1208, the department shall deny reissuance of such license plate or placard for a period of at least five years after the date of the second or each subsequent revocation. The department shall provide written notification to the person with a disability of such revocation, which notification shall contain a demand for the return of the license plate or placard to the department and a warning that continued use by any person shall be subject to the penalty set forth in section 42-4-1208 (11).

(II) The department may hold hearings to revoke an identifying license plate or placard.

(III) A person who fails to return a revoked identifying placard or license plate or who attempts to obtain an identifying license plate or placard when under revocation pursuant to this paragraph (d) commits a class B traffic infraction.

(e) Repealed.

(3) (a) The department shall issue a temporary identifying placard to a person who is temporarily disabled upon presentation of a written statement, verified by a professional, that such person temporarily meets the definition of a person with a disability.

(b) The department shall issue a temporary identifying placard to a qualifying person who is a resident of another state and who becomes disabled while in this state. The department shall not issue the placard unless the applicant provides a driver's license or identification card issued pursuant to article 2 of this title or issued by another state or a federally issued identification card. The department shall print the last four digits of the driver's license number or identification card number on the face of the placard.

(c) A temporary identifying placard is valid until the last day of the month falling ninety days after the date of issuance and may continually be renewed for additional ninety-day periods during the term of such disability upon resubmission of such written and verified statements.

(d) The privileges granted to persons with disabilities apply to temporary identifying placards issued under this subsection (3).

(e) Temporary placards issued by states other than Colorado are valid so long as they are currently valid in the state of issuance and valid pursuant to 23 CFR 1235.

(f) (I) A temporary identifying placard shall have the last four digits of the person's identification number printed on the placard's face. The department shall place an expiration date on an identifying placard using a date system that removes a portion of the placard to indicate the expiration date. The department shall affix a validating sticker indicating the expiration date to the placard.

(II) Repealed.

(4) Upon the filing of an application for issuance or renewal of an identifying license plate or placard under this section, the department shall make available to the applicant an informational pamphlet or other informational source developed by the department in consultation with the Colorado advisory council for persons with disabilities, created in section 24-45.5-103, C.R.S., that describes the rights and responsibilities of the holders of such license plates or placards and the parking privileges set forth in section 42-4-1208.

(5) (a) An application for an identifying license plate or placard shall contain a notice of eligibility requirements and penalties for obtaining such license plate or placard when not eligible. The applicant shall sign the notice affirming knowledge of the information contained therein.

(b) The department, in consultation with the Colorado advisory council for persons with disabilities, created in section 24-45.5-103, C.R.S., shall promulgate a rule creating a form that is signed by a professional, under penalty of perjury, affirming knowledge of the contents of the notice created in paragraph (a) of this subsection (5) before verifying that a person has a disability. The form shall contain a notice of the eligibility requirement to obtain an identifying license plate or placard.

(6) Any person renewing an identifying license plate or placard shall affirm under penalty of perjury that the person to whom the license plate or placard is issued remains eligible to use the license plate or placard. The department shall require the person renewing the plate or placard to submit the person's date of birth and driver's license or identification card number.

(7) (a) The department shall maintain in its records for three years the registration information used to issue an identifying license plate or placard, any violations of section 42-4-1208 by the holder, and the application or an electronic or digital reproduction of the application.

(b) Upon the funds being available and appropriated from the disabled parking education and enforcement fund created in section 42-1-226, the department shall provide immediate electronic access to the records maintained pursuant to paragraph (a) of this subsection (8) to a peace officer working within the course and scope of the officer's official duties.

(8) An identifying placard issued in another state or country is not valid for more than ninety days after the holder becomes a resident of Colorado. A person who applies for an identifying placard in Colorado shall surrender any currently held identifying placard issued in another state or country.

42-3-205. Substitute plates - waiting period for reissuance of identical combination of numbers and letters. (1) If a number or personalized license plate issued under this article becomes lost, stolen, mutilated, or illegible, the person who is entitled thereto shall immediately apply for a substitute. Such application shall include evidence satisfactory to the department that such plate is lost, stolen, mutilated, or illegible and payment of the required fees. If the plate to be replaced is in the possession of the applicant, the plate shall be surrendered to the department along with the application.

(2) If an application made pursuant to subsection (1) of this section is accompanied by the personalized plate to be replaced, the department shall reissue a substitute plate bearing the identical sequential combination of letters and numbers that appears on the original plate.

42-3-206. Remanufacture of certain license plates. Persons who have been approved to be issued a license plate before July 1, 2003, pursuant to this section as it existed on July 1, 2003, shall be issued such plate, shall be authorized to continue using such plate, and shall not be required to pay additional fees beyond the existing taxes and fees imposed for motor vehicle registration. Such issuance of license plates that contain only two alphabetic figures and up to four numeric figures shall be issued as personalized license plates pursuant to section 42-3-211, which are a flat-style license plate. If the same alphanumeric combination is issued to multiple vehicles, the department shall compare the last four numbers of the vehicle identification number of the motor vehicles to which such plates are issued and issue such alphanumeric combination only to the vehicle with the lowest last four numbers.

42-3-207. Special plates - rules - new plates - retirement. (1) (a) Neither the department nor an authorized agent of the department shall collect any fee for the privilege of using a special plate unless such fee is expressly authorized by statute. The department or an authorized agent of the department shall not transfer money collected for the privilege of using a special plate unless such transfer is expressly authorized by statute.

(b) (I) A special license plate shall not be issued pursuant to this section unless such license plate was approved prior to January 1, 2001.

(II) Special license plates that have been approved pursuant to this section shall be retired, effective March 1, 2008, unless such plates are issued for at least three thousand vehicles. The executive director of the department shall promulgate rules to provide standards for the retirement of special license plates not issued for at least three thousand vehicles.

(2) Before a bill is introduced in the general assembly that contains, or any bill is amended to contain, a provision that establishes a new category or type of group special license plate, the person, group, or association proposing the special license plate shall submit to the department a proposal for a group special license plate and certify that at least three thousand of such special plates are to be issued within one year after the authorization of such plates. The department shall verify that any proposed group special license plates meet the three-thousand-plate requirement.

(3) A group special license plate shall not be issued to any business entity conducted for profit.

(4) The amount of taxes and fees for special license plates issued pursuant to this section shall be the same as the amount of taxes and fees specified for regular motor vehicle registration plus an additional one-time fee of twenty-five dollars. The additional fee shall be transmitted to the state treasurer, who shall credit the same to the highway users tax fund for allocation and expenditure as specified in section 43-4-205 (5.5) (b), C.R.S.

42-3-208. Special plates - qualifications for issuance of special license plates. (1) The following special license plates created by rule by the department under section 42-3-207, as such section existed when the plates were created, shall be subject to the requirement so specified:

(a) The department or an authorized agent shall not issue a Denver firefighters' special license plate to an applicant until such applicant has provided to the department or an authorized agent sufficient evidence to demonstrate that the applicant is an active or retired Denver firefighter.

(b) The department or an authorized agent shall not issue a raptor education special license plate to an applicant until such applicant has provided to the department or an authorized agent sufficient evidence to demonstrate that the applicant is a member in good standing of the raptor education foundation and qualified by such foundation to receive a special license plate or the applicant is a member of the rocky mountain raptor program and qualified by such program to receive a special license plate.

(c) (Deleted by amendment, L. 2008, p. 228, § 1, effective August 5, 2008.)

(d) The department or an authorized agent shall not issue an Elks special license plate to an applicant until such applicant has provided to the department or an authorized agent sufficient evidence to demonstrate that the applicant is a member of the Benevolent and Protective Order of Elks.

(2) (Deleted by amendment, L. 2008, p. 228, § 1, effective August 5, 2008.)

(3) Special license plates subject to the requirements of this section shall be retired, effective January 1, 2009, unless such plates are issued to at least three thousand vehicles.

42-3-209. Legislative license plates. (1) Upon the application of the owner of a passenger car, truck, or trailer classified as Class B or Class C personal property, as defined in section 42-3-106, or the duly authorized agent of such owner showing that such owner is a member of congress from the state of Colorado, the department may assign to such owner registration plates bearing a number together with appropriate words or letters indicating that such owner is a member of the congress of the United States, and a separate number series shall be used to further identify such license plates. Said license plates shall not be issued by the counties but shall be issued directly by the department.

(2) Upon application of an owner of either a passenger car or a truck not over sixteen thousand pounds empty weight showing that such owner is a member of the general assembly of the state of Colorado, the department may assign to such owner, in lieu of the distinct registration number specified in section 42-3-113 (1) (a), registration plates bearing a number together with appropriate words or letters indicating that such owner is a member of the general assembly of the state of Colorado and a separate number series, based on senatorial and representative districts, to further identify such license plates.

42-3-210. Radio and television license plates. (1) A person who is the holder of a valid renewable amateur radio, standard radio, FM, or television license issued by the federal communications commission shall, upon application and payment of the additional registration fee prescribed in subsection (4) of this section, be entitled to have passenger cars or trucks that do not exceed sixteen thousand pounds empty weight registered under the call sign letters assigned to such station by said commission and shall be furnished license plates bearing such call sign letters in lieu of the distinct registration number specified in section 42-3-113.

(2) A holder of an amateur radio license shall not be entitled to purchase more than one set of such special license plates for a registration period. A holder of a standard radio, FM, or television license shall not be entitled to purchase more than ten sets of such special license plates for a registration period.

(3) Such special registration and license plates shall be valid until the end of the registration period and may be renewed for the same term as any other renewal of registration upon application and payment of the prescribed registration fee so long as the holder of such radio or television license is licensed by the federal communications commission.

(4) An additional fee of two dollars shall be collected for each vehicle annually registered

that is furnished amateur radio call plates, and an additional fee of five dollars shall be collected for each vehicle annually registered that is furnished standard radio, FM, and television call plates.

42-3-211. Issuance of personalized plates authorized. (1) The department may issue personalized license plates for motor vehicles in accordance with this section.

(2) (a) "Personalized license plates", as used in this section, means license plates that have displayed upon them the registration number assigned to the motor vehicle for which such registration number was issued in a combination of letters or numbers requested by the owner of the vehicle, subject to the limitations of this section.

(b) "Personalized license plates", as used in this section, includes special license plates that bear the words "street rod" and that may be issued only to a street rod vehicle.

(3) (a) Personalized license plates shall be the same color and design as regular motor vehicle license plates, shall consist of any combination of numbers or letters not exceeding seven positions and not less than two positions, and shall not conflict with existing passenger, commercial, trailer, motorcycle, or other special license plates series; except that personalized license plates bearing the words "street rod" shall be of a design determined by the executive director of the department, which design shall be different from those used by the state for regular motor vehicle license plates.

(b) If number plates issued for vehicles include the county of vehicle registration, a vehicle owner shall have the option of obtaining a personalized license plate that does not include such county designation.

(4) Any person who is the registered owner of a motor vehicle registered with the department or who applies to register a motor vehicle or renew personalized license registration of a motor vehicle, upon payment of the fee prescribed in subsection (6) of this section, may apply to the department for personalized license plates in the manner prescribed in this section. Personalized license plates shall be issued for the annual registration period immediately following the year in which the application is made.

(5) An applicant for issuance of personalized license plates or renewal of such plates shall apply in such form and by such date as the department may require, indicating thereon the combination of letters or numbers requested as a registration number. There shall be no duplication of registration numbers, and the department may refuse to issue any combination of letters or numbers that carry connotations offensive to good taste and decency, are misleading, or duplicate any other license plates provided for in this article.

(6) (a) A fee of thirty-five dollars shall be charged in addition to the registration fee normally due upon the vehicle for the issuance of the same number of personalized license plates for a vehicle as are specified in section 42-3-201 for the issuance of number plates. Upon reissuance of the same personalized license plates in subsequent years, the additional fee shall be twenty-five dollars. Such fee shall be due upon the original issuance or reissuance of personalized license plates other than a renewal of registration under paragraph (b) of this subsection (6).

(b) The department may provide for renewals of personalized license plates whereby such plates are retained by the applicant in subsequent years upon the payment, in addition to the normal registration fee, of an annual renewal fee of twenty-five dollars for which the department shall provide a distinctive tag or insignia to be affixed to such plates to signify that such vehicle has been properly registered for the year for which such license plate was renewed.

(c) The fee for transferring previously issued personalized license plates to another vehicle shall be twelve dollars in addition to other applicable fees.

(d) A person who fails to apply for the renewal or transfer of issued personalized license plates according to subsection (5) of this section shall lose the priority right to use the combination of letters or numbers displayed on the personalized license plates.

(e) Notwithstanding paragraphs (a) to (d) of this subsection (6), in lieu of such fees, the fee for a license plate that contains only two alphabetic figures and up to four numeric figures shall be the actual cost of issuing such plate.

(7) All applications for special registration of motor vehicles shall be made directly to the department, and shall be administered by the department. All fees received from special registrations shall be credited to the highway users tax fund created in section 43-4-201, C.R.S., and allocated and expended as specified in section 43-4-205 (5.5) (b), C.R.S.; except that two dollars of each such special registration fee collected pursuant to paragraphs (a) to (d) of subsection (6) of this section shall be remitted to the county general fund.

(8) The executive director of the department may prepare any special forms and issue any rules necessary to implement this section.

(9) (a) A person who has been issued personalized license plates may retain the unique combination of letters or numbers of such plate, notwithstanding that the person no longer has a registered motor vehicle, if the person pays an annual fee of twenty-five dollars, which shall be transferred to the highway users tax fund.

(b) This subsection (9) shall not be construed to authorize a person to reserve license plates for which no motor vehicle has ever been registered according to this article. This subsection (9) shall not be construed to require the department to send a renewal notice to the person who retains the unique combination of letters or numbers.

42-3-212. Issuance of optional plates authorized - retirement. (1) The department may issue optional license plates for passenger cars or trucks not over sixteen thousand pounds empty weight.

(2) Optional license plates shall have a background consisting of a graphic design representing the state flag of Colorado and shall consist of numbers or letters approved in accordance with rules of the department.

(3) An applicant may apply for personalized optional license plates. If the applicant complies with section 42-3-211, the department may issue such plates upon payment of the additional fee required by section 42-3-211 (6) for personalized license plates. If the applicant has existing personalized license plates for a motor vehicle, the applicant may transfer the combination of letters or numbers to a new set of optional license plates for the vehicle upon paying the fee imposed by section 42-3-211 (6) (a) and upon turning in such existing plates to the department as required by the department. A person who has obtained personalized optional license plates under this subsection (3) shall pay the annual fee imposed by section 42-3-211 (6) (b) to renew such plates. The fees imposed by this subsection (3) shall be in addition to all other taxes and fees imposed for optional license plates.

(4) The amount of the taxes and fees for optional license plates shall be the same as the amount of the taxes and fees specified for regular motor vehicle plates plus an additional annual fee of twenty-five dollars. The additional fee shall be transmitted to the state treasurer, who shall credit the same to the highway users tax fund for allocation and expenditure as specified in section 43-4-205 (5.5) (b), C.R.S.

(5) All applications for optional license plates shall be made directly to the department.

(6) The executive director of the department may prepare any special forms and issue any rules necessary to implement this section.

(7) The optional license plates authorized by this section shall be retired unless such plates have been issued for at least three thousand vehicles by July 1, 2007.

42-3-213. Special plates - military veterans - rules - retirement. (1) (a) The department shall issue one or more sets of special license plates to the following persons who own a truck that does not exceed sixteen thousand pounds empty weight, a passenger car, a motorcycle, or a noncommercial or recreational vehicle:

(I) A recipient of the purple heart;
(II) A former prisoner of war;
(III) An honorably discharged or retired veteran of the armed forces of the United States;
(IV) A disabled veteran of the armed forces of the United States;
(V) A survivor of the attack on Pearl Harbor;
(VI) A recipient of the medal of honor;
(VII) An honorably discharged, retired, reserve, or active member of the United States Marine Corps;
(VIII) A veteran of the Korean war;
(IX) A recipient of a military award for valor;
(X) A veteran of the Vietnam war;
(XI) An honorably discharged, retired, reserve, or active member of the United States Army;
(XII) Effective July 1, 2006, an honorably discharged, retired, reserve, or active member of the United States Navy;
(XIII) A recipient of a bronze star medal;
(XIV) The current or past spouse, child, sibling, grandparent, or parent of a person who died in the line of duty while serving in the armed forces and deployed to a combat zone;
(XV) An honorably discharged, retired, reserve, auxiliary, or active member of the United States Coast Guard;
(XVI) A serving member or honorably discharged or retired member of any component of the United States Air Force;
(XVII) An honorably discharged, retired, reserve, or active member of the special forces of the United States armed forces;
(XVIII) A person who supports the North American aerospace defense command;
(XIX) On or after January 1, 2009, a person who supports the United States Army fourth infantry division;
(XX) A veteran of the Afghanistan war;
(XXI) A veteran of the Iraq war; or
(XXII) A veteran of world war II.

(b) (I) Except as provided in subparagraph (II) of this paragraph (b), the amount of taxes and fees for special license plates issued pursuant to this section shall be the same as that specified for regular motor vehicle registration plus an additional one-time issuance or replacement fee. The additional one-time fee shall be twenty-five dollars and shall be transmitted to the state treasurer, who shall credit the same to the highway users tax fund for allocation and expenditure as specified in section 43-4-205 (5.5) (b), C.R.S.

(II) Notwithstanding subparagraph (I) of this paragraph (b):

(A) No fee shall be charged for one set of prisoner of war special license plates issued pursuant to subsection (3) of this section for a passenger car, a truck, a motorcycle, or a noncommercial or recreational vehicle.

(B) No fee shall be charged for one set of disabled veteran special license plates issued pursuant to subsection (5) of this section for a passenger car, a truck, a motorcycle, or a noncommercial or recreational vehicle.

(C) No fee shall be charged for one set of medal of honor special license plates issued pursuant to subsection (7) of this section for a passenger car, a truck, a motorcycle, or a noncommercial or recreational vehicle.

(D) No fee shall be charged for one set of purple heart special license plates issued pursuant to subsection (2) of this section.

(E) No fee shall be charged for one set of military valor special license plates issued pursuant to subsection (10) of this section.

(F) No fee shall be charged for one set of survivors of the attack on Pearl Harbor special license plates issued pursuant to subsection (6) of this section.

(G) The one-time issuance fee imposed pursuant to subparagraph (I) of this paragraph (b) shall not be charged for one set, per applicant, of fallen service member special license plates issued pursuant to subsection (15) of this section.

(H) The department shall not charge the one-time issuance fee imposed pursuant to subparagraph (I) of this paragraph (b) for one set, per applicant, of world war II special license plates issued pursuant to subsection (23) of this section.

(III) Except as provided in subparagraphs (IV) and (V) of this paragraph (b), the fees collected pursuant to this paragraph (b) shall be transmitted to the state treasurer, who shall credit the fees to the highway users tax fund.

(IV) One dollar of each additional fee collected from purchasers of special license plates issued pursuant to subsections (4) and (5) of this section shall be retained by the authorized agent, and one dollar and fifteen cents of each such additional fee shall be credited to the special purpose account established under section 42-1-211.

(V) One dollar of each additional fee collected from purchasers of special license plates issued pursuant to subsection (8) of this section shall be retained by the authorized agent.

(c) All applications for the special license plates described in this section shall be made directly to the department and shall include such information as the department may require.

(d) The executive director of the department may prepare such special forms and issue such rules as may be necessary to carry out the provisions of this section.

(e) Notwithstanding the weight limitation imposed by paragraph (a) of this subsection (1), a natural person eligible for a military veteran special license plate issued pursuant to this section may apply for such a license plate for a motor home, as defined in section 42-1-102 (57), upon the payment of the fees or taxes required by this article.

(f) A person who meets the conditions stated in subparagraph (XIV) of paragraph (a) of this subsection (1) is authorized to be issued a fallen service member special license plate. Except as provided by sub-subparagraph (G) of subparagraph (II) of paragraph (b) of this subsection (1), this paragraph (f) shall not be construed to authorize the spouse, child, sibling, grandparent, or parent to receive a license plate without paying the applicable fees or if such plate signifies more than that the deceased served in a branch of the armed forces.

(g) The department shall issue a special license plate authorized pursuant to this section for a motor vehicle owned by a trust if:

(I) The trust is created for the benefit of a natural person who is qualified to receive the special license plate under paragraph (a) of this subsection (1); and

(II) The trust name includes a natural person who is qualified to receive the special license plate under paragraph (a) of this subsection (1).

(2) **Recipient of a purple heart.** (a) The purple heart special license plate shall be designed to indicate that an owner of a motor vehicle to which such license plate is attached is a recipient of the purple heart.

(b) A natural person who has been awarded a purple heart for wounds received in combat at the hands of an enemy of the United States may use a purple heart special license plate. When applying for such a license plate, the applicant shall submit to the department a letter of verification from the appropriate branch of the armed forces of the United States that the applicant has been awarded a purple heart.

(3) **Former prisoner of war.** (a) The former prisoner of war special license plate shall be designed to indicate that an owner of a motor vehicle to which such license plate is attached is a former prisoner of war.

(b) A natural person who, while serving in the armed forces of the United States, was incarcerated by an enemy of the United States during a period of conflict with the United States may use the former prisoner of war special license plate.

(c) If a deceased former prisoner of war was authorized under this section to use a former prisoner of war special license plate, the surviving spouse of such former prisoner of war may apply to the department to retain any set or sets of such special plates that such former prisoner of war had obtained. Such surviving spouse shall be eligible to use such special plates upon the payment of any fees or taxes required by this article.

(4) **Honorably discharged or retired veteran of the U.S. armed forces.** (a) The veteran of the United States armed forces special license plate shall indicate that an owner of a motor vehicle to which such plate is attached is a veteran of the armed forces of the United States.

(b) A natural person who has received an honorable discharge or is retired from a branch of the armed services of the United States may use a veteran of the United States armed forces special license plate. When applying for such a license plate, an applicant shall submit as proof of honorable discharge either a department of defense form 214 or an honorable discharge from an armed forces branch of the United States.

(5) **Disabled veterans.** (a) (I) The disabled veteran special license plate shall indicate that the owner of the motor vehicle to which such license plate is attached is a disabled veteran of the United States armed forces.

(II) In addition to the requirements of subparagraph (I) of this paragraph (a), if the applicant demonstrates that he or she has a physical impairment affecting mobility under the standards provided in section 42-3-204 (1), then such special license plate shall have an additional identifying figure, as determined by the department, to indicate that the owner of the vehicle is authorized to make use of parking privileges for persons with disabilities.

(b) A natural person who has received an honorable discharge from a branch of the armed services of the United States and meets the requirements of section 42-3-304 (3) (a) may use a disabled veteran special license plate. When applying for such a license plate, the applicant shall submit proof of honorable discharge from an armed forces branch of the United States.

(c) License plates qualifying for the exemption granted in sub-subparagraph (B) of subparagraph (II) of paragraph (b) of subsection (1) of this section shall be issued only by the department and shall bear the inscription "D.V.", and a separate number series shall be used for such license plates. Additional license plates bearing such inscription may be issued by the department to eligible persons upon the payment of any fees or taxes required by this article.

(6) **Survivors of the attack on Pearl Harbor.** (a) The survivors of the attack on Pearl Harbor special license plates shall be designed to indicate that the owner of the motor vehicle to which such license plates are attached is a survivor of the attack on Pearl Harbor.

(b) Any natural person may use a survivors of the attack on Pearl Harbor special license plate if such person:

(I) Was a member of the United States armed forces on December 7, 1941;

(II) Was on station on December 7, 1941, during the hours of 7:55 a.m. to 9:45 a.m. Hawaii time at Pearl Harbor, the island of Oahu, or offshore at a distance not to exceed three miles therefrom;

(III) Received an honorable discharge from the United States armed forces; and

(IV) Holds a current membership in a national organization of survivors of the attack on Pearl Harbor.

(7) **Recipient of a medal of honor.** (a) The department shall design the medal of honor special license plate to indicate that an owner of a motor vehicle to which such license plate is attached is a recipient of the medal of honor.

(b) A natural person who has been awarded a medal of honor may use a medal of honor special license plate. When applying for such a license plate, the applicant shall submit to the department a letter of verification from the appropriate branch of the armed forces of the United States that the applicant has been awarded a medal of honor.

(8) **Honorably discharged, retired veteran, or active member of the U.S. Marine Corps.** (a) The United States Marine Corps special license plate shall indicate that an owner of a motor vehicle to which such plate is attached is a veteran, reserve member, or an active member of the United States Marine Corps.

(b) A natural person who has received an honorable discharge, is retired, or is an active or reserve member of the United States Marine Corps may use a United States Marine Corps special license plate. When applying for such a license plate, an applicant shall submit proof of an honorable discharge or proof that the applicant is currently an active or reserve member of the United States Marine Corps.

(9) **Veteran of the Korean war.** (a) The veteran of the Korean war special license plate shall be designed to indicate that the owner of the motor vehicle to which such license plate is attached is a veteran of the Korean war.

(b) A natural person may use a veteran of the Korean war special license plate if such person was a member of the United States armed forces between June 27, 1950, and January 31, 1955.

(10) **Recipient of a military valor award.** (a) The military valor special license plate shall be designed to indicate that an owner of a motor vehicle bearing such license plate has received a military award for valor.

(b) A natural person who has been awarded a military award for valor may use a military valor special license plate. When applying for such a license plate, the applicant shall submit to the department a copy of the military order awarding the military award for valor.

(c) For the purposes of this section,"military award for valor" or "military valor award" means the following awards:

(I) Navy cross;

(II) Distinguished service cross;

(III) Air Force cross; or

(IV) Silver star.

(11) **Veteran of the Vietnam war.** (a) The veteran of the Vietnam war special license plate shall be designed to indicate that the owner of the motor vehicle to which such license plate is attached is a veteran of the Vietnam war.

(b) A natural person may use a veteran of the Vietnam war special license plate if such person was a member of the United States armed services between August 7, 1964, and January 27, 1973.

(c) The department or an authorized agent shall not issue a veteran of the Vietnam war special license plate to an applicant until the applicant provides a DD214 form issued by the United States government or other evidence sufficient to demonstrate that the applicant is a veteran of the armed services who served between August 7, 1964, and January 27, 1973.

(12) **Honorably discharged, retired veteran, reserve, or active member of the United States Army.** (a) The United States Army special license plate shall be designed to indicate that the owner of the motor vehicle to which such license plate is attached is an honorably discharged, retired, reserve, or active member of the United States Army.

(b) A natural person may use a United States Army special license plate if such person is an honorably discharged, retired, reserve, or active member of the United States Army.

(c) The department or an authorized agent shall not issue an United States Army special license plate to an applicant until the applicant provides a DD214 form issued by the United

States government or other evidence sufficient to demonstrate that the applicant is an honorably discharged, retired, reserve, or active member of the United States Army.

(d) Repealed.

(13) **Honorably discharged, retired veteran, or active member of the United States Navy.** (a) The United States Navy special license plate shall indicate that an owner of a motor vehicle to which such plate is attached is a veteran, a reserve member, or an active member of the United States Navy.

(b) A natural person who has received an honorable discharge, is retired, or is an active or reserve member of the United States Navy shall be authorized to use a United States Navy special license plate. When applying for such a license plate, an applicant shall submit a DD214 form issued by the United States government or other evidence sufficient to demonstrate that the applicant has an honorable discharge or proof that the applicant is currently an active or reserve member of the United States Navy.

(c) This subsection (13) shall take effect July 1, 2006.

(14) **Recipient of a bronze star medal.** (a) The bronze star special license plate shall be designed to indicate that an owner of a motor vehicle bearing such license plate has received a bronze star medal. The bronze star for valor license plate shall be designed to indicate that an owner of a motor vehicle bearing such license plate has received the bronze star medal with the "V" for valor distinction.

(b) On or after January 1, 2007, a natural person who has been awarded a bronze star may use a bronze star special license plate. A natural person who has been awarded a bronze star with the "V" for valor distinction may use a bronze star for valor special license plate. When applying for such a license plate, the applicant shall submit to the department a copy of the military order awarding the bronze star and a DD214 form issued by the United States government showing that the award was received by the applicant.

(15) **Fallen service member special license plate.** (a) The fallen service member special license plate shall be designed to indicate that the owner of the motor vehicle to which the plate is attached is a family member of a person who died in the line of duty while serving in the armed forces and deployed to a combat zone. The plate shall bear the word "fallen" and the title of a person who serves in the branch of the armed forces in which the deceased served.

(b) A person who meets the conditions stated in subparagraph (XIV) of paragraph (a) of subsection (1) of this section may use a fallen service member special license plate. The department or an authorized agent shall not issue a fallen service member special license plate to an applicant until the applicant provides a DD214 form issued by the United States government and other evidence sufficient to demonstrate that the applicant is qualified to be issued the plate as determined by the department.

(16) **Honorably discharged, retired veteran, auxiliary, or active member of the United States Coast Guard.** (a) The United States Coast Guard special license plate shall indicate that an owner of a motor vehicle to which such plate is attached is a veteran, a reserve member, an auxiliary member, or an active member of the United States Coast Guard.

(b) On or after January 1, 2008, a natural person who has received an honorable discharge, is retired, or is an active, auxiliary, or reserve member of the United States Coast Guard shall be authorized to use a United States Coast Guard special license plate.

(c) When applying for such a license plate, an applicant shall submit a DD214 form issued by the United States government or other evidence sufficient to demonstrate that the applicant has an honorable discharge or proof that the applicant is currently an active, auxiliary, or reserve member of the United States Coast Guard.

(17) **Honorably discharged, retired veteran, or active member of the United States Air Force.** (a) Beginning January 1, 2008, the United States Air Force special license plate shall indicate that an owner of a motor vehicle to which such plate is attached is a veteran, reserve member, or active member of the United States Air Force.

(b) A natural person who has received an honorable discharge, is retired, or is an active or reserve member of any component of the United States Air Force shall be authorized to use a United States Air Force special license plate.

(c) When applying for such a license plate, an applicant shall submit a DD214 form issued by the United States government or other evidence sufficient to demonstrate that the applicant is a veteran, reserve member, or active member of any component of the United States Air Force.

(18) **Honorably discharged, retired veteran, or active member of the United States Army special forces.** (a) The United States Army special forces license plate shall indicate that an owner of a motor vehicle to which such plate is attached is a veteran, a reserve member, or an active member of the special forces of the United States Army.

(b) Beginning January 1, 2008, a natural person who has received an honorable discharge or is an active or reserve member of the United States Army special forces may use a United States Army special forces license plate. When applying for such a license plate, an applicant shall submit:

(I) Proof of an honorable discharge or retirement or proof that the applicant is currently an active or reserve member of the United States Army special forces;

(II) Orders or a DD214 form that shows an awarded prefix "3" or suffix "S" or a designation of "5G", 18/180 series MOS, special forces tab, OSS, or UNPIK-8240.

(19) **North American aerospace defense command commemorative special license plate.** (a) The North American aerospace defense command commemorative special license plate shall be designed to indicate that the owner of the motor vehicle to which the license plate is attached wishes to commemorate the North American aerospace defense command's fiftieth anniversary.

(b) The department shall issue North American aerospace defense command commemorative special license plates until January 1, 2010, or when the available inventory is depleted, whichever is later. This paragraph (b) shall not be deemed to prohibit the use of the plate after January 1, 2010, nor to require the plate to be recalled by the department.

(20) **Honorably discharged, retired veteran, reserve, or active member of the United States Army - fourth infantry division.** The United States Army fourth infantry division special license plate shall be designed to indicate that the owner of the motor vehicle to which such license plate is attached supports the United States Army fourth infantry division.

(21) **Veteran of the Afghanistan war.** (a) The veteran of the Afghanistan war special license plate shall be designed to indicate that the owner of the motor vehicle to which such license plate is attached is a veteran of the Afghanistan war.

(b) Effective January 1, 2011, a natural person may use a veteran of the Afghanistan war special license plate if such person was a member of the United States armed services between October 7, 2001, and the end of the conflict.

(c) The department or an authorized agent shall not issue a veteran of the Afghanistan war special license plate to an applicant until the applicant provides a DD214 form issued by the United States government or other evidence sufficient to demonstrate that the applicant is a veteran of the armed services who served between October 7, 2001, and the end of the conflict.

(22) **Veteran of the Iraq war.** (a) The veteran of the Iraq war special license plate shall be designed to indicate that the owner of the motor vehicle to which such license plate is attached is a veteran of the Iraq war.

(b) Effective January 1, 2011, a natural person may use a veteran of the Iraq war special license plate if such person was a member of the United States armed services between March 20, 2003, and the end of the conflict.

(c) The department or an authorized agent shall not issue a veteran of the Iraq war special license plate to an applicant until the applicant provides a DD214 form issued by the United States government or other evidence sufficient to demonstrate that the applicant is a veteran of the armed services who served between March 20, 2003, and the end of the conflict.

(23) **Veteran of world war II.** (a) The department shall design the veteran of world war II special license plate to indicate that the owner of the motor vehicle to which the license plate is attached is a veteran of world war II.

(b) Effective January 1, 2012, a natural person may use a world war II special license plate if the person was a member of the United States armed services between September 16, 1940, and July 25, 1947.

(c) The department or an authorized agent shall not issue a world war II special license plate to an applicant until the applicant provides a DD214 form issued by the United States government or other evidence sufficient to demonstrate that the applicant is a veteran of the armed services who served between September 16, 1940, and July 25, 1947.

42-3-214. Special plates - alumni associations - retirement. (1) The department shall issue one or more sets of special alumni license plates to applicants under this section for passenger cars or trucks that do not exceed sixteen thousand pounds empty weight. For the purposes of this section, recreational vehicles that do not exceed sixteen thousand pounds empty weight shall be classified as passenger cars.

(2) (a) An alumni association for a private or public college or university located within Colorado may apply directly to the department for the establishment of a special license plate for the alumni association. The department shall accept applications to establish special alumni license plates annually according to the schedule established by the department. An alumni association shall not apply for a license plate until the alumni association has commitments for license plate purchases from at least five hundred persons and provides a list of the names and addresses of such persons to the department.

(b) An alumni association applying for the establishment of a special alumni license plate is responsible for all costs of designing such plate and shall pay such costs before the license plate is produced. Any design for a special alumni license plate shall conform with standards established by the department and shall be approved by the department.

(c) For the purpose of this section, "college or university" means an institution of higher education that offers at least a bachelor degree in an educational program and that is accredited by a nationally recognized accrediting agency or association.

(3) (a) A person may apply for a special alumni license plate for a motor vehicle if the person pays the taxes and fees required under this section and provides the department or authorized agent a certificate issued by the alumni association confirming that such person meets the qualifications for the license plate established by the alumni association pursuant to paragraph (b) of this subsection (3). The department shall prepare a certificate form to be used by alumni

associations when confirming that a person is eligible to obtain special alumni license plates.

(b) An alumni association may establish the following qualifications to use the special alumni license plates:

(I) Membership in the alumni association; or

(II) Specified levels of contributions to the college or university.

(III) (Deleted by amendment, L. 2008, p. 1286, § 1, effective May 27, 2008.)

(c) An alumni association establishing qualifications to use special license plates shall set a one-time fee to qualify for the special license plates, which fee shall be used for the following purposes:

(I) Scholarships for students attending the university or college; or

(II) Support of academic programs at the university or college.

(4) The amount of the taxes and fees for special alumni license plates under this section is the same as the amount of the taxes and fees specified for regular motor vehicle license plates plus a one-time fee of twenty-five dollars for each motor vehicle to issue or replace such license plates. The department shall transmit the additional one-time fee to the state treasurer, who shall credit the fee to the highway users tax fund for allocation and expenditure as specified in section 43-4-205 (5.5) (b), C.R.S.

(5) An applicant may apply for personalized special alumni license plates. Upon payment of the additional fee required by section 42-3-211 (6) (a) for personalized license plates, the department may issue such plates if the applicant complies with section 42-3-211. If any applicant has existing personalized license plates for a motor vehicle, the applicant may transfer the combination of letters or numbers to a new set of special alumni license plates for the vehicle upon paying the fee imposed by section 42-3-211 (6) (a) and upon turning such existing plates in to the department as required by the department. A person who has obtained personalized special alumni license plates under this subsection (5) shall pay the annual fee imposed by section 42-3-211 (6) (b) for renewal of such personalized plates. The fees under this subsection (5) are in addition to all other taxes and fees imposed for the special alumni license plates.

(6) Special alumni license plates shall be renewed in the same manner as other license plates under section 42-3-113 or, for personalized plates, under section 42-3-211.

(7) The department shall retire the special alumni license plates authorized by this section unless the plates have been issued for at least five hundred vehicles by July 1, 2016. A person who was issued a special alumni license plate on or before July 1, 2016, may continue to use the plate after July 1, 2016.

42-3-215. Special plates - United States olympic committee - retirement. (1) The department shall issue one or more sets of olympic committee special license plates to applicants under this section for passenger cars or trucks that do not exceed sixteen thousand pounds empty weight.

(2) (a) There is hereby established the United States olympic committee special license plate. The department may begin issuance of such license plate when the United States olympic committee has commitments for license plate purchases from at least five hundred persons and provides a list of the names and addresses of such persons to the department.

(b) The United States olympic committee is responsible for the costs of designing the United States olympic committee special license plate and shall pay such costs before the license plate is produced. The design for the special license plate shall conform with standards established by the department and shall be approved by the department.

(3) (a) A person may apply for an olympic committee special license plate for a motor vehicle if the person pays the taxes and fees required under this section and provides the department or authorized agent a certificate issued by the committee confirming that such person meets the qualifications for the license plate established by the committee pursuant to paragraph (b) of this subsection (3). The department shall prepare a certificate form to be used by the committee when confirming that a person is eligible to obtain olympic committee special license plates.

(b) The committee may establish the following qualifications for persons seeking to obtain special license plates under this section:

(I) Specified levels of contributions to the United States olympic committee; or

(II) Payment of specified dues, including special dues established for the special license plates. If the olympic committee collects special dues for special license plates, the moneys may be expended only for support of the United States olympic committee program.

(4) (a) The amount of the taxes and fees for olympic committee special license plates under this section is the same as the amount of the taxes and fees specified for regular motor vehicle license plates plus a one-time fee of twenty-five dollars for each motor vehicle for issuance or replacement of such license plates. The department shall transmit the additional one-time fee to the state treasurer, who shall credit the fee to the highway users tax fund for allocation and expenditure as specified in section 43-4-205 (5.5) (b), C.R.S.

(b) An applicant may apply for personalized olympic committee special license plates. Upon payment of the additional fee required by section 42-3-211 (6) (a) for personalized license plates, the department may issue such plates if the applicant complies with section 42-3-211. If an applicant has existing personalized license plates for a motor vehicle, the applicant may transfer the combination of letters or numbers to a new set of special license plates for the vehicle upon paying the fee imposed by section 42-3-211 (6) (a) and upon turning such existing plates in to the department as required by the department. A person who has obtained personalized olympic committee special license plates under this paragraph (b) is required to pay the annual fee imposed by section 42-3-211 (6) (b) for renewal of such personalized plates. The fees under this paragraph (b) are in addition to all other taxes and fees imposed for the special license plates.

(5) Special license plates issued under this section shall be renewed in the same manner as other license plates under section 42-3-113 or, for personalized plates, under section 42-3-211.

(6) For the purposes of this section, "committee" means the United States olympic committee.

(7) The special license plates authorized by this section shall be retired unless such plates have been issued for at least three thousand vehicles by July 1, 2007.

42-3-216. Special plates - Colorado foundation for agriculture and natural resources - definitions - retirement. (1) For the purposes of this section:

(a) "Foundation" means the Colorado foundation for agriculture.

(b) "Special license plate" means the special agriculture and natural resources license plate.

(2) The department shall issue one or more sets of special license plates to applicants under this section for passenger cars or trucks that do not exceed sixteen thousand pounds empty weight.

(3) (a) There is hereby established the special agriculture and natural resources license plate. The department may begin issuance of such special license plate when the foundation has commitments for special license plate purchases for at least two hundred fifty special license plates and provides a list of the names and addresses of persons purchasing such plates to the department.

(b) The foundation is responsible for the costs of designing the special license plate and shall pay such costs before the license plate is produced. The design for the special license plate shall conform with standards established by the department and shall be approved by the department.

(4) (a) A person may apply for a special license plate for a motor vehicle if the person pays the taxes and fees required under this section and provides a certificate, issued by the foundation, confirming that such person meets the qualifications for the license plate established by the foundation pursuant to paragraph (b) of this subsection (4). The department shall prepare a certificate form to be used by the foundation when confirming that a person is eligible to obtain a special license plate.

(b) The foundation may establish the following qualifications for persons seeking to obtain special license plates under this section:

(I) Specified levels of contributions to the foundation; or

(II) Payment of specified special dues established for the special license plates. If the foundation collects special dues for special license plates, the moneys shall be expended only for support of the foundation's programs.

(5) (a) The amount of the taxes and fees for special license plates under this section is the same as the amount of the taxes and fees specified for regular motor vehicle license plates plus a one-time fee of twenty-five dollars for each motor vehicle for issuing or replacing such license plates. The department shall transmit the additional one-time fee to the state treasurer, who shall credit the same to the highway users tax fund for allocation and expenditure as specified in section 43-4-205 (5.5) (b), C.R.S.

(b) An applicant may apply for personalized special license plates. Upon payment of the additional fee required by section 42-3-211 (6) (a) for personalized license plates, the department may issue such plates if the applicant complies with section 42-3-211. If any applicant has existing personalized license plates for a motor vehicle, the applicant may transfer the combination of letters or numbers to a new set of special license plates for the vehicle upon paying the fee imposed by section 42-3-211 (6) (a) and upon turning such existing plates in to the department as required by the department. Any person who has obtained personalized special license plates under this paragraph (b) is required to pay the annual fee imposed by section 42-3-211 (6) (b) for renewal of such personalized plates. The fees under this paragraph (b) are in addition to all other taxes and fees imposed for the special license plates.

(6) Special license plates issued under this section shall be renewed in the same manner as other license plates under section 42-3-113 or, for personalized plates, under section 42-3-211.

(7) The special license plates authorized by this section shall be retired unless such plates have been issued for at least three thousand vehicles by March 1, 2008.

42-3-217. Special plates - Colorado commission of Indian affairs. (1) The department shall issue one or more sets of special license plates to applicants under this section for passenger cars, motorcycles, or trucks that do not exceed sixteen thousand pounds empty weight. The American Indian special license plate shall not be issued for motorcycles until January 1, 2007.

(2) (a) There is hereby established the American Indian special license plate. The department may begin issuance of such special license plate when the Rocky Mountain Indian chamber of commerce has commitments for special license plate purchases for at least two thousand special license plates and provides a list of the names and addresses of persons purchasing such plates to the department.

(b) The Rocky Mountain Indian chamber of commerce is responsible for the costs of designing the special license plate and shall pay such costs before the license plate is produced. The design for the special license plate shall conform with standards established by the department.

(3) (a) A person may apply for an American Indian special license plate for a motor vehicle if the person pays the taxes and fees required under this section and provides a certificate issued by the Rocky Mountain Indian chamber of commerce confirming that such person meets the qualifications for the license plate established pursuant to this subsection (3).

(b) The Colorado commission of Indian affairs shall establish a specific level of contribution to a scholarship fund that qualifies a person to obtain special license plates under this section and shall set appropriate qualifications in order for an applicant to receive a scholarship. The scholarship fund shall be administered by a nonprofit organization, association, or corporation selected and supervised by the Colorado commission of Indian affairs. Such scholarship shall not be awarded to an applicant unless the applicant can demonstrate that he or she is a Colorado resident and such scholarship will be used to attend an institution of higher education within Colorado. Such nonprofit organization shall issue a report to the Colorado commission of Indian affairs accounting for revenues and expenditures at least every other year.

(4) The amount of the taxes and fees for special license plates under this section is the same as the amount of the taxes and fees specified for regular motor vehicle license plates plus a one-time fee of twenty-five dollars for each motor vehicle for issuing or replacing such license plates. The department shall transmit the additional one-time fee to the state treasurer, who shall credit the same to the highway users tax fund, created in section 43-4-201, C.R.S., for allocation and expenditure as specified in section 43-4-205 (5.5) (b), C.R.S.

(5) On or after January 1, 2007, an applicant may apply for personalized American Indian special license plates. If the applicant complies with section 42-3-211, the department may issue such plates upon payment of the additional fee required by section 42-3-211 (6) for personalized license plates. If the applicant has existing personalized license plates for a motor vehicle, the applicant may transfer the combination of letters or numbers to a new set of American Indian special license plates for the vehicle upon paying the fee imposed by section 42-3-211 (6) (a) and upon turning such existing plates in to the department as required by the department. A person who has obtained personalized license plates under this subsection (5) shall pay the annual fee imposed by section 42-3-211 (6) (b) to renew such plates. The fees imposed by this subsection (5) shall be in addition to all other taxes and fees imposed for license plates issued pursuant to this section.

(6) Special license plates issued under this section shall be renewed in the same manner as other license plates under section 42-3-113 or, for personalized plates, under section 42-3-211.

42-3-217.5. Special plates - breast cancer awareness - retirement. (1) There is hereby established the breast cancer awareness special license plate. The department shall issue breast cancer special license plates to applicants for passenger cars, trucks, or motorcycles that do not exceed sixteen thousand pounds empty weight.

(2) The department shall work with interested parties to design the breast cancer awareness special license plate. The design for the special license plate shall conform with standards established by the department.

(3) (a) A person may apply for a breast cancer awareness special license plate if the person pays the taxes and fees required under this section.

(b) The amount of the taxes and fees for special license plates issued under this section is the same as the amount of the taxes and fees specified for regular motor vehicle license plates; except that the department shall collect a one-time fee of twenty-five dollars for issuing or replacing each such special license plate. The department shall transmit the additional one-time fee to the state treasurer, who shall credit the same to the highway users tax fund for allocation and expenditure as specified in section 43-4-201, C.R.S.

(c) In addition to the taxes and fees specified in paragraph (b) of this subsection (3), a person applying for a new or replacement breast cancer awareness special license plate shall pay a surcharge of twenty-five dollars. A person applying on or before June 30, 2012, to renew a breast cancer awareness special license plate shall have the option to pay the twenty-five dollar surcharge but shall not be required to pay the surcharge in order to renew the special plate. On or after July 1, 2012, a person applying to renew a breast cancer awareness special license plate shall pay the twenty-five dollar surcharge required by this paragraph (c). The department shall transmit the surcharge to the state treasurer, who shall credit the surcharge to the eligibility expansion account of the breast and cervical cancer prevention and treatment fund created in section 25.5-5-308 (8) (c), C.R.S., for use in accordance with that section; except that once the eligibility expansion account is dissolved pursuant to section 25.5-5-308 (8) (c) (III), C.R.S., the state treasurer shall credit the surcharge to the breast and cervical cancer prevention and treatment fund created in section 25.5-5-308 (8) (a), C.R.S. The department shall ensure implementation of this paragraph (c) no later than October 31, 2009.

(4) Any renewal of a special license plate issued under this section shall be handled in the same manner as other license plates under the provisions of section 42-3-113 or, for personal-

ized plates, under the provisions of section 42-3-211.

(5) An applicant may apply for personalized breast cancer awareness special plates. If the applicant complies with the requirements of section 42-3-211, the department may issue such plates upon payment of the additional fee required by section 42-3-211 (6) for personalized license plates. If the applicant has existing personalized license plates for a motor vehicle, the applicant may transfer the combination of letters or numbers to a new set of breast cancer awareness special license plates for the vehicle upon paying the fee imposed by section 42-3-211 (6) and upon turning in such existing plates to the department. A person who has obtained personalized license plates under this subsection (5) shall pay the annual fee imposed by section 42-3-211 (6) to renew such plates. The fees imposed by this subsection (5) shall be in addition to all other taxes and fees imposed for breast cancer awareness special license plates.

(6) and (7) Repealed.

42-3-218. Special plates - active and retired members of the Colorado National Guard - retirement. (1) The department shall issue special license plates for a passenger car or a truck that does not exceed sixteen thousand pounds empty weight owned by an active or retired member of the Colorado National Guard, as defined in section 28-3-101 (12), C.R.S.

(2) The special license plates shall have a white background with blue lettering and shall be of a design determined by the executive director of the department. Such plates shall indicate that the owner of the motor vehicle is a member of the Colorado National Guard.

(3) A natural person who is an active or retired member of the Colorado National Guard may use the special license plates provided for by this section.

(4) The amount of taxes and fees for such special license plates shall be the same as the amount of taxes and fees specified for regular motor vehicle registration plus an additional one-time fee of twenty-five dollars. The additional fee shall be transmitted to the state treasurer, who shall credit the fee to the highway users tax fund for allocation and expenditure as specified in section 43-4-205 (5.5) (b), C.R.S.

(5) Applications for special license plates provided for in this section shall include such information as the department may require. At the time of application, the applicant shall submit a proof of eligibility form prepared by the department of military and veterans affairs verifying active or retired status. If the owner of a vehicle registered pursuant to this section ceases to be an active member of the Colorado National Guard and has not qualified for retirement from the Colorado National Guard, such person shall return the special license plates to the department upon expiration of the registration. Upon retiring from the Colorado National Guard, a person wishing to retain such special license plates shall submit a verification of retired status that is issued by the department of military and veterans affairs to establish eligibility for retention of the plates. A retired member of the Colorado National Guard is required to verify retired status only once under this section.

(6) The executive director of the department may prepare any special forms and issue such rules as may be necessary to implement this section.

42-3-219. Special registration of collector's items. (Repealed)

42-3-220. Temporary special event license plates. (1) The department may issue a temporary special event license plate to a person or group of people in connection with a special event for a passenger vehicle or a truck that does not exceed sixteen thousand pounds empty weight.

(2) An applicant for a special event license plate shall submit to the department the name, date or dates, and location of the special event to which the request for the license plate is connected; the dates the license plate is needed; the quantity of license plates requested; a list of vehicle information including the vehicle identification number, make, model, and year of each vehicle; a certified letter stating that insurance coverage will be in place for each vehicle during its use for the period for which the temporary plate is issued; and any other information required by the department.

(3) The department may determine the amount of an application fee for special event license plates and determine the fee, not to exceed twenty-five dollars, for the issuance of each temporary special event license plate. Such fee shall be transmitted to the state treasurer, who shall credit the same to the license plate cash fund, created in section 42-3-301 (1).

(4) The executive director of the department may prepare any special forms and issue any rules necessary to carry out the purposes of this section.

42-3-221. Special plates - Denver Broncos. (1) Beginning January 1, 2007, the department shall issue special license plates to qualified applicants in accordance with this section for motorcycles, passenger cars, trucks, or noncommercial or recreational motor vehicles that do not exceed sixteen thousand pounds empty weight.

(2) (a) There is hereby established the Denver Broncos special license plate.

(b) The Denver Broncos may design the special license plate. The design for the special license plate shall conform with standards established by the department and shall be subject to the department's approval.

(3) A person may apply for a Denver Broncos special license plate if the person pays the taxes and fees required under this section and provides to the department or an authorized agent a certificate, issued by the Denver Broncos Charities or a successor organization, confirming that such person has donated thirty dollars to the Denver Broncos Charities.

(4) The amount of the taxes and fees for special license plates under this section is the same as the amount of the taxes and fees specified for regular motor vehicle license plates; except that the department shall collect a one-time fee of twenty-five dollars for issuance or replacement of each such license plate. The department shall transmit the additional one-time fee to the state treasurer, who shall credit the same to the highway users tax fund created in section 43-4-201, C.R.S.

(5) An applicant may apply for personalized Denver Broncos special license plates. Upon payment of the additional fee required by section 42-3-211 (6) (a) for personalized license plates, the department may issue such plates if the applicant complies with section 42-3-211. If an applicant has existing personalized license plates for a motor vehicle, the applicant may transfer the combination of letters or numbers to a new set of Denver Broncos special license plates for the vehicle upon payment of the fee imposed by section 42-3-211 (6) and upon turning in such existing plates to the department. A person who has obtained personalized Denver Broncos special license plates under this subsection (5) shall pay the annual fee imposed by section 42-3-211 (6) (b) for renewal of such personalized plates. The fees under this subsection (5) are in addition to all other taxes and fees imposed for personalized Denver Broncos special license plates.

(6) The Denver Broncos license plate shall be retired if three thousand plates are not issued by July 1, 2009.

42-3-222. Special plates - support public education. (1) Beginning January 1, 2007, the department shall issue special license plates to qualified applicants in accordance with this section for motorcycles, passenger cars, trucks, and noncommercial or recreational motor vehicles that do not exceed sixteen thousand pounds empty weight.

(2) (a) There is hereby established the support public education special license plate.

(b) The design for the special license plate shall conform with standards established by the department and shall be subject to the department's approval.

(3) (a) A person may apply for a support public education special license plate if the person pays the taxes and fees required under this section and provides to the department or an authorized agent a certificate, issued by impact on education, inc., Colorado legacy foundation, or either entity's successor, confirming that the person has donated twenty dollars to either organization or either entity's successor. When receiving the donation, impact on education, inc., Colorado legacy foundation, or either entity's successor shall ask the donor to specify in writing which nonprofit education organization qualified under paragraph (c) of this subsection (3) should receive the moneys. Impact on education, inc., Colorado legacy foundation, or either entity's successor shall compile and provide to the donor and the department a list of organizations that the entity has verified qualify for donations under paragraph (c) of this subsection (3).

(b) Impact on education, inc., Colorado legacy foundation, or either entity's successor shall use the moneys collected under this subsection (3) to support programs that focus on student learning in public schools located in Colorado.

(c) Impact on education, inc., Colorado legacy foundation, or either entity's successor shall transmit the entire donation to the nonprofit education organization pursuant to paragraph (a) of this subsection (3) if the organization:

(I) Exists;

(II) Is affiliated with a school district or the state charter institute;

(III) Is a nonprofit entity exempt from federal income taxes pursuant to section 501 (c) (3) of the federal "Internal Revenue Code of 1986", as amended; and

(IV) Agrees to spend all of the donation on programs that focus on student learning in Colorado.

(d) Impact on education, inc., Colorado legacy foundation, or either entity's successor shall not use the moneys collected under this subsection (3) to support political parties, candidates for public office, ballot initiatives, referenda, or any other political activities.

(4) The amount of the taxes and fees for the support public education special license plates under this section is the same as the amount of the taxes and fees specified for regular motor vehicle license plates; except that the department shall collect a one-time fee of twenty-five dollars for issuance or replacement of each such license plate. The department shall transmit the additional one-time fee to the state treasurer, who shall credit the same to the highway users tax fund created in section 43-4-201, C.R.S.

(5) An applicant may apply for personalized support public education special license plates. Upon payment of the additional fee required by section 42-3-211 (6) (a) for personalized license plates, the department may issue such plates if the applicant complies with section 42-3-211. If an applicant has existing personalized license plates for a motor vehicle, the applicant may transfer the combination of letters or numbers to a new set of support public education special license plates for the vehicle upon payment of the fee imposed by section 42-3-211 (6) and upon turning in such existing plates to the department. A person who has obtained personalized support public education special license plates under this

subsection (5) shall pay the annual fee imposed by section 42-3-211 (6) for renewal of such personalized plates. The fees under this subsection (5) are in addition to all other taxes and fees imposed for personalized support public education special license plates.

(6) The department may stop issuing the support public education special license plate if three thousand license plates are not issued by July 1, 2016. A person who was issued a support public education special license plate on or before July 1, 2016, may continue to use the plate after July 1, 2016.

42-3-223. Special plates - support the troops - retirement. (1) On or after July 1, 2007, the department shall issue one or more sets of support the troops special license plates to applicants under this section for passenger cars, trucks, motorcycles, and noncommercial or recreational motor vehicles that do not exceed sixteen thousand pounds empty weight.

(2) There is hereby established the United States support the troops special license plate. The plate shall be the design that was submitted to the department during the proposal and certification process under section 42-3-207 (2); except that the plate shall conform with standards established by the department, and the plate shall feature the statement "Support The Troops".

(3) (a) A person may apply for and shall be issued a support the troops special license plate for a motor vehicle if the person pays the taxes and fees required under this subsection (3) and provides a certificate issued by the nonprofit organization selected by the adjutant general pursuant to subsection (4) of this section showing that the person has donated twenty-five dollars to such organization.

(b) The amount of the taxes and fees for support the troops special license plates under this section is the same as the amount of the taxes and fees specified for regular motor vehicle license plates plus a one-time fee of twenty-five dollars for each motor vehicle for issuance of such license plates. The department shall transmit the additional one-time fee to the highway users tax fund for allocation and expenditure as specified in section 43-4-205 (5.5) (b), C.R.S.

(c) Upon payment of the additional fee required by section 42-3-211 (6) (a) for personalized license plates, the department may issue personalized support the troops special license plates if the applicant complies with section 42-3-211. If an applicant has existing personalized license plates for a motor vehicle, the applicant may transfer the combination of letters or numbers to a new set of special license plates for the vehicle upon paying the fee imposed by section 42-3-211 (6) (a) and upon turning such existing plates in to the department as required by the department. A person who has obtained personalized support the troops special license plates under this paragraph (c) is required to pay the annual fee imposed by section 42-3-211 (6) (b) for renewal of such personalized plates. The fees under this paragraph (c) are in addition to all other taxes and fees imposed for the special license plates.

(4) The adjutant general, appointed pursuant to section 28-3-105, C.R.S., shall select a nonprofit organization that aids veterans, active service members, and the families thereof to administer the donations collected pursuant to subsection (3) of this section. The adjutant general shall select the organization in consultation with the Colorado board of veterans affairs, created in section 28-5-702, C.R.S. The organization shall use the moneys to aid veterans, active service members, and the families thereof but may keep up to seven percent of the moneys for administrative costs. The organization may use the moneys to aid veterans, active service members, and the families thereof by making grants to or selecting other nonprofit organizations to provide the aid so long as no more than seven percent of the moneys are used for administrative costs. Once an organization is selected, it shall continue to administer the funds unless good cause is shown for removal.

(5) Special license plates issued under this section shall be renewed in the same manner as other license plates under section 42-3-113 or, for personalized plates, under section 42-3-211.

(6) The special license plates authorized by this section shall not be renewed unless such plates have been issued for at least three thousand vehicles by July 1, 2009.

42-3-224. Special plates - Colorado "Kids First". (1) The department shall issue special license plates to qualified applicants in accordance with this section for motorcycles, passenger cars, trucks, or noncommercial or recreational motor vehicles that do not exceed sixteen thousand pounds empty weight.

(2) (a) There is hereby established the Colorado "Kids First" special license plate. The department may stop issuing the Colorado "Kids First" special license plate if three thousand license plates are not issued by July 1, 2016. A person who was issued a Colorado "Kids First" special license plate on or before July 1, 2016, may continue to use the plate after July 1, 2016.

(b) (Deleted by amendment, L. 2009, (SB 09-175), ch. 226, p. 1027, § 3, effective July 1, 2009.)

(c) The Rocky Mountain research and prevention institute may design the special license plate. The design for the special license plate shall conform with standards established by the department and shall be subject to the department's approval.

(3) (a) A person may apply for a Colorado "Kids First" special license plate if the person pays the taxes and fees required under this section and provides to the department or an authorized agent a certificate, issued by the Rocky Mountain research and prevention institute or a

successor organization, confirming that such person meets the qualifications for the license plate established pursuant to this section.

(b) The Rocky Mountain research and prevention institute or a successor organization may establish a specific level of contribution to a health promotion and injury prevention fund that qualifies a person to obtain special license plates under this section. Such fund shall be used to fund programs, activities, and events that help promote the health of children and prevent injury to children.

(c) The Rocky Mountain research and prevention institute or its successor organization shall file an annual statement verifying that it is a nonprofit organization. The statement shall be filed under penalty of perjury with the department.

(4) The amount of the taxes and fees for special license plates under this section is the same as the amount of the taxes and fees specified for regular motor vehicle license plates; except that the department shall collect a one-time fee of twenty-five dollars for issuance or replacement of each such license plate. The department shall transmit the additional one-time fee to the state treasurer, who shall credit the same to the highway users tax fund created in section 43-4-201, C.R.S.

(5) An applicant may apply for personalized Colorado "Kids First" license plates. Upon payment of the additional fee required by section 42-3-211 (6) (a) for personalized license plates, the department may issue such plates if the applicant complies with section 42-3-211. If an applicant has existing personalized license plates for a motor vehicle, the applicant may transfer the combination of letters or numbers to a new set of Colorado "Kids First" license plates for the vehicle upon paying the fee imposed by section 42-3-211 (6) and upon turning in such existing plates to the department. A person who has obtained personalized Colorado "Kids First" license plates under this subsection (5) shall pay the annual fee imposed by section 42-3-211 (6) (b) for renewal of such personalized plates. The fees under this subsection (5) are in addition to all other taxes and fees imposed for Colorado "Kids First" license plates.

42-3-225. Special plates - Italian-American heritage. (1) Beginning January 1, 2008, the department shall issue special license plates to qualified applicants in accordance with this section for motorcycles, passenger cars, trucks, or noncommercial or recreational motor vehicles that do not exceed sixteen thousand pounds empty weight.

(2) (a) There is hereby established the Italian-American heritage special license plate, which shall be issued to any person who pays the taxes and fees required under this section.

(b) The department may stop issuing the Italian-American heritage special license plate if at least three thousand plates are not issued by July 1, 2016. A person who was issued an Italian-American heritage special license plate on or before July 1, 2016, may continue to use the plate after July 1, 2016.

(c) The Italian-American heritage special license plate shall be designed:

(I) To celebrate Italian-American heritage; and

(II) In accordance with standards established by the department and be subject to the department's approval.

(3) The amount of the taxes and fees for special license plates under this section is the same as the amount of the taxes and fees specified for regular motor vehicle license plates; except that the department shall collect a one-time fee of twenty-five dollars for issuance or replacement of each such license plate. The department shall transmit the additional one-time fee to the state treasurer, who shall credit the same to the highway users tax fund created in section 43-4-201, C.R.S.

(4) An applicant may apply for personalized Italian-American heritage special license plates. Upon payment of the additional fee required by section 42-3-211 (6) (a) for personalized license plates, the department may issue such plates if the applicant complies with section 42-3-211. If an applicant has existing personalized license plates for a motor vehicle, the applicant may transfer the combination of letters or numbers to a new set of Colorado Italian-American heritage license plates for the vehicle upon paying the fee imposed by section 42-3-211 (6) and upon turning in such existing plates to the department. A person who has obtained personalized Italian-American heritage special license plates under this subsection (4) shall pay the annual fee imposed by section 42-3-211 (6) (b) for renewal of such personalized plates. The fees under this subsection (4) are in addition to all other taxes and fees imposed for the Italian-American heritage special license plates.

42-3-226. Special plates - share the road. (1) Beginning January 1, 2008, the department shall issue special license plates to qualified applicants in accordance with this section for motorcycles, passenger cars, trucks, or noncommercial or recreational motor vehicles that do not exceed sixteen thousand pounds empty weight.

(2) (a) There is hereby established the share the road special license plate. The department may stop issuing the share the road special license plate if three thousand license plates are not issued by July 1, 2011. A person may continue to use the share the road special license plate after July 1, 2011.

(b) (Deleted by amendment, L. 2009, (SB 09-175), ch. 226, p. 1028, § 5, effective July 1, 2009.)

(c) The design for the special license plate shall conform with standards established by the department and shall be subject to approval by bicycle Colorado, inc.

(3) (a) A person may apply for a share the road special license plate if the person pays the taxes and fees required under this section and provides to the department or an authorized agent a certificate, issued by bicycle Colorado, inc., or a successor organization, confirming that such person meets the qualifications for the license plate established pursuant to this section.

(b) Bicycle Colorado, inc., or a successor organization, may establish a specific level of contribution to a share the road education fund that qualifies a person to obtain special license plates under this section. Such fund shall be used to fund programs, activities, and events that educate bicyclists, motorists, law enforcement, and transportation officials on the rights and responsibilities of bicycling, safely sharing the road, and reducing bicycle crashes.

(c) Bicycle Colorado, inc., or its successor organization, shall file with the department an annual statement verifying that it is a nonprofit organization.

(4) The amount of the taxes and fees for special license plates under this section is the same as the amount of the taxes and fees specified for regular motor vehicle license plates; except that the department shall collect a one-time fee of twenty-five dollars for issuance or replacement of each such license plate. The department shall transmit the additional one-time fee to the state treasurer, who shall credit the same to the highway users tax fund created in section 43-4-201, C.R.S.

(5) An applicant may apply for personalized share the road license plates. Upon payment of the additional fee required by section 42-3-211 (6) (a) for personalized license plates, the department may issue such plates if the applicant complies with section 42-3-211. If an applicant has existing personalized license plates for a motor vehicle, the applicant may transfer the combination of letters or numbers to a new set of share the road license plates for the vehicle upon paying the fee imposed by section 42-3-211 (6) and upon turning in such existing plates to the department. A person who has obtained personalized share the road license plates under this subsection (5) shall pay the annual fee imposed by section 42-3-211 (6) (b) for renewal of such personalized plates. The fees under this subsection (5) are in addition to all other taxes and fees imposed for share the road license plates.

42-3-227. Special plates - Colorado horse development authority. (1) On or after January 1, 2009, the department shall issue Colorado horse development authority special license plates to qualified applicants in accordance with this section for motorcycles, passenger cars, trucks, or noncommercial or recreational motor vehicles that do not exceed sixteen thousand pounds empty weight.

(2) The Colorado horse development authority may design the special license plates. The design for the special license plates shall conform with standards established by the department and shall be subject to the department's approval.

(3) A person may apply for Colorado horse development authority special license plates if the person pays the taxes and fees required under this section and provides to the department or an authorized agent a certificate, issued by the Colorado horse development authority or a successor organization, confirming that the person has donated thirty dollars to the Colorado horse development authority.

(4) The amount of the taxes and fees for special license plates under this section is the same as the amount of the taxes and fees specified for regular motor vehicle license plates; except that the department shall collect a one-time fee of twenty-five dollars for issuance or replacement of each such license plate. The department shall transmit the one-time fee to the state treasurer, who shall credit the same to the highway users tax fund created in section 43-4-201, C.R.S.

(5) An applicant may apply for personalized Colorado horse development authority special license plates. Upon payment of the additional fee required by section 42-3-211 (6) (a) for personalized license plates, the department may issue such license plates if the applicant complies with section 42-3-211. If an applicant has existing personalized license plates for a motor vehicle, the applicant may transfer the combination of letters or numbers to a new set of Colorado horse development authority special license plates for the vehicle upon payment of the fee imposed by section 42-3-211 (6) and upon turning in such existing plates to the department. A person who has obtained personalized Colorado horse development authority special license plates under this subsection (5) shall pay the annual fee imposed by section 42-3-211 (6) (b) for renewal of the personalized license plates. The fees imposed under this subsection (5) are in addition to all other taxes and fees imposed for personalized Colorado horse development authority special license plates.

(6) The department may stop issuing the Colorado horse development authority special license plate if three thousand license plates are not issued by July 1, 2016. A person who was issued a Colorado horse development authority special license plate on or before July 1, 2016, may continue to use the plate after July 1, 2016.

42-3-228. Special plates - Colorado carbon fund. (1) The department shall issue Colorado carbon fund special license plates to qualified applicants in accordance with this section for motorcycles, passenger cars, trucks, or noncommercial or recreational motor vehicles that do not exceed sixteen thousand pounds empty weight.

(2) The Colorado carbon fund, established by the governor's energy office, may design the Colorado carbon fund special license plates. The design for the special license plates shall conform with standards established by the department

and shall be subject to the department's approval.

(3) A person may apply for the Colorado carbon fund special license plates if the person pays the taxes and fees required under this section and provides to the department or an authorized agent a certificate, issued by the governor's energy office, or a successor office, confirming that such person has made to the Colorado carbon fund, or its successor, the donation required to qualify for the special license plates.

(4) The amount of the taxes and fees for special license plates under this section is the same as the amount of the taxes and fees specified for regular motor vehicle license plates; except that the department shall collect a one-time fee of twenty-five dollars for issuance or replacement of each such license plate. The department shall transmit the additional one-time fee to the state treasurer, who shall credit the same to the highway users tax fund created in section 43-4-201, C.R.S.

(5) An applicant may apply for personalized Colorado carbon fund special license plates. Upon payment of the additional fee required by section 42-3-211 (6) (a) for personalized license plates, the department may issue such personalized license plates if the applicant complies with section 42-3-211. If an applicant has existing personalized license plates for a motor vehicle, the applicant may transfer the combination of letters or numbers to a new set of Colorado carbon fund special license plates for the vehicle upon payment of the fee imposed by section 42-3-211 (6) (a) and upon turning in the existing license plates to the department. A person who has obtained personalized Colorado carbon fund special license plates under this subsection (5) shall pay the annual fee imposed by section 42-3-211 (6) (b) for renewal of such personalized license plates. The fees under this subsection (5) are in addition to all other taxes and fees imposed for personalized Colorado carbon fund special license plates.

(6) The department may stop issuing the Colorado carbon fund special license plate if three thousand license plates are not issued by July 1, 2016. A person who was issued a Colorado carbon fund special license plate on or before July 1, 2016, may continue to use the plate after July 1, 2016.

42-3-229. Special plates - boy scouts. (1) Beginning July 15, 2009, the department shall issue special license plates to qualified applicants in accordance with this section for motorcycles, passenger cars, trucks, or noncommercial or recreational motor vehicles that do not exceed sixteen thousand pounds empty weight.

(2) (a) There is hereby established the boy scouts centennial special license plate, which shall be issued from July 15, 2009, to June 30, 2016, or so long as the department has the special license plates in stock, whichever occurs later.

(b) A person may continue to use the boy scouts centennial special license plate after June 30, 2011, in accordance with this section.

(c) The department is authorized to begin issuance of the special license plate authorized by this subsection (2) if the boy scouts obtain commitments for the purchase of at least three thousand special license plates and provide to the department a list of the names and addresses of persons requesting such plates by January 15, 2009.

(d) Repealed.

(e) The design for the special license plate shall conform with standards established by the department.

(3) A person may apply for a special license plate created by this section if the person pays the taxes and fees required under this section.

(4) The amount of the taxes and fees for special license plates under this section is the same as the amount of the taxes and fees specified for regular motor vehicle license plates; except that the department shall collect a one-time fee of twenty-five dollars for issuance or replacement of each such license plate. The department shall transmit the additional one-time fee to the state treasurer, who shall credit the same to the highway users tax fund created in section 43-4-201, C.R.S.

(5) An applicant may apply for personalized special license plates created by this section. Upon payment of the additional fee required by section 42-3-211 (6) (a) for personalized license plates, the department may issue such plates if the applicant complies with section 42-3-211. If an applicant has existing personalized license plates for a motor vehicle, the applicant may transfer the combination of letters or numbers to a new set of special license plates created by this section for the vehicle upon paying the fee imposed by section 42-3-211 (6) and upon turning in such existing plates to the department. A person who has obtained personalized special license plates under this subsection (5) shall pay the annual fee imposed by section 42-3-211 (6) (b) for renewal of such personalized plates. The fees under this subsection (5) are in addition to all other taxes and fees imposed for the special license plates created by this section.

42-3-230. Special plates - "Alive at Twenty-five". (1) Beginning January 1, 2010, the department shall issue special license plates to qualified applicants in accordance with this section for motorcycles, passenger cars, trucks, or noncommercial or recreational motor vehicles that do not exceed sixteen thousand pounds empty weight.

(2) (a) There is hereby established the "Alive at Twenty-five" special license plate.

(b) The Colorado state patrol family foundation may design the special license plate. The design for the special license plate shall conform with standards established by the department and shall be subject to the department's approval.

(3) A person may apply for an "Alive at Twenty-five" special license plate if the person pays the taxes and fees required under this section and provides to the department or an authorized agent a certificate, issued by the Colorado state patrol family foundation or a successor organization, confirming that such person has donated thirty dollars to the Colorado state patrol family foundation.

(4) The amount of the taxes and fees for special license plates under this section is the same as the amount of the taxes and fees specified for regular motor vehicle license plates; except that the department shall collect a one-time fee of twenty-five dollars for issuance or replacement of each such license plate. The department shall transmit the additional one-time fee to the state treasurer, who shall credit the same to the highway users tax fund created in section 43-4-201, C.R.S.

(5) An applicant may apply for personalized "Alive at Twenty-five" special license plates. Upon payment of the additional fee required by section 42-3-211 (6) (a) for personalized license plates, the department may issue such plates if the applicant complies with section 42-3-211. If an applicant has existing personalized license plates for a motor vehicle, the applicant may transfer the combination of letters or numbers to a new set of "Alive at Twenty-five" special license plates for the vehicle upon payment of the fee imposed by section 42-3-211 (6) and upon turning in such existing plates to the department. A person who has obtained personalized "Alive at Twenty-five" special license plates under this subsection (5) shall pay the annual fee imposed by section 42-3-211 (6) (b) for renewal of such personalized plates. The fees under this subsection (5) are in addition to all other taxes and fees imposed for personalized "Alive at Twenty-five" special license plates.

(6) The department shall retire the "Alive at Twenty-five" license plate if three thousand plates are not issued by July 1, 2016. A person who was issued an "Alive at Twenty-five" license plate on or before July 1, 2016, may continue to use the plate after July 1, 2016.

42-3-231. Special plates - Colorado ski country. (1) On or after January 1, 2010, the department shall issue Colorado ski country special license plates to qualified applicants in accordance with this section for motorcycles, passenger cars, trucks, or noncommercial or recreational motor vehicles that do not exceed sixteen thousand pounds empty weight.

(2) Colorado ski country USA, inc., may design the special license plates. The design that was submitted to the department during the proposal and certification process under section 42-3-207 (2) shall be used for the special license plate; except that the plate shall conform with standards established by the department and be subject to approval by the department. The plate shall feature the tagline "Ski Country USA".

(3) A person shall be issued Colorado ski country special license plates if the person pays the taxes and fees required under this section.

(4) The amount of the taxes and fees for special license plates under this section is the same as the amount of the taxes and fees specified for regular motor vehicle license plates; except that the department shall collect a one-time fee of twenty-five dollars for issuance or replacement of each such license plate. The department shall transmit the one-time fee to the state treasurer, who shall credit the same to the highway users tax fund created in section 43-4-201, C.R.S.

(5) An applicant may apply for personalized Colorado ski country special license plates. Upon payment of the additional fee required by section 42-3-211 (6) (a) for personalized license plates, the department may issue such license plates if the applicant complies with section 42-3-211. If an applicant has existing personalized license plates for a motor vehicle, the applicant may transfer the combination of letters or numbers to a new set of Colorado ski country special license plates for the vehicle upon payment of the fee imposed by section 42-3-211 (6) and upon turning in such existing plates to the department. A person who has obtained personalized Colorado ski country special license plates under this subsection (5) shall pay the annual fee imposed by section 42-3-211 (6) (b) for renewal of the personalized license plates. The fees imposed under this subsection (5) are in addition to all other taxes and fees imposed for personalized Colorado ski country special license plates.

(6) (a) The department shall retire the Colorado ski country special license plate if three thousand license plates are not issued by July 1, 2016. A person who was issued a Colorado ski country special license plate on or before July 1, 2016, may continue to use the plate after July 1, 2016.

(b) (Deleted by amendment, L. 2011, (HB 11-1236), ch. 98, p. 288, § 10, effective April 8, 2011.)

42-3-232. Special plates - donate life. (1) On or after January 1, 2010, the department shall issue donate life special license plates to qualified applicants in accordance with this section for motorcycles, passenger cars, trucks, or noncommercial or recreational motor vehicles that do not exceed sixteen thousand pounds empty weight.

(2) The American transplant foundation, inc., may design the special license plates. The design for the special license plates shall conform with standards established by the department and shall be subject to the department's approval.

(3) A person shall be issued donate life special license plates if the person pays the taxes and fees required under this section.

(4) The amount of the taxes and fees for special license plates under this section is the same as the amount of the taxes and fees specified for regular motor vehicle license plates; except that the department shall collect a one-time fee of twenty-five dollars for issuance or replacement of each such license plate. The department shall transmit the one-time fee to the state treasurer, who shall credit the same to the highway users tax fund created in section 43-4-201, C.R.S.

(5) An applicant may apply for personalized donate life special license plates. Upon payment of the additional fee required by section 42-3-211 (6) (a) for personalized license plates, the department may issue such license plates if the applicant complies with section 42-3-211. If an applicant has existing personalized license plates for a motor vehicle, the applicant may transfer the combination of letters or numbers to a new set of donate life special license plates for the vehicle upon payment of the fee imposed by section 42-3-211 (6) and upon turning in the existing plates to the department. A person who has obtained personalized donate life special license plates under this subsection (5) shall pay the annual fee imposed by section 42-3-211 (6) (b) for renewal of personalized license plates. The fees imposed under this subsection (5) are in addition to all other taxes and fees imposed for personalized donate life special license plates.

(6) (a) The department shall retire the donate life special license plate if three thousand license plates are not issued by July 1, 2016. A person who was issued a donate life special license plate on or before July 1, 2016, may continue to use the plate after July 1, 2016.

(b) (Deleted by amendment, L. 2011, (HB 11-1236), ch. 98, p. 289, § 11, effective April 8, 2011.)

42-3-233. Special plates - Colorado state parks. (1) On or after January 1, 2011, the department shall issue Colorado state parks special license plates to qualified applicants in accordance with this section for motorcycles, passenger cars, trucks, or noncommercial or recreational motor vehicles that do not exceed sixteen thousand pounds empty weight.

(2) The foundation for Colorado state parks may design the special license plates. The design for the special license plates shall conform with standards established by the department and shall be subject to the department's approval.

(3) A person may apply for Colorado state parks special license plates if the person pays the taxes and fees required under this section and provides to the department or an authorized agent a certificate, issued by the foundation for Colorado state parks or a successor organization, confirming that the person has donated forty-four dollars to the foundation for Colorado state parks or a successor organization. All moneys collected pursuant to this subsection (3) and all interest and income earned on the investment of such moneys shall be expended on Colorado state parks projects and shall not be used for the administration of the foundation for Colorado state parks or a successor organization. The foundation for Colorado state parks or a successor organization shall hold the moneys collected pursuant to this subsection (3) in a separate account from all other moneys and retain the records of the expenditures of moneys collected pursuant to this subsection (3) for at least three years after the expenditure is made.

(4) The amount of the taxes and fees for special license plates under this section is the same as the amount of the taxes and fees specified for regular motor vehicle license plates; except that the department shall collect a one-time fee of twenty-five dollars for issuance or replacement of each such license plate. The department shall transmit the one-time fee to the state treasurer, who shall credit the same to the highway users tax fund created in section 43-4-201, C.R.S.

(5) An applicant may apply for personalized Colorado state parks special license plates. Upon payment of the additional fee required by section 42-3-211 (6) (a) for personalized license plates, the department may issue such license plates if the applicant complies with section 42-3-211. If an applicant has existing personalized license plates for a motor vehicle, the applicant may transfer the combination of letters or numbers to a new set of Colorado state parks special license plates for the vehicle upon payment of the fee imposed by section 42-3-211 (6) and upon turning in such existing plates to the department. A person who has obtained personalized Colorado state parks special license plates under this subsection (5) shall pay the annual fee imposed by section 42-3-211 (6) (b) for renewal of the personalized license plates. The fees imposed under this subsection (5) are in addition to all other taxes and fees imposed for personalized Colorado state parks special license plates.

(6) The department may stop issuing the Colorado state parks special license plate if three thousand license plates are not issued by July 1, 2016. A person who was issued a Colorado state parks special license plate on or before July 1, 2016, may continue to use the plate after July 1, 2016.

42-3-234. Special plates - adopt a shelter pet. (1) Beginning the earlier of January 1, 2011, or when the department is able to issue the plates created by this section, the department shall issue special license plates to qualified applicants in accordance with this section for motorcycles, passenger cars, trucks, and noncommercial or recreational motor vehicles that do not exceed sixteen thousand pounds empty weight.

(2) (a) There is hereby established the adopt a shelter pet special license plate.

(b) The design for the special license plate shall conform with standards established by the department and shall be subject to the department's approval.

(3) A person may apply for an adopt a shelter pet special license plate if the person pays the taxes and fees required under this section.

(4) The amount of the taxes and fees for special license plates under this section is the same as the amount of the taxes and fees specified for regular motor vehicle license plates; except that the department shall collect the following fees and donations:

(a) A one-time, twenty-five-dollar fee for issuance or replacement of the license plate, which fee shall be transmitted to the state treasurer, who shall credit the same to the highway users tax fund created in section 43-4-201, C.R.S.;

(b) A one-time, thirty-dollar donation for issuance or replacement of the license plate, which donation shall be transmitted to the state treasurer, who shall credit the same to the adopt a shelter pet account in the pet overpopulation fund created in section 35-80-116.5, C.R.S.; and

(c) An annual twenty-five-dollar license plate renewal donation, which donation shall be transmitted to the state treasurer, who shall credit the same to the adopt a shelter pet account in the pet overpopulation fund created in section 35-80-116.5, C.R.S.; except that the department and its authorized agents may retain the portion of the donation necessary to offset implementing this paragraph (c), up to a maximum of two dollars.

(5) An applicant may apply for personalized adopt a shelter pet special license plates. Upon payment of the additional fee required by section 42-3-211 (6) (a) for personalized license plates, the department may issue such plates if the applicant complies with section 42-3-211. If an applicant has existing personalized license plates for a motor vehicle, the applicant may transfer the combination of letters or numbers to a new set of adopt a shelter pet special license plates for the vehicle upon payment of the fee imposed by section 42-3-211 (6) and upon turning in such existing plates to the department. A person who has obtained personalized adopt a shelter pet special license plates under this subsection (5) shall pay the annual fee imposed by section 42-3-211 (6) (b) for renewal of such personalized plates. The fees under this subsection (5) are in addition to all other taxes and fees imposed for personalized adopt a shelter pet special license plates.

(6) (a) The department shall retire the adopt a shelter pet license plate if three thousand plates are not issued by July 1, 2016. A person who was issued an adopt a shelter pet license plate on or before July 1, 2016, may continue to use the plate after July 1, 2016.

(b) (Deleted by amendment, L. 2011, (HB 11-1236), ch. 98, p. 289, § 13, effective April 8, 2011.)

42-3-235. Livery license plates - luxury limousines - repeal. (1) The livery license plate is hereby established. The plate consists of red letters on a white background and features the words "Colorado" across the top and "Livery" across the bottom of the plate.

(2) (a) Except as provided in paragraphs (b) to (d) of this subsection (2), a person providing luxury limousine service under article 10.1 of title 40, C.R.S., shall register the motor vehicle used for such purposes pursuant to this article and display livery license plates on the vehicle. Upon registration, the department shall issue livery license plates for the vehicles in accordance with this section. The department shall not issue a livery license plate unless the person either submits a verification document issued pursuant to section 40-10.1-303, C.R.S., or the public utilities commission electronically verifies the authorization to provide luxury limousine service under section 40-10.1-303, C.R.S.

(b) A person providing luxury limousine service under article 10.1 of title 40, C.R.S., may provide such services without registering the motor vehicle or using livery license plates if the motor vehicle is rented, but the person shall not provide such services using a rented motor vehicle for more than thirty days.

(c) A person providing services requiring a livery plate pursuant to paragraph (a) of this subsection (2) with a motor vehicle that was registered on January 1, 2011, is not required to obtain livery plates until the vehicle is scheduled for renewal of the current registration. Upon renewing a registration for a luxury limousine registered pursuant to this article, the department shall issue livery license plates for the vehicle in accordance with this section. This paragraph (c) is repealed, effective January 1, 2012.

(d) If a motor vehicle is used to provide both taxicab services and luxury limousine services, the department shall issue the motor vehicle a taxicab license plate in accordance with section 42-3-236.

(3) Upon payment of the additional fee required by section 42-3-211 (6) (a) for personalized license plates, the department may issue personalized livery license plates if the applicant complies with section 42-3-211. If an applicant has existing personalized license plates, the applicant may transfer the combination of letters or numbers to a new set of special livery license plates upon paying the fee imposed by section 42-3-211 (6) (a) and upon turning the existing plates in to the department. A person who has obtained personalized livery license plates under this subsection (3) shall pay the annual fee imposed by section 42-3-211 (6) (b) for renewal of such personalized plates. The fees under this subsection (3) are in addition to all other taxes and fees imposed for the livery license plates.

(4) No person shall operate a motor vehicle with a livery license plate or temporary livery license plate unless the motor vehicle to which the plates are attached is required by subsection (2) of this section to bear livery license plates. A person who violates this section commits a class B traffic infraction, punishable by a fine of seventy-five dollars.

(5) If the person who owns the motor vehicle with livery plates is not the same person under whose authority the motor vehicle operates pursuant to article 10.1 of title 40, C.R.S., the person with such authority may request that the department of revenue require the plate to be replaced.

Upon a request being made, the department shall require the owner to return the livery license plate and be issued a new license plate.

(6) This section is effective January 1, 2011.

42-3-236. Taxicab license plates - taxicabs - repeal. (1) The taxicab license plate is hereby established. The plate consists of black letters on a yellow background and features the words "Colorado" across the top and "taxicab" across the bottom of the plate.

(2) A person who is authorized to provide taxicab service under article 10.1 of title 40, C.R.S., shall register a motor vehicle used for taxicab purposes under this article and display taxicab license plates on the vehicle. Upon registration, the department shall issue taxicab license plates for the vehicle in accordance with this section. The department shall not issue a taxicab license plate unless the person either submits a verification document or the public utilities commission electronically verifies the authorization as provided in section 40-10.1-207, C.R.S.

(3) A person providing taxicab services using a motor vehicle that was registered on January 1, 2012, is not required to obtain taxicab license plates until the vehicle is scheduled for renewal of the current registration. Upon renewing a registration for a taxicab registered under this article, the department shall issue taxicab license plates for the vehicle in accordance with this section. This subsection (3) is repealed, effective January 1, 2013.

(4) A person shall not operate a motor vehicle with a taxicab license plate or temporary taxicab license plate unless the motor vehicle to which the plates are attached is required by subsection (2) of this section to bear taxicab license plates.

(5) If the person who owns the motor vehicle with taxicab license plates is not the person under whose authority the motor vehicle operates under article 10.1 of title 40, C.R.S., the person with the authority may request that the department of revenue require the plate to be replaced. Within thirty days after receiving the request, the department shall require the owner of the motor vehicle to return the taxicab license plate and be issued a new license plate. The owner of the motor vehicle shall surrender the taxicab license plate to the department within ten days after receiving notice from the department unless the owner of the motor vehicle obtains authority to operate a taxicab under part 2 of article 10.1 of title 40, C.R.S., either directly or as an agent, and either the person submits a verification document or the public utilities commission electronically verifies the authorization as provided in section 40-10.1-207, C.R.S.

(6) A person who violates this section commits a class B traffic infraction, punishable by a fine of seventy-five dollars.

(7) This section is effective January 1, 2012.

42-3-237. Special plates - girl scouts. (1) Beginning January 1, 2012, the department shall issue special license plates to qualified applicants in accordance with this section for motorcycles, passenger cars, trucks, or noncommercial or recreational motor vehicles that do not exceed sixteen thousand pounds empty weight.

(2) (a) There is hereby established the girl scouts centennial special license plate.

(b) The girl scouts of Colorado may design the girl scouts centennial special license plate, but the plate must conform with standards established by the department.

(3) A person may apply for a special license plate under this section if the person pays the taxes and fees required by this section.

(4) The amount of the taxes and fees for special license plates under this section is the same as the amount of the taxes and fees specified for regular motor vehicle license plates; except that the department shall collect a one-time fee of twenty-five dollars for the issuance or replacement of each such license plate. The department shall transmit the additional one-time fee to the state treasurer, who shall credit the same to the highway users tax fund created in section 43-4-201, C.R.S.

(5) An applicant may apply for personalized special license plates created by this section. Upon payment of the additional fee required by section 42-3-211 (6) (a) for personalized license plates, the department may issue such plates if the applicant complies with section 42-3-211. If an applicant has existing personalized license plates for a motor vehicle, the applicant may transfer the combination of letters or numbers to a new set of special license plates created by this section for the vehicle upon paying the fee imposed by section 42-3-211 (6) (a) and upon turning in such existing plates to the department. A person who has obtained personalized special license plates under this subsection (5) shall pay the annual fee imposed by section 42-3-211 (6) (b) for renewal of such personalized plates. The fees under this subsection (5) are in addition to all other taxes and fees imposed for the special license plates created by this section.

(6) The department may stop issuing the girl scouts centennial special license plate if three thousand license plates are not issued by July 1, 2017. A person who was issued the plate on or before July 1, 2017, may continue to use the plate after July 1, 2017.

42-3-238. Special plates - type 1 diabetes. (1) Beginning the earlier of January 1, 2012, or when the department is able to issue the plates, the department shall issue special license plates to qualified applicants under this section for motorcycles, passenger cars, trucks, or noncommercial or recreational motor vehicles that do not exceed sixteen thousand pounds empty weight.

(2) (a) There is hereby established the juvenile diabetes special license plate. The department may stop issuing the juvenile diabetes special license plate if three thousand license plates are not issued by July 1, 2014. A person may con-

tinue to use the juvenile diabetes special license plate after July 1, 2014.

(b) The juvenile diabetes research foundation may design the special license plate. The design for the special license plate must conform with standards established by the department and is subject to the department's approval.

(3) A person may apply for a juvenile diabetes special license plate if the person pays the taxes and fees required under this section.

(4) The amount of the taxes and fees for special license plates under this section is the same as the amount of the taxes and fees for regular motor vehicle license plates; except that the department shall collect a one-time fee of twenty-five dollars for issuance or replacement of each such license plate. The department shall transmit the additional one-time fee to the state treasurer, who shall credit the fee to the highway users tax fund created in section 43-4-201, C.R.S.

(5) An applicant may apply for personalized juvenile diabetes special license plates. Upon payment of the additional fee required by section 42-3-211 (6) (a) for personalized license plates, the department may issue such plates if the applicant complies with section 42-3-211. If an applicant has existing personalized license plates for a motor vehicle, the applicant may transfer the combination of letters or numbers to a new set of juvenile diabetes special license plates for the vehicle upon paying the fee required by section 42-3-211 (6) (a) and upon turning in the existing plates to the department. A person who has obtained personalized juvenile diabetes special license plates under this subsection (5) shall pay the annual fee imposed by section 42-3-211 (6) (b) for renewal of such personalized plates. The fees under this subsection (5) are in addition to all other applicable taxes and fees.

42-3-239. Special plates - Colorado Avalanche or Denver Nuggets. (1) Beginning the earlier of January 1, 2012, or when the department is able to issue the plates, the department shall issue special license plates to qualified applicants under this section for motorcycles, passenger cars, trucks, or noncommercial or recreational motor vehicles that do not exceed sixteen thousand pounds empty weight.

(2) (a) There is hereby established the Colorado Avalanche and Denver Nuggets special license plates. The department may stop issuing either the Colorado Avalanche or Denver Nuggets special license plate if a total of three thousand license plates, of either design, are not issued by July 1, 2016. A person may continue to use either the Colorado Avalanche or Denver Nuggets special license plate after July 1, 2016.

(b) Kroenke sports charities may design the special license plates, but the design must conform with standards established by the department.

(3) (a) A person may apply for a Colorado Avalanche or Denver Nuggets special license plate if the person pays the taxes and fees required under this section and provides to the department or an authorized agent a certificate, issued by Kroenke sports charities or its successor organization, confirming that the applicant has donated forty-five dollars to Kroenke sports charities.

(b) Kroenke sports charities, or its successor organization, shall file with the department an annual statement verifying that it is a nonprofit organization.

(4) The amount of the taxes and fees for special license plates under this section is the same as the amount of the taxes and fees for regular motor vehicle license plates; except that the department shall collect a one-time fee of twenty-five dollars for issuance or replacement of each such license plate. The department shall transmit the additional one-time fee to the state treasurer, who shall credit the fee to the highway users tax fund created in section 43-4-201, C.R.S.

(5) An applicant may apply for personalized Colorado Avalanche or Denver Nuggets special license plates. Upon payment of the additional fee required by section 42-3-211 (6) (a) for personalized license plates, the department may issue the plates if the applicant complies with section 42-3-211. If an applicant has existing personalized license plates for a motor vehicle, the applicant may transfer the combination of letters or numbers to a new set of Colorado Avalanche or Denver Nuggets special license plates for the vehicle upon paying the fee required by section 42-3-211 (6) (a) and upon turning in the existing plates to the department. A person who has obtained personalized Colorado Avalanche or Denver Nuggets special license plates under this subsection (5) shall pay the annual fee imposed by section 42-3-211 (6) (b) for renewal of the personalized plates. The fees under this subsection (5) are in addition to all other applicable taxes and fees.

42-3-240. Special plates - Craig hospital. (1) Beginning the earlier of January 1, 2012, or when the department is able to issue the plates, the department shall issue special license plates to qualified applicants under this section for motorcycles, passenger cars, trucks, or noncommercial or recreational motor vehicles that do not exceed sixteen thousand pounds empty weight.

(2) (a) There is hereby established the Craig hospital special license plate. The department may stop issuing the Craig hospital special license plate if three thousand license plates are not issued by July 1, 2016. A person may continue to use the Craig hospital special license plate after July 1, 2016.

(b) Craig hospital may design the special license plates, but the design must conform with standards established by the department.

(3) (a) A person may apply for a Craig hospital special license plate if the person pays the taxes and fees required under this section and provides to the department or an authorized agent a certificate, issued by Craig hospital or its successor organization, confirming that the

applicant has donated twenty dollars to Craig hospital.

(b) Craig hospital, or its successor organization, shall file with the department an annual statement verifying that it is a nonprofit organization.

(4) The amount of the taxes and fees for special license plates under this section is the same as the amount of the taxes and fees for regular motor vehicle license plates; except that the department shall collect a one-time fee of twenty-five dollars for issuance or replacement of each such license plate. The department shall transmit the additional one-time fee to the state treasurer, who shall credit the fee to the highway users tax fund created in section 43-4-201, C.R.S.

(5) An applicant may apply for personalized Craig hospital license plates. Upon payment of the additional fee required by section 42-3-211 (6) (a) for personalized license plates, the department may issue such plates if the applicant complies with section 42-3-211. If an applicant has existing personalized license plates for a motor vehicle, the applicant may transfer the combination of letters or numbers to a new set of Craig hospital special license plates for the vehicle upon paying the fee required by section 42-3-211 (6) (a) and upon turning in such existing plates to the department. A person who has obtained personalized Craig hospital special license plates under this subsection (5) shall pay the annual fee imposed by section 42-3-211 (6) (b) for renewal of such personalized plates. The fees under this subsection (5) are in addition to all other applicable taxes and fees.

PART 3

FEES AND CASH FUNDS

42-3-301. License plate cash fund - license plate fees. (1) (a) In addition to the payment of any fees for motor vehicle registration or for the issuance of license plates, decals, or validating tabs, each owner of a motor vehicle issued a license plate, decal, or validating tab for a motor vehicle pursuant to this article shall also pay a fee to cover the direct costs of such plates, decals, or tabs. The amount of the fee imposed pursuant to this section shall be as specified in paragraph (b) of subsection (2) of this section.

(b) Fees collected pursuant to this section shall be transmitted to the state treasurer, who shall credit the same to the license plate cash fund, which fund is hereby created. The fund shall be administered by the department through June 30, 2005, and by the state treasurer thereafter. Moneys in the fund shall be appropriated by the general assembly for the direct costs incurred by the department in purchasing, as provided in section 17-24-109.5 (2), C.R.S., license plates, decals, and validating tabs from the division of correctional industries, referred to in this section as the "division", in the department of corrections, and issuing license plates pursuant to this article. At the end of each fiscal year, any unexpended and unencumbered moneys remaining in the fund shall revert to the highway users tax fund created in section 43-4-201 (1) (a), C.R.S., and shall be allocated and expended as specified in section 43-4-205 (5.5) (b), C.R.S.

(2) (a) The fees imposed pursuant to subsection (1) of this section shall be limited to the amount necessary to recover the costs of the production and distribution of any license plates, decals, or validating tabs issued pursuant to this article and the related support functions provided to the department of revenue by the division. The correctional industries advisory committee, established pursuant to section 17-24-104 (2), C.R.S., shall annually review and recommend to the director of the division the amounts of the fees to be imposed pursuant to subsection (1) of this section. The director of the division, in cooperation and consultation with the department of revenue and the office of state planning and budgeting, shall annually establish the amounts of the fees imposed pursuant to subsection (1) of this section to recover the division's costs pursuant to this subsection (2). On or before March 1, 2010, and on or before March 1 every five years thereafter, the director of the division shall file a written report with the transportation and energy committee of the house of representatives, or any successor committee, and the transportation committee of the senate, or any successor committee, concerning any change within the preceding five years in the amount of the fee imposed pursuant to subsection (1) of this section and the reason for the change in the fee.

(b) Notwithstanding any other provision of this article, with the exception of special license plates issued pursuant to section 42-3-213 for purple heart recipients, medal of valor recipients, former prisoners of war, survivors of the attack on Pearl Harbor, disabled veterans, or recipients of a medal of honor, the fees imposed by this subsection (2) shall apply to all other special license plates issued in accordance with this article.

42-3-302. Special plate fees. (1) The fees collected pursuant to sections 42-3-213 and 42-3-217 for the issuance of a license plate pursuant to sections 42-3-213 (9) and 42-3-217 shall be transmitted to the state treasurer, who shall credit the same to the license plate cash fund created in section 42-3-301.

(2) The executive director of the department shall make an annual report by March 1 of each year to the general assembly. Such report shall be open for public inspection and shall include:

(a) A summary of the department's activities for the previous year;

(b) A statement of plate revenues;

(c) Information regarding special plate purchases;

(d) Expenses of the department;

(e) Allocation of remaining revenues; and

(f) Any recommendations for changes in statutes that the executive director deems necessary or desirable.

42-3-303. Persistent drunk driver cash fund - programs to deter persistent drunk drivers. (1) There is hereby created in the state treasury the persistent drunk driver cash fund, which shall be composed of moneys collected for penalty surcharges under section 42-4-1307 (10) (b). The moneys in such fund are subject to annual appropriation by the general assembly:

(a) To pay the costs incurred by the department concerning persistent drunk drivers under sections 42-2-126 (10) and 42-7-406 (1.5);

(b) To pay for costs incurred by the department for computer programing changes related to treatment compliance for persistent drunk drivers pursuant to section 42-2-144;

(c) (I) To support programs that are intended to deter persistent drunk driving or intended to educate the public, with particular emphasis on the education of young drivers, regarding the dangers of persistent drunk driving.

(II) The departments of transportation, revenue, and human services and the judicial branch shall coordinate programs intended to accomplish the goals described in subparagraph (I) of this paragraph (c).

(d) On and after July 1, 2007, to pay a portion of the costs for intervention or treatment services required under sections 42-2-125, 42-2-126, 42-2-132, 42-2-132.5, and 42-4-1301.3 for a persistent drunk driver, as defined in section 42-1-102 (68.5), who is unable to pay for the required intervention or treatment services;

(e) To assist in providing court-ordered alcohol treatment programs for indigent and incarcerated offenders;

(f) To assist in providing approved ignition interlock devices, as defined in section 42-2-132.5 (7) (a), for indigent offenders; and

(g) To assist in providing continuous monitoring technology or devices for indigent offenders.

42-3-304. Registration fees - passenger and passenger-mile taxes - clean screen fund - repeal. (1) (a) In addition to other fees specified in this section, an applicant shall pay a motorist insurance identification fee in an amount determined by paragraph (d) of subsection (18) of this section when applying for registration or renewal of registration of a motor vehicle under this article.

(b) The following vehicles are exempt from the motorist insurance identification fee:

(I) Vehicles that are exempt from registration fees under this section or are owned by persons who have qualified as self-insured pursuant to section 10-4-624, C.R.S.

(II) Repealed.

(c) (Deleted by amendment, L. 2009, (SB 09-274), ch. 210, p. 955, § 8, effective May 1, 2009.)

(2) With respect to passenger-carrying motor vehicles, the weight used in computing annual registration fees shall be that weight published by the manufacturer in approved manuals, and, in case of a dispute over the weight of such vehicle, the actual weight determined by weighing such vehicle on a certified scale, as provided in section 35-14-122 (6), C.R.S., shall be conclusive. With respect to all other vehicles, the weight used in computing annual registration fees shall be the empty weight, determined by weighing such vehicle on a certified scale or in the case of registration fees imposed pursuant to section 42-3-306 (5), the declared gross vehicle weight of the vehicle declared by the owner at the time of registration.

(3) No fee shall be payable for the annual registration of a vehicle when:

(a) The owner of such vehicle is a veteran who in an application for registration shows that the owner has established such owner's rights to benefits under the provisions of Public Law 663, 79th Congress, as amended, and Public Law 187, 82nd Congress, as amended, or is a veteran of the armed forces of the United States who incurred a disability and who is, at the date of such application, receiving compensation from the veterans administration or any branch of the armed forces of the United States for a fifty percent or more, service-connected, permanent disability, or for loss of use of one or both feet or one or both hands, or for permanent impairment or loss of vision in both eyes that constitutes virtual or actual blindness. The exemption provided in this paragraph (a) shall apply to the original qualifying vehicle and to any vehicle subsequently purchased and owned by the same veteran but shall not apply to more than one vehicle at a time.

(b) The application for registration shows that the owner of such vehicle is a foreign government or a consul or other official representative of a foreign government duly recognized by the department of state of the United States government. License plates for the vehicles qualifying for the exemption granted in this paragraph (b) shall be issued only by the department and shall bear such inscription as may be required to indicate their status.

(c) The owner of such vehicle is the state or a political or governmental subdivision thereof; but any such vehicle that is leased, either by the state or any political or governmental subdivision thereof, shall be exempt from payment of an annual registration fee only if the agreement under which it is leased has been first submitted to the department and approved, and such vehicle shall remain exempt from payment of an annual registration fee only so long as it is used and operated in strict conformity with such approved agreement.

(d) The owner of such vehicle is a former prisoner of war being issued special plates pursuant to section 42-3-213 (3) or is the surviving spouse of a former prisoner of war retaining the special plates that were issued to such former prisoner of war pursuant to section 42-3-213 (3).

(e) The owner of such vehicle is the recipient of a purple heart being issued special plates pursuant to section 42-3-213 (2).

(f) The owner of such vehicle is a recipient of a medal of honor issued special plates pursuant to section 42-3-213 (7).

(g) The owner of the vehicle is a recipient of a medal of valor and is issued special license plates pursuant to section 42-3-213 (10).

(h) The owner of the vehicle survived the attack on Pearl Harbor and is issued special license plates pursuant to section 42-3-213 (6).

(4) Upon registration, the owner of each motorcycle shall pay a surcharge of four dollars, which shall be credited to the motorcycle operator safety training fund created in section 43-5-504, C.R.S.

(5) In lieu of registering each vehicle separately, a dealer in motorcycles shall pay to the department an annual registration fee of twenty-five dollars for the first license plate issued pursuant to section 42-3-116 (1), a fee of seven dollars and fifty cents for each additional license plate so issued up to and including five such plates, and a fee of ten dollars for each license plate so issued in excess of five.

(6) In lieu of registering each vehicle separately:

(a) A dealer in motor vehicles, trailers, and semitrailers, except dealers in motorcycles, shall pay to the department an annual fee of thirty dollars for the first license plate issued pursuant to section 42-3-116 (1), and a fee of seven dollars and fifty cents for each additional license plate so issued up to and including five, and a fee of ten dollars for each license plate so issued in excess of five; and

(b) A manufacturer of motor vehicles shall pay to the department an annual fee of thirty dollars for the first license plate issued pursuant to section 42-3-116 (1), and a fee of seven dollars and fifty cents for each additional license plate so issued up to and including five, and a fee of ten dollars for each additional license plate issued.

(7) (a) Every drive-away or tow-away transporter shall apply to the department for the issuance of license plates that may be transferred from one vehicle or combination to another vehicle or combination for delivery without further registration. The annual fee payable for the issuance of such plates shall be thirty dollars for the first set and ten dollars for each additional set. No transporter shall permit such license plates to be used upon a vehicle that is not in transit, or upon a work or service vehicle, including a service vehicle utilized regularly to haul vehicles, or by any other person.

(b) Each such transporter shall keep a written record of all vehicles transported, including the description thereof and the names and addresses of the consignors and consignees, and a copy of such record shall be carried in every driven vehicle; except that, when a number of vehicles are being transported in convoy, such copy, listing all the vehicles in the convoy, may be carried in only the lead vehicle in the convoy.

(c) This subsection (7) shall not apply to a nonresident engaged in interstate or foreign commerce if such nonresident is in compliance with the in-transit laws of the state of his or her residence and if such state grants reciprocal exemption to Colorado residents. The department may enter into reciprocal agreements with any other state or states containing such reciprocal exemptions or may issue written declarations as to the existence of any such reciprocal agreements.

(8) (a) Subsections (5), (6) (a), and (7) of this section shall not apply to a motor vehicle, trailer, or semitrailer operated by a dealer or transporter for such dealer's or transporter's private use or to a motor vehicle bearing full-use dealer plates issued pursuant to section 42-3-116 (6) (d).

(b) Paragraph (b) of subsection (6) of this section shall only apply to a motor vehicle if owned and operated by a manufacturer, a representative of a manufacturer, or a person so authorized by the manufacturer. A motor vehicle bearing manufacturer plates shall be of a make and model of the current or a future year and shall have been manufactured by or for the manufacturer to which such plates were issued.

(9) In addition to the registration fees imposed by section 42-3-306 (4) (a), the following additional registration fee shall be imposed on such vehicles:

(a) For farm trucks less than seven years old, twelve dollars;

(b) For farm trucks seven years old but less than ten years old, ten dollars;

(c) For farm trucks ten years old or older, seven dollars.

(10) (a) In addition to the registration fees imposed by section 42-3-306 (5) (a) and (13), for motor vehicles described in section 42-3-306 (5) (a) and (13), the following additional registration fee shall be imposed:

(I) For light trucks and recreational vehicles less than seven years old, twelve dollars;

(II) For light trucks and recreational vehicles seven years old but less than ten years old, ten dollars;

(III) For light trucks and recreational vehicles ten years old or older, seven dollars.

(b) In addition to the registration fees imposed by section 42-3-306 (5) (b), (5) (c), or (12) (b), an additional registration fee of ten dollars shall be assessed.

(c) The department shall adopt rules that allow a vehicle owner or a vehicle owner's agent to apply for apportioned registration for a vehicle that is used in interstate commerce and that qualifies for the registration fees provided in section 42-3-306 (5). In establishing the amount of such apportioned registration, such rules shall take into account the length of time such item may be operated in Colorado or the number of miles such item may be driven in Colorado. The apportioned registration, if based upon the length of time such item may be operated in Colorado, shall be valid for a period of between two and eleven months. Such rules shall also allow for extensions of apportioned registration periods. During such rule-making, the department shall confer with its authorized agents regarding enhanced communications with the authorized agents and the coordination of enforcement efforts.

(11) The additional fees collected pursuant to section 42-3-306 (2) (b) (II) and subsection (9) of this section and paragraphs (a) and (b) of subsection (10) of this section shall be transmitted to the state treasurer, who shall credit the same to the highway users tax fund to be allocated pursuant to section 43-4-205 (6) (b), C.R.S.

(12) An owner or operator that desires to make an occasional trip into this state with a truck, truck tractor, trailer, or semitrailer that is registered in another state shall obtain a permit from the public utilities commission as provided in article 10.1 of title 40, C.R.S. This subsection (12) does not apply to the vehicles of a public utility that are temporarily in this state to assist in the construction, installation, or restoration of utility facilities used in serving the public.

(13) In addition to the annual registration fees prescribed in this section for vehicles with a seating capacity of more than fourteen and operated for the transportation of passengers for compensation, the owner or operator of every such vehicle operated over the public highways of this state shall pay a passenger-mile tax equal to one mill for each passenger transported for a distance of one mile. The tax shall be credited to the highway users tax fund created in section 43-4-201, C.R.S., as required by section 43-4-203 (1) (c), C.R.S., and allocated and expended as specified in section 43-4-205 (5.5) (d), C.R.S. The tax assessed by this subsection (13) shall not apply to passenger service rendered within the boundaries of a city, city and county, or incorporated town by a company engaged in the mass transportation of persons by buses or trolley coaches.

(14) (a) The owner or operator of special mobile machinery having an empty weight not in excess of sixteen thousand pounds that the owner or operator desires to operate over the public highways of this state shall register such vehicle under section 42-3-306 (5) (a).

(b) The owner or operator of special mobile machinery with an empty weight exceeding sixteen thousand pounds that the owner or operator desires to operate over the public highways of this state shall register the vehicle under section 42-3-306 (5) (b).

(15) The owner of special mobile machinery, except that mentioned in sections 42-1-102 (44) and 42-3-104 (3), that is not registered for operation on the highway shall pay a fee of one dollar and fifty cents, which shall not be subject to any quarterly reduction.

(16) Nothing in this section shall be construed to prevent a farmer or rancher from occasionally exchanging transportation with another farmer or rancher when the sole consideration involved is the exchange of personal services and the use of vehicles.

(17) (a) At the time of registration of such vehicle, the owner of a truck subject to registration under section 42-3-306 (5) having a weight in excess of four thousand five hundred pounds, but not in excess of ten thousand pounds, including mounted equipment other than that of a recreational type, shall present to the authorized agent a copy of the manufacturer's statement or certificate of origin that specifies the shipping weight of such vehicle, or if such documentation is not available, a certified scale ticket showing the weight of such vehicle.

(b) The department shall furnish appropriate identification, by means of tags or otherwise, to indicate that a vehicle registered under this section is not subject to clearance by a port of entry weigh station.

(18) (a) In addition to any other fee imposed by this section, the owner shall pay, at the time of registration, a fee of fifty cents on every item of Class A, B, or C personal property required to be registered pursuant to this article. Such fee shall be transmitted to the state treasurer, who shall credit the same to a special account within the highway users tax fund, to be known as the AIR account, and such moneys shall be used, subject to appropriation by the general assembly, to cover the direct costs of the motor vehicle emissions activities of the department of public health and environment in the presently defined nonattainment area, and to pay for the costs of the commission in performing its duties under section 25-7-106.3, C.R.S. In the program areas within counties affected by this article, the authorized agent shall impose and retain an additional fee of up to seventy cents on every such registration to cover reasonable costs of administration of the emissions compliance aspect of vehicle registration. The department of public health and environment may accept and expend grants, gifts, and moneys from any source for the purpose of implementing its duties and functions under this section or section 25-7-106.3, C.R.S.

(b) In addition to any other fee imposed by this section, at the time of registration of any motor vehicle in the program area subject to inspection and not exempt from registration, the owner shall pay a fee of one dollar and fifty cents. Such fee shall be transmitted to the state treasurer, who shall credit the same to the AIR account within the highway users tax fund, and such moneys shall be expended only to cover the costs of administration and enforcement of the automobile inspection and readjustment program by the department of revenue and the department of public health and environment, upon appropriation by the general assembly. For such purposes, the revenues attributable to one dollar of such fee shall be available for appropriation to the department of revenue, and the revenues attributable to the remaining fifty cents of such fee shall be available for appropriation to the department of public health and environment.

(c) There shall be established two separate subaccounts within the AIR account, one for the revenues available for appropriation to the department of public health and environment pursuant to paragraphs (a) and (b) of this subsection (18) and one for the revenues available for appropriation to the department of revenue pursuant to paragraph (b) of this subsection (18) and section 42-4-305. After the state treasurer transfers moneys in the department of revenue subaccount to the department of revenue equal to the amount appropriated to the department of revenue from the AIR account for the fiscal year, the state treasurer shall transfer from the balance in the department of revenue subaccount to the department of public health and environment subaccount any amount needed to cover appropriations made to the department of public health and environment from the AIR account for that fiscal year for the administration and enforcement of the automobile inspection and readjustment program. Transfers from the department of revenue subaccount to the department of public health and environment subaccount shall be made on a monthly basis after the transfers to the department of revenue equal to the department of revenue's appropriation for that fiscal year have been made. The state treasurer shall not transfer to the department of public health and environment an amount that exceeds the amount of the appropriation made to the department of public health and environment from the AIR account for the fiscal year. Any transfer made pursuant to this paragraph (c) shall be subject to any limits imposed or appropriations made by the general assembly for other purposes and any limitations imposed by section 18 of article X of the state constitution.

(d) (I) In addition to any other fee imposed by this section, the owner shall pay, at the time of registration of a motor vehicle or low-power scooter, a motorist insurance identification fee. The fee shall be adjusted annually by the department, based upon moneys appropriated by the general assembly for the operation of the motorist insurance identification database program. Prior to July 1, 2011, in no event shall the fee exceed fifty cents. On and after July 1, 2011, in no event shall the fee exceed ten cents. The fee shall be transmitted to the state treasurer, who shall credit it to a special account within the highway users tax fund, to be known as the motorist insurance identification account, which is hereby created. Moneys in the motorist insurance identification account shall be used, subject to appropriation by the general assembly, to cover the costs of administration and enforcement of the motorist insurance identification database program, created in section 42-7-604 and, for state fiscal years 2010-11 and 2011-12, for expenses incurred in connection with the administration of article 2 of this title by the division of motor vehicles within the department; except that:

(A) For the 2010-11 and 2011-12 fiscal years, the state treasurer shall transfer moneys in the account in excess of the amount of moneys appropriated from the account to the Colorado state titling and registration account in the highway users tax fund for allocation and expenditure as required by section 42-1-211 (2). This sub-subparagraph (A) is repealed, effective July 1, 2012.

(B) For the fiscal year commencing July 1, 2012, the state treasurer shall transfer moneys in the account in excess of the amount of moneys appropriated from the account to the highway users tax fund for allocation and expenditure as specified in section 43-4-205 (5.5) (c), C.R.S.

(II) (Deleted by amendment, L. 2009, (SB 09-274), ch. 210, p. 955, § 8, effective May 1, 2009; (HB 09-1026), ch. 281, p. 1268, § 30, effective July 1, 2010.)

(19) (a) If the air quality control commission determines pursuant to section 42-4-306 (23) (b) to implement an expanded clean screen program in the enhanced emissions program area, on and after the specific dates determined by the commission for each of the following subparagraphs:

(I) In addition to any other fee imposed by this section, county clerks and recorders, acting as agents for the clean screen authority, shall collect at the time of registration an emissions inspection fee in an amount determined by section 42-4-311 (6) (a) or, after implementation of the plan by the commission as prescribed by House Bill 06-1302, as enacted at the second regular session of the sixty-fifth general assembly, in accordance with section 42-4-311 (6) (c), on every motor vehicle that the department of revenue has determined from data provided by its contractor to have been clean screened; except that the motorist shall not be required to pay such emissions inspection fee if the county clerk and recorder determines that a valid certification of emissions compliance has already been issued for the vehicle being registered indicating that the vehicle passed the applicable emissions test at an enhanced inspection center, inspection and readjustment station, motor vehicle dealer test facility, or fleet inspection station.

(II) County clerks and recorders shall be entitled to retain three and one-third percent of the fee so collected to cover the clerks' expenses in the collection and remittance of such fee. County treasurers shall, no later than ten days after the last business day of each month, remit the remainder of such fee to the clean screen authority created in section 42-4-307.5. The clean screen authority shall transmit such fee to the state treasurer, who shall deposit the same in the clean screen fund, which fund is hereby created. The clean screen fund shall be a pass-through trust account to be held in trust solely for the purposes and the beneficiaries specified in this subsection (19). Moneys in the clean screen fund shall not constitute fiscal year spending of the state for purposes of section 20 of article X of the state constitution, and such moneys shall be deemed custodial funds that are not subject to appropriation by the general assembly. Interest earned from the deposit and investment of moneys in the clean screen fund shall be credited to the clean screen fund, and the clean screen authority may also expend interest earned on the deposit and investment of the clean screen fund to pay for its costs associated with the implementation of House Bill 01-1402, enacted at the first regular session of the sixty-third general assembly. The clean screen authority may also expend interest earned on the deposit and investment of the clean screen fund to pay for its costs associated with the implementation of House Bill 06-1302, enacted at the second regular session of the sixty-fifth general assembly.

(III) The clean screen authority shall transmit moneys from the clean screen fund monthly to the contractor in accordance with the fees determined by section 42-4-311 (6) (a) within one week after receipt by the authority from the department of revenue of a notification of the number of registrations of clean-screened vehicles during the previous month.

(IV) The commission shall establish a pay-upon-registration program as a part of the plan to substantially increase the use of clean screen testing pursuant to section 42-4-307.7 and shall set a date to implement the pay-upon-registration program. The emissions inspection fee imposed in accordance with this subsection (19) shall not exceed nine dollars annually and shall be assessed on every motor vehicle in the program area. The commission shall have the authority to reduce, but not increase, emissions inspection fees. The fee, in addition to any other fee imposed by this section, shall be collected by the county clerk and recorder, acting as agent for the clean screen authority, at the time of registration each year. The contractor shall be paid on the basis of the number of vehicles inspected at enhanced inspection centers, which payment shall include payment for duplicate inspections when required for emissions compliance verification. The contractor shall also be paid based on the number of unique vehicles tested by remote sensing for the high emitter program. The contractor shall not be paid for vehicle remote sensing tests more than once for the same vehicle in any twelve-month vehicle registration period, but shall furnish duplicate vehicle test data to the department of public health and environment.

(b) In specifying dates for the implementation of the clean screen program pursuant to paragraph (a) of this subsection (19), the commission may specify different dates for the enhanced and basic emissions program areas.

(c) This subsection (19) shall not apply to El Paso county if the commission has excluded such county from the clean screen program pursuant to section 42-4-306 (23) (a).

(d) Any moneys remaining in the clean screen fund upon termination of the AIR program shall revert to the AIR account established in paragraph (a) of subsection (18) of this section.

(20) In addition to any other fee imposed by this section, there shall be collected, at the time of registration, a fee of ten dollars on every light and heavy duty diesel-powered motor vehicle in the program area registered pursuant to this article in Colorado. Such fee shall be transmitted to the state treasurer, who shall credit the same to the AIR account in the highway users tax fund, and such moneys shall be used, subject to appropriation by the general assembly, to cover the costs of the diesel-powered motor vehicle emissions control activities of the departments of public health and environment and revenue.

(21) In order to promote an effective emergency medical network and thus the maintenance and supervision of the highways throughout the state, in addition to any other fees imposed by this section, there shall be assessed an additional fee of two dollars at the time of registration of any motor vehicle. Such fee shall be transmitted to the state treasurer, who shall credit the same to the emergency medical services account created by section 25-3.5-603, C.R.S., within the highway users tax fund.

(22) In addition to any other fees imposed by this section, the authorized agent may collect and retain, and an applicant for registration shall pay at the time of registration, a reasonable fee, as determined from time to time by the authorized agent, that approximates the direct and indirect costs incurred, not to exceed five dollars, by the authorized agent in shipping and handling those license plates that the applicant has, pursuant to section 42-3-105 (1) (a), requested that the department mail to the owner.

(23) Repealed.

(24) In addition to any other fee imposed by this section, at the time of registration, the owner shall pay a fee of sixty cents on every item of Class A, B, or C personal property required to be registered pursuant to this article. Notwithstanding the requirements of section 43-4-203, C.R.S., such fee shall be transmitted to the state treasurer, who shall credit the same to the peace officers standards and training board cash fund, created in section 24-31-303 (2) (b), C.R.S.; except that county clerks and recorders shall be entitled to retain five percent of the fee collected to cover the clerks' expenses in the collection and remittance of such fee. All of the moneys in the fund that are collected pursuant to this subsection (24) shall be used by the peace officers standards and training board for the purposes specified in section 24-31-310, C.R.S.

Editor's note: Section 5 of chapter 136, Session Laws of Colorado 2011, provides that the act repealing subsection (1)(b)(II) applies to applications for registration filed on or after January 1, 2012.

42-3-305. Registration fees - passenger and passenger-mile taxes - fee schedule for years of TABOR surplus revenue - applicability. (Repealed)

42-3-306. Registration fees - passenger and passenger-mile taxes - fee schedule. (1) This section shall apply in any fiscal year beginning on or after July 1, 2010.

(2) Fees for the annual registration of passenger-carrying motor vehicles shall be as follows:

(a) Motorcycles, three dollars;

(b) (I) Passenger cars, station wagons, taxicabs, ambulances, motor homes, and hearses:

(A) Weighing two thousand pounds or less, six dollars;

(B) Weighing forty-five hundred pounds or less, six dollars plus twenty cents per one hundred pounds, or fraction thereof, of weight over two thousand pounds;

(C) Weighing more than forty-five hundred pounds, twelve dollars and fifty cents plus sixty cents per one hundred pounds, or fraction thereof, of weight over forty-five hundred pounds; except that, for motor homes weighing more than sixty-five hundred pounds, such fees shall be twenty-four dollars and fifty cents plus thirty cents per one hundred pounds, or fraction thereof, of weight over sixty-five hundred pounds.

(II) In addition to the registration fees imposed by subparagraph (I) of this paragraph (b), an additional registration fee shall be imposed on the motor vehicles described in the introductory portion to this paragraph (b), based on the age of the motor vehicle, as follows:

(A) For motor vehicles less than seven years old, twelve dollars;

(B) For motor vehicles seven years old but less than ten years old, ten dollars;

(C) For motor vehicles ten years old or older, seven dollars.

(III) The additional fees collected pursuant to subparagraph (II) of this paragraph (b) shall be transmitted to the state treasurer, who shall credit the same to the highway users tax fund to be allocated pursuant to section 43-4-205 (6) (b), C.R.S.

(IV) If a regional transportation plan is implemented within the regional transportation district, residents of the E-470 highway authority area shall be exempt from the first ten dollars of any motor vehicle registration fee increase in such plan.

(c) Passenger buses:

(I) All such vehicles used for the transportation of passengers for compensation having a seating capacity of fourteen or less passengers, twenty-five dollars plus one dollar and seventy cents for each seat capacity; and all such vehicles having a seating capacity of more than fourteen passengers, twenty-five dollars plus one dollar and twenty-five cents for each seat capacity in excess of fourteen;

(II) All such vehicles owned by a private owner and used for the transportation of school pupils having a juvenile seating capacity (meaning fourteen lineal inches of seat space) of twenty-five or less, fifteen dollars; and for all such vehicles having a juvenile seating capacity of more than twenty-five, fifteen dollars plus fifty cents for each juvenile seat capacity in excess of twenty-five.

(3) Fees for the annual registration of the following vehicles shall be:

(a) Trailer coaches, three dollars;

(b) Trailers, utility trailers, and camper trailers having an empty weight of two thousand pounds or less, three dollars;

(c) Trailers, utility trailers, and camper trailers having an empty weight exceeding two thousand pounds, seven dollars and fifty cents;

(d) Semitrailers, seven dollars and fifty cents.

(4) (a) The annual registration fee for trucks and truck tractors owned by a farmer or rancher that are operated over the public highways and are only commercially used to transport to market or place of storage raw agricultural products actually produced or livestock actually raised by such farmer or rancher or to transport commodities and livestock purchased by such farmer or rancher for personal use and used in such person's farming or ranching operations, shall be as follows:

(I) Each such vehicle having an empty weight of five thousand pounds or less, an amount computed to the nearest pound of the empty weight of such vehicle, according to the following schedule:

Empty Weight (Pounds)	Range		Registration Fee
2,000	and	under	$ 6.20
2,001	but not more than	2,100	6.40
2,101	but not more than	2,200	6.60
2,201	but not more than	2,300	6.80
2,301	but not more than	2,400	7.00
2,401	but not more than	2,500	7.20
2,501	but not more than	2,600	7.40
2,601	but not more than	2,700	7.60
2,701	but not more than	2,800	7.80
2,801	but not more than	2,900	8.00
2,901	but not more than	3,000	8.20
3,001	but not more than	3,100	8.40
3,101	but not more than	3,200	8.60
3,201	but not more than	3,300	8.80
3,301	but not more than	3,400	9.00
3,401	but not more than	3,500	9.20
3,501	but not more than	3,600	9.40
3,601	but not more than	3,700	9.60
3,701	but not more than	3,800	9.80
3,801	but not more than	3,900	10.00
3,901	but not more than	4,000	10.20
4,001	but not more than	4,100	10.40
4,101	but not more than	4,200	10.60
4,201	but not more than	4,300	10.80
4,301	but not more than	4,400	11.00
4,401	but not more than	4,500	11.20
4,501	but not more than	4,600	13.10
4,601	but not more than	4,700	13.70
4,701	but not more than	4,800	14.30
4,801	but not more than	4,900	14.90
4,901	but not more than	5,000	15.50

(II) Each such vehicle having an empty weight of ten thousand pounds or less but more than five thousand pounds, fifteen dollars and fifty cents plus forty-five cents per one hundred pounds, or fraction thereof, of empty weight over five thousand pounds;

(III) Each such vehicle having an empty weight of more than ten thousand pounds but not more than sixteen thousand pounds, thirty-eight dollars plus one dollar and twenty cents per one hundred pounds, or fraction thereof, of empty weight exceeding ten thousand pounds;

(IV) Each such vehicle having an empty weight of more than sixteen thousand pounds, one hundred ten dollars, plus one dollar and fifty cents per one hundred pounds, or fraction thereof, of empty weight exceeding sixteen thousand pounds.

(b) Nothing in this subsection (4) shall be construed to prevent a farmer or rancher from occasionally exchanging transportation with another farmer or rancher, but only if the sole consideration involved is the exchange of personal services or the use of equipment.

(c) A person applying for registration under this subsection (4) shall certify to the licensing authority on forms furnished by the department that the vehicle will be used in conformity with paragraph (a) of this subsection (4).

(d) No vehicle carrying mounted equipment other than a camper or other purely recreational equipment shall be registered under this subsection (4), and a vehicle registered under this subsection (4) shall be reregistered under the proper classification whenever equipment designed for commercial use is mounted upon such vehicle.

(e) The department or its authorized agent shall not require a person registering a farm truck or truck tractor under this subsection (4) to demonstrate that the owner's primary business or source of income is agriculture if the farm truck or truck tractor is used primarily for agricultural production on a farm or ranch owned or leased by the owner of the truck or truck tractor, and the land on which it is used is classified as agricultural land for the purposes of levying and collecting property tax under section 39-1-103, C.R.S.

(5) The annual registration fee for those trucks and truck tractors operated over the public highways of this state, except trucks that are registered under subsections (4) and (13) of this section and section 42-12-401 (1) (c), is as follows:

(a) For each such vehicle having an empty weight of up to and including sixteen thousand pounds, such registration fee shall be based upon the empty weight of such vehicle, computed to the nearest pound, according to the following schedule:

Empty Weight (Pounds)		Range	Registration Fee
2,000	and	under	$ 7.60
2,001	but not more than	2,100	7.80
2,101	but not more than	2,200	8.00
2,201	but not more than	2,300	8.20
2,301	but not more than	2,400	8.40
2,401	but not more than	2,500	8.60
2,501	but not more than	2,600	8.80
2,601	but not more than	2,700	9.00
2,701	but not more than	2,800	9.20
2,801	but not more than	2,900	9.40
2,901	but not more than	3,000	9.60
3,001	but not more than	3,100	10.20
3,101	but not more than	3,200	10.40
3,201	but not more than	3,300	10.60
3,301	but not more than	3,400	10.80
3,401	but not more than	3,500	11.00
3,501	but not more than	3,600	16.10
3,601	but not more than	3,700	16.70
3,701	but not more than	3,800	17.30
3,801	but not more than	3,900	17.90
3,901	but not more than	4,000	18.50
4,001	but not more than	4,100	19.10
4,101	but not more than	4,200	19.70
4,201	but not more than	4,300	20.30
4,301	but not more than	4,400	20.90
4,401	but not more than	4,500	21.50
4,501	but not more than	4,600	35.00
4,601	but not more than	4,700	37.00
4,701	but not more than	4,800	39.00
4,801	but not more than	4,900	41.00
4,901	but not more than	5,000	43.00
5,001	but not more than	5,100	45.00
5,101	but not more than	5,200	47.00
5,201	but not more than	5,300	49.00
5,301	but not more than	5,400	51.00
5,401	but not more than	5,500	53.00
5,501	but not more than	5,600	55.00
5,601	but not more than	5,700	57.00
5,701	but not more than	5,800	59.00
5,801	but not more than	5,900	61.00
5,901	but not more than	6,000	63.00
6,001	but not more than	6,100	65.00
6,101	but not more than	6,200	67.00
6,201	but not more than	6,300	69.00
6,301	but not more than	6,400	71.00
6,401	but not more than	6,500	73.00
6,501	but not more than	6,600	75.00
6,601	but not more than	6,700	77.00
6,701	but not more than	6,800	79.00
6,801	but not more than	6,900	81.00
6,901	but not more than	7,000	83.00
7,001	but not more than	7,100	85.00
7,101	but not more than	7,200	87.00
7,201	but not more than	7,300	89.00
7,301	but not more than	7,400	91.00
7,401	but not more than	7,500	93.00
7,501	but not more than	7,600	95.00
7,601	but not more than	7,700	97.00
7,701	but not more than	7,800	99.00
7,801	but not more than	7,900	101.00
7,901	but not more than	8,000	103.00
8,001	but not more than	8,100	105.00
8,101	but not more than	8,200	107.00

Empty Weight (Pounds)	Range		Registration Fee
8,201	but not more than	8,300	109.00
8,301	but not more than	8,400	111.00
8,401	but not more than	8,500	113.00
8,501	but not more than	8,600	115.00
8,601	but not more than	8,700	117.00
8,701	but not more than	8,800	119.00
8,801	but not more than	8,900	121.00
8,901	but not more than	9,000	123.00
9,001	but not more than	9,100	125.00
9,101	but not more than	9,200	127.00
9,201	but not more than	9,300	129.00
9,301	but not more than	9,400	131.00
9,401	but not more than	9,500	133.00
9,501	but not more than	9,600	135.00
9,601	but not more than	9,700	137.00
9,701	but not more than	9,800	139.00
9,801	but not more than	9,900	141.00
9,901	but not more than	10,000	143.00
10,001	but not more than	10,100	144.50
10,101	but not more than	10,200	146.00
10,201	but not more than	10,300	147.50
10,301	but not more than	10,400	149.00
10,401	but not more than	10,500	150.50
10,501	but not more than	10,600	152.00
10,601	but not more than	10,700	153.50
10,701	but not more than	10,800	155.00
10,801	but not more than	10,900	156.50
10,901	but not more than	11,000	158.00
11,001	but not more than	11,100	159.50
11,101	but not more than	11,200	161.00
11,201	but not more than	11,300	162.50
11,301	but not more than	11,400	164.00
11,401	but not more than	11,500	165.50
11,501	but not more than	11,600	167.00
11,601	but not more than	11,700	168.50
11,701	but not more than	11,800	170.00
11,801	but not more than	11,900	171.50
11,901	but not more than	12,000	173.00
12,001	but not more than	12,100	174.50
12,101	but not more than	12,200	176.00
12,201	but not more than	12,300	177.50
12,301	but not more than	12,400	179.00
12,401	but not more than	12,500	180.50
12,501	but not more than	12,600	182.00
12,601	but not more than	12,700	183.50
12,701	but not more than	12,800	185.00
12,801	but not more than	12,900	186.50
12,901	but not more than	13,000	188.00
13,001	but not more than	13,100	189.50
13,101	but not more than	13,200	191.00
13,201	but not more than	13,300	192.50
13,301	but not more than	13,400	194.00
13,401	but not more than	13,500	195.50
13,501	but not more than	13,600	197.00
13,601	but not more than	13,700	198.50
13,701	but not more than	13,800	200.00
13,801	but not more than	13,900	201.50
13,901	but not more than	14,000	203.00
14,001	but not more than	14,100	204.50
14,101	but not more than	14,200	206.00
14,201	but not more than	14,300	207.50
14,301	but not more than	14,400	209.00
14,401	but not more than	14,500	210.50

Empty Weight (Pounds)		Range	Registration Fee
14,501	but not more than	14,600	212.00
14,601	but not more than	14,700	213.50
14,701	but not more than	14,800	215.00
14,801	but not more than	14,900	216.50
14,901	but not more than	15,000	218.00
15,001	but not more than	15,100	219.50
15,101	but not more than	15,200	221.00
15,201	but not more than	15,300	222.50
15,301	but not more than	15,400	224.00
15,401	but not more than	15,500	225.50
15,501	but not more than	15,600	227.00
15,601	but not more than	15,700	228.50
15,701	but not more than	15,800	230.00
15,801	but not more than	15,900	231.50
15,901	but not more than	16,000	233.00

(b) (I) Except as provided in subparagraphs (II) and (III) of this paragraph (b), for each vehicle registered under this subsection (5) having an empty weight exceeding sixteen thousand pounds, the registration fee shall be based upon the declared gross vehicle weight of the vehicle registered, according to the following schedule:

Declared Gross Vehicle Weight (Pounds)	Registration Fee
16,001 but not more than 20,000	$ 330
20,001 but not more than 24,000	410
24,001 but not more than 30,000	490
30,001 but not more than 36,000	630
36,001 but not more than 42,000	770
42,001 but not more than 48,000	940
48,001 but not more than 54,000	1,150
54,001 but not more than 60,000	1,370
60,001 but not more than 66,000	1,570
66,001 but not more than 74,000	1,850
Over 74,000	1,975

(II) For each vehicle registered under this subsection (5) that has an empty weight exceeding sixteen thousand pounds and that is used in the operations of a common or contract carrier for hire, such registration fee shall be based upon the declared gross vehicle weight of the vehicle registered, according to the following schedule:

Declared Gross Vehicle Weight (Pounds)	Registration Fee
16,001 but not more than 20,000	$ 440
20,001 but not more than 24,000	550
24,001 but not more than 30,000	660
30,001 but not more than 36,000	770
36,001 but not more than 42,000	930
42,001 but not more than 48,000	1,130
48,001 but not more than 54,000	1,430
54,001 but not more than 60,000	1,700
60,001 but not more than 66,000	1,980
66,001 but not more than 74,000	2,260
Over 74,000	2,350

(III) (A) For each vehicle registered under this subsection (5) that has an empty weight exceeding sixteen thousand pounds and that is operated less than ten thousand miles in all jurisdictions during each year, such registration fee shall be based upon the declared gross vehicle weight of the vehicle registered, according to the following schedule:

Declared Gross Vehicle Weight (Pounds)	Registration Fee
16,001 but not more than 20,000	$ 330
20,001 but not more than 24,000	360
24,001 but not more than 30,000	380
30,001 but not more than 36,000	440
36,001 but not more than 42,000	500
42,001 but not more than 48,000	580
48,001 but not more than 54,000	600
54,001 but not more than 60,000	640
60,001 but not more than 66,000	660
66,001 but not more than 74,000	690
Over 74,000	710

(B) If a vehicle qualifies for both a registration fee provided in this subparagraph (III) and a registration fee provided in subparagraph (I) or (II) of this paragraph (b), the lesser registration fee shall apply.

(C) If a person replaces a registered vehicle with another vehicle, the mileage history of the vehicle being replaced may be used to qualify the new vehicle for the fees assessed under this subparagraph (III).

(D) If a person purchases an established business that is located in this state and the purchase of the business includes the purchase of vehicles, the mileage history of a vehicle so purchased may be used to qualify for the fees assessed under this subparagraph (III) if the business operations remain the same after the purchase and if, during the twelve-month period immediately preceding the date of purchase, the vehicle has been registered in Colorado and has been in operation in the business. A person purchasing a business shall present a copy of the current vehicle registration of the previous owner for each vehicle to be registered pursuant to this sub-subparagraph (D).

(E) If a truck or truck tractor having an empty weight exceeding sixteen thousand pounds is purchased by a person owning one or more other such vehicles and the other such vehicles owned by the purchaser all qualify for the fees assessed under this subparagraph (III), the purchased truck or truck tractor also qualifies for the fees assessed under this subparagraph (III). A person seeking to register a truck or truck tractor pursuant to this sub-subparagraph (E) shall present a copy of the current vehicle registration for each of the other trucks and truck tractors with empty weights exceeding sixteen thousand pounds that are owned by such person.

(c) For each vehicle registered under this subsection (5) that is exempt from the registration fees assessed under paragraph (b) of this subsection (5) under paragraph (d), (f), (g), or (h) of subsection (9) of this section and that weighs more than sixteen thousand pounds empty weight, the registration fee shall be one hundred seventy-five dollars plus one dollar and fifteen cents for each one hundred pounds, or fraction thereof, in excess of sixteen thousand pounds.

(d) For each vehicle registered under this subsection (5) that is exempt from the registration fees assessed under paragraph (b) of this subsection (5) pursuant to paragraph (d), (f), or (g) of subsection (9) of this section and that weighs more than sixteen thousand pounds empty weight, the registration fee shall be two hundred thirty-three dollars plus one dollar and fifty cents for each one hundred pounds, or fraction thereof, in excess of sixteen thousand pounds.

(e) Each vehicle registered under this subsection (5) having an empty weight not in excess of sixteen thousand pounds that is operated in combination with a trailer or semitrailer, which is commonly referred to as a tractor-trailer, shall be assessed according to paragraph (b) of this subsection (5).

(6) In lieu of the payment of registration fees specified in subsections (3) and (5) of this section, the owner of a truck, truck tractor, trailer, or semitrailer operating in interstate commerce may apply to the department for a special unladen weight registration. The registration shall be valid for a period of thirty days from issuance and shall authorize the operation of the vehicle only when empty. The fee for registration of a truck or truck tractor shall be five dollars. The fee for registration of a trailer or semitrailer shall be three dollars. The moneys from the fees shall be transmitted to the state treasurer, who shall credit the same to the highway users tax fund for allocation and expenditure as specified in section 43-4-205 (5.5) (c), C.R.S.

(7) In lieu of the payment of registration fees specified in subsections (3) and (5) of this section, the owner of a truck or truck tractor operating in interstate commerce shall apply to the department for a special laden weight registration. The registration shall be valid for seventy-two hours after issuance and shall authorize the operation of the vehicle when loaded. The moneys collected by the department from the fees shall be transmitted to the state treasurer, who shall credit the same to the highway users tax fund for allocation and expenditure as specified in section 43-4-205 (5.5) (c), C.R.S. The fee for the special registration of a truck or a truck tractor shall be based on the actual gross vehicle weight of the vehicle and its cargo, computed to the nearest pound, according to the following schedule:

Declared Gross Vehicle Weight (Pounds)	Registration Fee
10,001 but not more than 30,000	$ 60
30,001 but not more than 60,000	70
Over 60,000	80

(8) (a) The owner or operator of a motor vehicle that is exempt from the registration fees assessed under paragraph (b) or (c) of subsection (9) of this section may apply to the department for a temporary commercial registration permit for such motor vehicle. Such temporary commercial registration permit shall authorize the operation of such motor vehicle in commerce so long as the motor vehicle is operated solely in agricultural harvest operations within Colorado.

(b) A temporary commercial registration permit issued pursuant to this subsection (8) shall be valid for a period not to exceed sixty days. A maximum of two such temporary commercial registration permits may be issued for a motor vehicle in a twelve-month period. The fee for issuance of a temporary commercial registration permit for a motor vehicle shall be based upon the configuration and number of axles of such motor vehicle according to the following schedule:

Configuration	Registration permit
Single unit (two axles)	$ 80.00
Single unit (three or more axles)	120.00
Combination unit (any number of axles)	200.00

(c) The moneys collected by the department from the fees for temporary commercial registration permits shall be transmitted to the state treasurer, who shall credit the same to the highway users tax fund.

(d) This subsection (8) shall not be interpreted to affect the authority of a dealer in motor vehicles to use a dealer plate obtained under section 42-3-116 to demonstrate a truck or truck tractor by allowing a prospective buyer to operate such truck or truck tractor when loaded.

(9) The registration fees imposed by paragraph (b) of subsection (5) of this section shall not apply:

(a) To a motor vehicle operated by a manufacturer, dealer, or transporter issued plates pursuant to section 42-3-304 (6) and (7);

(b) To a farm truck or truck tractor registered under subsection (4) of this section;

(c) To a farm tractor or to a farm tractor and trailer or wagon combination;

(d) To a vehicle specially constructed for towing, wrecking, and repairing that is not otherwise used for transporting cargo;

(e) To a vehicle owned by the state or any political or governmental subdivision thereof;

(f) To an operator-owned vehicle transporting racehorses to and from the stud or to and from a racing meet in Colorado;

(g) To a veterinary mobile truck unit;

(h) To a mobile mixing concrete truck or trash compacting truck or to trucks designated by the executive director of the department as special use trucks;

(i) To a noncommercial or recreational vehicle registered under subsection (13) of this section.

(10) The owner or operator of a truck, truck tractor, trailer, or semitrailer operating over the public highways of this state and rendering service pursuant to a temporary certificate of public convenience and necessity issued by the public utilities commission shall pay for the issuance or renewal of such temporary certificate a fee of ten dollars.

(11) (a) The owner or operator of a passenger bus operating over the public highways of this state and rendering service pursuant to a temporary certificate of public convenience and necessity issued by the public utilities commission shall pay for the issuance or renewal of such temporary certificate a fee of ten dollars, which fee shall be in lieu of the tax assessed under this subsection (11), shall be credited to the highway users tax fund created in section 43-4-201, C.R.S., as required by section 43-4-203 (1) (c), C.R.S., and shall be allocated and expended as specified in section 43-4-205 (5.5) (d), C.R.S.

(b) The owner or operator of a passenger bus that is registered in another state and that is used to make an occasional trip into this state need not obtain a permit from the public utilities commission as provided in article 10.1 of title 40, C.R.S., but may instead apply to the department for the issuance of a trip permit and shall pay to the department for the issuance of such trip permit a fee of twenty-five dollars or the amount of passenger-mile tax becoming due and payable under paragraph (a) of this subsection (11) by reason of such trip, whichever amount is greater. The fee or passenger-mile tax shall be credited to the highway users tax fund created in section 43-4-201, C.R.S., as required by section 43-4-203 (1) (c), C.R.S., and allocated and expended as specified in section 43-4-205 (5.5) (d), C.R.S.

(12) (a) In lieu of registration under section 42-3-304 (14), the owner or operator of special mobile machinery that the owner or operator desires to operate over the public highways of this state may elect to pay an annual fee computed at the rate of two dollars and fifty cents per ton of vehicle weight for operation not to exceed a distance of two thousand five hundred miles in any registration period.

(b) In lieu of registration under section 42-3-304 (14), a public utility, as defined by section 40-1-103, C.R.S., owning or operating a utility truck having an empty weight in excess of ten thousand pounds that it desires to operate over the public highways of this state may elect to pay an annual registration fee for such a vehicle computed at the rate of ten dollars per ton of vehicle weight.

(13) The annual registration fee for a noncommercial or recreational vehicle, except a motor home, operated on the public highways of this state with an empty weight of ten thousand pounds or less shall be computed according to the schedule provided in subsection (5) of this section, and, for a noncommercial or recreational vehicle exceeding ten thousand pounds, the fee shall be twenty-four dollars and fifty cents plus sixty cents for each one hundred pounds in excess of four thousand five hundred pounds.

(14) (a) In addition to any other fee required by this section, on and after July 1, 2011, each authorized agent shall collect a fee of:

(I) Fifty cents per paid registration of any motor vehicle that is not exempt from the motor insurance identification fee pursuant to section 42-3-304 (1) (b); or

(II) Ten cents per paid registration of any motor vehicle that is exempt from the motor insurance identification fee pursuant to section 42-3-304 (1) (b).

(b) The fee required by paragraph (a) of this subsection (14) shall apply to every registration of a motor vehicle that is designed primarily to be operated or drawn on any highway in the state and shall be in addition to the annual registration fee for the vehicle; except that the fee shall not apply to a vehicle that is exempt from payment of the registration fees imposed by this article. The fee shall be credited to the Colorado state titling and registration account in the highway users tax fund created in section 42-1-211 (2).

Editor's note: (4) Section 5 of chapter 136, Session Laws of Colorado 2011, provides that the act adding subsection (4)(e) applies to applications for registration filed on or after January 1, 2012.

42-3-307. Enforcement powers of department. (1) The department may administer and enforce sections 42-3-304 and 42-3-306, including the right to inspect and audit the books, records, and documents of an owner or operator of a vehicle operated upon the public highways who is required to pay any registration fee or tax imposed, and the executive director of the department may promulgate such reasonable rules as the director deems necessary or suitable for such administration and enforcement.

(2) The powers granted in this section shall be separate, apart, and distinct from any powers or duties conferred prior to January 1, 1955, upon the public utilities commission with respect

to the issuance of certificates of public convenience and necessity, contract carrier permits, and the regulation and supervision of motor carriers.

42-3-308. Taxpayer statements - payment of tax - estimates - penalties - deposits - delinquency proceedings. (1) (a) Every owner or operator of a motor vehicle operated on a public highway of this state and required to pay the passenger-mile tax imposed by sections 42-3-304 and 42-3-306 shall, on or before the twenty-fifth day of each month, file with the department, on forms prescribed by the department and the public utilities commission, a statement, subject to the penalties for perjury in the second degree, showing the name and address of the owner of the motor vehicle, total miles traveled, and total number of passengers carried in this state during the preceding month and such other information as required by the department and the commission and shall compute and pay such tax; except that the executive director of the department may authorize the filing of statements and the payment of tax for periods in excess of one month but not to exceed a period of twelve months.

(b) If payment of the tax so computed is not made on or before the due date, there shall be added a penalty of three percent per month until such time as the full amount has been paid; but the executive director of the department may waive all or any portion of the penalty for good cause.

(2) If the owner or operator of a motor vehicle, required to file a statement as provided in subsection (1) of this section, fails, neglects, or refuses to file the statement and to pay the tax due, the department may estimate the amount of tax due for the period for which no statement was filed, add a penalty of ten percent plus one-half of one percent per month after the date when due, not to exceed eighteen percent in the aggregate, and mail the estimate to the last-known address of such owner or operator. The amount so estimated, together with the penalty, shall become fixed, due, and payable ten days after the date of mailing, unless such owner or operator, within the ten days, files and pays a true and correct statement of the tax due for the period.

(3) (a) If an owner or operator of a vehicle knowingly makes and files with the department a false or fraudulent statement with intent to evade payment of any passenger-mile tax due, the department shall, as soon as it discovers the false or fraudulent nature of such statement, make an investigation and determine the correct amount of tax due, add a penalty of one hundred percent, and proceed to collect the total amount by distraint and sale as provided in section 39-21-114, C.R.S. If an owner or operator disputes the amount asserted to be due and payable, that owner or operator shall be entitled to a hearing before the executive director of the department, and the decision of the executive director shall be subject to judicial review.

(b) A person who willfully fails or refuses to make the report required by this section, or who makes a false or fraudulent return, or who willfully fails to pay any tax owed by such person, shall be punished as provided by section 39-21-118, C.R.S.

(4) All passenger-mile taxes and penalties determined to be due from an owner or operator of a motor vehicle and not paid on the date when the same are due and payable shall become and remain a prior and perpetual lien upon all the personal property of such owner or operator until the full amount of the tax determined to be due, together with all penalties, has been paid. Nothing in this section shall be construed to abrogate or diminish the rights of bona fide purchasers, lienors, or pledgees for value and without notice.

(5) Taxes collected pursuant to this section and any penalties or interest charges imposed pursuant to this section shall be credited to the highway users tax fund created in section 43-4-201, C.R.S., as required by section 43-4-203 (1) (c), C.R.S., and allocated and expended as specified in section 43-4-205 (5.5) (d), C.R.S.

42-3-309. Permit to be secured - records kept - penalties. (1) Every owner or operator of a motor vehicle operated over any public highway of this state who is required to pay the passenger-mile tax imposed by sections 42-3-304 and 42-3-306 shall apply to the department and secure a passenger-mile tax permit and shall keep and maintain true and correct records of the operations of such motor vehicles, including the number of miles operated and the number of passengers carried, in such form as to reflect the actual activity of all such motor vehicles and as may be prescribed by the department and the public utilities commission. Such owner or operator shall preserve all such records for a period of four years. The passenger-mile tax permit shall remain effective until the owner advises the department of a change in ownership or a discontinuance of business or until such owner has failed to file tax reports and pay any applicable passenger-mile tax for four successive tax periods.

(2) For failure to apply for and secure a permit, the executive director of the department may impose a penalty in an amount equal to twenty-five percent of any tax found to be due and payable or twenty-five dollars, whichever is greater.

(3) Failure or refusal of an owner or operator to keep and maintain such records shall, upon certification by the department to the public utilities commission, be cause for suspension or revocation of a certificate of public convenience and necessity or a contract carrier permit.

(4) (a) If an examination of the financial responsibility of an owner or operator of a motor vehicle subject to the payment of the passenger-

mile tax indicates that a financial guarantee in the form of cash, a certified check, a bank money order, a bond, or a negotiable certificate of deposit issued by a commercial bank doing business in this state and acceptable to the executive director is necessary to guarantee payment of the tax, the owner or operator may be required to deposit such guarantee with the department in an amount no greater than twice the amount of tax estimated by the executive director to become due and payable each tax period. If the deposit is in cash or a negotiable certificate of deposit, it shall be subject to forfeiture upon failure of the owner or operator to comply with sections 42-3-304 to 42-3-308, this section, articles 10 and 11 of title 40, C.R.S., or the rules of the department or the public utilities commission; if it is a surety bond, it shall be conditioned upon the insured's faithful compliance with all applicable statutes and rules.

(b) Failure or refusal of an owner or operator to provide or to continue in effect the guarantee when required in paragraph (a) of this subsection (4) shall, upon certification by the department to the public utilities commission, be cause for denial, suspension, or revocation of a certificate of public convenience and necessity or a contract carrier permit.

(c) All cash, certified checks, bank money orders, negotiable certificates of deposit, and surety bonds deposited in compliance with this section shall be delivered into the custody of the state treasurer and held by the state treasurer subject to further order of the department. If an owner or operator ceases operations, the deposit or any balance thereof shall be returned to the owner or operator after all taxes, penalties, fees, and charges owed by such owner or operator pursuant to this article have been paid.

(5) The following penalties shall be imposed if a person negligently or knowingly includes an error in records required by subsection (1) of this section and such error is contained in a previously filed statement under section 42-3-308:

(a) Twenty-five percent of the deficiency assessed; and

(b) Interest of one-half of one percent per month on the deficiency assessed, which shall be in addition to the interest due under section 39-21-109, C.R.S.

42-3-310. Additional registration fees - apportionment of fees. (1) Every owner of a motor vehicle, trailer, or semitrailer that is primarily designed to be operated or drawn upon a highway, except the vehicles specifically exempted from payment of registration fees by this article, shall, within the registration period prescribed by law or within ten days after the date of purchase of any such vehicle, pay an annual registration fee of one dollar and fifty cents, which annual fee shall be in addition to the annual registration fee prescribed by law for such vehicle.

(2) The additional registration fee provided for in this section shall not be transmitted to the department, but the aggregate amount of all such fees paid over by the authorized agent to the county treasurer shall be retained by the treasurer and allocated by the treasurer to the county and to the cities and incorporated towns located within the boundaries of the county on the basis of the record of rural and urban registrations that indicates the place of residence of each vehicle owner paying registration fees.

(3) The owner of a vehicle specified in subsection (1) of this section who is required to pay an annual registration fee for such vehicle to the department shall also pay the additional annual registration fee provided for in this section to the department, and the department shall transmit such additional fee to the proper county treasurer, as indicated by the place of residence of such owner, and such county treasurer shall allocate such fee in the manner prescribed in subsection (2) of this section.

(4) Two dollars and fifty cents of each annual vehicle registration fee imposed by sections 42-3-304 to 42-3-306, exclusive of the annual registration fees prescribed for motorcycles, trailer coaches, special mobile machinery, and trailers having an empty weight of two thousand pounds or less and exclusive of a registration fee paid for a fractional part of a year, shall not be transmitted to the department but shall be paid over by the authorized agent, as collected, to the county treasurer, who shall credit the same to an account entitled "apportioned vehicle registration fees". On the tenth day of each month, the county treasurer shall apportion the balance in the account existing on the last day of the immediately preceding month between the county and the cities and incorporated towns located within the boundaries of the county on the basis of the record of rural and urban registrations that indicates the place of residence of each vehicle owner.

(5) All amounts allocated to the county shall be credited to the county road and bridge fund, and all amounts allocated to a city or incorporated town shall be credited to an appropriate fund and expended by such city or incorporated town only for the construction and maintenance of highways, roads, and streets located within its boundaries.

42-3-311. Low-power scooter registration - fee. (1) Every low-power scooter sold in this state shall have an identification number stamped on its frame, which number shall be recorded upon registration. A low-power scooter shall be registered with the department, which registration shall be evidenced by a number decal that is securely affixed to the low-power scooter frame in a conspicuous place. Registration shall be valid for a period of three years, and the fee for such registration shall be five dollars. Retail sellers of low-power scooters shall retain one dollar from each such fee, and four dollars of each such fee shall be forwarded monthly to the department for deposit in the state treasury to the credit of the highway users tax fund.

(2) The general assembly shall make appropriations from the fund for the expenses of the administration of this section, and any fees credited to the fund pursuant to subsection (1) of this section in excess of the amount of the appropriations shall be allocated and expended as specified in section 43-4-205 (5.5) (f), C.R.S. The department shall promulgate rules authorizing retail sellers of low-power scooters to be agents of the department for such registration.

42-3-312. Special license plate surcharge. In addition to any other fee imposed by this article, an applicant for a special license plate created by rule in accordance with section 42-3-207, as such section existed when the plate was created, or license plates issued pursuant to sections 42-3-211 to 42-3-218, sections 42-3-221 to 42-3-234, and sections 42-3-237 to 42-3-240 shall pay an issuance fee of twenty-five dollars; except that the fee is not imposed on special license plates exempted from additional fees for the issuance of a military special license plate by section 42-3-213 (1) (b) (II). The department shall transfer the fee to the state treasurer, who shall credit it to the licensing services cash fund created in section 42-2-114.5.

REGULATION OF VEHICLES AND TRAFFIC

ARTICLE 4
Regulation of Vehicles and Traffic

PART 1
TRAFFIC REGULATION - GENERALLY

42-4-101.	Short title.
42-4-102.	Legislative declaration.
42-4-103.	Scope and effect of article - exceptions to provisions.
42-4-104.	Adoption of traffic control manual.
42-4-105.	Local traffic control devices.
42-4-106.	Who may restrict right to use highways.
42-4-107.	Obedience to police officers.
42-4-108.	Public officers to obey provisions - exceptions for emergency vehicles.
42-4-109.	Low-power scooters, animals, skis, skates, and toy vehicles on highways.
42-4-109.5.	Low-speed electric vehicles.
42-4-109.6.	Class B low-speed electric vehicles - effective date - rules.
42-4-110.	Provisions uniform throughout state.
42-4-110.5.	Automated vehicle identification systems.
42-4-111.	Powers of local authorities.
42-4-112.	Noninterference with the rights of owners of realty.
42-4-113.	Appropriations for administration of article.
42-4-114.	Removal of traffic hazards.
42-4-115.	Information on traffic law enforcement - collection - profiling - annual report - repeal. (Repealed)
42-4-116.	Restrictions for minor drivers - definitions.
42-4-117.	Personal mobility devices.
42-4-118.	Establishment of wildlife crossing zones - report - repeal.

PART 2
EQUIPMENT

42-4-201.	Obstruction of view or driving mechanism - hazardous situation.
42-4-202.	Unsafe vehicles - penalty - identification plates.
42-4-203.	Unsafe vehicles - spot inspections.
42-4-204.	When lighted lamps are required.
42-4-205.	Head lamps on motor vehicles.
42-4-206.	Tail lamps and reflectors.
42-4-207.	Clearance and identification.
42-4-208.	Stop lamps and turn signals.
42-4-209.	Lamp or flag on projecting load.
42-4-210.	Lamps on parked vehicles.
42-4-211.	Lamps on farm equipment and other vehicles and equipment.
42-4-212.	Spot lamps and auxiliary lamps.
42-4-213.	Audible and visual signals on emergency vehicles.
42-4-214.	Visual signals on service vehicles.
42-4-215.	Signal lamps and devices - additional lighting equipment.
42-4-215.5.	Signal lamps and devices - street rod vehicles and custom motor vehicles. (Repealed)
42-4-216.	Multiple-beam road lights.
42-4-217.	Use of multiple-beam lights.
42-4-218.	Single-beam road-lighting equipment.
42-4-219.	Number of lamps permitted.
42-4-220.	Low-power scooters - lighting equipment - department control - use and operation.
42-4-221.	Bicycle and personal mobility device equipment.
42-4-222.	Volunteer firefighters - volunteer ambulance attendants - special lights and alarm systems.
42-4-223.	Brakes.
42-4-224.	Horns or warning devices.
42-4-225.	Mufflers - prevention of noise.
42-4-226.	Mirrors - exterior placements.
42-4-227.	Windows unobstructed - certain materials prohibited - windshield wiper requirements.
42-4-228.	Restrictions on tire equipment.
42-4-229.	Safety glazing material in motor vehicles.
42-4-230.	Emergency lighting equipment - who must carry.
42-4-231.	Parking lights.
42-4-232.	Minimum safety standards for motorcycles and low-power scooters.
42-4-233.	Alteration of suspension system.

42-4-234.	Slow-moving vehicles - display of emblem.		- emissions mechanics - requirements.
42-4-235.	Minimum standards for commercial vehicles - rules - repeal.	42-4-309.	Vehicle fleet owners - motor vehicle dealers - authority to conduct inspections - fleet inspection stations - motor vehicle dealer test facilities - contracts with licensed inspection-only entities.
42-4-236.	Child restraint systems required - definitions - exemptions.		
42-4-237.	Safety belt systems - mandatory use - exemptions - penalty.		
42-4-238.	Blue and red lights - illegal use or possession.	42-4-310.	Periodic emissions control inspection required.
42-4-239.	Misuse of a wireless telephone - definitions - penalty - preemption.	42-4-311.	Operation of inspection and readjustment stations - inspection-only facilities - fleet inspection stations - motor vehicle dealer test facilities - enhanced inspection centers.
42-4-240.	Low-speed electric vehicle equipment requirements.		
42-4-241.	Unlawful removal of tow-truck signage - unlawful usage of tow-truck signage.		
		42-4-312.	Improper representation as emissions inspection and readjustment station - inspection-only facility - fleet inspection station - motor vehicle dealer test facility - enhanced inspection center.

PART 3
EMISSIONS INSPECTION

42-4-301.	Legislative declarations - enactment of enhanced emissions program not waiver of state right to challenge authority to require specific loaded mode transient dynamometer technology in automobile emissions testing.		
		42-4-313.	Penalties.
		42-4-314.	Automobile air pollution control systems - tampering - operation of vehicle - penalty.
		42-4-315.	Warranties.
		42-4-316.	AIR program - demonstration of compliance with ambient air quality standards and transportation conformity.
42-4-302.	Commencement of basic emissions program - authority of commission.		
42-4-303.	Sunrise review of registration of repair facilities. (Repealed)	42-4-316.5.	Termination of vehicle emissions testing program - repeal.
42-4-304.	Definitions relating to automobile inspection and readjustment program.	42-4-317.	Purchase or lease of new motor vehicles by state agencies - clean-burning alternative fuels - definitions. (Repealed)
42-4-305.	Powers and duties of executive director - automobile inspection and readjustment program - basic emissions program - enhanced emissions program - clean screen program.		

PART 4
DIESEL INSPECTION PROGRAM

		42-4-401.	Definitions.
		42-4-402.	Administration of inspection program.
42-4-306.	Powers and duties of commission - automobile inspection and readjustment program - basic emissions program - enhanced emissions program - clean screen program.	42-4-403.	Powers and duties of the commission.
		42-4-404.	Powers and duties of the executive director of the department of public health and environment.
42-4-307.	Powers and duties of the department of public health and environment - division of administration - automobile inspection and readjustment program - basic emissions program - enhanced emissions program - clean screen program.	42-4-405.	Powers and duties of executive director.
		42-4-406.	Requirement of certification of emissions control for registration - testing for diesel smoke opacity compliance.
		42-4-407.	Requirements for a diesel emission-opacity inspection - licensure as diesel emissions inspection station - licensure as emissions inspector.
42-4-307.5.	Clean screen authority - enterprise - revenue bonds.		
42-4-307.7.	Vehicle emissions testing - remote sensing - rules.		
42-4-308.	Inspection and readjustment stations - inspection-only facilities - fleet inspection stations - motor vehicle dealer test facilities - contractor - emissions inspectors	42-4-408.	Operation of diesel inspection station.
		42-4-409.	Improper representation of a diesel inspection station.
		42-4-410.	Inclusion in the diesel inspection program.

42-4-411.	Applicability of this part to heavy-duty diesel fleets of nine or more.	42-4-615.	School zones - increase in penalties for moving traffic violations.
42-4-412.	Air pollution violations.	42-4-616.	Wildlife crossing zones - increase in penalties for moving traffic violations.
42-4-413.	Visible emissions from diesel-powered motor vehicles unlawful - penalty.		
42-4-414.	Heavy-duty diesel fleet inspection and maintenance program - penalty - rules.		

PART 7
RIGHTS-OF-WAY

42-4-701.	Vehicles approaching or entering intersection.
42-4-702.	Vehicle turning left.
42-4-703.	Entering through highway - stop or yield intersection.
42-4-704.	Vehicle entering roadway.
42-4-705.	Operation of vehicle approached by emergency vehicle - operation of vehicle approaching stationary emergency vehicle or stationary towing carrier vehicle.
42-4-706.	Obedience to railroad signal.
42-4-707.	Certain vehicles must stop at railroad grade crossings.
42-4-708.	Moving heavy equipment at railroad grade crossing.
42-4-709.	Stop when traffic obstructed.
42-4-710.	Emerging from or entering alley, driveway, or building.
42-4-711.	Driving on mountain highways.
42-4-712.	Driving in highway work area.
42-4-713.	Yielding right-of-way to transit buses - definitions - penalty.

PART 5
SIZE - WEIGHT - LOAD

42-4-501.	Size and weight violations - penalty.
42-4-502.	Width of vehicles.
42-4-503.	Projecting loads on passenger vehicles.
42-4-504.	Height and length of vehicles.
42-4-505.	Longer vehicle combinations - rules.
42-4-506.	Trailers and towed vehicles.
42-4-507.	Wheel and axle loads.
42-4-508.	Gross weight of vehicles and loads.
42-4-509.	Vehicles weighed - excess removed.
42-4-510.	Permits for excess size and weight and for manufactured homes - rules - repeal.
42-4-511.	Permit standards - state and local.
42-4-511.2.	Authority for cooperative agreements with regional states on excess size or weight vehicles - regulations.
42-4-512.	Liability for damage to highway.

PART 8
PEDESTRIANS

42-4-801.	Pedestrian obedience to traffic control devices and traffic regulations.
42-4-802.	Pedestrians' right-of-way in crosswalks.
42-4-803.	Crossing at other than crosswalks.
42-4-804.	Pedestrian to use right half of crosswalk. (Repealed)
42-4-805.	Pedestrians walking or traveling in a wheelchair on highways.
42-4-806.	Driving through safety zone prohibited.
42-4-807.	Drivers to exercise due care.
42-4-808.	Drivers and pedestrians, other than persons in wheelchairs, to yield to persons with disabilities.

PART 6
SIGNALS - SIGNS - MARKINGS

42-4-601.	Department to sign highways, where.
42-4-602.	Local traffic control devices.
42-4-603.	Obedience to official traffic control devices.
42-4-604.	Traffic control signal legend.
42-4-605.	Flashing signals.
42-4-606.	Display of unauthorized signs or devices.
42-4-607.	Interference with official devices.
42-4-608.	Signals by hand or signal device.
42-4-609.	Method of giving hand and arm signals.
42-4-610.	Unauthorized insignia.
42-4-611.	Paraplegic persons or persons with disabilities - distress flag.
42-4-612.	When signals are inoperative or malfunctioning.
42-4-613.	Failure to pay toll established by regional transportation authority.
42-4-614.	Designation of highway maintenance, repair, or construction zones - signs - increase in penalties for speeding violations.

PART 9
TURNING - STOPPING

42-4-901.	Required position and method of turning.
42-4-902.	Limitations on turning around.
42-4-903.	Turning movements and required signals.

PART 10
DRIVING - OVERTAKING - PASSING

42-4-1001.	Drive on right side - exceptions.
42-4-1002.	Passing oncoming vehicles.

42-4-1003.	Overtaking a vehicle on the left.		42-4-1301.2.	Refusal of test - effect on driver's license - revocation - reinstatement. (Repealed)
42-4-1004.	When overtaking on the right is permitted.		42-4-1301.3.	Alcohol and drug driving safety program.
42-4-1005.	Limitations on overtaking on the left.		42-4-1301.4.	Useful public service - definitions - local programs - assessment of cost.
42-4-1006.	One-way roadways and rotary traffic islands.		42-4-1302.	Stopping of suspect.
42-4-1007.	Driving on roadways laned for traffic.		42-4-1303.	Records - prima facie proof.
42-4-1008.	Following too closely.		42-4-1304.	Samples of blood or other bodily substance - duties of department of public health and environment.
42-4-1008.5.	Crowding or threatening bicyclist.			
42-4-1009.	Coasting prohibited.			
42-4-1010.	Driving on divided or controlled-access highways.		42-4-1305.	Open alcoholic beverage container - motor vehicle - prohibited.
42-4-1011.	Use of runaway vehicle ramps.		42-4-1306.	Interagency task force on drunk driving - creation.
42-4-1012.	High occupancy vehicle (HOV) and high occupancy toll (HOT) lanes.		42-4-1307.	Penalties for traffic offenses involving alcohol and drugs - repeal.
42-4-1013.	Passing lane - definitions - penalty.			

PART 11
SPEED REGULATIONS

42-4-1101.	Speed limits.
42-4-1102.	Altering of speed limits.
42-4-1103.	Minimum speed regulation.
42-4-1104.	Speed limits on elevated structures.
42-4-1105.	Speed contests - speed exhibitions - aiding and facilitating - immobilization of motor vehicle - definitions.
42-4-1106.	Minimum speed in left lane - interstate 70.

PART 12
PARKING

42-4-1201.	Starting parked vehicle.
42-4-1202.	Parking or abandonment of vehicles.
42-4-1203.	Ski areas to install signs.
42-4-1204.	Stopping, standing, or parking prohibited in specified places.
42-4-1205.	Parking at curb or edge of roadway.
42-4-1206.	Unattended motor vehicle.
42-4-1207.	Opening and closing vehicle doors.
42-4-1208.	Parking privileges for persons with disabilities - applicability - rules.
42-4-1209.	Owner liability for parking violations.
42-4-1210.	Designated areas on private property for authorized vehicles.
42-4-1211.	Limitations on backing.
42-4-1212.	Pay parking access for disabled.

PART 13
ALCOHOL AND DRUG OFFENSES

42-4-1300.3.	Definitions. (Repealed)
42-4-1301.	Driving under the influence - driving while impaired - driving with excessive alcoholic content - definitions - penalties.
42-4-1301.1.	Expressed consent for the taking of blood, breath, urine, or saliva sample - testing.

PART 14
OTHER OFFENSES

42-4-1401.	Reckless driving - penalty.
42-4-1402.	Careless driving - penalty.
42-4-1403.	Following fire apparatus prohibited.
42-4-1404.	Crossing fire hose.
42-4-1405.	Riding in trailers.
42-4-1406.	Foreign matter on highway prohibited.
42-4-1407.	Spilling loads on highways prohibited - prevention of spilling of aggregate, trash, or recyclables.
42-4-1407.5.	Splash guards - when required.
42-4-1408.	Operation of motor vehicles on property under control of or owned by parks and recreation districts.
42-4-1409.	Compulsory insurance - penalty - legislative intent.
42-4-1410.	Proof of financial responsibility required - suspension of license.
42-4-1411.	Use of earphones while driving.
42-4-1412.	Operation of bicycles and other human-powered vehicles.
42-4-1413.	Eluding or attempting to elude a police officer.
42-4-1414.	Use of dyed fuel on highways prohibited.
42-4-1415.	Radar jamming devices prohibited - penalty.

PART 15
MOTORCYCLES

42-4-1501.	Traffic laws apply to persons operating motorcycles - special permits.
42-4-1502.	Riding on motorcycles - protective helmet.
42-4-1503.	Operating motorcycles on roadways laned for traffic.
42-4-1504.	Clinging to other vehicles.

PART 16
ACCIDENTS AND ACCIDENT REPORTS

42-4-1601. Accidents involving death or personal injuries - duties.
42-4-1602. Accident involving damage - duty.
42-4-1603. Duty to give notice, information, and aid.
42-4-1604. Duty upon striking unattended vehicle or other property.
42-4-1605. Duty upon striking highway fixtures or traffic control devices.
42-4-1606. Duty to report accidents.
42-4-1607. When driver unable to give notice or make written report.
42-4-1608. Accident report forms.
42-4-1609. Coroners to report.
42-4-1610. Reports by interested parties confidential.
42-4-1611. Tabulation and analysis of reports.
42-4-1612. Accidents in state highway work areas - annual reporting by department of transportation and Colorado state patrol.

PART 17
PENALTIES AND PROCEDURE

42-4-1701. Traffic offenses and infractions classified - penalties - penalty and surcharge schedule - repeal.
42-4-1702. Alcohol- or drug-related traffic offenses - collateral attack.
42-4-1703. Parties to a crime.
42-4-1704. Offenses by persons controlling vehicles.
42-4-1705. Person arrested to be taken before the proper court.
42-4-1706. Juveniles - convicted - arrested and incarcerated - provisions for confinement.
42-4-1707. Summons and complaint or penalty assessment notice for misdemeanors, petty offenses, and misdemeanor traffic offenses - release - registration.
42-4-1708. Traffic infractions - proper court for hearing, burden of proof - appeal - collateral attack.
42-4-1709. Penalty assessment notice for traffic infractions - violations of provisions by officer - driver's license.
42-4-1710. Failure to pay penalty for traffic infractions - failure of parent or guardian to sign penalty assessment notice - procedures.
42-4-1711. Compliance with promise to appear.
42-4-1712. Procedure prescribed not exclusive.
42-4-1713. Conviction record inadmissible in civil action.
42-4-1714. Traffic violation not to affect credibility of witness.
42-4-1715. Convictions, judgments, and charges recorded - public inspection.
42-4-1716. Notice to appear or pay fine - failure to appear - penalty.
42-4-1717. Conviction - attendance at driver improvement school - rules.
42-4-1718. Electronic transmission of data - standards.
42-4-1719. Violations - commercial driver's license - compliance with federal regulation.

PART 18
VEHICLES ABANDONED ON PUBLIC PROPERTY

42-4-1801. Legislative declaration.
42-4-1802. Definitions.
42-4-1803. Abandonment of motor vehicles - public property.
42-4-1804. Report of abandoned motor vehicles - owner's opportunity to request hearing.
42-4-1805. Appraisal of abandoned motor vehicles - sale.
42-4-1806. Liens upon towed motor vehicles.
42-4-1807. Perfection of lien.
42-4-1808. Foreclosure of lien.
42-4-1809. Proceeds of sale.
42-4-1810. Transfer and purge of certificates of title.
42-4-1811. Penalty.
42-4-1812. Exemptions.
42-4-1813. Local regulations.
42-4-1814. Violation of motor vehicle registration or inspection laws - separate statutory provision.

PART 19
SCHOOL BUS REQUIREMENTS

42-4-1901. School buses - equipped with supplementary brake retarders.
42-4-1902. School vehicle drivers - special training required.
42-4-1903. School buses - stops - signs - passing.
42-4-1904. Regulations for school buses - regulations on discharge of passengers - penalty - exception.

PART 20
HOURS OF SERVICE

42-4-2001. Maximum hours of service - ready-mix concrete truck operators.

PART 21
VEHICLES ABANDONED ON PRIVATE PROPERTY

42-4-2101. Legislative declaration.
42-4-2102. Definitions.
42-4-2103. Abandonment of motor vehicles - private property.
42-4-2104. Appraisal of abandoned motor vehicles - sale.

42-4-2104.5. Abandonment of motor vehicles of limited value at repair shops - legislative declaration - definitions. (Repealed)
42-4-2105. Liens upon towed motor vehicles.
42-4-2106. Perfection of lien.
42-4-2107. Foreclosure of lien.
42-4-2108. Proceeds of sale.
42-4-2109. Transfer and purge of certificates of title.
42-4-2110. Penalty.

PART 22
RECYCLING MOTOR VEHICLES

42-4-2201. Definitions.
42-4-2202. Transfer for recycling.
42-4-2203. Vehicle verification system - fees - rules.
42-4-2204. Theft discovered - duties - liability.

PART 23
EDUCATION REGARDING USE OF NONMOTORIZED WHEELED TRANSPORTATION BY MINORS

42-4-2301. Comprehensive education.

PART 1

TRAFFIC REGULATION - GENERALLY

42-4-101. Short title. Parts 1 to 3, 5 to 19, and 21 of this article, part 1 of article 2 of this title, and part 5 of article 5 of title 43, C.R.S., shall be known and may be cited as the "Uniform Safety Code of 1935".

42-4-102. Legislative declaration. The general assembly recognizes the many conflicts which presently exist between the state's traffic laws and many of the municipal traffic codes, which conflicts lead to uncertainty in the movement of traffic on the state's highways and streets. These conflicts are compounded by the fact that today's Americans are extremely mobile and that while this state enjoys a large influx of traffic from many areas, there is some lack of uniformity existing between the "rules of the road" of this state and those of other states of the nation. The general assembly, therefore, declares it the purpose of this article to alleviate these conflicts and lack of uniformity by conforming, as nearly as possible, certain of the traffic laws of this state with the recommendations of the national committee of uniform traffic laws and ordinances as set forth in the committee's "Uniform Vehicle Code".

42-4-103. Scope and effect of article - exceptions to provisions. (1) This article constitutes the uniform traffic code throughout the state and in all political subdivisions and municipalities therein.

(2) The provisions of this article relating to the operation of vehicles and the movement of pedestrians refer exclusively to the use of streets and highways except:

(a) Where a different place is specifically referred to in a given section;

(b) For provisions of sections 42-2-128, 42-4-1301 to 42-4-1303, 42-4-1401, 42-4-1402, and 42-4-1413 and part 16 of this article which shall apply upon streets and highways and elsewhere throughout the state.

42-4-104. Adoption of traffic control manual. The department of transportation shall adopt a manual and specifications for a uniform system of traffic control devices consistent with the provisions of this article for use upon highways within this state. Such uniform system shall correlate with and insofar as possible conform to the system set forth in the most recent edition of the "Manual on Uniform Traffic Control Devices for Streets and Highways" and other related standards issued or endorsed by the federal highway administrator. For compliance with this section, the said department shall either publish and distribute a state manual and specifications approved by the transportation commission or shall, by the issuance of a traffic control manual supplement approved by the transportation commission, adopt the said national manual and other related standards subject to such exceptions, additions, and adaptations as are necessary for lawful and uniform application in this state. Said state manual or supplement shall be made available to all municipal and county road authorities and to other concerned agencies in the state.

42-4-105. Local traffic control devices. Local authorities in their respective jurisdictions shall place and maintain such traffic control devices upon highways under their jurisdiction as they may deem necessary to indicate and to carry out the provisions of this article or local traffic ordinances or to regulate, warn, or guide traffic, subject in the case of state highways to the provisions of sections 42-4-110 and 43-2-135 (1) (g), C.R.S. All such traffic control devices shall conform to the state manual and specifications for statewide uniformity as provided in section 42-4-104.

42-4-106. Who may restrict right to use highways. (1) Local authorities with respect to highways under their jurisdiction may by ordinance or resolution prohibit the operation of vehicles upon any such highway or impose restrictions as to the weight of vehicles to be operated upon any such highway, for a total period of not to exceed ninety days in any one calendar year, whenever any said highway by reason of deterioration, rain, snow, or other climatic conditions will be seriously damaged or destroyed unless the use of vehicles thereon is prohibited or the permissible weights thereof reduced.

(2) The local authority enacting any such ordinance or resolution shall erect or cause to be erected and maintained signs designating the permissible weights.

(3) Local authorities, with respect to highways under their jurisdiction, may also, by ordinance or resolution, prohibit the operation of trucks or commercial vehicles on designated highways or may impose limitations as to the weight thereof, which prohibitions and limitations shall be designated by appropriate signs placed on such highways.

(4) The department of transportation shall likewise have authority as granted in this section to local authorities to determine by resolution and to impose restrictions as to the weight of vehicles operated upon any highway under the jurisdiction of said department, and such restrictions shall be effective when signs giving notice thereof are erected upon the highways or portion of any highway affected by such resolution.

(5) (a) (I) The department of transportation shall also have authority to close any portion of a state highway to public travel or to prohibit the use thereof unless motor vehicles using the same are equipped with tire chains, four-wheel drive with adequate tires for the existing conditions, or snow tires with a "mud and snow" or all weather rating from the manufacturer having a tread of sufficient abrasive or skid-resistant design or composition and depth to provide adequate traction under existing driving conditions during storms or when other dangerous driving conditions exist or during construction or maintenance operations whenever the department considers such closing or restriction of use necessary for the protection and safety of the public. Such prohibition or restriction of use shall be effective when signs, including temporary or electronic signs, giving notice thereof are erected upon such portion of said highway, and it shall be unlawful to proceed in violation of such notice. The Colorado state patrol shall cooperate with the department of transportation in the enforcement of any such closing or restriction of use. "Tire chains", as used in this subsection (5), means metal chains which consist of two circular metal loops, one on each side of the tire, connected by not less than nine evenly spaced chains across the tire tread and any other traction devices differing from such metal chains in construction, material, or design but capable of providing traction equal to or exceeding that of such metal chains under similar conditions. The operator of a commercial vehicle with four or more drive wheels other than a bus shall affix tire chains to at least four of the drive wheel tires of such vehicle when such vehicle is required to be equipped with tire chains under this subsection (5). The operator of a bus shall affix tire chains to at least two of the drive wheel tires of such vehicle when such vehicle is required to be equipped with tire chains under this subsection (5).

(II) Any person who operates a motor vehicle in violation of restrictions imposed by the department of transportation or the state patrol under subparagraph (I) of this paragraph (a), where the result of the violation is an incident that causes the closure of a travel lane in one or both directions, shall be subject to an enhanced penalty as set forth in section 42-4-1701 (4) (a) (I) (F).

(III) A person who violates subparagraph (I) of this paragraph (a) while operating a commercial vehicle shall be subject to an enhanced penalty as set forth in section 42-4-1701 (4) (a) (I) (F).

(IV) A person who violates subparagraph (I) of this paragraph (a) while operating a commercial vehicle and the violation causes a closure in a travel lane shall be subject to an enhanced penalty as set forth in section 42-4-1701 (4) (a) (I) (F).

(V) If a fine is enhanced under subparagraphs (III) and (IV) of this paragraph (a), the portion of the fine that exceeds the fine imposed under subparagraph (I) for an enhancement under subparagraph (III), or subparagraph (II) for an enhancement under subparagraph (IV), that is allocated to the state by sections 42-1-217 and 43-4-205, C.R.S., shall be transferred to the state treasurer, who shall deposit it in the highway construction workers' safety account within the highway users tax fund created by section 42-4-1701 (4) (c) (II) (B), to be continuously appropriated to the department of transportation for work zone safety equipment, signs, and law enforcement.

(VI) Subparagraphs (III) and (IV) of this paragraph (a) shall not apply to a tow operator who is towing a motor vehicle or traveling to a site from which a motor vehicle shall be towed.

(VII) The Colorado department of transportation shall identify an appropriate place for commercial vehicles to apply chains, if necessary, to comply with subparagraph (I) of this paragraph (a) and provide adequate notice to commercial vehicle operators of such places.

(b) The transportation commission may promulgate rules to implement the provisions of this subsection (5).

(6) (a) The department of transportation and local authorities, within their respective jurisdictions, may, for the purpose of road construction and maintenance, temporarily close to through traffic or to all vehicular traffic any highway or portion thereof for a period not to exceed a specified number of workdays for project completion and shall, in conjunction with any such road closure, establish appropriate detours or provide for an alternative routing of the traffic affected when, in the opinion of said department or concerned local authorities, as evidenced by resolution or ordinance, such temporary closing of the highway or portion thereof and such rerouting of traffic is necessary for traffic safety and for the protection of work crews and road equipment. Such temporary closing of the high-

way or portion thereof and the routing of traffic along other roads shall not become effective until official traffic control devices are erected giving notice of the restrictions, and, when such devices are in place, no driver shall disobey the instructions or directions thereof.

(b) Local authorities, within their respective jurisdictions, may provide for the temporary closing to vehicular traffic of any portion of a highway during a specified period of the day for the purpose of celebrations, parades, and special local events or civic functions when in the opinion of said authorities such temporary closing is necessary for the safety and protection of persons who are to use that portion of the highway during the temporary closing.

(c) The department of transportation, local municipal authorities, and local county authorities shall enter into agreements with one another for the establishment, signing, and marking of appropriate detours and alternative routes which jointly affect state and local road systems and which are necessary to carry out the provisions of paragraphs (a) and (b) of this subsection (6). Any temporary closing of a street which is a state highway and any rerouting of state highway traffic shall have the approval of the department of transportation before such closing and rerouting becomes effective.

(7) (a) The transportation commission may also by resolution and within the reasonable exercise of the police power of the state adopt rules and regulations concerning the operation of any motor vehicle in any tunnel which is a part of the state highway system.

(b) In promulgating such rules and regulations, the transportation commission shall consider the regulations of the public utilities commission and the United States department of transportation relating to the transportation of dangerous articles and may prohibit or regulate the operation of any motor vehicle which transports any article, deemed to be dangerous, in any tunnel which is a part of the state highway system.

(8) (a) Except as provided in paragraph (b) of this subsection (8), a person who violates any provision of this section commits a class B traffic infraction.

(b) A person who violates paragraph (a) of subsection (5) of this section while operating a commercial vehicle commits a class B traffic infraction and shall be punished as provided in section 42-4-1701 (4) (a) (I) (F); except that this paragraph (b) shall not apply to a tow operator who is towing a motor vehicle or traveling to a site from which a motor vehicle shall be towed.

42-4-107. Obedience to police officers. No person shall willfully fail or refuse to comply with any lawful order or direction of any police officer invested by law with authority to direct, control, or regulate traffic. Any person who violates any provision of this section commits a class 2 misdemeanor traffic offense.

42-4-108. Public officers to obey provisions - exceptions for emergency vehicles. (1) The provisions of this article applicable to the drivers of vehicles upon the highways shall apply to the drivers of all vehicles owned or operated by the United States, this state, or any county, city, town, district, or other political subdivision of the state, subject to such specific exceptions as are set forth in this article with reference to authorized emergency vehicles.

(2) The driver of an authorized emergency vehicle, when responding to an emergency call, or when in pursuit of an actual or suspected violator of the law, or when responding to but not upon returning from a fire alarm, may exercise the privileges set forth in this section, but subject to the conditions stated in this article. The driver of an authorized emergency vehicle may:

(a) Park or stand, irrespective of the provisions of this title;

(b) Proceed past a red or stop signal or stop sign, but only after slowing down as may be necessary for safe operation;

(c) Exceed the lawful speeds set forth in section 42-4-1101 (2) or exceed the maximum lawful speed limits set forth in section 42-4-1101 (8) so long as said driver does not endanger life or property;

(d) Disregard regulations governing directions of movement or turning in specified directions.

(3) The exemptions and conditions provided in paragraphs (b) to (d), in their entirety, of subsection (2) of this section for an authorized emergency vehicle shall continue to apply to section 24-10-106 (1) (a), C.R.S., only when such vehicle is making use of audible or visual signals meeting the requirements of section 42-4-213, and the exemption granted in paragraph (a) of subsection (2) of this section shall apply only when such vehicle is making use of visual signals meeting the requirements of section 42-4-213 unless using such visual signals would cause an obstruction to the normal flow of traffic; except that an authorized emergency vehicle being operated as a police vehicle while in actual pursuit of a suspected violator of any provision of this title need not display or make use of audible or visual signals so long as such pursuit is being made to obtain verification of or evidence of the guilt of the suspected violator. Nothing in this section shall be construed to require an emergency vehicle to make use of audible signals when such vehicle is not moving, whether or not the vehicle is occupied.

(4) The provisions of this section shall not relieve the driver of an authorized emergency vehicle from the duty to drive with due regard for the safety of all persons, nor shall such provisions protect the driver from the consequences of such driver's reckless disregard for the safety of others.

(5) The state motor vehicle licensing agency shall designate any particular vehicle as an authorized emergency vehicle upon a finding that the designation of that vehicle is necessary

42-4-109. Low-power scooters, animals, skis, skates, and toy vehicles on highways. (1) A person riding a low-power scooter upon a roadway where low-power scooter travel is permitted shall be granted all of the rights and shall be subject to all of the duties and penalties applicable to the driver of a vehicle as set forth in this article except those provisions of this article that, by their very nature, can have no application.

(2) A person riding a low-power scooter shall not ride other than upon or astride a permanent and regular seat attached thereto.

(3) No low-power scooter shall be used to carry more persons at one time than the number for which it is designed and equipped.

(4) No person riding upon any low-power scooter, coaster, roller skates, sled, or toy vehicle shall attach the same or himself or herself to any vehicle upon a roadway.

(5) A person operating a low-power scooter upon a roadway shall ride as close to the right side of the roadway as practicable, exercising due care when passing a standing vehicle or one proceeding in the same direction.

(6) Persons riding low-power scooters upon a roadway shall not ride more than two abreast.

(6.5) A person under the age of eighteen years may not operate or carry a passenger who is under eighteen years of age on a low-power scooter unless the person and the passenger are wearing protective helmets in accordance with the provisions of section 42-4-1502 (4.5).

(7) For the sake of uniformity and bicycle, electrical assisted bicycle, and low-power scooter safety throughout the state, the department in cooperation with the department of transportation shall prepare and make available to all local jurisdictions for distribution to bicycle, electrical assisted bicycle, and low-power scooter riders a digest of state regulations explaining and illustrating the rules of the road, equipment requirements, and traffic control devices that are applicable to such riders and their bicycles, electrical assisted bicycles, or low-power scooters. Local authorities may supplement this digest with a leaflet describing any additional regulations of a local nature that apply within their respective jurisdictions.

(8) Persons riding or leading animals on or along any highway shall ride or lead such animals on the left side of said highway, facing approaching traffic. This shall not apply to persons driving herds of animals along highways.

(9) No person shall use the highways for traveling on skis, toboggans, coasting sleds, skates, or similar devices. It is unlawful for any person to use any roadway of this state as a sled or ski course for the purpose of coasting on sleds, skis, or similar devices. It is also unlawful for any person upon roller skates or riding in or by means of any coaster, toy vehicle, or similar device to go upon any roadway except while crossing a highway in a crosswalk, and when so crossing such person shall be granted all of the rights and shall be subject to all of the duties applicable to pedestrians. This subsection (9) does not apply to any public way which is set aside by proper authority as a play street and which is adequately roped off or otherwise marked for such purpose.

(10) Every person riding or leading an animal or driving any animal-drawn conveyance upon a roadway shall be granted all of the rights and shall be subject to all of the duties applicable to the driver of a vehicle by this article, except those provisions of this article which by their very nature can have no application.

(11) Where suitable bike paths, horseback trails, or other trails have been established on the right-of-way or parallel to and within one-fourth mile of the right-of-way of heavily traveled streets and highways, the department of transportation may, subject to the provisions of section 43-2-135, C.R.S., by resolution or order entered in its minutes, and local authorities may, where suitable bike paths, horseback trails, or other trails have been established on the right-of-way or parallel to it within four hundred fifty feet of the right-of-way of heavily traveled streets, by ordinance, determine and designate, upon the basis of an engineering and traffic investigation, those heavily traveled streets and highways upon which shall be prohibited any bicycle, electrical assisted bicycle, animal rider, animal-drawn conveyance, or other class or kind of nonmotorized traffic that is found to be incompatible with the normal and safe movement of traffic, and, upon such a determination, the department of transportation or local authority shall erect appropriate official signs giving notice thereof; except that, with respect to controlled access highways, section 42-4-1010 (3) shall apply. When such official signs are erected, no person shall violate any of the instructions contained thereon.

(12) The parent of any child or guardian of any ward shall not authorize or knowingly permit any child or ward to violate any provision of this section.

(13) (a) Except as otherwise provided in paragraph (b) of this subsection (13), any person who violates a provision of this section commits a class B traffic infraction.

(b) Any person who violates subsection (6.5) of this section commits a class A traffic infraction.

42-4-109.5. Low-speed electric vehicles. (1) A low-speed electric vehicle may be operated only on a roadway that has a speed limit equal to or less than thirty-five miles per hour; except that it may be operated to directly cross a roadway that has a speed limit greater than thirty-five miles per hour at an at-grade crossing to continue traveling along a roadway with a speed limit equal to or less than thirty-five miles per hour.

(2) No person shall operate a low-speed electric vehicle on a limited-access highway.

(3) Any person who violates subsection (1) or (2) of this section commits a class B traffic infraction.

(4) (Deleted by amendment, L. 2009, (SB 09-075), ch. 418, p. 2321, § 5, effective August 5, 2009.)

(5) The Colorado department of transportation may regulate the operation of a low-speed electric vehicle on a state highway located outside of a municipality. The regulation shall take effect when the Colorado department of transportation places an appropriate sign that provides adequate notice of the regulation.

42-4-109.6. Class B low-speed electric vehicles - effective date - rules. (1) A class B low-speed electric vehicle may be operated only on a roadway that has a speed limit equal to or less than forty-five miles per hour; except that it may be operated to directly cross a roadway that has a speed limit greater than forty-five miles per hour at an at-grade crossing to continue traveling along a roadway with a speed limit equal to or less than forty-five miles per hour.

(2) No person shall operate a class B low-speed electric vehicle on a limited-access highway.

(3) Any person who violates subsection (1) or (2) of this section commits a class B traffic infraction.

(4) For the purposes of this section, "class B low-speed electric vehicle" means a low-speed electric vehicle that is capable of traveling at greater than twenty-five miles per hour but less than forty-five miles per hour.

(5) (a) The department of revenue shall not register or issue a title for a class B low-speed electric vehicle until after the United States department of transportation, through the national highway traffic safety administration, has adopted a federal motor vehicle safety standard for low-speed electric vehicles that authorizes operation at greater than twenty-five miles per hour but less than forty-five miles per hour.

(b) After the United States department of transportation, through the national highway traffic safety administration, has adopted a federal motor vehicle safety standard for low-speed electric vehicles that authorizes operation at greater than twenty-five miles per hour but less than forty-five miles per hour, the department of revenue shall promulgate rules authorizing the operation of class B low-speed electric vehicles in compliance with this section and shall notify the revisor of statutes in writing. Upon the promulgation of rules authorizing the operation of such vehicles, subsections (1) to (3) of this section shall take effect.

(6) The Colorado department of transportation may regulate the operation of a class B low-speed electric vehicle on a state highway located outside of a municipality. The regulation shall take effect when the Colorado department of transportation places an appropriate sign that provides adequate notice of the regulation.

42-4-110. Provisions uniform throughout state. (1) The provisions of this article shall be applicable and uniform throughout this state and in all political subdivisions and municipalities therein. Cities and counties, incorporated cities and towns, and counties shall regulate and enforce all traffic and parking restrictions on streets which are state highways as provided in section 43-2-135 (1) (g), C.R.S., and all local authorities may enact and enforce traffic regulations on other roads and streets within their respective jurisdictions. All such regulations shall be subject to the following conditions and limitations:

(a) All local authorities may enact, adopt, or enforce traffic regulations which cover the same subject matter as the various sections of this article and such additional regulations as are included in section 42-4-111, except as otherwise stated in paragraphs (c) to (e) of this subsection (1).

(b) All local authorities may, in the manner prescribed in article 16 of title 31, C.R.S., or in article 15 of title 30, C.R.S., adopt by reference all or any part of a model traffic code which embodies the rules of the road and vehicle requirements set forth in this article and such additional regulations as are provided for in section 42-4-111; except that, in the case of state highways, any such additional regulations shall have the approval of the department of transportation.

(c) No local authority shall adopt, enact, or enforce on any street which is a state highway any ordinance, rule, or resolution which alters or changes the meaning of any of the "rules of the road" or is otherwise in conflict with the provisions of this article. For the purpose of this section, the "rules of the road" shall be construed to mean any of the regulations on the operation of vehicles set forth in this article which drivers throughout the state are required to obey without the benefit or necessity of official traffic control devices as declared in section 42-4-603 (2).

(d) In no event shall local authorities have the power to enact by ordinance regulations governing the driving of vehicles by persons under the influence of alcohol or of a controlled substance, as defined in section 12-22-303 (7), C.R.S., or under the influence of any other drug to a degree which renders any such person incapable of safely operating a vehicle, or whose ability to operate a vehicle is impaired by the consumption of alcohol or by the use of a controlled substance, as defined in section 12-22-303 (7), C.R.S., or any other drug, the registration of vehicles and the licensing of drivers, the duties and obligations of persons involved in traffic accidents, and vehicle equipment requirements in conflict with the provisions of this article; but said local authorities within their respective jurisdictions shall enforce the state laws pertaining to these subjects, and in every charge of violation the complaint shall specify the section of state law under which the charge is made and the state court having jurisdiction.

(e) Pursuant to section 43-2-135 (1) (g), C.R.S., no regulation of a local authority shall apply to or become effective for any streets which are state highways, including any part of the national system of interstate and defense highways, until such regulation has been presented to and approved in writing by the department of transportation; except that such regulations shall become effective on such streets sixty days after receipt for review by the department of transportation if not disapproved in writing by said department during that sixty-day period.

(2) The municipal courts have jurisdiction over violations of traffic regulations enacted or adopted by municipalities. However, the provisions of sections 42-4-1701, 42-4-1705, and 42-4-1707 shall not be applicable to municipalities, except for the provisions of section 42-4-1701 (4) (e) (II).

(3) No person convicted of or pleading guilty to a violation of a municipal traffic ordinance shall be charged or tried in a state court for the same or a similar offense.

(4) (a) Any municipality, city, county, or city and county located within the program area of the AIR program area as defined in section 42-4-304 may adopt ordinances or resolutions pertaining to the enforcement of the emissions control inspection requirements set forth in section 42-4-310.

(b) An officer coming upon an unattended vehicle in the program area which is in apparent violation of an ordinance or resolution adopted as authorized in paragraph (a) of this subsection (4) may place upon such vehicle a penalty assessment notice indicating the offense and directing the owner or operator of such vehicle to remit the penalty assessment as set forth in such ordinance to the local jurisdiction in whose name the penalty assessment notice was issued.

(c) The aggregate amount of fines, penalties, or forfeitures collected pursuant to ordinances or resolutions adopted as authorized in paragraph (a) of this subsection (4) shall be retained by the local jurisdiction in whose name such penalty notice was issued.

(5) The general assembly declares that the adjudication of class A and class B traffic infractions through the county court magistrate system was not intended to create a conflict between the provisions of this article and municipal ordinances covering the same subject matter as this article nor was it intended to require or prohibit the decriminalization of municipal ordinances covering the same subject matter as this article. Municipalities may continue to enforce violations of such ordinances through municipal court even though similar state offenses are enforced through the magistrate system established under this article.

42-4-110.5. Automated vehicle identification systems. (1) The general assembly hereby finds and declares that the enforcement of traffic laws through the use of automated vehicle identification systems under this section is a matter of statewide concern and is an area in which uniform state standards are necessary.

(1.5) Except for the authorization contained in subsection (1.7) of this section, nothing in this section shall apply to a violation detected by an automated vehicle identification device for driving twenty-five miles per hour or more in excess of the reasonable and prudent speed or twenty-five miles per hour or more in excess of the maximum speed limit of seventy-five miles per hour detected by the use of an automated vehicle identification device.

(1.7) (a) Upon request from the department of transportation, the department of public safety shall utilize an automated vehicle identification system to detect speeding violations under part 11 of this article within a highway maintenance, repair, or construction zone designated pursuant to section 42-4-614 (1) (a), if the department of public safety complies with subsections (2) to (6) of this section. An automated vehicle identification system shall not be used under this subsection (1.7) unless maintenance, repair, or construction is occurring at the time the system is being used. The department of public safety may contract with a vendor to implement this subsection (1.7). If the department of public safety contracts with a vendor, the contract shall incorporate the processing elements specified by department of public safety. The department of public safety may contract with the vendor to notify violators, collect and remit the penalties and surcharges to the state treasury less the vendor's expenses, reconcile payments against outstanding violations, implement collection efforts, and notify the department of public safety of unpaid violations for possible referral to the judicial system. No penalty assessment or summons and complaint or a penalty or surcharge for a violation detected by an automated vehicle identification system under this subsection (1.7) shall be forwarded to the department for processing.

(b) The department of transportation shall reimburse the department of public safety for the direct and indirect costs of complying with this subsection (1.7).

(2) A municipality may adopt an ordinance authorizing the use of an automated vehicle identification system to detect violations of traffic regulations adopted by the municipality, or the state, a county, a city and county, or a municipality may utilize an automated vehicle identification system to detect traffic violations under state law, subject to the following conditions and limitations:

(a) (I) (Deleted by amendment, L. 2002, p. 570, § 1, effective May 24, 2002.)

(II) If the state, a county, a city and county, or a municipality detects any alleged violation of a municipal traffic regulation or a traffic violation under state law through the use of an automated vehicle identification system, then the state, county, city and county, or municipality shall serve the penalty assessment notice or summons and complaint for the alleged violation on the defendant no later than ninety days after the alleged violation occurred. If a penalty assessment notice or summons and complaint for a violation detected using an automated vehicle identification system is personally served, the state, a county, a city and county, or a municipality may only charge the actual costs of service of process that shall be no more than the amount usually charged for civil service of process.

(b) Notwithstanding any other provision of the statutes to the contrary, the state, a county, a city and county, or a municipality may not report to the department any conviction or entry of judgment against a defendant for violation of a municipal traffic regulation or a traffic violation under state law if the violation was detected through the use of an automated vehicle identification system.

(c) The state, a county, a city and county, or a municipality may not report to the department any outstanding judgment or warrant for purposes of section 42-2-107 (5) or 42-2-118 (3) based upon any violation or alleged violation of a municipal traffic regulation or traffic violation under state law detected through the use of an automated vehicle identification system.

(d) (I) The state, a county, a city and county, or a municipality may not use an automated vehicle identification system to detect a violation of part 11 of this article or a local speed ordinance unless there is posted an appropriate temporary sign in a conspicuous place not fewer than three hundred feet before the area in which the automated vehicle identification device is to be used notifying the public that an automated vehicle identification device is in use immediately ahead. The requirement of this subparagraph (I) shall not be deemed satisfied by the posting of a permanent sign or signs at the borders of a county, city and county, or municipality, nor by the posting of a permanent sign in an area in which an automated vehicle identification device is to be used, but this subparagraph (I) shall not be deemed a prohibition against the posting of such permanent signs.

(II) Except as provided in subparagraph (I) of this paragraph (d), an automated vehicle identification system designed to detect disobedience to a traffic control signal or another violation of this article or a local traffic ordinance shall not be used unless the state, county, city and county, or municipality using such system conspicuously posts a sign notifying the public that an automated vehicle identification device is in use immediately ahead. The sign shall:

(A) Be placed in a conspicuous place not fewer than two hundred feet nor more than five hundred feet before the automated vehicle identification system; and

(B) Use lettering that is at least four inches high for upper case letters and two and nine-tenths inches high for lower case letters.

(e) The state, a county, a city and county, or a municipality may not require a registered owner of a vehicle to disclose the identity of a driver of the vehicle who is detected through the use of an automated vehicle identification system. However, the registered owner may be required to submit evidence that the owner was not the driver at the time of the alleged violation.

(f) The state, a county, a city and county, or a municipality shall not issue a penalty assessment notice or summons for a violation detected using an automated vehicle identification system unless, at the time the violation is alleged to have occurred, an officer or employee of the state, the county, the city and county, or the municipality is present during the operation of the automated vehicle identification device; except that this paragraph (f) shall not apply to an automated vehicle identification system designed to detect violations for disobedience to a traffic control signal.

(g) (I) The state, a county, a city and county, or a municipality shall not issue a penalty assessment notice or summons for a violation detected using an automated vehicle identification system unless the violation occurred within a school zone, as defined in section 42-4-615; within a residential neighborhood; within a maintenance, construction, or repair zone designated pursuant to section 42-4-614; or along a street that borders a municipal park.

(II) For purposes of this paragraph (g), unless the context otherwise requires, "residential neighborhood" means any block on which a majority of the improvements along both sides of the street are residential dwellings and the speed limit is thirty-five miles per hour or less.

(III) This paragraph (g) shall not apply to an automated vehicle identification system designed to detect disobedience to a traffic control signal.

(3) The department has no authority to assess any points against a license under section 42-2-127 upon entry of a conviction or judgment for a violation of a municipal traffic regulation or a traffic violation under state law if the violation was detected through the use of an automated vehicle identification system. The department may not keep any record of such violation in the official records maintained by the department under section 42-2-121.

(4) (a) If the state, a county, a city and county, or a municipality detects a speeding violation of less than ten miles per hour over the reasonable and prudent speed under a municipal traffic regulation or under state law through the use of an automated vehicle identification system and the violation is the first violation by such driver that the state, county, city and county, or municipality has detected using an automated vehicle identification system, then the state, county, city and county, or municipality shall mail such driver a warning regarding the violation and the state,

county, city and county, or municipality may not impose any penalty or surcharge for such first violation.

(b) (I) If the state, a county, a city and county, or a municipality detects a second or subsequent speeding violation under a municipal traffic regulation or under state law by a driver, or a first such violation by the driver if the provisions of paragraph (a) of this subsection (4) do not apply, through the use of an automated vehicle identification system, then, except as may be permitted in subparagraph (II) of this paragraph (b), the maximum penalty that the state, county, city and county, or municipality may impose for such violation, including any surcharge, is forty dollars.

(II) If any violation described in subparagraph (I) of this paragraph (b) occurs within a school zone, as defined in section 42-4-615, the maximum penalty that may be imposed shall be doubled.

(III) Subparagraph (I) of this paragraph (b) shall not apply within a maintenance, construction, or repair zone designated pursuant to section 42-4-614.

(4.5) If the state, a county, a city and county, or a municipality detects a violation under a municipal traffic regulation or under state law for disobedience to a traffic control signal through the use of an automated vehicle identification system, the maximum penalty that the state, a county, a city and county, or a municipality may impose for such violation, including any surcharge, is seventy-five dollars.

(4.7) If a driver fails to pay a penalty imposed for a violation detected using an automated vehicle identification device, the state, a county, a city and county, or a municipality shall not attempt to enforce such a penalty by immobilizing the driver's vehicle.

(5) If the state, a county, a city and county, or a municipality has established an automated vehicle identification system for the enforcement of municipal traffic regulations or state traffic laws, then no portion of any fine collected through the use of such system may be paid to the manufacturer or vendor of the automated vehicle identification system equipment. The compensation paid by the state, county, city and county, or municipality for such equipment shall be based upon the value of such equipment and may not be based upon the number of traffic citations issued or the revenue generated by such equipment.

(6) As used in this section, the term "automated vehicle identification system" means a system whereby:

(a) A machine is used to automatically detect a violation of a traffic regulation and simultaneously record a photograph of the vehicle, the operator of the vehicle, and the license plate of the vehicle; and

(b) A penalty assessment notice or summons and complaint is issued to the registered owner of the motor vehicle.

42-4-111. Powers of local authorities. (1) This article shall not be deemed to prevent local authorities, with respect to streets and highways under their jurisdiction and within the reasonable exercise of the police power, except those streets and highways that are parts of the state highway system that are subject to section 43-2-135, C.R.S., from:

(a) Regulating or prohibiting the stopping, standing, or parking of vehicles, consistent with the provisions of this article;

(b) Establishing parking meter zones where it is determined upon the basis of an engineering and traffic investigation that the installation and operation of parking meters is necessary to aid in the regulation and control of the parking of vehicles during the hours and on the days specified on parking meter signs;

(c) Regulating traffic by means of police officers or official traffic control devices, consistent with the provisions of this article;

(d) Regulating or prohibiting processions or assemblages on the highways, consistent with the provisions of this article;

(e) Designating particular highways or roadways for use by traffic moving in one direction, consistent with the provisions of this article;

(f) Designating any highway as a through highway or designating any intersection as a stop or yield intersection, consistent with the provisions of this article;

(g) Designating truck routes and restricting the use of highways, consistent with the provisions of this article;

(h) Regulating the operation of bicycles or electrical assisted bicycles and requiring the registration and licensing of same, including the requirement of a registration fee, consistent with the provisions of this article;

(i) Altering or establishing speed limits, consistent with the provisions of this article;

(j) Establishing speed limits for vehicles in public parks, consistent with the provisions of this article;

(k) Determining and designating streets, parts of streets, or specific lanes thereon upon which vehicular traffic shall proceed in one direction during one period and the opposite direction during another period of the day, consistent with the provisions of this article;

(l) Regulating or prohibiting the turning of vehicles, consistent with the provisions of this article;

(m) Designating no-passing zones, consistent with the provisions of this article;

(n) Prohibiting or regulating the use of controlled-access roadways by nonmotorized traffic or other kinds of traffic, consistent with the provisions of this article;

(o) Establishing minimum speed limits, consistent with the provisions of this article;

(p) Designating hazardous railroad crossings, consistent with the provisions of this article;

(q) Designating and regulating traffic on play streets, consistent with the provisions of this article;

(r) Prohibiting or restricting pedestrian crossing, consistent with the provisions of this article;

(s) Regulating the movement of traffic at school crossings by official traffic control devices or by duly authorized school crossing guards, consistent with the provisions of this article;

(t) Regulating persons propelling push carts;

(u) Regulating persons upon skates, coasters, sleds, or similar devices, consistent with the provisions of this article;

(v) Adopting such temporary or experimental regulations as may be necessary to cover emergencies or special conditions;

(w) Adopting such other traffic regulations as are provided for by this article;

(x) Closing a street or portion thereof temporarily and establishing appropriate detours or an alternative routing for the traffic affected, consistent with the provisions of this article;

(y) Regulating the local movement of traffic or the use of local streets where such is not provided for in this article;

(z) Regulating the operation of low-power scooters, consistent with the provisions of this article; except that local authorities shall be prohibited from establishing any requirements for the registration and licensing of low-power scooters;

(aa) Regulating the operation of low-speed electric vehicles, including, without limitation, establishing a safety inspection program, on streets and highways under their jurisdiction by resolution or ordinance of the governing body, if such regulation is consistent with the provisions of this title;

(bb) Authorizing and regulating the operation of golf cars on roadways by resolution or ordinance of the governing body, if the authorization or regulation is consistent with this title and does not authorize:

(I) An unlicensed driver of a golf car to carry a passenger who is under twenty-one years of age;

(II) Operation of a golf car by a person under fourteen years of age; or

(III) Operation of a golf car on a state highway.

(cc) Authorizing, prohibiting, or regulating the use of an EPAMD on a roadway, sidewalk, bike path, or pedestrian path consistent with section 42-4-117 (1) and (3);

(dd) Authorizing the use of the electrical motor on an electrical assisted bicycle on a bike or pedestrian path;

(ee) Enacting the idling standards in conformity with section 42-14-103.

(2) No ordinance or regulation enacted under paragraph (a), (b), (e), (f), (g), (i), (j), (k), (l), (m), (n), (o), (p), (q), (r), (v), (x), (y), (aa), or (cc) of subsection (1) of this section shall be effective until official signs or other traffic control devices conforming to standards as required by section 42-4-602 and giving notice of such local traffic regulations are placed upon or at the entrances to the highway or part thereof affected as may be most appropriate.

(3) (a) A board of county commissioners may by resolution authorize the use of designated portions of unimproved county roads within the unincorporated portion of the county for motor vehicles participating in timed endurance events and for such purposes shall make such regulations relating to the use of such roads and the operation of vehicles as are consistent with public safety in the conduct of such event and with the cooperation of county law enforcement officials.

(b) Such resolution by a board of county commissioners and regulations based thereon shall designate the specific route which may be used in such event, the time limitations imposed upon such use, any necessary restrictions in the use of such route by persons not participating in such event, special regulations concerning the operation of vehicles while participating in such event in which case any provisions of this article to the contrary shall not apply to such event, and such requirements concerning the sponsorship of any such event as may be reasonably necessary to assure adequate responsibility therefor.

Editor's note: (3) Section 3 of chapter 215, Session Laws of Colorado 2011, provides that the act adding subsection (1)(ee) applies to offenses committed on or after July 1, 2011.

42-4-112. Noninterference with the rights of owners of realty. Subject to the exception provided in section 42-4-103 (2), nothing in this article shall be construed to prevent the owner of real property used by the public for purposes of vehicular travel by permission of the owner and not as matter of right from prohibiting such use, or from requiring other or different or additional conditions than those specified in this article, or from otherwise regulating such use as may seem best to such owner.

42-4-113. Appropriations for administration of article. The general assembly shall make appropriations from the highway users tax fund for the expenses of the administration of this article.

42-4-114. Removal of traffic hazards. (1) The department of transportation and local authorities, within their respective jurisdictions, may by written notice sent by certified mail require the owner of real property abutting on the right-of-way of any highway, sidewalk, or other public way to trim or remove, at the expense of said property owner, any tree limb or any shrub, vine, hedge, or other plant which projects beyond the property line of such owner onto or over the public right-of-way and thereby obstructs the view of traffic, obscures any traffic control device, or otherwise constitutes a hazard to drivers or pedestrians.

(2) It is the duty of the property owner to remove any dead, overhanging boughs of trees located on the premises of such property owner that endanger life or property on the public right-of-way.

(3) In the event that any property owner fails or neglects to trim or remove any such tree limb or any such shrub, vine, hedge, or other plant within ten days after receipt of written notice from said department or concerned local authority to do so, said department or local authority may do or cause to be done the necessary work incident thereto, and said property owner shall reimburse the state or local authority for the cost of the work performed.

42-4-115. Information on traffic law enforcement - collection - profiling - annual report - repeal. (Repealed)

42-4-116. Restrictions for minor drivers - definitions. (1) (a) Except as provided in paragraph (c) of this subsection (1), a minor driver shall not operate a motor vehicle containing a passenger who is under twenty-one years of age and who is not a member of the driver's immediate family until such driver has held a valid driver's license for at least six months.

(b) Except as provided in paragraph (c) of this subsection (1), a minor driver shall not operate a motor vehicle containing more than one passenger who is under twenty-one years of age and who is not a member of the driver's immediate family until such driver has held a valid driver's license for at least one year.

(c) Paragraphs (a) and (b) of this subsection (1) shall not apply if:

(I) The motor vehicle contains the minor's parent or legal guardian or other responsible adult described in section 42-2-108;

(II) The motor vehicle contains an adult twenty-one years of age or older who currently holds a valid driver's license and has held such license for at least one year;

(III) The passenger who is under twenty-one years of age is in the vehicle on account of a medical emergency;

(IV) All passengers who are under twenty-one years of age are members of the driver's immediate family and all such passengers are wearing a seatbelt.

(2) (a) Except as provided in paragraph (b) of this subsection (2), a minor driver shall not operate a motor vehicle between 12 midnight and 5 a.m. until such driver has held a driver's license for at least one year.

(b) This subsection (2) shall not apply if:

(I) The motor vehicle contains the minor's parent or legal guardian or other responsible adult described in section 42-2-108;

(II) The motor vehicle contains an adult twenty-one years of age or older who currently holds a valid driver's license and has held such license for at least one year;

(III) The minor is driving to school or a school-authorized activity when the school does not provide adequate transportation, so long as the driver possesses a signed statement from the school official containing the date the activity will occur;

(IV) The minor is driving on account of employment when necessary, so long as the driver possesses a signed statement from the employer verifying employment;

(V) The minor is driving on account of a medical emergency; or

(VI) The minor is an emancipated minor.

(3) A violation of this section is a traffic infraction, and, upon conviction, the violator may be punished as follows:

(a) By the imposition of not less than eight hours nor more than twenty-four hours of community service for a first offense and not less than sixteen hours nor more than forty hours of community service for a subsequent offense;

(b) By the levying of a fine of not more than fifty dollars for a first offense, a fine of not more than one hundred dollars for a second offense, and a fine of one hundred fifty dollars for a subsequent offense;

(c) By an assessment of two license suspension points pursuant to section 42-2-127 (5) (kk).

(4) For the purposes of this section:

(a) "Emancipated minor" means an individual under eighteen years of age whose parents or guardian has surrendered parental responsibilities, custody, and the right to the care and earnings of such person, and are no longer under a duty to support such person.

(b) "Minor driver" means a person who is operating a motor vehicle and who is under eighteen years of age.

(5) No driver in a motor vehicle shall be cited for a violation of this section unless such driver was stopped by a law enforcement officer for an alleged violation of articles 1 to 4 of this title other than a violation of this section.

42-4-117. Personal mobility devices. (1) A rider of an EPAMD shall have all the same rights and duties as an operator of any other vehicle under this article, except as to those provisions that by their nature have no application.

(2) Unless prohibited under section 42-4-111 (1) (cc), an EPAMD may be operated on a roadway in conformity with vehicle use.

(3) An EPAMD shall not be operated:

(a) On a limited-access highway;

(b) On a bike or pedestrian path; or

(c) At a speed of greater than twelve and one-half miles per hour.

(4) A person who violates this section commits a class B traffic infraction.

42-4-118. Establishment of wildlife crossing zones - report - repeal. (1) The department of transportation created in section 43-1-103, C.R.S., in consultation with both the Colorado state patrol created pursuant to section 24-33.5-

201, C.R.S., and the division of wildlife created pursuant to section 24-1-124 (3) (h), C.R.S., in the department of natural resources, may establish areas within the public highways of the state as wildlife crossing zones.

(2) (a) If the department of transportation establishes an area within a public highway of the state as a wildlife crossing zone, the department of transportation may erect signs:

(I) Identifying the zone in accordance with the provisions of section 42-4-616; and

(II) Establishing a lower speed limit for the portion of the highway that lies within the zone.

(b) Notwithstanding the provisions of paragraph (a) of this subsection (2) to the contrary, the department of transportation shall not establish a lower speed limit for more than one hundred miles of the public highways of the state that have been established as wildlife crossing zones.

(3) (a) The department of transportation may establish an area within the federal highways of the state as a wildlife crossing zone if the department of transportation receives authorization from the federal government.

(b) If the department of transportation establishes an area within the federal highways of the state as a wildlife crossing zone pursuant to paragraph (a) of this subsection (3), the department of transportation may erect signs:

(I) Identifying the zone in accordance with the provisions of section 42-4-616; and

(II) Establishing a lower speed limit for the portion of the highway that lies within the zone.

(4) If the department of transportation erects a new wildlife crossing zone sign pursuant to subsection (2) or (3) of this section, it shall ensure that the sign indicates, in conformity with the state traffic control manual, that increased traffic penalties are in effect within the wildlife crossing zone. For the purposes of this section, it shall be sufficient that the sign states "increased penalties in effect".

(5) In establishing a lower speed limit within a wildlife crossing zone, the department of transportation shall give due consideration to factors including, but not limited to, the following:

(a) The percentage of traffic accidents that occur within the area that involve the presence of wildlife on the public highway;

(b) The relative levels of traffic congestion and mobility in the area; and

(c) The relative numbers of traffic accidents that occur within the area during the daytime and evening hours and involve the presence of wildlife on the public highway.

(6) As used in this section, unless the context otherwise requires, "wildlife" shall have the same meaning as "big game" as set forth in section 33-1-102 (2), C.R.S.

(7) (a) On or before March 1, 2012, the department of transportation shall prepare and submit to the transportation and energy committee of the house of representatives and the transportation committee of the senate, or any successor committees, a report concerning the implementation of this section. The report, at a minimum, shall include:

(I) The location and length of each wildlife crossing zone that the department of transportation has established pursuant to this section;

(II) The total number of miles within the public highways of the state that the department of transportation has established as wildlife crossing zones pursuant to this section;

(III) The total number of wildlife crossing zones within the state for which the department of transportation has established a lower speed limit, including identification of each wildlife crossing zone for which the department has established a lower speed limit;

(IV) The effect, if any, that the establishment of each wildlife crossing zone has had in reducing the frequency of traffic accidents within the area of the public highway that has been established as a wildlife crossing zone; and

(V) A recommendation by the department of transportation as to whether the general assembly should:

(A) Discontinue the establishment of wildlife crossing zones;

(B) Continue the establishment of wildlife crossing zones, as limited by the provisions of paragraph (b) of subsection (1) of this section; or

(C) Expand the establishment of wildlife crossing zones beyond the limits described in paragraph (b) of subsection (1) of this section.

(b) This subsection (7) is repealed, effective March 2, 2012.

(8) Notwithstanding any other provision of this section, the department of transportation shall not establish any area of any interstate highway as a wildlife crossing zone.

PART 2

EQUIPMENT

42-4-201. Obstruction of view or driving mechanism - hazardous situation. (1) No person shall drive a vehicle when it is so loaded or when there are in the front seat such number of persons, exceeding three, as to obstruct the view of the driver to the front or sides of the vehicle or as to interfere with the driver's control over the driving mechanism of the vehicle.

(2) No person shall knowingly drive a vehicle while any passenger therein is riding in any manner which endangers the safety of such passenger or others.

(3) No person shall drive any motor vehicle equipped with any television viewer, screen, or other means of visually receiving a television broadcast which is located in the motor vehicle at any point forward of the back of the driver's seat or which is visible to the driver while operating the motor vehicle. The provisions of this subsection (3) shall not be interpreted to prohibit the usage of any computer, data terminal, or other similar device in a motor vehicle.

(4) No vehicle shall be operated upon any highway unless the driver's vision through any required glass equipment is normal and unobstructed.

(5) No passenger in a vehicle shall ride in such position as to create a hazard for such passenger or others, or to interfere with the driver's view ahead or to the sides, or to interfere with the driver's control over the driving mechanism of the vehicle; nor shall the driver of a vehicle permit any passenger therein to ride in such manner.

(6) No person shall hang on or otherwise attach himself or herself to the outside, top, hood, or fenders of any vehicle, or to any other portion thereof, other than the specific enclosed portion of such vehicle intended for passengers or while in a sitting position in the cargo area of a vehicle if such area is fully or partially enclosed on all four sides, while the same is in motion; nor shall the operator knowingly permit any person to hang on or otherwise attach himself or herself to the outside, top, hood, or fenders of any vehicle, or any other portion thereof, other than the specific enclosed portion of such vehicle intended for passengers or while in a sitting position in the cargo area of a vehicle if such area is fully or partially enclosed on all four sides, while the same is in motion. This subsection (6) shall not apply to parades, caravans, or exhibitions which are officially authorized or otherwise permitted by law.

(7) The provisions of subsection (6) of this section shall not apply to a vehicle owned by the United States government or any agency or instrumentality thereof, or to a vehicle owned by the state of Colorado or any of its political subdivisions, or to a privately owned vehicle when operating in a governmental capacity under contract with or permit from any governmental subdivision or under permit issued by the public utilities commission of the state of Colorado, when in the performance of their duties persons are required to stand or sit on the exterior of the vehicle and said vehicle is equipped with adequate handrails and safeguards.

(8) Any person who violates any provision of this section commits a class A traffic infraction.

42-4-202. Unsafe vehicles - penalty - identification plates. (1) It is unlawful for any person to drive or move or for the owner to cause or knowingly permit to be driven or moved on any highway any vehicle or combination of vehicles which is in such unsafe condition as to endanger any person, or which does not contain those parts or is not at all times equipped with such lamps and other equipment in proper condition and adjustment as required in this section and sections 42-4-204 to 42-4-231 and part 3 of this article, or which is equipped in any manner in violation of said sections and part 3 or for any person to do any act forbidden or fail to perform any act required under said sections and part 3.

(2) The provisions of this section and sections 42-4-204 to 42-4-231 and part 3 of this article with respect to equipment on vehicles shall not apply to implements of husbandry or farm tractors, except as made applicable in said sections and part 3.

(3) Nothing in this article shall be construed to prohibit the use of additional parts and accessories on any vehicle, consistent with the provisions of this article.

(4) (a) Upon its approval, the department shall issue an identification plate for each vehicle, motor vehicle, trailer, or item of special mobile machinery, or similar implement of equipment, used in any type of construction business which shall, when said plate is affixed, exempt any such item of equipment, machinery, trailer, or vehicle from all or part of this section and sections 42-4-204 to 42-4-231 and part 3 of this article.

(b) The department is authorized to promulgate written rules and regulations governing the application for, issuance of, and supervision, administration, and revocation of such identification plates and exemption authority and to prescribe the terms and conditions under which said plates may be issued for each item as set forth in paragraph (a) of this subsection (4), and the department, in so doing, shall consider the safety of users of the public streets and highways and the type, nature, and use of such items set forth in paragraph (a) of this subsection (4) for which exemption is sought.

(c) Each exempt item may be moved on the roads, streets, and highways during daylight hours and at such time as vision is not less than five hundred feet. No cargo or supplies shall be hauled upon such exempt item except cargo and supplies used in normal operation of any such item.

(d) The identification plate shall be of a size and type designated and approved by the department. A fee of one dollar shall be charged and collected by the department for the issuance of each such identification plate. All such fees so collected shall be paid to the state treasurer who shall credit the same to the highway users tax fund for allocation and expenditure as specified in section 43-4-205 (5.5) (b), C.R.S.

(e) Each such identification plate shall be issued for a calendar year. Application for such identification plates shall be made by the owner, and such plates shall be issued to the owner of each such item described in paragraph (a) of this subsection (4). Whenever the owner transfers, sells, or assigns the owner's interest therein, the exemption of such item shall expire and the owner shall remove the identification plate therefrom and forward the same to the department.

(f) An owner shall report a lost or damaged identification plate to the department, and, upon application to and approval by the department, the department shall issue a replacement plate upon payment to it of a fee of fifty cents.

(g) Notwithstanding the amount specified for any fee in this subsection (4), the executive director of the department by rule or as otherwise provided by law may reduce the amount of one or more of the fees if necessary pursuant to section 24-75-402 (3), C.R.S., to reduce the uncommitted reserves of the fund to which all or any portion of one or more of the fees is credited. After the uncommitted reserves of the fund are sufficiently reduced, the executive director of the department by rule or as otherwise provided by law may increase the amount of one or more of the fees as provided in section 24-75-402 (4), C.R.S.

(5) Any person who violates any provision of this section commits a class A traffic infraction.

42-4-203. Unsafe vehicles - spot inspections. (1) Uniformed police officers, at any time upon reasonable cause, may require the driver of a vehicle to stop and submit such vehicle and its equipment to an inspection and such test with reference thereto as may be appropriate. The fact that a vehicle is an older model vehicle shall not alone constitute reasonable cause. In the event such vehicle is found to be in an unsafe condition or the required equipment is not present or is not in proper repair and adjustment, the officer may give a written notice and issue a summons to the driver. Said notice shall require that such vehicle be placed in safe condition and properly equipped or that its equipment be placed in proper repair and adjustment, the particulars of which shall be specified on said notice.

(2) In the event any such vehicle is, in the reasonable judgment of such police officer, in such condition that further operation would be hazardous, the officer may require, in addition to the instructions set forth in subsection (1) of this section, that the vehicle be moved at the operator's expense and not operated under its own power or that it be driven to the nearest garage or other place of safety.

(3) Every owner or driver upon receiving the notice and summons issued pursuant to subsection (1) of this section or mailed pursuant to paragraph (b) of subsection (4) of this section shall comply therewith and shall secure a certification upon such notice by a law enforcement officer that such vehicle is in safe condition and its equipment has been placed in proper repair and adjustment and otherwise made to conform to the requirements of this article. Said certification shall be returned to the owner or driver for presentation in court as provided for in subsection (4) of this section.

(4) (a) (I) Except as provided for in subparagraph (II) or subparagraph (III) of this paragraph (a), any owner receiving written notice and a summons pursuant to this section is guilty of a misdemeanor traffic offense and, upon conviction thereof, shall be punished by a fine of one hundred dollars, payable within thirty days after conviction.

(II) If the owner repairs the unsafe condition or installs or adjusts the required equipment within thirty days after issuance of the notice and summons and presents the certification required in subsection (3) of this section to the court of competent jurisdiction, the owner shall be punished by a fine of five dollars.

(III) If the owner submits to the court of competent jurisdiction within thirty days after the issuance of the summons proof that the owner has disposed of the vehicle for junk parts or immobilized the vehicle and also submits to the court the registration and license plates for the vehicle, the owner shall be punished by a fine of five dollars. If the owner wishes to relicense the vehicle in the future, the owner must obtain the certification required in subsection (3) of this section.

(b) (I) Except as provided for in subparagraph (II) of this paragraph (b), any nonowner driver receiving written notice and a summons pursuant to this section is guilty of a misdemeanor traffic offense and, upon conviction thereof, shall be punished by a fine of one hundred dollars, payable within thirty days after conviction.

(II) If the driver submits to the court of competent jurisdiction within thirty days after the issuance of the summons proof that the driver was not the owner of the car at the time the summons was issued and that the driver mailed, within five days of issuance thereof, a copy of the notice and summons by certified mail to the owner of the vehicle at the address on the registration, the driver shall be punished by a fine of five dollars.

(c) Upon a showing of good cause that the required repairs or adjustments cannot be made within thirty days after issuance of the notice and summons, the court of competent jurisdiction may extend the period of time for installation or adjustment of required equipment as may appear justified.

(d) The owner may, in lieu of appearance, submit to the court of competent jurisdiction, within thirty days after the issuance of the notice and summons, the certification specified in subsection (3) of this section and the fine of five dollars.

42-4-204. When lighted lamps are required. (1) Every vehicle upon a highway within this state, between sunset and sunrise and at any other time when, due to insufficient light or unfavorable atmospheric conditions, persons and vehicles on the highway are not clearly discernible at a distance of one thousand feet ahead, shall display lighted lamps and illuminating devices as required by this article for different classes of vehicles, subject to exceptions with respect to parked vehicles.

(2) Whenever requirement is declared by this article as to distance from which certain lamps and devices shall render objects visible or within which such lamps or devices shall be visible, said provisions shall apply during the times stated in subsection (1) of this section in respect to a vehicle without load when upon a straight, level, unlighted highway under normal atmos-

pheric conditions, unless a different time or condition is expressly stated.

(3) Whenever requirement is declared by this article as to the mounted height of lamps or devices, it shall mean from the center of such lamp or device to the level ground upon which the vehicle stands when such vehicle is without a load.

(4) Any person who violates any provision of this section commits a class A traffic infraction.

42-4-205. Head lamps on motor vehicles. (1) Every motor vehicle other than a motorcycle shall be equipped with at least two head lamps with at least one on each side of the front of the motor vehicle, which head lamps shall comply with the requirements and limitations set forth in sections 42-4-202 and 42-4-204 to 42-4-231 and part 3 of this article where applicable.

(2) Every motorcycle shall be equipped with at least one and not more than two head lamps that shall comply with the requirements and limitations of sections 42-4-202 and 42-4-204 to 42-4-231 and part 3 of this article where applicable.

(3) Every head lamp upon every motor vehicle, including every motorcycle, shall be located at a height measured from the center of the head lamp of not more than fifty-four inches nor less than twenty-four inches, to be measured as set forth in section 42-4-204 (3).

(4) Any person who violates any provision of this section commits a class B traffic infraction.

42-4-206. Tail lamps and reflectors. (1) To be operated on a road, every motor vehicle, trailer, semitrailer, and pole trailer and any other vehicle that is being drawn at the end of a train of vehicles must be equipped with at least one tail lamp mounted on the rear, which, when lighted as required in section 42-4-204, emits a red light plainly visible from a distance of five hundred feet to the rear; except that, in the case of a train of vehicles, only the tail lamp on the rear-most vehicle need actually be seen from the distance specified, except as provided in section 42-12-204. Furthermore, every vehicle registered in this state and manufactured or assembled after January 1, 1958, must be equipped with at least two tail lamps mounted on the rear, on the same level and as widely spaced laterally as practicable, which, when lighted as required in section 42-4-204, comply with this section.

(2) Every tail lamp upon every vehicle shall be located at a height of not more than seventy-two inches nor less than twenty inches, to be measured as set forth in section 42-4-204 (3).

(3) Either a tail lamp or a separate lamp shall be so constructed and placed as to illuminate with a white light the rear registration plate and render it clearly legible from a distance of fifty feet to the rear. Any tail lamp, together with any separate lamp for illuminating the rear registration plate, shall be so wired as to be lighted whenever the head lamps or auxiliary driving lamps are lighted.

(4) To be operated on a road, every motor vehicle must carry on the rear, either as part of a tail lamp or separately, one red reflector meeting the requirements of this section; except that vehicles of the type mentioned in section 42-4-207 must be equipped with reflectors as required by law unless otherwise provided in section 42-12-204.

(5) Every new motor vehicle sold and operated on and after January 1, 1958, upon a highway shall carry on the rear, whether as a part of the tail lamps or separately, two red reflectors; except that every motorcycle shall carry at least one reflector meeting the requirements of this section, and vehicles of the type mentioned in section 42-4-207 shall be equipped with reflectors as required in those sections applicable thereto.

(6) Every reflector shall be mounted on the vehicle at a height of not less than twenty inches nor more than sixty inches, measured as set forth in section 42-4-204 (3) and shall be of such size and characteristics and so mounted as to be visible at night from all distances within three hundred fifty feet to one hundred feet from such vehicle when directly in front of lawful upper beams and head lamps; except that visibility from a greater distance is required by law of reflectors on certain types of vehicles.

(7) Any person who violates any provision of this section commits a class B traffic infraction.

42-4-207. Clearance and identification. (1) Every vehicle designed or used for the transportation of property or for the transportation of persons shall display lighted lamps at the times mentioned in section 42-4-204 when and as required in this section.

(2) **Clearance lamps.** (a) Every motor vehicle or motor-drawn vehicle having a width at any part in excess of eighty inches shall be equipped with four clearance lamps located as follows:

(I) Two on the front and one at each side, displaying an amber light visible from a distance of five hundred feet to the front of the vehicle;

(II) Two on the rear and one at each side, displaying a red light visible only to the rear and visible from a distance of five hundred feet to the rear of the vehicle, which said rear clearance lamps shall be in addition to the rear red lamp required in section 42-4-206.

(b) All clearance lamps required shall be placed on the extreme sides and located on the highest stationary support; except that, when three or more identification lamps are mounted on the rear of a vehicle on the vertical center line and at the extreme height of the vehicle, rear clearance lamps may be mounted at optional height.

(c) Any trailer, when operated in conjunction with a vehicle which is properly equipped with front clearance lamps as provided in this section, may be, but is not required to be, equipped with front clearance lamps if the towing vehicle is of equal or greater width than the towed vehicle.

(d) All clearance lamps required in this section shall be of a type approved by the department.

(3) **Side marker lamps.** (a) Every motor vehicle or motor-drawn vehicle or combination of such vehicles which exceeds thirty feet in overall length shall be equipped with four side marker lamps located as follows:

(I) One on each side near the front displaying an amber light visible from a distance of five hundred feet to the side of the vehicle on which it is located;

(II) One on each side near the rear displaying a red light visible from a distance of five hundred feet to the side of the vehicle on which it is located; but the rear marker light shall not be so placed as to be visible from the front of the vehicle.

(b) Each side marker lamp required shall be located not less than fifteen inches above the level on which the vehicle stands.

(c) If the clearance lamps required by this section are of such a design as to display lights visible from a distance of five hundred feet at right angles to the sides of the vehicles, they shall be deemed to meet the requirements as to marker lamps in this subsection (3).

(d) All marker lamps required in this section shall be of a type approved by the department.

(4) **Clearance reflectors.** (a) Every motor vehicle having a width at any part in excess of eighty inches shall be equipped with clearance reflectors located as follows:

(I) Two red reflectors on the rear and one at each side, located not more than one inch from the extreme outside edges of the vehicle;

(II) All such reflectors shall be located not more than sixty inches nor less than fifteen inches above the level on which the vehicle stands.

(b) One or both of the required rear red reflectors may be incorporated within the tail lamp or tail lamps if any such tail lamps meet the location limits specified for reflectors.

(c) All such clearance reflectors shall be of a type approved by the department.

(5) **Side marker reflectors.** (a) Every motor vehicle or motor-drawn vehicle or combination of vehicles which exceeds thirty feet in overall length shall be equipped with four side marker reflectors located as follows:

(I) One amber reflector on each side near the front;

(II) One red reflector on each side near the rear.

(b) Each side marker reflector shall be located not more than sixty inches nor less than fifteen inches above the level on which the vehicle stands.

(c) All such side marker reflectors shall be of a type approved by the department.

(6) Any person who violates any provision of this section commits a class B traffic infraction.

(7) Nothing in this section shall be construed to supersede any federal motor vehicle safety standard established pursuant to the "National Traffic and Motor Vehicle Safety Act of 1966", Public Law 89-563, as amended.

42-4-208. Stop lamps and turn signals. (1) Every motor vehicle or motor-drawn vehicle shall be equipped with a stop light in good working order at all times and shall meet the requirements of section 42-4-215 (1).

(2) No person shall sell or offer for sale or operate on the highways any motor vehicle registered in this state and manufactured or assembled after January 1, 1958, unless it is equipped with at least two stop lamps meeting the requirements of section 42-4-215 (1); except that a motorcycle manufactured or assembled after said date shall be equipped with at least one stop lamp meeting the requirements of section 42-4-215 (1).

(3) No person shall sell or offer for sale or operate on the highways any motor vehicle, trailer, or semitrailer registered in this state and manufactured or assembled after January 1, 1958, and no person shall operate any motor vehicle, trailer, or semitrailer on the highways when the distance from the center of the top of the steering post to the left outside limit of the body, cab, or load of such motor vehicle exceeds twenty-four inches, unless it is equipped with electrical turn signals meeting the requirements of section 42-4-215 (2). This subsection (3) shall not apply to any motorcycle or low-power scooter.

(4) Any person who violates any provision of this section commits a class B traffic infraction.

42-4-209. Lamp or flag on projecting load. Whenever the load upon any vehicle extends to the rear four feet or more beyond the bed or body of such vehicle, there shall be displayed at the extreme rear end of the load, at the time specified in section 42-4-204, a red light or lantern plainly visible from a distance of at least five hundred feet to the sides and rear. The red light or lantern required under this section shall be in addition to the red rear light required upon every vehicle. At any other time, there shall be displayed at the extreme rear end of such load a red flag or cloth not less than twelve inches square and so hung that the entire area is visible to the driver of a vehicle approaching from the rear. Any person who violates any provision of this section commits a class A traffic infraction.

42-4-210. Lamps on parked vehicles. (1) Whenever a vehicle is lawfully parked upon a highway during the hours between sunset and sunrise and in the event there is sufficient light to reveal any person or object within a distance of one thousand feet upon such highway, no lights need be displayed upon such parked vehicle.

(2) Whenever a vehicle is parked or stopped upon a roadway or shoulder adjacent thereto, whether attended or unattended, during the hours between sunset and sunrise and there is not sufficient light to reveal any person or object within a distance of one thousand feet upon such highway, such vehicle so parked or stopped shall

be equipped with one or more operating lamps meeting the following requirements: At least one lamp shall display a white or amber light visible from a distance of five hundred feet to the front of the vehicle, and the same lamp or at least one other lamp shall display a red light visible from a distance of five hundred feet to the rear of the vehicle, and the location of said lamp or lamps shall always be such that at least one lamp or combination of lamps meeting the requirements of this section is installed as near as practicable to the side of the vehicle that is closer to passing traffic. This subsection (2) shall not apply to a low-power scooter.

(3) Any lighted head lamps upon a parked vehicle shall be depressed or dimmed.

(4) Any person who violates any provision of this section commits a class B traffic infraction.

(5) This section shall not apply to low-speed electric vehicles.

42-4-211. Lamps on farm equipment and other vehicles and equipment. (1) Every farm tractor and every self-propelled farm equipment unit or implement of husbandry not equipped with an electric lighting system shall, at all times mentioned in section 42-4-204, be equipped with at least one lamp displaying a white light visible from a distance of not less than five hundred feet to the front of such vehicle and shall also be equipped with at least one lamp displaying a red light visible from a distance of not less than five hundred feet to the rear of such vehicle.

(2) Every self-propelled unit of farm equipment not equipped with an electric lighting system shall, at all times mentioned in section 42-4-204, in addition to the lamps required in subsection (1) of this section, be equipped with two red reflectors visible from all distances within six hundred feet to one hundred feet to the rear when directly in front of lawful upper beams of head lamps.

(3) Every combination of farm tractor and towed unit of farm equipment or implement of husbandry not equipped with an electric lighting system shall, at all times mentioned in section 42-4-204, be equipped with the following lamps:

(a) At least one lamp mounted to indicate as nearly as practicable to the extreme left projection of said combination and displaying a white light visible from a distance of not less than five hundred feet to the front of said combination;

(b) Two lamps each displaying a red light visible when lighted from a distance of not less than five hundred feet to the rear of said combination or, as an alternative, at least one lamp displaying a red light visible from a distance of not less than five hundred feet to the rear thereof and two red reflectors visible from all distances within six hundred feet to one hundred feet to the rear thereof when illuminated by the upper beams of head lamps.

(4) Every farm tractor and every self-propelled unit of farm equipment or implement of husbandry equipped with an electric lighting system shall, at all times mentioned in section 42-4-204, be equipped with two single-beam head lamps meeting the requirements of section 42-4-216 or 42-4-218, respectively, and at least one red lamp visible from a distance of not less than five hundred feet to the rear; but every such self-propelled unit of farm equipment other than a farm tractor shall have two such red lamps or, as an alternative, one such red lamp and two red reflectors visible from all distances within six hundred feet to one hundred feet when directly in front of lawful upper beams of head lamps.

(5) (a) Every combination of farm tractor and towed farm equipment or towed implement of husbandry equipped with an electric lighting system shall, at all times mentioned in section 42-4-204, be equipped with lamps as follows:

(I) The farm tractor element of every such combination shall be equipped as required in subsection (4) of this section.

(II) The towed unit of farm equipment or implement of husbandry element of such combination shall be equipped with two red lamps visible from a distance of not less than five hundred feet to the rear or, as an alternative, two red reflectors visible from all distances within six hundred feet to the rear when directly in front of lawful upper beams of head lamps.

(b) Said combinations shall also be equipped with a lamp displaying a white or amber light, or any shade of color between white and amber, visible from a distance of not less than five hundred feet to the front and a lamp displaying a red light visible when lighted from a distance of not less than five hundred feet to the rear.

(6) The lamps and reflectors required in this section shall be so positioned as to show from front and rear as nearly as practicable the extreme projection of the vehicle carrying them on the side of the roadway used in passing such vehicle. If a farm tractor or a unit of farm equipment, whether self-propelled or towed, is equipped with two or more lamps or reflectors visible from the front or two or more lamps or reflectors visible from the rear, such lamps or reflectors shall be so positioned that the extreme projections, both to the right and to the left of said vehicle, shall be indicated as nearly as practicable.

(7) Every vehicle, including animal-drawn vehicles and vehicles referred to in section 42-4-202 (2), not specifically required by the provisions of this article to be equipped with lamps or other lighting devices shall at all times specified in section 42-4-204 be equipped with at least one lamp displaying a white light visible from a distance of not less than five hundred feet to the front of said vehicle and shall also be equipped with two lamps displaying red lights visible from a distance of not less than five hundred feet to the rear of said vehicle or, as an alternative, one lamp displaying a red light visible from a distance of not less than five hundred feet to the rear and two red reflectors visible for distances of one hundred feet to six hundred feet to the rear when illuminated by the upper beams of head lamps.

(8) Any person who violates any provision of this section commits a class B traffic infraction.

42-4-212. Spot lamps and auxiliary lamps. (1) Any motor vehicle may be equipped with not more than two spot lamps, and every lighted spot lamp shall be so aimed and used upon approaching another vehicle that no part of the high-intensity portion of the beam will be directed to the left of the prolongation of the extreme left side of the vehicle nor more than one hundred feet ahead of the vehicle.

(2) Any motor vehicle may be equipped with not more than two fog lamps mounted on the front at a height of not less than twelve inches nor more than thirty inches above the level surface upon which the vehicle stands and so aimed that, when the vehicle is not loaded, none of the high-intensity portion of the light to the left of the center of the vehicle shall at a distance of twenty-five feet ahead project higher than a level of four inches below the level of the center of the lamp from which it comes. Lighted fog lamps meeting the requirements of this subsection (2) may be used with lower head-lamp beams as specified in section 42-4-216 (1) (b).

(3) Any motor vehicle may be equipped with not more than two auxiliary passing lamps mounted on the front at a height of not less than twenty inches nor more than forty-two inches above the level surface upon which the vehicle stands. The provisions of section 42-4-216 shall apply to any combination of head lamps and auxiliary passing lamps.

(4) Any motor vehicle may be equipped with not more than two auxiliary driving lamps mounted on the front at a height of not less than sixteen inches nor more than forty-two inches above the level surface upon which the vehicle stands. The provisions of section 42-4-216 shall apply to any combination of head lamps and auxiliary driving lamps.

(5) Any person who violates any provision of this section commits a class B traffic infraction.

42-4-213. Audible and visual signals on emergency vehicles. (1) Except as otherwise provided in this section or in section 42-4-222 in the case of volunteer fire vehicles and volunteer ambulances, every authorized emergency vehicle shall, in addition to any other equipment and distinctive markings required by this article, be equipped as a minimum with a siren and a horn. Such devices shall be capable of emitting a sound audible under normal conditions from a distance of not less than five hundred feet.

(2) Every authorized emergency vehicle, except those used as undercover vehicles by governmental agencies, shall, in addition to any other equipment and distinctive markings required by this article, be equipped with at least one signal lamp mounted as high as practicable, which shall be capable of displaying a flashing, oscillating, or rotating red light to the front and to the rear having sufficient intensity to be visible at five hundred feet in normal sunlight. In addition to the required red light, flashing, oscillating, or rotating signal lights may be used which emit blue, white, or blue in combination with white.

(3) A police vehicle, when used as an authorized emergency vehicle, may but need not be equipped with the red lights specified in this section.

(4) Any authorized emergency vehicle, including those authorized by section 42-4-222, may be equipped with green flashing lights, mounted at sufficient height and having sufficient intensity to be visible at five hundred feet in all directions in normal daylight. Such lights may only be used at the single designated command post at any emergency location or incident and only when such command post is stationary. The single command post shall be designated by the on-scene incident commander in accordance with local or state government emergency plans. Any other use of a green light by a vehicle shall constitute a violation of this section.

(5) The use of either the audible or the visual signal equipment described in this section shall impose upon drivers of other vehicles the obligation to yield right-of-way and stop as prescribed in section 42-4-705.

(6) Any person who violates any provision of this section commits a class A traffic infraction.

42-4-214. Visual signals on service vehicles. (1) Except as otherwise provided in this section, on or after January 1, 1978, every authorized service vehicle shall, in addition to any other equipment required by this article, be equipped with one or more warning lamps mounted as high as practicable, which shall be capable of displaying in all directions one or more flashing, oscillating, or rotating yellow lights. Only yellow and no other color or combination of colors shall be used as a warning lamp on an authorized service vehicle; except that an authorized service vehicle snowplow operated by a general purpose government may also be equipped with and use no more than two flashing, oscillating, or rotating blue lights as warning lamps. Lighted directional signs used by police and highway departments to direct traffic need not be visible except to the front and rear. Such lights shall have sufficient intensity to be visible at five hundred feet in normal sunlight.

(2) The warning lamps authorized in subsection (1) of this section shall be activated by the operator of an authorized service vehicle only when the vehicle is operating upon the roadway so as to create a hazard to other traffic. The use of such lamps shall not relieve the operator from the duty of using due care for the safety of others or from the obligation of using any other safety equipment or protective devices that are required by this article. Service vehicles authorized to operate also as emergency vehicles shall also be equipped to comply with signal requirements for emergency vehicles.

(3) Whenever an authorized service vehicle is performing its service function and is displaying lights as authorized in subsection (1) of this section, drivers of all other vehicles shall exercise more than ordinary care and caution in approaching, overtaking, or passing such service vehicle and, in the case of highway and traffic maintenance equipment engaged in work upon the highway, shall comply with the instructions of section 42-4-712.

(4) On or after January 1, 1978, only authorized service vehicles shall be equipped with the warning lights authorized in subsection (1) of this section.

(5) The department of transportation shall determine by rule which types of vehicles render an essential public service when operating on or along a roadway and warrant designation as authorized service vehicles under specified conditions, including, without limitation, vehicles that sell or apply chains or other equipment to motor vehicles necessary to enable compliance with section 42-4-106.

(6) Any person who violates any provision of this section commits a class B traffic infraction.

42-4-215. Signal lamps and devices - additional lighting equipment. (1) To be operated on a road, any motor vehicle may be equipped, and when required under this article must be equipped, with a stop lamp or lamps on the rear of the vehicle that, except as provided in section 42-12-204, display a red or amber light, or any shade of color between red and amber, visible from a distance of not less than one hundred feet to the rear in normal sunlight, that are actuated upon application of the service (foot) brake, and that may but need not be incorporated with one or more other rear lamps. Such stop lamp or lamps may also be automatically actuated by a mechanical device when the vehicle is reducing speed or stopping. If two or more stop lamps are installed on any motor vehicle, any device actuating such lamps must be so designed and installed that all stop lamps are actuated by such device.

(2) Any motor vehicle may be equipped, and when required under this article must be equipped, with lamps showing to the front and rear for the purpose of indicating an intention to turn either to the right or to the left. The lamps showing to the front must be located on the same level and as widely spaced laterally as practicable and when in use display a white or amber light, or any shade of color between white and amber, visible from a distance of not less than one hundred feet to the front in normal sunlight, and the lamps showing to the rear must be located at the same level and as widely spaced laterally as practicable and, except as provided in section 42-12-204, when in use must display a red or amber light, or any shade of color between red and amber, visible from a distance of not less than one hundred feet to the rear in normal sunlight. When actuated, the lamps must indicate the intended direction of turning by flashing the light showing to the front and rear on the side toward which the turn is made.

(3) No stop lamp or signal lamp shall project a glaring or dazzling light.

(4) Any motor vehicle may be equipped with not more than two side cowl or fender lamps which shall emit an amber or white light without glare.

(5) Any motor vehicle may be equipped with not more than one runningboard courtesy lamp on each side thereof, which shall emit a white or amber light without glare.

(6) Any motor vehicle may be equipped with not more than two back-up lamps either separately or in combination with other lamps, but no such back-up lamp shall be lighted when the motor vehicle is in forward motion.

(7) Any vehicle may be equipped with lamps that may be used for the purpose of warning the operators of other vehicles of the presence of a vehicular traffic hazard requiring the exercise of unusual care in approaching, overtaking, or passing and, when so equipped and when the vehicle is not in motion or is being operated at a speed of twenty-five miles per hour or less and at no other time, may display such warning in addition to any other warning signals required by this article. The lamps used to display such warning to the front must be mounted at the same level and as widely spaced laterally as practicable and display simultaneously flashing white or amber lights, or any shade of color between white and amber. The lamps used to display the warning to the rear must be mounted at the same level and as widely spaced laterally as practicable and, except as provided in section 42-12-204, show simultaneously flashing amber or red lights, or any shade of color between amber and red. These warning lights must be visible from a distance of not less than five hundred feet under normal atmospheric conditions at night.

(8) Any vehicle eighty inches or more in overall width may be equipped with not more than three identification lamps showing to the front which shall emit an amber light without glare and not more than three identification lamps showing to the rear which shall emit a red light without glare. Such lamps shall be mounted horizontally.

(9) Any person who violates any provision of this section commits a class B traffic infraction.

42-4-215.5. Signal lamps and devices - street rod vehicles and custom motor vehicles. (Repealed)

42-4-216. Multiple-beam road lights. (1) Except as provided in this article, the head lamps or the auxiliary driving lamp or the auxiliary passing lamp or combination thereof on motor vehicles, other than motorcycles or low-power scooters, shall be so arranged that the driver may select at will between distributions of light projected to different elevations, and such lamps may, in addition, be so arranged that such selection can be made automatically, subject to the following limitations:

(a) There shall be an uppermost distribution of light or composite beam so aimed and of such intensity as to reveal persons and vehicles at a distance of at least three hundred fifty feet ahead for all conditions of loading.

(b) There shall be a lowermost distribution of light or composite beam so aimed and of sufficient intensity to reveal persons and vehicles at a distance of at least one hundred feet ahead; and on a straight level road under any condition of loading, none of the high-intensity portion of the beam shall be directed to strike the eyes of an approaching driver.

(1.5) Head lamps arranged to provide a single distribution of light not supplemented by auxiliary driving lamps shall be permitted for low-speed electric vehicles in lieu of multiple-beam, road-lighting equipment specified in this section if the single distribution of light complies with paragraph (b) of subsection (1) of this section.

(2) A new motor vehicle, other than a motorcycle or low-power scooter, that has multiple-beam road-lighting equipment, shall be equipped with a beam indicator, which shall be lighted whenever the uppermost distribution of light from the head lamps is in use and shall not otherwise be lighted. Said indicator shall be so designed and located that when lighted it will be readily visible without glare to the driver of the vehicle so equipped.

(3) Any person who violates any provision of this section commits a class B traffic infraction.

42-4-217. Use of multiple-beam lights. (1) Whenever a motor vehicle is being operated on a roadway or shoulder adjacent thereto during the times specified in section 42-4-204, the driver shall use a distribution of light, or composite beam, directed high enough and of sufficient intensity to reveal persons and vehicles at a safe distance in advance of the vehicle, subject to the following requirements and limitations:

(a) Whenever a driver of a vehicle approaches an oncoming vehicle within five hundred feet, such driver shall use a distribution of light or composite beam so aimed that the glaring rays are not projected into the eyes of the oncoming driver. The lowermost distribution of light or composite beam specified in section 42-4-216 (1) (b) shall be deemed to avoid glare at all times, regardless of road contour and loading.

(b) Whenever the driver of a vehicle follows another vehicle within two hundred feet to the rear, except when engaged in the act of overtaking and passing, such driver shall use a distribution of light permissible under this title other than the uppermost distribution of light specified in section 42-4-216 (1) (a).

(c) A low-speed electric vehicle may use the distribution of light authorized in section 42-4-216 (1.5).

(2) Any person who violates any provision of this section commits a class A traffic infraction.

42-4-218. Single-beam road-lighting equipment. (1) Head lamps arranged to provide a single distribution of light not supplemented by auxiliary driving lamps shall be permitted on motor vehicles manufactured and sold prior to July 15, 1936, in lieu of multiple-beam road-lighting equipment specified in section 42-4-216 if the single distribution of light complies with the following requirements and limitations:

(a) The head lamps shall be so aimed that when the vehicle is not loaded none of the high-intensity portion of the light shall, at a distance of twenty-five feet ahead, project higher than a level of five inches below the level of the center of the lamp from which it comes and in no case higher than forty-two inches above the level on which the vehicle stands at a distance of seventy-five feet ahead.

(b) The intensity shall be sufficient to reveal persons and vehicles at a distance of at least two hundred feet.

(2) Any person who violates any provision of this section commits a class B traffic infraction.

42-4-219. Number of lamps permitted. Whenever a motor vehicle equipped with head lamps as required in this article is also equipped with any auxiliary lamps or a spot lamp or any other lamp on the front thereof projecting a beam of an intensity greater than three hundred candlepower, not more than a total of four of any such lamps on the front of a vehicle shall be lighted at any one time when upon a highway. Any person who violates any provision of this section commits a class B traffic infraction.

42-4-220. Low-power scooters - lighting equipment - department control - use and operation. (1) (a) A low-power scooter when in use at the times specified in section 42-4-204 shall be equipped with a lamp on the front that shall emit a white light visible from a distance of at least five hundred feet to the front and with a red reflector on the rear, of a type approved by the department, that shall be visible from all distances from fifty feet to three hundred feet to the rear when directly in front of lawful upper beams of head lamps on a motor vehicle. A lamp emitting a red light visible from a distance of five hundred feet to the rear may be used in addition to the red reflector.

(b) No person shall operate a low-power scooter unless it is equipped with a bell or other device capable of giving a signal audible for a distance of at least one hundred feet; except that a low-power scooter shall not be equipped with nor shall any person use upon a low-power scooter a siren or whistle.

(c) A low-power scooter shall be equipped with a brake that will enable the operator to make the braked wheels skid on dry, level, clean pavement.

(2) (Deleted by amendment, L. 2009, (HB 09-1026), ch. 281, p. 1274, § 44, effective October 1, 2009.)

(3) (a) Any lighted lamp or illuminating device upon a motor vehicle, other than head lamps, spot lamps, auxiliary lamps, flashing turn signals, emergency vehicle warning lamps, and school bus warning lamps, which projects a beam of light of an intensity greater than three hundred candlepower shall be so directed that no part of the high-intensity portion of the beam will strike the level of the roadway on which the vehicle stands at a distance of more than seventy-five feet from the vehicle.

(b) Repealed.

(c) This subsection (3) shall not be construed to prohibit the use on any vehicle of simultaneously flashing hazard warning lights as provided by section 42-4-215 (7).

(4) No person shall have for sale, sell, or offer for sale, for use upon or as a part of the equipment of a motor vehicle, trailer, or semitrailer or for use upon any such vehicle, any head lamp, auxiliary or fog lamp, rear lamp, signal lamp, or reflector, which reflector is required under this article, or parts of any of the foregoing which tend to change the original design or performance thereof, unless of a type which has been approved by the department.

(5) No person shall have for sale, sell, or offer for sale, for use upon or as a part of the equipment of a motor vehicle, trailer, or semitrailer, any lamp or device mentioned in this section which has been approved by the department unless such lamp or device bears thereon the trademark or name under which it is approved so as to be legible when installed.

(6) No person shall use upon any motor vehicle, trailer, or semitrailer any lamps mentioned in this section unless said lamps are mounted, adjusted, and aimed in accordance with instructions of the department.

(7) The department is authorized to approve or disapprove lighting standards and specifications for the approval of such lighting devices and their installation, adjustment, and aiming and their adjustment when in use on motor vehicles.

(8) The department is required to approve or disapprove any lighting device, of a type on which approval is specifically required in this article, within a reasonable time after such device has been submitted.

(9) The department is authorized to provide the procedure which shall be followed when any device is submitted for approval.

(10) The department upon approving any such lamp or device shall issue to the applicant a certificate of approval, together with any instructions determined by the department to be reasonably necessary.

(11) The department shall provide lists of all lamps and devices by name and type which have been approved by it.

(12) When the department has reason to believe that an approved device as being sold commercially does not comply with the requirements of this article, the executive director of the department or the director's designated representatives may, after giving thirty days' previous notice to the person holding the certificate of approval for such device in the state, conduct a hearing upon the question of compliance of said approved device. After said hearing, said executive director shall determine whether said approved device meets the requirements of this article. If said device does not meet the requirements of this article, the director shall give notice to the person holding the certificate of approval for such device in this state.

(13) If, at the expiration of ninety days after such notice, the person holding the certificate of approval for such device has failed to establish to the satisfaction of the executive director of the department that said approved device as thereafter to be sold meets the requirements of this article, said executive director shall suspend or revoke the approval issued therefor and may require that all said devices sold since the notification following the hearing be replaced with devices that do comply with the requirements of this article, until or unless such device, at the sole expense of the applicant, shall be resubmitted to and retested by an authorized testing agency and is found to meet the requirements of this article. The department may, at the time of the retest, purchase in the open market and submit to the testing agency one or more sets of such approved devices, and, if such device upon such retest fails to meet the requirements of this article, the department may refuse to renew the certificate of approval of such device.

(14) Any person who violates any provision of this section commits a class B traffic infraction.

42-4-221. Bicycle and personal mobility device equipment. (1) No other provision of this part 2 and no provision of part 3 of this article shall apply to a bicycle, electrical assisted bicycle, or EPAMD or to equipment for use on a bicycle, electrical assisted bicycle, or EPAMD except those provisions in this article made specifically applicable to such a vehicle.

(2) Every bicycle, electrical assisted bicycle, or EPAMD in use at the times described in section 42-4-204 shall be equipped with a lamp on the front emitting a white light visible from a distance of at least five hundred feet to the front.

(3) Every bicycle, electrical assisted bicycle, or EPAMD shall be equipped with a red reflector of a type approved by the department, which shall be visible for six hundred feet to the rear when directly in front of lawful lower beams of head lamps on a motor vehicle.

(4) Every bicycle, electrical assisted bicycle, or EPAMD when in use at the times described in section 42-4-204 shall be equipped with reflective material of sufficient size and reflectivity to be visible from both sides for six hundred feet when directly in front of lawful lower beams of head lamps on a motor vehicle or, in lieu of such reflective material, with a lighted lamp visible

from both sides from a distance of at least five hundred feet.

(5) A bicycle, electrical assisted bicycle, or EPAMD or its rider may be equipped with lights or reflectors in addition to those required by subsections (2) to (4) of this section.

(6) A bicycle or electrical assisted bicycle shall not be equipped with, nor shall any person use upon a bicycle or electrical assisted bicycle, any siren or whistle.

(7) Every bicycle or electrical assisted bicycle shall be equipped with a brake or brakes that will enable its rider to stop the bicycle or electrical assisted bicycle within twenty-five feet from a speed of ten miles per hour on dry, level, clean pavement.

(8) A person engaged in the business of selling bicycles or electrical assisted bicycles at retail shall not sell any bicycle or electrical assisted bicycle unless the bicycle or electrical assisted bicycle has an identifying number permanently stamped or cast on its frame.

(9) Any person who violates any provision of this section commits a class B traffic infraction.

42-4-222. Volunteer firefighters - volunteer ambulance attendants - special lights and alarm systems. (1) (a) All members of volunteer fire departments regularly attached to the fire departments organized within incorporated towns, counties, cities, and fire protection districts and all members of a volunteer ambulance service regularly attached to a volunteer ambulance service within an area that the ambulance service would be reasonably expected to serve may have their private automobiles equipped with a signal lamp or a combination of signal lamps capable of displaying flashing, oscillating, or rotating red lights visible to the front and rear at five hundred feet in normal sunlight. In addition to the red light, flashing, oscillating, or rotating signal lights may be used that emit white or white in combination with red lights. At least one of such signal lamps or combination of signal lamps shall be mounted on the top of the automobile. Said automobiles may be equipped with audible signal systems such as sirens, whistles, or bells. Said lights, together with any signal systems authorized by this subsection (1), may be used only as authorized by subsection (3) of this section or when a member of a fire department is responding to or attending a fire alarm or other emergency or when a member of an ambulance service is responding to an emergency requiring the member's services. Except as authorized in subsection (3) of this section, neither such lights nor such signals shall be used for any other purpose than those set forth in this subsection (1). If used for any other purpose, such use shall constitute a violation of this subsection (1), and the violator commits a class B traffic infraction.

(b) Notwithstanding the provisions of paragraph (a) of this subsection (1), a member of a volunteer fire department or a volunteer ambulance service may equip his or her private automobile with the equipment described in paragraph (a) of this subsection (1) only after receiving a permit for the equipment from the fire chief of the fire department or chief executive officer of the ambulance service through which the volunteer serves.

(2) (Deleted by amendment, L. 96, p. 957, § 3, effective July 1, 1996.)

(3) A fire engine collector or member of a fire department may use the signal system authorized by subsection (1) of this section in a funeral, parade, or for other special purposes if the circumstances would not lead a reasonable person to believe that such vehicle is responding to an actual emergency.

42-4-223. Brakes. (1) Brake equipment required:

(a) Every motor vehicle, other than a motorcycle, when operated upon a highway shall be equipped with brakes adequate to control the movement of and to stop and hold such vehicle, including two separate means of applying the brakes, each of which means shall be effective to apply the brakes to at least two wheels. If these two separate means of applying the brakes are connected in any way, they shall be so constructed that failure of any one part of the operating mechanism shall not leave the motor vehicle without brakes on at least two wheels.

(b) Every motorcycle and low-power scooter, when operated upon a highway, shall be equipped with at least one brake, which may be operated by hand or foot.

(c) Every trailer or semitrailer of a gross weight of three thousand pounds or more, when operated upon a highway, shall be equipped with brakes adequate to control the movement of and to stop and to hold such vehicle and so designed as to be applied by the driver of the towing motor vehicle from the cab, and said brakes shall be so designed and connected that in case of an accidental breakaway of the towed vehicle the brakes shall be automatically applied. The provisions of this paragraph (c) shall not be applicable to any trailer which does not meet the definition of "commercial vehicle" as that term is defined in section 42-4-235 (1) (a) and which is owned by a farmer when transporting agricultural products produced on the owner's farm or supplies back to the farm of the owner of the trailer, tank trailers not exceeding ten thousand pounds gross weight used solely for transporting liquid fertilizer or gaseous fertilizer under pressure, or distributor trailers not exceeding ten thousand pounds gross weight used solely for transporting and distributing dry fertilizer when hauled by a truck capable of stopping within the distance specified in subsection (2) of this section.

(d) Every motor vehicle, trailer, or semitrailer constructed or sold in this state or operated upon the highways shall be equipped with service brakes upon all wheels of every such vehicle; except that:

(I) Any trailer or semitrailer of less than three thousand pounds gross weight, or any horse trailer of a capacity of two horses or less, or any trailer which does not meet the definition of "commercial vehicle" as that term is defined in section 42-4-235 (1) (a) and which is owned by a farmer when transporting agricultural products produced on the owner's farm or supplies back to the farm of the owner of the trailer, or tank trailers not exceeding ten thousand pounds gross weight used solely for transporting liquid fertilizer or gaseous fertilizer under pressure, or distributor trailers not exceeding ten thousand pounds gross weight used solely for transporting and distributing dry fertilizer when hauled by a truck capable of stopping with loaded trailer attached in the distance specified by subsection (2) of this section need not be equipped with brakes, and any two-wheel motor vehicle need have brakes on only one wheel.

(II) Any truck or truck tractor, manufactured before July 25, 1980, and having three or more axles, need not have brakes on the wheels of the front or tandem steering axles if the brakes on the other wheels meet the performance requirements of subsection (2) of this section.

(III) Every trailer or semitrailer of three thousand pounds or more gross weight must have brakes on all wheels.

(e) Provisions of this subsection (1) shall not apply to manufactured homes.

(2) Performance ability of brakes:

(a) The service brakes upon any motor vehicle or combination of vehicles shall be adequate to stop such vehicle when traveling twenty miles per hour within a distance of forty feet when upon dry asphalt or concrete pavement surface free from loose material where the grade does not exceed one percent.

(b) Under the conditions stated in paragraph (a) of this subsection (2), the hand brakes shall be adequate to stop such vehicle within a distance of fifty-five feet, and said hand brake shall be adequate to hold such vehicle stationary on any grade upon which operated.

(c) Under the conditions stated in paragraph (a) of this subsection (2), the service brakes upon a motor vehicle equipped with two-wheel brakes only, when permitted under this section, shall be adequate to stop the vehicle within a distance of fifty-five feet.

(d) All braking distances specified in this section shall apply to all vehicles mentioned, whether such vehicles are not loaded or are loaded to the maximum capacity permitted under this title.

(e) All brakes shall be maintained in good working order and shall be so adjusted as to operate as equally as possible with respect to the wheels on opposite sides of the vehicle.

(2.5) The department of public safety is specifically authorized to adopt rules relating to the use of surge brakes.

(3) Any person who violates any provision of this section commits a class A traffic infraction.

42-4-224. Horns or warning devices. (1) Every motor vehicle, when operated upon a highway, shall be equipped with a horn in good working order and capable of emitting sound audible under normal conditions from a distance of not less than two hundred feet, but no horn or other warning device shall emit an unreasonably loud or harsh sound, except as provided in section 42-4-213 (1) in the case of authorized emergency vehicles or as provided in section 42-4-222. The driver of a motor vehicle, when reasonably necessary to ensure safe operation, shall give audible warning with the horn but shall not otherwise use such horn when upon a highway.

(2) No vehicle shall be equipped with nor shall any person use upon a vehicle any audible device except as otherwise permitted in this section. It is permissible but not required that any vehicle be equipped with a theft alarm signal device which is so arranged that it cannot be used by the driver as a warning signal unless the alarm device is a required part of the vehicle. Nothing in this section is meant to preclude the use of audible warning devices that are activated when the vehicle is backing. Any authorized emergency vehicle may be equipped with an audible signal device under section 42-4-213 (1), but such device shall not be used except when such vehicle is operated in response to an emergency call or in the actual pursuit of a suspected violator of the law or for other special purposes, including, but not limited to, funerals, parades, and the escorting of dignitaries. Such device shall not be used for such special purposes unless the circumstances would not lead a reasonable person to believe that such vehicle is responding to an actual emergency.

(3) No bicycle, electrical assisted bicycle, or low-power scooter shall be equipped with nor shall any person use upon such vehicle a siren or whistle.

(4) Snowplows and other snow-removal equipment shall display flashing yellow lights meeting the requirements of section 42-4-214 as a warning to drivers when such equipment is in service on the highway.

(5) (a) When any snowplow or other snow-removal equipment displaying flashing yellow lights is engaged in snow and ice removal or control, drivers of all other vehicles shall exercise more than ordinary care and caution in approaching, overtaking, or passing such snowplow.

(b) The driver of a snowplow, while engaged in the removal or control of snow and ice on any highway open to traffic and while displaying the required flashing yellow warning lights as provided by section 42-4-214, shall not be charged with any violation of the provisions of this article relating to parking or standing, turning, backing, or yielding the right-of-way. These exemptions shall not relieve the driver of a snowplow from the duty to drive with due regard for the safety of all persons, nor shall these exemptions protect the driver of a snowplow from the consequences of a reckless or careless disregard for the safety of others.

(6) Any person who violates any provision of this section commits a class B traffic infraction.

42-4-225. Mufflers - prevention of noise. (1) Every motor vehicle subject to registration and operated on a highway shall at all times be equipped with an adequate muffler in constant operation and properly maintained to prevent any excessive or unusual noise, and no such muffler or exhaust system shall be equipped with a cut-off, bypass, or similar device. No person shall modify the exhaust system of a motor vehicle in a manner which will amplify or increase the noise emitted by the motor of such vehicle above that emitted by the muffler originally installed on the vehicle, and such original muffler shall comply with all of the requirements of this section.

(1.5) Any commercial vehicle, as defined in section 42-4-235 (1) (a), subject to registration and operated on a highway, that is equipped with an engine compression brake device is required to have a muffler.

(2) A muffler is a device consisting of a series of chamber or baffle plates or other mechanical design for the purpose of receiving exhaust gas from an internal combustion engine and effective in reducing noise.

(3) Any person who violates subsection (1) of this section commits a class B traffic infraction. Any person who violates subsection (1.5) of this section shall, upon conviction, be punished by a fine of five hundred dollars. Fifty percent of any fine for a violation of subsection (1.5) of this section occurring within the corporate limits of a city or town, or within the unincorporated area of a county, shall be transmitted to the treasurer or chief financial officer of said city, town, or county, and the remaining fifty percent shall be transmitted to the state treasurer, credited to the highway users tax fund, and allocated and expended as specified in section 43-4-205 (5.5) (a), C.R.S.

(4) This section shall not apply to electric motor vehicles.

42-4-226. Mirrors - exterior placements. (1) Every motor vehicle shall be equipped with a mirror or mirrors so located and so constructed as to reflect to the driver a free and unobstructed view of the highway for a distance of at least two hundred feet to the rear of such vehicle.

(2) Whenever any motor vehicle is not equipped with a rear window and rear side windows or has a rear window and rear side windows composed of, covered by, or treated with any material or component that, when viewed from the position of the driver, obstructs the rear view of the driver or makes such window or windows nontransparent, or whenever any motor vehicle is towing another vehicle or trailer or carrying any load or cargo or object that obstructs the rear view of the driver, such vehicle shall be equipped with an exterior mirror on each side so located with respect to the position of the driver as to comply with the visual requirement of subsection (1) of this section.

(3) Any person who violates any provision of this section commits a class B traffic infraction.

42-4-227. Windows unobstructed - certain materials prohibited - windshield wiper requirements. (1) (a) (I) Except as otherwise provided in this paragraph (a), no person shall operate a motor vehicle registered in Colorado on which any window, except the windshield, is composed of, covered by, or treated with any material or component that presents an opaque, nontransparent, or metallic or mirrored appearance in such a way that it allows less than twenty-seven percent light transmittance. The windshield shall allow at least seventy percent light transmittance.

(II) Notwithstanding subparagraph (I) of this paragraph (a), the windows to the rear of the driver, including the rear window, may allow less than twenty-seven percent light transmittance if the front side windows and the windshield on such vehicles allow at least seventy percent light transmittance.

(III) A law enforcement vehicle may have its windows, except the windshield, treated in such a manner so as to allow less than twenty-seven percent light transmittance only for the purpose of providing a valid law enforcement service. A law enforcement vehicle with such window treatment shall not be used for any traffic law enforcement operations, including operations concerning any offense in article 4 of this title. For purposes of this subparagraph (III), "law enforcement vehicle" means a vehicle owned or leased by a state or local law enforcement agency. The treatment of the windshield of a law enforcement vehicle is subject to the limits described in paragraph (b) of this subsection (1).

(b) Notwithstanding any provision of paragraph (a) of this subsection (1), nontransparent material may be applied, installed, or affixed to the topmost portion of the windshield subject to the following:

(I) The bottom edge of the material extends no more than four inches measured from the top of the windshield down;

(II) The material is not red or amber in color, nor does it affect perception of primary colors or otherwise distort vision or contain lettering that distorts or obstructs vision;

(III) The material does not reflect sunlight or headlight glare into the eyes of occupants of oncoming or preceding vehicles to any greater extent than the windshield without the material.

(c) Nothing in this subsection (1) shall be construed to prevent the use of any window which is composed of, covered by, or treated with any material or component in a manner approved by federal statute or regulation if such window was included as a component part of a vehicle at the time of the vehicle manufacture, or the replacement of any such window by such covering which meets such guidelines.

(d) No material shall be used on any window in the motor vehicle that presents a metallic or mirrored appearance.

(e) Nothing in this subsection (1) shall be construed to deny or prevent the use of certificates or other papers which do not obstruct the view of the driver and which may be required by law to be displayed.

(2) The windshield on every motor vehicle shall be equipped with a device for cleaning rain, snow, or other moisture from the windshield, which device shall be so constructed as to be controlled or operated by the driver of the vehicle.

(3) (a) Except as provided in paragraph (b) of this subsection (3), any person who violates any provision of this section commits a class B traffic infraction.

(b) Any person who installs, covers, or treats a windshield or window so that the windshield or window does not meet the requirements of paragraph (a) of subsection (1) of this section is guilty of a misdemeanor and shall be punished by a fine of not less than five hundred dollars nor more than five thousand dollars.

(4) This section shall apply to all motor vehicles; except that subsection (2) of this section shall not apply to low-speed electric vehicles.

42-4-228. Restrictions on tire equipment. (1) Every solid rubber tire on a vehicle shall have rubber on its entire traction surface at least one inch thick above the edge of the flange of the entire periphery.

(2) No person shall operate or move on any highway any motor vehicle, trailer, or semitrailer having any metal tire in contact with the roadway, and it is unlawful to operate upon the highways of this state any motor vehicle, trailer, or semitrailer equipped with solid rubber tires.

(3) No tire on a vehicle moved on a highway shall have on its periphery any block, stud, flange, cleat, or spike or any other protuberances of any material other than rubber which projects beyond the tread on the traction surface of the tire; except that, on single-tired passenger vehicles and on other single-tired vehicles with rated capacities up to and including three-fourths ton, it shall be permissible to use tires containing studs or other protuberances which do not project more than one-sixteenth of an inch beyond the tread of the traction surface of the tire; and except that it shall be permissible to use farm machinery with tires having protuberances which will not injure the highway; and except also that it shall be permissible to use tire chains of reasonable proportions upon any vehicle when required for safety because of snow, ice, or other conditions tending to cause a vehicle to skid.

(4) The department of transportation and local authorities in their respective jurisdictions, in their discretion, may issue special permits authorizing the operation upon a highway of traction engines or tractors having movable tracks with transverse corrugations upon the periphery of such movable tracks or farm tractors or other farm machinery, the operation of which upon a highway would otherwise be prohibited under this article.

(5) (a) No person shall drive or move a motor vehicle on any highway unless such vehicle is equipped with tires in safe operating condition in accordance with this subsection (5) and any supplemental rules and regulations promulgated by the executive director of the department.

(b) The executive director of the department shall promulgate such rules as the executive director deems necessary setting forth requirements of safe operating conditions for tires. These rules shall be utilized by law enforcement officers for visual inspection of tires and shall include methods for simple gauge measurement of tire tread depth.

(c) A tire shall be considered unsafe if it has:

(I) Any bump, bulge, or knot affecting the tire structure;

(II) A break which exposes a tire body cord or is repaired with a boot or patch;

(III) A tread depth of less than two thirty-seconds of an inch measured in any two tread grooves at three locations equally spaced around the circumference of the tire, or, on those tires with tread wear indicators, a tire shall be considered unsafe if it is worn to the point that the tread wear indicators contact the road in any two-tread grooves at three locations equally spaced around the circumference of the tire; except that this subparagraph (III) shall not apply to tires on a commercial vehicle as such term is defined in section 42-4-235 (1) (a); or

(IV) Such other conditions as may be reasonably demonstrated to render it unsafe.

(6) No passenger car tire shall be used on any motor vehicle which is driven or moved on any highway if such tire was designed or manufactured for nonhighway use.

(7) No person shall sell any motor vehicle for highway use unless the vehicle is equipped with tires that are in compliance with subsections (5) and (6) of this section and any rules of safe operating condition promulgated by the department.

(8) (a) Any person who violates any provision of subsection (1), (2), (3), (5), or (6) of this section commits a class A traffic infraction.

(b) Any person who violates any provision of subsection (7) of this section commits a class 2 misdemeanor traffic offense.

42-4-229. Safety glazing material in motor vehicles. (1) No person shall sell any new motor vehicle, nor shall any new motor vehicle be registered, unless such vehicle is equipped with safety glazing material of a type approved by the department for any required front windshield and wherever glazing material is used in doors and windows of said motor vehicle. This section shall apply to all passenger-type motor vehicles, including passenger buses and school vehicles, but, in respect to camper coaches and trucks, including truck tractors, the requirements as to safety glazing material shall apply only to all glazing material used in required front windshields and that used in doors and windows in the drivers' compartments and such other compartments as are lawfully occupied by passengers in said vehicles.

(2) The term "safety glazing materials" means such glazing materials as will reduce substantially, in comparison with ordinary sheet glass or plate glass, the likelihood of injury to persons by objects from exterior sources or by these safety glazing materials when they may be cracked or broken.

(3) The department shall compile and publish a list of types of glazing material by name approved by it as meeting the requirements of this section, and the department shall not, after January 1, 1958, register any motor vehicle which is subject to the provisions of this section unless it is equipped with an approved type of safety glazing material, and the department shall suspend the registration of any motor vehicle subject to this section which is found to be not so equipped until it is made to conform to the requirements of this section.

(4) A person shall not operate a motor vehicle on a highway unless the vehicle is equipped with a front windshield as provided in this section, except as provided in section 42-4-232 (1) and except for motor vehicles registered as collector's items under section 42-12-301 or 42-12-302.

(5) Any person who violates any provision of this section commits a class B traffic infraction.

42-4-230. Emergency lighting equipment - who must carry. (1) No motor vehicle carrying a truck license and weighing six thousand pounds or more and no passenger bus shall be operated over the highways of this state at any time without carrying in an accessible place inside or on the outside of the vehicle three bidirectional emergency reflective triangles of a type approved by the department, but the use of such equipment is not required in municipalities where there are street lights within not more than one hundred feet.

(2) Whenever a motor vehicle referred to in subsection (1) of this section is stopped upon the traveled portion of a highway or the shoulder of a highway for any cause other than necessary traffic stops, the driver of the stopped motor vehicle shall immediately activate the vehicular hazard warning signal flashers and continue the flashing until the driver places the bidirectional emergency reflective triangles as directed in subsection (3) of this section.

(3) Except as provided in subsection (2) of this section, whenever a motor vehicle referred to in subsection (1) of this section is stopped upon the traveled portion of a highway or the shoulder of a highway for any cause other than necessary traffic stops, the driver shall, as soon as possible, but in any event within ten minutes, place the bidirectional emergency reflective triangles in the following manner:

(a) One at the traffic side of the stopped vehicle, within ten feet of the front or rear of the vehicle;

(b) One at a distance of approximately one hundred feet from the stopped vehicle in the center of the traffic lane or shoulder occupied by the vehicle and in the direction toward traffic approaching in that lane; and

(c) One at a distance of approximately one hundred feet from the stopped vehicle in the opposite direction from those placed in accordance with paragraphs (a) and (b) of this subsection (3) in the center of the traffic lane or shoulder occupied by the vehicle; or

(d) If the vehicle is stopped within five hundred feet of a curve, crest of a hill, or other obstruction to view, the driver shall place the emergency equipment required by this subsection (3) in the direction of the obstruction to view at a distance of one hundred feet to five hundred feet from the stopped vehicle so as to afford ample warning to other users of the highway; or

(e) If the vehicle is stopped upon the traveled portion or the shoulder of a divided or one-way highway, the driver shall place the emergency equipment required by this subsection (3), one at a distance of two hundred feet and one at a distance of one hundred feet in a direction toward approaching traffic in the center of the lane or shoulder occupied by the vehicle, and one at the traffic side of the vehicle within ten feet of the rear of the vehicle.

(4) No motor vehicle operating as a wrecking car at the scene of an accident shall move or attempt to move any wrecked vehicle without first complying with those sections of the law concerning emergency lighting.

(5) Any person who violates any provision of this section commits a class B traffic infraction.

42-4-231. Parking lights. When lighted lamps are required by section 42-4-204, no vehicle shall be driven upon a highway with the parking lights lighted except when the lights are being used as signal lamps and except when the head lamps are lighted at the same time. Parking lights are those lights permitted by section 42-4-215 and any other lights mounted on the front of the vehicle, designed to be displayed primarily when the vehicle is parked. Any person who violates any provision of this section commits a class B traffic infraction.

42-4-232. Minimum safety standards for motorcycles and low-power scooters. (1) No person shall operate any motorcycle or low-power scooter on any public highway in this state unless such person and any passenger thereon is wearing goggles or eyeglasses with lenses made of safety glass or plastic; except that this subsection (1) shall not apply to a person wearing a helmet containing eye protection made of safety glass or plastic.

(2) The department shall adopt standards and specifications for the design of goggles and eyeglasses.

(3) Any motorcycle carrying a passenger, other than in a sidecar or enclosed cab, shall be equipped with footrests for such passengers.

(4) Any person who violates any provision of this section commits a class A traffic infraction.

42-4-233. Alteration of suspension system. (1) No person shall operate a motor vehicle of a type required to be registered under the laws of this state upon a public highway with either the rear or front suspension system altered or changed from the manufacturer's original design except in accordance with specifications permitting such alteration established by the department. Nothing contained in this section shall prevent the installation of manufactured heavy duty equipment to include shock absorbers and overload springs, nor shall anything contained in this section prevent a person from operating a motor vehicle on a public highway with normal wear of the suspension system if normal wear shall not affect the control of the vehicle.

(2) This section shall not apply to motor vehicles designed or modified primarily for off-highway racing purposes, and such motor vehicles may be lawfully towed on the highways of this state.

(3) Any person who violates any provision of this section commits a class 2 misdemeanor traffic offense.

42-4-234. Slow-moving vehicles - display of emblem. (1) (a) All machinery, equipment, and vehicles, except bicycles, electrical assisted bicycles, and other human-powered vehicles, designed to operate or normally operated at a speed of less than twenty-five miles per hour on a public highway shall display a triangular slow-moving vehicle emblem on the rear.

(b) The department shall set standards for a triangular slow-moving emblem for use on low-speed electric vehicles.

(c) Bicycles, electrical assisted bicycles, and other human-powered vehicles shall be permitted but not required to display the emblem specified in this subsection (1).

(2) The executive director of the department shall adopt standards and specifications for such emblem, position of the mounting thereof, and requirements for certification of conformance with the standards and specifications adopted by the American society of agricultural engineers concerning such emblems. The requirements of such emblem shall be in addition to any lighting device required by law.

(3) The use of the emblem required under this section shall be restricted to the use specified in subsection (1) of this section, and its use on any other type of vehicle or stationary object shall be prohibited.

(4) Any person who violates any provision of this section commits a class B traffic infraction.

42-4-235. Minimum standards for commercial vehicles - rules - repeal. (1) As used in this section, unless the context otherwise requires:

(a) "Commercial vehicle" means:

(I) Any self-propelled or towed vehicle bearing an apportioned plate or having a manufacturer's gross vehicle weight rating or gross combination rating of ten thousand one pounds or more, which vehicle is used in commerce on the public highways of this state or is designed to transport sixteen or more passengers, including the driver, unless such vehicle is a school bus regulated pursuant to section 42-4-1904 or any vehicle that does not have a gross vehicle weight rating of twenty-six thousand one or more pounds and that is owned or operated by a school district so long as such school district does not receive remuneration for the use of such vehicle, not including reimbursement for the use of such vehicle;

(II) Any motor vehicle designed or equipped to transport other motor vehicles from place to place by means of winches, cables, pulleys, or other equipment for towing, pulling, or lifting, when such motor vehicle is used in commerce on the public highways of this state; and

(III) A motor vehicle that is used on the public highways and transports materials determined by the secretary of transportation to be hazardous under 49 U.S.C. sec. 5103 in such quantities as to require placarding under 49 CFR parts 172 and 173.

(b) "Department" means the department of public safety.

(c) "Motor carrier" means every person, lessee, receiver, or trustee appointed by any court whatsoever owning, controlling, operating, or managing any commercial vehicle as defined in paragraph (a) of this subsection (1).

(2) (a) No person shall operate a commercial vehicle, as defined in subsection (1) of this section, on any public highway of this state unless such vehicle is in compliance with the rules adopted by the department pursuant to subsection (4) of this section. Any person who violates such rules, including intrastate motor carriers, shall be subject to the civil penalties authorized pursuant to 49 CFR part 386, subpart G, as such subpart existed on October 1, 2001. Persons who utilize an independent contractor shall not be liable for penalties imposed on the independent contractor for equipment, acts, and omissions within the independent contractor's control or supervision. All civil penalties collected pursuant to this article by a state agency or by a court shall be transmitted to the state treasurer, who shall credit the same to the highway users tax fund created in section 43-4-201, C.R.S., for allocation and expenditure as specified in section 43-4-205 (5.5) (a), C.R.S.

(b) Notwithstanding paragraph (a) of this subsection (2):

(I) Intrastate motor carriers shall not be subject to any provisions in 49 CFR, part 386, subpart G that relate the amount of a penalty to a violator's ability to pay, and such penalties shall be based upon the nature and gravity of the violation, the degree of culpability, and such other matters as justice and public safety may require;

(II) When determining the assessment of a civil penalty for safety violations, the period of a motor carrier's safety compliance history that a compliance review officer may consider shall not exceed three years; and

(III) The intrastate operation of implements of husbandry shall not be subject to the civil penalties provided in 49 CFR, part 386, subpart G. Nothing in this subsection (2) shall be construed to repeal, preempt, or negate any existing regulatory exemption for agricultural operations, intrastate farm vehicle drivers, intrastate vehicles or combinations of vehicles with a gross vehicle weight rating of not more than twenty-six thousand pounds that do not require a commercial driver's license to operate, or any successor or analogous agricultural exemptions, whether based on federal or state law.

(c) The Colorado state patrol shall have exclusive enforcement authority to conduct safety compliance reviews, as defined in 49 CFR 385.3, as such section existed on October 1, 2001, and to impose civil penalties pursuant to such reviews. Nothing in this paragraph (c) shall expand or limit the ability of local governments to conduct roadside safety inspections.

(d) (I) Upon notice from the department of public safety, the department shall, pursuant to section 42-3-120, cancel the registration of a motor carrier who fails to pay in full a civil penalty imposed pursuant to this subsection (2) within thirty days after notification of the penalty.

(II) Repealed.

(3) Any motor carrier operating a commercial vehicle within Colorado must declare knowledge of the rules and regulations adopted by the department pursuant to subsection (4) of this section. Such declaration of knowledge shall be in writing on a form provided by the department. Such form must be signed and returned by a motor carrier according to regulations adopted by the department.

(4) (a) The department shall adopt rules for the operation of all commercial vehicles. In adopting such rules, the department shall use as general guidelines the standards contained in the current rules and regulations of the United States department of transportation relating to safety regulations, qualifications of drivers, driving of motor vehicles, parts and accessories, notification and reporting of accidents, hours of service of drivers, inspection, repair and maintenance of motor vehicles, financial responsibility, insurance, and employee safety and health standards; except that rules regarding financial responsibility and insurance do not apply to a commercial vehicle as defined in subsection (1) of this section that is also subject to regulation by the public utilities commission under article 10.1 of title 40, C.R.S. On and after September 1, 2003, all commercial vehicle safety inspections conducted to determine compliance with rules promulgated by the department pursuant to this paragraph (a) shall be performed by an enforcement official, as defined in section 42-20-103 (2), who has been certified by the commercial vehicle safety alliance, or any successor organization thereto, to perform level I inspections.

(b) The Colorado public utilities commission may enforce safety rules of the department governing commercial vehicles described in subparagraphs (I) and (II) of paragraph (a) of subsection (1) of this section pursuant to its authority to regulate motor carriers as defined in section 40-10.1-101, C.R.S., including the issuance of civil penalties for violations of the rules as provided in section 40-7-113, C.R.S.

(5) Any person who violates a rule or regulation promulgated by the department pursuant to this section or fails to comply with subsection (3) of this section commits a class 2 misdemeanor traffic offense.

42-4-236. Child restraint systems required - definitions - exemptions. (1) As used in this section, unless the context otherwise requires:

(a) "Child care center" means a facility required to be licensed under the "Child Care Licensing Act", article 6 of title 26, C.R.S.

(a.3) (Deleted by amendment, L. 2010, (SB 10-110), ch. 294, p. 1365, § 3, effective August 1, 2010.)

(a.5) "Child restraint system" means a specially designed seating system that is designed to protect, hold, or restrain a child in a motor vehicle in such a way as to prevent or minimize injury to the child in the event of a motor vehicle accident that is either permanently affixed to a motor vehicle or is affixed to such vehicle by a safety belt or a universal attachment system, and that meets the federal motor vehicle safety standards set forth in section 49 CFR 571.213, as amended.

(a.7) (Deleted by amendment, L. 2010, (SB 10-110), ch. 294, p. 1365, § 3, effective August 1, 2010.)

(a.8) "Motor vehicle" means a passenger car; a pickup truck; or a van, minivan, or sport utility vehicle with a gross vehicle weight rating of less than ten thousand pounds. "Motor vehicle" does not include motorcycles, low-power scooters, motorscooters, motorbicycles, motorized bicycles, and farm tractors and implements of husbandry designed primarily or exclusively for use in agricultural operations.

(b) "Safety belt" means a lap belt, a shoulder belt, or any other belt or combination of belts installed in a motor vehicle to restrain drivers and passengers, except any such belt that is physically a part of a child restraint system. "Safety belt" includes the anchorages, the buckles, and all other equipment directly related to the operation of safety belts. Proper use of a safety belt means the shoulder belt, if present, crosses the shoulder and chest and the lap belt crosses the hips, touching the thighs.

(c) "Seating position" means any motor vehicle interior space intended by the motor vehicle manufacturer to provide seating accommodation while the motor vehicle is in motion.

(2) (a) (I) Unless exempted pursuant to subsection (3) of this section and except as otherwise provided in subparagraphs (II) and (III) of this paragraph (a), every child who is under eight years of age and who is being transported in this state in a motor vehicle or in a vehicle operated

by a child care center, shall be properly restrained in a child restraint system, according to the manufacturer's instructions.

(II) If the child is less than one year of age and weighs less than twenty pounds, the child shall be properly restrained in a rear-facing child restraint system in a rear seat of the vehicle.

(III) If the child is one year of age or older, but less than four years of age, and weighs less than forty pounds, but at least twenty pounds, the child shall be properly restrained in a rear-facing or forward-facing child restraint system.

(b) Unless excepted pursuant to subsection (3) of this section, every child who is at least eight years of age but less than sixteen years of age who is being transported in this state in a motor vehicle or in a vehicle operated by a child care center, shall be properly restrained in a safety belt or child restraint system according to the manufacturer's instructions.

(c) If a parent is in the motor vehicle, it is the responsibility of the parent to ensure that his or her child or children are provided with and that they properly use a child restraint system or safety belt system. If a parent is not in the motor vehicle, it is the responsibility of the driver transporting a child or children, subject to the requirements of this section, to ensure that such children are provided with and that they properly use a child restraint system or safety belt system.

(3) Except as provided in section 42-2-105.5 (4), subsection (2) of this section does not apply to a child who:

(a) Repealed.

(b) Is less than eight years of age and is being transported in a motor vehicle as a result of a medical or other life-threatening emergency and a child restraint system is not available;

(c) Is being transported in a commercial motor vehicle, as defined in section 42-2-402 (4) (a), that is operated by a child care center;

(d) Is the driver of a motor vehicle and is subject to the safety belt requirements provided in section 42-4-237;

(e) (Deleted by amendment, L. 2011, (SB 11-227), ch. 295, p. 1399, § 1, effective June 7, 2011.)

(f) Is being transported in a motor vehicle that is operated in the business of transporting persons for compensation or hire by or on behalf of a common carrier or a contract carrier as those terms are defined in section 40-10.1-101, C.R.S., or an operator of a luxury limousine service as defined in section 40-10.1-301, C.R.S.

(4) The division of highway safety shall implement a program for public information and education concerning the use of child restraint systems and the provisions of this section.

(5) No person shall use a safety belt or child restraint system, whichever is applicable under the provisions of this section, for children under sixteen years of age in a motor vehicle unless it conforms to all applicable federal motor vehicle safety standards.

(6) Any violation of this section shall not constitute negligence per se or contributory negligence per se.

(7) (a) Except as otherwise provided in paragraph (b) of this subsection (7), any person who violates any provision of this section commits a class B traffic infraction.

(b) A minor driver under eighteen years of age who violates this section shall be punished in accordance with section 42-2-105.5 (5) (b).

(8) The fine may be waived if the defendant presents the court with satisfactory evidence of proof of the acquisition, purchase, or rental of a child restraint system by the time of the court appearance.

(9) (Deleted by amendment, L. 2010, (SB 10-110), ch. 294, p. 1365, § 3, effective August 1, 2010.)

(10) and (11) Repealed.

42-4-237. Safety belt systems - mandatory use - exemptions - penalty. (1) As used in this section:

(a) "Motor vehicle" means a self-propelled vehicle intended primarily for use and operation on the public highways, including passenger cars, station wagons, vans, taxicabs, ambulances, motor homes, and pickups. The term does not include motorcycles, low-power scooters, passenger buses, school buses, and farm tractors and implements of husbandry designed primarily or exclusively for use in agricultural operations.

(b) "Safety belt system" means a system utilizing a lap belt, a shoulder belt, or any other belt or combination of belts installed in a motor vehicle to restrain drivers and passengers, which system conforms to federal motor vehicle safety standards.

(2) Unless exempted pursuant to subsection (3) of this section, every driver of and every front seat passenger in a motor vehicle equipped with a safety belt system shall wear a fastened safety belt while the motor vehicle is being operated on a street or highway in this state.

(3) Except as provided in section 42-2-105.5, the requirement of subsection (2) of this section shall not apply to:

(a) A child required by section 42-4-236 to be restrained by a child restraint system;

(b) A member of an ambulance team, other than the driver, while involved in patient care;

(c) A peace officer as described in section 16-2.5-101, C.R.S., while performing official duties so long as the performance of said duties is in accordance with rules and regulations applicable to said officer which are at least as restrictive as subsection (2) of this section and which only provide exceptions necessary to protect the officer;

(d) A person with a physically or psychologically disabling condition whose physical or psychological disability prevents appropriate restraint by a safety belt system if such person possesses a written statement by a physician certifying the condition, as well as stating the reason why such restraint is inappropriate;

(e) A person driving or riding in a motor vehicle not equipped with a safety belt system due to the fact that federal law does not require such vehicle to be equipped with a safety belt system;

(f) A rural letter carrier of the United States postal service while performing duties as a rural letter carrier; and

(g) A person operating a motor vehicle which does not meet the definition of "commercial vehicle" as that term is defined in section 42-4-235 (1) (a) for commercial or residential delivery or pickup service; except that such person shall be required to wear a fastened safety belt during the time period prior to the first delivery or pickup of the day and during the time period following the last delivery or pickup of the day.

(4) (a) Except as otherwise provided in paragraph (b) of this subsection (4), any person who operates a motor vehicle while such person or any passenger is in violation of the requirement of subsection (2) of this section commits a class B traffic infraction. Penalties collected pursuant to this subsection (4) shall be transmitted to the appropriate authority pursuant to the provisions of section 42-1-217 (1) (e) and (2).

(b) A minor driver under eighteen years of age who violates this section shall be punished in accordance with section 42-2-105.5 (5) (b).

(5) No driver in a motor vehicle shall be cited for a violation of subsection (2) of this section unless such driver was stopped by a law enforcement officer for an alleged violation of articles 1 to 4 of this title other than a violation of this section.

(6) Testimony at a trial for a violation charged pursuant to subsection (4) of this section may include:

(a) Testimony by a law enforcement officer that the officer observed the person charged operating a motor vehicle while said operator or any passenger was in violation of the requirement of subsection (2) of this section; or

(b) Evidence that the driver removed the safety belts or knowingly drove a vehicle from which the safety belts had been removed.

(7) Evidence of failure to comply with the requirement of subsection (2) of this section shall be admissible to mitigate damages with respect to any person who was involved in a motor vehicle accident and who seeks in any subsequent litigation to recover damages for injuries resulting from the accident. Such mitigation shall be limited to awards for pain and suffering and shall not be used for limiting recovery of economic loss and medical payments.

(8) The office of transportation safety in the department of transportation shall continue its program for public information and education concerning the benefits of wearing safety belts and shall include within such program the requirements and penalty of this section.

42-4-238. Blue and red lights - illegal use or possession. (1) A person shall not be in actual physical control of a vehicle, except an authorized emergency vehicle as defined in section 42-1-102 (6), that the person knows contains a lamp or device that is designed to display, or that is capable of displaying if affixed or attached to the vehicle, a red or blue light visible directly in front of the center of the vehicle.

(2) It shall be an affirmative defense that the defendant was:

(a) A peace officer as described in section 16-2.5-101, C.R.S.; or

(b) In actual physical control of a vehicle expressly authorized by a chief of police or sheriff to contain a lamp or device that is designed to display, or that is capable of displaying if affixed or attached to the vehicle, a red or blue light visible from directly in front of the center of the vehicle; or

(c) A member of a volunteer fire department or a volunteer ambulance service who possesses a permit from the fire chief of the fire department or chief executive officer of the ambulance service through which the volunteer serves to operate a vehicle pursuant to section 42-4-222 (1) (b); or

(d) A vendor who exhibits, sells, or offers for sale a lamp or device designed to display, or that is capable of displaying, if affixed or attached to the vehicle, a red or blue light; or

(e) A collector of fire engines, fire suppression vehicles, or ambulances and the vehicle to which the red or blue lamps were affixed is valued for the vehicle's historical interest or as a collector's item.

(3) A violation of this section is a class 1 misdemeanor.

42-4-239. Misuse of a wireless telephone - definitions - penalty - preemption. (1) As used in this section, unless the context otherwise requires:

(a) "Emergency" means a situation in which a person:

(I) Has reason to fear for such person's life or safety or believes that a criminal act may be perpetrated against such person or another person, requiring the use of a wireless telephone while the car is moving; or

(II) Reports a fire, a traffic accident in which one or more injuries are apparent, a serious road hazard, a medical or hazardous materials emergency, or a person who is driving in a reckless, careless, or otherwise unsafe manner.

(b) "Operating a motor vehicle" means driving a motor vehicle on a public highway, but "operating a motor vehicle" shall not mean maintaining the instruments of control while the motor vehicle is at rest in a shoulder lane or lawfully parked.

(c) "Use" means talking on or listening to a wireless telephone or engaging the wireless telephone for text messaging or other similar forms of manual data entry or transmission.

(d) "Wireless telephone" means a telephone that operates without a physical, wireline connection to the provider's equipment. The term includes, without limitation, cellular and mobile telephones.

(2) A person under eighteen years of age shall not use a wireless telephone while operating a motor vehicle.

(3) A person eighteen years of age or older shall not use a wireless telephone for the purpose of engaging in text messaging or other similar forms of manual data entry or transmission while operating a motor vehicle.

(4) Subsection (2) or (3) of this section shall not apply to a person who is using the wireless telephone:

(a) To contact a public safety entity; or
(b) During an emergency.

(5) (a) A person who operates a motor vehicle in violation of subsection (2) or (3) of this section commits a class A traffic infraction as defined in section 42-4-1701 (3), and the court or the department of revenue shall assess a fine of fifty dollars.

(b) A second or subsequent violation of subsection (2) or (3) of this section shall be a class A traffic infraction as defined in section 42-4-1701 (3), and the court or the department of revenue shall assess a fine of one hundred dollars.

(6) (a) An operator of a motor vehicle shall not be cited for a violation of subsection (2) of this section unless the operator was under eighteen years of age and a law enforcement officer saw the operator use, as defined in paragraph (c) of subsection (1) of this section, a wireless telephone.

(b) An operator of a motor vehicle shall not be cited for a violation of subsection (3) of this section unless the operator was eighteen years of age or older and a law enforcement officer saw the operator use a wireless telephone for the purpose of engaging in text messaging or other similar forms of manual data entry or transmission.

(7) The provisions of this section shall not be construed to authorize the seizure and forfeiture of a wireless telephone, unless otherwise provided by law.

(8) This section does not restrict operation of an amateur radio station by a person who holds a valid amateur radio operator license issued by the federal communications commission.

(9) The general assembly finds and declares that use of wireless telephones in motor vehicles is a matter of statewide concern.

42-4-240. Low-speed electric vehicle equipment requirements. A low-speed electric vehicle shall conform with applicable federal manufacturing equipment standards. Any person who operates a low-speed electric vehicle in violation of this section commits a class B traffic infraction.

42-4-241. Unlawful removal of tow-truck signage - unlawful usage of tow-truck signage. (1) (a) A person, other than a towing carrier or peace officer as described in section 16-2.5-101, C.R.S., commits the crime of unlawful removal of tow-truck signage if:

(I) A towing carrier has placed a tow-truck warning sign on the driver-side window of a vehicle to be towed or, if window placement is impracticable, in another location on the driver-side of the vehicle; and

(II) The vehicle to be towed is within fifty feet of the towing carrier vehicle; and

(III) The person removes the tow-truck warning sign from the vehicle before the tow is completed.

(b) A person commits the crime of unlawful usage of tow-truck signage if the person places a tow-truck warning sign on a vehicle when the vehicle is not in the process of being towed or when the vehicle is occupied.

(c) A towing carrier may permit an owner of the vehicle to be towed to retrieve any personal items from the vehicle before the vehicle is towed.

(2) A person who violates subsection (1) of this section commits a class 3 misdemeanor.

(3) For purposes of this section, "tow-truck warning sign" means a sign that is at least eight inches by eight inches, is either yellow or orange, and states the following:

WARNING: This vehicle is in tow. Attempting to operate or operating this vehicle may result in criminal prosecution and may lead to injury or death to you or another person.

Editor's note: Section 4 of chapter 298, Session Laws of Colorado 2011, provides that the act adding this section applies to offenses committed on or after July 1, 2011.

PART 3

EMISSIONS INSPECTION

42-4-301. Legislative declarations - enactment of enhanced emissions program not waiver of state right to challenge authority to require specific loaded mode transient dynamometer technology in automobile emissions testing. (1) The general assembly hereby finds and declares that sections 42-4-301 to 42-4-316 are enacted pursuant to, and that the program created by said sections is designed to meet, the requirements of the federal "Clean Air Act", as amended by the federal "Clean Air Act Amendments of 1990", 42 U.S.C. sec. 7401 et seq., as the same is in effect on November 15, 1990.

(2) (a) The general assembly further finds and declares that:

(I) The provisions of sections 42-4-301 to 42-4-316 related to the enhanced emissions program are enacted to comply with administrative requirements of rules and regulations of the federal environmental protection agency;

(II) Insofar as such rules and regulations require the use of loaded mode transient dynamometer technology utilizing a system commonly known as the IM 240 in motor vehicle emissions testing, the general assembly finds that reliable scientific data questions the effectiveness of such technology to measure motor vehicle emissions at the high altitude of the Denver metropolitan area;

(III) Less costly automobile emission testing systems may be available which are as effective or more effective at a lower cost to consumers than the loaded mode transient dynamometer test required by the federal environmental protection agency.

(b) (I) The general assembly, therefore, declares that the enactment of sections 42-4-301 to 42-4-316 in no way forecloses or limits the rights of the general assembly or any other appropriate entity of the state of Colorado to retain legal counsel as provided by law to request the federal environmental protection agency to consider alternative automobile emission inspection technology which may relieve Colorado of the requirements of the federal rules and regulations or change such rules and regulations to require a different technology in automobile emissions testing at a substantial savings in cost to consumers and jobs for Coloradans employed in the testing of motor vehicles for emissions compliance.

(II) If the federal agency refuses to alter its policies related to this issue, the general assembly hereby declares that it or any other appropriate entity of the state of Colorado does not waive the right to bring appropriate legal action in a court of competent jurisdiction to determine the validity of the federal environmental protection agency's authority to require the use of the loaded mode transient dynamometer test for automobile emissions inspection commonly known as the IM 240 when such requirement may be in excess of the federal agency's authority under the federal "Clean Air Act Amendments of 1990".

42-4-302. Commencement of basic emissions program - authority of commission. Notwithstanding the provisions of sections 42-4-301 to 42-4-316, if the commission is unable to implement the basic emissions program by January 1, 1994, the commission by rule and regulation shall establish the date for the commencement of said program as soon as practicable after January 1, 1994, and the provisions of sections 42-4-301 to 42-4-316 applicable to the basic emissions program shall be effective on and after the date determined by the commission by rule and regulation. Until such date, emission inspection activity in El Paso, Larimer, and Weld counties shall comply with the requirements applicable to inspection and readjustment stations in sections 42-4-301 to 42-4-316, and El Paso, Larimer, and Weld counties shall be deemed to continue to be included in the inspection and readjustment program until implementation of the basic emissions program by the commission pursuant to this section.

42-4-303. Sunrise review of registration of repair facilities. (Repealed)

42-4-304. Definitions relating to automobile inspection and readjustment program. As used in sections 42-4-301 to 42-4-316, unless the context otherwise requires:

(1) "AIR program" or "program" means the automobile inspection and readjustment program until replaced as provided in sections 42-4-301 to 42-4-316, the basic emissions program, and the enhanced emissions program established pursuant to sections 42-4-301 to 42-4-316.

(2) "Basic emissions program" means the inspection and readjustment program, established pursuant to the federal act, in the counties set forth in paragraph (b) of subsection (20) of this section.

(3) (a) "Certification of emissions control" means one of the following certifications, to be issued to the owner of a motor vehicle which is subject to the automobile inspection and readjustment program to indicate the status of inspection requirement compliance of said vehicle:

(I) "Certification of emissions waiver", indicating that the emissions of other than chlorofluorocarbons from the vehicle do not comply with the applicable emissions standards and criteria after inspection, adjustment, and emissions-related repairs in accordance with section 42-4-310.

(II) "Certification of emissions compliance", indicating that the emissions from said vehicle comply with applicable emissions and opacity standards and criteria at the time of inspection or after required adjustments or repairs.

(b) (I) The certification of emissions control will be issued to the vehicle owner at the time of sale or transfer except as provided in section 42-4-310 (1) (a) (I). The certification of emissions control will be in effect for twenty-four months for 1982 and newer model vehicles as defined in section 42-3-106 (4). Except as provided in paragraph (c) of this subsection (3), 1981 and older model vehicles and all vehicles inspected by the fleet-only air inspection stations shall be issued certifications of emissions control valid for twelve months.

(II) Except as provided in paragraph (c) of this subsection (3) and in section 42-4-309, a biennial inspection schedule shall be established for 1982 and newer model vehicles and an annual schedule shall be established for 1981 and older model vehicles.

(c) Repealed.

(d) Subject to section 42-4-310 (4), the certification of emissions control shall be obtained by the seller and transferred to the new owner at the time of vehicle sale or transfer.

(e) For purposes of this subsection (3), "sale or transfer" shall not include a change only in the legal ownership as shown on the vehicle's documents of title, whether for purposes of refinancing or otherwise, that does not entail a change in the physical possession or use of the vehicle.

(3.5) "Clean screen program" means the remote sensing system or other emission profiling system established and operated pursuant to sections 42-4-305 (12), 42-4-306 (23), 42-4-307 (10.5), and 42-4-310 (5).

(4) "Commission" means the air quality control commission, created in section 25-7-104, C.R.S.

(5) "Contractor" means any person, partnership, entity, or corporation that is awarded a contract by the state of Colorado through a competitive bid process conducted by the division in consultation with the executive director and in accordance with the "Procurement Code", articles 101 to 112 of title 24, C.R.S., and section 42-4-306, to provide inspection services for vehicles required to be inspected pursuant to section 42-4-310 within the enhanced program area, as set forth in subsection (9) of this section, to operate enhanced inspection centers necessary to perform inspections, and to operate the clean screen program within the program area.

(6) "Division" means the division of administration in the department of public health and environment.

(7) "Emissions inspector" means:

(a) An individual trained and licensed in accordance with section 42-4-308 to inspect motor vehicles at an inspection-only facility, fleet inspection station, or motor vehicle dealer test facility subject to the enhanced emissions program set forth in this part 3; or

(b) An individual employed by an enhanced inspection center who is authorized by the contractor to inspect motor vehicles subject to the enhanced emissions program set forth in this part 3 and subject to the direction of said contractor.

(8) "Emissions mechanic" means an individual licensed in accordance with section 42-4-308 to inspect and adjust motor vehicles subject to the automobile inspection and readjustment program until such program is replaced as provided in sections 42-4-301 to 42-4-316 and to the basic emissions program after such replacement.

(8.5) "Enhanced emissions inspection" means a motor vehicle emissions inspection conducted pursuant to the enhanced emissions program, including a detection of high emissions by remote sensing, an identification of high emitters, a clean screen inspection, or an inspection conducted at an enhanced inspection center.

(9) (a) "Enhanced emissions program" means the emissions inspection program established pursuant to the federal requirements set forth in the federal performance standards, 40 CFR, part 51, subpart S, in the locations set forth in paragraph (c) of subsection (20) of this section.

(b) (Deleted by amendment, L. 2009, (SB 09-003), ch. 322, p. 1714, § 1, effective June 1, 2009.)

(10) "Enhanced inspection center" means a strategically located, single- or multi-lane, high-volume, inspection-only facility operated in the enhanced emissions program area by a contractor not affiliated with any other automotive-related service, which meets the requirements of sections 42-4-305 and 42-4-306, which is equipped to enable vehicle exhaust gas and evaporative and chlorofluorocarbon emissions inspections, and which the owner or operator is authorized to operate by the executive director as an inspection-only facility.

(11) "Environmental protection agency" means the federal environmental protection agency.

(12) "Executive director" means the executive director of the department of revenue or the designee of such executive director.

(13) "Federal act" means the federal "Clean Air Act", 42 U.S.C. sec. 7401 et seq., as in effect on November 15, 1990, and any federal regulation promulgated pursuant to said act.

(14) "Federal requirements" means regulations of the environmental protection agency pursuant to the federal act.

(15) "Fleet inspection station" means a facility which meets the requirements of section 42-4-308, which is equipped to enable appropriate emissions inspections as prescribed by the commission and which the owner or operator is licensed to operate by the executive director as an inspection station for purposes of emissions testing on vehicles pursuant to section 42-4-309.

(15.5) "High emitter program" means a program to identify motor vehicles whose emissions or air pollutants are substantially higher than the levels deemed acceptable under the AIR program. Such vehicles shall be repaired in compliance with the AIR program or shall be subject to administrative suspension of vehicle registration.

(16) "Inspection and readjustment station" means:

(a) Repealed.

(b) (I) A facility within the basic emissions program area as defined in subsection (20) of this section which meets the requirements of section 42-4-308, which is equipped to enable vehicle exhaust, evaporative, and chlorofluorocarbon emissions inspections and any necessary adjustments and repairs to be performed, and which facility the owner or operator is licensed by the executive director to operate as an inspection and readjustment station.

(II) This paragraph (b) is effective January 1, 1994.

(17) (a) "Inspection-only facility" means a facility operated by an independent owner-operator within the enhanced program area as defined in subsection (20) of this section which meets the requirements of section 42-4-308 and which is equipped to enable vehicle exhaust, evaporative, and chlorofluorocarbon emissions

inspections and which facility the operator is licensed to operate by the executive director as an inspection-only facility. Such inspection-only facility shall be authorized to conduct inspections on model year 1981 and older vehicles.

(b) This subsection (17) is effective January 1, 1995.

(18) "Motor vehicle", as applicable to the AIR program, includes only a motor vehicle that is operated with four wheels or more on the ground, self-propelled by a spark-ignited engine burning gasoline, gasoline blends, gaseous fuel, blends of liquid gasoline and gaseous fuels, alcohol, alcohol blends, or other similar fuels, having a personal property classification of A, B, or C pursuant to section 42-3-106, and for which registration in this state is required for operation on the public roads and highways or which motor vehicle is owned or operated or both by a nonresident who meets the requirements set forth in section 42-4-310 (1) (c). "Motor vehicle" does not include kit vehicles; vehicles registered pursuant to section 42-12-301 or 42-3-306 (4); vehicles registered pursuant to section 42-12-401 that are of model year 1975 or earlier or that have two-stroke cycle engines manufactured prior to 1980; or vehicles registered as street-rods pursuant to section 42-3-201.

(19) (a) "Motor vehicle dealer test facility" means a stationary or mobile facility which is operated by a state trade association for motor vehicle dealers which is licensed to operate by the executive director as a motor vehicle dealer test facility to conduct emissions inspections.

(b) (I) Inspections conducted pursuant to section 42-4-309 (3) by a motor vehicle dealer test facility shall only be conducted on used motor vehicles inventoried or consigned in this state for retail sale by a motor vehicle dealer licensed pursuant to article 6 of title 12, C.R.S., and which is a member of the state trade association operating the motor vehicle dealer test facility.

(II) Inspection procedures used by a motor vehicle dealer test facility pursuant to this paragraph (b) shall include a loaded mode transient dynamometer test cycle in combination with appropriate idle short tests pursuant to rules and regulations of the commission.

(20) (a) "Program area" means the counties of Adams, Arapahoe, Boulder, Douglas, El Paso, Jefferson, Larimer, and Weld, and the cities and counties of Broomfield and Denver, excluding the following areas and subject to paragraph (d) of this subsection (20):

(I) That portion of Adams county that is east of Kiowa creek (Range sixty-two west, townships one, two, and three south) between the Adams-Arapahoe county line and the Adams-Weld county line;

(II) That portion of Arapahoe county that is east of Kiowa creek (Range sixty-two west, townships four and five south) between the Arapahoe-Elbert county line and the Arapahoe-Adams county line;

(III) That portion of El Paso county that is east of the following boundary, defined on a south-to-north axis: From the El Paso-Pueblo county line north (upstream) along Chico creek (Ranges 63 and 64 West, Township 17 South) to Hanover road, then east along Hanover road (El Paso county route 422) to Peyton highway, then north along Peyton highway (El Paso county route 463) to Falcon highway, then west on Falcon highway (El Paso county route 405) to Peyton highway, then north on Peyton highway (El Paso county route 405) to Judge Orr road, then west on Judge Orr road (El Paso county route 108) to Elbert road, then north on Elbert road (El Paso county route 91) to the El Paso-Elbert county line;

(IV) That portion of Larimer county that is west of the boundary defined on a north-to-south axis by Range seventy-one west and north of the boundary defined on an east-to-west axis by township five north, that portion that is west of the boundary defined on a north-to-south axis by range seventy-three west, and that portion that is north of the boundary latitudinal line 40 degrees, 42 minutes, 47.1 seconds north;

(V) That portion of Weld county that is north of the boundary defined on an east-to-west axis by Weld county road 78; that portion that is east of the boundary defined on a north-to-south axis by Weld county road 43 and north of the boundary defined on an east-to-west axis by Weld county road 62; that portion that is east of the boundary defined on a north-to-south axis by Weld county road 49, south of the boundary defined on an east-to-west axis by Weld county road 62 and north of the boundary defined on an east-to-west axis by Weld county road 46; that portion that is east of the boundary defined on a north-to-south axis by Weld county road 27, south of the boundary defined on an east-to-west axis by Weld county road 46 and north of the boundary defined on an east-to-west axis by Weld county road 36; that portion that is east of the boundary defined on a north-to-south axis by Weld county road 19, south of the boundary defined on an east-to-west axis by Weld county road 36 and north of the boundary defined on an east-to-west axis by Weld county road 20; and that portion that is east of the boundary defined on a north-to-south axis by Weld county road 39 and south of the boundary defined on an east-to-west axis by Weld county road 20.

(b) Effective January 1, 2010, the basic emissions program area shall consist of the county of El Paso, as described in paragraph (a) of this subsection (20).

(c) (I) Effective January 1, 2010, the enhanced emissions program area shall consist of the counties of Adams, Arapahoe, Boulder, Douglas, Jefferson, Larimer, and Weld, and the cities and counties of Broomfield and Denver as described in paragraph (a) of this subsection (20) and subject to paragraph (d) of this subsection (20). Notwithstanding any other provision of this section, vehicles registered in the counties of

Larimer and Weld shall not be required to obtain a certificate of emissions control prior to July 1, 2010, in order to be registered or reregistered.

(II) (Deleted by amendment, L. 2003, p. 1357, 1, effective August 6, 2003.)

(III) Only those counties included in the basic emissions program area pursuant to paragraph (b) of this subsection (20) that violate national ambient air quality standards for carbon monoxide or ozone as established by the environmental protection agency may, on a case-by-case basis, be incorporated into the enhanced emissions program by final order of the commission.

(d) The commission shall review the boundaries of the program area and may, by rule promulgated on or before December 31, 2011, adjust such boundaries to exclude particularly identified regions from either the basic program area, the enhanced area, or both, based on an analysis of the applicable air quality science and the effects of the program on the population living in such regions.

(21) "Registered repair facility or technician" means an automotive repair business which has registered with the division, agrees to have its emissions-related cost effectiveness monitored based on inspection data, and is periodically provided performance statistics for the purpose of improving emissions-related repairs. Specific repair effectiveness information shall subsequently be provided to motorists at the time of inspection failure.

(22) "State implementation plan" or "SIP" means the plan required by and described in section 110 (a) of the federal act.

(23) "Technical center" means any facility operated by the division or its designee to support AIR program activities including but not limited to licensed emissions inspectors or emissions mechanics, motorists, repair technicians, or small business technical assistance.

(23.5) "Vehicle" means a motor vehicle as defined in subsection (18) of this section.

(24) "Verification of emissions test" means a certificate to be attached to a motor vehicle's windshield verifying that the vehicle has been issued a valid certification of emissions control.

42-4-305. Powers and duties of executive director - automobile inspection and readjustment program - basic emissions program - enhanced emissions program - clean screen program. (1) (a) The executive director is authorized to issue, deny, cancel, suspend, or revoke licenses for, and shall furnish instructions to, inspection and readjustment stations, inspection-only facilities, fleet inspection stations, motor vehicle dealer test facilities, and enhanced inspection centers. The executive director shall provide all necessary forms for inspection and readjustment stations, inspection-only facilities, and fleet inspection stations. Motor vehicle dealer test facilities and enhanced inspection centers shall purchase necessary inspection forms from the vendor or vendors identified by the executive director. Said inspection and readjustment stations, inspection-only facilities, fleet inspection stations, motor vehicle dealer test facilities, and enhanced inspection centers shall be responsible for the issuance of certifications of emissions control. The executive director is authorized to furnish forms and instructions and issue or deny licenses to, or cancel, suspend, or revoke licenses of, emissions inspectors and emissions mechanics. The initial biennial fee for an inspection and readjustment station license, an inspection-only facility license, a fleet inspection station license, a motor vehicle dealer test facility license, and an enhanced inspection center authorization shall be thirty-five dollars, and the biennial renewal fee shall be twenty dollars. The initial biennial fee for issuance of an emissions inspector license or an emissions mechanic license shall be fifteen dollars, and the biennial renewal fee shall be ten dollars. The fee for each transfer of an emissions inspector license or an emissions mechanic license shall be ten dollars. The moneys received from such fees shall be deposited to the credit of the AIR account in the highway users tax fund, and such moneys shall be expended by the department of revenue only for the administration of the inspection and readjustment program upon appropriation by the general assembly.

(b) Notwithstanding the amount specified for any fee in paragraph (a) of this subsection (1), the executive director of the department by rule or as otherwise provided by law may reduce the amount of one or more of the fees if necessary pursuant to section 24-75-402 (3), C.R.S., to reduce the uncommitted reserves of the fund to which all or any portion of one or more of the fees is credited. After the uncommitted reserves of the fund are sufficiently reduced, the executive director of the department by rule or as otherwise provided by law may increase the amount of one or more of the fees as provided in section 24-75-402 (4), C.R.S.

(2) The executive director shall supervise the activities of licensed inspection and readjustment stations, inspection-only facilities, fleet inspection stations, motor vehicle dealer test facilities, authorized enhanced inspection centers, licensed emissions inspectors, and licensed emissions mechanics and shall cause inspections to be made of such stations, facilities, centers, inspectors, and mechanics and appropriate records for compliance with licensing requirements.

(3) The executive director shall require the surrender of any license issued under section 42-4-308 upon cancellation, suspension, or revocation action taken for a violation of any of the provisions of sections 42-4-301 to 42-4-316 or of any of the regulations promulgated pursuant thereto. In any such actions affecting licenses, the executive director may conduct hearings as a result of which such action is to be taken. Any such hearing may be conducted by a hearing officer appointed at the request of the executive

director in accordance with the "State Administrative Procedure Act", article 4 of title 24, C.R.S., which shall govern the conduct of such hearings and action on said licenses, except as provided in section 42-4-312 (4).

(4) The executive director shall promulgate rules and regulations consistent with those of the commission for the administration and operation of inspection and readjustment stations, inspection-only facilities, fleet inspection stations, motor vehicle dealer test facilities, and enhanced inspection centers and for the issuance, identification, and use of certifications of emissions control and shall promulgate such rules and regulations as may be necessary to the effectiveness of the automobile inspection and readjustment program.

(5) The executive director shall promulgate rules and regulations which require that each licensed inspection and readjustment station, inspection-only facility, or enhanced inspection center post in a clearly legible fashion in a conspicuous place in such station, facility, or center the fee charged by such station, facility, or center for performing an emissions inspection and, within the basic program area, the fee charged by any such inspection and readjustment station for performing the adjustments and any repairs required for the issuance of a certification of emissions waiver.

(6) (a) The executive director shall promulgate such rules and regulations as may be necessary to implement an ongoing quality assurance program to discover, correct, and prevent fraud, waste, and abuse and to determine whether proper procedures are being followed, whether the emissions test equipment is calibrated as specified, and whether other problems exist which would impede the success of the program.

(b) Overt performance audits shall be conducted as follows:

(I) Every ninety days at each inspection and readjustment station, inspection-only facility, and motor vehicle dealer test facility;

(II) Every ninety days at each fleet inspection station;

(III) Every ninety days for each test lane at each enhanced inspection center.

(c) Covert audits using unmarked motor vehicles shall be conducted as follows:

(I) Once per year at each inspection and readjustment station;

(II) At least twice per year for each test lane at each inspection-only facility and enhanced inspection center to include observation of inspector performance.

(d) Record audits to review the performance of inspection-only facilities, motor vehicle dealer test facilities, and enhanced inspection centers, including compliance with record-keeping and reporting requirements, shall be performed on a monthly basis.

(e) Equipment audits shall be performed to verify quality control and calibration of the required test equipment as follows:

(I) Twice per year at each inspection and readjustment station;

(II) Every ninety days for each test lane at each inspection-only facility, motor vehicle dealer test facility, and enhanced inspection center to be done contemporaneously with the overt performance audit;

(III) Once per year at each fleet inspection station.

(f) The executive director shall transfer quality assurance activity results to the department of public health and environment at least quarterly.

(7) The executive director shall implement and enforce the emissions test requirements as prescribed in section 42-4-310 by utilizing a registration denial-based enforcement program as required in the federal act including an electronic data transfer of inspection data through the use of a computer modem or similar technology for vehicle registration and program enforcement purposes. All inspection data generated at licensed inspection and readjustment stations, inspection-only facilities, fleet inspection stations, motor vehicle dealer test facilities, and enhanced inspection centers shall be provided to the department of public health and environment on a timely basis.

(8) The executive director shall, by regulation, establish a method for the owners of motor vehicles which are exempt pursuant to section 42-4-304 (20) from the AIR program to establish their entitlement to such exemption. No additional fee or charge for establishing entitlement to such exemption shall be collected by the department.

(9) The executive director shall be responsible for the issuance of certifications of emissions waiver as prescribed by section 42-4-310 and shall be responsible for the resolution of all formal public complaints concerning test results or test requirements in the most convenient and cost-effective manner possible.

(10) (a) The executive director and the department of public health and environment are authorized to enter into a contract or service agreement with a contractor to provide inspection services at enhanced inspection centers for vehicles within the enhanced program area required to be inspected pursuant to section 42-4-310. Any such contract or service agreement shall include such terms and conditions as are necessary to ensure that the contractor shall operate enhanced inspection centers in accordance with the requirements of this article and the federal act, shall include provisions establishing liquidated damages and penalties for failure to comply with the terms and conditions of the contract, and shall be in accordance with regulations adopted by the commission and the department of revenue. Any such contract or service agreement shall include provisions specifying that inspection and readjustment stations, inspection-only facilities, fleet inspection stations, and motor vehicle dealer test facilities shall

have complete access to electronic data transfer of inspection data through computer services of the contractor at a cost equal to that of enhanced inspection centers.

(b) Upon the approval of the executive director and the department of public health and environment, the contractor shall provide inspection services for vehicles within the enhanced program area required to be inspected pursuant to section 42-4-310.

(11) The executive director shall report to the transportation legislation review committee annually on the effectiveness of the quality assurance and enforcement measures contained in this section, the overall motorist compliance rates with inspections for registration denial, and the status of state implementation plan compliance pertaining to quality assurance. This annual report shall be submitted to the commission in May of each year for incorporation into appropriate annual and biennial reporting requirements. Reports shall cover the previous calendar year.

(12) The executive director shall promulgate such rules consistent with those of the commission as may be necessary for implementation, enforcement, and quality assurance and for procedures and policies that allow data collected from the clean screen program to be matched with vehicle ownership information and for such information to be transferred to county clerks and recorders. Such rules shall set forth the procedures for the executive director to inform county clerks and recorders of the emission inspection status of vehicles up for registration renewal.

42-4-306. Powers and duties of commission - automobile inspection and readjustment program - basic emissions program - enhanced emissions program - clean screen program. (1) The commission shall develop and evaluate motor vehicle inspection and readjustment programs for the enhanced program area and basic program area and may promulgate such regulations as may be necessary to implement and maintain the necessary performance of said programs consistent with the federal act.

(2) The commission shall develop and formulate training and qualification programs for state-employed motor vehicle emissions compliance officers to include annual auditor proficiency evaluations.

(3) (a) (I) (A) The commission shall promulgate rules and regulations for the training, testing, and licensing of emissions inspectors and emissions mechanics and the licensing of inspection and readjustment stations, inspection-only facilities, fleet inspection stations, motor vehicle dealer test facilities, and the authorization of enhanced inspection centers; the standards and specifications for the approval, operation, calibration, and certification of exhaust gas and evaporative emissions measuring instrumentation or test analyzer systems; and the procedures and practices to ensure the proper performance of inspections, adjustments, and required repairs.

(B) Specifications adopted by the commission for exhaust gas measuring instrumentation in the program areas shall conform to the federal act and federal requirements, including electronic data transfer, and may include bar code capabilities.

(C) Upon the adoption of specifications for measuring instruments and test analyzer systems, the division in consultation with the executive director may let bids for the procurement of instruments that meet federal requirements or guidelines and the standards of the federal act. The invitation for bids for test analyzer systems for the basic program and the inspection-only facilities in the enhanced program shall include, but shall not be limited to, the requirements for data collection and electronic transfer of data as established by the commission, service and maintenance requirements for such instruments for the period of the contract, requirements for replacement or loan instruments in the event that the purchased or leased instruments do not function, and the initial purchase or lease price. On and after June 5, 2001, each contract for the purchase of such instruments shall have a term of no more than four years.

(II) Points of no greater than five percent shall be assigned to those respondents that make the greatest use of Colorado goods, services, and the participation of small business. Licensed inspection and readjustment stations, inspection-only facilities, fleet inspection stations, and motor vehicle dealer test facilities, if applicable, which are required to purchase commission-approved test analyzer systems shall purchase them pursuant to the bid procedure of the department of personnel.

(III) Mobile test analyzer systems for motor vehicle dealer test facilities shall comply with commission specifications developed pursuant to subparagraph (I) of this paragraph (a).

(b) (I) For the enhanced emissions program, the commission shall develop system design standards, performance standards, and contractor requirements. Upon the adoption of such criteria, the division in consultation with the executive director may, according to procedures and protocol established in the "Procurement Code", articles 101 to 112 of title 24, C.R.S., enter into a contract for the design, construction, equipment, maintenance, and operation of enhanced inspection centers to serve affected motorists. The criteria for the award of such contract shall include, but shall not be limited to, such criteria as the contractor's qualifications and experience in providing emissions inspection services, financial and personnel resources available for start-up, technical or management expertise, and capacity to satisfy such requirements for the life of the contract.

(II) Inspection procedures, equipment calibration and maintenance, and data storage and transfer shall comply with federal requirements and may include bar code capability. The system shall provide reasonable convenience to the public.

(III) Points of no greater than five percent shall be assigned to those respondents who make the greatest use of Colorado goods, services, and participation of small businesses.

(IV) On and after May 26, 1998, any contract for inspection services shall have a term of no more than five years and shall be subject to rebidding under the provisions of this paragraph (b).

(V) (A) Notwithstanding any contrary provision in the "Procurement Code", articles 101 to 112 of title 24, C.R.S., or this article, any contract for inspection services may be renewed for a term not to exceed two years, after which the contract may be renewed for a single term of up to four years or rebid; except that inspection fees during any such four-year renewal contract shall be as determined under section 42-4-311 (6).

(B) The commission shall have rule-making authority to implement any environmental protection agency-approved alternative emissions inspection services or technologies, including on-board diagnostics, so long as such inspection technologies provide SIP credits equal to or greater than those currently in the SIP.

(4) (a) The commission shall develop a program to train and examine all applicants for an emissions inspector or emissions mechanic license. Training of emissions inspectors who are employed at enhanced inspection centers within the enhanced emissions program area shall be administered by the contractor subject to the commission's oversight. Emissions mechanic training shall be performed by instructors certified in accordance with commission requirements. Training classes shall be funded by tuition charged to the participants unless private or federal funds are available for such training. The qualifications and licensing examination for emissions inspectors, excluding such inspectors at enhanced inspection centers, who shall be authorized by and under the direction of the contractor, shall include a test of the applicant's knowledge of the technical and legal requirements for emissions testing, knowledge of data and emissions testing systems, and an actual demonstration of the applicant's ability to perform emissions inspection procedures.

(b) Emissions inspector and emissions mechanic licenses shall expire two years after issuance. The commission shall establish technical standards for renewing emissions inspector and emissions mechanic licenses to include requirements for retraining on a biennial schedule.

(c) The commission shall establish minimum performance criteria for licensed emissions inspectors and emissions mechanics.

(5) The commission shall perform its duties, as provided in sections 42-4-301 to 42-4-316, with the cooperation and aid of the division.

(6) (a) The commission shall develop and adopt, and may from time to time revise, regulations providing inspection procedures for detection of tampering with emissions-related equipment and on-board diagnostic systems and emissions standards for vehicle exhaust and evaporative gases, the detection of chlorofluorocarbons, and smoke opacity, as prescribed in section 42-4-412, with which emissions standards vehicles inspected in accordance with section 42-4-310 would be required to comply prior to issuance of certification of emissions compliance. Such inspection procedures and emissions standards shall be proven cost-effective and air pollution control-effective on the basis of detailed research conducted by the department of public health and environment in accordance with section 25-7-130, C.R.S., and shall be designed to assure compliance with the federal act, federal requirements, and the state implementation plan. Emissions standards shall be established for carbon monoxide, exhaust and evaporative hydrocarbons, oxides of nitrogen, and chlorofluorocarbons.

(b) (I) The commission shall adopt regulations which provide standards for motor vehicles and shall adopt by December 1 of each subsequent year standards for motor vehicles of one additional model year.

(II) Standards for carbon monoxide, exhaust and evaporative hydrocarbons, and oxides of nitrogen shall be no more stringent than those established pursuant to the federal act and federal requirements. The cut-points established for such standards prior to December 1, 1998, shall not be increased until on or after January 1, 2000.

(c) The commission shall recommend to the general assembly no later than December 1, 1998, adjustment or repair procedures to be followed for motor vehicles of the model year 1984 or a later model year which do not meet the applicable emissions standards. Notwithstanding the provisions of subsection (7) of this section, such recommended procedures may require the replacement or repair of emissions control components of such motor vehicles.

(d) Test procedures may authorize emissions inspectors or emissions mechanics to refuse testing of a vehicle that would be unsafe to test or that cannot physically be inspected, as specified by the commission; except that refusal to test a vehicle for such reasons shall not excuse or exempt such vehicle from compliance with all applicable requirements of this part 3.

(7) (a) The commission shall by regulation require the owner of a motor vehicle for which a certification of emissions control is required to obtain such certification. Such regulation shall provide:

(I) That a certification of emissions compliance be issued for the vehicle if, at the time of inspection or, after completion of required adjustments or repairs, the exhaust and evaporative gases and visible emissions from said vehicle comply with the applicable emissions standards adopted pursuant to subsection (6) of this section, and that applicable emissions control equipment and diagnostic systems are intact and operable, and, for model year 1995 and later vehicles, compliance with each applicable emissions-related recall campaign, or remedial action, as defined by the federal act, has been demonstrated.

(II) (A) That a certification of emissions waiver be issued for the motor vehicle if, at the time of inspection, the exhaust gas or evaporative emissions from said vehicle do not comply with the applicable emissions standards but said vehicle is adjusted or repaired by a registered repair technician or at a registered repair facility within the enhanced program area, or at a licensed inspection and repair station within the basic program area, whichever is appropriate, to motor vehicle manufacturer specifications and repair procedures as provided by regulation of the commission.

(B) Such specifications shall require that such motor vehicles be retested for exhaust gas emissions and evaporative emissions, if applicable, after such adjustments or repairs are performed, but, except as provided in section 42-4-310 (1) (d), no motor vehicle shall be required to receive additional repairs, maintenance, or adjustments beyond such specifications or repairs following such retest as a condition for issuance of a certification of emissions waiver.

(C) A time extension not to exceed the period of one inspection cycle may be granted in accordance with commission regulation to obtain needed repairs on a vehicle in the case of economic hardship when waiver requirements pursuant to commission regulation have not been met, but such extension may be granted only once per vehicle.

(D) Notwithstanding any provisions of this section, a temporary certificate of emissions control may be issued by state AIR program personnel for vehicles required to be repaired, if such repairs are delayed due to unavailability of needed parts.

(E) The results of the initial test, retests, and final test shall be given to the owner of the motor vehicle.

(F) The issuance of temporary certificates shall be entered into the main computer data base for the AIR program through the use of electronic records.

(G) The commission is authorized to reduce the emissions-related repair expenditure limit established in section 42-4-310 (1) (d) (III) for hydrocarbons and oxides of nitrogen if applicable federal requirements are met, and the environmental protection agency has approved a maintenance plan submitted by the state to ensure continued compliance with such federal requirements.

(b) (I) The commission shall by regulation provide that no vehicle shall be issued a certificate of emissions compliance or waiver if emissions control equipment and diagnostic or malfunction indicator systems, including microprocessor control systems, are not present, intact, and operational, if repairs were not appropriate and did not address the reason for the emissions failure, or if the vehicle emits visible smoke.

(II) The commission shall provide by regulation that no model year 1995 or later vehicle shall be issued a certificate of emissions control unless compliance with each applicable emissions-related recall campaign or remedial action, as defined in the federal act, has been demonstrated.

(8) (a) The commission may exempt motor vehicles of any make, model, or model year from the periodic inspection requirements of section 42-4-310.

(b) Pursuant to section 42-4-310 (1), the commission may increase the effective duration of certifications of emissions compliance issued for new motor vehicles without inspection.

(9) (a) (I) The commission shall continuously evaluate the entire AIR program to ensure compliance with the state implementation plan and federal law. Such evaluation shall be based on continuing research conducted by the department of public health and environment in accordance with section 25-7-130, C.R.S. Such evaluation shall include assessments of the cost-effectiveness and air pollution control-effectiveness of the program.

(II) The commission shall establish on a case-by-case basis and pursuant to final order any area of a county included in the basic emissions program area pursuant to section 42-4-304 (2) which shall be incorporated into the enhanced emissions program because it violates national ambient air quality standards on or after January 1, 1996, as established by the environmental protection agency.

(b) Such evaluation shall include a determination of the number of motor vehicles that fail to meet the applicable emissions standards after the adjustments and repairs required by subsection (7) of this section are made. If the commission finds that a significant number of motor vehicles do not meet the applicable emissions standards after such adjustments or repairs are made, the commission shall develop recommendations designed to improve the air pollution control-effectiveness of the program in a cost-effective manner.

(c) The evaluation shall also include an assessment of the methods of controlling or reducing exhaust gas emissions from motor vehicles of the model year 1981 or a later model year that are equipped with microprocessor-based emissions control systems and on-board diagnostic systems. Such evaluation shall include, if necessary for such motor vehicles, the development of more accurate alternative procedures to include the adjustments and repairs specified in subparagraph (II) of paragraph (a) of subsection (7) of this section, and such alternative procedures may require the replacement of inoperative or malfunctioning emissions control components. Such alternative procedures shall be designed to achieve control of emissions from such motor vehicles which is equivalent to or greater than the control performance level provided by performance standards established pursuant to the federal act.

(d) Such evaluation shall also include an annual assessment of in-use vehicle emissions performance levels by random testing of a representative sample of at least one-tenth of one percent of the vehicles subject to the enhanced emissions program requirements.

(10) The commission shall develop and implement, and shall revise as necessary, inspection procedures to detect tampering, poor maintenance, mis-fueling, and contamination of emissions control systems to include proper operation of on-board diagnostic systems.

(11) (a) The commission, with the cooperation of the department of public health and environment, the department of revenue, the contractor, and the owners or operators of the inspection and readjustment stations, inspection-only facilities, and motor vehicle dealer test facilities, shall implement an ongoing project designed to inform the public concerning the operation of the program and the benefits to be derived from such program.

(b) (I) The commission shall, as part of such project and with the cooperation of the department of public health and environment, the department of revenue, the contractor, and the owners or operators of the inspection and readjustment stations and inspection-only facilities prepare and cause the distribution of consumer protection information for the benefit of the owners of vehicles required to be inspected pursuant to section 42-4-310.

(II) This information shall include an explanation of the program, the owner's responsibilities under the program, the procedures to be followed in performing the inspection, the adjustments and repairs required for vehicles to pass inspection, cost expenditure limits pursuant to section 42-4-310 (1) (d) for such adjustments or repairs, the availability of diagnostic information to aid repairs, and a listing of registered repair facilities and technicians, and the package may include information on other aspects of the program as the commission determines to be appropriate.

(c) In addition to distribution of such information, the commission shall actively seek the assistance of the electronic and print media in communicating such information to the public and shall utilize such other means and manners of disseminating the information as are likely to effectuate the purpose of the program.

(12) (a) The commission, with the cooperation of the executive director of the department of public health and environment, shall conduct or cause to be conducted research concerning the presence of pollutants in the ambient air, which research shall include continuous monitoring of ambient air quality and modeling of sources concerning their impacts on air quality. Such research shall identify pollutants in the ambient air which originate from motor vehicle exhaust gas emissions and shall identify, quantify, and evaluate the ambient air quality benefit derived from the automobile inspection and readjustment program, from the federal new motor vehicle exhaust emissions standards, and from changes in vehicle miles traveled due to economic or other factors. Each such evaluation shall be reported separately to assess the air pollution control-effectiveness and cost-effectiveness of the pollution control strategy.

(b) (I) The commission with the cooperation of the department of public health and environment shall cause to be conducted a pilot study of the feasibility and costs of implementing remote sensing emissions detection technology as a potential supplemental maintenance strategy for areas that have attained applicable standards. This pilot study shall be conducted in the metropolitan Greeley, Weld county area with results and recommendations to be made available in January, 1998.

(II) The executive director of the department of public health and environment is authorized to enter into an agreement with a contractor in accordance with section 42-4-307 (10) (a) for the purchase of equipment and any assistance necessary for this study.

(13) The commission shall identify vehicle populations contributing significantly to ambient pollution inventories utilizing mobile source computer models approved by the environmental protection agency. The commission shall develop and implement more stringent or frequent, or both, inspection criteria for those vehicles with such significant pollution contributions.

(14) (a) Consistent with section 42-4-305, the commission shall promulgate technical rules and regulations governing quality control and audit procedures to be performed by the department of revenue as provided in section 42-4-305. Such regulations shall address all technical aspects of program oversight and quality assurance to include covert and overt performance audits and state implementation plan compliance.

(b) To ensure compliance with the state implementation plan and federal requirements the commission shall promulgate technical rules and regulations to address motor vehicle fleet and motor vehicle dealer inspection protocol and quality control and audit procedures.

(15) The commission shall provide for additional enforcement of the inspection programs by encouraging the adoption of local ordinances and active participation by local law enforcement personnel, parking control, and code enforcement officers against vehicles suspected to be out of compliance with inspection requirements.

(16) (a) (I) The commission shall promulgate rules and regulations governing the issuance of emissions-related repair waivers consistent with section 42-4-310.

(II) Within the enhanced program area waivers shall only be issued by authorized state personnel and enhanced inspection center personnel specifically authorized by the executive director.

(b) The issuance of all waivers shall be controlled and accountable to the main computer database for the AIR program by electronic record to ensure that maximum allowable waiver rate limits for both program types, as defined by the federal act, are not exceeded.

(17) For the enhanced emissions program, the commission shall promulgate rules and regulations establishing a network of enhanced inspection centers and inspection-only facilities within the enhanced emissions program area consistent with the following:

(a) (I) Owners, operators, and employees of enhanced inspection centers and independent inspection-only facilities within the enhanced program area are prohibited from engaging in any motor vehicle repair, service, parts sales, or the sale or leasing of motor vehicles and are prohibited from referring vehicle owners to particular providers of motor vehicle repair services; except that minor repair of components damaged by center or facility personnel during inspection at the center or facility, such as the reconnection of hoses, vacuum lines, or other measures pursuant to commission regulation that require no more than five minutes to complete, may be undertaken at no charge to the vehicle owner or operator if authorized.

(II) The operation of a motor vehicle dealer test facility shall not be considered to be engaging in any motor vehicle repair service, parts sales, or the sale or leasing of motor vehicles by a member of the state trade association operating such motor vehicle dealer test facility.

(b) Owners, operators, and employees of enhanced inspection centers shall ensure motorists and other affected parties reasonable convenience. Inspection services shall be available prior to, during, and after normal business hours on weekdays, and at least five hours on a weekend day.

(c) Owners, operators, and employees of enhanced inspection centers shall take appropriate actions, such as opening additional lanes, to avoid exceeding average motorist wait times of greater than fifteen minutes by designing optimized single- or multi-lane high-volume throughput systems.

(d) Owners or operators of enhanced inspection centers may develop, and are encouraged to develop, and implement alternate strategies including but not limited to off-peak pricing to reduce end-of-the-month wait times.

(e) The network of enhanced inspection centers shall be located to provide adequate coverage and convenience. At a minimum, the number of enhanced inspection centers shall be equivalent to the network that existed on January 1, 2000, and the hours of operation shall be determined by the contract.

(f) Within the enhanced emissions program area the commission shall provide for the operation of licensed inspection-only facilities. Applicable facility and inspector licensing, inspection procedures, and criteria shall be pursuant to rule and regulation of the commission and compliance with federal requirements. Inspection-only facilities shall be authorized to provide inspection services for all classes of motor vehicles as defined in section 42-4-304 (18) of the model year 1981 and older. Inspection-only owners or operators, or both, shall comply with paragraph (a) of this subsection (17).

(18) For the basic emissions program, inspection stations within the basic emissions program area which are licensed in accordance with section 42-4-308 may conduct inspections or provide motor vehicle repairs as well as offer emissions inspection services.

(19) The commission shall give at least sixty days' notice to the executive director prior to conducting any rule-making hearing pursuant to this article, except where the commission finds that an emergency exists under section 24-4-103 (6), C.R.S. The executive director shall participate as a party in any such hearing. Prior to promulgating any rule under this article, the commission shall consider the potential budgetary and personnel impacts any such rule may have on the department of revenue.

(20) (a) The commission shall develop and maintain a small business technical assistance program through the automobile inspection and repair program to provide information and to aid automotive businesses and technicians. As an element of this program, the commission shall develop a voluntary program for the training of registered repair technicians, to be funded by tuition charged to the participants, unless federal or private funds are made available for such training.

(b) For the enhanced emissions program, the commission shall provide for the voluntary registration of repair facilities and repair technicians within the enhanced emissions program area. Emissions-related repair effectiveness shall be monitored and periodically reported to participating facilities and technicians. Technical assistance shall be provided to those repair technicians and repair facilities needing improvement in repair effectiveness. The commission shall require that emissions-related repair effectiveness information regarding registered repair facilities be made available to the public.

(21) (a) The commission shall investigate and develop other supplemental or alternative motor vehicle related emissions reduction strategies, including but not limited to "cash for clunkers", which may complement or enhance the performance of the AIR program. Such strategies must be creditable under the state implementation plan and be proven cost-effective.

(b) (Deleted by amendment, L. 2002, p. 870, § 5, effective August 7, 2002.)

(22) The commission shall develop rules and regulations with respect to emissions inspection procedures and standards of motor vehicles

which operate on alternative motor fuels including but not limited to compressed natural gas, liquid petroleum gas, methanol, and ethanol. Such rules and regulations shall be developed for both the basic emissions program and the enhanced emissions program. The commission shall evaluate whether dual fuel motor vehicles should be inspected on both fuels and whether such vehicles shall be charged for one or two inspections.

(23) (a) The commission shall promulgate rules governing the operation of the clean screen program. Such rules shall authorize the division to commence the clean screen program in the basic emissions program area commencing as expeditiously as possible. Such rules shall authorize the division to extend, if feasible, the clean screen program to other parts of the state upon request of the lead air quality planning agencies for each respective area. Such rules shall govern operation of the clean screen program pursuant to the contract or service agreement entered into under section 42-4-307 (10.5). Such rules shall determine the percentage of the vehicle fleet targeted for the clean screen program, which percentage shall develop a target of the eligible vehicle fleet that meets air quality needs. Such rules shall specify emission levels for vehicles in the same manner as for other vehicles in the emissions program. The commission may, upon written request of the Pikes Peak area council of governments, exclude the El Paso county portion of the basic emissions program area from the clean screen program if the department of public health and environment receives written notification from the Pikes Peak area council of governments to such effect by June 1, 2001.

(b) The rules promulgated pursuant to paragraph (a) of this subsection (23) may also authorize the division to commence the clean screen program in the enhanced emissions program area commencing January 1, 2002, or as soon thereafter as is practical. The clean screen program may be implemented in the enhanced emissions program area only if the commission makes such a determination on or after July 1, 2001.

42-4-307. Powers and duties of the department of public health and environment - division of administration - automobile inspection and readjustment program - basic emissions program - enhanced emissions program - clean screen program. (1) The division shall establish and provide for the operation of a system, which may include a telephone answering service, to answer questions concerning the automobile inspection and readjustment programs from emissions inspectors, emissions mechanics, repair technicians, and the public.

(2) The division shall administer the licensing test for emissions inspectors, except for such inspectors at enhanced inspection centers, and emissions mechanics and shall oversee training.

(3) The division shall establish and operate such technical or administrative centers as may be necessary for the proper administration and ongoing support of the automobile inspection and readjustment program, for enhanced inspection centers, for the small business technical assistance program, and for the state smoking vehicle programs provided for in sections 42-4-412 to 42-4-414, and for affected motorists. The division is authorized to enter into a contract or service agreement in accordance with paragraph (a) of subsection (10) of this section for this purpose.

(4) The division shall develop and recommend to the commission, as necessary, vehicle emissions inspection procedure requirements to ensure compliance with the state implementation plan and the federal act.

(5) The division shall identify and recommend to the commission, as necessary, revisions to vehicle eligibility and the schedule of inspection frequency.

(6) (a) (I) The division shall administer, in accordance with federal requirements, the on-road remote sensing program.

(II) Pursuant to commission rule and based on confirmatory tests at an emissions technical center or emissions inspection facility that identify such vehicles as exceeding applicable emissions standards, off-cycle repairs may be required for noncomplying vehicles.

(b) Additional studies of the feasibility and appropriateness of on-road remote sensing technology as a potential emissions control strategy shall be pursued as available funding permits.

(c) The division is authorized to enter into a contract or service agreement in accordance with paragraph (a) of subsection (10) of this section for the purpose of this subsection (6).

(7) The division shall monitor and periodically report to the commission on the performance of the mobile sources state implementation plan provisions as they pertain to the basic emissions program area and the enhanced emissions program area.

(8) (a) The division shall administer the emissions inspector, emissions mechanic, and repair technician qualification and periodic requalification procedures, if applicable, and remedial training provisions in a manner consistent with department of revenue enforcement activities.

(b) The division, in consultation with the executive director, is authorized to bring enforcement actions in accordance with article 7 of title 25, C.R.S., for violations of regulations promulgated pursuant to section 42-4-306 which would cause violations of the state implementation plan.

(9) The division shall maintain inspection data from the AIR program pursuant to the federal act. Data analysis and reporting shall be submitted to the commission by the departments of public health and environment and revenue by July 1 of each year for the period of January through December of the previous year. Data analysis, state implementation plan compliance,

and program performance reporting shall be submitted to the environmental protection agency by the department of public health and environment by July 1 of each year for the period of January through December of the previous year. The division shall develop and maintain the data processing system necessary for the AIR program in compliance with federal reporting requirements.

(10) (a) For the enhanced emissions program, the department of public health and environment and the executive director are authorized to enter into a contract or service agreement with a contractor to provide inspection services at enhanced inspection centers for vehicles required to be inspected pursuant to section 42-4-310 within the enhanced program area. Any such contract or service agreement shall include such terms and conditions as are necessary to ensure that such enhanced inspection contractor will operate any such enhanced inspection center in compliance with this article and the federal act. Any such contract or service agreement shall also include provisions establishing liquidated damages and penalties for failure to comply with the terms and conditions of the contract and shall be in accordance with regulations adopted by the commission.

(b) Upon approval by the department of public health and environment and the executive director, the contractor shall provide inspection services for vehicles within the enhanced program area required to be inspected pursuant to section 42-4-310. Notwithstanding any contrary provision in the "Procurement Code", articles 101 to 112 of title 24, C.R.S., or this article, any contract for inspection services may be renewed for a term not to exceed two years to ensure that, on or after December 31, 2001, inspection services in the enhanced program area will not be interrupted by the expiration of the previous contract, after which the contract may be renewed for a single term of up to four years as provided in section 42-4-306 (3) (b) (V) (A). Any new contract entered into or renewed after the two-year renewal shall require the contractor to provide any necessary alternative inspection services or technologies so approved.

(10.5) (a) For the clean screen program and the Denver clean screening pilot study, the department of public health and environment and the department of revenue may, pursuant to the "Procurement Code", articles 101 to 112 of title 24, C.R.S., enter into a contract with a contractor for the purchase of equipment, the collection of remote sensing and other data and operation of remote sensing and support equipment, data processing and vehicle ownership matching in cooperation with the executive director, and collection of remote sensing and other data for the Denver clean screening pilot study, including analysis of the results of such study and report preparation. Under any such contract the department of public health and environment and the department of revenue may purchase approved remote sensing and support equipment or authorize the use of a qualified contractor or contractors to purchase approved remote sensing and support equipment for use in the clean screen program. Notwithstanding any contrary provision in the "Procurement Code", articles 101 to 112 of title 24, C.R.S., the clean screen contract may be incorporated into any contract or renewed contract pursuant to subsection (10) of this section. The contractor retained pursuant to this subsection (10.5) shall be the same as the contractor retained pursuant to subsection (10) of this section. The contractor shall make one-time transfers into the clean screen fund created in section 42-3-304 (19) in a total amount necessary to cover computer programming costs associated with implementation of House Bill 01-1402, enacted at the first regular session of the sixty-third general assembly, in the following order:

(I) Up to thirty thousand dollars from the contractor's revenues;

(II) Up to thirty thousand dollars from the public relations account provided for in the contract; and

(III) Up to forty thousand dollars from the technical center account provided for in the contract.

(b) Repealed.

(11) The department of public health and environment shall conduct studies on the development, effectiveness, and cost of evolving technologies in mobile source emission inspection for consideration by March of each even-numbered year. In the event that alternative technologies become available, cost and air quality effectiveness shall be considered prior to adoption by the commission as inspection technology.

(12) The department of public health and environment shall work with the contractor to develop a high emitter program that is acceptable to the environmental protection agency.

(13) Beginning July 1, 2007, and on or before October 15 of each year thereafter through October 15, 2009, and no later than October 15, 2011, and each October 15 thereafter, the department of public health and environment, in cooperation with the contractor, shall brief the transportation legislation review committee on the cost and effectiveness of the high emitter program. The briefing shall compare the effectiveness of the high emitter program to other emissions reduction options, including, but not limited to, the elimination of the AIR program, the elimination of the requirement for regular motor vehicle emissions inspections, and the appropriate reduction of the emissions inspection fee.

(14) For fiscal year 2006-07, the contractor shall make a payment from their high emitter account to the clean screen fund created in section 42-3-304 (19) (a) (II) in an amount of three hundred fifty thousand dollars. The department of public health and environment shall provide the contractor with an itemized report of the costs associated with the implementation of

House Bill 06-1302, enacted at the second regular session of the sixty-fifth general assembly, if an additional amount is necessary to cover the costs associated with the implementation of House Bill 06-1302.

(15) The department of public health and environment may enter into a contract extension with the contractor as necessary in order to implement House Bill 06-1302, enacted at the second regular session of the sixty-fifth general assembly. In evaluating a contract extension, the department of public health and environment and the commission shall consider a reduction in the fees set forth in section 42-3-304, C.R.S.

42-4-307.5. Clean screen authority - enterprise - revenue bonds. (1) If the commission determines pursuant to section 42-4-306 (23) (b) to implement an expanded clean screen program in the enhanced emissions program area, there shall be created a clean screen authority consisting of the executive director of the department of public health and environment and executive director of the department of revenue or their designees and any necessary support staff. The authority shall constitute an enterprise for the purposes of section 20 of article X of the state constitution so long as it retains the authority to issue revenue bonds and receives less than ten percent of its total annual revenues in grants, as defined in section 24-77-102 (7), C.R.S., from all Colorado state and local governments combined. So long as it constitutes an enterprise pursuant to the provisions of this section, the authority shall not be a district for purposes of section 20 of article X of the state constitution.

(2) (a) The authority may, by resolution that meets the requirements of subsection (3) of this section, authorize and issue revenue bonds in an amount not to exceed five million dollars in the aggregate for expenses of the authority. Such bonds may be issued only after approval by both houses of the general assembly acting either by bill or joint resolution and after approval by the governor in accordance with section 39 of article V of the state constitution. Such bonds shall be payable only from moneys allocated to the authority for expenses of the division and the commission pursuant to sections 42-4-306 and 42-4-307.

(b) All bonds issued by the authority shall provide that:

(I) No holder of any such bond may compel the state or any subdivision thereof to exercise its appropriation or taxing power; and

(II) The bond does not constitute a debt of the state and is payable only from the net revenues allocated to the authority for expenses as designated in such bond.

(3) (a) Any resolution authorizing the issuance of bonds under the terms of this section shall state:

(I) The date of issuance of the bonds;

(II) A maturity date or dates during a period not to exceed thirty years from the date of issuance of the bonds;

(III) The interest rate or rates on, and the denomination or denominations of, the bonds; and

(IV) The medium of payment of the bonds and the place where the bonds will be paid.

(b) Any resolution authorizing the issuance of bonds under the terms of this section may:

(I) State that the bonds are to be issued in one or more series;

(II) State a rank or priority of the bonds; and

(III) Provide for redemption of the bonds prior to maturity, with or without premium.

(4) Any bonds issued pursuant to the terms of this section may be sold at public or private sale. If bonds are to be sold at a public sale, the authority shall advertise the sale in such manner as the authority deems appropriate. All bonds issued pursuant to the terms of this section shall be sold at a price not less than the par value thereof, together with all accrued interest to the date of delivery.

(5) Notwithstanding any provisions of law to the contrary, all bonds issued pursuant to this section are negotiable.

(6) (a) A resolution pertaining to issuance of bonds under this section may contain covenants as to:

(I) The purpose to which the proceeds of sale of the bonds may be applied and to the use and disposition thereof;

(II) Such matters as are customary in the issuance of revenue bonds including, without limitation, the issuance and lien position of other or additional bonds; and

(III) Books of account and the inspection and audit thereof.

(b) Any resolution made pursuant to the terms of this section shall be deemed a contract with the holders of the bonds, and the duties of the authority under such resolution shall be enforceable by any appropriate action in a court of competent jurisdiction.

(7) Bonds issued under this section and bearing the signatures of the authority in office on the date of the signing shall be deemed valid and binding obligations regardless of whether, prior to delivery and payment, any or all of the persons whose signatures appear thereon have ceased to be members of the authority.

(8) (a) Except as otherwise provided in the resolution authorizing the bonds, all bonds of the same issue under this section shall have a prior and paramount lien on the net revenues pledged therefor. The authority may provide for preferential security for any bonds, both principal and interest, to be issued under this section to the extent deemed feasible and desirable by such authority over any bonds that may be issued thereafter.

(b) Bonds of the same issue or series issued under this section shall be equally and ratably secured, without priority by reason of number, date, sale, execution, or delivery, by a lien on the net revenue pledged in accordance with the terms of the resolution authorizing the bonds.

(9) The clean screen authority shall be a government-owned business that provides financial

services to all entities providing inspection services, the department, and the department of public health and environment with regard to the revenues subject to section 42-3-304 (19).

(10) The clean screen authority may accept grants from any source and shall deposit such moneys in the clean screen fund created in section 42-3-304 (19).

(11) The clean screen authority may contract with the department and expend moneys from the clean screen fund for computer programming costs associated with implementation of House Bill 01-1402, enacted at the first regular session of the sixty-third general assembly. The department is authorized to expend moneys pursuant to such contract, subject to annual appropriation by the general assembly, effective the fiscal year commencing July 1, 2000.

(12) Repealed.

42-4-307.7. Vehicle emissions testing - remote sensing - rules. (1) On or before December 31, 2006, the department of public health and environment and the contractor shall develop a plan, subject to approval by the commission, that shall provide for a phased increase in clean screen testing. The plan shall provide for the substantially increased use of remote sensing devices for the identification of vehicles whose emissions comply with the air quality criteria determined by the commission and those vehicles that exceed the air quality criteria determined by the commission. The commission shall use best efforts to eliminate the requirement for regular emissions inspections and to replace the regularly scheduled basic and enhanced emissions testing program with a high emitter program.

(2) If model year exemptions or clean screen testing is expanded, the department of public health and environment may reduce the number of lanes at enhanced inspection centers or the number of enhanced inspection centers in the program area. The department of public health and environment shall consider such reductions when establishing or adjusting compensation paid to the contractor.

(3) The Colorado department of transportation shall work with the department of public health and environment to identify locations that may accommodate unmanned remote sensing devices without causing a safety hazard.

(4) The commission shall evaluate options for increasing the number of vehicles passing a test under the clean screen program, including, but not limited to:

(a) The reduction of the number of remote sensing measurements per vehicle;

(b) Additional remote sensing devices and sites;

(c) Expanded hours of operation; and

(d) Additional staffing.

(5) The department of public health and environment shall work with the contractor to minimize false test results and shall track and report to the commission its progress in minimizing false test results on or before March 31 of each year.

(6) The commission shall determine the criteria used for the measurement of vehicle emissions needed to comply with the clean screen program and the high emitter program, which criteria shall include, but are not limited to, the pollutants measured, acceptable levels of the measured pollutants, and failure rates. Criteria adopted by the commission for the clean screen program shall meet environmental protection agency requirements.

(7) Vehicles identified as exceeding acceptable emission limitations, as determined by the commission pursuant to subsection (6) of this section, shall be required to report to an enhanced inspection center or other approved facility within thirty days and shall be subject to an approved emissions test to confirm that the vehicle has failed the emissions test. Thereafter, the owner of the vehicle shall have thirty days to repair and test the vehicle successfully.

(8) The commission shall adopt, by rule, emissions test methods to confirm the identification of a high emitting vehicle that was previously identified, by remote sensing, as a high emitting vehicle.

(9) Notwithstanding any other provision of law, vehicles operating within the program area but registered outside the program area that are repeatedly detected under the clean screen program shall be subject to enforcement under a program adopted by the commission to identify vehicles that exceed acceptable emissions limitations.

(10) The commission shall adopt, by rule, an enforcement program to identify vehicles that regularly operate within the program area but are registered outside the program area and shall require their compliance with acceptable emissions limitations determined by the commission.

(11) If the identified high emitting vehicle fails an enhanced emissions test at an enhanced inspection center or other approved test pursuant to subsection (8) of this section, repairs shall be completed and the vehicle shall pass a subsequent approved emissions test pursuant to this part 3 before the vehicle may be registered or reregistered.

(12) Photographs of a vehicle taken by a remote sensing device in order to capture an image of a vehicle's license plate shall be limited to the rear of the vehicle. No attempts shall be made by a remote sensing device to photograph a vehicle's driver.

(13) Repealed.

42-4-308. Inspection and readjustment stations - inspection-only facilities - fleet inspection stations - motor vehicle dealer test facilities - contractor - emissions inspectors - emissions mechanics - requirements. (1) (a) Applications for an inspection and readjustment station license, an inspection-only facility license, a fleet inspection station license, a motor vehicle dealer test facility license, an emissions inspector license, an enhanced inspection center license, or an emissions mechanic's license shall be made on forms prescribed by the executive director.

(b) No inspection and readjustment station license, inspection-only facility license, fleet inspection station license, motor vehicle dealer test facility license, or enhanced inspection center license shall be issued unless the executive director finds that the facilities of the applicant are of adequate size and properly equipped as provided in subsection (3) of this section, that a licensed inspector or emissions mechanic, whichever is applicable, is or will be available to make such inspection, and that the inspection and readjustment procedures will be properly followed based upon established performance criteria pursuant to section 42-4-306 (4) (c).

(2) No inspection or adjustments shall be made pursuant to the automobile inspection and readjustment program nor certification of emissions control issued unless the owner or operator of the inspection and readjustment station, inspection-only facility, fleet inspection station, motor vehicle dealer test facility, or enhanced inspection center at which such inspection is made or such adjustments or repairs are performed as required has been issued, and is then operating under, a valid inspection and readjustment station license, inspection-only facility license, fleet inspection station license, motor vehicle dealer test facility license, or a contract for an authorized enhanced inspection center and has one or more licensed emissions inspectors or emissions mechanics employed as required, one of whom shall have made the inspection for which said certification has been issued.

(3) No inspection and readjustment station license, inspection-only facility license, fleet inspection station license, motor vehicle dealer test facility license, or contractor's contract shall be issued or executed unless the station or contractor has proper equipment to meet licensing, facility, or contractor approval requirements. Such equipment shall include all test equipment approved by the commission to perform emissions inspections corresponding to the type of licensed or approved facility together with such auxiliary tools, equipment, and testing devices as are required by the commission by rule.

(4) (a) No emissions inspector license or emissions mechanic license shall be issued to any applicant unless said applicant has completed the required training, has demonstrated necessary skills and competence in the inspection of motor vehicles by passing the written certification test developed by the commission and administered by the department of public health and environment, and has demonstrated such skill and competence as a prerequisite to initial licensing by the department of revenue.

(b) The department of revenue shall monitor emissions inspector and emissions mechanic activities at inspection and readjustment stations, inspection-only facilities, fleet inspection stations, motor vehicle dealer test facilities, and enhanced inspection centers during periodic performance audits conducted as prescribed by section 42-4-305.

(c) An emissions inspector or emissions mechanic license may be revoked in accordance with section 42-4-305 if the licensee is not in compliance with the minimum performance criteria set forth by the commission or the department of revenue.

(d) Licenses shall be valid for two years.

(e) Emissions inspector and emissions mechanic license renewal shall be subject to the requirements set forth by the commission through rule and regulation.

42-4-309. Vehicle fleet owners - motor vehicle dealers - authority to conduct inspections - fleet inspection stations - motor vehicle dealer test facilities - contracts with licensed inspection-only entities. (1) (a) Any person in whose name twenty or more motor vehicles, required to be inspected, are registered in this state or to whom said number of vehicles are leased for a period of not less than six continuous months and who operates a motor vehicle repair garage or shop adequately equipped and manned, as required by section 42-4-308 and the rules and regulations issued pursuant thereto, may be licensed to perform said inspections as a fleet inspection station. Said inspections shall be made by licensed emissions inspectors or emissions mechanics. Such stations shall be subject to all licensing regulations and supervision applicable to inspection and readjustment stations. Fleet inspection stations shall inspect fleet vehicles in accordance with applicable requirements pursuant to rules and regulations promulgated by the commission. No person licensed pursuant to this section may conduct emissions inspections on motor vehicles owned by employees of such person or the general public, but only on those vehicles owned or operated by the person subject to the fleet inspection requirements. Any such motor vehicles are not eligible for a certificate of emissions waiver and shall be inspected annually. The commission shall promulgate such rules as may be necessary to establish non-loaded mode static idle inspection procedures, standards, and criteria under this section.

(b) Each fleet operator licensed or operating within the enhanced program area who is also licensed to operate a fleet inspection station shall assure that a representative sample of one-half of one percent or one vehicle, whichever is greater, of such operator's vehicle fleet is inspected annually at an inspection-only facility or enhanced inspection center. An analysis of the data gathered from any such inspection shall be performed by the department of public health and environment and provided to the department of revenue to determine compliance by such fleet with the self-inspection requirements of this section. An inspection is not required prior to the sale of a motor vehicle with at least twelve months remaining before the vehicle's certification of emissions compliance expires if such certification was issued when the vehicle was new.

(2) (a) As an alternative to subsection (1) of this section, any person having twenty or more vehicles registered in this state that are required to be inspected pursuant to section 42-4-310 may contract for periodic inspection services with a contractor or an inspection-only facility. Such inspections shall be in compliance with non-fleet vehicle requirements as specified in this part 3 and shall be performed by an authorized or licensed emissions inspector who shall be subject to all requirements and oversight as applicable.

(b) Upon retail sale of any vehicle subject to fleet inspection to a party other than a fleet operator, such vehicle shall be inspected at an authorized enhanced inspection center, licensed inspection-only facility, or licensed inspection and readjustment station, as applicable. A certificate of emissions compliance shall be required as a condition of the retail sale of any such vehicle.

(3) (a) Any person licensed as a motor vehicle dealer pursuant to article 6 of title 12, C.R.S., in whose name twenty or more motor vehicles are registered or inventoried or consigned for retail sale in this state which are required to be inspected shall comply with the requirements of section 42-4-310 for the issuance of a certificate of emissions compliance at the time of the retail sale of any such vehicle.

(b) Within the enhanced emissions program, motor vehicle dealers licensed pursuant to article 6 of title 12, C.R.S., may contract for used motor vehicle inspection services by a licensed motor vehicle dealer test facility. Pursuant to regulations of the commission, inspection procedures shall include a loaded mode transient dynamometer test cycle in combination with appropriate idle short tests pursuant to rules and regulations of the commission.

(c) 1981 and older model vehicles held in inventory and offered for retail sale by a used vehicle dealer may be inspected by a licensed inspection-only facility.

(d) Within the basic emissions program, any person licensed as a motor vehicle dealer pursuant to article 6 of title 12, C.R.S., may be licensed to conduct inspections pursuant to subsections (1) and (2) of this section.

(4) Nothing in this section shall preclude a fleet or motor vehicle dealer test facility from participating in the basic or enhanced emissions program pursuant to this part 3 with the requirements of such program being determined by the county of residence or operation.

(5) (a) Motor vehicle dealers selling any vehicle to be registered in the enhanced program area shall comply with the enhanced program requirements.

(b) Motor vehicle dealers selling any vehicle to be registered in the basic program area shall comply with the basic program requirements.

(c) If used motor vehicles for sale have been inspected by a motor vehicle dealer test facility, the motor vehicle dealer shall comply with the standards and requirements established for motor vehicle dealer test facilities.

(6) (a) On and after June 1, 1996, a motor vehicle dealer or a used motor vehicle dealer licensed pursuant to article 6 of title 12, C.R.S., that sells any vehicle subject to the provisions of the enhanced emissions program may comply with the provisions of sections 42-4-304 (3) (d) and 42-4-310 by providing the consumer of the vehicle a voucher purchased by the dealer from the contractor for the centralized enhanced emissions program, with or without charge to the consumer, up to the maximum amount charged for an emissions inspection at an enhanced inspection center. Such voucher shall cover the cost of an emissions inspection of the vehicle at an enhanced inspection center and shall entitle the consumer to such an emissions inspection.

(b) If a vehicle inspected with a voucher as authorized in this paragraph (b) fails a test at an enhanced inspection center and is returned within three business days after its purchase, the dealer, at its option, shall repair the motor vehicle to pass the emissions test, pay the consumer to obtain such repairs to pass the emissions test from a third party, or repurchase the vehicle at the vehicle's purchase price. After such payment, repair, or repurchase, a dealer shall have no further liability to the consumer for compliance with the requirements of the enhanced emissions program.

(c) The voucher to be delivered at time of sale shall set forth the conditions described in paragraph (b) of this subsection (6) on a form prescribed by the department of revenue.

(7) A motor vehicle dealer shall have a motor vehicle inspected annually pursuant to section 42-4-310, but shall not be required to have such vehicle inspected more than once a year.

42-4-310. Periodic emissions control inspection required. (1) (a) (I) Subject to subsection (4) of this section, a motor vehicle that is required to be registered in the program area shall not be sold, registered for the first time without a certification of emissions compliance, or reregistered unless such vehicle has passed a clean screen test or has a valid certification of emissions control as required by the appropriate county. The provisions of this paragraph (a) shall not apply to motor vehicle transactions at wholesale between motor vehicle dealers licensed pursuant to article 6 of title 12, C.R.S. An inspection is not required prior to the sale of a motor vehicle with at least twelve months remaining before the vehicle's certification of emissions compliance expires if such certification was issued when the vehicle was new.

(II) (A) If title to a roadworthy motor vehicle, as defined in section 42-6-102 (15), for which a certification of emissions compliance or emissions waiver must be obtained pursuant to this paragraph (a) is being transferred to a new owner, the new owner may require at the time of sale that the prior owner provide said certification as required for the county of residence of the new owner.

(B) The new owner shall submit such certification to the department of revenue or an authorized agent thereof with application for registration of the motor vehicle.

(C) If such vehicle is being registered in the program area for the first time, the owner shall obtain any certification required for the county where registration is sought and shall submit such certification to the department of revenue or an authorized agent thereof with such owner's application for the registration of the motor vehicle. A motor vehicle being registered in the program area for the first time may be registered without an inspection or certification if the vehicle has not yet reached its fourth model year or a later model year established by the commission pursuant to section 42-4-306 (8) (b).

(b) (I) (A) Effective July 1, 1987, and until May 28, 1999, those motor vehicles that are owned by the United States government or an agency thereof or by the state of Colorado or any agency or political subdivision thereof that would be registered in the program area shall be inspected once each year, and a valid certification of emissions compliance shall be obtained.

(B) New motor vehicles owned by the United States government or an agency thereof or by the state of Colorado or any agency or political subdivision thereof that would be registered in the program area shall be issued a certification of emissions compliance without inspection that shall expire on the anniversary of the day of the issuance of such certification when such vehicle has reached its fourth model year or a later model year established by the commission pursuant to section 42-4-306 (8) (b). Prior to the expiration of such certification such vehicle shall be inspected and a certification of emissions control shall be obtained therefor.

(C) Effective May 28, 1999, 1982 and newer model motor vehicles that are owned by the United States government or an agency thereof or by the state of Colorado or any agency or political subdivision thereof that would be registered in the program area shall be inspected every two years, and shall be issued a certification of emissions compliance that shall be valid for twenty-four months; except that vehicles owned or operated by any agency or political subdivision that is authorized and licensed pursuant to section 42-4-309 to inspect fleet vehicles shall be inspected annually.

(D) Effective May 28, 1999, 1981 and older model motor vehicles that are owned by the United States government or an agency thereof or by the state of Colorado or any agency or political subdivision thereof that would be registered in the program area shall be inspected once each year, and shall be issued a certification of emissions compliance that shall be valid for twelve months.

(E) Any vehicle subject to this subparagraph (I) that is suspected of having an emissions problem may undergo a voluntary inspection as provided in subparagraph (IV) of paragraph (c) of this subsection (1).

(II) (A) Motor vehicle dealers shall purchase verification of emissions test forms for the sum of twenty-five cents per form from the department or persons authorized by the department to make such sales to be used only on new motor vehicles. No refund or credit shall be allowed for any unused verification of emissions test forms. New motor vehicles required under this section to have a verification of emissions test form shall be issued a certification of emissions compliance without inspection, which shall expire on the anniversary of the day of the issuance of such certification when such vehicle has reached its fourth model year or a later model year established by the commission pursuant to section 42-4-306 (8) (b). Prior to the expiration of such certification such vehicle shall pass a clean screen test or be inspected and a certification of emissions control shall be obtained therefor.

(B) 1982 and newer model motor vehicles required pursuant to this section to have a certification of emissions control shall be inspected at the time of the sale or transfer of any such vehicle and, prior to registration renewal, shall be issued a certification of emissions control that shall be valid for twenty-four months except as provided under section 42-4-309. An inspection is not required prior to the sale of a motor vehicle with at least twelve months remaining before the vehicle's certification of emissions compliance expires if such certification was issued when the vehicle was new. This sub-subparagraph (B) does not apply to the sale of a motor vehicle that is inoperable or otherwise cannot be tested in accordance with regulations promulgated by the department of revenue if the seller of the motor vehicle provides a written notice to the purchaser pursuant to the requirements of subsection (4) of this section.

(C) 1981 and older model motor vehicles required pursuant to this section to have a certification of emissions control shall be inspected at the time of the sale or transfer of any such vehicle and, prior to registration renewal, shall be issued a certification of emissions control that shall be valid for twelve months. This sub-subparagraph (C) does not apply to the sale of a motor vehicle which is inoperable or otherwise cannot be tested in accordance with regulations promulgated by the department of revenue if the seller of the motor vehicle provides a written notice to the purchaser pursuant to the requirements of subsection (4) of this section.

(III) Upon registration or renewal of registration of a motor vehicle required to have a certification of emissions control, the department shall issue a tab identifying the vehicle as requiring certification of emissions control. The tab shall be displayed from the time of registration. The verification of emissions test shall also be displayed on the motor vehicle in a location prescribed by the department of revenue consistent with federal regulations.

(c) (I) Effective October 1, 1989, those motor vehicles owned by nonresidents who reside in either the basic or enhanced emissions program areas or by residents who reside outside the program area who are employed for at least ninety days in any twelve-month period in a program area or who are attending school in a program area, and are operated in either the basic or enhanced emissions program areas for at least ninety days, shall be inspected as required by this section and a valid certification of emissions compliance or emissions waiver shall be obtained as required for the county where said person is employed or attends school. Such nonresidents include, but are not limited to, all military personnel, temporarily assigned employees of business enterprises, and persons engaged in activities at the olympic training center.

(II) Any person owning or operating a business and any postsecondary educational institution located in a program area shall inform all persons employed by such business or attending classes at such institution that they are employed or attending classes in a program area and are required to comply with the provisions of subparagraph (I) of this paragraph (c).

(III) Vehicles that are registered in a program area and are being operated outside such area but within another program area shall comply with all program requirements of the area where such vehicles are being operated. Vehicles registered in a program area that are being temporarily operated outside the state at the time of registration or registration renewal may apply to the department of revenue for a temporary exemption from program requirements. Upon return to the program area, such vehicles must be in compliance with all requirements within fifteen days. A temporary exemption shall not be granted if the vehicle will be operated in an emissions testing area in another state unless proof of emissions from that area is submitted.

(IV) Nothing in this section shall be deemed to prevent or shall be interpreted so as to hinder the voluntary inspection of any motor vehicle in the enhanced emissions program. A certificate of emissions control issued under the provisions of the enhanced emissions program shall be acceptable as a demonstration of compliance within the basic program for vehicle registration purposes. In order to provide motorist protection, those vehicles voluntarily inspected and that fail said inspection but that are warrantable under manufacturers' emissions control warranties pursuant to section 207 (A) and (B) of the federal act shall comply with the emissions-related repair requirements of this part 3.

(V) Motor vehicles operated in the enhanced emissions program area, and required to be inspected pursuant to subparagraph (I) of this paragraph (c), shall comply with the inspection requirements of the enhanced emissions program area and are not required to comply with the inspection requirements of the basic emissions program area.

(d) (I) Repealed.

(II) (A) For the basic emissions program, effective January 1, 1994, for businesses which operate nineteen or fewer motor vehicles and for 1981 or older private motor vehicles required to be registered in the basic emissions program area, after any adjustments or repairs required pursuant to section 42-4-306, if total expenditures of at least seventy-five dollars have been made to bring the vehicle into compliance with applicable emissions standards and the vehicle still does not meet such standards, a certification of emissions waiver shall be issued for such vehicle.

(B) (Deleted by amendment, L. 2011, (SB 11-031), ch. 86, p. 246, § 11, effective August 10, 2011.)

(III) Repealed.

(IV) For the basic emissions program, effective January 1, 1994, for businesses that operate nineteen or fewer vehicles and for private motor vehicles only of a model year 1982 or later required to be registered in the basic emissions program area, after any adjustments or repairs required pursuant to section 42-4-306, if total expenditures of at least two hundred dollars have been made to bring the vehicle into compliance with the applicable emissions standards and the vehicle still does not meet such standards, a certification of emissions waiver shall be issued for such vehicle. For vehicles not older than two years or that have not more than twenty-four thousand miles, or such period of time and mileage as established for warranty protection by amendments to federal regulations, no emissions-related repair waivers shall be issued due to the provisions and enforcement of section 207 (A) and (B) of the federal act relating to emissions control systems components and performance warranties. Vehicles that are owned by the state of Colorado or any agency or political subdivision thereof are not eligible for emissions-related repair waivers under this subparagraph (IV).

(V) Repealed.

(VI) For the enhanced emissions program, effective January 1, 1995, for businesses that operate nineteen or fewer vehicles and for private motor vehicles only of a model year 1968 and later required to be registered in the enhanced emissions program area, after any adjustments or repairs required pursuant to section 42-4-306, if total expenditures of at least four hundred fifty dollars have been made to bring the vehicle into compliance with applicable emissions standards and the vehicle does not meet such standards, a certification of emissions waiver shall be issued for such vehicle except as prescribed in subparagraph (XII) of this paragraph (d) pertaining to vehicle warranty. The four-hundred-fifty-dollar minimum expenditure may be adjusted annually by an amount not to exceed the percentage, if any, by which the consumer price index for all urban consumers (CPIU) for the Denver-Boulder metropolitan statistical area for the preceding year differs from such index for 1989. Vehicles that are owned by the state of Colorado or any agency or political subdivision thereof are not eligible for emissions-related repair waivers under this subparagraph (VI).

(VII) Repealed.

(VIII) (A) For the enhanced emissions program except as provided in sub-subparagraph (B) of this subparagraph (VIII), for businesses that operate nineteen or fewer vehicles and for private motor vehicles only of a model year 1967 or earlier required to be registered in the enhanced emissions program area, after any adjustments or repairs required under section 42-4-306, if total expenditures of at least seventy-five dollars have been made to bring the vehicle into compliance with applicable emissions standards and the vehicle still does not meet the standards, a certification of emissions waiver shall be issued for the vehicle.

(B) This subparagraph (VIII) shall apply in Boulder county, effective July 1, 1995.

(IX) (A) For the enhanced emissions program except as provided in sub-subparagraph (B) of this subparagraph (IX) effective January 1, 1995, for vehicles subject to a transient, loaded mode dynamometer inspection procedure under the enhanced program as determined by the commission, a certificate of waiver may be issued by an authorized state representative, if after failing a retest, at which point the minimum repair cost limit of four hundred fifty dollars has not been met, a complete and documented physical and functional diagnosis of the vehicle performed at an emissions technical center indicates that no additional emissions-related repairs would be effective or needed.

(B) This subparagraph (IX) shall apply in Boulder county, effective July 1, 1995.

(X) Subject to the provisions of subparagraph (V) of this paragraph (d), a certificate of emissions control shall not be issued for vehicles in the program area exhibiting smoke or indications of tampering with or poor maintenance of emissions control systems including on-board diagnostic systems.

(XI) As used in this paragraph (d), "total expenditures" means those expenditures directly related to adjustment or repair of a motor vehicle to reduce exhaust or evaporative emissions to a level which complies with applicable emissions standards. The term does not include an inspection fee, or any costs of adjustment, repair, or replacement necessitated by the disconnection of, tampering with, or abuse of air pollution control equipment, improper fuel use, or visible smoke.

(XII) No certification of emissions waiver shall be issued for vehicles not older than two years or which have not more than twenty-four thousand miles, or are of such other age and mileage as established for warranty protection under the federal act in accordance with the provisions and enforcement of section 207 (A) and (B) of the federal act relating to emissions control component and systems performance warranties.

(2) (a) The emissions inspection required under this section shall include an analysis of tail pipe and evaporative emissions. After January 1, 1994, such inspection shall include an analysis of emissions control equipment including on-board diagnostic systems, chlorofluorocarbons, and visible smoke emissions for the basic emissions program area and the enhanced emissions program area and emissions testing that meets the performance standards set by federal requirements for the enhanced emissions program area by means of procedures specified by regulation of the commission to determine whether the motor vehicle qualifies for issuance of a certification of emissions compliance. For motor vehicles of the model year 1975 or later, not tested under a transient load on a dynamometer, said inspection shall also include a visual inspection of emissions control equipment pursuant to rules of the commission.

(b) and (c) Repealed.

(d) (I) In the basic emissions program area, effective January 1, 1994, in order to be issued a certificate of emissions waiver, appropriate adjustments and repairs must have been performed at a licensed inspection and readjustment station by a licensed emissions mechanic.

(II) In the enhanced emissions program area, effective January 1, 1995, in order to be issued a certificate of emissions waiver, appropriate adjustments and repairs must have been performed by a technician at a registered repair facility within the enhanced emissions program area.

(III) Adjustments and repairs performed by a registered repair facility and technician within the enhanced emissions program area shall be sufficient for compliance with the provisions of this paragraph (d) in the basic program area.

(3) (a) Effective July 1, 1993, any home rule city, city, town, or county shall, after holding a public hearing and receiving public comment and upon request by the governing body of such local government to the department of public health and environment and the department of revenue and after approval by the general assembly acting by bill pursuant to paragraph (e) of this subsection (3), be included in the program area established pursuant to sections 42-4-301 to 42-4-316. When such a request is made, said departments and governing body shall agree to a start-up date for the program in such area, and, on or after such date, all motor vehicles, as defined in section 42-4-304 (18), which are registered in the area shall be inspected and required to comply with the provisions of sections 42-4-301 to 42-4-316 and rules and regulations adopted pursuant thereto as if such area was included in the program area. Except as provided in paragraph (c) of this subsection (3), the department of public health and environment and the department of revenue, the executive director, and the commission shall perform all functions and exercise all powers related to the program in areas included

in the program pursuant to this subsection (3) that they are otherwise required to perform under sections 42-4-301 to 42-4-316.

(b) Effective July 1, 1993, notwithstanding the provisions of section 42-4-304 (20), a local government with jurisdiction over an area excluded from the program area pursuant to section 42-4-304 (20) may request inclusion in the program area, and the exclusion under section 42-4-304 (20) shall not apply to vehicles registered within such area.

(c) Effective July 1, 1993, the inclusion pursuant to paragraph (a) or (b) of this subsection (3) of any home rule city, city, town, or county in the program area shall not be submitted to the United States environmental protection agency as a revision to the state implementation plan or otherwise included in such plan. Any governing body which requests inclusion of an area pursuant to paragraph (a) or (b) of this subsection (3) in the program area may, after a minimum period of five years, request termination of the program in such area, and the program in such area shall be terminated thirty days after the receipt by the department of revenue of such a request.

(d) Effective January 1, 1994, except for those entities included within the program area pursuant to section 42-4-304 (20), for inclusion in the program area, any home rule city, city, town, or county shall have the basic emissions program test requirements and standards implemented as its emissions inspection program.

(e) Unless a home rule city, city, town, or county violates national ambient air quality standards as established by the environmental protection agency, the inclusion pursuant to paragraph (a) or (b) of this subsection (3) of any home rule city, city, town, or county in the program area shall be contingent upon approval by the general assembly acting by bill to include any such home rule city, city, town, or county in the program area.

(4) (a) The seller of a motor vehicle that is inoperable or otherwise cannot be tested in accordance with rules promulgated by the department of revenue or that is being sold pursuant to part 18 or part 21 of this article is not required to obtain a certification of emissions control prior to the sale of the vehicle if the seller provides a written notice to the purchaser prior to completion of the sale that clearly indicates the following:

(I) The vehicle does not currently comply with the emissions requirements for the program area;

(II) The seller does not warrant that the vehicle will comply with emissions requirements; and

(III) The purchaser is responsible for complying with emissions requirements prior to registering the vehicle in the emissions program area.

(b) The department shall prepare a form to comply with the provisions of paragraph (a) of this subsection (4) and shall make such form available to dealers and other persons who are selling motor vehicles which are inoperable or otherwise cannot be tested in accordance with regulations promulgated by the department of revenue.

(c) If a motor vehicle is exempted from the requirement for obtaining a certification of emissions control prior to sale pursuant to this subsection (4), the new owner of the motor vehicle is required to obtain a certification of emissions control for such motor vehicle before registering it in the program area.

(5) (a) Notwithstanding any other provision of this section, any eligible motor vehicle registered in a clean screen program county that complies with the requirements of the clean screen program under the provisions of sections 42-4-305 (12), 42-4-306 (23), and 42-4-307 (10.5) (a), by passing the requirements of such program and applicable rules shall be deemed to have complied with the inspection requirements of this section for the applicable emissions inspection cycle. For purposes of this subsection (5), "eligible motor vehicle" means a motor vehicle, including trucks, for model years 1978 and earlier having a gross vehicle weight rating of six thousand pounds or less and for model years 1979 and newer having a gross vehicle weight rating of eight thousand five hundred pounds or less.

(b) (I) If the commission does not specify a date for the county clerks and recorders in the basic emissions program area to begin collecting emissions inspection fees at the time of registration pursuant to section 42-3-304 (19) (a), or if the contractor determines that the motor vehicle required to be registered in the basic program area has complied with the inspection requirements pursuant to this subsection (5), a notice shall be sent to the owner of the vehicle identifying the owner of the vehicle, the license plate number, and other pertinent registration information, and stating that the vehicle has successfully complied with the applicable emission requirements. Such notice shall also include a notification that the registered owner of the vehicle may return the notice to the contractor with the payment as set forth on the notice to pay for the clean screen program. Upon receipt of the payment from the motor vehicle owner, the county clerk shall be notified that the motor vehicle has complied with the inspection requirements pursuant to this subsection (5).

(II) For vehicles with registration renewals coming due on or after the dates specified by the commission for county clerks and recorders to collect emissions inspection fees at the time of registration, if the contractor determines that a motor vehicle required to be registered in the program area has complied with the inspection requirements pursuant to this subsection (5), the contractor shall send a notice to the department of revenue identifying the owner of the vehicle, the license plate number, and any other pertinent registration information, stating that the vehicle has successfully complied with the applicable emission requirements.

(c) The department shall, by contract with a private vendor or by rule, establish a procedure for a vehicle owner to obtain the necessary emissions-related documents for the registration and operation of a vehicle that has complied with the inspection requirements pursuant to this subsection (5).

42-4-311. Operation of inspection and readjustment stations - inspection-only facilities - fleet inspection stations - motor vehicle dealer test facilities - enhanced inspection centers. (1) (a) No inspection and readjustment station license, inspection-only facility license, fleet inspection station license, motor vehicle dealer test facility license, or enhanced inspection center contract may be assigned or transferred or used at any other than the station, facility, or center therein designated, and every such license or authorization for an enhanced inspection center shall be posted in a conspicuous place at the facility designated.

(b) Beginning January 1, 1995, no emissions inspector license or authorization shall be assigned or transferred except to a licensed inspection-only facility, fleet inspection station, or enhanced inspection center.

(c) No emissions inspector or emissions mechanic license or authorization may be assigned or transferred, nor shall the inspection and adjustment be made by such emissions inspector or emissions mechanic except at a licensed inspection and readjustment station, inspection-only facility, fleet inspection station, or motor vehicle dealer test facility or authorized enhanced inspection center.

(2) A licensed inspection and readjustment station, inspection-only facility, fleet inspection station, motor vehicle dealer test facility, or authorized enhanced inspection center shall not issue a certification of emissions control to a motor vehicle except upon forms prescribed by the executive director. Such station, facility, or center shall not issue a certification of emissions compliance or emission waiver unless the licensed or authorized emissions inspector or emissions mechanic performing the inspection determines that:

(a) The exhaust gas and, if applicable, evaporative emissions from the motor vehicle comply with the applicable emissions standards and there is no evidence of emissions system tampering nor visible smoke, in which case a certification of emissions compliance shall be issued;

(b) The exhaust gas and, if applicable, evaporative emissions from the motor vehicle do not comply with the applicable emissions standards after the adjustments and repairs required by section 42-4-306 have been performed and there is no evidence of emissions system tampering or visible smoke, in which case a certification of emissions waiver shall be issued. A fleet emission inspector shall not issue a certification of emissions waiver within the enhanced program area.

(3) (a) (I) A verification of emissions test shall be issued to a motor vehicle by a licensed inspection and readjustment station, inspection-only facility, fleet inspection station, or motor vehicle dealer test facility or authorized enhanced inspection center at the time such vehicle is issued a certification of emissions control.

(II) No verification of emissions test is required to be issued to or required for any motor vehicle that is registered as a collector's item pursuant to section 42-12-401.

(III) (A) Repealed.

(B) Commencing July 1, 2001, every inspection and readjustment station, fleet inspection station, and inspection-only facility shall monthly transmit to the department the sum of twenty-five cents per motor vehicle inspection performed by such entity pursuant to this part 3 if the motor vehicle passes such inspection or is granted a waiver. No refund or credit shall be allowed for any unused verification of emissions test forms.

(C) The contractor shall monthly transmit to the department the sum of twenty-five cents per motor vehicle inspection performed by the contractor pursuant to this part 3 if the motor vehicle passes such inspection or is granted a waiver. No refund or credit shall be allowed for any unused verification of emissions test forms.

(b) The moneys collected by the department from the sale of verification forms shall be transmitted to the state treasurer, who shall credit such moneys to the AIR account, which account is created within the highway users tax fund. Moneys from the AIR account, upon appropriation by the general assembly, shall be expended only to pay the costs of administration and enforcement of the automobile inspection and readjustment program by the department and the department of public health and environment.

(4) (a) (I) A licensed inspection and readjustment station, inspection-only facility, or motor vehicle dealer test facility shall charge a fee not to exceed fifteen dollars for the inspection of vehicles, model year 1981 and older, at facilities licensed or authorized within either the basic or enhanced emissions program; except that for 1982 model and newer vehicles a test facility may charge a fee not to exceed twenty-five dollars.

(II) In no case shall any such fee exceed the maximum fee established by and posted by the station or facility pursuant to section 42-4-305 (5) for the inspection of any motor vehicle required to be inspected under section 42-4-310.

(b) A licensed emissions inspection and readjustment station shall charge a fee for performing the adjustments or repairs required for issuance of a certification of emissions waiver not to exceed the maximum charge established in section 42-4-310 and posted by the station pursuant to section 42-4-305.

(5) The fee charged in paragraph (a) of subsection (4) or subsection (6) of this section will be charged to all nonresident vehicle owners subject to the inspection requirement of section 42-4-310 and depending on the county of operation.

(6) (a) The fee charged for enhanced emissions inspections performed within the enhanced emissions program area on 1982 and later motor vehicles shall not be any greater than that determined by the contract and in no case greater than twenty-five dollars. The fee charged for clean screen inspections performed on vehicles registered in the basic area shall not be any greater than that determined by the contract and in no case greater than fifteen dollars. Such fee shall not exceed the maximum fee required to be posted by the enhanced inspection center pursuant to section 42-4-305 for the inspection of any motor vehicle required to be inspected under section 42-4-310.

(b) During the two-year renewal of the contract entered into pursuant to section 42-4-307 (10), the commission shall hold a hearing to determine the maximum fee that may be charged pursuant to the contract for inspections during any subsequent renewal term. Such maximum fee shall be based on estimated actual operating costs during the life of the contract, determined pursuant to the proceeding and an audit conducted by the office of the state auditor on the contractor, plus a percentage to be determined by the commission, not to exceed ten percent and not to exceed twenty-five dollars.

(c) Notwithstanding paragraphs (a) and (b) of this subsection (6), at such time that the plan developed pursuant to section 42-4-307.7 is implemented, the emissions inspection fee charged pursuant to the clean screen program shall not exceed nine dollars. Such fee shall be in accordance with section 42-3-304 (19) (a) (I).

(7) At least one free reinspection shall be provided for those vehicles initially failed at the inspection and readjustment station, inspection-only facility, or enhanced inspection center which conducted the initial inspection, within ten calendar days of such initial inspection.

42-4-312. Improper representation as emissions inspection and readjustment station - inspection-only facility - fleet inspection station - motor vehicle dealer test facility - enhanced inspection center. (1) No person shall in any manner represent any place as an inspection and readjustment station, inspection-only facility, fleet inspection station, motor vehicle dealer test facility, or enhanced inspection center or shall claim to be a licensed emissions inspector or licensed emissions mechanic unless such station, facility, center, or person has been issued and operates under a valid license issued by the department or contract with the state. If the license or contract is cancelled, suspended, or revoked, all evidence designating the station, facility, or center as a licensed inspection and readjustment station, inspection-only facility, fleet inspection station, or motor vehicle dealer test facility or authorized enhanced inspection center and indicative of licensed status of the station, facility, or center or emissions inspector or emissions mechanic shall be removed within five days after receipt of notice of such action.

(2) (a) The department shall have authority to suspend or revoke the inspection and readjustment station license, inspection-only facility license, fleet inspection license, or motor vehicle dealer test facility license or to seek termination of the contractor's contract and require surrender of said license and unused certification of emissions control forms and verification of emissions test forms held by such licensee or contractor when such station, facility, or center is not equipped as required, when such station, facility, or center is not operating from a location for which the license or contract was issued, when the approved location has been altered so that it will no longer qualify as a licensed station or facility or authorized center, or when inspections, repairs, or adjustments are not being made in accordance with applicable laws and the rules and regulations of the department or commission.

(b) The department shall also have authority to suspend or revoke the license of an emissions inspector or emissions mechanic and require surrender of said license when it determines that said inspector or mechanic is not qualified to perform the inspections, repairs, or adjustments or when inspections, repairs, or adjustments are not being made in accordance with applicable laws and the rules and regulations of the department or the commission.

(3) In addition to any other grounds for revocation or suspension, authority to suspend and revoke inspection and readjustment station licenses, inspection-only facility licenses, fleet inspection station licenses, motor vehicle dealer test facility licenses, or enhanced inspection center contracts, or to seek termination of a contractor's contract or an emissions inspector's or emissions mechanic's license and to require surrender of said licenses and unused certification of inspection forms and records of said station shall also exist upon a showing that:

(a) A vehicle which had been inspected and issued a certification of emissions compliance by said station, facility, or center or by said inspector or mechanic was in such condition that it did not, at the time of such inspection, comply with the law or the rules and regulations for issuance of such a certification; or

(b) An inspection and readjustment station, or emissions mechanic has demonstrated a pattern of issuing certifications of emissions waivers to vehicles which, at the time of issuance of such certifications, did not comply with the law or the rules and regulations for issuance of such certifications.

(4) Upon suspending the license of an inspection and readjustment station, inspection-only facility, fleet inspection station, or motor vehicle dealer test facility or an enhanced inspection center contract or of an emissions inspector or emissions mechanic as authorized in this section, the executive director shall immediately notify the licensee or contractor in writing and, upon request therefor, shall grant the licensee or contractor a hearing within thirty days after

receipt of such request, such hearing to be held in the county wherein the licensee or contractor resides, unless the executive director and the licensee or contractor agree that such hearing may be held in some other county. The executive director may request a hearing officer to act in the executive director's behalf. Upon such hearing, the executive director or the hearing officer may administer oaths and may issue subpoenas for the attendance of witnesses and the production of relevant books, records, and papers. Upon such hearing, the order of suspension or revocation may be rescinded, or, for good cause shown, the suspension may be extended for such period of time as the hearing person or body may determine, not exceeding one year, or the revocation order may be affirmed or reversed. The licensee shall not perform under the license pending the hearing and decision.

(5) Upon the final cancellation or termination of a contractor's contract, the executive director shall invoke the provisions of such contract to continue service until a new contract can be secured with qualified persons as supervised by the department of revenue.

42-4-313. Penalties. (1) (a) No person shall make, issue, or knowingly use any imitation or deceptively similar or counterfeit certification of emissions control form.

(b) No person shall possess a certification of emissions control if such person knows the same is fictitious, or was issued for another motor vehicle, or was issued without an emissions inspection having been made when required.

(c) Any person who violates any provision of this subsection (1) is guilty of a misdemeanor and, upon conviction thereof, shall be punished by a fine of not less than twenty-five dollars nor more than one thousand dollars, or by imprisonment in the county jail for not more than ninety days, or by both such fine and imprisonment.

(2) (a) No emissions inspector or emissions mechanic shall issue a certification of emissions control for a motor vehicle which does not qualify for the certification or verification issued.

(b) Any emissions inspector or emissions mechanic who issues a certification of emissions control in violation of paragraph (a) of this subsection (2) is guilty of a misdemeanor and, upon conviction thereof, shall be punished by a fine of not less than one hundred dollars nor more than one thousand dollars, or by imprisonment in the county jail for not more than ninety days, or by both such fine and imprisonment.

(3) (a) No person shall operate a motor vehicle registered or required to be registered in this state, nor shall any person allow such a motor vehicle to be parked on public property or on private property available for public use, without such vehicle having passed any necessary emissions test. The owner of any motor vehicle that is in violation of this paragraph (a) shall be responsible for payment of any penalty imposed under this section unless such owner proves that the motor vehicle was in the possession of another person without the owner's permission at the time of the violation.

(b) (Deleted by amendment, L. 2001, p. 1025, § 11, effective June 5, 2001.)

(c) Any vehicle owner who violates any provision of this section is guilty of a misdemeanor traffic offense and, upon conviction thereof, shall be punished by a fine of fifty dollars payable within thirty days after conviction.

(d) Any nonowner driver who violates any provision of this section is guilty of a misdemeanor traffic offense and, upon conviction thereof, shall be punished by a fine of fifteen dollars, payable within thirty days after conviction.

(e) The owner or driver may, in lieu of appearance, submit to the court of competent jurisdiction, within thirty days after the issuance of the notice and summons, the certification or proof of mailing specified in this subsection (3).

(f) Any fine collected pursuant to the provisions of this subsection (3) shall be retained by the jurisdiction in whose name such penalty was assessed.

(g) Nothing in this section shall be construed to limit the authority of any municipality, city, county, or city and county to adopt and enforce an ordinance or resolution pertaining to the enforcement of emissions control inspection requirements.

(h) Notwithstanding any other provision of this section, an owner of a vehicle that has failed under the high emitter program is in violation of this part 3 and shall be notified by mail by the contractor that his or her vehicle is not in compliance. The owner shall have thirty days to repair and test the vehicle successfully.

(i) A violator whose vehicle fails to comply with emission limits adopted by the commission pursuant to this part 3 shall be fined one hundred dollars per violation.

(j) After ninety days, registration shall be administratively suspended on a vehicle that remains out of compliance with this part 3. The registration shall not be reinstated until the vehicle owner provides proof of compliance with this part 3 and pays any applicable fines.

(4) (a) For the emissions program, a contractor who is awarded a contract to perform emissions inspections within the emissions program area shall be held accountable to the department of public health and environment and the department of revenue. Any such contractor shall be subject to civil penalties in accordance with this section or article 7 of title 25, C.R.S., as appropriate, for any violation of applicable laws or rules and regulations of the department of revenue or the commission.

(b) (I) Pursuant to the provisions of article 4 of title 24, C.R.S., the executive director may suspend for a period not less than six months the license of any operator or employee operating an inspection-only facility, fleet inspection station, or motor vehicle dealer test facility or may impose an administrative fine pursuant to subparagraph (II) of this paragraph (b), or may both suspend a license and impose a fine, if any such operator or employee, inspection-only facility, fleet inspection station, or motor vehicle dealer test facility engages in any of the following:

(A) Intentionally passing a failing vehicle;
(B) Performing any test by an unlicensed inspector;
(C) Performing a test on falsified test equipment;
(D) Failing a passing vehicle;
(E) Flagrantly misusing control documents; or
(F) Engaging in a pattern of noncompliance with any regulations of the department of revenue or the commission.

(II) The contract for operation of enhanced inspection centers shall specify administrative fines to be imposed for the violations enumerated in subparagraph (I) of this paragraph (b).

(c) Pursuant to the provisions of article 4 of title 24, C.R.S., the executive director shall impose administrative fines in amounts set by the executive director of not less than twenty-five dollars and not more than one thousand dollars against any operator or employee operating an inspection and readjustment station, an inspection-only facility, or a motor vehicle dealer test facility, or any contractor operating an enhanced inspection center or clean screen contractor that engages in two or more incidents per person, station, facility, or center, of any of the following:

(I) Test data entry violations;
(II) Test sequence violations;
(III) Emission retest procedural violations;
(IV) Vehicle emissions tag replacement test procedural violations;
(V) Performing any emissions test on non-certified equipment;
(VI) Wait-time and lane availability violations;
(VII) Physical emissions test examination violations;
(VIII) Knowingly passing failing vehicles; or
(IX) Knowingly failing passing vehicles.

42-4-314. Automobile air pollution control systems - tampering - operation of vehicle - penalty. (1) No person shall knowingly disconnect, deactivate, or otherwise render inoperable any air pollution control system which has been installed by the manufacturer of any automobile of a model year of 1968 or later, except to repair or replace a part or all of the system.

(2) No person shall operate on any highway in this state any automobile described in subsection (1) of this section knowing that any air pollution control system installed on such automobile has been disconnected, deactivated, or otherwise rendered inoperable.

(3) Any person who violates any provision of this section commits a class A traffic infraction. The department shall not assess any points under section 42-2-127 for a conviction pursuant to this section.

(4) The air quality control commission may adopt rules and regulations pursuant to sections 25-7-109 and 25-7-110, C.R.S., which permit or allow for the alteration, modification, or disconnection of manufacturer-installed air pollution control systems or manufacturer tuning specifications on motor vehicles for the purpose of controlling vehicle emissions. Nothing in this section shall prohibit the alteration or the conversion of a motor vehicle to operate on a gaseous fuel, if the resultant emissions are at levels complying with state and federal standards for that model year of motor vehicle.

(5) Nothing in this section shall be construed to prevent the adjustment or modification of motor vehicles to reduce vehicle emissions pursuant to section 215 of the federal "Clean Air Act", as amended, 42 U.S.C. sec. 7549.

42-4-315. Warranties. No provision of sections 42-4-301 to 42-4-316 shall be deemed to prevent, or interpreted so as to hinder, the enforcement of any applicable motor vehicle part or emissions control systems performance warranty.

42-4-316. AIR program - demonstration of compliance with ambient air quality standards and transportation conformity. (1) If the commission and the lead air quality planning agency of any portion of the program area agree that it has been demonstrated that any portion of the program meets ambient air quality standards and transportation conformity requirements, in compliance with federal acts, the commission may specify that the AIR program will no longer apply in that portion of the program area.

(2) The legislative audit committee shall cause to be conducted performance audits of the program, including the clean screen program. The first of such audits shall be completed not later than January 1, 2000, and shall be completed not later than January 1, 2004, and January 1 of each third year thereafter. Upon completion of the audit report, the legislative audit committee shall hold a public hearing for the purposes of a review of the report.

(3) (a) (Deleted by amendment, L. 2001, p. 1022, § 9, effective June 5, 2001.)

(b) In such audits, the determination as to whether an ongoing public need for the program has been demonstrated shall take into consideration the following factors, among others:

(I) The demonstrable effect on ambient air quality of the program;
(II) The cost to the public of the program;
(III) The cost-effectiveness of the program relative to other air pollution control programs;
(IV) The need, if any, for further reduction of air pollution caused by mobile sources to attain or maintain compliance with national ambient air quality standards;
(V) The application of the program to assure compliance with legally required warranties covering air pollution control equipment.

42-4-316.5. Termination of vehicle emissions testing program - repeal. The commission shall have the authority to eliminate all requirements for regularly scheduled basic or enhanced emissions inspections of motor vehicles. Notwithstanding any other provision of this part 3 and if the commission finds that this action does not violate federal air quality standards, the vehicle emissions inspection program set forth in sections 42-4-301 to 42-4-316 is repealed, effective December 31, 2010.

42-4-317. Purchase or lease of new motor vehicles by state agencies - clean-burning alternative fuels - definitions. (Repealed)

PART 4

DIESEL INSPECTION PROGRAM

42-4-401. Definitions. As used in this part 4, unless the context otherwise requires:

(1) "Certification of emissions control" means one of the following certifications, issued to the owner of a diesel vehicle which is subject to the diesel inspection program in order to indicate the status of inspection requirement compliance of such vehicle:

(a) "Certification of diesel smoke opacity compliance" is a document which indicates that the smoke emissions from the vehicle comply with applicable smoke opacity limits at the time of inspection or after required adjustments or repairs;

(b) "Certification of diesel smoke opacity waiver" is a document which indicates that the smoke emissions from the vehicle does not comply with the applicable smoke opacity limits after inspection, adjustment, and emissions related repairs.

(2) "Commission" means the air quality control commission.

(3) "Diesel emissions inspection station" means a facility which meets the requirements established by the commission, is licensed by the executive director, and is so equipped as to enable a diesel vehicle emissions-opacity inspection to be performed.

(4) "Diesel emissions inspector" means a person possessing a valid license to perform diesel emissions-opacity inspections in compliance with the requirements of the commission.

(5) "Diesel powered motor vehicle" or "diesel vehicle" as applicable to opacity inspections, includes only a motor vehicle with four wheels or more on the ground, powered by an internal combustion, compression ignition, diesel fueled engine, and also includes any motor vehicle having a personal property classification of A, B, or C, pursuant to section 42-3-106, as specified on its vehicle registration, and for which registration in this state is required for operation on the public roads and highways. "Diesel vehicle" does not include: Vehicles registered under section 42-12-301; vehicles taxed under section 42-3-306 (4); or off-the-road diesel powered vehicles or heavy construction equipment.

(6) "Executive director" means the executive director of the department of revenue or the executive director's designee.

(6.3) "Heavy-duty diesel vehicle" means a vehicle that is greater than fourteen thousand pounds gross vehicle weight rating.

(6.7) "Light-duty diesel vehicle" means a vehicle that is less than or equal to fourteen thousand pounds gross vehicle weight rating.

(7) "Opacity meter" means an optical instrument that is designed to measure the opacity of diesel exhaust gases.

(8) "Program area" means the counties of Adams, Arapahoe, Boulder, Douglas, El Paso, Jefferson, Larimer, and Weld, and the cities and counties of Broomfield and Denver, excluding the following areas:

(a) That portion of Adams county which is east of Kiowa creek (Range 62 West, Townships 1, 2, and 3 South) between the Adams-Arapahoe county line and the Adams-Weld county line;

(b) That portion of Arapahoe county which is east of Kiowa creek (Range 62 West, Townships 4 and 5 South) between the Arapahoe-Elbert county line and the Arapahoe-Adams county line;

(c) That portion of El Paso county which is east of the following boundary, defined on a south-to-north axis: From the El Paso-Pueblo county line north (upstream) along Chico creek (Ranges 63 and 64 West, Township 17 South) to Hanover road, then east along Hanover road (El Paso county route 422) to Peyton highway, then north along Peyton highway (El Paso county route 463) to Falcon highway, then west on Falcon highway (El Paso county route 405) to Peyton highway, then north on Peyton highway (El Paso county route 405) to Judge Orr road, then west on Judge Orr road (El Paso county route 108) to Elbert road, then north on Elbert road (El Paso county route 91) to the El Paso-Elbert county line;

(d) That portion of Larimer county which is west of the boundary defined on a north-to-south axis by Range 71 West and that portion which is north of the boundary defined on an east-to-west axis by Township 10 North;

(e) That portion of Weld county which is outside the corporate boundaries of Greeley, Evans, La Salle, and Garden City and, in addition, is outside the following boundary: Beginning at the point of intersection of the west boundary line of section 21, township six north, range sixty-six west and state highway 392, east along state highway 392 to the point of intersection with Weld county road 37; then south along Weld county road 37 to the point of intersection with Weld county road 64; then east along Weld county road 64 to the point of intersection with Weld county road 43; then south along Weld county road 43 to the point of intersection with Weld county road 62; then east along Weld county road 62 to the point of intersection with Weld county road 49; then south along Weld county road 49 to the point of intersection with the south boundary line of section 13, township five north, range sixty-five west; then west along the south boundary line of section 13, township five north, range sixty-five west, section 14, township five north, range sixty-five west, and section 15, township five north, range sixty-five west; then, from the southwest corner of section 15, township five west, range sixty-five west, south along the east boundary line of section 21, township five north, range sixty-five west, and section 28, township five north, range sixty-five west; then west along the south boundary line of section 28, township five north, range sixty-five west; then south along the east boundary line of section 32, township five north, range sixty-five west, and section 5, township four north, range sixty-five west; then west along the south boundary line of section 5, township four north, range sixty-five west, section 6, township four north, range sixty-five west, and section 1, township four north, range sixty-six west; then north along the west boundary line of section 1, township four north, range sixty-six west, and section 36, township five north, range sixty-six west; then, from the point of intersection of the west boundary line of section 36, township five north, range sixty-six west and Weld county road 52, west along Weld county road 52 to the point of intersection with Weld county road 27; then north along Weld county road 27 to the point of intersection with the south boundary line of section 18, township five north, range sixty-six west; then west along the south boundary line of section 18, township five north, range sixty-six west, section 13, township five north, range sixty-seven west, and section 14, township five north, range sixty-seven west; then north along the west boundary line of section 14, township five north, range sixty-seven west, section 11, township five north, range sixty-seven west, and section 2, township five north, range sixty-seven west; then east along the north boundary line of section 2, township five north, range sixty-seven west, section 1, township five north, range sixty-seven west, section 6, township five north, range sixty-six west, and section 5, township five north, range sixty-six west; then, from the northeast corner of section 5, township five north, range sixty-six west, north along the west boundary line of section 33, township six north, range sixty-six west, section 28, township six north, range sixty-six west, and section 21, township six north, range sixty-six west, to the point of beginning.

(9) "Smoke limit" means the maximum amount of allowable smoke opacity level as established by the commission.

42-4-402. Administration of inspection program. The department shall have responsibility for administering the diesel inspection program in accordance with the authority exercised by the executive director under the provisions of this part 4.

42-4-403. Powers and duties of the commission. (1) The commission shall be responsible for the adoption of rules and regulations which are necessary to implement the diesel inspection program including:

(a) Regulations governing procedures for:

(I) Testing and licensing of diesel emissions inspectors;

(II) Licensure of diesel emission inspection stations;

(III) Standards and specifications for the approval, operation, calibration, and certification of exhaust smoke opacity meters;

(IV) Proper performance of diesel opacity inspections and emissions system control inspections;

(b) Issuance of the following types of certifications of emissions control by licensed diesel emission inspectors:

(I) A certification of diesel smoke opacity compliance if, at the time of inspection, the smoke opacity from a diesel vehicle is in compliance with the applicable smoke opacity limits;

(II) A certification of diesel smoke opacity waiver if, at the time of inspection, the smoke opacity from a diesel vehicle does not comply with the applicable smoke opacity limits but such vehicle is adjusted or repaired to specifications as provided by regulation of the commission;

(III) A temporary certification of diesel smoke opacity compliance for diesel vehicles required to be repaired, if such repairs are delayed due to the unavailability of needed parts. The results of the initial smoke opacity test and final test shall be given to the owner of the diesel vehicle and reported to the department of public health and environment.

(2) (a) The commission shall promulgate and from time to time revise regulations on inspection procedures and smoke opacity limits when such procedures and limits have been proven cost-effective and air pollution control-effective on the basis of best available scientific research.

(b) Smoke limits shall not require unreasonable levels of emissions performance for a properly operated and maintained diesel vehicle of a given model year and technology, and such smoke limits shall be no less than twenty percent for five seconds minimum.

(c) The commission may also develop peak smoke opacity limits, but such limits shall not be less than forty percent for less than one second.

(d) Notwithstanding any other provisions of this subsection (2), for inspections conducted between January 1, 1990, and December 31, 1990, the smoke opacity limits shall be forty percent for five seconds minimum, and no diesel vehicle shall fail the smoke opacity inspection for peak limits.

(3) (a) The commission shall annually evaluate the diesel inspection program to determine but not limit the number of diesel vehicles which fail to meet the applicable smoke opacity limits after adjustments and repairs.

(b) If the commission finds that a significant number of diesel vehicles do not meet the applicable smoke opacity limits after adjustments or repairs are made, the commission shall develop recommendations designed to improve the air pollution control-effectiveness of the diesel inspection program in a cost-effective manner and shall submit such recommendations to the general assembly.

(4) In addition to any other authority granted under this section, the commission shall adopt regulations requiring each licensed diesel emissions inspection station to post, at the station, in a clearly legible manner and in a conspicuous place, the fee which shall be charged for performing a diesel emission-opacity inspection.

(5) The commission may exempt diesel vehicles of any make, model, or model year from the provisions of the diesel inspection program when inspection would be inappropriate for such vehicles. The exemption may include diesel vehicles which are required to be registered and inspected January, 1990.

(6) (a) Notwithstanding any other provisions to the contrary, the commission shall not have authority to adopt emission standards or implement an inspection and maintenance program that would result in emission requirements or an in-use testing or compliance demonstration that would be more stringent than the emission standards and test procedures adopted by the United States environmental protection agency for the corresponding model year and class of vehicle or engine.

(b) The commission shall determine by accepted scientific analysis that any emission standards and in-use test procedures it may adopt shall be designed so that any engine or vehicle which would pass the appropriate federal certification test shall also pass the inspection and maintenance test adopted by the commission for that engine or vehicle.

42-4-404. Powers and duties of the executive director of the department of public health and environment. (1) (a) The executive director of the department of public health and environment, referred to in this section as the "executive director", shall develop a program for the training, testing, and retesting of diesel emissions inspectors, which program may be funded by tuition charged to the participants.

(b) Those persons who successfully complete the testing set forth in paragraph (a) of this subsection (1) shall be recommended to the department of revenue for licensure.

(2) The executive director shall instruct the department of revenue to issue a license as a diesel inspection station to one or more parties with either new or existing diesel emissions inspection facilities. Such instruction shall be based on, among other factors:

(a) Any requirements for licensure set by the commission by rule and regulation pursuant to section 42-4-403;

(b) The requirements set forth in section 42-4-407;

(c) The geographical coverage which would result for licensing the station.

(d) Repealed.

(3) (a) The executive director shall continuously evaluate the diesel emissions inspection program. Such evaluation shall be based on continuing research conducted by the department of public health and environment and other engineering data and shall include assessments of the cost-effectiveness and air pollution control effectiveness of the program.

(b) The executive director shall submit such evaluation and any recommendations for program changes to the general assembly by December 1 of each year, in order that the general assembly may annually review the diesel emissions inspection program.

(4) The executive director shall implement an ongoing project designed to inform the public concerning the operation of the diesel emissions inspection program and the benefits to be derived from such program. The executive director shall also prepare a handbook which shall explain the diesel emissions inspection program, the owner's or operator's responsibilities under the program, the licensure of stations and inspectors, and any other aspects of the program which the executive director determines would be beneficial to the public. In addition to the distribution of such handbook, the executive director shall actively seek the assistance of the electronic and print media in communicating information to the public on the operation of the inspection program and shall utilize any other means of disseminating such information which may be likely to effectuate the purpose of such program.

(5) The executive director may establish and operate technical or administrative centers, if necessary, for the proper administration of the diesel inspection program or may utilize existing centers established for the AIR program pursuant to section 42-4-307.

(6) Repealed.

42-4-405. Powers and duties of executive director. (1) The executive director is authorized to issue, deny, cancel, suspend, or revoke licensure for, and shall furnish instructions and all necessary forms to, diesel emissions inspection stations and inspectors. Fees for such licenses shall be established by regulations promulgated by the executive director.

(2) The executive director shall supervise the activities of licensed diesel emissions inspection stations and inspectors and shall cause inspections to be made of such stations and records and such inspectors for compliance with licensure requirements. The accuracy of a licensed station's smoke opacity meters shall be inspected not less than once every sixty days.

(3) The executive director shall require the surrender of any license which has been issued upon the cancellation, suspension, or revocation of the license for a violation of any of the provisions or of any of the regulations of the diesel emissions inspection program established pursuant to this part 4.

(4) The executive director shall adopt regulations for the administration and operation of

diesel emissions inspection stations and for the issuance, identification, and use of certifications of emissions control and shall adopt such rules and regulations as may be necessary to improve the effectiveness of the diesel emissions inspection program.

(5) (a) On and after January 1, 1991, the executive director shall hold hearings annually concerning the maximum inspection fee in order to ascertain whether such fee provides fair compensation for performing diesel emission-opacity inspections and represents an equitable charge to the consumer for such inspection.

(b) Repealed.

42-4-406. Requirement of certification of emissions control for registration - testing for diesel smoke opacity compliance. (1) (a) A diesel vehicle in the program area that is registered or required to be registered pursuant to article 3 of this title, routinely operates in the program area, or is principally operated from a terminal, maintenance facility, branch, or division located within the program area shall not be sold, registered for the first time, or reregistered unless such vehicle has been issued a certification of emissions control within:

(I) The past twelve months if the motor vehicle is a heavy-duty diesel vehicle that is over ten model years old;

(II) The last twenty-four months if the motor vehicle is a heavy-duty diesel vehicle that is ten model years old or newer;

(III) The last twelve months if the motor vehicle is a light-duty diesel vehicle that is at least ten model years old or that is model year 2003 or older; or

(IV) The last twenty-four months if the motor vehicle is a light-duty diesel vehicle that is ten model years old or newer and that is model year 2004 or newer.

(b) (I) A certification of emissions control shall be issued to any diesel vehicle that has been inspected and tested pursuant to subsection (2) of this section for diesel smoke opacity compliance and was found at such time to be within the smoke opacity limits established by the commission.

(II) Notwithstanding the provisions of subparagraph (I) of this paragraph (b), new diesel vehicles, required under this section to have a certification of emissions control, shall be issued a certification of emissions compliance without inspection or testing. Prior to the expiration of such certification, such vehicle shall be inspected and a certification of emissions control shall be obtained for diesel smoke opacity compliance. Such certificate shall expire on the earliest to occur of the following:

(A) The anniversary of the day of the issuance of such certification when such vehicle has reached its fourth model year if it is a light-duty diesel vehicle;

(B) The anniversary of the day of the issuance of such certification when such vehicle has reached its fourth model year if it is a heavy-duty diesel vehicle; or

(C) On the date of the transfer of ownership if such date is within twelve months before such certification would expire pursuant to sub-subparagraph (A) or (B) of this subparagraph (II), unless such transfer of ownership is a transfer from the lessor to the lessee.

(2) (a) On or after January 1, 1990, all heavy duty diesel vehicles in the program area not subject to the provisions of section 42-4-414, with fleets of nine or more, shall be required to be tested for diesel smoke opacity compliance at a licensed diesel inspection station by submitting to loaded mode opacity testing utilizing dynamometers or on-road tests as prescribed by the commission.

(b) Light-duty diesel vehicles in the program area shall be required to be tested for diesel smoke opacity compliance at a licensed diesel inspection station by submitting to loaded mode opacity testing utilizing dynamometers.

42-4-407. Requirements for a diesel emission-opacity inspection - licensure as diesel emissions inspection station - licensure as emissions inspector. (1) A diesel emission-opacity inspection shall not be performed, nor shall a certification of emissions control be issued unless such inspection was performed at a licensed diesel inspection station or self-certification fleet station as defined in section 42-4-414 by a licensed diesel emissions inspector.

(2) No station shall be licensed as a diesel emissions inspection station unless the executive director finds that:

(a) The facilities of the station are of adequate size and the station is properly equipped. Such equipment shall include:

(I) A smoke opacity meter which may be owned or leased and which has been approved as being in good working order by the executive director and has been registered with the department of public health and environment;

(II) Any other equipment or testing devices which are required by rule or regulation of the commission;

(b) The owner or operator of the station has one or more licensed diesel emission inspectors employed or under contract and such inspectors are responsible for all diesel emission-opacity inspections and the issuance of all certifications of emissions control;

(c) Inspection procedures shall be properly conducted and shall include a smoke opacity inspection. For model years 1991 and newer, inspection procedures shall include evaluation of applicable emissions control systems.

(3) Applications for licensure as a diesel inspection station shall be made on forms prescribed by the executive director.

(4) No person shall be licensed as a diesel emissions inspector unless the person has demonstrated necessary skills and competence in the performance of diesel inspection by passing a qualification test developed and administered by

42-4-408. Operation of diesel inspection station. (1) (a) A licensed diesel inspection station shall issue a certification of diesel emissions control to a diesel vehicle only upon forms issued by the executive director.

(b) A certification of diesel emissions control shall be issued by a licensed diesel inspection station to a diesel vehicle only after the licensed diesel emission inspector performing the inspection determines that:

(I) The smoke opacity levels from the diesel vehicle comply with the applicable smoke opacity limits, in which case a certification of diesel emission compliance shall be issued;

(II) The smoke opacity levels from the diesel vehicle do not comply with the applicable smoke opacity limits after adjustment or repair required in accordance to commission rules have been performed, in which case a certification of diesel smoke opacity waiver shall be issued.

(2) Notwithstanding the provisions of subsection (1) of this section, no certification of diesel emissions control may be issued to a diesel vehicle of model year 1991 and newer if there is evidence of diesel emissions control system tampering.

(3) A licensed diesel emissions inspection station shall charge a fee as set by the commission for the inspection of any diesel vehicle pursuant to this section. Such fee shall be intended to encompass all costs related to the inspection, including those costs incurred by the inspection station, the department of revenue, and the department of public health and environment. No fee that is charged pursuant to this section shall exceed the posted hourly shop rate for one hour. Such fee shall be posted by the inspection station pursuant to regulations set by the commission. Personnel within the testing inspection station shall notify the owner of the diesel vehicle to be tested of the fee before commencing any testing activities.

42-4-409. Improper representation of a diesel inspection station. (1) The executive director shall have the authority to suspend or revoke the diesel inspection license and unused certification of diesel emissions control forms held by a licensed inspection station for the following reasons:

(a) The station is not equipped as required;

(b) The station is not operating from a location for which licensure was granted;

(c) The licensed location has been altered so that it no longer qualifies as a diesel inspection station;

(d) Diesel inspections are not being performed with applicable laws, rules, or regulations of the commission or the executive director.

(2) The executive director shall also have authority to suspend or revoke the license of a diesel emissions inspector and require surrender of such license when the executive director determines that the inspector is not qualified to perform the diesel inspection or when inspections do not comply with applicable laws and the rules and regulations of the executive director or commission.

42-4-410. Inclusion in the diesel inspection program. (1) (a) Any home rule city, town, or county shall be included in the diesel inspection program set forth in this part 4 upon request by the governing body of such local government to the department of revenue and the department of public health and environment.

(b) When such a request is made, the departments and governing body shall agree to a start-up date for the diesel inspection program in such areas. Such a date shall be administratively practical and agreed to by the departments.

(c) On or after the dates agreed to pursuant to paragraph (b) of this subsection (1), diesel vehicles which are registered in the area shall be inspected and shall be required to comply with the provisions of this part 4 and rules and regulations adopted pursuant thereto as if such area was included in the program area.

(2) The executive directors of the departments of revenue and health and the commission shall perform all functions and exercise all phases related to the diesel emissions inspection program that they are otherwise required to perform under this part 4 in areas included in the program pursuant to this section.

42-4-411. Applicability of this part to heavy-duty diesel fleets of nine or more. Diesel-powered motor vehicles subject to the provisions of section 42-4-414 shall not be subject to the diesel emissions inspection program set forth in this part 4 unless the conditions set forth in section 42-4-414 (3) (c) have been met.

42-4-412. Air pollution violations. (1) (a) A person commits a class 2 petty offense, as specified in section 18-1.3-503, C.R.S., if the person causes or permits the emission into the atmosphere from:

(I) Any motor vehicle, including a motorcycle, powered by gasoline or any fuel except diesel of any visible air pollutant as defined in section 25-7-103 (1.5), C.R.S.;

(II) Any diesel-powered motor vehicle, of any visible air pollutant, as defined in section 25-7-103 (1.5), C.R.S., which creates an unreasonable nuisance or danger to the public health, safety, or welfare.

(b) Violations of this section may be determined by visual observations, including the snap acceleration opacity test, or by test procedures using opacity measurements.

(c) The provisions of paragraph (a) of this subsection (1) shall not apply to emissions caused by cold engine start-up.

(2) (a) The air quality control commission shall determine the minimum emission level of

visible air pollutants from diesels which shall be considered to create an unreasonable nuisance or danger to the public health, safety, and welfare. Such minimum emission level shall be based on smoke levels attainable by correctly operated and maintained in-use diesel vehicles, considering altitude and other reasonable factors affecting visible smoke levels. In no case shall such level be less than twenty percent opacity when observed for five seconds or more. On interstate highways, opacity may be observed for ten seconds. Standards for transient conditions with no time limit shall also be established. Not later than December 1, 1979, the division shall develop a training course and qualification test designed to enable peace officers and environmental officers to ascertain violations of such standards without reference to opacity levels and to distinguish between air pollutants as defined in section 25-7-103 (1.5), C.R.S., and steam or water vapor.

(b) (I) The Colorado state patrol of the department of public safety shall offer the training course and qualification test.

(II) (Deleted by amendment, L. 96, p. 1263, § 171, effective August 7, 1996.)

(3) (a) This section shall apply only to motor vehicles intended, designed, and manufactured primarily for use in carrying passengers or cargo on roads, streets, and highways.

(b) Subparagraph (II) of paragraph (a) of subsection (1) of this section shall apply to all areas of the state except the program area, which program area shall be subject to section 42-4-413.

(4) (a) Effective January 1, 1980, the offense of causing air pollution pursuant to this section, upon conviction, is punishable by a fine of twenty-five dollars.

(b) Subsequent offenses involving the same motor vehicle within one year of a conviction under the provisions of paragraph (a) of this subsection (4), upon conviction, shall be punishable by a fine of one hundred dollars.

(c) Any owner who receives a citation under the provisions of this section may continue to use the vehicle for which the offense is alleged, without restriction, until such owner's conviction.

(d) Any fines collected pursuant to the provisions of this subsection (4) shall be divided in equal amounts and transmitted to the treasurer of the local jurisdiction in whose name the penalty was assessed and to the state treasurer for credit to the general fund.

42-4-413. Visible emissions from diesel-powered motor vehicles unlawful - penalty. (1) (a) Effective January 1, 1987, no owner or operator of a diesel-powered vehicle shall cause or knowingly permit the emission from the vehicle of any visible air contaminants that exceed the emission level as described in section 42-4-412 (2) (a) within the program area.

(b) As used in this section:

(I) "Air contaminant" means any fume, odor, smoke, particulate matter, vapor, gas, or combination thereof, except water vapor or steam condensate.

(II) "Emission" means a discharge or release of one or more air contaminants into the atmosphere.

(III) "Opacity" means the degree to which an air contaminant emission obscures the view of a trained observer, expressed in percentage of the obscuration or the percentage to which transmittance of light is reduced by an air contaminant emission.

(IV) "Trained observer" means a person who is certified by the department of public health and environment as trained in the determination of opacity.

(2) (a) A police officer or other peace officer who is a trained observer, or an environmental officer employed by a local government and certified by the department of public health and environment to determine opacity, at any time upon reasonable cause, may issue a summons personally to the operator of a motor vehicle emitting visible air contaminants in violation of paragraph (a) of subsection (1) of this section.

(b) (I) Any owner or operator of a diesel-powered motor vehicle receiving the summons issued pursuant to paragraph (a) of this subsection (2) or mailed pursuant to subparagraph (II) of paragraph (d) of this subsection (2) shall comply therewith and shall secure a certification of opacity compliance from a state emissions technical center that such vehicle conforms to the requirements of this section. Said certification shall be returned to the owner or operator for presentation in court as provided in paragraph (c) of this subsection (2).

(II) A fee of not more than six dollars and fifty cents shall be charged by emission technical centers for a certification of opacity compliance inspection and the certificate of no-smoke. Such fee shall be transmitted to the state treasurer, who shall credit the same to the AIR account established in section 42-4-311 (3) (b).

(c) (I) Any owner who violates any provision of this section is guilty of a misdemeanor traffic offense and, upon conviction thereof, except as provided in subparagraph (II) of this paragraph (c), shall be punished by a fine of one hundred dollars, payable within thirty days after conviction.

(II) If the owner submits to the court of competent jurisdiction within thirty days after the issuance of the summons proof that the owner has disposed of the vehicle for junk parts or immobilized the vehicle and if the owner also submits to the court within such time the registration and license plates for the vehicle, the owner shall be punished by a fine of twenty-five dollars. If the owner wishes to relicense the vehicle in the future, the owner shall obtain the certification required in paragraph (b) of this subsection (2).

(d) (I) Any nonowner operator who violates any provision of this section is guilty of a misdemeanor traffic offense and, upon conviction thereof, except as provided in subparagraph (II) of this paragraph (d), shall be punished by a fine of one hundred dollars, payable within thirty days after conviction.

(II) If the operator submits to the court of competent jurisdiction within thirty days after the issuance of the summons proof that the operator was not the owner of the vehicle at the time the summons was issued and that the operator mailed, within five days after issuance thereof, a copy of the notice and summons by certified mail to the owner of the vehicle at the address on the registration, the operator shall be punished by a fine of twenty-five dollars.

(e) Upon a showing of good cause that compliance with this section cannot be made within thirty days after issuance of the notice and summons, the court of competent jurisdiction may extend the period of time for compliance as may appear justified.

(f) The owner or operator, in lieu of appearance, may submit to the court of competent jurisdiction, within thirty days after the issuance of the notice and summons, the certification or proof of mailing specified in this subsection (2) together with the fine of twenty-five dollars.

(3) Any fine collected pursuant to the provisions of this section shall be transmitted to the treasurer of the local jurisdiction in which the violation occurred.

42-4-414. Heavy-duty diesel fleet inspection and maintenance program - penalty - rules. (1) The commission shall develop and implement, effective January 1, 1987, a fleet inspection and maintenance program for diesel-powered motor vehicles of more than fourteen thousand pounds gross vehicle weight rating. Regional transportation district buses, state, county, and municipal vehicles, and private diesel fleets shall participate in the program through self-certification inspection procedures as developed by the commission.

(2) (a) The commission shall promulgate rules requiring owners of diesel-powered motor vehicles, registered in the program area, routinely operated in the program area or principally operated from a terminal, maintenance facility, branch, or division located within the program area, and subject to the provisions of this section, to bring such vehicles into compliance with existing opacity standards set forth in section 42-4-412. Such rules and regulations shall be strictly construed, shall require no more than normal and reasonable maintenance practices, and shall not require additional fees or loaded mode testing equipment. Owners of fleets shall test opacity standards on a periodic basis.

(b) Such test shall use an opacity meter for such vehicles that are greater than ten model years old, but may use an automated opacity metering protocol for such vehicles that are less than or equal to ten model years old and of model year 1995 or newer.

(c) Such rules shall exempt a new diesel vehicle from testing until such vehicle has reached its second model year if it is a light-duty diesel vehicle, its fourth model year if it is a heavy-duty diesel vehicle, or until the date of the transfer of ownership prior to such expiration if such transfer is within twelve months before such exemption ends.

(d) Such rules shall provide for the testing of diesel vehicles every:

(I) Twelve months unless subparagraph (II) of this paragraph (d) applies; or

(II) The last twenty-four months if such vehicle is a heavy-duty diesel vehicle, equal to or less than ten model years old, and of model year 1995 or newer.

(2.5) An owner of a fleet registered in the program area may certify to the executive director or the executive director's designee, in a form and manner required by the executive director, that a diesel vehicle registered in the program area is physically based and principally operated from a terminal, division, or maintenance facility outside the program area. Any diesel vehicle registered in the program area, but certified to be physically based and principally operated from a terminal, division, or maintenance facility outside the program area, is exempt from this section. The commission shall promulgate rules to administer this subsection (2.5).

(3) (a) and (b) (Deleted by amendment, L. 2003, p. 1023, § 1, effective August 6, 2003.)

(c) On or after January 1, 1990, in addition to any other penalty set forth in this subsection (3), any owner who is subject to the provisions of this section and who commits an excessive violation of this section twice in a twelve-month period shall be subject to the provisions of this part 4. For purposes of this paragraph (c), "excessive violation" shall be that definition recommended by the governor's blue ribbon diesel task force in 1988 and thereafter adopted by the air quality control commission, or, if such task force does not make a recommendation, "excessive violation" shall be that definition adopted by the air quality control commission.

(4) As used in this section, "fleet" means nine or more diesel-powered motor vehicles.

Editor's note: Section 3 of chapter 259, Session Laws of Colorado 2011, provides that the act adding subsection (2.5) applies to heavy-duty diesel fleet vehicles registered in the program area of the diesel emission inspection program on or after January 1, 2012.

PART 5

SIZE - WEIGHT - LOAD

42-4-501. Size and weight violations - penalty. Except as provided in section 42-4-509, it is a traffic infraction for any person to drive or move or for the owner to cause or knowingly permit to be driven or moved on any highway any vehicle or vehicles of a size or weight exceeding the limitations stated in sections 42-4-502 to 42-4-512 or otherwise in violation of said sections or section 42-4-1407, except as permitted in section 42-4-510. The maximum size and weight of vehicles specified in said sections shall be lawful throughout this state, and local authorities shall have no power or authority to alter said limitations, except as express authority may be granted in section 42-4-106.

42-4-502. Width of vehicles. (1) The total outside width of any vehicle or the load thereon shall not exceed eight feet six inches, except as otherwise provided in this section.

(2) (a) A load of loose hay, including loosely bound, round bales, whether horse drawn or by motor, shall not exceed twelve feet in width.

(b) A vehicle and trailer may transport a load of rectangular hay bales if such vehicle and load do not exceed ten feet six inches in width.

(3) It is unlawful for any person to operate a vehicle or a motor vehicle which has attached thereto in any manner any chain, rope, wire, or other equipment which drags, swings, or projects in any manner so as to endanger the person or property of another.

(4) The total outside width of buses and coaches used for the transportation of passengers shall not exceed eight feet six inches.

(5) (a) The total outside width of vehicles as included in this section shall not be construed so as to prohibit the projection beyond such width of clearance lights, rearview mirrors, or other accessories required by federal, state, or city laws or regulations.

(b) The width requirements imposed by subsection (1) of this section shall not include appurtenances on recreational vehicles, including but not limited to motor homes, travel trailers, fifth wheel trailers, camping trailers, recreational park trailers, multipurpose trailers, and truck campers, all as defined in section 24-32-902, C.R.S., so long as such recreational vehicle, including such appurtenances, does not exceed a total outside width of nine feet six inches.

(6) Any person who violates any provision of this section commits a class B traffic infraction.

42-4-503. Projecting loads on passenger vehicles. No passenger-type vehicle, except a motorcycle, a bicycle, or an electrical assisted bicycle shall be operated on any highway with any load carried thereon extending beyond the line of the fenders on the left side of such vehicle nor extending more than six inches beyond the line of the fenders on the right side thereof. Any person who violates this section commits a class B traffic infraction.

42-4-504. Height and length of vehicles. (1) No vehicle unladen or with load shall exceed a height of thirteen feet; except that vehicles with a height of fourteen feet six inches shall be operated only on highways designated by the department of transportation.

(2) No single motor vehicle shall exceed a length of forty-five feet extreme overall dimension, inclusive of front and rear bumpers. The length of vehicles used for the mass transportation of passengers wholly within the limits of a town, city, or municipality or within a radius of fifteen miles thereof may extend to sixty feet. The length of school buses may extend to forty feet.

(3) Buses used for the transportation of passengers between towns, cities, and municipalities in the state of Colorado may be sixty feet extreme overall length, inclusive of front and rear bumpers but shall not exceed a height of thirteen feet six inches, if such buses are equipped to conform with the load and weight limitations set forth in section 42-4-508; except that buses with a height of fourteen feet six inches which otherwise conform to the requirements of this subsection (3) shall be operated only on highways designated by the department of transportation.

(4) No combination of vehicles coupled together shall consist of more than four units, and no such combination of vehicles shall exceed a total overall length of seventy feet. Said length limitation shall not apply to unladen truck tractor-semitrailer combinations when the semitrailer is fifty-seven feet four inches or less in length or to unladen truck tractor-semitrailer-trailer combinations when the semitrailer and the trailer are each twenty-eight feet six inches or less in length. Said length limitations shall also not apply to vehicles operated by a public utility when required for emergency repair of public service facilities or properties or when operated under special permit as provided in section 42-4-510, but, in respect to night transportation, every such vehicle and the load thereon shall be equipped with a sufficient number of clearance lamps on both sides and marker lamps upon the extreme ends of any projecting load to clearly mark the dimensions of such load.

(4.5) Notwithstanding the provisions of subsection (4) of this section, the following combinations of vehicles shall not exceed seventy-five feet in total overall length:

(a) Saddlemount combinations consisting of no more than four units;

(b) Laden truck tractor-semitrailer combinations; and

(c) Specialized equipment used in combination for transporting automobiles or boats. The overall length of such combination shall be exclusive of:

(I) Safety devices; however, such safety devices shall not be designed or used for carrying cargo;

(II) Automobiles or boats being transported;

(III) Any extension device that may be used for loading beyond the extreme front or rear ends of a vehicle or combination of vehicles; except that the projection of a load, including any extension devices loaded to the front of the vehicle, shall not extend more than four feet beyond the extreme front of the grill of such vehicle and no load or extension device may extend more than six feet to the extreme rear of the vehicle.

(5) The load upon any vehicle operated alone or the load upon the front vehicle of a

combination of vehicles shall not extend beyond the front wheels of such vehicles or vehicle or the front most point of the grill of such vehicle; but a load may project not more than four feet beyond the front most point of the grill assembly of the vehicle engine compartment of such a vehicle at a point above the cab of the driver's compartment so long as that part of any load projecting ahead of the rear of the cab or driver's compartment shall be so loaded as not to obscure the vision of the driver to the front or to either side.

(6) The length limitations of vehicles and combinations of vehicles provided for in this section as they apply to vehicles being operated and utilized for the transportation of steel, fabricated beams, trusses, utility poles, and pipes shall be determined without regard to the projection of said commodities beyond the extreme front or rear of the vehicle or combination of vehicles; except that the projection of a load to the front shall be governed by the provisions of subsection (5) of this section, and no load shall project to the rear more than ten feet.

(7) Any person who violates any provision of this section commits a class B traffic infraction.

42-4-505. Longer vehicle combinations - rules. (1) (a) Notwithstanding any other provision of this article to the contrary, the department of transportation, in the exercise of its discretion, may issue permits for the use of longer vehicle combinations. An annual permit for such use may be issued to each qualified carrier company. The carrier company shall maintain a copy of such annual permit in each vehicle operating as a longer vehicle combination; except that, if a peace officer, as described in section 16-2.5-101, C.R.S., or an authorized agent of the department of transportation may determine that the permit can be electronically verified at the time of contact, a copy of the permit need not be in each vehicle. The fee for the permit shall be two hundred fifty dollars per year.

(b) Notwithstanding the amount specified for the fee in paragraph (a) of this subsection (1), the executive director of the department by rule or as otherwise provided by law may reduce the amount of the fee if necessary pursuant to section 24-75-402 (3), C.R.S., to reduce the uncommitted reserves of the fund to which all or any portion of the fee is credited. After the uncommitted reserves of the fund are sufficiently reduced, the executive director of the department by rule or as otherwise provided by law may increase the amount of the fee as provided in section 24-75-402 (4), C.R.S.

(c) The department shall provide the option to a company filing for a permit under this section to file an express consent waiver that enables the company to designate a company representative to be a party of interest for a violation of this section. The appearance of the company representative in a court hearing without the operator when the operator has signed such waiver shall not be deemed the practice of law in violation of article 5 of title 12, C.R.S.

(2) The permits shall allow operation, over designated highways, of the following vehicle combinations of not more than three cargo units and neither fewer than six axles nor more than nine axles:

(a) An unladen truck tractor, a semitrailer, and two trailers. A semitrailer used with a converter dolly shall be considered a trailer. Semitrailers and trailers shall be of approximately equal lengths not to exceed twenty-eight feet six inches in length.

(b) An unladen truck tractor, a semitrailer, and a single trailer. A semitrailer used with a converter dolly shall be considered a trailer. Semitrailers and trailers shall be of approximately equal lengths not to exceed forty-eight feet in length. Notwithstanding any other restriction set forth in this section, such combination may have up to eleven axles when used to transport empty trailers.

(c) An unladen truck tractor, a semitrailer, and a single trailer, one trailer of which is not more than forty-eight feet long, the other trailer of which is not more than twenty-eight feet six inches long. A semitrailer used with a converter dolly shall be considered a trailer. The shorter trailer shall be operated as the rear trailer.

(d) A truck and single trailer, having an overall length of not more than eighty-five feet, the truck of which is not more than thirty-five feet long and the trailer of which is not more than forty feet long. For the purposes of this paragraph (d), a semitrailer used with a converter dolly shall be considered a trailer.

(3) (a) The long combinations are limited to interstate highway 25, interstate highway 76, interstate highway 70 west of its intersection with state highway 13 in Garfield county, interstate highway 70 east of its intersection with U.S. 40 and state highway 26, the circumferential highways designated I-225 and I-270, and state highway 133 in Delta county from mile marker 8.9 to mile marker 9.7. The department of transportation shall promulgate rules to provide carriers with reasonable ingress to and egress from such designated highway segments.

(b) Upon action by the congress of the United States to lift the freeze imposed by the federal "Intermodal Surface Transportation Efficiency Act of 1991", Pub.L. 102-240, as amended, concerning the use of longer vehicle combinations, either by the total freeze being lifted by congress or by the approval of pilot projects to expand the use of longer vehicle combinations by the states, the department of transportation shall undertake a process to evaluate both interstate and state highways for possible authorization by the department of additional highway segments for inclusion by the general assembly in paragraph (a) of this subsection (3). During the review process, the department shall solicit input from all relevant stakeholders and shall work within existing statutory and regulatory guidelines. The department shall commence the review process within ninety days after action by congress that would allow expansion of the longer vehicle combination route network in Colorado.

(4) The department of transportation shall promulgate rules and regulations governing the issuance of the permits, including, but not limited to, selection of carriers, driver qualifications, equipment selection, hours of operation, and safety considerations; except that they shall not include hazardous materials subject to regulation by the provisions of article 20 of this title.

(5) Any person who violates any provision of this section commits a class B traffic infraction.

42-4-506. Trailers and towed vehicles. (1) When one vehicle is towing another, the drawbar or other connection shall be of sufficient strength to pull all weight towed thereby, and said drawbar or other connection shall not exceed fifteen feet from one vehicle to the other, except the connection between any two vehicles transporting poles, pipe, machinery, or other objects of a structural nature which cannot readily be dismembered and except connections between vehicles in which the combined lengths of the vehicles and the connection does not exceed an overall length of fifty-five feet and the connection is of rigid construction included as part of the structural design of the towed vehicle.

(2) When one vehicle is towing another and the connection consists of a chain, rope, or cable, there shall be displayed upon such connection a white flag or cloth not less than twelve inches square.

(3) Whenever one vehicle is towing another, in addition to the drawbar or other connection, except a fifth wheel connection meeting the requirements of the department of transportation, safety chains or cables arranged in such a way that it will be impossible for the vehicle being towed to break loose from the vehicle towing in the event the drawbar or other connection were to be broken, loosened, or otherwise damaged shall be used. This subsection (3) shall apply to all motor vehicles, to all trailers, except semitrailers connected by a proper fifth wheel, and to any dolly used to convert a semitrailer to a full trailer.

(4) Any person who violates any provision of this section commits a class B traffic infraction.

42-4-507. Wheel and axle loads. (1) The gross weight upon any wheel of a vehicle shall not exceed the following:

(a) When the wheel is equipped with a solid rubber or cushion tire, eight thousand pounds;

(b) When the wheel is equipped with a pneumatic tire, nine thousand pounds.

(2) The gross weight upon any single axle or tandem axle of a vehicle shall not exceed the following:

(a) When the wheels attached to said axle are equipped with solid rubber or cushion tires, sixteen thousand pounds;

(b) Except as provided in paragraph (b.5) of this subsection (2), when the wheels attached to a single axle are equipped with pneumatic tires, twenty thousand pounds;

(b.5) When the wheels attached to a single axle are equipped with pneumatic tires and the vehicle or vehicle combination is a digger derrick or bucket boom truck operated by an electric utility on a highway that is not on the interstate system as defined in section 43-2-101 (2), C.R.S., twenty-one thousand pounds;

(c) When the wheels attached to a tandem axle are equipped with pneumatic tires, thirty-six thousand pounds for highways on the interstate system and forty thousand pounds for highways not on the interstate system.

(3) (a) Vehicles equipped with a self-compactor and used solely for the transporting of trash are exempted from the provisions of paragraph (b) of subsection (2) of this section.

(b) After January 1, 1987, the provisions of this subsection (3) shall be reviewed at a joint meeting of the senate transportation committee and the house transportation and energy committee in order to determine the effects of such provisions.

(4) For the purposes of this section:

(a) A single axle is defined as all wheels, whose centers may be included within two parallel transverse vertical planes not more than forty inches apart, extending across the full width of the vehicle.

(b) A tandem axle is defined as two or more consecutive axles, the centers of which may be included between parallel vertical planes spaced more than forty inches and not more than ninety-six inches apart, extending across the full width of the vehicle.

(5) The gross weight upon any one wheel of a steel-tired vehicle shall not exceed five hundred pounds per inch of cross-sectional width of tire.

(6) Any person who drives a vehicle or owns a vehicle in violation of any provision of this section commits a class 2 misdemeanor traffic offense.

42-4-508. Gross weight of vehicles and loads. (1) Except as provided in subsection (1.5) of this section, no vehicle or combination of vehicles shall be moved or operated on any highway or bridge when the gross weight thereof exceeds the limits specified below:

(a) (I) The gross weight upon any one axle of a vehicle shall not exceed the limits prescribed in section 42-4-507.

(II) Subject to the limitations prescribed in section 42-4-507, the gross weight of a vehicle having two axles shall not exceed thirty-six thousand pounds.

(III) Subject to the limitations prescribed in section 42-4-507, the gross weight of a single vehicle having three or more axles shall not exceed fifty-four thousand pounds.

(b) Subject to the limitations prescribed in section 42-4-507, the maximum gross weight of any vehicle or combination of vehicles shall not exceed that determined by the formula W equals 1,000 (L plus 40), W = the gross weight in pounds, L = the length in feet between the centers of the first and last axles of such vehicle or combination of vehicles, but in computation of this formula no gross vehicle weight shall exceed eighty-five thousand pounds. For the purposes of this section, where a combination of vehicles is used, no vehicle shall carry a gross weight of less than ten percent of the overall gross weight of the combination of vehicles; except that these limitations shall not apply to specialized trailers of fixed public utilities whose axles may carry less than ten percent of the weight of the combination. The limitations provided in this section shall be strictly construed and enforced.

(c) Notwithstanding any other provisions of this section, except as may be authorized under section 42-4-510, no vehicle or combination of vehicles shall be moved or operated on any highway or bridge which is part of the national system of interstate and defense highways, also known as the interstate system, when the gross weight of such vehicle or combination of vehicles exceeds the following specified limits:

(I) Subject to the limitations prescribed in section 42-4-507, the gross weight of a vehicle having two axles shall not exceed thirty-six thousand pounds.

(II) Subject to the limitations prescribed in section 42-4-507, the gross weight of a single vehicle having three or more axles shall not exceed fifty-four thousand pounds.

(III) (A) Subject to the limitations prescribed in section 42-4-507, the maximum gross weight of any vehicle or combination of vehicles shall not exceed that determined by the formula $W = 500 [(LN/N-1) + 12N + 36]$.

(B) In using the formula in sub-subparagraph (A) of this subparagraph (III), W equals overall gross weight on any group of two or more consecutive axles to the nearest 500 pounds, L equals distance in feet between the extreme of any group of two or more consecutive axles, and N equals number of axles in the group under consideration; but in computations of this formula no gross vehicle weight shall exceed eighty thousand pounds, except as may be authorized under section 42-4-510.

(IV) For the purposes of this subsection (1), where a combination of vehicles is used, no vehicle shall carry a gross weight of less than ten percent of the overall gross weight of the combination of vehicles; except that this limitation shall not apply to specialized trailers whose specific use is to haul poles and whose axles may carry less than ten percent of the weight of the combination.

(1.5) The gross weight limits provided in subsection (1) of this section are increased by one thousand pounds for any vehicle or combination of vehicles if the vehicle or combination of vehicles contains an alternative fuel system and operates on alternative fuel or both alternative and conventional fuel. The provisions of this subsection (1.5) apply only when the vehicle or combination of vehicles is operated on a highway that is not on the interstate system as defined in section 43-2-101 (2), C.R.S. For the purposes of this subsection (1.5), "alternative fuel" has the same meaning provided in section 25-7-106.8 (1) (a), C.R.S.

(2) The department upon registering any vehicle under the laws of this state, which vehicle is designed and used primarily for the transportation of property or for the transportation of ten or more persons, may acquire such information and may make such investigation or tests as necessary to enable it to determine whether such vehicle may safely be operated upon the highways in compliance with all the provisions of this article. The department shall not register any such vehicle for a permissible gross weight exceeding the limitations set forth in sections 42-4-501 to 42-4-512 and 42-4-1407. Every such vehicle shall meet the following requirements:

(a) It shall be equipped with brakes as required in section 42-4-223;

(b) Every motor vehicle to be operated outside of business and residence districts shall have motive power adequate to propel at a reasonable speed such vehicle and any load thereon or to be drawn thereby.

(3) If the federal highway administration or the United States congress prescribes or adopts vehicle size or weight limits greater than those now prescribed by the "Federal-Aid Highway Act of 1956", which limits exceed in full or in part the provisions of section 42-4-504 or paragraph (b) or (c) of subsection (1) of this section, the transportation commission, upon determining that Colorado highways have been constructed to standards which will accommodate such additional size or weight and that the adoption of said size and weight limitations will not jeopardize any distribution of federal highway funds to the state, may adopt size and weight limits comparable to those prescribed or adopted by the federal highway administration or the United States congress and may authorize said limits to be used by owners or operators of vehicles while said vehicles are using highways within this state; but no vehicle size or weight limit so adopted by the commission shall be less in any respect than those now provided for in section 42-4-504 or paragraph (b) or (c) of subsection (1) of this section.

(4) Any person who drives a vehicle or owns a vehicle in violation of any provision of this section commits a class 2 misdemeanor traffic offense.

42-4-509. Vehicles weighed - excess removed. (1) Any police or peace officer, as described in section 16-2.5-101, C.R.S., having reason to believe that the weight of a vehicle and load is unlawful is authorized to require the driver to stop and submit to a weighing of the same by means of either portable or stationary scales or shall require that such vehicle be driven to the nearest public scales in the event such scales are within five miles.

(2) (a) Except as provided in paragraph (b) of this subsection (2), whenever an officer upon

weighing a vehicle and load as provided in subsection (1) of this section determines that the weight is unlawful, such officer shall require the driver to stop the vehicle in a suitable place and remain standing until such portion of the load is removed as may be necessary to reduce the gross weight of such vehicle to such limit as permitted under sections 42-4-501 to 42-4-512 and 42-4-1407. All material so unloaded shall be cared for by the owner or operator of such vehicle at the risk of such owner or operator.

(b) Whenever an officer upon weighing a vehicle and load as provided in subsection (1) of this section determines that the weight is unlawful and the load consists solely of either explosives or hazardous materials as defined in section 42-1-102 (32), such officer shall permit the driver of such vehicle to proceed to the driver's destination without requiring the driver to unload the excess portion of such load.

(3) Any driver of a vehicle who fails or refuses to stop and submit the vehicle and load to a weighing or who fails or refuses when directed by an officer upon a weighing of the vehicle to stop the vehicle and otherwise comply with the provisions of this section commits a class 2 misdemeanor traffic offense.

42-4-510. Permits for excess size and weight and for manufactured homes - rules - repeal. (1) (a) The department of transportation, the motor carrier services division of the department of revenue, or the Colorado state patrol with respect to highways under its jurisdiction or any local authority with respect to highways under its jurisdiction may, upon application in writing and good cause being shown therefor, issue a single trip, a special, or an annual permit in writing authorizing the applicant to operate or move a vehicle or combination of vehicles of a size or weight of vehicle or load exceeding the maximum specified in this article or otherwise not in conformity with the provisions of this article upon any highway under the jurisdiction of the party granting such permit and for the maintenance of which said party is responsible; except that permits for the movement of any manufactured home shall be issued as provided in subsection (2) of this section.

(b) (I) The application for any permit shall specifically describe the vehicle and load to be operated or moved and the particular highways for which the permit to operate is requested, and whether such permit is for a single trip, a special, or an annual operation, and the time of such movement. All state permits shall be issued in the discretion of the department of transportation, subject to rules adopted by the transportation commission in accordance with this section and section 42-4-511. All local permits shall be issued in the discretion of the local authority pursuant to ordinances or resolutions adopted in accordance with section 42-4-511. Any ordinances or resolutions of local authorities shall not conflict with this section.

(II) An overweight permit issued pursuant to this section shall be available for overweight divisible loads if:

(A) The vehicle has a quad axle grouping and the maximum gross weight of the vehicle does not exceed one hundred ten thousand pounds; or

(B) The vehicle is operated in combination with a trailer or semitrailer, the trailer has two or three axles, and the maximum gross weight of the vehicle does not exceed ninety-seven thousand pounds; and

(C) The owner and operator of the motor vehicle are in compliance with the federal "Motor Carrier Safety Improvement Act of 1999", Pub.L. 106-159, as amended, as applicable to commercial vehicles; and

(D) The vehicle complies with rules promulgated by the department of transportation concerning the distribution of the load upon the vehicle's axles.

(III) A permit issued pursuant to this paragraph (b) shall not authorize the operation or movement of a motor vehicle on the interstate highway in violation of federal law.

(c) (I) A single trip or annual permit shall be issued pursuant to this section for a self-propelled fixed load crane that exceeds legal weight limits if it does not exceed the weight limits authorized by the department of transportation. A boom trailer or boom dolly shall not be permitted unless the boom trailer or boom dolly is attached to the crane in a manner and for the purpose of distributing load to meet the weight requirements established by the department. A self-propelled fixed load crane may be permitted with counterweights when a boom trailer or boom dolly is used if the counterweights do not exceed the manufacturer's rated capacity of the self-propelled fixed load crane and do not cause the vehicle to exceed permitted axle or gross weight limits. A permit issued pursuant to this paragraph (c) shall not authorize movement on interstate highways if not approved by federal law.

(II) For the purposes of this paragraph (c), "self-propelled fixed load crane" means a self-powered mobile crane designed with equipment or parts permanently attached to the body of the crane. A self-propelled fixed load crane includes, without limitation, the crane's shackles and slings.

(1.5) (a) The department of transportation may, upon application in writing or electronically made and good cause being shown therefor, issue an annual fleet permit authorizing the applicant to operate or move any two or more vehicles owned by the applicant of a size or weight of vehicle or load exceeding the maximum specified in this article or otherwise not in conformity with the provisions of this article upon any highway.

(b) The application for any annual fleet permit shall specifically describe the vehicles, loads, and estimated number of loads to be operated or moved and the particular highways for which the permit to operate is requested, as defined by rules of the department of transportation. Permits issued pursuant to this subsection (1.5) shall not authorize the operation of vehicles that exceed the maximum dimensions allowed for vehicles operating under annual permits issued pursuant to the rules of the department pertaining to transport permits for the movement of extra-legal vehicles or loads.

(c) The department shall provide the option to a company filing for a permit under this subsection (1.5) to file an express consent waiver that enables the company to designate a company representative to be a party of interest for a violation of this section. The appearance of the company representative in a court hearing without the operator when the operator has signed such waiver shall not be deemed the practice of law in violation of article 5 of title 12, C.R.S.

(1.7) (a) The department of transportation may issue super-load permits for:

(I) A combination vehicle with a weight of five hundred thousand pounds or more that occupies two lanes to haul the load; or

(II) An unladen combination vehicle with an expandable dual-lane transport trailer that occupies two lanes.

(b) (I) The department of transportation may place restrictions on the use of a permit. A person shall obey the restrictions contained in a permit.

(II) (A) The department of transportation may refuse to issue a permit to a person who has been held by an administrative law judge to have disobeyed permit restrictions or to have violated this section or rules promulgated under this section in a hearing held in accordance with article 4 of title 24, C.R.S.

(B) The department shall create a system that tracks the compliance of permit holders and use the system to determine if a permit holder has a pattern of noncompliance. The department shall promulgate rules establishing standards to deny permits to persons who show a pattern of noncompliance, which standards include the length of time a permit is denied based upon the number and type of noncomplying events.

(III) The department of transportation shall include in a super-load permit a speed restriction, not to exceed twenty-five miles per hour on the highway and ten miles per hour on structures; except that the department of transportation may modify the speed restriction when necessary for safety or to prevent structural damage.

(c) When filing an application, an applicant for a super-load permit shall provide the department of transportation with documentation, acceptable to the department of transportation, from a third party establishing the gross weight of the load. The driver shall carry the documentation in the vehicle during the permitted move and produce, upon request, the documentation for any state agency or law enforcement personnel.

(d) The department of transportation may refuse to issue a super-load permit under this section for an unladen combination vehicle unless the applicant breaks the load down to the smallest dimensions possible. The department of transportation may refuse to issue a super-load permit under this section for an unladen vehicle unless the applicant renders the dual lane trailer into legal loads.

(e) The department of transportation, Colorado state patrol, or port of entry shall inspect the load of a super-load permit holder, at the permit holder's expense, at the nearest point where the shipment enters the state, at a location specified by the department of transportation, or at the load's point of origin to ensure compliance with the permit requirements and safety statutes and rules, including:

(I) Height, width, and length;
(II) Number of axles;
(III) Date of move;
(IV) Correct route;
(V) Documentation of load weight;
(VI) Use of signs and pilot cars; and
(VII) Weight, if the vehicle can be weighed within two hours.

(f) The department of transportation shall notify the port of entry of the permit's issuance and the location and date of the move.

(g) Until the department of transportation promulgates rules to implement this subsection (1.7), the department may issue permits conforming to the requirements of this section under existing rules. This paragraph (g) is repealed, effective July 1, 2012.

(2) (a) An authentication of paid ad valorem taxes, after notification of such movement to the county treasurer, may serve as a permit for movement of manufactured homes on public streets or highways under the county's jurisdiction. An authentication of paid ad valorem taxes from the county treasurer of the county from which the manufactured home is to be moved, after notification of such movement has been provided to the county assessor of the county to which the manufactured home is to be moved, pursuant to section 39-5-205, C.R.S., may also serve as a permit for the movement of manufactured homes from one adjoining county to an adjoining county on streets and highways under local jurisdiction. The treasurer shall issue along with the authentication of paid ad valorem taxes a transportable manufactured home permit. The treasurer may establish and collect a fee, which shall not exceed ten dollars, for issuing the authentication of paid ad valorem taxes and the transportable manufactured home permit. Such transportable manufactured home permit shall be printed on an eleven inch by six inch fluorescent orange card and shall contain the following information: The name and address of the owner of the mobile home; the name and address of the mover; the transport number of the mover, a description of the mobile home including the make, year, and identification or serial number; the county authentication number; and an expiration date. The expiration date shall be set by the treasurer, but in no event shall the expiration date be more than thirty days after the date of

issue of the permit. Such transportable manufactured home permit shall be valid for a single trip only. The transportable manufactured home permit shall be prominently displayed on the rear of the mobile home during transit of the mobile home. Peace officers and local tax and assessment officials may request, and upon demand shall be shown, all moving permits, tax receipts, or certificates required by this subsection (2). Nothing in this section shall require a permit from a county treasurer for the movement of a new manufactured home. For the purposes of this section, a new manufactured home is one in transit under invoice or manufacturer's statement of origin which has not been previously occupied for residential purposes.

(b) All applications for permits to move manufactured homes over state highways shall comply with the following special provisions:

(I) Each such application shall be for a single trip, a special permit, an annual permit, or, subject to the requirements of paragraph (a) of subsection (1.5) of this section, an annual fleet permit. The application shall be accompanied by a certificate or other proof of public liability insurance in amounts of not less than one hundred thousand dollars per person and three hundred thousand dollars per accident for all manufactured homes moved within this state by the permit holder during the effective term of the permit. Each application for a single trip permit shall be accompanied by an authentication of paid ad valorem taxes on the used manufactured home.

(II) Holders of permits shall keep and maintain, for not less than three calendar years, records of all manufactured homes moved in whole or in part within this state, which records shall include the plate number of the towing vehicle; the year, make, serial number, and size of the unit moved, together with date of the move; the place of pickup; and the exact address of the final destination and the county of final destination and the name and address of the landowner of the final destination. These records shall be available upon request within this state for inspection by the state of Colorado or any of its ad valorem taxing governmental subdivisions.

(III) Holders of permits shall obtain an authentication of paid ad valorem taxes through the date of the move from the owner of a used manufactured home or from the county treasurer of the county from which the used manufactured home is being moved. Permit holders shall notify the county treasurer of the county from which the manufactured home is being moved of the new exact address of the final destination and the county of final destination of the manufactured home and the name and address of the landowner of the final destination, and, if within the state, the county treasurer shall forward copies of the used manufactured home tax certificate to the county assessor of the destination county. County treasurers may compute ad valorem manufactured home taxes due based upon the next preceding year's assessment prorated through the date of the move and accept payment of such as payment in full.

(IV) No owner of a manufactured home shall move the manufactured home or provide for the movement of the manufactured home without being the holder of a paid ad valorem tax certificate and a transportable manufactured home permit thereon, and no person shall assist such an owner in the movement of such owner's manufactured home, including a manufactured home dealer. Except as otherwise provided in this paragraph (b), a permit holder who moves any manufactured home within this state shall be liable for all unpaid ad valorem taxes thereon through the date of such move if movement is made prior to payment of the ad valorem taxes due on the manufactured home moved.

(V) In the event of an imminent natural or man-made disaster or emergency, including, but not limited to, rising waters, flood, or fire, the owner, owner's representative or agent, occupant, or tenant of a manufactured home or the mobile home park owner or manager, lienholder, or manufactured home dealer is specifically exempted from the need to obtain a permit pursuant to this section and may move the endangered manufactured home out of the danger area to a temporary or new permanent location and may move such manufactured home back to its original location without a permit or penalty or fee requirement. Upon any such move to a temporary location as a result of a disaster or emergency, the person making the move or such person's agent or representative shall notify the county assessor in the county to which the manufactured home has been moved, within twenty days after such move, of the date and circumstances pertaining to the move and the temporary or permanent new location of the manufactured home. If the manufactured home is moved to a new permanent location from a temporary location as a result of a disaster or emergency, a permit for such move shall be issued but no fee shall be assessed.

(3) The department of transportation, the motor carrier services division of the department of revenue, or the Colorado state patrol or any local authority is authorized to issue or withhold a permit, as provided in this section, and, if such permit is issued, to limit the number of trips, or to establish seasonal or other time limitations within which the vehicles described may be operated on the highways indicated, or otherwise to limit or prescribe conditions of operation of such vehicles, when necessary to protect the safety of highway users, to protect the efficient movement of traffic from unreasonable interference, or to protect the highways from undue damage to the road foundations, surfaces, or structures and may require such undertaking or other security as may be deemed necessary to compensate for any injury to any highway or highway structure.

(4) The original or a copy of every such permit shall be carried in the vehicle or combination of vehicles to which it refers and shall be open to inspection by any police officer or

authorized agent of any authority granting such permit; except that, if a peace officer, as described in section 16-2.5-101, C.R.S., or an authorized agent of the authority that granted a permit may determine that the permit can be electronically verified at the time of contact, a copy of the permit need not be carried in the vehicle or combination of vehicles to which it refers. No person shall violate any of the terms or conditions of such permit.

(5) The department of transportation, the motor carrier services division of the department of revenue, or the Colorado state patrol shall, unless such action will jeopardize distribution of federal highway funds to the state, authorize the operation or movement of a vehicle or combination of vehicles on the interstate highway system of Colorado at a maximum weight of eighty-five thousand pounds.

(6) No vehicle having a permit under this section shall be remodeled, rebuilt, altered, or changed except in such a way as to conform to those specifications and limitations established in sections 42-4-501 to 42-4-507 and 42-4-1407.

(7) Any person who has obtained a valid permit for the movement of any oversize vehicle or load may attach to such vehicle or load or to any vehicle accompanying the same not more than three illuminated flashing yellow signals as warning devices.

(8) (a) The department of transportation shall have a procedure to allow those persons who are transporting loads from another state into Colorado and who would require a permit under the provisions of this section to make advance arrangements by telephone or other means of communication for the issuance of a permit if the load otherwise complies with the requirements of this section.

(b) Effective July 1, 1996, the motor carrier services division in the department of revenue shall have available for issuance at each fixed port of entry weigh station permits for extralegal vehicles or loads; except that special permits for extralegal vehicles or loads that are considered extraordinary in dimensions or weight, or both, and that require additional safety precautions while in transit shall be issued only by the department of transportation. A port of entry may issue such special permits if authorized to do so by the department of transportation and under such rules as the department of transportation may establish, and may deliver from a fixed port of entry weigh station any permit issued by the department of transportation.

(c) Repealed.

(9) No permit shall be necessary for the operation of authorized emergency vehicles, public transportation vehicles operated by municipalities or other political subdivisions of the state, county road maintenance and county road construction equipment temporarily moved upon the highway, implements of husbandry, and farm tractors temporarily moved upon the highway, including transportation of such tractors or implements by a person dealing therein to such person's place of business within the state or to the premises of a purchaser or prospective purchaser within the state; nor shall such vehicles or equipment be subject to the size and weight provisions of this part 5.

(10) The Colorado state patrol, the personnel in any port of entry weigh station, and local law enforcement officials shall verify the validity of permits issued under this section whenever feasible. Upon determination by any of such officials or by any personnel of a county assessor's or county treasurer's office indicating that a manufactured home has been moved without a valid permit, the district attorney shall investigate and prosecute any alleged violation as authorized by law.

(11) (a) The department of transportation, the motor carrier services division of the department of revenue, or the Colorado state patrol may charge permit applicants permit fees as follows:

(I) For overlength, overwidth, and overheight permits on loads or vehicles which do not exceed legal weight limits:

(A) Annual permit, two hundred fifty dollars;

(B) Single trip permit, fifteen dollars;

(II) For overlength, including front or rear overhang, annual fleet permits on loads or vehicles which do not exceed legal weight limits, one thousand five hundred dollars plus fifteen dollars per fleet vehicle. For purposes of this subparagraph (II), "fleet" means any group of two or more vehicles owned by one person. This subparagraph (II) shall only apply for public utility vehicles and loads.

(III) For overweight permits for vehicles or loads exceeding legal weight limits up to two hundred thousand pounds:

(A) Annual permit, four hundred dollars;

(B) Single trip permit, fifteen dollars plus five dollars per axle;

(C) Annual fleet permits, one thousand five hundred dollars plus twenty-five dollars per vehicle to be permitted. For purposes of this sub-subparagraph (C), "fleet" means any group of two or more vehicles owned by one person. This sub-subparagraph (C) shall apply only to longer vehicle combinations as defined in section 42-4-505.

(IV) Special permits for structural, oversize, or overweight moves requiring extraordinary action or moves involving weight in excess of two hundred thousand pounds, one hundred twenty-five dollars for a permit for a single trip, including a super-load permit issued under subsection (1.7) of this section; except that a super-load permit fee is four hundred dollars;

(V) The fee for an annual fleet permit issued pursuant to subsection (1.5) or (2) of this section is three thousand dollars for a fleet of from two to ten vehicles plus three hundred dollars for each additional vehicle in the fleet;

(VI) For overweight permits for vehicles that have a quad axle grouping for divisible vehicles or loads exceeding legal weight limits issued pursuant to subparagraph (II) of paragraph (b) of subsection (1) of this section:

(A) Annual permit, five hundred dollars;

(B) Single trip permit, thirty dollars plus ten dollars per axle; and

(C) Annual fleet permits, two thousand dollars plus thirty-five dollars per vehicle to be permitted;

(D) (Deleted by amendment, L. 2009, (HB 09-1318), ch. 316, p. 1704, § 2, effective January 1, 2010.)

(VII) For overweight permits for vehicle combinations with a trailer that has two or three axles for divisible vehicles or loads exceeding legal weight limits established pursuant to sub-subparagraph (B) of subparagraph (II) of paragraph (b) of subsection (1) of this section:

(A) Annual permit, five hundred dollars;

(B) Six-month permit, two hundred fifty dollars; and

(C) Single trip permit, fifteen dollars plus ten dollars per axle.

(b) Any local authority may impose a fee, in addition to but not to exceed the amounts required in subparagraphs (I) and (III) of paragraph (a) of this subsection (11), as provided by the applicable local ordinance or resolution; and, in the case of a permit under subparagraph (IV) of paragraph (a) of this subsection (11), the amount of the fee shall not exceed the actual cost of the extraordinary action.

(12) (a) Any person holding a permit issued pursuant to this section or any person operating a vehicle pursuant to such permit who violates any provision of this section, any ordinance or resolution of a local authority, or any standards or rules or regulations promulgated pursuant to this section, except the provisions of subparagraph (IV) of paragraph (b) of subsection (2) of this section, commits a class 2 misdemeanor traffic offense.

(b) Any person who violates the provisions of subparagraph (IV) of paragraph (b) of subsection (2) of this section commits a class 2 petty offense and, upon conviction thereof, shall be fined two hundred dollars; except that, upon conviction of a second or subsequent such offense, such person commits a class 3 misdemeanor and shall be punished as provided in section 18-1.3-501, C.R.S.

(c) The department of transportation or the Colorado state patrol with regard to any state permit and the local authority with regard to a local permit may, after a hearing under section 24-4-105, C.R.S., revoke, suspend, refuse to renew, or refuse to issue any permit authorized by this section upon a finding that the holder of the permit has violated the provisions of this section, any ordinance or resolution of a local authority, or any standards or rules or regulations promulgated pursuant to this section.

(d) A driver or holder of a permit issued under subsection (1.7) of this section who fails to comply with the terms of the permit or subsection (1.7) of this section commits a class 1 misdemeanor traffic offense and shall be punished as provided in section 42-4-1701 (3) (a) (II).

42-4-511. Permit standards - state and local. (1) The transportation commission shall adopt such rules and regulations as are necessary for the proper administration and enforcement of section 42-4-510 with regard to state permits.

(2) (a) Any permits which may be required by local authorities shall be issued in accordance with ordinances and resolutions adopted by the respective local authorities after a public hearing at which testimony is received from affected motor vehicle owners and operators. Notice of such public hearing shall be published in a newspaper having general circulation within the local authority's jurisdiction. Such notice shall not be less than eight days prior to the date of hearing. The publication shall not be placed in that portion of the newspaper in which legal notices or classified advertisements appear. Such notice shall state the purpose of the hearing, the time and place of the hearing, and that the general public, including motor vehicle owners and operators to be affected, may attend and make oral or written comments regarding the proposed ordinance or resolution. Notice of any subsequent hearing shall be published in the same manner as for the original hearing.

(b) At least thirty days prior to such public hearing, the local authority shall transmit a copy of the proposed ordinance or resolution to the department of transportation for its comments, and said department shall make such comments in writing to the local authority prior to such public hearing.

(c) Effective July 1, 1996, any local authority that adopts or has adopted an ordinance or resolution governing permits for the movement of oversize or overweight vehicles or loads shall file a copy of such ordinance or resolution with the department of transportation and the motor carrier services division of the department of revenue.

42-4-511.2. Authority for cooperative agreements with regional states on excess size or weight vehicles - regulations. (1) **Purpose.** The purpose of this section is to authorize the negotiation and execution of agreements in cooperation with other states to:

(a) Establish a regional permit system to allow nondivisible oversize or overweight vehicles to operate between and among two or more states under one single trip permit, instead of requiring such vehicles to stop and obtain a separate permit before entering each state;

(b) Promote uniformity concerning administrative and enforcement procedures for applicable vehicle size and weight standards to facilitate regional movement of such vehicles, to eliminate unnecessary bureaucratic barriers, and to improve the highway operating environment and vehicle safety under the applicable laws of the respective states; and

(c) Encourage and utilize research that will facilitate the achievement of the purposes described in this subsection (1).

(2) **Authority.** (a) In addition to any other powers granted by law, the executive director of the department of transportation, or the executive director's designee, is hereby authorized to negotiate and enter into appropriate agreements with other states concerning the regional operation or movement of nondivisible oversize or overweight vehicles and to facilitate the uniform application, administration, and enforcement of applicable laws concerning such vehicles.

(b) A cooperative agreement under this section may include, but shall not be limited to, the establishment of a regional permit system authorizing the operation or movement of nondivisible oversize or overweight vehicles from one state in the region to or through another state or states in the region under a single trip permit in accordance with the applicable requirements of each of the states.

(c) For the purposes of a regional permit agreement, the department of transportation is authorized to:

(I) Delegate to other states its authority under section 42-4-510 (1) to issue permits for nondivisible oversize or overweight vehicles to operate on Colorado state highways; except that any such issuance by another state shall conform, at a minimum, to the applicable Colorado permit standards and legal requirements as described in this part 5 and to the regulations implementing this part 5. The department of transportation may also impose additional standards concerning such regional permits as it deems appropriate.

(II) Accept a delegation of authority from other states to issue permits for the operation of vehicles on the highways of such states in accordance with the applicable standards and requirements of such states, pursuant to the terms of the regional permit agreement; and

(III) Collect any fees, taxes, and penalties on behalf of other states that are parties to the regional permit agreement and to remit such fees, taxes, and penalties to such states. Such fees, taxes, and penalties shall not be considered taxes or funds of the state of Colorado for any purpose.

(d) For the purposes of a regional permit agreement, the Colorado state patrol, ports of entry, and local law enforcement authorities are authorized to enforce the terms of any regional permit concerning the operation of the permitted vehicle on state highways in Colorado. The Colorado state patrol, ports of entry, and local law enforcement authorities are also permitted to take necessary actions in Colorado to enforce the applicable requirements of the permitting state or states which shall include, but shall not be limited to, monitoring licenses and other credential usage; enforcing tax restraint, distraint, or levy orders; issuing civil citations; and conducting necessary safety and equipment inspections.

(e) The executive director of the department of transportation, or the executive director's designee, is hereby authorized to appoint employees and officials of other states as agents of the department for the limited purpose of enforcing the laws of Colorado under the terms of the cooperative agreements entered into under the provisions of this section. The executive director or the designee may promulgate such regulations as are necessary for the implementation of the provisions of this section.

(f) Any agreement entered into under the provisions of this section shall contain provisions that express the understanding that any employees and officials of any other state who enforce the laws of Colorado under the terms of such agreement, or who otherwise act under the terms of such agreement, shall not be eligible for compensation, employee rights, or benefits from the state of Colorado and shall not be considered to be employees or officials of the state of Colorado.

(g) A cooperative agreement under this section may also provide for uniformity concerning enforcement procedures, safety inspection standards, operational standards, permit and application form procedures, driver qualifications, and such other matters that may be pertinent to said matters.

(h) Notwithstanding any provision of this section to the contrary, all existing statutes and rules and regulations prescribing size or weight vehicle requirements, or relating to permits for such vehicles, shall continue to be in full force and effect until amended or repealed by law, and any cooperative agreement must comply with such statutes and rules and regulations. The transportation commission shall ratify any cooperative agreement entered into under the provisions of this section.

42-4-512. Liability for damage to highway. (1) No person shall drive, operate, or move upon or over any highway or highway structure any vehicle, object, or contrivance in such a manner so as to cause damage to said highway or highway structure. When the damage sustained to said highway or highway structure is the result of the operating, driving, or moving of such vehicle, object, or contrivance weighing in excess of the maximum weight authorized by sections 42-4-501 to 42-4-512 and 42-4-1407, it shall be no defense to any action, either civil or criminal, brought against such person that the weight of the vehicle was authorized by special permit issued in accordance with sections 42-4-501 to 42-4-512 and 42-4-1407.

(2) Every person violating the provisions of subsection (1) of this section shall be liable for all damage which said highway or highway structure may sustain as a result thereof. Whenever the driver of such vehicle, object, or contrivance is not the owner thereof but is operating, driving, or moving such vehicle, object, or contrivance with the express or implied consent of the owner

thereof, then said owner or driver shall be jointly and severally liable for any such damage. The liability for damage sustained by any such highway or highway structure may be enforced by a civil action by the authorities in control of such highway or highway structure. No satisfaction of such civil liability, however, shall be deemed to be a release or satisfaction of any criminal liability for violation of the provisions of subsection (1) of this section.

(3) Any person who violates any provision of this section commits a class A traffic infraction.

PART 6

SIGNALS - SIGNS - MARKINGS

42-4-601. Department to sign highways, where. (1) The department of transportation shall place and maintain such traffic control devices, conforming to its manual and specifications, upon state highways as it deems necessary to indicate and to carry out the provisions of this article or to regulate, warn, or guide traffic.

(2) No local authority shall place or maintain any traffic control device upon any highway under the jurisdiction of the department of transportation except by the latter's permission.

42-4-602. Local traffic control devices. (1) No local authority shall erect or maintain any stop sign or traffic control signal at any location so as to require the traffic on any state highway to stop before entering or crossing any intersecting highway unless approval in writing has first been obtained from the department of transportation.

(2) Where practical no local authority shall maintain three traffic control signals located on a roadway so as to be within one minute's driving time (to be determined by the speed limit) from any one of the signals to the other without synchronizing the lights to enhance the flow of traffic and thereby reduce air pollution.

42-4-603. Obedience to official traffic control devices. (1) No driver of a vehicle shall disobey the instructions of any official traffic control device including any official hand signal device placed or displayed in accordance with the provisions of this article unless otherwise directed by a police officer subject to the exceptions in this article granted the driver of an authorized emergency vehicle.

(2) No provision of this article for which official traffic control devices are required shall be enforced against an alleged violator if at the time and place of the alleged violation an official device is not in proper position and sufficiently legible to be seen by an ordinarily observant person. Whenever a particular section does not state that official traffic control devices are required, such section shall be effective even though no devices are erected or in place.

(3) Whenever official traffic control devices are placed in position approximately conforming to the requirements of this article, such devices shall be presumed to have been so placed by the official act or direction of lawful authority unless the contrary is established by competent evidence.

(4) Any official traffic control device placed pursuant to the provisions of this article and purporting to conform to the lawful requirements pertaining to such devices shall be presumed to comply with the requirements of this article unless the contrary is established by competent evidence.

(5) Any person who violates any provision of this section commits a class A traffic infraction.

42-4-604. Traffic control signal legend. (1) If traffic is controlled by traffic control signals exhibiting different colored lights, or colored lighted arrows, successively one at a time or in combination as declared in the traffic control manual adopted by the department of transportation, only the colors green, yellow, and red shall be used, except for special pedestrian-control signals carrying a word or symbol legend as provided in section 42-4-802, and said lights, arrows, and combinations thereof shall indicate and apply to drivers of vehicles and pedestrians as follows:

(a) Green indication:

(I) Vehicular traffic facing a circular green signal may proceed straight through or turn right or left unless a sign at such place prohibits such turn; but vehicular traffic, including vehicles turning right or left, shall yield the right-of-way to other vehicles and to pedestrians lawfully within the intersection and to pedestrians lawfully within an adjacent crosswalk at the time such signal is exhibited.

(II) Vehicular traffic facing a green arrow signal, shown alone or in combination with another indication, may cautiously enter the intersection only to make the movement indicated by such arrow or such other movement as is permitted by other indications shown at the same time. Such vehicular traffic shall yield the right-of-way to pedestrians lawfully within an adjacent crosswalk and to other traffic lawfully using the intersection.

(III) Unless otherwise directed by a pedestrian-control signal as provided in section 42-4-802, pedestrians facing any green signal, except when the sole green signal is a turn arrow, may proceed across the roadway within any marked or unmarked crosswalk.

(b) Steady yellow indication:

(I) Vehicular traffic facing a steady circular yellow or yellow arrow signal is thereby warned that the related green movement is being terminated or that a red indication will be exhibited immediately thereafter.

(II) Pedestrians facing a steady circular yellow or yellow arrow signal, unless otherwise directed by a pedestrian-control signal as provided in section 42-4-802, are thereby advised that there is insufficient time to cross the roadway before a red indication is shown, and no pedestrian shall then start to cross the roadway.

(c) Steady red indication:

(I) Vehicular traffic facing a steady circular red signal alone shall stop at a clearly marked stop line but, if none, before entering the crosswalk on the near side of the intersection or, if none, then before entering the intersection and shall remain standing until an indication to proceed is shown; except that:

(A) Such vehicular traffic, after coming to a stop and yielding the right-of-way to pedestrians lawfully within an adjacent crosswalk and to other traffic lawfully using the intersection, may make a right turn, unless state or local road authorities within their respective jurisdictions have by ordinance or resolution prohibited any such right turn and have erected an official sign at each intersection where such right turn is prohibited.

(B) Such vehicular traffic, when proceeding on a one-way street and after coming to a stop, may make a left turn onto a one-way street upon which traffic is moving to the left of the driver. Such turn shall be made only after yielding the right-of-way to pedestrians and other traffic proceeding as directed. No turn shall be made pursuant to this sub-subparagraph (B) if local authorities have by ordinance prohibited any such left turn and erected a sign giving notice of any such prohibition at each intersection where such left turn is prohibited.

(C) To promote uniformity in traffic regulation throughout the state and to protect the public peace, health, and safety, the general assembly declares that no local authority shall have any discretion other than as expressly provided in this subparagraph (I).

(II) Pedestrians facing a steady circular red signal alone shall not enter the roadway, unless otherwise directed by a pedestrian-control signal as provided in section 42-4-802.

(III) Vehicular traffic facing a steady red arrow signal may not enter the intersection to make the movement indicated by such arrow and, unless entering the intersection to make such other movement as is permitted by other indications shown at the same time, shall stop at a clearly marked stop line but, if none, before entering the crosswalk on the near side of the intersection or, if none, then before entering the intersection and shall remain standing until an indication to make the movement indicated by such arrow is shown.

(IV) Pedestrians facing a steady red arrow signal shall not enter the roadway, unless otherwise directed by a pedestrian-control signal as provided in section 42-4-802.

(d) Nonintersection signal: In the event an official traffic control signal is erected and maintained at a place other than at an intersection, the provisions of this section shall be applicable except as to those provisions which by their nature can have no application. Any stop required shall be made at a sign or pavement marking indicating where the stop should be made, but in the absence of any such sign or marking the stop shall be made at the signal.

(e) Lane-use-control signals: Whenever lane-use-control signals are placed over the individual lanes of a street or highway, as declared in the traffic control manual adopted by the department of transportation, such signals shall indicate and apply to drivers of vehicles as follows:

(I) Downward-pointing green arrow (steady): A driver facing such signal may drive in any lane over which said green arrow signal is located.

(II) Yellow "X" (steady): A driver facing such signal is warned that the related green arrow movement is being terminated and shall vacate in a safe manner the lane over which said steady yellow signal is located to avoid if possible occupying that lane when the steady red "X" signal is exhibited.

(III) Yellow "X" (flashing): A driver facing such signal may use the lane over which said flashing yellow signal is located for the purpose of making a left turn or a passing maneuver, using proper caution, but for no other purpose.

(IV) Red "X" (steady): A driver facing such signal shall not drive in any lane over which said red signal is exhibited.

(2) Any person who violates any provision of this section commits a class A traffic infraction.

42-4-605. Flashing signals. (1) Whenever an illuminated flashing red or yellow signal is used in conjunction with a traffic sign or a traffic signal or as a traffic beacon, it shall require obedience by vehicular traffic as follows:

(a) When a red lens is illuminated with rapid intermittent flashes, drivers of vehicles shall stop at a clearly marked stop line but, if none, before entering the crosswalk on the near side of the intersection or, if none, then at the point nearest the intersecting roadway where the driver has a view of approaching traffic on the intersecting roadway before entering the intersection, and the right to proceed shall be subject to the rules applicable after making a stop at a stop sign.

(b) When a yellow lens is illuminated with rapid intermittent flashes, drivers of vehicles may proceed past such signal and through the intersection or other hazardous location only with caution.

(2) This section shall not apply at railroad grade crossings. Conduct of drivers of vehicles approaching railroad crossings shall be governed by the provisions of sections 42-4-706 to 42-4-708.

(3) Any person who violates any provision of this section commits a class A traffic infraction.

42-4-606. Display of unauthorized signs or devices. (1) No person shall place, maintain, or display upon or in view of any highway any unauthorized sign, signal, marking, or device which purports to be or is an imitation of or resembles an official traffic control device or railroad sign or signal, or which attempts to direct the movement of traffic, or which hides from view or interferes with the effectiveness of any official traffic control device or any railroad sign or signal, and no person shall place or maintain nor shall any public authority permit upon any highway any traffic sign or signal bearing thereon any commercial advertising. The provisions of this section shall not be deemed to prohibit the use of motorist services information of a general nature on official highway guide signs if such signs do not indicate the brand, trademark, or name of any private business or commercial enterprise offering the service, nor shall this section be deemed to prohibit the erection upon private property adjacent to highways of signs giving useful directional information and of a type that cannot be mistaken for official signs.

(2) Every such prohibited sign, signal, or marking is declared to be a public nuisance, and the authority having jurisdiction over the highway is empowered to remove the same or cause it to be removed without notice.

(3) Any person who violates any provision of this section commits a class A traffic infraction.

(4) The provisions of this section shall not be applicable to informational sites authorized under section 43-1-405, C.R.S.

(5) The provisions of this section shall not be applicable to specific information signs authorized under section 43-1-420, C.R.S.

42-4-607. Interference with official devices. (1) (a) No person shall, without lawful authority, attempt to or in fact alter, deface, injure, knock down, remove, or interfere with the effective operation of any official traffic control device or any railroad sign or signal or any inscription, shield, or insignia thereon or any other part thereof. Except as otherwise provided in subsection (2) of this section, any person who violates any provision of this paragraph (a) commits a class B traffic infraction.

(b) No person shall possess or sell, without lawful authority, an electronic device that is designed to cause a traffic light to change. A person who violates any provision of this paragraph (b) commits a class B traffic infraction.

(2) (a) No person shall use an electronic device, without lawful authority, that causes a traffic light to change. Except as otherwise provided in paragraph (b) of this subsection (2), a person who violates any provision of this paragraph (a) commits a class A traffic infraction.

(b) A person who violates any provision of paragraph (a) of this subsection (2) and thereby proximately causes bodily injury to another person commits a class 1 misdemeanor traffic offense. In addition to any other penalty imposed by law, the court shall impose a fine of one thousand dollars.

42-4-608. Signals by hand or signal device. (1) Any stop or turn signal when required as provided by section 42-4-903 shall be given either by means of the hand and arm as provided by section 42-4-609 or by signal lamps or signal device of the type approved by the department, except as otherwise provided in subsection (2) of this section.

(2) Any motor vehicle in use on a highway shall be equipped with, and the required signal shall be given by, signal lamps when the distance from the center of the top of the steering post to the left outside limit of the body, cab, or load of such motor vehicle exceeds twenty-four inches or when the distance from the center of the top of the steering post to the rear limit of the body or load thereof exceeds fourteen feet. The latter measurement shall apply to any single vehicle, also to any combination of vehicles.

(3) Any person who violates any provision of this section commits a class A traffic infraction.

42-4-609. Method of giving hand and arm signals. (1) All signals required to be given by hand and arm shall be given from the left side of the vehicle in the following manner, and such signals shall indicate as follows:

(a) Left-turn, hand and arm extended horizontally;

(b) Right-turn, hand and arm extended upward;

(c) Stop or decrease speed, hand and arm extended downward.

(2) Any person who violates any provision of this section commits a class A traffic infraction.

42-4-610. Unauthorized insignia. No owner shall display upon any part of the owner's vehicle any official designation, sign, or insignia of any public or quasi-public corporation or municipal, state, or national department or governmental subdivision without authority of such agency or any insignia, badge, sign, emblem, or distinctive mark of any organization or society of which the owner is not a bona fide member or otherwise authorized to display such sign or insignia. Any person who violates any provision of this section commits a class B traffic infraction.

42-4-611. Paraplegic persons or persons with disabilities - distress flag. (1) Any paraplegic person or person with a disability when in motor vehicle distress is authorized to display by the side of such person's disabled vehicle a white flag of approximately seven and one-half inches in width and thirteen inches in length, with the letter "D" thereon in red color with an irregular one-half inch red border. Said flag shall be of reflective material so as to be readily discernible under darkened conditions, and said reflective material must be submitted to and approved by the department of transportation before the same is used.

(2) Any person desiring to use such display shall make application to the department, and the department may in its discretion issue to such person with a disability upon application a card that sets forth the applicant's name, address, and date of birth, the physical apparatus needed to operate a motor vehicle, if any, and any other

pertinent facts that the department deems desirable, and in its discretion the department may issue a permit for the use of and issue to such person a display flag. Each such flag shall be numbered, and in the event of loss or destruction, a duplicate may be issued upon the payment of the sum of one dollar by such applicant. The department shall maintain a list of such applicants and persons to whom permits and flags have been issued and furnish a copy thereof to the Colorado state patrol upon request.

(3) Any person who is not a paraplegic person or a person with a disability who uses such flag as a signal or for any other purpose is guilty of a misdemeanor, and, upon conviction thereof, shall be punished by a fine of not less than one hundred dollars nor more than three hundred dollars, or by imprisonment in the county jail for not less than ten days nor more than ninety days, or by both such fine and imprisonment.

42-4-612. When signals are inoperative or malfunctioning. (1) Whenever a driver approaches an intersection and faces a traffic control signal which is inoperative or which remains on steady red or steady yellow during several time cycles, the rules controlling entrance to a through street or highway from a stop street or highway, as provided under section 42-4-703, shall apply until a police officer assumes control of traffic or until normal operation is resumed. In the event that any traffic control signal at a place other than an intersection should cease to operate or should malfunction as set forth in this section, drivers may proceed through the inoperative or malfunctioning signal only with caution, as if the signal were one of flashing yellow.

(2) Whenever a pedestrian faces a pedestrian-control signal as provided in section 42-4-802 which is inoperative or which remains on "Don't Walk" or "Wait" during several time cycles, such pedestrian shall not enter the roadway unless the pedestrian can do so safely and without interfering with any vehicular traffic.

(3) Any person who violates any provision of this section commits a class A traffic infraction.

42-4-613. Failure to pay toll established by regional transportation authority. Any person who fails to pay a required fee, toll, rate, or charge established by a regional transportation authority created pursuant to part 6 of article 4 of title 43, C.R.S., for the privilege of traveling on or using any property included in a regional transportation system pursuant to part 6 of article 4 of title 43, C.R.S., commits a class A traffic infraction.

42-4-614. Designation of highway maintenance, repair, or construction zones - signs - increase in penalties for speeding violations. (1) (a) If maintenance, repair, or construction activities are occurring or will occur within four hours on a portion of a state highway, the department of transportation may designate such portion of the highway as a highway maintenance, repair, or construction zone. Any person who commits certain violations listed in section 42-4-1701 (4) in a maintenance, repair, or construction zone that is designated pursuant to this section is subject to the increased penalties and surcharges imposed by section 42-4-1701 (4) (c).

(b) If maintenance, repair, or construction activities are occurring or will occur within four hours on a portion of a roadway that is not a state highway, the public entity conducting the activities may designate such portion of the roadway as a maintenance, repair, or construction zone. A person who commits certain violations listed in section 42-4-1701 (4) in a maintenance, repair, or construction zone that is designated pursuant to this section is subject to the increased penalties and surcharges imposed by section 42-4-1701 (4) (c).

(2) The department of transportation or other public entity shall designate a maintenance, repair, or construction zone by erecting or placing an appropriate sign in a conspicuous place before the area where the maintenance, repair, or construction activity is taking place or will be taking place within four hours. Such sign shall notify the public that increased penalties for certain traffic violations are in effect in such zone. The department of transportation or other public entity shall erect or place a second sign after such zone indicating that the increased penalties for certain traffic violations are no longer in effect. A maintenance, repair, or construction zone begins at the location of the sign indicating that increased penalties are in effect and ends at the location of the sign indicating that the increased penalties are no longer in effect.

(3) Signs used for designating the beginning and end of a maintenance, construction, or repair zone shall conform to department of transportation requirements. The department of transportation or other public entity may display such signs on any fixed, variable, or movable stand. The department of transportation or other public entity may place such a sign on a moving vehicle if required for certain activities, including, but not limited to, highway painting work.

42-4-615. School zones - increase in penalties for moving traffic violations. (1) Any person who commits a moving traffic violation in a school zone is subject to the increased penalties and surcharges imposed by section 42-4-1701 (4) (d).

(2) For the purposes of this section, "school zone" means an area that is designated as a school zone and has appropriate signs posted indicating that the penalties and surcharges will be doubled. The state or local government having jurisdiction over the placement of traffic signs and traffic control devices in the school zone area shall designate when the area will be deemed to be a school zone for the purposes of this section. In making such designation, the state or local government shall consider when increased penalties are necessary to protect the safety of school children.

(3) This section does not apply if the penalty and surcharge for a violation has been doubled pursuant to section 42-4-614 because such violation also occurred within a highway maintenance, repair, or construction zone.

42-4-616. Wildlife crossing zones - increase in penalties for moving traffic violations. (1) Except as described by subsection (4) of this section, a person who commits a moving traffic violation in a wildlife crossing zone is subject to the increased penalties and surcharges imposed by section 42-4-1701 (4) (d.5).

(2) For the purposes of this section, "wildlife crossing zone" means an area on a public highway that:

(a) Begins at a sign that conforms to the state traffic control manual, was erected by the department of transportation pursuant to section 42-4-118, and indicates that a person is about to enter a wildlife crossing zone; and

(b) Extends to:

(I) A sign that conforms to the state traffic control manual, was erected by the department of transportation pursuant to section 42-4-118, and indicates that a person is about to leave a wildlife crossing zone; or

(II) If no sign exists that complies with subparagraph (I) of this paragraph (b), the distance indicated on the sign indicating the beginning of the wildlife crossing zone; or

(III) If no sign exists that complies with subparagraph (I) or (II) of this paragraph (b), one-half mile beyond the sign indicating the beginning of the wildlife crossing zone.

(3) (a) If the department of transportation erects a sign that indicates that a person is about to enter a wildlife crossing zone pursuant to section 42-4-118, the department of transportation shall:

(I) Establish the times of day and the periods of the calendar year during which the area will be deemed to be a wildlife crossing zone for the purposes of this section; and

(II) Ensure that the sign indicates the times of day and the periods of the calendar year during which the area will be deemed to be a wildlife crossing zone for the purposes of this section.

(b) In erecting signs as described in paragraph (a) of this subsection (3), the department of transportation, pursuant to section 42-4-118, shall not erect signs establishing a lower speed limit for more than one hundred miles of the public highways of the state that have been established as wildlife crossing zones.

(4) This section shall not apply if:

(a) The person who commits a moving traffic violation in a wildlife crossing zone is already subject to increased penalties and surcharges for said violation pursuant to section 42-4-614 or 42-4-615;

(b) The sign indicating that a person is about to enter a wildlife crossing zone does not indicate that increased traffic penalties are in effect in the zone; or

(c) The person who commits a moving traffic violation in a wildlife crossing zone commits the violation during a time that the area is not deemed by the department of transportation to be a wildlife crossing zone for the purposes of this section.

PART 7

RIGHTS-OF-WAY

42-4-701. Vehicles approaching or entering intersection. (1) When two vehicles approach or enter an intersection from different highways at approximately the same time, the driver of the vehicle on the left shall yield the right-of-way to the vehicle on the right.

(2) The foregoing rule is modified at through highways and otherwise as stated in sections 42-4-702 to 42-4-704.

(3) Any person who violates any provision of this section commits a class A traffic infraction.

42-4-702. Vehicle turning left. The driver of a vehicle intending to turn to the left within an intersection or into an alley, private road, or driveway shall yield the right-of-way to any vehicle approaching from the opposite direction which is within the intersection or so close thereto as to constitute an immediate hazard. Any person who violates any provision of this section commits a class A traffic infraction.

42-4-703. Entering through highway - stop or yield intersection. (1) The department of transportation and local authorities, within their respective jurisdictions, may erect and maintain stop signs, yield signs, or other official traffic control devices to designate through highways or to designate intersections or other roadway junctions at which vehicular traffic on one or more of the roadways is directed to yield or to stop and yield before entering the intersection or junction. In the case of state highways, such regulations shall be subject to the provisions of section 43-2-135 (1) (g), C.R.S.

(2) Every sign erected pursuant to subsection (1) of this section shall be a standard sign adopted by the department of transportation.

(3) Except when directed to proceed by a police officer, every driver of a vehicle approaching a stop sign shall stop at a clearly marked stop line, but if none, before entering the crosswalk on the near side of the intersection, or if none, then at the point nearest the intersecting roadway where the driver has a view of approaching traffic on the intersecting roadway before entering it. After having stopped, the driver shall yield the right-of-way to any vehicle in the intersection or approaching on another roadway so closely as to constitute an immediate hazard during the time when such driver is moving across or within the intersection or junction of roadways.

(4) The driver of a vehicle approaching a yield sign, in obedience to such sign, shall slow to a speed reasonable for the existing conditions and, if required for safety to stop, shall stop at a clearly marked stop line, but if none, before entering the crosswalk on the near side of the intersection, or if none, then at the point nearest the intersecting roadway where the driver has a view of approaching traffic on the intersecting roadway before entering it. After slowing or stopping, the driver shall yield the right-of-way to any vehicle in the intersection or approaching on another roadway so closely as to constitute an immediate hazard during the time such driver is moving across or within the intersection or junction of roadways; except that, if a driver is involved in a collision with a vehicle in the intersection or junction of roadways after driving past a yield sign without stopping, such collision shall be deemed prima facie evidence of the driver's failure to yield right-of-way.

(5) Any person who violates any provision of this section commits a class A traffic infraction.

42-4-704. Vehicle entering roadway. The driver of a vehicle about to enter or cross a roadway from any place other than another roadway shall yield the right-of-way to all vehicles approaching on the roadway to be entered or crossed. Any person who violates any provision of this section commits a class A traffic infraction.

42-4-705. Operation of vehicle approached by emergency vehicle - operation of vehicle approaching stationary emergency vehicle or stationary towing carrier vehicle. (1) Upon the immediate approach of an authorized emergency vehicle making use of audible or visual signals meeting the requirements of section 42-4-213 or 42-4-222, the driver of every other vehicle shall yield the right-of-way and where possible shall immediately clear the farthest left-hand lane lawfully available to through traffic and shall drive to a position parallel to, and as close as possible to, the right-hand edge or curb of a roadway clear of any intersection and shall stop and remain in that position until the authorized emergency vehicle has passed, except when otherwise directed by a police officer.

(2) (a) A driver in a vehicle that is approaching or passing a stationary authorized emergency vehicle that is giving a visual signal by means of flashing, rotating, or oscillating red, blue, or white lights as permitted by section 42-4-213 or 42-4-222 or a stationary towing carrier vehicle that is giving a visual signal by means of flashing, rotating, or oscillating yellow lights shall exhibit due care and caution and proceed as described in paragraphs (b) and (c) of this subsection (2).

(b) On a highway with at least two adjacent lanes proceeding in the same direction on the same side of the highway where a stationary authorized emergency vehicle or stationary towing carrier vehicle is located, the driver of an approaching or passing vehicle shall proceed with due care and caution and yield the right-of-way by moving into a lane at least one moving lane apart from the stationary authorized emergency vehicle or stationary towing carrier vehicle, unless directed otherwise by a peace officer or other authorized emergency personnel. If movement to an adjacent moving lane is not possible due to weather, road conditions, or the immediate presence of vehicular or pedestrian traffic, the driver of the approaching vehicle shall proceed in the manner described in paragraph (c) of this subsection (2).

(c) On a highway that does not have at least two adjacent lanes proceeding in the same direction on the same side of the highway where a stationary authorized emergency vehicle or stationary towing carrier vehicle is located, or if movement by the driver of the approaching vehicle into an adjacent moving lane, as described in paragraph (b) of this subsection (2), is not possible, the driver of an approaching vehicle shall reduce and maintain a safe speed with regard to the location of the stationary authorized vehicle or stationary towing carrier vehicle, weather conditions, road conditions, and vehicular or pedestrian traffic and proceed with due care and caution, or as directed by a peace officer or other authorized emergency personnel.

(2.5) (a) A driver in a vehicle that is approaching or passing a maintenance, repair, or construction vehicle that is moving at less than twenty miles per hour shall exhibit due care and caution and proceed as described in paragraphs (b) and (c) of this subsection (2.5).

(b) On a highway with at least two adjacent lanes proceeding in the same direction on the same side of the highway where a stationary or slow-moving maintenance, repair, or construction vehicle is located, the driver of an approaching or passing vehicle shall proceed with due care and caution and yield the right-of-way by moving into a lane at least one moving lane apart from the vehicle, unless directed otherwise by a peace officer or other authorized emergency personnel. If movement to an adjacent moving lane is not possible due to weather, road conditions, or the immediate presence of vehicular or pedestrian traffic, the driver of the approaching vehicle shall proceed in the manner described in paragraph (c) of this subsection (2.5).

(c) On a highway that does not have at least two adjacent lanes proceeding in the same direction on the same side of the highway where a stationary or slow-moving maintenance, repair, or construction vehicle is located, or if movement by the driver of the approaching vehicle into an adjacent moving lane, as described in paragraph (b) of this subsection (2.5), is not possible, the driver of an approaching vehicle shall reduce and maintain a safe speed with regard to the location of the stationary or slow-moving maintenance, repair, or construction vehicle, weather conditions, road conditions, and vehicular or pedestrian traffic, and shall proceed with due care and caution, or as directed by a peace officer or other authorized emergency personnel.

(2.6) (a) A driver in a vehicle that is approaching or passing a motor vehicle where the tires are being equipped with chains on the side of the highway shall exhibit due care and caution and proceed as described in paragraphs (b) and (c) of this subsection (2.6).

(b) On a highway with at least two adjacent lanes proceeding in the same direction on the same side of the highway where chains are being applied to the tires of a motor vehicle, the driver of an approaching or passing vehicle shall proceed with due care and caution and yield the right-of-way by moving into a lane at least one moving lane apart from the vehicle, unless directed otherwise by a peace officer or other authorized emergency personnel. If movement to an adjacent moving lane is not possible due to weather, road conditions, or the immediate presence of vehicular or pedestrian traffic, the driver of the approaching vehicle shall proceed in the manner described in paragraph (c) of this subsection (2.6).

(c) On a highway that does not have at least two adjacent lanes proceeding in the same direction on the same side of the highway where chains are being applied to the tires of a motor vehicle, or if movement by the driver of the approaching vehicle into an adjacent moving lane, as described in paragraph (b) of this subsection (2.6), is not possible, the driver of an approaching vehicle shall reduce and maintain a safe speed with regard to the location of the motor vehicle where chains are being applied to the tires, weather conditions, road conditions, and vehicular or pedestrian traffic, and shall proceed with due care and caution, or as directed by a peace officer or other authorized emergency personnel.

(3) (a) Any person who violates subsection (1) of this section commits a class A traffic infraction.

(b) Any person who violates subsection (2), (2.5), or (2.6) of this section commits careless driving as described in section 42-4-1402.

42-4-706. Obedience to railroad signal. (1) Any driver of a motor vehicle approaching a railroad crossing sign shall slow down to a speed that is reasonable and safe for the existing conditions. If required to stop for a traffic control device, flagperson, or safety before crossing the railroad grade crossing, the driver shall stop at the marked stop line, if any. If no such stop line exists, the driver shall:

(a) Stop not less than fifteen feet nor more than fifty feet from the nearest rail of the railroad grade crossing and shall not proceed until the railroad grade can be crossed safely; or

(b) In the event the driver would not have a reasonable view of approaching trains when stopped pursuant to paragraph (a) of this subsection (1), stop before proceeding across the railroad grade crossing at the point nearest such crossing where the driver has a reasonable view of approaching trains and not proceed until the railroad grade can be crossed safely.

(2) No person shall drive any vehicle through, around, or under any crossing gate or barrier at a railroad crossing while such gate or barrier is closed or is being opened or closed, nor shall any pedestrian pass through, around, over, or under any crossing gate or barrier at a railroad grade crossing while such gate or barrier is closed or is being opened or closed.

(3) Any person who violates any provision of this section commits a class A traffic infraction.

42-4-707. Certain vehicles must stop at railroad grade crossings. (1) Except as otherwise provided in this section, the driver of a school bus, as defined in paragraph (b) of subsection (5) of this section, carrying any schoolchild, the driver of a vehicle carrying hazardous materials that is required to be placarded in accordance with regulations issued pursuant to section 42-20-108, or the driver of a commercial vehicle, as defined in section 42-4-235, that is transporting passengers, before crossing at grade any tracks of a railroad, shall stop such vehicle within fifty feet but not less than fifteen feet from the nearest rail of such railroad and while so stopped shall listen and look in both directions along such track for any approaching train and for signals indicating the approach of a train and shall not proceed until the driver can do so safely. After stopping as required in this section and upon proceeding when it is safe to do so, the driver of any said vehicle shall cross only in such gear of the vehicle that there will be no necessity for changing gears while traversing such crossing, and the driver shall not manually shift gears while crossing the tracks.

(2) This section shall not apply at street railway grade crossings within a business district.

(3) When stopping as required at such railroad crossing, the driver shall keep as far to the right of the roadway as possible and shall not form two lanes of traffic unless the roadway is marked for four or more lanes of traffic.

(4) Subsection (1) of this section shall not apply at:

(a) (Deleted by amendment, L. 2006, p. 42, § 1, effective July 1, 2006.)

(b) Any railroad grade crossing at which traffic is regulated by a traffic control signal;

(c) Any railroad grade crossing at which traffic is controlled by a police officer or human flagperson;

(d) Any railroad crossing where state or local road authorities within their respective jurisdictions have determined that trains are not operating during certain periods or seasons of the year and have erected an official sign carrying the legend "exempt", which shall give notice when so posted that such crossing is exempt from the stopping requirement provided for in this section.

(5) For the purposes of this section:

(a) The definition of hazardous materials shall be the definition contained in the rules adopted by the chief of the Colorado state patrol pursuant to section 42-20-108.

(b) "School bus" means a school bus that is required to bear on the front and rear of such school bus the words "SCHOOL BUS" and display visual signal lights pursuant to section 42-4-1903 (2) (a).

(6) Any person who violates any provision of this section commits a class A traffic infraction.

42-4-708. Moving heavy equipment at railroad grade crossing. (1) No person shall operate or move any crawler-type tractor, steam shovel, derrick, or roller or any equipment or structure having a normal operating speed of ten or less miles per hour or a vertical body or load clearance of less than nine inches above the level surface of a roadway upon or across any tracks at a railroad grade crossing without first complying with this section.

(2) Notice of any such intended crossing shall be given to a superintendent of such railroad and a reasonable time be given to such railroad to provide proper protection at such crossing.

(3) Before making any such crossing, the person operating or moving any such vehicle or equipment shall first stop the same not less than fifteen feet nor more than fifty feet from the nearest rail of such railroad, and while so stopped shall listen and look in both directions along such track for any approaching train and for signals indicating the approach of a train, and shall not proceed until the crossing can be made safely.

(4) No such crossing shall be made when warning is given by automatic signal or crossing gates or a flagperson or otherwise of the immediate approach of a railroad train or car.

(5) Subsection (3) of this section shall not apply at any railroad crossing where state or local road authorities within their respective jurisdictions have determined that trains are not operating during certain periods or seasons of the year and have erected an official sign carrying the legend "exempt", which shall give notice when so posted that such crossing is exempt from the stopping requirement provided in this section.

(6) Any person who violates any provision of this section commits a class B traffic infraction.

42-4-709. Stop when traffic obstructed. No driver shall enter an intersection or a marked crosswalk or drive onto any railroad grade crossing unless there is sufficient space on the other side of the intersection, crosswalk, or railroad grade crossing to accommodate the vehicle the driver is operating without obstructing the passage of other vehicles, pedestrians, or railroad trains, notwithstanding the indication of any traffic control signal to proceed. Any person who violates any provision of this section commits a class A traffic infraction.

42-4-710. Emerging from or entering alley, driveway, or building. (1) The driver of a vehicle emerging from an alley, driveway, building, parking lot, or other place, immediately prior to driving onto a sidewalk or into the sidewalk area extending across any such alleyway, driveway, or entranceway, shall yield the right-of-way to any pedestrian upon or about to enter such sidewalk or sidewalk area extending across such alleyway, driveway, or entranceway, as may be necessary to avoid collision, and when entering the roadway shall comply with the provisions of section 42-4-704.

(2) The driver of a vehicle entering an alley, driveway, or entranceway shall yield the right-of-way to any pedestrian within or about to enter the sidewalk or sidewalk area extending across such alleyway, driveway, or entranceway.

(3) No person shall drive any vehicle other than a bicycle, electric assisted bicycle, or any other human-powered vehicle upon a sidewalk or sidewalk area, except upon a permanent or duly authorized temporary driveway.

(4) Any person who violates any provision of this section commits a class A traffic infraction.

42-4-711. Driving on mountain highways. (1) The driver of a motor vehicle traveling through defiles or canyons or on mountain highways shall hold such motor vehicle under control and as near to the right-hand edge of the highway as reasonably possible and, except when driving entirely to the right of the center of the roadway, shall give audible warning with the horn of such motor vehicle upon approaching any curve where the view is obstructed within a distance of two hundred feet along the highway.

(2) On narrow mountain highways with turnouts having a grade of six percent or more, ascending vehicles shall have the right-of-way over descending vehicles, except where it is more practicable for the ascending vehicle to return to a turnout.

(3) Any person who violates any provision of this section commits a class A traffic infraction.

42-4-712. Driving in highway work area. (1) The driver of a vehicle shall yield the right-of-way to any authorized vehicle or pedestrian engaged in work upon a highway within any highway construction or maintenance work area indicated by official traffic control devices.

(2) The driver of a vehicle shall yield the right-of-way to any authorized service vehicle engaged in work upon a highway whenever such vehicle displays flashing lights meeting the requirements of section 42-4-214.

(3) State and local road authorities, within their respective jurisdictions and in cooperation with law enforcement agencies, may train and appoint adult civilian personnel for special traffic duty as highway flagpersons within any highway maintenance or construction work area. Whenever such duly authorized flagpersons are wearing the badge, insignia, or uniform of their office, are engaged in the performance of their respective duties, and are displaying any official hand signal device of a type and in the manner prescribed in the adopted state traffic control manual or supplement thereto for signaling traffic in such areas

to stop or to proceed, no person shall willfully fail or refuse to obey the visible instructions or signals so displayed by such flagpersons. Any alleged willful failure or refusal of a driver to comply with such instructions or signals, including information as to the identity of the driver and the license plate number of the vehicle alleged to have been so driven in violation, shall be reported by the work area supervisor in charge at the location to the district attorney for appropriate penalizing action in a court of competent jurisdiction. Any person who violates any provision of this section commits a class A traffic infraction.

42-4-713. Yielding right-of-way to transit buses - definitions - penalty. (1) As used in this section, unless the context otherwise requires:

(a) "Public mass transit operator" has the same meaning as in section 43-1-102 (5), C.R.S.

(b) "Transit bus" means a bus operated by a public mass transit operator.

(2) Drivers of vehicles in the same lane of traffic and behind a transit bus shall yield the right-of-way to the bus if:

(a) The driver of the transit bus, after stopping to allow passengers to board or exit, is signaling an intention to enter a traffic lane; and

(b) A yield sign as described in subsection (3) of this section is displayed and illuminated on the back of the transit bus.

(3) The yield sign referred to in paragraph (b) of subsection (2) of this section shall:

(a) Warn a driver of a vehicle behind the transit bus that the driver is required to yield when the bus is entering a traffic lane; and

(b) Be illuminated when the driver of the transit bus is attempting to enter a traffic lane.

(4) This section does not require a public mass transit operator to install yield signs as described in subsection (3) of this section on transit buses operated by the public mass transit operator.

(5) This section does not relieve a driver of a transit bus from the duty to drive with due regard for the safety of all persons using the roadway.

PART 8

PEDESTRIANS

42-4-801. Pedestrian obedience to traffic control devices and traffic regulations. (1) A pedestrian shall obey the instructions of any official traffic control device specifically applicable to the pedestrian, unless otherwise directed by a police officer.

(2) Pedestrians shall be subject to traffic and pedestrian-control signals as provided in sections 42-4-604 and 42-4-802 (5).

(3) At all other places, pedestrians shall be accorded the privileges and shall be subject to the restrictions stated in this title.

(4) Any person who violates any provision of this section commits a class B traffic infraction.

42-4-802. Pedestrians' right-of-way in crosswalks. (1) When traffic control signals are not in place or not in operation, the driver of a vehicle shall yield the right-of-way, slowing down or stopping if need be to so yield, to a pedestrian crossing the roadway within a crosswalk when the pedestrian is upon the half of the roadway upon which the vehicle is traveling or when the pedestrian is approaching so closely from the opposite half of the roadway as to be in danger.

(2) Subsection (1) of this section shall not apply under the conditions stated in section 42-4-803.

(3) No pedestrian shall suddenly leave a curb or other place of safety and ride a bicycle, ride an electrical assisted bicycle, walk, or run into the path of a moving vehicle that is so close as to constitute an immediate hazard.

(4) Whenever any vehicle is stopped at a marked crosswalk or at any unmarked crosswalk at an intersection to permit a pedestrian to cross the roadway, the driver of any other vehicle approaching from the rear shall not overtake and pass such stopped vehicle.

(5) Whenever special pedestrian-control signals exhibiting "Walk" or "Don't Walk" word or symbol indications are in place, as declared in the traffic control manual adopted by the department of transportation, such signals shall indicate and require as follows:

(a) "Walk" (steady): While the "Walk" indication is steadily illuminated, pedestrians facing such signal may proceed across the roadway in the direction of the signal indication and shall be given the right-of-way by the drivers of all vehicles.

(b) "Don't Walk" (steady): While the "Don't Walk" indication is steadily illuminated, no pedestrian shall enter the roadway in the direction of the signal indication.

(c) "Don't Walk" (flashing): Whenever the "Don't Walk" indication is flashing, no pedestrian shall start to cross the roadway in the direction of such signal indication, but any pedestrian who has partly completed crossing during the "Walk" indication shall proceed to a sidewalk or to a safety island, and all drivers of vehicles shall yield to any such pedestrian.

(d) Whenever a signal system provides for the stopping of all vehicular traffic and the exclusive movement of pedestrians and "Walk" and "Don't Walk" signal indications control such pedestrian movement, pedestrians may cross in any direction between corners of the intersection offering the shortest route within the boundaries of the intersection while the "Walk" indication is exhibited, if signals and other official devices direct pedestrian movement in such manner consistent with section 42-4-803 (4).

(6) Any person who violates any provision of this section commits a class A traffic infraction.

42-4-803. Crossing at other than crosswalks. (1) Every pedestrian crossing a roadway at any point other than within a marked crosswalk or within an unmarked crosswalk at an intersection shall yield the right-of-way to all vehicles upon the roadway.

(2) Any pedestrian crossing a roadway at a point where a pedestrian tunnel or overhead pedestrian crossing has been provided shall yield the right-of-way to all vehicles upon the roadway.

(3) Between adjacent intersections at which traffic control signals are in operation, pedestrians shall not cross at any place except in a marked crosswalk.

(4) No pedestrian shall cross a roadway intersection diagonally unless authorized by official traffic control devices; and, when authorized to cross diagonally, pedestrians shall cross only in accordance with the official traffic control devices pertaining to such crossing movements.

(5) Any person who violates any provision of this section commits a class B traffic infraction.

42-4-804. Pedestrian to use right half of crosswalk. (Repealed)

42-4-805. Pedestrians walking or traveling in a wheelchair on highways. (1) Pedestrians walking or traveling in a wheelchair along and upon highways where sidewalks are not provided shall walk or travel only on a road shoulder as far as practicable from the edge of the roadway. Where neither a sidewalk nor road shoulder is available, any pedestrian walking or traveling in a wheelchair along and upon a highway shall walk as near as practicable to an outside edge of the roadway and, in the case of a two-way roadway, shall walk or travel only on the left side of the roadway facing traffic that may approach from the opposite direction; except that any person lawfully soliciting a ride may stand on either side of such two-way roadway where there is a view of traffic approaching from both directions.

(2) No person shall stand in a roadway for the purpose of soliciting a ride from the driver of any private vehicle. For the purposes of this subsection (2), "roadway" means that portion of the road normally used by moving motor vehicle traffic.

(3) It is unlawful for any person who is under the influence of alcohol or of any controlled substance, as defined in section 12-22-303 (7), C.R.S., or of any stupefying drug to walk or be upon that portion of any highway normally used by moving motor vehicle traffic.

(4) This section applying to pedestrians shall also be applicable to riders of animals.

(5) Any city or town may, by ordinance, regulate the use by pedestrians of streets and highways under its jurisdiction to the extent authorized under subsection (6) of this section and sections 42-4-110 and 42-4-111, but no ordinance regulating such use of streets and highways in a manner differing from this section shall be effective until official signs or devices giving notice thereof have been placed as required by section 42-4-111 (2).

(6) No person shall solicit a ride on any highway included in the interstate system, as defined in section 43-2-101 (2), C.R.S., except at an entrance to or exit from such highway or at places specifically designated by the department of transportation; or, in an emergency affecting a vehicle or its operation, a driver or passenger of a disabled vehicle may solicit a ride on any highway.

(7) Pedestrians shall only be picked up where there is adequate road space for vehicles to pull off and not endanger and impede the flow of traffic.

(8) Upon the immediate approach of an authorized emergency vehicle making use of audible or visual signals meeting the requirements of section 42-4-213 or of a police vehicle properly and lawfully making use of an audible signal only, every pedestrian shall yield the right-of-way to the authorized emergency vehicle and shall leave the roadway and remain off the same until the authorized emergency vehicle has passed, except when otherwise directed by a police officer. This subsection (8) shall not relieve the driver of an authorized emergency vehicle from the duty to use due care as provided in sections 42-4-108 (4) and 42-4-807.

(9) Any person who violates any provision of this section commits a class B traffic infraction.

42-4-806. Driving through safety zone prohibited. No vehicle at any time shall be driven through or within a safety zone. Any person who violates any provision of this section commits a class A traffic infraction.

42-4-807. Drivers to exercise due care. Notwithstanding any of the provisions of this article, every driver of a vehicle shall exercise due care to avoid colliding with any pedestrian upon any roadway and shall give warning by sounding the horn when necessary and shall exercise proper precaution upon observing any child or any obviously confused or incapacitated person upon a roadway. Any person who violates any provision of this section commits a class A traffic infraction.

42-4-808. Drivers and pedestrians, other than persons in wheelchairs, to yield to persons with disabilities. (1) Any pedestrian, other than a person in a wheelchair, or any driver of a vehicle who approaches a person who has an obviously apparent disability of blindness, deafness, or mobility impairment shall immediately come to a full stop and take such precautions before proceeding as are necessary to avoid an accident or injury to said person. A disability shall be deemed to be obviously apparent if, by way of example and without limitation, the person is using a cane or crutches, is assisted by an assistance dog, as defined in section 24-34-803 (7), C.R.S., is being assisted by another person, is in a wheelchair, or is walking with an obvious physical impairment. Any person who violates any provision of this section commits a class A traffic offense.

(2) The department has no authority to assess any points under section 42-2-127 to any

pedestrian who is convicted of a violation of subsection (1) of this section.

PART 9

TURNING - STOPPING

42-4-901. Required position and method of turning. (1) The driver of a motor vehicle intending to turn shall do so as follows:

(a) **Right turns.** Both the approach for a right turn and a right turn shall be made as close as practicable to the right-hand curb or edge of the roadway.

(b) **Left turns.** The driver of a vehicle intending to turn left shall approach the turn in the extreme left-hand lane lawfully available to traffic moving in the direction of travel of such vehicle. Whenever practicable, the left turn shall be made to the left of the center of the intersection so as to leave the intersection or other location in the extreme left-hand lane lawfully available to traffic moving in the same direction as such vehicle on the roadway being entered.

(c) **Two-way left-turn lanes.** Where a special lane for making left turns by drivers proceeding in opposite directions has been indicated by official traffic control devices in the manner prescribed in the state traffic control manual, a left turn shall not be made from any other lane, and a vehicle shall not be driven in said special lane except when preparing for or making a left turn from or into the roadway or when preparing for or making a U-turn when otherwise permitted by law.

(2) The department of transportation and local authorities in their respective jurisdictions may cause official traffic control devices to be placed and thereby require and direct that a different course from that specified in this section be traveled by turning vehicles, and, when such devices are so placed, no driver shall turn a vehicle other than as directed and required by such devices. In the case of streets which are a part of the state highway system, the local regulation shall be subject to the approval of the department of transportation as provided in section 43-2-135 (1) (g), C.R.S.

(3) Any person who violates any provision of this section commits a class A traffic infraction.

42-4-902. Limitations on turning around. (1) No vehicle shall be turned so as to proceed in the opposite direction upon any curve or upon the approach to or near the crest of a grade where such vehicle cannot be seen by the driver of any other vehicle approaching from either direction within such distance as is necessary to avoid interfering with or endangering approaching traffic.

(2) The driver of any vehicle shall not turn such vehicle at an intersection or any other location so as to proceed in the opposite direction unless such movement can be made in safety and without interfering with or endangering other traffic.

(3) Local and state authorities, within their respective jurisdictions, subject to the provisions of section 43-2-135 (1) (g), C.R.S., in the case of streets which are state highways, may erect "U-turn" prohibition or restriction signs at intersections or other locations where such movements are deemed to be hazardous, and, whenever official signs are so erected, no driver of a vehicle shall disobey the instructions thereof.

(4) Any person who violates any provision of this section commits a class A traffic infraction.

42-4-903. Turning movements and required signals. (1) No person shall turn a vehicle at an intersection unless the vehicle is in proper position upon the roadway as required in section 42-4-901, or turn a vehicle to enter a private road or driveway, or otherwise turn a vehicle from a direct course or move right or left upon a roadway unless and until such movement can be made with reasonable safety and then only after giving an appropriate signal in the manner provided in sections 42-4-608 and 42-4-609.

(2) A signal of intention to turn right or left shall be given continuously during not less than the last one hundred feet traveled by the vehicle before turning in urban or metropolitan areas and shall be given continuously for at least two hundred feet on all four-lane highways and other highways where the prima facie or posted speed limit is more than forty miles per hour. Such signals shall be given regardless of existing weather conditions.

(3) No person shall stop or suddenly decrease the speed of a vehicle without first giving an appropriate signal in the manner provided in sections 42-4-608 and 42-4-609 to the driver of any vehicle immediately to the rear when there is opportunity to give such signal.

(4) The signals provided for in section 42-4-608 (2) shall be used to indicate an intention to turn, change lanes, or start from a parked position and shall not be flashed on one side only on a parked or disabled vehicle or flashed as a courtesy or "do pass" signal to operators of other vehicles approaching from the rear.

(5) Any person who violates any provision of this section commits a class A traffic infraction.

PART 10

DRIVING - OVERTAKING - PASSING

42-4-1001. Drive on right side - exceptions. (1) Upon all roadways of sufficient width, a vehicle shall be driven upon the right half of the roadway, except as follows:

(a) When overtaking and passing another vehicle proceeding in the same direction under the rules governing such movement;

(b) When an obstruction exists making it necessary to drive to the left of the center of the highway; but any person so doing shall yield the right-of-way to all vehicles traveling in the proper direction upon the unobstructed portion of the highway within such distance as to constitute an immediate hazard;

(c) Upon a roadway divided into three lanes for traffic under the rules applicable thereon; or

(d) Upon a roadway restricted to one-way traffic as indicated by official traffic control devices.

(2) Upon all roadways any vehicle proceeding at less than the normal speed of traffic at the time and place and under the conditions then existing shall be driven in the right-hand lane then available for traffic or as close as practicable to the right-hand curb or edge of the roadway, except when overtaking and passing another vehicle proceeding in the same direction or when preparing for a left turn at an intersection or into a private road or driveway.

(3) Upon any roadway having four or more lanes for moving traffic and providing for two-way movement of traffic, no vehicle shall be driven to the left of the center line of the roadway, except when authorized by official traffic control devices designating certain lanes to the left side of the center of the roadway for use by traffic not otherwise permitted to use such lanes or except as permitted under subsection (1) (b) of this section. However, this subsection (3) does not prohibit the crossing of the center line in making a left turn into or from an alley, private road, or driveway when such movement can be made in safety and without interfering with, impeding, or endangering other traffic lawfully using the highway.

(4) Any person who violates any provision of this section commits a class A traffic infraction.

42-4-1002. Passing oncoming vehicles. (1) Drivers of vehicles proceeding in opposite directions shall pass each other to the right, and, upon roadways having width for not more than one lane of traffic in each direction, each driver shall give to the other at least one-half of the main-traveled portion of the roadway as nearly as possible.

(2) A driver shall not pass a bicyclist moving in the same direction and in the same lane when there is oncoming traffic unless the driver can simultaneously:

(a) Allow oncoming vehicles at least one-half of the main-traveled portion of the roadway in accordance with subsection (1) of this section; and

(b) Allow the bicyclist at least a three-foot separation between the right side of the driver's vehicle, including all mirrors or other projections, and the left side of the bicyclist at all times.

(3) Any person who violates any provision of this section commits a class A traffic infraction.

42-4-1003. Overtaking a vehicle on the left. (1) The following rules shall govern the overtaking and passing of vehicles proceeding in the same direction, subject to the limitations, exceptions, and special rules stated in this section and sections 42-4-1004 to 42-4-1008:

(a) The driver of a vehicle overtaking another vehicle proceeding in the same direction shall pass to the left of the vehicle at a safe distance and shall not again drive to the right side of the roadway until safely clear of the overtaken vehicle.

(b) The driver of a motor vehicle overtaking a bicyclist proceeding in the same direction shall allow the bicyclist at least a three-foot separation between the right side of the driver's vehicle, including all mirrors or other projections, and the left side of the bicyclist at all times.

(c) Except when overtaking and passing on the right is permitted, the driver of an overtaken vehicle shall give way to the right in favor of the overtaking vehicle on audible signal and shall not increase the speed of the driver's vehicle until completely passed by the overtaking vehicle.

(2) Any person who violates any provision of this section commits a class A traffic infraction.

42-4-1004. When overtaking on the right is permitted. (1) The driver of a vehicle may overtake and pass upon the right of another vehicle only under the following conditions:

(a) When the vehicle overtaken is making or giving indication of making a left turn;

(b) Upon a street or highway with unobstructed pavement not occupied by parked vehicles and marked for two or more lanes of moving vehicles in each direction; or

(c) Upon a one-way street or upon any roadway on which traffic is restricted to one direction of movement where the roadway is free from obstructions and marked for two or more lanes of moving vehicles.

(1.5) The driver of a motor vehicle upon a one-way roadway with two or more marked traffic lanes, when overtaking a bicyclist proceeding in the same direction and riding on the left-hand side of the road, shall allow the bicyclist at least a three-foot separation between the left side of the driver's vehicle, including all mirrors or other projections, and the right side of the bicyclist at all times.

(2) The driver of a vehicle may overtake and pass another vehicle upon the right only under conditions permitting such movement in safety. In no event shall such movement be made by driving off the pavement or main-traveled portion of the roadway.

(3) Any person who violates any provision of this section commits a class A traffic infraction.

42-4-1005. Limitations on overtaking on the left. (1) No vehicle shall be driven to the left side of the center of the roadway in overtaking and passing another vehicle proceeding in the same direction unless authorized by the provisions of this article and unless such left side is clearly visible and is free of oncoming traffic for a sufficient distance ahead to permit such overtaking and passing to be completed without interfering with the operation of any vehicle approaching from the opposite direction or any vehicle overtaken. In every event the overtaking vehicle must return to an authorized lane of travel as soon as practicable and, in the event the passing movement involves the use of a lane authorized for vehicles approaching from the opposite direction, before coming within two hundred feet of any approaching vehicle.

(2) No vehicle shall be driven on the left side of the roadway under the following conditions:

(a) When approaching or upon the crest of a grade or a curve in the highway where the driver's view is obstructed within such distance as to create a hazard in the event another vehicle might approach from the opposite direction;

(b) When approaching within one hundred feet of or traversing any intersection or railroad grade crossing; or

(c) When the view is obstructed upon approaching within one hundred feet of any bridge, viaduct, or tunnel.

(3) The department of transportation and local authorities are authorized to determine those portions of any highway under their respective jurisdictions where overtaking and passing or driving on the left side of the roadway would be especially hazardous and may by appropriate signs or markings on the roadway indicate the beginning and end of such zones. Where such signs or markings are in place to define a no-passing zone and such signs or markings are clearly visible to an ordinarily observant person, no driver shall drive on the left side of the roadway within such no-passing zone or on the left side of any pavement striping designed to mark such no-passing zone throughout its length.

(4) The provisions of this section shall not apply:

(a) Upon a one-way roadway;

(b) Under the conditions described in section 42-4-1001 (1) (b);

(c) To the driver of a vehicle turning left into or from an alley, private road, or driveway when such movement can be made in safety and without interfering with, impeding, or endangering other traffic lawfully using the highway; or

(d) To the driver of a vehicle passing a bicyclist moving the same direction and in the same lane when such movement can be made in safety and without interfering with, impeding, or endangering other traffic lawfully using the highway.

(5) Any person who violates any provision of this section commits a class A traffic infraction.

42-4-1006. One-way roadways and rotary traffic islands. (1) Upon a roadway restricted to one-way traffic, a vehicle shall be driven only in the direction designated at all or such times as shall be indicated by official traffic control devices.

(2) A vehicle passing around a rotary traffic island shall be driven only to the right of such island.

(3) The department of transportation and local authorities with respect to highways under their respective jurisdictions may designate any roadway, part of a roadway, or specific lanes upon which vehicular traffic shall proceed in one direction at all or such times as shall be indicated by official traffic control devices. In the case of streets which are a part of the state highway system, the regulation shall be subject to the approval of the department of transportation pursuant to section 43-2-135 (1) (g), C.R.S.

(4) Any person who violates any provision of this section commits a class A traffic infraction.

42-4-1007. Driving on roadways laned for traffic. (1) Whenever any roadway has been divided into two or more clearly marked lanes for traffic, the following rules in addition to all others consistent with this section shall apply:

(a) A vehicle shall be driven as nearly as practicable entirely within a single lane and shall not be moved from such lane until the driver has first ascertained that such movement can be made with safety.

(b) Upon a roadway which is divided into three lanes and provides for two-way movement of traffic, a vehicle shall not be driven in the center lane except when overtaking and passing another vehicle traveling in the same direction where the roadway is clearly visible and such center lane is clear of traffic within a safe distance, or in preparation for a left turn, or where such center lane is at the time allocated exclusively to the traffic moving in the direction the vehicle is proceeding and is designated by official traffic control devices to give notice of such allocation. Under no condition shall an attempt be made to pass upon the shoulder or any portion of the roadway remaining to the right of the indicated right-hand traffic lane.

(c) Official traffic control devices may be erected directing specified traffic to use a designated lane or designating those lanes to be used by traffic moving in a particular direction regardless of the center of the roadway, and drivers of vehicles shall obey the directions of every such device.

(d) Official traffic control devices may be installed prohibiting the changing of lanes on sections of roadway, and drivers of vehicles shall obey the directions of every such device.

(2) Any person who violates any provision of this section commits a class A traffic infraction.

42-4-1008. Following too closely. (1) The driver of a motor vehicle shall not follow another vehicle more closely than is reasonable and prudent, having due regard for the speed of such vehicles and the traffic upon and the condition of the highway.

(2) The driver of any motor truck or motor vehicle drawing another vehicle when traveling upon a roadway outside of a business or residence district and which is following another motor truck or motor vehicle drawing another vehicle shall, whenever conditions permit, leave sufficient space so that an overtaking vehicle may enter and occupy such space without danger;

except that this shall not prevent a motor truck or motor vehicle drawing another vehicle from overtaking and passing any like vehicle or other vehicle.

(3) Motor vehicles being driven upon any roadway outside of a business or residence district in a caravan or motorcade, whether or not towing other vehicles, shall be so operated as to allow sufficient space between each such vehicle or combination of vehicles so as to enable any other vehicle to enter and occupy such space without danger. This provision shall not apply to funeral processions.

(4) Any person who violates any provision of this section commits a class A traffic infraction.

42-4-1008.5. Crowding or threatening bicyclist. (1) The driver of a motor vehicle shall not, in a careless and imprudent manner, drive the vehicle unnecessarily close to, toward, or near a bicyclist.

(2) Any person who violates subsection (1) of this section commits careless driving as described in section 42-4-1402.

42-4-1009. Coasting prohibited. (1) The driver of any motor vehicle when traveling upon a downgrade shall not coast with the gears or transmission of such vehicle in neutral.

(2) The driver of a truck or bus when traveling upon a downgrade shall not coast with the clutch disengaged.

(3) Any person who violates any provision of this section commits a class A traffic infraction.

42-4-1010. Driving on divided or controlled-access highways. (1) Whenever any highway has been divided into separate roadways by leaving an intervening space or by a physical barrier or clearly indicated dividing section so constructed as to impede vehicular traffic, every vehicle shall be driven only upon the right-hand roadway, unless directed or permitted to use another roadway by official traffic control devices. No vehicle shall be driven over, across, or within any such dividing space, barrier, or section, except through an opening in such physical barrier or dividing section or space or at a crossover or intersection as established, unless specifically prohibited by official signs and markings or by the provisions of section 42-4-902. However, this subsection (1) does not prohibit a left turn across a median island formed by standard pavement markings or other mountable or traversable devices as prescribed in the state traffic control manual when such movement can be made in safety and without interfering with, impeding, or endangering other traffic lawfully using the highway.

(2) (a) No person shall drive a vehicle onto or from any controlled-access roadway except at such entrances and exits as are established by public authority.

(b) Wherever an acceleration lane has been provided in conjunction with a ramp entering a controlled-access highway and the ramp intersection is not designated or signed as a stop or yield intersection as provided in section 42-4-703 (1), drivers may use the acceleration lane to attain a safe speed for merging with through traffic when conditions permit such acceleration with safety. Traffic so merging shall be subject to the rule governing the changing of lanes as set forth in section 42-4-1007 (1) (a).

(c) Wherever a deceleration lane has been provided in conjunction with a ramp leaving a controlled-access highway, drivers shall use such lane to slow to a safe speed for making an exit turn after leaving the mainstream of faster-moving traffic.

(3) The department of transportation may by resolution or order entered in its minutes and local authorities may by ordinance consistent with the provisions of section 43-2-135 (1) (g), C.R.S., with respect to any controlled-access highway under their respective jurisdictions, prohibit the use of any such highway by any class or kind of traffic which is found to be incompatible with the normal and safe movement of traffic. The department of transportation or the local authority adopting such prohibitory regulations shall install official traffic control devices in conformity with the standards established by sections 42-4-601 and 42-4-602 at entrance points or along the highway on which such regulations are applicable. When such devices are so in place, giving notice thereof, no person shall disobey the restrictions made known by such devices. This subsection (3) shall not be construed to give the department authority to regulate pedestrian use of highways in a manner contrary to the provisions of section 42-4-805.

(4) Any person who violates any provision of this section commits a class A traffic infraction.

42-4-1011. Use of runaway vehicle ramps. (1) No person shall use a runaway vehicle ramp unless such person is in an emergency situation requiring use of the ramp to stop such person's vehicle.

(2) No person shall stop, stand, or park a vehicle on a runaway vehicle ramp or in the pathway of the ramp.

(3) Any person who violates any provision of this section commits a class A traffic infraction.

42-4-1012. High occupancy vehicle (HOV) and high occupancy toll (HOT) lanes. (1) (a) The department of transportation and local authorities, with respect to streets and highways under their respective jurisdictions, may designate exclusive or preferential lanes for vehicles that carry a specified number of persons. The occupancy level of vehicles and the time of day when lane usage is restricted to high occupancy vehicles, if applicable, shall be designated by official traffic control devices.

(b) (I) On or before July 1, 2001, the department shall issue a request for proposals to private entities for the purpose of entering into a contract with such an entity for the conversion of an existing high occupancy vehicle lane described in paragraph (a) of this subsection (1) to a high occupancy toll lane and for the purpose of entering into a contract for the operation of the high occupancy toll lane by a private entity; except that the department may convert or operate the high occupancy toll lane, or both, in the event that no proposal by a private entity for such conversion or operation, or both, is acceptable.

(II) The high occupancy toll lane shall be a lane for use by vehicles carrying less than the specified number of persons for such high occupancy vehicle lane that pay a specified toll or fee.

(III) Any contract entered into between the department and a private entity pursuant to subparagraph (I) of this paragraph (b) shall:

(A) Authorize the private entity to impose tolls for use of the high occupancy toll lane;

(B) Require that over the term of such contract only toll revenues be applied to payment of the private entity's capital outlay costs for the project, the costs associated with operations, toll collection, administration of the high occupancy toll lane, if any, and a reasonable return on investment to the private entity, as evidenced by and consistent with the returns on investment to private entities on similar public and private projects;

(C) Require that any excess toll revenue either be applied to any indebtedness incurred by the private entity with respect to the project or be paid into the state highway fund created pursuant to section 43-1-219, C.R.S., for exclusive use in the corridor where the high occupancy toll lane is located including for maintenance and enforcement purposes in the high occupancy toll lane and for other traffic congestion relieving options including transit. Such contract shall define or provide a method for calculating excess toll revenues and shall specify the amount of indebtedness that the private entity may incur and apply excess toll revenues to before such revenues must be paid into the state highway fund. It is not the intent of the general assembly that the conversion of a high occupancy vehicle lane to a high occupancy toll lane shall detract in any way from the possible provision of mass transit options by the regional transportation district or any other agency in the corridor where the high occupancy toll lane is located.

(IV) The department shall structure a variable toll or fee to ensure a level of service C and unrestricted access to the lanes at all times by eligible vehicles, including buses, carpools, and EPA certified low-emitting vehicles with a gross vehicle weight rating over ten thousand pounds.

(V) The department shall not enter into a contract for the conversion of a high occupancy vehicle lane to a high occupancy toll lane if such a conversion will result in the loss or refund of federal funds payable, available, or paid to the state for construction, reconstruction, repairs, improvement, planning, supervision, and maintenance of the state highway system and other public highways.

(VI) The department shall require the private entity entering into a contract pursuant to this section to provide such performance bond or other surety for the project as the department may reasonably require.

(c) Whenever practicable, a high occupancy toll lane described in paragraph (b) of this subsection (1) shall be physically separated from the other lanes of a street or highway so as to minimize the interference between traffic in the designated lanes and traffic in the other lanes.

(d) The department shall develop and adopt functional specifications and standards for an automatic vehicle identification system for use on high occupancy vehicle lanes, high occupancy toll lanes, any public highway constructed and operated under the provisions of part 5 of article 4 of title 43, C.R.S., and any other street or highway where tolls or charges are imposed for the privilege of traveling upon such street or highway. The specifications and standards shall ensure that:

(I) Automatic vehicle identification systems utilized by the state, municipality, or other entity having jurisdiction over the street or highway are compatible with one another;

(II) A vehicle owner shall not be required to purchase or install more than one device to use on all toll facilities;

(III) Toll facility operators have the ability to select from different manufacturers and vendors of automatic vehicle identification systems; and

(IV) There is compatibility between any automatic vehicle identification system in operation on August 4, 1999, and any automatic vehicle identification system designed and installed on and after said date; except that the operator of an automatic vehicle identification system in operation on August 4, 1999, may replace such system with a different system that is not compatible with the system in operation on August 4, 1999, subject to the approval of the department. After the department approves such replacement, the specifications and standards developed pursuant to this paragraph (d) shall be amended to require compatibility with the replacement system.

(2) A motorcycle may be operated upon high occupancy vehicle lanes pursuant to section 163 of Public Law 97-424 or upon high occupancy toll lanes, unless prohibited by official traffic control devices.

(2.5) (a) (I) Except as otherwise provided in paragraph (d) of this subsection (2.5), a motor vehicle with a gross vehicle weight of twenty-six thousand pounds or less that is either an inherently low-emission vehicle or a hybrid vehicle may be operated upon high occupancy vehicle lanes without regard to the number of persons in the vehicle and without payment of a special toll or fee. The exemption relating to hybrid vehicles shall apply only if such exemption does not affect the receipt of federal funds and does not violate any federal laws or regulations.

(II) As used in this subsection (2.5), "inherently low-emission vehicle" or "ILEV" means:

(A) A light-duty vehicle or light-duty truck, regardless of whether such vehicle or truck is part of a motor vehicle fleet, that has been certified by the federal environmental protection agency as conforming to the ILEV guidelines, procedures, and standards as published in the federal register at 58 FR 11888 (March 1, 1993) and 59 FR 50042 (September 30, 1994), as amended from time to time; and

(B) A heavy-duty vehicle powered by an engine that has been certified as set forth in subsubparagraph (A) of this subparagraph (II).

(III) As used in this subsection (2.5), "hybrid vehicle" means a motor vehicle with a hybrid propulsion system that uses an alternative fuel by operating on both an alternative fuel, including electricity, and a traditional fuel.

(b) No person shall operate a vehicle upon a high occupancy vehicle lane pursuant to this subsection (2.5) unless the vehicle:

(I) Meets all applicable federal emission standards set forth in 40 CFR sec. 88.311-93, as amended from time to time, or, subject to subparagraph (I) of paragraph (a) of this subsection (2.5), is a hybrid vehicle; and

(II) Is identified by means of a circular sticker or decal at least four inches in diameter, made of bright orange reflective material, and affixed either to the windshield, to the front of the sideview mirror on the driver's side, or to the front bumper of the vehicle. Said sticker or decal shall be approved by the Colorado department of transportation.

(c) The department of transportation and local authorities, with respect to streets and highways under their respective jurisdictions, shall provide information via official traffic control devices to indicate that ILEVs and, subject to subparagraph (I) of paragraph (a) of this subsection (2.5), hybrid vehicles may be operated upon high occupancy vehicle lanes pursuant to this section. Such information may, but need not, be added to existing printed signs, but as existing printed signs related to high occupancy vehicle lane use are replaced or new ones are erected, such information shall be added. In addition, whenever existing electronic signs are capable of being reprogrammed to carry such information, they shall be so reprogrammed by September 1, 2003.

(d) (I) In consultation with the regional transportation district, the department of transportation and local authorities, with respect to streets and highways under their respective jurisdictions, shall, in connection with their periodic level-of-service evaluation of high occupancy vehicle lanes, perform a level-of-service evaluation of the use of high occupancy vehicle lanes by ILEVs and hybrid vehicles. If the use of high occupancy vehicle lanes by ILEVs or hybrid vehicles is determined to cause a significant decrease in the level of service for other bona fide users of such lanes, then the department of transportation or a local authority may restrict or eliminate use of such lanes by ILEVs or hybrid vehicles.

(II) If the United States secretary of transportation makes a formal determination that, by giving effect to paragraph (a) of this subsection (2.5) on a particular highway or lane, the state of Colorado would disqualify itself from receiving federal highway funds the state would otherwise qualify to receive or would be required to refund federal transportation grant funds it has already received, then said paragraph (a) shall not be effective as to such highway or lane.

(3) (a) Any person who uses a high occupancy vehicle lane in violation of restrictions imposed by the department of transportation or local authorities commits a class A traffic infraction.

(b) Any person convicted of a third or subsequent offense of paragraph (a) of this subsection (3) committed within a twelve-month period shall be subject to an increased penalty pursuant to section 42-4-1701 (4) (a) (I) (K).

42-4-1013. Passing lane - definitions - penalty. (1) A person shall not drive a motor vehicle in the passing lane of a highway if the speed limit is sixty-five miles per hour or more unless such person is passing other motor vehicles that are in a nonpassing lane or turning left, or unless the volume of traffic does not permit the motor vehicle to safely merge into a nonpassing lane.

(2) For the purposes of this section:

(a) "Nonpassing lane" means any lane that is to the right of the passing lane if there are two or more adjacent lanes of traffic moving in the same direction in one roadway.

(b) "Passing lane" means the farthest to the left lane if there are two or more adjacent lanes of traffic moving in the same direction in one roadway; except that, if such left lane is restricted to high occupancy vehicle use or is designed for left turns only, the passing lane shall be the lane immediately to the right of such high occupancy lane or left-turn lane.

(3) A person who violates this section commits a class A traffic infraction.

PART 11

SPEED REGULATIONS

42-4-1101. Speed limits. (1) No person shall drive a vehicle on a highway at a speed greater than is reasonable and prudent under the conditions then existing.

(2) Except when a special hazard exists that requires a lower speed, the following speeds shall be lawful:

(a) Twenty miles per hour on narrow, winding mountain highways or on blind curves;

(b) Twenty-five miles per hour in any business district, as defined in section 42-1-102 (11);

(c) Thirty miles per hour in any residence district, as defined in section 42-1-102 (80);

(d) Forty miles per hour on open mountain highways;

(e) Forty-five miles per hour for all single rear axle vehicles in the business of transporting trash that exceed twenty thousand pounds, where higher speeds are posted, when said vehicle is loaded as an exempted vehicle pursuant to section 42-4-507 (3);

(f) Fifty-five miles per hour on other open highways which are not on the interstate system, as defined in section 43-2-101 (2), C.R.S., and are not surfaced, four-lane freeways or expressways;

(g) Sixty-five miles per hour on surfaced, four-lane highways which are on the interstate system, as defined in section 43-2-101 (2), C.R.S., or are freeways or expressways;

(h) Any speed not in excess of a speed limit designated by an official traffic control device.

(3) No driver of a vehicle shall fail to decrease the speed of such vehicle from an otherwise lawful speed to a reasonable and prudent speed when a special hazard exists with respect to pedestrians or other traffic or by reason of weather or highway conditions.

(4) Except as otherwise provided in paragraph (c) of subsection (8) of this section, any speed in excess of the lawful speeds set forth in subsection (2) of this section shall be prima facie evidence that such speed was not reasonable or prudent under the conditions then existing. As used in this subsection (4), "prima facie evidence" means evidence which is sufficient proof that the speed was not reasonable or prudent under the conditions then existing, and which will remain sufficient proof of such fact, unless contradicted and overcome by evidence bearing upon the question of whether or not the speed was reasonable and prudent under the conditions then existing.

(5) In every charge of violating subsection (1) of this section, the complaint, summons and complaint, or penalty assessment notice shall specify the speed at which the defendant is alleged to have driven and also the alleged reasonable and prudent speed applicable at the specified time and location of the alleged violation.

(6) The provisions of this section shall not be construed to relieve the party alleging negligence under this section in any civil action for damages from the burden of proving that such negligence was the proximate cause of an accident.

(7) Notwithstanding paragraphs (a), (b), and (c) of subsection (2) of this section, any city or town may by ordinance adopt absolute speed limits as the maximum lawful speed limits in its jurisdiction, and such speed limits shall not be subject to the provisions of subsection (4) of this section.

(8) (a) (Deleted by amendment, L. 96, p. 578, § 2, effective May 25, 1996.)

(b) Notwithstanding any other provisions of this section, no person shall drive a vehicle on a highway at a speed in excess of a maximum lawful speed limit of seventy-five miles per hour.

(c) The speed limit set forth in paragraph (b) of this subsection (8) is the maximum lawful speed limit and is not subject to the provisions of subsection (4) of this section.

(d) State and local authorities within their respective jurisdictions shall not authorize any speed limit which exceeds seventy-five miles per hour on any highway.

(e) The provisions of this subsection (8) are declared to be matters of both local and statewide concern requiring uniform compliance throughout the state.

(f) In every charge of a violation of paragraph (b) of this subsection (8), the complaint, summons and complaint, or penalty assessment notice shall specify the speed at which the defendant is alleged to have driven and also the maximum lawful speed limit of seventy-five miles per hour.

(g) Notwithstanding any other provision of this section, no person shall drive a low-power scooter on a roadway at a speed in excess of forty miles per hour. State and local authorities shall not authorize low-power scooters to exceed forty miles per hour on a roadway.

(9) The conduct of a driver of a vehicle which would otherwise constitute a violation of this section is justifiable and not unlawful when:

(a) It is necessary as an emergency measure to avoid an imminent public or private injury which is about to occur by reason of a situation occasioned or developed through no conduct of said driver and which is of sufficient gravity that, according to ordinary standards of intelligence and morality, the desirability and urgency of avoiding the injury clearly outweigh the desirability of avoiding the consequences sought to be prevented by this section; or

(b) With respect to authorized emergency vehicles, the applicable conditions for exemption, as set forth in section 42-4-108, exist.

(10) The minimum requirement for commission of a traffic infraction or misdemeanor traffic offense under this section is the performance by a driver of prohibited conduct, which includes a voluntary act or the omission to perform an act which said driver is physically capable of performing.

(11) It shall not be a defense to prosecution for a violation of this section that:

(a) The defendant's conduct was not performed intentionally, knowingly, recklessly, or with criminal negligence; or

(b) The defendant's conduct was performed under a mistaken belief of fact, including, but not limited to, a mistaken belief of the defendant regarding the speed of the defendant's vehicle; or

(c) The defendant's vehicle has a greater operating or fuel-conserving efficiency at speeds greater than the reasonable and prudent speed under the conditions then existing or at speeds greater than the maximum lawful speed limit.

(12) (a) A violation of driving one to twenty-four miles per hour in excess of the reasonable and prudent speed or in excess of the maximum lawful speed limit of seventy-five miles per hour is a class A traffic infraction.

(b) A violation of driving twenty-five or more miles per hour in excess of the reasonable and prudent speed or in excess of the maximum lawful speed limit of seventy-five miles per hour is a class 2 misdemeanor traffic offense; except that such violation within a maintenance, repair, or construction zone, designated pursuant to section 42-4-614, is a class 1 misdemeanor traffic offense.

(c) A violation under subsection (3) of this section is a class A traffic infraction.

42-4-1102. Altering of speed limits. (1) (a) Whenever the department of transportation determines upon the basis of a traffic investigation or survey or upon the basis of appropriate design standards and projected traffic volumes in the case of newly constructed highways or segments thereof that any speed specified or established as authorized under sections 42-4-1101 to 42-4-1104 is greater or less than is reasonable or safe under the road and traffic conditions at any intersection or other place or upon any part of a state highway under its jurisdiction, said department shall determine and declare a reasonable and safe speed limit thereat which shall be effective when appropriate signs giving notice thereof are erected at such intersection or other place or upon the approaches thereto; except that no speed limit in excess of seventy-five miles per hour shall be authorized by said department.

(b) Repealed.

(2) Whenever county or municipal authorities within their respective jurisdictions determine upon the basis of a traffic investigation or survey, or upon the basis of appropriate design standards and projected traffic volumes in the case of newly constructed highways or segments thereof, that any speed specified or established as authorized under sections 42-4-1101 to 42-4-1104 is greater or less than is reasonable or safe under the road and traffic conditions at any intersection or other place or upon any part of a street or highway in its jurisdiction, said local authority shall determine and declare a reasonable and safe speed limit thereat which shall be effective when appropriate signs giving notice thereof are erected at such intersection or other place or upon the approaches thereto. No such local authority shall have the power to alter the basic rules set forth in section 42-4-1101 (1) or in any event to authorize by resolution or ordinance a speed in excess of seventy-five miles per hour.

(3) Local municipal authorities within their respective jurisdictions shall determine upon the basis of a traffic investigation or survey the proper speed for all arterial streets and shall declare a reasonable and safe speed limit thereon which may be greater or less than the speed specified under section 42-4-1101 (2) (b) or (2) (c). Such speed limit shall not exceed seventy-five miles per hour and shall become effective when appropriate signs are erected giving notice thereof. For purposes of this subsection (3), an "arterial street" means any United States or state-numbered route, controlled-access highway, or other major radial or circumferential street or highway designated by local authorities within their respective jurisdictions as part of a major arterial system of streets or highways.

(4) No alteration of speed limits on state highways within cities, cities and counties, and incorporated towns shall be effective until such alteration has been approved in writing by the department of transportation. Upon the request of any incorporated city or town having a population of five thousand or less, the department of transportation shall conduct any traffic investigation or survey that is deemed to be warranted for determination of a safe and reasonable speed limit on any street or portion thereof that is a state highway. Any speed limit so determined by said department shall then become effective when declared by the local authority and made known by official signs conforming to the state traffic control manual.

(5) Whenever the department of transportation or local authorities, within their respective jurisdictions, determine upon the basis of a traffic investigation or survey that a reduced speed limit is warranted in a school or construction area or other place during certain hours or periods of the day when special or temporary hazards exist, the department or the concerned local authority may erect or display official signs of a type prescribed in the state traffic control manual giving notice of the appropriate speed limit for such conditions and stating the time or period the regulation is effective. When such signs are erected or displayed, the lawful speed limit at the particular time and place shall be that which is then indicated upon such signs; except that no such speed limit shall be less than twenty miles per hour on a state highway or other arterial street as defined in subsection (3) of this section nor less than fifteen miles per hour on any other road or street, nor shall any such reduced speed limit be made applicable at times when the special conditions for which it is imposed cease to exist. Such reduced speed limits on streets which are state highways shall be subject to the written approval of the department of transportation before becoming effective.

(6) In its discretion, a municipality, by ordinance, or a county, by resolution of the board of county commissioners, may impose and enforce stop sign regulations and speed limits, not inconsistent with the provisions of sections 42-4-1101 to 42-4-1104, upon any way which is open to travel by motor vehicles and which is privately maintained in mobile home parks, when appropriate signs giving notice of such enforcement are erected at the entrances to such ways. Unless there is an agreement to the contrary, the jurisdiction ordering the regulations shall be responsible for the erection and maintenance of the signs.

(7) Any powers granted in this section to county or municipal authorities may be exercised by such authorities or by any municipal officer or employee who is designated by ordinance to exercise such powers.

(8) The department of transportation shall not set a speed limit on interstate 70 for commercial vehicles or any other motor vehicle that differs from the highest authorized speed for any other type of motor vehicle on the same

portion of a highway by more than twenty-five miles per hour.

42-4-1103. Minimum speed regulation. (1) No person shall drive a motor vehicle on any highway at such a slow speed as to impede or block the normal and reasonable forward movement of traffic, except when a reduced speed is necessary for safe operation of such vehicle or in compliance with law.

(2) Whenever the department of transportation or local authorities within their respective jurisdictions determine, on the basis of an engineering and traffic investigation as described in the state traffic control manual, that slow speeds on any part of a highway consistently impede the normal and reasonable movement of traffic, said department or such local authority may determine and declare a minimum speed limit below which no person shall drive a vehicle, except when necessary for safe operation or in compliance with law.

(3) Notwithstanding any minimum speed that may be authorized and posted pursuant to this section, if any person drives a motor vehicle on a highway outside an incorporated area or on any controlled-access highway at a speed less than the normal and reasonable speed of traffic under the conditions then and there existing and by so driving at such slower speed impedes or retards the normal and reasonable movement of vehicular traffic following immediately behind, then such driver shall:

(a) Where the width of the traveled way permits, drive in the right-hand lane available to traffic or on the extreme right side of the roadway consistent with the provisions of section 42-4-1001 (2) until such impeded traffic has passed by; or

(b) Pull off the roadway at the first available place where such movement can safely and lawfully be made until such impeded traffic has passed by.

(4) Wherever special uphill traffic lanes or roadside turnouts are provided and posted, drivers of all vehicles proceeding at less than the normal and reasonable speed of traffic shall use such lanes or turnouts to allow other vehicles to pass or maintain normal traffic flow.

(5) Any person who violates any provision of this section commits a class A traffic infraction.

42-4-1104. Speed limits on elevated structures. (1) No person shall drive a vehicle over any bridge or other elevated structure constituting a part of a highway at a speed which is greater than the maximum speed which can be maintained with safety to such bridge or structure, when such structure is signposted as provided in this section.

(2) The department of transportation upon request from any local authority shall, or upon its own initiative may, conduct an investigation of any bridge or other elevated structure constituting a part of a highway, and, if it finds that such structure cannot with safety to itself withstand vehicles traveling at the speed otherwise permissible under sections 42-4-1101 to 42-4-1104, said department shall determine and declare the maximum speed of vehicles which such structure can withstand and shall cause or permit suitable standard signs stating such maximum speed to be erected and maintained before each end of such structure in conformity with the state traffic control manual.

(3) Upon the trial of any person charged with a violation of this section, proof of said determination of the maximum speed by said department and the existence of said signs shall constitute conclusive evidence of the maximum speed which can be maintained with safety to such bridge or structure.

(4) Any person who violates any provision of this section commits a class A traffic infraction.

42-4-1105. Speed contests - speed exhibitions - aiding and facilitating - immobilization of motor vehicle - definitions. (1) (a) Except as otherwise provided in subsection (4) of this section, it is unlawful for a person to knowingly engage in a speed contest on a highway.

(b) For purposes of this section, "speed contest" means the operation of one or more motor vehicles to conduct a race or a time trial, including but not limited to rapid acceleration, exceeding reasonable and prudent speeds for highways and existing traffic conditions, vying for position, or performing one or more lane changes in an attempt to gain advantage over one or more of the other race participants.

(c) A person who violates any provision of this subsection (1) commits a class 1 misdemeanor traffic offense.

(2) (a) Except as otherwise provided in subsection (4) of this section, it is unlawful for a person to knowingly engage in a speed exhibition on a highway.

(b) For purposes of this section, "speed exhibition" means the operation of a motor vehicle to present a display of speed or power. "Speed exhibition" includes, but is not limited to, squealing the tires of a motor vehicle while it is stationary or in motion, rapid acceleration, rapid swerving or weaving in and out of traffic, producing smoke from tire slippage, or leaving visible tire acceleration marks on the surface of the highway or ground.

(c) A person who violates any provision of this subsection (2) commits a class 2 misdemeanor traffic offense.

(3) (a) Except as otherwise provided in subsection (4) of this section, a person shall not, for the purpose of facilitating or aiding or as an incident to any speed contest or speed exhibition upon a highway, in any manner obstruct or place a barricade or obstruction, or assist or participate in placing any such barricade or obstruction, upon a highway.

(b) A person who violates any provision of this subsection (3) commits, pursuant to section 42-4-1703, the offense that the person aided in or facilitated the commission of. Nothing in this subsection (3) shall be construed to preclude charging a person under section 42-4-1703 for otherwise being a party to the crime of engaging in a speed contest or engaging in a speed exhibition.

(4) The provisions of this section shall not apply to the operation of a motor vehicle in an organized competition according to accepted rules on a designated and duly authorized race track, race course, or drag strip.

(5) (a) In addition to a sentence imposed pursuant to this section or pursuant to any other provision of law:

(I) Upon the second conviction for an offense specified in subsection (1) or (2) of this section, or any other crime, the underlying factual basis of which has been found by the court to include an act of operating a motor vehicle in violation of subsection (1) or (2) of this section, the court may, in its discretion, order the primary law enforcement agency involved with the case to place an immobilization device on the motor vehicle or motor vehicles so operated for a period of up to fourteen days.

(II) Upon the third or subsequent conviction for an offense specified in subsection (1) or (2) of this section, or any other crime, the underlying factual basis of which has been found by the court to include an act of operating a motor vehicle in violation of subsection (1) or (2) of this section, the court may, in its discretion, order the primary law enforcement agency involved with the case to place an immobilization device on the motor vehicle or motor vehicles so operated for a period of up to thirty days but more than fourteen days.

(b) The period during which a motor vehicle may be fitted with an immobilization device pursuant to paragraph (a) of this subsection (5) shall be in addition to any period during which the motor vehicle was impounded prior to sentencing.

(c) An order issued under this subsection (5) shall state the requirements included in subsections (7) and (8) of this section.

(d) For purposes of this section, "immobilization device" means a device locked into place over a wheel of a motor vehicle that prevents the motor vehicle from being moved. "Immobilization device" includes but is not limited to a device commonly referred to as a "traffic boot" or "boot".

(6) (a) Except as otherwise provided in subsection (9) of this section, a law enforcement agency that is ordered to place an immobilization device on a motor vehicle pursuant to subsection (5) of this section shall attempt to locate the motor vehicle within its jurisdiction. The law enforcement agency may, in its discretion, attempt to locate the motor vehicle outside of its jurisdiction.

(b) Nothing in this subsection (6) shall be construed to:

(I) Prohibit a law enforcement agency from seeking the assistance of another law enforcement agency for the purpose of placing an immobilization device on a motor vehicle or removing the device in accordance with this section; or

(II) Require a law enforcement agency to expend excessive time or commit excessive staff to the task of locating a motor vehicle subject to immobilization under this section.

(c) The time spent by a law enforcement agency in locating a motor vehicle in accordance with this subsection (6) shall not alter the immobilization period ordered by the court under subsection (5) of this section.

(d) A law enforcement agency that places an immobilization device on a motor vehicle pursuant to this section shall affix a notice to the immobilized motor vehicle stating the information described in subsections (7) and (8) of this section.

(e) A peace officer who locates or attempts to locate a motor vehicle, or who places or removes, or assists with the placement or removal of, an immobilization device in accordance with the provisions of this section shall be immune from civil liability for damages, except for damages arising from willful and wanton conduct.

(7) (a) The owner of a motor vehicle immobilized under this section shall be assessed a fee of thirty-five dollars for each day the motor vehicle is ordered immobilized and, except as otherwise provided in paragraph (d) of this subsection (7), thirty-five dollars for each day up to fourteen days after the immobilization period that the fee for the immobilization period is not paid. The owner shall pay the fee to the law enforcement agency that places the immobilization device on the motor vehicle.

(b) The owner, within fourteen days after the end of the immobilization period ordered by the court, may obtain removal of the immobilization device by the law enforcement agency that placed it by requesting the removal and paying the fee required under paragraph (a) of this subsection (7).

(c) The failure of the owner of the immobilized motor vehicle to request removal of the immobilization device and pay the fee within fourteen days after the end of the immobilization period ordered by the court or within the additional time granted by the court pursuant to paragraph (d) of this subsection (7), whichever is applicable, shall result in the motor vehicle being deemed an "abandoned motor vehicle", as defined in sections 42-4-1802 (1) (d) and 42-4-2102 (1) (d), and subject to the provisions of part 18 or 21 of this article, whichever is applicable. The law enforcement agency entitled to payment of the fee under this subsection (7) shall be eligible to recover the fee if the abandoned motor vehicle is sold, pursuant to section 42-4-1809 (2) (b.5) or 42-4-2108 (2) (a.5).

(d) Upon application of the owner of an immobilized motor vehicle, the court that ordered the immobilization may, in its discretion, grant additional time to pay the immobilization fee required under paragraph (a) of this subsection (7). If additional time is granted, the court shall notify the law enforcement agency that placed the immobilization device.

(8) (a) A person may not remove an immobilization device that is placed on a motor vehicle pursuant to this section during the immobilization period ordered by the court.

(b) No person may remove the immobilization device after the end of the immobilization period except the law enforcement agency that placed the immobilization device and that has been requested by the owner to remove the device and to which the owner has properly paid the fee required by subsection (7) of this section. Nothing in this subsection (8) shall be construed to prevent the removal of an immobilization device in order to comply with the provisions of part 18 or 21 of this article.

(c) A person who violates any provision of this subsection (8) commits a class 2 misdemeanor traffic offense.

(9) (a) A law enforcement agency that is ordered to place an immobilization device on a motor vehicle pursuant to subsection (5) of this section shall inform the court at sentencing if it is unable to comply with the court's order either because the law enforcement agency is not yet equipped with an immobilization device or because it does not have a sufficient number of immobilization devices. The court, upon being so informed, shall, in lieu of ordering immobilization, order the law enforcement agency to impound the motor vehicle for the same time period that the court initially ordered the motor vehicle to be immobilized.

(b) If a motor vehicle is ordered to be impounded pursuant to paragraph (a) of this subsection (9), the provisions of subsections (6) to (8) of this section shall not apply.

42-4-1106. Minimum speed in left lane - interstate 70. (1) Where the average grade is six percent or more uphill for at least one mile, no person shall operate a motor vehicle in the far left lane of traffic of interstate 70 at a speed of less than the lower of ten miles per hour below the speed limit or the minimum speed set by the department of transportation, except if:

(a) Necessary to obey traffic control devices;

(b) Necessary to exit or enter interstate 70;

(c) Weather or traffic conditions require speeds slower than the speed limit necessary under section 42-4-1101; or

(d) Necessary because of a lane closure or blockage.

(2) The department of transportation shall post signs giving the public notice of this section.

PART 12

PARKING

42-4-1201. Starting parked vehicle. No person shall start a vehicle which is stopped, standing, or parked unless and until such movement can be made with reasonable safety. Any person who violates any provision of this section commits a class A traffic infraction.

42-4-1202. Parking or abandonment of vehicles. (1) No person shall stop, park, or leave standing any vehicle, either attended or unattended, outside of a business or a residential district, upon the paved or improved and main-traveled part of the highway. Nothing contained in this section shall apply to the driver of any vehicle which is disabled while on the paved or improved and main-traveled portion of a highway in such manner and to such extent that it is impossible to avoid stopping and temporarily leaving such disabled vehicle in such position, subject, when applicable, to the emergency lighting requirements set forth in section 42-4-230.

(2) Any person who violates any provision of this section commits a class B traffic infraction.

42-4-1203. Ski areas to install signs. (1) Colorado ski areas shall install traffic control signs as provided in this section on both sides of that segment of every highway which is within one mile of and which leads to the recognized entrances to the ski area parking lots if it is found that:

(a) The ski area has insufficient parking capacity as evidenced by the practice of parking by motor vehicles on such highways; and

(b) Such parking constitutes a hazard to traffic or an obstacle to snow removal or the movement or passage of emergency equipment.

(2) The findings required by subsection (1) of this section shall be made by the department of transportation for the state highway system, by the chairman of the board of county commissioners for county roads, and by the chief executive officer of a municipality for a municipal street system. Such findings shall be based upon a traffic investigation.

(3) Such signs shall conform to any and all specifications of the department of transportation adopted pursuant to section 42-4-601. All such signs shall contain a statement that there is no parking allowed on a highway right-of-way so as to obstruct traffic or highway maintenance and that offending vehicles will be towed away.

42-4-1204. Stopping, standing, or parking prohibited in specified places. (1) Except as otherwise provided in subsection (4) of this section, no person shall stop, stand, or park a vehicle, except when necessary to avoid conflict with other traffic or in compliance with the directions of a police officer or an official traffic control device, in any of the following places:

(a) On a sidewalk;

(b) Within an intersection;

(c) On a crosswalk;

(d) Between a safety zone and the adjacent curb or within thirty feet of points on the curb immediately opposite the ends of a safety zone, unless the traffic authority indicates a different length by signs or markings;

(e) Alongside or opposite any street excavation or obstruction when stopping, standing, or parking would obstruct traffic;

(f) On the roadway side of any vehicle stopped or parked at the edge or curb of a street;

(g) Upon any bridge or other elevated structure upon a highway or within a highway tunnel;

(h) On any railroad tracks;

(i) On any controlled-access highway;

(j) In the area between roadways of a divided highway, including crossovers;

(k) At any other place where official signs prohibit stopping.

(2) Except as otherwise provided in subsection (4) of this section, in addition to the restrictions specified in subsection (1) of this section, no person shall stand or park a vehicle, except when necessary to avoid conflict with other traffic or in compliance with the directions of a police officer or an official traffic control device, in any of the following places:

(a) Within five feet of a public or private driveway;

(b) Within fifteen feet of a fire hydrant;

(c) Within twenty feet of a crosswalk at an intersection;

(d) Within thirty feet upon the approach to any flashing beacon or signal, stop sign, yield sign, or traffic control signal located at the side of a roadway;

(e) Within twenty feet of the driveway entrance to any fire station or, on the side of a street opposite the entrance to any fire station, within seventy-five feet of said entrance when properly signposted;

(f) At any other place where official signs prohibit standing.

(3) In addition to the restrictions specified in subsections (1) and (2) of this section, no person shall park a vehicle, except when necessary to avoid conflict with other traffic or in compliance with the directions of a police officer or official traffic control device, in any of the following places:

(a) Within fifty feet of the nearest rail of a railroad crossing;

(b) At any other place where official signs prohibit parking.

(4) (a) Paragraph (a) of subsection (1) of this section shall not prohibit persons from parking bicycles or electrical assisted bicycles on sidewalks in accordance with the provisions of section 42-4-1412 (11) (a) and (11) (b).

(b) Paragraph (f) of subsection (1) of this section shall not prohibit persons from parking two or more bicycles or electrical assisted bicycles abreast in accordance with the provisions of section 42-4-1412 (11) (d).

(c) Paragraphs (a), (c), and (d) of subsection (2) of this section shall not apply to bicycles or electrical assisted bicycles parked on sidewalks in accordance with section 42-4-1412 (11) (a) and (11) (b).

(5) No person shall move a vehicle not lawfully under such person's control into any such prohibited area or away from a curb such distance as is unlawful.

(6) The department of transportation, with respect to highways under its jurisdiction, may place official traffic control devices prohibiting, limiting, or restricting the stopping, standing, or parking of vehicles on any highway where it is determined, upon the basis of a traffic investigation or study, that such stopping, standing, or parking is dangerous to those using the highway or where the stopping, standing, or parking of vehicles would unduly interfere with the free movement of traffic thereon. No person shall stop, stand, or park any vehicle in violation of the restrictions indicated by such devices.

(7) Any person who violates any provision of this section commits a class B traffic infraction.

(8) A political subdivision may not adopt or enforce an ordinance or regulation that prohibits the parking of more than one motorcycle within a space served by a single parking meter.

42-4-1205. Parking at curb or edge of roadway. (1) Except as otherwise provided in this section, every vehicle stopped or parked upon a two-way roadway shall be so stopped or parked with the right-hand wheels parallel to and within twelve inches of the right-hand curb or as close as practicable to the right edge of the right-hand shoulder.

(2) Except as otherwise provided by local ordinance, every vehicle stopped or parked upon a one-way roadway shall be so stopped or parked parallel to the curb or edge of the roadway in the direction of authorized traffic movement, with its right-hand wheels within twelve inches of the right-hand curb or as close as practicable to the right edge of the right-hand shoulder or with its left-hand wheels within twelve inches of the left-hand curb or as close as practicable to the left edge of the left-hand shoulder.

(3) Local authorities may by ordinance permit angle parking on any roadway; except that angle parking shall not be permitted on any state highway unless the department of transportation has determined by resolution or order entered in its minutes that the roadway is of sufficient width to permit angle parking without interfering with the free movement of traffic.

(4) Any person who violates any provision of this section commits a class B traffic infraction.

42-4-1206. Unattended motor vehicle. No person driving or in charge of a motor vehicle shall permit it to stand unattended without first stopping the engine, locking the ignition, removing the key from the ignition, and effectively setting the brake thereon, and, when standing upon any grade, said person shall turn the front wheels to the curb or side of the highway in such a manner as to prevent the vehicle from rolling onto the traveled way. Any person who violates any provision of this section commits a class B traffic infraction.

42-4-1207. Opening and closing vehicle doors. No person shall open the door of a motor vehicle on the side available to moving traffic unless and until it is reasonably safe to do so and can be done without interfering with the movement of other traffic; nor shall any person leave a door open on the side of a vehicle available to moving traffic for a period of time longer than necessary to load or unload passengers. Any person who violates any provision of this section commits a class B traffic infraction.

42-4-1208. Parking privileges for persons with disabilities - applicability - rules. (1) As used in this section:

(a) "Disability" or "disabled" means a physical impairment that meets the standards of 23 CFR 1235, which impairment is verified, in writing, by a professional. To be valid, the verifying professional shall certify to the department that the person meets the standards established by the executive director of the department.

(b) "Identifying figure" means a figure that provides notice that a person is authorized to use a reserved parking space.

(c) "Identifying license plate" means a license plate bearing an identifying figure.

(d) "Identifying placard" means a placard bearing an identifying figure.

(e) "Professional" means a physician licensed to practice medicine or practicing medicine pursuant to section 12-36-106 (3) (i), C.R.S., a podiatrist licensed under article 32 of title 12, C.R.S., or an advanced practice nurse registered pursuant to section 12-38-111.5, C.R.S.

(f) "Reserved parking space" means a parking space reserved for a person with a disability.

(2) In a jurisdiction recognizing the privilege defined by this subsection (2), a vehicle with an identifying license plate or a placard obtained pursuant to section 42-3-204 or as otherwise authorized by subsection (4) of this section may be parked in public parking areas along public streets regardless of any time limitation imposed upon parking in such area; except that a jurisdiction shall not limit such a privilege to park on any public street to less than four hours. The respective jurisdiction shall clearly post the appropriate time limits in such area. Such privilege need not apply to zones in which:

(a) Stopping, standing, or parking of all vehicles is prohibited;

(b) Only special vehicles may be parked;

(c) Parking is not allowed during specific periods of the day in order to accommodate heavy traffic.

(3) (a) A person with a disability may park in a parking space identified as being reserved for use by persons with disabilities whether on public property or private property available for public use. An identifying license plate or placard obtained pursuant to section 42-3-204 or as otherwise authorized by subsection (4) of this section shall be displayed in accordance with 23 CFR 1235 at all times on the vehicle while parked in such space.

(b) The owner of private property available for public use may request the installation of official signs identifying reserved parking spaces. Such a request shall be a waiver of any objection the owner may assert concerning enforcement of this section by peace officers of any political subdivision of this state, and the officers are hereby authorized and empowered to enforce this section, provisions of law to the contrary notwithstanding. No person shall impose restrictions on the use of disabled parking unless specifically authorized by a statute, resolution, or ordinance of the state of Colorado or a political subdivision thereof and notice of the restriction is prominently posted by a sign clearly visible at the parking space.

(c) Each parking space reserved for use by persons with disabilities whether on public property or private property shall be marked with an official upright sign, which sign may be stationary or portable, identifying such parking space as reserved for use by persons with disabilities.

(4) Persons with disabilities from states other than Colorado shall be allowed to use parking spaces for persons with disabilities in Colorado so long as such persons have valid license plates or placards from their home state that are also valid pursuant to 23 CFR 1235.

(5) It is unlawful for any person other than a person with a disability to park in a parking space on public or private property that is clearly identified by an official sign as being reserved for use by persons with disabilities unless:

(a) Such person is parking the vehicle for the direct benefit of a person with a disability to enter or exit the vehicle while it is parked in the reserved parking space; and

(b) An identifying license plate or placard obtained pursuant to section 42-3-204 or as otherwise authorized by subsection (4) of this section is displayed in such vehicle.

(6) (a) A person who does not have a disability and who exercises the privilege defined in subsection (2) of this section or who violates subsection (5) or (10) of this section commits a class B traffic infraction punishable by a surcharge of thirty-two dollars pursuant to sections 24-4.1-119 (1) (f) and 24-4.2-104 (1) (b) (I), C.R.S., and a minimum fine of three hundred fifty dollars, not to exceed one thousand dollars, for the first offense and a minimum fine of six hundred dollars, not to exceed one thousand dollars, for a second offense. A person who violates this subsection (6) three or more times commits a misdemeanor punishable by a minimum fine of one thousand dollars, not to exceed five thousand dollars, and not more than ten hours of community service. The state or local authority issuing a citation under this subsection (a) or any local ordinance of a substantially equivalent offense shall transfer one-half of the fine to the state treasurer, who shall credit the fine to the disabled parking education and enforcement fund created in section 42-1-226.

(b) A person who violates this subsection (6) by parking a vehicle owned by a commercial carrier, as defined in section 42-1-102 (17), shall be subject to a fine of up to twice the penalty imposed in paragraph (a) of this subsection (6).

(7) A person who does not have a disability and who uses an identifying license plate or placard in order to receive the benefits or privileges available to a person with a disability under this section commits a misdemeanor punishable by a surcharge of thirty-two dollars pursuant to sections 24-4.1-119 (1) (f) and 24-4.2-104 (1) (b) (I), C.R.S., and a minimum fine of three hundred fifty dollars, not to exceed one thousand dollars, for the first offense and a minimum fine of six hundred dollars, not to exceed one thousand dollars, for a second offense. A person who violates this subsection (7) three or more times commits a misdemeanor punishable by a minimum fine of one thousand dollars, not to exceed five thousand dollars, and not more than ten hours of community service. The state or local authority issuing a citation under this subsection (7) or any local ordinance of a substantially equivalent offense shall transfer one-half of the fine to the state treasurer, who shall credit the fine to the disabled parking education and enforcement fund created in section 42-1-226.

(8) (a) A peace officer or authorized and uniformed parking enforcement official may check the identification of any person using an identifying license plate or placard in order to determine whether such use is authorized.

(b) A peace officer or authorized and uniformed parking enforcement official may confiscate an identifying placard that is being used in violation of this section. The peace officer shall transmit the placard to the department unless it is being held for prosecution of a violation of this section. The department shall hold a confiscated placard for thirty days and may dispose of the placard after thirty days. Upon the person with a disability signing a statement under penalty of perjury that he or she was unaware that the violator used, or intended to use, the placard in violation of this section, the department shall release the placard to the person with a disability to whom it was issued.

(c) A peace officer may investigate an allegation that a person is violating this section.

(9) Any state agency or division thereof that transports persons with disabilities may obtain an identifying placard for persons with disabilities in the same manner provided in this section for any other person. If an identifying placard is used by any employee of such state agency or division when not transporting persons with disabilities, the executive director of such agency and the offending employee shall be subject to a fine of one hundred fifty dollars. This subsection (9) applies to any corporation or independent contractor as determined by rule of the department to be eligible to transport persons with disabilities; except that the chief executive officer or an equivalent of the corporation or independent contractor and the offending employee are subject to the fine.

(10) Regardless of whether the person displays an identifying license plate or placard, it is unlawful for any person to park a vehicle so as to block reasonable access to curb ramps, passenger loading zones, or accessible routes, as identified in 28 CFR 36 (appendix A), that are clearly identified unless such person is loading or unloading a person with a disability.

(11) (a) A person who knowingly and fraudulently obtains, possesses, uses, or transfers an identifying placard issued to a person with a disability; who knowingly makes, possesses, uses, or transfers what purports to be, but is not, an identifying placard; or who knowingly creates or uses a device intended to give the impression that it is an identifying placard when viewed from outside the vehicle is guilty of a misdemeanor and is subject to the criminal and civil penalties provided under section 42-6-139 (3) and (4).

(b) A person who knowingly and willfully receives remuneration for committing a misdemeanor pursuant to this subsection (11) is subject to twice the civil and criminal penalties that would otherwise be imposed.

(12) (a) Certification of the entry of judgment for each violation of subsection (6), (7), or (11) of this section shall be sent by the entering court to the department.

(b) (Deleted by amendment, L. 2010, (HB 10-1019), ch. 400, p. 1923, § 3, effective January 1, 2011.)

(c) Upon receipt of certification of an entry of judgment for a violation of subsection (6), (7), or (11) of this section by any person, the department shall withhold that person's vehicle registration until such time as any fines imposed for the violations have been paid.

(d) Upon receipt of certification or independent verification of an entry of judgment, the department shall revoke an identifying license plate or placard as provided in section 42-3-204 (2) (d).

(e) (Deleted by amendment, L. 2010, (HB 10-1019), ch. 400, p. 1923, § 3, effective January 1, 2011.)

(13) (a) For purposes of this subsection (13), "holder" means a person with a disability as defined in section 42-3-204 who has lawfully obtained an identifying license plate or placard issued pursuant to section 42-3-204 (2) or as otherwise authorized by subsection (4) of this section.

(b) Notwithstanding any other provision of this section to the contrary, a holder is liable for any penalty or fine as set forth in this section or section 42-3-204 or for any misuse of an identifying license plate or placard, including the use of such plate or placard by any person other than a holder, unless the holder can furnish sufficient evidence that the license plate or placard was, at the time of the violation, in the care, custody, or control of another person without the holder's knowledge or consent.

(c) A holder may avoid the liability described in paragraph (b) of this subsection (13) if, within a reasonable time after notification of the violation, the holder furnishes to the prosecutorial division of the appropriate jurisdiction the name and address of the person who had the care, custody, or control of the identifying license plate or placard at the time of the violation or the holder reports said license plate or placard lost or stolen to both the appropriate local law enforcement agency and the department.

(14) (a) A person who observes a violation of this section may submit evidence, along with a sworn statement of a violation of this section, to any law enforcement agency.

(b) No employer shall forbid an employee from reporting violations of this section. No person shall initiate or administer any disciplinary action against an employee on account of the employee notifying the authorities of a possible violation of this section if the employee has a good faith belief that a violation has occurred.

(c) No landlord shall retaliate against a tenant on account of the tenant notifying the authorities of a possible violation of this section if the tenant has a good faith belief that a violation has occurred.

(15) (a) No person, after using a reserved parking space that has a time limit, shall switch motor vehicles or move the motor vehicle to another reserved parking space within one hundred yards of the original parking space within the same eight hours in order to exceed the time limit.

(b) Parking in a time-limited reserved parking space for more than three hours for at least three days a week for at least two weeks shall create a rebuttable presumption that the person is violating this subsection (15).

(c) This subsection (15) does not apply to privately owned parking lots.

(d) A person who violates this subsection (15) commits a class B traffic infraction. Upon conviction or the plea of guilty or nolo contendere for a violation of this subsection (15), the court shall send a certification of the entry of judgment to the department. Upon receiving a certification of entry of judgment or independent verification, the department shall revoke the identifying license plate or placard of a person who violates this subsection (15) a second or subsequent time pursuant to section 42-3-204 (2).

(16) (a) No person shall use parking privileges obtained by an identifying license plate or placard for a commercial purpose unless the purpose relates to transacting business with a business the reserved parking space is intended to serve.

(b) A person who violates this subsection (16) commits a class B traffic infraction. Upon conviction or the plea of guilty or nolo contendere for a violation of this subsection (16), the court shall send a certification of the entry of judgment to the department. Upon receiving a certification of entry of judgment or independent verification, the department shall revoke the identifying license plate or placard of a person who violates this subsection (16) a second or subsequent time pursuant to section 42-3-204 (2).

(17) (a) A peace officer may issue a penalty assessment notice for a violation of subsection (9), (15), or (16) of this section by sending it by certified mail to the registered owner of the motor vehicle. The peace officer shall include in the penalty assessment notice the offense or infraction, the time and place where it occurred, and a statement that the payment of the penalty assessment and surcharge is due within twenty days from the issuance of the notice. Receipt of the payment of the penalty assessment postmarked by the twentieth day after the receipt of the penalty assessment notice by the defendant is receipt on or before the date the payment was due.

(b) If the penalty assessment and surcharge are not paid within the twenty days from the date of mailing of the notice, the peace officer who issued the original penalty assessment notice shall file a complaint with a court having jurisdiction and issue and serve upon the registered owner of the vehicle a summons to appear in court at the time and place specified therein.

42-4-1209. Owner liability for parking violations. (1) In addition to any other liability provided for in this article, the owner of a motor vehicle who is engaged in the business of leasing or renting motor vehicles is liable for payment of a parking violation fine unless the owner of the leased or rented motor vehicle can furnish sufficient evidence that the vehicle was, at the time of the parking violation, in the care, custody, or control of another person. To avoid liability for payment the owner of the motor vehicle is required, within a reasonable time after notification of the parking violation, to furnish to the prosecutorial division of the appropriate jurisdiction the name and address of the person or company who leased, rented, or otherwise had the care, custody, or control of such vehicle. As a condition to avoid liability for payment of a parking violation, any person or company who leases or rents motor vehicles to another person shall attach to the leasing or rental agreement a notice stating that, pursuant to the requirements of this section, the operator of the vehicle is liable for payment of a parking violation fine incurred when the operator has the care, custody, or control of the motor vehicle. The notice shall inform the operator that the operator's name and address shall be furnished to the prosecutorial division of the appropriate jurisdiction when a parking violation fine is incurred by the operator.

(2) The provisions of this section may be adopted by local authorities pursuant to section 42-4-110 (1).

42-4-1210. Designated areas on private property for authorized vehicles. (1) The owner or lessee of any private property available for public use in the unincorporated areas of a county may request in writing that specified areas on such property be designated by the board of county commissioners for use only by authorized vehicles and that said areas, upon acceptance in writing by the board of county commissioners, shall be clearly marked by the owner or lessee with official traffic control devices, as defined in section 42-1-102 (64). Such a request shall be a waiver of any objection the owner or lessee may assert concerning enforcement of this section by peace officers of this state, and such officers are hereby authorized and empowered to so enforce this section, provisions of law to the contrary notwithstanding. When the owner or lessee gives written notice to the board of county commissioners that said request is withdrawn, and the owner or lessee removes all traffic control devices, the provisions of this section shall no longer be applicable.

(2) It is unlawful for any person to park any vehicle other than an authorized vehicle in any area designated and marked for such use as provided in this section.

(3) Any person who violates the provisions of subsection (2) of this section is guilty of a class 2 petty offense and, upon conviction thereof, shall be punished by a fine of twenty-five dollars. The disposition of fines and forfeitures shall be paid into the treasury of the county at such times and in such manner as may be prescribed by the board of county commissioners.

42-4-1211. Limitations on backing. (1) (a) The driver of a vehicle, whether on public property or private property which is used by the general public for parking purposes, shall not back the same unless such movement can be made with safety and without interfering with other traffic.

(b) The driver of a vehicle shall not back the same upon any shoulder or roadway of any controlled-access highway.

(2) Any person who violates any provision of this section commits a class A traffic infraction.

42-4-1212. Pay parking access for disabled. (1) Unless the method of remuneration is reasonably accessible to a person with a disability as defined in section 42-3-204, no person who owns, operates, or manages a parking space that requires remuneration shall tow, boot, or otherwise take adverse action against a person or motor vehicle parking in such space for failure to pay the remuneration if the motor vehicle bears a placard or license plate bearing an identifying figure issued pursuant to section 42-3-204 or a similar law in another state that is valid under 23 CFR 1235.

(2) Notwithstanding any statute, resolution, or ordinance of the state of Colorado or a political subdivision thereof, parking in a space without paying the required remuneration shall not be deemed a violation of such statute, resolution, or ordinance if:

(a) The motor vehicle bears a placard or license plate bearing the identifying figure issued pursuant to section 42-3-204 or a similar law in another state that is valid under 23 CFR 1235; and

(b) The method of remuneration is not reasonably accessible to a person with a disability as defined in section 42-3-204.

(3) A law enforcement agency shall withdraw any penalty assessment notice or summons and complaint that is deemed not to be a violation under subsection (2) of this section.

(4) For the purposes of this section, "reasonably accessible" means meeting the standards of 28 CFR 36 (appendix A) or substantially similar standards.

PART 13

ALCOHOL AND DRUG OFFENSES

42-4-1300.3. Definitions. (Repealed)

42-4-1301. Driving under the influence - driving while impaired - driving with excessive alcoholic content - definitions - penalties. (1) (a) It is a misdemeanor for any person who is under the influence of alcohol or one or more drugs, or a combination of both alcohol and one or more drugs, to drive a motor vehicle or vehicle.

(b) It is a misdemeanor for any person who is impaired by alcohol or by one or more drugs, or by a combination of alcohol and one or more drugs, to drive a motor vehicle or vehicle.

(c) It is a misdemeanor for any person who is an habitual user of any controlled substance defined in section 12-22-303 (7), C.R.S., to drive a motor vehicle, vehicle, or low-power scooter in this state.

(d) For the purposes of this subsection (1), one or more drugs shall mean all substances defined as a drug in section 12-22-303 (13), C.R.S., and all controlled substances defined in section 12-22-303 (7), C.R.S., and glue-sniffing, aerosol inhalation, and the inhalation of any other toxic vapor or vapors.

(e) The fact that any person charged with a violation of this subsection (1) is or has been entitled to use one or more drugs under the laws of this state, including, but not limited to, the medical use of marijuana pursuant to section 18-18-406.3, C.R.S., shall not constitute a defense against any charge of violating this subsection (1).

(f) "Driving under the influence" means driving a motor vehicle or vehicle when a person has consumed alcohol or one or more drugs, or a combination of alcohol and one or more drugs, that affects the person to a degree that the person is substantially incapable, either mentally or physically, or both mentally and physically, to exercise clear judgment, sufficient physical control, or due care in the safe operation of a vehicle.

(g) "Driving while ability impaired" means driving a motor vehicle or vehicle when a person has consumed alcohol or one or more drugs, or a combination of both alcohol and one or more drugs, that affects the person to the slightest degree so that the person is less able than the person ordinarily would have been, either mentally or physically, or both mentally and physically, to exercise clear judgment, sufficient physical control, or due care in the safe operation of a vehicle.

(h) Pursuant to section 16-2-106, C.R.S., in charging the offense of DUI, it shall be sufficient to describe the offense charged as "drove a vehicle under the influence of alcohol or drugs or both".

(i) Pursuant to section 16-2-106, C.R.S., in charging the offense of DWAI, it shall be sufficient to describe the offense charged as "drove a vehicle while impaired by alcohol or drugs or both".

(2) (a) It is a misdemeanor for any person to drive a motor vehicle or vehicle when the person's BAC is 0.08 or more at the time of driving or within two hours after driving. During a trial, if the state's evidence raises the issue, or if a defendant presents some credible evidence, that the defendant consumed alcohol between the time that the defendant stopped driving and the time that testing occurred, such issue shall be an affirmative defense, and the prosecution must establish beyond a reasonable doubt that the minimum 0.08 blood or breath alcohol content required in this paragraph (a) was reached as a result of alcohol consumed by the defendant before the defendant stopped driving.

(a.5) (I) It is a class A traffic infraction for any person under twenty-one years of age to drive a motor vehicle or vehicle when the person's BAC, as shown by analysis of the person's breath, is at least 0.02 but not more than 0.05 at the time of driving or within two hours after driving. The court, upon sentencing a defendant pursuant to this subparagraph (I), may, in addition to any penalty imposed under a class A traffic infraction, order that the defendant perform up to twenty-four hours of useful public service, subject to the conditions and restrictions of section 18-1.3-507, C.R.S., and may further order that the defendant submit to and complete an alcohol evaluation or assessment, an alcohol education program, or an alcohol treatment program at such defendant's own expense.

(II) A second or subsequent violation of this paragraph (a.5) shall be a class 2 traffic misdemeanor.

(b) In any prosecution for the offense of DUI per se, the defendant shall be entitled to offer direct and circumstantial evidence to show that there is a disparity between what the tests show and other facts so that the trier of fact could infer that the tests were in some way defective or inaccurate. Such evidence may include testimony of nonexpert witnesses relating to the absence of any or all of the common symptoms or signs of intoxication for the purpose of impeachment of the accuracy of the analysis of the person's blood or breath.

(c) Pursuant to section 16-2-106, C.R.S., in charging the offense of DUI per se, it shall be sufficient to describe the offense charged as "drove a vehicle with excessive alcohol content".

(3) The offenses described in subsections (1) and (2) of this section are strict liability offenses.

(4) No court shall accept a plea of guilty to a non-alcohol-related or non-drug-related traffic offense or guilty to the offense of UDD from a person charged with DUI, DUI per se, or habitual user; except that the court may accept a plea of guilty to a non-alcohol-related or non-drug-related traffic offense or to UDD upon a good faith representation by the prosecuting attorney that the attorney could not establish a prima facie case if the defendant were brought to trial on the original alcohol-related or drug-related offense.

(5) Notwithstanding the provisions of section 18-1-408, C.R.S., during a trial of any person accused of both DUI and DUI per se, the court shall not require the prosecution to elect between the two violations. The court or a jury may consider and convict the person of either DUI or DWAI, or DUI per se, or both DUI and DUI per se, or both DWAI and DUI per se. If the person is convicted of more than one violation, the sentences imposed shall run concurrently.

(6) (a) In any prosecution for DUI or DWAI, the defendant's BAC at the time of the commission of the alleged offense or within a reasonable time thereafter gives rise to the following presumptions or inferences:

(I) If at such time the defendant's BAC was 0.05 or less, it shall be presumed that the defendant was not under the influence of alcohol and that the defendant's ability to operate a motor vehicle or vehicle was not impaired by the consumption of alcohol.

(II) If at such time the defendant's BAC was in excess of 0.05 but less than 0.08, such fact gives rise to the permissible inference that the defendant's ability to operate a motor vehicle or vehicle was impaired by the consumption of alcohol, and such fact may also be considered with other competent evidence in determining whether or not the defendant was under the influence of alcohol.

(III) If at such time the defendant's BAC was 0.08 or more, such fact gives rise to the permissible inference that the defendant was under the influence of alcohol.

(b) The limitations of this subsection (6) shall not be construed as limiting the introduction, reception, or consideration of any other competent evidence bearing upon the question of whether or not the defendant was under the influence of alcohol or whether or not the defendant's ability to operate a motor vehicle or vehicle was impaired by the consumption of alcohol.

(c) In all actions, suits, and judicial proceedings in any court of this state concerning alcohol-related or drug-related traffic offenses, the court shall take judicial notice of methods of testing a person's alcohol or drug level and of the design and operation of devices, as certified by the department of public health and environment, for testing a person's blood, breath, saliva, or urine to determine such person's alcohol or drug level. The department of public health and environment may, by rule, determine that, because of the reliability of the results from certain devices, the collection or preservation of a second sample of a person's blood, saliva, or urine or the collection and preservation of a delayed breath alcohol specimen is not required. This paragraph (c) shall not prevent the necessity of establishing during a trial that the testing devices used were working properly and that such testing devices were properly operated. Nothing in this paragraph (c) shall preclude a defendant from offering evidence concerning the accuracy of testing devices.

(d) If a person refuses to take or to complete, or to cooperate with the completing of, any test or tests as provided in section 42-4-1301.1 and such person subsequently stands trial for DUI or DWAI, the refusal to take or to complete, or to cooperate with the completing of, any test or tests shall be admissible into evidence at the trial, and a person may not claim the privilege against self-incrimination with regard to admission of refusal to take or to complete, or to cooperate with the completing of, any test or tests.

(e) **Involuntary blood test - admissibility.** Evidence acquired through an involuntary blood test pursuant to section 42-4-1301.1 (3) shall be admissible in any prosecution for DUI, DUI per se, DWAI, habitual user, or UDD, and in any prosecution for criminally negligent homicide pursuant to section 18-3-105, C.R.S., vehicular homicide pursuant to section 18-3-106 (1) (b), C.R.S., assault in the third degree pursuant to section 18-3-204, C.R.S., or vehicular assault pursuant to section 18-3-205 (1) (b), C.R.S.

(f) **Chemical test - admissibility.** Strict compliance with the rules and regulations prescribed by the department of public health and environment shall not be a prerequisite to the admissibility of test results at trial unless the court finds that the extent of noncompliance with a board of health rule has so impaired the validity and reliability of the testing method and the test results as to render the evidence inadmissible. In all other circumstances, failure to strictly comply with such rules and regulations shall only be considered in the weight to be given to the test results and not to the admissibility of such test results.

(g) It shall not be a prerequisite to the admissibility of test results at trial that the prosecution present testimony concerning the composition of any kit used to obtain blood, urine, saliva, or breath specimens. A sufficient evidentiary foundation concerning the compliance of such kits with the rules and regulations of the department of public health and environment shall be established by the introduction of a copy of the manufacturer's or supplier's certificate of compliance with such rules and regulations if such certificate specifies the contents, sterility, chemical makeup, and amounts of chemicals contained in such kit.

(h) In any trial for a violation of this section, the testimony of a law enforcement officer that he or she witnessed the taking of a blood specimen by a person who the law enforcement officer reasonably believed was authorized to withdraw blood specimens shall be sufficient evidence that such person was so authorized, and testimony from the person who obtained the blood specimens concerning such person's authorization to obtain blood specimens shall not be a prerequisite to the admissibility of test results concerning the blood specimens obtained.

(i) (I) Following the lawful contact with a person who has been driving a motor vehicle or vehicle and when a law enforcement officer reasonably suspects that a person was driving a motor vehicle or vehicle while under the influence of or while impaired by alcohol, the law enforcement officer may conduct a preliminary screening test using a device approved by the executive director of the department of public health and environment after first advising the driver that the driver may either refuse or agree to provide a sample of the driver's breath for such preliminary test; except that, if the driver is under twenty-one years of age, the law enforcement officer may, after providing such advisement to the person, conduct such preliminary screening test if the officer reasonably suspects that the person has consumed any alcohol.

(II) The results of this preliminary screening test may be used by a law enforcement officer in determining whether probable cause exists to believe such person was driving a motor vehicle or vehicle in violation of this section and whether to administer a test pursuant to section 42-4-1301.1 (2).

(III) Neither the results of such preliminary screening test nor the fact that the person refused such test shall be used in any court action except in a hearing outside of the presence of a jury, when such hearing is held to determine if a law enforcement officer had probable cause to believe that the driver committed a violation of this section. The results of such preliminary screening test shall be made available to the driver or the driver's attorney on request.

(7) Repealed.

(8) A second or subsequent violation of this section committed by a person under eighteen years of age may be filed in juvenile court.

42-4-1301.1. Expressed consent for the taking of blood, breath, urine, or saliva sample - testing. (1) Any person who drives any motor vehicle upon the streets and highways and elsewhere throughout this state shall be deemed to have expressed such person's consent to the provisions of this section.

(2) (a) (I) A person who drives a motor vehicle upon the streets and highways and elsewhere throughout this state shall be required to take and complete, and to cooperate in the tak-

ing and completing of, any test or tests of the person's breath or blood for the purpose of determining the alcoholic content of the person's blood or breath when so requested and directed by a law enforcement officer having probable cause to believe that the person was driving a motor vehicle in violation of the prohibitions against DUI, DUI per se, DWAI, habitual user, or UDD. Except as otherwise provided in this section, if a person who is twenty-one years of age or older requests that the test be a blood test, then the test shall be of his or her blood; but, if the person requests that a specimen of his or her blood not be drawn, then a specimen of the person's breath shall be obtained and tested. A person who is under twenty-one years of age shall be entitled to request a blood test unless the alleged violation is UDD, in which case a specimen of the person's breath shall be obtained and tested, except as provided in subparagraph (II) of this paragraph (a).

(II) Except as otherwise provided in paragraph (a.5) of this subsection (2), if a person elects either a blood test or a breath test, the person shall not be permitted to change the election, and, if the person fails to take and complete, and to cooperate in the completing of, the test elected, the failure shall be deemed to be a refusal to submit to testing. If the person is unable to take, or to complete, or to cooperate in the completing of a breath test because of injuries, illness, disease, physical infirmity, or physical incapacity, or if the person is receiving medical treatment at a location at which a breath testing instrument certified by the department of public health and environment is not available, the test shall be of the person's blood.

(III) If a law enforcement officer requests a test under this paragraph (a), the person must cooperate with the request such that the sample of blood or breath can be obtained within two hours of the person's driving.

(a.5) (I) If a law enforcement officer who requests a person to take a breath or blood test under paragraph (a) of this subsection (2) determines there are extraordinary circumstances that prevent the completion of the test elected by the person within the two-hour time period required by subparagraph (III) of paragraph (a) of this subsection (2), the officer shall inform the person of the extraordinary circumstances and request and direct the person to take and complete the other test described in paragraph (a) of this subsection (2). The person shall then be required to take and complete, and to cooperate in the completing of, the other test.

(II) A person who initially requests and elects to take a blood or breath test, but who is requested and directed by the law enforcement officer to take the other test because of the extraordinary circumstances described in subparagraph (I) of this paragraph (a.5), may change his or her election for the purpose of complying with the officer's request. The change in the election of which test to take shall not be deemed to be a refusal to submit to testing.

(III) If the person fails to take and complete, and to cooperate in the completing of, the other test requested by the law enforcement officer pursuant to subparagraph (I) of this paragraph (a.5), the failure shall be deemed to be a refusal to submit to testing.

(IV) (A) As used in this paragraph (a.5), "extraordinary circumstances" means circumstances beyond the control of, and not created by, the law enforcement officer who requests and directs a person to take a blood or breath test in accordance with this subsection (2) or the law enforcement authority with whom the officer is employed.

(B) "Extraordinary circumstances" includes, but shall not be limited to, weather-related delays, high call volume affecting medical personnel, power outages, malfunctioning breath test equipment, and other circumstances that preclude the timely collection and testing of a blood or breath sample by a qualified person in accordance with law.

(C) "Extraordinary circumstances" does not include inconvenience, a busy workload on the part of the law enforcement officer or law enforcement authority, minor delay that does not compromise the two-hour test period specified in subparagraph (III) of paragraph (a) of this subsection (2), or routine circumstances that are subject to the control of the law enforcement officer or law enforcement authority.

(b) (I) Any person who drives any motor vehicle upon the streets and highways and elsewhere throughout this state shall be required to submit to and to complete, and to cooperate in the completing of, a test or tests of such person's blood, saliva, and urine for the purpose of determining the drug content within the person's system when so requested and directed by a law enforcement officer having probable cause to believe that the person was driving a motor vehicle in violation of the prohibitions against DUI, DWAI, or habitual user and when it is reasonable to require such testing of blood, saliva, and urine to determine whether such person was under the influence of, or impaired by, one or more drugs, or one or more controlled substances, or a combination of both alcohol and one or more drugs, or a combination of both alcohol and one or more controlled substances.

(II) If a law enforcement officer requests a test under this paragraph (b), the person must cooperate with the request such that the sample of blood, saliva, or urine can be obtained within two hours of the person's driving.

(3) Any person who is required to take and to complete, and to cooperate in the completing of, any test or tests shall cooperate with the person authorized to obtain specimens of such person's blood, breath, saliva, or urine, including the signing of any release or consent forms required by any person, hospital, clinic, or association authorized to obtain such specimens. If such per-

son does not cooperate with the person, hospital, clinic, or association authorized to obtain such specimens, including the signing of any release or consent forms, such noncooperation shall be considered a refusal to submit to testing. No law enforcement officer shall physically restrain any person for the purpose of obtaining a specimen of such person's blood, breath, saliva, or urine for testing except when the officer has probable cause to believe that the person has committed criminally negligent homicide pursuant to section 18-3-105, C.R.S., vehicular homicide pursuant to section 18-3-106 (1) (b), C.R.S., assault in the third degree pursuant to section 18-3-204, C.R.S., or vehicular assault pursuant to section 18-3-205 (1) (b), C.R.S., and the person is refusing to take or to complete, or to cooperate in the completing of, any test or tests, then, in such event, the law enforcement officer may require a blood test.

(4) Any driver of a commercial motor vehicle requested to submit to a test as provided in paragraph (a) or (b) of subsection (2) of this section shall be warned by the law enforcement officer requesting the test that a refusal to submit to the test shall result in an out-of-service order as defined under section 42-2-402 (8) for a period of twenty-four hours and a revocation of the privilege to operate a commercial motor vehicle for one year as provided under section 42-2-126.

(5) The tests shall be administered at the direction of a law enforcement officer having probable cause to believe that the person had been driving a motor vehicle in violation of section 42-4-1301 and in accordance with rules and regulations prescribed by the department of public health and environment concerning the health of the person being tested and the accuracy of such testing.

(6) (a) No person except a physician, a registered nurse, a paramedic, as certified in part 2 of article 3.5 of title 25, C.R.S., an emergency medical technician, as defined in part 1 of article 3.5 of title 25, C.R.S., or a person whose normal duties include withdrawing blood samples under the supervision of a physician or registered nurse shall be entitled to withdraw blood for the purpose of determining the alcoholic or drug content therein.

(b) No civil liability shall attach to any person authorized to obtain blood, breath, saliva, or urine specimens or to any hospital, clinic, or association in or for which such specimens are obtained as provided in this section as a result of the act of obtaining such specimens from any person submitting thereto if such specimens were obtained according to the rules and regulations prescribed by the department of public health and environment; except that this provision shall not relieve any such person from liability for negligence in the obtaining of any specimen sample.

(7) A preliminary screening test conducted by a law enforcement officer pursuant to section 42-4-1301 (6) (i) shall not substitute for or qualify as the test or tests required by subsection (2) of this section.

(8) Any person who is dead or unconscious shall be tested to determine the alcohol or drug content of the person's blood or any drug content within such person's system as provided in this section. If a test cannot be administered to a person who is unconscious, hospitalized, or undergoing medical treatment because the test would endanger the person's life or health, the law enforcement agency shall be allowed to test any blood, urine, or saliva that was obtained and not utilized by a health care provider and shall have access to that portion of the analysis and results of any tests administered by such provider that shows the alcohol or drug content of the person's blood, urine, or saliva or any drug content within the person's system. Such test results shall not be considered privileged communications, and the provisions of section 13-90-107, C.R.S., relating to the physician-patient privilege shall not apply. Any person who is dead, in addition to the tests prescribed, shall also have the person's blood checked for carbon monoxide content and for the presence of drugs, as prescribed by the department of public health and environment. Such information obtained shall be made a part of the accident report.

42-4-1301.2. Refusal of test - effect on driver's license - revocation - reinstatement. (Repealed)

42-4-1301.3. Alcohol and drug driving safety program. (1) (a) Upon conviction of a violation of section 42-4-1301, the court shall sentence the defendant in accordance with the provisions of this section and other applicable provisions of this part 13. The court shall consider the alcohol and drug evaluation required pursuant to this section prior to sentencing; except that the court may proceed to immediate sentencing without considering such alcohol and drug evaluation:

(I) (A) If the defendant has no prior convictions or pending charges under this section; or

(B) If the defendant has one or more prior convictions, the prosecuting attorney and the defendant have stipulated to such conviction or convictions; and

(II) If neither the defendant nor the prosecuting attorney objects.

(b) If the court proceeds to immediate sentencing, without considering an alcohol and drug evaluation, the alcohol and drug evaluation shall be conducted after sentencing, and the court shall order the defendant to complete the education and treatment program recommended in the alcohol and drug evaluation. If the defendant disagrees with the education and treatment program recommended in the alcohol and drug evaluation, the defendant may request the court to hold a hearing to determine which education and treatment program should be completed by the defendant.

(2) (Deleted by amendment, L. 2011, (HB 11-1268), ch. 267, p. 1217, § 1, effective June 2, 2011.)

(3) (a) The judicial department shall administer in each judicial district an alcohol and drug driving safety program that provides presentence and postsentence alcohol and drug evaluations on all persons convicted of a violation of section 42-4-1301. The alcohol and drug driving safety program shall further provide supervision and monitoring of all such persons whose sentences or terms of probation require completion of a program of alcohol and drug driving safety education or treatment.

(b) The presentence and postsentence alcohol and drug evaluations shall be conducted by such persons determined by the judicial department to be qualified to provide evaluation and supervision services as described in this section.

(c) (I) An alcohol and drug evaluation shall be conducted on all persons convicted of a violation of section 42-4-1301, and a copy of the report of the evaluation shall be provided to such person. The report shall be made available to and shall be considered by the court prior to sentencing unless the court proceeds to immediate sentencing pursuant to the provisions of subsection (1) of this section.

(II) The report shall contain the defendant's prior traffic record, characteristics and history of alcohol or drug problems, and amenability to rehabilitation. The report shall include a recommendation as to alcohol and drug driving safety education or treatment for the defendant.

(III) The alcohol evaluation shall be conducted and the report prepared by a person who is trained and knowledgeable in the diagnosis of chemical dependency. Such person's duties may also include appearing at sentencing and probation hearings as required, referring defendants to education and treatment agencies in accordance with orders of the court, monitoring defendants in education and treatment programs, notifying the probation department and the court of any defendant failing to meet the conditions of probation or referral to education or treatment, appearing at revocation hearings as required, and providing assistance in data reporting and program evaluation.

(IV) For the purpose of this section, "alcohol and drug driving safety education or treatment" means either level I or level II education or treatment programs that are approved by the unit in the department of human services that administers behavioral health programs and services, including those related to mental health and substance abuse. Level I programs are to be short-term, didactic education programs. Level II programs are to be therapeutically oriented education, long-term outpatient, and comprehensive residential programs. Any defendant sentenced to level I or level II programs shall be instructed by the court to meet all financial obligations of such programs. If such financial obligations are not met, the sentencing court shall be notified for the purpose of collection or review and further action on the defendant's sentence. Nothing in this section shall prohibit treatment agencies from applying to the state for funds to recover the costs of level II treatment for defendants determined to be indigent by the court.

(4) (a) There is hereby created an alcohol and drug driving safety program fund in the office of the state treasurer to the credit of which shall be deposited all moneys as directed by this paragraph (a). The assessment in effect on July 1, 1998, shall remain in effect unless the judicial department and the unit in the department of human services that administers behavioral health programs and services, including those related to mental health and substance abuse, have provided to the general assembly a statement of the cost of the program, including costs of administration for the past and current fiscal year to include a proposed change in the assessment. The general assembly shall then consider the proposed new assessment and approve the amount to be assessed against each person during the following fiscal year in order to ensure that the alcohol and drug driving safety program established in this section shall be financially self-supporting. Any adjustment in the amount to be assessed shall be so noted in the appropriation to the judicial department and the unit in the department of human services that administers behavioral health programs and services, including those related to mental health and substance abuse, as a footnote or line item related to this program in the general appropriation bill. The state auditor shall periodically audit the costs of the programs to determine that they are reasonable and that the rate charged is accurate based on these costs. Any other fines, fees, or costs levied against such person shall not be part of the program fund. The amount assessed for the alcohol and drug evaluation shall be transmitted by the court to the state treasurer to be credited to the alcohol and drug driving safety program fund. Fees charged under sections 27-81-106 (1) and 27-82-103 (1), C.R.S., to approved alcohol and drug treatment facilities that provide level I and level II programs as provided in paragraph (c) of subsection (3) of this section shall be transmitted to the state treasurer, who shall credit the fees to the alcohol and drug driving safety program fund. Upon appropriation by the general assembly, these funds shall be expended by the judicial department and the unit in the department of human services that administers behavioral health programs and services, including those related to mental health and substance abuse, for the administration of the alcohol and drug driving safety program. In administering the alcohol and drug driving safety program, the judicial department is authorized to contract with any agency for such services as the judicial department deems necessary. Moneys deposited in the alcohol and drug driving safety program fund shall remain in said fund to be used for the purposes set forth in this section and shall not revert or transfer to the general fund except by further act of the general assembly.

(b) The judicial department shall ensure that qualified personnel are placed in the judicial districts. The judicial department and the unit in the department of human services that administers behavioral health programs and services, including those related to mental health and substance abuse, shall jointly develop and maintain criteria for evaluation techniques, treatment referral, data reporting, and program evaluation.

(c) The alcohol and drug driving safety program shall cooperate in providing services to a defendant who resides in a judicial district other than the one in which the arrest was made. Alcohol and drug driving safety programs may cooperate in providing services to any defendant who resides at a location closer to another judicial district's program. The requirements of this section shall not apply to persons who are not residents of Colorado at the time of sentencing.

(d) Notwithstanding any provision of paragraph (a) of this subsection (4) to the contrary, on March 5, 2003, the state treasurer shall deduct one million dollars from the alcohol and drug driving safety program fund and transfer such sum to the general fund.

(5) The provisions of this section are also applicable to any defendant who receives a deferred prosecution in accordance with section 18-1.3-101, C.R.S., or who receives a deferred sentence in accordance with section 18-1.3-102, C.R.S., and the completion of any stipulated alcohol evaluation, level I or level II education program, or level I or level II treatment program to be completed by the defendant shall be ordered by the court in accordance with the conditions of such deferred prosecution or deferred sentence as stipulated to by the prosecution and the defendant.

(6) An approved alcohol or drug treatment facility that provides level I or level II programs as provided in paragraph (c) of subsection (3) of this section shall not require a person to repeat any portion of an alcohol and drug driving safety education or treatment program that he or she has successfully completed while he or she was imprisoned for the current offense.

42-4-1301.4. Useful public service - definitions - local programs - assessment of costs. (1) This section applies to any person convicted of a violation of section 42-4-1301 and who is ordered to complete useful public service.

(2) (a) For the purposes of this section and section 42-4-1301, "useful public service" means any work that is beneficial to the public and involves a minimum of direct supervision or other public cost. "Useful public service" does not include any work that would endanger the health or safety of any person convicted of a violation of any of the offenses specified in section 42-4-1301.

(b) The sentencing court, the probation department, the county sheriff, and the board of county commissioners shall cooperate in identifying suitable work assignments. An offender sentenced to such work assignment shall complete the same within the time established by the court.

(3) There may be established in the probation department of each judicial district in the state a useful public service program under the direction of the chief probation officer. It is the purpose of the useful public service program: To identify and seek the cooperation of governmental entities and political subdivisions thereof, as well as corporations organized not for profit or charitable trusts, for the purpose of providing useful public service jobs; to interview and assign persons who have been ordered by the court to perform useful public service to suitable useful public service jobs; and to monitor compliance or noncompliance of such persons in performing useful public service assignments within the time established by the court.

(4) (a) Any general public liability insurance policy obtained pursuant to this section shall be in a sum of not less than the current limit on government liability under the "Colorado Governmental Immunity Act", article 10 of title 24, C.R.S.

(b) For the purposes of the "Colorado Governmental Immunity Act", article 10 of title 24, C.R.S., "public employee" does not include any person who is sentenced pursuant to section 42-4-1301 to participate in any type of useful public service.

(c) No governmental entity shall be liable under the "Workers' Compensation Act of Colorado", articles 40 to 47 of title 8, C.R.S., or under the "Colorado Employment Security Act", articles 70 to 82 of title 8, C.R.S., for any benefits on account of any person who is sentenced pursuant to section 42-4-1301 to participate in any type of useful public service, but nothing in this paragraph (c) shall prohibit a governmental entity from electing to accept the provisions of the "Workers' Compensation Act of Colorado" by purchasing and keeping in force a policy of workers' compensation insurance covering such person.

(5) In accordance with section 42-4-1307 (14), in addition to any other penalties prescribed in this part 13, the court shall assess an amount, not to exceed one hundred twenty dollars, upon any person required to perform useful public service. Such amount shall be used by the operating agency responsible for overseeing such person's useful public service program to pay the cost of administration of the program, a general public liability policy covering such person, and, if such person will be covered by workers' compensation insurance pursuant to paragraph (c) of subsection (4) of this section or an insurance policy providing such or similar coverage, the cost of purchasing and keeping in force such insurance coverage. Such amount shall be adjusted from time to time by the general assembly in order to ensure that the useful public service program established in this section shall be financially self-supporting. The proceeds from such amounts shall be used by the operating agency only for defraying the cost of personal services and other operating expenses related to the administration of the program and the cost of purchasing and

keeping in force policies of general public liability insurance, workers' compensation insurance, or insurance providing such or similar coverage and shall not be used by the operating agency for any other purpose.

(6) The provisions of this section relating to the performance of useful public service are also applicable to any defendant who receives a deferred prosecution in accordance with section 18-1.3-101, C.R.S., or who receives a deferred sentence in accordance with section 18-1.3-102, C.R.S., and the completion of any stipulated amount of useful public service hours to be completed by the defendant shall be ordered by the court in accordance with the conditions of such deferred prosecution or deferred sentence as stipulated to by the prosecution and the defendant.

42-4-1302. Stopping of suspect. A law enforcement officer may stop any person who the officer reasonably suspects is committing or has committed a violation of section 42-4-1301 (1) or (2) and may require the person to give such person's name, address, and an explanation of his or her actions. The stopping shall not constitute an arrest.

42-4-1303. Records - prima facie proof. Official records of the department of public health and environment relating to certification of breath test instruments, certification of operators and operator instructors of breath test instruments, certification of standard solutions, and certification of laboratories shall be official records of the state, and copies thereof, attested by the executive director of the department of public health and environment or the director's deputy and accompanied by a certificate bearing the official seal for said department that the executive director or the director's deputy has custody of said records, shall be admissible in all courts of record and shall constitute prima facie proof of the information contained therein. The department seal required under this section may also consist of a rubber stamp producing a facsimile of the seal stamped upon the document.

42-4-1304. Samples of blood or other bodily substance - duties of department of public health and environment. (1) The department of public health and environment shall establish a system for obtaining samples of blood or other bodily substance from the bodies of all pilots in command, vessel operators in command, or drivers and pedestrians fifteen years of age or older who die within four hours after involvement in a crash involving a motor vehicle, a vessel, or an aircraft. For purposes of this section, "vessel" has the meaning set forth in section 33-13-102, C.R.S. No person having custody of the body of the deceased shall perform any internal embalming procedure until a blood and urine specimen to be tested for alcohol, drug, and carbon monoxide concentrations has been taken by an appropriately trained person certified by the department of public health and environment. Whenever the driver of the vehicle cannot be immediately determined, the samples shall be obtained from all deceased occupants of the vehicle.

(2) All samples so collected shall be placed in containers of a type designed to preserve the integrity of a sample from the time of collection until it is subjected to analysis.

(3) All samples shall be tested and analyzed in the laboratories of the department of public health and environment, or in any other laboratory approved for this purpose by the department of public health and environment, to determine the amount of alcohol, drugs, and carbon monoxide contained in such samples or the amount of any other substance contained therein as deemed advisable by the department of public health and environment.

(4) The state board of health shall establish and promulgate such administrative regulations and procedures as are necessary to ensure that collection and testing of samples is accomplished to the fullest extent. Such regulations and procedures shall include but not be limited to the following:

(a) The certification of laboratories to ensure that the collection and testing of samples is performed in a competent manner; and

(b) The designation of responsible state and local officials who shall have authority and responsibility to collect samples for testing.

(5) All records of the results of such tests shall be compiled by the department of public health and environment and shall not be public information, but shall be disclosed on request to any interested party in any civil or criminal action arising out of the collision.

(6) All state and local public officials, including investigating law enforcement officers, have authority to and shall follow the procedures established by the department of public health and environment pursuant to this section, including the release of all information to the department of public health and environment concerning such samples and the testing thereof. The Colorado state patrol and the county coroners and their deputies shall assist the department of public health and environment in the administration and collection of such samples for the purposes of this section.

(7) The office of the highway safety coordinator, the department, and the Colorado state patrol shall have access to the results of the tests of such samples taken as a result of a traffic crash for statistical analysis. The division of parks and outdoor recreation shall have access to the results of the tests of such samples taken as a result of a boating accident for statistical analysis.

(8) Failure to perform the required duties as prescribed by this section and by the administrative regulations and procedures resulting therefrom shall be deemed punishable under section 18-8-405, C.R.S.

42-4-1305. Open alcoholic beverage container - motor vehicle - prohibited. (1) **Definitions.** As used in this section, unless the context otherwise requires:

(a) "Alcoholic beverage" means a beverage as defined in 23 CFR 1270.3 (a).

(b) "Motor vehicle" means a vehicle driven or drawn by mechanical power and manufactured primarily for use on public highways but does not include a vehicle operated exclusively on a rail or rails.

(c) "Open alcoholic beverage container" means a bottle, can, or other receptacle that contains any amount of alcoholic beverage and:

(I) That is open or has a broken seal; or

(II) The contents of which are partially removed.

(d) "Passenger area" means the area designed to seat the driver and passengers while a motor vehicle is in operation and any area that is readily accessible to the driver or a passenger while in his or her seating position, including but not limited to the glove compartment.

(2) (a) Except as otherwise permitted in paragraph (b) of this subsection (2), a person while in the passenger area of a motor vehicle that is on a public highway of this state or the right-of-way of a public highway of this state may not knowingly:

(I) Drink an alcoholic beverage; or

(II) Have in his or her possession an open alcoholic beverage container.

(b) The provisions of this subsection (2) shall not apply to:

(I) Passengers, other than the driver or a front seat passenger, located in the passenger area of a motor vehicle designed, maintained, or used primarily for the transportation of persons for compensation;

(II) The possession by a passenger, other than the driver or a front seat passenger, of an open alcoholic beverage container in the living quarters of a house coach, house trailer, motor home, as defined in section 42-1-102 (57), or trailer coach, as defined in section 42-1-102 (106) (a);

(III) The possession of an open alcoholic beverage container in the area behind the last upright seat of a motor vehicle that is not equipped with a trunk; or

(IV) The possession of an open alcoholic beverage container in an area not normally occupied by the driver or a passenger in a motor vehicle that is not equipped with a trunk.

(c) A person who violates the provisions of this subsection (2) commits a class A traffic infraction and shall be punished by a fine of fifty dollars and a surcharge of seven dollars and eighty cents as provided in section 42-4-1701 (4) (a) (I) (N).

(3) Nothing in this section shall be construed to preempt or limit the authority of any statutory or home rule town, city, or city and county to adopt ordinances that are no less restrictive than the provisions of this section.

42-4-1306. Interagency task force on drunk driving - creation. (1) The general assembly finds and declares that:

(a) Drunk and impaired driving continues to cause needless deaths and injuries, especially among young people;

(b) In 2003, there were over thirty thousand arrests for driving under the influence or driving while ability-impaired;

(c) Although Colorado has taken many measures to reduce the incidents of drunk and impaired driving, the persistent regularity of these incidents continues to be a problem, as evidenced by the case of Sonja Marie Devries who was killed in 2004 by a drunk driver who had been convicted of drunk driving on six previous occasions; and

(d) According to the federal national highway transportation safety administration, other states with a statewide interagency task force on drunk driving have seen a decrease in incidents of drunk and impaired driving.

(2) There is hereby created an interagency task force on drunk driving, referred to in this section as the "task force". The task force shall meet regularly to investigate methods of reducing the incidents of drunk and impaired driving and develop recommendations for the state of Colorado regarding the enhancement of government services, education, and intervention to prevent drunk and impaired driving.

(3) (a) The task force shall consist of:

(I) The executive director of the department of transportation or his or her designee who shall also convene the first meeting of the task force;

(II) Two representatives appointed by the executive director of the department of revenue, with the following qualifications:

(A) One representative with expertise in driver's license sanctioning; and

(B) One representative with expertise in enforcement of the state's liquor sales laws;

(III) The state court administrator or his or her designee;

(IV) The chief of the Colorado state patrol or his or her designee;

(V) The state public defender or his or her designee;

(VI) The director of the division of behavioral health in the department of human services;

(VII) The director of the division of probation services or his or her designee;

(VIII) The executive director of the department of public health and environment, or his or her designee;

(IX) The following members selected jointly by the member serving pursuant to subparagraph (I) of this paragraph (a):

(A) A representative of a statewide association of chiefs of police with experience in making arrests for drunk or impaired driving;

(B) A representative of a statewide organization of county sheriffs with experience in making arrests for drunk or impaired driving;

(C) A victim or a family member of a victim of drunk or impaired driving;

(D) A representative of a statewide organization of victims of drunk or impaired driving;

(E) A representative of a statewide organization of district attorneys with experience in prosecuting drunk or impaired driving offenses;

(F) A representative of a statewide organization of criminal defense attorneys with experience in defending persons charged with drunk or impaired driving offenses;

(G) A representative of a statewide organization that represents persons who sell alcoholic beverages for consumption on-premises;

(G.5) A representative of a statewide organization that represents persons who sell alcoholic beverages for consumption off-premises;

(H) A representative of a statewide organization that represents distributors of alcoholic beverages in Colorado;

(I) A manufacturer of alcoholic beverages in Colorado;

(J) A person under twenty-four years of age who is enrolled in a secondary or postsecondary school; and

(K) A representative of a statewide organization that represents alcohol and drug addiction counselors.

(b) Members selected pursuant to subparagraph (IX) of paragraph (a) of this subsection (3) shall serve terms of two years but may be selected for additional terms.

(c) Members of the task force shall not be compensated for or reimbursed for their expenses incurred in attending meetings of the task force.

(d) The initial meeting of the task force shall be convened on or before August 1, 2006, by the member serving pursuant to subparagraph (I) of paragraph (a) of this subsection (3). At the first meeting, the task force shall elect a chair and vice-chair from the members serving pursuant to subparagraphs (I) to (VIII) of paragraph (a) of this subsection (3), who shall serve a term of two years but who may be reelected for additional terms.

(e) The task force shall meet not less frequently than bimonthly and may adopt policies and procedures necessary to carry out its duties.

(4) The task force shall report its findings and recommendations to the judiciary committees of the house of representatives and the senate, or any successor committees, on or before January 15, 2007, and on or before each January 15 thereafter.

(5) (Deleted by amendment, L. 2011, (SB 11-093), ch. 41, p. 108, § 2, effective March 21, 2011.)

42-4-1307. Penalties for traffic offenses involving alcohol and drugs - repeal. (1) **Legislative declaration.** The general assembly hereby finds and declares that, for the purposes of sentencing as described in section 18-1-102.5, C.R.S., each sentence for a conviction of a violation of section 42-4-1301 shall include:

(a) A period of imprisonment, which, for a repeat offender, shall include a mandatory minimum period of imprisonment and restrictions on where and how the sentence may be served; and

(b) For a second or subsequent offender, a period of probation. The imposition of a period of probation upon the conviction of a first-time offender shall be subject to the court's discretion as described in paragraph (c) of subsection (3) and paragraph (c) of subsection (4) of this section. The purpose of probation is to help the offender change his or her behavior to reduce the risk of future violations of section 42-4-1301. If a court imposes imprisonment as a penalty for a violation of a condition of his or her probation, the penalty shall constitute a separate period of imprisonment that the offender shall serve in addition to the imprisonment component of his or her original sentence.

(2) **Definitions.** As used in this section, unless the context otherwise requires:

(a) "Conviction" means a verdict of guilty by a judge or jury or a plea of guilty or nolo contendere that is accepted by the court for an offense or adjudication for an offense that would constitute a criminal offense if committed by an adult. "Conviction" also includes having received a deferred judgment and sentence or deferred adjudication; except that a person shall not be deemed to have been convicted if the person has successfully completed a deferred sentence or deferred adjudication.

(b) "Driving under the influence" or "DUI" means driving a motor vehicle or vehicle when a person has consumed alcohol or one or more drugs, or a combination of alcohol and one or more drugs, that affects the person to a degree that the person is substantially incapable, either mentally or physically, or both mentally and physically, of exercising clear judgment, sufficient physical control, or due care in the safe operation of a vehicle.

(c) "Driving while ability impaired" or "DWAI" means driving a motor vehicle or vehicle when a person has consumed alcohol or one or more drugs, or a combination of both alcohol and one or more drugs, that affects the person to the slightest degree so that the person is less able than the person ordinarily would have been, either mentally or physically, or both mentally and physically, to exercise clear judgment, sufficient physical control, or due care in the safe operation of a vehicle.

(d) "UDD" shall have the same meaning as provided in section 42-1-102 (109.7).

(3) **First offenses - DUI, DUI per se, and habitual user.** (a) Except as otherwise provided in subsections (5) and (6) of this section, a person who is convicted of DUI, DUI per se, or habitual user shall be punished by:

(I) Imprisonment in the county jail for at least five days but no more than one year, the minimum period of which shall be mandatory; except that the court may suspend the mandatory minimum period if, as a condition of the suspended sentence, the offender undergoes a presentence or postsentence alcohol and drug evaluation and satisfactorily completes and meets all financial obligations of a level I or level II program as is determined to be appropriate by the alcohol and drug evaluation that is required pursuant to section 42-4-1301.3;

(II) A fine of at least six hundred dollars but no more than one thousand dollars, and the court shall have discretion to suspend the fine; and

(III) At least forty-eight hours but no more than ninety-six hours of useful public service, and the court shall not have discretion to suspend the mandatory minimum period of performance of such service.

(b) Notwithstanding the provisions of subparagraph (I) of paragraph (a) of this subsection (3), and except as described in paragraphs (a) and (b) of subsection (5) and paragraph (a) of subsection (6) of this section, a person who is convicted of DUI or DUI per se when the person's BAC was 0.20 or more at the time of driving or within two hours after driving shall be punished by imprisonment in the county jail for at least ten days but not more than one year; except that the court shall have the discretion to employ the sentencing alternatives described in section 18-1.3-106, C.R.S.

(c) In addition to any penalty described in paragraph (a) of this subsection (3), the court may impose a period of probation that shall not exceed two years, which probation may include any conditions permitted by law.

(4) **First offenses - DWAI.** (a) Except as otherwise provided in subsections (5) and (6) of this section, a person who is convicted of DWAI shall be punished by:

(I) Imprisonment in the county jail for at least two days but no more than one hundred eighty days, the minimum period of which shall be mandatory; except that the court may suspend the mandatory minimum period if, as a condition of the suspended sentence, the offender undergoes a presentence or postsentence alcohol and drug evaluation and satisfactorily completes and meets all financial obligations of a level I or level II program as is determined to be appropriate by the alcohol and drug evaluation that is required pursuant to section 42-4-1301.3; and

(II) A fine of at least two hundred dollars but no more than five hundred dollars, and the court shall have discretion to suspend the fine; and

(III) At least twenty-four hours but no more than forty-eight hours of useful public service, and the court shall not have discretion to suspend the mandatory minimum period of performance of such service.

(b) Notwithstanding the provisions of subparagraph (I) of paragraph (a) of this subsection (4), and except as described in paragraphs (a) and (b) of subsection (5) and paragraph (a) of subsection (6) of this section, a person who is convicted of DWAI when the person's BAC was 0.20 or more at the time of driving or within two hours after driving shall be punished by imprisonment in the county jail for at least ten days but not more than one year; except that the court shall have the discretion to employ the sentencing alternatives described in section 18-1.3-106, C.R.S.

(c) In addition to any penalty described in paragraph (a) of this subsection (4), the court may impose a period of probation that shall not exceed two years, which probation may include any conditions permitted by law.

(5) **Second offenses.** (a) Except as otherwise provided in subsection (6) of this section, a person who is convicted of DUI, DUI per se, DWAI, or habitual user who, at the time of sentencing, has a prior conviction of DUI, DUI per se, DWAI, habitual user, vehicular homicide pursuant to section 18-3-106 (1) (b), C.R.S., vehicular assault pursuant to section 18-3-205 (1) (b), C.R.S., aggravated driving with a revoked license pursuant to section 42-2-206 (1) (b) (I) (A) or (1) (b) (I) (B), or driving while the person's driver's license was under restraint pursuant to section 42-2-138 (1) (d), shall be punished by:

(I) Imprisonment in the county jail for at least ten consecutive days but no more than one year; except that the court shall have discretion to employ the sentencing alternatives described in section 18-1.3-106, C.R.S. During the mandatory ten-day period of imprisonment, the person shall not be eligible for earned time or good time pursuant to section 17-26-109, C.R.S., or for trusty prisoner status pursuant to section 17-26-115, C.R.S.; except that the person shall receive credit for any time that he or she served in custody for the violation prior to his or her conviction.

(II) A fine of at least six hundred dollars but no more than one thousand five hundred dollars, and the court shall have discretion to suspend the fine;

(III) At least forty-eight hours but no more than one hundred twenty hours of useful public service, and the court shall not have discretion to suspend the mandatory minimum period of performance of the service; and

(IV) A period of probation of at least two years, which period shall begin immediately upon the commencement of any part of the sentence that is imposed upon the person pursuant to this section, and a suspended sentence of imprisonment in the county jail for one year, as described in subsection (7) of this section.

(b) If a person is convicted of DUI, DUI per se, DWAI, or habitual user and the violation occurred less than five years after the date of a previous violation for which the person was convicted of DUI, DUI per se, DWAI, habitual user, vehicular homicide pursuant to section 18-3-106 (1) (b), C.R.S., vehicular assault pursuant to section 18-3-205 (1) (b), C.R.S., aggravated driving with a revoked license pursuant to section 42-2-206 (1) (b) (I) (A) or (1) (b) (I) (B), or driving while the person's driver's license was under restraint pursuant to section 42-2-138 (1) (d), the court shall not have discretion to employ any sentencing alternatives described in section 18-1.3-106, C.R.S., during the minimum period of imprisonment described in subparagraph (I) of paragraph (a) of this subsection (5); except that a court may allow the person to participate in a program pursuant to section 18-1.3-106 (1) (a) (II), (1) (a) (IV), or (1) (a) (V), C.R.S., only if the program is available through the county in which the person is imprisoned and only for the purpose of:

(I) Continuing a position of employment that the person held at the time of sentencing for said violation;

(II) Continuing attendance at an educational institution at which the person was enrolled at the time of sentencing for said violation; or

(III) Participating in a court-ordered level II alcohol and drug driving safety education or treatment program, as described in section 42-4-1301.3 (3) (c) (IV).

(c) Notwithstanding the provisions of section 18-1.3-106 (12), C.R.S., if, pursuant to paragraph (a) or (b) of this subsection (5), a court allows a person to participate in a program pursuant to section 18-1.3-106, C.R.S., the person shall not receive one day credit against his or her sentence for each day spent in such a program, as provided in said section 18-1.3-106 (12), C.R.S.

(6) **Third and subsequent offenses.** (a) A person who is convicted of DUI, DUI per se, DWAI, or habitual user who, at the time of sentencing, has two or more prior convictions of DUI, DUI per se, DWAI, habitual user, vehicular homicide pursuant to section 18-3-106 (1) (b), C.R.S., vehicular assault pursuant to section 18-3-205 (1) (b), C.R.S., aggravated driving with a revoked license pursuant to section 42-2-206 (1) (b) (I) (A) or (1) (b) (I) (B), or driving while the person's driver's license was under restraint pursuant to section 42-2-138 (1) (d) shall be punished by:

(I) Imprisonment in the county jail for at least sixty consecutive days but no more than one year. During the mandatory sixty-day period of imprisonment, the person shall not be eligible for earned time or good time pursuant to section 17-26-109, C.R.S., or for trusty prisoner status pursuant to section 17-26-115, C.R.S.; except that a person shall receive credit for any time that he or she served in custody for the violation prior to his or her conviction. During the mandatory period of imprisonment, the court shall not have any discretion to employ any sentencing alternatives described in section 18-1.3-106, C.R.S.; except that the person may participate in a program pursuant to section 18-1.3-106 (1) (a) (II), (1) (a) (IV), or (1) (a) (V), C.R.S., only if the program is available through the county in which the person is imprisoned and only for the purpose of:

(A) Continuing a position of employment that the person held at the time of sentencing for said violation;

(B) Continuing attendance at an educational institution at which the person was enrolled at the time of sentencing for said violation; or

(C) Participating in a court-ordered level II alcohol and drug driving safety education or treatment program, as described in section 42-4-1301.3 (3) (c) (IV);

(II) A fine of at least six hundred dollars but no more than one thousand five hundred dollars, and the court shall have discretion to suspend the fine;

(III) At least forty-eight hours but no more than one hundred twenty hours of useful public service, and the court shall not have discretion to suspend the mandatory minimum period of performance of the service; and

(IV) A period of probation of at least two years, which period shall begin immediately upon the commencement of any part of the sentence that is imposed upon the person pursuant to this section, and a suspended sentence of imprisonment in the county jail for one year, as described in subsection (7) of this section.

(b) Notwithstanding the provisions of section 18-1.3-106 (12), C.R.S., if, pursuant to paragraph (a) of this subsection (6), a court allows a person to participate in a program pursuant to section 18-1.3-106 (1) (a) (II), (1) (a) (IV), or (1) (a) (V), C.R.S., the person shall not receive one day credit against his or her sentence for each day spent in such a program, as provided in said section 18-1.3-106 (12), C.R.S.

(7) **Probation-related penalties.** When a person is sentenced to a period of probation pursuant to subparagraph (IV) of paragraph (a) of subsection (5) of this section or subparagraph (IV) of paragraph (a) of subsection (6) of this section:

(a) The court shall impose, in addition to any other condition of probation, a sentence to one year of imprisonment in the county jail, which sentence shall be suspended, and against which sentence the person shall not receive credit for any period of imprisonment to which he or she is sentenced pursuant to subparagraph (I) of paragraph (a) of subsection (5) of this section or subparagraph (I) of paragraph (a) of subsection (6) of this section;

(b) The court:

(I) Shall include, as a condition of the person's probation, a requirement that the person complete a level II alcohol and drug driving safety education or treatment program, as described in section 42-4-1301.3 (3) (c) (IV), at the person's own expense;

(II) May impose an additional period of probation for the purpose of monitoring the person or ensuring that the person continues to receive court-ordered alcohol or substance abuse treatment, which additional period shall not exceed two years;

(III) May require that the person commence the alcohol and drug driving safety education or treatment program described in subparagraph (I) of this paragraph (b) during any period of imprisonment to which the person is sentenced;

(IV) May require the person to appear before the court at any time during the person's period of probation;

(V) May require the person to use an approved ignition interlock device, as defined in section 42-2-132.5 (7) (a), during the period of probation at the person's own expense;

(VI) May require the person to submit to continuous alcohol monitoring using such technology or devices as are available to the court for such purpose; and

(VII) May impose such additional conditions of probation as may be permitted by law.

(c) (I) The court may impose all or part of the suspended sentence described in subparagraph (IV) of paragraph (a) of subsection (5) of this section or subparagraph (IV) of paragraph (a) of subsection (6) of this section at any time during the period of probation if the person violates a condition of his or her probation. During the period of imprisonment, the person shall continue serving the probation sentence with no reduction in time for the sentence to probation. A cumulative period of imprisonment imposed pursuant to this paragraph (c) shall not exceed one year.

(II) In imposing a sentence of imprisonment pursuant to subparagraph (I) of this paragraph (c), the court shall consider the nature of the violation, the report or testimony of the probation department, the impact on public safety, the progress of the person in any court-ordered alcohol and drug driving safety education or treatment program, and any other information that may assist the court in promoting the person's compliance with the conditions of his or her probation. Any imprisonment imposed upon a person by the court pursuant to subparagraph (I) of this paragraph (c) shall be imposed in a manner that promotes the person's compliance with the conditions of his or her probation and not merely as a punitive measure.

(d) The prosecution, the person, the person's counsel, or the person's probation officer may petition the court at any time for an early termination of the period of probation, which the court may grant upon a finding of the court that:

(I) The person has successfully completed a level II alcohol and drug driving safety education or treatment program pursuant to subparagraph (I) of paragraph (b) of this subsection (7);

(II) The person has otherwise complied with the terms and conditions of his or her probation; and

(III) Early termination of the period of probation will not endanger public safety.

(8) **Ignition interlock devices.** In sentencing a person pursuant to this section, courts are encouraged to require the person to use an approved ignition interlock device, as defined in section 42-2-132.5 (7) (a), as a condition of bond, probation, and participation in programs pursuant to section 18-1.3-106, C.R.S.

(9) **Previous convictions.** (a) For the purposes of subsections (5) and (6) of this section, a person shall be deemed to have a previous conviction for DUI, DUI per se, DWAI, habitual user, vehicular homicide pursuant to section 18-3-106 (1) (b), C.R.S., vehicular assault pursuant to section 18-3-205 (1) (b), C.R.S., aggravated driving with a revoked license pursuant to section 42-2-206 (1) (b) (I) (A) or (1) (b) (I) (B), or driving while the person's driver's license was under restraint pursuant to section 42-2-138 (1) (d), if the person has been convicted under the laws of this state or under the laws of any other state, the United States, or any territory subject to the jurisdiction of the United States, of an act that, if committed within this state, would constitute the offense of DUI, DUI per se, DWAI, habitual user, vehicular homicide pursuant to section 18-3-106 (1) (b), C.R.S., vehicular assault pursuant to section 18-3-205 (1) (b), C.R.S., aggravated driving with a revoked license pursuant to section 42-2-206 (1) (b) (I) (A) or (1) (b) (I) (B), or driving while the person's driver's license was under restraint pursuant to section 42-2-138 (1) (d).

(b) (I) For sentencing purposes concerning convictions for second and subsequent offenses, prima facie proof of a person's previous convictions shall be established when:

(A) The prosecuting attorney and the person stipulate to the existence of the prior conviction or convictions;

(B) The prosecuting attorney presents to the court a copy of the person's driving record provided by the department of revenue or by a similar agency in another state, which record contains a reference to the previous conviction or convictions; or

(C) The prosecuting attorney presents an authenticated copy of the record of the previous conviction or judgment from a court of record of this state or from a court of any other state, the United States, or any territory subject to the jurisdiction of the United States.

(II) The court shall not proceed to immediate sentencing if the prosecuting attorney and the person have not stipulated to previous convictions or if the prosecution has requested an opportunity to obtain a driving record or a copy of a court record. The prosecuting attorney shall not be required to plead or prove any previous convictions at trial.

(10) **Additional costs and surcharges.** In addition to the penalties prescribed in this section:

(a) Persons convicted of DUI, DUI per se, DWAI, habitual user, and UDD are subject to the costs imposed by section 24-4.1-119 (1) (c), C.R.S., relating to the crime victim compensation fund;

(b) Persons convicted of DUI, DUI per se, DWAI, and habitual user are subject to a surcharge of at least one hundred dollars but no more than five hundred dollars to fund programs to reduce the number of persistent drunk drivers. The surcharge shall be mandatory, and the court shall not have discretion to suspend or waive the surcharge; except that the court may suspend or waive the surcharge if the court determines that a person is indigent. Moneys collected for the surcharge shall be transmitted to the state treasurer, who shall credit the amount collected to the persistent drunk driver cash fund created in section 42-3-303.

(c) Persons convicted of DUI, DUI per se, DWAI, habitual user, and UDD are subject to a surcharge of twenty dollars to be transmitted to the state treasurer who shall deposit moneys collected for the surcharge in the Colorado traumatic brain injury trust fund created pursuant to section 26-1-309, C.R.S.;

(d) (I) Persons convicted of DUI, DUI per se, DWAI, and habitual user are subject to a surcharge of at least one dollar but no more than ten dollars for programs to fund efforts to address alcohol and substance abuse problems among persons in rural areas. The surcharge shall be mandatory, and the court shall not have discretion to suspend or waive the surcharge; except that the court may suspend or waive the surcharge if the court determines that a person is indigent. Any moneys collected for the surcharge shall be transmitted to the state treasurer, who shall credit the same to the rural alcohol and substance abuse cash fund created in section 27-80-117 (3), C.R.S.

(II) This paragraph (d) is repealed, effective July 1, 2016, unless the general assembly extends the repeal of the rural alcohol and substance abuse prevention and treatment program created in section 27-80-117, C.R.S.

(11) **Restitution.** As a condition of any sentence imposed pursuant to this section, the sentenced person shall be required to make restitution in accordance with the provisions of section 18-1.3-205, C.R.S.

(12) **Victim impact panels.** In addition to any other penalty provided by law, the court may sentence a person convicted of DUI, DUI per se, DWAI, habitual user, or UDD to attend and pay for one appearance at a victim impact panel approved by the court, for which the fee assessed to the person shall not exceed twenty-five dollars.

(13) **Alcohol and drug evaluation and supervision costs.** In addition to any fines, fees, or costs levied against a person convicted of DUI, DUI per se, DWAI, habitual user, or UDD, the judge shall assess each such person for the cost of the presentence or postsentence alcohol and drug evaluation and supervision services.

(14) **Public service penalty.** In addition to any other penalties prescribed in this part 13, the court shall assess an amount, not to exceed one hundred twenty dollars, upon a person required to perform useful public service.

(15) If a defendant is convicted of aggravated driving with a revoked license based upon the commission of DUI, DUI per se, or DWAI pursuant to section 42-2-206 (1) (b) (I) (A) or (1) (b) (I) (B):

(a) The court shall convict and sentence the offender for each offense separately;

(b) The court shall impose all of the penalties for the alcohol-related driving offense, as such penalties are described in this section;

(c) The provisions of section 18-1-408, C.R.S, shall not apply to the sentences imposed for either conviction;

(d) Any probation imposed for a conviction under section 42-2-206 may run concurrently with any probation required by this section; and

(e) The department shall reflect both convictions on the defendant's driving record.

PART 14

OTHER OFFENSES

42-4-1401. Reckless driving - penalty. (1) A person who drives a motor vehicle, bicycle, electrical assisted bicycle, or low-power scooter in such a manner as to indicate either a wanton or a willful disregard for the safety of persons or property is guilty of reckless driving. A person convicted of reckless driving of a bicycle or electrical assisted bicycle shall not be subject to the provisions of section 42-2-127.

(2) Any person who violates any provision of this section commits a class 2 misdemeanor traffic offense. Upon a second or subsequent conviction, such person shall be punished by a fine of not less than fifty dollars nor more than one thousand dollars, or by imprisonment in the county jail for not less than ten days nor more than six months, or by both such fine and imprisonment.

42-4-1402. Careless driving - penalty. (1) A person who drives a motor vehicle, bicycle, electrical assisted bicycle, or low-power scooter in a careless and imprudent manner, without due regard for the width, grade, curves, corners, traffic, and use of the streets and highways and all other attendant circumstances, is guilty of careless driving. A person convicted of careless driving of a bicycle or electrical assisted bicycle shall not be subject to the provisions of section 42-2-127.

(2) (a) Except as otherwise provided in paragraphs (b) and (c) of this subsection (2), any person who violates any provision of this section commits a class 2 misdemeanor traffic offense.

(b) If the person's actions are the proximate cause of bodily injury to another, such person commits a class 1 misdemeanor traffic offense.

(c) If the person's actions are the proximate cause of death to another, such person commits a class 1 misdemeanor traffic offense.

42-4-1403. Following fire apparatus prohibited. The driver of any vehicle other than one on official business shall not follow any fire apparatus traveling in response to a fire alarm closer than five hundred feet or drive into or park such vehicle within the block where fire apparatus has stopped in answer to a fire alarm. Any person who violates any provision of this section commits a class A traffic infraction.

42-4-1404. Crossing fire hose. No vehicle shall be driven over any unprotected hose of a fire department used at any fire, alarm of fire, or practice runs or laid down on any street, private driveway, or highway without the consent of the fire department official in command. Any person who violates any provision of this section commits a class B traffic infraction.

42-4-1405. Riding in trailers. No person shall occupy a trailer while it is being moved upon a public highway. Any person who violates any provision of this section commits a class B traffic infraction.

42-4-1406. Foreign matter on highway prohibited. (1) (a) No person shall throw or deposit upon or along any highway any glass bottle, glass, stones, nails, tacks, wire, cans, container of human waste, or other substance likely to injure any person, animal, or vehicle upon or along such highway.

(b) No person shall throw, drop, or otherwise expel a lighted cigarette, cigar, match, or other burning material from a motor vehicle upon any highway.

(2) Any person who drops, or permits to be dropped or thrown, upon any highway or structure any destructive or injurious material or lighted or burning substance shall immediately remove the same or cause it to be removed.

(3) Any person removing a wrecked or damaged vehicle from a highway shall remove any glass or other injurious substance dropped upon the highway from such vehicle.

(4) No person shall excavate a ditch or other aqueduct, or construct any flume or pipeline or any steam, electric, or other railway, or construct any approach to a public highway without written consent of the authority responsible for the maintenance of that highway.

(5) (a) Except as provided in paragraph (b) of this subsection (5), any person who violates any provision of this section commits a class B traffic infraction.

(b) (I) Any person who violates any provision of paragraph (b) of subsection (1) of this section commits a class 2 misdemeanor and shall be punished as provided in section 18-1.3-501, C.R.S.

(II) Any person who violates paragraph (a) of subsection (1) of this section by throwing or depositing a container of human waste upon or along any highway shall be punished by a fine of five hundred dollars in lieu of the penalty and surcharge prescribed in section 42-4-1701 (4) (a) (I) (N).

(6) As used in this section:

(a) "Container" includes, but is not limited to, a bottle, a can, a box, or a diaper.

(b) "Human waste" means urine or feces produced by a human.

42-4-1407. Spilling loads on highways prohibited - prevention of spilling of aggregate, trash, or recyclables. (1) No vehicle shall be driven or moved on any highway unless such vehicle is constructed or loaded or the load thereof securely covered to prevent any of its load from blowing, dropping, sifting, leaking, or otherwise escaping therefrom; except that material may be dropped for the purpose of securing traction or water or other substance may be sprinkled on a roadway in cleaning or maintaining such roadway.

(2) (Deleted by amendment, L. 99, p. 295, § 1, effective July 1, 1999.)

(2.4) (a) A vehicle shall not be driven or moved on a highway if the vehicle is transporting trash or recyclables unless at least one of the following conditions is met:

(I) The load is covered by a tarp or other cover in a manner that prevents the load from blowing, dropping, shifting, leaking, or otherwise escaping from the vehicle;

(II) The vehicle utilizes other technology that prevents the load from blowing, dropping, shifting, leaking, or otherwise escaping from the vehicle;

(III) The load is required to be secured under and complies with 49 CFR parts 392 and 393; or

(IV) The vehicle is loaded in such a manner or the load itself has physical characteristics such that the contents will not escape from the vehicle. Such a load may include, but is not limited to, heavy scrap metal or hydraulically compressed scrap recyclables.

(b) Paragraph (a) of this subsection (2.4) shall not apply to a motor vehicle in the process of collecting trash or recyclables within a one-mile radius of the motor vehicle's last collection point.

(2.5) (a) No vehicle shall be driven or moved on any highway for a distance of more than two miles if the vehicle is transporting aggregate material with a diameter of one inch or less unless:

(I) The load is covered by a tarp or other cover in a manner that prevents the aggregate material from blowing, dropping, sifting, leaking, or otherwise escaping from the vehicle; or

(II) The vehicle utilizes other technology that prevents the aggregate material from blowing, dropping, sifting, leaking, or otherwise escaping from the vehicle.

(b) Nothing in this subsection (2.5) shall apply to a vehicle:

(I) Operating entirely within a marked construction zone;

(II) Involved in maintenance of public roads during snow or ice removal operations; or

(III) Involved in emergency operations when requested by a law enforcement agency or an emergency response authority designated in or pursuant to section 29-22-102, C.R.S.

(2.7) For the purposes of this section:

(a) "Aggregate material" means any rock, clay, silts, gravel, limestone, dimension stone, marble, and shale; except that "aggregate material" does not include hot asphalt, including asphalt patching material, wet concrete, or other materials not susceptible to blowing.

(b) "Recyclables" means material or objects that can be reused, reprocessed, remanufactured, reclaimed, or recycled.

(c) "Trash" means material or objects that have been or are in the process of being discarded or transported.

(3) (a) Except as otherwise provided in paragraph (b) or (c) of this subsection (3), any person

who violates any provision of this section commits a class B traffic infraction.

(b) Any person who violates any provision of this section while driving or moving a car or pick-up truck without causing bodily injury to another person commits a class A traffic infraction.

(c) Any person who violates any provision of this section while driving or moving a car or pick-up truck and thereby proximately causes bodily injury to another person commits a class 2 misdemeanor traffic offense.

42-4-1407.5. Splash guards - when required. (1) As used in this section, unless the context otherwise requires:

(a) "Splash guards" means mud flaps, rubber, plastic or fabric aprons, or other devices directly behind the rear-most wheels, designed to minimize the spray of water and other substances to the rear.

(b) "Splash guards" must, at a minimum, be wide enough to cover the full tread of the tire or tires being protected, hang perpendicular from the vehicle not more than ten inches above the surface of the street or highway when the vehicle is empty, and generally maintain their perpendicular relationship under normal driving conditions.

(2) Except as otherwise permitted in this section, no vehicle or motor vehicle shall be driven or moved on any street or highway unless the vehicle or motor vehicle is equipped with splash guards. However, vehicles and motor vehicles with splash guards that violate this section shall be allowed to remain in service for the time necessary to continue to a place where the deficient splash guards will be replaced. Such replacement shall occur at the first reasonable opportunity.

(3) This section does not apply to:

(a) Passenger-carrying motor vehicles registered pursuant to section 42-3-306 (2);

(b) Trucks and truck tractors registered pursuant to section 42-3-306 (4) or (5) having an empty weight of ten thousand pounds or less;

(c) Trailers equipped with fenders or utility pole trailers;

(d) Vehicles while involved in chip and seal or paving operations or road widening equipment;

(e) Truck tractors or converter dollies when used in combination with other vehicles;

(f) Vehicles drawn by animals; or

(g) Bicycles or electrical assisted bicycles.

(4) Any person who violates any provision of this section commits a class B traffic infraction.

42-4-1408. Operation of motor vehicles on property under control of or owned by parks and recreation districts. (1) Any metropolitan recreation district, any park and recreation district organized pursuant to article 1 of title 32, C.R.S., or any recreation district organized pursuant to the provisions of part 7 of article 20 of title 30, C.R.S., referred to in this section as a "district", shall have the authority to designate areas on property owned or controlled by the district in which the operation of motor vehicles shall be prohibited. Areas in which it shall be prohibited to operate motor vehicles shall be clearly posted by a district.

(2) It is unlawful for any person to operate a motor vehicle in an area owned or under the control of a district if the district has declared the operation of motor vehicles to be prohibited in such area, as provided in subsection (1) of this section.

(3) Any person who violates any provision of this section commits a class B traffic infraction.

42-4-1409. Compulsory insurance - penalty - legislative intent. (1) No owner of a motor vehicle or low-power scooter required to be registered in this state shall operate the vehicle or permit it to be operated on the public highways of this state when the owner has failed to have a complying policy or certificate of self-insurance in full force and effect as required by law.

(2) No person shall operate a motor vehicle or low-power scooter on the public highways of this state without a complying policy or certificate of self-insurance in full force and effect as required by law.

(3) When an accident occurs, or when requested to do so following any lawful traffic contact or during any traffic investigation by a peace officer, no owner or operator of a motor vehicle or low-power scooter shall fail to present to the requesting officer immediate evidence of a complying policy or certificate of self-insurance in full force and effect as required by law.

(4) (a) Any person who violates the provisions of subsection (1), (2), or (3) of this section commits a class 1 misdemeanor traffic offense. The minimum fine imposed by section 42-4-1701 (3) (a) (II) (A) shall be mandatory, and the defendant shall be punished by a minimum mandatory fine of not less than five hundred dollars. The court may suspend up to one half of the fine upon a showing that appropriate insurance as required pursuant to section 10-4-619 or 10-4-624, C.R.S., has been obtained. Nothing in this paragraph (a) shall be construed to prevent the court from imposing a fine greater than the minimum mandatory fine.

(b) Upon a second or subsequent conviction under this section within a period of five years following a prior conviction under this section, in addition to any imprisonment imposed pursuant to section 42-4-1701 (3) (a) (II) (A), the defendant shall be punished by a minimum mandatory fine of not less than one thousand dollars, and the court shall not suspend such minimum fine. The court or the court collections' investigator may establish a payment schedule for a person convicted of the provisions of subsection (1), (2), or (3) of this section, and the provisions of section 16-11-101.6, C.R.S., shall apply. The court may suspend up to one half of the fine upon a showing that appropriate insurance as required pursuant to section 10-4-619 or 10-4-624, C.R.S., has been obtained.

(c) In addition to the penalties prescribed in paragraphs (a) and (b) of this subsection (4), any person convicted pursuant to this section may, at the discretion of the court, be sentenced to perform not less than forty hours of community service, subject to the provisions of section 18-1.3-507, C.R.S.

(5) Testimony of the failure of any owner or operator of a motor vehicle or low-power scooter to present immediate evidence of a complying policy or certificate of self-insurance in full force and effect as required by law, when requested to do so by a peace officer, shall constitute prima facie evidence, at a trial concerning a violation charged under subsection (1) or (2) of this section, that such owner or operator of a motor vehicle violated subsection (1) or (2) of this section.

(6) No person charged with violating subsection (1), (2), or (3) of this section shall be convicted if the person produces in court a bona fide complying policy or certificate of self-insurance that was in full force and effect as required by law at the time of the alleged violation.

(7) The owner of a motor vehicle or low-power scooter, upon receipt of an affirmation of insurance as described in section 42-3-113 (2) and (3), shall sign and date such affirmation in the space provided.

(8) (Deleted by amendment, L. 2003, p. 2648, § 7, effective July 1, 2003.)

(9) It is the intent of the general assembly that the moneys collected as fines imposed pursuant to paragraphs (a) and (b) of subsection (4) of this section are to be used for the supervision of the public highways. The general assembly determines that law enforcement agencies that patrol and maintain the public safety on public highways are supervising the public highways. The general assembly further determines that a clerk and recorder for a county is supervising the public highways through his or her enforcement of the requirements for demonstration of proof of motor vehicle insurance pursuant to section 42-3-105 (1) (d). Therefore, of the moneys collected from fines pursuant to paragraphs (a) and (b) of subsection (4) of this section, fifty percent of these moneys shall be transferred to the law enforcement agency that issued the ticket for a violation of this section. The remaining fifty percent of the moneys collected from fines for violations of paragraph (a) or (b) of subsection (4) of this section shall be transmitted to the clerk and recorder for the county in which the violation occurred.

42-4-1410. Proof of financial responsibility required - suspension of license. (1) Any person convicted of violating section 42-4-1409 (1) shall file and maintain proof of financial responsibility for the future as prescribed in sections 42-7-408 to 42-7-412. Said proof of insurance shall be maintained for a period of three years from the date of conviction.

(2) The clerk of a court or the judge of a court which has no clerk shall forward to the executive director of the department of revenue a certified record of any conviction under section 42-4-1409 (1). Upon receipt of any such certified record, the director shall give written notice to the person convicted that such person shall be required to provide proof of financial responsibility for the future for a period of three years from the date of conviction and advising such person of the manner in which proof is to be provided. If no proof as required is provided to the director within a period of twenty days from the time notice is given or if at any time when proof is required to be maintained it is not so maintained or becomes invalid, the director shall suspend the driver's license of the person from whom proof is required and shall not reinstate the license of such person until proof of financial responsibility is provided.

(3) Repealed.

42-4-1411. Use of earphones while driving. (1) (a) No person shall operate a motor vehicle while wearing earphones.

(b) For purposes of this subsection (1), "earphones" includes any headset, radio, tape player, or other similar device which provides the listener with radio programs, music, or other recorded information through a device attached to the head and which covers all of or a portion of the ears. "Earphones" does not include speakers or other listening devices which are built into protective headgear.

(2) Any person who violates this section commits a class B traffic infraction.

42-4-1412. Operation of bicycles and other human-powered vehicles. (1) Every person riding a bicycle or electrical assisted bicycle shall have all of the rights and duties applicable to the driver of any other vehicle under this article, except as to special regulations in this article and except as to those provisions which by their nature can have no application. Said riders shall comply with the rules set forth in this section and section 42-4-221, and, when using streets and highways within incorporated cities and towns, shall be subject to local ordinances regulating the operation of bicycles and electrical assisted bicycles as provided in section 42-4-111.

(2) It is the intent of the general assembly that nothing contained in House Bill No. 1246, enacted at the second regular session of the fifty-sixth general assembly, shall in any way be construed to modify or increase the duty of the department of transportation or any political subdivision to sign or maintain highways or sidewalks or to affect or increase the liability of the state of Colorado or any political subdivision under the "Colorado Governmental Immunity Act", article 10 of title 24, C.R.S.

(3) No bicycle or electrical assisted bicycle shall be used to carry more persons at one time than the number for which it is designed or equipped.

(4) No person riding upon any bicycle or electrical assisted bicycle shall attach the same or

himself or herself to any motor vehicle upon a roadway.

(5) (a) Any person operating a bicycle or an electrical assisted bicycle upon a roadway at less than the normal speed of traffic shall ride in the right-hand lane, subject to the following conditions:

(I) If the right-hand lane then available for traffic is wide enough to be safely shared with overtaking vehicles, a bicyclist shall ride far enough to the right as judged safe by the bicyclist to facilitate the movement of such overtaking vehicles unless other conditions make it unsafe to do so.

(II) A bicyclist may use a lane other than the right-hand lane when:

(A) Preparing for a left turn at an intersection or into a private roadway or driveway;

(B) Overtaking a slower vehicle; or

(C) Taking reasonably necessary precautions to avoid hazards or road conditions.

(III) Upon approaching an intersection where right turns are permitted and there is a dedicated right-turn lane, a bicyclist may ride on the left-hand portion of the dedicated right-turn lane even if the bicyclist does not intend to turn right.

(b) A bicyclist shall not be expected or required to:

(I) Ride over or through hazards at the edge of a roadway, including but not limited to fixed or moving objects, parked or moving vehicles, bicycles, pedestrians, animals, surface hazards, or narrow lanes; or

(II) Ride without a reasonable safety margin on the right-hand side of the roadway.

(c) A person operating a bicycle or an electrical assisted bicycle upon a one-way roadway with two or more marked traffic lanes may ride as near to the left-hand curb or edge of such roadway as judged safe by the bicyclist, subject to the following conditions:

(I) If the left-hand lane then available for traffic is wide enough to be safely shared with overtaking vehicles, a bicyclist shall ride far enough to the left as judged safe by the bicyclist to facilitate the movement of such overtaking vehicles unless other conditions make it unsafe to do so.

(II) A bicyclist shall not be expected or required to:

(A) Ride over or through hazards at the edge of a roadway, including but not limited to fixed or moving objects, parked or moving vehicles, bicycles, pedestrians, animals, surface hazards, or narrow lanes; or

(B) Ride without a reasonable safety margin on the left-hand side of the roadway.

(6) (a) Persons riding bicycles or electrical assisted bicycles upon a roadway shall not ride more than two abreast except on paths or parts of roadways set aside for the exclusive use of bicycles.

(b) Persons riding bicycles or electrical assisted bicycles two abreast shall not impede the normal and reasonable movement of traffic and, on a laned roadway, shall ride within a single lane.

(7) A person operating a bicycle or electrical assisted bicycle shall keep at least one hand on the handlebars at all times.

(8) (a) A person riding a bicycle or electrical assisted bicycle intending to turn left shall follow a course described in sections 42-4-901 (1), 42-4-903, and 42-4-1007 or may make a left turn in the manner prescribed in paragraph (b) of this subsection (8).

(b) A person riding a bicycle or electrical assisted bicycle intending to turn left shall approach the turn as closely as practicable to the right-hand curb or edge of the roadway. After proceeding across the intersecting roadway to the far corner of the curb or intersection of the roadway edges, the bicyclist shall stop, as much as practicable, out of the way of traffic. After stopping, the bicyclist shall yield to any traffic proceeding in either direction along the roadway that the bicyclist had been using. After yielding and complying with any official traffic control device or police officer regulating traffic on the highway along which the bicyclist intends to proceed, the bicyclist may proceed in the new direction.

(c) Notwithstanding the provisions of paragraphs (a) and (b) of this subsection (8), the transportation commission and local authorities in their respective jurisdictions may cause official traffic control devices to be placed on roadways and thereby require and direct that a specific course be traveled.

(9) (a) Except as otherwise provided in this subsection (9), every person riding a bicycle or electrical assisted bicycle shall signal the intention to turn or stop in accordance with section 42-4-903; except that a person riding a bicycle or electrical assisted bicycle may signal a right turn with the right arm extended horizontally.

(b) A signal of intention to turn right or left when required shall be given continuously during not less than the last one hundred feet traveled by the bicycle or electrical assisted bicycle before turning and shall be given while the bicycle or electrical assisted bicycle is stopped waiting to turn. A signal by hand and arm need not be given continuously if the hand is needed in the control or operation of the bicycle or electrical assisted bicycle.

(10) (a) A person riding a bicycle or electrical assisted bicycle upon and along a sidewalk or pathway or across a roadway upon and along a crosswalk shall yield the right-of-way to any pedestrian and shall give an audible signal before overtaking and passing such pedestrian. A person riding a bicycle in a crosswalk shall do so in a manner that is safe for pedestrians.

(b) A person shall not ride a bicycle or electrical assisted bicycle upon and along a sidewalk or pathway or across a roadway upon and along a crosswalk where such use of bicycles or electrical assisted bicycles is prohibited by official traffic control devices or local ordinances. A person riding a bicycle or electrical assisted bicycle shall dismount before entering any crosswalk where required by official traffic control devices or local ordinances.

(c) A person riding or walking a bicycle or electrical assisted bicycle upon and along a sidewalk or pathway or across a roadway upon and along a crosswalk shall have all the rights and duties applicable to a pedestrian under the same circumstances, including, but not limited to, the rights and duties granted and required by section 42-4-802.

(d) (Deleted by amendment, L. 2005, p. 1353, § 1, effective July 1, 2005.)

(11) (a) A person may park a bicycle or electrical assisted bicycle on a sidewalk unless prohibited or restricted by an official traffic control device or local ordinance.

(b) A bicycle or electrical assisted bicycle parked on a sidewalk shall not impede the normal and reasonable movement of pedestrian or other traffic.

(c) A bicycle or electrical assisted bicycle may be parked on the road at any angle to the curb or edge of the road at any location where parking is allowed.

(d) A bicycle or electrical assisted bicycle may be parked on the road abreast of another such bicycle or bicycles near the side of the road or any location where parking is allowed in such a manner as does not impede the normal and reasonable movement of traffic.

(e) In all other respects, bicycles or electrical assisted bicycles parked anywhere on a highway shall conform to the provisions of part 12 of this article regulating the parking of vehicles.

(12) (a) Any person who violates any provision of this section commits a class 2 misdemeanor traffic offense; except that section 42-2-127 shall not apply.

(b) Any person riding a bicycle or electrical assisted bicycle who violates any provision of this article other than this section which is applicable to such a vehicle and for which a penalty is specified shall be subject to the same specified penalty as any other vehicle; except that section 42-2-127 shall not apply.

(13) Upon request, the law enforcement agency having jurisdiction shall complete a report concerning an injury or death incident that involves a bicycle or electrical assisted bicycle on the roadways of the state, even if such accident does not involve a motor vehicle.

(14) Except as authorized by section 42-4-111, the rider of an electrical assisted bicycle shall not use the electrical motor on a bike or pedestrian path.

42-4-1413. Eluding or attempting to elude a police officer. Any operator of a motor vehicle who the officer has reasonable grounds to believe has violated a state law or municipal ordinance, who has received a visual or audible signal such as a red light or a siren from a police officer driving a marked vehicle showing the same to be an official police, sheriff, or Colorado state patrol car directing the operator to bring the operator's vehicle to a stop, and who willfully increases his or her speed or extinguishes his or her lights in an attempt to elude such police officer, or willfully attempts in any other manner to elude the police officer, or does elude such police officer commits a class 2 misdemeanor traffic offense.

42-4-1414. Use of dyed fuel on highways prohibited. (1) No person shall operate a motor vehicle upon any highway of the state using diesel fuel dyed to show that no taxes have been collected on the fuel.

(2) (a) Any person who violates subsection (1) of this section commits a class B traffic infraction.

(b) Any person who commits a second violation of subsection (1) of this section within a twelve-month period shall be subject to an increased penalty pursuant to section 42-4-1701 (4) (a) (I) (N).

(c) Any person who commits a third or subsequent violation of subsection (1) of this section within a twelve-month period shall be subject to an increased penalty pursuant to section 42-4-1701 (4) (a) (I) (N).

(3) Any person violating any provision of this section shall be subject to audit by the department regarding payment of motor fuel tax.

42-4-1415. Radar jamming devices prohibited - penalty. (1) (a) No person shall use, possess, or sell a radar jamming device.

(b) No person shall operate a motor vehicle with a radar jamming device in the motor vehicle.

(2) (a) For purposes of this section, "radar jamming device" means any active or passive device, instrument, mechanism, or equipment that is designed or intended to interfere with, disrupt, or scramble the radar or laser that is used by law enforcement agencies and peace officers to measure the speed of motor vehicles. "Radar jamming device" includes but is not limited to devices commonly referred to as "jammers" or "scramblers".

(b) For purposes of this section, "radar jamming device" shall not include equipment that is legal under FCC regulations, such as a citizens' band radio, ham radio, or any other similar electronic equipment.

(3) Radar jamming devices are subject to seizure by any peace officer and may be confiscated and destroyed by order of the court in which a violation of this section is charged.

(4) A violation of subsection (1) of this section is a class 2 misdemeanor traffic offense, punishable as provided in section 42-4-1701 (3) (a) (II) (A).

(5) The provisions of subsection (1) of this section shall not apply to peace officers acting in their official capacity.

PART 15

MOTORCYCLES

42-4-1501. Traffic laws apply to persons operating motorcycles - special permits. (1) Every person operating a motorcycle shall be granted all of the rights and shall be subject to all of the duties applicable to the driver of any other vehicle under this article, except as to special regulations in this article and except as to those provisions of this article which by their nature can have no application.

(2) For the purposes of a prearranged organized special event and upon a showing that safety will be reasonably maintained, the department of transportation may grant a special permit exempting the operation of a motorcycle from any requirement of this part 15.

42-4-1502. Riding on motorcycles - protective helmet. (1) A person operating a motorcycle shall ride only upon the permanent and regular seat attached thereto, and such operator shall not carry any other person nor shall any other person ride on a motorcycle unless such motorcycle is designed to carry more than one person, in which event a passenger may ride upon the permanent seat if designed for two persons or upon another seat firmly attached to the motorcycle at the rear or side of the operator.

(2) A person shall ride upon a motorcycle only while sitting astride the seat, facing forward, with one leg on either side of the motorcycle.

(3) No person shall operate a motorcycle while carrying packages, bundles, or other articles which prevent the person from keeping both hands on the handlebars.

(4) No operator shall carry any person nor shall any person ride in a position that will interfere with the operation or control of the motorcycle or the view of the operator.

(4.5) (a) A person shall not operate or ride as a passenger on a motorcycle or low-power scooter on a roadway unless:

(I) Each person under eighteen years of age is wearing a protective helmet of a type and design manufactured for use by operators of motorcycles;

(II) The protective helmet conforms to the design and specifications set forth in paragraph (b) of this subsection (4.5); and

(III) The protective helmet is secured properly on the person's head with a chin strap while the motorcycle is in motion.

(b) A protective helmet required to be worn by this subsection (4.5) shall:

(I) Be designed to reduce injuries to the user resulting from head impacts and to protect the user by remaining on the user's head, deflecting blows, resisting penetration, and spreading the force of impact;

(II) Consist of lining, padding, and chin strap; and

(III) Meet or exceed the standards established in the United States department of transportation federal motor vehicle safety standard no. 218, 49 CFR 571.218, for motorcycle helmets.

(5) Any person who violates any provision of this section commits a class A traffic infraction.

42-4-1503. Operating motorcycles on roadways laned for traffic. (1) All motorcycles are entitled to full use of a traffic lane, and no motor vehicle shall be driven in such a manner as to deprive any motorcycle of the full use of a traffic lane. This subsection (1) shall not apply to motorcycles operated two abreast in a single lane.

(2) The operator of a motorcycle shall not overtake or pass in the same lane occupied by the vehicle being overtaken.

(3) No person shall operate a motorcycle between lanes of traffic or between adjacent lines or rows of vehicles.

(4) Motorcycles shall not be operated more than two abreast in a single lane.

(5) Subsections (2) and (3) of this section shall not apply to police officers in the performance of their official duties.

(6) Any person who violates any provision of this section commits a class A traffic infraction.

42-4-1504. Clinging to other vehicles. No person riding upon a motorcycle shall attach himself, herself, or the motorcycle to any other vehicle on a roadway. Any person who violates any provision of this section commits a class A traffic infraction.

PART 16

ACCIDENTS AND ACCIDENT REPORTS

42-4-1601. Accidents involving death or personal injuries - duties. (1) The driver of any vehicle directly involved in an accident resulting in injury to, serious bodily injury to, or death of any person shall immediately stop such vehicle at the scene of such accident or as close to the scene as possible but shall immediately return to and in every event shall remain at the scene of the accident until the driver has fulfilled the requirements of section 42-4-1603 (1). Every such stop shall be made without obstructing traffic more than is necessary.

(1.5) It shall not be an offense under this section if a driver, after fulfilling the requirements of subsection (1) of this section and of section 42-4-1603 (1), leaves the scene of the accident for the purpose of reporting the accident in accordance with the provisions of sections 42-4-1603 (2) and 42-4-1606.

(2) Any person who violates any provision of this section commits:

(a) A class 1 misdemeanor traffic offense if the accident resulted in injury to any person;

(b) A class 5 felony if the accident resulted in serious bodily injury to any person;

(c) A class 3 felony if the accident resulted in the death of any person.

(3) The department shall revoke the driver's license of the person so convicted.

(4) As used in this section and sections 42-4-1603 and 42-4-1606:

(a) "Injury" means physical pain, illness, or any impairment of physical or mental condition.

(b) "Serious bodily injury" means injury that involves, either at the time of the actual injury or at a later time, a substantial risk of death, a substantial risk of serious permanent disfigurement, or a substantial risk of protracted loss or impairment of the function of any part or organ of the body, or breaks, fractures, or burns of the second or third degree.

42-4-1602. Accident involving damage - duty. (1) The driver of any vehicle directly involved in an accident resulting only in damage to a vehicle which is driven or attended by any person shall immediately stop such vehicle at the scene of such accident or as close thereto as possible but shall immediately return to and in every event shall remain at the scene of such accident, except in the circumstances provided in subsection (2) of this section, until the driver has fulfilled the requirements of section 42-4-1603. Every such stop shall be made without obstructing traffic more than is necessary. Any person who violates any provision of this subsection (1) commits a class 2 misdemeanor traffic offense.

(2) When an accident occurs on the traveled portion, median, or ramp of a divided highway and each vehicle involved can be safely driven, each driver shall move such driver's vehicle as soon as practicable off the traveled portion, median, or ramp to a frontage road, the nearest suitable cross street, or other suitable location to fulfill the requirements of section 42-4-1603.

42-4-1603. Duty to give notice, information, and aid. (1) The driver of any vehicle involved in an accident resulting in injury to, serious bodily injury to, or death of any person or damage to any vehicle which is driven or attended by any person shall give the driver's name, the driver's address, and the registration number of the vehicle he or she is driving and shall upon request exhibit his or her driver's license to the person struck or the driver or occupant of or person attending any vehicle collided with and where practical shall render to any person injured in such accident reasonable assistance, including the carrying, or the making of arrangements for the carrying, of such person to a physician, surgeon, or hospital for medical or surgical treatment if it is apparent that such treatment is necessary or if the carrying is requested by the injured person.

(2) In the event that none of the persons specified are in condition to receive the information to which they otherwise would be entitled under subsection (1) of this section and no police officer is present, the driver of any vehicle involved in such accident after fulfilling all other requirements of subsection (1) of this section, insofar as possible on the driver's part to be performed, shall immediately report such accident to the nearest office of a duly authorized police authority as required in section 42-4-1606 and submit thereto the information specified in subsection (1) of this section.

42-4-1604. Duty upon striking unattended vehicle or other property. The driver of any vehicle which collides with or is involved in an accident with any vehicle or other property which is unattended resulting in any damage to such vehicle or other property shall immediately stop and either locate and notify the operator or owner of such vehicle or other property of such fact, the driver's name and address, and the registration number of the vehicle he or she is driving or attach securely in a conspicuous place in or on such vehicle or other property a written notice giving the driver's name and address and the registration number of the vehicle he or she is driving. The driver shall also make report of such accident when and as required in section 42-4-1606. Every stop shall be made without obstructing traffic more than is necessary. This section shall not apply to the striking of highway fixtures or traffic control devices which shall be governed by the provisions of section 42-4-1605. Any person who violates any provision of this section commits a class 2 misdemeanor traffic offense.

42-4-1605. Duty upon striking highway fixtures or traffic control devices. The driver of any vehicle involved in an accident resulting only in damage to fixtures or traffic control devices upon or adjacent to a highway shall notify the road authority in charge of such property of that fact and of the driver's name and address and of the registration number of the vehicle he or she is driving and shall make report of such accident when and as required in section 42-4-1606. Any person who violates any provision of this section commits a class 2 misdemeanor traffic offense.

42-4-1606. Duty to report accidents. (1) The driver of a vehicle involved in a traffic accident resulting in injury to, serious bodily injury to, or death of any person or any property damage shall, after fulfilling the requirements of sections 42-4-1602 and 42-4-1603 (1), give immediate notice of the location of such accident and such other information as is specified in section 42-4-1603 (2) to the nearest office of the duly authorized police authority and, if so directed by the police authority, shall immediately return to and remain at the scene of the accident until said police have arrived at the scene and completed their investigation thereat.

(2) Repealed.

(3) The department may require any driver of a vehicle involved in an accident of which report must be made as provided in this section to file supplemental reports whenever the origi-

nal report is insufficient in the opinion of the department and may require witnesses of accidents to render reports to the department.

(4) (a) (I) It is the duty of all law enforcement officers who receive notification of traffic accidents within their respective jurisdictions or who investigate such accidents either at the time of or at the scene of the accident or thereafter by interviewing participants or witnesses to submit reports of all such accidents to the department on the form provided, including insurance information received from any driver, within five days of the time they receive such information or complete their investigation. The law enforcement officer shall indicate in such report whether the inflatable restraint system in the vehicle, if any, inflated and deployed in the accident. For the purposes of this section, "inflatable restraint system" has the same meaning as set forth in 49 CFR sec. 507.208 S4.1.5.1 (b).

(II) Repealed.

(b) The law enforcement officer shall not be required to complete an investigation or file an accident report:

(I) In the case of a traffic accident involving a motor vehicle, if the law enforcement officer has a reasonable basis to believe that damage to the property of any one person does not exceed one thousand dollars and if the traffic accident does not involve injury to or death of any person; except that the officer shall complete an investigation and file a report if specifically requested to do so by one of the participants or if one of the participants cannot show proof of insurance; or

(II) In the case of a traffic accident not involving a motor vehicle, if the traffic accident does not involve serious bodily injury to or death of any person.

(5) The person in charge at any garage or repair shop to which is brought any motor vehicle which shows evidence of having been struck by any bullet shall report to the nearest office of the duly authorized police authority within twenty-four hours after such motor vehicle is received, giving the vehicle identification number, registration number, and, if known, the name and address of the owner and operator of such vehicle together with any other discernible information.

(6) Any person who violates any provision of this section commits a class 2 misdemeanor traffic offense.

42-4-1607. When driver unable to give notice or make written report. (1) Whenever the driver of a vehicle is physically incapable of giving an immediate notice of an accident as required in section 42-4-1606 (1) and there was another occupant in the vehicle at the time of the accident capable of doing so, such occupant shall give or cause to be given the notice not given by the driver.

(2) Repealed.

(3) Any person who violates any provision of this section commits a class 2 misdemeanor traffic offense.

42-4-1608. Accident report forms. (1) The department shall prepare and upon request supply to police departments, coroners, sheriffs, and other suitable agencies or individuals forms for accident reports required under this article, which reports shall call for sufficiently detailed information to disclose, with reference to a traffic accident, the contributing circumstances, the conditions then existing, and the persons and vehicles involved.

(2) Every required accident report shall be made on a form approved by the department, where such form is available.

42-4-1609. Coroners to report. Every coroner or other official performing like functions shall on or before the tenth day of each month report in writing to the department the death of any person within such official's jurisdiction during the preceding calendar month as the result of an accident involving a motor vehicle and the circumstances of such accident.

42-4-1610. Reports by interested parties confidential. All accident reports and supplemental reports required by law to be made by any driver, owner, or person involved in any accident shall be without prejudice to the individual so reporting and shall be for the confidential use of the department; except that the department may disclose the identity of a person involved in an accident when such identity is not otherwise known or when such person denies his or her presence at such accident. Except as provided in section 42-7-504 (2), no such report shall be used as evidence in any trial, civil or criminal, arising out of an accident; except that the department shall furnish, upon demand of any person who has, or claims to have, made such a report or upon demand of any court, a certificate showing that a specified accident report has or has not been made to the department solely to prove a compliance or failure to comply with the requirement that such a report be made to the department. This section shall not be construed to mean that reports of investigation or other reports made by sheriffs, police officers, coroners, or other peace officers shall be confidential, but the same shall be public records and shall be subject to the provisions of section 42-1-206.

42-4-1611. Tabulation and analysis of reports. The department shall tabulate and may analyze all accident reports and shall publish annually or at more frequent intervals statistical information based thereon as to the number and circumstances of traffic accidents and in such a way that the information may be of value to the department of transportation in eliminating roadway hazards. The statistical information shall be issued in accordance with the provisions of section 24-1-136, C.R.S.

42-4-1612. Accidents in state highway work areas - annual reporting by department of transportation and Colorado state patrol. (1) On or before February 15, 2011, and on or before February 15 of each succeeding year, the department of transportation and the Colorado state patrol shall present a joint report to the transportation and energy committee of the house of representatives and the transportation committee of the senate, or any successor committees, regarding fatal accidents in state highway work areas during the preceding year. The report shall include, at a minimum:

(a) A summary of the total number of fatal accidents and the total number of individuals killed;

(b) A categorization of the total number of individuals killed that identifies the individuals as employees of the department of transportation, employees of contractors or subcontractors working on a project for the department, or other individuals;

(c) A copy of the accident reporting form for each fatal accident;

(d) A description of both ongoing and newly implemented measures taken by the department of transportation to prevent fatal accidents in state highway work areas.

(2) For purposes of this section, "state highway work area" includes any area where an employee of the department of transportation is working at the time a fatal accident occurs.

(3) Nothing in this section shall be construed to require the department of transportation or the Colorado state patrol to specifically identify by name any individual killed, injured, or otherwise involved in an accident.

PART 17

PENALTIES AND PROCEDURE

42-4-1701. Traffic offenses and infractions classified - penalties - penalty and surcharge schedule - repeal. (1) It is a traffic infraction for any person to violate any of the provisions of articles 1 to 3 of this title and parts 1 to 3 and 5 to 19 of this article unless such violation is, by articles 1 to 3 of this title and parts 1 to 3 and 5 to 19 of this article or by any other law of this state, declared to be a felony, misdemeanor, petty offense, or misdemeanor traffic offense. Such a traffic infraction shall constitute a civil matter.

(2) (a) For the purposes of this part 17, "judge" shall include any county court magistrate who hears traffic infraction matters, but no person charged with a traffic violation other than a traffic infraction or class 2 misdemeanor traffic offense shall be taken before a county court magistrate.

(b) For the purposes of this part 17, "magistrate" shall include any county court judge who is acting as a county court magistrate in traffic infraction and class 2 misdemeanor traffic offense matters.

(3) (a) (I) Except as provided in subsections (4) and (5) of this section or the section creating the infraction, traffic infractions are divided into two classes which shall be subject to the following penalties which are authorized upon entry of judgment against the defendant:

Class	Minimum Penalty	Maximum Penalty
A	$15 penalty	$100 penalty
B	$15 penalty	$100 penalty

(II) (A) Except as otherwise provided in sub-subparagraph (B) of this subparagraph (II), subsections (4) and (5) of this section, and sections 42-4-1301.3, 42-4-1301.4, and 42-4-1307, or the section creating the offense, misdemeanor traffic offenses are divided into two classes that are distinguished from one another by the following penalties that are authorized upon conviction:

Class	Minimum Sentence	Maximum Sentence
1	Ten days imprisonment, or $300 fine, or both	Ninety days imprisonment, or $1,000 fine, or both
2	Ten days imprisonment, or $150 fine, or both	Ninety days imprisonment, or $300 fine, or both

(B) Any person convicted of a class 1 or class 2 misdemeanor traffic offense shall be required to pay restitution as required by article 18.5 of title 16, C.R.S., and may be sentenced to perform a certain number of hours of community or useful public service in addition to any other sentence provided by sub-subparagraph (A) of this subparagraph (II), subject to the conditions and restrictions of section 18-1.3-507, C.R.S.

(b) Any traffic infraction or misdemeanor traffic offense defined by law outside of articles 1 to 4 of this title shall be punishable as provided in the statute defining it or as otherwise provided by law.

(c) The department has no authority to assess any points under section 42-2-127 upon entry of judgment for any class B traffic infractions.

(4) (a) (I) Except as provided in paragraph (c) of subsection (5) of this section, every person who is convicted of, who admits liability for, or against whom a judgment is entered for a violation of any provision of this title to which paragraph (a) or (b) of subsection (5) of this section apply shall be fined or penalized, and have a surcharge levied thereon pursuant to sections 24-4.1-119 (1) (f) and 24-4.2-104 (1) (b) (I), C.R.S., in accordance with the penalty and surcharge schedule set forth in sub-subparagraphs (A) to (P) of this subparagraph (I); or, if no penalty or surcharge is specified in the schedule, the penalty for class A and class B traffic infractions shall be fifteen dollars, and the surcharge shall be four

dollars. These penalties and surcharges shall apply whether the defendant acknowledges the defendant's guilt or liability in accordance with the procedure set forth by paragraph (a) of subsection (5) of this section or is found guilty by a court of competent jurisdiction or has judgment entered against the defendant by a county court magistrate. Penalties and surcharges for violating specific sections shall be as follows:

Section Violated	Penalty	Surcharge
(A) **Drivers' license violations:**		
42-2-101 (1) or (4)	$ 35.00	$ 10.00
42-2-101 (2), (3), or (5)	15.00	6.00
42-2-103	15.00	6.00
42-2-105	70.00	10.00
42-2-105.5 (4)	65.00	10.00
42-2-106	70.00	10.00
42-2-116 (6) (a)	30.00	6.00
42-2-119	15.00	6.00
42-2-134	35.00	10.00
42-2-136	35.00	10.00
42-2-139	35.00	10.00
42-2-140	35.00	10.00
42-2-141	35.00	10.00
(B) **Registration and taxation violations:**		
42-3-103	$ 50.00	$ 16.00
42-3-113	15.00	6.00
42-3-202	15.00	6.00
42-3-116	50.00	16.00
42-3-121 (1)(a)	75.00	24.00
42-3-121 (1)(c)	35.00	10.00
42-3-121 (1)(f), (1)(g), and (1)(h)	75.00	24.00
42-3-304 to 42-3-306	50.00	16.00
(C) **Traffic regulation generally:**		
42-4-1412	$ 15.00	$ 6.00
42-4-109 (13)(a)	15.00	6.00
42-4-109 (13)(b)	100.00	15.00
42-4-1211	30.00	6.00
42-4-1405	15.00	6.00
(D) **Equipment violations:**		
42-4-201	$ 35.00	$ 10.00
42-4-202	35.00	10.00
42-4-204	15.00	6.00
42-4-205	15.00	6.00
42-4-206	15.00	6.00
42-4-207	15.00	6.00
42-4-208	15.00	6.00
42-4-209	15.00	6.00
42-4-210	15.00	6.00
42-4-211	15.00	6.00
42-4-212	15.00	6.00
42-4-213	15.00	6.00
42-4-214	15.00	6.00
42-4-215	15.00	6.00
42-4-216	15.00	6.00
42-4-217	15.00	6.00
42-4-218	15.00	6.00
42-4-219	15.00	6.00
42-4-220	15.00	6.00
42-4-221	15.00	6.00
42-4-222 (1)	15.00	6.00
42-4-223	15.00	6.00
42-4-224	15.00	6.00

42-4-225 (1)	15.00	6.00
42-4-226	15.00	6.00
42-4-227 (1)	50.00	16.00
42-4-227 (2)	15.00	6.00
42-4-228 (1), (2), (3), (5), or (6)	15.00	6.00
42-4-229	15.00	6.00
42-4-230	15.00	6.00
42-4-231	15.00	6.00
42-4-232	15.00	6.00
42-4-233	75.00	24.00
42-4-234	15.00	6.00
42-4-235	50.00	16.00
42-4-236	65.00	16.00
42-4-237	65.00	6.00
42-4-1411	15.00	6.00
42-4-1412	15.00	6.00
42-4-1901	35.00	10.00

(E) **Emissions inspections:**

42-4-313 (3)(c)	$ 50.00	$ 16.00
42-4-313 (3)(d)	15.00	6.00

(F) **Size, weight, and load violations:**

42-4-502	$ 75.00	$ 24.00
42-4-503	15.00	6.00
42-4-504	75.00	24.00
42-4-505	75.00	24.00
42-4-506	15.00	6.00
42-4-509	50.00	16.00
42-4-510 (12)(a)	35.00	10.00
42-4-106 (1), (3), (4), (6), or (7)	35.00	10.00
42-4-106 (5)(a)(I)	100.00	32.00
42-4-106 (5)(a)(II)	500.00	156.00
42-4-106 (5)(a)(III)	500.00	78.00
42-4-106 (5)(a)(IV)	1,000.00	156.00
42-4-512	75.00	24.00
42-8-105 (1) to (5)	50.00	16.00
42-8-106	50.00	16.00

(G) **Signals, signs, and markings violations:**

42-4-603	$ 100.00	$ 10.00
42-4-604	100.00	10.00
42-4-605	70.00	10.00
42-4-606	15.00	6.00
42-4-607 (1)	50.00	16.00
42-4-607 (2)(a)	100.00	32.00
42-4-608 (1)	70.00	6.00
42-4-608 (2)	15.00	6.00
42-4-609	15.00	6.00
42-4-610	15.00	6.00
42-4-612	70.00	10.00
42-4-613	35.00	10.00

(H) **Rights-of-way violations:**

42-4-701	$ 70.00	$ 10.00
42-4-702	70.00	10.00
42-4-703	70.00	10.00
42-4-704	70.00	10.00
42-4-705	70.00	16.00
42-4-706	70.00	10.00
42-4-707	70.00	10.00
42-4-708	35.00	10.00
42-4-709	70.00	10.00

42-4-710	70.00	10.00
42-4-711	100.00	10.00
42-4-712	70.00	10.00

(I) Pedestrian violations:

42-4-801	$ 15.00	$ 6.00
42-4-802 (1)	30.00	6.00
42-4-802 (3)	15.00	6.00
42-4-802 (4)	30.00	6.00
42-4-802 (5)	30.00	6.00
42-4-803	15.00	6.00
42-4-805	15.00	6.00
42-4-806	70.00	10.00
42-4-807	70.00	10.00
42-4-808	70.00	10.00

(J) Turning and stopping violations:

42-4-901	$ 70.00	$ 10.00
42-4-902	70.00	10.00
42-4-903	70.00	10.00

(K) Driving, overtaking, and passing violations:

42-4-1001	$ 70.00	$ 10.00
42-4-1002	100.00	10.00
42-4-1003	100.00	10.00
42-4-1004	100.00	10.00
42-4-1005	100.00	10.00
42-4-1006	70.00	10.00
42-4-1007	100.00	10.00
42-4-1008	100.00	10.00
42-4-1009	70.00	10.00
42-4-1010	70.00	10.00
42-4-1011	200.00	32.00
42-4-1012 (3)(a)	65.00	(NONE)
42-4-1012 (3)(b)	125.00	(NONE)
42-4-1013	100.00	(NONE)

(L) Speeding violations:

42-4-1101 (1) or (8) (b) (1 to 4 miles per hour over the reasonable and prudent speed or over the maximum lawful speed limit of 75 miles per hour)	$ 30.00	$ 6.00
42-4-1101 (1) or (8) (b) (5 to 9 miles per hour over the reasonable and prudent speed or over the maximum lawful speed limit of 75 miles per hour)	70.00	10.00
42-4-1101 (1) or (8) (b) (10 to 19 miles per hour over the reasonable and prudent speed or over the maximum lawful speed limit of 75 miles per hour)	135.00	16.00
42-4-1101 (1) or (8) (b) (20 to 24 miles per hour over the reasonable and prudent speed or over the maximum lawful speed limit of 75 miles per hour)	200.00	32.00
42-4-1101 (8) (g) (1 to 4 miles per hour over the maximum lawful speed limit of 40 miles per hour driving a low-power scooter)	50.00	6.00
42-4-1101 (8) (g) (5 to 9 miles per hour over the maximum lawful speed limit of 40 miles per hour driving a low-power scooter)	75.00	10.00
42-4-1101 (8) (g) (greater than 9 miles per hour over the maximum lawful speed limit of 40 miles per hour driving a low-power scooter)	100.00	16.00
42-4-1101 (3)	100.00	10.00
42-4-1103	50.00	6.00
42-4-1104	30.00	6.00

(M) **Parking violations:**

Section	Fine	Surcharge
42-4-1201	$ 30.00	$ 6.00
42-4-1202	30.00	6.00
42-4-1204	15.00	6.00
42-4-1205	15.00	6.00
42-4-1206	15.00	6.00
42-4-1207	15.00	6.00
42-4-1208 (9), (15), or (16)	150.00	32.00

(N) **Other offenses:**

Section	Fine	Surcharge
42-4-1301 (2)(a.5)	$ 100.00	$ 16.00
42-4-1305	50.00	16.00
42-4-1402	150.00	16.00
42-4-1403	30.00	6.00
42-4-1404	15.00	6.00
42-4-1406	35.00	10.00
42-4-1407 (3)(a)	35.00	10.00
42-4-1407 (3)(b)	100.00	30.00
42-4-1407 (3)(c)	500.00	200.00
42-4-314	35.00	10.00
42-4-1408	15.00	6.00
42-4-1414 (2)(a)	500.00	156.00
42-4-1414 (2)(b)	1,000.00	312.00
42-4-1414 (2)(c)	5,000.00	1,560.00
42-20-109 (2)	250.00	66.00

(O) **Motorcycle violations:**

Section	Fine	Surcharge
42-4-1502 (1), (2), (3), or (4)	$ 30.00	$ 6.00
42-4-1502 (4.5)	100.00	15.00
42-4-1503	30.00	6.00
42-4-1504	30.00	6.00

(P) **Offenses by persons controlling vehicles:**

Section	Fine	Surcharge
42-4-239 (5)(a)	$ 50.00	$ 6.00
42-4-239 (5)(b)	100.00	6.00
42-4-1704	15.00	6.00

(II) (A) A person convicted of violating section 42-4-507 or 42-4-508 shall be fined pursuant to this sub-subparagraph (A), whether the defendant acknowledges the defendant's guilt pursuant to the procedure set forth in paragraph (a) of subsection (5) of this section or is found guilty by a court of competent jurisdiction. A person who violates section 42-4-507 or 42-4-508 shall be punished by a fine and surcharge as follows:

Excess Weight - Pounds	Penalty	Surcharge
1 - 1,000	$ 20.00	$ 14.00
1,001 - 3,000	25.00	14.00
3,001 - 5,000	0.03 per pound overweight rounded to the nearest dollar	48.00
5,001 - 7,000	0.05 per pound overweight rounded to the nearest dollar	108.00
7,001 - 10,000	0.07 per pound overweight rounded to the nearest dollar	384.00
10,001 - 15,000	0.10 per pound overweight rounded to the nearest dollar	1,892.00
15,001 - 19,750	0.15 per pound rounded to the nearest dollar	2,438.00
Over 19,750	0.25 per pound rounded to the nearest dollar	28.00 for each 250 pounds additional overweight, plus $ 492.00

(B) The state, county, city, or city and county issuing a citation that results in the assessment of the penalties in sub-subparagraph (A) of this subparagraph (II) may retain and distribute the following amount of the penalty according to the law of the jurisdiction that assesses the penalty, but the remainder of the penalty shall be transmitted to the state treasurer, who shall credit the moneys to the commercial vehicle enterprise tax fund created in section 42-1-225:

Excess Weight - Pounds	Penalty Retained
1 - 3,000	$ 15.00
3,001 - 4,250	25.00
4,251 - 4,500	50.00
4,501 - 4,750	55.00
4,751 - 5,000	60.00
5,001 - 5,250	65.00
5,251 - 5,500	75.00
5,501 - 5,750	85.00
5,751 - 6,000	95.00
6,001 - 6,250	105.00
6,251 - 6,500	125.00
6,501 - 6,750	145.00
6,751 - 7,000	165.00
7,001 - 7,250	185.00
7,251 - 7,500	215.00
7,501 - 7,750	245.00
7,751 - 8,000	275.00
8,001 - 8,250	305.00
8,251 - 8,500	345.00
8,501 - 8,750	385.00
8,751 - 9,000	425.00
9,001 - 9,250	465.00
9,251 - 9,500	515.00
9,501 - 9,750	565.00
9,751 - 10,000	615.00
10,001 - 10,250	665.00
Over 10,250	$ 30.00 for each 250 pounds additional overweight, plus $ 665.00

(III) Any person convicted of violating any of the rules promulgated pursuant to section 42-4-510, except section 42-4-510 (2) (b) (IV), shall be fined as follows, whether the violator acknowledges the violator's guilt pursuant to the procedure set forth in paragraph (a) of subsection (5) of this section or is found guilty by a court of competent jurisdiction:

(A) Except as provided in sub-subparagraph (D) of this subparagraph (III), any person who violates the maximum permitted weight on an axle or on gross weight shall be punished by a fine and surcharge as follows:

Excess Weight Above Maximum Permitted Weight - Pounds	Penalty	Surcharge
1 - 2,500	$ 50.00	$ 46.00
2,501 - 5,000	100.00	96.00
5,001 - 7,500	200.00	192.00
7,501 - 10,000	400.00	384.00
Over 10,000	$ 150.00 for each 1,000 pounds additional overweight, plus $ 400.00	$ 144.00 for each 1,000 pounds additional overweight, plus $ 296.00

(B) Any person who violates any of the requirements of the rules and regulations pertaining to transport permits for the movement of overweight or oversize vehicles or loads, other than those violations specified in sub-subparagraph (A) or (C) of this subparagraph (III), shall be punished by a fine of fifty dollars.

(C) Any person who fails to have an escort vehicle when such vehicle is required by the rules and regulations pertaining to transport permits for the movement of overweight or oversize vehicles or loads or who fails to reduce speed when such speed reduction is required by said rules and regulations shall be punished by a fine of two hundred fifty dollars.

(D) The fines for a person who violates the maximum permitted weight on an axle or on gross weight under a permit issued pursuant to section 42-4-510 (1) (b) (II) shall be doubled.

(IV) (A) Any person convicted of violating section 42-3-114 who has not been convicted of a violation of section 42-3-114 in the twelve months preceding such conviction shall be fined as follows, whether the defendant acknowledges the defendant's guilt pursuant to the procedure set forth in paragraph (a) of subsection (5) of this section or is found guilty by a court of competent jurisdiction:

Number of days beyond renewal period that registration has been expired	Penalty	Surcharge
1 - 29	$ 35.00	$ 8.00
30 - 59	50.00	12.00
60 and over	75.00	18.00

(B) Any person convicted of violating section 42-3-114 who has been convicted of violating said section within the twelve months preceding such conviction shall be fined pursuant to subparagraph (I) of paragraph (a) of subsection (3) of this section.

(V) Any person convicted of violating section 42-20-204 (2) shall be fined twenty-five dollars, whether the violator acknowledges guilt pursuant to the procedure set forth in paragraph (a) of subsection (5) of this section or is found guilty by a court of competent jurisdiction.

(VI) (A) Except as provided in paragraph (c) of subsection (5) of this section, every person who is convicted of, who admits liability for, or against whom a judgment is entered for a violation of any provision of this title to which the provisions of paragraph (a) or (b) of subsection (5) of this section apply, shall, in addition to any other fine or penalty or surcharge, be assessed a surcharge of one dollar, which amount shall be transmitted to the state treasurer for deposit in the family-friendly court program cash fund created in section 13-3-113 (6), C.R.S. This surcharge shall apply whether the defendant acknowledges the defendant's guilt or liability in accordance with the procedure set forth by paragraph (a) of subsection (5) of this section or is found guilty by a court of competent jurisdiction or has judgment entered against the defendant by a county court magistrate.

(B) Repealed.

(VII) The penalties and surcharges for a second or subsequent violation of section 42-20-109 (2) within twelve months shall be doubled.

(b) (I) The schedule in subparagraph (I) of paragraph (a) of this subsection (4) shall not apply when the provisions of paragraph (c) of subsection (5) of this section prohibit the issuance of a penalty assessment notice for a violation of the aforesaid traffic violation.

(II) The schedules in subparagraphs (II) and (III) of paragraph (a) of this subsection (4) shall apply whether the violator is issued a penalty assessment notice or a summons and complaint.

(c) (I) The penalties and surcharges imposed for speeding violations under subsection (4) (a) (I) (L) of this section shall be doubled if a speeding violation occurs within a maintenance, repair, or construction zone that is designated by the department of transportation pursuant to section 42-4-614 (1) (a); except that the penalty for violating section 42-4-1101 (1) or (8) (b) by twenty to twenty-four miles per hour over the reasonable and prudent speed or over the maximum lawful speed limit of seventy-five miles per hour shall be five hundred forty dollars.

(II) (A) The penalties and surcharges imposed for violations under sub-subparagraphs (C), (G), (H), (I), (J), (K), (N), and (O) of subparagraph (I) of paragraph (a) of this subsection (4) shall be doubled if a violation occurs within a maintenance, repair, or construction zone that is designated by the department of transportation pursuant to section 42-4-614 (1) (a); except that the fines for violating sections 42-4-314, 42-4-610, 42-4-613, 42-4-706, 42-4-707, 42-4-708, 42-4-709, 42-4-710, 42-4-1011, 42-4-1012, 42-4-1404, 42-4-1408, and 42-4-1414 shall not be doubled under this subparagraph (II).

(B) There is hereby created, within the highway users tax fund, the highway construction workers' safety account.

(C) If a fine is doubled under subparagraph (I) or (II) of this paragraph (c), one-half of the fine allocated to the state by sections 42-1-217 and 43-4-205, C.R.S., shall be transferred to the state treasurer, who shall deposit it in the highway construction workers' safety account within the highway users tax fund to be continuously appropriated to the department of transportation for work zone safety equipment, signs, and law enforcement.

(D) This subparagraph (II) is effective July 1, 2006.

(III) The penalties and surcharges imposed for speeding violations under sub-subparagraph (L) of subparagraph (I) of paragraph (a) of this subsection (4) shall be doubled if a speeding violation occurs within a maintenance, repair, or construction zone that is designated by a public entity pursuant to section 42-4-614 (1) (b).

(IV) The penalties and surcharges imposed for violations under sub-subparagraphs (C), (G), (H), (I), (J), (K), (N), and (O) of subparagraph (I) of paragraph (a) of this subsection (4) shall be doubled if a violation occurs within a maintenance, repair, or construction zone that is designated by a public entity pursuant to section 42-4-614 (1) (b); except that the fines for violating sections 42-4-314, 42-4-610, 42-4-613, 42-4-706, 42-4-707, 42-4-708, 42-4-709, 42-4-710, 42-4-1011, 42-4-1012, 42-4-1404, 42-4-1408, and 42-4-1414 shall not be doubled under this subparagraph (IV).

(d) The penalty and surcharge imposed for any moving traffic violation under subparagraph (I) of paragraph (a) of this subsection (4) are doubled if the violation occurs within a school zone pursuant to section 42-4-615.

(d.5) (I) The penalty and surcharge imposed for any moving traffic violation under subparagraph (I) of paragraph (a) of this subsection (4) are doubled if the violation occurs within a wildlife crossing zone pursuant to section 42-4-616.

(II) (A) There is hereby created, within the highway users tax fund, the wildlife crossing zones safety account.

(B) If a penalty and surcharge are doubled pursuant to subparagraph (I) of this paragraph (d.5), one-half of the penalty and surcharge allocated to the state by sections 42-1-217 and 43-4-205, C.R.S., shall be transferred to the state treasurer, who shall deposit the moneys in the wildlife crossing zones safety account within the highway users tax fund to be continuously appropriated to the department of transportation for wildlife crossing zones signs and law enforcement.

(e) (I) An additional fifteen dollars shall be assessed for speeding violations under sub-subparagraph (L) of subparagraph (I) of paragraph (a) of this subsection (4) in addition to the penalties and surcharge stated in said sub-subparagraph (L). Moneys collected pursuant to this paragraph (e) shall be transmitted to the state treasurer who shall deposit such moneys in the Colorado traumatic brain injury trust fund created pursuant to section 26-1-309, C.R.S., within fourteen days after the end of each quarter, to be used for the purposes set forth in sections 26-1-301 to 26-1-310, C.R.S.

(II) If the surcharge is collected by a county or municipal court, the surcharge shall be seventeen dollars of which two dollars shall be retained by the county or municipality and the remaining fifteen dollars shall be transmitted to the state treasurer and credited to the Colorado traumatic brain injury trust fund created pursuant to section 26-1-309, C.R.S., within fourteen days after the end of each quarter, to be used for the purposes set forth in sections 26-1-301 to 26-1-310, C.R.S.

(III) An additional fifteen dollars shall be assessed for a violation of a traffic regulation under sub-subparagraph (C) of subparagraph (I) of paragraph (a) of this subsection (4) for a violation of section 42-4-109 (13) (b), in addition to the penalties stated in said sub-subparagraph (C). An additional fifteen dollars shall be assessed for a motorcycle violation under sub-subparagraph (O) of subparagraph (I) of paragraph (a) of this subsection (4) for a violation of section 42-4-1502 (4.5), in addition to the penalties stated in said sub-subparagraph (O). Moneys collected pursuant to this subparagraph (III) shall be transmitted to the state treasurer, who shall deposit the moneys in the Colorado traumatic brain injury trust fund created pursuant to section 26-1-309, C.R.S., to be used for the purposes set forth in sections 26-1-301 to 26-1-310, C.R.S.

(f) (I) In addition to the surcharge specified in sub-subparagraph (N) of subparagraph (I) of paragraph (a) of this subsection (4), an additional surcharge of five dollars shall be assessed for a violation of section 42-4-1301 (2) (a.5). Moneys collected pursuant to this paragraph (f) shall be transmitted to the state treasurer who shall deposit such moneys in the rural alcohol and substance abuse cash fund created in section 27-80-117 (3), C.R.S., within fourteen days after the end of each quarter, to be used for the purposes set forth in section 27-80-117, C.R.S.

(II) If the additional surcharge is collected by a county court, the additional surcharge shall be six dollars of which one dollar shall be retained by the county and the remaining five dollars shall be transmitted to the state treasurer and credited to the rural alcohol and substance abuse cash fund created in section 27-80-117 (3), C.R.S., within fourteen days after the end of each quarter, to be used for the purposes set forth in section 27-80-117, C.R.S.

(III) This paragraph (f) is repealed, effective July 1, 2016, unless the general assembly extends the repeal of the rural alcohol and substance abuse prevention and treatment program created in section 27-80-117, C.R.S.

(5) (a) (I) At the time that any person is arrested for the commission of any misdemeanors, petty offenses, or misdemeanor traffic offenses set forth in subsection (4) of this section,

the arresting officer may, except when the provisions of paragraph (c) of this subsection (5) prohibit it, offer to give a penalty assessment notice to the defendant. At any time that a person is charged with the commission of any traffic infraction, the peace officer shall, except when the provisions of paragraph (c) of this subsection (5) prohibit it, give a penalty assessment notice to the defendant. Such penalty assessment notice shall contain all the information required by section 42-4-1707 (3) or by section 42-4-1709, whichever is applicable. The fine or penalty specified in subsection (4) of this section for the violation charged and the surcharge thereon may be paid at the office of the department of revenue, either in person or by postmarking such payment within twenty days from the date the penalty assessment notice is served upon the defendant; except that the fine or penalty charged and the surcharge thereon shall be paid to the county if it relates to a traffic offense authorized by county ordinance. The department of revenue shall accept late payment of any penalty assessment up to twenty days after such payment becomes due. Except as otherwise provided in subparagraph (II) of this paragraph (a), in the case of an offense other than a traffic infraction, a defendant who otherwise would be eligible to be issued a penalty assessment notice but who does not furnish satisfactory evidence of identity or who the officer has reasonable and probable grounds to believe will disregard the summons portion of such notice may be issued a penalty assessment notice if the defendant consents to be taken by the officer to the nearest mailbox and to mail the amount of the fine or penalty and surcharge thereon to the department. The peace officer shall advise the person arrested or cited of the points to be assessed in accordance with section 42-2-127. Except as otherwise provided in section 42-4-1710 (1) (b), acceptance of a penalty assessment notice and payment of the prescribed fine or penalty and surcharge thereon to the department shall be deemed a complete satisfaction for the violation and the defendant shall be given a receipt which so states when such fine or penalty and surcharge thereon is paid in currency or other form of legal tender. Checks tendered by the defendant to and accepted by the department and on which payment is received by the department shall be deemed sufficient receipt.

(II) In the case of an offense other than a traffic infraction that involves a minor under the age of eighteen years, the officer shall proceed in accordance with the provisions of section 42-4-1706 (2) or 42-4-1707 (1) (b) or (3) (a.5). In no case may an officer issue a penalty assessment notice to a minor under the age of eighteen years and require or offer that the minor consent to be taken by the officer to the nearest mailbox to mail the amount of the fine or penalty and surcharge thereon to the department.

(b) In the case of an offense other than a traffic infraction, should the defendant refuse to accept service of the penalty assessment notice when such notice is tendered, the peace officer shall proceed in accordance with section 42-4-1705 or 42-4-1707. Should the defendant charged with an offense other than a traffic infraction accept service of the penalty assessment notice but fail to post the prescribed penalty and surcharge thereon within twenty days thereafter, the notice shall be construed to be a summons and complaint unless payment for such penalty assessment has been accepted by the department of revenue as evidenced by receipt. Should the defendant charged with a traffic infraction accept the notice but fail to post the prescribed penalty and surcharge thereon within twenty days thereafter, and should the department of revenue not accept payment for such penalty and surcharge as evidenced by receipt, the defendant shall be allowed to pay such penalty and surcharge thereon and the docket fee in the amount set forth in section 42-4-1710 (4) to the clerk of the court referred to in the summons portion of the penalty assessment notice during the two business days prior to the time for appearance as specified in the notice. If the penalty for a misdemeanor, misdemeanor traffic offense, or a petty offense and surcharge thereon is not timely paid, the case shall thereafter be heard in the court of competent jurisdiction prescribed on the penalty assessment notice in the same manner as is provided by law for prosecutions of the misdemeanors not specified in subsection (4) of this section. If the penalty for a traffic infraction and surcharge thereon is not timely paid, the case shall thereafter be heard in the court of competent jurisdiction prescribed on the penalty assessment notice in the manner provided for in this article for the prosecution of traffic infractions. In either case, the maximum penalty that may be imposed shall not exceed the penalty set forth in the applicable penalty and surcharge schedule in subsection (4) of this section.

(b.5) The provisions of section 42-4-1710 (1) (b) shall govern any case described in paragraph (b) of this subsection (5) in which a minor under the age of eighteen years submits timely payment for an infraction or offense in a penalty assessment notice but such payment is not accompanied by the penalty assessment notice signed and notarized in the manner required by section 42-4-1707 (3) (a.5) or 42-4-1709 (1.5).

(c) (I) The penalty and surcharge schedules of subsection (4) of this section and the penalty assessment notice provisions of paragraphs (a) and (b) of this subsection (5) shall not apply to violations constituting misdemeanors, petty offenses, or misdemeanor traffic offenses not specified in said subsection (4) of this section, nor shall they apply to the violations constituting misdemeanors, petty offenses, misdemeanor traffic offenses, or traffic infractions specified in said subsection (4) of this section when it appears that:

(A) (Deleted by amendment, L. 96, p. 580, § 4, effective May 25, 1996.)

(B) In a violation of section 42-4-1101 (1) or (8) (b), the defendant exceeded the reasonable and prudent speed or the maximum lawful speed of seventy-five miles per hour by more than twenty-four miles per hour;

(C) The alleged violation has caused, or contributed to the cause of, an accident resulting in appreciable damage to property of another or in injury or death to any person;

(D) The defendant has, in the course of the same transaction, violated one of the provisions of this title specified in the penalty and surcharge schedules in subsection (4) of this section and has also violated one or more provisions of this title not so specified, and the peace officer charges such defendant with two or more violations, any one of which is not specified in the penalty and surcharge schedules in subsection (4) of this section.

(II) In all cases where this paragraph (c) prohibits the issuance of a penalty assessment notice, the penalty and surcharge schedule contained in subparagraph (I) of paragraph (a) of subsection (4) of this section shall be inapplicable; except that the penalty and surcharge provided in the schedule contained in sub-subparagraph (B) of subparagraph (I) of paragraph (a) of subsection (4) of this section for any violation of section 42-3-121 (1) (a) shall always apply to such a violation. In all cases where the penalty and surcharge schedule contained in subparagraph (I) of paragraph (a) of subsection (4) of this section is inapplicable, the provisions of subsection (3) of this section shall apply.

(d) In addition to any other cases governed by this section, the penalty and surcharge schedule contained in subparagraph (I) of paragraph (a) of subsection (4) of this section shall apply in the following cases:

(I) In all cases in which a peace officer was authorized by the provisions of this subsection (5) to offer a penalty assessment notice for the commission of a misdemeanor, petty offense, or misdemeanor traffic offense but such peace officer chose not to offer such penalty assessment notice;

(II) In all cases involving the commission of a misdemeanor, petty offense, or misdemeanor traffic offense in which a penalty assessment notice was offered by a peace officer but such penalty assessment notice was refused by the defendant.

(6) An officer coming upon an unattended vehicle that is in apparent violation of any provision of the state motor vehicle law may place upon the vehicle a penalty assessment notice indicating the offense or infraction and directing the owner or operator of the vehicle to remit the penalty assessment provided for by subsection (4) of this section and the surcharges thereon pursuant to sections 24-4.1-119 (1) (f) and 24-4.2-104 (1), C.R.S., to the Colorado department of revenue within ten days. If the penalty assessment and surcharge thereon is not paid within ten days of the issuance of the notice, the department shall mail a notice to the registered owner of the vehicle, setting forth the offense or infraction and the time and place where it occurred and directing the payment of the penalty assessment and surcharge thereon within twenty days from the issuance of the notice. If the penalty assessment and surcharge thereon is not paid within the twenty days from the date of mailing of such notice, the department shall request the police officer who issued the original penalty assessment notice to file a complaint with a court having jurisdiction and issue and serve upon the registered owner of the vehicle a summons to appear in court at a time and place specified therein as in the case of other offenses or infractions.

(7) Notwithstanding the provisions of paragraph (b) of subsection (5) of this section, receipt of payment by mail by the department or postmarking such payment on or prior to the twentieth day after the receipt of the penalty assessment notice by the defendant shall be deemed to constitute receipt on or before the date the payment was due.

(8) The surcharges described in subsections (4) to (6) of this section are separate and distinct from a surcharge levied pursuant to section 24-33.5-415.6, C.R.S.

42-4-1702. Alcohol- or drug-related traffic offenses - collateral attack. (1) Except as otherwise provided in paragraph (b) of this subsection (1), no person against whom a judgment has been entered for DUI, DUI per se, DWAI, habitual user, or UDD shall collaterally attack the validity of that judgment unless such attack is commenced within six months after the date of entry of the judgment.

(2) In recognition of the difficulties attending the litigation of stale claims and the potential for frustrating various statutory provisions directed at repeat offenders, former offenders, and habitual offenders, the only exceptions to the time limitations specified in paragraph (a) of this subsection (1) shall be:

(a) A case in which the court entering judgment did not have jurisdiction over the subject matter of the alleged infraction;

(b) A case in which the court entering judgment did not have jurisdiction over the person of the violator;

(c) Where the court hearing the collateral attack finds by a preponderance of the evidence that the failure to seek relief within the applicable time period was caused by an adjudication of incompetence or by commitment of the violator to an institution for treatment as a person with a mental illness; or

(d) Where the court hearing the collateral attack finds that the failure to seek relief within the applicable time period was the result of circumstances amounting to justifiable excuse or excusable neglect.

42-4-1703. Parties to a crime. Every person who commits, conspires to commit, or aids or abets in the commission of any act declared in this article and part 1 of article 2 of this title to be a crime or traffic infraction, whether individually or in connection with one or more other persons or as principal, agent, or accessory, is guilty of such offense or liable for such infraction, and every person who falsely, fraudulently, forcibly, or willfully induces, causes, coerces, requires, permits, or directs another to violate any provision of this article is likewise guilty of such offense or liable for such infraction.

42-4-1704. Offenses by persons controlling vehicles. It is unlawful for the owner or any other person employing or otherwise directing the driver of any vehicle to require or knowingly to permit the operation of such vehicle upon a highway in any manner contrary to law. Any person who violates any provision of this section commits a class 2 misdemeanor traffic offense.

42-4-1705. Person arrested to be taken before the proper court. (1) Whenever a person is arrested for any violation of this article punishable as a misdemeanor, the arrested person shall be taken without unnecessary delay before a county judge who has jurisdiction of such offense as provided by law, in any of the following cases:

(a) When a person arrested demands an appearance without unnecessary delay before a judge;

(b) When the person is arrested and charged with an offense under this article causing or contributing to an accident resulting in injury or death to any person;

(c) When the person is arrested and charged with DUI, DUI per se, habitual user, or UDD;

(d) When the person is arrested upon a charge of failure to stop in the event of an accident causing death, personal injuries, or damage to property;

(e) In any other event when the provisions of section 42-4-1701 (5) (b) and (5) (c) apply and the person arrested refuses to give a written promise to appear in court as provided in section 42-4-1707.

(2) Whenever any person is arrested by a police officer for any violation of this article punishable as a misdemeanor and is not required to be taken before a county judge as provided in subsection (1) of this section, the arrested person shall, in the discretion of the officer, either be given a written notice or summons to appear in court as provided in section 42-4-1707 or be taken without unnecessary delay before a county judge who has jurisdiction of such offense when the arrested person does not furnish satisfactory evidence of identity or when the officer has reasonable and probable grounds to believe the person will disregard a written promise to appear in court. The court shall provide a bail bond schedule and available personnel to accept adequate security for such bail bonds.

(2.5) In any case in which the arrested person that is taken before a county judge pursuant to subsection (1) or (2) of this section is a child, as defined in section 19-1-103 (18), C.R.S., the provisions of section 42-4-1706 (2) shall apply.

(3) Any other provision of law to the contrary notwithstanding, a police officer may place a person who has been arrested and charged with DUI, DUI per se, or UDD and who has been given a written notice or summons to appear in court as provided in section 42-4-1707 in a state-approved treatment facility for alcoholism even though entry or other record of such arrest and charge has been made. Such placement shall be governed by article 81 of title 27, C.R.S., except where in conflict with this section.

42-4-1706. Juveniles - convicted - arrested and incarcerated - provisions for confinement. (1) Notwithstanding any other provision of law, a child, as defined in section 19-1-103 (18), C.R.S., convicted of a misdemeanor traffic offense under this article, violating the conditions of probation imposed under this article, or found in contempt of court in connection with a violation or alleged violation under this article shall not be confined in a jail, lockup, or other place used for the confinement of adult offenders if the court with jurisdiction is located in a county in which there is a juvenile detention facility operated by or under contract with the department of human services that shall receive and provide care for such child or if the jail is located within forty miles of such facility. The court imposing penalties under this section may confine a child for a determinate period of time in a juvenile detention facility operated by or under contract with the department of human services. If a juvenile detention facility operated by or under contract with the department of human services is not located within the county or within forty miles of the jail, a child may be confined for up to forty-eight hours in a jail pursuant to section 19-2-508 (4), C.R.S.

(2) (a) Notwithstanding any other provision of law, a child, as defined in section 19-1-103 (18), C.R.S., arrested and incarcerated for an alleged misdemeanor traffic offense under this article, and not released on bond, shall be taken before a county judge who has jurisdiction of such offense within forty-eight hours for fixing of bail and conditions of bond pursuant to section 19-2-508 (4) (d), C.R.S. Such child shall not be confined in a jail, lockup, or other place used for the confinement of adult offenders for longer than seventy-two hours, after which the child may be further detained only in a juvenile detention facility operated by or under contract with the department of human services. In calculating time under this subsection (2), Saturdays, Sundays, and court holidays shall be included.

(b) In any case in which a child is taken before a county judge pursuant to paragraph (a) of this subsection (2), the child's parent or legal guardian shall immediately be notified by the court in which the county judge sits. Any person so notified by the court under this paragraph (b) shall comply with the provisions of section 42-4-1716 (4).

42-4-1707. Summons and complaint or penalty assessment notice for misdemeanors, petty offenses, and misdemeanor traffic offenses - release - registration. (1) (a) Whenever a person commits a violation of this title punishable as a misdemeanor, petty offense, or misdemeanor traffic offense, other than a violation for which a penalty assessment notice may be issued in accordance with the provisions of section 42-4-1701 (5) (a), and such person is not required by the provisions of section 42-4-1705 to be arrested and taken without unnecessary delay before a county judge, the peace officer may issue and serve upon the defendant a summons and complaint which shall contain the name and address of the defendant, the license number of the vehicle involved, if any, the number of the defendant's driver's license, if any, a citation of the statute alleged to have been violated, a brief description of the offense, the date and approximate location thereof, and the date the summons and complaint is served on the defendant; shall direct the defendant to appear in a specified county court at a specified time and place; shall be signed by the peace officer; and shall contain a place for the defendant to execute a written promise to appear at the time and place specified in the summons portion of the summons and complaint.

(b) A summons and complaint issued and served pursuant to paragraph (a) of this subsection (1) on a minor under the age of eighteen years shall also contain or be accompanied by a document containing an advisement to the minor that the minor's parent or legal guardian, if known, shall be notified by the court from which the summons is issued and be required to appear with the minor at the minor's court hearing or hearings.

(2) If a peace officer issues and serves a summons and complaint to appear in any court upon the defendant as described in subsection (1) of this section, any defect in form in such summons and complaint regarding the name and address of the defendant, the license number of the vehicle involved, if any, the number of the defendant's driver's license, if any, the date and approximate location thereof, and the date the summons and complaint is served on the defendant may be cured by amendment at any time prior to trial or any time before verdict or findings upon an oral motion by the prosecuting attorney after notice to the defendant and an opportunity for a hearing. No such amendment shall be permitted if substantial rights of the defendant are prejudiced. No summons and complaint shall be considered defective so as to be cause for dismissal solely because of a defect in form in such summons and complaint as described in this subsection (2).

(3) (a) Whenever a penalty assessment notice for a misdemeanor, petty offense, or misdemeanor traffic offense is issued pursuant to section 42-4-1701 (5) (a), the penalty assessment notice that shall be served upon the defendant by the peace officer shall contain the name and address of the defendant, the license number of the vehicle involved, if any, the number of the defendant's driver's license, if any, a citation of the statute alleged to have been violated, a brief description of the offense, the date and approximate location thereof, the amount of the penalty prescribed for the offense, the amount of the surcharges thereon pursuant to sections 24-4.1-119 (1) (f), 24-4.2-104 (1), and 24-33.5-415.6, C.R.S., the number of points, if any, prescribed for the offense pursuant to section 42-2-127, and the date the penalty assessment notice is served on the defendant; shall direct the defendant to appear in a specified county court at a specified time and place in the event the penalty and surcharges thereon are not paid; shall be signed by the peace officer; and shall contain a place for the defendant to elect to execute a signed acknowledgment of guilt and an agreement to pay the penalty prescribed and surcharges thereon within twenty days, as well as such other information as may be required by law to constitute the penalty assessment notice to be a summons and complaint, should the prescribed penalty and surcharges thereon not be paid within the time allowed in section 42-4-1701.

(a.5) A penalty assessment notice issued and served pursuant to paragraph (a) of this subsection (3) on a minor under the age of eighteen years shall also contain or be accompanied by a document containing:

(I) A preprinted declaration stating that the minor's parent or legal guardian has reviewed the contents of the penalty assessment notice with the minor;

(II) Preprinted signature lines following the declaration on which the reviewing person described in subparagraph (I) of this paragraph (a.5) shall affix his or her signature and for a notary public to duly acknowledge the reviewing person's signature; and

(III) An advisement to the minor that:

(A) The minor shall, within seventy-two hours after service of the penalty assessment notice, inform his or her parent or legal guardian that the minor has received a penalty assessment notice;

(B) The parent or legal guardian of the minor is required by law to review and sign the penalty assessment notice and to have his or her signature duly acknowledged by a notary public; and

(C) Noncompliance with the requirement set forth in sub-subparagraph (B) of this subparagraph (III) shall result in the minor and the parent or legal guardian of the minor being required to appear in court pursuant to sections 42-4-1710 (1) (b), 42-4-1710 (1.5), and 42-4-1716 (4).

(b) One copy of said penalty assessment notice shall be served upon the defendant by the peace officer and one copy sent to the supervisor within the department and such other copies sent as may be required by rule of the department to govern the internal administration of this article between the department and the Colorado state patrol.

(4) (a) The time specified in the summons portion of said summons and complaint must be at least twenty days after the date such summons and complaint is served, unless the defendant shall demand an earlier court appearance date.

(b) The time specified in the summons portion of said penalty assessment notice shall be at least thirty days but not more than ninety days after the date such penalty assessment notice is served, unless the defendant shall demand an earlier court appearance date.

(5) The place specified in the summons portion of said summons and complaint or of the penalty assessment notice must be a county court within the county in which the offense is alleged to have been committed.

(6) If the defendant is otherwise eligible to be issued a summons and complaint or a penalty assessment notice for a violation of this title punishable as a misdemeanor, petty offense, or misdemeanor traffic offense and if the defendant does not possess a valid Colorado driver's license, the defendant, in order to secure release, as provided in this section, must either consent to be taken by the officer to the nearest mailbox and to mail the amount of the penalty and surcharges thereon to the department or must execute a promise to appear in court on the penalty assessment notice or on the summons and complaint. If the defendant does possess a valid Colorado driver's license, the defendant shall not be required to execute a promise to appear on the penalty assessment notice or on the summons and complaint. The peace officer shall not require any person who is eligible to be issued a summons and complaint or a penalty assessment notice for a violation of this title to produce or divulge such person's social security number.

(7) Any officer violating any of the provisions of this section is guilty of misconduct in office and shall be subject to removal from office.

42-4-1708. Traffic infractions - proper court for hearing, burden of proof - appeal - collateral attack. (1) Every hearing in county court for the adjudication of a traffic infraction, as provided by this article, shall be held before a county court magistrate appointed pursuant to part 5 of article 6 of title 13, C.R.S., or before a county judge acting as a magistrate; except that, whenever a crime and a class A or class B traffic infraction or a crime and both such class A and class B traffic infractions are charged in the same summons and complaint, all charges shall be made returnable before a judge or magistrate having jurisdiction over the crime and the rules of criminal procedure shall apply. Nothing in this part 17 or in part 5 of article 6 of title 13, C.R.S., shall be construed to prevent a court having jurisdiction over a criminal charge relating to traffic law violations from lawfully entering a judgment on a case dealing with a class A or class B traffic infraction.

(2) When a court of competent jurisdiction determines that a person charged with a class 1 or class 2 misdemeanor traffic offense is guilty of a lesser-included offense which is a class A or class B traffic infraction, the court may enter a judgment as to such lesser charge.

(3) The burden of proof shall be upon the people, and the traffic magistrate shall enter judgment in favor of the defendant unless the people prove the liability of the defendant beyond a reasonable doubt. The district attorney or the district attorney's deputy may, in the district attorney's discretion, enter traffic infraction cases for the purpose of attempting a negotiated plea or a stipulation to deferred prosecution or deferred judgment and sentence but shall not be required to so enter by any person, court, or law, nor shall the district attorney represent the state at hearings conducted by a magistrate or a county judge acting as a magistrate on class A or class B traffic infraction matters. The magistrate or county judge acting as a magistrate shall be permitted to call and question any witness and shall also act as the fact finder at hearings on traffic infraction matters.

(4) Appeal from final judgment on a traffic infraction matter shall be taken to the district court for the county in which the magistrate or judge acting as magistrate is located.

(5) (a) Except as otherwise provided in paragraph (b) of this subsection (5), no person against whom a judgment has been entered for a traffic infraction as defined in section 42-4-1701 (3) (a) shall collaterally attack the validity of that judgment unless such attack is commenced within six months after the date of entry of the judgment.

(b) In recognition of the difficulties attending the litigation of stale claims and the potential for frustrating various statutory provisions directed at repeat offenders, former offenders, and habitual offenders, the only exceptions to the time limitations specified in paragraph (a) of this subsection (5) shall be:

(I) A case in which the court entering judgment did not have jurisdiction over the subject matter of the alleged infraction;

(II) A case in which the court entering judgment did not have jurisdiction over the person of the violator;

(III) Where the court hearing the collateral attack finds by a preponderance of the evidence that the failure to seek relief within the applicable time period was caused by an adjudication of incompetence or by commitment of the violator to an institution for treatment as a person with a mental illness; or

(IV) Where the court hearing the collateral attack finds that the failure to seek relief within the applicable time period was the result of circumstances amounting to justifiable excuse or excusable neglect.

42-4-1709. Penalty assessment notice for traffic infractions - violations of provisions by officer - driver's license. (1) Whenever a penalty assessment notice for a traffic infraction is issued pursuant to section 42-4-1701 (5) (a), the penalty assessment notice that shall be served upon the defendant by the peace officer shall contain the name and address of the defendant, the license number of the vehicle involved, if any, the number of the defendant's driver's license, if any, a citation of the statute alleged to have been violated, a brief description of the traffic infraction, the date and approximate location thereof, the amount of the penalty prescribed for the traffic infraction, the amount of the surcharges thereon pursuant to sections 24-4.1-119 (1) (f), 24-4.2-104 (1), and 24-33.5-415.6, C.R.S., the number of points, if any, prescribed for the traffic infraction pursuant to section 42-2-127, and the date the penalty assessment notice is served on the defendant; shall direct the defendant to appear in a specified county court at a specified time and place in the event the penalty and surcharges thereon are not paid; shall be signed by the peace officer; and shall contain a place for the defendant to elect to execute a signed acknowledgment of liability and an agreement to pay the penalty prescribed and surcharges thereon within twenty days, as well as such other information as may be required by law to constitute the penalty assessment notice to be a summons and complaint, should the prescribed penalty and surcharges thereon not be paid within the time allowed in section 42-4-1701.

(1.5) A penalty assessment notice issued and served pursuant to subsection (1) of this section on a minor under the age of eighteen years shall also contain or be accompanied by a document containing:

(a) A preprinted declaration stating that the minor's parent or legal guardian has reviewed the contents of the penalty assessment notice with the minor;

(b) Preprinted signature lines following the declaration on which the reviewing person described in paragraph (a) of this subsection (1.5) shall affix his or her signature and for a notary public to duly acknowledge the reviewing person's signature; and

(c) An advisement to the minor that:

(I) The minor shall, within seventy-two hours after service of the penalty assessment notice, inform his or her parent or legal guardian that the minor has received a penalty assessment notice;

(II) The parent or legal guardian of the minor is required by law to review and sign the penalty assessment notice and to have his or her signature duly acknowledged by a notary public; and

(III) Noncompliance with the requirement set forth in subparagraph (II) of this paragraph (c) shall result in the minor and the parent or legal guardian of the minor being required to appear in court pursuant to sections 42-4-1710 (1) (b), 42-4-1710 (1.5), and 42-4-1716 (4).

(2) One copy of said penalty assessment notice shall be served upon the defendant by the peace officer and one copy sent to the supervisor within the department and such other copies sent as may be required by rule of the department to govern the internal administration of this article between the department and the Colorado state patrol.

(3) The time specified in the summons portion of said penalty assessment notice must be at least thirty days but not more than ninety days after the date such penalty assessment notice is served, unless the defendant shall demand an earlier hearing.

(4) The place specified in the summons portion of said penalty assessment notice must be a county court within the county in which the traffic infraction is alleged to have been committed.

(5) Whenever the defendant refuses to accept service of the penalty assessment notice, tender of such notice by the peace officer to the defendant shall constitute service thereof upon the defendant.

(6) Any officer violating any of the provisions of this section is guilty of misconduct in office and shall be subject to removal from office.

(7) (a) No person shall be allowed or permitted to obtain or renew a permanent driver's, minor driver's, or probationary license if such person has, at the time of making application for obtaining or renewing such driver's license:

(I) An outstanding judgment entered against such person on and after January 1, 1983, pursuant to section 42-4-1710 (2) or (3);

(II) An outstanding judgment entered against such person by a county or municipal court for a violation of a statute or ordinance relating to the regulation of motor vehicles or traffic, excluding traffic infractions defined by state statute or ordinance and violations relating to parking;

(III) A bench warrant issued against such person by a county or municipal court for failure to appear to answer a citation for an alleged violation of a statute or ordinance relating to the regulation of motor vehicles or traffic, excluding traffic infractions defined by state statute or ordinance and violations relating to parking;

(IV) An outstanding judgment entered against such person by a municipal court for a violation of any municipal ordinance which occurred when such person was under eighteen years of age, excluding traffic infractions defined by state statute or ordinance and violations related to parking;

(V) A bench warrant issued against such person by a municipal court for failure to appear to answer a summons or summons and complaint for an alleged violation of any municipal ordinance that occurred when such person was under eighteen years of age, excluding traffic infractions defined by state statute or ordinance and violations relating to parking;

(VI) Issued a check or order to the department to pay a penalty assessment, a driver's license fee, a license reinstatement fee, or a motor vehicle record fee and such check or order is returned for insufficient funds or a closed account and remains unpaid. For the purposes of this subparagraph (VI), the term "insufficient funds" means having an insufficient balance on account with a bank or other drawee for the payment of a check or order when the check or order is presented for payment within thirty days after issue.

(VII) Repealed.

(b) The restrictions in paragraph (a) of this subsection (7) shall not apply in cases where an appeal from any determination of liability and penalty is pending and not disposed of at the time of such application for obtaining or renewing a driver's license.

42-4-1710. Failure to pay penalty for traffic infractions - failure of parent or guardian to sign penalty assessment notice - procedures. (1) (a) Unless a person who has been cited for a traffic infraction pays the penalty assessment as provided in this article and surcharge thereon pursuant to sections 24-4.1-119 (1) (f) and 24-4.2-104 (1), C.R.S., the person shall appear at a hearing on the date and time specified in the citation and answer the complaint against such person.

(b) Notwithstanding the provisions of paragraph (a) of this subsection (1) and section 42-4-1701 (5), a minor under the age of eighteen years shall be required to appear at a hearing on the date and time specified in the citation and answer the complaint if the penalty assessment was timely paid but not signed and notarized in the manner required by section 42-4-1707 (3) (a.5) or 42-4-1709 (1.5).

(1.5) If a minor under the age of eighteen years is required to appear at a hearing pursuant to subsection (1) of this section, the minor shall so inform his or her parent or legal guardian, and the parent or legal guardian shall also be required to appear at the hearing.

(2) If the violator answers that he or she is guilty or if the violator fails to appear for the hearing, judgment shall be entered against the violator.

(3) If the violator denies the allegations in the complaint, a final hearing on the complaint shall be held subject to the provisions regarding a speedy trial which are contained in section 18-1-405, C.R.S. If the violator is found guilty or liable at such final hearing or if the violator fails to appear for a final hearing, judgment shall be entered against the violator.

(4) (a) (I) (A) If judgment is entered against a violator, the violator shall be assessed an appropriate penalty and surcharge thereon, a docket fee of sixteen dollars, and other applicable costs authorized by section 13-16-122 (1), C.R.S. If the violator had been cited by a penalty assessment notice, the penalty shall be assessed pursuant to section 42-4-1701 (4) (a). If a penalty assessment notice is prohibited by section 42-4-1701 (5) (c), the penalty shall be assessed pursuant to section 42-4-1701 (3) (a).

(B) On and after July 1, 2008, all docket fees collected under this subparagraph (I) shall be transmitted to the state treasurer for deposit in the judicial stabilization cash fund created in section 13-32-101 (6), C.R.S.

(II) On and after June 6, 2003, the docket fee assessed in subparagraph (I) of this paragraph (a) shall be increased by three dollars. The additional revenue generated by the docket fee shall be transmitted to the state treasurer for deposit in the state commission on judicial performance cash fund created in section 13-5.5-107, C.R.S.

(a.5) Pursuant to section 13-1-204 (1) (b), C.R.S., a five-dollar surcharge, in addition to the original surcharge described in paragraph (a) of this subsection (4), shall be assessed and collected on each docket fee that is described in paragraph (a) of this subsection (4) concerning penalties assessed on and after July 1, 2007.

(b) In no event shall a bench warrant be issued for the arrest of any person who fails to appear for a hearing pursuant to subsection (1.5) or (2) of this section or for a final hearing pursuant to subsection (3) of this section. Except as otherwise provided in section 42-4-1716, entry of judgment and assessment of the penalty and surcharge pursuant to paragraph (a) of this subsection (4) and any penalties imposed pursuant to section 42-2-127 shall constitute the sole penalties for failure to appear for either the hearing or the final hearing.

42-4-1711. Compliance with promise to appear. A written promise to appear in court may be complied with by an appearance by counsel.

42-4-1712. Procedure prescribed not exclusive. The foregoing provisions of this article shall govern all police officers in making arrests without a warrant or issuing citations for violations of this article, for offenses or infractions committed in their presence, but the procedure prescribed in this article shall not otherwise be exclusive of any other method prescribed by law for the arrest and prosecution of a person for an offense or infraction of like grade.

42-4-1713. Conviction record inadmissible in civil action. Except as provided in sections 42-2-

201 to 42-2-208, no record of the conviction of any person for any violation of this article shall be admissible as evidence in any court in any civil action.

42-4-1714. Traffic violation not to affect credibility of witness. The conviction of a person upon a charge of violating any provision of this article or other traffic regulation less than a felony shall not affect or impair the credibility of such person as a witness in any civil or criminal proceeding.

42-4-1715. Convictions, judgments, and charges recorded - public inspection. (1) (a) Every judge of a court not of record and every clerk of a court of record shall keep a full record of every case in which a person is charged with any violation of this article or any other law regulating the operation of vehicles on highways.
(b) (I) Upon application by a person, the court shall expunge all records concerning a conviction of the person for UDD with a BAC of at least 0.02 but not more than 0.05 if:
(A) Such person presents a request for expungement to the court and provides all information required by the court to process such request;
(B) Such person is over twenty-one years of age and the court action regarding the offense has been concluded;
(C) The person has not been convicted for any other offense under section 42-4-1301 that was committed while such person was under twenty-one years of age;
(D) Such person pays the fine and surcharge for such conviction and completes any other requirements of the court with regard to such conviction, including, but not limited to, any order to pay restitution to any party;
(E) Such person has never held a commercial driver's license as defined in section 42-2-402; and
(F) Such person was not operating a commercial motor vehicle as defined in section 42-2-402.
(II) Upon receiving a request for expungement, the court may delay consideration of such request until sufficient time has elapsed to ensure that the person is not convicted for any additional offense of DUI, DUI per se, DWAI, habitual user, or UDD committed while the person was under twenty-one years of age.
(2) (a) Subject to paragraph (b) of this subsection (2), within ten days after the entry of a judgment, conviction, or forfeiture of bail of a person upon a charge of violating this article or other law regulating the operation of vehicles on highways, the judge or clerk of the court in which the entry of a judgment was made, the conviction was had, or bail was forfeited shall prepare and forward to the department an abstract of the record of the court covering every case in which the person had a judgment entered against him or her, was convicted, or forfeited bail, which abstract shall be certified by the preparer to be true and correct.
(b) For the holder of a commercial driver's license as defined in section 42-2-402 or an offense committed by a person operating a commercial motor vehicle as defined in section 42-2-402, within five days after conviction of a person upon a charge of violating this article or other law regulating the operation of vehicles on highways, the judge or clerk of the court in which the person was convicted shall prepare and forward to the department an abstract of the record of the court covering every case in which the person was convicted, which abstract shall be certified by the preparer to be true and correct.
(3) Said abstract must be made upon a form furnished by the department and shall include the name, address, and driver's license number of the party charged, the registration number of the vehicle involved, the nature of the offense, the date of hearing, the plea, the judgment or whether bail forfeited, and the amount of the fine or forfeiture.
(4) (a) Every court of record shall also forward a like report to the department:
(I) Upon the conviction of any person of vehicular homicide or any other felony in the commission of which a vehicle was used; and
(II) Upon the dismissal of a charge for DUI, DUI per se, DWAI, habitual user, or UDD or if the original charge was for DUI, DUI per se, DWAI, habitual user, or UDD and the conviction was for a nonalcohol- or nondrug-related traffic offense.
(b) (Deleted by amendment, L. 2008, p. 475, § 6, effective July 1, 2008.)
(5) The department shall keep all abstracts received under this section, as well as a record of penalty assessments received, at the main office, and the same shall be public records and subject to the provisions of section 42-1-206.

42-4-1716. Notice to appear or pay fine - failure to appear - penalty. (1) For the purposes of this part 17, tender by an arresting officer of the summons or penalty assessment notice shall constitute notice to the violator to appear in court at the time specified on such summons or to pay the required fine and surcharge thereon.
(2) Except as otherwise provided in subsection (4) of this section, a person commits a class 2 misdemeanor traffic offense if the person fails to appear to answer any offense other than a traffic infraction charged under this part 17.
(3) (Deleted by amendment, L. 2004, p. 1335, § 9, effective July 1, 2005.)
(4) (a) (I) Except as otherwise provided in subparagraph (II) of this paragraph (a), a person who is a parent or legal guardian of a minor under the age of eighteen years and who is required to appear in court with the minor pursuant to the provisions of this part 17 including but not limited to section 42-4-1706 (2) (b), 42-4-

1707 (1) (b), or 42-4-1710 (1.5), shall appear in court at the location and on the date stated in the penalty assessment notice or in the summons and complaint or as instructed by the court.

(II) The provisions of subparagraph (I) of this paragraph (a) concerning the appearance of a parent or legal guardian shall not apply in a case where the minor under the age of eighteen years or the parent of the minor demonstrates to the court by clear and convincing evidence that the minor is an emancipated minor.

(III) For purposes of this subsection (4), "emancipated minor" means a minor under the age of eighteen years who has no legal guardian and whose parents have entirely surrendered the right to the care, custody, and earnings of the minor, no longer are under any duty to support or maintain the minor, and have made no provision for the support of the minor.

(b) A person who violates any provision of paragraph (a) of subparagraph (I) of this subsection (4) commits a class 1 petty offense and shall be punished pursuant to section 18-1.3-503, C.R.S.

42-4-1717. Conviction - attendance at driver improvement school - rules. (1) Except as otherwise provided in subsection (2) of this section, if a person has been convicted of violating this article or any other law regulating the operation of motor vehicles other than a violation of section 42-4-1301, the court may require the defendant, or, if the defendant has not been convicted of a violation of this article or any other law regulating the operation of motor vehicles within the last eighteen months, the court shall offer the defendant an opportunity, at the defendant's expense, to attend and satisfactorily complete a course of instruction at any designated driver improvement school providing instruction in the traffic laws of this state, instruction in recognition of hazardous traffic situations, and instruction in traffic accident prevention. Upon completion of the course, the court may suspend all or a portion of the fine or sentence of imprisonment. Unless otherwise provided by law, such school shall be approved by the court.

(2) Whenever a minor under eighteen years of age has been convicted of violating any provision of this article or other law regulating the operation of vehicles on highways, other than a traffic infraction, the court shall require the minor to attend and satisfactorily complete a course of instruction at any designated driver improvement school providing instruction in the traffic laws of this state, instruction in recognition of hazardous traffic situations, and instruction in traffic accident prevention. The court shall impose the driver improvement school requirement in addition to the penalty provided for the violation or as a condition of either the probation or the suspension of all or any portion of any fine or sentence of imprisonment for the violation. The minor, or the minor's parent or parents who appear in court with the minor in accordance with section 42-4-1716 (4), shall pay the cost of attending the designated driver improvement school. The courts shall make available information on scholarships and other financial assistance available to help minors or their parents offset the costs of driver improvement school. Unless otherwise provided by law, such school shall be approved by the court.

(3) (a) Effective January 1, 2010, a person who is required to attend a course of instruction pursuant to subsection (1) or (2) of this section shall pay, in addition to any other penalties, a penalty surcharge as determined by rules promulgated by the department. The driver improvement school shall collect the penalty surcharge and remit it to the department at least monthly in accordance with rules promulgated by the department. The department shall set the penalty surcharge in an amount to offset the direct and indirect cost of implementing section 42-1-223. The penalty surcharge shall be transferred to the state treasurer and credited to the defensive driving school fund created in section 42-1-223.

(b) The court shall include on the referral form information concerning the amount and purpose of the penalty surcharge. If the court determines that a person is unable to pay the cost of the penalty surcharge, the court may waive the surcharge and the driver improvement school shall not collect nor remit the penalty surcharge to the department.

(c) A person who is required to attend a course of instruction pursuant to subsection (1) or (2) of this section shall register with the entity that monitors the driver improvement school pursuant to section 42-1-223. If the person satisfactorily completes the course, the driver improvement school shall electronically notify the entity.

42-4-1718. Electronic transmission of data - standards. (1) The department, the judicial department, and the department of public safety shall jointly develop standards for the electronic transmission of any penalty assessment notice or summons and complaint issued pursuant to the provisions of this article or issued pursuant to any county ordinance adopted under section 30-15-401 (1) (h), C.R.S. Such agencies shall consult with county sheriffs, municipal police departments, municipal courts, and the office of transportation safety in the department of transportation in developing such standards. Such standards shall be consistent with requirements of the department for reporting convictions under the provisions of this article and with the requirements of the department of public safety for reporting criminal information under article 21 of title 16, C.R.S. The provisions of this section shall not be interpreted to require any municipality, county, or other government entity to transmit traffic data electronically.

(2) A municipal court, county court, district court, or any court with jurisdiction over violations of traffic rules and laws shall not dismiss any charges or refuse to enforce any traffic law or rule solely because a penalty assessment notice or summons and complaint issued pursuant to the standards established in this section is in electronic form or contains an electronic signature.

42-4-1719. Violations - commercial driver's license - compliance with federal regulation. As to a holder of a commercial driver's license as defined in section 42-2-402 or the operator of a commercial motor vehicle as defined in section 42-2-402, a court shall not defer imposition of judgment or allow a person to enter into a diversion program that would prevent a driver's conviction for any violation, in any type of motor vehicle, of a traffic control law from appearing on the driver's record.

PART 18

VEHICLES ABANDONED ON PUBLIC PROPERTY

42-4-1801. Legislative declaration. The general assembly hereby declares that the purpose of this part 18 is to provide procedures for the removal, storage, and disposal of motor vehicles that are abandoned on public property.

42-4-1802. Definitions. As used in this part 18, unless the context otherwise requires:

(1) "Abandoned motor vehicle" means:

(a) Any motor vehicle left unattended on public property, including any portion of a highway right-of-way, outside the limits of any incorporated town or city for a period of forty-eight hours or longer;

(b) Any motor vehicle left unattended on public property, including any portion of a highway right-of-way, within the limits of any incorporated town or city for a period longer than any limit prescribed by any local ordinance concerning the abandonment of motor vehicles or, if there is no such ordinance, for a period of forty-eight hours or longer;

(c) Any motor vehicle stored in an impound lot at the request of a law enforcement agency and not removed from the impound lot within seventy-two hours after the time the law enforcement agency notifies the owner or agent that the vehicle is available for release upon payment of any applicable charges or fees;

(d) A motor vehicle fitted with an immobilization device that is on public property and deemed to be abandoned pursuant to section 42-4-1105 (7) (c); or

(e) Any motor vehicle left unattended at a regional transportation district parking facility, as defined in section 32-9-119.9 (6), C.R.S., that is deemed to be abandoned pursuant to section 32-9-119.9 (4) (b), C.R.S.

(2) "Agency employee" means any employee of the department of transportation or other municipal, county, or city and county agency responsible for highway safety and maintenance.

(3) (Deleted by amendment, L. 2009, (HB 09- 1279), ch. 170, p. 763, § 1, effective August 5, 2009.)

(4) "Appraisal" means a bona fide estimate of reasonable market value made by any motor vehicle dealer licensed in this state or by any employee of the Colorado state patrol or of any sheriff's or police department whose appointment for such purpose has been reported by the head of the appointing agency to the executive director of the department.

(5) "Disabled motor vehicle" means any motor vehicle that is stopped or parked, either attended or unattended, upon a public right-of-way and that is, due to any mechanical failure or any inoperability because of a collision, a fire, or any other such injury, temporarily inoperable under its own power.

(6) "Impound lot" means a parcel of real property that is owned or leased by a government or operator at which motor vehicles are stored under appropriate protection.

(7) "Operator" means a person or a firm licensed by the public utilities commission as a towing carrier.

(8) "Public property" means any real property having its title, ownership, use, or possession held by the federal government; this state; or any county, municipality, as defined in section 31-1-101 (6), C.R.S., or other governmental entity of this state.

(9) "Responsible law enforcement agency" means the law enforcement agency authorizing the original tow of an abandoned motor vehicle, whether or not the vehicle is towed to another law enforcement agency's jurisdiction.

42-4-1803. Abandonment of motor vehicles - public property. (1) (a) No person shall abandon any motor vehicle upon public property. Any sheriff, undersheriff, deputy sheriff, police officer, marshal, Colorado state patrol officer, or agent of the Colorado bureau of investigation who finds a motor vehicle that such officer has reasonable grounds to believe has been abandoned shall require such motor vehicle to be removed or cause the same to be removed and placed in storage in any impound lot designated or maintained by the law enforcement agency employing such officer.

(b) If an operator is used by the responsible law enforcement agency to tow or impound the motor vehicle pursuant to paragraph (a) of this subsection (1), the operator shall be provided with written authorization to possess the motor vehicle on a document that includes, without limitation, the year, make, model, vehicle identification number, and storage location.

(2) Whenever any sheriff, undersheriff, deputy sheriff, police officer, marshal, Colorado state patrol officer, agent of the Colorado bureau of investigation, or agency employee finds a motor vehicle, vehicle, cargo, or debris, attended or unattended, standing upon any portion of a highway right-of-way in such a manner as to constitute an obstruction to traffic or proper highway maintenance, such officer or agency employee is authorized to cause the motor vehicle, vehicle, cargo, or debris to be moved to eliminate any such obstruction; and neither the officer, the agency employee, nor anyone acting under the direction of such officer or employee shall be liable for any damage to such motor vehicle, vehicle, cargo, or debris occasioned by such removal. The removal process is intended to clear the obstruction, but such activity should create as little damage as possible to the vehicle, or cargo, or both. No agency employee shall cause any motor vehicle to be moved unless such employee has obtained approval from a local law enforcement agency of a municipality, county, or city and county, the Colorado bureau of investigation, or the Colorado state patrol.

(3) The operator shall be responsible for removing the motor vehicle and the motor vehicle debris from the site pursuant to this section, but shall not be required to remove or clean up any hazardous or commercial cargo the motor vehicle carried. The commercial carrier shall be responsible for removal or clean-up of the hazardous or commercial cargo.

42-4-1804. Report of abandoned motor vehicles - owner's opportunity to request hearing. (1) (a) Upon having an abandoned motor vehicle towed, the responsible law enforcement agency shall ascertain, if possible, whether or not the motor vehicle has been reported stolen, and, if so reported, such agency shall recover and secure the motor vehicle and notify its rightful owner and terminate the abandonment proceedings under this part 18. The responsible law enforcement agency and the towing carrier shall have the right to recover from the owner their reasonable costs and fees for recovering and securing the motor vehicle. Nothing in this section shall be construed to authorize fees for services that were not provided or that were provided by another person or entity.

(b) As soon as possible, but in no event later than ten working days after having an abandoned motor vehicle towed, the responsible law enforcement agency shall report the same to the department by first-class or certified mail, by personal delivery, or by internet communication. The report shall be on a form prescribed and supplied by the department.

(c) The report shall contain the following information:

(I) The fact of possession, including the date possession was taken, the location of storage of the abandoned motor vehicle and the location from which it was towed, the identity of the responsible law enforcement agency, and the business address, telephone number, and name and signature of a representative from the responsible law enforcement agency;

(II) If applicable, the identity of the operator possessing the abandoned motor vehicle, together with the operator's business address and telephone number and the carrier number assigned by the public utilities commission; and

(III) A description of the abandoned motor vehicle, including the make, model, color, and year, the number, issuing state, and expiration date of the license plate, and the vehicle identification number.

(2) Upon its receipt of such report, the department shall search its records to ascertain the last-known owner of record for the abandoned motor vehicle and any lienholder as those persons are represented in department records. In the event the vehicle is determined by the department not to be registered in the state of Colorado, the report required by this section shall state that no Colorado title record exists regarding the vehicle. Within ten working days after such receipt, the department shall complete its search and shall transmit such report, together with all relevant information, to the responsible law enforcement agency.

(3) The responsible law enforcement agency, upon its receipt of the report required under subsection (2) of this section, shall determine, from all available information and after reasonable inquiry, whether the abandoned motor vehicle has been reported stolen, and, if so reported, such agency shall recover and secure the motor vehicle and notify its rightful owner and terminate the abandonment proceedings under this part 18. The responsible law enforcement agency and the operator shall have the right to recover from the owner their reasonable costs to recover and secure the motor vehicle.

(4) (a) If the responsible law enforcement agency does not use an operator to store the motor vehicle, the responsible law enforcement agency, within ten working days after the receipt of the report from the department required in subsection (2) of this section, shall notify by certified mail the owner of record, if ascertained, and any lienholder, if ascertained, of the fact of such report and the claim of any lien under section 42-4-1806. The notice shall contain information that the identified motor vehicle has been reported abandoned to the department, the location of the motor vehicle and the location from where it was towed, and that, unless claimed within thirty calendar days after the date the notice was sent as determined from the postmark on the notice, the motor vehicle is subject to sale.

(b) If the responsible law enforcement agency uses an operator to store the motor vehicle, the responsible law enforcement agency, within ten working days after the receipt of the report from the department required in subsection (2) of this section, shall notify by first-class mail the owner of record, if ascertained, and any lienholder, if ascertained, of the fact of the report and the claim of any lien under section 42-4-1806. The notice shall contain information that the identified motor vehicle has been reported abandoned to the department, the location of the motor vehicle and the location from where it was towed, and that, unless claimed within thirty calendar days after the date the notice was sent as determined from the postmark on the notice, the motor vehicle is subject to sale.

(c) The responsible law enforcement agency shall include in the notices sent pursuant to either paragraph (a) or (b) of this subsection (4) a statement informing the owner of record of the opportunity to request a hearing concerning the legality of the towing of the abandoned motor vehicle, and the responsible law enforcement agency to contact for that purpose.

(d) If an owner or lienholder requests a hearing, the owner or lienholder shall make the request in writing to the responsible law enforcement agency within ten days after the notice was sent, as determined by the postmark. Such hearing, if requested, shall be conducted pursuant to section 24-4-105, C.R.S., if the responsible law enforcement agency is the Colorado state patrol. If a local political subdivision is the responsible law enforcement agency, such hearing shall be conducted pursuant to local hearing procedures. If it is determined at the hearing that the motor vehicle was illegally towed upon request from a law enforcement agency, all towing charges and storage fees assessed against the vehicle shall be paid by such law enforcement agency.

(5) The department shall maintain department-approved notice forms satisfying the requirements of subsection (4) of this section and shall make them available for use by local law enforcement agencies.

(6) (a) An operator or its agent shall, no less than two days, but no more than ten days after a motor vehicle has been towed, determine if there is an owner and a lienholder represented in department records and send a notice by certified mail, return receipt requested, to the last address of the owner, as shown on the motor vehicle's registration, and the lienholder, as shown on the title, if either is shown in department records. The cost of complying with this paragraph (a) shall be considered a cost of towing; except that the total of such costs shall not exceed one hundred fifty dollars. The notice to the owner and lienholder shall be sent within three days after the operator receives the information from the department. Such notice shall contain the following information:

(I) The fact of possession, including the date possession was taken, the location of storage of the motor vehicle, and the location from which it was towed;

(II) The identity of the operator possessing the abandoned motor vehicle, together with the operator's business address and telephone number and the carrier number assigned by the public utilities commission; and

(III) A description of the motor vehicle, including the make, model, color, and year and the number, issuing state, and expiration date of the license plate, or any other indicia of the motor vehicle's state of origin.

(b) The operator shall not be entitled to recover any daily storage fees from the day the vehicle is towed until the day the owner and lienholder are notified, unless the operator reasonably attempts to notify the owner and lienholder by the date specified in paragraph (a) of this subsection (6). Sending a notice by certified mail, return receipt requested, to the owner and the lienholder as represented in department records shall be deemed a reasonable attempt to notify the owner and the lienholder. Failure to notify the owner and the lienholder due to the receipt of erroneous information from the department or a failure of the law enforcement agency to comply with this section shall not cause the loss of such storage fees accrued from the date the vehicle is towed until the owner and the lienholder receive such notice.

42-4-1805. Appraisal of abandoned motor vehicles - sale. (1) (a) Abandoned motor vehicles or motor vehicles abandoned in an impound lot subsequent to a tow from public property shall be appraised by a law enforcement officer or an independent motor vehicle dealer and sold by the responsible law enforcement agency at a public or private sale held not less than thirty days nor more than sixty days after the date the notice required by section 42-4-1804 (4) was mailed.

(b) Subject to section 42-4-1804, the operator may continue to charge for daily storage fees until the responsible law enforcement agency complies with this section.

(2) If the appraised value of an abandoned motor vehicle sold pursuant to this section is three hundred fifty dollars or less, the sale shall be made only for the purpose of junking, scrapping, or dismantling such motor vehicle, and the purchaser thereof shall not, under any circumstances, be entitled to a Colorado certificate of title. The responsible law enforcement agency making the sale shall cause to be executed and delivered a bill of sale, together with a copy of the report described in section 42-4-1804 (2), to the person purchasing such motor vehicle. The bill of sale shall state that the purchaser acquires no right to a certificate of title for such vehicle. The responsible law enforcement agency making the sale shall promptly submit a report of sale, with a copy of the bill of sale, to the department and shall deliver a copy of such report of sale to the purchaser of the motor vehicle. Upon receipt of any report of sale with supporting documents on any sale made pursuant to this subsection (2), the department shall purge the records for such

vehicle as provided in section 42-4-1810 (1) (b) and shall not issue a new certificate of title for such vehicle. Any certificate of title issued in violation of this subsection (2) shall be void.

(3) If the appraised value of an abandoned motor vehicle sold pursuant to this section is more than three hundred fifty dollars, the sale may be made for any intended use by the purchaser. The responsible law enforcement agency making the sale shall cause to be executed and delivered a bill of sale, together with a copy of the report described in section 42-4-1804 (2), and an application for a Colorado certificate of title signed by a legally authorized representative of the responsible law enforcement agency conducting the sale, to the person purchasing such motor vehicle. The purchaser of the abandoned motor vehicle shall be entitled to a Colorado certificate of title upon application and proof of compliance with the applicable provisions of the "Certificate of Title Act", part 1 of article 6 of this title, within fourteen days after the sale; except that, if such vehicle is less than five years old, including the current year model, and if the department does not provide the name of an owner of record to the law enforcement agency, the purchaser shall apply for a bonded title and the department shall issue such bonded title upon the applicant meeting the qualifications for such title pursuant to rules promulgated by the department.

(4) (a) Transferring the title of a motor vehicle to an operator to satisfy a debt created pursuant to this part 18 shall not be deemed to be the sale of a motor vehicle.

(b) Nothing in this section shall be deemed to require an operator to be licensed pursuant to article 6 of title 12, C.R.S., for purposes of conducting activities under this part 18.

42-4-1806. Liens upon towed motor vehicles. (1) Whenever an operator who is registered with the department in accordance with subsection (2) of this section recovers, removes, or stores a motor vehicle upon instructions from any duly authorized law enforcement agency or peace officer who has determined that such motor vehicle is an abandoned motor vehicle, such operator shall have a possessory lien, subject to the provisions of section 42-4-1804 (6), upon such motor vehicle and its attached accessories or equipment for all fees for recovering, towing, and storage as authorized in section 42-4-1809 (2) (a). Such lien shall be a first and prior lien on the motor vehicle, and such lien shall be satisfied before all other charges against such motor vehicle.

(2) (a) No operator shall have a possessory lien upon a motor vehicle described in subsection (1) of this section unless said operator is registered with the department. Such registration shall include the following information:

(I) The location of the operator's tow business;

(II) The hours of operation of the operator's tow business;

(III) The location of the impound lot where vehicles may be claimed by the owner of record; and

(IV) Any information relating to a violation of any provision contained in this part 18 or of any other state law or rule relating to the operation, theft, or transfer of motor vehicles.

(b) The executive director of the department may cancel the registration of any operator if an administrative law judge finds, after affording the operator due notice and an opportunity to be heard, that the operator has violated any of the provisions set forth in this part 18.

42-4-1807. Perfection of lien. The lien provided for in section 42-4-1806 shall be perfected by taking physical possession of the motor vehicle and its attached accessories or equipment and by sending to the department within ten working days after the time possession was taken a notice containing the information required in the report to be made under the provisions of section 42-4-1804. In addition, such report shall contain a declaration by the operator that a possessory lien is claimed for all past, present, and future charges, up to the date of redemption, and that the lien is enforceable and may be foreclosed pursuant to the provisions of this part 18.

42-4-1808. Foreclosure of lien. Any motor vehicle and its attached accessories and equipment or personal property within or attached to such vehicle that are not redeemed by the last-known owner of record or lienholder after such owner or lienholder has been sent notice of such lien by the operator or responsible law enforcement agency shall be sold in accordance with the provisions of section 42-4-1805.

42-4-1809. Proceeds of sale. (1) If the sale of any motor vehicle, personal property, and its attached accessories or equipment under the provisions of section 42-4-1805 produces an amount less than or equal to the sum of all charges of the operator who has perfected his or her lien, then the operator shall have a valid claim against the owner for the full amount of such charges, less the amount received upon the sale of such motor vehicle. Failure to register such vehicle in accordance with this title shall constitute a waiver of such owner's right to be notified pursuant to this part 18 for the purposes of foreclosure of the lien pursuant to section 42-4-1808. Such charges shall be assessed in the manner provided for in paragraph (a) of subsection (2) of this section.

(2) If the sale of any motor vehicle and its attached accessories or equipment under the provisions of section 42-4-1805 produces an amount greater than the sum of all charges of the operator who has perfected his or her lien:

(a) The proceeds shall first satisfy the operator's reasonable fee arising from the sale of the motor vehicle and the cost and fees of towing and storing the abandoned motor vehicle with a maximum charge that is specified in rules promulgated by the public utilities commission that govern nonconsensual tows by towing carriers. In the case of an abandoned motor vehicle weighing in excess of ten thousand pounds, the operator's charges shall be determined by negotiated agreement between the operator and the responsible law enforcement agency.

(b) Any balance remaining after payment pursuant to paragraph (a) of this subsection (2) shall be paid to the responsible law enforcement agency to satisfy the cost of mailing notices, having an appraisal made, advertising and selling the motor vehicle, and any other costs of the responsible law enforcement agency including administrative costs, taxes, fines, and penalties due.

(b.5) In the case of the sale of an abandoned motor vehicle described in section 42-4-1802 (1) (d), any balance remaining after payment pursuant to paragraph (b) of this subsection (2) shall be paid to the law enforcement agency that is owed a fee for the court-ordered placement of an immobilization device on the motor vehicle pursuant to section 42-4-1105.

(c) Any balance remaining after payment pursuant to paragraphs (b) and (b.5) of this subsection (2) shall be forwarded to the department, and the department may recover from such balance any taxes, fees, and penalties due and payable to it with respect to such motor vehicle.

(d) Any balance remaining after payment pursuant to paragraph (c) of this subsection (2) shall be paid by the department: First, to any lienholder of record as the lienholder's interest may appear upon the records of the department; second, to any owner of record as the owner's interest may so appear; and then to any person submitting proof of such person's interest in such motor vehicle upon the application of such lienholder, owner, or person. If such payments are not requested and made within one hundred twenty days after the sale of the abandoned motor vehicle, the balance shall be transmitted to the state treasurer, who shall credit the same to the highway users tax fund for allocation and expenditure as specified in section 43-4-205 (5.5) (e), C.R.S.

(3) The provisions of paragraphs (a) and (b) of subsection (2) of this section shall not apply to a responsible law enforcement agency operating under a towing contract.

42-4-1810. Transfer and purge of certificates of title. (1) Whenever any motor vehicle is abandoned and removed and sold in accordance with the procedures set forth in this part 18, the department shall transfer the certificate of title or issue a new certificate of title or shall purge such certificate of title in either of the following cases:

(a) Upon a person's submission to the department of the necessary documents indicating the abandonment, removal, and subsequent sale or transfer of a motor vehicle, the department shall transfer the certificate of title or issue a new certificate of title for such abandoned motor vehicle.

(b) Upon a person's submission of documents indicating the abandonment, removal, and subsequent wrecking or dismantling of a motor vehicle, including all sales of abandoned motor vehicles with an appraised value under three hundred fifty dollars that are conducted pursuant to section 42-4-1805 (2), the department shall keep the records for one year and then purge the records for such abandoned motor vehicle; except that the department shall not be required to wait before purging the records if the purchaser is a licensed motor vehicle dealer.

42-4-1811. Penalty. Unless otherwise specified in this part 18, any person who knowingly violates any of the provisions of this part 18 commits a class 2 misdemeanor and shall be punished as provided in section 18-1.3-501, C.R.S.

42-4-1812. Exemptions. (1) Nothing in this part 18 shall be construed to include or apply to the driver of any disabled motor vehicle who temporarily leaves such vehicle on the paved or improved and main-traveled portion of a highway, subject, when applicable, to the emergency lighting requirements set forth in section 42-4-230.

(2) Nothing in this part 18 shall be construed to include or apply to authorized emergency motor vehicles while such vehicles are actually and directly engaged in, coming from, or going to an emergency.

42-4-1813. Local regulations. (1) The state or any county, municipality as defined in section 31-1-101 (6), C.R.S., or other governmental entity of the state may execute a contract or contracts for the removal, storage, or disposal of abandoned motor vehicles within the area of its authority to effectuate the provisions of this part 18.

(2) The provisions of this part 18 may be superseded by ordinance or resolution of a municipality, as defined in section 31-1-101, C.R.S., or any county that sets forth procedures for the removal, storage, and disposal of abandoned or illegally parked motor vehicles on public property; except that such ordinance or resolution shall not deprive an operator of a lien attached and perfected under this part 18.

42-4-1814. Violation of motor vehicle registration or inspection laws - separate statutory provision. Owners of motor vehicles impounded by the Colorado state patrol for violation of motor vehicle registration or inspection laws shall receive notice and the opportunity for a hearing pursuant to the provisions of section 42-13-106. If such a motor vehicle is found to be abandoned in accordance with the provisions of said section 42-13-106, the notice and hearing provisions to owners of motor vehicles under other sections of this part 18 shall be deemed to have been met for purposes of proper disposition of the motor vehicle under the terms of this part 18. Nevertheless, the notice and hearing provisions of the other sections of this part 18 as to lienholders are applicable and shall not be deemed to have been met by the provisions of section 42-13-106 or this section.

PART 19

SCHOOL BUS REQUIREMENTS

42-4-1901. School buses - equipped with supplementary brake retarders. (1) (a) On and after July 1, 1991, except as provided in paragraph (a) of subsection (2) of this section, passengers of any school bus being used on mountainous terrain by any school district of the state shall not occupy the front row of seats and any seats located next to the emergency doors of such school bus during the period of such use.

(b) For purposes of this section, mountainous terrain shall include, but shall not be limited to, any road or street which the department of transportation has designated as being located on mountainous terrain.

(2) (a) The provisions of paragraph (a) of subsection (1) of this section shall not apply to:

(I) Passengers of any school bus which is equipped with retarders of appropriate capacity for purposes of supplementing any service brake systems of such school bus; or

(II) Any passenger who is adequately restrained in a fixed position pursuant to federal and state standards.

(b) The general assembly encourages school districts to consider installing only electromagnetic retarders or state-of-the-art retarders for purposes of supplementing service brake systems of school buses when such retarders are acquired on or after April 17, 1991. The general assembly also encourages school districts to consider purchasing only those new school buses which are equipped with external public address systems and retarders of appropriate capacity for purposes of supplementing any service brake systems of such school buses.

(3) For purposes of this section and section 42-4-1902:

(a) "Mountainous terrain" means that condition where longitudinal and transverse changes in the elevation of the ground with respect to a road or street are abrupt and where benching and sidehill excavation are frequently required to obtain acceptable horizontal and vertical alignment.

(b) Repealed.

42-4-1902. School vehicle drivers - special training required. On and after July 1, 1992, the driver of any school vehicle as defined in section 42-1-102 (88.5) owned or operated by or for any school district in this state shall have successfully completed training, approved by the department of education, concerning driving on mountainous terrain, as defined in section 42-4-1901 (3) (a), and driving in adverse weather conditions.

42-4-1903. School buses - stops - signs - passing. (1) (a) The driver of a motor vehicle upon any highway, road, or street, upon meeting or overtaking from either direction any school bus that has stopped, shall stop the vehicle at least twenty feet before reaching the school bus if visual signal lights as specified in subsection (2) of this section have been actuated on the school bus. The driver shall not proceed until the visual signal lights are no longer being actuated. The driver of a motor vehicle shall stop when a school bus that is not required to be equipped with visual signal lights by subsection (2) of this section stops to receive or discharge schoolchildren.

(b) (I) A driver of any school bus who observes a violation of paragraph (a) of this subsection (1) shall notify the driver's school district transportation dispatcher. The school bus driver shall provide the school district transportation dispatcher with the color, basic description, and license plate number of the vehicle involved in the violation, information pertaining to the identity of the alleged violator, and the time and the approximate location at which the violation occurred. Any school district transportation dispatcher who has received information by a school bus driver concerning a violation of paragraph (a) of this subsection (1) shall provide such information to the appropriate law enforcement agency or agencies.

(II) A law enforcement agency may issue a citation on the basis of the information supplied to it pursuant to subparagraph (I) of this paragraph (b) to the driver of the vehicle involved in the violation.

(2) (a) Every school bus as defined in section 42-1-102 (88), other than a small passenger-type vehicle having a seating capacity of not more than fifteen, used for the transportation of schoolchildren shall:

(I) Bear upon the front and rear of such school bus plainly visible and legible signs containing the words "SCHOOL BUS" in letters not less than eight inches in height; and

(II) Display eight visual signal lights meeting the requirements of 49 CFR 571.108 or its successor regulation.

(b) (I) The red visual signal lights shall be actuated by the driver of the school bus whenever the school bus is stopped for the purpose of receiving or discharging schoolchildren, is stopped because it is behind another school bus that is receiving or discharging passengers, or, except as provided in subsection (4) of this section, is stopped because it has met a school bus traveling in a different direction that is receiving or discharging passengers and at no other time;

but such lights need not be actuated when a school bus is stopped at locations where the local traffic regulatory authority has by prior written designation declared such actuation unnecessary.

(II) A school bus shall be exempt from the provisions of subparagraph (I) of this paragraph (b) when stopped for the purpose of discharging or loading passengers who require the assistance of a lift device only when no passenger is required to cross the roadway. Such buses shall stop as far to the right off the roadway as possible to reduce obstruction to traffic.

(c) The alternating flashing yellow lights shall be actuated at least two hundred feet prior to the point where the bus is to be stopped for the purpose of receiving or discharging schoolchildren, and the red lights shall be actuated only at the time the bus is actually stopped.

(3) Every school bus used for the transportation of schoolchildren, except those small passenger-type vehicles described in subsection (1) of this section, shall be equipped with school bus pedestrian safety devices that comply with 49 CFR 571.131 or its successor regulation.

(4) The driver of a vehicle upon a highway with separate roadways need not stop upon meeting or passing a school bus which is on a different roadway. For the purposes of this section, "highway with separate roadways" means a highway that is divided into two or more roadways by a depressed, raised, or painted median or other intervening space serving as a clearly indicated dividing section or island.

(5) Every school bus shall stop as far to the right of the roadway as possible before discharging or loading passengers; except that the school bus may block the lane of traffic when a passenger being received or discharged is required to cross the roadway. When possible, a school bus shall not stop where the visibility is obscured for a distance of two hundred feet either way from the bus. The driver of a school bus that has stopped shall allow time for any vehicles that have stopped behind the school bus to pass the school bus, if such passing is legally permissible where the school bus is stopped, after the visual signal lights, if any, are no longer being displayed or actuated and after all children who have embarked or disembarked from the bus are safe from traffic.

(6) (a) Except as provided in paragraph (b) of this subsection (6), any person who violates any provision of paragraph (a) of subsection (1) of this section commits a class 2 misdemeanor traffic offense.

(b) Any person who violates the provisions of paragraph (a) of subsection (1) of this section commits a class 1 misdemeanor traffic offense if such person has been convicted within the previous five years of a violation of paragraph (a) of subsection (1) of this section.

(7) The provisions of this section shall not apply in the case of public transportation programs for pupil transportation under section 22-51-104 (1) (c), C.R.S.

42-4-1904. Regulations for school buses - regulations on discharge of passengers - penalty - exception. (1) The state board of education, by and with the advice of the executive director of the department, shall adopt and enforce regulations not inconsistent with this article to govern the operation of all school buses used for the transportation of schoolchildren and to govern the discharge of passengers from such school buses. Such regulations shall prohibit the driver of any school bus used for the transportation of schoolchildren from discharging any passenger from the school bus which will result in the passenger's immediately crossing a major thoroughfare, except for two-lane highways when such crossing can be done in a safe manner, as determined by the local school board in consultation with the local traffic regulatory authority, and shall prohibit the discharging or loading of passengers from the school bus onto the side of any major thoroughfare whenever access to the destination of the passenger is possible by the use of a road or street which is adjacent to the major thoroughfare. For the purposes of this section, a "major thoroughfare" means a freeway, any U.S. highway outside any incorporated limit, interstate highway, or highway with four or more lanes, or a highway or road with a median separating multiple lanes of traffic. Every person operating a school bus or responsible for or in control of the operation of school buses shall be subject to said regulations.

(2) Any person operating a school bus under contract with a school district who fails to comply with any of said regulations is guilty of breach of contract, and such contract shall be cancelled after notice and hearing by the responsible officers of such district.

(3) Any person who violates any provision of this section is guilty of a misdemeanor and, upon conviction thereof, shall be punished by a fine of not less than five dollars nor more than one hundred dollars, or by imprisonment in the county jail for not more than one year, or by both such fine and imprisonment.

(4) The provisions of this section shall not apply in the case of public transportation programs for pupil transportation under section 22-51-104 (1) (c), C.R.S.

PART 20

HOURS OF SERVICE

42-4-2001. Maximum hours of service - ready-mix concrete truck operators. (1) Any person who operates a commercial motor vehicle solely in intrastate commerce for the purpose of transporting wet, ready-mix concrete need not comply with 49 CFR sec. 395.3 (b). No such person shall drive for any period after:

(a) Having been on duty seventy hours in any seven consecutive days if the employing motor carrier does not operate every day in the week; or

(b) Having been on duty eighty hours in any period of eight consecutive days if the employing motor carrier operates motor vehicles every day of the week.

(2) Within a seven day work week all hours of service after sixty hours are voluntary starting the next scheduled work day.

(3) Twenty-four consecutive hours off duty shall constitute the end of any seven or eight consecutive-day period.

(4) Any commercial motor vehicle that transports hazardous materials shall be exempt from this section and shall be subject to the federal hours-of-service limitations in 49 CFR secs. 395 and 350.

PART 21

VEHICLES ABANDONED ON PRIVATE PROPERTY

42-4-2101. Legislative declaration. The general assembly hereby declares that the purpose of this part 21 is to provide procedures for the removal, storage, and disposal of motor vehicles that are abandoned on private property.

42-4-2102. Definitions. As used in this part 21, unless the context otherwise requires:

(1) "Abandoned motor vehicle", except as otherwise defined in section 38-20-116 (2.5) (b) (I), C.R.S., for purposes of section 38-20-116 (2.5), C.R.S., means:

(a) Any motor vehicle left unattended on private property for a period of twenty-four hours or longer or for such other period as may be established by local ordinance without the consent of the owner or lessee of such property or the owner's or lessee's legally authorized agent;

(b) Any motor vehicle stored in an impound lot at the request of its owner or the owner's agent and not removed from the impound lot according to the agreement with the owner or agent;

(c) Any motor vehicle that is left on private property without the property owner's consent, towed at the request of the property owner, and not removed from the impound lot by the vehicle owner within forty-eight hours; or

(d) A motor vehicle fitted with an immobilization device that is on private property and deemed to be abandoned pursuant to section 42-4-1105 (7) (c).

(2) "Appraisal" means a bona fide estimate of reasonable market value made by any motor vehicle dealer licensed in this state or by any employee of the Colorado state patrol or of any sheriff's or police department whose appointment for such purpose has been reported by the head of the appointing agency to the executive director of the department.

(3) (Deleted by amendment, L. 2009, (HB 09-1279), ch. 170, p. 766, § 7, effective August 5, 2009.)

(4) "Impound lot" means a parcel of real property that is owned or leased by an operator at which motor vehicles are stored under appropriate protection.

(5) "Operator" means a person or a firm licensed by the public utilities commission as a towing carrier.

(6) "Private property" means any real property that is not public property.

(7) "Public property" means any real property having its title, ownership, use, or possession held by the federal government; this state; or any county, municipality, as defined in section 31-1-101 (6), C.R.S., or other governmental entity of this state.

(8) "Responsible law enforcement agency" means the law enforcement agency having jurisdiction over the private property where the motor vehicle becomes abandoned.

42-4-2103. Abandonment of motor vehicles - private property. (1) (a) Motor vehicles abandoned at repair shops shall be removed as set forth in section 38-20-116 (2.5), C.R.S.

(b) No person shall abandon any motor vehicle upon private property other than his or her own. Any owner or lessee, or the owner's or lessee's agent authorized in writing, may have an abandoned motor vehicle removed from his or her property by having it towed and impounded by an operator. Motor vehicles abandoned upon the property of a motor vehicle recycler may be recycled in accordance with part 22 of this article if the vehicle's appraisal value is less than three hundred fifty dollars.

(2) Any operator having in his or her possession any motor vehicle that was abandoned on private property shall notify, within thirty minutes, the department, the sheriff, or the sheriff's designee, of the county in which the motor vehicle is located or the chief of police, or the chief's designee, of the municipality in which the motor vehicle is located as to the name of the operator and the location of the impound lot where the vehicle is located and a description of the abandoned motor vehicle, including the make, model, color, and year, the number, issuing state, and expiration date of the license plate, and the vehicle identification number. Upon such notification, the law enforcement agency that receives such notice shall assign the vehicle a tow report number immediately, shall enter the vehicle and the fact that it has been towed in the Colorado crime information center computer system, and shall ascertain, if possible, whether or not the vehicle has been reported stolen and, if so

reported, such agency shall recover and secure the motor vehicle and notify its rightful owner and terminate the abandonment proceedings under this part 21. Upon the release of the vehicle to the owner or lienholder, the operator shall notify the responsible law enforcement agent who shall adjust or delete the entry in the Colorado crime information center computer system. The responsible law enforcement agency and operator shall have the right to recover from the owner their reasonable fees for recovering and securing the vehicle. Nothing in this section shall be construed to authorize fees for services that were not provided or that were provided by another person or entity.

(3) (a) An operator shall, no less than two days, but no more than ten days after a motor vehicle has been towed or abandoned, report such motor vehicle tow to the department by first-class or certified mail, by personal delivery, or by internet communication, which report shall be on a form prescribed and supplied by the department.

(b) The report shall contain the following information:

(I) The fact of possession, including the date possession was taken, the location of storage of the abandoned motor vehicle and the location from which it was towed, the tow report number, and the identity of the law enforcement agency determining that the vehicle was not reported stolen;

(II) The identity of the operator possessing the abandoned motor vehicle, together with the operator's business address and telephone number and the carrier number assigned by the public utilities commission; and

(III) A description of the abandoned motor vehicle, including the make, model, color, and year, the number, issuing state, and expiration date of the license plate, or any other indicia of the motor vehicle's state of origin, and the vehicle identification number.

(c) (I) An operator or its agent shall, no less than two days, but no more than ten days after a motor vehicle has been towed or abandoned, determine if there is an owner and a lienholder represented in department records and send a notice by certified mail, return receipt requested, to the address of the owner, as shown on the motor vehicle's registration, and the lienholder if either is shown in department records. Such notice shall include the information required by the report set forth in paragraph (b) of this subsection (3). The cost of complying with the provisions of this paragraph (c) shall be considered a cost of towing; except that the total of such costs shall not exceed one hundred fifty dollars. The notice to the owner and lienholder shall be sent within three days after receiving the information from the department.

(II) The operator shall not be entitled to recover any daily storage fees from the day the vehicle is towed until the day the owner and lienholder are notified, unless the operator reasonably attempts to notify the owner and lienholder by the date specified in subparagraph (I) of this paragraph (c). Sending a notice by certified mail, return receipt requested, to the owner and the lienholder as represented in department records shall be deemed a reasonable attempt to notify the owner and the lienholder. Failure to notify the owner and the lienholder due to the receipt of erroneous information from the department shall not cause the loss of such storage fees accrued from the date the vehicle is towed until the owner and the lienholder receive such notice.

(III) The department shall implement an electronic system whereby an operator registered under section 42-4-1806 (2) or the agent of such operator shall have access to correct information relating to any owner and lienholder of a vehicle towed by the operator as represented in the department records. The department shall ensure that the information available to an operator or its agent is correct and is limited solely to that information necessary to contact the owner and lienholder of such vehicle.

(4) Within ten days after the receipt of the report set forth in paragraph (b) of subsection (3) of this section from the department, the operator shall notify by certified mail the owner of record including an out-of-state owner of record. The operator shall make a reasonable effort to ascertain the address of the owner of record. Such notice shall contain the following information:

(a) That the identified motor vehicle has been reported abandoned to the department;

(b) The claim of any lien under section 42-4-2105;

(c) The location of the motor vehicle and the location from which it was towed; and

(d) That, unless claimed within thirty calendar days after the date the notice was sent, as determined from the postmark on the notice, the motor vehicle is subject to sale.

(5) The department shall maintain department-approved notice forms satisfying the requirements of subsection (4) of this section and shall make them available for use by operators and local law enforcement agencies.

42-4-2104. Appraisal of abandoned motor vehicles - sale. (1) (a) Motor vehicles that are abandoned on private property shall be appraised and sold by the operator in a commercially reasonable manner at a public or private sale held not less than thirty days nor more than sixty days after the postmarked date the notice was mailed pursuant to section 42-4-2103 (4) or the date the operator receives notice that no record exists for such vehicle. Such sale shall be made to a licensed motor vehicle dealer or wholesaler, or wholesale motor vehicle auction dealer, or through a classified newspaper advertisement published in Colorado. For purposes of this section, a sale shall not be considered commercially reasonable if the vehicle's appraisal value is more than three hundred fifty dollars and the vehicle is sold to an officer or partner of the operator that has possession of the vehicle or to any other person with a proprietary interest in such operator.

(b) Nothing in this section shall require that an operator must be a licensed dealer pursuant to article 6 of title 12, C.R.S., for purposes of selling a motor vehicle pursuant to this part 21.

(c) Subject to section 42-4-2103 and if an operator conducts a commercially reasonable sale but fails to sell the motor vehicle, the operator may continue to collect daily storage fees for such vehicle actually accrued for up to one hundred twenty days.

(2) If the appraised value of an abandoned motor vehicle sold pursuant to this section is three hundred fifty dollars or less, the sale shall be made only for the purpose of junking, scrapping, or dismantling such motor vehicle, and the purchaser thereof shall not, under any circumstances, be entitled to a Colorado certificate of title. The operator making the sale shall cause to be executed and delivered a bill of sale, together with a copy of the report described in section 42-4-2103 (3), to the person purchasing such motor vehicle. The bill of sale shall state that the purchaser acquires no right to a certificate of title for such vehicle. The operator making the sale shall promptly submit a report of sale, with a copy of the bill of sale, to the department and shall deliver a copy of such report of sale to the purchaser of the motor vehicle. Upon receipt of any report of sale with supporting documents on any sale made pursuant to this subsection (2), the department shall purge the records for such vehicle as provided in section 42-4-2109 (1) (b) and shall not issue a new certificate of title for such vehicle. Any certificate of title issued in violation of this subsection (2) shall be void.

(3) If the appraised value of an abandoned motor vehicle sold pursuant to this section is more than three hundred fifty dollars, the sale may be made for any intended use by the purchaser. The operator making the sale shall cause to be executed and delivered a bill of sale, together with a copy of the report described in section 42-4-2103 (3), and an application for a Colorado certificate of title signed by a legally authorized representative of the operator conducting the sale, to the person purchasing such motor vehicle. The purchaser of the abandoned motor vehicle shall be entitled to a Colorado certificate of title upon application and proof of compliance with the applicable provisions of the "Certificate of Title Act", part 1 of article 6 of this title; except that, if such vehicle is less than five years old, including the current year models, and if the department does not provide the name of an owner of record to the operator, the buyer shall apply for a bonded title and the department shall issue such bonded title upon the applicant meeting the qualifications for such title pursuant to rules promulgated by the department.

(4) Transferring the title of a motor vehicle to an operator to satisfy a debt covered by a lien created pursuant to this part 21 shall not be deemed to be the sale of a motor vehicle.

42-4-2104.5. Abandonment of motor vehicles of limited value at repair shops - legislative declaration - definitions. (Repealed)

42-4-2105. Liens upon towed motor vehicles. (1) Whenever an operator who is registered with the department in accordance with subsection (2) of this section recovers, removes, or stores a motor vehicle upon instructions from the owner of record, any other legally authorized person in control of such motor vehicle, or from the owner or lessee of real property upon which a motor vehicle is illegally parked or such owner's or lessee's agent authorized in writing, such operator shall have a possessory lien, subject to the provisions of section 42-4-2103 (3), upon such motor vehicle and its attached accessories, equipment, and personal property for all the costs and fees for recovering, towing, and storage as authorized in section 42-4-2108. Such lien shall be a first and prior lien on the motor vehicle, and such lien shall be satisfied before all other charges against such motor vehicle. This subsection (1) shall not apply to personal property if subsection (3) of this section applies to such personal property.

(2) (a) No operator shall have a possessory lien upon a motor vehicle described in subsection (1) of this section unless said operator is registered with the department. Such registration shall include the following information:

(I) The location of the operator's tow business;

(II) The hours of operation of the operator's tow business;

(III) The location of the impound lot where vehicles may be claimed by the owner of record; and

(IV) Any information relating to a violation of any provision contained in this part 21 or of any other state law or rule relating to the operation, theft, or transfer of motor vehicles.

(b) The executive director of the department may cancel the registration of any operator if an administrative law judge finds, after affording the operator due notice and an opportunity to be heard, that the operator has violated any of the provisions set forth in this part 21.

(3) If the operator obtains personal property from an abandoned vehicle that has been towed pursuant to this part 21 and if the serial or identification number of such property has been visibly altered or removed, the operator shall not have a lien upon such property and shall destroy or discard such property within five days after disposing of such vehicle pursuant to sections 42-4-2104 and 42-4-2107.

42-4-2106. Perfection of lien. The lien provided for in section 42-4-2105 shall be perfected by taking physical possession of the motor vehicle and its attached accessories, equipment, or personal property and by sending to the department, within ten working days after the time possession was taken, a notice containing the information required in the report to be made under the provisions of section 42-4-2103. In addition, such report shall contain a declaration by the operator that a possessory lien is claimed for all past, present, and future charges, up to the date of redemption, and that the lien is enforceable and may be foreclosed pursuant to the provisions of this part 21.

42-4-2107. Foreclosure of lien. (1) Any motor vehicle and its attached accessories and equipment or personal property within or attached to such vehicle that are not redeemed by the last-known owner of record or lienholder after such owner or lienholder has been sent notice of such lien by the operator shall be sold in accordance with the provisions of section 42-4-2104.

(2) Within five days after foreclosure of the lien pursuant to this section, the operator shall send a notice to the law enforcement agency having jurisdiction over the operator. Such notice shall contain a list of personal property found within the abandoned vehicle that has an intact serial or identification number and such serial or identification number. Such notification shall be made by certified mail, facsimile machine, or personal delivery.

42-4-2108. Proceeds of sale. (1) If the sale of any motor vehicle, personal property, and attached accessories or equipment under the provisions of section 42-4-2104 produces an amount less than or equal to the sum of all charges of the operator who has perfected his or her lien, then the operator shall have a valid claim against the owner for the full amount of such charges, less the amount received upon the sale of such motor vehicle. Failure to register such vehicle in accordance with this title shall constitute a waiver of such owner's right to be notified pursuant to this part 21 for the purposes of foreclosure of the lien pursuant to section 42-4-2107. Such charges shall be assessed in the manner provided for in paragraph (a) of subsection (2) of this section.

(2) If the sale of any motor vehicle and its attached accessories or equipment under the provisions of section 42-4-2104 produces an amount greater than the sum of all charges of the operator who has perfected his or her lien:

(a) The proceeds shall first satisfy the operator's reasonable costs and fees arising from the sale of the motor vehicle pursuant to section 42-4-2104 and the cost and fees of towing and storing the abandoned motor vehicle with a maximum charge that is specified in rules promulgated by the public utilities commission that govern nonconsensual tows by towing carriers.

(a.5) In the case of the sale of an abandoned motor vehicle described in section 42-4-2102 (1) (d), any balance remaining after payment pursuant to paragraph (a) of this subsection (2) shall be paid to the law enforcement agency that is owed a fee for the court-ordered placement of an immobilization device on the motor vehicle pursuant to section 42-4-1105.

(b) Any balance remaining after payment pursuant to paragraphs (a) and (a.5) of this subsection (2) shall be forwarded to the department, and the department may recover from such balance any taxes, fees, and penalties due to it with respect to such motor vehicle. The department shall provide a receipt to the operator within seven days after receiving the money if the operator provides the department with a postage-paid, self-addressed envelope.

(c) Any balance remaining after payment pursuant to paragraph (b) of this subsection (2) shall be paid by the department: First, to any lienholder of record as the lienholder's interest may appear upon the records of the department; second, to any owner of record as the owner's interest may so appear; and then to any person submitting proof of such person's interest in such motor vehicle upon the application of such lienholder, owner, or person. If such payments are not requested and made within one hundred twenty days after the sale of the abandoned motor vehicle, the balance shall be transmitted to the state treasurer, who shall credit the same to the highway users tax fund for allocation and expenditure as specified in section 43-4-205 (5.5) (e), C.R.S.

42-4-2109. Transfer and purge of certificates of title. (1) Whenever any motor vehicle is abandoned and removed and sold in accordance with the procedures set forth in this part 21, the department shall transfer the certificate of title or issue a new certificate of title or shall purge such certificate of title in either of the following cases:

(a) Upon a person's submission to the department of the necessary documents indicating the abandonment, removal, and subsequent sale or transfer of a motor vehicle with an appraised value of more than two hundred dollars, the department shall transfer the certificate of title or issue a new certificate of title for such abandoned motor vehicle.

(b) Upon a person's submission of documents indicating the abandonment, removal, and subsequent wrecking or dismantling of a motor vehicle, including all sales of abandoned motor vehicles with an appraised value of three hundred fifty dollars or less that are conducted pursuant to section 42-4-2104 (2) and all sales of abandoned motor vehicles, as defined in section 38-20-116 (2.5) (b) (I), C.R.S., with a retail fair market value of three hundred fifty dollars or less that are conducted pursuant to section 38-20-116 (2.5) (d) (I), C.R.S., the department shall keep the records for one year and then purge the records for such abandoned motor vehicle;

except that the department shall not be required to wait before purging the records if the purchaser is a licensed motor vehicle dealer.

42-4-2110. Penalty. Unless otherwise specified in this part 21, any person who knowingly violates any of the provisions of this part 21 commits a class 2 misdemeanor and shall be punished as provided in section 18-1.3-501, C.R.S.

PART 22

RECYCLING MOTOR VEHICLES

42-4-2201. Definitions. As used in this part 22, unless the context otherwise requires:

(1) "Auto parts recycler" means any person that purchases motor vehicles for the purpose of dismantling and selling the components thereof and that complies with all federal, state, and local laws and regulations.

(2) "Licensed motor vehicle dealer" means a motor vehicle dealer that is licensed pursuant to part 1 of article 6 of title 12, C.R.S.

(3) "Operator" means a person or a firm licensed by the public utilities commission as a towing carrier.

(4) "Recycling" means:

(a) Crushing or shredding a motor vehicle to produce scrap metal that may be used to produce new products; or

(b) Dismantling a motor vehicle to remove reusable parts prior to recycling the remainder of the vehicle.

(5) "System" means the Colorado motor vehicle verification system created in section 42-4-2203.

42-4-2202. Transfer for recycling. (1) No person who is not a licensed motor vehicle dealer shall purchase or otherwise receive a motor vehicle to recycle the vehicle, unless:

(a) The seller or transferor is the owner on the certificate of title, an operator, or a licensed motor vehicle dealer;

(b) The seller or transferor provides a completed bill of sale on a form prescribed by the department of revenue; or

(c) The receiver or purchaser complies with subsection (2) of this section.

(2) (a) A person other than a licensed motor vehicle dealer who purchases or otherwise receives a motor vehicle for the purpose of recycling the vehicle shall keep the vehicle for seven business days before recycling unless the seller or transferor:

(I) Is the owner on the certificate of title, an operator, or a licensed motor vehicle dealer; or

(II) If the purchaser or transferee is an operator selling an abandoned motor vehicle pursuant to part 18 or 21 of this article or a licensed motor vehicle dealer or used motor vehicle dealer, provides a completed bill of sale on a form prescribed by the department of revenue.

(b) During the seven-day waiting period:

(I) The motor vehicle, the bill of sale, a copy of the system inquiry results, and, if applicable, the daily record required pursuant to section 42-5-105 shall be open at all times during regular business hours to inspection by the department of revenue or any peace officer; and

(II) The receiver or purchaser shall submit the vehicle identification number to the system.

(3) Any person who violates this section is guilty of a misdemeanor and, upon conviction thereof, shall be punished by a fine of not more than five hundred dollars for the first offense and one thousand dollars for each subsequent offense.

42-4-2203. Vehicle verification system - fees - rules. (1) The Colorado motor vehicle verification system is hereby created within the Colorado bureau of investigation. The system shall be a database system that uses a motor vehicle's vehicle identification number to ascertain whether the motor vehicle has been stolen. The system shall be accessible through the internet by motor vehicle dealers, motor vehicle recyclers, automobile repair shops, licensed tow operators, the department of revenue and its authorized agents, and the general public.

(2) The system shall use the latest information that the department of public safety possesses on stolen motor vehicles.

(3) Users of the system shall pay a fee as established by the department of public safety in an amount necessary to fund the direct and indirect costs of administering the system; except that neither the department of revenue nor its authorized agent shall pay a fee for the use of the system.

(4) The department of public safety may register the persons who use the system and promulgate any rules reasonably necessary to implement the system.

42-4-2204. Theft discovered - duties - liability. (1) If a motor vehicle is identified as stolen by the system, the person submitting the inquiry shall report the incident to the nearest law enforcement agency with jurisdiction within one business day.

(2) A person who, acting in good faith, recycles a motor vehicle or reports an incident to a law enforcement agency shall be immune from civil liability and criminal prosecution for such acts if made in reliance on the system. The department of public safety shall not be subject to civil liability for failing to identify a stolen vehicle.

(3) A person who fails to comply with subsection (1) of this section commits a class 3 misdemeanor and, upon conviction thereof, shall be punished in accordance with section 18-1.3-501, C.R.S. A person who fails to comply with subsection (1) of this section two times within five years commits a class 2 misdemeanor and, upon conviction thereof, shall be punished in accordance

with section 18-1.3-501, C.R.S. A person who fails to comply with subsection (1) of this section three or more times within five years commits a class 1 misdemeanor and, upon conviction thereof, shall be punished in accordance with section 18-1.3-501, C.R.S.

PART 23

EDUCATION REGARDING USE OF NONMOTORIZED WHEELED TRANSPORTATION BY MINORS

42-4-2301. Comprehensive education. (1) The department of transportation, in collaboration with the departments of education and public safety and appropriate nonprofit organizations and advocacy groups, shall notify schools of the availability of and make available to schools existing educational curriculum for individuals under eighteen years of age regarding the safe use of public streets and premises open to the public by users of nonmotorized wheeled transportation and pedestrians. The curriculum shall focus on, at a minimum, instruction regarding:

(a) The safe use of bicycles;
(b) High risk traffic situations;
(c) Bicycle and traffic handling skills;
(d) On-bike training;
(e) Proper use of bicycle helmets;
(f) Traffic laws and regulations;
(g) The use of hiking and bicycling trails; and
(h) Safe pedestrian practices.

AUTOMOBILE THEFT LAW

ARTICLE 5

Automobile Theft Law - Inspection of Motor Vehicle Identification Numbers

PART 1
AUTOMOBILE THEFT

42-5-101.	Definitions.
42-5-102.	Stolen motor vehicle parts - buying, selling - removed or altered motor vehicle parts - possession.
42-5-103.	Tampering with a motor vehicle.
42-5-104.	Theft of motor vehicle parts - theft of license plates.
42-5-105.	Daily record.
42-5-106.	Duties of dealers - assembled motor vehicles.
42-5-107.	Seizure of motor vehicles or component parts by peace officers.
42-5-108.	Penalty.
42-5-109.	Report of stored or parked motor vehicles - when.
42-5-110.	Possession of removed, defaced, altered, or destroyed motor vehicle identification numbers.
42-5-111.	Proof of authorized possession.
42-5-112.	Automobile theft prevention authority - board - creation - duties - rules - fund - repeal.
42-5-113.	Colorado auto theft prevention cash fund - audit

PART 2
VEHICLE IDENTIFICATION NUMBER INSPECTION

42-5-201.	Definitions.
42-5-202.	Vehicle identification number inspection.
42-5-203.	Inspections - street rod vehicles. (Repealed)
42-5-204.	Inspection fees - vehicle number inspection funds.
42-5-205.	Assignment of a special vehicle identification number by the department of revenue. (Repealed)
42-5-206.	Certification of inspectors.
42-5-207.	Rules.

PART 1
AUTOMOBILE THEFT

42-5-101. Definitions. As used in this part 1, unless the context otherwise requires:

(1) "Calendar year" means the twelve calendar months beginning January first and ending December thirty-first of any year.

(2) "Dealer" means all persons, firms, partnerships, associations, or corporations engaged in the business or vocation of manufacturing, buying, selling, trading, dealing in, destroying, disposing of, or salvaging motor vehicles or in secondhand or used motor vehicle parts, equipment, attachments, accessories, or appurtenances common to or a part of motor vehicles.

(3) "Driver" means the person operating or driving a motor vehicle.

(4) "Garage" means any public building or place of business for the storage or repair of motor vehicles.

(5) "Motor vehicle" means any vehicle of whatever description propelled by any power other than muscular except a vehicle running on rails.

(6) "Officer" means any duly constituted peace officer of this state, or of any town, city, county, or city and county in this state.

(7) "Owner" means any person, firm, partnership, association, or corporation.

(8) "Peace officer" means every officer authorized to direct or regulate traffic or to make arrests for violations of traffic regulations.

(9) "Person" includes a partnership, company, corporation, or association.

(10) "Public highway" means any public street, thoroughfare, roadway, alley, lane, or bridge in any county or city and county in the state.

(11) "Vehicle identification number" means any identifying number, serial number, engine number, or other distinguishing number or mark, including letters, if any, that is unique to the identity of a given vehicle or component part thereof that was placed on a vehicle or engine by its manufacturer or by authority of the department of revenue pursuant to section 42-12-202 or in accordance with the laws of another state or country.

42-5-102. Stolen motor vehicle parts - buying, selling - removed or altered motor vehicle parts - possession. (1) Any person who buys, sells, exchanges, trades, receives, conceals, or alters the appearance of a motor vehicle or any motor vehicle part, equipment, attachment, accessory, or appurtenance which is the property of another or any person who aids or abets in the commission or attempted commission of any such act, knowing or having reasonable cause to know and believe that such motor vehicle or motor vehicle part, equipment, attachment, accessory, or appurtenance is stolen property, commits a class 5 felony and shall be punished as provided in section 18-1.3-401, C.R.S.

(2) Except as necessary to effect legitimate repairs, any person who intentionally removes, changes, alters, or obliterates the vehicle identification number, manufacturer's number, or engine number of a motor vehicle or motor vehicle part or who possesses a motor vehicle or a motor vehicle part and knows or has reasonable cause to know that it contains such a removed, changed, altered, or obliterated vehicle identification number, manufacturer's number, or engine number commits a class 5 felony and shall be punished as provided in section 18-1.3-401, C.R.S. Any person who commits any of said acts for the purpose of legitimately repairing the motor vehicle shall provide evidence of such legitimate repair to the investigating law enforcement agency. Such evidence shall include, but need not be limited to, prerepair and postrepair photographs of the affected motor vehicle part and vehicle identification number and a signed affidavit describing the required repairs.

42-5-103. Tampering with a motor vehicle. (1) Any person who with criminal intent does any of the following to a motor vehicle or to any part, equipment, attachment, accessory, or appurtenance contained in or forming a part thereof without the knowledge and consent of the owner of such motor vehicle commits tampering with a motor vehicle:

(a) Tightens or loosens any bolt, bracket, wire, screw, or other fastening contained in, contained on, or forming a part of such motor vehicle; or

(b) Shifts or changes the gears or brakes of such motor vehicle; or

(c) Scratches, mars, marks, or otherwise damages such motor vehicle or any part thereof; or

(d) Adds any substance or liquid to the gas tank, carburetor, oil, radiator, or any other part of such motor vehicle; or

(e) Aids, abets, or assists in the commission or attempted commission of any such unlawful act or acts enumerated in this subsection (1).

(2) Tampering with a motor vehicle is:

(a) A class 1 misdemeanor if the damage is less than one thousand dollars;

(b) A class 5 felony if the damage is one thousand dollars or more but less than twenty thousand dollars;

(c) A class 3 felony if the damage is twenty thousand dollars or more or causes bodily injury to a person.

42-5-104. Theft of motor vehicle parts - theft of license plates. (1) Any person who with criminal intent removes, detaches, or takes from a motor vehicle which is the property of another any part, equipment, attachment, accessory, or appurtenance contained therein, contained thereon, or forming a part thereof or any person who aids, abets, or assists in the commission of any such act or acts is guilty of theft of motor vehicle parts.

(2) Theft of motor vehicle parts is:

(a) A class 1 misdemeanor if the value of the thing involved is less than one thousand dollars;

(b) A class 5 felony if the value of the thing involved is one thousand dollars or more but less than twenty thousand dollars;

(c) A class 3 felony if the value of the thing involved is twenty thousand dollars or more.

(3) When a person commits theft of motor vehicle parts two times or more within a period of six months without having been placed in jeopardy for the prior offense or offenses and the aggregate value of the things involved is one thousand dollars or more but less than twenty thousand dollars, it is a class 5 felony; however, if the aggregate value of the things involved is twenty thousand dollars or more, it is a class 4 felony.

(4) Any person who steals a license plate shall be in violation of paragraph (a) of subsection (2) of this section.

42-5-105. Daily record. (1) (a) It is the duty of every dealer, and of the proprietor of every garage, to keep and maintain in such person's place of business an easily accessible and permanent daily record of all secondhand or used motor vehicle equipment, attachments, accessories, and appurtenances bought, sold, traded, exchanged, dealt in, repaired, or received or disposed of in any manner or way by or through the dealer or proprietor. The record may be created, recorded, stored, or reproduced physically or electronically.

(b) The record shall be kept in a good businesslike manner in the form of invoices or in a book by the dealer or proprietor and shall contain the following:

(I) A description of any and all such articles of property of every class or kind sufficient for the ready identification thereof by a peace officer;

(II) The name and address, legibly written, of the owner, vendor, and vendee;

(III) The time and date of such transactions;

(IV) The name, address, and a copy of the identification document of the driver and the owner of a motor vehicle received for any purpose; except that a licensed motor vehicle dealer or used motor vehicle dealer is not required to obtain or retain a copy of an identification document if such dealer complies with article 6 of title 12, C.R.S.;

(V) The model year, make and style, and engine or vehicle identification number and state registration license number of such motor vehicle if registered; and

(VI) The purpose the motor vehicle was received and the disposition made thereof.

(c) The record shall be open and the motor vehicle shall be available at all times during regular business hours to the inspection by the department of revenue or any peace officer and available for use as evidence.

(2) It is the duty of every person offering to a dealer, or to the proprietor of a garage, for any purpose, a motor vehicle or secondhand or used motor vehicle equipment, attachment, accessory, or appurtenance to:

(a) Write or register, as legibly as possible, the full and true name and address of the person and the name and address of the owner in the record kept by such dealer or proprietor of a garage as provided for in this section; and

(b) Present a valid identification document verifiable by federal or state law enforcement. The following documents, without limitation, shall be deemed to comply with this paragraph (b):

(I) An identification document issued by the state of Colorado;

(II) An identification document issued by any other state;

(III) An identification document issued by the United States government;

(IV) A passport issued by the United States government or another jurisdiction.

(3) It is the duty of every driver, upon taking a motor vehicle to any dealer's place of business or to any garage for storage, repair, sale, trade, or any other purpose, to write or register, as legibly as possible, with ink or indelible pencil, the full and true name and address of the driver and the name and address of the owner of such motor vehicle in the record provided for in this section. Such driver shall not be required, however, to so register the same motor vehicle more than once in the same garage in any calendar year when the driver is personally known to the dealer or the proprietor of the garage to be in the rightful and lawful possession of such motor vehicle. Such driver, on request or demand of such dealer or proprietor of a garage, or his or her agent, shall produce for examination the motor vehicle state registration license certificate issued to such driver or to the owner of such motor vehicle.

(4) Any person violating any provision of this section is guilty of a misdemeanor and, upon conviction thereof, shall be punished by a fine of not more than five hundred dollars.

42-5-106. Duties of dealers - assembled motor vehicles. It is the duty of every dealer and of every proprietor of a garage to examine, without charge, the engine or vehicle identification number of every motor vehicle bought, taken in trade, repaired, or stored by them. Such dealer shall not be required to examine the engine or vehicle identification number of the same motor vehicle more than once in the same calendar year when such dealer knows that the person in possession of such motor vehicle is the lawful owner thereof. It is the further duty of the dealer, proprietor of a garage, or his or her agent, promptly and without delay, to report to or notify in person, or by telephone or telegraph, or by special messenger the nearest police station or peace officer if the engine or vehicle identification number of said motor vehicle has been altered, changed, or so obliterated as to make the number indecipherable or if the engine or vehicle identification number or the state registration license number of said motor vehicle does not correspond with the engine or vehicle identification number of the motor vehicle state registration certificate of the driver of said motor vehicle. Any person violating any of the provisions of this section commits a class 1 petty offense and shall be punished as provided in section 18-1.3-503, C.R.S.

42-5-107. Seizure of motor vehicles or component parts by peace officers. All peace officers are authorized to take and hold possession of any motor vehicle or component part if its engine number, vehicle identification number, or manufacturer's serial number has been altered, changed, or obliterated or if such officer has good and sufficient reason to believe that the motor vehicle or component part is not in the rightful possession of the driver or person in charge thereof.

42-5-108. Penalty. Any person violating any of the provisions of this part 1, unless otherwise specifically provided for in this part 1, commits a class 3 misdemeanor and shall be punished as provided in section 18-1.3-501, C.R.S.

42-5-109. Report of stored or parked motor vehicles - when. Whenever any motor vehicle of a type subject to registration in this state has been stored, parked, or left in a garage, a trailer park, or any type of storage or parking lot for a period of over thirty days, the owner of such garage, trailer park, or lot shall report the make, engine number, vehicle identification number, and serial number of such motor vehicle in writing to the Colorado state patrol auto theft section, Denver, Colorado, and the sheriff of the county in which the garage, trailer park, or lot is located. Nothing in this section shall apply where arrangements have been made for continuous storage or parking by the owner of the motor vehicle so parked or stored and where the owner of said motor vehicle so parked or stored is personally known to the owner or operator of such garage, trailer park, or storage or parking lot. Any person who fails to submit the report required under this section at the end of thirty days shall forfeit all claims for storage of such motor vehicles and shall be subject to a fine of not more than twenty-five dollars, and each day's failure to make such a report as required under this section shall constitute a separate offense.

42-5-110. Possession of removed, defaced, altered, or destroyed motor vehicle identification numbers. (1) No person shall knowingly buy, sell, offer for sale, receive, or possess any motor vehicle or component part thereof from which the vehicle identification number or any number placed on said vehicle or component part for its identification by the manufacturer has been removed, defaced, altered, or destroyed unless such vehicle or component part has attached thereto a special identification number assigned or approved by the department in lieu of the manufacturer's number.

(2) Whenever such motor vehicle or component part comes into the custody of a peace officer, it shall be destroyed, sold, or otherwise disposed of under the conditions provided in an order by the court having jurisdiction. No court order providing for disposition shall be issued unless the person from whom the property was seized and all claimants to the property whose interest or title is on the records in the department of revenue are provided a postseizure hearing by the court having jurisdiction within a reasonable period after the seizure. This postseizure hearing shall be held on those motor vehicles or component parts for which true ownership is in doubt, including, but not limited to, those motor vehicles or component parts that are altered to the extent that they cannot be identified, those motor vehicles or component parts that are composed of parts belonging to several different claimants, and those motor vehicles or component parts for which there are two or more existing titles. This subsection (2) shall not apply with respect to such motor vehicle or component part used as evidence in any criminal action or proceeding. Nothing in this section shall, however, preclude the return of such motor vehicle or component part to the owner by the seizing agency following presentation of satisfactory evidence of ownership and, if it is determined to be necessary, upon assignment of an identification number to the vehicle or component part by the department of revenue. There shall be no special identification number issued for a component part unless it is a component part of a complete motor vehicle.

(3) Whenever such motor vehicle or component part comes into the custody of a peace officer, the person from whom the property was seized and all claimants to the property whose interest or title is noted on the records of the department of revenue shall be notified within ninety days of seizure of the seizing agency's intent to commence a postseizure hearing as described in subsection (2) of this section. Such notice shall contain the following information:

(a) The name and address of the person or persons from whom the motor vehicle or component part was seized;

(b) A statement that the motor vehicle or component part has been seized for investigation as provided in this section and that the property will be released upon a determination that the identification number has not been removed, defaced, altered, or destroyed or upon the presentation of satisfactory evidence of the ownership of such motor vehicle or component part if no other person claims an interest in the property within thirty days of the date the notice is mailed; otherwise, a hearing regarding the disposition of such motor vehicle or component part shall take place in the court having jurisdiction;

(c) A statement that the person from whom the property was seized and all claimants to the motor vehicle or component part whose interest or title is on the records in the department of revenue will have notification of the seizing agency's intention to commence a postseizure hearing, and such notice shall be sent to the last-known address by registered mail within ninety days of the date of seizure;

(d) The name and address of the law enforcement agency where the evidence of ownership of such motor vehicle or component part may be presented;

(e) A statement or copy of the text contained in this section.

(4) (a) A hearing on the disposition of the motor vehicle or component part shall be held by the court having jurisdiction within a reasonable time after the seizure. The hearing shall be before the court without a jury.

(b) If the evidence reveals either that the identification number has not been removed, altered, or destroyed or that the identification has been removed, altered, or destroyed but satisfactory evidence of ownership has been presented, then the motor vehicle or component part shall be released to the person entitled thereto. Nothing in this section shall preclude the return of such motor vehicle or component part to a good faith purchaser following the presentation of satisfactory evidence of ownership thereof, and, if necessary, said good faith purchaser may be required to obtain an assigned identification number from the motor vehicle group.

(c) If the evidence reveals that the identification number of the motor vehicle or the component part has been removed, altered, or destroyed and satisfactory evidence of ownership has not been presented, then the property shall be destroyed, sold, or converted to the use of the seizing agency or otherwise disposed of as provided by court order.

(d) At the hearing, the seizing agency shall have the burden of establishing that the identification number of the motor vehicle or the component part has been removed, defaced, altered, or destroyed.

(e) At the hearing, any claimant to the property shall have the burden of providing satisfactory evidence of ownership.

42-5-111. Proof of authorized possession. Whenever any motor vehicle or major component part of a motor vehicle is transported, shipped, towed, or hauled by any means in this state, said vehicle or component part shall be accompanied by proper authorization of possession from the legal owner or a law enforcement agency. Such authorization may include, but need not be limited to, bills of lading, shipment invoices, towing requests, or other specific authorization which readily identifies the rightful owner and conveys said owner's authorization of possession to the person transporting the motor vehicle or component part.

42-5-112. Automobile theft prevention authority - board - creation - duties - rules - fund - repeal. (1) There is hereby created in the department of public safety the automobile theft prevention authority, referred to in this section as the "authority". Under the authority, a law enforcement agency or other qualified applicant may apply for grants to assist in improving and supporting automobile theft prevention programs or programs for the enforcement or prosecution of automobile theft crimes through statewide planning and coordination.

(2) (a) There is hereby created the automobile theft prevention board, referred to in this section as the "board", which shall consist of eleven members as follows:

(I) The executive director of the department of public safety, or the executive director's designee;

(II) The executive director of the department of revenue, or the executive director's designee; and

(III) Nine members appointed by the governor as follows:

(A) Five representatives of insurance companies who are authorized to issue motor vehicle insurance policies pursuant to part 6 of article 4 of title 10, C.R.S.;

(B) Two representatives of law enforcement;

(C) A representative of a statewide association of district attorneys; and

(D) A representative of the public who may also be a representative of a consumer group.

(b) The governor shall appoint members of the board within thirty days after the governor receives notification pursuant to subsection (5) of this section that moneys in the fund exceed the sum of three hundred thousand dollars. The appointed members of the board shall serve terms of six years; except that, of the members first appointed pursuant to sub-subparagraph (A) of subparagraph (III) of paragraph (a) of this subsection (2), the governor shall select one member who shall serve an initial term of four years and one member who shall serve an initial term of two years. Of the members first appointed pursuant to sub-subparagraph (B) of subparagraph (III) of paragraph (a) of this subsection (2), the governor shall select one member who shall serve an initial term of two years. The member first appointed pursuant to sub-subparagraph (C) of subparagraph (III) of paragraph (a) of this subsection (2) shall serve an initial term of four years. No appointed member shall serve more than two consecutive six-year terms.

(b.5) Notwithstanding the provisions of paragraph (b) of this subsection (2), of the two additional members appointed to the board pursuant to Senate Bill 08-060, enacted at the second regular session of the sixty-sixth general assembly, one member shall serve an initial term of four years and one member shall serve an initial term of two years.

(c) The members of the board shall serve without compensation; except that the members of the board shall be reimbursed from moneys in the fund created in subsection (4) of this section for their actual and necessary expenses incurred in the performance of their duties pursuant to this section.

(3) (a) The board shall solicit and review applications for grants pursuant to this section. The board may award grants for one to three years. The board shall give priority to applications representing multijurisdictional programs. Each application, at a minimum, shall describe the type of theft prevention, enforcement, prosecution, or offender rehabilitation program to be implemented. Such programs may include, but need not be limited to:

(I) Multi-agency law enforcement and national insurance crime bureau task force programs using proactive investigative methods to reduce the incidents of motor vehicle theft and related crimes and to increase the apprehension of motor vehicle thieves and persons who attempt to defraud insurance companies in order to:

(A) Direct proactive investigative and enforcement efforts toward the reduction of motor vehicle thefts;

(B) Increase recoveries of stolen motor vehicles, including farm and construction equipment; and

(C) Increase the arrests of perpetrators;

(II) Programs that engage in crime prevention efforts, activities, and public awareness campaigns that are intended to reduce the public's victimization by motor vehicle theft, fraud, and related crimes;

(III) Programs that provide or develop specialized training for motor vehicle theft investigations personnel, including but not limited to law enforcement personnel, county title and registration clerks, division of revenue title clerks, and port-of-entry officials, in order to enhance knowledge, skills, procedures, and systems to detect, prevent, and combat motor vehicle theft and fraud and related crimes;

(IV) Programs to provide for the support and maintenance of one or more dedicated prosecutors who have the specific mission and expertise to provide legal guidance and prosecutorial continuity to complex criminal cases arising from the activities of a multi-agency law enforcement program; and

(V) Programs to prevent future criminal behavior by first time offenders who have been charged, convicted, or adjudicated for motor vehicle theft.

(b) Subject to available moneys, the board shall approve grants pursuant to this section. In selecting grant recipients, the board, to the extent possible, shall ensure that grants are awarded to law enforcement agencies or other qualified applicants in a variety of geographic areas of the state. The board shall not require as a condition of receipt of a grant that an agency, political subdivision, or other qualified applicant provide any additional moneys to operate an automobile theft prevention program or a program for the enforcement or prosecution of automobile theft crimes.

(c) Subject to available moneys, the board may appoint a director for the authority who may employ such staff as may be necessary to operate and administer the authority.

(d) No more than eight percent of the moneys in the fund created pursuant to subsection (4) of this section may be used for operational or administrative expenses of the authority.

(e) The FTE authorization for any staff necessary to support the authority shall be eliminated should sufficient moneys from gifts, grants, or donations no longer be available for the authority.

(f) The executive director of the department of public safety shall promulgate rules for the administration of this section, including but not limited to:

(I) Requirements for an entity other than a law enforcement agency to be a qualified applicant;

(II) Application procedures by which law enforcement agencies or other qualified applicants may apply for grants pursuant to this section;

(III) The criteria for selecting those agencies or other qualified applicants that shall receive grants and the criteria for determining the amount to be granted to the selected agencies or applicants and the duration of the grants; and

(IV) Procedures for reviewing the success of the programs that receive grants pursuant to this section.

(g) On or before December 1, 2006, any law enforcement agency or other qualified applicant that receives a grant pursuant to this section shall submit a report to the board concerning the implementation of the program funded through the grant.

(h) On or before February 1, 2007, the board shall report to the judiciary committees of the senate and the house of representatives on the implementation of the programs receiving grants pursuant to this section and the authority. The report shall include but need not be limited to:

(I) The number and geographic jurisdiction of law enforcement agencies or other qualified applicants that received grants under the authority and the amount and duration of the grants;

(II) The effect that the programs that received grants had on the number of automobile thefts in areas of the state; and

(III) Recommendations for legislative changes to assist in the prevention, enforcement, and prosecution of automobile-theft-related criminal activities.

(4) (a) The department of public safety is authorized to accept gifts, grants, or donations from private or public sources for the purposes of this section. All private and public funds received through gifts, grants, or donations shall be transmitted to the state treasurer, who shall credit the same to the Colorado auto theft prevention cash fund, which fund is hereby created and referred to in this section as the "fund". The fund shall also include the moneys deposited in the fund pursuant to section 10-4-617, C.R.S. The moneys in the fund shall be subject to annual appropriation by the general assembly for the direct and indirect costs associated with the implementation of this section. Any moneys in the fund not expended for the purpose of this section may be invested by the state treasurer as provided in section 24-36-113, C.R.S. All interest and income derived from the investment and deposit of moneys in the fund shall be credited to the fund. Any unexpended and unencumbered moneys remaining in the fund at the end of any fiscal year shall remain in the fund and shall not be credited or transferred to the general fund or any other fund.

(b) It is the intent of the general assembly that the department of public safety not be required to solicit gifts, grants, or donations from any source for the purposes of this section and that no general fund moneys be used to pay for grants awarded pursuant to this section or for any expenses of the authority.

(5) (a) The state treasurer shall notify the governor and the executive directors of the departments of public safety and revenue the first time that the moneys in the fund reach or exceed the sum of three hundred thousand dollars.

(b) If by June 1, 2008, moneys in the fund have never reached or exceeded three hundred thousand dollars, the state treasurer shall return from the fund to the grantee or donee the amount of all gifts, grants, or donations. If gifts, grants, and donations are returned pursuant to this paragraph (b), on July 1, 2008, the treasurer shall transfer to the general fund any interest or income earned on moneys in the fund.

(6) (a) This section is repealed, effective September 1, 2018.
(b) Prior to said repeal, the authority created pursuant to subsection (1) of this section and the board created pursuant to subsection (2) of this section shall be reviewed as provided for in section 24-34-104, C.R.S.

42-5-113. Colorado auto theft prevention cash fund - audit. Beginning in the 2008-09 fiscal year, and every two years thereafter, the state auditor shall cause an audit to be made of the Colorado auto theft prevention cash fund created in section 42-5-112 (4) to include procedures to test distributions from the fund for compliance with program requirements and guidelines. The auditor shall review a sample of distributions and expenditures from the Colorado auto theft prevention cash fund for the purposes described in section 42-5-112. The state auditor shall prepare a report of each audit conducted and file the report with the audit committee of the general assembly. Following the release of the audit report, the state auditor shall file the audit report with the judiciary committees of the house of representatives and the senate, or any successor committees.

PART 2

VEHICLE IDENTIFICATION NUMBER INSPECTION

42-5-201. Definitions. As used in this part 2, unless the context otherwise requires:
(1) "Bonded title vehicle" means a vehicle the owner of which has posted a bond for title pursuant to the provisions of section 42-6-115.
(2) "Commercial vehicle" means any trailer as defined in section 42-1-102 (105), truck as defined in section 42-1-102 (108), or truck tractor as defined in section 42-1-102 (109).
(3) (Deleted by amendment, L. 2000, p. 1647, § 36, effective June 1, 2000.)
(4) "Homemade vehicle" means a vehicle which is constructed by a manufacturer not licensed by the state of Colorado and which is not recognizable as a commercially manufactured vehicle.
(5) "Inspector" means a duly constituted peace officer of a law enforcement agency or other individual who has been certified pursuant to section 42-5-206 to inspect vehicle identification numbers.
(6) "Law enforcement agency" means the Colorado state patrol or the agency of a local government authorized to enforce the laws of the state of Colorado.
(7) "Local government" means a town, a city, a county, or a city and county.
(8) "Rebuilt vehicle" means a vehicle which has been assembled from parts of two or more commercially manufactured vehicles or which has been altered in such a manner that it is not readily recognizable as a commercially manufactured vehicle of a given year. "Rebuilt vehicle" includes a street rod vehicle.
(9) "Reconstructed vehicle" means a vehicle constructed from two or more commercially manufactured vehicles of the same type and year which has not been altered and which is recognizable as a commercially manufactured vehicle of a given year.
(10) "State" includes the territories and the federal districts of the United States.
(11) "Street rod vehicle" means a vehicle with a body design manufactured in 1948 or earlier or with a reproduction component that resembles a 1948 or earlier model which has been modified for safe road use, including, but not limited to, modifications of the drive train, suspension, and brake systems, modifications to the body through the use of materials such as steel or fiber glass, and other safety or comfort features.
(12) "Vehicle" means a motor vehicle subject to the certificate of title provisions of part 1 of article 6 of this title but does not include commercial vehicles as defined in subsection (2) of this section.
(13) "Vehicle identification number" means any identifying number, serial number, engine number, or other distinguishing number or mark, including letters, if any, that is unique to the identity of a given vehicle or commercial vehicle or component part thereof that was placed on a vehicle, commercial vehicle, or engine by its manufacturer or by authority of the department of revenue under section 42-12-202 or in accordance with the laws of another state or country.

42-5-202. Vehicle identification number inspection. (1) No bonded title vehicle, homemade vehicle, rebuilt vehicle, reconstructed vehicle, or vehicle assembled from a kit shall be sold in the state of Colorado or issued a Colorado certificate of title unless the seller or owner of such vehicle has had its vehicle identification number inspected and recorded by an inspector on the inspection form approved by the department of revenue.
(2) No bonded title commercial vehicle, homemade commercial vehicle, rebuilt commercial vehicle, reconstructed commercial vehicle, or commercial vehicle assembled from a kit shall be issued a Colorado certificate of title unless an inspector inspects the vehicle identification number and records the number on the inspection form approved by the department of revenue.
(2.5) The department is authorized to perform a vehicle identification number inspection on any motor vehicle subject to this article that the department determines is necessary or convenient in carrying out its duties pursuant to this article and to charge and receive an inspection fee pursuant to section 42-5-204 for such inspection.
(3) The inspections required by this section include a physical inspection of the vehicle or commercial vehicle and a computer check of the

state and national compilations of wanted and stolen vehicles or commercial vehicles. If the inspector determines that the vehicle identification number has not been removed, changed, altered, or obliterated and that it is not the identification number of a wanted or stolen vehicle or commercial vehicle, the inspection form shall be transmitted to the executive director of the department of revenue, who shall then act upon the application for a Colorado certificate of title for such vehicle or commercial vehicle.

(4) If the inspector determines that the vehicle identification number has been removed, changed, altered, or obliterated or if the inspector has good and sufficient reason to believe that the vehicle or commercial vehicle is wanted or was stolen in the state of Colorado or another state, the inspector shall proceed according to the provisions of part 1 of this article.

42-5-203. Inspections - street rod vehicles. (Repealed)

42-5-204. Inspection fees - vehicle number inspection funds. (1) (a) A fee of twenty dollars shall be charged for each inspection performed pursuant to this part 2. Upon payment of the fee, the owner of the vehicle or commercial vehicle inspected shall be issued a receipt as evidence of payment.

(b) Notwithstanding the amount specified for the fee in paragraph (a) of this subsection (1), the executive director of the department of revenue by rule or as otherwise provided by law may reduce the amount of the fee if necessary pursuant to section 24-75-402 (3), C.R.S., to reduce the uncommitted reserves of the fund to which all or any portion of the fee is credited. After the uncommitted reserves of the fund are sufficiently reduced, the executive director of the department of revenue by rule or as otherwise provided by law may increase the amount of the fee as provided in section 24-75-402 (4), C.R.S.

(2) (a) All inspection fees collected by the Colorado state patrol shall be transmitted to the state treasurer, who shall credit the same to the vehicle identification number inspection fund, which fund is hereby created. The moneys in the fund shall be subject to annual appropriation by the general assembly for the administration and enforcement of this article, including the direct and indirect costs of the Colorado state patrol in performing inspections pursuant to this part 2. The moneys in the fund shall not be transferred or credited to the general fund or to any other fund; except that, at the end of each fiscal year, any unexpended and unencumbered moneys remaining in the fund shall be credited to the general fund.

(b) All inspection fees collected by a law enforcement agency of a local government shall be credited to a special fund in the office of the treasurer of the local government. Such fund shall be separate and apart from the general fund of the local government and shall be made available for use by the law enforcement agency for the administration and enforcement of this part 2, including the training and certification of inspectors; except that the governing body of the local government, acting by resolution or ordinance, may order that the inspection fees be paid into the general fund of the local government.

42-5-205. Assignment of a special vehicle identification number by the department of revenue. (Repealed)

42-5-206. Certification of inspectors. (1) Except as otherwise provided in subsection (2) of this section, no peace officer shall be an inspector of vehicle identification numbers unless the peace officer has been certified by the peace officers standards and training board pursuant to section 24-31-303 (1) (e), C.R.S. In order to be certified, the peace officer must satisfactorily complete a vehicle identification number inspection training course approved by said board and pay a certification fee to the board not to exceed twenty-five dollars. The cost of the training course shall include all necessary and actual expenses but shall not exceed fifty dollars per peace officer.

(2) In lieu of the requirement for certification in subsection (1) of this section, any peace officer shall be certified as an inspector of vehicle identification numbers if the peace officer is able to demonstrate to the peace officers standards and training board that the peace officer has had sixteen hours or more of vehicle identification number inspection training which is acceptable to the board and which was received between January 1, 1986, and January 1, 1988.

(3) The sheriff of any county and the police chief of any municipality may certify individuals in addition to peace officers to serve as inspectors in accordance with the provisions of this part 2. Such individuals shall be employees or bona fide representatives of a county or municipality and shall satisfactorily complete fingerprint and background checks. Such individuals must satisfactorily complete a vehicle identification number inspection training course approved by the peace officers standards and training board and pay a fee to the board for the cost of the certification not to exceed twenty-five dollars. The cost of the training course shall include all necessary and actual expenses but shall not exceed fifty dollars per individual.

42-5-207. Rules. The executive director of the department of revenue may adopt rules necessary to implement this part 2.

CERTIFICATES OF TITLE

ARTICLE 6

Certificates of Title - Used Motor Vehicle Sales

PART 1
CERTIFICATES OF TITLE

42-6-101.	Short title.
42-6-102.	Definitions.
42-6-103.	Application.
42-6-104.	Administration.
42-6-105.	Authorized agents.
42-6-106.	Certificates of registration - plates.
42-6-107.	Certificates of title - contents.
42-6-108.	Identification number - title - street rod vehicles. (Repealed)
42-6-108.5.	Rebuilder's certificate of title. (Repealed)
42-6-109.	Sale or transfer of vehicle.
42-6-110.	Certificate of title - transfer.
42-6-111.	Sale to dealers - certificate need not issue.
42-6-112.	Initial registration of a motor vehicle - dealer responsibility to timely forward certificate of title to purchaser or holder of a chattel mortgage.
42-6-113.	New vehicles - bill of sale - certificate of title.
42-6-114.	Transfers by bequest, descent, law.
42-6-115.	Furnishing bond for certificates.
42-6-116.	Applications for filing of certificates of title.
42-6-117.	Filing of certificate.
42-6-118.	Amended certificate.
42-6-119.	Certificates for vehicles registered in other states.
42-6-120.	Security interests upon motor vehicles.
42-6-121.	Filing of mortgage.
42-6-122.	Disposition of mortgages by agent.
42-6-123.	Disposition after mortgaging.
42-6-124.	Disposition of certificates of title.
42-6-125.	Release of mortgages.
42-6-126.	New certificate upon release of mortgage - rules.
42-6-127.	Duration of lien of mortgage - extensions.
42-6-128.	Validity of mortgage between parties.
42-6-129.	Second or other junior mortgages.
42-6-130.	Priority of secured interests.
42-6-131.	Mechanics', warehouse, and other liens.
42-6-132.	Existing mortgages not affected. (Repealed)
42-6-133.	Foreign mortgages and liens.
42-6-134.	Where application for certificates of title made.
42-6-135.	Lost certificates of title.
42-6-136.	Surrender and cancellation of certificate - penalty for violation.
42-6-137.	Fees.
42-6-138.	Disposition of fees.
42-6-139.	Registration - where made.
42-6-140.	Registration upon becoming resident.
42-6-141.	Director's records to be public.
42-6-142.	Penalties.
42-6-143.	Altering or using altered certificate.
42-6-144.	False oath.
42-6-145.	Use of vehicle identification numbers in applications - rules.
42-6-146.	Repossession of motor vehicle - owner must notify law enforcement agency - penalty.
42-6-147.	Central registry - rules.

PART 2
USED MOTOR VEHICLE SALES

42-6-201.	Definitions.
42-6-202.	Prohibited acts.
42-6-203.	Penalty.
42-6-204.	Private civil action.
42-6-205.	Consumer protection.
42-6-206.	Disclosure requirements upon transfer of ownership of a salvage vehicle.

PART 1
CERTIFICATES OF TITLE

42-6-101. Short title. This part 1 shall be known and may be cited as the "Certificate of Title Act".

42-6-102. Definitions. As used in this part 1, unless the context otherwise requires:

(1) "Authorized agents" means the county clerk and recorder in each of the counties of the state, including the city and county of Broomfield, and the manager of revenue or such other official of the city and county of Denver as may be appointed by the mayor to perform functions related to the registration of motor vehicles.

(2) "Dealer" means any person, firm, partnership, corporation, or association licensed under the laws of this state to engage in the business of buying, selling, exchanging, or otherwise trading in motor vehicles.

(3) "Department" means the department of revenue.

(4) "Director" means the executive director of the department of revenue.

(5) (a) "Electronic record" means a record generated, created, communicated, received, sent, or stored by electronic means.

(b) A record covered by this article may not be denied legal effect, validity, or enforceability solely because it is in the form of an electronic record. Except as otherwise provided in this article, if a rule of law requires a record to be in writing or provides consequences if it is not, an electronic record satisfies that rule of law.

(6) "File" means the creation of or addition to an electronic record maintained for a certificate of title by the director or an authorized agent of the director, as defined in section 42-6-105.

(6.5) "Kit vehicle" means a passenger-type motor vehicle assembled, by other than a licensed manufacturer, from a manufactured kit that includes a prefabricated body and chassis and is accompanied by a manufacturer's statement of origin.

(7) "Lien" means a security interest in a motor vehicle under article 9 of title 4, C.R.S., and this article.

(8) "Manufacturer" means a person, firm, partnership, corporation, or association engaged in the manufacture of new motor vehicles, trailers, or semitrailers.

(9) "Mortgage" or "chattel mortgage" means a security agreement as defined in section 4-9-102 (76), C.R.S.

(10) "Motor vehicle" means any self-propelled vehicle that is designed primarily for travel on the public highways and is generally and commonly used to transport persons and property over the public highways, including trailers, semitrailers, and trailer coaches, without motive power. "Motor vehicle" does not include the following:

(a) A low-power scooter, as defined in section 42-1-102;

(b) A vehicle that operates only upon rails or tracks laid in place on the ground or that travels through the air or that derives its motive power from overhead electric lines;

(c) A farm tractor, farm trailer, and any other machines and tools used in the production, harvesting, and care of farm products; or

(d) Special mobile machinery or industrial machinery not designed primarily for highway transportation.

(11) "New vehicle" means a motor vehicle being transferred for the first time from a manufacturer or importer, or dealer or agent of a manufacturer or importer, to the end user or customer. A motor vehicle that has been used by a dealer for the purpose of demonstration to prospective customers shall be considered a "new vehicle" unless such demonstration use has been for more than one thousand five hundred miles. Motor vehicles having a gross vehicle weight rating of sixteen thousand pounds or more shall be exempt from this definition.

(12) "Owner" means a person or firm in whose name the title to a motor vehicle is registered.

(13) "Person" means natural persons, associations of persons, firms, limited liability companies, partnerships, or corporations.

(14) "Record" means information that is inscribed on a tangible medium or that is stored in an electronic or other medium and is retrievable in a perceivable form.

(15) "Roadworthy" means a condition in which a motor vehicle has sufficient power and is fit to operate on the roads and highways of this state after visual inspection by appropriate law enforcement authorities. In order to be roadworthy, such vehicle, in accord with its design and use, shall have all major parts and systems permanently attached and functioning and shall not be repaired in such a manner as to make the vehicle unsafe. For purposes of this subsection (15), "major parts and systems" shall include, but not be limited to, the body of a motor vehicle with related component parts, engine, transmission, tires, wheels, seats, exhaust, brakes, and all other equipment required by Colorado law for the particular vehicle.

(15.5) (a) "Rolling chassis" means that:

(I) For a motorcycle, the motorcycle has a frame, a motor, front forks, a transmission, and wheels;

(II) For a motor vehicle that is not a motorcycle, the motor vehicle has a frame, a body, a suspension, an axle, a steering mechanism, and wheels.

(b) Nothing in this subsection (15.5) shall be construed to require any listed parts to be operable, in working order, or roadworthy.

(16) "Salvage certificate of title" means a document issued under the authority of the director to indicate ownership of a salvage vehicle.

(17) (a) "Salvage vehicle" means a vehicle that is damaged by collision, fire, flood, accident, trespass, or other occurrence, excluding hail damage, to the extent that the cost of repairing the vehicle to a roadworthy condition and for legal operation on the highways exceeds the vehicle's retail fair market value immediately prior to such damage, as determined by the person who owns the vehicle at the time of such occurrence or by the insurer or other person acting on behalf of such owner.

(b) In assessing whether a vehicle is a "salvage vehicle" under this section, the retail fair market value shall be determined by reference to sources generally accepted within the insurance industry including price guide books, dealer quotations, computerized valuation services, newspaper advertisements, and certified appraisals, taking into account the condition of the vehicle prior to the damage. When assessing the repairs, the assessor shall consider the actual retail cost of the needed parts and the reasonable and customary labor rates for needed labor.

(c) This subsection (17) shall not apply to a vehicle whose model year of manufacture is six years or older at the time of damage.

(18) "Signature" means either a written signature or an electronic signature.

(19) "State" includes the territories and the federal districts of the United States.

(20) "Street rod vehicle" means a vehicle manufactured in 1948 or earlier with a body design that has been modified for safe road use, including, but not limited to, modifications of the drive train, suspension, and brake systems, modifications to the body through the use of materials such as steel or fiberglass, and modifications to any other safety or comfort features.

(21) "Transfer by inheritance" means the transfer of ownership after the death of an owner by means of a will, a written statement, a list as described in section 15-11-513, C.R.S., or upon lawful descent and distribution upon the death intestate of the owner of the vehicle.

(22) "Used vehicle" means a motor vehicle that has been sold, bargained, exchanged, or given away, or has had the title transferred from the person who first took title from the manufacturer or importer, dealer, or agent of the manufacturer or importer, or has been so used as to have become what is commonly known as a secondhand motor vehicle. A motor vehicle that has been used by a dealer for the purpose of demonstration to prospective customers shall be considered a "used vehicle" if such demonstration use has been for more than one thousand five hundred miles.

(23) "Vehicle" means any motor vehicle as defined in subsection (10) of this section.

42-6-103. Application. The provisions of this part 1 shall apply to motor vehicles as defined in section 42-6-102.

42-6-104. Administration. The director is charged with the duty of administering this part 1. For that purpose the director is vested with the power to make such reasonable rules and require the use of such forms and procedures as are reasonably necessary for the efficient administration of this part 1.

42-6-105. Authorized agents. The county clerk and recorder in each of the counties of the state, including the city and county of Broomfield, and the manager of revenue or such other official of the city and county of Denver as may be appointed by the mayor to perform functions related to the registration of motor vehicles is designated to be the authorized agent of the director and, under the direction of the director, is charged with the administration of this part 1 and the rules that may be adopted for the administration of this part 1 in the county where the authorized agent holds office.

42-6-106. Certificates of registration - plates. (1) No certificate of registration or license plates shall be issued for a motor vehicle by the director or an authorized agent except in the following cases:

(a) The applicant exhibits to the director or the authorized agent, or the director or the authorized agent has on file, an official Colorado certificate of title for such vehicle in which it appears that the applicant is the owner of the vehicle sought to be registered and licensed.

(b) The applicant submits satisfactory evidence to the director or the authorized agent that an official Colorado certificate of title to such motor vehicle has been issued or is on file or from which it otherwise appears that the applicant is the owner of the vehicle sought to be registered and licensed. Any evidence submitted to the director or the authorized agent may be maintained in a paper or electronic version.

(c) The applicant applies for an official certificate of title for such motor vehicle pursuant to section 42-6-116.

(d) A member of the armed forces of the United States has purchased a vehicle in a foreign country and registered such vehicle in accordance with the directives of the department of defense of the United States government and is unable to supply proof of ownership in the form customarily required by this state and evidence of ownership is supplied by submitting an executed document prescribed by the secretary of defense concerning the vehicle and authenticated by an officer of the armed forces who has authority to administer oaths under 10 U.S.C. sec. 936.

(e) (I) The vehicle is a commercial vehicle that is registered as part of a fleet based in Colorado and is leased from the owner of such vehicle;

(II) The owner of the commercial vehicle is not a resident of Colorado; and

(III) The applicant applies for apportioned registration pursuant to article 3 of this title and provides the following to the director or authorized agent:

(A) A copy of a current registration or a copy of a current title for such vehicle from a foreign jurisdiction; and

(B) A copy of a lease agreement between the owner and the applicant.

42-6-107. Certificates of title - contents. (1) (a) All certificates of title to motor vehicles issued under this part 1 shall be mailed to the applicant, except as provided in section 42-6-124, and information appearing and concerning the issuance thereof shall be retained by the director and appropriately indexed and filed in the director's office. Such certificates may be electronic records pursuant to rules adopted by the director and, in addition to other information that the director may by rule require, shall contain the make and model of the motor vehicle for which the certificate is issued or the record is created, where such information is available, together with the motor and any serial number of the vehicle, and a description of such other marks or symbols as may be placed upon the vehicle by the vehicle manufacturer for identification purposes. The year that is listed on the certificate of title of a kit vehicle shall be the year of manufacture of the kit from which the vehicle was assembled, as indicated in the manufacturer's statement of origin.

(b) The department may require those vehicle-related entities specified by regulation to verify information concerning a vehicle through the physical inspection of such vehicle. The information required to be verified by such a physical inspection shall include the vehicle identification number or numbers, the make of vehicle, the vehicle model, the type of vehicle, the year of manufacture of such vehicle, the type of fuel used by such vehicle, the odometer reading of such vehicle, and such other information as may be required by the department. For the purposes of this paragraph (b), "vehicle-related entity" means an authorized agent or designated employee of such agent, a Colorado law enforcement officer, a licensed Colorado dealer, a licensed inspection and readjustment station, or a licensed diesel inspection station.

(2) The electronic record of the certificate or the paper version of the certificate shall contain a description of every lien to which the motor vehicle is subject, as appears in the application for the certificate of title or as is noted and shown to be unreleased upon a certificate of title issued after August 1, 1949, for such vehicle, including the date of such lien, the original amount secured by the vehicle, the named lienee, and the county in which the lien appears of record if it is of public record. The certificates and electronic records shall be numbered consecutively by counties, beginning with number one. The certificate of title filed with the authorized agent shall be prima facie evidence of the contents of the record and that the person in whose name the certificate is registered is the lawful owner of the vehicle. Except as provided in section 42-6-118, said certificate shall be effective after filing until the vehicle described in the record is sold or ownership is otherwise transferred.

42-6-108. Identification number - title - street rod vehicles. (Repealed)

42-6-108.5. Rebuilder's certificate of title. (Repealed)

42-6-109. Sale or transfer of vehicle. (1) Except as provided in section 42-6-113, no person shall sell or otherwise transfer a motor vehicle to a purchaser or transferee without delivering to such purchaser or transferee a certificate of title, which may be electronic, to such vehicle duly transferred in the manner prescribed in section 42-6-110. No purchaser or transferee shall acquire any right, title, or interest in and to a motor vehicle purchased by such purchaser or transferee unless and until he or she obtains from the transferor the certificate of title duly transferred in accordance with this part 1. A lienholder may request either a paper or electronic version of a certificate of title.

(2) A paper copy of a certificate of title shall be necessary for any transaction in which:

(a) Either party to the transaction is located outside Colorado; or

(b) The purchaser pays for a motor vehicle entirely with cash.

42-6-110. Certificate of title - transfer. (1) Upon the sale or transfer of a motor vehicle for which a certificate of title has been issued or filed, the person in whose name the certificate of title is registered, if such person is other than a dealer, shall execute a formal transfer of the vehicle described in the certificate. Such transfer shall be affirmed by a statement signed by the person in whose name the certificate of title is registered or by such person's authorized agent or attorney and shall contain or be accompanied by a written declaration that it is made under the penalties of perjury in the second degree, as defined in section 18-8-503, C.R.S. The purchaser or transferee, within sixty days thereafter, shall present such certificate, together with an application for a new certificate of title, to the director or one of the authorized agents, accompanied by the fee required in section 42-6-137 to be paid for the filing of a new certificate of title; except that, if no title can be found and the motor vehicle is not roadworthy, the purchaser or transferee may wait until twenty-four months after the motor vehicle was purchased to apply for a certificate of title.

(2) A person who violates subsection (1) of this section is guilty of a misdemeanor and, upon conviction, shall be punished by a fine of not less than ten dollars nor more than five hundred dollars, or by imprisonment in the county jail for not less than ten days nor more than six months, or by both such fine and imprisonment.

42-6-111. Sale to dealers - certificate need not issue. (1) Upon the sale or transfer to a dealer of a motor vehicle for which a Colorado certificate of title has been issued, the certificate of title to the motor vehicle shall be transferred and filed; except that, so long as the vehicle remains in the dealer's possession and at the dealer's place of business for sale and for no other purpose, such dealer shall not be required to procure or file a new certificate of title as is otherwise required in this part 1.

(2) If a motor vehicle dealer wishes to obtain a new certificate of title to a motor vehicle, such dealer may present the old certificate of title to the director with the fee imposed by section 42-6-137 (6), whereupon, the director shall issue a new certificate of title to such dealer within one working day after application. This subsection (2) shall not apply to a motor vehicle subject to a lien.

(3) (a) A wholesale motor vehicle auction dealer who does not buy, sell, or own the motor vehicles transferred at auction shall disclose the identity of the wholesale motor vehicle auction dealer, the date of the auction, and the license number of the auction on a form and in a manner prescribed by the executive director. A wholesale motor vehicle auction dealer does not become an owner by reason of such disclosure nor as a result solely of the guarantee of title, guarantee of payment, or reservation of a security interest.

(b) A wholesale motor vehicle auction dealer may buy or sell motor vehicles at wholesale in such dealer's own name and, in such instances, shall comply with the provisions of this part 1 applicable to dealers, including licensing.

42-6-112. Initial registration of a motor vehicle - dealer responsibility to timely forward certificate of title to purchaser or holder of a chattel mortgage. In order to facilitate initial registration of a vehicle, a dealer of motor vehicles shall have not more than thirty days after the date of sale of such vehicle to deliver or facilitate the delivery of the certificate of title to a purchaser or the holder of a chattel mortgage on such motor vehicle, subject to section 42-6-109.

42-6-113. New vehicles - bill of sale - certificate of title. Upon the sale or transfer by a dealer of a new motor vehicle, such dealer shall, upon delivery, make, execute, and deliver to the purchaser or transferee a sufficient bill of sale and the manufacturer's certificate of origin. The bill of sale shall be affirmed by a statement signed by such dealer, shall contain or be accompanied by a written declaration that it is made under the penalties of perjury in the second degree, as defined in section 18-8-503, C.R.S., shall be in such form as the director may require, and shall contain, in addition to other information that the director may by rule require, the make and model of the motor vehicle so sold or transferred, the identification number placed upon the vehicle by the manufacturer for identification purposes, the manufacturer's suggested retail price, and the date of the sale or transfer, together with a description of any mortgage or lien on the vehicle that secures any part of the purchase price. Upon presentation of such a bill of sale to the director or an authorized agent, a new certificate of title for the vehicle described in the bill of sale shall be filed. A new motor vehicle that is used by a dealer for demonstration shall be transferred in accordance with this section.

42-6-114. Transfers by bequest, descent, law. Upon the transfer of ownership of a motor vehicle by inheritance or by operation of law, as in proceedings in bankruptcy, insolvency, replevin, attachment, execution, or other judicial sale, or whenever such vehicle is sold to satisfy storage or repair charges or repossessed to satisfy a secured debt, the director or the authorized agent may issue, upon the surrender of any available certificate of title and presentation of such proof of ownership as the director may reasonably require or a court order, a new certificate of title on behalf of the new owner, and disposition shall be made as in other cases.

42-6-115. Furnishing bond for certificates. (1) If the applicant for a certificate of title to a motor vehicle is unable to provide the director or the authorized agent with a certificate of title duly transferred to such applicant, a bill of sale, or other evidence of ownership that satisfies the director that the applicant owns the vehicle, a certificate of title for such vehicle may be filed by the director or the authorized agent upon the applicant furnishing the director or the authorized agent with a statement, in such form as required by the director. The statement shall contain a recital of the facts and circumstances by which the applicant acquired the ownership and possession of such vehicle, the source of the title to the vehicle, and such other information as the director may require to determine whether any liens are attached to such motor vehicle, the date of the liens, the amount secured by the vehicle, where such liens are of public record, and the right of the applicant to have a certificate of title filed on behalf of the applicant. The statement shall contain or be accompanied by a written declaration that it is made under the penalties of perjury in the second degree, as defined in section 18-8-503, C.R.S., and shall accompany the application for the certificate as required in section 42-6-116. Any evidence submitted to and maintained by the director or the authorized agent may be maintained in a paper or electronic version.

(2) If the director or the authorized agent finds that the applicant is the same person to whom a certificate of title for the vehicle has previously been issued or filed and to whom a license was issued for the year during which the application for such certificate of title is made and that a certificate of title should be filed on behalf of the applicant, such certificate may be filed and disposition of such certificate shall be made as in other cases.

(3) (a) Except as provided by paragraph (b) of this subsection (3) or section 42-12-402, the department or an authorized agent shall not file a certificate of title under this section until the applicant furnishes evidence of a savings account, deposit, or certificate of deposit meeting the requirements of section 11-35-101, C.R.S., or a good and sufficient bond with a corporate surety, to the state, in an amount to be fixed by the director, not less than twice the reasonable value of the vehicle determined as of the time of application. The applicant and the applicant's surety shall hold harmless any person who suffers loss or damage by reason of the filing of a certificate under this section.

(b) If the vehicle for which the certificate is filed is twenty-five years old or older, the applicant has had a certified vehicle identification number inspection performed on the vehicle, and the applicant presents a notarized bill of sale within twenty-four months after the sale with the title application, then the applicant need not furnish surety under this subsection (3). To be excepted from the surety requirement, an applicant shall submit an affidavit to the department that is sworn to under penalty of perjury that states that the required documents submitted are true and correct.

(4) If any person suffers loss or damage by reason of the filing of the certificate of title as provided in this section, such person shall have a right of action against the applicant and the surety on the applicant's bond against either of whom the person damaged may proceed independently of the other.

42-6-116. Applications for filing of certificates of title. If a person who desires or who is entitled to a filing of a certificate of title to a motor vehicle is required to apply to the director or the authorized agent, such applicant shall apply upon a form provided by the director in which appears a description of the motor vehicle including the make and model, the manufacturer's number, and a description of any other distinguishing mark, number, or symbol placed on said vehicle by the vehicle manufacturer for identification purposes, as may be required by the director by rule adopted in accordance with article 4 of title 24, C.R.S. The application shall also show the name and correct address of the owner determined pursuant to section 42-6-139, a class A, class B, class C, class D, or class F vehicle owner's personal identification number as provided on a state-issued driver's license or assigned by the department, and the applicant's source of title and shall include a description of all known mortgages and liens upon the motor vehicle, the holder of the lien, the amount originally secured, and the name of the county and state in which such mortgage or lien is recorded or filed. Such application shall be verified by a statement signed by the applicant and shall contain or be accompanied by a written declaration that it is made under the penalties of perjury in the second degree, as defined in section 18-8-503, C.R.S.

42-6-117. Filing of certificate. (1) The director or the authorized agent shall use reasonable diligence to ascertain whether the facts stated in an application and other documents submitted to the director or the authorized agent are true. In appropriate cases, the director or authorized agent may require the applicant to furnish additional information regarding ownership of the vehicle and the right to file on behalf of the applicant a certificate of title for the vehicle. The director or the authorized agent may refuse to file a certificate of title to such vehicle if the director or the authorized agent determines that the applicant is not entitled to such certificate.

(2) No certificate of title may be filed for a vehicle required to have its vehicle identification number inspected pursuant to section 42-5-202 unless a vehicle identification number inspection form has been transmitted to the director or the authorized agent showing the number recorded from the vehicle or the number assigned to the vehicle under section 42-12-202.

(3) At the request of the title owner, lienholder, or mortgagee, a paper copy of a filed certificate of title may be issued by the director or the authorized agent.

42-6-118. Amended certificate. If the owner of a motor vehicle for which a Colorado certificate of title has been issued or filed replaces any part of the motor vehicle on which appears the identification number or symbol described in the certificate of title and such identification number or symbol no longer appears on the motor vehicle, or incorporates the part containing the identification number or symbol into another motor vehicle, such owner shall immediately apply to the director or an authorized agent for an assigned identification number and an amended filing of a certificate of title to such vehicle.

42-6-119. Certificates for vehicles registered in other states. (1) When a resident of the state acquires the ownership of a motor vehicle for which a certificate of title has been issued by a state other than Colorado, the person acquiring such vehicle shall apply to the director or an authorized agent for the filing of a certificate of title as in other cases.

(2) If a dealer acquires the ownership of a motor vehicle by lawful means and the motor vehicle is titled under the laws of a state other than Colorado, such dealer shall not be required to file a Colorado certificate of title for the vehicle so long as such vehicle remains in the dealer's possession and at the dealer's place of business solely for the purpose of sale.

(3) Upon the sale by a dealer of a motor vehicle, the certificate of title to which was issued in a state other than Colorado, the dealer shall, within thirty days after the date of sale, deliver or facilitate the delivery to the purchaser such certificate of title from a state other than Colorado duly and properly endorsed or assigned to the purchaser with a statement by the dealer that shall contain or be accompanied by a written declaration that it is made under the penalties of perjury in the second degree, as defined in section 18-8-503, C.R.S., and that shall set forth the following:

(a) That such dealer has warranted and, by the execution of such affidavit, does warrant to the purchaser and all persons who shall claim through the purchaser named that, at the time of the sale, transfer, and delivery by the dealer, the vehicle described was free and clear of all liens and mortgages except as might therein appear;

(b) That the vehicle is not a stolen vehicle; and

(c) That such dealer had good, sure, and adequate title to, and full right and authority to sell and transfer, the vehicle.

(4) If the purchaser of the vehicle completes and includes the vehicle identification number inspection form as part of the application for filing of a Colorado certificate of title to such vehicle and accompanies the application with the affidavit required by subsection (3) of this section and the duly endorsed or assigned certificate of title from a state other than Colorado, a Colorado certificate of title may be filed in the same manner as upon the sale or transfer of a motor vehicle for which a Colorado certificate of title has been issued or filed. Upon the filing by the director or the authorized agent of such certificate of title, the director or the authorized agent may dispose of such certificate of title and shall record such certificate of title as provided in section 42-6-124.

42-6-120. Security interests upon motor vehicles. (1) Except as provided in this section and section 42-6-130, the provisions of the "Uniform Commercial Code", title 4, C.R.S., relating to the filing, recording, releasing, renewal, priority, and extension of chattel mortgages, as the term is defined in section 42-6-102 (9), shall not apply to motor vehicles. Any mortgage or refinancing of a mortgage intended by the parties to the mortgage or refinancing to encumber or create a lien on a motor vehicle, or to be perfected as a valid lien against the rights of third persons, purchasers for value without notice, mortgagees, or creditors of the owner, shall be filed for public record. The fact of filing shall be noted on the owner's certificate of title or bill of sale substantially in the manner provided in section 42-6-121.

(2) The provisions of this section and section 42-6-121 shall not apply to any mortgage or security interest upon any vehicle or motor vehicle held for sale or lease which constitutes inventory as defined in section 4-9-102, C.R.S. As to such mortgages or security interests, the provisions of article 9 of title 4, C.R.S., shall apply, and perfection of such mortgages or security interests shall be made pursuant thereto, and the rights of the parties shall be governed and determined thereby.

(3) Notwithstanding any provision of law to the contrary, in the case of motor vehicles or trailers, a lease transaction does not create a sale or security interest solely because it permits or requires the rental price to be adjusted either upward or downward under the agreement by reference to the amount realized upon sale or other disposition of the motor vehicle or trailer.

(4) The rights of a buyer, lessee, or lien creditor that arise after a mortgage attaches to a motor vehicle and before perfection under this article shall be determined by section 4-9-317, C.R.S.

42-6-121. Filing of mortgage. (1) The holder of a chattel mortgage on a motor vehicle desiring to secure the rights provided for in this part 1 and to have the existence of the mortgage and the fact of the filing of the mortgage for public record noted in the filing of the certificate of title to the encumbered motor vehicle shall present the signed original or signed duplicate of the mortgage or copy thereof certified by the holder of the mortgage or the holder's agent to be a true copy of the signed original mortgage and the certificate of title or application for certificate of title to the motor vehicle encumbered to the authorized agent of the director in the county or city and county in which the mortgagor of such motor vehicle resides or where the property is located. The filings may be made either with paper documents or electronically. The mortgage or refinancing of a loan secured by a mortgage shall state the name and address of the debtor; the name and address of the mortgagee or name of the mortgagee's assignee; the make, vehicle identification number, and year of manufacture of the mortgaged vehicle; and the date and amount of the loan secured by the mortgage.

(2) Upon the receipt of the electronic, original, or duplicate mortgage or certified copy thereof and certificate of title or application for certificate of title, the authorized agent, if satisfied that the vehicle described in the mortgage is the same as that described in the certificate of title or filed title, shall file within the director's authorized agent's motor vehicle database notice of such mortgage or lien in which shall appear the day on which the mortgage was received for filing, the name and address of the mortgagee named and the name and address of the holder of such mortgage, if such person is other than the mortgagee named, the amount secured by the vehicle, the date of the mortgage, the day and year on which the mortgage was filed for public record, and such other information regarding the filing of the mortgage in the office of the director's authorized agent as may be required by the director by rule. The director's authorized agent shall electronically transmit, when the director's authorized agent uses an electronic filing system, the certificate of title, application for certificate of title, and mortgage information to the database of the director for maintenance of a central registry of motor vehicle title information pursuant to section 42-6-147.

(3) A mortgage is deemed to be a signed original or a signed duplicate if the signature appearing on a certificate of title or application for certificate of title was affixed personally by the mortgagor or the mortgagor's attorney-in-fact, in ink, in carbon, or by any other means.

(4) For purposes of liens created pursuant to section 14-10-122 (1.5), C.R.S., the lien shall contain the information set forth in this section as well as any additional information required in section 14-10-122 (1.5) (f), C.R.S.

(5) The lien or mortgage shall be perfected pursuant to section 42-6-120 on the date all documents required by subsection (1) of this section, including, without limitation, the signed original or signed duplicate of the mortgage or a copy containing the information required by subsection (1) of this section, are received by the authorized agent and payment is tendered on the fee imposed by section 42-6-137 (2).

42-6-122. Disposition of mortgages by agent. (1) The authorized agent, upon receipt of the mortgage, shall file the mortgage in the agent's office. Such mortgage shall be appropriately indexed and cross-indexed:

(a) Under one or more of the following headings in accordance with the rules adopted by the director:

(I) Make or vehicle identification number of motor vehicles mortgaged;

(II) Names of owners of mortgaged motor vehicles as the same appear on the certificates of title thereto;

(III) The numbers of the certificates of title for motor vehicles mortgaged;

(IV) The numbers or other identification marks assigned to registration certificates issued upon the licensing of mortgaged vehicles;

(b) Under the name of the mortgagee, the holder of such mortgage, or the owner of such vehicle; or

(c) Under such other system as the director may devise and determine to be necessary for the efficient administration of this part 1.

(2) All records of mortgages affecting motor vehicles shall be public and may be inspected and copies thereof made, as is provided by law respecting public records affecting real property.

42-6-123. Disposition after mortgaging. After a mortgage on a motor vehicle has been filed in the authorized agent's office, the authorized agent shall mail or electronically transfer to the director the certificate of title or bill of sale which the authorized agent has filed in the record. Upon the receipt thereof, the director shall maintain completed electronic records transferred by the authorized agent. The director shall issue a new certificate of title containing, in addition to the other matters and things required to be set forth in certificates of title, a description of the mortgage and all information respecting said mortgage and the filing thereof as may appear in the certificate of the authorized agent, and the director or the director's authorized agent shall thereafter dispose of said new certificate of title containing said notation as provided in section 42-6-124.

42-6-124. Disposition of certificates of title. (1) All certificates of title issued by the director or the director's authorized agent shall be disposed of by the director in the following manner:

(a) If the certificate of title that is filed by the director's authorized agent is maintained in an electronic format within the director's and the director's authorized agent's motor vehicle databases as required by the standards established pursuant to article 71.3 of title 24, C.R.S., the certificate of title shall be disposed of in accordance with paragraphs (b) and (c) of this subsection (1).

(b) If it appears from the records in the director's or the director's authorized agent's office and from an examination of the certificate of title that the motor vehicle therein described is not subject to a mortgage filed subsequent to August 1, 1949, or if such vehicle is encumbered by a mortgage filed in any county of a state other than the state of Colorado, the certificate of title shall be delivered to the person who therein appears to be the owner of the vehicle described, or such certificate shall be mailed to the owner thereof at his or her address as the same may appear in the application, the certificate of title, or other records in the director's or the director's authorized agent's office.

(c) If it appears from the records in the office of the director or the director's authorized agent and from the certificate of title that the motor vehicle therein described is subject to one or more mortgages filed subsequent to August 1, 1949, the director or the director's authorized agent shall electronically maintain or deliver the certificate of title issued by the director to the mortgagee named therein or the holder thereof whose mortgage was first filed in the office of an authorized agent.

42-6-125. Release of mortgages. (1) Upon the payment or discharge of the undertaking secured by any mortgage on a motor vehicle that has been filed for record in the manner prescribed in section 42-6-121, the legal holder, on a form approved by the director, shall make and execute the notice of the discharge of the obligation and release of the mortgage securing the obligation and set forth in the notice the facts concerning the right of the holder to release the mortgage as the director by appropriate rule may require, which satisfaction and release shall be affirmed by a statement signed by the legal lienholder noted in the certificate of title on file with the director or the director's authorized agent and that shall contain or be accompanied by a written declaration that it is made under the penalties of perjury in the second degree, as defined in section 18-8-503, C.R.S. Thereupon, the holder of the mortgage so released shall dispose of the certificate of title as follows:

(a) If it appears that the motor vehicle is encumbered by a mortgage filed in the manner prescribed in section 42-6-121 subsequent to the date on which the mortgage so released was filed for record, the holder of such certificate of title shall deliver the title to the person shown to be the holder of the mortgage noted on the title, filed earliest after the filing of the mortgage released, or to the person or agent of the person shown to be the assignee or other legal holder of the mortgage or shall mail the title to the mortgagee or holder at his or her address. If the certificate is returned unclaimed, it shall be sent by mail to the director.

(b) If it appears from an examination of the certificate of title that there are no other outstanding mortgages against the motor vehicle in the title, upon the release of the mortgage as provided in this section, the holder of the mortgage shall deliver the certificate of title to the owner of the vehicle or shall mail the title to the owner at his or her address, and, if for any reason the certificate of title is not delivered to the owner of the vehicle or is returned unclaimed, it shall immediately be mailed to the director.

(c) The director's authorized agent shall note in the electronic record of the lien such satisfaction or release of such lien or mortgage and shall file such satisfaction or release of such lien as required in section 42-6-122.

(2) (a) (I) Except when a lienholder can show extenuating circumstances, within fifteen calendar days after a lien or mortgage on a motor

vehicle is paid and satisfied, a lienholder shall release the lien or mortgage as required by subsection (1) of this section.

(II) As used in this subsection (2), "extenuating circumstances" means a situation where access to the title is impaired, making good faith compliance with this subsection (2) impossible within the time frame required by this paragraph (a). "Extenuating circumstances" does not include intentional or negligent acts by a lienholder that result in delay beyond the time frame required in this subsection (2).

(b) Any person aggrieved by a violation of this subsection (2) may bring a civil action in a court of competent jurisdiction to bring about compliance with this subsection (2) and for any damages arising from the violation.

42-6-126. New certificate upon release of mortgage - rules. (1) (a) Upon the satisfaction of the debt and release of a mortgage on a motor vehicle filed for record in the manner prescribed in section 42-6-121:

(I) The owner of the vehicle encumbered by the mortgage, the purchaser from or transferee of the owner as appears on the certificate of title, or the holder of any mortgage that was junior to the mortgage released, upon the receipt of the certificate of title, as provided in section 42-6-125, shall deliver the title to the authorized agent who shall transmit the title to the director; or

(II) The lienholder shall notify the authorized agent of the satisfaction of the debt and release of the mortgage, setting forth any facts concerning the right of the holder to release the mortgage as the director may require. The satisfaction and release shall be affirmed by a statement signed by the lienholder noted in the certificate of title and shall contain or be accompanied by a written declaration that it is made under the penalties of perjury in the second degree, as defined in section 18-8-503, C.R.S. Upon receiving a valid satisfaction and release, the director or authorized agent shall note the release of the lien and shall issue a certificate of title for the motor vehicle, omitting all reference to the mortgage.

(b) Upon the receipt by the director of a statement of mortgage release, the director shall:

(I) Note on the records in the director's office to show the release of the lien of the mortgage;

(II) Issue a new certificate of title to the motor vehicle, omitting all reference to the released mortgage; and

(III) Dispose of the new certificate of title in the manner prescribed in other cases unless directed otherwise.

(2) For certificates of title that are maintained in an electronic format, any release of lien, mortgage, or encumbrance shall be filed prior to the issuance of a new certificate of title. In the event the holder of the lien, mortgage, or other encumbrance has filed bankruptcy or is no longer in business, the person seeking issuance of a new certificate of title reflecting the release of the lien, mortgage, or other encumbrance, which has been maintained electronically, shall either post a bond with the director in a reasonable amount determined by the director or shall wait until the period of the lien, mortgage, or other encumbrance expires.

42-6-127. Duration of lien of mortgage - extensions. (1) The lien of a mortgage or refinancing of a mortgage filed in the manner prescribed in section 42-6-121 or 42-6-129 shall remain valid and enforceable for a period of ten years after the filing of the certificate in the office of the director's authorized agent or until the discharge of the mortgage on the vehicle, if the discharge occurs sooner, except in the case of trailer coaches; truck tractors; multipurpose trailers, if known when filed; and motor homes, that are subject to the provisions of subsection (3) of this section. During the ten-year period or any extension of such period, the lien of the mortgage may be extended for successive three-year periods upon the holder of the mortgage presenting to the director's authorized agent of the county where the mortgage is filed or in the county where the owner resides a certification of extension of chattel mortgage, subscribed by the holder of the mortgage and acknowledged by the holder before an officer authorized to acknowledge deeds to real property, in which shall appear a description of the mortgage on the vehicle, to what extent it has been discharged or remains unperformed, and such other information respecting the mortgage as may be required by appropriate rule of the director to enable the director's authorized agent to properly record the extension.

(2) Upon receipt of a mortgage extension, the director's authorized agent shall make and complete the electronic record of the extension as the director by rule may require within the director's or the director's authorized agent's motor vehicle database, and shall note the fact of the extension of the mortgage on the certificate of title, which may be filed electronically. Thereafter the certificate of title shall be returned to the person shown on the certificate to be entitled to the certificate. If any mortgage other than one on a trailer coach; truck tractor; multipurpose trailer, if known when filed; or motor home, that has been filed for record and noted on the certificate of title, has not been released or extended within ten years after the date on which the mortgage was filed in the office of the director's authorized agent, the person shown by the records in the director's office to be the owner of the motor vehicle described in the certificate of title, upon making an appropriate application therefor, may request that any references to the mortgages shown on the records of the director's authorized agent be removed by the authorized agent. The director's authorized agent shall

remove all reference to mortgages shown in the director's authorized agent's records to have been of record in the office of the authorized agent for more than ten years, which mortgages have been neither released nor extended as provided in this section.

(3) The duration of the lien of any mortgage on a trailer coach, as defined in section 42-1-102 (106) (a), a truck tractor, as defined in section 42-1-102 (109), a multipurpose trailer, as defined in section 42-1-102 (60.3), or a motor home, as defined in section 42-1-102 (57), shall be for the full term of the mortgage, but the lien of the mortgage may be extended beyond the original term of the mortgage for successive three-year periods by following the procedure prescribed in subsection (1) of this section during the term of the mortgage or any extension thereof.

42-6-128. Validity of mortgage between parties. Nothing in this part 1 shall be construed to impair the validity of a mortgage on a motor vehicle between the parties thereto as long as no purchaser for value, mortgagee, or creditor without actual notice of the existence thereof has acquired an interest in the motor vehicle described therein, notwithstanding that the parties to said mortgage have failed to comply with the provisions of this part 1.

42-6-129. Second or other junior mortgages. (1) On and after July 1, 1977, any person who takes a second or other junior mortgage on a motor vehicle for which a Colorado certificate of title has been issued or filed may file said mortgage for public record and have the existence thereof noted or filed on the certificate of title with like effect as in other cases, in the manner prescribed in this section.

(2) Such second or junior mortgagee or the holder thereof shall file said mortgage pursuant to the requirements of section 42-6-121 with the director's authorized agent of the county wherein the mortgagor of said motor vehicle resides or where the motor vehicle is located and shall accompany said mortgage with a written request to have the existence thereof noted or filed on the certificate of title records of the director's authorized agent pertaining to the motor vehicle covered by the junior or second mortgage. Upon the filing of such mortgage, the director's authorized agent shall note in the record of the subject vehicle the day and hour on which such mortgage was received by the agent and shall make and deliver a receipt for the mortgage to the person filing the mortgage, and shall file the second or junior mortgage as required under section 42-6-122.

(3) The director's authorized agent, by registered mail, return receipt requested, shall make a written demand on the holder of the certificate of title, addressed to such person at the person's address as the same may appear in said written request, that such certificate be delivered to the authorized agent for the purpose of having noted on the certificate such second or junior mortgage. Within fifteen days after the receipt of such demand, the person holding such certificate shall either mail or deliver the same to such director's authorized agent or, if the person no longer has possession of the certificate, shall so notify the agent and, if the person knows, shall likewise inform the agent where and from whom such certificate may be procured. Upon the receipt of such certificate, the director's authorized agent shall complete an application for a new title and record the number thereof on the mortgage, as in the case of a first mortgage, and shall, as in the case of a first mortgage, issue and file a new certificate of title on which record the existence of all mortgages on the motor vehicle, including such second or junior mortgage, have been noted.

(4) If any person lawfully in possession of a certificate of title to any motor vehicle upon whom demand is made for the delivery thereof to the authorized agent omits, for any reason whatsoever, to deliver or mail the same to the authorized agent, such person shall be liable to the holder of such second or junior mortgage for all damage sustained by reason of such omission.

42-6-130. Priority of secured interests. The liens or mortgages filed for record or noted on a certificate of title to a motor vehicle, as provided in section 42-6-121, shall take priority in the same order that they were filed in the office of the authorized agent; except that the priority of a purchase-money security interest, as defined in section 4-9-103, C.R.S., shall be determined in accordance with sections 4-9-317 (e) and 4-9-324 (a), C.R.S.

42-6-131. Mechanics', warehouse, and other liens. Nothing in this part 1 shall be construed to impair the rights of lien claimants arising under any mechanics' lien law or the lien of a warehouse or other person claimed for repairs on or storage of any motor vehicle, when a mechanic's lien or storage lien originated prior to a mortgage or lien on the motor vehicle being filed for record and such motor vehicle has remained continuously in the possession of the person claiming such mechanic's lien or lien for storage.

42-6-132. Existing mortgages not affected. (Repealed)

42-6-133. Foreign mortgages and liens. No mortgage or lien on a motor vehicle filed for record in a state other than Colorado shall be valid and enforceable against the rights of subsequent purchasers for value, creditors, lienholders, or mortgagees having no actual notice of the existence of such mortgage or lien. If the certificate of title for such vehicle bears any notation adequate to apprise a purchaser, creditor, lienholder, or mortgagee of the existence of a mortgage or lien at the time a third party acquires a right in the motor vehicle, such mortgage or lien and the rights of the holder of the mortgage or lien shall be enforceable in this state as though such mortgage were filed in Colorado and noted on the certificate of title or noted in the record of the authorized agent pertaining to that vehicle pursuant to section 42-6-121.

42-6-134. Where application for certificates of title made. Except as otherwise provided in this part 1, all applications for recording of certificates of title upon the sale or transfer of a motor vehicle described in the certificate of title shall be directed to and filed with the authorized agent of the county where such vehicle will be registered and licensed for operation.

42-6-135. Lost certificates of title. (1) If data is lost transmitting an application for a certificate of title and accompanying documentation, which may be transmitted by the authorized agent to the director and upon an appropriate application of the owner or other person entitled to such certificate of title, such certificate of title may be reissued or recorded bearing such notations respecting existing unreleased mortgages or liens on the vehicle as indicated by the director's or authorized agent's records. Such certificate of title shall be issued without charge.

(2) If the title owner, lienholder, or mortgagee of a certificate of title loses, misplaces, or accidentally destroys a certificate of title to a motor vehicle that such person holds as described in the certificate of title, upon application, the director or the authorized agent may issue a duplicate copy of the recorded certificate of title as in other cases.

(3) (a) Upon the issuance of a copy of the recorded certificate of title as provided for in this section, the director or the authorized agent shall note on the copy every mortgage shown to be unreleased and the lien that is in effect as disclosed by the records of the director or authorized agent and shall dispose of such certificate as in other cases.

(b) Upon the payment or discharge of the debt secured by a mortgage on a motor vehicle that has been filed for record in the manner prescribed in section 42-6-121, the lienholder shall notify the authorized agent of the satisfaction and release of the mortgage, setting forth any facts concerning the right of the holder to release the mortgage as the director may require. The satisfaction and release shall be affirmed by a statement signed by the lienholder noted in the certificate of title and shall contain or be accompanied by a written declaration that it is made under the penalties of perjury in the second degree, as defined in section 18-8-503, C.R.S. Upon receiving a valid satisfaction and release, the director or authorized agent shall note the release of the lien and shall issue a certificate of title for the motor vehicle, omitting all reference to the mortgage.

42-6-136. Surrender and cancellation of certificate - penalty for violation. (1) The owner of a motor vehicle for which a Colorado certificate of title has been issued, upon the destruction or dismantling of said motor vehicle, upon its being changed so that it is no longer a motor vehicle, or upon its being sold or otherwise disposed of as salvage, shall surrender the certificate of title to the motor vehicle to the director or the authorized agent to be canceled or notify the director or the authorized agent on director-approved forms indicating the loss, destruction or dismantling, or sale for salvage. Upon the owner's procuring the consent of the holders of any unreleased mortgages or liens noted on or recorded as part of the certificate of title, such certificate shall be canceled. A person who violates this section commits a class 1 petty offense and shall be punished as provided in section 18-1.3-503, C.R.S.

(2) Upon the sale or transfer of a motor vehicle for which a current Colorado certificate of title has been issued or filed and that has become a salvage vehicle, as defined in section 42-6-102 (17), the purchaser or transferee shall apply for a salvage certificate of title. The owner of such a motor vehicle may apply for a salvage certificate of title before the sale or transfer of such vehicle. An owner applying for a salvage certificate of title shall provide the director evidence of ownership that satisfies the director of the right of the applicant to have a salvage certificate of title filed in favor of the owner.

(3) (a) An owner of a salvage motor vehicle that has been made roadworthy who applies for a certificate of title as provided in section 42-6-116 shall include such information regarding the vehicle as the director may require by rule. The owner shall provide to the director evidence of ownership that satisfies the director that the applicant is entitled to filing of a certificate of title. The director or the authorized agent shall designate in a conspicuous place in the record for a vehicle that it is a salvage vehicle that has been made roadworthy. Such designation shall include the words "REBUILT FROM SALVAGE" and shall become a permanent part of the certificate of title for such vehicle and shall appear on all subsequent certificates of title for such vehicle.

(b) (I) An owner of a salvage motor vehicle that has been made roadworthy who applies for a certificate of title as provided in section 42-6-116 shall include a certified VIN inspection, DR2704, performed by a law enforcement officer certified as a VIN inspector.

(II) Prior to the inspection, the applicant shall stamp into the motor vehicle the words "REBUILT FROM SALVAGE" with each letter being not less than one-fourth inch in size. Such words shall be a salvage brand and be stamped in the following locations:

(A) In a motorcycle, on the frame in a visible location;

(B) In a class A manufactured motor home, on the main entrance door jamb;

(C) In a trailer, adjacent to the public vehicle identification number;

(D) In all other motor vehicles, on the body post to which the driver's door latches, also known as the driver's door B pillar.

(III) The law enforcement officer shall not complete the inspection required by this paragraph (b) unless the salvage brand complies with this paragraph (b).

(c) (I) Except as provided in subparagraph (II) of this paragraph (c), a person commits a class 1 misdemeanor and, upon conviction, shall be punished as provided in section 18-1.3-501, C.R.S., if such person:

(A) Intentionally removes or alters a salvage brand; or

(B) Possesses a motor vehicle without retitling the vehicle with a salvage brand for forty-five days after learning that the motor vehicle's salvage brand may have been removed or altered.

(II) A person may remove or alter a salvage brand if necessary to legitimately repair a motor vehicle. Such person shall provide evidence of such repair to the investigating law enforcement authority, including pre-repair and post-repair photographs of the affected motor vehicle part and the salvage brand and a signed affidavit describing the repairs. Upon repair, or subsequent repair, the vehicle shall be restamped.

42-6-137. Fees. (1) (a) Upon filing with the authorized agent an application for a certificate of title, the applicant shall pay to the agent a fee of seven dollars and twenty cents, which shall be in addition to the fees for the registration of such motor vehicle.

(b) Repealed.

(2) Upon the receipt by an authorized agent of a mortgage for filing under section 42-6-121, 42-6-125, or 42-6-129, the authorized agent shall be paid such fees as are imposed by law for the filing of like instruments in the office of the county clerk and recorder in the county where such mortgage is filed and shall also receive a fee of seven dollars and twenty cents for the issuance or recording of the certificate of title and the notation in the record of the director or the authorized agent of the existence of the mortgage.

(3) Upon application to the authorized agent to have noted or recorded on a certificate of title the extension of a mortgage described in the certificate of title and noted or recorded on the certificate, such authorized agent shall receive a fee of one dollar and fifty cents.

(4) Upon the release and satisfaction of a mortgage and upon application to the authorized agent for the notation on the certificate of title pursuant to section 42-6-125, such authorized agent shall be paid a fee of seven dollars and twenty cents.

(5) For the issuance of a copy of a recorded certificate of title, except as may be otherwise provided in this part 1, the authorized agent shall be paid a fee of eight dollars and twenty cents. If the department assigns a new identifying number to any motor vehicle, the fee charged for such assignment shall be three dollars and fifty cents.

(6) Upon filing with the director an application for a certificate of title, a motor vehicle dealer who applies to receive a certificate of title within one working day after application shall pay to such director a fee of twenty-five dollars.

(7) An authorized agent shall, if possible, provide the following recording of titles on the same day as the date of request by an applicant:

(a) A title issued pursuant to a transfer of a motor vehicle currently titled in Colorado;

(b) A title issued for a new motor vehicle upon filing of a manufacturer's statement of origin without liens; and

(c) Any other title issued or recorded by the director or the authorized agent. The director and authorized agents shall take into account the best service for citizens in the most cost-effective manner, the use of electronic issuance of titles, and consideration of the business plan for issuing titles at county offices.

(8) Notwithstanding the amount specified for any fee in this section, the director by rule or as otherwise provided by law may reduce the amount of one or more of the fees if necessary pursuant to section 24-75-402 (3), C.R.S., to reduce the uncommitted reserves of the fund to which all or any portion of one or more of the fees is credited. After the uncommitted reserves of the fund are sufficiently reduced, the director by rule or as otherwise provided by law may increase the amount of one or more of the fees as provided in section 24-75-402 (4), C.R.S.

42-6-138. Disposition of fees. (1) (a) All fees received by the authorized agent under section 42-6-137 (1) (a), (2), or (4) or 38-29-138 (1) (a), (2), or (4), C.R.S., upon application for a certificate of title, shall be disposed of as follows: Four dollars shall be retained by the authorized agent and disposition made as provided by law; three dollars and twenty cents shall be credited to the special purpose account established by section 42-1-211.

(b) Repealed.

(2) All fees collected by the authorized agent under section 42-6-137 (5) or 38-29-138 (5), C.R.S., shall be disposed of as follows:

(a) For a copy of a recorded certificate of title, six dollars and fifty cents shall be retained by the authorized agent and disposition made as provided by law; and one dollar and seventy cents shall be credited to the special purpose account established by section 42-1-211; and

(b) For assignment of a new identifying number to a motor vehicle or manufactured home, two dollars and fifty cents shall be retained by the authorized agent and disposition made as provided by law; and one dollar shall be credited to the special purpose account established by section 42-1-211. All fees collected by the department under the provisions of section 42-6-137 (1) (a), (4), or (5) or 38-29-138 (1) (a),

(4), or (5), C.R.S., shall be credited to such special purpose account.

(3) All fees paid to the authorized agent under section 42-6-137 (3) for the extension of a mortgage or lien on a motor vehicle filed in the authorized agent's office shall be retained by the authorized agent to defray the cost of such extension or release and shall be disposed of by the authorized agent as provided by law; except that fees for this service that are paid to the authorized agent in the city and county of Denver shall, by such agent, be disposed of in the same manner as fees retained by the agent that were paid upon application being made for a certificate of title.

(4) The fee paid by a motor vehicle dealer to the director pursuant to section 42-6-137 (6) for a certificate of title issued within one working day of application shall be credited to the special purpose account established by section 42-1-211 (2).

42-6-139. Registration - where made. (1) For purposes of this section, a person's residence shall be the person's principal or primary home or place of abode, to be determined in the same manner as residency for voter registration purposes as provided in sections 1-2-102 and 31-10-201, C.R.S.; except that "voter registration" shall be substituted for "motor vehicle registration" as a circumstance to be taken into account in determining such principal or primary home or place of abode.

(2) Except as may be otherwise provided by rule of the director, it is unlawful for any person who is a resident of the state to register, to obtain a license for, or to procure a certificate of title to, a motor vehicle at any address other than:

(a) For a motor vehicle that is owned by a business and operated primarily for business purposes, the address where such vehicle is principally operated and maintained; or

(b) For any motor vehicle for which the provisions of paragraph (a) of this subsection (2) do not apply, the address of the owner's residence; except that, if a motor vehicle is permanently maintained at an address other than the address of the owner's residence, such motor vehicle shall be registered at the address where such motor vehicle is permanently maintained.

(3) A person who knowingly violates any of the provisions of subsection (2) of this section, section 42-3-103 (4) (a), or section 42-6-140 or any rule of the director promulgated pursuant to this part 1 is guilty of a misdemeanor and, upon conviction, shall be punished by a fine of one thousand dollars.

(4) In addition to any other applicable penalty, a person who registers a motor vehicle in violation of the provisions of subsection (2) of this section, section 42-3-103 (4) (a), or section 42-6-140 shall be subject to a civil penalty of five hundred dollars. Such violation shall be determined by, assessed by, and paid to the municipality or county where the motor vehicle is or should have been registered, subject to judicial review pursuant to rule 106 (a) (4) of the Colorado rules of civil procedure.

(5) A person subject to the penalties imposed by this section continues to be liable for unpaid registration fees, specific ownership taxes, or other taxes and fees concerning the registration of a vehicle owed by such person.

42-6-140. Registration upon becoming resident. Within ninety days after becoming a resident of Colorado, the owner of a motor vehicle shall apply for a Colorado certificate of title, a license, and registration for the vehicle that is registered, that is licensed, or for which a certificate of title is issued in another state. Any person who violates the provisions of this section is subject to the penalties provided in sections 42-6-139 and 43-4-804 (1) (d), C.R.S.

42-6-141. Director's records to be public. All records in the director's office pertaining to the title to a motor vehicle shall be public records and shall be subject to the provisions of section 42-1-206. This shall include any records regarding ownership of and mortgages or liens on a vehicle for which a Colorado certificate of title has been issued.

42-6-142. Penalties. (1) No person may sell, transfer, or in any manner dispose of a motor vehicle in this state without complying with this part 1.

(2) A person who violates subsection (1) of this section for which no other penalty is expressly provided is guilty of a misdemeanor and, upon conviction, shall be punished by a fine of not less than one hundred dollars nor more than five hundred dollars, or by imprisonment in the county jail for not less than ten days nor more than six months, or by both such fine and imprisonment.

42-6-143. Altering or using altered certificate. A person who causes to be altered or forged a certificate of title issued by the director pursuant to this part 1, or a written transfer of a title, or any other notation placed on the title by the director or under the director's authority concerning a mortgage or lien or who uses or attempts to use any such certificate to transfer the vehicle, knowing it to be altered or forged, commits a class 6 felony and shall be punished as provided in section 18-1.3-401, C.R.S.

42-6-144. False oath. A person who applies for a certificate of title, written transfer of a title, satisfaction and release, oath, affirmation, affidavit, statement, report, or deposition required to be made or taken under any of the provisions of this article, and who, upon such application, transfer, satisfaction and release, oath, affirmation, affidavit, statement, report, or deposition, swears or affirms willfully and falsely in a matter material to any issue, point, or subject matter in question, in addition to any other penalties provided in this article, is guilty of perjury in the second degree, as defined in section 18-8-503, C.R.S.

42-6-145. Use of vehicle identification numbers in applications - rules. (1) A person required to apply for a certificate of title or registration of a motor vehicle shall use the identification number placed upon the motor vehicle by the manufacturer or the special vehicle identification number assigned to the motor vehicle by the department pursuant to section 42-12-202. The certificate of title and registration card issued by the department shall use the identification number of the motor vehicle.

(2) The identification number provided for in this section shall be accepted in lieu of any motor number or serial number provided for in this title.

(3) (a) After receiving an application for a certificate of title, the department or its authorized agent shall electronically verify with the department of public safety that the motor vehicle has not been reported stolen. The department shall not register a motor vehicle reported stolen in the system until the vehicle is recovered by the owner.

(b) The department shall promulgate rules setting forth procedures to notify the local law enforcement agency upon discovery that a person is attempting to obtain a certificate of title for a stolen motor vehicle.

(c) This subsection (3) is effective July 1, 2009.

42-6-146. Repossession of motor vehicle - owner must notify law enforcement agency - penalty. (1) If a mortgagee, lienholder, or the mortgagee's or lienholder's assignee or the agent of either repossesses a motor vehicle because of default in the terms of a secured debt, the repossessor shall notify, either verbally or in writing, a law enforcement agency, as provided in this section, of the fact of such repossession, the name of the owner, the name of the repossessor, and the name of the mortgagee, lienholder, or assignee. Such notification shall be made at least one hour before or no later than one hour after the repossession occurs. If such repossession takes place in an incorporated city or town, the repossessor shall notify the police department, town marshal, or other local law enforcement agency of such city or town. If such repossession takes place in the unincorporated area of a county, the repossessor shall notify the county sheriff.

(2) A repossessor who violates subsection (1) of this section is guilty of a class 2 misdemeanor and, upon conviction, shall be punished as provided in section 18-1.3-501, C.R.S.

(3) If a motor vehicle being repossessed is subject to the "Uniform Commercial Code - Secured Transactions", article 9 of title 4, C.R.S., the repossession shall be governed by the provisions of section 4-9-629, C.R.S.

(4) As used in this section, the term "repossessor" means the party who physically takes possession of the motor vehicle and drives, tows, or transports the motor vehicle for delivery to the mortgagee, lienholder, or assignee or the agent of such mortgagee, lienholder, or assignee.

42-6-147. Central registry - rules. (1) The director shall maintain a central registry of electronic files for all certificates of title, mortgages, liens, releases of liens or mortgages, and extensions. The authorized agents shall transmit all electronic filing information to the director for maintenance of the registry. The director shall promulgate rules:

(a) To determine when an electronic signature is acceptable for the purposes of filing certificate of title documents; and

(b) As may be necessary for the administration of electronic filing of certificates of title and all related documents.

(2) The director shall develop a plan to implement electronic filing on a statewide basis. The director shall encourage participation by the counties in an electronic filing system. The director shall begin the implementation of the electronic filing system no later than July 1, 2001, and shall complete the statewide implementation of electronic filing no later than July 1, 2006. The director may grant an exclusion from participation in the electronic filing system upon application by an individual county that demonstrates reasonable cause why electronic filing would be burdensome to the county.

PART 2

USED MOTOR VEHICLE SALES

42-6-201. Definitions. As used in this part 2, unless the context otherwise requires:

(1) "Owner" means the person who holds the legal title of a motor vehicle, but, in the event a motor vehicle is the subject of an agreement for the conditional sale or lease thereof, with the right to purchase upon the performance of the conditions stated in the agreement and with an immediate right to possession vested in the conditional vendee or lessee, or in the event a mortgagor of a vehicle is entitled to possession, then such conditional vendee, lessee, or mortgagor shall be deemed the owner.

(2) "Person" means an individual, firm, association, corporation, or partnership.

(3) "Private sale" means a sale or transfer of a used motor vehicle between two persons neither of whom is a used motor vehicle dealer.

(4) "Retail used motor vehicle sale" means a sale or transfer of a used motor vehicle from a used motor vehicle dealer to a person other than a used motor vehicle dealer.

(5) "Sale" means that the buyer of the used motor vehicle has paid the purchase price or, in lieu thereof, has signed a purchase contract or security agreement and has taken physical possession or delivery of the used motor vehicle.

(6) "Sale between used motor vehicle dealers" means a sale or transfer of a used motor vehicle from one used motor vehicle dealer to another.

(7) "Sale from an owner other than a used motor vehicle dealer to a used motor vehicle dealer" means any sale, trade-in, or other transfer of a used motor vehicle from a person other than a used motor vehicle dealer to a used motor vehicle dealer.

(8) "Used motor vehicle" means every self-propelled motor vehicle having a gross weight of less than sixteen thousand pounds that has been sold, bargained for, exchanged, given away, leased, loaned, or driven as a "company executive car" or the title to which has been transferred from the person who first acquired it from the manufacturer or importer and it is so used as to have become what is commonly known as "secondhand" within the ordinary meaning thereof. A previously untitled motor vehicle that has been driven by the dealer for more than one thousand five hundred miles, excluding mileage incurred in the transit of the motor vehicle from the manufacturer to the dealer or from another dealer to the dealer, shall be considered a "used motor vehicle". This shall not apply to any automobile manufactured before January 1, 1942.

(9) "Used motor vehicle dealer" means any licensed motor vehicle dealer, used motor vehicle dealer, or wholesaler as defined by the introductory portions to section 12-6-102 (13) and (17) and section 12-6-102 (18), C.R.S.

42-6-202. Prohibited acts. (1) It is unlawful for any person to advertise for sale, to sell, to use, or to install or to have installed any device which causes an odometer to register any mileage other than the true mileage driven. For purposes of this section, the true mileage driven is that mileage driven by the vehicle as registered by the odometer within the manufacturer's designed tolerance.

(2) It is unlawful for any person or the person's agent to disconnect, reset, or alter the odometer of any motor vehicle with the intent to change the number of miles indicated thereon.

(3) It is unlawful for any person, with the intent to defraud, to operate a motor vehicle on any street or highway knowing that the odometer of such vehicle is disconnected or nonfunctional.

(4) Nothing in this part 2 shall prevent the service, repair, or replacement of an odometer, if the mileage indicated thereon remains the same as before the service, repair, or replacement. When the odometer is incapable of registering the same mileage as before such service, repair, or replacement, the odometer shall be adjusted to read zero, and a notice in writing shall be attached to the left door frame of the vehicle by the owner or the owner's agent specifying the mileage prior to repair or replacement of the odometer and the date on which it was repaired or replaced. Any removal or alteration of such notice so affixed is unlawful.

(5) It is unlawful for any transferor to fail to comply with 49 U.S.C. sec. 32705 and any rule concerning odometer disclosure requirements or to knowingly give a false statement to a transferee in making any disclosure required by such law.

42-6-203. Penalty. A violation of any of the provisions of section 42-6-202 is a class 1 misdemeanor.

42-6-204. Private civil action. (1) Any person who, with intent to defraud, violates any requirement imposed under this part 2 shall be liable in an amount equal to the sum of:

(a) Three times the amount of actual damages sustained or three thousand dollars, whichever is greater; and

(b) In the case of any successful action to enforce said liability, the costs of the action together with reasonable attorney fees as determined by the court.

(2) An action to enforce any liability created under subsection (1) of this section must be brought within the time period prescribed in section 13-80-102, C.R.S.

(3) There shall be no liability under this section if a judgment has been entered in federal court pursuant to section 409 of the "Motor Vehicle Information and Cost Savings Act", Public Law 92-513.

42-6-205. Consumer protection. All provisions of section 6-1-708, C.R.S., concerning deceptive trade practices in the sale of motor vehicles shall apply to the sale of used motor vehicles.

42-6-206. Disclosure requirements upon transfer of ownership of a salvage vehicle. (1) Prior to sale of a vehicle rebuilt from salvage to a prospective purchaser for the purpose of selling or transferring ownership of such vehicle, the owner shall prepare a disclosure affidavit stating that the vehicle was rebuilt from salvage. The disclosure affidavit shall also contain a statement of the owner stating the nature of the damage which resulted in the determination that the vehicle is a salvage vehicle. The words "rebuilt from salvage" shall appear in bold print at the top of each such affidavit.

(2) Any person who sells a vehicle rebuilt from salvage for the purpose of transferring ownership of such vehicle shall:

(a) Provide a copy of a disclosure affidavit prepared in accordance with the provisions of subsection (1) of this section to each prospective purchaser; and

(b) Obtain a signed statement from each such purchaser clearly stating that the purchaser has received a copy of the disclosure affidavit and has read and understands the provisions contained therein.

(3) (a) Any person who purchases a vehicle rebuilt from salvage who was not provided with a

copy of a disclosure affidavit prepared in accordance with the provisions of subsection (1) of this section and who, subsequent to sale, discovers that the vehicle purchased was rebuilt from salvage shall be entitled to a full and immediate refund of the purchase price from the prior owner.

(b) In the event a person is entitled to a refund under this subsection (3), the prior owner shall be required to make an immediate refund of the full purchase price to the purchaser. A signed statement from the purchaser prepared in accordance with the provisions of paragraph (b) of subsection (2) of this section shall relieve the prior owner of the obligation to make such refund.

(4) Any owner, seller, or transferor of a vehicle rebuilt from salvage who fails to comply with the provisions of this section shall be guilty of a misdemeanor and, upon conviction thereof, shall be punished by a fine for a first offense not to exceed one thousand five hundred dollars and a fine of five thousand dollars for each subsequent offense.

(5) The executive director of the department of revenue shall prescribe rules and regulations for the purpose of implementing the provisions of this section.

(6) As used in this section, unless the context otherwise requires:

(a) "Sale" means any sale or transfer of a vehicle rebuilt from salvage.

(b) "Salvage vehicle" shall have the same meaning as set forth in section 42-6-102 (17).

MOTOR VEHICLE FINANCIAL RESPONSIBILITY LAW

ARTICLE 7

Motor Vehicle Financial Responsibility Law

PART 1
GENERAL PROVISIONS

42-7-101.	Short title.
42-7-102.	Legislative declaration.
42-7-103.	Definitions.

PART 2
ADMINISTRATION

42-7-201.	Director to administer article.
42-7-202.	Report of accident required. (Repealed)

PART 3
SECURITY AND PROOF OF FINANCIAL RESPONSIBILITY IN CONNECTION WITH ACCIDENTS

42-7-301.	Security and proof of financial responsibility for the future required under certain circumstances.
42-7-301.5.	Proof of financial responsibility.
42-7-302.	Exemptions from requirement of filing security and proof of financial responsibility for the future.
42-7-303.	Duration of suspension.
42-7-304.	Custody and disposition of security.

PART 4
PROOF OF FINANCIAL RESPONSIBILITY - JUDGMENTS AND CONVICTIONS

42-7-401.	Proof required on judgments.
42-7-402.	Suspension, duration, bankruptcy.
42-7-403.	Sufficiency of payments.
42-7-404.	Payment of judgment in installments.
42-7-405.	Suspension upon second judgment.
42-7-406.	Proof required under certain conditions.
42-7-407.	Duty of courts to report.
42-7-408.	Proof of financial responsibility - methods of giving proof - duration - exception.
42-7-409.	Proof for member of family or chauffeur.
42-7-410.	Certificate for insurance policy.
42-7-411.	Restrictions in certain type of policy.
42-7-412.	Certificate furnished by nonresident.
42-7-413.	Motor vehicle liability policy.
42-7-414.	Requirements to be complied with.
42-7-415.	When insurance carrier to issue certificate.
42-7-416.	Notice required upon cancellation.
42-7-417.	Article not to affect other policies.
42-7-418.	Money - securities for financial responsibility.
42-7-419.	Substitution of proof.
42-7-420.	Failure of proof - other proof.
42-7-421.	When director may release proof of financial responsibility.
42-7-422.	No proof when proof required.

PART 5
GENERAL

42-7-501.	Self-insurers.
42-7-502.	Action against nonresident - reciprocity with other states.
42-7-503.	Director to furnish operating record.
42-7-504.	Matters not to be evidence in litigation.
42-7-505.	Forging ability to respond in damages.
42-7-506.	Surrender of license.
42-7-507.	Penalty.
42-7-508.	No repeal of motor vehicle laws.
42-7-509.	Article does not prevent other process.
42-7-510.	Insurance or bond required.

PART 6
UNINSURED MOTORIST IDENTIFICATION DATABASE PROGRAM

42-7-601. Short title.
42-7-602. Uninsured motorist identification database program - creation.
42-7-603. Definitions.
42-7-604. Motorist insurance identification database program - creation - administration - selection of designated agent - legislative declaration.
42-7-605. Notice of lack of financial responsibility. (Repealed)
42-7-606. Disclosure of insurance information - penalty.
42-7-607. Part 6 not to supersede other provisions.
42-7-608. Review by department of regulatory agencies - repeal. (Repealed)
42-7-609. Report.

PART 1
GENERAL PROVISIONS

42-7-101. Short title. This article shall be known and may be cited as the "Motor Vehicle Financial Responsibility Act".

42-7-102. Legislative declaration. (1) The general assembly is acutely aware of the toll in human suffering and loss of life, limb, and property caused by negligence in the operation of motor vehicles in our state. Although it recognizes that this basic problem can be and is being dealt with by direct measures designed to protect our people from the ravages of irresponsible drivers, the general assembly is also very much concerned with the financial loss visited upon innocent traffic accident victims by negligent motorists who are financially irresponsible. In prescribing the sanctions and requirements of this article, it is the policy of this state to induce and encourage all motorists to provide for their financial responsibility for the protection of others, and to assure the widespread availability to the insuring public of insurance protection against financial loss caused by negligent financially irresponsible motorists.

(2) (a) The general assembly hereby finds that motor vehicle accidents cause a substantial economic impact in lost wages, medical bills, and property destruction exacerbated by the following:

(I) Some negligent motorists are uninsured or flee the scene of an accident.

(II) Negligent motorists often attempt to avoid financial responsibility by means such as fleeing the state, concealing their whereabouts, or failing to update the address on their driver's license with the department of revenue, thereby frustrating service of process and preventing the innocent victim from accessing either the negligent driver's liability insurance policy or the uninsured motorist coverage the victim has purchased.

(III) When innocent traffic accident victims cannot access either the negligent driver's automobile liability policy or their own uninsured motorist coverage, the burden of the uncompensated losses are borne by the taxpayer in the form of taxes for medicaid, by trauma facilities in the form of uncompensated hospital-related costs, and by the innocent victim.

(b) (I) The state of Colorado encourages the widespread availability of uninsured or underinsured motorist insurance by requiring every motor vehicle liability policy delivered or issued in this state to contain uninsured motorist coverage unless the named insured rejects such coverage in writing.

(II) Because insurance benefits have been paid for by either the negligent driver or the innocent victim for the purpose of compensating the innocent victim for injuries or losses, the general assembly declares that it is necessary to simplify the process for an innocent victim to access the negligent driver's liability insurance policy or his or her own uninsured motorist coverage in order to prevent the burden from being borne by the taxpayer or the health care system.

(c) Therefore, the general assembly declares that the policy of Colorado is that all motor vehicle liability policies shall require policyholders of an automobile liability policy to appoint their insurance carrier as an agent for the purpose of service of process in certain limited instances in accordance with section 42-7-414 (3), and to deem a defendant to be uninsured for purposes of uninsured or underinsured motorist coverage if the court deems service on the defendant's insurance company to be ineffective or insufficient.

42-7-103. Definitions. As used in this article, unless the context otherwise requires:

(1) "Accident" means a motor vehicle accident occurring on public or private property within this state.

(2) "Automobile liability policy" or "bond" means a liability policy or bond subject, if the accident has resulted in bodily injury or death, to a limit, exclusive of interest and costs, of not less than twenty-five thousand dollars because of bodily injury to or death of one person in any one accident and, subject to said limit for one person, to a limit of not less than fifty thousand dollars because of bodily injury to or death of two or more persons in any one accident, and, if the accident has resulted in injury to or destruction of property, to a limit of not less than fifteen thousand dollars because of injury to or destruction of property of others in any one accident.

(3) "Conviction" means conviction in any court of record or municipal court, and such conviction shall include a plea of guilty, a plea of

nolo contendere accepted by the court, the forfeiture of any bail or collateral deposited to secure a defendant's appearance in court which forfeiture has not been vacated, and the acceptance and payment of a penalty assessment under the provisions of section 42-4-1701 or under the similar provisions of any town or city ordinance.

(4) "Department" means the department of revenue acting directly or through its duly authorized officers and agents.

(5) "Director" means the executive director of the department of revenue.

(6) "Driver" means every person who is in actual physical control of a motor vehicle upon a highway.

(6.5) (a) "Evidence of insurance" means proof given by the insured in person to the department that the insured has a complying policy in full force and effect. Proof may be made through presentation of a copy of such complying policy or a card issued to the insured as evidence that a complying policy is in full force and effect.

(b) For purposes of this subsection (6.5), "complying policy" means a policy of insurance as required by part 6 of article 4 of title 10, C.R.S.

(7) "License" means any license, temporary instruction permit, or temporary license issued under laws of this state pertaining to the licensing of persons to operate motor vehicles, or, with respect to any person not licensed, the term means any operating privilege or privileges to apply for such license.

(8) "Motor vehicle" means every vehicle which is self-propelled, including trailers and semitrailers designed for use with such vehicles and every vehicle which is propelled by electric power obtained from overhead trolley wires but not operated upon rails.

(9) "Motor vehicle liability policy", "operators' policy of liability insurance", or "financial responsibility bond" means a policy or bond certified as proof of financial responsibility for the future.

(10) "Nonresident" means every person who is not a resident of this state.

(11) "Nonresident's operating privilege" means the privilege conferred upon a nonresident by the laws of this state pertaining to the operation by the nonresident of a motor vehicle.

(12) "Owner" means a person who holds the legal title of the vehicle; or in the event a vehicle is the subject of an agreement for the conditional sale or lease thereof with the right of purchase upon performance of the conditions stated in the agreement and with an immediate right of possession vested in the conditional vendee or lessee, or in the event a mortgagor of a vehicle is entitled to possession, then such conditional vendee or lessee or mortgagor shall be deemed the owner for the purpose of this article.

(13) "Person" means every natural person, firm, partnership, association, or corporation.

(14) (a) "Proof of financial responsibility for the future", also referred to in this article as proof of financial responsibility, means proof of ability to respond in damages for liability, on account of accidents occurring after the effective date of said proof, arising out of the ownership, maintenance, or use of a motor vehicle, in the amount of twenty-five thousand dollars because of bodily injury to or death of one person in any one accident, and, subject to said limit for one person, in the amount of fifty thousand dollars because of bodily injury to or death of two or more persons in any one accident, and in the amount of fifteen thousand dollars because of injury to or destruction of property of others in any one accident.

(b) For purposes of this title, the form known as the "SR-22" furnished to the department may be used as proof of financial responsibility in compliance with this article.

(15) "State" means any state of the United States, the District of Columbia, or any province of Canada.

PART 2

ADMINISTRATION

42-7-201. Director to administer article. (1) The director shall administer and enforce the provisions of this article and may make rules and regulations in writing necessary for the administration of this article.

(2) (a) The director shall provide for a hearing upon request of any person affected by an order or act of the director under the provisions of this article. Such hearing need not be a matter of record.

(b) A request for a hearing, made within the twenty-day period prescribed in section 42-7-301 (3) and (4), shall operate during the pendency of such hearing to postpone the effective date of any order or act of the director pursuant to this article.

(c) If the person, for the protection of the public interest and safety, files or has filed with the director evidence of current liability insurance in the driver's name, or has made a deposit as provided in section 42-7-418, the request for hearing shall also postpone the date on which the affected person's license or nonresident's operating privilege would otherwise be suspended.

(d) The decision as rendered by the director upon a hearing, or an order or act of the director when no hearing is requested, shall be final unless the affected person seeks judicial review.

(e) In any action for judicial review of the action of the director, the court, upon application for a hearing on the question of irreparable injury with three days' notice to the director of such hearing and upon a finding by the court at such hearing that irreparable injury to the affected person would otherwise result, may order that the filing of the action shall operate to postpone the effective date of the director's order or act, in which event the court may also impose the condition, for the protection of the public interest and safety, that the person bringing the action shall obtain and maintain during the pendency of the action an automobile liability policy or bond or deposit of security as provided in section 42-7-418. The procedure in all other respects upon review shall be in accordance with the applicable provision of section 24-4-106, C.R.S.

42-7-202. Report of accident required. (Repealed)

PART 3

SECURITY AND PROOF OF FINANCIAL RESPONSIBILITY IN CONNECTION WITH ACCIDENTS

42-7-301. Security and proof of financial responsibility for the future required under certain circumstances. (1) Unless exempt under section 42-7-302, an operator or owner named in an accident report required to be filed pursuant to section 42-4-1606 shall file with the director, according to the procedure provided by this section, both:

(a) Security, in an amount specified after consideration of the accident report and written substantiation of such report as provided in paragraph (b) of subsection (3) of this section, which is sufficient to satisfy any judgments for damages or injuries resulting from the accident as may be recovered against such operator or owner but which in no event shall exceed the sum of thirty-five thousand dollars; and

(b) Proof of financial responsibility for the future.

(2) Based upon a report filed pursuant to section 42-4-1606, the director shall determine whether an operator or owner is required to comply with the provisions of this article and, if so, shall:

(a) Within fifteen days after receipt of the accident report, inform each such operator and each such owner of such requirement and that the operator or owner's license or nonresident's operating privilege will be suspended if the operator or owner fails to comply with the provisions of this article;

(b) Within sixty days after receipt of the accident report, send written notice of the requirement of filing security and proof of financial responsibility for the future to each such owner and each such operator at his or her last-known address, by first-class mail pursuant to section 42-2-119 (2).

(3) The notice specified in paragraph (b) of subsection (2) of this section shall state that:

(a) The license or nonresident's operating privilege of the person so notified is subject to suspension and shall be suspended unless such person, within twenty days after the mailing of such notice by the director, establishes that the requirements of this section are not applicable to such person or that such person previously filed or then files both security and proof of financial responsibility for the future as provided in paragraphs (a) and (b) of subsection (1) of this section.

(b) Any person having a claim for property damage or personal injury may be required by the director to substantiate such claim by written statement sworn to by a person experienced in estimating the cost of repairing the property damaged and a written report as to the personal injury sworn to by a licensed physician.

(c) The person notified is entitled to a hearing and judicial review as provided in section 42-7-201.

(d) The date on which such person's license or nonresident's operating privilege would otherwise be suspended shall be postponed during the pendency of such hearing if the request for a hearing is made within twenty days after the mailing of said notice and if the person files security and evidence of current liability insurance in the respondent's name.

(4) Upon expiration of such twenty-day period without a request for hearing or compliance with the contents of the notice as specified in subsection (3) of this section, such person's license or nonresident's operating privilege shall be suspended unless and until such person files security and proof of financial responsibility for the future as provided in paragraphs (a) and (b) of subsection (1) of this section.

(5) When no accident report is filed or when erroneous or incomplete information is given, the director, with regard to the matters set forth in this article, shall, after receipt of correct information with respect to said matters, take whatever appropriate action is indicated, consistent with the provisions of this article.

(6) No policy or bond shall be effective under this section unless issued by an insurance company or surety company authorized to do business in this state, but the surety requirements of this section may be satisfied by evidence of a savings account, deposit, or certificate of deposit meeting the requirements of section 11-35-101, C.R.S. However, if a motor vehicle was not registered in this state, or if a motor vehicle was registered elsewhere than in this state at the effective date of the policy or bond, or the most recent renewal thereof, such policy or bond shall not be effective under this section unless the insurance company or surety company, if not authorized to do business in this state, executes a power of attorney authorizing the director to accept, on its behalf, service of notice or process in any action upon such policy or bond arising out of such accident.

(7) (a) (I) The security required pursuant to paragraph (a) of subsection (1) of this section may, in whole or in part, take the form of a con-

tract between a person having a claim for property damage or personal injury and the operator or owner. Any such contract shall require notice by first-class mail to any obligor in default at the obligor's last-known address and allowing at least a ten-day period after mailing for the obligor to cure the default before remedies become available.

(II) The director shall prescribe the form of any contract authorized by subparagraph (I) of this paragraph (a).

(b) The director shall immediately suspend the license of a person obligated under a contract used as security pursuant to paragraph (a) of this subsection (7), upon receipt of evidence from the creditor in the form of an affidavit that:

(I) The obligor has defaulted on any payment obligation under the contract;

(II) Notice of the default has been sent to the obligor by certified mail; and

(III) The obligor has failed to cure the default within fifteen days after the date of mailing of the notice.

42-7-301.5. Proof of financial responsibility. (1) Any person who presents an altered or counterfeit letter or altered or counterfeit insurance identification card from an insurer or agent for the purpose of proving financial responsibility for purposes of this article shall be in violation of section 18-5-104, C.R.S., and the minimum fine shall be one thousand dollars. A second or subsequent presentation is a violation of section 18-5-104, C.R.S., and the minimum fine shall be one thousand five hundred dollars.

(2) Any person who alters or creates a counterfeit letter or insurance identification card for another violates section 18-5-104, C.R.S., and shall be punished by a minimum fine of one thousand dollars. A second or subsequent alteration or creation of a counterfeit letter or insurance identification card is a violation of section 18-5-104, C.R.S., and the fine shall be one thousand five hundred dollars.

(3) It shall be an affirmative defense that the person did not know or could not have known that the presented document was altered or counterfeit.

(4) Repealed.

42-7-302. Exemptions from requirement of filing security and proof of financial responsibility for the future. (1) The requirement of filing security and proof of financial responsibility for the future pursuant to section 42-7-301 shall not apply:

(a) To any person who qualifies as a self-insurer under section 42-7-501 or who operates a motor vehicle for a self-insurer under section 42-7-501;

(b) To any person who has been released from liability, or finally adjudicated not liable, prior to the date the director would otherwise suspend a license or a nonresident's operating privilege under section 42-7-301 (4);

(c) To the state of Colorado or any political subdivision thereof or any municipality therein;

(d) To the operation by any employee of the federal government of any motor vehicle while acting within the scope of such employment;

(e) Repealed.

(f) To the operator or owner if such owner had in effect at the time of such accident an automobile liability policy with respect to the motor vehicle involved in such accident;

(g) To the operator, if not the owner of such motor vehicle, if there was in effect at the time of such accident an automobile liability policy or bond with respect to the operation of motor vehicles not owned by that person;

(h) To the operator or owner if the liability of such operator or owner for damages resulting from such accident is, in the judgment of the director, covered by any other form of liability insurance policy or bond or deposit as provided in section 42-7-418;

(i) To the owner of a motor vehicle if at the time of the accident the vehicle was being operated without the owner's express or implied permission, or was parked by a person who had been operating such motor vehicle without such permission.

(2) In determining whether any person is exempt from the requirements of section 42-7-301, the director shall rely upon reports or other information submitted and, when requested by any person affected by an accident to make a finding of fact, shall consider the report of the investigating officer, if any, the accident reports, and any affidavits of persons having knowledge of the facts.

42-7-303. Duration of suspension. (1) The license or nonresident's operating privilege suspended under section 42-7-301 shall remain so suspended and not be renewed, nor shall any such license be issued to such person, unless there is filed with the director evidence satisfactory to the director that such person has been released from liability, has entered into a contract used as security pursuant to section 42-7-301 (7), or has been finally adjudicated not liable, or until:

(a) Such person deposits and files or there has been deposited and filed on behalf of such person the security and proof of financial responsibility for the future required under section 42-7-301; or

(b) Three years have elapsed following the date of such accident and evidence satisfactory to the director has been filed with the director that during such period no action for damages arising out of such accident has been instituted, and such person has filed or then files and maintains proof of financial responsibility for the future as provided in section 42-7-408; except that a contract used as security pursuant to section 42-7-301 (7) may provide for a different period of time; or

(c) Three years have elapsed since the failure to timely cure any default, after notice, under a contract used as security pursuant to section 42-7-301 (7) and evidence satisfactory to the director has been filed with the department showing that no civil action to enforce the contract has been filed during such period.

(2) If the director determines that the driver is not responsible for any damages to any other party as a result of the accident, the driver may:

(a) Prevent a suspension from occurring by filing future proof of liability insurance pursuant to section 42-7-408; or

(b) Reinstate a license, if a suspension has already occurred, by filing future proof of liability insurance pursuant to section 42-7-408 and paying the reinstatement fee.

42-7-304. Custody and disposition of security. (1) Security deposited in compliance with the requirements of section 42-7-301 shall be placed by the director in the custody of the state treasurer and shall be applied only to the payment of a judgment rendered against the person on whose behalf the deposit was made, for damages arising out of the accident in question in an action at law begun not later than one year after the date of such accident. Such deposit or any balance thereof shall be returned to the depositor or the depositor's personal representative, or the person designated by either of them, when evidence satisfactory to the director has been filed with the director that there has been a release from liability, or a final adjudication of nonliability, or a warrant for confession of judgment, or a duly acknowledged agreement, or whenever, after the expiration of one year from the date of the accident, or within one year after the date of deposit of any security, the director shall be given reasonable evidence that there is no such action pending and no judgment rendered in such action left unpaid.

(2) The director may reduce the amount of security ordered in any case within six months after the date of the accident if, in the director's judgment, the amount originally ordered is excessive. In case the security originally ordered has been deposited, the excess deposit over the reduced amount ordered shall be returned immediately to the depositor or the depositor's personal representative, regardless of any other provisions of this article.

(3) (a) It is the duty of any person having a claim against the security deposited under the provisions of section 42-7-301, on or before the expiration of one year from the date of the accident, to notify the director in writing under oath that there has been a release of liability, or a final adjudication of nonliability, or a warrant for confession of judgment, or a duly acknowledged agreement or that there is no action pending and no judgment rendered in any such action left unpaid or of any action taken on said claim which has not been finally determined.

(b) If any claimant fails to notify the director in writing under oath as provided in paragraph (a) of this subsection (3), the director shall notify the state treasurer to that effect and the state treasurer may, upon receipt of said notification, void the obligation provided for in section 42-7-301 and release and return the security to the depositor. The state treasurer shall then be fully and completely released from any further obligation or liability in relation thereto.

(c) Where said depositor cannot be located, the state treasurer shall notify the depositor by registered or certified mail, return receipt requested, addressed to the last-known address of said depositor, advising said depositor that the depositor must either appear and claim the security deposited within thirty days from the date of receipt of said letter, or said security will escheat to the general fund of the state of Colorado. If said depositor does not appear within the thirty-day period, the state treasurer shall void the obligation as provided in section 42-7-301, and the security shall escheat to the general fund of the state of Colorado, relieving the state treasurer of any further obligation or liability in relation thereto.

PART 4

PROOF OF FINANCIAL RESPONSIBILITY - JUDGMENTS AND CONVICTIONS

42-7-401. Proof required on judgments. (1) The director shall also suspend the license issued to any person upon receiving an affidavit from the judgment creditor that such person has failed for a period of thirty days to satisfy any final judgment in amounts and upon a cause of action as stated in this article, or, in a criminal proceeding arising from the use or operation of a motor vehicle, has failed to comply with the terms of any order of restitution made as a condition of probation pursuant to section 18-1.3-205, C.R.S.

(2) The judgment referred to means a final judgment of any court of competent jurisdiction in any state or of the United States against a person as defendant upon a cause of action as stated in this article.

(3) The judgment referred to means any final judgment for damage to property in excess of one hundred dollars or for damages in any amount for or on account of bodily injury to or death of any person resulting from the operation of any motor vehicle upon a highway.

(4) This article shall not apply to any such judgment rendered against this state or any political subdivision thereof or any municipality therein.

42-7-402. Suspension, duration, bankruptcy. (1) The suspension required in section 42-7-401 shall remain in effect and no new license shall be issued to such person unless and until such judgment is satisfied or vacated or execution therein stayed and proof of financial responsibility given, except under the conditions stated in this article.

(2) A discharge in bankruptcy following the rendering of any such judgment shall relieve the judgment debtor from any of the requirements of this article.

42-7-403. Sufficiency of payments. (1) Every judgment referred to in this article and for the purposes of this article shall be deemed satisfied:

(a) When twenty-five thousand dollars has been credited upon any judgment rendered in excess of that amount for or on account of bodily injury to or the death of one person as the result of any one accident; or

(b) When, subject to said limit of twenty-five thousand dollars as to one person, the sum of fifty thousand dollars has been credited upon any judgment rendered in excess of that amount for or on account of bodily injury to or the death of more than one person as the result of any one accident; or

(c) When fifteen thousand dollars has been credited upon any judgment rendered in excess of that amount for damage to property of others in excess of one hundred dollars as a result of any one accident; or

(d) When six years have elapsed since the date that such judgment became final; or

(e) When three years, or such other period as authorized pursuant to section 42-7-408 (1), have elapsed since the judgment debtor gives proof of financial responsibility; except that this paragraph (e) shall not apply to any judgment debtor subject to paragraph (d) of this subsection (1).

(2) Credit for such amounts shall be deemed a satisfaction of any such judgment in excess of said amounts only for the purposes of this article.

(3) Whenever payment has been made in settlement of any claims for bodily injury, death, or property damage arising from a motor vehicle accident resulting in injury, death, or property damage to two or more persons in such accident, any such payment shall be credited in reduction of the amounts provided for in this section.

42-7-404. Payment of judgment in installments. (1) The director shall not suspend a license and shall restore any suspended license following nonpayment of a final judgment when the judgment debtor gives proof of financial responsibility and obtains an order from the trial court in which such judgment was rendered permitting the payment of such judgment in installments of not less than twenty-five dollars per month, while the payment of any said installment is not in default.

(2) A judgment debtor upon five days' notice to the judgment creditor may apply to the trial court in which the judgment was obtained for the privilege of paying such judgment in installments, and the court, in its discretion and without prejudice to any other legal remedies which the judgment creditor may have, may so order, fixing the amounts and times of, and the person to receive, payment of the installments.

(3) In the event the judgment debtor fails to pay any installment as permitted by the order of the court, upon notice of such default supported by an appropriate document from the court or by sworn affidavit of either the judgment creditor or the person designated to receive payments, the director shall immediately suspend the license of the judgment debtor until said judgment is satisfied as provided in this article.

42-7-405. Suspension upon second judgment. After one judgment is satisfied and proof of financial responsibility is given as required in this article and another such judgment is rendered against the judgment debtor for any accident occurring prior to the date of the giving of said proof and such person fails to satisfy the latter judgment within the amounts specified in this article within thirty days after the same becomes final, the director shall again suspend the license of such judgment debtor and shall not renew the same nor issue to the judgment debtor any license while such latter judgment remains in effect and unsatisfied within the amounts specified in this article.

42-7-406. Proof required under certain conditions. (1) Whenever the director revokes the license of any person under section 42-2-125 or 42-2-126, or cancels any license under section 42-2-122 because of the licensee's inability to operate a motor vehicle because of physical or mental incompetence, or cancels any probationary license under section 42-2-127, the director shall not issue to or continue in effect for any such person any new or renewal of license until permitted under the motor vehicle laws of this state, and not then until and unless such person files or has filed and maintains proof of financial responsibility as provided in this article; except that persons whose licenses are canceled pursuant to section 42-2-122 (2.5), revoked pursuant to section 42-2-125 (1) (m), or revoked for a first offense under section 42-2-125 (1) (g.5) or a first offense under section 42-2-126 (3) (b) or (3) (e) shall not be required to file proof of financial responsibility in order to be relicensed.

(1.5) (a) Whenever the director revokes the license of a person under section 42-2-126 (3) (a), (3) (c), or (3) (d) for a second or subsequent offense and such person was driving the same vehicle in two or more of such offenses but did not own such vehicle, the director shall mail a notice to the owner of the vehicle pursuant to section 42-2-119 (2). In such notice, the director shall inform the owner that:

(I) The operator of the motor vehicle owned by the owner has been involved in multiple alcohol-related driving violations while operating the owner's vehicle;

(II) Because of the risks to the public connected with the use of the vehicle in alcohol-related driving violations, it is necessary for the motor vehicle owner to establish proof of financial responsibility;

(III) Within thirty days after the date of mailing of the notice, the owner is required to file proof of financial responsibility for the future pursuant to the requirements of section 42-7-408 or to request a hearing regarding the applicability of this requirement to the owner;

(IV) The vehicle owner is entitled to a hearing and judicial review pursuant to section 42-7-201;

(V) If the owner has not filed proof of financial responsibility or requested a hearing within thirty days after the date of mailing of the notice, the department will suspend the driver's license or nonresident operating privilege of the owner.

(b) If proof of financial responsibility for the future is required under this subsection (1.5), such proof shall be maintained for a period of three years as required by section 42-7-408 (1) (b).

(c) This subsection (1.5) does not apply to a motor vehicle that is:

(I) Rented from a person, firm, corporation, or other business entity whose primary business is the rental of motor vehicles; or

(II) Rented or loaned from a person, firm, corporation, or other business entity whose primary business is operation as a motor vehicle repair facility and who is providing such motor vehicle to the person while a motor vehicle is being repaired.

(2) (a) Whenever the director suspends the license of any person under section 42-2-127, the director shall not issue a probationary license to such person, nor shall the director at the termination of such person's period of suspension reinstate, reissue, renew, or issue a new license to such person unless such person furnishes the director evidence of insurance to show that the person is then insured, unless such person has deposited or deposits money or securities as provided in section 42-7-418.

(b) Evidence of insurance required pursuant to this subsection (2) does not require the use of the form known as the "SR-22" or any substantially similar form.

42-7-407. Duty of courts to report. The clerk of a court or the judge of a court which has no clerk shall forward to the director a certified record of any judgment for damages, the rendering and nonpayment of which judgment requires the director to suspend the license and registrations in the name of the judgment debtor under this article. This record shall be forwarded to the director immediately upon the expiration of thirty days after such judgment becomes final and when such judgment has not been stayed or satisfied within the amounts specified in this article, as shown by the records of the court.

42-7-408. Proof of financial responsibility - methods of giving proof - duration - exception. (1) (a) Proof of financial responsibility for the future, when required under this article, may be given by the following alternate methods:

(I) Proof that a policy of liability insurance has been obtained and is in full force and effect or that a bond has been duly executed or that deposit has been made of money; or

(II) Securities as provided in section 42-7-418.

(b) Proof of financial responsibility for the future in the amounts provided in section 42-7-103 (14) shall be maintained for three years from the date last required and shall be furnished for each motor vehicle registered during that period; except that, if during such three-year period the insured has not been licensed to drive pursuant to this title, the insured shall be credited with the nonlicensed time toward the three-year period.

(c) Notwithstanding the three-year requirement in paragraph (b) of this subsection (1):

(I) If an insured has been found guilty of DUI, DUI per se, DWAI, or habitual user or if the insured's license has been revoked pursuant to section 42-2-126, other than a revocation under section 42-2-126 (3) (b) or (3) (e), only one time and no accident was involved in such offense, proof of financial responsibility for the future shall be required to be maintained only for as long as the insured's driving privilege is ordered to be under restraint, up to a maximum of three years. The time period for maintaining the future proof of liability insurance shall begin at the time the driver reinstates his or her driving privilege.

(II) If an insured has been found guilty of a second or subsequent offense of UDD with a BAC of at least 0.02 but not more than 0.05 or if the insured's driver's license has been revoked because of a second or subsequent offense pursuant to section 42-2-126 (3) (b) or (3) (e), proof of financial responsibility for the future shall be required to be maintained only for as long as the insured's driving privilege is ordered to be under restraint. The time period for maintaining the future proof of liability insurance shall begin at the time the driver reinstates his or her driving privilege.

(2) The term of the policy of liability insurance or the bond submitted as proof of financial responsibility for the future shall be for a minimum of three months.

(3) If an insured's driver's license is cancelled pursuant to section 42-2-125 (4), and after such cancellation neither a court of competent jurisdiction nor an administrative hearing officer determines that the charges have been proved, the insured shall not be required to comply with the proof of financial responsibility requirements stated in this section.

(4) If at any time when insurance is required to be maintained in accordance with section 42-4-1409 or this article it is not so maintained or becomes invalid, the director shall suspend the driver's license of the person who has not maintained the required insurance and shall not reinstate the license of such person until future proof of financial responsibility is provided in accordance with section 42-7-406 (1).

(5) Repealed.

(6) (a) Upon receipt of evidence from an agency of another state or foreign jurisdiction that a former Colorado resident has obtained a license in such state or foreign jurisdiction, the director shall suspend the requirement for proof of financial responsibility for the future until such time as the former resident has made application for a new Colorado license.

(b) If such former resident makes application for a Colorado driver's license, the director shall reinstate the requirement for proof of financial responsibility for the future until such time as the original requirement to maintain proof of financial responsibility for the future has expired.

42-7-409. Proof for member of family or chauffeur. Whenever the director determines that any person required to give proof by reason of a conviction is not the owner of a motor vehicle but was at the time of such conviction a chauffeur or motor vehicle operator, however designated, in the employ of an owner of a motor vehicle or a member of the immediate family or household of the owner of a motor vehicle, the director shall accept proof of financial responsibility given by such owner in lieu of proof given by such other person so long as such latter person is operating a motor vehicle for which the owner has given proof as provided in this article. No such license shall be reinstated and no new license issued until otherwise permitted under the laws of this state.

42-7-410. Certificate for insurance policy. (1) Proof of financial responsibility may be made by filing with the director the written certificate of any insurance carrier duly authorized to do business in this state, certifying that it has issued to or for the benefit of the person furnishing such proof and named as the insured a motor vehicle liability policy or in certain events an operator's policy, meeting the requirements of this article, and that said policy is then in full force and effect. Such certificate shall give the dates of issuance and expiration of such policy and shall explicitly describe all motor vehicles covered thereby, unless the policy is issued to a person who is not the owner of a motor vehicle.

(2) The director shall not accept any certificate unless the same covers all motor vehicles registered in the name of the person furnishing such proof as owner and an additional certificate shall be required as a condition precedent to the subsequent registration of any motor vehicle or motor vehicles in the name of the person giving such proof as owner.

42-7-411. Restrictions in certain type of policy. (1) When a certificate is filed showing that a policy has been issued covering all motor vehicles owned by the insured but not insuring such person when operating any motor vehicle not owned by that person, it is unlawful for such person to operate any motor vehicle not owned by that person or not covered by such certificate.

(2) In the event the owner of the motor vehicle desires to be relieved of the restriction stated in subsection (1) of this section and to be permitted to drive any other motor vehicle, the owner may have such restrictions removed upon filing a certificate showing that there has been issued to the owner a policy of insurance insuring the owner as insured against liability imposed by law upon such an insured for bodily injury to or death of any person or damage to property to the amounts and limits as provided under section 42-7-103 (14) with respect to any motor vehicle operated by the insured and which otherwise complies with the requirements of this article with respect to such type of policy. Such policy is referred to in this article as an operator's policy.

(3) When the person required to give proof of financial responsibility is not the owner of a motor vehicle, then an operator's policy of the type and coverage described in subsection (2) of this section shall be sufficient under this article.

42-7-412. Certificate furnished by nonresident. (1) The nonresident owner of a foreign vehicle may give proof of financial responsibility by filing with the director a written certificate of an insurance carrier authorized to transact business in the state in which the motor vehicle described in such certificate is registered or if such nonresident does not own a motor vehicle then in the state in which the insured resides and otherwise conforming to the provisions of this article, and the director shall accept the same upon condition that said insurance carrier complies with the following provisions of this section:

(a) Said insurance carrier shall execute a power of attorney authorizing the director to accept service on its behalf of notice or process in any action arising out of a motor vehicle accident in this state.

(b) Said insurance carrier shall duly adopt a resolution which shall be binding upon it, declaring that its policies shall be deemed to be varied to comply with the law of this state relating to the terms of motor vehicle liability policies issued in this article.

(c) Said insurance carrier shall also agree to accept as final and binding any final judgment of any court of competent jurisdiction in this state duly rendered in any action arising out of a motor vehicle accident.

(2) If any foreign insurance carrier which has qualified to furnish proof of financial responsibility defaults in any of said undertakings or agreements, the director shall not subsequently accept any certificate of said carrier, whether previously filed or subsequently tendered, as proof of financial responsibility so long as such default continues.

42-7-413. Motor vehicle liability policy. (1) "Motor vehicle liability policy", as used in this article, means a policy of liability insurance issued by an insurance carrier authorized to transact business in this state to or for the benefit of the person named therein as insured, which policy shall meet the following requirements:

(a) The policy of liability insurance shall designate by explicit description or by appropriate reference all motor vehicles with respect to which coverage is thereby intended to be granted.

(b) The policy of liability insurance shall insure the person named therein and any other person using or responsible for the use of said motor vehicle with the express or implied permission of said insured.

(c) The policy of liability insurance shall insure every such person on account of the maintenance, use, or operation of the motor vehicle within the continental limits of the United States or Canada against loss from the liability imposed by law; for damages, including damages for care and loss of services arising from such maintenance, use, or operation to the extent and aggregate amount, exclusive of interest and costs, with respect to each such motor vehicle, in the amounts specified in section 42-7-103 (2).

(2) When an operator's policy of liability insurance is required, it shall insure the person named therein as insured against the liability imposed by law upon the insured for bodily injury to or death of any person or damage to property to the amounts and limits set forth in paragraph (c) of subsection (1) of this section and growing out of the use or operation by the insured within the continental limits of the United States or Canada of any motor vehicle not owned by the insured.

(3) Any liability policy issued under this section need not cover any liability of the insured assumed by or imposed upon said insured under any workers' compensation law nor any liability for damage to property in charge of the insured or the insured's employees.

(4) Any such policy of liability insurance may grant any lawful coverage in excess of or in addition to the coverage specified in this section or contain any agreements, provisions, or stipulations not in conflict with the provisions of this article and not otherwise contrary to law.

(5) Any motor vehicle liability policy which by endorsement contains the provisions required under this section shall be sufficient proof of ability to respond in damages.

(6) The department may accept several policies of one or more such carriers which together meet the requirements of this section.

(7) Any binder pending the issuance of any policy of liability insurance, which binder contains or by reference includes the provisions under this section, shall be sufficient proof of ability to respond in damages.

42-7-414. Requirements to be complied with. (1) Except as provided in section 42-7-417, no motor vehicle liability policy or operator's policy of liability insurance shall be issued in this state unless and until all of the requirements of subsection (2) of this section are met.

(2) Every motor vehicle liability policy and every operator's policy of liability insurance accepted as proof under this article shall be subject to the following provisions whether or not contained therein:

(a) The liability of the insurance carrier under any such policy shall become absolute whenever loss or damage covered by such policy occurs, and the satisfaction by the insured of a final judgment for such loss or damage shall not be a condition precedent to the right or obligation of the carrier to make payment on account of such loss or damage. No fraud, misrepresentation, or other act of the insured in obtaining or retaining any such policy, or in adjusting a claim under any such policy, and no failure of the insured to give any notice, forward any paper, or otherwise cooperate with the insurance carrier shall constitute a defense as against the judgment creditor on any such judgment. The insurance carrier shall not be liable on any such judgment if it has not had reasonable notice of an opportunity to appear in and defend the action in which such judgment was rendered or if the judgment was obtained through collusion between the judgment creditor and the insured.

(b) The insurance carrier shall have the right to settle any claim covered by the policy, and if such settlement is made in good faith, the amount thereof shall be deductible from the limits of liability specified in the policy.

(c) No such policy shall be cancelled except as provided in this section and section 42-7-416. The notice of cancellation shall be delivered to the named insured in person or mailed by certified mail, post-office receipt secured, or by registered mail prior to such cancellation. Unless the contract or policy of insurance provides for a shorter period of notice, said notice shall be so delivered or mailed to the address shown in the policy not less than thirty days prior to the date of cancellation. Proof of such mailing shall be sufficient proof of cancellation. Failure by any insurer to comply with the provisions for cancellation in this section and section 42-7-416 shall render invalid any such cancellation.

(d) No such policy shall be cancelled or annulled as respects any loss or damage by any agreement between the carrier and the insured after the said insured has become responsible for such loss or damage, and any such cancellation or annulment shall be void.

(e) The policy may provide that the insured, or any other person covered by the policy, shall reimburse the insurance carrier for payment made on account of any loss or damage claim or suit involving a breach of the terms, provisions, or conditions of the policy. If the policy provides for limits in excess of the limits specified in section 42-7-103 (14), the insurance carrier may plead against any plaintiff, with respect to the amount of such excess limits of liability, any defenses which it may be entitled to plead against the insured, and any such policy may further provide for the prorating of the insurance thereunder with other applicable valid and collectible insurance.

(f) The policy, the written application therefor, if any, and any rider or endorsement which does not conflict with the provisions of this article shall constitute the entire contract between the parties.

(g) When any insurance carrier authorized to do business within the state of Colorado issues a policy of automobile insurance insuring against bodily injury, death, or injury to or destruction of property or showing financial responsibility, except a binder, a complete copy of the insurance policy shall be transmitted to the purchaser within thirty days of the purchase thereof; except that, when such policy is renewed, only a copy of the notice of renewal shall be required. Mailing of the copy of the policy to the address of the purchaser as given at the time of purchase shall be deemed to be a transmittal as required by this section.

(3) (a) The insurance carrier that issues a motor vehicle liability policy accepted as proof under this article shall include the following provision in the policy contract: "If the insured's whereabouts for service of process cannot be determined through reasonable effort, the insured agrees to designate and irrevocably appoint the insurance carrier as the agent of the insured for service of process, pleadings, or other filings in a civil action brought against the insured or to which the insured has been joined as a defendant or respondent in any Colorado court if the cause of action concerns an incident for which the insured can possibly claim coverage. Subsequent termination of the insurance policy does not affect the appointment for an incident that occurred when the policy was in effect. The insured agrees that any such civil action may be commenced against the insured by the service of process upon the insurance carrier as if personal service had been made directly on the insured. The insurance carrier agrees to forward all communications related to service of process to the last-known e-mail and mailing address of the policyholder in order to coordinate any payment of claims or defense of claims that are required."

(b) If service of process is made on the insurance carrier under this subsection (3), the plaintiff shall cause the service of process to be made on the insurance carrier's registered agent.

(c) If service is obtained under this section, the venue for the underlying claim is the same as if the defendant is a nonresident.

(d) Except as expressly provided in this subsection (3), this subsection (3) does not alter or expand the terms and conditions of the insurance policy or liability coverage.

(e) In the contract provision required by this subsection (3), the name of the insurance carrier issuing the policy shall be substituted for the phrase "The insurance carrier."

(f) If service of process is made on the insurance carrier under this subsection (3) and the court enters judgment or the insurance carrier agrees to a settlement for the damages caused by the absent insured, the amount of the insurance carrier's liability shall not exceed the policy limits of the coverage. A judgment or settlement obtained using service of process on the carrier shall not bar the injured person from subsequently making personal service on the person who caused the injury and seeking additional remedies provided by law.

(g) Payment under the policy pursuant to this section shall not be deemed to be an admission of liability by the alleged tortfeasor and shall not prejudice the right of the alleged tortfeasor to contest his or her liability or the extent of damages owed to the injured party.

(h) As used in this subsection (3), "reasonable effort" means service at the defendant's last-known address, an address obtained from the insurance policy, an address obtained from a driver's license or motor vehicle registration, or any readily ascertainable successor address.

42-7-415. When insurance carrier to issue certificate. An insurance carrier which has issued a motor vehicle liability policy or an operator's policy of liability insurance meeting the requirements of this article shall upon request of the insured therein deliver to the insured for filing or at the request of the insured shall file directly with the director an appropriate certificate showing that such policy has been issued, which certificate shall meet the requirements of this article. The issuance and delivery or filing of such a certificate shall be conclusive evidence that every policy therein recited has been duly issued and complies with the requirements of this article.

42-7-416. Notice required upon cancellation. When an insurance carrier has certified a motor vehicle liability policy under this article, it shall give written notice to the director during the ten-day period immediately following the effective date of the cancellation of such policy stating that the policy has been cancelled.

42-7-417. Article not to affect other policies. (1) This article shall not be held to apply to or affect policies of automobile insurance against liability which may be required by any other law of this state, and such policies, if endorsed to conform to the requirements of this article, shall be accepted as proof of financial responsibility when required under this article.

(2) This article shall not be held to apply to or affect policies insuring solely the insured named in the policy against liability resulting from the maintenance, operation, or use of motor vehicles not owned by the insured by persons in the insured's employ or on the insured's behalf.

42-7-418. Money - securities for financial responsibility. (1) A person may give proof of financial responsibility by delivering to the director money in an amount or securities approved by said director and of a market value in a total amount as would be required for coverage in a motor vehicle liability policy furnished by the person giving such proof under this article. Such securities shall be of a type which may legally be purchased by savings banks or for trust funds.

(2) All money or securities so deposited shall be subject to execution to satisfy any judgment mentioned in this article but shall not otherwise be subject to attachment or execution.

42-7-419. Substitution of proof. The director shall cancel any bond or return any certificate of insurance or the director shall direct and the state treasurer shall return any money or securities to the person entitled thereto, upon the substitution and acceptance of other adequate proof of financial responsibility pursuant to this article.

42-7-420. Failure of proof - other proof. Whenever any evidence of proof of ability to respond in damages filed by any person under the provisions of this article no longer fulfills the purpose for which required, the director, for the purpose of this article, shall require other evidence of ability to respond in damages as required by this article and shall suspend the license of such person pending such proof.

42-7-421. When director may release proof of financial responsibility. (1) The director, upon request, shall cancel any bond or return any certificate of insurance, or the director shall direct and the state treasurer shall return to the person entitled thereto any money or securities deposited pursuant to this article as proof of financial responsibility, or waive the requirement of filing proof of financial responsibility in any of the following events:

(a) At any time after three years from the date such proof was required, or after any other period during which proof was required pursuant to section 42-7-408 (1) in the case of certain violations for an alcohol-related driving offense, if, during such three-year or other period preceding the request, the person furnishing such proof has not been convicted of any offense referred to in section 42-7-406; or

(b) In the event of the death of the person on whose behalf such proof was filed, or the permanent incapacity of such person to operate a motor vehicle; or

(c) In the event the person who has given proof of financial responsibility surrenders the person's license to the director, but the director shall not release such proof in the event any action for damages upon a liability referred to in this article is then pending or any judgment upon any such liability is then outstanding and unsatisfied or in the event the director has received notice that such person has within the period of three months immediately preceding been involved as a driver in any motor vehicle accident. An affidavit of the applicant of the nonexistence of such facts shall be sufficient evidence thereof in the absence of evidence to the contrary in the records of the department.

(2) Whenever any person to whom proof has been surrendered, as provided in paragraph (c) of subsection (1) of this section, applies for a license within a period of three years from the date proof of financial responsibility was originally required, or within any other period during which proof of financial responsibility was required pursuant to section 42-7-408 (1), any such application shall be refused unless the applicant establishes such proof for the remainder of such period.

42-7-422. No proof when proof required. Any person whose license or other privilege to operate a motor vehicle has been suspended, cancelled, or revoked, and restoration thereof or issuance of a new license is contingent upon the furnishing of proof of financial responsibility for the future, and who, during such suspension or revocation or in the absence of proper authorization from the director, drives any motor vehicle upon any highway in Colorado except as permitted under this article, is guilty of a misdemeanor and, upon conviction thereof, shall be punished by imprisonment in the county jail for not less than five days nor more than six months and, in the discretion of the court, a fine of not less than fifty dollars nor more than five hundred dollars may be imposed. The minimum sentence imposed by this section shall be mandatory, and the court shall not grant probation or a suspended sentence, in whole or in part, or reduce or suspend the fine, except in a case where the defendant has established that the defendant had to drive the motor vehicle in violation of this section because of an emergency, in which case the mandatory jail sentence does not apply. Such minimum sentence need not be five consecutive days but may be served during any thirty-day period.

PART 5

GENERAL

42-7-501. Self-insurers. (1) Any person in whose name more than twenty-five motor vehicles are registered may qualify as a self-insurer by obtaining a certificate of self-insurance issued by the commissioner of insurance.

(2) The commissioner of insurance may, in his or her discretion, upon the application of such person, issue a certificate of self-insurance when the commissioner of insurance is satisfied that such person is possessed and will continue to be possessed of ability to pay all judgments that may be obtained against such person. Upon not less than five days' notice and a hearing pursuant to such notice, the commissioner of insurance may, upon reasonable grounds, cancel a certificate of self-insurance. Failure to pay any judgment within thirty days after such judgment has become final shall constitute a reasonable ground for the cancellation of a certificate of self-insurance.

42-7-502. Action against nonresident - reciprocity with other states. (1) All of the provisions of this article shall apply to any person who is not a resident of this state, and if such nonresident has been convicted of an offense which would require the suspension or revocation of the license of a resident, or if such nonresident has failed to satisfy a judgment within thirty days after the same became final which would require suspension or revocation under this article in respect to a resident, then in either such event such nonresident shall not operate any motor vehicle in this state, and the director shall not issue to such nonresident any license unless and until such nonresident gives proof of financial responsibility and satisfies any such judgment as is required with respect to a resident of this state.

(2) The director shall transmit a certified copy of any record of any such conviction of a nonresident to the motor vehicle commissioner or state officer performing the functions of a commissioner in the state in which such nonresident resides and shall likewise forward to such officer a certified record of any unsatisfied judgment rendered against such nonresident which requires suspension of such nonresident's driving privileges in this state.

(3) When a nonresident's operating privilege is suspended pursuant to section 42-7-301, the director shall transmit a certified copy of the record of such action to the official in charge of the issuance of licenses in the state in which such nonresident resides, if the law of such other state provides for action in relation thereto similar to that provided for in subsection (4) of this section.

(4) Upon receipt of certification that the operating privilege of a resident of this state has been suspended or revoked in any such other state pursuant to a law providing for its suspension or revocation for failure to deposit security for the payment of judgments arising out of a motor vehicle accident or for failure to deposit security and furnish a statement evidencing that the resident is insured under an automobile liability insurance policy or bond or for failure to file and maintain proof of financial responsibility, under circumstances which would require the director to suspend a nonresident's operating privilege had the accident occurred in this state, the director shall suspend the license of such resident. Such suspension shall continue until such resident furnishes evidence of compliance with the law of such other state relating to the deposit of such security and until such resident furnishes the statement evidencing automobile liability insurance or a bond, or, as the case may be, files proof of financial responsibility, if required by such law.

42-7-503. Director to furnish operating record. The director shall, upon request, furnish any insurance carrier or any person or surety the record of any person subject to the provisions of this article, which record shall fully designate the motor vehicles, if any, registered in the name of such person, and if there is no record of any conviction of such person of a violation of any provision of any statute relating to the operation of a motor vehicle or of any injury or damage caused by such person as provided in this article, the director shall so certify. Such records shall be public records and subject to the provisions of section 42-1-206. No information required to be confidential by the provisions of section 24-72-204 (3.5) (a), C.R.S., shall be released by the director except as provided by that section. The director shall collect for each such certificate the sum of seventy-five cents.

42-7-504. Matters not to be evidence in litigation. (1) Except as provided in subsection (2) of this section, neither action taken by the director pursuant to this article, any judgment or court decision on appeal therefrom, the findings of the director in such action, nor the security deposited, statement evidencing automobile liability insurance or bond, or proof of financial responsibility filed as provided in this article shall be referred to nor be evidence of the negligence or due care of either party of an action at law to recover damages or in a criminal proceeding arising out of a motor vehicle accident. This section shall not apply to an action brought by the director to enforce the provisions of this article.

(2) For the purposes of any civil trial, civil hearing, or arbitration held in relation to uninsured or underinsured motorist insurance coverage where the question of the existence of automobile liability insurance is an issue or when the amount of such insurance is an issue, the director shall issue, upon request, a certificate under seal. The certificate shall contain the motor vehicle operator's name, address, date of birth, and driver's license number; the date of the accident; and a statement indicating whether or not the records indicate that the owner or operator had in effect at the time of the accident an effective automobile liability policy and, if such a policy was in effect, the amount of coverage, the name of the insurer, and the number of the policy. Such certificate shall be prima facie evidence of the facts contained therein. The director shall collect for each such certificate an amount sufficient to defray the costs of administration of this section. Such amount shall be included as a cost of the action.

42-7-505. Forging ability to respond in damages. Any person who forges or without authority signs any evidence of ability to respond in damages or who furnishes the director with a false statement evidencing that such person is insured under an automobile liability policy or bond, as required by the director in the administration of this article, is guilty of a misdemeanor and, upon conviction thereof, shall be punished by a fine of not less than one hundred dollars nor more than one thousand dollars, or by imprisonment in the county jail for not more than ninety days, or by both such fine and imprisonment.

42-7-506. Surrender of license. (1) Any person whose license has been suspended as provided in this article and has not been reinstated shall immediately return such license held by such person to the director. Any person willfully failing to comply with this requirement is guilty of a misdemeanor.

(2) The director is authorized to take possession of any license upon the suspension thereof under the provisions of this article or to direct any peace officer to take possession thereof and to return the same to the office of the director.

42-7-507. Penalty. Any person who violates any provision of this article for which another penalty is not prescribed by law is guilty of a misdemeanor and, upon conviction thereof, shall be punished by a fine of not less than one hundred dollars nor more than one thousand dollars, or by imprisonment in the county jail for not more than ninety days, or by both such fine and imprisonment.

42-7-508. No repeal of motor vehicle laws. This article shall in no respect be considered as a repeal of the provisions of the state motor vehicle laws, but shall be construed as supplemental thereto.

42-7-509. Article does not prevent other process. This article shall not be construed to prevent the plaintiff in any action at law from relying for security upon the other processes provided by law.

42-7-510. Insurance or bond required. (1) An owner of a truck that is subject to the registration fee imposed pursuant to section 42-3-306 (5) (b) or (7) and that is not subject to article 10.1 of title 40, C.R.S., before operating or permitting the operation of the vehicle upon a public highway in this state, shall have in each vehicle a motor vehicle liability policy or a certificate evidencing the policy issued by an insurance carrier or insurer authorized to do business in Colorado, or a copy of a valid certificate of self-insurance issued pursuant to section 10-4-624, C.R.S., or a surety bond issued by a company authorized to do a surety business in Colorado in the sum of fifty thousand dollars for damages to property of others; the sum of one hundred thousand dollars for damages for or on account of bodily injury or death of one person as a result of any one accident; and, subject to such limit as to one person, the sum of three hundred thousand dollars for or on account of bodily injury to or death of all persons as a result of any one accident.

(2) (a) Every owner of a motor vehicle designed and used for the nonemergency transportation of individuals with disabilities as defined in paragraph (b) of this subsection (2), before operating or permitting the operation of such vehicle upon any public highway in this state, shall file with the department a certificate evidencing a motor vehicle liability insurance policy issued by an insurance carrier or insurer authorized to do business in the state of Colorado or a surety bond issued by a company authorized to do a surety business in the state of Colorado with a minimum sum of fifty thousand dollars for damages to property of others; a minimum sum of one hundred thousand dollars for damages for or on account of bodily injury or death of one person as a result of any one accident; and, subject to such limit as to one person, a minimum sum of three hundred thousand dollars for or on account of bodily injury to or death of all persons as a result of any one accident.

(b) As used in this subsection (2), a "motor vehicle designed and used for the nonemergency transportation of individuals with disabilities" means any motor vehicle designed to facilitate the loading of individuals with physical disabilities confined to a wheelchair except vehicles owned by the United States government, vehicles owned and operated by any special transportation district, or privately owned vehicles when such privately owned vehicles are used by the owner to transport the owner or members of the owner's family who are confined to a wheelchair.

(3) Any person who violates any provision of this section is guilty of a misdemeanor and shall be punished according to the provisions of section 42-7-507. If any violation of this section is committed on behalf of a partnership or corporation, any director, officer, partner, or high managerial agent thereof who authorized, ordered, permitted, or otherwise participated in, by commission or omission, such violation is also guilty of a misdemeanor and shall be punished according to the provisions of section 42-7-507.

PART 6

UNINSURED MOTORIST
IDENTIFICATION DATABASE
PROGRAM

42-7-601. Short title. (1) This part 6 shall be known and may be cited as the "Motorist Insurance Identification Database Program Act".

(2) Repealed.

42-7-602. Uninsured motorist identification database program - creation. The general assembly hereby directs the transportation legislation review committee to conduct an examination of the problem of uninsured motorists in this state and to propose legislation which shall alleviate if not eliminate the problem. The general assembly further directs the transportation legislation review committee to examine Colorado's compulsory motor vehicle insurance system. Such examination shall include a review of whether such system should be maintained or repealed and whether there are more effective enforcement mechanisms that might be employed. The committee shall also study the effectiveness of other enforcement mechanisms including, but not limited to, uninsured motorist database programs that have been employed in other compulsory insurance states.

42-7-603. Definitions. As used in this part 6, unless the context otherwise requires:

(1) "Database" means the motorist insurance identification database described in section 42-7-604 (5).

(2) "Department" means the department of revenue.

(3) "Designated agent" means the party with which the department contracts under section 42-7-604.

(4) (Deleted by amendment, L. 2000, p. 1649, § 43, effective June 1, 2000.)

(5) "Program" means the motorist insurance identification database program created in section 42-7-604.

42-7-604. Motorist insurance identification database program - creation - administration - selection of designated agent - legislative declaration. (1) The general assembly hereby finds, determines, and declares that the purpose of this section is to help reduce the uninsured motorist population in this state and measure the effectiveness of the motorist insurance identification database created herein.

(2) The general assembly further recognizes that the information and data required to be disclosed by insurers in creating and maintaining the motorist insurance identification database is proprietary in nature. Accordingly, the parties handling such information and data shall at all times maintain their confidential and proprietary nature.

(3) The motorist insurance identification database program is hereby created for the purpose of establishing a database to use when verifying compliance with the motor vehicle security requirements in this article and in articles 3 and 4 of this title. The program shall be administered by the department.

(4) (a) The department shall monitor compliance with the financial security requirements of this article and may contract with a designated agent to monitor such compliance with the financial security requirements of this article. If the department contracts with a designated agent, the agent shall be authorized to perform all functions of the department delegated to the agent in the contract.

(b) After a contract has been entered into with a designated agent, the department shall convene a working group for the purpose of facilitating the implementation of the program. The working group shall consist of representatives of the insurance industry, the division of insurance, the department of public safety, and the department.

(5) (a) The department or its designated agent, using its own computer network, shall develop and maintain a computer database with information provided by:

(I) Insurers, pursuant to section 10-4-615, C.R.S.; except that any person who qualifies as self-insured pursuant to section 10-4-624, C.R.S., shall not be required to provide information to the department; and

(II) The department shall compare the make, year, and vehicle identification number of all registered vehicles to policy information provided by insurers.

(b) The department shall establish guidelines for the development and maintenance of a database so that the database can easily be accessed by state and local law enforcement agencies.

(c) The department shall:

(I) Provide an internet option that allows insurers and their agents, including commercial insurers, to submit insurance information directly to the designated agent. Each insurer shall cooperate with the verification process.

(II) Provide a reasonable and adequate quality control process to ensure the accurate input of data, including the vehicle identification numbers and insurance information;

(III) (Deleted by amendment, L. 2006, p. 1011, § 7, effective July 1, 2006.)

(IV) Provide each county clerk access to the most currently available data from the database of insurance information.

(6) The department shall, at least weekly:

(a) Update the database with information provided by insurers in accordance with section 10-4-615, C.R.S.;

(b) Compare then-current motor vehicle registrations against the database.

(6.5) and (7) Repealed.

(8) The department, in cooperation with the division of insurance, shall promulgate rules and develop procedures for administering and enforcing this part 6. Such rules shall specify the reporting requirements that are necessary and appropriate for commercial lines of insurance and shall be developed with input by insurers and the designated agent.

42-7-605. Notice of lack of financial responsibility. (Repealed)

42-7-606. Disclosure of insurance information - penalty. (1) Information provided by insurers and the department for inclusion in the database established pursuant to section 42-7-604 is the property of the insurer or the department, as the case may be, and may not be disclosed except as follows:

(a) The department shall verify a motor vehicle's insurance coverage upon request by any state or local government agency investigating, litigating, or enforcing such motor vehicle's compliance with the financial security requirements.

(b) The department shall disclose whether a motor vehicle has the required insurance coverage upon request by the following individuals and agencies only:

(I) The owner;

(II) The parent or legal guardian of the owner if the owner is an unemancipated minor;

(III) The legal guardian of the owner if the owner is legally incapacitated;

(IV) Any person who has power of attorney from the owner;

(V) Any person who submits a notarized release from the owner that is dated no more than ninety days before the date the request is made;

(VI) Any person suffering loss or injury in a motor vehicle accident, but only as part of an accident report authorized in part 16 of article 4 of this title; or

(VII) The office of the state auditor, for the purpose of conducting any audit authorized by law.

(2) Any person or agency who knowingly discloses information from the database for a purpose or to a person other than those authorized in this section commits a class 1 misdemeanor and shall be punished as provided in section 18-1.3-501, C.R.S.

(3) The state shall not be liable to any person for gathering, managing, or using information in the database pursuant to this part 6.

(4) The designated agent shall not be liable to any person for performing its duties under this part 6, unless and to the extent said agent commits a willful and wanton act or omission. The designated agent shall be liable to any insurer damaged by the designated agent's negligent failure to protect the confidential and proprietary nature of the information and data disclosed by the insurer to the designated agent.

(5) The designated agent shall provide to this state an errors and omissions insurance policy covering said designated agent in an appropriate amount.

(6) No insurer shall be liable to any person for performing its duties under this part 6, unless and to the extent the insurer commits a willful and wanton act or omission.

42-7-607. Part 6 not to supersede other provisions. This part 6 shall not supersede other actions or penalties that may be taken or imposed for violation of the financial security requirements of this article.

42-7-608. Review by department of regulatory agencies - repeal. (Repealed)

42-7-609. Report. The department of revenue shall submit a report, in consultation with the division of insurance, regarding the effectiveness of the motorist insurance database, including without limitation the department's recommendations on whether the program should be continued and on whether enforcement mechanisms should be instituted or changed. The report shall be submitted to the house business affairs and labor committee of the general assembly by January 1, 2008.

PORT OF ENTRY WEIGH STATIONS

ARTICLE 8
Port of Entry Weigh Stations

42-8-101.	Legislative declaration.
42-8-102.	Definitions.
42-8-103.	Motor carrier services division.
42-8-104.	Powers and duties.
42-8-105.	Clearance of motor vehicles at port of entry weigh stations.
42-8-106.	Issuance of clearance receipts.
42-8-107.	Construction and rights-of-way.
42-8-108.	Cooperation among departments.
42-8-109.	Fines and penalties.
42-8-110.	Expenses of administration appropriated from the highway users tax fund.
42-8-111.	Cooperative agreements with contiguous states for operations of ports of entry - regulations.

42-8-101. Legislative declaration. In order to facilitate enforcement of the laws of the state of Colorado concerning motor carriers and the owners and operators of motor vehicles; to equally distribute the payments of any fees, licenses, or taxes imposed by the laws of this state on motor carriers and the owners and operators of motor vehicles, and to effect the collection thereof; and to assist motor carriers and the owners and operators of motor vehicles to comply with all tax laws, rules, and regulations pertaining to them, it is declared necessary to establish port of entry weigh stations on the public highways of this state.

42-8-102. Definitions. As used in this article, unless the context otherwise requires:

(1) "Motor vehicles" means trucks, truck tractors, trailers, and semitrailers or combinations thereof.

(2) "Person" means an individual, a partnership, a corporation, a company, or an association.

42-8-103. Motor carrier services division. (1) There is hereby created within the department of revenue a motor carrier services division, which division, acting under the authority and direction of the executive director of the department of revenue, shall be further subdivided into enforcement functions and service functions. Enforcement functions shall include, but need not be limited to, the ports of entry section. Service functions shall include, but need not be limited to, personnel and facilities for dealing with interstate and international motor vehicle registrations.

(2) The executive director shall be responsible for establishing and operating port of entry weigh stations at such points along the public

highways of this state as are determined to be necessary to carry out the purposes of this article. The executive director shall authorize permanent port of entry weigh stations and mobile port of entry weigh stations to be established and operated by the division. The location or relocation of such stationary or mobile port of entry weigh stations shall be determined by the executive director. Wherever any provision of this article refers to a motor vehicle inspection station or to a motor carrier inspection station, such provision shall be deemed to refer to a port of entry weigh station established and operated by the motor carrier services division.

42-8-104. Powers and duties. (1) The executive director of the department of revenue shall issue such rules and regulations as the executive director deems necessary to implement this article and carry out its purposes. Said executive director shall, to the fullest extent possible, house department field offices at such places as port of entry weigh stations are established. All permanent port of entry weigh stations established under the authority of this article shall be operated on a twenty-four-hour-a-day basis, except for certain holidays or other times determined by the executive director of the department of revenue, and in such manner as to reasonably allow owners and operators of motor vehicles subject to fees, licenses, or taxes or to regulations imposed by the state of Colorado to comply with all such laws and regulations issued pursuant thereto by clearance at a port of entry weigh station. All port of entry weigh stations, either permanent or mobile, shall be equipped with weighing equipment approved as to accuracy by the division of inspection and consumer services of the department of agriculture.

(2) The personnel of a port of entry weigh station, during the time that they are actually engaged in performing their duties as such and while acting under proper orders or regulations issued by the executive director of the department of revenue, shall have and exercise all the powers invested in peace officers in connection with the enforcement of the provisions of this article, article 2 of this title, parts 2, 3, and 5 of article 20 of this title, part 5 of article 4 of this title, and sections 42-3-107 (17) and 42-4-1409; except that they shall not have the power to serve civil writs and process and, in the exercise of their duties, such personnel shall have the authority to restrain and detain persons or vehicles and may impound any vehicle until any tax or license fee imposed by law is paid or until compliance is had with any tax or regulatory law or regulation issued thereunder.

42-8-105. Clearance of motor vehicles at port of entry weigh stations. (1) Every owner or operator of a motor vehicle that is subject to payment of registration fees under the provisions of section 42-3-306 (5) (b) and every owner or operator of a motor vehicle or combination of vehicles having a manufacturer's gross vehicle weight rating or gross combination weight rating of twenty-six thousand one pounds or more shall secure a valid clearance from an office of the department of revenue, from an officer of the Colorado state patrol, or from a port of entry weigh station before operating such vehicle or combination of vehicles or causing such vehicle or combination of vehicles to be operated on the public highways of this state, but an owner or operator shall be deemed to have complied with the provisions of this subsection (1) if the owner or operator secures a valid clearance from the first port of entry weigh station located within five road miles of the route that the owner or operator would normally follow from the point of departure to the point of destination. An owner or operator shall not be required to seek out a port of entry weigh station not located on the route such owner or operator is following if the owner or operator secures a special revocable permit from the department of revenue in accordance with the provisions of subsection (4) of this section. A vehicle with a seating capacity of fourteen or more passengers registered under the provisions of section 42-3-304 (13) or 42-3-306 (2) (c) (I) shall not be required to secure a valid clearance pursuant to this section.

(2) It is unlawful for any owner or operator of a motor vehicle subject to the provisions of subsection (1) of this section to permit the travel of such motor vehicle on the public highways of this state without first having secured a valid clearance as provided in said subsection (1), and every such owner or operator shall be required to seek out a port of entry weigh station for the purpose of securing such valid clearance, whether or not such port of entry weigh station is located on the route that the owner or operator is following, unless a valid clearance or a special permit in accordance with subsection (4) of this section has previously been secured.

(3) Every owner or operator of a motor vehicle subject to the provisions of subsection (1) of this section shall secure a valid clearance at each port of entry weigh station located on the route that the owner or operator would normally follow from the point of departure to the point of destination for verification of its previously secured clearance.

(3.5) Every owner or operator of a motor vehicle subject to the provisions of subsection (1) of this section, when stopped for a lawful inspection, shall permit personnel of a port of entry weigh station to inspect the fuel tank of the vehicle for the purpose of ensuring that the vehicle is not operating on the public highways of the state using tax-exempt diesel fuel in violation of section 42-4-1414.

(4) The department of revenue may issue a special revocable permit to the owner or operator of any vehicle being operated over a regularly scheduled route waiving the requirement that the owner or operator seek out and secure a valid clearance at a port of entry weigh station not located directly on the route being followed.

In order for the permit to be effective, the vehicle must be operating over a regularly scheduled route that has previously been cleared with the department of revenue.

(5) Any owner or operator of a motor vehicle that is subject to the provisions of sections 42-3-304 to 42-3-306, who is found guilty of violating the provisions and requirements of this section, shall be subject to the fines and penalties prescribed in section 42-8-109.

(6) To facilitate the proper identification and handling of all motor vehicles requiring clearance through the port of entry weigh stations of the state, every vehicle requiring such clearance shall have affixed to it a distinct marking conforming to specifications set by the executive director. Such marking shall include the name or company logo of the owner or operator of the motor vehicle and such other information as the executive director shall require.

42-8-106. Issuance of clearance receipts. All owners and operators of motor vehicles subject to the payment of fees, licenses, or taxes imposed by the laws of this state, including foreign vehicles, that have not been properly certificated or permitted by the public utilities commission or that have not been approved by the department of revenue for monthly or periodic payment of such fees, licenses, or taxes shall be issued a clearance receipt at a port of entry weigh station only after such fees, licenses, or taxes that may be due are paid or compliance is had with regulatory acts. A clearance receipt issued under this section shall specify the date upon which issued and amounts of fees, licenses, or taxes to be paid. Such receipt shall be valid only for the dates and trips specified thereon and for the length of time specified thereon. The executive director of the department of revenue, through the port of entry weigh stations, may also issue permits for oversize and overweight commercial hauls pursuant to rules and regulations governing such hauls established by the department of transportation. Failure to secure such clearance receipt shall subject the owner or operator to a penalty of double the amount of any tax, license, or fee due that shall be in addition to and distinct from the penalty provided for in section 42-8-109.

42-8-107. Construction and rights-of-way. Within thirty days after receiving notification from the executive director of the department of revenue, the department of transportation shall make available without charge to the department of revenue such rights-of-way upon or adjacent to the public highways of this state as are needed for the construction or reconstruction of port of entry weigh stations. If such rights-of-way are not available, the department of transportation shall acquire such rights-of-way as are needed to carry out the purposes of this article out of money in the state highway fund provided for right-of-way acquisition. If possible, the construction, reconstruction, and maintenance of port of entry weigh stations shall be accomplished with forces of the department of transportation within thirty days after notification by the executive director of the department of revenue requesting such work.

42-8-108. Cooperation among departments. The governor of Colorado shall require the executive director of the department of revenue, the chief of the Colorado state patrol, the chief engineer of the division of highways, the commissioner of agriculture, the director of the division of commerce and development, and the chairman of the public utilities commission to cooperate to the fullest extent possible to the end that port of entry weigh stations established under authority of this article shall serve the broadest possible functions.

42-8-109. Fines and penalties. (1) Any person who drives a vehicle or owns a vehicle in violation of the provisions of section 42-8-105 (1) to (5) or 42-8-106 commits a class 2 misdemeanor traffic offense.

(2) Notwithstanding the provisions of section 42-1-217, all fines and penalties imposed under this article shall be transmitted to the state treasurer, who shall credit the same to the state highway fund; except that, fifty percent of any fine or penalty imposed under this article for a violation occurring within the corporate limits of a city, town, or city and county or outside the corporate limits of a city, town, or city and county, which violation is cited by a law enforcement officer of such city, town, county, or city and county, shall be transmitted to the treasurer or chief financial officer of such city, town, county, or city and county, and the remaining fifty percent shall be transmitted to the state treasurer, who shall credit the same to the state highway fund.

(3) In addition to the penalties imposed pursuant to subsection (1) of this section, the executive director of the department of revenue shall, upon the conviction of any owner or operator or of any agent, officer, or employee, after a third offense within one calendar year, notify the public utilities commission of such conviction, and the commission may suspend any license or permit for a period not to exceed six months or revoke all such certificates and permits issued to the owner or operator of such vehicles by the public utilities commission. Such certificate or permit can be suspended or revoked only after due notice and hearing and for good cause shown. The executive director of the department of revenue shall file a complaint with the public utilities commission, and the commission must hold a hearing within thirty days after filing of a complaint by the said executive director. If at the hearing the commission finds that the facts as stated in the complaint by the said executive director are substantially correct, the commission may immediately revoke all intrastate certificates and permits issued by it to such violator.

(4) (Deleted by amendment, L. 96, p. 386, § 4, effective April 17, 1996.)

42-8-110. Expenses of administration appropriated from the highway users tax fund. For the purpose of administering this article and for the operation, maintenance, and future construction of the port of entry weigh stations established pursuant to this article, there shall be appropriated from the highway users tax fund for each fiscal year such moneys as the general assembly may determine, upon presentation of a budget for that purpose in form and content in accordance with the provisions for submission of budget requests by state agencies.

42-8-111. Cooperative agreements with contiguous states for operations of ports of entry - regulations. (1) In addition to any other powers granted by law, the executive director of the department of revenue is hereby authorized to negotiate and enter into cooperative agreements with the designated representatives of contiguous states for the operations of ports of entry at the borders between Colorado and such contiguous states.

(2) An agreement with a contiguous state or contiguous states for the operation of ports of entry at the borders between Colorado and such contiguous state or states entered into under the provisions of this section may include, but shall not be limited to, the following provisions:

(a) The joint operation of ports of entry by Colorado and a contiguous state or contiguous states;

(b) A grant of authority to the port of entry employees and officials of Colorado and to the port of entry employees and officials of each other state which is a party to such agreement to:

(I) Collect any fees, taxes, and penalties which are imposed by other states which are parties to such agreement on behalf of such states and to remit such fees, taxes, and penalties to such states; and

(II) Take actions to enforce the laws of other states that are parties to the agreement, including, but not limited to, the monitoring of licenses and other credential usage, the enforcement of tax restraint, distraint, or levy orders, the issuance of civil citations, and the conduct of any necessary equipment inspections. Port of entry personnel shall have and maintain the authority to enforce the provisions of section 42-4-1414 regarding the prohibition on the use of dyed fuel on Colorado highways.

(c) The assignment of Colorado ports of entry employees and officials at jointly operated ports of entry outside of Colorado and the assignment of ports of entry employees and officials of contiguous states at ports of entry within Colorado; and

(d) The allowance of such access to the data bases of Colorado and other states which are parties to such agreement by the employees and officials of each state as is necessary to enforce the laws of each such state and to operate under the terms of such agreement.

(3) Any agreement entered into under the provisions of this section shall contain provisions which express the understanding that any employees and officials of any other state who are assigned to jointly operated ports of entry, who enforce the laws of Colorado under the terms of such agreement, or who otherwise act under the terms of such agreement shall not be compensated by Colorado and shall not be considered to be employees or officials of Colorado for the purposes of any employee rights or benefits.

(4) The executive director of the department of revenue is hereby authorized to appoint employees and officials of a contiguous state as agents of the ports of entry section of the department of revenue with the powers to enforce the laws of Colorado under the terms of cooperative agreements entered into under the provisions of this section.

(5) The executive director of the department of revenue may promulgate such regulations as are necessary for the implementation of the provisions of this section.

MOTOR VEHICLE REPAIRS

ARTICLE 9

Motor Vehicle Repair Act

42-9-101.	Short title.
42-9-102.	Definitions.
42-9-103.	Applicability.
42-9-104.	When consent and estimate required - original transaction - disassembly.
42-9-105.	When consent and estimate required - additional repairs - changed completion date.
42-9-106.	Amounts over estimate - storage charges - cancellation of authorized repairs.
42-9-107.	Used, reconditioned, or rebuilt parts.
42-9-108.	Invoice.
42-9-108.5.	Warranty completion date.
42-9-108.7.	Motor vehicle repair facility warranties.
42-9-109.	Return of replaced parts.
42-9-109.5.	Inflatable restraint systems - replacement.
42-9-110.	Exemption - antique motor vehicles.
42-9-111.	Prohibited acts.
42-9-112.	Criminal penalties.
42-9-113.	Civil penalties.

42-9-101. Short title. This article shall be known and may be cited as the "Motor Vehicle Repair Act of 1977".

42-9-102. Definitions. As used in this article, unless the context otherwise requires:

(1) "Auto parts recycler" means any person who purchases motor vehicles for the purpose of dismantling and selling the components thereof and who complies with all federal, state, and

local regulations. "Auto parts recycler" includes a vehicle dismantler.

(1.2) "Customer" means the owner, the agent of the owner, or a family member, employee, or any other person whose use of the vehicle is authorized by the owner.

(1.5) "Estimate" means a written or oral assessment that describes structural damage to or mechanical needs of a motor vehicle. The estimate shall include total estimated costs of repair, excluding sales taxes and towing charges, together with a statement as to whether any parts to be installed are new original equipment manufacturer, new nonoriginal equipment manufacturer, used, reconditioned, or rebuilt.

(1.6) "Inflatable restraint system" has the same meaning as is set forth in 49 CFR sec. 507.208 S4.1.5.1 (b).

(1.7) "Invoice" means the final statement for services rendered.

(2) "Motor vehicle" means every self-propelled vehicle intended primarily for use and operation on the public highways. The term does not include trucks and truck tractors having a gross vehicle weight of more than eight thousand five hundred pounds, nor does it include farm tractors and other machines and tools used in the production, harvesting, and care of farm products, nor does it include motorcycles.

(3) "Motor vehicle repair facility" means any natural person, partnership, corporation, trust, association, or group of persons associated in fact although not a legal entity which, with intent to make a profit or a gain of money or other thing of value, engages in the business or occupation of performing repairs on a motor vehicle, including repairs on body parts. The term "motor vehicle repair facility" includes a motor vehicle repair garage.

(4) "Necessary" means essential to a desired or projected end as stated by the customer or indispensable to avoid loss or damage.

(5) "Repairs on a motor vehicle" or "repairs" includes maintenance, diagnosis, repairs, service, and parts replacement but does not include washing the vehicle or adding gasoline or oil to the vehicle.

(6) "Work order" means a document that a customer signs to authorize repairs. "Work order" may include an estimate.

42-9-103. Applicability. The provisions of sections 42-9-104, 42-9-105, and 42-9-106 shall not apply where the total cost of the labor and parts is one hundred dollars or less.

42-9-104. When consent and estimate required - original transaction - disassembly. (1) (a) No repairs on a motor vehicle shall be performed by a motor vehicle repair facility unless the facility obtains the written consent of the customer.

(b) The required written consent is waived by the customer only when the motor vehicle has been towed to the motor vehicle repair facility or the customer has left the motor vehicle with the motor vehicle repair facility outside of normal business hours or when the customer has signed a waiver in compliance with paragraph (b) of subsection (2) of this section. The waiver established by this paragraph (b) for any vehicle that is towed to a motor vehicle repair facility or left with the motor vehicle repair facility outside of normal business hours is limited to a maximum of one hundred dollars for all labor and parts.

(c) When the customer has not given the motor vehicle repair facility written consent to perform repairs, no repairs shall be performed unless the facility first communicates orally to the customer the written estimate of the total cost of such repairs and the customer then consents to the required repairs. A record of such communication and consent shall be made on the work order by the motor vehicle repair facility and shall include the date, time, manner of consent, telephone number called, if any, and the names of the persons giving and receiving such consent. If more than one such communication occurs between the motor vehicle repair facility and the customer, a record of the telephone number need not be made for each subsequent communication if the telephone number is the same as on the initial consent.

(2) (a) (I) Except as provided in paragraph (b) of this subsection (2), no repairs shall be performed by a motor vehicle repair facility unless said facility first submits in writing or, where allowed by this section, orally communicates to the customer an estimate of the total cost of any such repairs. The written estimate shall include the expected completion date of such repairs. A copy of the completed written estimate of the total cost of repair shall be provided to the customer.

(II) (A) Except as provided in sub-subparagraph (B) of this subparagraph (II), storage charges may accrue, beginning on the fourth day, if the customer has not picked up the motor vehicle within three days, exclusive of Saturday, Sunday, any legal holiday, and any days the repair facility is closed for business, after notification of the completion of authorized repairs or if the customer failed to authorize repairs to be performed within three days, exclusive of Saturday, Sunday, any legal holiday, and any days the repair facility is closed for business, after the date of communication of an estimate.

(B) Storage charges shall be assessed in accordance with section 38-20-109, C.R.S., if the facility chooses to sell the customer's property in accordance with article 20 of title 38, C.R.S.

(C) The amounts that a customer may be charged for storage charges shall be conspicuously printed on the separate written authorization provided to the customer.

(III) The work order provided to the customer shall state conspicuously that, except for body shop repair parts and exchanged or warranty parts that shall only be presented to the customer for examination and not returned, and except for inflatable restraint system components, the customer is entitled to the return of the replaced parts if the customer so requests at the time of consenting to or authorizing the repairs.

(IV) The work order, or a legible copy thereof, shall be retained by the motor vehicle repair facility for at least three years.

(b) A customer may waive the right to receive any estimate, either written or oral, prior to authorizing repairs by signing the customer's name and the date below the following statement that shall be in bold type: **"I DO NOT WISH TO RECEIVE ANY ESTIMATE, EITHER WRITTEN OR ORAL, TO WHICH I AM ENTITLED BY LAW, BEFORE REPAIRS ARE AUTHORIZED."** The signing of such waiver does not constitute an authorization of repairs, which shall be a separate statement.

(c) (I) In the event that it is necessary to disassemble, or partially disassemble, a motor vehicle or a motor vehicle part in order to provide the customer with an estimate for required repairs, the written estimate required in paragraph (a) of this subsection (2) shall show the cost of reassembly in the event that the customer elects not to proceed with the repairs of the motor vehicle or motor vehicle part. The estimate shall also include the total cost of labor and parts to replace those expendable items that are normally destroyed by such disassembly. No act of disassembly that would prevent the restoration of the same unit to its former condition may be undertaken unless the motor vehicle repair facility has fully informed the customer of that fact in writing on the work order and the customer consents to the disassembly.

(II) Any estimate of required repairs given after a disassembly shall comply with the requirements of paragraph (a) of this subsection (2); except that such written estimate may then be communicated orally to the customer. A record of such communication shall be made on the work order by the motor vehicle repair facility, including the date, time, manner of communication, telephone number called, if any, and names of persons giving and receiving such consent. If more than one such communication occurs between the motor vehicle repair facility and the customer, a record of the telephone number need not be made for each subsequent communication if the telephone number is the same as on the initial consent.

(d) Towing charges are excluded from the written or oral estimate and consent requirements of this section.

42-9-105. When consent and estimate required - additional repairs - changed completion date. (1) Except when an estimate has been waived pursuant to section 42-9-104 (2) (b), no charge shall be made for labor and parts in excess of the estimate, plus ten percent thereof or twenty-five dollars, whichever is less, without the consent of the customer to the additional charge before performance of the labor or installation of the parts not included in the estimate. Consent by the customer to additional charges may be written or oral. In either case, a record of such consent shall be made on the work order by the motor vehicle repair facility and shall include the date, time, manner of consent, telephone number called, if any, and names of the persons giving and receiving the consent. If more than one such communication occurs between the motor vehicle repair facility and the customer, a record of the telephone number need not be made for each subsequent communication if the telephone number is the same as on the initial consent.

(2) (a) The customer shall be notified in writing on the work order of any changes in the expected completion date of the repairs and of the new expected completion date. Such notification may be communicated to the customer orally, but such communication, written or oral, shall be made no more than twenty-four hours after the original completion date, exclusive of Saturday, Sunday, and any legal holiday. If communicated orally, a record of such communication shall be made on the work order by the motor vehicle repair facility and shall include the date, time, telephone number called, if any, and names of the persons giving and receiving such communication. If the name of the person receiving such communication is different than the original customer, the name and telephone number called, if any, shall be recorded on the work order.

(b) No additional changes in the completion date shall be made unless the consent of the customer to the additional change is obtained. If the required consent is given orally, the motor vehicle repair facility shall make a record of such consent on the work order and shall include the date, time, manner of consent, and the names of the persons giving and receiving such consent.

(c) If the motor vehicle repair facility fails to notify the customer of the change in the completion date or if the customer refuses to consent to an additional change in the completion date, the contract may be cancelled at the option of either the customer or the motor vehicle repair facility. Once the contract has been cancelled in this manner, the motor vehicle repair facility shall be required to reassemble the motor vehicle in substantially the same condition in which it was delivered to the motor vehicle repair facility without cost to the customer unless the customer has been previously notified as to the impracticality of such reassembly; except that the customer shall be required to pay for any repairs already completed as specified in section 42-9-106 (3) (a).

42-9-106. Amounts over estimate - storage charges - cancellation of authorized repairs. (1) Except when an estimate has been waived pursuant to section 42-9-104 (2) (b), if the charge for labor and parts is over the original estimate or any subsequent estimate by ten percent thereof or twenty-five dollars, whichever is less, and unless further oral or written consent is given by the customer pursuant to section 42-9-105 (1), the motor vehicle repair facility shall return the motor vehicle to the customer upon the payment of the amount of the original estimate or any subsequent estimate plus ten percent thereof or twenty-five dollars, whichever is less, and the motor vehicle repair facility shall not be entitled to a lien for said excess pursuant to section 38-20-106, C.R.S.

(2) No charge shall be made for storage of the motor vehicle unless the motor vehicle is not picked up by the customer within three days, exclusive of Saturday, Sunday, legal holidays, and any days the repair facility is closed for business, after the customer is notified that the repairs have been completed and the customer was notified, as required by section 42-9-104 (2) (a), that such storage charges would accrue. Storage charges may accrue pursuant to a written agreement, separate from any other repair document, between the motor vehicle repair facility and the customer. The written authorization, in bold type, shall state the following:

Storage Fee Policy

A storage fee may not be charged unless a written agreement, separate from any other repair document, for an amount is reached. A storage fee may be charged, beginning on the fourth day, if a motor vehicle is not removed within three days after the customer is notified that repairs have been completed, excluding Saturdays, Sundays, legal holidays, and any days the repair facility is closed for business.

The motor vehicle repair facility shall make a record of the notice of completion on the work order. The record shall include the date and time of the notice of completion, the manner of communication of the notice, the telephone number called, if any, and the name of the person receiving the notice.

(3) (a) If the customer cancels previously authorized repairs prior to their completion, the motor vehicle repair facility shall be entitled to charge the customer for repairs, including labor and parts, which have already been performed so long as said charge does not exceed the original estimate or any subsequent estimate for the repairs already performed.

(b) In requesting the return of the motor vehicle subsequent to the cancellation of previously authorized repairs, the customer shall specify whether it should be reassembled in substantially the same condition in which it was delivered to the motor vehicle repair facility or in such a lesser condition of assembly as the customer shall designate. Reassembly shall be completed by the motor vehicle repair facility within three days of the customer's request, excluding Saturday, Sunday, any legal holiday, and any days the repair facility is closed for business.

(c) All charges for reassembly, whether or not the requested repairs are completed, shall be included in the original estimate or in any subsequent estimate.

(4) Nothing in this section shall require a motor vehicle repair facility to give an estimate if such facility does not agree to perform the requested repairs.

(5) Payment by the customer of any amount in excess of those allowed by this article or for unauthorized repairs is not a waiver of any of the rights granted by this article to the customer, nor shall such payment be construed as consent to additional repairs or excess charges.

(6) All written estimates and other information required by this section shall be recorded on or attached to the invoice described in section 42-9-108.

42-9-107. Used, reconditioned, or rebuilt parts. The motor vehicle repair facility shall specify in the original estimate whether any parts to be installed are new original equipment manufacturer, new nonoriginal equipment manufacturer, used, reconditioned, or rebuilt and then shall obtain the consent of the customer before any new original equipment manufacturer, new nonoriginal equipment manufacturer, used, reconditioned, or rebuilt parts are installed in the motor vehicle. If such consent is oral, the motor vehicle repair facility shall make a record of such consent on the work order and shall include the date, time, and manner of consent. The telephone number called, if any, and the name of the person giving and receiving the consent, if different than the original customer, shall be recorded on the work order. The motor vehicle repair facility shall adjust the original estimate for new parts to reflect the altered cost if used, reconditioned, or rebuilt parts are authorized and installed.

42-9-108. Invoice. (1) All repairs done by a motor vehicle repair facility shall be recorded on a customer's invoice. A legible copy of the customer's invoice shall be given to the customer when the motor vehicle is returned to the customer. The original or a legible copy of the customer's invoice shall be retained for at least three years by the motor vehicle repair facility.

(2) The customer's invoice shall include the following:

(a) The name and address of the customer;

(b) The year, make, odometer reading on the date the motor vehicle was brought in for repairs, and license number of the motor vehicle;

(c) The date the motor vehicle was received for repairs;

(d) An itemization of each part added to or replaced in the motor vehicle; a description of each part by name and identifying number; clear identification of which parts are used, reconditioned, or rebuilt; and the charges levied for each part added or replaced;

(e) The amount charged for labor, the full name or employee number of each mechanic or repairer who in whole or in part performed repairs, and the identification of the specific stage of repair for which each mechanic or repairer named was partially or wholly responsible;

(f) An itemized statement of all additional charges, including storage, service and handling, and taxes;

(g) An identification of any repairs subcontracted to another repair facility;

(h) The legible initials of the person filling out any portion of the invoice not specified in this subsection (2); and

(i) A copy of any warranty issued by the motor vehicle repair facility setting forth the terms and conditions of such warranty.

(3) Itemization of a particular part is not required on the customer's invoice if no charge is levied for that part.

(4) Miscellaneous designations such as "shop supplies", "paint and paint supplies", and "shop materials" may be used on the customer's invoice.

(5) Designation of mechanics, repairers, parts, or labor is not required on the customer's invoice if the customer has been given a flat-rate price, if such repairs are customarily done and billed on a flat-rate price basis and agreed upon by the customer, and if such flat rates are conspicuously posted by the motor vehicle repair garage or otherwise made available to the customer prior to rendering the estimate.

42-9-108.5. Warranty completion date. When a motor vehicle is returned under a warranty issued by the repair facility, the facility shall give the customer a written notice that specifies that the work is under warranty and that provides the customer with a completion date for the repair, as required by section 42-9-104.

42-9-108.7. Motor vehicle repair facility warranties. If a motor vehicle repair facility issues a motor vehicle repair facility warranty, such warranty shall appear with the invoice and shall set forth all terms and conditions of such warranty. The facility warranty shall be limited to the terms and conditions set forth in such warranty.

42-9-109. Return of replaced parts. Except for body shop repair parts, inflatable restraint system components, and parts that the motor vehicle repair facility is required to return to the manufacturer or distributor under a manufacturer warranty or exchange arrangement, the motor vehicle repair facility shall return replaced parts to the customer at the time of the completion of the repairs if the customer so requests at the time of consenting to or authorizing the repairs. A motor vehicle repair facility is not authorized to return any components of an inflatable restraint system to the consumer.

42-9-109.5. Inflatable restraint systems - replacement. (1) (a) A motor vehicle repair garage may replace an inflatable restraint system only with an inflatable restraint system that is newly manufactured or an inflatable restraint system salvaged and sold by a vehicle dismantler or auto parts recycler.

(b) A motor vehicle repair garage is not required to install a salvaged inflatable restraint system and may do so only upon obtaining specific written authorization from the customer. A motor vehicle repair garage installing a salvaged inflatable restraint system shall include the phrase "salvaged inflatable restraint system" prominently on the face of the invoice. A motor vehicle repair garage may not use other terms, including but not limited to "used" or "as is", to describe a salvaged inflatable restraint system on an invoice.

(2) (a) If a vehicle dismantler or auto parts recycler sells a salvaged inflatable restraint system, the vehicle dismantler or auto parts recycler shall state the following information on the invoice:

(I) The date of sale of the salvaged inflatable restraint system;

(II) The vehicle identification number of the vehicle from which the inflatable restraint system was salvaged; and

(III) The part number of the salvaged inflatable restraint system, if such number is available.

(b) A vehicle dismantler or auto parts recycler shall maintain the bill of sale for any sale of a salvaged inflatable restraint system for at least three years after the date of the sale.

42-9-110. Exemption - antique motor vehicles. This article does not apply to repairs of any motor vehicle twenty-five or more years old or of any motor vehicle that is a collector's item as defined in section 42-12-101.

42-9-111. Prohibited acts. (1) No motor vehicle repair facility or any employee or contract laborer of such facility shall:

(a) Charge for repairs which have not been consented to by the customer or charge for repairs in excess of amounts allowed by this article;

(b) Represent that repairs are necessary when such is not a fact;

(c) Represent that repairs have been performed when such is not a fact;

(d) Represent that a motor vehicle or motor vehicle part being diagnosed is in dangerous condition when such is not a fact;

(e) Perform emissions repairs to bring motor vehicles into compliance with the provisions of sections 42-4-301 to 42-4-316 when such repairs are not indicated by the identified emissions failure;

(f) Fail to issue an invoice as required by section 42-9-108;

(g) Fail to give notice as required by section 42-9-105;

(h) Require a customer to sign a work order that does not state the repairs that are requested by the customer;

(i) Fail to state the motor vehicle odometer reading, unless such reading is unfeasible due to the condition of the odometer; or

(j) Install or reinstall, as part of a vehicle inflatable restraint system, any object in lieu of an air bag that was designed in accordance with federal safety regulations for the make, model, and year of the vehicle.

42-9-112. Criminal penalties. (1) Except as provided in subsection (2) of this section, any motor vehicle repair facility or any employee of such facility that fails to provide a completed written or oral estimate as required under section 42-9-104 (2), or an invoice as required under section 42-9-108, is guilty of a misdemeanor and, upon conviction thereof, shall be punished by a fine of not less than five hundred dollars nor more than two thousand dollars per violation. No portion of the minimum fine for repeat offenders shall be suspended.

(2) Except as otherwise provided in subsection (4) of this section, any motor vehicle repair facility or any employee of such facility who violates section 42-9-111 is guilty of a misdemeanor and, upon conviction thereof, shall be punished by a fine of not less than five hundred dollars nor more than one thousand dollars per violation. No portion of the minimum fine for repeat offenders shall be suspended.

(2.5) Any motor vehicle repair facility or any employee of such facility who violates any provision of this article other than the provisions for which penalties are provided in subsections (1), (2), and (4) of this section is guilty of a misdemeanor and, upon conviction thereof, shall be punished by a fine of five hundred dollars per violation.

(2.7) A violation of this article shall also constitute a deceptive trade practice in violation of the "Colorado Consumer Protection Act", article 1 of title 6, C.R.S., and shall subject the motor vehicle repair facility or any employee of such facility to the remedies or penalties contained in article 1 of title 6.

(3) (Deleted by amendment, L. 97, p. 863, § 11, effective May 21, 1997.)

(4) Any motor vehicle repair facility or any employee of such facility who violates the provisions of section 42-9-111 (1) (j) is guilty of a misdemeanor and, upon conviction thereof, shall be punished by a fine of not less than two thousand five hundred dollars and not more than five thousand dollars per violation, or imprisonment in the county jail for up to one year, or both.

42-9-113. Civil penalties. In any civil action for the enforcement of this article, the court may award reasonable attorney fees and costs to the prevailing party, and a customer shall be entitled to treble damages for failure of any motor vehicle repair facility or any employee of such facility to comply with this article, except for clerical errors or omissions; but in no event shall such damages be less than two hundred fifty dollars. The customer shall first make written demand for the customer's damages from the motor vehicle repair facility by certified mail at least ten days prior to the filing of any such action, exclusive of Saturday, Sunday, and any legal holiday. Such action shall be brought within the time period prescribed in section 13-80-103, C.R.S.

ARTICLE 9.5

Vehicle Protection Products

42-9.5-101. Short title.
42-9.5-102. Definitions.
42-9.5-103. Vehicle protection products.
42-9.5-104. Warranty reimbursement insurance policies.
42-9.5-105. Warranties - insurance.
42-9.5-106. Applicability.

42-9.5-101. Short title. This article shall be known and may be cited as the "Vehicle Protection Products Act".

42-9.5-102. Definitions. As used in this article, unless the context otherwise requires:

(1) "Incidental costs" means expenses incurred by the warranty holder that concern the failure of the vehicle protection product and that are specified in the vehicle protection product warranty. Incidental costs may include, without limitation, insurance policy deductibles, rental vehicle charges, the difference between the actual value of the stolen vehicle at the time of theft and the cost of a replacement vehicle, sales taxes, registration fees, transaction fees, and mechanical inspection fees.

(2) "Vehicle protection product" means a vehicle protection device, system, or service that:

(a) Is installed on or applied to a vehicle;

(b) Is designed to prevent loss or damage to a vehicle from a specific cause;

(c) Includes a written warranty by a warrantor stating that, if the vehicle protection product fails to prevent loss or damage to a vehicle from a specific cause, the warranty holder shall be paid specified incidental costs by the warrantor as a result of such failure; and

(d) Comes with a warranty reimbursement insurance policy covering the warrantor's liability from such product.

(3) "Vehicle protection product warrantor" or "warrantor" means a person who is contractually obligated to the warranty holder under the terms of the vehicle protection product warranty agreement. "Warrantor" does not include an authorized insurer.

(4) "Warranty" means an express warranty and shall not include an insurance policy.

(5) "Warranty reimbursement insurance policy" means a policy of insurance issued to the

vehicle protection product warrantor to pay, on behalf of the warrantor, all covered contractual obligations incurred by the warrantor under the vehicle protection product warranty.

42-9.5-103. Vehicle protection products. (1) A warranty contract accompanying a vehicle protection product that is sold or offered for sale shall:

(a) Identify in the contract the warrantor, the seller, the warranty holder, and the terms of the sale;

(b) Conspicuously state that the obligations of the warrantor are guaranteed under a warranty reimbursement insurance policy;

(c) Conspicuously state that, if the payment due under the terms of the warranty is not provided by the warrantor within sixty days after proof of loss has been filed by the warranty holder pursuant to the terms of the warranty, the warranty holder may file a claim for reimbursement directly with the warranty reimbursement insurance company;

(d) Conspicuously state the name and address of the warranty reimbursement insurance company;

(e) Conspicuously state: "This agreement is a product warranty and is not insurance.";

(f) Guarantee the warrantor's product with a warranty reimbursement insurance policy; and

(g) Authorize the warranty holder to file a claim directly with the warranty reimbursement insurance company if the payment due under the terms of the warranty is not provided by the warrantor within sixty days after proof of loss has been filed pursuant to the terms of the warranty.

42-9.5-104. Warranty reimbursement insurance policies. (1) A warranty reimbursement insurance policy shall state that the warranty reimbursement insurance company will reimburse or pay on behalf of the vehicle protection product warrantor all covered sums that the warrantor is legally obligated to pay, or will provide the service that the warrantor is legally obligated to perform, according to the warrantor's contractual obligations under the vehicle protection product warranty.

(2) A warranty reimbursement insurance policy shall state that, if the payment due under the terms of the warranty is not provided by the warrantor within sixty days after proof of loss has been filed according to the terms of the warranty by the warranty holder, the warranty holder may file directly with the warranty reimbursement insurance company for reimbursement.

42-9.5-105. Warranties - insurance. A vehicle protection warranty that complies with this section shall not be deemed to be insurance and shall be exempt from regulation as insurance pursuant to title 10, C.R.S.

42-9.5-106. Applicability. This article shall not apply to contracts regulated by article 11 of this title, which concerns motor vehicle service contract insurance.

ARTICLE 10
Motor Vehicle Warranties

42-10-101. Definitions.
42-10-102. Repairs to conform vehicle to warranty.
42-10-103. Failure to conform vehicle to warranty - replacement or return of vehicle.
42-10-104. Affirmative defenses.
42-10-105. Limitations on other rights and remedies.
42-10-106. Applicability of federal procedures.
42-10-107. Statute of limitations.

42-10-101. Definitions. As used in this article, unless the context otherwise requires:

(1) "Consumer" means the purchaser, other than for purposes of resale, of a motor vehicle normally used for personal, family, or household purposes, any person to whom such motor vehicle is transferred for the same purposes during the duration of a manufacturer's express warranty for such motor vehicle, and any other person entitled by the terms of such warranty to enforce the obligations of the warranty.

(2) "Motor vehicle" means a self-propelled private passenger vehicle, including pickup trucks and vans, designed primarily for travel on the public highways and used to carry not more than ten persons, which is sold to a consumer in this state; except that the term does not include motor homes as defined in section 42-1-102 (57) or vehicles designed to travel on three or fewer wheels in contact with the ground.

(3) "Warranty" means the written warranty, so labeled, of the manufacturer of a new motor vehicle, including any terms or conditions precedent to the enforcement of obligations under that warranty.

42-10-102. Repairs to conform vehicle to warranty. If a motor vehicle does not conform to a warranty and the consumer reports the nonconformity to the manufacturer, its agent, or its authorized dealer during the term of such warranty or during a period of one year following the date of the original delivery of the motor vehicle to a consumer, whichever is the earlier date, the manufacturer, its agent, or its authorized dealer shall make such repairs as are necessary to conform the vehicle to such warranty, notwithstanding the fact that such repairs are made after the expiration of such term or such one-year period.

42-10-103. Failure to conform vehicle to warranty - replacement or return of vehicle. (1) If the manufacturer, its agent, or its authorized dealer is unable to conform the motor vehicle to the warranty by repairing or correcting the defect or condition which substantially impairs the use and market value of such motor vehicle after a reasonable number of attempts, the manufacturer shall, at its option, replace the motor vehicle with a comparable motor vehicle or accept return of the motor vehicle from the consumer and refund to the consumer the full purchase price, including the sales tax, license fees, and registration fees and any similar governmental charges, less a reasonable allowance for the consumer's use of the motor vehicle. Refunds shall be made to the consumer and lienholder, if any, as their interests may appear. A reasonable allowance for use shall be that amount directly attributable to use by the consumer and any previous consumer prior to the consumer's first written report of the nonconformity to the manufacturer, agent, or dealer and during any subsequent period when the vehicle is not out of service by reason of repair.

(2) (a) It shall be presumed that a reasonable number of attempts have been undertaken to conform a motor vehicle to the warranty if:

(I) The same nonconformity has been subject to repair four or more times by the manufacturer, its agent, or its authorized dealer within the warranty term or during a period of one year following the date of the original delivery of the motor vehicle to the consumer, whichever is the earlier date, but such nonconformity continues to exist; or

(II) The motor vehicle is out of service by reason of repair for a cumulative total of thirty or more business days of the repairer during the term specified in subparagraph (I) of this paragraph (a) or during the period specified in said subparagraph (I), whichever is the earlier date.

(b) For the purposes of this subsection (2), the term of a warranty, the one-year period, and the thirty-day period shall be extended by any period of time during which repair services are not available to the consumer because of war, invasion, strike, or fire, flood, or other natural disaster.

(c) In no event shall a presumption under paragraph (a) of this subsection (2) apply against a manufacturer unless the manufacturer has received prior written notification by certified mail from or on behalf of the consumer and has been provided an opportunity to cure the defect alleged. Such defect shall count as one nonconformity subject to repair under subparagraph (I) of paragraph (a) of this subsection (2).

(d) Every authorized motor vehicle dealer shall include a form, containing the manufacturer's name and business address, with each motor vehicle owner's manual on which the consumer may give written notification of any defect, as such notification is required by paragraph (c) of this subsection (2), and the form shall clearly and conspicuously disclose that written notification by certified mail of the nonconformity is required, in order for the consumer to obtain remedies under this article.

(3) The court shall award reasonable attorney fees to the prevailing side in any action brought to enforce the provisions of this article.

42-10-104. Affirmative defenses. (1) It shall be an affirmative defense to any claim under this article that:

(a) An alleged nonconformity does not substantially impair the use and market value of a motor vehicle; or

(b) A nonconformity is the result of abuse, neglect, or unauthorized modifications or alterations of the motor vehicle by a consumer.

42-10-105. Limitations on other rights and remedies. Nothing in this article shall in any way limit the rights or remedies which are otherwise available to a consumer under any other state law or any federal law. Nothing in this article shall affect the other rights and duties between the consumer and a seller, lessor, or lienholder of a motor vehicle or the rights between any of them. Nothing in this article shall be construed as imposing a liability on any authorized dealer with respect to a manufacturer or creating a cause of action by a manufacturer against its authorized dealer; except that failure by an authorized dealer to properly prepare a motor vehicle for sale, to properly install options on a motor vehicle, or to properly make repairs on a motor vehicle, when such preparation, installation, or repairs would have prevented or cured a nonconformity, shall be actionable by the manufacturer.

42-10-106. Applicability of federal procedures. If a manufacturer has established or participates in an informal dispute settlement procedure which substantially complies with the provisions of part 703 of title 16 of the code of federal regulations, as from time to time amended, the provisions of section 42-10-103 (1) concerning refunds or replacement shall not apply to any consumer who has not first resorted to such procedure.

42-10-107. Statute of limitations. Any action brought to enforce the provisions of this article shall be commenced within six months following the expiration date of any warranty term or within one year following the date of the original delivery of a motor vehicle to a consumer, whichever is the earlier date; except that the statute of limitations shall be tolled during the period the consumer has submitted to arbitration under section 42-10-106.

ARTICLE 11
Motor Vehicle Service Contract Insurance

42-11-101. Definitions.
42-11-102. Reimbursement policy required for sale of service contract.
42-11-103. Reimbursement policy - required provisions.
42-11-104. Service contract - required statements.
42-11-105. Manufacturers' express warranties and service contracts excluded.
42-11-106. Deceptive trade practices prohibited.
42-11-107. Enforcement.
42-11-108. Remedies.

42-11-101. Definitions. As used in this article, unless the context otherwise requires:

(1) "Mechanical breakdown insurance" means an insurance policy, contract, or agreement, as defined in section 10-1-102 (12), C.R.S., that undertakes to perform or provide repair or replacement service, or indemnification for that service, for the operational or structural failure of a motor vehicle due to a defect in materials or skill of work or normal wear and tear, and that is issued by an insurance company authorized to do business in this state.

(2) "Motor vehicle" means any vehicle subject to registration under section 42-1-102 (58).

(3) "Motor vehicle service contract" or "service contract" means a contract or agreement between a provider and a service contract holder given for consideration over and above the lease or purchase price of a motor vehicle that undertakes to perform or provide repair or replacement service, or indemnification for that service, for the operational or structural failure of a motor vehicle due to a defect in materials or skill of work or normal wear and tear, but does not include mechanical breakdown insurance.

(4) (a) "Motor vehicle service contract provider" or "provider" means a person who, in connection with a motor vehicle service contract:

(I) Incurs the obligations and liabilities to the service contract holder as set forth in the contract; and

(II) Issues, makes, provides, sells, or offers to sell the contract.

(b) A motor vehicle dealer who sells a motor vehicle that is the subject of a motor vehicle service contract is not a "provider" unless the dealer also satisfies both of the conditions set forth in paragraph (a) of this subsection (4).

(5) "Motor vehicle service contract reimbursement insurance policy" or "reimbursement insurance policy" means a policy of insurance providing coverage for all obligations and liabilities incurred by a motor vehicle service contract provider under the terms of a motor vehicle service contract issued by the provider.

(6) "Service contract holder" means a person who purchases a motor vehicle service contract.

42-11-102. Reimbursement policy required for sale of service contract. A motor vehicle service contract shall not be issued, made, provided, sold, or offered for sale in this state unless the provider of the service contract is insured under a motor vehicle service contract reimbursement insurance policy issued by an insurer or administrator authorized to do business in this state.

42-11-103. Reimbursement policy - required provisions. A motor vehicle service contract reimbursement insurance policy shall not be issued, made, provided, sold, or offered for sale in this state unless the reimbursement insurance policy conspicuously states that the issuer of the policy shall pay on behalf of the provider all sums which the provider is legally obligated to pay for failure to perform according to the provider's contractual obligations under the motor vehicle service contracts issued or sold by the provider.

42-11-104. Service contract - required statements. A motor vehicle service contract shall not be issued, made, provided, sold, or offered for sale in this state unless the contract conspicuously states that the obligations of the provider to the service contract holder are guaranteed under a service contract reimbursement policy, and unless the contract conspicuously states the name and address of the issuer of the reimbursement policy, the applicable policy number, and the means by which a service contract holder may file a claim under the policy.

42-11-105. Manufacturers' express warranties and service contracts excluded. This article does not apply to motor vehicle manufacturers' express warranties and service contracts as defined in section 42-10-101 (3).

42-11-106. Deceptive trade practices prohibited. Failure to comply with the provisions of this article in the course of a business, vocation, or occupation is a deceptive trade practice and is subject to the provisions of the "Colorado Consumer Protection Act", article 1 of title 6, C.R.S.

42-11-107. Enforcement. The attorney general and the district attorneys of the judicial districts of the state are concurrently responsible for the enforcement of this article.

42-11-108. Remedies. The provisions of this article shall be available to any service contract holder in a civil action for any claim against a motor vehicle service contract provider. The court shall award reasonable attorney fees and costs to a prevailing party in any civil action brought to enforce the provisions of this article.

COLLECTOR'S ITEMS

ARTICLE 12
Motor Vehicles as Collector's Items

PART 1
GENERAL PROVISIONS

42-12-101. Definitions.
42-12-102. Rebuilder's certificate of title.
42-12-103. Furnishing bond for certificates.
42-12-104. Applicability of articles 1, 3, 4, 5, and 6.

PART 2
STREET-ROD VEHICLES

42-12-201. Inspections - street-rod vehicles.
42-12-202. Assignment of a special vehicle identification number by the department.
42-12-203. Identification number - title - street-rod vehicles.
42-12-204. Signal lamps and devices - street-rod vehicles and custom motor vehicles - definition.

PART 3
SPECIAL REGISTRATION OF HORSELESS CARRIAGES AND ORIGINAL PLATES

42-12-301. Special registration of horseless carriages - rules.
42-12-302. Original plates.

PART 4
COLLECTOR'S ITEMS

42-12-401. Registration of collector's items - fees - definition.
42-12-402. Storage.
42-12-403. Special equipment or modification.
42-12-404. Emissions.
42-12-405. Registration penalty.

PART 1

GENERAL PROVISIONS

42-12-101. Definitions. As used in this article, unless the context otherwise requires:

(1) "Collector" means an individual or person who is:

(a) The owner of one or more vehicles of historic or special interest who collects, purchases, acquires, trades, or disposes of these vehicles or parts thereof for such owner's use in order to preserve, restore, and maintain a vehicle for hobby purposes or use; or

(b) A bona fide member of a national automobile club or association whose charter recognizes in membership a sincere demonstration of interest in the history of automotive engineering, in the preservation of antique, vintage, or special interest motor vehicles, in a sharing of knowledge and experience with other automotive enthusiasts, or in the promotion of good fellowship among such members or collectors.

(2) "Collector's item" means a motor vehicle, including a truck or truck tractor, that is of:

(a) Model year 1975 or earlier; or

(b) Model year 1976 or later that was registered as a collector's item prior to September 1, 2009; except that a vehicle so registered is not eligible for registration as a collector's item upon sale or transfer to a new owner.

(3) "Commercial vehicle" means a trailer, truck, or truck tractor, as those terms are defined in section 42-1-102.

(4) "Dealer" means a person who is engaged in the business or vocation of manufacturing, buying, selling, trading, destroying, or salvaging motor vehicles, motor vehicle parts, motor vehicle equipment, or motor vehicle accessories.

(5) "Department" means the department of revenue.

(6) "Director" means the executive director of the department of revenue.

(7) "Garage" means a building or business place used for the storage or repair of motor vehicles.

(8) "Inspector" means a peace officer of a law enforcement agency who has been certified under section 42-5-206 to inspect vehicle identification numbers.

(9) "Law enforcement agency" means the Colorado state patrol or the agency of a local government authorized to enforce the laws of Colorado.

(10) "Motor vehicle" means a self-propelled vehicle designed for operation on the highway and not running on rails.

(11) "Parts car" means a motor vehicle, generally in inoperable condition, that is owned by a collector to furnish or to supply parts that are usually unobtainable from normal sources, thus enabling a collector or other collectors to preserve, restore, complete, and maintain a vehicle of historic or special interest.

(12) "Rebuilt vehicle" means a vehicle that was assembled from parts of two or more commercially manufactured vehicles or that has been altered in such a manner that it is not readily recognizable as a commercially manufactured vehicle of a given year. "Rebuilt vehicle" includes a kit car and a street-rod vehicle.

(13) "State" includes the territories and the federal districts of the United States.

(14) "Street-rod vehicle" means a vehicle with a body design manufactured in 1948 or earlier or with a reproduction component that resembles a 1948 or earlier model that has been modified for safe road use, including modifications to the drive train, suspension, and brake systems, modifications to the body through the use of materials such as steel or fiberglass, and modifications to other safety or comfort features.

(15) "Vehicle" means a motor vehicle required to have a certificate of title under part 1

of article 6 of this title but does not include commercial vehicles.

(16) "Vehicle identification number" means the identifying number, serial number, engine number, or other distinguishing number or mark, including any letters, that is unique to the identity of a given vehicle or vehicle part and that was placed on a vehicle or vehicle part by its manufacturer or by the department under either section 42-12-202 or the laws of another state or country.

42-12-102. Rebuilder's certificate of title. (1) (a) If the applicant for a certificate of title to a motor vehicle is unable to provide the director or the authorized agent with a certificate of title duly transferred to the applicant or other evidence of ownership that satisfies the director that the applicant owns the vehicle, the director may issue a rebuilder's title for a motor vehicle valued principally because of the vehicle's early date of manufacture, design, or historical interest or valued as a collector's item if:

(I) The motor vehicle is not roadworthy;

(II) The motor vehicle is at least twenty-five years old;

(III) The components of the motor vehicle include at least a rolling chassis;

(IV) The application contains or is accompanied by a statement that complies with paragraph (b) of this subsection (1);

(V) The applicant obtains a certified vehicle identification number inspection; and

(VI) The applicant provides surety that complies with subsection (3) of this section.

(b) The statement required by subparagraph (IV) of paragraph (a) of this subsection (1) must contain an account of the facts by which the applicant acquired ownership of the vehicle, the source of the title to the vehicle, and such other information as the director may require. The statement must contain a written declaration that it is made under the penalties of perjury in the second degree, as defined in section 18-8-503, C.R.S.

(2) If a motor vehicle titled under this section is later made roadworthy, the department shall issue to an applicant a standard certificate of title if the applicant:

(a) Obtains a certified vehicle identification number inspection; and

(b) Furnishes a bond under subsection (3) of this section.

(3) (a) To convert a rebuilder's title to a standard certificate of title, the applicant shall furnish evidence of a savings account, deposit, or certificate of deposit meeting the requirements of section 11-35-101, C.R.S., or a good and sufficient bond with a corporate surety. The account, deposit, certificate, or bond must be in an amount fixed by the director, but not less than twice the reasonable value of the vehicle, determined as of the time of application. The applicant and the applicant's surety shall hold harmless any person who suffers loss or damage by reason of the filing of a certificate of title under this section.

(b) If a person suffers loss or damage by reason of the filing of a certificate of title under this section, the person has a right of action against the applicant and the surety on the applicant's bond, against either of whom the person damaged may proceed independently of the other.

(4) (a) A person shall not drive a motor vehicle titled under this section on the highways until it complies with subsection (5) of this section.

(b) The department or its authorized agent shall not classify a vehicle issued a title under this section as a salvage vehicle.

(5) (a) If the motor vehicle's frame and body identification numbers do not match the manufacturer's numbering system as being originally mated or if the motor vehicle is reconstructed from salvage parts or other motor vehicles or reproduction parts, an application for title using subsection (1) or (2) of this section must include evidence of ownership of the parts, other motor vehicles, or reproduction components used in the reconstruction. If the evidence is not acceptable to the director, the director shall reject the application for certificate of title.

(b) The evidence required by paragraph (a) of this subsection (5) must include or be accompanied by an affidavit stating the facts concerning the reconstruction and an affidavit of physical inspection that includes a computer check of the state and national compilations of wanted and stolen vehicles.

(c) Before issuing a certificate of title under paragraph (a) of this subsection (5), the department shall issue a special vehicle identification number to the vehicle.

42-12-103. Furnishing bond for certificates. (1) If a collector's item, street-rod vehicle, or horseless carriage is twenty-five years old or older, the applicant has had a certified vehicle identification number inspection performed on the vehicle, and the applicant presents a notarized bill of sale within twenty-four months after the sale with the title application, then the applicant need not furnish surety under section 42-6-115 (3). To be excepted from the surety requirement, an applicant shall submit to the department a sworn affidavit, under penalty of perjury, stating that the required documents submitted are true and correct.

(2) If any person suffers loss or damage by reason of the filing of the certificate of title as provided in this section, the person shall have a right of action against the applicant and the surety on the applicant's bond, against either of whom the person damaged may proceed independently of the other.

42-12-104. Applicability of articles 1, 3, 4, 5, and 6. Except as otherwise provided in this article, articles 1, 3, 4, 5, and 6 of this title apply to the titling and registration of a motor vehicle.

PART 2

STREET-ROD VEHICLES

42-12-201. Inspections - street-rod vehicles. When an inspector performs a vehicle identification number inspection on a street-rod vehicle, the inspector shall accept the serial number of such street-rod vehicle as the vehicle's identification number or, if the street-rod vehicle has frame and body identification numbers that do not match or is reconstructed from salvage parts, other vehicles, or reproduction parts, the inspector shall accept the special vehicle identification number assigned to such vehicle by the department by section 42-12-202 as the vehicle identification number.

42-12-202. Assignment of a special vehicle identification number by the department. The department may assign a special vehicle identification number to any street-rod vehicle whenever required by section 42-12-203 and to any vehicle or commercial vehicle whenever no vehicle identification number is found on the vehicle or whenever a vehicle identification number has been removed, changed, altered, or obliterated. The special number must be affixed to the vehicle or commercial vehicle in the manner and position determined by the department. The special number is the vehicle identification number required to be recorded by an inspector on the inspection form that is transmitted to the department, which shall register and title the motor vehicle using the special vehicle identification number.

42-12-203. Identification number - title - street-rod vehicles. (1) When a person applies for a certificate of title for a street-rod vehicle, the department shall accept the serial number of the street-rod vehicle as its vehicle identification number or the special vehicle identification number assigned to such vehicle by the department under section 42-12-202.

(2) A person who applies for a certificate of title for a street-rod vehicle having frame and body identification numbers that do not match the manufacturer's numbering system as being originally mated or that is reconstructed from salvage parts or other motor vehicles or reproduction parts shall furnish evidence of ownership, acceptable to the director, of such salvage parts, other motor vehicles, or reproduction components used in the reconstruction of such vehicle. In addition, the applicant shall furnish an affidavit stating the facts concerning the reconstruction and an affidavit of physical inspection that includes a computer check of the state and national compilations of wanted and stolen vehicles. The department may issue a special vehicle identification number and title the street-rod vehicle as a rebuilt vehicle. The model year and the year of manufacture that are listed on the certificate of title of a street-rod vehicle are the model year and the year of manufacture that the body of such vehicle resembles.

42-12-204. Signal lamps and devices - street-rod vehicles and custom motor vehicles - definition. (1) As used in this section, "blue dot tail light" means a red lamp installed in the rear of a motor vehicle containing a blue or purple insert that is not more than one inch in diameter.

(2) A street-rod vehicle or custom motor vehicle may use blue dot tail lights for stop lamps, rear turning indicator lamps, rear hazard lamps, and rear reflectors if the lamps comply with all requirements of part 2 of article 4 of this title.

PART 3

SPECIAL REGISTRATION OF HORSELESS CARRIAGES AND ORIGINAL PLATES

42-12-301. Special registration of horseless carriages - rules. (1) (a) The department may specially register and issue a horseless carriage special license plate for motor vehicles valued principally because of the vehicles' early date of manufacture, design, or historical interest or valued as collector's items.

(b) For the purposes of this section, "early date of manufacture" means that a motor vehicle was manufactured at least fifty years before the current date of registration.

(2) The plates issued under subsection (1) of this section must be of a design, determined by the director, that is different from that used by the state for regular motor vehicle registration.

(3) (a) The director shall register the vehicles and issue plates for a period not exceeding five years, but all the registrations and plates shall expire on the same date regardless of the date of issue.

(b) Upon the expiration of the five-year period ending with the year 1959, and each five years thereafter, the registration plate originally issued for each vehicle must remain with the vehicle. The director shall issue a tab to be securely fastened to the plate showing the five years for which the motor vehicle is registered.

(c) A person who has registered a vehicle under this section shall renew the registration within thirty days prior to its expiration date. If the application for renewal, together with the fees, is not received by the director prior to the expiration date, the director shall notify the registered owner, at the address shown by the department's records, by regular mail, to reregister the vehicle or surrender the registration plate within ten days after the expiration date of the registration. If the notice is not complied with, the director shall secure the return of the plate.

(4) The fee for issuing such registration and special registration plate or tab is five dollars for

each five-year period or fraction thereof. In addition to the five-dollar registration fee, the director shall collect the one-dollar-and-fifty-cent annual specific ownership fee provided by law for each year of registration, which additional fee shall be collected for the number of years remaining at the time of registration and issuance or renewal of the registration.

(5) A person may drive a motor vehicle with the special registration plates authorized by this section or section 42-12-302 on the streets and highways, but only:

(a) To and from assemblies, conventions, or other meetings where such vehicles and their ownership are the primary interest;

(b) On special occasions, for demonstrations and parades;

(c) On occasions when the operation of the vehicle on the streets and highways will not constitute a traffic hazard; and

(d) To, from, and during local, state, or national tours held primarily for the exhibition and enjoyment of such vehicles.

(6) Upon the sale or transfer of a motor vehicle bearing a special registration plate, the plate remains with the vehicle and is transferred to the new owner. The new owner shall title such motor vehicle as provided by law and give notice of the transfer of ownership to the department.

(7) Applications for special registration of motor vehicles are made directly to the department. The department shall administer all matters concerning such registration. The department shall transfer fees received from special registrations to the state treasurer, who shall credit the fees to the highway users tax fund.

(8) The director may prepare any special forms and issue any rules necessary to implement this section.

(9) When the director receives an application for a title to a vehicle under subsection (1) of this section, the director shall accept the original motor or serial number on the vehicle and shall not require or issue a special identification number for the vehicle.

42-12-302. Original plates. (1) In addition to any other registration, the department may approve use of the style of original plates from the vehicle's year of manufacture for motor vehicles valued principally because of the vehicles' early date of manufacture, design, or historical interest or valued as collector's items. Original plates must meet the following criteria in order to qualify for use under this section:

(a) The plates were made at least thirty years prior to registration under this section;

(b) The plates are embossed with the year of original issue;

(c) The plates are legible;

(d) The plates were issued contemporaneously with the year of manufacture of the vehicle upon which they are displayed, as determined by the department; and

(e) The plates do not exceed seven characters.

(2) A person shall not drive the vehicle bearing the original plates except as authorized in section 42-12-301 (5).

PART 4

COLLECTOR'S ITEMS

42-12-401. Registration of collector's items - fees - definition. (1) Except for motor vehicles that are entitled to registration under section 42-12-301, owners of collector's items shall apply for a title, register, and pay a specific ownership tax in the same manner as provided in this title for other motor vehicles, with the following exceptions:

(a) Such collector's items are registered for periods of five years. The taxes and fees imposed for registration of a collector's item for each five-year registration period is equal to five times the annual taxes and fees that would otherwise be imposed for the registration of the motor vehicle under this title and under title 43, C.R.S.; except that the amount of a surcharge imposed pursuant to section 43-4-804 (1) (a) or 43-4-805 (5) (g), C.R.S., is the amount specified in the applicable section. In addition to any other taxes and fees, if a collector's item is registered in a county that is a member of a highway authority and the authority has imposed an annual motor vehicle registration fee pursuant to section 43-4-506 (1) (k), C.R.S., then five times such annual motor vehicle registration fee is imposed and remitted to the authority.

(b) The motor vehicle's compliance with emissions standards is governed by section 42-12-404.

(c) The annual registration fee for a truck or truck tractor that has an empty weight of six thousand one pounds or more, or a declared gross vehicle weight of sixteen thousand one pounds or more and is a collector's item, is sixty-five dollars if such vehicle is used exclusively for noncommercial transportation and only used to drive:

(I) To and from assemblies, conventions, or other meetings where such vehicles and their ownership are the primary interest;

(II) For special occasions, demonstrations, and parades and on occasions when their operation on the streets and highways will not constitute a traffic hazard; or

(III) Traveling to, from, and during local, state, or national tours held primarily for the exhibition and enjoyment of such vehicles by their owners.

(d) For purposes of paragraph (c) of this subsection (1), "noncommercial transportation" means a truck or truck tractor used exclusively for private transportation of passengers or cargo for purposes unrelated in any way to a business or commercial enterprise.

(2) (a) An owner of a collector's item that is not operated upon the highways of this state and that is kept on private property for the purpose of maintenance, repair, restoration, rebuilding, or any other similar purpose shall pay an annual specific ownership tax as provided in section 42-3-106 on any such motor vehicle owned by the owner, except owners of parts cars or licensed garages or licensed automobile dealers. The owner shall pay the specific ownership tax in the manner provided in section 42-12-301.

(b) Upon payment of the specific ownership tax as provided in this subsection (2), the department shall issue to the owner of the motor vehicle for which the tax has been paid a license, sticker, decal, or other device evidencing such payment, as may be prescribed by the director. When such device or license is affixed to the motor vehicle for which it is issued, the owner of that motor vehicle is permitted to keep such motor vehicle on private property for the purposes of maintenance, repair, restoration, rebuilding, or renovation.

(3) Notwithstanding the amount specified for any fee in subsection (1) of this section, the director by rule or as otherwise provided by law may reduce the amount of one or more of the fees if necessary pursuant to section 24-75-402 (3), C.R.S., to reduce the uncommitted reserves of the fund to which all or any portion of one or more of the fees is credited. After the uncommitted reserves of the fund are sufficiently reduced, the director by rule or as otherwise provided by law may increase the amount of one or more of the fees as provided in section 24-75-402 (4), C.R.S.

(4) An applicant may apply for personalized license plates issued for a motor vehicle registration issued pursuant to this section. If the applicant complies with section 42-3-211, the department may issue such plates upon payment of the additional fee required by section 42-3-211 (6) for personalized license plates. If the applicant has existing personalized license plates for a motor vehicle, the applicant may transfer the combination of letters or numbers to a new set of license plates for the vehicle upon paying the fee imposed by section 42-3-211 (6) (a) and upon turning in such existing plates to the department as required by the department. A person who has obtained personalized plates under this subsection (4) shall pay the annual fee imposed by section 42-3-211 (6) (b) to renew such plates. The fees imposed by this subsection (4) are in addition to all other taxes and fees imposed for collector's license plates.

42-12-402. Storage. A collector may store one or more motor vehicles or motor vehicle parts on the collector's property if the vehicle, motor vehicle part, and storage area are maintained so as to not constitute a health hazard, a safety hazard, or a fire hazard; are screened from ordinary public view by means of a solid fence, trees, shrubbery, or other appropriate means; and are kept free of weeds, trash, and objectionable items.

42-12-403. Special equipment or modification. (1) Unless the presence of special equipment was a prior condition for sale within Colorado at the time an historic or special interest vehicle was manufactured for first use, the presence of such equipment or device is not required as a condition for current legal use.

(2) Any safety device or safety equipment that was manufactured for and installed on a motor vehicle as original equipment must be in proper operating condition when the vehicle is operated on or for highway purposes.

42-12-404. Emissions. (1) A motor vehicle of historic or special interest manufactured prior to the date emission controls were standard equipment on that particular make or model of vehicle is exempted from statutes requiring the inspection and use of such emission controls. A motor vehicle using emission controls as standard equipment at the time of manufacture must have such equipment in proper operating condition at all times when the vehicle is operated on or for highway purposes.

(2) A certification of emissions control that has been issued for a motor vehicle that is registered as a collector's item before September 1, 2009, and that is of model year 1976 or later is valid until the motor vehicle is sold or transferred.

42-12-405. Registration penalty. In addition to any other penalties, the department shall cancel the registration of a noncommercial or recreational vehicle, truck, or truck tractor registered as a collector's item pursuant to section 42-12-401 that is used to transport cargo or passengers for profit or hire or in a business or commercial enterprise. The department shall cancel the registration of a truck or truck tractor registered as a collector's item pursuant to section 42-12-401 that is driven for any purpose other than those purposes allowed in section 42-12-401 (1) (c).

DISPOSITION OF PERSONAL PROPERTY

ARTICLE 13
Disposition of Personal Property

42-13-101. Scope and effect of article - exception to provisions.
42-13-102. Return of property.
42-13-103. Sale of unclaimed property.
42-13-104. Deposit of proceeds.
42-13-105. Release of impounded vehicles - penalty.
42-13-106. Impounded vehicles - notice - hearing.
42-13-107. Recovery of property - limitation.
42-13-108. Damages.
42-13-109. Local regulations.

42-13-101. Scope and effect of article - exception to provisions. This article shall apply to all personal property acquired or held by a law enforcement agency in the course of motor vehicle law enforcement or related highway duties and under circumstances supporting a reasonable belief that such property was abandoned, lost, stolen, or otherwise illegally possessed, including property left in abandoned vehicles or at vehicle accident locations, unclaimed property obtained by a search and seizure, and unclaimed property used as evidence in any criminal trial, except for such other personal property as shall be disposed of in a different manner in accordance with other Colorado statutes.

42-13-102. Return of property. Any personal property of the type described in section 42-13-101 and believed to be abandoned, lost, stolen, or otherwise illegally possessed shall be retained in custody by the sheriff, chief of police, or chief of the Colorado state patrol or by a designated representative within the law enforcement agency, who shall make reasonable inquiry and effort to identify and notify the owner or person entitled to possession thereof and shall return the property after such owner or person provides reasonable and satisfactory proof of ownership or right to possession and reimburses the law enforcement agency for all reasonable expenses of such custody and handling.

42-13-103. Sale of unclaimed property. If the identity or location of the owner or person entitled to possession of the property has not been ascertained within six months after the law enforcement agency obtains possession of the property described in section 42-13-101, the sheriff, chief of police, or chief of the Colorado state patrol or a designated representative within the law enforcement agency shall effectuate the sale of such property for cash to the highest bidder at a public auction, notice of which, including time, place, and a brief description of such property, shall be published at least once in a newspaper of general circulation in the county wherein such official has authority or jurisdiction or, in the case of the Colorado state patrol, in the county wherein said public auction is to be held at least ten days prior to such auction.

42-13-104. Deposit of proceeds. Proceeds from the sale of property at public auction, less reimbursement of the law enforcement agency for the reasonable expenses of custody and handling thereof, shall be deposited in the treasury of the county, city and county, city, town, or state of which government the law enforcement agency is a branch.

42-13-105. Release of impounded vehicles - penalty. Any owner, operator, or employee of any garage or service station or any appointed custodian who releases any vehicle impounded or ordered held by an officer of the Colorado state patrol without a release from an officer of the Colorado state patrol or a bona fide court order commits a class 3 misdemeanor and shall be punished as provided in section 18-1.3-501, C.R.S.

42-13-106. Impounded vehicles - notice - hearing. (1) Whenever a motor vehicle is impounded and ordered held by the Colorado state patrol for a violation of motor vehicle registration or inspection laws, said patrol shall notify the registered owner of record of the impoundment of such vehicle and of the owner's opportunity to request a hearing to determine the validity of the impoundment.

(2) Such notice shall be sent by certified mail to the owner of the motor vehicle within forty-eight hours of impoundment, excluding weekends and holidays, and shall include the following information:

(a) The address and telephone number of the Colorado state patrol;

(b) The location of storage of the motor vehicle;

(c) A description of the motor vehicle, which shall include, if available, the make, model, license plate number, mileage, and vehicle identification number;

(d) The reason for which the motor vehicle was ordered held;

(e) A citation to this section as the basis for the hearing provided for in subsection (1) of this section;

(f) That, if the owner fails to request a hearing or if the impoundment is determined to be valid and the owner does not comply with the appropriate statute within thirty days, the motor vehicle may be subject to sale; and

(g) That, in order to obtain a hearing concerning the validity of the impoundment, the owner must request such hearing in writing in the county court of the county in which the motor vehicle was impounded within ten days after the date appearing on the notice.

(3) Any notice sent to the owner of a motor vehicle pursuant to this section shall also include a form that the owner shall use when requesting a hearing in the county court of the county in which the motor vehicle is impounded. Such form shall include at least the following:

(a) The name and address of the owner of the impounded motor vehicle;

(b) A description of the motor vehicle as specified in paragraph (c) of subsection (2) of this section;

(c) The reason for which the motor vehicle was ordered held;

(d) A printed citation to this section as the basis for the requested hearing;

(e) A printed statement naming the Colorado state patrol as a party to the action;

(f) A printed statement that the hearing is requested to contest the legality of the impoundment; and

(g) A statement to the owner of the motor vehicle that a copy of the citation on which the impoundment was based and a copy of the notice served on the owner by the Colorado state patrol must be attached to the form to complete the owner's request for a hearing.

(4) Any such hearing shall be conducted within five days after the court's receipt of the owner's request for a hearing, excluding weekends and holidays. The clerk of the county court to which the request for hearing was made shall provide written notice of the scheduled date, time, and location of said hearing to both the requesting party and the Colorado state patrol, which notice shall be delivered at least two days prior to the hearing date. The failure of the owner to request or to attend a scheduled hearing shall satisfy the hearing requirement of this section.

(5) The sole issue of the hearing shall be the legality of the impoundment of the motor vehicle. The burden of proof shall be on the Colorado state patrol to establish probable cause for the impoundment.

(6) If the court determines that the impoundment was invalid, the Colorado state patrol shall be responsible only for the costs incurred in the towing and storage of the motor vehicle. If the court determines that the impoundment was valid and if the owner does not comply with the appropriate statute within ten days after the court's decision and refuses to remove the motor vehicle by means other than under its own power on a public highway, the Colorado state patrol shall have reasonable grounds to believe that the motor vehicle has been abandoned, and the provisions of part 18 or 21 of article 4 of this title shall apply; except that any notice or hearing requirements of said part 18 or 21 of article 4 of this title as to owners of motor vehicles shall be deemed to have been met by the notice and hearing provisions of this section. Nevertheless, the notice and hearing requirements of said part 18 or 21 of article 4 of this title as to lienholders, other than section 42-4-1814, shall not be deemed to have been met by the notice and hearing provisions of this section.

(7) The provisions of this section shall not apply to removal of motor vehicles for any purpose other than those specified in this section.

42-13-107. Recovery of property - limitation. The owner or person entitled to possession of the property described in section 42-13-101 may claim and recover possession of the property at any time before its sale at public auction upon providing reasonable and satisfactory proof of ownership or right to possession and after reimbursing the law enforcement agency for all reasonable expenses of custody and handling thereof.

42-13-108. Damages. No person or agency shall be responsible for consequent damages to another occasioned by an act or omission in compliance with this article.

42-13-109. Local regulations. The provisions of this article may be superseded by ordinance or resolution of a municipality or county which sets forth procedures for disposition of personal property.

IDLING STANDARD

ARTICLE 14

State Idling Standard

42-14-101. Legislative declaration.
42-14-102. Definitions.
42-14-103. Uniform standard - local governments.
42-14-104. Applicability.
42-14-105. Idling.
42-14-106. Penalties.

42-14-101. Legislative declaration. The general assembly hereby finds and determines that the operation of a motor vehicle in commerce has important statewide ramifications for commercial diesel vehicle operators because the transportation of people and property is not confined to one jurisdiction. Therefore, the general assembly hereby declares that idling standards are a matter of statewide concern.

42-14-102. Definitions. As used in this article, unless the context otherwise requires:
(1) "Covered vehicle" means a vehicle to which this article applies under section 42-3-104.
(2) "Idling" means when the primary propulsion engine of a covered vehicle is running but the vehicle is not in motion.
(3) "Loading location" means a place where a covered vehicle loads or unloads people or property.

42-14-103. Uniform standard - local governments. A local authority shall not adopt or enact a resolution, ordinance, or other law concerning idling of a covered vehicle that is more stringent than this article.

42-14-104. Applicability. (1) This article applies to:
(a) Commercial diesel vehicles with a gross vehicle weight rating of greater than fourteen thousand pounds that are designed to operate on highways; and
(b) Locations where commercial diesel vehicles load or unload if a local authority has adopted or enacted a resolution, ordinance, or other law consistent with this article.
(2) This article does not supersede an ordinance of a local authority if the authority has an average elevation of over six thousand feet and if the ordinance was in effect on January 1, 2011.

42-14-105. Idling. (1) **Standard.** The owner or operator of a covered vehicle shall not cause or permit the vehicle to idle for more than five minutes within any sixty-minute period except as authorized by subsection (2) of this section.

(2) **Exemptions.** Subsection (1) of this section does not apply to an idling, covered vehicle:

(a) When it remains motionless because of highway traffic, an official traffic control device or signal, or at the direction of a law enforcement officer;

(b) When the driver is operating defrosters, heaters, or air conditioners or is installing equipment only to prevent a safety or health emergency, and not for rest periods;

(c) In the case of a law enforcement, emergency, public safety, or military vehicle, or any other vehicle used to respond to an emergency, when it is responding to an emergency or being used for training for an emergency, and not for the convenience of the vehicle operator;

(d) When necessary for required maintenance, servicing, or repair of the vehicle;

(e) During a local, state, or federal inspection verifying that the equipment is in good working order if required for the inspection;

(f) During the operation of power take-off equipment if necessary for operating work-related mechanical or electrical equipment;

(g) In the case of an armored vehicle, when a person is inside the vehicle to guard its contents or during the loading or unloading of the vehicle;

(h) In the case of a passenger bus, when idling for up to five minutes in any sixty-minute period to maintain passenger comfort while non-driver passengers are on board;

(i) When used to heat or cool a sleeper berth compartment during a rest or sleep period at a safety rest area as defined under 23 CFR 752.3, fleet trucking terminal, commercial truck stop, or state-designated location designed to be a driver's rest area;

(j) When used to heat or cool a sleeper berth compartment during a rest or sleep period at a location where the vehicle is legally permitted to park and that is at least one thousand feet from residential housing, a school, a daycare facility, a hospital, a senior citizen center, or a medical outpatient facility providing primary, specialty, or respiratory care; or

(k) When idling for up to twenty minutes in any sixty-minute period if the ambient temperature is less then ten degrees.

42-14-106. Penalties. The owner or operator of a vehicle or the owner of a loading location that violates this article commits a class B traffic infraction, punishable by a fine of not more than one hundred fifty dollars for the first offense or a fine of not more than five hundred dollars for a second or subsequent offense and by a surcharge of twenty dollars in accordance with section 24-4.1-119, C.R.S.

HIGHWAY SAFETY

ARTICLE 20
Transportation of Hazardous and Nuclear Materials

PART 1
HAZARDOUS MATERIALS -
GENERAL PROVISIONS

42-20-101. Short title.
42-20-102. Legislative declaration.
42-20-103. Definitions.
42-20-104. General powers and duties of chief - department of public safety - cooperation from other state agencies.
42-20-105. Enforcement.
42-20-106. Regulatory authority of local governments - preemption - disposition of local fines and penalties.
42-20-107. Hazardous materials safety fund.
42-20-108. Rules and regulations for transportation of hazardous materials.
42-20-108.5. Materials used for agricultural production - exemption - legislative declaration.
42-20-109. Penalty for violations.
42-20-110. Immobilization of unsafe vehicles.
42-20-111. Additional penalties.
42-20-112. Reimbursement of local governments.
42-20-113. Hazardous materials spill - abandonment of vehicle containing hazardous material - penalty.

PART 2
PERMIT SYSTEM FOR
HAZARDOUS MATERIALS

42-20-201. Hazardous materials transportation permit required.
42-20-202. Transportation permit - application fee.
42-20-203. Carrying of permit and shipping papers.
42-20-204. Permit violations - penalties.
42-20-205. Permit suspension or revocation.
42-20-206. Local government preemption.

PART 3
ROUTE DESIGNATION FOR
HAZARDOUS MATERIALS

42-20-300.3. Definitions.
42-20-301. Route designation.
42-20-302. Application for route designation - procedure - approval.
42-20-303. Road signs required - uniform standards.
42-20-304. Emergency closure of public roads.
42-20-305. Deviation from authorized route - penalty.

PART 4
NUCLEAR MATERIALS - GENERAL PROVISIONS

42-20-401. Legislative declaration.
42-20-402. Definitions.
42-20-403. Chief to promulgate rules and regulations - motor vehicles.
42-20-404. Inspections.
42-20-405. Violations - criminal penalties.
42-20-406. Violations - civil penalties - motor vehicles.
42-20-407. Repeat violations - civil penalties.
42-20-408. Compliance orders - penalty.

PART 5
NUCLEAR MATERIALS PERMIT SYSTEM

42-20-501. Nuclear materials transportation permit required - application.
42-20-502. Permits - fees.
42-20-503. Carrying of shipping papers.
42-20-504. Rules and regulations.
42-20-505. Penalties - permit system.
42-20-506. Permit suspension and revocation.
42-20-507. Local government preemption.
42-20-508. Route designation - motor vehicles.
42-20-509. Strict liability for nuclear incidents.
42-20-510. Statute of limitations.
42-20-511. Nuclear materials transportation fund.

PART 1
HAZARDOUS MATERIALS - GENERAL PROVISIONS

42-20-101. Short title. Parts 1, 2, and 3 of this article shall be known and may be cited as the "Hazardous Materials Transportation Act of 1987".

42-20-102. Legislative declaration. The general assembly finds that the permitting and routing of motor vehicles transporting hazardous materials is a matter of statewide concern and is affected with a public interest and that the provisions of parts 1, 2, and 3 of this article are enacted in the exercise of the police powers of this state for the purpose of protecting the health, peace, safety, and welfare of the people of this state.

42-20-103. Definitions. As used in this article, unless the context otherwise requires:

(1) "Chief" means the chief of the Colorado state patrol.

(2) "Enforcement official" means, and is limited to, a peace officer who is an officer of the Colorado state patrol as described in sections 16-2.5-101 and 16-2.5-114, C.R.S., a certified peace officer who is a certified port of entry officer as described in sections 16-2.5-101 and 16-2.5-115, C.R.S., a peace officer who is an investigating official of the transportation section of the public utilities commission as described in sections 16-2.5-101 and 16-2.5-143, C.R.S., or any other peace officer as described in section 16-2.5-101, C.R.S.

(3) "Hazardous materials" means those materials listed in tables 1 and 2 of 49 CFR 172.504, excluding highway route controlled quantities of radioactive materials as defined in 49 CFR 173.403 (l), excluding ores, the products from mining, milling, smelting, and similar processing of ores, and the wastes and tailing therefrom, and excluding special fireworks as defined in 49 CFR 173.88 (d) when the aggregate amount of flash powder does not exceed fifty pounds.

(4) "Motor vehicle" means any device which is capable of moving from place to place upon public roads. The term includes, but is not limited to, any motorized vehicle or any such vehicle with a trailer or semitrailer attached thereto.

(5) "Patrol" means the Colorado state patrol within the department of public safety.

(6) "Person" means an individual, a corporation, a government or governmental subdivision or agency, a partnership, an association, or any other legal entity; except that separate divisions of the same corporation may, at their request, be treated as separate persons for the purposes of part 2 of this article.

(7) "Public road" means every way publicly maintained and opened to the use of the public for the purposes of vehicular travel, including, but not limited to, streets, bridges, toll roads, tunnels, and state and federal highways.

42-20-104. General powers and duties of chief - department of public safety - cooperation from other state agencies. (1) In addition to any other powers and duties granted to him or her in parts 1, 2, and 3 of this article, the chief shall promulgate such rules and regulations and conduct such hearings as may be necessary for the administration of this article.

(2) In addition to any other powers and duties granted to him or her in parts 1, 2, and 3 of this article and except as otherwise provided in parts 1, 2, and 3 of this article, the chief shall have the general authority and duty to carry out the provisions of parts 1, 2, and 3 of this article and shall promulgate such rules and regulations, subject to the provisions of article 4 of title 24, C.R.S., as may be necessary to clarify the enforcement provisions of parts 1, 2, and 3 of this article.

(3) Upon request, other agencies of state government, including but not limited to the department of public health and environment and the department of transportation, shall provide advice and assistance to the department of public safety relating to the program established by parts 1, 2, and 3 of this article.

42-20-105. Enforcement. (1) The provisions of parts 1, 2, and 3 of this article relating to the transportation of hazardous materials by motor vehicle may only be enforced by an enforcement official.

(2) Any enforcement official shall have the authority to issue penalty assessments for the misdemeanor traffic offenses specified in sections 42-20-204 (1) and 42-20-305 (2). At any time that a person is cited for a violation of any of the offenses specified, the person in charge of or operating the motor vehicle involved shall be given a notice in the form of a penalty assessment notice. Such notice shall be tendered by the enforcement official and shall contain the name and address of such person, the license number of the motor vehicle involved, if any, the number of such person's driver's license, the nature of the violation, the amount of the penalty prescribed for such violation, the date of the notice, a place for such person to execute a signed acknowledgment of receipt of the penalty assessment notice, a place for such person to execute a signed acknowledgment of guilt for the cited violation, and such other information as may be required by law to constitute such notice as a summons and complaint to appear in court should the prescribed penalty not be paid within twenty days. Every cited person shall execute the signed acknowledgment of receipt of the penalty assessment notice. The acknowledgment of guilt shall be executed at the time the cited person pays the prescribed penalty. The person cited shall pay the specified penalty at the office of the department of revenue, either in person or by postmarking such payment within twenty days after the citation. The department of revenue shall accept late payment of any penalty assessment up to twenty days after such payment becomes due. If the person cited does not pay the prescribed penalty within twenty days of the notice, the penalty assessment notice shall constitute a summons and complaint to appear in the county court of the county in which the penalty assessment was issued at a time and place specified by the notice, unless payment for such penalty assessment has been accepted by the department of revenue as evidenced by receipt.

(3) All enforcement officials may, at their discretion and in lieu of issuing the penalty assessments pursuant to subsection (2) of this section, issue warning citations to persons who violate the provisions of part 1, 2, or 3 of this article.

(4) Enforcement of any law relating to the fixed-site storage or use of hazardous materials shall not be affected by the provisions of part 1, 2, or 3 of this article.

42-20-106. Regulatory authority of local governments - preemption - disposition of local fines and penalties. (1) Except as specifically authorized in parts 1, 2, and 3 of this article, no county, town, city, or city and county shall have any authority to regulate the transportation of hazardous materials separate and apart from the regulation of other commodities. However, a county, town, city, or city and county may adopt and enforce regulations or ordinances which are no more stringent than the provisions of state law and regulations adopted pursuant thereto, if violations of such local regulations or ordinances carry penalties which are not more than the penalties imposed upon violations of state law and regulations adopted pursuant thereto. Any local government which adopts a regulation or ordinance pursuant to this section shall file a certified copy of such regulation or ordinance, and any amendment thereto, with the patrol.

(2) No person shall be prosecuted for a violation of both the provisions of part 1, 2, or 3 of this article and the provisions of such local ordinance or regulation when such prosecution arises out of the same incident.

42-20-107. Hazardous materials safety fund. (1) There is hereby created in the state treasury the hazardous materials safety fund, which shall consist of:

(a) Such moneys as may be appropriated thereto by the general assembly from time to time;

(b) Any permit fees collected pursuant to section 42-20-202;

(c) Any penalties collected by a state agency or by a court, as provided in section 42-20-305 (3);

(d) Any penalties collected pursuant to section 42-20-204 (4);

(e) Any gifts or donations made to the state of Colorado or any agency thereof specifically for the purpose of carrying out the provisions of parts 1, 2, and 3 of this article;

(f) Any federal funds made available to the state of Colorado or any agency thereof specifically for the purpose of carrying out the provisions of parts 1, 2, and 3 of this article;

(g) Any excess moneys credited to the fund in accordance with section 40-2-110.5 (9), C.R.S.

(2) The moneys in the hazardous materials safety fund shall be subject to appropriation by the general assembly for the purposes of parts 1, 2, and 3 of this article.

(3) At the end of each fiscal year, any moneys remaining in the hazardous materials safety fund shall not revert to the general fund but shall be subject to appropriation by the general assembly to the executive director of the department of public safety for disbursement to local governments for purposes related to the preparation and training for and response to hazardous materials incidents.

42-20-108. Rules and regulations for transportation of hazardous materials. (1) The chief shall promulgate rules and regulations pursuant to section 24-4-103, C.R.S., for the safe transportation of hazardous materials by motor vehicle, both in interstate and intrastate transportation. Such rules and regulations shall be applicable to any person who transports or ships, or who causes to be transported or shipped, a hazardous material by motor vehicle. Such rules and regulations may govern any safety aspect of the transportation of hazardous materials which the chief deems appropriate, including, but not limited to, the packaging, handling, labeling, marking, and placarding of hazardous materials and motor vehicles transporting hazardous materials, the qualifications of drivers of motor vehicles transporting hazardous materials, financial responsibility requirements, and the use of any package or container in the transportation of hazardous materials which is not manufactured, fabricated, marked, labeled, maintained, reconditioned, repaired, or tested in accordance with such rules and regulations.

(2) The chief shall also promulgate rules and regulations pursuant to section 24-4-103, C.R.S., for the permitting and routing of hazardous materials transportation by motor vehicle within this state and the inspection of vehicles transporting hazardous materials.

(3) In adopting such rules and regulations, the chief shall use as general guidelines the standards and specifications for the safe transportation of hazardous materials contained in federal statutes, and in the rules and regulations promulgated thereunder, as amended from time to time. The rules and regulations adopted by the chief shall not unduly burden interstate or intrastate commerce and shall be no more stringent than federal statutes and the rules and regulations promulgated thereunder.

(4) The rules and regulations adopted by the chief pursuant to subsection (2) of this section shall not apply to farm machinery which is exempted from registration requirements pursuant to section 42-3-103, agricultural distribution equipment attached to or conveyed by such farm machinery, or vehicles used to transport to or from the farm or ranch site products necessary for agricultural production, except when such vehicles are used in the furtherance of any commercial business other than agriculture.

(5) The rules and regulations adopted by the chief shall provide for the issuance of a certificate of inspection which shall exempt inspected vehicles from additional inspections for a period of at least sixty days unless there is probable cause to assume that the vehicle is in an unsafe condition.

42-20-108.5. Materials used for agricultural production - exemption - legislative declaration. (1) The general assembly hereby finds, determines, and declares that the federal government has extended federal hazardous materials rules to agricultural producers in 49 CFR 173.5 in a way that would be unduly burdensome to agriculture without contributing significantly to public safety. The general assembly further finds, determines, and declares that the federal rules give explicit authority to the states to exempt themselves from the federal rules, and that this section is intended to exempt Colorado agriculture from such rules. The general assembly further finds, determines, and declares that it is imperatively necessary for the chief to adopt the rules required by this section in time to meet the deadline imposed by the federal rules.

(2) As used in this section, unless the context otherwise requires:

(a) "Agricultural product" means a hazardous material, other than hazardous waste, whose end use directly supports the production of an agricultural commodity including, but not limited to, a fertilizer, pesticide, soil amendment, or fuel. An agricultural product is limited to a material in class 3, 8, or 9, division 2.1, 2.2, 5.1, or 6.1, or an ORM-D material as set forth in 49 CFR 172 and 173.

(b) "Farmer" means a person or such person's agent or contractor engaged in the production or raising of crops, poultry, or livestock.

(3) The transportation of an agricultural product other than a class 2 material, as such term is used in 49 CFR 172 and 173, over local roads between fields of the same farm, is excepted from the requirements of this part 1 when it is transported by a farmer who is an intrastate private motor carrier and the movement of the agricultural product conforms to rules of the chief, in consultation with the department of agriculture regarding such movement. The chief shall, in consultation with the director of the department of agriculture, promulgate rules and regulations pursuant to section 24-4-103, C.R.S., for the intrastate transportation of agricultural products.

(4) The transportation of an agricultural product to or from a farm, within one hundred fifty miles of such farm, is excepted from the emergency response information and training requirements in subparts G and H of 49 CFR 172, and this article when:

(a) It is transported by a farmer who is an intrastate private motor carrier;

(b) The total amount of agricultural product being transported on a single vehicle does not exceed:

(I) Seven thousand three hundred kilograms or sixteen thousand ninety-four pounds of ammonium nitrate fertilizer properly classed as division 5.1.PG III in a bulk packaging; or

(II) One thousand nine hundred liters or five hundred two gallons for liquids or gasses, or two thousand three hundred kilograms or five thousand seventy pounds for solids of any other agricultural product;

(c) The packaging conforms to rules adopted by the chief in consultation with the department of agriculture. Such rules shall be adopted by September 30, 1998. Such products are hereby authorized for transportation.

(d) Each person having any responsibility for transporting the agricultural product for shipment pursuant to this subsection (4) is instructed in the applicable requirements of this section.

(5) The rules and regulations adopted by the chief pursuant to this section shall be no more stringent than the federal statutes or regulations require.

(6) Any rules and regulations required to be adopted by the chief pursuant to this section shall be promulgated no later than September 30, 1998. If the chief finds that such rules cannot be promulgated by that date pursuant to the regular rule-making process set forth in section 24-4-103, C.R.S., the chief shall adopt temporary or emergency rules pursuant to section 24-4-103 (6), C.R.S.

(7) The chief shall send a copy of the notification of proposed rule-making for rules adopted pursuant to this section, including temporary or emergency rule-making sent pursuant to section 24-4-103 (3) (b), C.R.S., to the office of legislative legal services.

42-20-109. Penalty for violations. (1) Any person who violates a rule or regulation promulgated by the chief pursuant to section 42-20-104 commits a class 3 misdemeanor and shall be punished as provided in section 18-1.3-501, C.R.S.

(2) Any person who violates a rule promulgated by the chief pursuant to section 42-20-108 commits a class 2 misdemeanor traffic offense and shall be punished as provided in section 42-4-1701.

(3) No conviction pursuant to this section shall bar enforcement by the public utilities commission of any provision of title 40, C.R.S., with respect to violations by persons subject to said title.

42-20-110. Immobilization of unsafe vehicles. Any enforcement official shall have the power to immobilize, impound, or otherwise direct the disposition of motor vehicles transporting hazardous materials when the enforcement official deems that the motor vehicle or the operation thereof is unsafe and when such immobilization, impoundment, or disposition is appropriate under or required by rules and regulations promulgated by the chief pursuant to section 42-20-104.

42-20-111. Additional penalties. Any person, corporation, partnership, or other entity which intentionally or knowingly authorizes, solicits, requests, commands, conspires in, or aids and abets in the violation of any of the provisions of part 1, 2, or 3 of this article commits a class 1 misdemeanor and shall be punished as provided in section 18-1.3-501, C.R.S.

42-20-112. Reimbursement of local governments. (1) A public entity, political subdivision of the state, or other unit of local government is hereby given the right to claim reimbursement for the costs resulting from action taken to remove, contain, or otherwise mitigate the effects of a hazardous materials abandonment or a hazardous materials spill.

(2) Nothing contained in this section shall be construed to change or impair any right of recovery or subrogation arising under any other provision of law.

(3) Claims for reimbursement made pursuant to this section shall be in accordance with article 22 of title 29, C.R.S.

42-20-113. Hazardous materials spill - abandonment of vehicle containing hazardous material - penalty. (1) No person shall abandon any vehicle containing any hazardous material excluding that which is considered fuel and is contained within the vehicle's fuel tank or shall intentionally spill hazardous materials upon a street, highway, right-of-way, or any other public property or upon any private property without the express consent of the owner or person in lawful charge of that private property.

(2) (a) As used in this section, "abandon" means to leave a thing with the intention not to retain possession of or assert ownership or control over it. The intent need not coincide with the act of leaving.

(b) It is prima facie evidence of the necessary intent that:

(I) The vehicle has been left for more than three days unattended and unmoved; or

(II) License plates or other identifying marks have been removed from the vehicle; or

(III) The vehicle has been damaged or is deteriorated so extensively that it has value only for junk or salvage; or

(IV) The owner has been notified by a law enforcement agency to remove the vehicle and it has not been removed within twenty-four hours after notification.

(3) The driver of a motor vehicle transporting hazardous materials as cargo which is involved in a hazardous materials spill, whether intentional or unintentional, shall give immediate notice of the location of such spill and such other information as necessary to the nearest law enforcement agency.

(4) Any person who violates the provisions of subsection (3) of this section commits a class 3 misdemeanor and shall be punished as provided in section 18-1.3-501, C.R.S.

PART 2

PERMIT SYSTEM FOR
HAZARDOUS MATERIALS

42-20-201. Hazardous materials transportation permit required. Except as otherwise provided in this part 2, no transportation of hazardous materials by motor vehicle which requires placarding under 49 CFR 172 or 173 shall take place in, to, from, or through this state until the public utilities commission issues a permit, in accordance with the provisions of this part 2, authorizing the applicant to operate or move upon the public roads of this state a motor vehicle or a combination of motor vehicles which carries hazardous materials. This part 2 shall not apply to motor vehicles owned by the federal government, motor vehicles when used to transport to or from the farm or ranch site products used for agricultural production, or farm machinery which is exempted from registration requirements by section 42-3-103, unless such vehicles are used in furtherance of any commercial business other than agriculture. This part 2 shall apply to motor vehicles owned by the state or any political subdivision thereof; except that such vehicles shall be exempt from the fees provided in section 42-20-202. The requirements of this part 2 shall be in addition to, and not in substitution for, any other provisions of law.

42-20-202. Transportation permit - application fee. (1) (a) Except as otherwise provided in this section, each person desiring to transport hazardous materials which require placarding under 49 CFR 172 or 173 in, to, from, or through this state shall submit a permit application for an annual permit to the public utilities commission prior to beginning such transportation. Permit applications shall be in a form designated by the public utilities commission, and the public utilities commission shall maintain records of all such applications.

(b) Each annual permit shall be valid for one year following its issuance and shall be issued after the approval of the permit application by the public utilities commission and upon the payment of a permit fee, which fee shall be based on the number of motor vehicles the applicant operates within this state, as follows:

Number of Motor Vehicles	Permit Fee
1 - 5	$ 10
6 - 10	25
11 - 50	125
51 - 100	200
101 - 300	350
over 300	400

(c) Single trip permits may be obtained at all port of entry weigh stations and from the Colorado state patrol. Each person transporting such hazardous materials in, to, from, or through this state who has not obtained an annual permit from the public utilities commission shall apply at the closest possible port of entry weigh station or to an officer or office of the Colorado state patrol for a single trip permit. Each single trip permit shall be valid for a single continuous business venture, but in no event shall the permit be valid for more than seventy-two hours, unless extended by any enforcement official for any reason the official deems advisable, including mechanical difficulties and road and weather conditions. The single trip permit shall be issued upon the approval of the permit application and upon the payment of a twenty-five-dollar permit fee.

(d) The public utilities commission shall provide the option to a company filing for a permit under this subsection (1) to file an express consent waiver that enables the company to designate a company representative to be a party of interest for a violation of this section. The appearance of the company representative in a court hearing without the operator when the operator has signed such waiver shall not be deemed the practice of law in violation of article 5 of title 12, C.R.S.

(2) No annual permit application shall be approved unless the applicant:

(a) Supplies proof of having obtained liability insurance as required by the United States department of transportation pursuant to 49 CFR 387. Proof of such liability insurance policy shall be filed with the public utilities commission. The insurance carrier shall give thirty days' written notice for nonpayment of premium and ninety days' notice for nonrenewal of policy to the public utilities commission before the cancellation of such policy. At any time that the insurance policy lapses, the permit shall be automatically revoked.

(b) Agrees to comply with the rules and regulations promulgated pursuant to section 42-20-108.

(3) No single trip permit application shall be approved unless the applicant:

(a) Supplies proof of having liability insurance as required by the United States department of transportation pursuant to 49 CFR 387 or signs a verification under the penalty of perjury as provided in section 42-3-122 that the applicant has the liability insurance as required by the United States department of transportation pursuant to 49 CFR 387;

(b) Agrees to comply with the rules and regulations promulgated pursuant to section 42-20-108.

(4) The chief is authorized to promulgate such reasonable rules and regulations as may be necessary or desirable in governing the issuance of permits, if such rules and regulations are not in conflict with other provisions of state law.

(5) Any fees collected pursuant to this section shall be transmitted to the state treasurer, who shall credit the same to the hazardous materials safety fund created in section 42-20-107.

42-20-203. Carrying of permit and shipping papers. (1) Any person transporting hazardous materials that require placarding under 49 CFR 172 or 173 in this state shall carry a copy of the shipping papers required in 49 CFR 172.200 and a copy of the hazardous materials transportation permit issued by the public utilities commission or the port of entry weigh station in the transporting motor vehicle while in this state; except that, if a peace officer, as described in section 16-2.5-101, C.R.S., or any other enforcement official may determine that the hazardous materials transportation permit can be electronically verified at the time of contact, a copy of the permit need not be carried by the person transporting hazardous materials. Such permit shall be open to inspection or electronic verification by any enforcement official.

(2) In the event of an accident involving hazardous materials, the operator of the motor vehicle shall provide the shipping papers to the emergency response authorities designated in or pursuant to article 22 of title 29, C.R.S., and immediately bring to their attention the fact that the motor vehicle is carrying hazardous materials.

42-20-204. Permit violations - penalties. (1) Any person who transports hazardous materials without a permit in violation of any of the provisions of section 42-20-201 commits a misdemeanor traffic offense and shall be assessed a penalty of two hundred fifty dollars in accordance with the procedure set forth in section 42-20-105 (2). Any person who intentionally transports hazardous materials without a permit in violation of any of the provisions of section 42-20-201 commits a class 1 misdemeanor and shall be punished as provided in section 18-1.3-501, C.R.S. For the purposes of this subsection (1), if any person who previously has acknowledged guilt or has been convicted of a misdemeanor pursuant to this subsection (1) subsequently transports hazardous materials without a permit in violation of any of the provisions of section 42-20-201, a permissive inference is created that such subsequent transportation without a permit was intentional.

(2) Any person who has obtained an annual or a single trip hazardous materials transportation permit but fails to have a copy of said permit in the cab of the motor vehicle while transporting hazardous materials in, to, from, or through this state commits a class B traffic infraction and shall be assessed a penalty of twenty-five dollars in accordance with the procedure set forth in section 42-4-1701 (4) (a) (V); except that, if a peace officer, as described in section 16-2.5-101, C.R.S., or any other enforcement official may determine that the permit can be electronically verified at the time of contact, a copy of the permit need not be in the cab of the motor vehicle.

(3) Any person who knowingly violates any of the terms and conditions of an annual or single trip hazardous materials transportation permit commits a class 1 misdemeanor and shall be punished as provided in section 18-1.3-501, C.R.S.

(4) All penalties collected pursuant to this section by a state agency or by a court shall be transmitted to the state treasurer, who shall credit the same to the hazardous materials safety fund created in section 42-20-107.

(5) Every court having jurisdiction over offenses committed under this section shall forward to the chief in said court a record of the conviction of any person in said court for a violation of any said laws within forty-eight hours after such conviction. The term "conviction" means a final conviction.

42-20-205. Permit suspension or revocation. In addition to any other civil or criminal penalties, the public utilities commission may suspend the hazardous materials transportation annual permit for a period not to exceed six months or may revoke such permit for failure to comply with the terms and conditions of such permit, for failure to pay a civil penalty assessed pursuant to section 42-20-204, or for continuing violations of the regulations promulgated pursuant to part 1, 2, or 3 of this article. The permit may be suspended or revoked only for good cause shown after due notice and an opportunity for a hearing as provided in article 4 of title 24, C.R.S., if requested by the permit holder.

42-20-206. Local government preemption. No county, city and county, city, or town shall establish any permit or fee system for the transportation of hazardous materials by motor vehicle.

PART 3

ROUTE DESIGNATION FOR HAZARDOUS MATERIALS

42-20-300.3. Definitions. As used in this part 3, unless the context otherwise requires:

(1) "Route designation" means a designation of a route by the state patrol under this part 3.

Editor's note: Section 4 of chapter 56, Session Laws of Colorado 2011, provides that the act adding this section applies to petitions made on or after August 10, 2011.

42-20-301. Route designation. (1) (a) The patrol, after consultation with local governmental authorities, has the sole authority to designate which public roads are to be used and which are not to be used by motor vehicles transporting hazardous materials. The patrol shall exercise its authority in accordance with section 42-20-302. Gasoline, diesel fuel, and liquefied petroleum gas are exempt from route designation unless the petitioning authority specified in section 42-20-302 requests their inclusion. The patrol may exempt crude oil from route designation after a request from the petitioning authority.

(b) The patrol may include, as part of designated route restrictions, the closing of streets and highways and other conditions or restrictions the patrol deems advisable, except for hours of operation and curfews.

(c) Routes designated by the patrol in accordance with this part 3 do not apply to motor vehicles when used to transport to or from the farm or ranch site products necessary for agricultural production.

(d) No city, county, or city and county may impose restrictions on hours of operation on designated routes; except that this paragraph (d) does not apply to any city, county, or city and county that, by resolution or ordinance, had routes or hours of operation restrictions in effect on July 1, 1985.

(2) The patrol may approve route designations only for those materials listed in table 1 of 49 CFR 172.504, in any quantities, and those

materials listed in table 2 of 49 CFR 172.504, when carried in quantities of five hundred gallons or more; except that the patrol may not accept or approve route designations for those materials listed in table 2 when packaged in containers of five gallons or less or when packaged as consumer commodities as defined in 49 CFR 173.1200.

(3) Notwithstanding any other provision of this part 3 or part 1 or 2 of this article to the contrary, the transportation commission may regulate hours of operation of the Eisenhower-Johnson tunnels, structure numbers F13Y and F13X, respectively, on interstate 70.

Editor's note: Section 4 of chapter 56, Session Laws of Colorado 2011, provides that the act amending subsection (1) applies to petitions made on or after August 10, 2011.

42-20-302. Application for route designation - procedure - approval. (1) Petitions for new route designations or for a change in an existing route designation may be submitted to the patrol no more than once a year:

(a) By a county, with respect to any public road maintained by the county, upon approval of the petition by the board of county commissioners of such county;

(b) By a town, city, or city and county, with respect to any public road located within such town, city, or city and county, upon approval of the petition by the governing body of such town, city, or city and county;

(c) By the department of transportation, with respect to any public road maintained by the state, except for any public road located within a town, city, or city and county, upon approval of the petition by the transportation commission.

(2) A county, town, city, or city and county, with approval of the patrol, may adopt and enforce regulations or ordinances concerning the parking of motor vehicles, if such regulations and ordinances, as enforced or applied, do not prohibit or exclude motor vehicles carrying hazardous materials from the enforcing jurisdiction and do not unreasonably limit parking on or near the designated routes through the enforcing jurisdiction or for pickup and delivery.

(3) The petition shall describe specifically the designation sought, shall identify any local business or industry which is known to be significantly reliant on hazardous materials transportation and which would be affected by the designation, and shall include any other information which is necessary for the patrol to act upon the petition and which is required by rule and regulation of the patrol.

(4) Upon the filing of a complete petition with the patrol, the patrol shall give adequate public notice of such petition, including at least the following:

(a) Notification by certified mail to the governing body of any county, town, city, or city and county which would be affected by the route designation; and

(b) Publication in a newspaper having general circulation in each affected community once each week for three consecutive weeks.

(5) If the petitioner is not the department of transportation, the patrol shall provide a copy of the petition to the department of transportation for its review and comment.

(6) No sooner than thirty days after the requirements of subsections (3) and (4) of this section have been met and after reasonable notice to the petitioner, to the department of transportation, and to any persons requesting such notice, the patrol shall hold an informal public conference on the petition. At such conference, representatives of the petitioner and the department of transportation and any interested persons shall be afforded the opportunity to comment on the petition, and the petitioner shall have the opportunity to amend the petition. The patrol shall approve the designation if there is no opposition to the petition and if the requirements of subsection (8) of this section have been met.

(7) If there is opposition to the petition at the informal public conference and no agreement can be reached, the patrol shall hold a formal public hearing and act on the petition in accordance with the provisions of article 4 of title 24, C.R.S.

(8) No route designation shall be approved by the patrol unless it finds that:

(a) The routes available for the transportation of hazardous materials by motor vehicle:

(I) Are feasible, practicable, and not unreasonably expensive for such transportation;

(II) Are continuous within a jurisdiction and from one jurisdiction to another;

(III) Provide greater safety to the public than other feasible routes; and

(IV) Do not unreasonably burden interstate or intrastate commerce;

(b) The designation is not arbitrary or intended by the petitioner merely to divert the transportation of hazardous materials to other communities;

(c) Reasonable provision is made for signs along the affected public roads giving adequate notice of the designation to the public, to affected industry, and to transporters of hazardous materials. Such signs shall not be required in jurisdictions where the governmental authority has provided the patrol with professional quality maps which indicate the route designations in that jurisdiction.

(d) The designation will not interfere with the pickup or delivery of hazardous materials; and

(e) The designation is consistent with all applicable federal laws and regulations.

(9) Any town, city, city and county, or county may request the department of transportation to submit a petition to the patrol for a route designation on any highway maintained by the state within the jurisdiction of said local entity.

(10) The patrol shall make a final decision to approve or deny any petition for a route designation within six months of the filing of the petition.

(11) (a) The patrol shall base the approval or denial of a petition to exempt crude oil upon due consideration of the factors listed in subsection (8) of this section.

(b) The patrol shall approve route designations for gasoline, diesel fuel, and liquefied petroleum gas requested by petitioning authorities under section 42-20-301 (1) where the designations follow routes approved by the patrol for other hazardous materials under this section.

42-20-303. Road signs required - uniform standards. Signs giving adequate notice of route designations shall be placed and maintained along public roads affected by such designations. In accordance with part 6 of article 4 of this title and section 42-4-105, the department of transportation shall adopt uniform standards for highway signs giving notice of route designations. The requirements of this section shall not apply to jurisdictions in which the governmental authority has provided the patrol with professional quality maps which indicate the route designations in that jurisdiction.

42-20-304. Emergency closure of public roads. Nothing in part 1, 2, or 3 of this article shall limit the authority of state and local authorities to close public roads temporarily if necessary because of any road construction or maintenance, an accident, a natural disaster, the weather conditions, or any other emergency circumstances resulting in making road conditions unsafe for travel by motor vehicles transporting hazardous materials.

42-20-305. Deviation from authorized route - penalty. (1) No person shall transport hazardous materials by motor vehicle contrary to any route designation approved by the patrol pursuant to this part 3 unless such action is necessary to service a motor vehicle or to make a local pickup or delivery of hazardous materials or unless such action is so required by emergency conditions which would make continued use of authorized routes unsafe or by the closure of an authorized route pursuant to section 42-20-304, and, in such circumstances, the motor vehicle shall remain on authorized routes whenever possible and shall minimize the distance traveled on restricted routes. A person transporting hazardous materials by motor vehicle may make successive local pickups and deliveries without returning to the authorized route between each pickup or delivery when such return would be unreasonable. A person transporting hazardous materials shall not utilize residential streets unless there is no other reasonable route available to reach the destination.

(2) Any person who transports hazardous materials by motor vehicle in a manner inconsistent with the provisions of subsection (1) of this section commits a misdemeanor traffic offense and shall be assessed a penalty of two hundred fifty dollars for each separate violation in accordance with the procedure set forth in section 42-20-105 (2). A person who commits a second or subsequent violation within a twelve-month period of transporting hazardous materials by motor vehicle in a manner inconsistent with the provisions of subsection (1) of this section commits a misdemeanor traffic offense and shall be issued a summons and complaint in accordance with the provisions of section 42-4-1707 (1), and, upon conviction thereof, shall be punished by a fine of not less than two hundred fifty dollars nor more than five hundred dollars.

(3) All penalties collected pursuant to this section by a state agency or by a court shall be transmitted to the state treasurer, who shall credit the same to the hazardous materials safety fund created in section 42-20-107.

(4) Every court having jurisdiction over offenses committed under subsection (2) of this section shall forward to the chief a record of the conviction of any person in said court for a violation of any said laws within forty-eight hours after such conviction. The term "conviction" means a final conviction.

PART 4

NUCLEAR MATERIALS - GENERAL PROVISIONS

42-20-401. Legislative declaration. It is hereby determined and declared that nuclear materials create a potential risk to the public health, safety, and welfare of the people of the state of Colorado. As an origination point of nuclear waste and a corridor state through which nuclear materials pass, the state has a duty to protect its citizens and environment from all hazards created by the transportation of nuclear materials within its borders. State and public participation in planning for the transport of nuclear materials and in the development of a plan to cope with all phases of the nuclear materials problem is essential in order to adequately prepare for potential nuclear incidents. To that end, it is the purpose of this part 4 and part 5 of this article to require safe and environmentally acceptable methods of transporting nuclear materials within this state in a manner consistent with the laws of the United States and the rules and regulations promulgated by agencies of the United States.

42-20-402. Definitions. As used in this part 4 and part 5 of this article, unless the context otherwise requires:

(1) "Carrier" means any person transporting goods or property on the public roads of this state in, to, from, or through this state, whether or not such transportation is for hire.

(2) "Commission" means the public utilities commission.

(3) (a) "Nuclear materials" means highway route controlled quantities of radioactive materials as defined in 49 CFR 173.403 (l).

(b) "Nuclear materials" does not include nuclear materials used for research or medical purposes within Colorado. For the purpose of this paragraph (b), highway route controlled quantities of radioactive materials used to irradiate medical supplies and equipment are not considered to be used for medical purposes.

(c) (I) "Nuclear materials" includes radioactive materials being transported to the waste isolation pilot plant in New Mexico and radioactive materials being transported to any facility provided pursuant to section 135 of the federal "Nuclear Waste Policy Act of 1982", 42 U.S.C. 10101 et seq., or any repository licensed by the United States nuclear regulatory commission that is used for the permanent deep geologic disposal of high-level radioactive waste and spent nuclear fuel.

(II) Except as provided in subparagraph (I) of this paragraph (c), "nuclear materials" does not include radioactive materials utilized in national security activities under the direct control of the United States department of defense, nor does it include radioactive materials under the direct control of the United States department of energy which are utilized in carrying out atomic energy defense activities, as defined in the federal "Nuclear Waste Policy Act of 1982", 42 U.S.C. 10101 et seq., or wastes from mining, milling, smelting, or similar processing of ores and mineral-bearing material.

(III) Notwithstanding the provisions of subparagraph (I) of this paragraph (c), "nuclear materials" does not include ores or products from mining, milling, smelting, or similar processing of ores, or the transportation thereof.

42-20-403. Chief to promulgate rules and regulations - motor vehicles. The chief shall promulgate rules and regulations for the safe transportation of nuclear materials by motor vehicle. Such rules shall not be inconsistent with any federal rule or regulation governing the transportation of the nuclear materials subject to parts 4 and 5 of this article. Such rules shall be applicable to any person who transports or ships, or who causes to be transported or shipped, a nuclear material by motor vehicle.

42-20-404. Inspections. All vehicles carrying nuclear materials entering the state on the public highways shall be inspected by Colorado state patrol officers at the nearest point at which the shipment enters the state or at a location specified by the Colorado state patrol. For all shipments originating within the state, inspection shall be made at the point of origination by Colorado state patrol officers. All such inspections conducted by Colorado state patrol officers shall be in accordance with the rules promulgated pursuant to sections 42-4-235, 42-20-108 (2), and 42-20-403.

42-20-405. Violations - criminal penalties. (1) Notwithstanding the provisions of section 40-7-107, C.R.S., any person who violates any provision of this part 4 or part 5 of this article or rule or regulation promulgated by the chief pursuant to this part 4 and part 5 of this article commits a class 2 misdemeanor and shall be punished as provided in section 18-1.3-501, C.R.S. No conviction pursuant to this section shall bar enforcement by the commission of any provision of title 40, C.R.S., with respect to violations by persons subject to said title.

(2) Every court having jurisdiction over offenses committed under subsection (1) of this section shall forward to the chief a record of the conviction of any person in said court for a violation of any provision of part 4 or 5 of this article or any rule or regulation promulgated pursuant thereto within forty-eight hours after such conviction. As used in this subsection (2), "conviction" means a final conviction.

42-20-406. Violations - civil penalties - motor vehicles. (1) Any person who violates any provision of this part 4 or part 5 of this article or a rule or regulation promulgated by the chief pursuant to this part 4 and part 5 of this article, except for the violations enumerated in subsection (3) of this section and section 42-20-505, shall be subject to a civil penalty of not more than ten thousand dollars per day for each day during which such violation occurs. The penalty shall be assessed by the chief upon receipt of a complaint by any investigative personnel of the commission or Colorado state patrol officer and after written notice and an opportunity for a hearing pursuant to section 24-4-105, C.R.S. Payment of a civil penalty under this section shall not relieve any person from liability pursuant to article 11 of title 25, part 3 of article 15 of title 25, or article 22 of title 29, C.R.S. Any person who is assessed a penalty pursuant to this subsection (1) shall have the right to appeal the chief's decision by filing a notice of appeal with the court of appeals as specified in section 24-4-106 (11), C.R.S.

(2) Any person who commits any of the acts enumerated in subsection (3) of this section shall be subject to the civil penalty listed in said subsection (3). Investigative personnel of the commission, and officers of the Colorado state patrol shall have the authority to issue civil penalty assessments for the enumerated violations. At any time that a person is cited for a violation enumerated in subsection (3) of this section, the person in charge of or operating the motor vehicle involved shall be given a notice in the form of a civil penalty assessment notice. Such notice shall be tendered by the enforcement official and shall contain the name and address of such person, the license number of the motor vehicle involved, if any, the number of such person's driver's license, the nature of the violation, the amount of the penalty prescribed for such violation, the date of the notice, a place for such person to execute a signed acknowledgment of his

or her receipt of the civil penalty assessment notice, a place for such person to execute a signed acknowledgment of liability for the cited violation, and such other information as may be required by law to constitute such notice as a complaint to appear in court should the prescribed penalty not be paid within ten days. Every cited person shall execute the signed acknowledgment of his or her receipt of the civil penalty assessment notice. The acknowledgment of liability shall be executed at the time the cited person pays the prescribed penalty. The person cited shall pay the civil penalty specified in subsection (3) of this section for the violation involved at the office of the department of revenue either in person or by postmarking such payment within ten days of the citation. The department of revenue shall accept late payment of any penalty assessment up to twenty days after such payment becomes due. If the person cited does not pay the prescribed penalty within ten days of the notice, the civil penalty assessment notice shall constitute a complaint to appear in court unless payment for such penalty assessment has been accepted by the department of revenue as evidenced by receipt, and the person cited shall, within the time specified in the civil penalty assessment notice, file an answer to this complaint with the county court for the county in which the penalty assessment was issued. The attorney general shall represent the state agency that issued the civil penalty assessment notice if so requested by the agency.

(3) The following penalties shall apply only to the transportation of nuclear materials by motor vehicle and shall be assessed against drivers, shippers, carriers, operators, brokers, and other persons, as appropriate:

(a) Any person who operates a motor vehicle without a driver's log book in his or her possession, as required by 49 CFR 395.8, shall be assessed a civil penalty of one hundred dollars.

(b) Any person who operates a motor vehicle without maintaining a driver's log book in current condition, in accordance with 49 CFR 395.8, shall be assessed a civil penalty of one hundred dollars.

(c) Any person who enters false information in a driver's log book in violation of 49 CFR 395.8 (e) shall be assessed a civil penalty of two hundred fifty dollars.

(d) Any person who exceeds maximum driving or on duty time, as established by 49 CFR 395.3, shall be assessed a civil penalty of two hundred fifty dollars.

(e) Any person who fails to produce his or her driver's log book on demand of any law enforcement official, port of entry personnel, or investigative personnel of the commission in violation of 49 CFR 395.8 shall be assessed a civil penalty of two hundred fifty dollars.

(f) Any person who fails to have a valid medical certificate in his or her possession, in accordance with 49 CFR 391.43, shall be assessed a civil penalty of one hundred dollars.

(g) Any person who operates a motor vehicle without meeting driver qualifications, as established in 49 CFR 177.825 (d) and section 42-20-501, shall be assessed a civil penalty of five hundred dollars.

(h) Any person who carries an unauthorized passenger, as defined in 49 CFR 392.60, shall be assessed a civil penalty of one hundred dollars.

(i) Any person who operates a motor vehicle while that person is declared to be out of service, as defined in 49 CFR 395.13, shall be assessed a civil penalty of five hundred dollars.

(j) Any person who operates an unsafe vehicle, as defined in 49 CFR 396, shall be assessed a civil penalty of one hundred fifty dollars.

(k) Any person who operates a motor vehicle without correcting defects as noted on a safety inspection report in violation of 49 CFR 396.9 shall be assessed a civil penalty of five hundred dollars.

(l) Any person who operates a motor vehicle while that vehicle is declared to be out of service, as defined in 49 CFR 396.9 (c) (2), shall be assessed a civil penalty of one thousand dollars.

(m) Any person who transports nuclear materials without proper visibility and display of placards in violation of 49 CFR 172.504 shall be assessed a civil penalty of two hundred dollars.

(n) Any person who transports nuclear materials without proper placards, as provided in 49 CFR 172.504, shall be assessed a civil penalty of five hundred dollars.

(o) Any person who displays nuclear materials placards on vehicles not transporting nuclear materials in violation of 49 CFR 172.502 shall be assessed a civil penalty of one hundred dollars.

(p) Any person who fails to have hazardous materials shipping papers in conformance with 49 CFR 177.817 shall be assessed a civil penalty of five hundred dollars.

(q) Any person who parks a motor vehicle transporting nuclear materials in violation of 49 CFR 397.7 shall be assessed a civil penalty of five hundred dollars.

(r) Any person who violates a provision of section 42-20-508 or the rules adopted pursuant thereto shall be assessed a civil penalty of five hundred dollars.

(s) Any person who improperly fills out the shipping papers required by 49 CFR 172, subpart C, shall be assessed a civil penalty of five hundred dollars.

(t) Any person who fails to report a nuclear incident, or fails to take necessary response actions, as required by 49 CFR 171.15 and 171.16 and 49 CFR 177.861, shall be assessed a civil penalty of five hundred dollars.

(u) Any person who supplies inaccurate information in, or who fails to comply with, the route plan required by 49 CFR 177.825 (c) shall be assessed a civil penalty of five hundred dollars.

(v) Any person who transports nuclear materials in violation of the radiation level limitations established in 49 CFR 173.441 shall be assessed a civil penalty of one thousand dollars.

(w) Any person who transports nuclear materials in excess of the maximum permissible transport index, as provided in 49 CFR 173, shall be assessed a civil penalty of one thousand dollars.

42-20-407. Repeat violations - civil penalties. (1) If any person receives two penalty assessments within one year for a violation of section 42-20-406 and the first penalty assessment has not been reversed by a court of competent jurisdiction, the penalty for the second violation shall be two times the amount of the penalty listed for the violation in section 42-20-406.

(2) If any person receives three or more penalty assessments within one year for a violation of section 42-20-406 and if two or more of the previous penalty assessments have not been reversed by a court of competent jurisdiction, the penalty for each of the third and subsequent violations shall be three times the amount of the penalty listed for the violation in section 42-20-406.

42-20-408. Compliance orders - penalty. (1) Whenever the chief finds that any person is in violation of any rule, regulation, or requirement of part 4 or 5 of this article, the chief may issue an order requiring such person to comply with any such rule, regulation, or requirement and may request the attorney general to bring suit for injunctive relief or for penalties pursuant to section 42-20-406.

(2) Any person who violates any compliance order of the chief which is not subject to a stay pending judicial review and which has been issued pursuant to this part 4 shall be subject to a civil penalty of not more than ten thousand dollars per day for each day during which such violation occurs.

PART 5

NUCLEAR MATERIALS PERMIT SYSTEM

42-20-501. Nuclear materials transportation permit required - application. (1) No transportation of nuclear materials shall take place in, to, from, or through this state until the commission issues a permit, in accordance with the provisions of this section, which is not inconsistent with federal law, authorizing the applicant to operate or move upon public roads of this state a motor vehicle or combination of motor vehicles which carry nuclear materials.

(2) Each carrier desiring to transport nuclear materials shall submit a permit application, in the form designated by the commission, to the commission prior to beginning such transportation.

42-20-502. Permits - fees. Each permit issued pursuant to section 42-20-501 shall be valid for one year following its issuance and shall be issued after approval of the carrier's permit application and upon payment of a five-hundred-dollar permit fee. In addition to the permit fee, each carrier shall pay a two-hundred-dollar fee for each shipment. The shipment fee shall be paid either by mail, in which case it must be postmarked at least seven days before the shipment is to be made, or at the time the shipment enters the state at the port of entry weigh station nearest the point at which the shipment enters the state. If the shipment originates in this state, payment shall be made at the port of entry weigh station nearest the point of origination of the shipment.

42-20-503. Carrying of shipping papers. Any person transporting nuclear materials in this state shall carry a copy of the shipping papers required in 49 CFR 172, subpart C.

42-20-504. Rules and regulations. The chief is authorized to promulgate reasonable rules and regulations which are necessary or desirable in governing the issuance of permits if such rules and regulations are not in conflict with or inconsistent with federal rules and regulations.

42-20-505. Penalties - permit system. (1) The investigative personnel of the commission, the ports of entry personnel, and the officers of the Colorado state patrol may assess a civil penalty of one thousand dollars against every carrier who transports nuclear materials without first obtaining a nuclear materials transportation permit.

(2) Every carrier who misrepresents information in the carrier's application for a nuclear materials transportation permit, violates the terms of the permit, or commits a second violation of subsection (1) of this section within one calendar year shall be assessed a civil penalty of not less than five hundred dollars nor more than three thousand dollars.

(3) The penalties in subsection (1) of this section shall be assessed upon an action brought by the commission, the motor carrier services division of the department of revenue, or the Colorado state patrol in accordance with the procedure set forth in section 42-20-406.

42-20-506. Permit suspension and revocation. In addition to any other civil or criminal penalties, the commission may suspend the nuclear materials transportation permit of any carrier for a period not to exceed six months or revoke such permit for failure to comply with the permit terms, misrepresentation of information in the permit application, failure to pay a civil penalty assessed pursuant to section 42-20-406, or failure to comply with the regulations promulgated pursuant to parts 4 and 5 of this article. The permit may be suspended or revoked only for good cause shown after due notice and opportunity for a hearing pursuant to section 24-4-105, C.R.S., if requested by the carrier.

42-20-507. Local government preemption. No county, city and county, city, or town shall establish any permit or fee system for the transportation of nuclear materials by motor vehicle or railcar in, to, from, or through this state.

42-20-508. Route designation - motor vehicles. (1) The chief of the Colorado state patrol shall have the authority to adopt rules to designate which state highways shall be used and which shall not be used by motor vehicles transporting nuclear materials in this state.

(2) The carrier shall not deviate from the routes designated pursuant to subsection (1) of this section except in order to make local pickups and deliveries and in cases of emergency conditions which would make continued use of the designated route unsafe, or to refuel, or when the designated route is closed due to road conditions, road construction, or maintenance operations. When making local pickups and deliveries or when refueling, the carrier shall remain on the routes designated by the Colorado state patrol and shall minimize the distance traveled on nondesignated routes.

42-20-509. Strict liability for nuclear incidents. Any person who causes the release of any nuclear material being transported shall be strictly liable for all injuries and damages resulting therefrom. The conduct of the claimant shall not be a defense to liability; except that this section does not waive any defense based on the claimant's failure to mitigate damages or related to any injury or damage to the claimant or the claimant's property which is intentionally sustained by the claimant or which results from the release of any nuclear material being transported intentionally and wrongfully caused by the claimant.

42-20-510. Statute of limitations. No person who has been injured or damaged as a result of a nuclear incident shall be precluded from bringing a suit against the person or persons responsible for causing the nuclear incident if such suit is instituted within three years after the date on which the injured person first knew, or reasonably could have known, of his or her injury or damage and the cause thereof; except that such suit must be brought within forty years after the date of the nuclear incident.

42-20-511. Nuclear materials transportation fund. All moneys collected pursuant to parts 4 and 5 of this article shall be transmitted to the state treasurer, who, in addition to any excess moneys transferred from the motor carrier fund pursuant to section 40-2-110.5 (9), C.R.S., shall credit the same to the nuclear materials transportation fund, which fund is hereby created. The moneys in the fund shall be subject to annual appropriation by the general assembly for the direct and indirect costs of the administration of parts 4 and 5 of this article.

TITLE 43
TRANSPORTATION

TITLE 43
TRANSPORTATION

HIGHWAY SAFETY

ARTICLE 5
Highway Safety

PART 1
COLORADO STATE PATROL

43-5-101 to
43-5-128.   (Repealed)

PART 2
AUTO AND TOURIST CAMPS,
HOTELS, AND MOTELS

43-5-201.   Definitions.
43-5-202.   Licenses - fee - penalty. (Repealed)
43-5-203.   Required records.
43-5-204.   Record open for inspection by officers.
43-5-205.   Allowing stolen motor vehicle to be stored - penalty.
43-5-206.   Revocation of license. (Repealed)
43-5-207.   Penalty.
43-5-208.   Effective date - applicability. (Repealed)

PART 3
OFFENSES

43-5-301.   Obstructing highway - penalty.
43-5-302.   Not to dam stream - penalty.
43-5-303.   Overflowing highways - penalty.
43-5-304.   Jurisdiction.
43-5-305.   Owners construct culverts - penalty.
43-5-306.   Transporting heavy machines.
43-5-307.   Injury to highway - penalty.

PART 4
IMPLEMENTATION OF FEDERAL
"HIGHWAY SAFETY ACT OF 1966"

43-5-401.   Duties and responsibility of governor.

PART 5
MOTORCYCLE OPERATOR
SAFETY TRAINING

43-5-501.   Definitions.
43-5-502.   Motorcycle operator safety training program.
43-5-503.   Instructor requirements and training.
43-5-504.   Motorcycle operator safety training fund.
43-5-505.   Advisory committee. (Repealed)

PART 1
COLORADO STATE PATROL

43-5-101 to 43-5-128.   (Repealed)

PART 2
AUTO AND TOURIST CAMPS,
HOTELS, AND MOTELS

Cross references: For penalty for false advertising of accommodations and rates of hotel facilities, see article 14 of title 18.

43-5-201.   Definitions. As used in this part 2, unless the context otherwise requires:

(1) "Auto camp" means any auto or tourist camp, park or campsite, tourist court, auto court, auto hotel, or trailer coach court owned, operated, controlled, or leased by any person, firm, association, or corporation for the purpose of renting, leasing, or otherwise providing parking sites or spaces for any motor vehicle, trailer, semitrailer, or trailer coach, irrespective of the number of parking sites or spaces provided. The term does not include mobile home parks with respect to spaces rented for the parking and hooking up of trailer coaches or mobile homes for use as residences.

(2) "Hotel" or "hotel facility" means an establishment engaged in the business of furnishing overnight room accommodations primarily for transient persons and which maintains or makes available, as a part of its services to its patrons, facilities for the parking or storage of motor vehicles.

(3) "Motor vehicle" includes all motor vehicles propelled by power other than muscular power, except road rollers, fire wagons, fire engines, police patrol wagons, police ambulances, and such vehicles as run only upon rails or tracks or travel through the air.

(4) "Owner" includes any person, firm, association, or corporation renting a motor vehicle or having the exclusive use thereof under a lease or otherwise for a period greater than thirty days.

43-5-202.   Licenses - fee - penalty. (Repealed)

43-5-203.   Required records. (1) It is the duty of every person, firm, association, or corporation owning, operating, controlling, or leasing an auto camp or hotel to keep and maintain in the auto camp or hotel an easily accessible and permanent daily record of all automobiles stored, kept, parked, or maintained in said auto camp and all automobiles of patrons of such hotel which are parked in facilities maintained and made available exclusively for such patrons by such hotel. The record shall be kept in a book or on cards, consecutively numbered, in a uniform manner approved by the Colorado state patrol. The record shall include the name and address of the owner of the automobile stored, parked, kept, or maintained in said auto camp or hotel facility, together with the make, body style, and year of said automobile and the license number, if any. All such records shall be preserved for a period of three years.

(2) Repealed.

43-5-204. Record open for inspection by officers. The books and records of every auto camp and hotel shall be open for inspection to members of the Colorado state patrol and all peace officers of the state.

43-5-205. Allowing stolen motor vehicle to be stored - penalty. Any person who knowingly allows or permits any stolen motor vehicle to be stored, kept, parked, or maintained in any licensed auto camp or hotel facility within the state of Colorado is guilty of a misdemeanor and, upon conviction thereof, shall be punished by a fine of not more than one hundred dollars. This provision shall not be exclusive of any other penalties prescribed by any existing or future laws for the theft or unauthorized taking of a motor vehicle.

43-5-206. Revocation of license. (Repealed)

43-5-207. Penalty. Any person violating any of the provisions of this part 2, except as set forth in section 43-5-205, is guilty of a class 2 petty offense and, upon conviction thereof, shall be punished by a fine of not more than one hundred dollars.

43-5-208. Effective date - applicability. (Repealed)

PART 3

OFFENSES

43-5-301. Obstructing highway - penalty. No person or corporation shall erect any fence, house, or other structure, or dig pits or holes in or upon any highway, or place thereon or cause or allow to be placed thereon any stones, timber, or trees or any obstruction whatsoever. No person or corporation shall tear down, burn, or otherwise damage any bridge of any highway, or cause wastewater or the water from any ditch, road, drain, flume, agricultural crop sprinkler system, or other source to flow or fall upon any road or highway so as to damage the same or to cause a hazard to vehicular traffic. Any person or corporation so offending is guilty of a misdemeanor and, upon conviction thereof, shall be punished by a fine of not less than ten dollars nor more than three hundred dollars and shall also be liable to any person, unit of government, or corporation in a civil action for any damages resulting therefrom. Upon a third conviction therefor, the offender shall be punished by a fine of not less than ten dollars nor more than three hundred dollars or by imprisonment in the county jail for not more than three days and shall also be liable to any person, unit of government, or corporation in a civil action for any damages resulting therefrom. Each day such condition is allowed to continue upon any highway shall be deemed a separate offense.

43-5-302. Not to dam stream - penalty. No person or corporation shall dam the waters of any stream so as to cause the same to overflow any road or damage or weaken the abutments, walls, or embankments of any bridge of any highway. Any person or corporation violating any of the provisions of this section shall forfeit the sum of fifty dollars to the county and shall be liable to any person or corporation in a civil action for any damages resulting therefrom.

43-5-303. Overflowing highways - penalty. No person or corporation shall repeatedly, willfully or negligently cause or allow water to flow, fall, or sprinkle from any ditch, lateral, canal, waste ditch, reservoir, pond, drain, flume, or agricultural crop sprinkler system upon any public road or highway so as to damage the same or to cause a hazard to vehicular traffic. Any person or corporation so offending is guilty of a misdemeanor and, upon conviction thereof, shall be punished by a fine of not less than ten dollars nor more than three hundred dollars. Upon a third conviction therefor, the offender shall be punished by a fine of not less than ten dollars nor more than three hundred dollars or by imprisonment in the county jail for not more than three days. Each day that water is so allowed to flow upon any public road or highway shall be deemed a separate offense. Agricultural crop sprinkler systems upon which generally accepted devices are installed or preventive practices are carried out and when due diligence has been exercised to prevent the end gun from discharging water upon the highway shall not be deemed to be in violation of this section, nor shall acts of God, including but not limited to wind, be deemed a violation of this section.

43-5-304. Jurisdiction. The county court of the county wherein any of the offenses described in sections 43-5-301 and 43-5-303 may be committed shall have jurisdiction of complaints coming within the provisions of sections 43-5-301 and 43-5-303.

43-5-305. Owners construct culverts - penalty. (1) Any person or corporation owning or constructing any ditch, race, drain, or flume in, upon, or across any highway shall keep the highway open for safe and convenient travel by constructing culverts, bridges, or similar structures over such ditch, race, drain, or flume. When any ditch is constructed across, in, or upon any highway, the person owning or constructing such ditch shall construct a culvert, bridge, or similar structure long enough to conduct the water from shoulder to shoulder from such road or highway or of such greater length as the board of county commissioners having jurisdiction thereover may require, plans for said culvert, bridge, or similar structure having been approved in advance by said board of county commissioners. The board of county commissioners shall maintain said culvert, bridge, or similar structure after construction, in accordance with the provisions of section 37-84-106, C.R.S.

(2) Any person or corporation who fails to construct a culvert, bridge, or similar structure across any ditch, race, drain, or flume, within a time limit to be specified by the board of county commissioners when the plans therefor are approved by said board as provided in subsection (1) of this section, shall forfeit the sum of twenty-five dollars to the county for each day of failure to construct such bridge, culvert, or similar structure together with the cost of construction thereof. Proceeds from such penalty shall be paid into the road fund of the district. It is the duty of the road supervisor of the district to construct such culvert, bridge, or similar structure if the owner of such ditch, race, drain, or flume fails to comply.

43-5-306. Transporting heavy machines. It is the duty of all persons, associations, and corporations operating threshing machines or vehicles or using the public roads for transporting such machines or other heavy machinery to use a sufficient number of heavy planks, wherever necessary, to protect all sidewalks, bridges, culverts, and causeways from being broken by said threshing machines or other heavy machinery in passing over the same.

43-5-307. Injury to highway - penalty. If any person, association, or corporation purposely destroys or injures any sidewalk, bridge, culvert, or causeway, or removes any of the timber or plank thereof, or obstructs the same, he shall forfeit a sum of not less than one hundred dollars nor more than three hundred dollars and shall be liable for all damages occasioned thereby and for all necessary cost for rebuilding or repairing the same. All forfeitures and sums of money recovered under this section and section 43-5-306 shall be turned into the county road fund.

PART 4

IMPLEMENTATION OF FEDERAL "HIGHWAY SAFETY ACT OF 1966"

43-5-401. Duties and responsibility of governor. The governor is hereby designated as the official of the state of Colorado having the ultimate responsibility for dealing with the federal government with respect to programs and activities pursuant to the federal "Highway Safety Act of 1966", and subsequent amendments thereto. To that end, he shall coordinate the activities of all departments and agencies of this state and its political subdivisions relating thereto.

PART 5

MOTORCYCLE OPERATOR SAFETY TRAINING

43-5-501. Definitions. As used in this part 5, unless the context otherwise requires:

(1) "Director" means the director of the office.

(2) "Fund" means the motorcycle operator safety training fund created in section 43-5-504.

(3) "Instructor training specialist" means a licensed motorcycle operator who meets the standards promulgated by the office to train and oversee instructors for the program.

(4) "Office" means the office of transportation safety in the department of transportation.

(5) "Program" means the motorcycle operator safety training program established pursuant to section 43-5-502.

43-5-502. Motorcycle operator safety training program. (1) (a) (I) The office shall establish a motorcycle operator safety training program which shall include courses to develop the knowledge, attitudes, habits, and skills necessary for the safe operation of a motorcycle. Such program shall include instruction relating to the effects of alcohol and drugs on the operation of motorcycles, and it shall include a course to train instructors. The office shall set standards for the certification of courses in the program. The office shall contract with vendors for the purpose of providing the program.

(II) The following individuals may enroll in a certified motorcycle operator safety training course:

(A) Any resident of the state who holds a current valid Colorado driver's license, a minor driver's license, or an instruction permit authorized by section 42-2-106, C.R.S.; or

(B) Any individual who is a member of the armed forces, who has moved to Colorado on a permanent change of station basis, and who holds a valid driver's licence issued by another state.

(III) The charge for enrollment in the certified motorcycle operator training course shall be the same regardless of whether an individual qualifies for the course pursuant to sub-subparagraph (A) or (B) of subparagraph (II) of this paragraph (a).

(b) The director may certify any person meeting the applicable standards as an instructor training specialist to assist in establishing motorcycle operator safety training courses throughout the state, in implementing the program, and in training and monitoring instructors.

(c) The director shall designate a program coordinator to implement and administer the program. In no event shall the office expend more than fifteen percent of the total cost of the program for administrative costs.

(d) The office shall adopt such rules and regulations as are necessary to carry out the provisions of the program pursuant to article 4 of title 24, C.R.S.

(2) The office shall begin implementation of this part 5 on November 1, 1990, or when the moneys in the fund are sufficient to pay for the costs of implementing the program, whichever is later. However, operation of courses in the program shall commence no later than July 1, 1991.

43-5-503. Instructor requirements and training. (1) The office shall establish standards for an approved instructor training course. Successful completion of the course shall require the participant to demonstrate knowledge of course material, knowledge of safe motorcycle operating practices, and the necessary aptitude for instructing students.

(2) Each applicant for an instructor certificate shall be at least twenty-one years of age and hold a valid Colorado driver's license endorsed for motorcycles, which license has not been revoked or suspended within the three years preceding the date on which the application for certification is made.

(3) No applicant shall be certified as an instructor if, within the three years preceding the date on which the application for certification is made:

(a) The applicant was convicted for an offense which is assigned eight or more points in the point system schedule, as specified in section 42-2-127 (5), C.R.S., or its equivalent in another state; or

(b) The applicant's driver's license from any other state was revoked or suspended.

(4) The office shall prescribe the form for an approved instructor certificate and shall provide for verification that a certified instructor is currently active in the program. No instructor shall participate in the program without a current certificate.

43-5-504. Motorcycle operator safety training fund. There is hereby created in the state treasury a motorcycle operator safety training fund which shall consist of moneys collected pursuant to sections 42-2-114 (2) (b) and (4) (b), 42-2-118 (1) (b) (II), and 42-3-304 (4), C.R.S. The moneys in the fund shall be available immediately, without further appropriation, for allocation by the transportation commission to the office of transportation safety to be used for the implementation and administration of the program. Moneys credited to the fund shall remain therein at the end of each fiscal year and shall not be transferred to any other fund.

43-5-505. Advisory committee. (Repealed)

TITLE 12
PROFESSIONS AND OCCUPATIONS

TITLE 12

PROFESSIONS AND OCCUPATIONS

GENERAL

Art.	6.	Automobiles, 12-6-101 to 12-6-403.
Art.	15.	Commercial Driving Schools, 12-15-101 to 12-15-121.

GENERAL

ARTICLE 6

Automobiles

PART 1
AUTOMOBILE DEALERS

12-6-101.	Legislative declaration.
12-6-102.	Definitions.
12-6-103.	Motor vehicle dealer board.
12-6-104.	Board - oath - meetings - powers and duties - rules.
12-6-105.	Powers and duties of executive director.
12-6-106.	Records as evidence.
12-6-107.	Attorney general to advise and represent.
12-6-108.	Classes of licenses.
12-6-108.5.	Temporary motor vehicle dealer license.
12-6-109.	Display, form, custody, and use of licenses.
12-6-110.	Fees - disposition - expenses - expiration of licenses.
12-6-111.	Bond of licensee.
12-6-112.	Motor vehicle salesperson's bond.
12-6-112.2.	Buyer agent bonds.
12-6-112.7.	Notice of claims honored against bond.
12-6-113.	Testing licensees.
12-6-114.	Filing of written warranties.
12-6-115.	Application - prelicensing education - rules.
12-6-116.	Notice of change of address or status.
12-6-117.	Principal place of business - requirements.
12-6-118.	Licenses - grounds for denial, suspension, or revocation.
12-6-119.	Procedure for denial, suspension, or revocation of license - judicial review.
12-6-119.5.	Sales activity following license denial, suspension, or revocation - unlawful act - penalty.
12-6-120.	Unlawful acts.
12-6-120.3.	New, reopened, or relocated dealer - notice required - grounds for refusal of dealer license - definitions - rules.
12-6-120.5.	Independent control of dealer - definitions.
12-6-120.7.	Successor under existing franchise agreement - duties of manufacturer.
12-6-121.	Penalty.
12-6-121.5.	Fines - disposition - unlicensed sales.
12-6-121.6.	Drafts not honored for payment - penalties.
12-6-122.	Right of action for loss.
12-6-122.5.	Contract disputes - venue - choice of law.
12-6-123.	Disposition of fees - auto dealers license fund.
12-6-124.	Repeal of article.
12-6-125.	Advertisement - inclusion of dealer name.
12-6-126.	Audit reimbursement limitations - dealer claims.
12-6-127.	Reimbursement for right of first refusal.
12-6-128.	Payout exemption to execution.
12-6-129.	Site control extinguishes.
12-6-130.	Modification voidable.
12-6-131.	Termination appeal.

PART 2
ANTIMONOPOLY FINANCING LAW

12-6-201.	Definitions.
12-6-202.	Exclusive finance agreements void - when.
12-6-203.	Threat prima facie evidence of violation.
12-6-204.	Threat by agent as evidence of violation.
12-6-205.	Offering consideration to eliminate competition.
12-6-206.	Accepting consideration to eliminate competition.
12-6-207.	Recipient of consideration shall not buy mortgages.
12-6-208.	Quo warranto action.
12-6-209.	Violation by foreign corporation - penalty.
12-6-210.	Penalty.
12-6-211.	Contract void.
12-6-212.	Provisions cumulative.
12-6-213.	Damages.

PART 3
SUNDAY CLOSING LAW

12-6-301.	Definitions.
12-6-302.	Sunday closing.
12-6-303.	Penalties.

PART 4
EVENT DATA RECORDERS

12-6-401.	Definitions.
12-6-402.	Event data recorders.
12-6-403.	Applicability.

PART 1

AUTOMOBILE DEALERS

12-6-101. Legislative declaration. (1) The general assembly hereby declares that:

(a) The sale and distribution of motor vehicles affects the public interest and a significant factor of inducement in making a sale of a motor vehicle is the trust and confidence of the purchaser in the retail dealer from whom the purchase is made and the expectancy that such dealer will remain in business to provide service for the motor vehicle purchased;

(b) Proper motor vehicle service is important to highway safety and the manufacturers and distributors of motor vehicles have an obligation to the public not to terminate or refuse to continue their franchise agreements with retail dealers unless the manufacturer or distributor has first established good cause for termination or noncontinuance of any such agreement, to the end that there shall be no diminution of locally available service;

(c) The licensing and supervision of motor vehicle dealers by the motor vehicle dealer board are necessary for the protection of consumers and therefore the sale of motor vehicles by unlicensed dealers or salespersons, or by licensed dealers or salespersons who have demonstrated unfitness, should be prevented; and

(d) Consumer education concerning the rules and regulations of the motor vehicle industry, the considerations when purchasing a motor vehicle, and the role, functions, and actions of the motor vehicle dealer board are necessary for the protection of the public and for maintaining the trust and confidence of the public in the motor vehicle dealer board.

12-6-102. Definitions. As used in this part 1 and in part 5 of this article, unless the context or section 12-6-502 otherwise requires:

(1) (Deleted by amendment, L. 92, p. 1841, § 2, effective July 1, 1992.)

(1.5) "Advertisement" means any commercial message in any newspaper, magazine, leaflet, flyer, or catalog, on radio, television, or a public address system, in direct mail literature or other printed material, on any interior or exterior sign or display, in any window display, on a computer display, or in any point-of-transaction literature or price tag that is delivered or made available to a customer or prospective customer in any manner whatsoever; except that such term does not include materials required to be displayed by federal or state law.

(2) "Board" means the motor vehicle dealer board.

(2.4) "Business incidental thereto" means a business owned by the motor vehicle dealer or used motor vehicle dealer related to the sale of motor vehicles, including, without limitation, motor vehicle part sales, motor vehicle repair, motor vehicle recycling, motor vehicle security interest assignment, and motor vehicle towing.

(2.5) (a) (I) "Buyer agent" means any person required to be licensed pursuant to this part 1 who is retained or hired by a consumer for a fee or other thing of value to assist, represent, or act on behalf of such consumer in connection with the purchase or lease of a motor vehicle.

(II) "Consumer", as used in this subsection (2.5), means a purchaser or lessee of a motor vehicle, which vehicle is primarily used for business, personal, family, or household purposes. "Consumer" does not include a purchaser of motor vehicles who purchases said motor vehicles primarily for resale.

(b) (I) "Buyer agent" does not include a person whose business includes the purchase of motor vehicles primarily for resale or lease; except that nothing in this subsection (2.5) shall be construed to prohibit a buyer agent from assisting a consumer regarding the disposal of a trade-in motor vehicle that is incident to the purchase or lease of a vehicle if the buyer agent does not advertise the sale of, or sell, such vehicle to the general public, directs interested dealers and wholesalers to communicate their offers directly to the consumer or to the consumer via the buyer agent, does not handle or transfer titles or funds between the consumer and the purchaser, receives no compensation from a dealer or wholesaler purchasing a consumer's vehicle, and identifies himself or herself as a buyer agent to dealers and wholesalers interested in the consumer's vehicle.

(II) A "buyer agent" licensed pursuant to this part 1 shall not be employed by or receive a fee from a person whose business includes the purchase of motor vehicles primarily for resale or lease, a motor vehicle manufacturer, a motor vehicle dealer, or a used motor vehicle dealer.

(3) "Coerce" means to compel or attempt to compel by threatening, retaliating, economic force, or by not performing or complying with any terms or provisions of the franchise or agreement; except that recommendation, exposition, persuasion, urging, or argument shall not be deemed to constitute coercion.

(4) "Community" means a franchisee's area of responsibility as set out in the franchise.

(4.5) (a) "Custom trailer" means any motor vehicle which is not driven or propelled by its own power and is designed to be attached to, become a part of, or be drawn by a motor vehicle and which is uniquely designed and manufactured for a specific purpose or customer.

(b) "Custom trailer" does not include manufactured housing, farm tractors, and other machines and tools used in the production, harvest, and care of farm products.

(5) "Distributor" means a person, resident or nonresident, who, in whole or in part, sells or distributes new motor vehicles to motor vehicle dealers or who maintains distributor representatives.

(6) and (7) (Deleted by amendment, L. 2003, p. 1300, § 1, effective April 22, 2003.)

(7.5) "Executive director" means the executive director of the department of revenue charged with the administration, enforcement, and issuance or denial of the licensing of buyer agents, distributors, manufacturer representatives, and manufacturers.

(8) and (9) (Deleted by amendment, L. 2003, p. 1300, § 1, effective April 22, 2003.)

(9.5) "Fire truck" means a vehicle intended for use in the extermination of fires, with features that may include, but shall not be limited to, a fire pump, a water tank, an aerial ladder, an elevated platform, or any combination thereof.

(9.7) "Franchise" means the authority to sell or service and repair motor vehicles of a designated line-make granted through a sales, service, and parts agreement with a manufacturer, distributor, or manufacturer representative.

(10) "Good faith" means the duty of each party to any franchise and all officers, employees, or agents thereof to act in a fair and equitable manner toward each other so as to guarantee the one party freedom from coercion, intimidation, or threats of coercion or intimidation from the other party. Recommendation, endorsement, exposition, persuasion, urging, or argument shall not be deemed to constitute a lack of good faith.

(10.5) "Line-make" means a group or series of motor vehicles that have the same brand identification or brand name, based upon the manufacturer's trademark, trade name, or logo.

(11) "Manufacturer" means any person, firm, association, corporation, or trust, resident or nonresident, who manufactures or assembles new and unused motor vehicles; except that "manufacturer" shall not include:

(a) Any person who only manufactures utility trailers that weigh less than two thousand pounds and does not manufacture any other type of motor vehicle; and

(b) Any person, other than a manufacturer operating a dealer pursuant to section 12-6-120.5, who is a licensed dealer selling motor vehicles that such person has manufactured.

(11.5) "Manufacturer representative" means a representative employed by a person who manufactures or assembles motor vehicles for the purpose of making or promoting the sale of its motor vehicles or for supervising or contacting its dealers or prospective dealers.

(12) "Motor vehicle" means every vehicle intended primarily for use and operation on the public highways which is self-propelled and every vehicle intended primarily for operation on the public highways which is not driven or propelled by its own power but which is designed to be attached to or become a part of or to be drawn by a self-propelled vehicle, not including farm tractors and other machines and tools used in the production, harvesting, and care of farm products. "Motor vehicle" includes, without limitation, a low-power scooter, as defined in section 42-1-102, C.R.S.

(12.5) (Deleted by amendment, L. 92, p. 1841, § 2, effective July 1, 1992.)

(12.6) "Motor vehicle auctioneer" means any person, not otherwise required to be licensed pursuant to this part 1, who is engaged in the business of offering to sell, or selling, used motor vehicles owned by persons other than the auctioneer at public auction only. Any auctioning of motor vehicles by an auctioneer shall be incidental to the primary business of auctioning goods.

(13) "Motor vehicle dealer" means a person who, for commission or with intent to make a profit or gain of money or other thing of value, sells, leases, exchanges, rents with option to purchase, offers, or attempts to negotiate a sale, lease, or exchange of an interest in new or new and used motor vehicles or who is engaged wholly or in part in the business of selling or leasing new or new and used motor vehicles, whether or not such motor vehicles are owned by such person. The sale or lease of three or more new or new and used motor vehicles or the offering for sale or lease of more than three new or new and used motor vehicles at the same address or telephone number in any one calendar year shall be prima facie evidence that a person is engaged in the business of selling or leasing new or new and used motor vehicles. "Motor vehicle dealer" includes an owner of real property who allows more than three new or new and used motor vehicles to be offered for sale or lease on such property during one calendar year unless said property is leased to a licensed motor vehicle dealer. "Motor vehicle dealer" does not include:

(a) Receivers, trustees, administrators, executors, guardians, or other persons appointed by or acting under the judgment or order of any court;

(b) Public officers while performing their official duties;

(c) Employees of persons enumerated in the definition of "motor vehicle dealer" when engaged in the specific performance of their duties as such employees;

(d) A wholesaler, as defined in subsection (18) of this section, or anyone selling motor vehicles solely to wholesalers;

(e) Any person engaged in the selling of a fire truck;

(f) A motor vehicle auctioneer, as defined in subsection (12.6) of this section.

(14) "Motor vehicle salesperson" means a natural person who, for a salary, commission, or compensation of any kind, is employed either directly or indirectly, regularly or occasionally, by a motor vehicle dealer or used motor vehicle dealer to sell, lease, purchase, or exchange or to negotiate for the sale, lease, purchase, or exchange of motor vehicles.

(15) "Person" means any natural person, estate, trust, limited liability company, partnership, association, corporation, or other legal entity, including, without limitation, a registered limited liability partnership.

(16) "Principal place of business" means a site or location devoted exclusively to the business for which the motor vehicle dealer or used motor vehicle dealer is licensed and businesses incidental thereto, sufficiently designated to admit of definite description, with space thereon or contiguous thereto adequate to permit the display of one or more new or used motor vehicles, and on which there shall be located or erected a permanent enclosed building or structure large enough to accommodate the office of the dealer and to provide a safe place to keep the books and other records of the business of such dealer, at which site or location the principal portion of such dealer's business shall be conducted and the books and records thereof kept and maintained; except that a dealer may keep its books and records at an off-site location in Colorado after notifying the board in writing of such location at least thirty days in advance.

(16.5) "Recreational vehicle" means a camping trailer, fifth wheel trailer, motor home, recreational park trailer, travel trailer, or truck camper, all as defined in section 24-32-902, C.R.S., or multipurpose trailer, as defined in section 42-1-102, C.R.S.

(16.6) "Sales, service, and parts agreement" means an agreement between a manufacturer, distributor, or manufacturer representative and a motor vehicle or powersports dealer authorizing the dealer to sell and service a line-make of motor or powersports vehicles or imposing any duty on the dealer in consideration for the right to have or competitively operate a franchise, including any amendments or additional related agreements thereto.

(16.7) "Site control provision" means an agreement that applies to real property owned or leased by the franchisee and that gives a motor vehicle or powersports vehicle manufacturer, distributor, or manufacturer representative the right to:

(a) Control the use and development of the real property;

(b) Require the franchisee to establish or maintain an exclusive dealership facility at the real property; or

(c) Restrict the franchisee from transferring, selling, leasing, developing, or changing the use of the real property.

(17) "Used motor vehicle dealer" means any person who, for commission or with intent to make a profit or gain of money or other thing of value, sells, exchanges, leases, or offers an interest in used motor vehicles, or attempts to negotiate a sale, exchange, or lease of used and new motor vehicles or who is engaged wholly or in part in the business of selling used motor vehicles, whether or not such motor vehicles are owned by such person. The sale of three or more used motor vehicles or the offering for sale of more than three used motor vehicles at the same address or telephone number in any one calendar year shall be prima facie evidence that a person is engaged in the business of selling used motor vehicles. "Used motor vehicle dealer" includes any owner of real property who allows more than three used motor vehicles to be offered for sale on such property during one calendar year unless said property is leased to a licensed used motor vehicle dealer. "Used motor vehicle dealer" does not include:

(a) Receivers, trustees, administrators, executors, guardians, or other persons appointed by or acting under the judgment or order of any court;

(b) Public officers while performing their official duties;

(c) Employees of persons enumerated in the definition of "used motor vehicle dealer" when engaged in the specific performance of their duties as such employees;

(d) A wholesaler, as defined in subsection (18) of this section, or anyone selling motor vehicles solely to wholesalers;

(e) Mortgagees or secured parties as to sales in any one year of not more than twelve motor vehicles constituting collateral on a mortgage or security agreement, if such mortgagees or secured parties shall not realize for their own account from such sales any moneys in excess of the outstanding balance secured by such mortgage or security agreement, plus costs of collection;

(f) Any person who only sells or exchanges no more than four motor vehicles that are collector's items under part 3 or 4 of article 12 of title 42, C.R.S.;

(g) A motor vehicle auctioneer, as defined in subsection (12.6) of this section;

(h) An operator, as defined in section 42-4-2102 (5), C.R.S., who sells a motor vehicle pursuant to section 42-4-2104, C.R.S.

(17.5) "Wholesale motor vehicle auction dealer" means any person or firm that provides auction services in wholesale transactions in which the purchasers are motor vehicle dealers licensed by this state or any other jurisdiction or in consumer transactions of government vehicles at a time and place that does not conflict with a wholesale motor vehicle auction conducted by that licensee.

(18) "Wholesaler" means a person who, for commission or with intent to make a profit or gain of money or other thing of value, sells, exchanges, or offers or attempts to negotiate a sale, lease, or exchange of an interest in new or new and used motor vehicles solely to motor vehicle dealers or used motor vehicle dealers.

12-6-103. Motor vehicle dealer board. (1) There is hereby created and established the motor vehicle dealer board, consisting of nine members who have been residents of this state for at least five years, three of whom shall be licensed motor vehicle dealers, three of whom shall be licensed used motor vehicle dealers, and three of whom shall be members from the public at large. The members representing the public at large shall not have a present or past financial interest in a motor vehicle dealership. The board shall assume its duties July 1, 1992, and all terms of the board members shall commence on that date. The terms of office of the board members shall be three years. Any vacancies shall be filled by appointment for the unexpired term.

(2) All board members shall be appointed by the governor.

(3) Each board member shall be reimbursed for actual and necessary expenses incurred while engaged in the discharge of official duties.

12-6-104. Board - oath - meetings - powers and duties - rules. (1) Each member of the board, before entering on the discharge of such member's duties and within thirty days after the effective date of such member's appointment, shall subscribe an oath for the faithful performance of such member's duties before any officer authorized to administer oaths in this state and shall file the same with the secretary of state.

(2) The board shall annually in the month of July elect from the membership thereof a president, a first vice-president, and a second vice-president. The board shall meet at such times as it deems necessary. A majority of the board shall constitute a quorum at any meeting or hearing.

(3) The board is authorized and empowered:

(a) To promulgate, amend, and repeal rules reasonably necessary to implement this part 1, including the administration, enforcement, issuance, and denial of licenses to motor vehicle dealers, motor vehicle salespersons, used motor vehicle dealers, wholesale motor vehicle auction dealers, and wholesalers, and the laws of the state of Colorado;

(a.5) To delegate to the board's executive secretary, employed pursuant to section 12-6-105 (1) (b), the authority to execute all actions within the power of the board, carry out the directives of the board, and make recommendations to the board on all matters within the authority of the board;

(a.7) To issue through the department of revenue a temporary license to any person applying for any license issued by the board. The temporary license shall permit the applicant to operate for a period not to exceed one hundred twenty days while the board is completing its investigation and determination of all facts relative to the qualifications of the applicant for such license. A temporary license is terminated when the applicant's license is issued or denied.

(b) and (c) (Deleted by amendment, L. 92, p. 1842, § 4, effective July 1, 1992.)

(d) (I) To issue through the department of revenue and, for reasonable cause shown or upon satisfactory proof of the unfitness of the applicant under standards established and set forth in this part 1, to refuse to issue to any applicant any license the board is authorized to issue by this part 1;

(II) To permit the executive director, or the executive director's designee, to issue licenses pursuant to rules and regulations adopted by the board pursuant to paragraph (a) of this subsection (3);

(e) (I) After due notice and a hearing, to review the findings of an administrative law judge or a hearing officer from a hearing conducted pursuant to this part 1 to revoke and suspend or to order the executive director to issue or to reinstate, on such terms and conditions and for such period of time as to the board shall appear fair and just, any license issued under and pursuant to the terms and provisions of this part 1. The board may direct a letter of admonition for minor violations or may issue a letter of reprimand to any licensee for a violation of this part 1. A letter of admonition does not become a part of the licensee's record with the board. A letter of reprimand is a part of the licensee's record with the board for a period of two years after issuance and may be considered in aggravation of any subsequent violation by the licensee. When a letter of reprimand is sent to a licensee of the board, such licensee shall be notified in writing regarding the right to request in writing, within twenty days after receipt of such letter, that formal disciplinary proceedings be initiated against such licensee to adjudicate the propriety of the conduct upon which the letter of reprimand is based. If a request is made within such time period, the letter of reprimand is deemed vacated and the matter shall be processed by means of formal disciplinary proceedings.

(II) The findings of the board pursuant to subparagraph (I) of this paragraph (e) shall be final.

(f) (I) To investigate through the executive director, on its own motion or upon the written and signed complaint of any person, any suspected or alleged violation by any motor vehicle dealer, motor vehicle salesperson, used motor vehicle dealer, wholesale motor vehicle auction dealer, or wholesaler licensee of any of the terms and provisions of this part 1 or of any rule or regulation promulgated by the board under the authority conferred upon it in this section. The board shall order an investigation of all written and signed complaints, shall have the authority to issue subpoenas and to delegate the authority to issue subpoenas to the executive director, and the executive director shall make an investigation of all such complaints transmitted by the board pursuant to section 12-6-105 (1) (d). The board has the authority to seek to resolve disputes before beginning an investigation or hearing through its own action or by direction to the executive director.

(II) After an investigation by the executive director or the executive director's designee, if the board determines that there is probable cause to believe a violation of this article has occurred, it may order that an administrative hearing be held pursuant to section 24-4-105, C.R.S., or may designate one of the board's members as a hearing officer to conduct a hearing pursuant to section 24-4-105, C.R.S.

(f.5) To summarily issue cease-and-desist orders on such terms and conditions and for such period of time as to the board appears fair and just to any person who is licensed by the board pursuant to this part 1 if such orders are followed by notice and a hearing pursuant to section 12-6-119;

(g) To prescribe the forms to be used for applications for motor vehicle dealers', motor vehicle salespersons', used motor vehicle dealers', wholesale motor vehicle auction dealers', and wholesalers' licenses to be issued and to require of such applicants, as a condition precedent to the issuance of such licenses, such information concerning their fitness to be licensed under this part 1 as it may consider necessary. Every application for a motor vehicle dealer's license or used motor vehicle dealer's license shall contain, in addition to such information as the board may require, a statement of the following facts:

(I) The name and residence address of the applicant and the trade name, if any, under which such applicant intends to conduct such applicant's business and, if the applicant is a copartnership, the name and residence address of each member thereof, whether a limited or general partner, and the name under which the partnership business is to be conducted and, if the applicant is a corporation, the name of the corporation and the name and address of each of its principal officers and directors;

(II) A complete description, including the city, town, or village, the street and number, if any, of the principal place of business, and such other and additional places of business as shall be operated and maintained by the applicant in conjunction with the principal place of business;

(III) If the application is for a motor vehicle dealer's license, the names of the new motor vehicles that the applicant has been enfranchised to sell or exchange and the name and address of the manufacturer or distributor who has enfranchised the applicant;

(IV) The names and addresses of the persons who shall act as salespersons under the authority of the license, if issued.

(h) To adopt a seal with the words "motor vehicle dealer board" and such other devices as the board may desire engraved thereon by which it shall authenticate the acts of its office;

(i) To require that a motor vehicle dealer's or used motor vehicle dealer's principal place of business and such other sites or locations as may be operated and maintained by such dealers in conjunction with their principal place of business have erected or posted thereon such signs or devices providing information relating to the dealer's name, the location and address of such dealer's principal place of business, the type of license held by the dealer, and the number thereof, as the board shall consider necessary to enable any person doing business with such dealer to identify such dealer properly, and for this purpose to determine the size and shape of such signs or devices, the lettering thereon, and other details thereof and to prescribe rules and regulations for the location thereof;

(j) (I) To conduct or cause to be conducted written examinations as prescribed by the board testing the competency of all first-time applicants for a motor vehicle dealer's license, motor vehicle salesperson's license, used motor vehicle dealer's license, wholesale motor vehicle auction dealer's license, or wholesaler's license;

(II) and (III) (Deleted by amendment, L. 98, p. 592, § 4, effective July 1, 1998.)

(k) (I) To prescribe a form or forms to be used as a part of a contract for the sale of a motor vehicle by any motor vehicle dealer or motor vehicle salesperson, other than a retail installment sales contract subject to the provisions of the "Uniform Consumer Credit Code", articles 1 to 9 of title 5, C.R.S., which shall include the following information in addition to any other disclosures or information required by state or federal law:

(A) In twelve-point bold-faced type or a size at least three points larger than the smallest type appearing in the contract, an instruction that the form is a legal instrument and that, if the purchaser of the motor vehicle does not understand the form, such purchaser should seek legal assistance;

(B) In bold-faced type, of the size specified in sub-subparagraph (A) of this subparagraph (I), an instruction that only those terms in written form embody the contract for sale of a motor vehicle and that any conflicting oral representations made to the purchaser are void;

(C) In bold-faced type, of the size specified in sub-subparagraph (A) of this subparagraph (I), a notice that fraud or misrepresentation in the sale of a motor vehicle is punishable under the laws of this state;

(D) In bold-faced type, of the size specified in sub-subparagraph (A) of this subparagraph (I), if the contract for the sale of a motor vehicle requires a single lump sum payment of the purchase price, a clear disclosure to the purchaser of that fact or, if the contract is contingent upon the approval of credit financing for the purchaser arranged by or through the motor vehicle dealer, in bold-faced type, a statement that the purchaser shall agree to purchase the motor vehicle which is the subject of the sale from the motor vehicle dealer at not greater than a certain annual percentage rate of financing, which annual percentage rate of financing shall be agreed upon by the parties and entered in writing on the contract;

(E) Except as otherwise provided under part 1 of article 1 of title 6, C.R.S., where the purchase price of the motor vehicle is not paid to the motor vehicle dealer in full at the time of consummation of the sale and the purchaser and motor vehicle dealer elect that the motor vehicle dealer shall deliver and the purchaser shall take possession of such motor vehicle at such time, in bold-faced type, a statement that in the event financing cannot be arranged in accordance with the provisions stated in the contract, and the sale is not consummated, the purchaser shall agree to pay a daily rate and a mileage rate for use of the motor vehicle until such time as financing of the purchase price of such motor vehicle is arranged for the obligor by or through the authorized motor vehicle dealer or until the purchase price is paid to the authorized motor vehicle dealer in full by or through the obligor, which daily rate and mileage rate shall be specified and agreed upon by the parties and entered in writing on the contract;

(II) The information required by subparagraph (I) of this paragraph (k) shall be read and initialed by both parties at the time of the consummation of the sale of a motor vehicle;

(III) The use of the contract form required by subparagraph (I) of this paragraph (k) shall be mandatory for the sale of any motor vehicle;

(IV) To require a licensee to include with a consumer sales contract a written notice that provides to the consumer the contact information of the board and information about the board's authority over consumer motor vehicle sales;

(l) (Deleted by amendment, L. 98, p. 592, § 4, effective July 1, 1998.)

(m) (I) (A) If a hearing is held before an administrative law judge or a hearing officer designated by the board from within the board's membership, after due notice and a hearing by such judge or hearing officer pursuant to section 24-4-105, C.R.S., to review the findings of law and fact and the fairness of any fine imposed and to uphold such fine, to impose an administrative fine upon its own initiative, which shall not exceed ten thousand dollars for each separate offense by any licensee, or to vacate the fine imposed by the judge or hearing officer; except that, for motor vehicle dealers who sell primarily vehicles that weigh under one thousand five hundred pounds, the fine for each separate offense shall not exceed one thousand dollars. Whenever a hearing is heard by an administrative law judge, the maximum fine that may be imposed is ten thousand dollars for each separate offense by any person licensed by the board pursuant to this part 1; except that, for motor vehicle dealers who sell primarily vehicles that weigh under one thousand five hundred pounds, the fine for each separate offense may not exceed one thousand dollars. Whenever a licensing hearing is conducted by a hearing officer, the sanctions that may be recommended by the hearing officer are limited to the denial or grant of an unrestricted license or a restricted license under such terms as the hearing officer deems appropriate. Whenever a disciplinary hearing is conducted by a hearing officer, the hearing officer may only recommend a probationary period of no more than twelve months, a fine of no more than five hundred dollars, or both such probationary period and fine for each separate violation committed by a person licensed by the board.

(B) The board shall promulgate rules regarding circumstances in which a board member should not act as a hearing officer in a particular matter before the board because of business competition issues connected with the parties involved in such matter.

(II) The findings of the board pursuant to subparagraph (I) of this paragraph (m) shall be final.

(n) (Deleted by amendment, L. 2007, p. 1578, § 4, effective July 1, 2007.)

(o) (I) To impose a fine of up to one thousand dollars per day per violation for any person found, after notice and hearing pursuant to section 24-4-105, C.R.S., to have violated the provisions of section 12-6-120 (2). For the purposes of this paragraph (o), the address for the notice to be given under section 24-4-105, C.R.S., is the last-known address for the person as indicated in the state motor vehicle records; the last-known address for the owner of the real property upon which motor vehicles are displayed in violation of section 12-6-120 (2) as indicated in the records of the county assessor's office; or an address for service of process in accordance with rule 4 of the Colorado rules of civil procedure.

(II) Any person who fails to pay a fine ordered by the board for a violation of section 12-6-120 (2) under this paragraph (o) shall be subject to enforcement proceedings, by the board through the attorney general, in the county or district court pursuant to the Colorado rules of civil procedure. Any fines collected under the provisions of this paragraph (o) shall be disposed of pursuant to section 12-6-123.

(4) The board shall promulgate rules by January 1, 2008, establishing enforcement and compliance standards to ensure that administrative penalties are equitably assessed and commensurate with the seriousness of the violation.

12-6-105. Powers and duties of executive director. (1) The executive director is hereby charged with the administration, enforcement, and issuance or denial of the licensing of buyer agents, distributors, manufacturer representatives, and motor vehicle manufacturers, and shall have the following powers and duties:

(a) To promulgate, amend, and repeal reasonable rules and regulations relating to those functions the executive director is mandated to carry out pursuant to this part 1 and the laws of the state of Colorado that the executive director deems necessary to carry out the duties of the office of the executive director pursuant to this part 1;

(b) To employ, subject to the laws of the state of Colorado and after consultation with the board, an executive secretary for the board. The executive secretary shall be accountable to the board and shall, pursuant to delegation by the board, discharge the responsibilities of the board under this part 1. The executive director may also employ such clerks, deputies, and assistants as the executive director considers necessary to discharge the duties imposed upon the executive director by this part 1 and to designate the duties of such clerks, deputies, and assistants.

(c) To issue and, for reasonable cause shown or upon satisfactory proof of the unfitness of the applicant under standards established and set forth in this part 1, to refuse to issue to any applicant any license the executive director is authorized to issue by this part 1;

(d) (I) To investigate upon the executive director's own initiative, upon the written and signed complaint of any person, or upon request by the board pursuant to section 12-6-104 (3) (f) (I), any suspected or alleged violation by any person licensed by the executive director pursuant to this part 1 of any of the terms and provisions of this part 1 or of any rule or regulation promulgated by the executive director under the authority conferred upon the executive director in this section;

(II) The investigators and their supervisors utilized by the executive director, pursuant to subparagraph (I) of this paragraph (d), while actually engaged in performing their duties, shall have the authority as delegated by the executive director to issue subpoenas in relation to performance of their duties relating to licensees who are under the jurisdiction of the executive director and the authority as delegated by the executive director to issue summonses for violations of sections 12-6-120 (2) and 42-6-142, C.R.S., to issue misdemeanor summonses for violations of section 12-6-119.5 (1) (a), and to procure criminal records during an investigation.

(e) To prescribe the forms to be used for applications for licenses to be issued by the executive director under the provisions of this part 1 and to require of such applicants, as a condition precedent to the issuance of such licenses, such information concerning the applicant's fitness to be licensed under this part 1 as the executive director considers necessary;

(f) (I) To summarily issue cease-and-desist orders on such terms and conditions and for such period of time as to the executive director appears fair and just to any person who is licensed by the executive director pursuant to this part 1 if such orders are followed by notice and a hearing pursuant to section 12-6-104 (3) (e) (I).

(II) To issue cease-and-desist orders to persons acting as motor vehicle manufacturers without the manufacturer's license required by this part 1.

(III) To impose a fine, not to exceed one thousand dollars per day, for each violation of section 12-6-120 (1) after a notice and hearing subject to section 24-4-105, C.R.S.

(g) (Deleted by amendment, L. 92, p. 1847, § 5, effective July 1, 1992.)

(2) In the event any person fails to comply with a cease-and-desist order issued pursuant to this section, the executive director may bring a suit for injunction to prevent any further and continued violation of such order. In any such suit the final proceedings of the executive director, based upon evidence in record, shall be prima facie evidence of the facts found therein.

(3) The executive director may impose a civil fine of not less than ten thousand dollars and not more than twenty-five thousand dollars on a motor vehicle manufacturer, distributor, or manufacturer representative who knowingly violates section 12-6-120.3 (5). Each day that a manufacturer, distributor, or manufacturer representative violates section 12-6-120.3 (5) by failing to offer the right of first refusal or failing to make a payment required by section 12-6-120.3 (5) is a separate offense.

12-6-106. Records as evidence. Copies of all records and papers in the office of the board or executive director, duly authenticated under the hand and seal of the board or executive director, shall be received in evidence in all cases equally and with like effect as the original thereof.

12-6-107. Attorney general to advise and represent. (1) The attorney general of this state shall represent the board and executive director and shall give opinions on all questions of law relating to the interpretation of this part 1 or arising out of the administration thereof and shall appear for and in behalf of the board and executive director in all actions brought by or against them, whether under the provisions of this part 1 or otherwise.

(2) The board may request the attorney general to make civil investigations and enforce rules and regulations of the board in cases of civil violations and to bring and defend civil suits and proceedings for any of the purposes necessary and proper for carrying out the functions of the board.

12-6-108. Classes of licenses. (1) Licenses issued under the provisions of this part 1 shall be of the following classes:

(a) Motor vehicle dealer's license shall permit the licensee to engage in the business of selling, exchanging, leasing, or offering new and used motor vehicles, and this form of license shall permit not more than two persons named therein who shall be owners or part owners of the business of the licensee to act as motor vehicle salespersons.

(b) Used motor vehicle dealer's license shall permit the licensee to engage in the business of selling, exchanging, leasing, or offering used motor vehicles only. Such license shall also permit a licensee to negotiate for a consumer the sale, exchange, or lease of used and new motor vehicles not owned by the licensee, except those vehicles defined in section 42-1-102 (55), C.R.S., as motorcycles and section 33-14.5-101 (3), C.R.S., as off-highway vehicles; however, prior to completion of such sale, exchange, or lease of a motor vehicle not owned by the licensee, the licensee shall disclose in writing to the consumer whether the licensee will receive any compensation from the consumer and whether the licensee will receive any compensation from the owner of the motor vehicle as a result of such transaction. If the licensee receives compensation from the owner of the motor vehicle as a result of the transaction, the licensee shall include in the written disclosure the name of such owner from whom the licensee will receive compensation. This form of license shall permit not more than two persons named therein who shall be owners or part owners of the business of the licensee to act as motor vehicle salespersons.

(c) Motor vehicle salesperson's license shall permit the licensee to engage in the activities of a motor vehicle salesperson.

(c.1) (Deleted by amendment, L. 92, p. 1849, § 8, effective July 1, 1992.)

(d) Manufacturer's or distributor's license shall permit the licensee to engage in the activities of a manufacturer, distributor, factory branch, or distributor branch and to sell fire trucks.

(e) Wholesaler's license shall permit the licensee to engage in the activities of a wholesaler.

(f) Manufacturer representative's license shall permit the licensee to engage in the activities of a manufacturer representative.

(g) Buyer agent's license shall permit the licensee to engage in the activities of a buyer agent.

(h) (I) Wholesale motor vehicle auction dealer's license shall permit a licensee to engage in the activities of a wholesale motor vehicle auction dealer if the licensee provides auction services solely in connection with wholesale transactions in which the purchasers are motor vehicle dealers licensed by this state or any other jurisdiction or in connection with the sale of government vehicles to consumers at a time and place that does not conflict with a wholesale motor vehicle auction conducted by that licensee. A wholesale motor vehicle auction dealer shall abide by all laws and rules of the state of Colorado.

(II) A wholesale motor vehicle auction dealer shall maintain a check and title insurance policy for the benefit of such dealer's customers or, alternatively, a wholesale motor vehicle auction dealer shall provide written guarantees of title to such dealer's purchasing customers and written guarantees of payment to such dealer's selling dealers with coverage and exclusions that are customary in check and title insurance policies available to wholesale motor vehicle auction dealers.

(2) Any license issued by the executive director pursuant to law in effect prior to July 1, 1992, shall be valid for the period for which issued.

(3) The licensing requirements of this part 1 shall not apply to banks, savings banks, savings and loan associations, building and loan associations, industrial banks, or credit unions or an affiliate or subsidiary of such entities in offering to sell, or in the sale of, a motor vehicle that was subject to a lease or that has been repossessed or foreclosed upon if the repossession or foreclosure is in connection with a loan made or originated in Colorado.

(4) The licensing requirements of this part 1 shall not apply to an insurance company selling or offering to sell a motor vehicle through a motor vehicle dealer or used motor vehicle dealer if the vehicle is obtained by the company as a result of an insurance claim.

12-6-108.5. Temporary motor vehicle dealer license. (1) If a licensed vehicle dealer has entered into a written agreement to sell a dealership to a purchaser and the purchaser has been awarded a new dealership franchise, the board may issue a temporary motor vehicle dealer's license to such purchaser or prospective purchaser. The executive director shall issue the temporary license only after the board has received the applications for both a temporary motor vehicle dealer's license and a motor vehicle dealer's license, the appropriate application fee for the motor vehicle dealer's application, evidence of a passing test score, and evidence that the franchise has been awarded to the applicant by the manufacturer. Such temporary motor vehicle dealer's license shall authorize the licensee to act as a motor vehicle dealer. Such temporary licensees shall be subject to all the provisions of this article and to all applicable rules and regulations adopted by the executive director or the board. Such temporary motor vehicle dealer's license shall be effective for up to sixty days or until the board acts on such licensee's application for a motor vehicle dealer's license, whichever is sooner.

(2) For the purpose of enabling an out-of-state dealer to sell vehicles on a temporary basis during specifically identified events, the executive director may issue, upon direction by the board, a temporary dealer's license which shall be effective for thirty days. Such temporary license shall subject the licensee to compliance with rules and regulations adopted by the executive director or the board.

12-6-109. Display, form, custody, and use of licenses. The board and the executive director shall prescribe the form of the license to be issued by the executive director, and each license shall have imprinted thereon the seal of their offices. The license of each motor vehicle salesperson shall be mailed to the business address where the salesperson is licensed under this article and shall be kept by the salesperson at such salesperson's place of employment for inspection by employers, consumers, the executive director, or the board. It is the duty of each motor vehicle dealer, manufacturer, distributor, wholesaler, manufacturer representative, wholesale motor vehicle auction dealer, or used motor vehicle dealer to display conspicuously such person's own license in such person's place of business. Each license issued pursuant to this part 1 is separate and distinct. It shall be a violation of this part 1 for a person to exercise any of the privileges granted under a license that such person does not hold, or for a licensee to knowingly allow such an exercise of privileges.

12-6-110. Fees - disposition - expenses - expiration of licenses. (1) There shall be collected with each application the fee established pursuant to subsection (5) of this section for each of the following licenses:

(a) (I) Motor vehicle dealer's or used motor vehicle dealer's license;

(II) Motor vehicle dealer's or used motor vehicle dealer's license, for each place of business in addition to the principal place of business;

(III) Renewal or reissue of motor vehicle dealer's or used motor vehicle dealer's license after change in location or lapse in principal place of business;

(b) Manufacturer's license;
(c) Distributor's license;
(d) Wholesaler's license;
(e) (Deleted by amendment, L. 2003, p. 1302, § 5, effective April 22, 2003.)
(f) Manufacturer representative's license;
(g) Motor vehicle salesperson's license including, but not limited to, reissuing a license;
(h) (Deleted by amendment, L. 92, p. 1851, § 11, effective July 1, 1992.)
(i) Buyer agent's license;
(j) Wholesale motor vehicle auction dealer's license.

(2) All such fees shall be paid to the state treasurer who shall credit the same to the auto dealers license fund.

(2.5) If an application for a buyer agent's, motor vehicle dealer's, used motor vehicle dealer's, wholesaler's, or salesperson's license is withdrawn by the applicant prior to issuance of the license, one-half of the license fee shall be refunded.

(3) (a) Such licenses, if the same have not been suspended or revoked as provided in this part 1, shall be valid until one year following the month of issuance thereof and shall then expire; except that any license issued under this part 1 shall expire upon the voluntary surrender thereof or upon the abandonment of the licensee's place of business for a period of more than thirty days.

(b) Thirty days prior to the expiration of such licenses, the executive director shall mail to any such licensee's business address of record a notice stating when such person's license is due to expire and the fee necessary to renew such license. For a salesperson or manufacturer representative, the notice shall be mailed to the address of the dealer or manufacturer where such person is licensed.

(c) Upon the expiration of such license, unless suspended or revoked, the same may be renewed upon the payment of the fees specified in this section, which shall accompany applications, and such renewal shall be made from year to year as a matter of right; except that, if a motor vehicle dealer, used motor vehicle dealer, or wholesaler voluntarily surrenders its license or abandons its place of business for a period of more than thirty days, the licensee is required to file a new application to renew its license.

(d) A transition procedure for licensees licensed prior to July 1, 1992, shall be established by the board or the executive director by rule and regulation.

(e) Notwithstanding paragraph (a) of this subsection (3), a person has a thirty-day grace period after his or her license expires, and the person may renew the license within such thirty days pursuant to paragraph (c) of this subsection (3), so long as the person has a bond in full force and effect that complies with the applicable bonding requirements of section 12-6-111, 12-6-112, or 12-6-112.2 during such thirty-day period. A person applying during the thirty-day grace period shall pay a late fee established pursuant to subsection (5) of this section.

(4) (Deleted by amendment, L. 92, p. 1851, § 11, effective July 1, 1992.)

(5) (a) The board shall propose, as part of its annual budget request, an adjustment in the amount of each fee which the board is authorized by law to collect. The budget request and the adjusted fees for the board shall reflect direct and indirect costs.

(b) Based upon the appropriation made and subject to the approval of the executive director, the board shall adjust the fees collected by the executive director so that the revenue generated from said fees covers the direct and indirect costs of administering this article. Such fees shall remain in effect for the fiscal year for which the appropriation is made.

(c) Whenever moneys appropriated to the board for its activities for the prior fiscal year are unexpended, said moneys shall be made a part of the appropriation to the board for the next fiscal year, and such amount shall not be raised from fees collected by the board or the executive director. If a supplemental appropriation is made to the board for its activities, the fees of the board and the executive director, when adjusted for the fiscal year next following that in which the supplemental appropriation was made, shall be adjusted by an additional amount which is sufficient to compensate for such supplemental appropriation. Moneys appropriated to the board in the annual general appropriation bill shall be from the fund provided in section 12-6-123.

12-6-111. Bond of licensee. (1) Before any motor vehicle dealer's, wholesaler's, wholesale motor vehicle auction dealer's, or used motor vehicle dealer's license shall be issued by the board through the executive director to any applicant therefor, the said applicant shall procure and file with the board evidence of a savings account, deposit, or certificate of deposit meeting the requirements of section 11-35-101, C.R.S., or a good and sufficient bond with corporate surety thereon duly licensed to do business within the state, approved as to form by the attorney general of the state, and conditioned that said applicant shall not practice fraud, make any fraudulent representation, or violate any of the provisions of this part 1 that are designated by the board by rule in the conduct of the business for which such applicant is licensed. A motor vehicle dealer or used motor vehicle dealer shall not be required to furnish an additional bond, savings account, deposit, or certificate of deposit under this section if such dealer furnishes a bond, savings account, deposit, or certificate of deposit under section 12-6-512.

(2) (a) The purpose of the bond procured by the applicant pursuant to subsection (1) of this section and section 12-6-112.2 (1) is to provide for the reimbursement for any loss or damage suffered by any retail consumer caused by violation of this part 1 by a motor vehicle dealer, used motor vehicle dealer, wholesale motor vehicle auction dealer, or wholesaler. For a wholesale transaction, the bond is available to each party to the transaction; except that, if a retail consumer is involved, such consumer shall have priority to recover from the bond. The amount of the bond shall be fifty thousand dollars for a motor vehicle dealer applicant, used motor vehicle dealer applicant, wholesale motor vehicle auction dealer applicant, or wholesaler applicant except the amount of the bond shall be five thousand dollars for those dealers who sell only small utility trailers that weigh less than two thousand pounds. The aggregate liability of the surety for all transactions shall not exceed the amount of the bond, regardless of the number of claims or claimants.

(b) No corporate surety shall be required to make any payment to any person claiming under such bond until a final determination of fraud or fraudulent representation has been made by the board or by a court of competent jurisdiction.

(3) All bonds required pursuant to this section shall be renewed annually at such time as the bondholder's license is renewed. Such renewal may be done through a continuation certificate issued by the surety.

(4) Nothing in this part 1 shall interfere with the authority of the courts to administer and conduct an interpleader action for claims against a licensee's bond.

12-6-112. Motor vehicle salesperson's bond. (1) Before any motor vehicle salesperson's license is issued by the board through the executive director to any applicant therefor, the applicant shall procure and file with the board evidence of a savings account, deposit, or certificate of deposit meeting the requirements of section 11-35-101, C.R.S., or a good and sufficient bond in the amount of fifteen thousand dollars with corporate surety thereon duly licensed to do business within the state, approved as to form by the attorney general of the state, and conditioned that said applicant shall perform in good faith as a motor vehicle salesperson without fraud or fraudulent representation and without the violation of any of the provisions of this part 1 that are designated by the board by rule. A motor vehicle salesperson shall not be required to furnish an additional bond, savings account, deposit, or certificate of deposit under this section if such dealer furnishes a bond, savings account, deposit, or certificate of deposit under section 12-6-513.

(2) No corporate surety shall be required to make any payment to any person claiming under such bond until a final determination of fraud or fraudulent representation has been made by the board or by a court of competent jurisdiction.

(3) All bonds required pursuant to this section shall be renewed annually at such time as the bondholder's license is renewed. Such renewal may be done through a continuation certificate issued by the surety.

12-6-112.2. Buyer agent bonds. (1) A buyer agent's license shall not be issued by the executive director to any applicant therefor until said applicant procures and files with the executive director evidence of a savings account, deposit, or certificate of deposit meeting the requirements of section 11-35-101, C.R.S., or a good and sufficient bond in the amount of five thousand dollars with a corporate surety duly licensed to do business within the state and approved as to form by the attorney general. The bond shall be available to ensure that said applicant shall perform in good faith as a buyer agent without fraud or fraudulent representation and without violating any of the provisions of this part 1 that are designated by the executive director by rule.

(2) All bonds required pursuant to this section shall be renewed annually at such time as the bondholder's license is renewed. Such renewal may be done through a continuation certificate issued by the surety.

(3) No corporate surety shall be required to make any payment to any person claiming under such bond until a final determination of fraud or fraudulent representation has been made by the executive director or by a court of competent jurisdiction.

12-6-112.7. Notice of claims honored against bond. (1) Any corporate surety which has provided a bond to a licensee pursuant to the requirements of section 12-6-111, 12-6-112, or 12-6-112.2 shall provide notice to the board and executive director of any claim which is honored against such bond. Such notice shall be provided to the board and executive director within thirty days after a claim is honored.

(2) A notice provided by a corporate surety pursuant to the requirement of subsection (1) of this section shall be in such form as required by the executive director subject to approval by the board and shall include, but shall not be limited to, the name of the licensee, the name and address of the claimant, the amount of the honored claim, and the nature of the claim against the licensee.

12-6-113. Testing licensees. Persons applying for a motor vehicle dealer's, used motor vehicle dealer's, wholesaler's, wholesale motor vehicle auction dealer's, or motor vehicle salesperson's license under this part 1 shall be examined for their knowledge of the motor vehicle laws of the state of Colorado and the rules promulgated pursuant to this part 1. If the applicant is a corporation, the managing officer shall take such examination, and, if the applicant is a partnership, all the general partners shall take such examination. No license shall be issued except upon successful passing of the examination. The board shall implement by January 1, 2008, a psychometrically valid and reliable salesperson examination that measures the minimum level of competence necessary to practice. This section shall not apply to a powersports vehicle dealer, used powersports vehicle dealer, or powersports salesperson licensed pursuant to part 5 of this article.

12-6-114. Filing of written warranties. All licensed manufacturers shall file with the executive director all written warranties and changes in written warranties that such manufacturer makes on any motor vehicle or parts thereof. All licensed manufacturers shall file with the executive director a copy of the delivery and preparation obligations of a manufacturer's dealer, and these warranties and obligations shall constitute the dealer's only responsibility for product liability as between the dealer and the manufacturer. Any mechanical, body, or parts defects arising from any express or implied warranties of the manufacturer shall constitute the manufacturer's product or warranty liability, and the manufacturer shall reasonably compensate any authorized dealer who performs work to rectify said manufacturer's product or warranty defects.

12-6-115. Application - prelicensing education - rules. (1) Application for a motor vehicle dealer's, motor vehicle salesperson's, used motor vehicle dealer's, wholesale motor vehicle auction dealer's, or wholesaler's license shall be made to the board.

(2) Application for distributor's, manufacturer representative's, or manufacturer's licenses shall be made to the executive director.

(3) All fees for licenses shall be paid at the time of the filing of application for license.

(4) All persons applying for a motor vehicle dealer's license shall file with the board a certified copy of a certificate of appointment as a dealer from a manufacturer.

(5) All persons applying for a manufacturer's or distributor's license shall file with the executive director a certified copy of their typical written agreement with all motor vehicle dealers, and also evidence of the appointment of an agent for process in the state of Colorado shall be included with the application.

(6) All persons applying for a motor vehicle dealer's license, a used motor vehicle dealer's license, a wholesaler's license, a motor vehicle auctioneer's license, or a motor vehicle salesman's license shall file with the board a good and sufficient instrument in writing in which he shall appoint the secretary of the board as the true and lawful agent of said applicant upon whom all process may be served in any action which may thereafter be commenced against said applicant arising out of any claim for damages suffered by any firm, person, association, or corporation by reason of the violation of said applicant of any of the terms and provisions of this part 1 or any condition of the applicant's bond.

(7) (a) A person applying for a used motor vehicle dealer's license, a wholesale motor vehicle auction dealer's license, or a wholesaler's license shall file with the board a certification that the applicant has met the educational requirements for licensure under this subsection (7). This subsection (7) shall not apply to a person who has held a license within the last three years as a motor vehicle dealer, used motor vehicle dealer, wholesaler, wholesale motor vehicle auction dealer, powersports vehicle dealer, or used powersports vehicle dealer under this part 1 or part 5 of this article.

(b) An applicant for a used motor vehicle dealer's license, a wholesale motor vehicle auction dealer's license, or a wholesaler's license shall not be licensed unless one of the following persons has completed an eight-hour prelicensing education program:

(I) The managing officer if the applicant is a corporation or limited liability company;

(II) All of the general partners if the applicant is any form of partnership; or

(III) The owner or managing officer if the applicant is a sole proprietorship.

(c) The prelicensing education program shall include, without limitation, state and federal statutes and rules governing the sale of motor vehicles.

(d) A prelicensing education program shall not fulfill the requirements of this section unless approved by the board. The board shall approve any program with a curriculum that reasonably covers the material required by this section within eight hours.

(e) The board may adopt rules establishing reasonable fees to be charged for the prelicensing education program.

(f) The board may adopt reasonable rules to implement this section, including, without limitation, rules that govern:

(I) The content and subject matter of education;

(II) The criteria, standards, and procedures for the approval of courses and course instructors;

(III) The training facility requirements; and

(IV) The methods of instruction.

(g) An approved prelicensing program provider shall issue a certificate to a person who successfully completes the approved prelicensing education program. The current certificate of completion, or a copy of the certificate, shall be posted conspicuously at the dealership's principal place of business.

(h) An approved prelicensing program provider shall submit a certificate to the executive director for each person who successfully completes the prelicensing education program. The certificate may be transmitted electronically.

12-6-116. Notice of change of address or status. (1) The board, through the executive director, shall not issue a motor vehicle dealer's license or used motor vehicle dealer's license to any applicant therefor who has no principal place of business as is defined in this part 1. Should the motor vehicle dealer or used motor vehicle dealer change the site or location of such dealer's principal place of business, such dealer shall immediately upon making such change so notify the board in writing, and thereupon a new license shall be granted for the unexpired portion of the term of such license at a fee established pursuant to section 12-6-110. Should a motor vehicle dealer or used motor vehicle dealer, for any reason whatsoever, cease to possess a principal place of business, as defined in this part 1, from and on which such dealer conducts the business for which such dealer is licensed, such dealer shall immediately so notify in writing the board and, upon demand therefor by the board, shall deliver to it such dealer's license, which shall be held and retained until it appears to the board that such licensee again possesses a principal place of business; whereupon, such dealer's license shall be reissued. Nothing in this part 1 shall be construed to prevent a motor vehicle dealer or used motor vehicle dealer from conducting the business for which such dealer is licensed at one or more sites or locations not contiguous to such dealer's principal place of business but operated and maintained in conjunction therewith.

(2) Should the motor vehicle dealer change to a new line of motor vehicles, add another franchise for the sale of new motor vehicles, or cancel or, for any cause whatever, otherwise lose a franchise for the sale of new motor vehicles, such dealer shall immediately so notify the board. In the case of a cancellation or loss of franchise, the board shall determine whether or not by reason thereof such dealer should be licensed as a used motor vehicle dealer, in which case the board shall take up and the motor vehicle dealer shall deliver to it such dealer's license, and the board shall direct the executive director to thereupon issue to such dealer a used motor vehicle dealer's license. Upon the cancellation or loss of a franchise to sell new motor vehicles and the relicensing of such dealer as a used motor vehicle dealer, such dealer may continue in the business for which a motor vehicle dealer is licensed for a time, not exceeding six months from the date of the relicensing of such dealer, to enable such dealer to dispose of the stock of new motor vehicles on hand at the time of such relicensing, but not otherwise.

(3) If a motor vehicle salesperson is discharged, leaves an employer, or changes a place of employment, the motor vehicle dealer or used motor vehicle dealer who last employed the salesperson shall confiscate and return such salesperson's license to the board. Upon being reemployed as a motor vehicle salesperson, the motor vehicle salesperson shall notify the board. Upon receiving such notification, the board shall issue a new license for the unexpired portion of such returned license after collecting a fee set pursuant to section 12-6-110 (5). It shall be unlawful for such salesperson to act as a motor vehicle salesperson until a new license is procured.

(4) Should a wholesaler, for any reason whatsoever, change such wholesaler's place of business or business address during any license year, such wholesaler shall immediately so notify the board.

(5) Any wholesale motor vehicle auction dealer who changes a place of business or business address during any license year shall notify the board immediately of such dealer's new business address.

12-6-117. Principal place of business - requirements. (1) The building or structure required to be located on a principal place of business shall have electrical service and adequate sanitary facilities.

(2) (a) In no event shall a room in a hotel, rooming house, or apartment house building or a part of any single or multiple unit dwelling house be considered a "principal place of business" within the terms and provisions of this part 1, unless the entire ground floor of such hotel, apartment house, or rooming house building or such dwelling house is devoted principally to and occupied for commercial purposes and the office of the dealer is located on the ground floor thereof.

(b) A motor vehicle dealer who operates such motor vehicle dealer's business from his or her primary residence and who has been a resident of Colorado for the immediately preceding twelve-month period and is a motor vehicle dealer only because such dealer sells custom trailers for one or more manufacturers and maintains an inventory of fewer than four vehicles at all times shall be exempt from paragraph (a) of this subsection (2). Any motor vehicle dealer who is issued dealer plates in accordance with this paragraph (b) pursuant to section 42-3-116, C.R.S., shall only use such plates on trailers.

(3) Repealed.

(4) Nothing in this section shall be construed to exempt a motor vehicle dealer from local zoning ordinances.

12-6-118. Licenses - grounds for denial, suspension, or revocation. (1) A manufacturer's or distributor's license may be denied, suspended, or revoked on the following grounds:

(a) (Deleted by amendment, L. 92, p. 1857, § 20, effective July 1, 1992.)

(b) Material misstatement in an application for a license;

(c) Willful failure to comply with this part 1, including the right of first refusal created in section 12-6-120.3 (5), or any rule or regulation promulgated by the executive director;

(d) Engaging, in the past or present, in any illegal business practice.

(2) A manufacturer representative's license may be denied, suspended, or revoked on the following grounds:

(a) (Deleted by amendment, L. 92, p. 1857, § 20, effective July 1, 1992.)

(b) Material misstatement in an application for a license;

(c) Willful failure to comply with any provision of this part 1 or any rule or regulation promulgated by the executive director under this part 1;

(d) Having indulged in any unconscionable business practice pursuant to title 4, C.R.S.;

(e) Having coerced or attempted to coerce any motor vehicle dealer to accept delivery of any motor vehicle, parts or accessories therefor, or any other commodities or services which have not been ordered by said dealer;

(f) Having coerced or attempted to coerce any motor vehicle dealer to enter into any agreement to do any act unfair to said dealer by threatening to cause the cancellation of the franchise of said dealer;

(g) Having withheld, threatened to withhold, reduced, or delayed without just cause an order for motor vehicles, parts or accessories therefor, or any other commodities or services which have been ordered by a motor vehicle dealer;

(h) Engaging, in the past or present, in any illegal business practice.

(3) A motor vehicle dealer's, wholesale motor vehicle auction dealer's, wholesaler's, buyer agent's, or used motor vehicle dealer's license may be denied, suspended, or revoked on the following grounds:

(a) (Deleted by amendment, L. 92, p. 1857, § 20, effective July 1, 1992.)

(b) Material misstatement in an application for a license;

(c) Violation of any of the terms and provisions of this part 1 or any rule or regulation promulgated by the board under this part 1;

(d) Having been convicted of or pled nolo contendere to any felony, or any crime pursuant to article 3, 4, or 5 of title 18, C.R.S., or any like crime pursuant to federal law or the law of any other state. A certified copy of the judgment of conviction by a court of competent jurisdiction shall be conclusive evidence of such conviction in any hearing held pursuant to this article.

(e) Defrauding any buyer, seller, motor vehicle salesperson, or financial institution to such person's damage;

(f) Intentional or negligent failure to perform any written agreement with any buyer or seller;

(g) Failure or refusal to furnish and keep in force any bond required under this part 1;

(h) Having made a fraudulent or illegal sale, transaction, or repossession;

(i) Willful misrepresentation, circumvention, or concealment of or failure to disclose, through whatsoever subterfuge or device, any of the material particulars or the nature thereof required to be stated or furnished to the buyer;

(j) Repealed.

(k) To intentionally publish or circulate any advertising which is misleading or inaccurate in any material particular or which misrepresents any of the products sold or furnished by a licensed dealer;

(l) To knowingly purchase, sell, or otherwise acquire or dispose of a stolen motor vehicle;

(m) For any licensed motor vehicle dealer or used motor vehicle dealer to engage in the business for which such dealer is licensed without at all times maintaining a principal place of business as required by this part 1 during reasonable business hours;

(n) Engaging in such business through employment of an unlicensed motor vehicle salesperson;

(o) To willfully violate any state or federal law respecting commerce or motor vehicles, or any lawful rule or regulation respecting commerce or motor vehicles promulgated by any licensing or regulating authority pertaining to motor vehicles, under circumstances in which the act constituting the violation directly and necessarily involves commerce or motor vehicles;

(p) (Deleted by amendment, L. 92, p. 1857, § 20, effective July 1, 1992.)

(q) Repealed.

(r) Representing or selling as a new and unused motor vehicle any motor vehicle which the dealer or salesperson knows has been used and operated for demonstration purposes or which the dealer or salesperson knows is otherwise a used motor vehicle;

(s) Violating any state or federal statute or regulation issued thereunder dealing with odometers;

(t) (I) Selling to a retail customer a motor vehicle which is not equipped or in proper condition and adjustment as required by part 2 of article 4 of title 42, C.R.S., unless such vehicle is sold as a tow away, not to be driven;

(II) Repealed.

(t.1) Repealed.

(u) Committing a fraudulent insurance act pursuant to section 10-1-128, C.R.S.;

(v) Failure to give notice to a prospective buyer of the acceptance or rejection of a motor vehicle purchase order agreement within a reasonable time period, as determined by the board, when the licensee is working with the prospective buyer on a finance sale or a consignment sale.

(4) A wholesaler's or wholesale motor vehicle auction dealer's license may be denied, suspended, or revoked for the selling, leasing, or offering or attempting to negotiate the sale, lease, or exchange of an interest in motor vehicles by such wholesaler or wholesale motor vehicle auction dealer to persons other than motor vehicle dealers, used motor vehicle dealers, or other wholesalers or wholesale motor vehicle auction dealers.

(5) The license of a motor vehicle salesperson may be denied, revoked, or suspended on the following grounds:

(a) (Deleted by amendment, L. 92, p. 1857, § 20, effective July 1, 1992.)

(b) Material misstatement in an application for a license;

(c) Failure to comply with any provision of this part 1 or any rule or regulation promulgated by the board or executive director under this part 1;

(d) To engage in the business for which such licensee is licensed without having in force and effect a good and sufficient bond with corporate surety as provided in this part 1;

(e) To intentionally publish or circulate any advertising which is misleading or inaccurate in any material particular or which misrepresents any motor vehicle products sold or attempted to be sold by such salesperson;

(f) Having indulged in any fraudulent business practice;

(g) Selling, offering, or attempting to negotiate the sale, exchange, or lease of motor vehicles for any motor vehicle dealer or used motor vehicle dealer for which such salesperson is not licensed; except that negotiation with a motor vehicle dealer for the sale, exchange, or lease of new and used motor vehicles, except those vehicles defined in section 42-1-102 (55), C.R.S., as motorcycles and section 33-14.5-101 (3), C.R.S., as off-highway vehicles, by a salesperson compensated for said negotiation by the used motor vehicle dealer for which such salesperson is licensed shall not be grounds for denial, revocation, or suspension;

(h) Representing oneself as a salesperson for any motor vehicle dealer or used motor vehicle dealer when such salesperson is not so employed and licensed;

(i) (Deleted by amendment, L. 92, p. 1857, § 20, effective July 1, 1992.)

(j) Having been convicted of or pled nolo contendere to any felony, or any crime pursuant to article 3, 4, or 5 of title 18, C.R.S., or any like crime pursuant to federal law or the law of any other state. A certified copy of the judgment of conviction by a court of competent jurisdiction shall be conclusive evidence of such conviction in any hearing held pursuant to this article.

(k) Having knowingly purchased, sold, or otherwise acquired or disposed of a stolen motor vehicle;

(l) Employing an unlicensed motor vehicle salesperson;

(m) Violating any state or federal statute or regulation issued thereunder dealing with odometers;

(n) Defrauding any retail buyer to such person's damage;

(o) Representing or selling as a new and unused motor vehicle any motor vehicle which the salesperson knows has been used and operated for demonstration purposes or which the salesperson knows is otherwise a used motor vehicle;

(p) (I) Selling to a retail customer a motor vehicle which is not equipped or in proper condition and adjustment as required by part 2 of article 4 of title 42, C.R.S., unless such vehicle is sold as a tow away, not to be driven;

(II) Repealed.

(p.1) Repealed.

(q) Willfully violating any state or federal law respecting commerce or motor vehicles, or any lawful rule or regulation respecting commerce or motor vehicles promulgated by any licensing or regulating authority pertaining to motor vehicles, under circumstances in which the act constituting the violation directly and necessarily involves commerce or motor vehicles;

(r) Improperly withholding, misappropriating, or converting to such salesperson's own use any money belonging to customers or other persons, received in the course of employment as a motor vehicle salesperson.

(6) Any license issued pursuant to this part 1 may be denied, revoked, or suspended if unfitness of such licensee or licensee applicant is shown in the following:

(a) The licensing character or record of the licensee or licensee applicant;

(b) The criminal character or record of the licensee or licensee applicant;

(c) The financial character or record of the licensee or licensee applicant;

(d) Violation of any lawful order of the board.

(7) (a) Any license issued or for which an application has been made pursuant to this part 1 shall be revoked or denied if the licensee or applicant has been convicted of or pleaded no contest to any of the following offenses in this state or any other jurisdiction during the previous ten years:

(I) A felony in violation of article 3, 4, or 5 of title 18, C.R.S., or any similar crime under federal law or the law of any other state; or

(II) A crime involving odometer fraud, salvage fraud, motor vehicle title fraud, or the defrauding of a retail consumer in a motor vehicle sale or lease transaction.

(b) A certified copy of a judgment of conviction by a court of competent jurisdiction of an offense under paragraph (a) of this subsection (7) is conclusive evidence of such conviction in any hearing held pursuant to this article.

12-6-119. Procedure for denial, suspension, or revocation of license - judicial review. (1) The denial, suspension, or revocation of licenses issued under this part 1 shall be in accordance with the provisions of sections 24-4-104 and 24-4-105, C.R.S.; except that the discovery available under rule 26 (b) (2) of the Colorado rules of civil procedure is available in any proceeding.

(2) (a) (I) The board shall appoint an administrative law judge pursuant to part 10 of article 30 of title 24, C.R.S., to conduct any hearing concerning the licensing or discipline of a motor vehicle dealer, used motor vehicle dealer, wholesaler, buyer's agent, or wholesale motor vehicle

auction dealer; except that the board may, upon a unanimous vote of the members present when the vote is taken, conduct the hearing in lieu of appointing an administrative law judge.

(II) Beginning July 1, 2008, the board shall issue an annual report to the executive director detailing the number of hearings held pursuant to this paragraph (a) and the number of such hearings conducted by the board. If the board conducts greater than forty percent of the hearings, the executive director shall analyze the hearing procedures and acts and issue a report to the general assembly, which shall include any recommendations of the executive director.

(b) The board shall assign a hearing concerning the licensing or discipline of a motor vehicle salesperson to the executive director who shall appoint an officer to conduct a hearing.

(3) Hearings conducted before an administrative law judge shall be in accordance with the rules of procedure of the office of administrative courts. Hearings conducted before an officer appointed by the executive director shall be in accordance with the rules of procedure established by the executive director.

(4) The board may summarily suspend a licensee required to post a bond under this article if such licensee does not have a bond in full force and effect as required by this article. The suspension shall become effective upon the earlier of the licensee receiving notice of the suspension or within three days after the notice of suspension is mailed to a licensee's last-known address on file with the board. The notice may be effected by certified mail or personal delivery.

(5) The court of appeals shall have initial jurisdiction to review all final actions and orders that are subject to judicial review of the board. Such proceedings shall be conducted in accordance with section 24-4-106 (11), C.R.S.

12-6-119.5. Sales activity following license denial, suspension, or revocation - unlawful act - penalty. (1) (a) It shall be unlawful and a violation of this part 1 for any person whose motor vehicle dealer's, used motor vehicle dealer's, motor vehicle wholesaler's, or motor vehicle salesperson's license has been denied, suspended, or revoked to exercise any of the privileges of the license that was denied, suspended, or revoked.

(b) A violation of paragraph (a) of this subsection (1) shall be punishable in accordance with section 12-6-121; except that a second or subsequent violation of said paragraph (a) shall be a class 6 felony.

(c) In any trial for a violation of paragraph (a) of this subsection (1):

(I) A duly authenticated copy of the board's order of denial, suspension, or revocation shall constitute prima facie evidence of such denial, suspension, or revocation;

(II) A duly authenticated invoice, buyer's order, or other customary, written sales or purchase document or instrument proven to be signed by the defendant and indicating the defendant's role in the purchase or sale of a motor vehicle at any motor vehicle auction, wholesale motor vehicle sales location, or retail motor vehicle sales location, as applicable, shall constitute prima facie evidence of the defendant's exercise of a privilege of licensure;

(III) It shall be an affirmative defense that the defendant bought or sold a motor vehicle that was, at all relevant times, intended for the defendant's own use and not bought or sold for the purpose of profit or gain; and

(IV) The fact that the defendant has a motor vehicle dealer's, used motor vehicle dealer's, motor vehicle wholesaler's, or motor vehicle salesperson's license, or any other license to buy and sell motor vehicles, that is issued by a state or jurisdiction other than Colorado shall not constitute a defense.

(2) Upon the defendant's conviction by entry of a plea of guilty or nolo contendere or judgment or verdict of guilt in connection with a violation of paragraph (a) of subsection (1) of this section or of section 12-6-120 (2) or 42-6-142 (1), C.R.S., the court shall immediately give the executive director written notice of such conviction. In addition, the court shall forward to the executive director copies of documentation of any conviction on a lesser included offense and any amended charge, plea bargain, deferred prosecution, deferred sentence, or deferred judgment in connection with the original charge.

(3) Upon receiving notice of a conviction or other disposition pursuant to subsection (2) of this section, the executive director or his or her designee shall forward such notice to the motor vehicle dealer board, which shall immediately examine its files to determine whether in fact the defendant's license was denied, suspended, or revoked at the time of the offense to which the conviction or other disposition relates. If in fact the defendant's license was denied, suspended, or revoked at the time of such offense, the board:

(a) Shall not issue or reinstate any license to the defendant until one year after the time the defendant would otherwise have been eligible to receive a new or reinstated license; and

(b) Shall revoke or suspend any other licenses held by the defendant until at least one year after the date of the conviction or other disposition.

12-6-120. Unlawful acts. (1) It is unlawful and a violation of this part 1 for any manufacturer, distributor, or manufacturer representative:

(a) To willfully fail to perform or cause to be performed any written warranties made with respect to any motor vehicle or parts thereof;

(b) To coerce or attempt to coerce any motor vehicle dealer to perform or allow to be performed any act that could be financially detrimental to the dealer or that would impair the dealer's goodwill or to enter into any agreement with a manufacturer or distributor that would be financially detrimental to the dealer or impair the dealer's goodwill, by threatening to cancel or not renew any franchise between a manufacturer or distributor and said dealer;

(c) To coerce or attempt to coerce any motor vehicle dealer to accept delivery of any motor vehicle, parts or accessories therefor, or any commodities or services which have not been ordered by said dealer;

(d) (I) To cancel or cause to be canceled, directly or indirectly, without just cause, the franchise of any motor vehicle dealer, and the nonrenewal of a franchise or selling agreement without just cause is a violation of this paragraph (d) and shall constitute an unfair cancellation.

(II) As used in this paragraph (d), "just cause" shall be determined in the context of all circumstances surrounding the cancellation or nonrenewal, including but not limited to:

(A) The amount of business transacted by the motor vehicle dealer;

(B) The investments necessarily made and obligations incurred by the motor vehicle dealer, including but not limited to goodwill, in the performance of its duties under the franchise agreement, together with the duration and permanency of such investments and obligations;

(C) The potential for harm to consumers as a result of disruption of the business of the motor vehicle dealer;

(D) The motor vehicle dealer's failure to provide adequate service of facilities, equipment, parts, and qualified service personnel;

(E) The motor vehicle dealer's failure to perform warranty work on behalf of the manufacturer, subject to reimbursement by the manufacturer; and

(F) The motor vehicle dealer's failure to substantially comply, in good faith, with requirements of the franchise that are determined to be reasonable and material.

(III) The following conduct by a motor vehicle dealer shall constitute just cause for termination without consideration of other factors:

(A) Conviction of, or a plea of guilty or nolo contendere to, a felony;

(B) A continuing pattern of fraudulent conduct against the manufacturer or consumers; or

(C) Continuing failure to operate for ten days or longer.

(e) To withhold, reduce, or delay unreasonably or without just cause delivery of motor vehicles, motor vehicle parts and accessories, commodities, or moneys due motor vehicle dealers for warranty work done by any motor vehicle dealer;

(f) To withhold, reduce, or delay unreasonably or without just cause services contracted for by motor vehicle dealers;

(g) To coerce any motor vehicle dealer to provide installment financing with a specified financial institution;

(h) To violate any duty imposed by, or fail to comply with, any provision of section 12-6-120.3, 12-6-120.5, or 12-6-120.7;

(i) (I) To fail to provide to the motor vehicle dealer, within twenty days after receipt of a notice of intent from a motor vehicle dealer, the list of documents and information necessary to approve the sale or transfer of the ownership of a dealership by sale of the business or by stock transfer or the change in executive management of the dealership;

(II) To fail to confirm within twenty days after receipt of all documents and information listed in subparagraph (I) of this paragraph (i) that such documentation and information has been received;

(III) To refuse to approve, unreasonably, the sale or transfer of the ownership of a dealership by sale of the business or by stock transfer within sixty days after the manufacturer has received all documents and information necessary to approve the sale or transfer of ownership, or to refuse to approve, unreasonably, the change in executive management of the dealership within sixty days after the manufacturer has received all information necessary to approve the change in management; except that nothing in this part 1 shall authorize the sale, transfer, or assignment of a franchise or a change of the principal operator without the approval of the manufacturer or distributor unless the manufacturer or distributor fails to send notice of the disapproval within sixty days after receiving all documents and information necessary to approve the sale or transfer of ownership; or

(IV) To condition the sale, transfer, relocation, or renewal of a franchise agreement, or to condition sales, services, parts, or finance incentives, upon site control or an agreement to renovate or make improvements to a facility; except that voluntary acceptance of such conditions by the dealer shall not constitute a violation;

(j) (I) To fail or refuse to offer to its same line-make franchised dealers all models manufactured for that line-make except as a result of a strike or labor difficulty, lack of manufacturing capacity, shortage of materials, freight embargo, or other cause over which the manufacturer has no control; or

(II) To require a dealer to pay an unreasonable fee, purchase unreasonable advertising displays or other materials, or comply with unreasonable training or facilities requirements as a prerequisite to receiving any particular model of that same line-make. For purposes of this subparagraph (II), reasonableness shall be judged based on the circumstances of the individual dealer and the conditions of the market served by the dealer.

(III) This paragraph (j) shall not apply to manufacturers of recreational vehicles nor to manufacturers of vehicles with a passenger capacity of thirty-two or more.

(k) To require, coerce, or attempt to coerce any motor vehicle dealer to refrain from participation in the management of, investment in, or acquisition of any other line-make of new motor vehicles or related products; except that this paragraph (k) shall not apply unless the motor vehicle dealer:

(I) Maintains a reasonable line of credit for each make or line of new motor vehicle;

(II) Remains in compliance with reasonable capital standards and reasonable facilities requirements specified by the manufacturer; except that "reasonable facilities requirements" shall not include a requirement that a motor vehicle dealer establish or maintain exclusive facilities, personnel, or display space; and

(III) Provides written notice to the manufacturer, distributor, or manufacturer's representative, no less than ninety days prior to the dealer's intent to participate in the management of, investment in, or acquisition of another line-make of new motor vehicles or related products;

(l) (I) To fail to pay to a motor vehicle dealer, within ninety days after the termination, cancellation, or nonrenewal of a franchise, all of the following:

(A) The dealer cost, plus any charges made by the manufacturer for distribution, delivery, and taxes, less all allowances paid or credited to the motor vehicle dealer by the manufacturer, of unused, undamaged, and unsold motor vehicles in the motor vehicle dealer's inventory that were acquired from the manufacturer or from another motor vehicle dealer of the same line-make in the ordinary course of business within the previous twelve months;

(B) The dealer cost, less all allowances paid or credited to the motor vehicle dealer by the manufacturer, for all unused, undamaged, and unsold supplies, parts, and accessories in original packaging and listed in the manufacturer's current parts catalog;

(C) The fair market value of each undamaged sign owned by the motor vehicle dealer and bearing a common name, trade name, or trademark of the manufacturer if acquisition of such sign was required by the manufacturer;

(D) The fair market value of all special tools and equipment that were acquired from the manufacturer or from sources approved and required by the manufacturer and that are in good and usable condition, excluding normal wear and tear; and

(E) The cost of transporting, handling, packing, and loading the motor vehicles, supplies, parts, accessories, signs, special tools, equipment, and furnishings described in this paragraph (l).

(II) This paragraph (l) shall only apply to manufacturers of recreational vehicles in cases where the manufacturer terminates, cancels, or fails to renew the recreational vehicle dealer franchise; and this paragraph (l) shall not apply to manufacturers of vehicles with a passenger capacity of thirty-two or more.

(m) To require, coerce, or attempt to coerce any motor vehicle dealer to close or change the location of the motor vehicle dealer, or to make any substantial alterations to the dealer premises or facilities when doing so would be unreasonable or without written assurance of a sufficient supply of motor vehicles so as to justify such changes, in light of the current market and economic conditions;

(n) (I) To authorize or permit a person to perform warranty service repairs on motor vehicles unless the person is:

(A) A motor vehicle dealer with whom the manufacturer has entered into a franchise agreement for the sale and service of the manufacturer's motor vehicles; or

(B) A person or government entity that has purchased new motor vehicles pursuant to a manufacturer's fleet discount program and is performing the warranty service repairs only on vehicles owned by such person or entity.

(II) This paragraph (n) shall not apply to manufacturers of recreational vehicles nor to manufacturers of vehicles with a passenger capacity of thirty-two or more.

(o) To require, coerce, or attempt to coerce any motor vehicle dealer to prospectively agree to a release, assignment, novation, waiver, or estoppel that would relieve any person of a duty or liability imposed under this article except in settlement of a bona fide dispute;

(p) To discriminate between or refuse to offer to its same line-make franchised dealers all models manufactured for that line-make based upon unreasonable sales and service standards;

(q) To fail to make practically available any incentive, rebate, bonus, or other similar benefit to a motor vehicle dealer that is offered to another motor vehicle dealer of the same line-make within this state;

(r) To fail to pay to a motor vehicle dealer:

(I) Within ninety days after the termination, cancellation, or nonrenewal of a franchise for the failure of a dealer to meet performance sales and service obligations or after the termination, elimination, or cessation of a line-make, the cost of the lease for the facilities used for the franchise or line-make for the unexpired term of the lease, not to exceed one year; except that:

(A) If the motor vehicle dealer owns the facilities, the value of renting such facilities for one year, prorated for each line-make based upon total sales volume for the previous twelve months before the involuntary termination;

(B) If the dealer sells recreational vehicles and a subsequent manufacturer or distributor that manufactures or distributes recreational vehicles replaces any portion of the vacated facilities, the lease or rental value shall be prorated on a monthly basis unless the dealer sells motor vehicles that are not recreational vehicles;

(C) Nothing in this subparagraph (I) shall be construed to limit the application of paragraph (d) of this subsection (1);

(II) Within ninety days after the termination, elimination, or cessation of a line-make or the termination of a franchise due to the insolvency of the manufacturer or distributor, the fair market value of the motor vehicle dealer's goodwill for the line-make as of the date the manufacturer or distributor announces the action that results in the termination, elimination, or cessation, not including any amounts paid under subsubparagraphs (A) to (E) of subparagraph (I) of paragraph (l) of this subsection (1);

(s) To condition a franchise agreement on improvements to a facility unless reasonably required by the technology of a motor vehicle being sold at the facility;

(t) To sell or offer for sale a low-speed electric vehicle, as defined by section 42-1-102, C.R.S., for use on a roadway unless the vehicle complies with part 2 of article 4 of title 42, C.R.S.;

(u) To charge back, deny motor vehicle allocation, withhold payments, or take other actions against a motor vehicle dealer if a motor vehicle sold by the motor vehicle dealer is exported from Colorado unless the manufacturer, distributor, or manufacturer representative proves that the motor vehicle dealer knew or reasonably should have known a motor vehicle was intended to be exported, which shall operate as a rebuttable presumption that the motor vehicle dealer did not have such knowledge;

(v) Within ninety days after the termination, elimination, or cessation of a line-make or the termination, cancellation, or nonrenewal of a franchise by the manufacturer, distributor, or manufacturer representative, for any reason other than that the motor vehicle dealer commits fraud, makes a misrepresentation, or commits any other crime within the scope of the franchise agreement or in the operation of the dealership, to fail to reimburse a motor vehicle dealer for the cost depreciated by five percent per year of any upgrades or alterations to the motor vehicle dealer's facilities required by the manufacturer, distributor, or manufacturer representative within the previous five years;

(w) To fail to notify a motor vehicle dealer at least ninety days before the following and to provide the specific reasons for the following:

(I) Directly or indirectly terminating, cancelling, or not renewing a franchise agreement; or

(II) Modifying, replacing, or attempting to modify or replace the franchise or selling agreement of a motor vehicle dealer, including a change in the dealer's geographic area upon which sales or service performance is measured, if the modification would substantially and adversely alter the rights or obligations of the dealer under the current franchise or selling agreement or would substantially impair the sales or service obligations or the dealer's investment; and

(x) To require, coerce, or attempt to coerce a motor vehicle dealer to substantially alter a facility or premises if:

(I) The facility or premises has been altered within the last seven years at a cost of more than two hundred fifty thousand dollars and the alteration was required and approved by the manufacturer, distributor, or manufacturer representative unless the motor vehicle dealer sells only motorcycles or motorcycles and powersports vehicles; except that this paragraph (x) does not apply to improvements made to comply with health or safety laws or to accommodate the technology requirements necessary to sell or service a line-make; or

(II) The motor vehicle dealer sells only motorcycles or motorcycles and powersports vehicles, the facility or premises has been altered within the last seven years at a cost of more than twenty-five thousand dollars, and the alteration was required and approved by the manufacturer, distributor, or manufacturer representative; except that this paragraph (x) does not apply to improvements made to comply with health or safety laws or to accommodate the technology requirements necessary to sell or service a line-make.

(2) It is unlawful for any person to act as a motor vehicle dealer, manufacturer, distributor, wholesaler, manufacturer representative, used motor vehicle dealer, buyer agent, wholesale motor vehicle auction dealer, or motor vehicle salesperson unless such person has been duly licensed under the provisions of this part 1, except for persons exempt from licensure as a manufacturer pursuant to section 12-6-102 (11); however, such persons shall comply with all other applicable requirements for manufacturers, including, but not limited to, those pertaining to vehicle identification numbers and manufacturers' statements of origin.

(3) It is unlawful and a violation of this part 1 for a buyer's agent to engage in the following:

(a) To make a material misstatement in an application for a license;

(b) To willfully fail to perform or cause to be performed any written agreement with respect to any motor vehicle or parts thereof;

(c) To defraud any buyer, seller, motor vehicle salesperson, or financial institution;

(d) To intentionally enter into a financial agreement with a seller of a motor vehicle for the buyer agent's own benefit;

(e) To coerce any motor vehicle dealer into providing installment financing with a specified financial institution.

12-6-120.3. New, reopened, or relocated dealer - notice required - grounds for refusal of dealer license - definitions - rules. (1) No manufacturer or distributor shall establish an additional new motor vehicle dealer, reopen a previously existing motor vehicle dealer, or relocate an existing motor vehicle dealer without first providing at least sixty days' notice to all of its franchised dealers and former dealers whose franchises were terminated, cancelled, or not renewed by a manufacturer, distributor, or manufacturer representative in the previous five years due to the insolvency of the manufacturer or distributor within whose relevant market area the new, reopened, or relocated dealer would be located. The notice shall state:

(a) The specific location at which the additional, reopened, or relocated motor vehicle dealer will be established;

(b) The date on or after which the manufacturer intends to be engaged in business with the additional, reopened, or relocated motor vehicle dealer at the proposed location;

(c) The identity of all motor vehicle dealers who are franchised to sell the same line-make of vehicles with licensed locations in the relevant market area where the additional, reopened, or relocated motor vehicle dealer is proposed to be located; and

(d) The names and addresses of the dealer-operator and principal investors in the proposed additional, reopened, or relocated motor vehicle dealer.

(1.5) A manufacturer shall reasonably approve or disapprove of a motor vehicle dealer facility initial site location or relocation request within sixty days after the request or after sending the notice required by subsection (1) of this section to all of its franchised dealers and former dealers whose franchises were terminated, cancelled, or not renewed in the previous five years due to the insolvency of the manufacturer or distributor, whichever is later, but not to exceed one hundred days.

(2) Subsection (1) of this section shall not apply to:

(a) The relocation of an existing dealer within two miles of its current location; or

(b) The establishment of a replacement dealer, within two years, either at the former location or within two miles of the former location.

(3) As used in this section:

(a) "Manufacturer" means a motor vehicle manufacturer, distributor, or manufacturer representative.

(b) "Relevant market area" means the greater of the following:

(I) The geographic area of responsibility defined in the franchise agreement of an existing dealer; or

(II) The geographic area within a radius of five miles of any existing dealer of the same line-make of vehicle that is located in a county with a population of more than one hundred fifty thousand or within a radius of ten miles of an existing dealer of the same line-make of vehicles that is located in a county with a population of one hundred fifty thousand or less.

(c) "Right of first refusal area" means a five-mile radius extending from the location of where a motor vehicle dealer had a franchise terminated, cancelled, or not renewed if the franchise was in a county with a population of more than one hundred fifty thousand or a ten-mile radius if the franchise was in a county with a population of one hundred fifty thousand or less.

(4) (a) If a licensee or former licensee whose franchise was terminated, cancelled, or not renewed by the manufacturer, distributor, or manufacturer representative in the previous five years due to the insolvency of the manufacturer or distributor brings an action or proceeding before the executive director or a court pursuant to this part 1, the manufacturer shall have the burden of proof on the following issues:

(I) The size and permanency of investment and obligations incurred by the existing motor vehicle dealers of the same line-make located in the relevant market area;

(II) Growth or decline in population and new motor vehicle registrations in the relevant market area;

(III) The effect on the consuming public in the relevant market area and whether the opening of the proposed additional, reopened, or relocated dealer is injurious or beneficial to the public welfare; and

(IV) Whether the motor vehicle dealers of the same line-make in the relevant market area are providing adequate and convenient customer care for motor vehicles of the same line-make in the relevant market area, including but not limited to the adequacy of sales and service facilities, equipment, parts, and qualified service personnel.

(b) (I) In addition to the powers specified in section 12-6-105, the executive director has jurisdiction to resolve actions or proceedings brought before the executive director pursuant to this part 1 that allege a violation of this part 1 or rules promulgated pursuant to this part 1. The executive director may promulgate rules to facilitate the administration of such actions or proceedings, including provisions specifying procedures for the executive director or the executive director's designee to:

(A) Conduct an investigation pursuant to section 12-6-105 (1) (d) of an alleged violation of this part 1 or rules promulgated pursuant to this part 1, including issuance of a notice of violation;

(B) Hold a hearing regarding the alleged violation to be held pursuant to section 24-4-105, C.R.S.;

(C) Issue an order, including a cease-and-desist order issued pursuant to section 12-6-105 (1) (f), to resolve the notice of violation; and

(D) Impose a fine pursuant to section 12-6-105 (1) (f) (III).

(II) The court of appeals has initial jurisdiction to review all final actions and orders that are subject to judicial review of the executive director made pursuant to this subsection (4). Such proceedings shall be conducted in accordance with section 24-4-106, C.R.S.

(5) (a) No manufacturer, distributor, or manufacturer representative shall offer or award a person a franchise or permit the relocation of an existing franchise to the right of first refusal area unless the manufacturer, distributor, or manufacturer representative has complied with paragraph (b) of this subsection (5) or unless paragraph (b) of this subsection (5) does not apply.

(b) If a manufacturer, distributor, or manufacturer representative, or the predecessor thereof, has terminated, cancelled, or not renewed a motor vehicle dealer's franchise for a line-make within the right of first refusal area due to the insolvency of the manufacturer or distributor that was held by the motor vehicle dealer immediately prior to the franchise being terminated, cancelled, or not renewed within the amount of time the right of first refusal is granted under paragraph (c) of this subsection (5), the manufacturer, distributor, or manufacturer representative, or the successor thereof, shall offer the former motor vehicle dealer whose franchise was terminated, cancelled, or not renewed a franchise within the first refusal area prior to making the offer to any other person for the same line-make unless the former motor vehicle dealer elects to receive the payments required by section 12-6-120 (1) (l) and (1) (r) in lieu of the right of first refusal or the motor vehicle dealer has accepted compensation from the manufacturer, distributor, or manufacturer representative for the termination, cancellation, or nonrenewal of the franchise agreement.

(c) The duration of the right of first refusal granted in paragraph (b) of this subsection (5) is equal to five years after the franchise is terminated, cancelled, or not renewed.

(d) If a manufacturer, distributor, or manufacturer representative, or the predecessor thereof, has made any payment to the motor vehicle dealer in consideration for the termination, cancellation, or nonrenewal of a franchise agreement and the motor vehicle dealer obtains a new franchise agreement through this subsection (5), the motor vehicle dealer shall reimburse the manufacturer, distributor, or manufacturer representative for such payments. The motor vehicle dealer may reimburse the manufacturer, distributor, or manufacturer representative with a commercially reasonable repayment installment plan.

(e) The right of first refusal survives a court voiding the payments required by section 12-6-120 (1) (l) and (1) (r).

(f) (I) The right of first refusal survives a manufacturer, distributor, or manufacturer representative, or predecessor thereof, awarding a franchise within the same right of first refusal for the same line-make to a person or entity other than the former motor vehicle dealer whose franchise was terminated, cancelled, or not renewed.

(II) If a manufacturer, distributor, or manufacturer representative, or predecessor thereof, has awarded the franchise to another motor vehicle dealer in the same right of first refusal area without granting the right of first refusal under this section, the former motor vehicle dealer may elect to either receive a franchise agreement in the same area or the payments required by section 12-6-120 (1) (l) and (1) (r) from the manufacturer, distributor, or manufacturer representative unless the manufacturer, distributor, or manufacturer representative, or predecessor thereof, has paid compensation in consideration of the initial termination, cancellation, or nonrenewal of the franchise agreement.

12-6-120.5. Independent control of dealer - definitions. (1) Except as otherwise provided in this section, no manufacturer shall own, operate, or control any motor vehicle dealer or used motor vehicle dealer in Colorado.

(2) Notwithstanding subsection (1) of this section, the following activities are not prohibited:

(a) (I) Except as provided in subparagraph (II) of this paragraph (a), operation of a dealer for a temporary period, not to exceed twelve months, during the transition from one owner or operator to another independent owner or operator; except that the executive director may extend the period, not to exceed twenty-four months, upon showing by the manufacturer or distributor of the need to operate the dealership for such time to achieve a transition from an owner or operator to another independent third-party owner or operator;

(II) Operation of a dealer that sells recreational vehicles for not more than eighteen months during the transition from one owner or operator to another independent owner or operator;

(b) Ownership or control of a dealer while the dealer is being sold under a bona fide contract or purchase option to the operator of the dealer;

(c) Participation in the ownership of the dealer solely for the purpose of providing financing or a capital loan that will enable the dealer to become the majority owner of the dealer in less than seven years;

(d) Operation of a motor vehicle dealer if the manufacturer has no other dealers of the same line-make in this state;

(e) Ownership, operation, or control of a used motor vehicle dealer if the manufacturer owned, operated, or controlled the used motor vehicle dealer on January 1, 2009, and has continuously operated or controlled the used motor vehicle facilities after January 1, 2009; and

(f) Operation of a motor vehicle dealer if the manufacturer was operating the dealer on January 1, 2009, so long as the dealer is in continuous operation after January 1, 2009.

(3) As used in this section:

(a) "Control" means to possess, directly, the power to direct or cause the direction of the management or policies of a person, whether through the ownership of voting securities, by contract, or otherwise; except that "control" does not include the relationship between a manufacturer and a motor vehicle dealer under a franchise agreement.

(b) "Manufacturer" means a motor vehicle manufacturer, distributor, or manufacturer representative.

(c) "Operate" means to directly or indirectly manage a motor vehicle dealer.

(d) "Own" means to hold any beneficial ownership interest of one percent or more of any class of equity interest in a dealer, whether as a shareholder, partner, limited liability company member, or otherwise. To "hold" an ownership interest means to have possession of, title to, or control of the ownership interest, either directly or through a fiduciary or agent.

(4) This section shall not apply to manufacturers of vehicles with a passenger capacity of thirty-two or more.

12-6-120.7. Successor under existing franchise agreement - duties of manufacturer. (1) If a licensed motor vehicle dealer under franchise by a manufacturer dies or becomes incapacitated, the manufacturer shall act in good faith to allow a successor, which may include a family member, designated by the deceased or incapacitated motor vehicle dealer to succeed to ownership and operation of the dealer under the existing franchise agreement if:

(a) Within ninety days after the motor vehicle dealer's death or incapacity, the designated successor gives the manufacturer written notice of an intent to succeed to the rights of the deceased or incapacitated motor vehicle dealer in the franchise agreement;

(b) The designated successor agrees to be bound by all of the terms and conditions of the existing franchise agreement; and

(c) The designated successor meets the criteria generally applied by the manufacturer in qualifying motor vehicle dealers.

(2) A manufacturer may refuse to honor the existing franchise agreement with the designated successor only for good cause. The manufacturer may request in writing from a designated successor the personal and financial data that is reasonably necessary to determine whether the existing franchise agreement should be honored, and the designated successor shall supply such data promptly upon request.

(3) (a) If a manufacturer believes that good cause exists for refusing to honor the requested succession, the manufacturer shall send the designated successor, by certified or overnight mail, notice of its refusal to approve the succession within sixty days after the later of:

(I) Receipt of the notice of the designated successor's intent to succeed the motor vehicle dealer in the ownership and operation of the dealer; or

(II) The receipt of the requested personal and financial data.

(b) Failure to serve the notice pursuant to paragraph (a) of this subsection (3) shall be considered approval of the designated successor, and the franchise agreement is considered amended to reflect the approval of the succession the day following the last day of the notice period specified in said paragraph (a).

(c) If the manufacturer gives notice of refusal to approve the succession, such notice shall state the specific grounds for the refusal and shall state that the franchise agreement shall be discontinued not less than ninety days after the date the notice of refusal is served unless the proposed successor files an action in the district court to enjoin such action.

(4) This section shall not be construed to prohibit a motor vehicle dealer from designating a person as the successor in advance, by written instrument filed with the manufacturer. If the motor vehicle dealer files such an instrument, that instrument governs the succession rights to the management and operation of the dealer subject to the designated successor satisfying the manufacturer's qualification requirements as described in this section.

(5) This section shall not apply to manufacturers of vehicles with a passenger capacity of thirty-two or more.

12-6-121. Penalty. Any person who willfully violates any of the provisions of this part 1 or who willfully commits any offense in this part 1 declared to be unlawful commits a class 1 misdemeanor and shall be punished as provided in section 18-1.3-501, C.R.S.; except that any person who violates the provisions of section 12-6-120 (2) commits a class 3 misdemeanor and, upon conviction thereof, shall be punished by a fine of not less than one hundred dollars or more than one thousand dollars for each separate offense; except that, if the violator is a corporation, the fine shall be not less than five hundred dollars or more than two thousand five hundred dollars for each separate offense. A second conviction shall be punished by a fine of two thousand five hundred dollars.

12-6-121.5. Fines - disposition - unlicensed sales. Any fine collected for a violation of section 12-6-120 (2) shall be awarded to the law enforcement agency which investigated and issued the citation for said violation.

12-6-121.6. Drafts not honored for payment - penalties. (1) If a motor vehicle dealer, wholesaler, or used motor vehicle dealer issues a draft or check to a motor vehicle dealer, wholesaler, used motor vehicle dealer, motor vehicle auction house, or consignor and fails to honor such draft or check, then the license of such licensee shall be subject to suspension pursuant to section 12-6-104 (3) (e) (I). The license suspension shall be effective upon the date of any final decision against such licensee based upon the unpaid draft or check. A licensee whose license has been suspended pursuant to the provisions of this subsection (1) shall not be eligible for reinstatement of such license and shall not be eligible to apply for any other license issued under this part 1 unless it is demonstrated to the board that the unpaid draft or check has been paid in full and that any fine imposed on the licensee pursuant to subsection (2) of this section has been paid in full.

(2) Any motor vehicle dealer, wholesaler, or used motor vehicle dealer which issues a draft or check to a motor vehicle dealer, wholesaler, used motor vehicle dealer, motor vehicle auction house, or consignor and who fails to honor such draft or check, causing loss to a third party, commits a misdemeanor and shall be punished by a fine of two thousand five hundred dollars. Any fine collected for a violation of this subsection (2)

12-6-122. Right of action for loss. (1) If any person suffers loss or damage by reason of any fraud practiced on such person or fraudulent representation made to such person by a licensed dealer or one of the dealer's salespersons acting for the dealer on such dealer's behalf or within the scope of the employment of the salesperson or suffers any loss or damage by reason of the violation by such dealer or salesperson of any of the provisions of this part 1 that are designated by the board by rule, whether or not such violation is the basis for denial, suspension, or revocation of a license, such person shall have a right of action against the dealer, such dealer's motor vehicle salespersons, and the sureties upon their respective bonds. The right of a person to recover for loss or damage as provided in this subsection (1) against the dealer or salesperson shall not be limited to the amount of their respective bonds.

(2) If any person suffers any loss or damage by reason of any unlawful act as provided in section 12-6-120 (1) (a), such person shall have a right of action against the manufacturer, distributor, or manufacturer representative. In any court action wherein a manufacturer, distributor, or manufacturer representative has been found liable in damages to any person under this part 1, the amount of damages so determined shall be trebled and shall be recoverable by the person so damaged. Any person so damaged shall also be entitled to recover reasonable attorney fees as part of his or her damages.

(3) If any licensee suffers any loss or damage because of a violation of section 12-6-120 (1) or 12-6-120.3 (5), the licensee shall have a right of action against the manufacturer, distributor, or manufacturer representative. In any court action wherein a manufacturer, distributor, or manufacturer representative has been found liable in damages to any licensee under this part 1, any licensee so damaged shall also be entitled to recover reasonable attorney fees and costs as part of his or her damages.

12-6-122.5. Contract disputes - venue - choice of law. (1) In the event of a dispute between a motor vehicle dealer and a manufacturer under a franchise agreement, notwithstanding any provision of the agreement to the contrary:

(a) At the option of the motor vehicle dealer, venue shall be proper in the county or judicial district where the dealer resides or has its principal place of business; and

(b) Colorado law shall govern, both substantively and procedurally.

12-6-123. Disposition of fees - auto dealers license fund. (1) All moneys received under this part 1, except fines awarded pursuant to section 12-6-121.5, shall be deposited with the state treasurer by the department of revenue, subject to the provisions of section 24-35-101, C.R.S., together with a detailed statement of such receipts, and such funds deposited with the state treasurer shall constitute a fund to be known as the auto dealers license fund, which fund is hereby created and which shall be used under the direction of the board in the following manner:

(a) Repealed.

(b) (I) For the payment of the expenses of the administration of the board as the general assembly deems necessary by making an appropriation therefor on an annual fiscal-year basis commencing July 1, 1971, and thereafter.

(II) Any money remaining in said fund on December 31, 1971, and at the close of each calendar year thereafter, after costs of administration of the law as provided in this part 1 shall remain in the auto dealers license fund to be used for educational and enforcement purposes as appropriated by the general assembly.

(c) To pay the department of revenue for the administration of actions or proceedings brought before the executive director pursuant to section 12-6-120.

(2) (a) Notwithstanding any provision of subsection (1) of this section to the contrary, on March 27, 2002, the state treasurer shall deduct one million one hundred thousand dollars from the auto dealers license fund and transfer such sum to the general fund; except that, if the balance of moneys in the auto dealers license fund on March 27, 2002, is less than one million one hundred thousand dollars, the state treasurer shall transfer the balance of moneys in the fund to the general fund.

(b) Notwithstanding any provision of subsection (1) of this section to the contrary and in addition to any amount transferred pursuant to paragraph (a) of this subsection (2):

(I) On May 28, 2002, the state treasurer shall transfer an amount equal to the balance of the auto dealers license fund as of April 30, 2002, to the general fund.

(II) Except as otherwise provided in this subparagraph (II), for each succeeding calendar month of the 2001-02 fiscal year, through June 30, 2002, the state treasurer shall transfer the amount of moneys credited to the auto dealers license fund during such calendar month to the general fund no later than the last day of the month in which such moneys were credited to the auto dealers license fund. However, the aggregate amount of moneys transferred from the auto dealers license fund to the general fund pursuant to paragraph (a) of this subsection (2), subparagraph (I) of this paragraph (b), and this subparagraph (II) shall not exceed one million one hundred thousand dollars.

12-6-124. Repeal of article. This article is repealed, effective July 1, 2017. Prior to such repeal, the motor vehicle dealer board and the functions of the executive director, including licensing, shall be reviewed as provided for in section 24-34-104, C.R.S.

12-6-125. Advertisement - inclusion of dealer name. No motor vehicle dealer or used motor vehicle dealer or any agent of either of said dealers shall advertise any offer for the sale, lease, or purchase of a motor vehicle or a used motor vehicle which creates the false impression that the vehicle is being offered by a private party or by a motor vehicle agent or which does not contain the name of the dealer or the word "dealer" or, if the name is contained in the offer and does not clearly reflect that the business is a dealer, both the name of the dealer and the word "dealer".

12-6-126. Audit reimbursement limitations - dealer claims. (1) (a) A manufacturer, distributor, or manufacturer representative shall have the right to audit warranty, sales, or incentive claims of a motor vehicle dealer for nine months after the date the claim was submitted.

(b) A manufacturer, distributor, or manufacturer representative shall not require documentation for warranty, sales, or incentive claims or audit warranty, sales, or incentive claims of a motor vehicle dealer more than fifteen months after the date the claim was submitted, nor shall the manufacturer require a charge back, reimbursement, or credit against a future transaction arising out of an audit or request for documentation arising more than nine months after the date the claim was submitted.

(2) The motor vehicle dealer shall have nine months after making a sale or providing service to submit warranty, sales, or incentive claims to the manufacturer, distributor, or manufacturer representative.

(3) Subsection (1) of this section shall not limit any action for fraud instituted in a court of competent jurisdiction.

(4) A motor vehicle dealer may request a determination from the executive director, within thirty days, that a charge back, reimbursement, or credit required violates subsection (1) of this section. If a determination is requested within the thirty-day period, then the charge back, reimbursement, or credit shall be stayed pending the decision of the executive director. If the executive director determines after a hearing that the charge back, reimbursement, or credit violates subsection (1) of this section, the charge back, reimbursement, or credit shall be void.

12-6-127. Reimbursement for right of first refusal. A manufacturer or distributor shall pay reasonable attorney fees, not to exceed the usual and customary fees charged for the transfer of a franchise, and reasonable expenses that are incurred by the proposed owner or transferee before the manufacturer or distributor exercised its right of first refusal in negotiating and implementing the contract for the proposed change of ownership or the transfer of assets. Payment of attorney fees and expenses is not required if the claimant has failed to submit an accounting of attorney fees and expenses within twenty days after the receipt of the manufacturer's or dealer's written request for an accounting. An expense accounting may be requested by the manufacturer or distributor before exercising its right of first refusal.

12-6-128. Payout exemption to execution. A motor vehicle dealer's right to receive payments from a manufacturer or distributor required by section 12-6-120 (1) (l) and (1) (r) is not liable to attachment or execution and may not otherwise be seized, taken, appropriated, or applied in a legal or equitable process or by operation of law to pay the debts or liabilities of the manufacturer or distributor. This section shall not prohibit a secured creditor from exercising rights accrued pursuant to a security agreement if the right arose as a result of the manufacturer or distributor voluntarily creating a security interest before paying existing debts or liabilities of the manufacturer or distributor. This section shall not prohibit a manufacturer or distributor from withholding a portion of such payments necessary to cover an amount of money owed to the manufacturer or distributor as an offset to such payments if the manufacturer or distributor provides the motor vehicle dealer written notice thereof.

12-6-129. Site control extinguishes. If a manufacturer, distributor, or manufacturer representative has terminated, eliminated, or not renewed a franchise agreement containing a site control provision, the motor vehicle dealer may void a site control provision of a franchise agreement by returning any money the dealer has accepted in exchange for site control prorated by the time remaining before the agreement expires over the time period between the agreement being signed and the agreement expiring. This section does not apply if the termination, elimination, or nonrenewal is for just cause in accordance with section 12-6-120 (1) (d).

Editor's note: Section 7 of chapter 175, Session Laws of Colorado 2011, provides that the act adding this section applies to offenses committed on or after May 13, 2011.

12-6-130. Modification voidable. If a manufacturer, distributor, or manufacturer representative fails to comply with section 12-6-120 (1) (w) (II), the motor vehicle dealer may void the modification or replacement of the franchise agreement.

Editor's note: Section 7 of chapter 175, Session Laws of Colorado 2011, provides that the act adding this section applies to offenses committed on or after May 13, 2011.

12-6-131. Termination appeal. A motor vehicle dealer who has reason to believe that a manufacturer, distributor, or manufacturer representative has violated section 12-6-120 (1) (d) or (1) (w) may appeal to the board by filing a complaint with the executive director. Upon receiving the complaint and upon a showing of specific facts that a violation has occurred, the executive director shall summarily issue a cease-and-desist order under section 12-6-105 (1) (f) staying the termination, elimination, modification, or nonrenewal of the franchise agreement. The cease-and-desist order remains in effect until the hearing required by section 12-6-105 (1) (f) is held. If a determination is made at the hearing required by section 12-6-105 (1) (f) that a violation occurred, the executive director shall make the cease-and-desist order permanent and take any actions authorized by section 12-6-104 (3). A motor vehicle dealer who appeals to the executive director maintains all rights under the franchise agreement until the later of the executive director issuing a decision or ninety days after the manufacturer, distributor, or manufacturer's representative provides the notice of termination unless the executive director finds that the termination, cancellation, or nonrenewal was for fraud, a misrepresentation, or committing a crime within the scope of the franchise agreement or in the operation of the dealership, in which case the franchise rights terminate immediately.

Editor's note: Section 7 of chapter 175, Session Laws of Colorado 2011, provides that the act adding this section applies to offenses committed on or after May 13, 2011.

PART 2

ANTIMONOPOLY FINANCING LAW

12-6-201. Definitions. As used in this part 2, unless the context otherwise requires:

(1) "Person" means any individual, firm, corporation, partnership, association, trustee, receiver, or assignee for the benefit of creditors.

(2) "Sell", "sold", "buy", and "purchase" include exchange, barter, gift, and offer or contract to sell or buy.

12-6-202. Exclusive finance agreements void - when. It is unlawful for any person who is engaged, either directly or indirectly, in the manufacture or distribution of motor vehicles, to sell or enter into contract to sell motor vehicles, whether patented or unpatented, to any person who is engaged or intends to engage in the business of selling such motor vehicles at retail in this state, on the condition or with an agreement or understanding, either express or implied, that such person so engaged in selling motor vehicles at retail in any manner shall finance the purchase or sale of any one or number of motor vehicles only with or through a designated person or class of persons or shall sell and assign the conditional sales contracts, chattel mortgages, or leases arising from the sale of motor vehicles or any one or number thereof only to a designated person or class of persons, when the effect of the condition, agreement, or understanding so entered into may be to lessen or eliminate competition, or create or tend to create a monopoly in the person or class of persons who are designated, by virtue of such condition, agreement, or understanding to finance the purchase or sale of motor vehicles or to purchase such conditional sales contracts, chattel mortgages, or leases. Any such condition, agreement, or understanding is declared to be void and against the public policy of this state.

12-6-203. Threat prima facie evidence of violation. Any threat, expressed or implied, made directly or indirectly to any person engaged in the business of selling motor vehicles at retail in this state by any person engaged, either directly or indirectly, in the manufacture or distribution of motor vehicles, that such person will discontinue or cease to sell, or refuse to enter into a contract to sell, or will terminate a contract to sell motor vehicles, whether patented or unpatented, to such person who is so engaged in the business of selling motor vehicles at retail, unless such person finances the purchase or sale of any one or number of motor vehicles only with or through a designated person or class of persons or sells and assigns the conditional sales contracts, chattel mortgages, or leases arising from his retail sales of motor vehicles or any one or number thereof only to a designated person or class of persons shall be prima facie evidence of the fact that such person so engaged in the manufacture or distribution of motor vehicles has sold or intends to sell the same on the condition or with the agreement or understanding prohibited in section 12-6-202.

12-6-204. Threat by agent as evidence of violation. Any threat, expressed or implied, made directly or indirectly to any person engaged in the business of selling motor vehicles at retail in this state by any person, or any agent of any such person, who is engaged in the business of financing the purchase or sale of motor vehicles or of buying conditional sales contracts, chattel mortgages, or leases on motor vehicles in this state and is affiliated with or controlled by any person engaged, directly or indirectly, in the manufacture or distribution of motor vehicles, that such person so engaged in such manufacture or distribution shall terminate his contract with or cease to sell motor vehicles to such person engaged in the sale of motor vehicles at retail in this state unless such person finances the purchase or sale of any one or number of motor vehicles only or through a designated person or class of persons or sells and assigns the conditional sales contracts, chattel mortgages, or leases arising from his retail sale of motor vehicles or any one or any number thereof only to such person so engaged in financing the purchase or sale of motor vehicles or in buying conditional sales contracts, chattel mortgages, or leases on motor vehicles, shall be presumed to be made at the direction of and with the authority of such person so engaged in such manufacture or distribution of motor vehicles, and shall be prima facie evidence of the fact that such person so engaged in the manufacture or distribution of motor vehicles has sold or intends to sell the same on the condition or with the agreement or understanding prohibited in section 12-6-202.

12-6-205. Offering consideration to eliminate competition. It is unlawful for any person who is engaged, directly or indirectly, in the manufacture or wholesale distribution only of motor vehicles, whether patented or unpatented, to pay or give, or contract to pay or give, any thing or service of value to any person who is engaged in the business of financing the purchase or sale of motor vehicles or of buying conditional sales contracts, chattel mortgages, or leases on motor vehicles sold at retail within this state if the effect of any such payment or the giving of any such thing or service of value may be to lessen or eliminate competition, or tend to create or create a monopoly in the person or class of persons who receive or accept such thing or service of value.

12-6-206. Accepting consideration to eliminate competition. It is unlawful for any person who is engaged in the business of financing the purchase or sale of motor vehicles or of buying conditional sales contracts, chattel mortgages, or leases on motor vehicles sold at retail within this state to accept or receive, or contract or agree to accept or receive, either directly or indirectly, any payment, thing, or service of value from any person who is engaged, either directly or indirectly, in the manufacture of or wholesale distribution only of motor vehicles, whether patented or unpatented, if the effect of the acceptance or receipt of any such payment, thing, or service of value may be to lessen or eliminate competition, or to create or tend to create a monopoly in the person who accepts or receives such payment, thing, or service of value or contracts or agrees to accept or receive the same.

12-6-207. Recipient of consideration shall not buy mortgages. It is unlawful for any person who hereafter so accepts or receives, either directly or indirectly, any payment, thing, or service of value, as set forth in section 12-6-206, or contracts, either directly or indirectly, to receive any such payment, or thing, or service of value to thereafter finance or attempt to finance the purchase or sale of any motor vehicle or buy or attempt to buy any conditional sales contracts, chattel mortgages, or leases on motor vehicles sold at retail in this state.

12-6-208. Quo warranto action. For a violation of any of the provisions of this part 2 by any corporation or association mentioned in this part 2, it is the duty of the attorney general or the district attorney of the proper county to institute proper suits or an action in the nature of quo warranto in any court of competent jurisdiction for the forfeiture of its charter rights, franchises, or privileges and powers exercised by such corporation or association, and for the dissolution of the same under the general statutes of the state.

12-6-209. Violation by foreign corporation - penalty. Every foreign corporation and every foreign association exercising any of the powers, franchises, or functions of a corporation in this state violating any of the provisions of this part 2 is denied the right and prohibited from doing any business in this state, and it is the duty of the attorney general to enforce this provision by bringing proper proceedings by injunction or otherwise. The secretary of state is authorized to revoke the license of any such corporation or association heretofore authorized by him to do business in this state.

12-6-210. Penalty. Any person who violates any of the provisions of this part 2, any person who is a party to any agreement or understanding, or to any contract prescribing any condition, prohibited by this part 2, and any employee, agent, or officer of any such person who participates, in any manner, in making, executing, enforcing, or performing, or in urging, aiding, or abetting in the performance of, any such contract, condition, agreement, or understanding and any person who pays or gives or contracts to pay or give any thing or service of value prohibited by this part 2, and any person who receives or accepts or contracts to receive or accept any thing or service of value prohibited by this part 2 commits a class 6 felony and shall be punished as provided in section 18-1.3-401, C.R.S. Each day's violation of this provision shall constitute a separate offense.

12-6-211. Contract void. Any contract or agreement in violation of the provisions of this part 2 shall be absolutely void and shall not be enforceable either in law or equity.

12-6-212. Provisions cumulative. The provisions of this part 2 shall be held cumulative of each other and of all other laws in any way affecting them now in force in this state.

12-6-213. Damages. In addition to the criminal and civil penalties provided in this part 2, any person who is injured in his business or property by any other person or corporation or association or partnership, by reason of any thing forbidden or declared to be unlawful by this part 2, may sue therefor in any court having jurisdiction thereof in the county where the defendant resides or is found, or any agent resides or is found, or where service may be obtained, without respect to the amount of controversy, and to recover twofold the damages sustained by him, and the costs of suit. When it appears to the court before which any proceedings under this part 2 are pending that the ends of justice require that other parties shall be brought before the court, the court may cause them to be made parties defendant and summoned, whether they reside in the county where such action is pending or not.

PART 3

SUNDAY CLOSING LAW

12-6-301. Definitions. As used in this part 3, unless the context otherwise requires:

(1) "Motor vehicle" means every self-propelled vehicle intended primarily for use and operation on the public highways and every vehicle intended primarily for operation on the public highways which is not driven or propelled by its own power, but which is designed either to be attached to or become a part of a self-propelled vehicle; it does not include farm tractors and other machines and tools used in the production, harvesting, and care of farm products.

12-6-302. Sunday closing. No person, firm, or corporation, whether owner, proprietor, agent, or employee, shall keep open, operate, or assist in keeping open or operating any place or premises or residences, whether open or closed, for the purpose of selling, bartering, or exchanging or offering for sale, barter, or exchange any motor vehicle, whether new, used, or secondhand, on the first day of the week commonly called Sunday. This part 3 shall not apply to the opening of an establishment or place of business on the said first day of the week for other purposes, such as the sale of petroleum products, tires, or automobile accessories, or for the purpose of operating and conducting a motor vehicle repair shop, or for the purpose of supplying such services as towing or wrecking. The provisions of this part 3 shall not apply to the opening of an establishment or place of business on the said first day of the week for the purpose of selling, bartering, or exchanging or offering for sale, barter, or exchange any boat, boat trailer, snowmobile, or snowmobile trailer.

12-6-303. Penalties. Any person, firm, partnership, or corporation who violates any of the provisions of this part 3 is guilty of a misdemeanor and, upon conviction thereof, shall be punished by a fine of not less than seventy-five dollars nor more than one thousand dollars, or by imprisonment in the county jail for not more than six months, or the court, in its discretion, may suspend or revoke the Colorado motor vehicle dealer's license issued under the provisions of part 1 of this article, or by such fine and imprisonment and suspension or revocation.

PART 4

EVENT DATA RECORDERS

12-6-401. Definitions. As used in this part 4, unless the context otherwise requires:

(1) "Event data" means records of one or more of the following categories of information concerning a motor vehicle, which records are captured by an event data recorder:
  (a) Whether the vehicle's air bag deployed;
  (b) Vehicle speed;
  (c) Vehicle direction;
  (d) Vehicle location;
  (e) Vehicle steering performance or use;
  (f) Vehicle brake performance or use; or
  (g) Vehicle seatbelt status or use.

(2) "Event data recorder" means a device or feature that is installed by the manufacturer of a motor vehicle for the purpose of capturing or transmitting retrievable event data.

(3) "Owner" means:
  (a) A person having all the incidents of ownership of a motor vehicle, including legal title to the motor vehicle, regardless of whether the person lends, rents, or creates a security interest in the vehicle;
  (b) A person entitled to possession of a motor vehicle as the purchaser under a security agreement; or
  (c) A person entitled to possession of a vehicle as lessee under a written lease agreement if the lease agreement is intended to last for more than three months at its inception.

(4) "Owner's agent" means a natural person authorized by the owner within the last thirty days or the owner's representative as defined by section 13-20-702 (3), C.R.S.

12-6-402. Event data recorders. (1) A manufacturer of a motor vehicle that is sold or leased in Colorado with an event data recorder shall in bold-faced type disclose, in the owner's manual, that the vehicle is so equipped and, if so, the type of data recorded. A disclosure made by means of an insert into the owner's manual shall be deemed a disclosure in the owner's manual.

(2) Event data that is recorded on an event data recorder is the personal information of the motor vehicle's owner, and therefore, such information shall not be retrieved by a person who is not the owner of the motor vehicle, except in the following circumstances:
  (a) The owner of the motor vehicle or the owner's agent has consented to the retrieval of the data within the last thirty days;
  (b) The data is retrieved by a motor vehicle dealer or by an automotive technician to diagnose, service, or repair the motor vehicle at the request of the owner or the owner's agent;
  (c) The data is subject to discovery pursuant to the rules of civil procedure in a claim arising out of a motor vehicle accident;

(d) A court or administrative agency having jurisdiction orders the data to be retrieved;

(e) The event data recorder is installed after the manufacturer or motor vehicle dealer sells the motor vehicle; or

(f) A peace officer retrieves the data pursuant to a court order as part of an investigation of a suspected violation of a law that has caused, or contributed to the cause of, an accident resulting in damage of property or injury to a person.

(3) (a) No person shall release event data unless authorized by paragraph (b) of this subsection (3).

(b) A person authorized to download or retrieve data from an event data recorder may release such data in the following circumstances:

(I) The owner of the motor vehicle or the owner's agent has consented to the release of the data within the last thirty days;

(II) The data is subject to discovery pursuant to the rules of civil procedure in a claim arising out of a motor vehicle accident;

(III) The data is released pursuant to a court order as part of an investigation of a suspected violation of a law that has caused, or contributed to the cause of, an accident resulting in appreciable damage of property or injury to a person;

(IV) If the identity of the owner or driver is not disclosed, the data is released to a motor vehicle safety and medical research entity in order to advance motor vehicle safety, security, or traffic management; or

(V) The data is released to a data processor solely for the purposes permitted by this section if the identity of the owner or driver is not disclosed.

(4) (a) If a motor vehicle is equipped with an event data recorder that is capable of recording or transmitting event data that is part of a subscription service, the fact that the data may be recorded or transmitted and instructions for discontinuing the subscription service or for disabling the event data recorder by a trained service technician shall be prominently disclosed in the subscription service agreement. A disclosure made by means of an insert into the service agreement shall be deemed a disclosure in the service agreement.

(b) Subsections (2) and (3) of this section shall not apply to subscription services meeting the requirements of paragraph (a) of this subsection (4).

(5) A person who violates subsection (2) or (3) of this section commits a class 1 misdemeanor and shall be punished as provided in section 18-1.3-501, C.R.S.

12-6-403. Applicability. This part 4 shall apply to motor vehicles manufactured on or after May 1, 2007.

ARTICLE 15

Commercial Driving Schools

12-15-101. Definitions.
12-15-102. License required. (Repealed)
12-15-103. Application - fee. (Repealed)
12-15-104. Qualifications for commercial driving schools. (Repealed)
12-15-105. Issuance of license. (Repealed)
12-15-106. Expiration of license - renewal - fee. (Repealed)
12-15-107. Commercial driving instructor license required. (Repealed)
12-15-108. Qualifications of commercial driving instructors. (Repealed)
12-15-109. Application for license - fee. (Repealed)
12-15-110. Examinations required. (Repealed)
12-15-111. License issues. (Repealed)
12-15-112. Possession and display requirements. (Repealed)
12-15-113. Expiration of license - renewal - fee. (Repealed)
12-15-114. Equipment of vehicles.
12-15-115. Registration and inspection. (Repealed)
12-15-115.1. Registration and inspection. (Repealed)
12-15-116. Rules and regulations.
12-15-117. Refusal to issue or renew or suspension or revocation of licenses - grounds. (Repealed)
12-15-118. Procedure - judicial review. (Repealed)
12-15-119. Department to be informed of cancellation of insurance. (Repealed)
12-15-120. Violations - penalty.
12-15-121. Repeal - review of functions. (Repealed)

12-15-101. Definitions. As used in this article, unless the context otherwise requires:

(1) "Clock hour" means a full hour consisting of sixty minutes.

(2) "Commercial driving instructor" means an individual who has been employed by a commercial driving school.

(3) "Commercial driving school" means any business or any person who, for compensation, provides or offers to provide instruction in the operation of a motor vehicle, with the exceptions of secondary schools and institutions of higher education offering programs approved by the department of education and private occupational schools offering programs approved by the private occupational school division. Such term shall not include any motorcycle operator safety training program established pursuant to section 43-5-502, C.R.S.

(4) "Department" means the department of revenue.

(5) "Laboratory instruction" means an extension of classroom instruction which provides students with opportunities for traffic experiences under real and simulated conditions.

(6) Repealed.

12-15-102. License required. (Repealed)

12-15-103. Application - fee. (Repealed)

12-15-104. Qualifications for commercial driving schools. (Repealed)

12-15-105. Issuance of license. (Repealed)

12-15-106. Expiration of license - renewal - fee. (Repealed)

12-15-107. Commercial driving instructor license required. (Repealed)

12-15-108. Qualifications of commercial driving instructors. (Repealed)

12-15-109. Application for license - fee. (Repealed)

12-15-110. Examinations required. (Repealed)

12-15-111. License issues. (Repealed)

12-15-112. Possession and display requirements. (Repealed)

12-15-113. Expiration of license - renewal - fee. (Repealed)

12-15-114. Equipment of vehicles. (1) Every motor vehicle used by a commercial driving school in the conduct of its course of driver training shall be equipped as follows:

(a) The vehicle shall be equipped as provided in article 4 of title 42, C.R.S.

(b) The vehicle shall be equipped with dual controls on the foot brake that will enable the commercial driving instructor to bring the car under control in case of emergency.

(c) The vehicle shall have an outside rear vision mirror on the commercial driving instructor's side of the vehicle.

(d) The vehicle shall be equipped with four-way emergency flashers.

(e) (Deleted by amendment, L. 2003, p. 862, § 2, effective August 6, 2003.)

(f) The vehicle shall be equipped with seat belts for the operator of the vehicle and for the commercial driving instructor.

12-15-115. Registration and inspection. (Repealed)

12-15-115.1. Registration and inspection. (Repealed)

12-15-116. Rules and regulations. (1) The department is authorized to promulgate such rules and regulations necessary to carry out the provisions of this article.

(2) Specifically, the department shall have power to adopt rules and regulations upon the following matters:

(a) Prescribe the content of courses of instruction;

(b) Prescribe the type of equipment to be used in said courses of instruction;

(c) Prescribe records to be kept by a commercial driving school;

(d) Prescribe the form of contracts and agreements used by commercial driving schools.

(3) In adopting such rules and regulations the department shall use the guidelines concerning commercial driving schools promulgated by the United States department of transportation.

(4) Rules and regulations adopted pursuant to this section shall be adopted in accordance with section 24-4-103, C.R.S.

12-15-117. Refusal to issue or renew or suspension or revocation of licenses - grounds. (Repealed)

12-15-118. Procedure - judicial review. (Repealed)

12-15-119. Department to be informed of cancellation of insurance. (Repealed)

12-15-120. Violations - penalty. Any person who violates any of the provisions of this article is guilty of a misdemeanor and, upon conviction thereof, shall be punished by a fine of not more than five hundred dollars, or by imprisonment in the county jail for not more than thirty days, or by both such fine and imprisonment.

12-15-121. Repeal - review of functions. (Repealed)

TITLE 24
GOVERNMENT - STATE

TITLE 24

GOVERNMENT - STATE

Cross references: For elections, see title 1; for peace officers and firefighters, see article 5 of title 29; for state engineer, see article 80 of title 37; for state chemist, see part 4 of article 1 of title 25; for offenses against government, see article 8 of title 18; for the "Uniform Records Retention Act", see article 17 of title 6.

INTERSTATE COMPACTS AND AGREEMENTS

Art. 60. Interstate Compacts and Agreements, 24-60-901 to 24-60-912; 24-60-1101 to 24-60-1107; 24-60-2101 to 24-60-2104.

INTERSTATE COMPACTS AND AGREEMENTS

ARTICLE 60

Interstate Compacts and Agreements

PART 9
VEHICLE EQUIPMENT
SAFETY COMPACT

24-60-901. Legislative declaration.
24-60-902. Compact approved and ratified.
24-60-903. Approval of compact.
24-60-904. Commissioner appointed - alternate.
24-60-905. Retirement benefits.
24-60-906. Other agencies cooperate.
24-60-907. State contribution limited.
24-60-908. Compact effective - when.
24-60-909. Filing of documents.
24-60-910. Budget submitted.
24-60-911. Inspection of accounts.
24-60-912. Governor executive head.

PART 11
DRIVER LICENSE COMPACT

24-60-1101. Compact approved and ratified.
24-60-1102. Definition of "licensing authority".
24-60-1103. Compact administrator - expenses.
24-60-1104. Executive head - definition.
24-60-1105. Offenses - assessment of points.
24-60-1106. Operator's license under compact.
24-60-1107. Review by district court.

PART 21
NONRESIDENT VIOLATOR COMPACT

24-60-2101. Compact approved and ratified.
24-60-2102. Licensing authority - definition.
24-60-2103. Compact administrator - expenses.
24-60-2104. Jurisdiction executive - definition.

PART 9
VEHICLE EQUIPMENT SAFETY
COMPACT

24-60-901. Legislative declaration. (1) The general assembly finds that:

(a) The public safety necessitates the continuous development, modernization, and implementation of standards and requirements of law relating to vehicle equipment in accordance with expert knowledge and opinion;

(b) The public safety further requires that such standards and requirements be uniform from jurisdiction to jurisdiction, except to the extent that specific and compelling evidence supports variation;

(c) The executive director of the department of revenue, acting upon recommendations of the vehicle equipment safety commission and pursuant to the vehicle equipment safety compact, provides a just, equitable, and orderly means of promoting the public safety in the manner and within the scope contemplated by this part 9.

24-60-902. Compact approved and ratified. The general assembly hereby approves and ratifies and the governor shall enter into a compact on behalf of the state of Colorado with any of the United States or other jurisdictions legally joining therein in the form substantially as follows:

ARTICLE I

Findings and Purpose

(a) The party states find that:

(1) Accidents and deaths on their streets and highways present a very serious human and economic problem with a major deleterious effect on the public welfare.

(2) There is a vital need for the development of greater interjurisdictional cooperation to achieve the necessary uniformity in the laws, rules, regulations and codes relating to vehicle equipment, and to accomplish this by such means as will minimize the time between the development of demonstrably and scientifically sound safety features and their incorporation into vehicles.

(b) The purposes of this compact are to:

(1) Promote uniformity in regulation of and standards for equipment.

(2) Secure uniformity of law and administrative practice in vehicular regulation and related safety standards to permit incorporation of desirable equipment changes in vehicles in the interest of greater traffic safety.

(3) To provide means for the encouragement and utilization of research which will facilitate the achievement of the foregoing purposes, with due regard for the findings set forth in subdivision (a) of this article.

(c) It is the intent of this compact to emphasize performance requirements and not to determine the specific detail of engineering in the manufacture of vehicles or equipment except to the extent necessary for the meeting of such performance requirements.

ARTICLE II
Definitions

As used in this compact:

(a) "Vehicle" means every device in, upon or by which any person or property is or may be transported or drawn upon a highway, excepting devices moved by human power or used exclusively upon stationary rails or tracks.

(b) "State" means a state, territory or possession of the United States, the District of Columbia, or the Commonwealth of Puerto Rico.

(c) "Equipment" means any part of a vehicle or any accessory for use thereon which affects the safety of operation of such vehicle or the safety of the occupants.

ARTICLE III
The Commission

(a) There is hereby created an agency of the party states to be known as the "Vehicle Equipment Safety Commission" hereinafter called the commission. The commission shall be composed of one commissioner from each party state who shall be appointed, serve and be subject to removal in accordance with the laws of the state which he represents. If authorized by the laws of his party state, a commissioner may provide for the discharge of his duties and the performance of his functions on the commission, either for the duration of his membership or for any lesser period of time, by an alternate. No such alternate shall be entitled to serve unless notification of his identity and appointment shall have been given to the commission in such form as the commission may require. Each commissioner, and each alternate, when serving in the place and stead of a commissioner, shall be entitled to be reimbursed by the commission for expenses actually incurred in attending commission meetings or while engaged in the business of the commission.

(b) The commissioners shall be entitled to one vote each on the commission. No action of the commission shall be binding unless taken at a meeting at which a majority of the total number of votes on the commission are cast in favor thereof. Action of the commission shall be only at a meeting at which a majority of the commissioners, or their alternates, are present.

(c) The commission shall have a seal.

(d) The commission shall elect annually, from among its members, a chairman, a vice-chairman and a treasurer. The commission may appoint an executive director and fix his duties and compensation. Such executive director shall serve at the pleasure of the commission, and together with the treasurer shall be bonded in such amount as the commission shall determine. The executive director also shall serve as secretary. If there be no executive director, the commission shall elect a secretary in addition to the other officers provided by this subdivision.

(e) Irrespective of the civil service, personnel or other merit system laws of any of the party states, the executive director with the approval of the commission, or the commission if there be no executive director, shall appoint, remove or discharge such personnel as may be necessary for the performance of the commission's functions, and shall fix the duties and compensation of such personnel.

(f) The commission may establish and maintain independently or in conjunction with any one or more of the party states, a suitable retirement system for its full time employees. Employees of the commission shall be eligible for social security coverage in respect of old age and survivor's insurance provided that the commission takes such steps as may be necessary pursuant to the laws of the United States, to participate in such program of insurance as a governmental agency or unit. The commission may establish and maintain or participate in such additional programs of employee benefits as may be appropriate.

(g) The commission may borrow, accept or contract for the services of personnel from any party state, the United States, or any subdivision or agency of the aforementioned governments, or from any agency of two or more of the party states or their subdivisions.

(h) The commission may accept for any of its purposes and functions under this compact any and all donations, and grants of money, equipment, supplies, materials, and services, conditional or otherwise, from any state, the United States, or any other governmental agency and may receive, utilize and dispose of the same.

(i) The commission may establish and maintain such facilities as may be necessary for the transacting of its business. The commission may acquire, hold, and convey real and personal property and any interest therein.

(j) The commission shall adopt bylaws for the conduct of its business and shall have the power to amend and rescind these bylaws. The commission shall publish its bylaws in convenient form and shall file a copy thereof and a copy of any amendment thereto, with the appropriate agency or officer in each of the party states. The bylaws shall provide for appropriate notice to the commissioners of all commission meetings and hearings and the business to be transacted at such meetings or hearings. Such notice shall also be given to such agencies or officers of each party state as the laws of such party state may provide.

(k) The commission annually shall make to the governor and legislature of each party state a report covering the activities of the commission for the preceding year, and embodying such recommendations as may have been issued by the commission. The commission may make such additional reports as it may deem desirable.

ARTICLE IV
Research and Testing

The commission shall have power to:

(a) Collect, correlate, analyze and evaluate information resulting or derivable from research and testing activities in equipment and related fields.

(b) Recommend and encourage the undertaking of research and testing in any aspect of equipment or related matters when, in its judgment, appropriate or sufficient research or testing has not been undertaken.

(c) Contract for such equipment research and testing as one or more governmental agencies may agree to have contracted for by the commission, provided that such governmental agency or agencies shall make available the funds necessary for such research and testing.

(d) Recommend to the party states changes in law or policy with emphasis on uniformity of laws and administrative rules, regulations or codes which would promote effective governmental action or coordination in the prevention of equipment-related highway accidents or the mitigation of equipment-related highway safety problems.

ARTICLE V
Vehicular Equipment

(a) In the interest of vehicular and public safety, the commission may study the need for or desirability of the establishment of or changes in performance requirements or restrictions for any item of equipment. As a result of such study, the commission may publish a report relating to any item or items of equipment, and the issuance of such a report shall be a condition precedent to any proceedings or other action provided or authorized by this article. No less than sixty days after the publication of a report containing the results of such study, the commission upon due notice shall hold a hearing or hearings at such place or places as it may determine.

(b) Following the hearing or hearings provided for in subdivision (a) of this article, and with due regard for standards recommended by appropriate professional and technical associations and agencies, the commission may issue rules, regulations or codes embodying performance requirements or restrictions for any item or items of equipment covered in the report, which in the opinion of the commission will be fair and equitable and effectuate the purposes of this compact.

(c) Each party state obligates itself to give due consideration to any and all rules, regulations and codes issued by the commission and hereby declares its policy and intent to be the promotion of uniformity in the laws of the several party states relating to equipment.

(d) The commission shall send prompt notice of its action in issuing any rule, regulation or code pursuant to this article to the appropriate motor vehicle agency of each party state and such notice shall contain the complete text of the rule, regulation or code.

(e) If the constitution of a party state requires, or if its statutes provide, the approval of the legislature by appropriate resolution or act may be made a condition precedent to the taking effect in such party state of any rule, regulation or code. In such event, the commissioner of such party state shall submit any commission rule, regulation or code to the legislature as promptly as may be in lieu of administrative acceptance or rejection thereof by the party state.

(f) Except as otherwise specifically provided in or pursuant to subdivisions (e) and (g) of this article, the appropriate motor vehicle agency of a party state shall in accordance with its constitution or procedural laws adopt the rule, regulation or code within six months of the sending of the notice, and, upon such adoption, the rule, regulation or code shall have the force and effect of law therein.

(g) The appropriate motor vehicle agency of a party state may decline to adopt a rule, regulation or code issued by the commission pursuant to this article if such agency specifically finds, after public hearing on due notice, that a variation from the commission's rule, regulation or code is necessary to the public safety, and incorporates in such finding the reasons upon which it is based. Any such finding shall be subject to review by such procedure for review of administrative determinations as may be applicable pursuant to the laws of the party state. Upon request, the commission shall be furnished with a copy of the transcript of any hearings held pursuant to this subdivision.

ARTICLE VI
Finance

(a) The commission shall submit to the executive head or designated officer or officers of each party state a budget of its estimated expenditures for such period as may be required by the laws of that party state for presentation to the legislature thereof.

(b) Each of the commission's budgets of estimated expenditures shall contain specific recommendations of the amount or amounts to be appropriated by each of the party states. The total amount of appropriations under any such budget shall be apportioned among the party states as follows: One-third in equal shares; and the remainder in proportion to the number of motor vehicles registered in each party state. In determining the number of such registrations, the commission may employ such source or sources of information as, in its judgment present the most equitable and accurate comparisons among the party states. Each of the commission's budgets of estimated expenditures and requests for appropriations shall indicate the source or sources used in obtaining information concerning vehicular registrations.

(c) The commission shall not pledge the credit of any party state. The commission may meet any of its obligations in whole or in part with funds available to it under article III (h) of this compact, provided that the commission takes specific action setting aside such funds prior to incurring any obligation to be met in whole or in part in such manner. Except where the commission makes use of funds available to it under article III (h) hereof, the commission shall not incur any obligation prior to the allotment of funds by the party states adequate to meet the same.

(d) The commission shall keep accurate accounts of all receipts and disbursements. The receipts and disbursements of the commission shall be subject to the audit and accounting procedures established under its rules. However, all receipts and disbursements of funds handled by the commission shall be audited yearly by a qualified public accountant and the report of the audit shall be included in and become part of the annual reports of the commission.

(e) The accounts of the commission shall be open at any reasonable time for inspection by duly constituted officers of the party states and by any persons authorized by the commission.

(f) Nothing contained herein shall be construed to prevent commission compliance with laws relating to audit or inspection of accounts by or on behalf of any government contributing to the support of the commission.

ARTICLE VII
Conflict of Interest

(a) The commission shall adopt rules and regulations with respect to conflict of interest for the commissioners of the party states, and their alternates, if any, and for the staff of the commission and contractors with the commission to the end that no member or employee or contractor shall have a pecuniary or other incompatible interest in the manufacture, sale or distribution of motor vehicles or vehicular equipment or in any facility or enterprise employed by the commission or on its behalf for testing, conduct of investigations or research. In addition to any penalty for violation of such rules and regulations as may be applicable under the laws of the violator's jurisdiction of residence, employment or business, any violation of a commission rule or regulation adopted pursuant to this article shall require the immediate discharge of any violating employee and the immediate vacating of membership, or relinquishing of status as a member on the commission by any commissioner or alternate. In the case of a contractor, any violation of any such rule or regulation shall make any contract of the violator with the commission subject to cancellation by the commission.

(b) Nothing contained in this article shall be deemed to prevent a contractor for the commission from using any facilities subject to his control in the performance of the contract even though such facilities are not devoted solely to work of or done on behalf of the commission; nor to prevent such a contractor from receiving remuneration or profit from the use of such facilities.

ARTICLE VIII
Advisory and Technical Committees

The commission may establish such advisory and technical committees as it may deem necessary, membership on which may include private citizens and public officials, and may cooperate with and use the services of any such committees and the organizations which the members represent in furthering any of its activities.

ARTICLE IX
Entry Into Force and Withdrawal

(a) This compact shall enter into force when enacted into law by any six or more states. Thereafter, this compact shall become effective as to any other state upon its enactment thereof.

(b) Any party state may withdraw from this compact by enacting a statute repealing the same, but no such withdrawal shall take effect until one year after the executive head of the withdrawing state has given notice in writing of the withdrawal to the executive heads of all other party states. No withdrawal shall affect any liability already incurred by or chargeable to a party state prior to the time of such withdrawal.

ARTICLE X
Construction and Severability

This compact shall be liberally construed so as to effectuate the purposes thereof. The provisions of this compact shall be severable and if any phrase, clause, sentence or provision of this compact is declared to be contrary to the Constitution of any state or of the United States or the applicability thereof to any government, agency, person or circumstance is held invalid, the validity of the remainder of this compact and the applicability thereof to any government, agency, person, or circumstance shall not be affected thereby. If this compact shall be held contrary to the constitution of any state participating herein, the compact shall remain in full force and effect as to the remaining party states and in full force and effect as to the state affected as to all severable matters.

24-60-903. Approval of compact. Pursuant to article V (e) of the vehicle equipment safety compact, it is the intention of this state and it is provided that no rule, regulation, or code issued by the vehicle equipment safety commission in accordance with article V of the compact shall take effect until approved by act of the general assembly.

24-60-904. Commissioner appointed - alternate. The commissioner of this state serving on the vehicle equipment safety commission shall be appointed by the governor from among the members of the legislative council, consistent with the provisions of section 2-3-311, C.R.S. The commissioner of this state, appointed pursuant to this section, may designate the executive director of the department of revenue to serve in his place and stead on the vehicle equipment safety commission. Subject to the provisions of the compact and bylaws of the vehicle equipment safety commission, the authority and responsibilities of the alternate shall be as determined by the commissioner designating such alternate.

24-60-905. Retirement benefits. The public employees' retirement association may make an agreement with the vehicle equipment safety commission for the coverage of said commission's employees pursuant to article III (f) of the compact. Any such agreement, as nearly as may be, shall provide for arrangements similar to those available to the employees of this state and shall be subject to amendment or termination in accordance with its terms.

24-60-906. Other agencies cooperate. Within appropriations available therefor, the departments, agencies, and officers of the government of this state may cooperate with and assist the vehicle equipment safety commission within the scope contemplated by article III (h) of the compact. The departments, agencies, and officers of the government of this state are authorized generally to cooperate with said commission.

24-60-907. State contribution limited. In no event shall the contribution of the state of Colorado exceed two thousand dollars as its share of the commission's budget.

24-60-908. Compact effective - when. Notwithstanding the provisions of article IX (a) of the compact, the participation of the state of Colorado in the compact shall not become effective until twenty-four or more states have enacted this compact into law; except that if twelve or more states have enacted this compact into law, then, upon request of the commissioner of the state vehicle equipment safety commission, the governor may enter into this compact on behalf of the state of Colorado.

24-60-909. Filing of documents. Filing of documents as required by article III (j) of the compact shall be with the executive director of the department of revenue.

24-60-910. Budget submitted. Pursuant to article VI (a) of the compact, the vehicle equipment safety commission shall submit its budgets to the executive director of the department of revenue for recommendation and submission to the office of state planning and budgeting pursuant to part 3 of article 37 of this title.

24-60-911. Inspection of accounts. Pursuant to article VI (e) of the compact, the executive director of the department of revenue may inspect the accounts of the vehicle equipment safety commission.

24-60-912. Governor executive head. The term "executive head" as used in article IX (b) of the compact shall, with reference to this state, mean the governor.

PART 11

DRIVER LICENSE COMPACT

24-60-1101. Compact approved and ratified. The general assembly hereby approves and ratifies and the governor shall enter into a compact on behalf of the state of Colorado with any of the United States or other jurisdictions legally joining therein in the form substantially as follows:

ARTICLE I
Findings and Declaration of Policy

(a) The party states find that:
(1) The safety of their streets and highways is materially affected by the degree of compliance with state laws and local ordinances relating to the operation of motor vehicles.
(2) Violation of such a law or ordinance is evidence that the violator engages in conduct which is likely to endanger the safety of persons and property.
(3) The continuance in force of a license to drive is predicated upon compliance with laws and ordinances relating to the operation of motor vehicles, in whichever jurisdiction the vehicle is operated.
(b) It is the policy of each of the party states to:
(1) Promote compliance with the laws, ordinances, and administrative rules and regulations relating to the operation of motor vehicles by their operators in each of the jurisdictions where such operators drive motor vehicles.
(2) Make the reciprocal recognition of licenses to drive and eligibility therefor more just and equitable by considering the over-all compliance with motor vehicle laws, ordinances and administrative rules and regulations as a condition precedent to the continuance or issuance of any license by reason of which the licensee is authorized or permitted to operate a motor vehicle in any of the party states.

ARTICLE II
Definitions

As used in this compact:

(a) "State" means a state, territory or possession of the United States, the District of Columbia, or the Commonwealth of Puerto Rico.

(b) "Home state" means the state which has issued and has the power to suspend or revoke the use of the license or permit to operate a motor vehicle.

(c) "Conviction" means a conviction of any offense related to the use or operation of a motor vehicle which is prohibited by state law, municipal ordinance or administrative rule or regulation, or a forfeiture of bail, bond or other security deposited to secure appearance by a person charged with having committed any such offense, and which conviction or forfeiture is required to be reported to the licensing authority.

ARTICLE III
Reports of Conviction

The licensing authority of a party state shall report each conviction of a person from another party state occurring within its jurisdiction to the licensing authority of the home state of the licensee. Such report shall clearly identify the person convicted; describe the violation specifying the section of the statute, code or ordinance violated; identify the court in which action was taken; indicate whether a plea of guilty or not guilty was entered, or the conviction was a result of the forfeiture of bail, bond or other security; and shall include any special findings made in connection therewith.

ARTICLE IV
Effect of Conviction

(a) The licensing authority in the home state, for the purposes of suspension, revocation or limitation of the license to operate a motor vehicle, shall give the same effect to the offense reported, pursuant to Article III of this compact, as it would if such offense had occurred in the home state, in the case of convictions for:

(1) Manslaughter or negligent homicide resulting from the operation of a motor vehicle;

(2) Driving a motor vehicle while under the influence of intoxicating liquor or a narcotic drug or under the influence of any other drug to a degree which renders the driver incapable of safely driving a motor vehicle;

(3) Any felony in the commission of which a motor vehicle is used;

(4) Failure to stop and render aid in the event of a motor vehicle accident resulting in the death or personal injury of another.

(b) As to other convictions, reported pursuant to Article III, the licensing authority in the home state shall give such effect to the offense as is provided by the laws of the home state.

(c) If the laws of a party state do not provide for offenses or violations denominated or described in precisely the words employed in subdivision (a) of this article, such party state shall construe the denominations and descriptions appearing in subdivision (a) hereof as being applicable to and identifying those offenses or violations of a substantially similar nature, and the laws of such party state shall contain such provisions as may be necessary to ensure that full force and effect is given to this article.

ARTICLE V
Applications for New Licenses

Upon application for a license to drive, the licensing authority in a party state shall ascertain whether the applicant has ever held, or is the holder of a license to drive issued by any other party state. The licensing authority in the state where application is made shall not issue a license to drive to the applicant if:

(1) The applicant has held such a license, but the same has been suspended by reason, in whole or in part, of a conviction for a violation and if such suspension period has not terminated.

(2) The applicant has held such a license, but the same has been revoked by reason, in whole or in part, of a conviction for a violation and if such revocation has not terminated, except that after the expiration of one year from the date the license was revoked, such person may make application for a new license if permitted by Colorado law. The licensing authority may refuse to issue a license to any such applicant if, after investigation, the licensing authority determines that it will not be safe to grant to such person the privilege of driving a motor vehicle on the public highways.

(3) The applicant is the holder of a license to drive issued by another party state and currently in force unless the applicant surrenders such license.

ARTICLE VI
Applicability of Other Laws

Except as expressly required by provisions of this compact, nothing contained herein shall be construed to affect the right of any party to apply any of its other laws relating to licenses to drive to any person or circumstance, nor to invalidate or prevent any driver license agreement or other cooperative arrangement between a party state and a nonparty state.

ARTICLE VII
Compact Administrator and Interchange of Information

(a) The head of the licensing authority of each party state shall be the administrator of this compact for his state. The administrators, acting jointly, shall have the power to formulate all necessary and proper procedures for the exchange of information under this compact.

(b) The administrator of each party state shall furnish to the administrator of each other party state any information or documents reasonably necessary to facilitate the administration of this compact.

ARTICLE VIII
Entry Into Force and Withdrawal

(a) This compact shall enter into force and become effective as to any state when it has enacted the same into law.

(b) Any party state may withdraw from this compact by enacting a statute repealing the same, but no such withdrawal shall take effect until six months after the executive head of the withdrawing state has given notice of the withdrawal to the executive heads of all other party states. No withdrawal shall affect the validity or applicability by the licensing authorities of states remaining party to the compact of any report of conviction occurring prior to the withdrawal.

ARTICLE IX
Construction and Severability

This compact shall be liberally construed so as to effectuate the purposes thereof. The provisions of this compact shall be severable and if any phrase, clause, sentence or provision of this compact is declared to be contrary to the constitution of any party state or of the United States or the applicability thereof to any government, agency, person or circumstance is held invalid, the validity of the remainder of this compact and the applicability thereof to any government, agency, person or circumstance shall not be affected thereby. If this compact shall be held contrary to the constitution of any state party thereto, the compact shall remain in full force and effect as to the remaining states and in full force and effect as to the state affected as to all severable matters.

24-60-1102. Definition of "licensing authority". (1) As used in the compact, the term "licensing authority", with reference to this state, means the executive director of the department of revenue. Said executive director shall furnish to the appropriate authorities of any other party state any information or documents reasonably necessary to facilitate the administration of articles III, IV, and V of the compact.

(2) The executive director of the department of revenue is authorized to administer the provisions of any driver license compact entered into between the state of Colorado and any other state and shall enforce any provisions thereof relative to licenses to operate motor vehicles issued by the department of revenue.

24-60-1103. Compact administrator - expenses. The compact administrator provided for in article VII of the compact shall not be entitled to any additional compensation on account of his service as such administrator but shall be entitled to expenses incurred in connection with his duties and responsibilities as such administrator in the same manner as for expenses incurred in connection with any other duties or responsibilities of his office or employment.

24-60-1104. Executive head - definition. As used in the compact, with reference to this state, the term "executive head" means the governor.

24-60-1105. Offenses - assessment of points. (1) Those offenses described in article IV (a) of the compact refer only to the following: As specified in sections 42-2-128, 42-4-1301, and 42-4-1603, C.R.S. "Felony" as used in article IV (a) (3) means only an offense which if committed in this state would constitute a felony. No conviction in another state for an offense described in article IV (a) of the compact shall be considered in this state unless the executive director of the department of revenue has made a finding with respect thereto that the prerequisites to such conviction in such other state with respect to trial by jury, burden of proof, and elements of the offense are not less stringent than such prerequisites to conviction for such offense in this state.

(2) The executive director of the department of revenue shall not assess points against the operator's license of any driver because of convictions reported from other states under article IV (b) of the compact.

24-60-1106. Operator's license under compact. The provisions of sections 42-1-102 (81), 42-2-101 (1), and 42-2-102 (1) (d) and (1) (e), C.R.S., requiring residents of other states to secure an operator's license from this state shall not apply to persons licensed to drive by other states party to the driver license compact. This state shall require a resident to secure an operator's license from the department of revenue and to surrender any outstanding license to drive issued by another state; except that, if the laws of such other state require the person to be licensed to drive thereby in order to engage in such person's regular trade or profession, no license shall be issued by this state so long as such other license to drive is in force, nor shall this state issue any license to drive in contravention of the driver license compact.

24-60-1107. Review by district court. Any act or omission of any official or employee of this state done or omitted pursuant to or in enforcing the provisions of the driver license compact shall be subject to review by the district court in accordance with sections 24-4-106 and 42-2-135, C.R.S., and the Colorado rules of civil procedure.

PART 21

NONRESIDENT VIOLATOR COMPACT

24-60-2101. Compact approved and ratified. The general assembly hereby approves and ratifies and the governor shall enter into a compact on behalf of the state of Colorado with any of the United States or other jurisdictions legally joining therein in the form substantially as follows:

ARTICLE I

Findings, Declaration of Policy, and Purpose

(a) The party jurisdictions find that:

(1) In most instances, a motorist who is cited for a traffic violation in a jurisdiction other than his home jurisdiction:

(i) Must post collateral or bond to secure appearance for trial at a later date; or

(ii) If unable to post collateral or bond, is taken into custody until the collateral or bond is posted; or

(iii) Is taken directly to court for his trial to be held.

(2) In some instances, the motorist's driver's license may be deposited as collateral to be returned after he has complied with the terms of the citation.

(3) The purpose of the practices described in paragraphs (1) and (2) above is to ensure compliance with the terms of a traffic citation by the motorist who, if permitted to continue on his way after receiving the traffic citation, could return to his home jurisdiction and disregard his duty under the terms of the traffic citation.

(4) A motorist receiving a traffic citation in his home jurisdiction is permitted, except for certain violations, to accept the citation from the officer at the scene of the violation and to immediately continue on his way after promising or being instructed to comply with the terms of the citation.

(5) The practice described in paragraph (1) above causes unnecessary inconvenience and, at times, a hardship for the motorist who is unable at the time to post collateral, furnish a bond, stand trial, or pay the fine, and thus is compelled to remain in custody until some arrangement can be made.

(6) The deposit of a driver's license as a bail bond, as described in paragraph (2) above, is viewed with disfavor.

(7) The practices described herein consume an undue amount of law enforcement time.

(b) It is the policy of the party jurisdictions to:

(1) Seek compliance with the laws, ordinances, and administrative rules and regulations relating to the operation of motor vehicles in each of the jurisdictions.

(2) Allow motorists to accept a traffic citation for certain violations and proceed on their way without delay whether or not the motorist is a resident of the jurisdiction in which the citation was issued.

(3) Extend cooperation to its fullest extent among the jurisdictions for obtaining compliance with the terms of a traffic citation issued in one jurisdiction to a resident of another jurisdiction.

(4) Maximize effective utilization of law enforcement personnel and assist court systems in the efficient disposition of traffic violations.

(c) The purpose of this compact is to:

(1) Provide a means through which the party jurisdictions may participate in a reciprocal program to effectuate the policies enumerated in paragraph (b) above in a uniform and orderly manner.

(2) Provide for the fair and impartial treatment of traffic violators operating within party jurisdictions in recognition of the motorist's right of due process and the sovereign status of a party jurisdiction.

ARTICLE II

Definitions

As used in this compact, unless the context requires otherwise:

(a) "Citation" means any summons, ticket, or other official document issued by a police officer for a traffic violation containing an order which requires the motorist to respond.

(b) "Collateral" means any cash or other security deposited to secure an appearance for trial, following the issuance by a police officer of a citation for a traffic violation.

(c) "Compliance" means the act of answering a citation, summons or subpoena through appearance at court, a tribunal, and/or payment of fines and costs.

(d) "Court" means a court of law or traffic tribunal.

(e) "Driver's license" means any license or privilege to operate a motor vehicle issued under the laws of the home jurisdiction.

(f) "Home jurisdiction" means the jurisdiction that issued the driver's license of the traffic violator.

(g) "Issuing jurisdiction" means the jurisdiction in which the traffic citation was issued to the motorist.

(h) "Jurisdiction" means a state, territory, or possession of the United States, the District of Columbia, Commonwealth of Puerto Rico, Provinces of Canada, or other countries.

(i) "Motorist" means a driver of a motor vehicle operating in a party jurisdiction other than the home jurisdiction.

(j) "Personal recognizance" means an agreement by a motorist made at the time of issuance of the traffic citation that he will comply with the terms of that traffic citation.

(k) "Police officer" means any individual authorized by the party jurisdiction to issue a citation for a traffic violation.

(l) "Terms of the citation" means those options expressly stated upon the citation.

ARTICLE III
Procedure for Issuing Jurisdiction

(a) When issuing a citation for a traffic violation, a police officer shall issue the citation to a motorist who possesses a driver's license issued by a party jurisdiction and shall not, subject to the exceptions noted in paragraph (b) of this article, require the motorist to post collateral to secure appearance, if the officer receives the motorist's personal recognizance that he or she will comply with the terms of the citation.

(b) Personal recognizance is acceptable only if not prohibited by law. If mandatory appearance is required, it must take place immediately following issuance of the citation.

(c) Upon failure of a motorist to comply with the terms of a traffic citation, the appropriate official shall report the failure to comply to the licensing authority of the jurisdiction in which the traffic citation was issued. The report shall be made in accordance with procedures specified by the issuing jurisdiction and shall contain information as specified in the compact manual as minimum requirements for effective processing by the home jurisdiction.

(d) Upon receipt of the report, the licensing authority of the issuing jurisdiction shall transmit to the licensing authority in the home jurisdiction of the motorist, the information in a form and content as contained in the compact manual.

(e) The licensing authority of the issuing jurisdiction need not suspend the privilege of a motorist for whom a report has been transmitted.

(f) The licensing authority of the issuing jurisdiction shall not transmit a report on any violation if the date of transmission is more than six months after the date on which the traffic citation was issued.

(g) The licensing authority of the issuing jurisdiction shall not transmit a report on any violation where the date of issuance of the citation predates the most recent of the effective dates of entry for the two jurisdictions affected.

ARTICLE IV
Procedure for Home Jurisdiction

(a) Upon receipt of a report of a failure to comply from the licensing authority of the issuing jurisdiction, the licensing authority of the home jurisdiction shall notify the motorist and initiate a suspension action, in accordance with the home jurisdiction's procedures, to suspend the motorist's driver's license until satisfactory evidence of compliance with the terms of the traffic citation has been furnished to the home jurisdiction licensing authority. Due process safeguards will be accorded.

(b) The licensing authority of the home jurisdiction shall maintain a record of actions taken and make reports to issuing jurisdictions as provided in the compact manual.

ARTICLE V
Applicability of Other Laws

Except as expressly required by provisions of this compact, nothing contained herein shall be construed to affect the right of any party jurisdiction to apply any of its other laws relating to license to drive to any person or circumstance, or to invalidate or prevent any driver license agreement or other cooperative arrangements between a party jurisdiction and a nonparty jurisdiction.

ARTICLE VI
Compact Administrator Procedures

(a) For the purpose of administering the provisions of this compact and to serve as a governing body for the resolution of all matters relating to the operation of this compact, a board of compact administrators is established. The board shall be composed of one representative from each party jurisdiction to be known as the compact administrator. The compact administrator shall be appointed by the jurisdiction executive and will serve and be subject to removal in accordance with the laws of the jurisdiction he represents. A compact administrator may provide for the discharge of his duties and the performance of his functions as a board member by an alternate. An alternate may not be entitled to serve unless written notification of his identity has been given to the board.

(b) Each member of the board of compact administrators shall be entitled to one vote. No action of the board shall be binding unless taken at a meeting at which a majority of the total number of votes on the board are cast in favor. Action by the board shall be only at a meeting at which a majority of the party jurisdictions are represented.

(c) The board shall elect annually, from its membership, a chairman and vice chairman.

(d) The board shall adopt bylaws, not inconsistent with the provisions of this compact or the laws of a party jurisdiction, for the conduct of its business and shall have the power to amend and rescind its bylaws.

(e) The board may accept for any of its purposes and functions under this compact any and all donations, and grants of money, equipment, supplies, materials, and services, conditional or otherwise, from any jurisdiction, the United States, or any other governmental agency, and may receive, utilize and dispose of the same.

(f) The board may contract with, or accept services or personnel from any governmental or intergovernmental agency, person, firm, or corporation, or any private nonprofit organization or institution.

(g) The board shall formulate all necessary procedures and develop uniform forms and documents for administering the provisions of this compact. All procedures and forms adopted pursuant to board action shall be contained in the compact manual.

ARTICLE VII
Entry into Compact and Withdrawal

(a) This compact shall become effective when it has been adopted by at least two jurisdictions.

(b) (1) Entry into the compact shall be made by a resolution of ratification executed by the authorized officials of the applying jurisdiction and submitted to the chairman of the board.

(2) The resolution shall be in a form and content as provided in the compact manual and shall include statements that in substance are as follows:

(i) A citation of the authority by which the jurisdiction is empowered to become a party to this compact.

(ii) Agreement to comply with the terms and provisions of the compact.

(iii) That compact entry is with all jurisdictions then party to the compact and with any jurisdiction that legally becomes a party to the compact.

(3) The effective date of entry shall be specified by the applying jurisdiction, but it shall not be less than sixty days after notice has been given by the chairman of the board of compact administrators or by the secretariat of the board to each party jurisdiction that the resolution from the applying jurisdiction has been received.

(c) A party jurisdiction may withdraw from this compact by official written notice to the other party jurisdictions, but a withdrawal shall not take effect until ninety days after notice of withdrawal is given. The notice shall be directed to the compact administrator of each member jurisdiction. No withdrawal shall affect the validity of this compact as to the remaining party jurisdictions.

ARTICLE VIII
Exceptions

The provisions of this compact shall not apply to parking or standing violations, highway weight limit violations, and violations of law governing the transportation of hazardous materials.

ARTICLE IX
Amendments to the Compact

(a) This compact may be amended from time to time. Amendments shall be presented in resolution form to the chairman of the board of compact administrators and may be initiated by one or more party jurisdictions.

(b) Adoption of an amendment shall require endorsement of all party jurisdictions and shall become effective thirty days after the date of the last endorsement.

(c) Failure of a party jurisdiction to respond to the compact chairman within one hundred twenty days after receipt of the proposed amendment shall constitute endorsement.

ARTICLE X
Construction and Severability

This compact shall be liberally construed so as to effectuate the purposes stated herein. The provisions of this compact shall be severable and if any phrase, clause, sentence, or provision of this compact is declared to be contrary to the constitution of any party jurisdiction or of the United States or the applicability thereof to any government, agency, person, or circumstance is held invalid, the compact shall not be affected thereby. If this compact shall be held contrary to the constitution of any jurisdiction party thereto, the compact shall remain in full force and effect as to the remaining jurisdictions and in full force and effect as to the jurisdiction affected as to all severable matters.

ARTICLE XI
Title

This compact shall be known as the Nonresident Violator Compact of 1977.

24-60-2102. Licensing authority - definition. As used in the compact, the term "licensing authority", with reference to this state, means the executive director of the department of revenue. Said executive director shall furnish to the appropriate authorities of any other party jurisdiction any information or documents reasonably necessary to facilitate the administration of articles III and IV of the compact.

24-60-2103. Compact administrator - expenses. The compact administrator provided for in article VI of the compact shall not be entitled to any additional compensation on account of his service as such administrator but shall be entitled to expenses incurred in connection with his duties and responsibilities as such administrator in the same manner as for expenses incurred in connection with any other duties or responsibilities of his office or employment.

24-60-2104. Jurisdiction executive - definition. As used in the compact, with reference to this state, the term "jurisdiction executive" means the governor.

GENERAL INDEX

A to Z

A

ABANDONED VEHICLES
Disposition of personal property, §§42-13-101 to 42-13-109.
Tow away warnings, §42-4-1202.
Stopping, standing, and parking.
  Presumption of abandonment, §42-4-1202.
Towing and storage.
  Abandoned on private property, §42-4-2103.
    Appraisal, §42-4-2104.
    Certificates of title, §§42-4-2104, 42-4-2109.
    Definitions, §42-4-2102.
    Legislative declaration, §42-4-2101.
    Liens.
      Establishment of, §42-4-2105.
      Perfection, §42-4-2106.
    Notice and reports, §42-4-2103.
    Sale.
      Appraisal, §42-4-2104.
      Foreclosure, §42-4-2107.
      Procedure, §42-4-2103.
      Proceeds, §42-4-2108.
    Violations, §42-4-2110.
  Abandoned on public property, §42-4-1803.
    Appraisal, §42-4-1805.
    Certificates of title, §§42-4-1805, 42-4-1810.
    Definitions, §42-4-1802.
    Exemptions, §42-4-1812.
    Hearings, §42-4-1804.
    Legislative declaration, §42-4-1801.
    Liens.
      Establishment of, §42-4-1806.
      Foreclosure, §42-4-1808.
      Perfection, §42-4-1807.
    Local regulations, §42-4-1813.
    Reports, §42-4-1804.
    Sale.
      Appraisal, §42-4-1805.
      Foreclosure, §42-4-1808.
      Procedure, §42-4-1805.
      Proceeds, §42-4-1809.
    Violations, §42-4-1812.
  Certificates of title, §§42-4-1681, 42-4-1810, 42-4-2109.

ACCIDENTS - MOTOR VEHICLE
Arrests.
  Immediate appearance before judge, §42-4-1705.
Confidentiality of information, §42-4-1610.
Death.
  Blood samples from crash victims, §42-4-1304.
  Express consent to blood test, §42-4-1301.1.
Department of revenue.
  Publication of information, §42-1-208.
Divided highways.
  Duty to move vehicle off traveled portion of divided highway, §42-4-1602.
Drivers' licenses.
  See DRIVERS' LICENSES.

ACCIDENTS - MOTOR VEHICLE-Cont'd
Duty of driver to stop, §42-4-1601.
Duty to give information or render aid, §42-4-1603.
Duty to remove glass or other foreign material from street or highway, §42-4-1406.
  Suspension, §§42-7-301, 42-7-303.
Financial responsibility, §§42-7-301 to 42-7-303.
Highway fixtures or traffic control devices.
  Duty of driver upon striking, §42-4-1605.
Hit and run, §§42-2-125, 42-4-1601, 42-4-1602.
Moving vehicle off traveled portion of divided highway, §42-4-1602.
Police.
  Duty to report, §42-4-1606.
Publication of information by department of revenue, §42-1-208.
Records, §42-1-216.
Removal of wrecked or damaged vehicle.
Reports.
  Bullet damage to motor vehicles.
    Garage manager to report, §42-4-1606.
  Confidentiality, §42-4-1610.
  Coroners, §42-4-1609.
  Duty of driver, §42-4-1606.
  Duty of occupant or owner, §42-4-1607.
  Expungement of records, §42-2-121.
  Filing by department, §42-2-121.
  Financial responsibility law.
    Requirement, §42-4-1404.
  Forms, §42-4-1608.
  Law enforcement officers.
    Duty to make reports, §42-4-1606.
  Physical incapacity to report.
  Police, §42-4-1606.
  Supplemental reports, §42-4-1606.
  Tabulation and analysis, §42-4-1611.
  Threshold amount of damage requiring report, §42-4-1406.
  Traffic violations occurring outside state, §42-2-121.
Signs, signals, and markings.
  Duty of driver upon striking, §42-4-1605.
Unattended vehicles.
  Duties upon striking, §42-4-1604.
AGE
Motor vehicle drivers' licenses.
  Age limits, §42-2-104.
  Penalties for forgery of penalty assessment notice issued to a minor under eighteen years of age, §42-2-127.4.
  Penalties, on minor drivers under seventeen, §42-2-127.
  Restrictions on minor drivers under seventeen, §42-2-105.5.
  Special restrictions on certain drivers, §42-2-105.
  Training for minor drivers, §42-4-104.
  Learners' permits, §42-2-106.
AGRICULTURE
Agricultural products.
  Transportation, §42-20-108.5.
Colorado foundation for agriculture.
  Special license plates, §42-3-216.

AGRICULTURE-Cont'd
Farm Equipment.
Exemption from registration, §42-3-104.
Lamps and reflectors, §42-4-211.
Proof of farm use not required for registration, §42-3-306.
Transporting heavy machines on public roads, §43-5-306.
Crop sprinkler systems.
Causing waters to damage highways, §43-5-301.

AIR PROGRAM
General provisions, §§42-4-301 to 42-4-316.

AIR QUALITY CONTROL
Emissions.
Criminal offenses related to emissions, §42-4-412.
Diesel emissions inspection program.
Administration of program, §42-4-402.
Air quality commission.
Regulatory powers, §§25-7-106, 42-4-403.
Certification of emissions control prior to registration, §42-4-406.
Definitions, §42-4-401.
Diesel fleets.
Applicability to, §§42-4-406, 42-4-411, 42-4-414.
Executive director of department of public health and environment.
Powers and duties, §§42-4-404, 42-4-405.
Inspection stations.
Improper representation, §42-4-409.
Operation, §42-4-408.
Inspectors.
Licensure, §§42-4-405, 42-4-407.
Program area.
Definition, §42-4-401.
Requests from localities for inclusion in program, §42-4-410.
Regulatory powers, §§25-7-106, 42-4-403.
Smoke opacity limits, §42-4-403.
Program area.
Motor vehicle registration, §42-3-113.
Purchase or lease of new vehicles.
Clean-burning alternative fuel vehicles, §42-4-317.
State fleet alternative fuels plan, §42-4-317.
Motor vehicles.
Alternative fuel conversion.
Study on use of alternative fuels.
Funding, §42-3-304.
Regulation.
Funding for study of costs and benefits of programs, §42-3-304.
Violations.
Criminal offenses, §42-4-412.

ALCOHOL BEVERAGES
Alcohol and drug driving safety program, §42-4-1301.3.

ALCOHOL BEVERAGES-Cont'd
Drivers' licenses.
Alcohol-related offenses.
Education and treatment program, §§42-4-1301.3, 42-2-144.
Electronic hearings, §§42-1-218.5, 42-2-125, 42-2-126, 42-2-127.
Habitual drunkards.
Persons not to be licensed, §42-2-104.
License to drive vehicle with ignition interlock device, §42-2-132.5.
Revocation, §§42-2-125, 42-2-126.
Suspension, §42-2-127.
Driving under the influence or while impaired, §42-4-1301.
Driving with excessive alcoholic content, §42-4-1301.
Expressed consent.
Blood tests for drivers under 21 years of age not required, §§42-2-126, 42-4-1301.1.
Chemical test for intoxication, §§42-2-126, 42-4-1301.1.
Open container, §42-4-1305.
Possession.
Minors.
Revocation of driver's license, §42-2-125.
Vehicular assault.
Revocation of driver's license, §42-2-125.
Vehicular homicide.
Revocation of driver's license, §§42-2-125, 42-2-128.

ALTERNATIVE FUELS
Alternative fuel vehicles.
Purchase or lease of new vehicles by state of Colorado, §42-4-317.

AMBULANCES
Exemption from registration, §42-3-104.

ANTIMONOPOLY FINANCING LAW
Contracts void.
Violation of provisions, §12-6-211.
Cumulative provisions, §12-6-212.
Damages.
Violation of provisions, §12-6-213.
Definitions, §12-6-201.
Elimination of competition.
Accepting consideration.
General provisions, §12-6-206.
Recipient not to buy mortgages, §12-6-207.
Offering consideration, §12-6-205.
Exclusive finance agreements.
Evidence of violation, §12-6-204.
Prima facie evidence of violation, §12-6-203.
Unlawful, §12-6-202.
Void, §12-6-202.
Foreign corporations.
Violations, §12-6-209.
Penalties, §12-6-210.
Quo warranto.
Actions for violation, §12-6-208.

ANATOMICAL GIFTS
Drivers' licenses.
Donor space on license, §42-2-107.

ANATOMICAL GIFTS-Cont'd
  Drivers' licenses.-Cont'd
    Voluntary donation to fund, §§42-2-107, 42-2-118.
  Minors, §§12-34-103, 42-2-108.
ANIMALS
  Animal-drawn vehicles.
    Traffic laws, §42-4-109.
ARBITRATION
  Motor vehicles.
    Warranties, §§42-10-106, 42-10-107.
ARREST
  Minors.
    Misdemeanor traffic offenses, §42-4-1706.
  Warrantless arrest, §§42-4-1705 to 42-4-1712.
ASSAULT
  Vehicular assault.
    Revocation of driver's license, §42-2-125.
ASSISTANCE DOGS
  Disabled persons.
    Failure to yield right-of-way to, §42-4-808.
ATTORNEY FEES
  Automobile dealers.
    Loss or damage by reason of unlawful acts, §12-6-122.
  Used motor vehicle sales.
    Intent to defraud, §42-6-204.
    Violations of regulatory provisions, §42-9-112.
  Warranties.
    Failure to conform vehicle to warranty, §42-10-103.
ATTORNEY GENERAL
  Motor vehicle dealers board, §12-6-107.
AUTOMOBILE INSPECTION AND READJUSTMENT PROGRAM
  General provisions, §§42-4-301 to 42-4-316.
AVIATION ACCIDENTS
  Blood tests from crash victims, §42-4-1304.

B

BAIL AND RECOGNIZANCE
  Traffic citations.
    Nonresident violator's driver's license as bail bond, §24-60-2101.
BANKRUPTCY AND INSOLVENCY
  Motor vehicle financial responsibility.
    Suspension of driver's license, §42-7-402.
BICYCLES
  Accidents.
    Reporting requirements, §42-4-1606.
  Brakes.
    Requirements, §42-4-223.
  Careless driving, §42-4-1402.
  Crowding or threatening bicyclist, §42-4-1008.5.
  Definitions, §42-1-102
  Electrical assisted bicycle, §42-1-102 (28.5).
  Equipment, §42-4-221.
  Motorized bicycles.
    Brake requirements, §42-4-223.
    Definition, §42-1-102.
    Drivers' licenses, §42-2-103.

BICYCLES-Cont'd
  Motorized bicycles.-Cont'd
    Equipment, §42-4-220.
    General provisions, §42-4-109.
    Operation on interstate highway, §42-2-103.
    Operation on sidewalks, §42-2-103.
    Registration, §42-3-311.
  Operation on streets and highways, §42-4-1412.
  Parking of bicycles, §§42-4-1204, 42-4-1412.
  Reckless driving, §42-4-1401.
  Riders.
    Attachment to vehicles prohibited, §42-4-1412.
    Driver's license suspension provisions not applicable to, §42-4-1412.
    Number of riders, §42-4-1412.
    Rights and duties, §42-4-1412.
  Sirens and whistles prohibited, §42-4-224.
  Slow-moving vehicle emblem.
    Optional display of, §42-4-234.
  Traffic laws.
    Applicability, §42-4-1412.
  Vehicle.
    Inclusion of bicycle within definition, §42-1-102.
  Violations.
    Careless driving, §42-4-1402.
    Reckless driving, §42-4-1401.
    Traffic regulations, §§42-4-1412, 42-4-1701.
BLIND PERSONS
  Rental of motor vehicles, §42-2-141.
BLOOD TESTS
  Accidents.
    Samples from crash victims, §42-4-1304.
  Expressed consent law.
    Driving after drinking alcohol, §§42-2-126, 42-4-1301.1.
  Intoxication.
    Drivers of motor vehicles, §42-4-1301.1.
    Blood tests for drivers under 21 years of age not required, §§42-2-126, 42-4-1301.1.
BLUE LAWS
  Motor vehicle sales on Sundays, §12-6-302.
BOARDS AND COMMISSIONS
  Interstate commissions.
    Vehicle equipment safety commission, §24-60-902.
  Motor vehicle dealer board, §12-6-103.
BRAIN INJURY
  Traumatic brain injury trust fund.
    Surcharge for convictions, §§30-15-402, 42-4-1301, 42-4-1701.
BREACH OF CONTRACTS
  Bus drivers for school districts.
    Failure to comply with regulations, §42-4-1904.
BRIDGES
  Motor vehicles.
    Stopping, standing, or parking on bridge prohibited, §42-4-1204.

BURDEN OF PROOF
Traffic infractions.
Proper court for hearing, §42-4-1708.

C

CAMPING TRAILERS AND MOTOR HOMES
Parking or storage provided by owner of camp or hotel.
Definitions, §43-5-201.
Records.
General requirements, §43-5-203.
Inspection by law enforcement officers, §43-5-204.
Violations of requirements for, §43-5-207.
Stolen vehicles.
Knowingly allowing storage or parking of such a vehicle.
Penalty, §43-5-205.
CARELESS DRIVING
Elements of offense and penalties, §42-4-1402.
Points, §42-2-127.
CEASE AND DESIST ORDERS
Motor vehicle dealers and manufacturers, §12-6-105.
CERTIFICATES OF TITLE - MOTOR VEHICLES
Altering or using altered certificate, §42-6-143.
Amended certificates.
Issuance, §42-6-118.
Applicability of provisions, §42-6-103.
Applications.
Filing application with registration, §42-3-105.
Forms, §42-6-116.
Granting application, §42-6-117.
Where made, §42-6-134.
Authorized agents, §42-6-105.
Bonds, surety.
Inadequate proof of ownership, §42-6-115.
Purchase of abandoned vehicle, §42-4-1805.
Cancellation of certificate, §42-6-136.
Central registry of electronic files, §42-6-147.
Contents, §42-6-107.
Electronic record.
Definitions, §42-4-102.
Generally, §42-6-107.
Loss of data transmission, §42-6-135.
When allowed, §42-6-109.
False oath, §42-6-144.
False statements, §42-6-142.
Fees.
Disposition, §42-6-138.
Mortgage filing fees, §42-6-137.
Felonies.
Altering or using altered certificate, §42-6-143.
Identification numbers.
Amendment to certificate, §42-6-118.
Application, §42-6-145.
Inadequate proof of ownership, §42-6-115.

CERTIFICATES OF TITLE - MOTOR VEHICLES-Cont'd
Issuance, §42-6-117.
Lost certificates, §42-6-135.
Misdemeanors.
Failure of mortgagee to give required repossession notice, §42-6-146.
General provisions, §42-6-142.
Mortgages.
Disposition after mortgaging, §§42-6-123, 42-6-124.
Disposition by authorized agent, §42-6-122.
Duration of lien of mortgage, §42-6-127.
Enforcement of foreign mortgages, §42-6-133.
Extension of mortgage, §42-6-127.
Fees, §42-6-137.
Filing of mortgage, §§42-6-120, 42-6-121.
Priority of mortgages, §42-6-130.
Records open to public inspection, §42-6-141.
Release of mortgages.
Central registry of electronic files, §42-6-147.
Electronic record, procedure for issuance of new certificate, §42-6-126.
Upon discharge of obligation, §42-6-125.
Repossession, §42-6-146.
Second or junior mortgages, §42-6-129.
Validity of mortgage between parties, §42-6-128.
New certificates, §42-6-126.
New vehicles, §42-6-113.
Nonresidents, §42-6-140.
Prerequisite to registration, §42-6-106.
Request for paper copy, §42-6-117.
Rules, §42-6-104.
Sale of vehicle.
To dealers, §42-6-111.
To purchasers, §42-6-109.
Transfer of title, §42-6-110.
Salvage certificates of title.
Application for certificate, §42-6-136.
Definitions, §42-6-102.
Street-rod vehicles, §§42-12-201 to 42-12-204.
Surrender of certificate, §42-6-136.
Title of act, §42-6-101.
Transfer.
Bequest, descent, or operation of law, §42-6-114.
General provisions, §§42-3-115, 42-6-109, 42-6-110.
Vehicles registered in other states, §42-6-119.
Wholesale motor vehicle auction dealers.
Transfer of vehicles not bought, sold, or owned by auction dealer, §42-6-111.
CHAUFFEURS
Definition, §42-1-102.
Drivers' license, suspension for points, §42-2-127.
Financial responsibility, §42-7-409.
CHECKS
Bad checks.
Motor vehicle registration.
Checks to pay fees, §42-3-202.

CHECKS-Cont'd
Bad checks.-Cont'd
Renewal of drivers' license denied, §§42-2-118, 42-4-1709.
CHILD SUPPORT ENFORCEMENT
Driver's license.
Suspension for nonpayment of child support, §42-2-127.5.
CIGARETTES
Traffic infractions related to.
Disgarding lighted cigarettes, cigars, or matches on any highway, §42-4-1406.
CIVIL PENALTIES
Commercial vehicles, §42-4-235.
Hazardous materials.
Transportation by motor vehicle.
  Route deviations, §42-20-305.
Nuclear materials transportation.
Penalty assessments.
  Acceptance of late payments, §42-20-406.
  Violations, §§42-20-406, 42-20-407.
COERCION
Motor vehicles dealers.
Penalties, §12-6-121.
Unlawful acts, §12-6-120.
COMMERCIAL DRIVING SCHOOLS
Definitions, §12-15-101.
Department of revenue.
Rules, §12-15-116.
Equipment of vehicles, §12-15-114.
Insurance.
Violations, §12-15-120.
Licenses.
Termination of licensing function, §12-15-121.
Rules, §12-15-116.
Violations.
Misdemeanor penalties, §12-15-120.
COMMERCIAL VEHICLES.
Commercial drivers' licenses, §§42-2-401 to 42-2-408.
Engine compression brake device muffler, §42-4-225.
Safety standards, §§42-4-235, 42-4-2001.
COMPACTS
Driver license compact, §§24-60-1101 to 24-60-1107.
Nonresident violator compact, §§24-60-2101 to 24-60-2104.
Vehicle equipment safety compact, §§24-60-901 to 24-60-912.
COMPUTERS
Use in motor vehicles, §42-4-201.
CONFIDENTIALITY OF INFORMATION
Motor vehicle accidents, §42-4-1610.
CONFISCATION
Motor vehicles.
Disposition of personal property, §§42-13-101 to 42-13-109.
CONSENT
Chemical test for intoxication, §§42-2-126, 42-4-1301.1.

CONSTRUCTION
Exemption of certain construction equipment from registration, §§42-3-104, 42-3-304.
CONSUMER AND COMMERCIAL AFFAIRS
Motor vehicles.
Nonconformity to warranties, §§42-10-101 to 42-10-107.
CONSUMER PROTECTION
Deceptive trade practices.
Automobile air bags, §42-9-111.
Motor vehicle repairs, §42-9-111.
Motor vehicle sales, §42-6-205.
CONTRACTS
Motor vehicles.
Antimonopoly financing.
  Violation of provisions, §12-6-211.
Dealers.
  Repair contracts with garages, §12-6-117.
CORONERS
Motor vehicle accident reports, §42-4-1609.
CORPORATIONS
Antimonopoly financing-motor vehicles.
Violations by foreign corporations, §12-6-209.
COUNTY ORDINANCES
Automated vehicle identification systems, §42-4-110.5.
COUNTY CLERK AND RECORDERS
Motor vehicles.
Agents of department of revenue for registering and titling of motor vehicles, §42-1-210.
Fees.
  Fees to defray expenses of issuance of plates and tabs, §42-1-210.
  Registration fees and cash funds, §§42-3-301 to 42-3-311.
  P.O.S.T. board cash fund surcharge, §42-3-304.
  Reports and disposition of fees, §42-1-214.
  Retention of registration fees, §42-1-210.
COURTS
Family-friendly courts act.
Family-friendly court program cash fund.
  Funding by surcharges, §42-4-1701.
Judicial department.
Electronic transmission of traffic infraction penalty assessment notice or summons and complaint, §42-4-1718.
CRIMINAL LAW AND PROCEDURE
Air pollution.
Prohibited acts, §42-4-412.
Convictions.
Attendance at driver improvement school, §42-4-1717.
Driver license compact.
  Assessment of points, §24-60-1105.
  General provisions, §24-60-1101.
Electronic transmission of data, §42-4-1718.

CRIMINAL LAW AND PROCEDURE-Cont'd
Convictions.-Cont'd
Evidence.
  Admissibility of conviction records, §42-4-1713.
  Recording by judge or clerk of court, §42-4-1715.
Reports.
  When court to report, §§42-2-124, 42-4-1208.
Criminal mischief.
  Mandatory revocation, §42-2-125.
Habitual criminals.
  Motor vehicles, §§42-2-201 to 42-2-208.
Parties to crime, §42-4-1703.
Perjury.
  Motor vehicle registration application.
    False statements, §§42-3-105, 42-3-113, 42-3-122.
Presumptions.
  Driving under the influence or while impaired, §42-4-1301.
CROSSWALKS
Pedestrians, §§42-4-802 to 42-4-804.

D

DATA PROCESSING
Motor vehicles.
  Colorado state titling and registration system, §42-1-211.
DECEDENTS' ESTATES
Motor vehicle title transfers, §42-6-114.
DECEPTIVE TRADE PRACTICES
Consumer protection act.
  Motor vehicles, §§42-6-205, 42-9-112, 42-11-106.
DEFACEMENT
Graffiti.
  Mandatory revocation of drivers' license, §42-2-125.
DEPARTMENT OF REVENUE
Accidents.
  Publication of information, §42-1-208.
Appropriations for expenses of administration of title, §42-1-219.
Director.
  Administration and enforcement of provisions, §42-1-201.
  Central registry of electronic files, §42-6-147.
  Coordination of enforcement throughout state, §42-1-203.
  Rule-making power, §42-1-204.
Oaths.
  Administration of oaths or affirmations, §42-1-215.
Powers.
  Registration fee enforcement powers, §42-3-307.
Records.
  Bulk electronic transfer of information open to inspection, §42-1-206.
  Confidential information, §42-1-206.

DEPARTMENT OF REVENUE-Cont'd
Records.-Cont'd
Copies, §42-1-206.
Filing by executive director, §42-1-205.
Public inspection, §§24-72-204, 42-1-206.
Seals, §42-1-205.
Supervisor, §§42-1-201, 42-1-202.
DEVELOPMENTALLY DISABLED
Restricted licenses, §42-2-116.
DISTRICT ATTORNEYS
Appeals, Drivers' licenses.
  Representation of department of revenue, §42-2-135.
Traffic infraction cases.
  Authority to enter cases for limited purposes, §42-4-1708.
DITCHES
Highways.
  Excavation of ditches.
    Written consent required, §42-4-1406.
DOMICILE
Drivers' licenses, §42-2-102.
DRAG RACING
General provisions, §42-4-1105.
DRIVER LICENSE COMPACT
Administrator.
  Expenses, §24-60-1103.
Appeals.
  Review by district court, §24-60-1107.
Applicability of provisions, §24-60-1106.
Approval, §24-60-1101.
Convictions.
  Assessment of points, §24-60-1105.
  General provisions, §24-60-1101.
Definitions, §§24-60-1101, 24-60-1102.
General provisions, §24-60-1101.
Governor as executive head, §24-60-1104.
Ratification, §24-60-1101.
Text, §24-60-1101.
DRIVERS' LICENSES.
Affidavits.
  False affidavit or knowingly swearing or affirming falsely, §42-2-137.
Age.
  General provisions, §42-2-104.
    Minor driver's license held by a child in foster care, §42-2-108.
    Training required for minor drivers, §42-2-104.
  Learners' permits and temporary licenses, §42-2-106.
  Penalties for forgery of penalty assessment notice issued to minor under eighteen, §42-2-127.4.
  Penalties for violation of restrictions on minor drivers under seventeen years of age, §§42-2-127, 42-4-1701.
  Restrictions on minor drivers under seventeen years of age, §42-2-105.5.
  Special restrictions on certain drivers, §42-2-105.
Anatomical gifts.
  Donor space on driver's license, §42-2-107.

DRIVERS' LICENSES.-Cont'd

Appeals.
Denial, cancellation, or revocation of license, §§42-2-126, 42-2-135.
Applications.
Compliance with Military Selective Service Act, §42-2-107.
Confidentiality, §42-2-121.
Contents, §42-2-107.
False application for new license, §42-2-132.
Fees, §42-2-107.
Forms, §42-2-107.
Minors, §§42-2-108 to 42-2-110.
Outstanding warrants or judgments, §§42-2-107, 42-4-1709.
Cancellation.
Grounds, §42-2-122.
Hearings, §42-2-122.
Restoration fee, §42-2-132.
Change of address or name, §42-2-119.
Commercial drivers' licenses.
Age requirement, §§42-2-105, 42-2-404.
Cancellation, §42-4-604.
Compliance with Military Selective Service Act, §42-2-403.
Definitions, §42-2-402.
Denial, §42-2-405.
Driving testers and testing units.
Acting as testing unit or driving tester without license, §42-2-408.
License fees, §42-2-406.
Operations, §42-4-407.
Revocation or suspension of license, §42-2-407.
Expiration, §42-2-114.
Federal requirements, §42-2-403.
Fees, §42-2-406.
Licensing procedure, §42-2-403.
Requirement, §42-2-404.
Revocation.
Alcohol offenses, §§42-2-126, 42-2-405.
Leaving scene of accident, §§42-2-125, 42-2-405.
Rules, §42-2-403.
Title of act, §42-2-401.
Violations of regulatory provisions.
Disciplinary actions, §42-2-405.
Driving without a license, §42-2-404.
Holding of more than one license, §42-2-404.
Construction and interpretation, §42-2-143.
Contents, §42-2-114.
Controlled substances.
Persons addicted not to be licensed, §42-2-104.
Copies.
Validity, §42-2-101.
Denial, §§42-2-104, 42-2-122.
Disabled persons.
Restricted licenses, §42-2-116.
Driving between the hours of 12 midnight and 5 a.m. for minor drivers under seventeen years of age.
Penalties, §§42-2-127, 42-4-1701.

DRIVERS' LICENSES.-Cont'd

Driving under the influence or while impaired.
Education and treatment program, §§42-2-144, 42-4-1301.3.
License to drive vehicle with ignition interlock device, §42-2-132.5.
Mandatory surrender of license, §42-2-129.
Revocation, §§42-2-125, 42-2-126.
Suspension, §42-2-127.
Driving with excessive alcoholic content.
Education and treatment program, §§42-2-144, 42-4-1301.3.
License to drive vehicle with ignition interlock device, §42-2-132.5.
Mandatory surrender of license, §42-2-129.
Revocation, §§42-2-125, 42-2-126.
Suspension, §42-2-127.
Driving with more passengers than seat belts.
Penalties, §§42-2-127, 42-4-1701.
Drug addiction.
Persons not to be licensed, §42-2-104.
Drug convictions.
Mandatory revocation.
Failure to surrender revoked license.
Penalty, §42-2-130.
General provisions, §42-2-125.
Period of revocation, §42-2-132.
Surrender of license, §42-2-130.
Drunkards.
Habitual drunkards.
Persons not to be licensed, §42-2-104.
Duplicates, §42-2-117.
Examinations.
Contents, §42-2-111.
Examiners, §42-2-113.
Rules, §42-2-111.
Special restrictions on certain drivers, §42-2-105.
Where given, §42-2-111.
Exemptions from requirements, §42-2-102.
Exhibition of license on demand, §42-2-115.
Expiration.
Date, §42-2-114.
Renewal period, §42-2-114.
Fees.
General provisions, §42-2-114.
Restoration fee, §42-2-132.
Financial responsibility.
Failure to prove.
Revocation, §42-2-125.
Surrender of license.
Failure to surrender revoked license.
Penalty, §42-2-124.
General provisions, §42-7-506.
Revoking court, §42-2-124.
Graffiti conviction resulting in revocation, §42-2-125.
Habitual offenders, §§42-2-201 to 42-2-208.
Hearings.
Cancellation, §42-2-122.
Habitual offenders, §42-2-203.
Restricted licenses.
Violation of restrictions, §42-2-116.

DRIVERS' LICENSES.-Cont'd
  Hearings.-Cont'd
    Revocation.
      Administrative determination based on alcohol offense, §42-2-125.
  Hit-and-run driving.
    Revocation of license, §§42-2-125, 42-4-1601.
  Identification cards for nondrivers, §§42-2-301 to 42-2-310.
  Identification security fund, §42-1-220.
  Identification verfication, §§42-2-106, 42-2-107.
  Image comparison technology, §42-2-114.
  Insurance.
    Proof of insurance, §42-7-406.
  Issuance.
    General provisions, §§42-2-104, 42-2-114.
    Information required to be on license, §42-2-114.
    Payment of outstanding judgments prior to renewal, §42-2-118.
    Restrictions, limitations, or conditions on, §42-2-116.
    Use of medical advice, §42-2-112.
  Learners' permits.
    Age limits, §42-2-106.
    Applications and fees, §42-2-107.
    Conditions, §42-2-106.
    Damages.
      Liability of parents or guardian.
        General provisions, §42-2-108.
        Release from liability, §42-2-109.
    Motorcycles and mopeds, §42-2-106.
    Proof of legal presence in the country, §42-2-107.
    Revocation upon death of signer for minor, §42-2-110.
    Surrender to court upon conviction, §42-2-124.
  Legal presence in the country.
    Illegal presence grounds for cancellation, §42-2-122.
    Proof for application, §42-2-107.
  Lost licenses and permits, §42-2-117.
  Low-power scooters, §42-2-103.
  Mentally ill.
    Restricted licenses, §42-2-116.
  Military affairs.
    Exemption of persons serving in armed forces, §42-2-102.
    Extension of period of validity, §42-2-118.
  Minors.
    Applications, §§42-2-108 to 42-2-110.
    Forgery of penalty assessment notice, §42-2-127.4.
    Liability of parents or guardians.
      General provisions, §42-2-108.
      Release from liability, §42-2-109.
    Permitting unauthorized minor to drive, §42-2-139.
    Restriction on more than one minor passenger, §42-4-116.
    Revocation upon death of signer for minor, §42-2-110.

DRIVERS' LICENSES.-Cont'd
  Minors.-Cont'd
    Restriction on ability to have more than one minor passenger, §42-4-116.
  Motorized bicycles, §42-2-103.
  Nonresidents.
    Exemptions from requirements, §42-2-102.
  Perjury.
    Revocation for perjury relating to ownership or operation of motor vehicle, §42-2-125.
  Photographs, §42-2-114.
  Physical or mental incompetence, §42-2-122.
  Point system, §42-2-127.
  Probationary licenses.
    License to drive vehicle with ignition interlock device, §42-2-132.5.
    Revoked licenses, §42-2-125.
    Suspended licenses, §42-2-127.
  Records.
    Admissibility of records in court proceedings, §42-2-121.
    General provisions, §42-2-121.
    Prohibition on maintenance of certain convictions, §42-2-121.
    Rentals, §42-2-141.
  Renewal.
    General provisions, §42-2-118.
    Information required to be on license, §42-2-114.
    Payment of outstanding judgments prior to renewal, §42-2-118.
    Restrictions, limitations, or conditions on, §42-2-116.
  Representation of department by district attorney, §42-2-135.
  Requirement of.
    Exemptions from requirements, §42-2-102.
    General provisions, §42-2-101.
  Restricted licenses, §§42-2-116, 42-2-122, 42-2-132.5.
  Revocation.
    Administrative revocation for alcohol-related offense, §42-2-126.
      Persons holding commercial drivers' licenses, §§42-2-126, 42-2-405.
      Restoration fee credited to special account to pay costs of revocation proceedings, §42-2-132.
    Aggravated motor vehicle theft, §§18-4-409, 42-2-125.
    Commercial drivers' licenses.
      Alcohol offenses, §§42-2-125, 42-2-405.
      Leaving scene of accident, §§42-2-125, 42-2-405.
    Criminal mischief, §§18-4-501, 42-2-125.
    Driving under the influence or while impaired or with excessive alcoholic content.
      Mandatory surrender of license, §42-2-129.
    Driving while license or driving privilege is under restraint, §42-2-138.
    Duration, §42-2-132.

DRIVERS' LICENSES.-Cont'd
Revocation.-Cont'd
  Electronic hearings, §§24-34-104, 42-1-218.5.
  Excess BAC, §42-2-126.
  Financial responsibility.
    Failure to prove, §42-2-125.
    Surrender of license.
      General provisions, §42-7-506.
      Penalty for failure to surrender revoked license, §42-2-124.
      Revoking court, §42-2-124.
  Foreign license invalid during revocation, §42-2-134.
  Habitual offenders, §42-2-203.
  Hearing, §§42-2-125, 42-2-126.
  Hit-and-run driving, §§42-2-125, 42-4-1601.
  Ignition interlock device, §42-2-132.
  Mandatory revocation, §42-2-125.
  Mandatory surrender of license, §42-2-129.
  Minors.
    Death of signer for minor, §42-2-110.
  Non-driving alcohol offenses, §42-2-131.
  Notice to vehicle owner of alcohol-related violation, §§42-2-126, 42-7-406.
  Report by revoking court, §42-2-124.
  Restoration fee, §42-2-132.
  Second degree criminal trespass, §42-2-125.
  Surrender of license to department of revenue, §42-2-133.
  Surrender of license to revoking court, §42-2-124.
  Tribal code.
    Colorado driving privileges, §42-2-126.5.
Signing by licensee, §42-2-114.
Social security number on license, §42-2-107.
Stored information, §42-2-114.
Surrender of license.
  Department of revenue, §42-2-133.
  Failure to surrender, §42-2-136.
  Financial responsibility, §42-7-506.
  Suspending or revoking court, §42-2-124.
Suspension.
  Accidents, §§42-7-301, 42-7-303.
  Driving while license or driving privilege is under restraint, §42-2-138.
  Driving without self-insurance.
    Electronic hearings, §42-1-218.5.
    Generally, §42-2-127.7.
  Duration, §42-2-132.
  Failure to maintain proof of financial responsibility, §§42-2-127.7, 42-4-1410.
  Failure to pay restitution, §42-7-401.
  Failure to satisfy judgment, §§42-7-401, 42-7-402, 42-7-405.
  Foreign license invalid during suspension, §42-2-134.
  Fuel piracy, §42-2-127.
  Hearing, §42-2-127.
  Nonpayment of child support, §§26-13-123, 42-2-127.5.
  Point system, §42-2-127.
  Probationary licenses, §42-2-127.
  Report by suspending court, §42-2-124.

DRIVERS' LICENSES.-Cont'd
Suspension.-Cont'd
  Restoration fee, §42-2-132.
  Return of license to licensee, §42-2-133.
  Type of conviction, §42-2-127.
  Underage drinking violations, §42-2-127.6.
Temporary licenses, §42-2-106.
Unlawful acts.
  Penalties, §42-2-142.
  Permitting unauthorized minor to drive, §42-2-139.
  Permitting unauthorized person to drive, §42-2-140.
  Unlawful duplication of license, §42-2-136.
  Unlawful possession or use of license, §42-2-136.
Violations.
  Point system, §42-2-127.

DRIVING SCHOOLS
  Commercial driving schools, §§12-15-101 to 12-15-121.

DRIVING UNDER THE INFLUENCE OR WHILE IMPAIRED.
Alcohol and drug driving safety program, §42-4-1300.
Arrest.
  Immediate appearance before judge, §42-4-1705.
Chemical tests for intoxication.
  Blood test for drivers under 21 years of age not required, §§42-2-126, 42-4-1301.1.
  General provisions, §42-4-1301.1.
  Records of testing methods.
    Prima facie proof, §42-4-1303.
  Refusal to take test.
    Admissibility in court, §42-4-1301.
    Revocation of driver's license, §42-2-126.
Collateral attack on judgment, §42-4-1702.
Definitions, §§42-1-102, 42-4-1300.
Designation of offenses as strict liability offenses, §42-4-1301.
Drivers' licenses.
  Habitual drunkards, §42-2-104.
  License to drive vehicle with ignition interlock device, §42-2-132.5.
  Mandatory surrender of license, §42-2-129.
  Notice to vehicle owner of alcohol-related violation, §§42-2-126, 42-7-406.
  Restricted license, §42-2-132.5.
  Revocation, §§42-2-125, 42-2-126.
  Suspension, §42-2-127.
Driving while an habitual user of controlled substances, §42-4-1301.
Interagency task force on drunk driving, §42-4-1306.
Penalties, §42-4-1301.
Public service requirement, §42-4-1301.4.
Repeat violation within five years, §42-4-1301.
Stopping of suspect, §42-4-1302.
Victim impact panel, §42-4-1301.

DRIVING WITH EXCESSIVE ALCOHOLIC CONTENT.
Alcohol and drug driving program, §42-4-1301.3.
Arrest.
　Immediate appearance before judge, §42-4-1705.
Chemical tests for intoxication.
　General provisions, §42-4-1301.1.
　Records of testing.
　　Prima facie proof, §42-4-1303.
Collateral attack on judgment, §42-4-1702.
Definitions, §42-4-1300.
Designation of offenses as strict liability offenses, §42-4-1301.
Drivers' licenses.
　License to drive vehicle with ignition interlock device, §42-2-132.5.
　Mandatory surrender of license, §42-2-129.
　Notice to vehicle owner of alcohol-related violation, §§42-2-126, 42-7-406.
　Revocation, §§42-2-125, 42-2-126.
　Suspension, §42-2-127.
Interagency task force on drunk driving, §42-4-1306.
Penalties, §42-4-1307.
Public service requirement, §42-4-1301.4.
Stopping of suspect, §42-4-1302.

DRUGS
Controlled substances.
　Criminal offenses.
　　Penalties, §§18-18-405, 18-18-406.3, 42-2-125.
　　Revocation or suspension of driver's license, §42-2-125.
　Driving under the influence or while impaired, §42-4-1301.
　Marijuana.
　　Revocation or suspension of driver's license, §42-2-125.
Drug addicts not to be licensed, §42-2-104.
Vehicular assault.
　Revocation of driver's license, §42-2-125.
Vehicular homicide.
　Revocation of driver's license, §§42-2-125, 42-2-128.

E

ELECTIONS
Data processing.
　Colorado state titling and registration system.
　　Establishment, §42-1-211.

EMERGENCY MEDICAL AND TRAUMA SERVICES
Local emergency medical services.
　Emergency medical services account.
　　Funding, §42-3-304.

EMERGENCY VEHICLES
Ambulance equipment.
　Signals on emergency vehicles generally.
　　Audible and visual signals, §42-4-213.
　Volunteer ambulance attendants.
　　Private vehicles to have identifying signals, §42-4-222.

EMERGENCY VEHICLES-Cont'd
General provisions.
　Exemption from traffic laws, §42-4-108.
　Pedestrian to yield to authorized emergency vehicle, §42-4-805.
　Registration exemption for ambulances, §42-3-104.
　Rights-of-way, §42-4-705.
　Safety belt systems.
　　Mandatory use, §42-4-237.

EMISSIONS CONTROL.
Antique motor vehicles.
　Collectors' items subject to, §42-12-404.
Audits.
　General provisions, §42-4-305.
　Legislative audit of emissions program, §42-4-316.
　Regulations, §42-4-306.
Basic emissions program.
　Commencement, §42-4-302.
　Regulations to implement program, §§42-4-306, 42-4-307.
Certification of emissions compliance.
　Definition, §42-4-304.
　Requirement prior to registration, §42-4-310.
Certification of emissions control.
　Duration, §42-4-304.
　Issuance, §§42-4-304, 42-4-311.
　Requirement upon sale and exemptions, §42-4-310.
Certification of emissions waiver.
　Definition, §42-4-304.
　Issuance, §42-4-311.
　Requirement prior to registration, §42-4-310.
Clean screen program.
　Clean screen enterprise, §42-4-307.5.
　Contracts for basic and enhanced program areas, §42-4-307.
　Inspection fee and waiver, §42-4-311.
　Registration and notice requirements, §42-4-310.
　Registration fee for emissions inspection, §42-3-304.
　Rules for basic and enhanced program areas, §42-4-306.
Commission.
　Powers and duties generally, §42-4-306.
Criminal offenses related to emissions, §42-4-412.
Definitions, §42-4-304.
Diesel emissions, §§42-4-401 to 42-4-411.
Director.
　Powers and duties generally, §42-4-305.
Enhanced emissions program.
　Contract to provide inspection services, §§42-4-305, 42-4-307.
　Inspections centers and inspection-only facilities.
　　Prohibition against making repairs, §42-4-306.
　Regulations to implement program, §§42-4-306, 42-4-307.
　Standards and contractor requirements, §42-4-306.

EMISSIONS CONTROL.-Cont'd
  Equipment.
    Tampering with emissions control equipment on vehicle prohibited, §42-4-314.
  Executive director of department of public health and environment.
    Powers and duties, §§42-4-305, 42-4-307.
  Exemptions, §§42-4-306, 42-4-307, 42-4-310.
  Fees.
    Inspection facilities, §42-4-311.
    Licenses, §42-4-305.
    Posting of charges, §42-4-305.
  Forms.
    Certification forms, §§42-4-310, 42-4-311.
  Government-owned motor vehicles, §42-4-310.
  Green truck grant program, §§42-1-301 to 42-1-305.
  Hearings.
    Licenses, §§42-4-305, 42-4-312.
  Inoperable or untestable vehicles, §42-4-310.
  Inspection and readjustment program.
    Definition, §42-4-304.
    Evidence of valid certification of emissions control, §42-4-313.
  Inspection facilities.
    Employment of emissions inspector or emissions mechanic, §42-4-308.
    Fees, §42-4-311.
    Licenses.
      Suspension or revocation, §42-4-312.
    Periodic inspections, §42-4-310.
    Requirements, §42-4-308.
  Legislative declarations, §42-4-301.
  Licenses.
    Cancellation, suspension, or revocation.
      Surrender of license, §42-4-305.
    Emissions inspectors and mechanics.
      Fees, §42-4-305.
      General provisions, §42-4-306.
      Qualifications, §42-4-308.
      Transfer prohibited, §42-4-311.
    Fees, §42-4-305.
    Hearings, §§42-4-305, 42-4-312.
    Inspection facilities.
      Applications, §42-4-308.
      Display, §42-4-311.
      Employment of emissions inspector or emissions mechanic, §42-4-308.
      Equipment requirements, §42-4-308.
      Fees, §42-4-305.
      Issuance, §42-4-308.
      Requirement, §42-4-308.
      Transfer prohibited, §42-4-311.
    Surrender, §§42-4-305, 42-4-312.
    Suspension or revocation, §42-4-312.
  Local authorities.
    Enforcement of emissions control inspection requirements, §42-4-110.
  Motor vehicle dealers.
    Authority to conduct inspections, §42-4-309.
    Vouchers for inspections, §42-4-309.
  Notice to purchaser of untestable vehicle, §42-4-310.

EMISSIONS CONTROL.-Cont'd
  On-road remote testing program, §42-4-307.
  Penalties.
    Violations of provisions, §42-4-313.
  Periodic inspections, §42-4-310.
  Program area.
    Definition, §42-4-304.
  Quality assurance program, §42-4-305.
  Registration, §42-3-113.
  Remote sensing emissions detection technology.
    Pilot program, §42-4-306.
  Repair facilities.
    Registration.
      Sunrise review of repair facility registration, §42-4-303.
  Repairs.
    Prohibition against performance of unnecessary repairs, §42-9-111.
  Reports.
    Audit report by legislative audit committee, §42-4-316.
  Reservation of state's right to challenge federal testing requirements, §42-4-301.
  Rules.
    Audits, §42-4-306.
    Clean screen, §42-4-306.
    Commencement date for basic emissions program, §42-4-302.
    Emissions-related repair waivers, §42-4-306.
    General provisions, §42-4-305.
    Implementation of basic and enhanced emissions programs, §§42-4-306, 42-4-307.
    Posting of charges, §42-4-305.
    Quality assurance program, §42-4-305.
    Tampering with emissions equipment, §42-4-306.
    Training of emissions inspectors and emissions mechanics, §42-4-306.
    Vehicle standards, §42-4-306.
  Small business technical assistance program, §42-4-306.
  Termination of program, §42-4-316.
  Vehicle fleet owners.
    Authority to conduct inspections, §42-4-309.
  Waivers.
    Emissions-related control waivers, §42-4-306.
  Warranties.
    Effect of enforcement of applicable warranty, §42-4-315.
EQUIPMENT - MOTOR VEHICLES
  Air bags, installation of false or incorrect unit, §§6-1-710, 42-9-111.
  Alarm systems.
    Volunteer ambulance services, §42-4-222.
    Volunteer fire departments, §42-4-222.
  Antique motor vehicles.
    Emission controls installed, §42-12-404.
    Special or safety equipment, §42-12-403.
  Brakes, §42-4-223.
  Child restraint systems, §42-4-236.
  Commercial driving schools, §12-15-114.
  Commercial vehicles, §42-4-235.

EQUIPMENT - MOTOR VEHICLES-Cont'd
Computers use in motor vehicles, §42-4-201.
Construction equipment.
   Exemptions of certain construction equipment from equipment requirements, §42-4-202.
Disabled persons.
   Distress flag, §42-4-611.
Emergency lighting equipment, §42-4-230.
Emergency vehicles, §42-4-213.
Emissions control.
   Tampering with emissions control equipment, §42-4-314.
Exemptions from provisions.
   Identification plates, §42-4-202.
   Regulation of exempt vehicles, §42-4-202.
Farm equipment.
   Exemptions from provisions, §42-4-202.
   Lamps, §42-4-211.
   Reflectors, §42-4-211.
Flags.
   Distress flag, §42-4-611.
Flares, §42-4-230.
Horns and warning devices, §42-4-224.
Lamps.
   Auxiliary driving and passing lamps, §42-4-212.
   Back-up lamps, §42-4-215.
   Clearance lamps, §42-4-207.
   Farm equipment, §42-4-211.
   Fender lamps, §42-4-215.
   Flashing lights, §42-4-215.
   Fog lamps, §42-4-212.
   Head lamps, §42-4-205.
   Height for mounting, §42-4-205.
   Motorcycles, §§42-4-205, 42-4-220.
   Motorized bicycles, §42-4-220.
   Multiple-beam lights.
      Requirements, §42-4-216.
      Use, §42-4-217.
   Number of lamps permitted, §42-4-219.
   Parked vehicles, §42-4-210.
   Parking lights, §42-4-231.
   Projecting load, §42-4-209.
   Running board courtesy lamps, §42-4-215.
   Side cowl lamps, §42-4-215.
   Side marker lamps, §42-4-207.
   Signal lamps and devices.
      Additional lighting equipment, §42-4-215.
      Custom motor vehicles, §42-12-204.
      Emergency vehicles, §42-4-213.
      Service vehicles, §42-4-214.
      Street-rod vehicles, §42-12-204.
   Single-beam road-lighting equipment, §42-4-218.
   Snow-removal equipment, §42-4-224.
   Spot lamps, §42-4-212.
   Stop lamps, §§42-4-208, 42-4-215.
   Tail lamps, §42-4-206.
   Turn signals, §§42-4-208, 42-4-215.
   Visibility distance, §42-4-204.
   Volunteer ambulance services, §42-4-222.
   Volunteer fire departments, §42-4-222.
   When illuminating devices required, §42-4-204.

EQUIPMENT - MOTOR VEHICLES-Cont'd
Mirrors, §42-4-226.
Motorcycles.
   Lamps, §§42-4-205, 42-4-220.
   Minimum safety standards, §42-4-232.
Mufflers, §42-4-225.
Odometers.
   Used motor vehicles, §§42-6-202, 42-6-203.
Optional equipment, §42-4-202.
Reflectors.
   Clearance reflectors, §42-4-207.
   Farm equipment, §42-4-211.
   Mounting, §42-4-206.
   Side marker reflectors, §42-4-207.
   Visibility, §42-4-206.
Safety.
   Air bags, installation of false or incorrect unit, §§6-1-710, 42-9-111.
   Vehicle equipment safety compact, §§24-60-901 to 24-60-912.
Seat belts, §42-4-237.
Service vehicles, §42-4-214.
Slow-moving vehicles.
   Emblem, §42-4-234.
Snow tires, §42-4-106.
Suspension systems, §42-4-233.
Television.
   Installation and use in motor vehicles, §42-4-201.
Tires.
   Mud, snow, and all weather tires, §42-4-106.
   Change of tires, §42-4-106.
   Restrictions, §42-4-228.
Traction devices, §42-4-106.
Trailers.
   Additional equipment required for the connection of towed vehicles, §42-4-506.
Trucks, §42-4-235.
Unsafe vehicles.
   Violations of provisions, §42-4-202.
Windows and windshields.
   Requirement, §42-4-229.
   Safety glazing materials, §42-4-229.
   Standard for light transmittance, §42-4-227.
   Stickers on windshields, §42-4-227.
   Tinted windows allowed on law enforcement vehicles, §42-4-227.
   Unobstructed view required, §42-4-227.
   Wipers, §42-4-227.

ESCHEAT
Motor vehicle financial responsibility law.
   Security deposited by operator or owner named in accident report.
      Unclaimed security will escheat to state, §42-7-304.

EVIDENCE
Insurance.
   Admissibility in motor vehicle negligence action, §42-7-504.
Motor vehicles.
   Admissibility of conviction records, §42-4-1713.

EVIDENCE-Cont'd
Motor vehicles.-Cont'd
Dealers.
  Boards' records, §12-6-106.
Distributors and manufacturers.
  Records of licensure, §12-6-106.
Driving under the influence or while impaired.
  Blood tests for drivers under 21 years of age not required, §§42-2-126, 42-4-1301.1.
  Percentage of alcohol in blood, §42-4-1301.
  Records.
    Prima facie proof, §42-4-1303.
Financial responsibility.
  Admissibility of evidence, §42-7-504.
Judgments, §42-7-504.
Official records and documents kept by the department of revenue, §42-2-121.
Witnesses.
  Effect of traffic violations on credibility of witness, §42-4-1714.
Reckless driving.
Conviction records, §42-4-1713.

F

FELONIES
Failure to stop at scene where serious bodily injury involved, §42-4-1601.
Motor vehicles.
Aggravated driving with a revoked license, §42-2-206.
Antimonopoly financing, §12-6-210.
Buying or selling stolen motor vehicle parts, §42-5-102.
Tampering with a motor vehicle, §42-5-103.
Theft of motor vehicle parts, §42-5-104.
Titles.
  Altering or using altered certificate, §42-6-143.

FENCES
Obstructing highways.
Penalty, §43-5-301.

FINANCIAL RESPONSIBILITY
Accidents.
Bond, surety, §42-7-301.
General provisions, §42-7-301.
Nonresidents.
  Failure to comply with provisions, §42-7-301.
Security and proof of financial responsibility under certain circumstances.
  Exemptions, §42-7-302.
Suspension of driver's license.
  Duration of suspension, §42-7-303.
  Hearings, §42-7-301.
Alcohol-related violations.
Notice to vehicle owner, §42-2-126.
Proof by vehicle owner, §42-7-406.
Altered or counterfeit letter or insurance identification card, §42-7-301.5.

FINANCIAL RESPONSIBILITY-Cont'd
Bankruptcy.
Suspension of driver's licenses, §42-7-402.
Bond, surety.
Custody and disposition of security, §42-7-304.
Deposit of money or securities, §42-7-301.
Failure of proof, §42-7-420.
Chauffeurs, §42-7-409.
Definitions, §42-7-103.
Department of revenue, director.
Administration of article, §42-7-201.
Drivers' licenses.
Revocation.
  Failure to provide proof of financial responsibility, §42-2-125.
Surrender of license.
  Failure to surrender revoked license.
    Penalty, §42-2-124.
    General provisions, §42-7-506.
    Revoking court, §42-2-124.
Evidence.
Admissibility of evidence, §42-7-504.
Forgery, §42-7-505.
Hearings, §42-7-201.
Insurance.
Certificate for insurance policy.
  General provisions, §42-7-410.
  When insurance carrier to issue certificate, §42-7-415.
Effect of article on other insurance policies, §42-7-417.
Former Colorado resident, §42-7-408.
Liability policy.
  Cancellation.
    Notice to director when policy is proof of financial responsibility, §42-7-416.
  Proof required, §42-7-414.
  Contents, §42-7-413.
  Definition, §§42-7-103, 42-7-413.
  Proof of financial responsibility, §42-7-414.
Minimum terms, §42-7-408.
Proof, §42-7-406.
Records.
  Confidential information, §42-7-503.
  Copies of drivers' records, §42-7-503.
  Restrictions in certain types of policy, §42-7-411.
Self-insurers, §42-7-501.
Judgments.
Bankruptcy, §42-7-402.
Deposit of money or other security, §§42-7-406, 42-7-418.
Failure of proof, §42-7-420.
Operation of motor vehicle without required proof, §42-7-422.
Release of proof, §42-7-421.
Satisfaction.
  General provisions, §42-7-403.
  Installment payments, §42-7-404.
Substitution of other proof, §42-7-419.
Suspension of driver's license.
  Duty of courts to report, §42-7-407.
  Effect of bankruptcy, §42-7-402.

FINANCIAL RESPONSIBILITY-Cont'd
Judgments.-Cont'd
Suspension of driver's license.-Cont'd
Effect of second judgment, §42-7-405.
Failure to satisfy judgment, §42-7-401.
Judicial review of actions, §42-7-201.
Legislative declaration, §42-7-102.
Methods.
Other methods not excluded by provisions of article, §42-7-509.
Misdemeanors.
Forgery, §42-7-505.
Insurance or bond required for certain vehicles, §42-7-510.
Proof of financial responsibility.
Operation of motor vehicle without required proof, §42-7-422.
Violations for which no penalty prescribed, §42-7-507.
Motorist insurance identification program.
Creation, §42-7-602.
Short title, §42-7-601.
Nonresidents.
Insurance.
Acceptance of certificate of foreign insurance carrier, §42-7-412.
Judgments.
Certified copy of unsatisfied judgment to state of nonresident, §42-7-502.
Owner other than operator, §42-7-409.
Proof.
Altered or counterfeit letter or insurance identification card, §42-7-301.5.
Chauffeur or family member, §42-7-409.
Failure of proof, §42-7-420.
Methods of giving proof, §42-7-408.
Operation without required proof, §42-7-422.
Release of proof, §42-7-421.
Required under certain conditions, §42-7-406.
Securities, §42-7-418.
Substitution of other proof, §42-7-419.
Records of drivers' open to public, §42-7-503.
Registration permits.
Requirements, §42-3-309.
Requirements under certain conditions, §42-7-406.
Savings clause, §42-7-508.
Securities, §42-7-418.
Signing, §42-7-505.
Title of act, §42-7-101.
FINES
Alcohol- or drug-related traffic offenses, §42-4-1301.
Traffic offenses, §42-4-1701.
FIRES AND FIRE PREVENTION
Motor vehicles.
Crossing fire hose, §42-4-1404.
Traffic violations.
Following fire apparatus, §42-4-1403.
FLAGS
Disabled persons.
Distress flags, §42-4-611.

FOREIGN CORPORATIONS
Antimonopoly financing.
Violations by foreign corporations, §12-6-209.
FORGERY
Certificates of title, §42-6-143.
Financial responsibility, §42-7-505.
FRAUD
Buyer agent, §12-6-120.
Motor vehicle dealers.
Right of action for loss, §12-6-122.
Used motor vehicles.
Private civil action, §42-6-204.
FREEWAYS
School buses.
Discharge of children on freeways, §42-4-1904.
FUNDS
Alcohol and drug driving safety program fund, §42-4-1301.3.
Auto dealer's license fund, §12-6-123.
Family-friendly court program cash fund, 42-4-1701.
Fuel piracy computer reprogramming cash fund, §42-1-221.
Hazardous materials safety fund, §42-20-107.
License plate cash fund, §42-3-301.
Motorcycle operator safety training fund, §43-5-504.
Nuclear materials transportation fund, §42-20-511.
Organ and tissue donation awareness fund, §42-2-107.
Persistent drunk driver cash fund, §42-3-303.
Vehicle identification number inspection fund, §42-5-204.

G

GRANTS OF RULE MAKING AUTHORITY
Education, department of.
School buses, §42-4-1904.
Public health and environment, department of.
Air quality control commission.
Diesel emissions program, §§42-4-403, 42-4-408, 42-4-414.
Motor vehicle emissions inspection, §§42-4-302, 42-4-306, 42-4-307, 42-4-309, 42-4-314.
Health, state board of.
Blood samples, collection and testing of, §42-4-1304.
Ignition interlock devices, §42-2-132.5.
Public safety, department of.
Colorado state patrol.
Chief, §§42-20-104, 42-20-108, 42-20-108.5, 42-20-202, 42-20-403, 42-20-504, 42-20-508.
Revenue, department of.
Commercial driving schools, §12-15-116.
Motor vehicles.
Automobile theft and inspection of vehicle identification numbers, §42-5-207.

GRANTS OF RULE MAKING AUTHORITY-Cont'd
Revenue, department of.-Cont'd
Commercial driving schools, §12-15-116.-Cont'd
- Motor vehicles.-Cont'd
  - Certificates of title and used motor vehicle sales, §42-6-107.
  - Drivers' licenses, §§42-2-111, 42-2-112, 42-2-114, 42-2-118, 42-2-122, 42-2-132.5, 42-2-144, 42-2-403, 42-2-406, 42-2-407.
  - Generally, §42-1-206.
  - Registration and taxation, §§42-3-102, 42-3-105, 42-3-107, 42-3-110, 42-3-301, 42-3-212, 42-3-304, 42-3-311.
  - Regulation of vehicles and traffic, §§42-4-202, 42-4-235, 42-4-310, 42-4-1208.
  - Uninsured motorist identification database program, §42-7-604.

Executive director.
- Automobile dealers, §§12-6-105, 12-6-110.
- Motor vehicle dealer board, §§12-6-104, 12-6-110, 12-6-122.
- Motor vehicles.
  - Automobile theft and inspection of vehicle identification numbers, §42-5-204.
  - Certificates of title and used motor vehicle sales, §§42-6-104, 42-6-107, 42-6-113, 42-6-122, 42-6-137, 42-6-147, 42-6-206.
  - Collectors' items, §42-12-401.
  - Drivers' licenses, §§42-2-107, 42-2-114, 42-2-117, 42-2-118, 42-2-127.7, 42-2-132, 42-2-406.
  - Generally, §§42-1-204, 42-1-206.
  - Motor vehicle financial responsibility, §42-7-201.
  - Port of entry weigh stations, §§42-8-104, 42-8-111.
  - Registration and taxation, §§42-3-107, 42-3-211, 42-3-212, 42-3-213, 42-3-218, 42-3-122, 42-3-124, 42-3-116, 42-3-304, 42-3-307, 42-12-301, 42-3-311.
  - Regulation of vehicles and traffic, §§42-4-202, 42-4-305, 42-4-405, 42-4-505, 42-4-511.2.
  - Temporary special event license plates, §42-3-220.

Transportation, department of.
- Department, §§42-4-414, 42-4-505, 42-4-510.
- Transportation commission, §§42-4-106, 42-4-511.

H

HABITUAL OFFENDERS
Appeals, §42-2-204.

HABITUAL OFFENDERS-Cont'd
Computation of number of offenses, §42-2-208.
Construction and interpretation, §42-2-207.
Drivers' licenses.
- Driving after revocation, §42-2-206.
- License to drive vehicle with ignition interlock device, §42-2-132.5.
- Persons not to be licensed, §42-2-205.
- Revocation, §42-2-203.

Elements of offense, §42-2-202.
Hearings prior to revocation, §42-2-203.
Legislative intent, §42-2-201.

HAZARDOUS MATERIALS TRANSPORTED BY MOTOR VEHICLES
Abandonment of motor vehicle.
- Prohibition against, §42-20-113.
- Reimbursement of expenses incurred by local governments, §42-20-112.

Agricultural product, §42-20-108.5.
Commercial vehicles.
- Standards, §42-4-235.

Definitions, §42-20-103.
Enforcement of regulatory provisions, §42-20-105.
Legislative declaration, §42-20-102.
Local government authority, §42-20-106.
Penalty assessments.
- Acceptance of late payments, §42-20-105.

Permits.
- Application, §42-20-202.
- Carrying of permit and shipping papers, §42-20-203.
- Fee, §42-20-202.
- Proof of liability insurance policy, §42-20-202.
- Regulation by local government.
  - Prohibition against, §42-20-206.
- Requirement of, §42-20-201.
- Suspension or revocation, §42-20-205.

Route designation.
- Application for, §42-20-302.
- Designation by state patrol, §§42-20-301, 42-20-302.
- Deviation from authorized routes, §42-20-305.
- Eisenhower-Johnson tunnels on interstate 70, §42-20-301.
- Emergency closure of public roads, §42-20-304.
- Road sign requirement, §42-20-303.
- Violations of.
  - Civil penalty, §42-20-305.

Rules.
- Applicability, §42-20-108.
- Criteria for adoption, §42-20-108.
- Penalty for violation of, §42-20-109.

Safety and instruction related to hazardous materials.
- Certification of enforcement officials, §§42-4-235, 42-20-105.

Safety fund, §42-20-107.
Spills.
- Duty of driver to provide notice of spill, §42-20-113.
- Prohibition against, §42-20-113.

HAZARDOUS MATERIALS TRANSPORTED BY MOTOR VEHICLES-Cont'd
Spills.-Cont'd
Reimbursement of expenses incurred by local governments, §42-20-112.
State patrol.
Chief.
Powers and duties, §42-20-104.
Rules, §§42-20-104, 42-20-108, 42-20-108.5.
Single trip permits.
Issuance, §42-20-202.
Title of act, §42-20-101.
Unsafe vehicles.
Certification of enforcement officials, §§42-4-235, 42-20-105.
Immobilization of, §42-20-110.
Standards for commercial vehicles, §42-4-235.
Violations.
Civil penalties, §§42-20-204, 42-20-305.
Failure of driver to provide notice of spill, §42-20-113.
General provisions, §§42-20-109, 42-20-111.
Permit violations, §42-20-204.

HIGHWAY USERS TAX FUND AIR ACCOUNT
Establishment, §42-3-304.
Use of moneys in account, §§42-3-304, 42-4-305.
Driver's license administrative revocation account, §42-2-132.
Special purpose account, §42-1-211.
Traffic laws.
Appropriations for expenses of administration of article, §42-4-113.
Weigh stations.
Appropriations for, §42-8-110.

HIGHWAYS
Animals and fowl.
Traffic laws, §42-4-109.
Bicycles.
Operation on highways, §42-4-1412.
Billboards.
Signs imitating or obscuring traffic signs, §42-4-606.
Bridges.
Penalty for failure of owners to construct culverts or bridges, §43-5-305.
Damages.
Crop sprinkler systems, §43-5-301.
Damaging bridges of highways, §43-5-301.
Motor vehicles.
Liability of driver for damage to highway or highway structures, §42-4-512.
Department of transportation.
Maintenance, repair, or construction zone designation, §42-4-613.
Ditches.
Written consent to excavate required, §43-5-1406.
Electric vehicles, §§42-4-109.5, 42-4-111.

HIGHWAYS-Cont'd
Federal highway safety act of 1966.
Implimentation, §43-5-401.
Fences, obstructing highways.
Penalty, §43-5-301.
Garbage and trash.
Littering prohibited, §42-4-1406.
High occupancy toll lanes, §42-4-1012.
Holes.
Digging pits or holes in or upon highways, §43-5-301.
Injury to highway, §43-5-307.
Intersections.
Rights-of-way, §§42-4-701 to 42-4-703.
Stop signs and yield signs, §42-4-703.
Turning.
Required position and method, §42-4-901.
Interstate highways.
Driving on.
Traffic laws, §42-4-1010.
Operation of motorized bicycles on, §42-2-103.
Lanes.
Acceleration lanes, §42-4-1010.
Deceleration lanes, §42-4-1010.
Driving on roadways laned for traffic, §42-4-1007.
Limited access roads.
Traffic laws, §42-4-1010.
Littering, §42-4-1406.
Low-power scooters.
Operation on highways, §42-4-109.
Machinery.
Transporting heavy machinery on public roads, §43-5-306.
Maintenance, repair, or construction zone designation, §42-4-613.
Motorized bicycles.
Operation on limited-access roads, §42-2-103.
Motor vehicles.
Restrictions on right to use highways, §42-4-106.
Traction devices, §42-4-106.
Transporting heavy machines.
Use of public roads, §43-5-306.
Mountain highways.
Rights-of-way, §42-4-711.
Obstruction.
Penalty, §43-5-301.
Pipelines.
Construction of pipelines.
Consent required, §42-4-1406.
Ports of entry.
Weigh stations, §§42-8-101 to 42-8-111.
Railroads.
Construction of railroads.
Consent required, §42-4-1406.
Rights-of-way.
Construction and maintenance.
Vehicles to yield, §42-4-712.
Intersections, §§42-4-701 to 42-4-703.
Mountain highways, §42-4-711.
Removal of traffic hazards on land abutting rights-of-way, §42-4-114.

HIGHWAYS-Cont'd
Signs.
Department of transportation.
Duty to sign state highways, §42-4-601.
Local authorities.
Permission of department of transportation required for signs, §42-4-602.
See also SIGNS, SIGNALS, AND MARKINGS.
Skates, skis, sleds and toboggans.
Use on highways, §42-4-109.
Toll roads.
High occupancy toll lanes, §42-4-1012.
Toy vehicles.
Use on highways, §42-4-109.
Trees and timber.
Obstructing highways, §43-5-301.
Waters and watercourses.
Causing water to overflow onto highways, §§43-5-301, 43-5-303.
Damming streams, §43-5-302.
Weigh stations, §§42-8-101 to 42-8-111.
Wildlife crossing zones, establishment, §42-4-118.
Increased penalties for moving traffic violations, §42-4-616.
Traffic offenses within, §42-4-1701.
HIT AND RUN DRIVING
Prohibition, §§42-4-1601, 42-4-1602.
HITCHHIKING
Restrictions, §42-4-805.
HOMICIDE
Vehicular homicide.
Revocation of driver's license, §§42-2-125, 42-2-128.
HOTELS, INNS, AND OTHER TRANSIENT LODGING PLACES
Definitions.
Auto and tourist camps, hotels and motels, §43-5-201.
Stolen vehicles.
Definitions, §43-5-201.
Penalties.
Allowing storage of stolen motor vehicles, §43-5-205.
Violation of part, §43-5-207.
Records.
Inspection of records by state patrol and peace officers, §43-5-204.
Owners required to keep records, §43-5-203.

I

IDENTIFICATION CARDS
Cancellation.
For failure to register vehicle, §42-2-304.5.
Generally, §42-2-302.
Change of address, §42-2-307.
Compliance with Military Selective Service Act, §42-2-302.
Contents, §§42-2-302, 42-2-303.
County jail processing unit, §§42-2-311 to 42-2-313.

IDENTIFICATION CARDS-Cont'd
Definitions, §42-2-301.
Duplicates.
Fees, §42-2-306.
General provisions, §42-2-305.
Expiration, §42-2-304.
Fees, §42-2-306.
Issuance, §42-2-302.
Liability of public entity, §42-2-308.
Photographs, §42-2-303.
Proof of legal presence in country required, §42-2-302.
Qualifications and limitations, §42-2-302.
Renewal, §42-2-304.
Stored information, §42-2-303.
Unlawful acts.
Enumeration, §42-2-309.
Penalties, §42-2-310.
Unlawful duplication of card, §42-2-309.
IDENTITIY THEFT.
Motor vehicle investigation unit established, §42-1-122.
IDLING STANDARDS
Applicablity, §42-14-104.
Definitions, §42-14-102.
Exemptions, §42-14-105.
Penalties for violation, §42-14-106.
Idling standard defined, §42-14-105.
Local government standards - how affected, §42-14-103.
INDIANS
Revocation of Colorado driving privileges, §42-2-126.5.
INSPECTIONS
Hotels, inns, and other transient lodging places.
Stolen vehicles.
Records open for inspection by state patrol and peace officers, §43-5-204.
INSURANCE - MOTOR VEHICLES
Commercial driving schools.
Violations.
Penalties, §12-15-120.
Compulsory insurance.
Penalty and assessment of points on driver's license when driver not complying, §§42-2-127, 42-4-1409.
Disabled persons.
Nonemergency transportation of individuals with disabilities, §42-7-510.
Motor vehicle service contract insurance, §§42-11-101 to 42-11-108.
Motorist insurance identification database program.
Administration of program, §42-7-604.
Confidentiality of database, §§42-7-604, 42-7-606.
Coordination with other financial responsibility requirements, §42-7-607.
Definitions, §42-7-603.
Fees, §42-3-304.
Liability for implementing program, §42-7-606.
Notice of lack of financial responsibility, §42-7-605.
Penalty, §42-7-605.

INSURANCE - MOTOR VEHICLES—Cont'd
  Motorist insurance identification database program.—Cont'd
    Release of insurance information, §42-7-606.
    Repeal of program, §§24-34-104, 42-7-609.
    Short title, §42-7-601.
    Suspension of drivers' license, §42-2-127.7.
  Proof of insurance.
    Relicensing, §42-7-406.
  Uninsured motorists.
    Identification program, §§42-7-601, 42-7-602.
INTOXICATION
  Chemical tests for intoxication.
    Blood alcohol level, §42-4-1301.1.
    Blood test for drivers under the age of 21 years not required, §§42-2-126, 42-4-1301.1.
  Driving under the influence or while impaired, §42-4-1301.
  Records of testing methods.
    Prima facie proof, §42-4-1303.
  Refusal to take test.
    Admissibility in court, §42-4-1301.
    Revocation of driver's license, §42-2-126.
  Samples from crash victims, §42-4-1304.

J

JAILS
  Juvenile prisoners.
    Confinement with adult offenders, §42-4-1706.
JUDICIAL NOTICE
  Administrative procedure act.
    Hearings.
      Agency may take notice of general, technical, or scientific fact, §§24-4-105, 42-2-122.1, 42-2-126.
  Alcohol- or drug-related traffic offenses.
    Testing methods, §42-4-1301.

L

LEMON LAW
  Nonconformity to warranties, §§42-10-101 to 42-10-107.
LIMITATION OF ACTIONS
  Motor vehicles.
    Repairs, §42-9-112.
    Used motor vehicles, §42-6-204.
    Warranties.
      Noncompliance to warranties, §42-10-107.
LITTERING
  Highways, §42-4-1406.
LOW-POWER SCOOTERS
  Careless driving, §42-4-1402.
  Compulsory insurance, §42-4-1409.
  Equipment, §42-4-220.
  Minimum safety standards, §42-4-232.
  Registration fee, §42-3-311.
  Regulation, §42-4-109.
  Speed regulations, §42-4-1101.

LOW-SPEED ELECTRIC VEHICLES
  Equipment requirements, §42-4-240.
  Traffic regulation, §42-4-109.5.
  Class B low-speed electric vehicles, §42-4-109.6.

M

MACHINERY
  Transportation of heavy machinery.
    Protection of sidewalks, bridges, and culverts, §43-5-306.
  Mobile machinery and self-propelled construction equipment.
    Certificates of title, §42-6-102.
    Definition, §42-1-102.
    License plates, §§42-3-201, 42-3-202.
    Registration, §§42-3-103, 42-3-104, 42-3-304.
    Requirement, §42-3-106.
    Specific ownership tax, §§42-3-106, 42-3-107, 42-3-304.
MANUFACTURED HOUSING
  Specific ownership tax.
    Exemption from classification, §42-3-106.
MECHANICS' LIENS
  Motor vehicle mortgages.
    Effect of mortgage on mechanics' and warehouse liens, §42-6-131.
    Towed vehicles, §§42-4-1806, 42-4-2105.
MENTAL HEALTH
  Mentally ill.
    Drivers' licenses.
      Restricted licenses, §42-2-116.
MILEAGE
  Specific ownership taxes.
    Apportionment to counties, §42-3-107.
MILITARY AFFAIRS
  Drivers' licenses.
    Exemption of person serving in armed forces, §42-2-102.
    Extension of period of validity, §42-2-118.
  Registration.
    Proof of ownership in lieu of title, §42-6-106.
    United States' vehicles registered in foreign countries.
      Exemption period upon return to country, §42-3-103.
  Special license plates.
    National guard, §42-3-218.
    Veterans, §42-3-213.
MINORS
  Alcohol beverages.
    Revocation of driver's license.
      Blood test for drivers under 21 years of age not required, §§42-2-126, 42-4-1301.1.
      Mandatory revocation, §42-2-125.
  Drivers' licenses.
    Liability of parents or guardians.
      General provisions, §42-2-108.
      Release from liability, §42-2-109.
    Revocation upon death of signer for minor, §42-2-110.

MINORS-Cont'd
  Jails.
    Misdemeanor traffic offenses.
      Confinement with adult offenders, §42-4-1706.
  Learners' permits.
    Revocation of permit upon death of signer for minor, §42-2-110.
    Permitting unauthorized minor to drive, §42-2-139.
    Restriction on ability to have more than one minor passenger, §42-4-116.
  Mandatory revocation of driver's license or permit.
    Aggravated motor vehicle theft, §42-2-125.
    Criminal mischief, §42-2-125.
    Criminal trespass, §42-2-125.
    Misuse of mobile communication devices, §42-4-239.
  Vehicular homicide.
    Revocation of driver's license, §§42-2-125, 42-2-128.

MIRRORS
  Motor vehicle requirements, §42-4-226.

MISCHIEF
  Criminal mischief.
    Mandatory revocation of driver's license, §42-2-125.

MISDEMEANOR TRAFFIC OFFENSES
  Accidents and accident reports.
    Failure of driver to stop at scene, §42-4-1601.
    Failure to exchange information or render aid, §42-4-1602.
    Failure to notify owner or operator when collision or property damage to unattended vehicle, §42-4-1604.
  Community or useful public service.
    Sentencing, §§18-1.3-507, 42-4-1701.
  Drivers' licenses.
    Failure to surrender revoked license.
      Driving under the influence or while impaired, §42-2-129.
      Drug convictions, §42-2-130.
      General provisions, §42-2-124.
    False affidavits or knowingly swearing or affirming falsely, §42-2-137.
    False application for new license, §42-2-132.
    Refusal to exhibit identification on demand, §42-2-115.
    Revocation due to non-driving alcohol offenses, §42-2-131.
    Unlawful possession or use of license, §42-2-136.
    Violation of license provision, §42-2-101.
  Equipment.
    Violation of regulatory provisions.
      Alteration of suspension system, §42-4-233.
      Minimum standards for commercial vehicles, §42-4-235.
      Restrictions on tire equipment, §42-4-228.

MISDEMEANOR TRAFFIC OFFENSES-Cont'd
  Hazardous materials.
    Transportation by motor vehicle.
      Permit violations, §42-20-204.
  Inspection.
    Failure to comply with safety requirements after spot inspection, §42-4-203.
    Violations of emissions control provisions, §§42-4-313, 42-4-413.
  Other offenses.
    Careless driving, §42-4-1402.
    Eluding or attempting to elude a police officer, §42-4-1413.
    Failure to comply with insurance requirements, §42-4-1409.
    Illegal use of distress flag for persons with disabilities, §42-4-611.
    Reckless driving, §42-4-1401.
    Use of radar jamming devices, §42-4-1415.
    Use of tax-exempt diesel fuel, §42-4-1414.
  Penalties and procedure.
    Classification of traffic offense penalties, §42-4-1701.
    Community or useful public service, §42-4-1701.
    Court hearings.
      Appeals, §42-4-1708.
      Burden of proof, §42-4-1708.
      Failure to appear, §42-4-1716.
    Eluding or attempting to elude a police officer, §42-4-1413.
    Offenses by persons controlling vehicles, §42-4-1704.
    Penalty assessments.
      Acceptance of late payments, §42-4-1701.
    Provisions for confinement of juveniles convicted of misdemeanor traffic offense, §42-4-1706.
    Summons and complaint or penalty assessment notice for offenses, §42-4-1707.
    Surcharges.
      Victims and witnesses assistance and law enforcement fund, §42-4-1701.
    Use of tax-exempt diesel fuel, §42-4-1414.
  Registration.
    Improper use of truck registered as collectors' item, §§42-3-121, 42-12-405.
    Misuse or forgery of special plate or placard, §42-4-1208.
    Violation of registration provisions.
      Deceptive use of certificate of title or registration materials, §42-3-121.
      Failure to surrender registration card upon demand, §42-3-121.
      Noncompliance with mandatory motor vehicle insurance coverage requirements, §§42-3-105, 42-3-113.
      Sale of invalid or stolen registration materials, §42-3-121.

MISDEMEANOR TRAFFIC OFFENSES-Cont'd
  Regulations of vehicles and traffic.
    Violations.
      Disobedience of rules governing operation of bicycles, §42-4-1412.
      Disobedience to police officer, §42-4-107.
  Reports upon conviction.
    Misuse or forgery of special plate or placard, §42-4-1208.
  Rights-of-way.
    Failure of vehicle to stop for flashing signals on school bus, §42-4-1903.
  Size, weight, and load violations.
    Gross weight of vehicles and loads, §42-4-508.
    Permits for excess size and weight and for mobile homes, §42-4-510.
    Vehicles weighed - excess removed, §42-4-509.
    Wheel and axle loads, §42-4-507.
  Speed regulations.
    Speed contests, §42-4-1105.
    Speed limits, §42-4-1101.

MISDEMEANORS
  Commercial driving schools.
    Violations, §12-15-120.
  Drivers' licenses.
    Commercial drivers' licenses.
      Driving testers.
        Acting as testing unit or driving tester without license, §42-2-408.
      Multiple drivers' licenses, §42-2-404.
      Operation of commercial vehicle without license, §42-2-404.
    Driving while license is under restraint, §42-2-138.
    Unlawful duplication of license, §42-2-136.
  Drugs.
    Controlled substances.
      Driving under the influence or while impaired, §42-4-1301.
      Habitual users prohibited from driving, §42-4-1301.
      Revocation or suspension of driver's license, §§42-2-125, 42-2-127.3.
    Marijuana.
      Revocation or suspension of driver's license, §§42-2-125, 42-2-127.3.
  Hazardous materials.
    Transportation by motor vehicle.
      Failure of driver to provide notice of spill, §42-20-113.
      General provisions, §§42-20-109, 42-20-111.
      Permit violations, §42-20-204.
  Hotels, inns, and other lodging places.
    Allowing storage of stolen motor vehicles, §43-5-205.
  Nuclear materials transportation.
    Violations, §42-20-405.
  Penalties and procedure.
    School zones, §42-4-615.
  Sales.
    Salvage vehicles, §42-6-206.

MISDEMEANORS-Cont'd
  School buses.
    Operation violations, §42-4-1904.
  Waters and watercourses.
    Causing water to overflow upon highways, §43-5-303.

MOBILE HOMES
  Permits.
    Prorated tax receipt as permit, §42-4-510.
    Transporting mobile homes, §42-4-511.

MOPEDS
  Applicability of traffic laws, §42-4-109.
  Learners' permits, §42-2-106.
  Lighting equipment, §42-4-220.

MORTGAGES AND DEEDS OF TRUST
  Mechanics' and warehouse liens.
    Motor vehicles.
      Effect of mortgage on lien, §42-6-131.

MOTORCYCLES
  Brakes, §42-4-223.
  Equipment.
    Lamps, §§42-4-205, 42-4-220.
    Minimum safety standards, §42-4-232.
  Learners' permits, §42-2-106.
  Operator safety training program.
    Advisory committee.
      Membership, §43-5-505.
      Sunset review, §§2-3-1203, 43-5-505.
    Definitions, §43-5-501.
    General provisions, §43-5-502.
    Instructor requirements and training, §43-5-503.
    Motorcycle operator safety training fund.
      Creation, §43-5-504.
      Surcharge on licenses to be deposited in fund, §§42-2-114, 42-2-118, 42-3-304.
  Overtaking and passing, §42-4-1503.
  Passengers, §42-4-1502.
  Riding on motorcycles.
    Carrying articles, §42-4-1502.
    Clinging to other vehicles, §42-4-1504.
    Group riding, §42-4-1503.
    Number of riders, §42-4-1502.
    Traffic lanes, §42-4-1503.
  Temporary licenses, §42-2-106.
  Traffic laws.
    Applicability of traffic laws, §42-4-1501.
    General provisions, §§42-4-1501 to 42-4-1504.

MOTOR CARRIERS
  Minimum standards for commercial vehicles, §2-3-306.
  Weigh stations, §§42-8-101 to 42-8-111.

MOTOR VEHICLE DEALERS
  Advertisements.
  Definition, §12-6-102.
  Board.
    Actions brought by or against.
      Attorney general to advise and represent, §12-6-107.
    Appointment, §12-6-103.
    Creation, §12-6-103.
    Membership, §12-6-104.
    Oath of office, §12-6-104.

MOTOR VEHICLE DEALERS-Cont'd
Powers and duties, §12-6-104.
Records as evidence, §12-6-106.
Rules, §12-6-104.
Seal, §12-6-104.
Termination, §12-6-124.
Change of status or address.
  Notice, §12-6-116.
Coercion.
  Elements of offense, §12-6-120.
  Penalties, §12-6-121.
Contract disputes with manufacturer, §12-6-122.5.
Criminal penalties, §§12-6-119.5, 12-6-121.
Definitions, §12-6-102.
Discharge of salesmen.
  Notification of board, §12-6-116.
Drafts or checks issued by licensee not honored for payment.
  Fine and suspension of license, §12-6-121.5.
Engine identification numbers.
  Duties of dealers and mechanics, §42-5-106.
Franchises.
  Definitions, §12-6-102.
  Unlawful acts by manufacturer or distributor.
    Violations and penalties, §§12-6-120, 12-6-130.
    Appeal to board, §42-6-131.
Fraud.
  Right of action for loss due to dealer's fraud or unlawful act, §12-6-122.
Lease form to be used for contract, §12-6-104.
Legislative declaration, §12-6-101.
Licensure.
  Applications, §12-6-115.
  Bonding requirement.
    Corporate surety to provide notice of claims to licensing board and executive director, §12-6-112.7.
    General provisions, §12-6-111.
  Classes of license, §12-6-108.
  Denial, suspension, or revocation.
    Appeal and judicial review, §12-6-119.
    Grounds, §§12-6-118, 12-6-303.
    Procedure, §12-6-119.
    Unlawful sales activity, §12-6-119.5.
  Display, §12-6-109.
  Examination requirement, §12-6-113.
  Fees, §12-6-110.
  Financial responsibility requirements, §§11-35-101, 12-6-111.
  Fund.
    Auto dealers license fund, §12-6-123.
  Principal place of business.
    Contracts with garages, §12-6-117.
    Structural requirements, §12-6-117.
  Renewal and expiration, §12-6-110.
  Temporary license, §12-6-108.5.
Manufacturers.
  Manufacturer representative, §12-6-102.
Motor vehicle agent.
  Definition, §12-6-102.

MOTOR VEHICLE DEALERS-Cont'd
Successor under existing franchise agreement, §12-6-120.7.
Unlawful acts.
  General provisions, §12-6-120.
  Penalties, §§12-6-119.5, 12-6-120, 12-6-303.
  Right of action for loss, §12-6-122.
  Unlawful sales activity, §12-6-119.5.
Vouchers for emissions inspections, §42-4-309.

MOTOR VEHICLE REGISTRATION
Address for motor vehicle registration, §42-6-139.
Amateur radio operators.
  Call letters on license plates, §42-3-210.
Antique motor vehicles.
  Collectors' items, §§42-12-101 to 42-12-405.
  Emissions control, §42-12-404.
  Original plates, §42-12-302.
  Special provisions, §42-12-301.
Applications.
  Contents, §42-3-105.
  Denial, §42-3-119.
  Filing, §42-3-113.
Cancellation.
  General provisions, §42-3-120.
  Use of noncommercial or recreational vehicle for commercial purposes, §42-3-121.
Card, §42-3-113.
Certificates of title.
  Application filed simultaneously, §42-3-105.
  Requirement, §42-6-106.
  Temporary registration certificates, §42-3-203.
  Transfer.
    Expiration of registration, §42-3-115.
Change of address or name, §42-2-119.
Change of primary body color, §42-3-126.
Compulsory insurance coverage.
  Affirmation clause, §§42-3-105, 42-3-113.
  False statements.
    Perjury, §§42-3-105, 42-3-113, 42-3-122.
  Noncompliance.
    Misdemeanor traffic offense, §§42-3-105, 42-3-112.
  Proof of insurance.
    Required coverage, §§42-3-105, 42-3-113.
  Seasonal coverage, §42-3-105.
Disabled persons.
  See within this subheading, "Persons with disabilities".
Drivers' licenses.
  Cancellation for failure to register vehicle, §42-2-122.
  Commercial drivers' licenses, §42-2-403.
  Statement of registration requirement on application, §42-2-107.
Exemptions.
  General provisions, §42-3-104.
Fees.
  Antique motor vehicles, §42-3-219.
  Apportioned registration, §42-3-304.

MOTOR VEHICLE REGISTRATION-Cont'd
Fees.-Cont'd
  County registration fee, §42-3-310.
  Emissions inspections, §42-3-304.
  Enforcement of provisions, §42-3-307.
  Foreign diplomats.
    Exemption of certain foreign diplomatic vehicles, §42-3-304.
  License plate fees, §42-3-301.
  Monthly report to the state controller, §42-3-304.
  Municipal corporation registration fee, §42-3-310.
  Passenger-mile tax.
    General provisions, §§42-3-304 to 42-3-306.
    Schedule of fees charged, §42-3-306.
    Taxpayer statement, §42-3-308.
  Passenger and passenger-mile taxes, §42-3-304.
  Payment by bad check.
    Recovery of plates, §42-3-123.
  Payment by installment for fleet vehicles, §42-3-110.
  Penalties for not filing, §42-3-308.
  P.O.S.T. board cash fund surcharge, §42-3-304.
  Schedule of fees charged, §§42-3-304 to 42-3-306.
  Special plate fees, §42-3-302.
  State of Colorado.
    Exemption of state owned vehicles, §42-3-304.
  Taxpayer statement, §42-3-308.
  Temporary commercial registration permits, §42-3-304.
  Veterans.
    Exemptions for disabled veterans, §§42-3-204, 42-3-304.
Filing.
  Payment of fees required, §42-3-105.
Fleet operators, §§42-3-107, 42-3-125.
Fleet vehicles in emissions program area, §42-3-113.
Funds.
  Clean screen fund, §42-3-304.
  Highway users tax fund, §42-3-304.
  License plate cash fund, §§42-3-301, 42-3-302.
  Peace officers standards and training board cash fund, §42-3-304.
  Persistent drunk driver cash fund, §42-3-303.
Identification cards for nondrivers.
  Cancellation for failure to register vehicle, §42-2-304.5.
  Statement of registration requirement on application, §42-2-302.
Identification numbers, §42-6-145.
Initial registration, §42-6-112.
Legislative intent, §42-3-101.
License plates.
  See within this subheading, "Plates".

MOTOR VEHICLE REGISTRATION-Cont'd
Military affairs.
  Proof of ownership in lieu of title, §42-6-106.
  United States' vehicles registered in foreign countries.
    Exemption period upon return to country, §42-3-103.
Motor vehicles in emissions program area, §42-3-113.
Motorized bicycles, §42-3-311.
New residents.
  Change in deadline for registration, §42-3-103.
Nonresidents, §§42-3-103, 42-3-117, 42-6-140.
Passenger-mile tax.
  Permits, §42-3-309.
Passenger buses.
  See this heading within MOTOR VEHICLES.
Periodic registration, §42-3-102.
Permits.
  Passenger-mile tax, §42-3-309.
Personal mobility devices, §42-4-117.
Persons with disabilities.
  Identification, §42-3-113.
  Misuse or forgery of special plate or placard, §42-4-1208.
Plates.
  Certificate of title required, §42-6-106.
  Confidential information, §24-72-204.
  Contents, §42-3-201.
  Dealer registration plates.
    General provisions, §42-3-116.
  Display, §42-3-202.
  Duplicates, §42-3-205.
  Expiration, §42-3-114.
  Fees, §42-3-113.
  Full-use dealer plates, §42-3-116.
  Lost plates, §42-3-205.
  Manufacturers, distributors, and dealers, §42-3-116.
  Number furnished, §42-3-201.
  Optional plates.
    Authorization for issuance, §42-3-212.
  Personalized license plates, §42-3-211.
  Remanufacturing, §42-3-206.
  Rental vehicles, §42-3-113.
  Revocation.
    Abuse of parking privileges, §§42-3-204, 42-4-1208.
    Payment by bad check, §42-3-123.
  Rules, §42-3-113.
Proof of insurance.
  Required coverage, §§42-3-105, 42-3-113.
  Seasonal coverage, §42-3-105.
Reciprocity, §42-3-103.
Records.
  Confidential information, §24-72-204.
Registration of motor vehicle at improper address, §42-6-139.
Rental vehicles, §42-3-113.
Requirement, §42-3-103.
Residence, §42-6-139.

MOTOR VEHICLE REGISTRATION-Cont'd
  Sales tax.
    Payment of tax as prerequisite, §39-26-113.
  Situs, §42-6-139.
  Special plates.
    Authorization, issuance, and revocation.
      Electric powered motor vehicles, §42-3-103.
      Fees, §42-3-302.
      Fleet vehicles, §42-3-125.
      Group plates, §42-3-207.
      Issuance by department, §42-3-208.
      License Plate Auctions, §§42-1-401 to 42-1-407; 42-3-213.
      Misuse or forgery of special plate or placard, §42-4-1208.
      Original plates, §42-3-219.
      Personalized plates, §42-3-211.
      Persons with disabilities, §§24-72-204, 42-3-204, 42-4-1208.
      Retirement of special plates, §§42-3-207, 42-3-212, 42-3-213, 42-3-214, 42-3-215, 42-3-216.
      Revocation, §§42-3-204, 42-4-1208.
      Special plates created by rule.
        Requirements for certain plates created by rule, §42-3-208.
        Rules relating to, §42-3-207.
      Taxes and fees, §42-3-207.
      Temporary plates, §42-3-115.
      Transferred from disposed vehicles, §42-3-115.
      Transport operators, §42-3-116.
      Validating tab or sticker, §42-3-201.
  Special plates allowed by statute.
    Adopt a shelter pet, §42-3-234.
    "Alive at Twenty-five", §42-3-230.
    Alumni associations, §42-3-214.
    Amateur radio operators, §42-3-210.
    American Indian, §42-3-217.
    Antique motor vehicles, §42-3-219.
    Boy Scouts, §42-3-229.
    Breast cancer awareness, §42-3-217.5.
    Colorado Avelanche, §42-3-239.
    Colorado foundation for agriculture, §42-3-216.
    Colorado carbon fund, §42-3-228.
    Colorado horse development authority, §42-3-227.
    Colorado "Kids first", §42-3-224.
    Colorado ski country, §42-3-231.
    Colorado state parks, §42-3-233.
    Craig hospital, §42-3-240.
    Denver Broncos, §42-3-221.
    Denver Nuggets, §42-3-239.
    Denver firefighter, §42-3-208.
    Diabetes - Type 1, §42-3-238.
    Disabled veterans, §§42-3-213, 42-3-304.
    Donate life, §42-3-232.
    Elks club, §42-3-208.
    Former prisoners of war or surviving spouses, §§42-3-213, 42-3-304.
    Girl Scouts, §42-3-237.
    Korean war veteran, §42-3-213.
    Legislative plates, §42-3-209.

MOTOR VEHICLE REGISTRATION-Cont'd
  Special plates allowed by statute.-Cont'd
    Luxury limousines, §42-3-235.
    Medal of honor recipients, §42-3-213.
    Military veterans, §§42-3-213.
    National guard members, §42-3-218.
    Pearl Harbor survivors, §42-3-213.
    Public education, §42-3-222.
    Purple heart recipients, §42-3-213.
    Raptor education, §42-3-208.
    Recipient of military valor award, §42-3-213.
    Rotary club, §42-3-208.
    Support the troops, §42-3-223.
    Taxicabs, §42-3-236.
    United States navy, §42-3-213.
    United States Olympic committee, §42-3-215.
    Vietnam war veteran, §§42-3-208, 42-3-213.
  Special registration of state and local government vehicles, §42-3-104.
  Specific ownership tax.
    Ad valorem property taxes.
      Imposition of specific ownership tax in lieu of, §42-3-101.
    Antique motor vehicles.
      Payment of tax, §42-12-401.
    Collection.
      Apportionment of tax collections, §42-3-107.
      County clerk and recorders, §§42-1-210, 42-1-213.
    Determination of taxable value, §42-3-106.
    Exemptions.
      Disabled veterans, §42-3-104.
      Manufactured homes, §42-3-106.
      Property which is exempt from ad valorem taxes, §42-3-104.
      Purple heart recipients, §42-3-104.
      United States government, §42-3-104.
    Imposition of tax, §42-3-106.
    Payment for twelve-month registration period, §42-3-109.
    Payment.
      Accompanying registration application, §42-3-105.
      Failure to pay tax, §42-3-112.
      Installments for fleet vehicles, §42-3-110.
      Time for payment, §42-3-107.
    Rate of tax.
      General provisions, §42-3-107.
      Minimum tax, §42-3-109.
    Tax year.
      Effective date of tax, §42-3-111.
    Trailer coaches, §42-3-111.
    Value.
      Classification of vehicles, §42-3-106.
      Determination of year model, §42-3-108.
      Phases for determining, §42-3-107.
  Stolen vehicles.
    Suspension of registration, §42-3-118.
  Taxpayer statement for passenger-mile tax, §42-3-308.

MOTOR VEHICLE REGISTRATION-Cont'd

Temporary commercial registration permits, §42-3-304.
Temporary registration certificates, §42-3-203.
Temporary special event license plates, §42-3-220.
Violations of provisions.
　Display of plates, §42-3-202.
　Penalties, §42-3-121.
　Penalty where no specific penalty provided, §42-3-124.
　Use of noncommercial or recreational vehicle for commercial purposes, §42-3-121.

MOTOR VEHICLES

Abandoned vehicles.
　See ABANDONED VEHICLES.
Accidents.
　See ACCIDENTS - MOTOR VEHICLES.
Age.
　See AGE
Agriculture.
　See AGRICULTURE
Air bags, installation of false or incorrect unit, §§6-1-710, 42-9-111.
Air pollution.
　Causing air pollution, §42-4-412.
AIR program, §§42-4-301 to 42-4-316.
Alarms.
　Volunteer ambulance services, §42-4-222.
　Volunteer fire departments, §42-4-222.
Alcohol beverages.
　See ALCOHOL BEVERAGES.
Antimonopoly financing.
　See ANTIMONOPOLY FINANCING LAW.
Antique motor vehicles.
　As collectors' items, 7sect;§42-12-101 to 42-12-405.
　Definitions, §42-12-101.
　Emissions control program.
　　Exemptions and requirements, §42-12-404.
　Equipment, §42-12-403.
　Horseless carriages, §42-12-301.
　Registration.
　　Collectors' item, §42-12-401.
　　Original plates, §42-12-302.
　　Special provisions, §42-12-301.
　　Violation of registration penalties, §§42-3-121, 42-12-405.
　Rebuilder's certificate of title, §42-12-102.
　Repairs.
　　Exemption from provisions, §42-9-110.
　Specific ownership tax.
　　Payment, §42-12-401.
　Storage, §42-12-402.
　Street-rod vehicles, §§42-12-201 to 204.
Apportioned registration.
　Classification of vehicles, §42-3-106.
　Definition, §42-1-102.
　Registration fees, §42-3-304.
Appropriations.
　Administration of title, §42-1-219.

MOTOR VEHICLES-Cont'd

Appropriations.-Cont'd
　Traffic laws.
　　Expenses for administration of article, §42-4-113.
　Weigh stations.
　　Expenses of administration, §42-8-111.
Appurtenance.
　Definitions, §42-1-102.
　Width requirements, §42-4-502.
Auction dealers.
　Licensing, §§12-6-108, 12-6-110.
Auctioneers.
　Definition, §12-6-102.
Automated vehicle identification systems, §42-4-110.5.
Automobile inspection and readjustment program, §§42-4-301 to 42-4-316.
Backing, §42-4-1211.
Bonds, surety.
　Buyer agent, §12-6-112.2.
　Dealers, §12-6-111.
　Titles.
　　Furnishing bond for certificates of title, §42-6-115.
Brakes.
　Bicycles, §42-4-221.
　Requirements, §42-4-223.
　Stopping distances, §42-4-223.
Buyer agents.
　Bonding requirement, §12-6-112.2.
　Definition, §12-6-102.
　Licensing.
　　Denial, suspension, or revocation.
　　　Grounds, §12-6-118.
　　Fees, §12-6-110.
　　General provisions, §§12-6-108, 12-6-110.
　Unlawful acts, §12-6-120.
Chemical tests for intoxication.
　See INTOXICATION.
Child restraint systems, §42-4-236.
Coasting, §42-4-1009.
Collector's items, §§42-12-101 to 42-12-405.
Commercial code.
　Secured transactions.
　　Repossession, §42-6-146.
　　Security interests, §42-6-120.
Commercial driving schools.
　See COMMERCIAL DRIVING SCHOOLS
Commercial vehicles.
　See COMMERCIAL VEHICLES
Compulsory insurance, §42-4-1409.
Confiscated vehicles.
　Disposition of personal property, §§42-13-101 to 42-13-109.
Construction and interpretation.
　Drivers' licenses, §42-2-143.
　Habitual offenders, §42-2-207.
Construction.
　Exemption of certain construction equipment from requirements, §42-4-202.
Exemption of certain construction equipment from registration, §42-3-104.

MOTOR VEHICLES–Cont'd
Counties.
See COUNTY CLERKS AND RECORDERS.
Custom motor vehicles.
Equipment, §42-4-215.5.
Data processing.
Colorado state titling and registration system.
Generally, §42-1-211.
Dealers.
See MOTOR VEHICLE DEALERS.
Definitions.
Antimonopoly financing, §12-6-201.
Antique motor vehicles, §42-12-101.
BAC, §42-1-102.
Clean screen program, §42-4-304.
Commercial drivers' licenses, §42-2-402.
Commercial driving schools, §12-15-101.
Driver license compact, §§24-60-1101, 24-60-1102.
Drivers' licenses.
Restraint, §42-2-138.
DUI per se, §42-1-102.
DUI, §42-1-102.
DWAI, §42-1-102.
Emissions control program, §42-4-304.
Financial responsibility, §42-7-103.
General definitions, §42-1-102.
Habitual offenders, §42-2-202.
Habitual user, §42-1-102.
Identification cards for nondrivers, §42-2-301.
Inherently low-emission vehicle (ILEV), §42-4-102.
Personalized license plates, §42-3-211.
Repairs, §42-9-102.
Stolen vehicles.
General definitions, §42-5-101.
Hotels, inns, tourist camps, etc.
Recordkeeping requirements, §43-5-201.
Sunday sales, §12-6-301.
Titles, §42-6-102.
Traffic administration, §42-1-102.
UDD, §42-1-102.
Used motor vehicle sales, §42-6-201.
Warranties.
Nonconformity to warranties, §42-10-101.
Weigh stations, §42-8-102.
Demonstrators.
Transfers, §42-6-113.
When deemed used vehicle, §§42-6-102, 42-6-201.
Department of revenue.
See DEPARTMENT OF REVENUE.
Diesel-powered vehicles.
Emissions control, §42-4-413.
Heavy duty diesel self-inspection and maintenance program, §42-4-414.
Disposition of personal property.
Damages, §42-13-108.
Effect of article, §42-13-101.
Return of property, §42-13-102.

MOTOR VEHICLES–Cont'd
Disposition of personal property.-Cont'd
Sale.
Disposition of proceeds, §42-13-104.
Recovery of property by true owner prior to sale, §42-13-107.
Unclaimed property, §42-13-103.
Scope of article, §42-13-101.
Supersession of provisions by local regulations, §42-13-109.
Drag racing, §42-4-1105.
Drivers' licenses.
See DRIVERS' LICENSES.
Driving under the influence or while impaired.
See DRIVING UNDER THE INFLUENCE OR WHILE IMPAIRED.
Driving while an habitual user of controlled substances, §42-4-1301.
Driving with excessive alcoholic content.
See DRIVING WITH EXCESSIVE ALCOLOLIC CONTENT.
Earphones.
Use while driving prohibited, §42-4-1411.
Electric vehicles, §§42-4-109.5, 42-4-111.
Emergency vehicles.
Equipment, §42-4-213.
Exemption from traffic laws, §42-4-108.
Pedestrian to yield to authorized emergency vehicle, §42-4-805.
Rights-of-way, §42-4-705.
Emissions control.
See EMISSIONS CONTROL.
Engine numbers.
Duties of dealers and mechanics, §42-5-106.
Removed, changed, altered, or obliterated.
General provisions, §42-5-102.
Seizure of autos or component parts by officers, §42-5-107.
Equipment.
See EQUIPMENT - MOTOR VEHICLES
Executive director, §§12-6-105 to 12-6-107.
Farm equipment.
Exemption from equipment provisions, §42-4-202.
Lamps, §42-4-211.
Reflectors, §42-4-211.
Registration exemption, §42-3-104.
Fees.
Dealers.
Disposition, §12-6-123.
Drivers' licenses.
General provisions, §42-2-114.
Restoration fee, §42-2-132.
Emissions control program.
Inspection facilities, §42-4-311.
Licenses, §42-4-305.
Posting of charges, §42-4-305.
Identification cards for nondrivers, §42-2-306.
Titles.
Certificates of title.
Application fees, §42-6-137.

MOTOR VEHICLES-Cont'd
  Fees.-Cont'd
    Titles.-Cont'd
      Certificates of title.-Cont'd
        Disposition of fees, §42-6-138.
        Mortgage filing fees, §42-6-137.
  Felonies.
    See FELONIES.
  Financial responsibility.
    See FINANCIAL RESPONSIBILITY - MOTOR VEHICLES
  Fines.
    Notice to appear or pay fine.
      Failure to appear, §42-4-1716.
  Fire apparatus.
    Following, §42-4-1403.
  Fire hose.
    Crossing, §42-4-1404.
  Flares, §42-4-230.
  Fleet operators.
    Fleet vehicles in emissions program area, §42-3-113.
    Registration, §§42-3-107, 42-3-125, 42-3-125.
  Forfeitures.
    Disposition of personal property, §§42-13-101 to 42-13-109.
  Forms.
    Certification forms, §§42-4-310, 42-4-311.
    Proof of service forms, §42-2-120.
  Fraud.
    Dealers.
      Right of action for loss due to dealer's fraud or unlawful acts, §12-6-122.
      Used motor vehicles.
        Private civil action, §42-6-204.
  Fullmount.
    Definition, §42-1-102.
  Funds.
    Dealers.
      Auto dealers license fund, §12-6-123.
    Fuel piracy computer reprogramming cash fund, §42-1-221.
  Government-owned motor vehicles.
    Certification of emissions compliance, §42-4-310.
  Hearings.
    Commercial drivers' licenses.
      Revocation or suspension of licenses of testing units and driving testers, §42-2-407.
    Drivers' licenses.
      Cancellation, §42-2-122.
      Habitual offenders, §42-2-203.
      Restricted licenses.
        Violation of restrictions, §42-2-116.
      Revocation.
        Administrative determination based on alcohol offense, §42-2-126.
        Mandatory, §42-2-125.
    Emissions control.
      Licenses, §§42-4-305, 42-4-312.
    Habitual offenders, §42-2-203.

MOTOR VEHICLES-Cont'd
  Hearings.-Cont'd
    Traffic infractions.
      Proper court for hearing, §42-4-1708.
    Weigh stations, §42-8-109.
  Highways.
    See HIGHWAYS
  Horns, §42-4-224.
  Identification cards for nondrivers.
    See IDENTIFICATION CARDS FOR NONDRIVERS.
  Identification numbers.
    Certificate title application, §42-6-145.
    Duties of dealers and mechanics, §42-5-106.
    Removed, changed, altered, or obliterated numbers.
      General provisions, §42-5-102.
      Seizure of autos or component parts by officers, §42-5-107.
    Street-rod vehicles, §42-12-203.
    Titles.
      Amendment to certificate, §42-6-118.
  Ignition interlock device.
    Restricted license, §§42-2-116, 42-2-132.5.
    Tampering with, §42-2-126.3.
  Inspections.
    Determination that vehicle is unsafe, §42-4-203.
    Spot inspections, §42-4-203.
    Verification of vehicle information, §§42-3-105, 42-6-107.
  Insurance.
    See INSURANCE - MOTOR VEHICLES.
  Liens.
    See "Liens" within this heading.
  Limitation of actions.
    Repairs, §§13-80-103, 42-9-112.
    Used motor vehicles, §§13-80-102, 42-6-204.
    Warranties.
      Nonconformity to warranties, §42-10-107.
  Loads.
    Length, §42-4-504.
    Operation with unsecured load.
      Prohibition, §42-4-1407.
    Projecting loads, §42-4-503.
    Splash guards.
      When required, §42-4-1407.5.
    Weight of vehicles and loads, §42-4-508.
    Wheel and axle loads, §42-4-507.
    Width, §42-4-502.
  Manufacturers and distributors.
    Contract disputes with dealer, §12-6-122.5.
    Definitions, §12-6-102.
    Duties.
      Successor under existing franchise agreement, §12-6-120.7.
    Licensure.
      Application, §12-6-115.
      Denial, suspension, or revocation.
        Grounds, §12-6-118.
        Judicial review, §12-6-119.

MOTOR VEHICLES-Cont'd
  Manufacturers and distributors.-Cont'd
    Licensure.-Cont'd
      Denial, suspension, or revocation.-Cont'd
        Procedure, §12-6-119.
      Display of license, §12-6-109.
      Executive director.
        Actions by or against director, §12-6-107.
        Powers and duties, §12-6-105.
        Records as evidence, §12-6-106.
        Rules, §12-6-105.
      Fees, §12-6-110.
      Renewal and expiration, §12-6-110.
    Notice required before new, reopened or relocated dealer established, §12-6-120.3.
    Ownership, operation, or control of dealer, §12-6-120.5.
    Unlawful acts.
      General provisions, §12-6-120.
      Penalty, §12-6-121.
      Right of action for loss, §12-6-122.
    Warranties.
      Compensation of dealers under warranties, §12-6-114.
      Filing of written warranties, §12-6-114.
  Mileage.
    Abandoned vehicles.
      Fee for towing, §42-4-710.
    Odometers.
      Prohibited acts, §§42-6-202, 42-6-203.
  Minors.
    See MINORS
  Mirrors, §42-4-226.
  Misdemeanors.
    See MISDEMEANORS.
  Mobile homes.
    Size and weight of vehicles.
      Permits for transporting of mobile homes, §42-4-510.
  Mopeds.
    See MOPEDS.
  Mortgages.
    Disposition after mortgaging, §§42-6-123, 42-6-124.
    Existing mortgages not affected, §42-6-132.
    Filing.
      Fees, §42-6-137.
    Liens.
      Mechanics' and warehouse liens.
        Effect of mortgage on mechanics' and warehouse liens, §42-6-131.
    Records.
      Open to public inspection, §42-6-141.
    Repossession.
      Misdemeanors.
        Failure of mortgagee to give required notice, §42-6-146.
  Motor vehicle service contract insurance, §§42-11-101 to 42-11-108.
  Motorcycles.
    See MOTORCYCLES.

MOTOR VEHICLES-Cont'd
  Motorist insurance identification database program.
    See INSURANCE - MOTOR VEHICLES. §42-2-127.7.
  Mufflers, §42-4-225.
  Nonresident violator compact.
    Administrator.
      Compensation, §24-60-2103.
    Definitions, §§24-60-2101, 24-60-2102.
    General provisions, §24-60-2101.
    Jurisdiction executive, §24-60-2104.
    Licensing authority, §24-60-2102.
    Text, §24-60-2101.
  Oaths.
    Administration of oaths or affirmations by officers.
      Department of revenue, §42-1-215.
      Dealer board, §12-6-104.
  Obstruction of roadway.
    Authority to tow vehicle obstructing highway, §42-4-1803.
    Racing.
      Obstructing streets or highways prohibited, §42-4-1105.
    Weigh stations, §42-8-107.
  Odometers.
    Used motor vehicles, §§42-6-202, 42-6-203.
    Verification through vehicle inspection, §§42-3-105, 42-6-107.
  Overtaking and passing.
    Bicycles, §§42-4-1002, 42-4-1005, 42-4-1006.
    Driving on right side of roadway, §42-4-1001.
    Motorcycles, §42-4-1503.
    Overtaking on the left.
      General provisions, §42-4-1003.
    Overtaking on the right, §42-4-1004.
    School buses, §42-4-1903.
    Signals.
      "Do pass" signal restrictions, §42-4-903.
    Vehicles proceeding in opposite directions, §42-4-1002.
  Parks and recreation Districts.
    Prohibition of motor vehicle, §42-4-1408.
  Passenger-mile tax.
    General provisions, §§42-3-304 to 42-3-306.
    Permits, §42-3-309.
  Passenger buses.
    Buses with a seating capacity of more than 14.
      Registration fees, §42-3-304.
      Trip permit in lieu of payment of tax, §42-3-304.
  Passengers.
    Motorcycles, §42-4-1502.
  Pedestrians.
    See PEDESTRIANS
  Penalties.
    Assessments.
      School zones, §42-4-615.
    Careless driving, §42-4-1402.
    Disposition of fines, penalties, and forfeitures, §42-1-217.

MOTOR VEHICLES-Cont'd
  Penalties.-Cont'd
    Drivers' license violations, §42-2-142.
    Hit-and-run driving, §§42-4-1601, 42-4-1602.
    Misuse or forgery of special plate or placard, §42-4-1208.
    Payment of fine.
      Notice to appear or pay fine, §42-4-1716.
    Point system, §42-2-127.
    Reckless driving, §42-4-1401.
    Registration of motor vehicle at improper address, §42-6-139.
    Specific ownership tax.
      Failure to pay tax, §42-3-112.
    Traffic laws.
      Assessments.
        Acceptance of late payments, §42-4-1701.
        General provisions, §§42-4-1701, 42-4-1707, 42-4-1709.
    Traffic offenses and infractions.
      Failure to pay penalty, §42-4-1710.
  Permits.
    See PERMITS.
  Personal property.
    Disposition of personal property, §§42-13-101 to 42-13-109.
  Persons with disabilities.
    Drivers and pedestrians to yield to persons with disabilities, §42-4-808.
    Flags.
      Distress flag, §42-4-611.
    Insurance.
      Vehicles used for nonemergency transportation, §42-7-510.
    License plate.
      Generally, §42-3-204.
      Misuse or forgery of special plate or placard, §42-4-1208.
      Parking privileges, §42-3-204.
      Registration, §42-3-204.
  Photographs.
    Drivers' licenses, §42-2-114.
    Identification cards, §42-2-303.
  Point system.
    Drivers' licenses, §42-2-127.
  Police.
    Accidents.
      Duty to report, §42-4-1606.
    Registration.
      Exemption of vehicles from registration, §42-3-104.
    Service of notices and orders, §42-2-120.
    Size and weight of vehicles.
      Failure or refusal to weigh at request of police or peace officer, §42-4-509.
  Presumptions.
    Delivery of notices by first-class mail, §42-2-119.
    Driving under the influence or while impaired, §42-4-1301.

MOTOR VEHICLES-Cont'd
  Quo warranto.
    Antimonopoly financing.
      Actions for violation, §12-6-208.
  Racing, §42-4-1105.
  Records.
    Accidents.
      Retention of accident records, §42-1-216.
    Commercial drivers' licenses.
      Duty of testing unit to keep records, §42-2-407.
    Confidential information.
      Insurance, §42-7-503.
      Records of the department of revenue, §42-1-206.
    Copies.
      Furnishing copies of drivers' records, §42-7-503.
    Dealers board.
      Evidence, §12-6-106.
    Department of revenue.
      Bulk electronic transfer of information open to inspection, §42-1-206.
      Confidential information, §42-1-206.
      Copies of records, §42-1-206.
      Filing of records, §42-1-205.
      Public inspection, §§24-72-204, 42-1-206, 42-7-503.
    Destruction of obsolete records, §42-1-216.
    Distributors and manufacturers.
      Executive director.
        Evidence, §12-6-106.
    Drivers' licenses.
      General provisions, §42-2-121.
      Public inspection of drivers' records, §42-7-503.
      Rentals, §42-2-141.
    Driving under the influence or while impaired, or with excessive alcoholic content.
      Prima facie proof of records, §42-4-1303.
    Evidence.
      Admissibility of conviction records, §42-4-1713.
    Expungement, §§42-2-121, 42-4-1715.
    Financial responsibility.
      Insurance.
        Copies of drivers' records, §42-7-503.
    Mortgages.
      Filing, §42-6-122.
      Public inspection, §42-6-141.
    Rentals, §42-2-141.
    Repairs.
      Duties of dealers and mechanics, §§42-5-105, 42-5-106.
    Service of process.
      Written notification of service, §42-2-120.
    Stolen vehicles.
      Auto and tourist camps, hotels, and motels.
        Duty of owner to keep records, §43-5-203.
        Inspection of owners' records by officers, §43-5-204.

MOTOR VEHICLES-Cont'd
  Records.-Cont'd
    Stolen vehicles.-Cont'd
      Repairs and auto parts, §42-5-105.
    Titles.
      Public inspection, §42-6-141.
  Registration.
    See MOTOR VEHICLE REGISTRATION.
  Rentals.
    Blind persons, §42-2-141.
    License plates, §42-3-201.
    Parking violations, §42-4-1209.
    Permitting unauthorized person to drive, §42-2-141.
    Records, §42-2-141.
    Specific ownership tax.
      Payment of, §42-3-107.
  Repairs.
    Air bags, installation of false or incorrect unit, §§6-1-710, 42-9-111.
    Antique motor vehicles.
      Exemption from provisions, §42-9-110.
    Applicability of certain regulatory provisions, §42-9-103.
    Authorized repairs.
      Additional charges, §42-9-105.
      Cancellation of, §42-9-106.
      Completion date.
        Change in, §42-9-105.
      Towing charges excluded, §42-9-104.
      Used, reconditioned, or rebuilt parts, §42-9-107.
      Written consent of customer required, §42-9-104.
    Damages.
      Civil remedies, §42-9-113.
      Violations of provisions, §42-9-112.
    Deceptive trade practices, §§6-1-105, 42-9-112.
    Definitions, §42-9-102.
    Emissions control.
      Prohibition against performance of unnecessary repairs, §42-9-111.
    Estimate.
      Amounts over estimate, §42-9-106.
      Requirement of, §42-9-104.
      Used, reconditioned, or rebuilt parts, §42-9-107.
    Facility warranties, §42-9-108.7.
    Inflatable restraint systems, §42-9-109.5, 42-9-111.
    Invoice.
      Penalty for failure to provide, §42-9-112.
      Requirements, §42-9-108.
    Limitation of actions, §42-9-112.
    Misdemeanors.
      Unfair practices, §42-9-112.
    Motor vehicle service contract insurance.
      Applicability.
        Exclusion of manufacturers' express warranties and service contracts, §42-11-105.
      Contents of service contracts, §42-11-104.

MOTOR VEHICLES-Cont'd
  Repairs.-Cont'd
    Motor vehicle service contract insurance.-Cont'd
      Definitions, §42-11-101.
      Failure to comply with statutory provisions.
        Deceptive trade practice, §42-11-106.
        Enforcement, §42-11-107.
        Remedies, §42-11-108.
      Reimbursement insurance policy.
        Provisions of policy, §42-11-103.
        Requirement of prior to sale of service contract, §42-11-102.
    Parts.
      Return of replaced parts, §42-9-109.
      Used, reconditioned, or rebuilt parts, §42-9-107.
    Prohibited acts.
      Enumeration of, §42-9-111.
      Penalties, §§42-9-112, 42-9-113.
    Reassembly, §42-9-104.
    Records.
      Duties of dealers and mechanics, §§42-5-105, 42-5-106.
      Requirement of, §42-9-104.
      Waiver, §42-9-104.
    Storage charges, §§42-9-104, 42-9-106.
    Title of act, §42-9-101.
    Unfair practices.
      Deceptive and unfair practices prohibited, §42-9-111.
      Penalty, §42-9-112.
    Warranty repairs, §42-9-108.5.
  Repossession.
    Failure of mortgagee to give required notice, §42-6-146.
  Right side of roadway.
    Divided or limited access highways, §42-4-1010.
    Driving on, §42-4-1001.
    Exceptions, §42-4-1001.
    Mountain highways, §42-4-711.
    Overtaking and passing.
      Exception to requirements, §42-4-1001.
    Passing oncoming vehicles, §42-4-1002.
    Rotary traffic islands, §42-4-1006.
  Rights-of-way.
    Disabled persons.
      Drivers and pedestrians to yield to persons with disabilities, §42-4-808.
    Emergency vehicles, §42-4-705.
    Entering highway, §42-4-704.
    Highway construction and maintenance, §42-4-712.
    Intersections.
      Approaching or entering intersection, §42-4-701.
      Signs, signals, and markings.
        Obedience to signs when entering intersections, §42-4-703.
      Turning left at intersection, §42-4-702.
    Mountain highways, §42-4-711.

MOTOR VEHICLES-Cont'd
Rights-of-way.-Cont'd
Pedestrians.
Authorized emergency vehicles.
Pedestrian to yield, §42-4-805.
Crosswalks.
Crossing at other than crosswalks, §42-4-803.
General provisions, §42-4-802.
Private road, alley, or driveway.
Vehicle to yield, §42-4-710.
Railroad grade crossings.
When pedestrian use prohibited, §42-4-706.
Private road, alley, or driveway.
Turning left into, §42-4-702.
Vehicle to yield to pedestrian, §42-4-710.
School buses, §42-4-1903.
Stop signs.
Entering through highway or intersection.
Obedience to stop signs, §42-4-703.
Through highways.
Signs, signals, and markings, §42-4-703.
Weigh stations, §42-8-107.
Yield signs.
Entering through highway or intersection.
Obedience to yield signs, §42-4-703.
Yielding to transit buses, §42-4-713.
Runaway vehicle ramps.
Unlawful use of, §42-4-1011.
Saddlemount combination.
Definition, §42-1-102.
Maximum length, §42-4-504.
Safety glazing material, §42-4-229.
Safety zones.
Pedestrians.
Driving vehicle through safety zone prohibited, §42-4-806.
Sales.
Deceptive trade practices, §§42-6-205, 42-9-111.
Disposition of personal property.
Disposition of proceeds, §42-13-104.
Recovery of property by true owner prior to sale, §42-13-107.
Unclaimed property, §42-13-103.
Salvage vehicles, §42-6-206.
Titles.
Dealers.
Exemption from procuring new certificate, §42-6-111.
Delivery of certificate of title, §42-6-109.

Electronic version.
When allowed, §42-6-109.
Transfer of title, §42-6-110.
Used motor vehicle sales, §§42-6-201 to 42-6-206.
Salvage vehicles.
Transfer of ownership, §42-6-206.

MOTOR VEHICLES-Cont'd
Searches and seizures.
Disposition of personal property, §§42-13-101 to 42-13-109.
Stolen vehicles.
Removal, change, alteration, or obliteration of engine numbers, §42-5-107.
Seat belts.
Definitions, §42-4-237.
Mandatory use requirement.
Drivers and front seat passengers in equipped motor vehicles, §42-4-237.
Exemptions, §42-4-237.
Restrictions on minor drivers under seventeen years of age, §42-2-105.5.
Violation of.
Disposition of fines, §42-1-217.
Penalties, §§42-2-127, 42-4-237, 42-4-1701.
Service of process, §42-2-120.
Service vehicles.
Equipment, §42-4-214.
Sidewalks.
Stopping, standing, or parking prohibited, §42-4-1204.
Vehicles prohibited, §42-4-710.
Signs, signals, and markings.
See SIGNS, SIGNALS, AND MARKINGS.
Size and weight of vehicles.
Cooperative agreements with regional states, §42-4-511.2.
Height.
Maximum height, §42-4-504.
Length.
Longer vehicle combinations, §42-4-505.
Maximum length, §42-4-504.
Mobile homes.
Permits to transport.
General provisions, §42-4-510.
Standards, §42-4-511.
Permits.
Issuance of special permit for nonconforming vehicles.
General provisions, §42-4-510.
Standards, §42-4-511.
Regional permit system, §42-4-511.2.
Port of entry weigh stations, §§42-8-101 to 42-8-111.
Regional permit system, §42-4-511.2.
Trailers.
Towing and coupling devices, §42-4-506.
Violations of provisions.
Failure or refusal to weigh vehicle, §42-4-509.
Penalties, §42-4-501.
Regional permit system, §42-4-511.2.
Weight.
Gross weight of vehicles and loads, §42-4-508.
Overweight vehicles.
Removal of excess weight, §42-4-509.
Weigh stations, §§42-8-101 to 42-8-111.
Weighing of vehicle at request of police or peace officer, §42-4-509.

MOTOR VEHICLES-Cont'd
  Size and weight of vehicles.-Cont'd
    Weight.-Cont'd
      Wheel and axle loads, §42-4-507.
    Width.
      Maximum width of vehicle or load, §42-4-502.
  Slow-moving vehicles.
    Emblem, §42-4-234.
  Snow-removal equipment.
    Lamps, §42-4-224.
  Specific ownership tax.
    See MOTOR VEHICLE REGISTRATION
  Starting.
    Parked vehicle, §42-4-1201.
  Stinger-steered vehicle.
    Definition, §42-1-102.
  Stolen vehicles.
    Buying or selling stolen vehicles or parts, §42-5-102.
    Definitions, §42-5-101.
    Forfeiture actions.
      General provisions, §42-5-107.
    Garages, trailer parks, and parking lots.
      Vehicles left more than thirty days.
        Reports, §42-5-109.
    Hotels, inns, and other transient lodging places.
      Allowing storage of stolen motor vehicles.
        Penalties, §43-5-205.
        Recordkeeping requirements, §43-5-201.
      Petty offenses.
        Violation of part, §43-5-207.
      Records.
        Duty of lodging owners to keep records, §43-5-203.
        Inspection of owners' records, §43-5-204.
    Identification numbers.
      Duties of dealers and mechanics, §42-5-106.
      Evidence of alteration for legitimate repair purposes, §42-5-102.
      Removed, changed, altered, or obliterated.
        Seizure of autos by officers, §42-5-107.
    Parts.
      Identification numbers.
        Evidence of alteration for legitimate repair purposes, §42-5-102.
        Possession of part with removed, defaced, altered, or destroyed identification number, §42-5-110.
      Removing or altering parts, §42-5-102.
      Theft of motor vehicle parts, §42-5-104.
    Proof of authorized possession of motor vehicle, §42-5-111.
    Records of vehicle repairs and auto parts, §42-5-105.

MOTOR VEHICLES-Cont'd
  Stolen vehicles.-Cont'd
    Registration.
      Suspension of registration, §42-3-118.
    Tampering with a motor vehicle, §42-5-103.
    Vehicle identification numbers.
      Inspection by officer.
        Definitions, §42-5-201.
        Fees, §42-5-204.
        Inspectors.
          Certification, §42-5-206.
        Requirement, §42-5-202.
        Rules, §42-5-207.
      Special vehicle identification number.
        Assignment by department of revenue, §42-12-202.
      Street-rod vehicles, §42-12-201.
      Vehicle number inspection funds, §42-5-204.
    Possession of motor vehicle or component part with removed, defaced, altered, or destroyed number, §42-5-110.
  Stop signs.
    Rights-of-way, §42-4-703.
  Stopping, standing, and parking.
    Abandoned vehicles.
      Presumption of abandonment, §42-4-1202.
    Accidents.
      Stopping for accident, §§42-4-1601 to 42-4-1604.
    Bridges, §42-4-1204.
    Fire apparatus.
      Vehicle parking within block, §42-4-1403.
    Opening and closing vehicle doors, §42-4-1207.
    Outside business or residence districts, §42-4-1202.
    Persons with disabilities.
      Parking privileges, §42-4-1208.
    Private property.
      Designated areas for authorized vehicles, §42-4-1210.
    Prohibitions.
      Stopping, standing, or parking in specified places, §42-4-1204.
    Railroad grade crossings.
      Certain vehicles to stop at all railroad grade crossings, §42-4-707.
      Heavy equipment, §42-4-708.
      Obstruction of traffic prohibited, §42-4-709.
      Signal indicating approach of train.
        Obedience to, §42-4-706.
    Rental vehicles.
      Liability of owner for parking violations, §42-4-1209.
    Right-hand curb.
      Parking at, §42-4-1205.
    Sidewalks, §42-4-1204.

MOTOR VEHICLES-Cont'd
  Stopping, standing, and parking.-Cont'd
    Signals.
      Mandatory under certain conditions, §§42-4-608, 42-4-903.
    Signs.
      Tow away warnings, §42-4-1202.
    Ski areas.
      Installation of traffic control signs, §42-4-1203.
    Starting parked vehicle, §42-4-1201.
    Unattended motor vehicles, §42-4-1206.
  Street-rod vehicles.
    Certificates of title, §42-12-203.
    Definition, §42-12-101.
    Equipment, §42-12-204.
    Identification number, §42-12-203.
  Sunday closing law.
    Definitions, §12-6-301.
    Exception of certain sales involving boats and snowmobiles, §12-6-302.
    General provisions, §12-6-302.
    Penalties, §12-6-303.
  Surcharges.
    Disposition of, §42-1-217.
  Tailgating, §42-4-1008.
  Tampering with a motor vehicle, §42-5-103.
  Taxation.
    Passenger-mile tax.
      General provisions, §§42-3-304 to 42-3-306.
      Permits, §42-3-309.
      Record-keeping errors.
        Penalty if errors due to negligence or disregard of the law, §42-3-309.
  Telephones.
    Misuse of a wireless telephone, §42-4-239.
  Tickets.
    Classification of traffic offenses and infractions, §42-4-1701.
    Payment of fine.
      Notice to appear or pay fine, §42-4-1716.
    Summons and complaint.
      Compliance with promise to appear, §42-4-1711.
      Defect in form.
        Cure by amendment prior to trial, §42-4-1709.
      General provisions, §42-4-1707.
      Release for traffic infractions, §42-4-1709.
    Traffic infractions.
      Proper court for hearing on traffic infractions, §42-4-1708.
      Penalty assessment.
        Failure to pay penalty for traffic infractions, §42-4-1710.
  Tires.
    Change of tires, §42-4-106.
    Types of tires, §42-4-106.
    Restrictions, §42-4-228.
  Title of act, §42-1-101.

MOTOR VEHICLES-Cont'd
  Titles.
    Certificates of title.
      See CERTIFICATES OF TITLE - MOTOR VEHICLES
  Tolls, §§42-4-613, 42-4-1701.
  Tourist camps.
    See TOURIST CAMPS.
  Towing.
    Abandoned vehicles.
      Obstructing traffic, §42-4-1803.
      Private property, §42-4-1805.
      Public property, §42-4-1803.
    Consent.
      Charges for towing excluded from consent requirement, §42-9-104.
    Equipment.
      Additional equipment requirements, §42-4-206.
      Emergency lighting, §42-4-230.
    Unlawful removal or usage of tow-truck signage, §42-4-241.
  Traffic lanes.
    Acceleration lanes, §42-4-1010.
    Deceleration lanes, §42-4-1010.
    Driving on roadways laned for traffic, §42-4-1007.
    High occupancy lanes, §42-4-1012.
    Use of runaway vehicle ramps, §42-4-1011.
  Traffic Laws.
    See TRAFFIC LAWS
  Trucks.
    Cement operators' hours of service, §42-4-2001.
    Collectors' item.
      Registration, §42-12-401.
      Violation of use limitations, §42-12-405.
    Equipment.
      Minimum safety standards, §42-4-235.
    Size and weight of vehicles.
      Port of entry weigh stations, §§42-8-101 to 42-8-111.
  Turning.
    See TRAFFIC INFRACTIONS.
  Unclaimed property.
    Disposition of personal property, §§42-13-101 to 42-13-109.
  Uninsured motorists.
    Motorist insurance identification program.
      Creation, §42-7-602.
      Generally, §§42-7-601 to 42-7-609.
  United States.
    Registration.
      Exemption for government-owned vehicles, §42-3-104.
  Used motor vehicle sales.
    Deceptive trade practices, §§6-1-708, 42-6-205.
    Definitions, §42-6-201.
    Demonstrators.
      Transfers, §42-6-113.
      When deemed used vehicle, §42-6-102.
    Enforcement of provisions, §42-6-204.

MOTOR VEHICLES-Cont'd
Used motor vehicle sales.-Cont'd
Fraud.
Limitation of actions, §§13-80-102, 42-6-204.
Penalties, §42-6-204.
Odometers.
Misdemeanors, §42-6-203.
Prohibited acts, §42-6-202.
Salvage vehicles, §42-6-206.
Vehicle equipment safety compact.
Approval, §§24-60-902, 24-60-903.
Budget submission, §24-60-910.
Commission.
Accounts.
Inspection, §24-60-911.
Appointment of Colorado commissioner, §24-60-904.
Cooperation by other agencies, §24-60-906.
General provisions, §24-60-902.
Retirement benefits for employees, §24-60-905.
Contributions.
Limitation on state contribution, §24-60-907.
Effective date, §24-60-908.
Filing of documents, §24-60-909.
General provisions, §24-60-902.
Governor as executive head, §24-60-912.
Legislative declaration, §24-60-901.
Veterans.
Exemption from registration, §§42-3-204, 42-3-304.
Exemption from specific ownership tax, §42-3-104.
Special plates, §42-3-304.
Generally, §42-3-213.
Warehouses.
Effect of mortgage on warehouseman's lien, §42-6-131.
Warranties.
Dealers.
Compensation of dealers under warranties, §12-6-114.
Failure to perform.
General provisions, §12-6-120.
Penalties, §12-6-121.
Right of action for loss, §12-6-122.
Licensed manufacturers.
Filing of written warranties, §12-6-114.
Emissions control program.
Effect of enforcement of applicable warranty, §42-4-315.
Nonconformity to warranties.
Affirmative defenses, §42-10-104.
Definitions, §42-10-101.
Federal procedures.
Applicability, §42-10-106.
Limitation of actions, §42-10-107.
Limitations on other rights and remedies, §42-10-105.
Repairs to conform vehicle to warranty, §§42-10-102,

MOTOR VEHICLES-Cont'd
Warranties.-Cont'd
Nonconformity to warranties.-Cont'd
42-10-103.
Warranty repairs, §42-9-108.5.
Weigh stations.
See WEIGH STATIONS.
Weight of vehicles.
Weigh stations, §§42-8-101 to 42-8-111.
Wholesale motor vehicle auction dealers.
Licensure, §§12-6-108, 12-6-110.
Wholesalers.
Licensure.
Application, §12-6-115.
Windows and windshields.
Light transmittance standards, §42-4-227.
Safety glazing material, §42-4-229.
Stickers on windshields, §42-4-227.
Unobstructed view required, §42-4-227.
Witnesses.
Effect of traffic violations on credibility of witness, §42-4-1714.
Wrecked vehicles.
Removal from highway, §42-4-1406.
MUFFLERS
Motor vehicles, §42-4-225.
MUNICIPAL CORPORATIONS
Motor vehicles.
Disposition of personal property.
Supersession of provisions by local regulations, §42-13-109.
Registration.
Vehicles owned and operated by municipal corporations, §42-3-104.
Ordinances.
Automated vehicle identification systems, §42-4-110.5.

N

NAMES
Change of name.
Drivers' licenses.
Notice of change of address or name, §42-2-119.
NEGLIGENCE
Criminally negligent homicide.
Revocation of driver's license, §42-2-125.
Motor vehicles.
Speed.
Proof of negligence required, §42-4-1101.
NONRESIDENTS
Convictions.
Certified copies to state of nonresident, §42-2-123.
Conviction reports, §§42-2-123, 42-2-124.
Drivers' licenses.
Exemptions from requirement, §42-2-102.
Financial responsibility.
Insurance.
Acceptance of certificate of foreign insurance carrier, §42-7-412.

NONRESIDENTS-Cont'd
  Judgments.
    Certified copy of unsatisfied judgment to state of nonresident, §42-7-502.
  Registration, §§42-3-103, 42-3-117, 42-6-140.
  Suspension or revocation of driving privileges, §42-2-123.
  Titles, §42-6-140.
NUCLEAR MATERIALS
  Transportation of.
    Carrying of shipping papers, §42-20-502.
    Compliance orders, §42-20-408.
    Definitions, §42-20-402.
    Inspections of vehicles, §42-20-404.
    Legislative declaration, §§40-2.2-102, 42-20-401.
    Nuclear incidents.
      Injuries or damages caused by.
        Statute of limitations, §42-20-510.
      Strict liability for, §42-20-509.
    Nuclear materials transportation fund, §42-20-511.
    Permit system.
      Application, §42-20-501.
      Fee, §42-20-502.
      Local government preemption, §42-20-507.
      Period of validity, §42-20-502.
      Requirement, §42-20-501.
      Rules, §42-20-504.
      Shipment fee, §42-20-502.
      Suspension or revocation, §42-20-506.
      Violations.
        Penalties, §42-20-505.
    Route designation.
      Deviation from route, §42-20-508.
      Rules, §42-20-508.
    Rules, §§42-20-403, 42-20-504, 42-20-508.
    Violations of regulatory provisions.
      Civil penalties, §§42-20-406, 42-20-407.
      Compliance orders, §42-20-408.
      Criminal penalties, §42-20-405.
      Penalty assessments.
        Acceptance of late payments, §42-20-406.
      Permit system, §42-20-505.
NUISANCES
  Traffic regulation.
    Unauthorized signs or devices, §42-4-606.

O

ODOMETERS
  Motor vehicles.
    Used motor vehicles, §§42-6-202, 42-6-203.

P

PARKS AND RECREATION
  Districts.
    Prohibition of motor vehicles, §42-4-1408.
PARTIES
  Motor vehicles violations, §42-4-1703.
PASSENGER-MILE TAX
  General provisions, §§42-3-304 to 42-3-306.

PASSENGER-MILE TAX-Cont'd
  Permits, §42-3-309.
PEACE OFFICERS
  Air pollution.
    Enforcement of criminal provisions, §42-4-412.
  Peace officers.
    Collection of information on traffic law enforcement, §42-4-115.
    Service of notices and orders, §42-2-120.
  Hotels, inns, tourist camps, and other transient lodging places.
    Stolen vehicles.
      Inspection of owners' records by officers, §43-5-204.
PEACE OFFICERS STANDARDS AND TRAINING BOARD
  Funding.
    Motor vehicle registration surcharge, §42-3-304.
  Training programs.
    Financial support, §42-3-304.
PEDESTRIANS.
  Crosswalks.
    Crossing at other than crosswalks, §42-4-803.
    Rights-of-way, §42-4-802.
  Drivers to exercise due care, §42-4-807.
  Emergency vehicles.
    Yielding to authorized emergency vehicles, §42-4-805.
  Hitchhiking, §42-4-805.
  Private road, alley, or driveway.
  Vehicle to yield, §42-4-710.
  Railroad crossings.
    When pedestrian use prohibited, §42-4-706.
  Roadways, walking on, §42-4-805.
  Safety zones.
    Driving vehicle through safety zone prohibited, §42-4-806.
  Signs, signals, and markings.
    Subject to, §42-4-801.
    Walk and don't walk signals, §42-4-802.
PERJURY
  Motor vehicle registration application.
    False statements, §§42-3-105, 42-3-113, 42-3-122.
  Motor vehicles.
    Drivers' licenses.
      Revocation for perjury, §42-2-125.
PERMITS
  Mobile homes.
    Transporting mobile homes.
      General provisions, §42-4-510.
      Standards, §42-4-511.
  Nuclear materials.
    Transportation of, §§42-20-501 to 42-20-511.
  Notice of local ordinances concerning permits for oversize or overweight vehicles, §42-4-511.
  Passenger-mile tax, §42-3-309.
  Special permit for nonconforming vehicles.
    General provisions, §42-4-510.
    Standards, §42-4-511.

PERMITS-Cont'd
  Weigh stations.
    Oversize and overweight commercial hauls, §42-8-106.
    Reciprocal permits, §42-8-105.
    Suspension or revocation, §42-8-109.
PERSONAL MOBILITY DEVICES
  Definition, §42-4-112.
  Equipment, §42-4-221.
  Regulation, §42-4-117.
PERSONAL PROPERTY
  Motor vehicles.
    Disposition of personal property, §§42-13-101 to 42-13-109.
PERSONNEL DEPARTMENT
  Controller duties.
    Monthly allocation of moneys to highway users tax fund, §42-3-304.
PERSONS WITH DISABILITIES
  Drivers' licenses, §42-2-116.
  Drivers and pedestrians to yield to persons with disabilities, §42-4-808.
  Flags.
    Distress flag, §42-4-611.
  Insurance.
    Vehicles used for nonemergency transportation, §42-7-510.
  License plates.
    Generally, §42-3-204.
  Parking privileges, §§42-3-204, 42-4-1208.
  Vehicle registration, §42-3-204.
PETTY OFFENSES
  Air pollution violations, §42-4-412.
  Manufactured homes.
    Moving a manufactured home without a permit, §42-4-510.
  Motor vehicle registration application.
    False statements, §§42-3-105, 42-3-113, 42-3-122.
  Motor vehicle dealers.
    Unlawful acts, §§12-6-119.5, 12-6-120, 12-6-302.
  Stolen vehicles.
    Hotels, inns, tourist camps, etc.
      Violation of part, §43-5-207.
PIPELINES
  Construction of pipelines.
    Consent required, §42-4-1406.
POINT SYSTEM
  Drivers' licenses, §42-2-127.
PORTS OF ENTRY
  Weigh stations, §§42-8-101 to 42-8-111.
PRESUMPTIONS
  Blood tests.
    Blood test for drivers under 21 years of age not required, §§42-2-126, 42-4-1301.1.
    Driving under the influence or while impaired, §42-4-1301.
PROFESSIONS AND OCCUPATIONS
  Motor vehicle dealers, §§12-6-101 to 12-6-126.
  Towing carriers, §§42-4-1802 to 42-4-1814, 42-4-2101 to 42-4-2110.
PROFILING
  Collection of information on traffic law enforcement, §42-4-115.

PROPERTY
  Abandoned property.
    Motor vehicles, §42-4-1805.
  Graffiti.
    Mandatory revocation of drivers' license, §42-2-125.
PUBLIC SAFETY DEPARTMENT
  Automobile theft prevention authority, §42-5-112.
  Development of standards.
    Electronic transmission of traffic infraction penalty assessment notice or summons and complaint, §42-4-1718.
PUBLIC SCHOOLS
  School crossing guards.
    Powers of local authorities, §42-4-111.
PUBLICATIONS
  Accident information to be published by department of revenue, §42-1-208.

Q

QUO WARRANTO
  Motor vehicles.
    Antimonopoly financing.
      Actions for violation, §12-6-208.

R

RADAR
  Radar jamming devices, §42-4-1415.
RADIO
  Amateur radio operators.
    Call letters on license plates, §42-3-210.
RAILROADS
  Crossings.
    Flashing signals, §42-4-605.
    Motor vehicle stopping requirements.
      Certain vehicles to stop at all crossings, §42-4-707.
      Exceptions from stopping at crossings, §42-4-707.
    Heavy equipment, §42-4-708.
    Obstruction of traffic, §§42-4-708, 42-4-709.
    Signals to be obeyed, §42-4-706.
    Pedestrians.
      Use by pedestrians, §42-4-706.
  Highways.
    Construction of railroad.
      Consent requirements, §42-4-1406.
REAL PROPERTY
  Real property owners right to limit use by vehicular traffic, §42-4-112.
  Sidewalks.
    Removal of traffic hazards on land abutting rights-of-way, §42-4-114.
RECIPROCITY
  Motor vehicles registration, §42-3-103.
RECKLESS DRIVING
  Elements of offense, §42-4-1401.
  Evidence, §42-4-1713.

REFUNDS
  Salvage vehicles.
    Failure to receive disclosure affidavit, §42-6-206.
REGISTRATION
  See MOTOR VEHICLE REGISTRATION.
REPOSSESSION
  Motor vehicles.
    Fraudulent or illegal repossessions by dealers or wholesalers, §12-6-118.
    Notification of law enforcement agency by repossessor, §42-6-146.
    Registration.
      Expiration upon transfer of title by act of repossession, §§42-3-115, 42-3-415.
    Payment of fee and tax by bad check.
      Repossession of tax receipt, license fee receipt, and plates, §42-3-123.
    Secured transactions.
      Liability of secured party when taking possession upon default, §§4-9-629, 42-6-146.
    Transfer of title, §42-6-114.
RESTRAINT OF TRADE
  Motor vehicles.
    Antimonopoly financing law, §§12-6-201 to 12-6-213.
RIGHTS-OF-WAY
  See MOTOR VEHICLES.
  Rights-of-way.

S

SAFETY
  Highways.
    Federal highway safety act of 1966.
      Implementation of act by governor, §43-5-401.
  Motor vehicles.
    Safety glazing materials, §42-4-229.
    Vehicle equipment safety compact, §§24-60-901 to 24-60-912.
SALES
  Motor vehicles.
    Antimonopoly financing law, §§12-6-201 to 12-6-213.
    Dealers, §§12-6-101 to 12-6-126.
    Sunday closing law, §§12-6-301 to 12-6-303.
SCHOOL BUSES
  Drivers.
    Training.
      Driving on mountainous terrain and in adverse weather conditions, §42-4-1902.
  Equipment.
    Supplementary brake retarders, §42-4-1901.
  Lights, §42-4-1903.
  Operation.
    Mountainous terrain, §42-4-1901.
  Overtaking and passing, §42-4-1903.
  Rights-of-way, §42-4-1903.
  Signals.
    Armed signal device, §42-4-1903.
    Flashing red lights, §42-4-1903.
    Flashing yellow lights, §42-4-1903.

SCHOOL BUSES-Cont'd
  Stops.
    Discharge of children.
      Prohibition against discharge onto major thoroughfares, §42-4-1904.
    Failure to stop for a stopped school bus.
      Assessment of points on driver's license, §42-2-127.
      Identification of violator.
        Driver of school bus to provide information, §42-4-1903.
      Misdemeanor traffic offense, §42-4-1903.
  Violations.
    Discharge onto major thoroughfares, §42-4-1904.
    Failure to stop for a stopped school bus.
      Misdemeanor traffic offense, §42-4-1903.
      Points on driver's license, §§42-2-127, 42-4-123.
    Operating a school bus, §42-4-1904.
SCHOOLS
  Commercial driving schools, §§12-15-101 to 12-15-121.
  Driving schools, §§12-15-101 to 12-15-121.
SEALS AND SEALED INSTRUMENTS
  Motor vehicle dealer board, §12-6-104.
  Motor vehicles.
    Department of revenue, §42-1-205.
  Revenue department, §42-1-205.
SEARCHES AND SEIZURES
  Motor vehicles.
    Disposition of personal property, §§42-13-101 to 42-13-109.
    Stolen vehicles.
      Removal, change, alteration, or obliteration of engine numbers, §42-5-107.
SECRETARY OF STATE
  Data processing, §42-1-211.
    Colorado state titling and registration system, §42-1-211.
SENTENCING
  Community or useful public service.
    Misdemeanor traffic offenses, §42-4-1701.
  Misdemeanor traffic offenses.
    Community or useful public service, §42-4-1701.
  Motor vehicles.
    Aggravated driving with a revoked license, §42-2-206.
    Attendance at driver improvement school, §42-4-1717.
    Driving after revocation, §42-2-206.
    Habitual offenders, §42-2-206.
SIDEWALKS
  Bicycles.
    Operation of motorized bicycle on sidewalk, §42-2-103.
    Operation or parking of bicycle on sidewalk, §42-4-1412.
  Motor vehicles.
    Stopping, standing, or parking prohibited, §42-4-1204.
    Vehicles prohibited, §42-4-710.

SIDEWALKS-Cont'd
  Rights-of-way.
    Removal of traffic hazards on land abutting rights-of-way, §42-4-114.
SIGNS, SIGNALS, AND MARKINGS
  Accidents.
    Duty of driver upon striking, §42-4-1605.
  Department of transportation.
    Duty to sign state highways, §42-4-601.
  Distress flag, §42-4-611.
  Flashing signals, §42-4-605.
  Inoperative signals, §42-4-612.
  Insignia.
    Display of unauthorized insignia prohibited, §42-4-610.
  Interference with official signs, signals, or markings, §42-4-607.
  Intersections.
    Stop signs and yield signs, §42-4-703.
  Lane use control signals, §42-4-604.
  Local authorities.
    State highways.
      Permission of department of transportation required for signs, §42-4-602.
  Maintenance, repair, or construction zones, §42-4-613.
  Malfunctioning signals, §42-4-612.
  Manual for uniform system of traffic control devices.
    Adoption, §42-4-104.
    Local authorities.
      Adherence to, §42-4-602.
    State highways.
      Conformity to manual required, §42-4-601.
  Mountain highways.
    Horn to be used, §42-4-711.
  Nonintersection signals, §42-4-604.
  Obedience to, §42-4-603.
  Parking ski areas, §42-4-1203.
  Pedestrians.
    Subject to, §42-4-801.
    Walk and don't walk signals, §42-4-802.
  Railroad grade crossings.
    Flashing signals, §42-4-605.
    Obedience to railroad signals, §42-4-706.
  Ski areas.
    Installation of traffic control signs, §42-4-1203.
  Stop signs.
    Rights-of-way, §42-4-703.
  Through highways.
    Stop signs and yield signs, §42-4-703.
  Tow away warnings, §42-4-1202.
  Traffic control signal legend, §42-4-604.
  Unauthorized signs, signals, or markings.
    Display prohibited, §42-4-606.
  Yield signs.
    Rights-of-way, §42-4-703.
SIRENS
  Bicycles.
    Prohibition, §42-4-224.
  Emergency vehicles.
    Equipment, §42-4-213.

SKATES
  Use on highways, §42-4-109.
SKIING
  Highways, §42-4-109.
SLEDS
  Use on highways, §42-4-109.
SOCIAL SERVICES
  Traumatic brain injury trust fund.
    Surcharge for convictions, §§42-4-1301, 42-4-1701.
SPEEDING
  Actions.
    Plaintiff in civil action must prove negligence, §42-4-1101.
  Drag racing, §42-4-1105.
  General provisions, §42-4-1101.
  Maximum speed limits.
    Elevated structures, §42-4-1104.
    Local authorities.
      Adoption of absolute speed limits by municipalities, §42-4-1101.
      Alteration of limits, §42-4-1102.
  Minimum speed limits.
    General provisions, §42-4-1103.
    Minimum speed in left lane - I-70, §42-4-1106.
STATE AUDITOR
  Duties.
    Study of existing air quality programs, §42-3-304.
STATE DEPARTMENTS AND AGENCIES
  Purchase or lease of new vehicles, §42-4-317.
STATE PATROL
  Hotels, inns, and other transient lodging places.
    Stolen vehicles.
      Inspection of innkeepers records by officers, §43-5-204.
  Motor vehicles reports.
    Garages, trailer parks, and parking lots.
      Vehicles left more than thirty days, §42-5-109.
  Nuclear materials.
    Designation of routes for transport, §42-20-508.
STOP SIGNS
  Rights-of-way, §42-4-703.
SUNSET LAW
  Functions of agencies and boards subject to.
    Revenue department.
      Licensing of commercial driving schools, §12-15-121.
      Licensing of motor vehicle dealers, §12-6-124.
      Operation of motorist insurance identification database program, §42-7-609.

T

TAXATION
  Special mobile machinery, §§42-3-107, 42-3-109, 42-3-304, 42-8-104.

TELEVISION
  Installation and use in motor vehicles, §42-4-201.
TIRES
  Change of tires, §42-4-106.
  Restrictions, §42-4-228.
  Snow, mud, and all weather tires, §42-4-106.
  Studs, §42-4-228.
TITLES
  See CERTIFICATES OF TITLE - MOTOR VEHICLES
TOBOGGANS
  Use on highways, §42-4-109.
TOLLS
  Rural transportation authorities, §§42-4-613, 42-4-1701.
TOURIST CAMPS
  Stolen vehicles.
    Allowing storage of stolen motor vehicles.
      Penalties, §43-5-205.
    Definitions.
      Recordkeeping requirements, §43-5-201.
    Inspections.
      Records of owners to be inspected by officers, §43-5-204.
    Petty offenses.
      Violation of part, §43-5-207.
TOWING CARRIERS
  Liens, §§42-4-1806, 42-4-2105.
  Permits.
    Registration with department of revenue, §§42-4-1806, 42-4-2105.
  Registration with department of revenue, §§42-4-1806, 42-4-2105.
  Rules.
    Subject to safety rules, §42-4-235.
  Unlawful removal or usage of tow-truck signage, §42-4-241.
TRAFFIC
  Information on traffic law enforcement.
    Annual report, §42-4-115.
TRAFFIC INFRACTIONS
  Automated vehicle identification systems, §42-4-110.5.
  Crossing fire hose, §42-4-1404.
  Drivers' licenses.
    Age restrictions on certain drivers, §42-2-105.
    Failure to provide notice of change of address or name, §42-2-119.
    Instruction permits and temporary licenses, §42-2-106.
    Permitting unauthorized minor to drive, §42-2-139.
    Permitting unauthorized person to drive, §42-2-140.
    Unlawful acts not otherwise classified, §42-2-142.
    Violation of driving restrictions on minor drivers under seventeen years of age, §42-2-105.5.
    Violation of license requirement, §42-2-101.
    Violation of restricted license provisions, §42-2-116.

TRAFFIC INFRACTIONS-Cont'd
  Equipment.
    Violation of regulatory provisions.
      Additional signal lamps and devices on vehicles, §42-4-215.
      Audible and visual signals on emergency vehicles, §42-4-213.
      Bicycle equipment, §42-4-221.
      Brakes, §42-4-223.
      Child restraint systems, §42-4-236.
      Clearance lamps and clearance reflectors, §42-4-207.
      Earphones used while driving, §42-4-1411.
      Emergency lighting equipment, §42-4-230.
      Engine compression brake device muffler, §42-4-225.
      Head lamps, §§42-4-204, 42-4-205.
      Horns or warning devices, §42-4-224.
      Lamp or flag on projecting load, §42-4-209.
      Lamps on farm equipment, §42-4-211.
      Lamps on parked vehicle, §42-4-210.
      Mirrors, §42-4-226.
      Motorized bicycles, §§42-4-220, 42-4-232.
      Mufflers, §42-4-225.
      Multiple-beam road lights, §§42-4-216, 42-4-217.
      Number of lamps permitted, §42-4-219.
      Operation of unsafe vehicles prohibited, §42-4-202.
      Parking lights, §42-4-231.
      Safety belt systems, §42-4-237.
      Side marker lamps and reflectors, §42-4-207.
      Signal lamps and devices, §42-4-215.5.
      Single-beam road-lights, §42-4-218.
      Slow-moving vehicles, §42-4-234.
      Spot lamps and auxiliary lamps, §42-4-212.
      Stop lamps, §§42-4-208, 42-4-215.
      Tail lamps, §42-4-206.
      Tampering with automobile air pollution control systems, §42-4-314.
      Tires, §42-4-228.
      Turn signals, §§42-4-208, 42-4-215.
      Visual signals on service vehicles, §42-4-214.
      Volunteer ambulance services and volunteer fire departments, §42-4-222.
      Windshields and windows, §42-4-229.
  Following fire apparatus prohibited, §42-4-1403.
  Foreign matter on highway prohibited.
    Disgarding cigarettes, cigars, or matches on the highway prohibited, §42-4-1406.
  Habitual offenders, §42-2-202.
  Low-power scooters speeding, §42-2-1101.
  Motorcycles.
    Clinging to other vehicles, §42-4-1504.
    Minimum safety standards for motorcycles and motor-driven cycles, §§42-4-232, 42-4-1502.

TRAFFIC INFRACTIONS-Cont'd
Motorcycles.-Cont'd
Operating motorcycles on roadways, §42-4-1503.
Obstruction of view of driver prohibited, §42-4-201.
Operation of motor vehicles on property under control of or owned by parks and recreation districts, §42-4-1408.
Overtaking and passing.
Coasting prohibited, §42-4-1009.
Driving on divided or controlled-access highways, §42-4-1010.
Exceptions to driving on right side, §42-4-1001.
Following too closely, §42-4-1008.
Overtaking a vehicle on the left, §§42-4-903, 42-4-905.
Overtaking a vehicle on the right, §42-4-1004.
Passing oncoming vehicles, §42-4-1002.
Roadways and rotary traffic islands, §§42-4-1006, 42-4-1007.
Parking.
Area or space reserved for persons with disabilities, §42-4-1208.
Opening vehicle doors, §42-4-1207.
Parking at curb or edge of roadway, §42-4-1205.
Parking or abandonment of vehicles, §42-4-1202.
Parking prohibited in specified places, §42-4-1204.
Runaway vehicle ramps, §42-4-1011.
Starting parked vehicle, §42-4-1201.
Unattended motor vehicle, §42-4-1206.
Pedestrians.
Disobedience to traffic control devices and regulations, §42-4-801.
Drivers to exercise due care, §42-4-807.
Driving through safety zone prohibited, §42-4-806.
Pedestrians' use of crosswalks, §§42-4-802 to 42-4-804.
Pedestrians on highways, §42-4-805.
Penalties and procedure.
Automated vehicle identification systems, §42-4-110.5.
Classification of traffic infraction penalties, §42-4-1701.
Failure to pay penalty assessment, §42-4-1710.
Payment of fine.
  Notice to appear or pay fine, §42-4-1716.
Penalty assessments.
  Acceptance of late payments, §42-4-1701.
  Electronic transmission of data, §42-4-1718.
Summons and complaint.
  Release, §42-4-1709.
Photo-radar, §42-4-110.5.

TRAFFIC INFRACTIONS-Cont'd
Registration and taxation.
License plate violations, §§42-3-202, 42-3-124.
Penalty where no specific penalty provided, §42-3-142.
Registration requirement violations, §§42-3-103, 42-3-121.
Use of license plate or placard for persons with disabilities by person who is not disabled, §42-4-1208.
Use of noncommercial or recreational vehicle for commercial purposes, §42-3-121.
Regulation of vehicles and traffic.
Driving with inoperable emission control system, §42-4-314.
Electric cars, §42-4-109.5.
High occupancy lanes, §42-4-1012.
Restrictions on right to use highways, §42-4-106.
Snow tires or tire chains, §42-4-106.
Use of runaway vehicle ramps, §42-4-1011.
Rights-of-way.
Disabled persons, §42-4-808.
Driving in highway work area, §42-4-712.
Driving on mountain highways, §42-4-711.
Emergency vehicles, §42-4-705.
Emerging from or entering alley, driveway, or building, §42-4-710.
Moving heavy equipment at railroad grade crossing, §42-4-708.
Obedience to railroad signal, §42-4-706.
Stop when traffic obstructed, §42-4-709.
Vehicle entering roadway, §42-4-704.
Vehicle entering through highway, §42-4-703.
Vehicles entering intersection, §§42-4-701, 42-4-702.
Vehicles required to stop at railroad grade crossings, §42-4-707.
School zones, §42-4-615.
Signals, signs, and markings.
Disobedience to traffic control devices, §§42-4-603 to 42-4-605.
Display of unauthorized signs or devices, §42-4-606.
Inoperative or malfunctioning traffic control devices, §42-4-612.
Interference with traffic control devices, §42-4-607.
Required use of hand signals or signals device, §§42-4-608, 42-4-609.
Unauthorized insignia on vehicle, §42-4-610.
Size and weight violations.
Causing damage to highway or highway structure, §42-4-512.
General provisions, §42-4-501.
Height and length of vehicles, §42-4-504.
Longer vehicle combinations, §42-4-505.
Projecting loads on passenger vehicles, §42-4-503.
Trailers and towed vehicles, §42-4-506.
Width of vehicles, §42-4-502.

TRAFFIC INFRACTIONS-Cont'd
Speed regulations.
Automated vehicle identification systems.
Generally, §42-4-110.5.
Maximum penalty, §42-4-110.5.
Service of citation, §42-4-110.5.
Sign posted notifying public of device in use, §42-4-110.5.
Photo-radar, §42-4-110.5.
Speed limits generally, §§42-4-1101, 42-4-1103.
Speed limits on elevated structures, §42-4-1104.
Spilling loads on highways prohibited, §42-4-1407.
Tolls, §§42-4-613, 42-4-1701.
Trailers.
Riding in trailers, §42-4-1405.
Turning.
Intersections.
Required position and method, §42-4-901.
Right-of-way.
Turning left at intersection, §42-4-702.
Limitations on turning around, §42-4-902.
Private road, alley, or driveway.
Right-of-way.
Turning left into, §42-4-702.
Signals.
Devices, §42-4-608.
Hand and arm signals.
General provisions, §42-4-608.
Method of giving, §42-4-609.
Land use control signals, §42-4-604.
Mandatory under certain conditions, §§42-4-608, 42-4-903.
Required position and method of turning, §42-4-901.
Turn signals required, §§42-4-208, 42-4-215.
Turning movements and required signals, §42-4-903.
U-turns, §42-4-902.
TRAFFIC LAWS.
Appropriations to administer article, §42-4-113.
Arrest.
Immediate appearance before judge, §42-4-1705.
Warrantless arrest.
General provisions, §§42-4-1705 to 42-4-1711.
Procedure not exclusive, §42-4-1712.
Automated vehicle identification systems, §42-4-110.5.
Backing, §42-4-1211.
Bicycles.
Applicability of motor vehicle laws, §42-4-1412.
Careless driving, §42-4-1402.
Classification of traffic offenses and infractions, §42-4-1701.
Coasting, §42-4-1009.
Collateral attack on judgment.
Alcohol-related or drug-related traffic offenses, §42-4-1702.

TRAFFIC LAWS.-Cont'd
Collateral attack on judgment.-Cont'd
Proper court for hearing, §42-4-1708.
Controlled-access or divided highways, §42-4-1010.
Convictions.
Attendance at driver improvement school, §42-4-1717.
Recording by judge or clerk of court, §42-4-1715.
Electric vehicles, §§42-4-109.5, 42-4-111.
Emergency vehicles.
Exemption from traffic laws, §42-4-108.
Emissions control systems.
Driving with inoperable emission control system prohibited, §42-4-314.
Equipment, §§42-4-201 to 42-4-1411.
Exemptions, §42-4-108.
Fire apparatus.
Following, §42-4-1403.
Fire hose.
Crossing, §42-4-1404.
Following too closely, §42-4-1008.
Interstate highways.
Driving on, §42-4-1010.
Legislative intent, §42-4-102.
Limited access highways.
Driving on, §42-4-1010.
Local authorities.
Enforcement of emissions control inspection requirements, §42-4-110.
Operation of electric vehicles, §42-4-111.
Powers.
General provisions, §42-4-111.
Limitation of powers, §42-4-110.
Misdemeanors.
Classification, §42-4-1701.
Mopeds.
Applicability of traffic laws, §42-4-109.
Motorcycles.
Applicability of traffic laws, §42-4-1501.
General provisions, §§42-4-1501 to 42-4-1504.
Motorized bicycles.
Applicability of traffic laws, §42-4-109.
Obstruction to driver's view or driving mechanism, §42-4-201.
Offenses by persons controlling vehicles, §42-4-1704.
One-way roadways, §42-4-1006.
Parties to a crime, §§42-4-1703, 42-4-1704.
Passengers.
Hazardous situations, §42-4-201.
Penalties.
Assessments.
Acceptance of late payments, §42-4-1701.
General provisions, §§42-4-1701, 42-4-1707, 42-4-1709.
Photo-radar, §42-4-110.5.
Point system, §42-2-127.
Police.
Compliance with orders required, §§42-4-107, 42-4-1413.

TRAFFIC LAWS.-Cont'd
Police.-Cont'd
Eluding or attempting to elude, §42-4-1413.
Public officers to obey provisions, §42-4-108.
Real property.
Removal of traffic hazards, §42-4-114.
Right of owner to regulate use of property by vehicular traffic, §42-4-112.
Reckless driving, §42-4-1401.
Roadways laned for traffic, §42-4-1007.
Safety zones.
Driving through safety zones prohibited, §42-4-806.
Scope of article, §42-4-103.
Skates, skis, and sleds.
Use on highways, §42-4-109.
Starting parked vehicles, §42-4-1201.
Summons and complaint.
Compliance with promise to appear, §42-4-1711.
General provisions, §42-4-1707.
Information on notice, §42-4-1707.
Issuance of, §§42-4-1701, 42-4-1707.
Release from custody contingent on written notice to appear, §42-4-1707.
Tailgating, §42-4-1008.
Title of law, §42-4-101.
Toboggans.
Use on highways, §42-4-109.
Toll evasion, § 42-4-1709.
Toy vehicles.
Use on highways, §42-4-109.
Trailers.
Riding in trailers, §42-4-1405.
Uniformity of provisions throughout state, §42-4-110.
TRANSPORTATION
Department of transportation.
Development of standards.
Electronic transmission of traffic infraction penalty assessment notice or summons and complaint, §42-4-1718.
Rural transportation authorities.
Tolls, §§42-4-613, 42-4-1701.
Traffic laws, §42-4-607.
TREES AND TIMBER
Highways.
Obstructing highways, §43-5-301.

U

UNCLAIMED PROPERTY
Motor vehicles.
Disposition of personal property, §§42-13-101 to 42-13-109.
UNITED STATES
Highways.
Federal highway safety act of 1966.
Implementation, §43-5-401.
Motor vehicles.
Automobile inspection and readjustment program, §42-4-310.

UNITED STATES-Cont'd
Motor vehicles.-Cont'd
Registration and specific ownership tax.
Exemption of government owned vehicles, §42-3-104.

V

VEHICLE EQUIPMENT SAFETY COMPACT
General provisions, §§24-60-901 to 24-60-912.
VEHICULAR ASSAULT
Revocation of driver's license, §42-2-125.
VEHICULAR HOMICIDE
Revocation of drivers' license, §§42-2-125, 42-2-128.
VENUE
Driver's licenses.
Denial, suspension, or revocation.
Judicial review, §42-2-135.
VETERANS
Motor vehicles.
Exemption from registration, §§42-3-204, 42-3-304.
Exemption from specific ownership tax, §42-3-104.
License plates, §42-3-213.
VOLUNTEER FIREFIGHTERS
Emergency vehicles, §42-4-222.

W

WAREHOUSES
Motor vehicles liens.
Effect of mortgage on warehouse liens, §42-6-131.
WARRANTIES
Motor vehicles.
Dealers.
Compensation of dealers under warranties, §12-6-114.
Failure to perform.
General provisions, §12-6-120.
Penalties, §12-6-121.
Right of action for loss, §12-6-122.
Licensed manufacturers.
Filing of written warranties, §12-6-114.
Emissions control.
Effect of enforcement of applicable warranty, §42-4-315.
Nonconformity to warranties, §§42-10-101 to 42-10-107.
WARRANTS
Warrantless arrest.
General provisions, §§42-4-1705 to 42-4-1711.
Procedure not exclusive, §42-4-1712.

WATERCOURSES
Highways.
  Agricultural crop sprinkler systems.
    Causing water to flow onto highways.
      Penalty, §§43-5-301, 43-5-303.
    Damming streams.
      Penalty, §43-5-302.
WEIGH STATIONS.
  Appropriations for expenses of administration, §42-8-111.
  Clearance certificates.
    Contents, §42-8-103.
    Suspension or revocation, §42-8-109.
  Clearances.
    Failure to obtain, §42-8-106.
    Issuance of receipts, §42-8-106.
    Special revocable permits, §42-8-105.
    Unlawful use of tax-exempt fuel, §42-8-105.
    Verification at each station on route, §42-8-105.
  Construction and maintenance, §42-8-107.
  Contiguous states.
    Operation of ports of entry at borders, §42-8-111.
  Definitions, §42-8-102.
  Hours of operation, §42-8-104.
  Interdepartmental cooperation required, §42-8-108.
  Legislative declaration, §42-8-101.
  Misdemeanors, §42-8-109.
  Motor carrier services division, §42-8-103.
  Obstruction, §42-8-107.
  Operation of ports of entry at borders.
    Cooperative agreements, §42-8-111.
  Passenger buses.
    Exemption from clearance requirement, §42-8-105.
  Permits.
    Oversize and overweight commercial hauls, §42-8-106.
    Special reciprocal permits, §42-8-105.
    Suspension or revocation, §42-8-109.
  Personnel.
    Powers and duties, §42-8-104.
  Rights-of-way, §42-8-107.
  Rules.
    General provisions, §42-8-104.
    Operation of ports of entry at borders, §42-8-111.
WHISTLES
  Bicycles.
    Prohibition of siren or whistle, §§42-4-221, 42-4-224.
  Motorized bicycles.
    Prohibition of siren or whistle, §§42-4-220, 42-4-224.
  Volunteer firemen and volunteer ambulance attendants.
    Audible signal systems on vehicles, §42-4-222.
WINDSHIELDS
  General provisions, §§42-4-227, 42-4-229.

WITNESSES
Effect of traffic violations on credibility of witness, §42-4-1714.

SHORT TITLES AND POPULAR NAMES

Blue Laws.
  Automobile dealers, §12-6-302.
Certificate of Title Act, §§42-6-101 to 42-6-143.
Chain Law, §42-4-106.
Commercial Driver's License Act, §§42-2-401 to 42-2-408.
Lemon Law, §§42-10-101 to 42-10-107.
Motor Vehicle Financial Responsibility Act, §§42-7-101 to 42-7-510.
Motor Vehicle Law, §§42-1-101 to 42-20-511.
Motor Vehicle Repair Act of 1977, §§42-9-101 to 42-9-112.
Safety Code of 1935, §§42-2-101 to 42-2-143, 42-4-101 to 42-4-1814, 42-4-2101 to 42-4-2110.
Uninsured Motorist Identification Database Program Act, §§42-7-601 to 42-7-609.

WORDS AND PHRASES

Acceleration lane, §42-1-102.
Accident.
  Motor vehicles, §42-7-103.
Advertisement.
  Automobile dealers, §12-6-102.
AIR program, §42-4-307.
All-terrain recreational vehicle, §42-1-102.
Alley, §42-1-102.
Antifreeze, §42-10-102.
Apportioned registration.
  Motor vehicle law, §42-1-102.
Approved ignition interlock device, §42-2-132.5.
Appurtenance, §42-1-102.
Auctioneers.
  Automobiles, §12-6-102.
Authorized agent.
  Certificates of title, §42-6-102.
Auto camp, §43-5-201.
Auto parts recycler, §§42-4-1802, 42-9-102.
Automated vehicle identification system, §42-4-110.5.
Automobile inspection and readjustment program, §42-4-307.
Automobile liability policy, §42-7-103.
Automobile.
  Definitions, §42-1-102.
  Sunday sales, §12-6-302.
BAC.
  Driving under the influence, §42-1-102.
Ballot box.
  DUI per se, §42-1-102.
Bicycle, §42-1-102.
Blue law, §§12-6-302, 12-47-901.
Bulk electronic transfer, §42-1-102.
Buyer agent, §12-6-102.

WORDS AND PHRASES-Cont'd

Camper coach.
  Motor vehicle law, §42-1-102.
Camper trailer.
  Motor vehicle law, §42-1-102.
Certification of emissions control, §42-4-307.
Chauffeur, §42-1-102.
Coerce.
  Automobile dealers, §12-6-102.
Commercial carrier.
  Motor vehicle law, §42-1-102.
Commercial vehicle.
  Motor vehicle law, §42-1-102.
  Safety standards, §42-4-234.
Community.
  Automobile dealers, §12-6-102.
Consumer.
  Motor vehicle warranties, §42-12-101.
Contractor.
  Emissions control, §42-4-307.
Controlled-access highway, §42-1-102.
Crosswalk, §42-1-102.
Custom trailer, §12-6-102.
Deceleration lane, §42-1-102.
Distributor branch.
  Automobile dealers, §12-6-102.
Distributor representative.
  Automobile dealers, §12-6-102.
Drive-away or tow-away transporter, §42-1-102.
Driver's license.
  Nonresident violator compact, §24-60-2101.
Driver, §§42-1-102, 42-7-103.
DUI per se.
  Driving under the influence, §42-1-102.
DUI, §42-1-102.
DWAI.
  Driving under the influence, §42-1-102.
Electrical assisted bicycle, §42-1-102.
Emissions inspector.
  Emissions control, §42-4-307.
Emissions mechanic, §42-4-307.
Empty weight.
  Motor vehicles, §42-1-102.
Enhanced inspection center.
  Emissions control, §42-4-307.
EPAMD.
  Electric personal assistive mobility device, §§42-4-102, 42-4-117.
Essential parts.
  Motor vehicles, §42-1-102.
Established place of business.
  Motor vehicles, §42-1-102.
Estimate.
  Motor vehicle repair act, §42-9-102.
Evidence of insurance.
  Motor vehicle financial responsibility act, §42-7-103.
Explosives and hazardous materials, §42-1-102.
Factory branch.
  Automobile dealers, §12-6-102.
Factory representative.
  Automobile dealers, §12-6-102.

WORDS AND PHRASES-Cont'd

Farm tractor, §42-1-102.
Financial responsibility bond.
  Motor vehicles, §42-7-103.
Flammable liquid, §42-1-102.
Fleet operator.
  Motor vehicles, §42-1-102.
Fleet vehicle.
  Motor vehicles, §42-1-102.
Foreign vehicle, §42-1-102.
Fullmount.
  Motor vehicle law, §42-1-102.
Garage, §42-1-102.
Golf car, §42-1-102.
Good faith.
  Automobile dealers, §12-6-102.
Graduated annual specific ownership tax, §42-1-102.
Gross dollar volume.
  Motor vehicles, §42-1-102.
Habitual user.
  Driving under the influence, §42-1-102.
Highway.
  Motor vehicle law, §42-1-102.
Holder.
  Disabled parking permit, §42-4-1208.
Homemade vehicle, §42-5-201.
Hotel.
  General definition, §43-5-201.
Identification card, §42-2-401.
Implement of husbandry.
  Motor vehicles, §42-1-102.
Inspection and readjustment station, §42-4-307.
Intersection, §42-1-102.
Invoice.
  Motor vehicle repair act, §42-9-102.
Laden truck tractor, §42-1-102.
Laned highway, §42-1-102.
License.
  Motor vehicles, §42-7-103.
Low-power scooter, §42-1-102.
Low-speed electric vehicle, §42-1-102.
Manufactured home.
  Motor vehicle law, §42-1-102.
Manufacturer.
  Automobile dealers, §12-6-102.
Mobile machinery, §42-1-102.
Motor-driven cycle, §42-1-102.
Motor vehicle agent, §12-6-102.
Motor vehicle dealer, §12-6-102.
Motor vehicle liability policy, §§42-7-103, 42-7-413.
Motor vehicle repair facility, §42-11-102.
Motor vehicle salesperson, §12-6-102.
Motor vehicle service contract, §42-13-101.
Motor vehicle.
  Auto and tourist camps, §43-5-201.
  Automobile dealers, §12-6-102.
  Certificates of title, §42-6-102.
  Emissions control, §42-4-307.
  Financial responsibility, §42-7-103.
  Motor vehicle law, §42-1-102.
  Repairs, §42-11-102.
  Sunday closing law, §12-6-301.

WORDS AND PHRASES-Cont'd
Motor vehicle.-Cont'd
  Warranties, §42-12-101.
  Weigh stations, §42-8-102.
Motorcycle, §42-1-102.
Motorized bicycle, §42-1-102.
Motorscooter, §42-1-102.
Muffler, §42-4-222.
Neighborhood electric vehicle, §42-1-102.
New vehicles.
  Certificates of title, §42-6-102.
Noncommercial or recreational vehicle, §42-1-102.
Nonresident's operating privilege, §42-7-103.
Nonresident.
  Motor vehicle financial responsibility act, §42-7-103.
Official records and documents.
  Motor vehicle law, §42-2-118.
Official traffic control devices, §42-1-102.
Official traffic control signal, §42-1-102.
Owner.
  Used motor vehicles sales, §42-6-201.
Pedestrian.
  Uniform motor vehicle law, §42-1-102.
Personal recognizance.
  Nonresident violator compact, §24-60-2101.
Personalized license plates, §42-3-211.
Photo-radar, §42-4-110.5.
Pneumatic tires, §42-1-102.
Police officer.
  Nonresident violator compact, §24-60-2101.
Primary user, §42-1-102.
Private road, §42-1-102.
Private sale, §42-6-201.
Program area.
  Emissions control, §42-4-307.
Proof of financial responsibility for the future, §42-7-103.
Provisional driver's license, §42-1-102.
Railroad sign or signal, §42-1-102.
Rebuilt vehicle, §42-5-201.
Reciprocal agreement.
  Motor vehicle law, §42-1-102.
Reciprocity.
  Motor vehicle law, §42-1-102.
Reconstructed vehicle, §§42-1-102, 42-5-201.
Registration period.
  Motor vehicles, §42-1-102.
Repairs on a motor vehicle, §42-11-102.
Residence district, §42-1-102.
Restraint.
  Motor vehicle law, §42-2-130.
Retail used motor vehicle sale, §42-6-201.
Right-of-way.
  Motor vehicle law, §42-1-102.
Road tractor, §42-1-102.
Roadway.
  Motor vehicle law, §42-1-102.
Roadworthy.
  Certificates of title, §42-6-102.
Road.
  Motor vehicle law, §42-1-102.

WORDS AND PHRASES-Cont'd
Saddlemount combination.
  Motor vehicle law, §42-1-102.
Safety zone, §42-1-102.
Sale.
  Used motor vehicles, §42-6-201.
Salvage certificate of title.
  Certificates of title, §42-6-102.
Salvage vehicle.
  Certificates of title, §42-6-102.
School bus.
  Uniform motor vehicle law, §42-1-102.
Semitrailer, §42-1-102.
Sidewalk.
  Motor vehicle law, §42-1-102.
Snowplow, §42-1-102.
Solid rubber tires, §42-1-102.
Specially constructed vehicle, §42-1-102.
State traffic control manual, §42-1-102.
Steam and electric trains, §42-1-102.
Stinger-steered.
  Motor vehicles, §42-1-102.
Stop line.
  Motor vehicles, §42-1-102.
Stop.
  Motor vehicles, §42-1-102.
Street-rod vehicle, §42-5-201.
Street-rod.
  Special license plates, §42-3-211.
Sunday sales, §12-6-302.
Surge brakes, §42-1-102.
Temporary special license plate, §42-1-102.
Through highway, §42-1-102.
Tire chains, §42-4-410.
Traffic, §42-1-102.
Trailer coach, §42-1-102.
Trailer, §42-1-102.
Transporter.
  Motor vehicle law, §42-1-102.
Truck tractor, §42-1-102.
Truck, §42-1-102.
UDD.
  Driving under the influence, §42-1-102.
Unladen truck tractor, §42-1-102.
Used motor vehicle dealer.
  Professions and occupations, §12-6-102.
  Sales, §42-6-201.
Used motor vehicle.
  Sales, §42-6-201.
Used vehicle.
  Certificates of title, §42-6-102.
  Motor vehicle law, §42-1-102.
Useful public service.
  Driving under the influence, §42-4-1301.4.
Utility trailer, §42-1-102.
Vehicle identification number, §42-5-201.
Vehicle.
  Certificates of title, §42-6-102.
  Motor vehicle law, §42-1-102.
  Vehicle equipment safety compact, §24-60-902.
Warranty, §42-12-101.
Wholesale motor vehicle auction dealer, §12-6-102.
Work order.
  Motor vehicle repair act, §42-9-102.

COMMON CODE

Provided by the
Colorado State Patrol

Common Codes
Title 42 and Related Laws
2011

Statutes referred to in this manual include subsections and paragraph numbers. The judicial system uses the subsection and paragraph numbers when a charge is filed. Please include all subsections and paragraphs on citations where indicated.

The Colorado Department of Revenue maintains the numeric Common Codes used with motor vehicle laws and are applied to traffic violations.

The Colorado State Patrol maintains codes for penal violations that are more criminal in nature. The codes start with the letters F, M, or P.

Any agency may use these codes. Should an agency need an additional code, the request must be coordinated with the Department of Revenue and the Colorado State Patrol.

Disclaimer: With respect to information or documents related to the enforcement of Colorado State Statutes, neither the Colorado State Patrol nor the Colorado Department of Public Safety, nor any of their employees, volunteers or members, makes any warranty, express or implied, or assumes any legal liability or responsibility for the accuracy, completeness, timeliness or usefulness of any opinions, advice, or other information contained or referenced in this document. This document has been provided as a reference guide only.

CSP Contents and Abbreviations

Legend of Abbreviations iii
Title 42 Index iv
Title 42 Related Law and Common Codes 1
    Alcohol / Drugs* / Under the Influence 1
    Auto Theft – Abandoned Vehicles 1
    Bicycles 3
    Bicycle Equipment 3
    Commercial Vehicle (D.P.S. & P.U.C. Rules & Regulations) 4
    Crimes Involving Assault 5
    Crimes Involving Child Abuse 5
    Crimes Involving Death 5
    Driver's License 6
    Drugs / Marijuana 7
    Emissions 9
    Equipment 9
    Financial Responsibility / Insurance 11
    Firearms / Weapons 11
    Hazardous Materials Violations 11
    Hit and Run / Failure to Report 12
    Identification Cards 12
    Improper / Reckless / Careless Driving and Actions 12
    Interference 13
    Lane Usage 14
    Lights / Reflectors 14
    Low-Power Scooters 16
    Motorcycles 16
    Obscured Vision / Interference With Driver 16
    Oversize / Overwidth / Overlength / Overweight / Projecting Load 17
    Parking Violations 18
    Passing 19
    Pedestrian / Animal Rider Violations 19
    Recreational Vehicles / Areas / Services 20
    Registration / Title 21
    Right-of-Way (Vehicle / Pedestrian) 22
    Safety Belts / Restraints 23
    School Bus 23
    Signaling 23
    Speed 23
    Spilling Loads / Damaging Highway / Littering 25
    Theft 25
    Towing 26
    Traffic Controls 26
    Turns 27
    Wrong Way / Wrong Side 27
Presumptive Penalty and Enforcement Guide 29
    Registration Violations Fine Schedule 29
    Penalty Chart for Weight in Excess of Weight Authorized by Special Permit 29
    PCC Codes (CSP Use Only) 29
    Patrol Codes (CSP Use Only) 29
    Felony Offenses 30

> Misdemeanor Offenses 31
> Misdemeanor Traffic Offenses 31
> Traffic Infractions 31
> Safety Zone Definitions 32

Drug Schedule Reference 33
> Schedule I 33
> Schedule II 34
> Schedule III 35
> Schedule IV 35
> Schedule V 36

NIBRS System Codes 37

Legend of Abbreviations

CLS	Class of offense
Comm. Code / Code	Common code of offense
Commercial Vehicle	Common codes for offenses committed by a commercial motor carrier
F1	Penalty Class is a class 1 felony
F2	Penalty Class is a class 2 felony
F3	Penalty Class is a class 3 felony
F4	Penalty Class is a class 4 felony
F5	Penalty Class is a class 5 felony
F6	Penalty Class is a class 6 felony
Fine + S.C / Fine	A penalty assessment citation should be issued with the **fine** being the first number and the **surcharge** being the second number
HB	Determine the actual charging of the offense by using the Colorado Peace Officer's Handbook, section IX: **Misdemeanor Summons and Complaint Charging Manual**
M	Penalty Class is misdemeanor
M1	Penalty Class is a class 1 misdemeanor
M2	Penalty Class is a class 2 misdemeanor
M3	Penalty Class is a class 3 misdemeanor
MT1	Class 1 Misdemeanor Traffic Infraction
MT2	Class 2 Misdemeanor Traffic Infraction
NIBR	National Incident Based Reporting System. The district attorney files all charges listed with the notation. A special entry should be made into the Colorado Crime Information Center (CCIC).
PO1	Penalty Class is a class 1 petty offense
PO2	Penalty Class is a class 2 petty offense
PT	Points Assessed
RA	Convictions of these offenses require the Department of Revenue, Motor Vehicle Division to take restraint action against the violator's driver's privilege or license.
Safety Zone	Indication of a different fine and surcharge schedule when offense is done within an active safety zone
SUM	A summons and complaint should be issued.
TI	Penalty Class is a traffic infraction with no penalty class stated.
TIA	Penalty Class is a class A traffic infraction
TIB	Penalty Class is a class B traffic infraction
VAR	Various penalty classes apply – refer to the statute for the actual class.

Index

A

Abandonment: Icebox, 2; Motor Vehicle, 2
Alcohol: Animal Rider Impaired, 1; AWOL Device, 1; Driving Under Restraint, 6; DUI, 1; DWAI, 1; Minor CDL/DUI, 1; Open Container, 1; Pedestrian, 1; Per Se, 1; Provided to Under 21, 1
Animals: Failed to Yield, 19; Rider Impaired, 1; Wrong Side of Highway, 20
Auto Parts: Illegal Sale / Purchase, 2; Prohibited Transportation, 3
AWOL Device: Unlawful Possession, 1

B

Backing: Highway, 13; Parking Lot, 13
Bicycle: Parking, 3
Bicycles: Handlebars, 3; Speeding, 4
Brake Lights, 15

C

Careless: Bicycle, 3; Driving, 13
CDL: Minor DUI, 1; Out of Service Order, 4; Port of Entry, 4; Right of Way (Vehicle Being Equipped with Chains), 22
Child Abuse, 5
CMV: Collector's Vehicle, 4; No Proof of Insurance, 4; Out of Service Order, 4; Port of Entry, 4; PUC Permit, 4; Railroad Crossing, 23; Splash Guards, 4; Tow Truck Signs, 26
Criminal Trespassing, 2

D

Death: Careless Driving, 13; Child Abuse, 5; Hit and Run, 12
Divided Highway: Turn, 27; Wrong Side, 27
Drawbar: Unlawful, 26
Driver's License: Alcohol Restraint, 6; Forgery, 6; FRA Suspension, 6; Interlock Bypassed, 1; Interlock Tampering, 1; Unlawful Use, 6
Driving: Habitual User, 1
Drugs: DUID, 1; DWAID, 1; Toxic Vapors, 9
DUI, 1; Animal Rider, 1; DUID, 1; DWAI, 1; DWAID, 1; Interlock Tampering, 1; Minor CDL/DUI, 1; Open Container, 1; Pedestrian, 1; Per Se, 1
DWAI, 1

E

Emissions: Counterfeit Certification, 9; Deactivated Equipment, 9
Equipment: Brake Lights, 15; Emissions, 9; Splash Guards, 4; Tires, 10

F

Firearms: Juvenile Possession, 11
Forgery: Driver's License, 6; Title, 3
Fraud: Emissions, 9
Fuel: Dyed Diesel, 11; Failed to Pay, 26

G

Gas Skip, 26

H

Habitual User: Driving Motor Vehicle, 1
Hand Signals, 23; Improper, 23
Handlebars: Bicycles, 3
Helmets: Motorcycle, 16; Motorized Bicycle, 16
Highway: Backing, 13; Divided Median, 27; Livestock, 13
Hit and Run, 12
HOV Lane, 14

I

Impeded: Flow of Traffic, 25
Impersonation of Police Officer, 13
Injury: Careless Driving, 13; Child Abuse, 5; Hit and Run, 12
Insurance, 11; Failed to Sign Affirmation, 22; FRA Suspension, 6, 11; No Proof - CMV, 4
Interlock, 1; Drove With Device Bypassed, 1; Tampering, 1
Intersection: Right of Way, 22

L

Lanes: HOV, 14; Passing Lane, 14; Unsafe Change, 14; Weaving, 14
Lights: School Bus, 23; Signals, 23
Littering: Icebox, 2
Livestock: Highway, 13

M

Median: Turn, 27
Motor Vehicle: Abandonment, 2; Rental Theft, 1; Tampering, 2; Theft, 1
Move Over Law, 14

N

No Proof of Insurance, 11

O

Open Container, 1
Out of Service Order, 4

P

Parking: Bicycle, 3
Parking Lot: Backing, 13
Passengers: In Trailers, 26
Passing Lane, 19
Pedestrian: Impaired, 1; In Path of Vehicle, 22; Safety Zone, 14; Traffic Control, 22
Per Se, 1; Driving Under Restraint, 6
Permits: PUC, 4
Police Officer: Directing Traffic, 14; Eluding, 25; Failed to Report Accident To, 12; Impersonation, 13
Port of Entry, 4
PUC: Permit, 4

R

Railroad Crossing: School Bus, 23
Reckless: Child Abuse, 5; Driving, 13; Eluding, 25; Endangerment, 13; Vehicular Homicide, 5
Records Inspection: Dealer / Garage Proprietor, 2; Refusal, 2
Rental Property: Theft, 1
Right of Way: Intersection, 22; School Bus, 23; Vehicle Being Equipped with Chains, 22

S

Safety Chains: Tires, 10; Towing, 26
School Bus: Lights, 23; Railroad Crossing, 23
Sidewalk: Driving a Motor Vehicle, 13
Signals: Hand, 23; Improper, 23; Improper Hand, 23
Signs: Tow Truck, 26
Speed: Contest, 24; Eluding, 25; Impeded Flow of Traffic, 24; Overweight Permit, 4
Speeding: Bicycle Common Code, 4

T

Tampering: Motor Vehicle, 2
Theft, 1; Auto Parts, 2; Fuel, 26; Motor Vehicle, 1; Receiving, 2; Rental Auto Theft, 1; Rental Property, 1
Tire Chains, 10
Tires: Illegal Transportation / Storage, 12; Unsafe, 10
Title: Forgery, 3
Tow Truck: Signs, 26
Towing: Passengers In Trailers, 26; Safety Chains, 26; Unlawful Drawbar, 26; White Flag, 26
Traffic Control: Bicycle, 3
Traffic Controls: Pedestrian, 26
Trespassing: See Criminal Trespassing
Turns: Divided Median, 27

W

Weaving, 14

COLORADO STATE PATROL
Title 42
Related Laws and Common Codes

STATUTE 2011	CHARGE	CLS	Comm. Code	Fine + S.C.	PT	Safety Zone Fine	Commercial Vehicle Code	Commercial Vehicle Fine
	Alcohol / Drugs / Under the Influence							
42-4-805 (4)	Animal Rider on Highway Under the Influence of (Alcohol/Controlled Substance)	TIB	802	15+7	0	30+13		
42-4-805 (3)	Pedestrian on Highway Under the Influence of (Alcohol/controlled Substance)	TIB	803	15+7	0	30+13		
42-4-1301 (1)(a)	Drove Vehicle While Under the Influence of Alcohol or Drugs or Both	M	800	SUM	12		753	SUM
42-4-1301 (1)(a)	Drove Vehicle While Under the Influence of Drugs	M	813	SUM	12		754	SUM
42-4-1301 (1)(b)	Drove Vehicle While Ability Impaired by Alcohol or Drugs or Both	M	801	SUM	8		753	SUM
42-4-1301 (1)(b)	Drove Vehicle While Ability Impaired by Drugs	M	814	SUM	8		754	SUM
42-4-1301 (1)(c)	Habitual User of Controlled Substance Drove (Motor Vehicle/Low-Power Scooter)	M	804	SUM	RA		754	SUM
42-4-1301 (2)(a)	Drove Vehicle With Blood Alcohol Content of 0.08 or More	M	812	SUM	12		755	SUM
42-4-1301 (2)(a.5)	Person or CMV Driver Under 21 Drove Vehicle with BAC of 0.02 but Less Than 0.05 (First Offense)	TIA	810	100 +32	4	200+48	785	4
42-4-1301 (2)(a.5)(I)	Person or CMV driver Under 21 Drove Vehicle With BAC of 0.02 but Less Than 0.05 (Second Offense)	MT2	810	SUM	4		785	4
42-4-1305 (2)(a)	(Drank From/Possessed) an Open Alcoholic Beverage Container in a Motor Vehicle	TIA	962	50+17	3	100+33		

42-2-116 (6)(b)	Drove Vehicle Other Than Vehicle Equipped With Approved Ignition Interlock Device	M	818	SUM		RA
42-2-126.3 (2)	Drove Vehicle Knowingly With Ignition Interlock Device (Intercepted/Bypassed/Interfered With)	M1	816	SUM		RA
42-2-126.3 (1)	Tampered With Ignition Interlock Device	M1	817	SUM		RA
18-13-122 (2)(a)	Illegal (Possession/Consumption) of Ethyl Alcohol by an Underage Person (Applicable Anywhere)	PO2	117	HB		RA
12-47-901 (1)(c)	Unlawful Possession of Alcohol Beverage by Person Under 21 Years of Age (Juvenile Court)	M2	117	SUM		RA
12-47-901 (1)(a.5)	Attempted to provide an alcoholic beverage to a person under 21years of age	M2	963	SUM		RA
12-47-901 (1)(k)	Allowed the Use of Personal Identification by a Person Under 21 Years of Age	M2	964	SUM		RA
12-47-902.5 (3)	Unlawful (Possession/Purchase/Sale/Use) of an AWOL Device	M2	MDL	SUM		RA

*Please see page 32 for Drug Schedule Reference Guide

Auto Theft – Abandonded Vehicles

18-4-401 (2)(b)	Theft: Value Less Than $500	M2	M8A	SUM		0
18-4-401 (2)(b.5)	Theft: Value $500 But Less Than $1,000	M1	M8A	NIBR		0
18-4-401 (2)(c)	Theft: Value $1,000 But Less Than $20,000	F4	F8A	NIBR		0
18-4-401 (d)	Theft: Value $20,000 or More	F3	F8A	NIBR		0
18-4-402 (3)	Theft of Rental Property (Auto) Less Than $500	M2	M8B	HB		0
18-4-402 (3.5)	Theft of Rental Property (Auto)($500 But Less Than $1,000)	M1	M8B	NIBR		0
18-4-402 (4)	Theft of Rental Property (Auto) $1,000 but less than $20,000	F5	F8B	NIBR		0
18-4-402 (5)	Theft of Rental Property (Auto) $20,000 or more	F3	F8B	NIBR		0

STATUTE 2011	CHARGE	CLS	Comm. Code	Fine + S.C.	PT	Safety Zone Fine	Commercial Vehicle Code	Commercial Vehicle Fine
	Auto Theft – Abandonded Vehicles (Continued)							
18-4-409 (3)(a)	1st Degree Aggravated Motor Vehicle Theft (Value Less Than $20,000)	F4	F8C	NIBR	0			
18-4-409 (3)(b)	1st Degree Aggravated Motor Vehicle Theft (Value More Than $20,000 or 2 Previous Motor Vehicle Theft)	F3	F8C	NIBR	0			
18-4-409 (4)(a)	2nd Degree Aggravated Motor Vehicle Theft (Value $20,000 or More)	F5	F8C	HB	0			
18-4-409 (4)(b)	2nd Degree Aggravated Motor Vehicle Theft (Value $1,000 But Less Than $20,000)	F6	F8C	HB	0			
18-4-409 (4)(c)	2nd Degree Aggravated Motor Vehicle Theft (Value Less Than $1,000)	M1	M8C	HB	0			
18-4-410 (3)	Theft by Receiving (Auto) Less Than $500	M2	M8D	HB	0			
18-4-410 (3.5)	Theft by Receiving (Auto) $500 but less than $1,000	M1	M8D	HB	0			
18-4-410 (4)	Theft by Receiving (Auto) $1,000 But Less Than $20,000	F4	F8D	NIBR	0			
18-4-410 (5)	Theft by Receiving (Auto) $20,000 or More	F3	F8D	NIBR	0			
18-4-410 (6)	Theft by Receiving (Auto) (Engaged in Business of Buying/Selling Stolen Goods (Value is $1,000 or More)	F3	F8D	NIBR	0			
18-4-502	1st Degree Criminal Trespass (Motor Vehicle)	F5	F8E	NIBR	0			
18-4-512	Abandonment of a Motor Vehicle	M3	M8E	HB	0			
18-13-106	Unlawfully Discarded a Motor Vehicle/Icebox/ Similar Items	PO1	PMB	HB	0			
42-5-102 (1)	(Bought/Sold/Altered/Removed) Auto Part(s) Which Are the Property of Another	F5	F8F	NIBR	0			

42-5-102 (1)	Aiding and Abetting the (Buying/Selling/Altering/Removing) of Auto Parts Which Are the Property of Another	F5	F8F	NIBR			0
42-5-102 (2)	(Removed/Changed/Altered/Obliterated) (Vehicle Identification Number/Mfg's Number/Engine Number)	F5	F8F	NIBR			0
42-5-102 (2)	Knowingly Possessed Automobile Part(s) With (Removed/Changed/Altered/Obliterated) (Vehicle Identification Number/Mfg's Number/Engine Number)	F5	F8F	NIBR			0
42-5-103 (2)(a)	Tampered With Motor Vehicle Where Damage is Less Than $1,000	M1	M8F	SUM			0
42-5-103 (2)(b)	Tampered With Motor Vehicle Where Damage is $1,000 But Less Than $20,000	F5	F8G	NIBR			0
42-5-103 (2)(c)	Tampered With Motor Vehicle (Where Damage is $20,000 or More/Caused Bodily Injury)	F3	F8G	NIBR			0
42-5-104 (2)(a)	(Theft/Removal) of Motor Vehicle Part(s) Where Value is Less Than $1,000	M1	M8G	SUM			0
42-5-104 (2)(b)	(Theft/Removal) of Motor Vehicle Part(s) Where Value is $1,000 but Less Than $20,000	F5	F8H	NIBR			0
42-5-104 (2)(c)	(Theft/Removal) of Motor Vehicle Part(s) Where Value is $20,000 or More	F3	F8H	NIBR			0
42-5-105 (1)	(Dealer/Garage Proprietor) Failed to Maintain Records as Required	M	M8H	SUM			0
42-5-105 (1)	(Dealer/Garage Proprietor) (Failed/Refused) to Submit Records for Inspection	M	M8H	SUM			0
42-5-105 (3)	(Driver/Person) Failed to Register Name and Address With (Dealer/Garage Proprietor) as Required	M	M8H	SUM			0
18-8-106 (1)(a)	(Dealership Owner/Garage Proprietor) Refused to Permit Inspection of Property	PO1	P8A	SUM			0

STATUTE 2011	CHARGE	CLS	Comm. Code	Fine + S.C.	PT	Safety Zone Fine	Commercial Vehicle Code	Commercial Vehicle Fine
Auto Theft – Abandoned Vehicles (Continued)								
42-5-106	(Dealer/Garage Proprietor) Failed to Examine VIN	PO1	P8B	SUM	0			
42-5-106	(Dealer/Garage Proprietor/Agent) Failed to Notify Police of (Altered VIN/Discrepancy Between VIN and Registration Certificate)	PO1	P8B	SUM	0			
42-5-109	Failed to Submit Report of Stored Motor Vehicle	M	M8J	SUM	0			
42-5-111	(Transported/Towed/Hauled) (Motor Vehicle/Parts) Without Proper Authorization	M3	M8K	SUM	0			
42-6-136	Failed to Surrender Title of Motor Vehicle Upon (Destruction/Dismantling/Changing/Sale/Disposal as Salvage)	PO1	P8C	SUM	0			
42-6-143	(Altered/Forged) Certificate of Title	F6	F8J	NIBR	0			
42-4-2202 (1)	Unlicensed Person Violated Restrictions on (Purchasing/Receiving) a Motor Vehicle for Scrap	M	RMV	SUM	0			
42-4-2202 (2)	Unlicensed Person Violated Restrictions on Scrapping a Motor Vehicle	M	SMV	SUM	0			
Bicycles								
42-4-1412 (3)	Unlawful Number of Persons on Bicycle	MT2	925	15+7	0	30+13		
42-4-1412 (4)	Bicycle Rider Attached Himself to Motor Vehicle	MT2	925	15+7	0	30+13		
42-4-1412 (5)	Bicycle Rider Failed to Ride in Right-hand Lane as Required	MT2	925	15+7	0	30+13		
42-4-1412 (5)	Bicycle Rider Failed to Ride on Right Side of Lane When Being Overtaken	MT2	925	15+7	0	30+13		

Statute	Description							
42-4-1412 (5)	Bicycle Rider Failed to Ride on Suitable Paved Shoulder	MT2	925	15+7	0	30+13		
42-4-1412 (6)(a)	Bicycle Rider Failed to Ride Single File When Required	MT2	925	15+7	0	30+13		
42-4-1412 (6)(b)	Bicycle Rider Failed to Ride in Single Lane When Riding Two Abreast	MT2	925	15+7	0	30+13		
42-4-1412 (7)	Bicycle Rider Failed to Keep at Least One Hand on Handlebars	MT2	925	15+7	0	30+13		
42-4-1412 (8)(a)	Bicycle Rider Made Improper Left Turn	MT2	925	15+7	0	30+13		
42-4-1412 (8)(b)	Bicycle Rider Intending to Turn Left Disregarded Official Traffic Control Device	MT2	924	15+7	0	30+13		
42-4-1412 (9)	Bicycle Rider Failed to Signal Intention to (Turn/Stop)	MT2	925	15+7	0	30+13		
42-4-1412 (10)(a)	Bicycle Rider on (Sidewalk/Roadway/Crosswalk/Pathway) Failed to Yield Right of Way to Pedestrian	MT2	925	15+7	0	30+13		
42-4-1412 (10)(b)	Rode Bicycle on (Sidewalk/Roadway/Pathway) When Prohibited by (Sign/Device)	MT2	925	15+7	0	30+13		
42-4-1412 (11)	Improper Parking of a Bicycle	MT2	924	15+7	0	30+13		
42-4-109 (11)	Failed to Use Bicycle Path When Directed by Official Signs	TIB	926	15+12	0	30+13		
42-4-1402 (1)	Rode Bicycle in Careless Manner	MT2	925	150+17	0	300+33		
Bicycle Equipment								
42-4-221 (2)	Bicycle Not Equipped With Front Lamp Visible 500 Feet to Front	TIB	931	15+7	0			
42-4-221 (3)	Bicycle Not Equipped With Red Reflector Visible 600 Feet to Rear	TIB	931	15+7	0			
42-4-221 (4)	Bicycle Not Equipped With Side Reflective Material or Lamps	TIB	931	15+7	0			

STATUTE 2011	CHARGE	CLS	Comm. Code	Fine + S.C.	PT	Safety Zone Fine	Commercial Vehicle Code	Commercial Vehicle Fine
Bicycle Equipment (Continued)								
Use the Following "Bicycle Common Codes" when a Citation is Issued to a Bicyclist for a Violation Other Than CRS 42-4-1412 or 42-4-221 (Utilize equivalent fine and surcharge, however assess 0 points)								
	Bicycle obedience to traffic control devices		924					
	Persons riding on bicycles - any violation pertaining to improper riding on a bicycle to include lane violation, passing violation, improper turn, and any other unspecified moving violation.		925					
	Riding on roadways and bicycle paths - any violation pertaining to use of designated roadways, lanes, bike paths, etc.		926					
	Speeding on a bicycle - any speeding violation.		927					
	Lamps and other equipment on bicycles - any equipment violation.		931					
Commercial Vehicle (D.P.S. & P.U.C. Rules & Regulations)								
40-10-108	Operated as Motor Vehicle Carrier Without Permit	M			0		MVF	SUM
40-10-113	Motor Vehicle Carrier Failed to Comply With PUC Rules and Regulations	M2			0		MVG	SUM
40-11-107	Operated as Contract Carrier Without PUC Permit	M			0		MVH	SUM
40-11-111	Contract Carrier Failed to Comply With PUC Rules and Regulations	M2			0		MVJ	SUM
42-3-121 (1)(g)	Operated Commercial Vehicle While Registered as Collector Vehicle	TIB			0		042	75+25

Statute	Description	Code			Number	Fine
42-4-235 (2)(a)	Commercial Vehicle Failed to Comply With D.P.S. Rules and Regulations Governing Safety Standards and Specifications	MT2		0	713	50+17
42-4-509 (3)	(Failed/Refused) to Stop for Weighing (Load/Vehicle)	MT2		0	525	50+17
42-4-106	Drove (Truck/Commercial Vehicle) Where Prohibited	TIB		0	920	35+11
42-4-106	Vehicle Exceeded Posted Weight Limitation (Specify Posted and Actual Weights)	TIB		0	530	35+11
42-4-225 (1.5)	(No/Inadequate) Muffler on Vehicle Equipped With an Engine Compression Brake (Jake Brake)	TIB		0	581	500+186
42-4-1407.5 (2)	(Truck/Tractor/Trailer) Did Not Have Splash Guards as Required	TIB		0	579	35+11
42-4-405.5 (1)	Commercial Vehicle Operator Violated Out-of Service Order	MT1		RA	788	SUM
42-4-405.5 (1)	Commercial Vehicle Operator Carrying (Hazardous Material/Passengers) Violated Out-of Service Order	MT1		RA	789	SUM
42-4-510	Failed Have Escort Vehicle When Required by Oversize/Overweight Permit	MT2		0	527	250+93.50
42-4-510	Failed to Reduce Speed When Required by Oversized/Overweight Permit	MT2		0	527	250+93.50
42-4-510 (12)(a)	Operated Vehicle in Violation of Overwidth/Overlength Permit. For weight violations see page 28	MT2		0	527	50+47
42-4-510 (12)(b)	Owner Moved Manufactured Home Without a Paid Ad Valorem Tax Certificate and a Transportable Manufactured Home Permit	PO2		0	531	SUM
42-4-510 (12)(b)	Owner Moved Manufactured Home Without a Paid Ad Valorem Tax Certificate and a Transportable Manufactured Home Permit 2 or More Times	M3		0	531	SUM
42-7-510	Failed to Have Proof of Insurance in Cab of Commercial Vehicle	M		0	953	SUM
42-8-105	Failed to Obtain Port of Entry Clearance	MT2		0	702	50+17

4

STATUTE 2011	CHARGE	CLS	Comm. Code	Fine + S.C.	PT	Safety Zone Fine	Commercial Vehicle Code	Commercial Vehicle Fine
	Crimes Involving Assault							
18-3-205 (1)(a)	Vehicular Assault - Operated a Motor Vehicle in a Reckless Manner Which was the Proximate Cause of Serious Bodily Injury to Another Person	F5	110	NIBR	0			
18-3-205 (1)(b)(I)	Vehicular Assault - While Driving Under the Influence of Alcohol or One or More Drugs or Both, Such Conduct was the Proximate Cause of Serious Bodily Injury to Another Person	F4	807	NIBR	0		754	NIBR
18-3-202 (1)(e)	1st Degree Assault on a (Peace Officer/Fireman) Without Deliberation	F5	FKF	NIBR	0			
18-3-202 (1)(e)	1st Degree Assault on a (Peace Officer/Fireman) With Deliberation	F3	FKF	NIBR	0			
18-3-203 (1)(c)	2nd Degree Assault on a (Peace Officer/Fireman) Without Deliberation	F6	FKG	NIBR	0			
18-3-203 (1)(c)	2nd Degree Assault on a (Peace Officer/Fireman) With Deliberation	F4	FKG	NIBR	0			
18-3-204	3rd Degree Assault	M1	MKA	HB	0			
18-9-115 (1)(a)/(d)	Endangering Public Transportation	F3	FNR	NIBR	0			
18-9-115.5	Endangering Public Transportation Violation of Restraining Order	M3	MNY	HB	0			
	Crimes Involving Child Abuse							
18-6-401 (7)(a)(I)	Child Abuse (Acted Knowingly or Recklessly Resulting in Death to a Child)	F2	FAC	NIBR	0			

Statute	Description	Class	Code				
18-6-401 (7)(a)(II)	Child Abuse (Acted With a Criminal Negligence Resulting in Death to a Child)	F3	FAC	NIBR	0		
18-6-401 (7)(a)(III)	Child Abuse (Acted knowingly or Recklessly Resulting in Serious Bodily Injury to a Child)	F3	FAC	NIBR	0		
18-6-401 (7)(a)(IV)	Child Abuse (Acted With Criminal Negligence Resulting in Serious Bodily Injury to a Child)	F4	FAC	NIBR	0		
18-6-401 (7)(a)(V)	Child Abuse (Acted Knowingly or Recklessly Resulting in Injury to a Child)	M1	MAA	HB	0		
18-6-401 (7)(a)(VI)	Child Abuse (Acted With Criminal Negligence Resulting in Injury to a Child)	M2	MAA	HB	0		
18-6-401 (7)(b)(I)	Child Abuse (Acted Knowingly or Recklessly Where No Death or Injury Results)	M2	MAA	HB	0		
18-6-401 (7)(b)(II)	Child Abuse (Acted With Criminal Negligence Where No Death or Injury Results)	M3	MAA	HB	0		
Crimes Involving Death							
18-3-104 (1)(a)	Manslaughter: Recklessly Caused the Death of Another Person (Auto Involved)	F4	105	NIBR	0	765	NIBR
18-3-104 (1)(a)	Manslaughter: Recklessly Caused the Death of Another Person	F4	FKC	NIBR	0		
18-3-104 (1)(b)	Manslaughter: Intentionally Causes or Aids Another Person to Commit Suicide	F4	FKC	NIBR	0		
18-3-105	Criminally Negligent Homicide (Auto Involved)	F5	108	NIBR	0	765	NIBR
18-3-105	Criminally Negligent Homicide	F5	FKD	NIBR	0		
18-3-106 (1)(a)	Vehicular Homicide - Operated a Motor Vehicle in a Reckless Manner Which was the Proximate Cause of Death of Another Person	F4	109	NIBR	0	765	NIBR
18-3-106 (1)(b)	Vehicular Homicide - While Driving Under the Influence of Alcohol or One or More Drugs or Both, Such Conduct was the Proximate Cause of a Death to Another Person	F3	806	NIBR	0	765	NIBR

STATUTE 2011	CHARGE	CLS	Comm. Code	Fine + S.C.	PT	Safety Zone Fine	Commercial Vehicle Code	Commercial Vehicle Fine
	Driver's License							
42-2-101 (1)	Drove Vehicle Without Valid Driver's License	MT2	060	35+11	3		060	35+11
42-2-101 (1)	Drove Vehicle Without Valid Driver's License (2nd/Subsequent Offense)	MT2	060	35+11	6		060	35+11
42-2-101 (1)	Drove Vehicle Without Valid Driver's License (Resident more than 30 days)	MT2	083	35+11	3			
42-2-101 (2)	Drove Vehicle When Driver's License Expired One Year or Less	TIB	069	15+7	0			
42-2-101 (4)	Drove Vehicle Without Proper Class of Driver's License	MT2	084	35+11	3		784	35+11
42-2-101 (4)	Provisional Driver (18 to 20 Years Old) (Not Qualified/No CDL)	MT2	084	35+11	3		784	35+11
42-2-101 (5)	Drove Vehicle Without Valid Driver's License on Person	TIB	063	15+7	0		783	15+7
42-2-105 (1)	Person Under 18 Transported (Explosives/Inflammable Material)	TIA	061	70+11	3		061	70+11
42-2-105 (1)	Person Under 18 Transported Children in School Bus	TIA	061	70+11	3		061	70+11
42-2-105 (1)	Person Under 18 Not Qualified to Operate Commercial Vehicle	TIA	061	70+11	3		061	70+11
42-2-106	Violated Restrictions on Temporary Instruction Permit	TIA	062	70+11	3			
42-2-116 (a)	Violated Restrictions on Driver's License	TIA	065	30+7	3			
42-2-116 (6)(b)	Violated Restrictions on Driver's License Regarding Interlock Device	MT1	818	SUM	RA			
42-2-119 (1)	Failed to Notify Authorities of Change of (Name/Address) Within 30 Days	TIB	066	15+7	0			

42-2-134	Used Foreign License During Suspension or Revocation of Colorado Driving Privileges	TIB	072	35+11	0	
42-2-136 (1)	Possessed Altered (Driver's License/Instruction Permit)	MT2	067	35+11	RA	
42-2-136 (2)	Possessed (Fictitious/Fraudulent) (Driver's License/Instruction Permit)	MT2	067	35+11	RA	
42-2-136 (3)	Displayed Driver's License that was Issued to Another Person	MT2	067	35+11	RA	
42-2-136 (5)	Permitted Unlawful Use of Driver's License	MT2	067	35+11	RA	
42-2-136 (5.5)	Reproduced Driver's License Without Authorization	M3	MN5	SUM	RA	
42-2-137	Made False Affidavit Concerning Driver's License	MT2	068	SUM	RA	
42-2-138 (1)(a)	Drove (Motor/Off-highway) Vehicle When License Under Restraint (Suspended)	M	076	SUM	RA	763	SUM
42-2-138 (1)(a)	Drove (Motor/Off-highway) Vehicle When License Under Restraint (Revoked)	M	077	SUM	RA	763	SUM
42-2-138 (1)(a)	Drove (Motor/Off-highway) Vehicle When License Under Restraint (Denied)	M	078	SUM	RA	763	SUM
42-7-422	Drove Vehicle While Under FRA Suspension	M	075	SUM	RA	075	SUM
42-2-138 (1)(d)(I)	Drove (Motor/Off-highway) Vehicle upon Highway When (License/Privilege to Drive) was Restrained for Express Consent or Alcohol/Drug Related Offense	M	085	SUM	RA	085	SUM
42-2-206 (1)(a)	Drove Vehicle When License Revoked as an Habitual Offender	M	090	SUM	RA	763	SUM
42-2-206 (1)(b)	Drove Vehicle When License Revoked as an Habitual Offender (Aggravated)	F6	080	NIBR	RA	763	SUM
42-2-139	Permitted Unlicensed Minor to Drive Vehicle	TIB	070	35+11	0	
42-2-140	Permitted Unlicensed Person to Drive Vehicle	TIB	071	35+11	0	
42-2-141 (1)	(Rented/Loaned) Vehicle to Unlicensed Person	TIB	073	35+11	0	

STATUTE 2011	CHARGE	CLS	Comm. Code	Fine + S.C.	PT	Safety Zone Fine	Commercial Vehicle Code	Commercial Vehicle Fine
Driver's License (Continued)								
42-2-141 (2)	Failed to Inspect License of Renter	TIB	073	35+11	0			
42-2-141 (3)	Failed to Keep Rental Records	TIB	073	35+11	0			
42-2-404 (1)	Drove Commercial Vehicle (When Not Qualified or Without CDL)	M	060	SUM	3		782	SUM
42-2-404 (2)	Driver of Commercial Vehicle had More Than One License	M	060	SUM	3		782	SUM
42-2-409 (1)(a)	Knowingly Possessed an Unlawfully Altered Commercial Driver's License	M	790	SUM	RA		790	SUM
42-2-409 (1)(b)	Fraudulently Obtained a Commercial Driver's License	M	790	SUM	RA		790	SUM
42-2-409 (1)(c)	Knowingly Possessed a (Document/Instrument) Pertaining to a Commercial Driver's License	M	790	SUM	RA			
42-2-409 (1)(d)	Displayed a Commercial Driver's License Issued to Another Person	M	790	SUM	RA			
42-2-409 (1)(e)	(Failed/Refused) to Surrender a Commercial Driver's License Issued to Another Person	M	790	SUM	RA			
42-2-409 (1)(f)	Permitted the Unlawful Use of a Commercial Driver's License	M	790	SUM	RA		790	SUM
42-2-409 (1)(g)	Unlawfully Reproduced a Commercial Driver's License	M	790	SUM	RA		790	SUM
42-4-116 (1)(a)	Minor Driver Operated a Motor Vehicle with an Unauthorized Passenger (secondary violation)	TIA	169	50+17	2			
42-4-116 (2)(a)	Minor Driver Operated Motor Vehicle Between 12 Midnight and 5 AM (secondary violation)	TIA	168	50+17	2			
42-4-1704	Directed Operator of Vehicle Contrary to Law	MT2	074	15+7	0			

		Drugs / Marijuana					
18-18-403.5 (2)(a)(I)	Unlawful Possession of Schedule I or II (except Methamphetamine), Flunitrazepan, or Ketamine (four grams or less)	F6	116	NIBR	RA		
18-18-403.5 (2)(a)(II)	Unlawful Possession of Schedule I or II (except Methamphetamine), Flunitrazepan, or Ketamine (over four grams)	F4	116	NIBR	RA		
18-18-403.5 (2)(b)(I)	Unlawful Possession of Methamphetamine (two grams or less)	F6	116	NIBR	RA		
18-18-403.5 (2)(b)(I)	Unlawful Possession of Methamphetamine (over two grams)	F4	116	NIBR	RA		
18-18-403.5 (2)(c)	Unlawful Possession of Schedule III, IV or V (except Flunitrazepan, or Ketamine)	M1	MCE	HB	RA		
18-18-404 (1)(a)	Unlawful Use of a Controlled Substance	M2	MCE	HB	RA		
18-18-405 (2)(a)(I)(A)	Unlawful Distribution, Manufacturing, Dispensing, Sale or Possession (With Intent) of Schedule I or II Controlled Substance	F3	116	NIBR	RA		
18-18-405 (2)(a)(II)(A)	Unlawful Distribution, Manufacturing, Dispensing, Sale or Possession (With Intent) of Schedule III Controlled Substance (Subsequent F3)	F4	116	NIBR	RA		
18-18-405 (2)(a)(III)(A)	Unlawful Distribution, Manufacturing, Dispensing, Sale or Possession (With Intent) of Schedule IV Controlled Substance (Subsequent F4)	F5	116	NIBR	RA		
18-18-405 (1)(a)	Unlawful Possession of One or More Chemicals/ Supplies/Equipment With Intent to Sell/Manufacture a Controlled Substance	F3	116	NIBR	RA		
18-18-405 (2)(a)(IV)(A)	Unlawful Distribution, Manufacturing, Dispensing, Sale or Possession of Schedule V Controlled Substance (Subsequent F5)	M1	MCF	HB	RA		
18-18-405 (7)	Unlawful Distribution, Dispensing, or Sale of a Controlled Substance (except Marijuana) to Person(s) Under 18 Years of Age	F3	116	NIBR	RA		

STATUTE 2011	CHARGE	CLS	Comm. Code	Fine + S.C.	PT	Safety Zone Fine	Commercial Vehicle Code	Commercial Vehicle Fine
	Drugs / Marijuana (Continued)							
18-18-406 (1)	Possession of 2 oz. or Less of Marijuana	PO2	PCA	HB	RA			
18-18-406 (1)	Minor/Provisional Driver Possessed 2 oz. or Less of Marijuana	PO2	811	HB	RA			
18-18-406 (3)(a)(I)	Open Public Display, Consumption, or Use of Not More Than 2 oz. of Marijuana	PO2	PCA	HB	RA			
18-18-406 (3)(a)(I)	Minor/Provisional Driver Openly Public Displayed, Consumed, or Used Not More Than 2 oz. of Marijuana	PO2	811	HB	RA			
18-18-406 (4)(a)(I)	Possession of Marijuana: More Than 2 oz. but Less Than 6 oz.	M2	MCG	HB	RA			
18-18-406 (4)(a)(I)	Minor/Provisional Driver Possessed More Than 2 oz. but Less Than 6 oz. of Marijuana	M2	811	HB	RA			
18-18-406 (4)(b)(I)	Possession of Marijuana More Than 6 oz. but Less Than 12 oz. or 3 oz. or Less of Marijuana Concentrate	M1	MCG	HB	RA			
18-18-406 (4)(c)	Possession of Marijuana More Than 12 oz. or More Than 3 oz. of Marijuana Concentrate	F6	116	NIBR	RA			
18-18-406 (5)	Unlawful Transferring or Dispensing 2 oz. or Less of Marijuana (No Consideration)	PO2	PCB	HB	RA			
18-18-406 (6)(a)(I)	Unlawful Process or Manufacture of Marijuana or Marijuana Concentrate (F3 Subsequent)	F4	116	HB	RA			
18-18-406 (6)(b)(III)(A)	Unlawful Distribution, Manufacturing, Dispensing, Sale or Possession With Intent of Sale Under 5 lbs. Marijuana or Under 1 lb. of Marijuana Concentrate (F3 Subsequent)	F5	116	HB	RA			

18-18-406 (6)(b)(III)(B)	Unlawful Distribution, Manufacturing, Dispensing, Sale or Possession With Intent of Sale 5 lbs. or More but Not More Than 100 lbs. Marijuana or 1 lb. or More but Not More Than 100 lbs. of Marijuana Concentrate (F3 Subsequent)	F4	116	HB	RA
18-18-406 (6)(b)(III)(C)	Unlawful Distribution, Manufacturing, Dispensing, Sale or Possession With Intent More Than 100 lbs. Marijuana or More Than 100 lbs. of Marijuana Concentrate (F3 Subsequent)	F3	116	HB	RA
18-18-406 (7)(a)	Dispensing of 2 oz. But Less Than Five lbs. of Marijuana or Less Than 1 lb. Marijuana Concentrate to a Minor At Least the Age of 15 but Under the Age of 18	F4	116	NIBR	RA
18-18-406 (7)(b)	Dispensing of More Than Five lbs. of Marijuana or More Than 1 lbs. Marijuana Concentrate to a Person At Least the Age of 15 but Under the Age of 18	F3	116	NIBR	RA
18-18-406 (7)(c)	Dispensing of Any Amount of Marijuana or Marijuana Concentrate to a Person Under the Age of 15	F3	116	NIBR	RA
18-18-406 (7.5)(a)	Unlawful Cultivation/Production of Six or Less Marijuana Plants	M1	MCC	HB	RA
18-18-406 (7.5)(b)	Unlawful Cultivation/Production of More Than Six but Less Than 30 Marijuana Plants	F5	116	HB	RA
18-18-406 (7.5)(c)	Unlawful Cultivation/Production of 30 or More Marijuana Plants	F4	116	HB	RA
18-18-406.1 (2)	Unlawful Possession of Synthetic Cannabinoid or Salvia Divinorum * Effective January 1, 2012 *	M2	MCG	HB	RA
18-18-406.2 (2)	Unlawful Distribution, Manufacturing, Dispensing, Sale or Possession With Intent of Sale Synthetic Cannabinoid or Salvia Divinorum	F5	116	HB	RA

STATUTE 2011	CHARGE	CLS	Comm. Code	Fine + S.C.	PT	Safety Zone Fine	Commercial Vehicle Code	Commercial Vehicle Fine
	Drugs / Marijuana (Continued)							
18-18-406.2 (3)	Unlawful Distribution, Dispensing or Sale of Synthetic Cannabinoid or Salvia Divinorum to a Person Under the Age of 18	F4	116	HB	RA			
18-18-412.5	Unlawful Possession of Materials to Make Methamphetamine or Amphetamine	F3	116	NIBR	RA			
18-18-413	Improper Authorized Possession of a Controlled Substance	PO1	PCC	HB	RA			
18-18-415	Unlawfully Obtained Prescription of a Controlled Substance by Fraud or Deceit	F6	116	HB	RA			
18-18-428	Possession of Drug Paraphernalia	PO2	PCD	HB	RA			
18-18-429	Manufacture/Sale/Delivery of Drug Paraphernalia	M2	MCL	HB	RA			
18-18-430	Advertisement of Drug Paraphernalia	M2	MCM	HB	RA			
18-18-412 (1)	Abuse of Toxic Vapors	PO1	PCB	HB	RA			
	Emissions							
42-4-313 (1)	Displayed (Certification of Emissions Control/ Verification of Emission Test) that was Counterfeit	M	674	SUM	0			
42-4-313 (2)	Issued a Certificate of Emissions Control to a Vehicle That Did Not Qualify	M	675	SUM	0			
42-4-313 (3)(a)	Owner Failed to Provide Valid Verification of Emissions Test	MT	673	50+17	0			
42-4-313 (3)(d)	Non-owner Driver Failed to Provide Valid Verification of Emissions Test	MT	673	15+17	0			

42-4-413 (1)	(Owner/Operator) Operated Diesel When Visible Diesel Exhaust Emissions Exceeded Maximum Lawful Limit in AIR Program Area *(Notice must accompany citation)*	MT	573	SUM	0			
42-4-412 (1)(a)(II)	Visible Diesel Exhaust Emission Exceeded Maximum Lawful Limit (Use outside air program area and include percentage)	PO2	573	SUM	0			
42-4-412 (1)(a)(I)	Vehicle Not Powered by Diesel Emitted Visible Air Pollutants	PO2	573	SUM	0			
42-4-314 (1)	(Deactivated/Disconnected) a Pollution Control Device	TIA	563	35+11	0			
42-4-314 (2)	Operated a Vehicle With a (Deactivated/ Disconnected) Pollution Control System	TIA	563	35+11	0			
42-14-106	Violation of Diesel Idling Standards	TIB	677	150+21	0			
Equipment								
42-4-109.5 (1)	Operated Low Speed Electric Vehicle Where Prohibited	TIB	233	15+7	0			
42-4-109.5 (2)	Operated Low Speed Electric Vehicle on Limited Access Highway	TIB	234	15+7	0			
42-4-109.6 (1)	Operated Low Speed Electric Vehicle (Class B) Where Prohibited	TIB	233	15+7	0			
42-4-109.6 (2)	Operated Low Speed Electric Vehicle (Class B) on Limited Access Highway	TIB	234	15+7	0			
42-4-240	Low Speed Electric Vehicle Failed to Conform to Equipment Requirements	TIB	559	15+7	0			
42-4-202 (1)	Drove a (Defective/Unsafe) Vehicle	TIA	542	35+11	2			
42-4-203	Drove a Defective or Unsafe Vehicle *(Notice Must Accompany Citation)*	MT	576	SUM	2			
42-4-202 (4)(c)	Moved Exempt Construction Equipment on Highway When Vision Less Than 500 Feet	TIA	999	35+11	0			

STATUTE 2011	CHARGE	CLS	Comm. Code	Fine + S.C.	PT	Safety Zone Fine	Commercial Vehicle Code	Commercial Vehicle Fine
	Equipment (Continued)							
42-4-202 (4)(e)	Owner of Identification Plate Failed to Remove Plate and Forward It to the Dept. of Revenue	TIA	999	35+11	0			
42-4-202 (4)(f)	Failed to Report Lost/Damaged/Stolen Identification Plate to the Dept. of Revenue	TIA	999	35+11	0			
42-4-209	(Improper/No) Red (Flag/Light) on Projecting Load	TIA	543	15+7	0			
42-4-233	Alteration of Suspension	MT2	564	75+26	0			
42-4-213 (1)	Defective (Audible/Visual Signal) on Emergency Vehicle	TIA	546	15+7	0			
42-4-213 (4)	(Unauthorized/Improper) Use of Green Light on (Motor/Emergency) Vehicle	TIA	539	15+7	0			
42-4-223 (1)(b)	(Motorcycle/Motorized Bicycle/Bicycle with Motor) Not Equipped With One Brake	TIA	548	15+7	2			
42-4-223 (1)(c)	(Trailer/Semi-trailer) Did Not Have Breakaway Brakes as Required	TIA	549	15+7	2			
42-4-223 (1)(d)	(Motor Vehicle/Trailer/Semi-Trailer) Did Not Have Service Brake as Required	TIA	548	15+7	2			
42-4-223 (2)	Performance of (Service/Hand) Brake Did Not Meet Requirements	TIA	548	15+7	2			
42-4-224	Vehicle Had (No/Defective) Horn	TIB	550	15+7	0			
42-4-224	Operated Vehicle With Unauthorized Audible Signal	TIB	551	15+7	0			
42-4-225	Vehicle Had (Defective/Improper/No) Mufflers	TIB	552	15+7	0			
42-4-226	Vehicle Did Not Have Rearview Mirror(s)	TIB	553	15+7	0			
42-4-226	Rearview Mirror Did Not Permit Minimum 200 Ft. Vision	TIB	554	15+7	0			

Code	Description	Col3	Col4	Col5	Col6	Col7	Col8
42-4-227 (2)	Vehicle Had (No/Defective) Windshield Wipers	TIB	555	15+7	0		
42-4-228 (1)	Solid Rubber Tire Failed to be at Least One Inch Thick	TIA	556	15+7	0		
42-4-228 (3)	Tire had (Block/Flange/Cleat/Spike) Protruding From Rubber	TIA	556	15+7	0		
42-4-228 (5)	Operated a Vehicle With (Improper/Unsafe) Tires	TIA	556	15+7	0		
42-4-228 (6)	Operated Vehicle on Highway with Tires Designed for Non-Highway Use	TIA	556	15+7	0		
42-4-228 (7)	Sold a Vehicle With (Improper/Unsafe) Tires	MT2	556	SUM	0		
42-4-229 (4)	Vehicle Not Equipped With (Front Windshield/ Safety Glass in Front Windshield)	TIB	572	15+7	0		
42-4-230	Vehicle Did Not Have Emergency Reflective Triangles as Required	TIB	640	15+7	0		
42-4-230	Failed to Use (Warning Signal Flashers/ Emergency Reflective Triangles) as Required	TIB	641	15+7	0		
42-4-234 (1)	Failed to Display Slow-Moving Vehicle Emblem	TIB	565	15+7	0		
42-4-234 (3)	Misused Slow-Moving Vehicle Emblem	TIB	565	15+7	0		
42-4-238 (1)	Knowingly Possessed Vehicle Equipped With a Red or Blue Light	M1	M9A	SUM	0		
42-4-502 (3)	Vehicle Had (Chains/Rope/Wire) (Swinging/ Dragging/Projecting)	TIB	561	75+25	0		
42-4-106 (5)(a)(I)	Failed to Comply With (Tire/Chain) Restrictions	TIB	562	100+33	0		
42-4-106 (5)(a)(II)	Failed to Comply With (Tire/Chain) Restrictions That Resulted in Road Closure of a Travel Lane in One or More Directions	TIB	562	500+157	0		
42-4-106 (5)(a)(III)	Commercial Vehicle Failed to Comply With (Tire/Chain) Restrictions (Safety Zone)	TIB			0	700	500+79
42-4-106 (5)(a)(IV)	Commercial Vehicle Failed to Comply with Tire Chain Restrictions Resulting in Road Closure of Travel Lane in one or More Direction (Safety Zone)	TIB			0	701	1000+ 157

STATUTE 2011	CHARGE	CLS	Comm. Code	Fine + S.C.	PT	Safety Zone Fine	Commercial Vehicle Code	Commercial Vehicle Fine
Equipment (Continued)								
42-4-608 (2)	Vehicle Not Equipped With Turn Signals as Required	TIA	540	15+7	0	30+13		
42-4-610	Displayed Unauthorized Insignia	TIB	541	15+7	0			
42-4-1414 (2)(a)	Unlawful Use of Dyed Diesel Fuel (First Offense)	TIB	710	500+157	0			
42-4-1414 (2)(b)	Unlawful Use of Dyed Diesel Fuel (Second Offense)	TIB	710	1000+313	0			
42-4-1414 (2)(c)	Unlawful Use of Dyed Diesel Fuel (Third or Subsequent Offense)	TIB	710	5000+1561	0			
42-4-1415 (1)(a)	(Offered for Sale/Possessed) Radar Jamming Device	MT2	584	150+17	0			
42-4-1415 (1)(b)	Operated a Vehicle with a Radar Jamming Device	MT2	583	150+17	0			
Financial Responsibility / Insurance								
42-4-1409 (1)	Owner Operated an Uninsured Motor Vehicle on a Public Roadway	MT1	954	SUM	4			
42-4-1409 (2)	Operated an Uninsured Motor Vehicle on a Public Roadway	MT1	956	SUM	4			
42-4-1409 (3)	Failed to Present Evidence of Insurance Upon Request	MT1	957	SUM	4			
42-7-422	Drove Vehicle While Under FRA Suspension	M	075	SUM	RA			
Firearms / Weapons								
18-12-105 (1)(a)	Carrying Concealed Knife	M2	MFF	HB	0			
18-12-105 (1)(b)	Carrying Concealed Firearm	M2	MFF	HB	0			
18-12-105 (1)(c)	Carrying a Firearm or other Dangerous device at Legislature Without Legal Authority	M2	MFF	HB	0			

18-12-106 (1)(d)	Possession of a Weapon While Under the Influence of Intoxicating Liquor or a Controlled Substance	M2	MFF	HB	0	
18-12-108.5 (1)	Illegal Possession of a Handgun by a Juvenile **	M2	MJA	NIBR	**	
18-12-108.5 (1)	Illegal Possession of a Handgun by a Juvenile (2nd Offense) **	F5	FJA	NIBR	**	

** Law requires the Juvenile be Taken into Temporary Custody. Notify Command Staff of Any Arrest

18-12-108.7 (1)	Person Unlawfully Provided or Permitted a Juvenile to Possess a Handgun	F4	FJB	NIBR	0	
18-12-108.7 (2)	(Parent/Guardian) Unlawfully Provided or Permitted a Juvenile to Possess a Handgun	F4	FJB	NIBR	0	
18-12-105.5	Unlawfully Carried a Weapon in or on Real Estate of Any Public or Private School, College, University, or Seminary	F6	MFF	HB	0	
18-12-106	Prohibited Use of Weapons (Refer to Statute)	M2	MFH	HB	0	
33-6-126	Shooting (From/Across) Public Highway	M	905	HB	0	

Hazardous Materials Violations

42-20-109 (1)	Violation of CSP Rules & Regulations Concerning the (Transporting/Shipping) of Hazardous Materials. (Specify HMS Rule)	M3	724	SUM	0	
42-20-109 (2)	Violation of CSP (Permitting/Routing) Rules & Regulations Concerning Hazardous Materials. (Specify HMR or HMP Rule)	MT2	722	250+67	0	500+133
42-20-111	Knowingly/Intentionally) (Conspired/Aiding & Abetting) in Violations of the Provisions of Title 42, Article 20, CRS	M1	720	SUM	0	
42-20-204 (1)	Transported Hazardous Materials Without a Permit as Required in 42-20-201	MT	720	250+1	0	720	SUM
42-20-204 (1)	Intentionally Transported Hazardous Materials Without a Permit as Required in 42-20-201	M1	720	SUM	0	

STATUTE 2011	CHARGE	CLS	Comm. Code	Fine + S.C.	PT	Safety Zone Fine	Commercial Vehicle Code	Commercial Vehicle Fine
\multicolumn{9}{c}{Hazardous Materials Violations (Continued)}							
42-20-204 (2)	No (Annual/Single Trip) Hazardous Materials Transportation Permit in Vehicle	TIB	721	25+0	0			
42-20-204 (3)	Knowingly Violated Hazardous Materials Transportation Permit Terms & Conditions	M1	724	SUM	0			
42-20-305 (2)	Unauthorized Deviation From Designated Route While Transporting Hazardous Materials	MT	723	250+1	0			
42-4-707	Vehicle Carrying Placarded Load of Hazardous Material Failed to Stop at Railroad Crossing.	TAI	317	70+11	4			
42-20-305 (2)	Unauthorized Deviation From Designated Route While Transporting Hazardous Materials. (2nd or Subsequent Offense Within a Twelve-Month Period)	MT	723	SUM	0			
18-8-110	Made False Report of (Explosives/Bomb/Weapons/ Biological or Chemical Agent/Poison/Radioactive Substance)	F6	FEB	NIBR	0			
18-13-112 (1)	Intentionally (Spilled/Abandoned Vehicle Containing) Hazardous Waste	F4	F3A	NIBR	0			
25-17-204 (1)	Illegal (Transportation/Storage) of Waste Tires	M	MST	SUM	0			
29-22-108 (1)	(Intentionally Caused/Substantially Contributed to) a Hazardous Substance Incident	F4	F3B	NIBR	0			
29-22-108 (2)	(Willfully/Recklessly/with Criminal Negligence) (Caused/Substantially Contributed to the Occurrence of) a Hazardous Materials Incident	F5	F3B	NIBR	0			

Hit and Run / Failure to Report							
42-4-1601 (2)(a)	Failed to (Remain at the Scene/Give Information and/or Aid) After Accident Involving Injury	MT1	120	SUM	RA	752	SUM
42-4-1601 (2)(b)	Failed to (Remain at the Scene/Give Information and/or Aid) After Accident Involving Serious Bodily Injury	F5	120	SUM	RA	752	SUM
42-4-1601 (2)(c)	Failed to (Remain at the Scene/Give Information and/or Aid) After Accident Involving Death	F3	120	NIBR	RA	752	NIBR
42-4-1602 (1)	Failed to Give Information and/or Aid After Damaging Another Vehicle	MT2	121	SUM	12	752	SUM
42-4-1603 (1)	Driver Failed to Provide Information After Accident Involving (Injury/Serious Injury/Death)	MT2	122	SUM	12	752	SUM
42-4-1604	Left Scene Without Providing Required Information After Striking Unattended (Vehicle/Property)	MT2	123	SUM	12	752	SUM
42-4-1605	Failed to Report Accident Involving Highway Fixture	MT2	124	SUM	12	752	SUM
42-4-1606 (1)	Failed to Notify Police of Accident	MT2	125	SUM	12	752	SUM
42-4-1606 (1)	Failed to (Remain at/Return to) Accident Scene as Directed by Police	MT2	126	SUM	12	752	SUM
42-4-1607 (1)	Passenger Failed to Provide Information After Accident Involving (Injury/Serious Injury/Death)	MT2	M9B	SUM	0		
Identification Cards							
42-2-307	Failed to Notify Authorities of change of (Name/Address) Within 30 Days	M3	MN3	SUM	0		
42-2-309	Improper Use/Reproduction of Identification Card *(Refer to Statute for Charging)*	M3	MN4	SUM	0		

STATUTE 2011	CHARGE	CLS	Comm. Code	Fine + S.C.	PT	Safety Zone Fine	Commercial Vehicle Code	Commercial Vehicle Fine
Improper / Reckless / Careless Driving and Actions								
12-28-102 (5)	Unlawful (Possession/Use/Sale) of Fireworks	M3	MPG	SUM	0			
18-7-301	Public Indecency	PO1	PCS	NIBR	RA			
18-7-302	Indecent Exposure	PO1	MSG	NIBR	RA			
42-4-1211 (1)(a)	Backed Vehicle in Parking Area (When Not Safe/and Interfered With Traffic)	TIA	153	30+7	2	60+13		
42-4-1211 (1)(b)	Backed Vehicle on (Shoulder/Roadway) of Controlled-Access Highway	TIA	154	30+7	2	60+13		
42-4-1201	Improper Starting From (Parked/Stopped) Position	TIA	144	30+7	3	60+13		
42-4-709	Driver Stopped Vehicle in (Intersection/Marked Crosswalk/Railroad Grade Crossing) When Prohibited	TIA	952	70+11	3	140+21		
42-4-710 (3)	Drove Vehicle Upon Sidewalk	TIA	166	70+11	3	140+21		
42-4-711 (1)	Drove Vehicle Improperly on Mountain Highway	TIA	146	100+11	3	200+21		
42-4-1008 (1)	Following Too Closely	TIA	142	100+11	4	200+21	774	100+11
42-4-1008 (2)	Unlawful Following By Vehicle Drawing Another Vehicle	TIA	165	100+11	4	200+21		
42-4-1008 (3)	Following Too Closely in Motorcade	TIA	143	100+11	4	200+21	774	100+11
42-4-1009 (1)	Coasted Vehicle Down Grade With Gears in Neutral	TIA	147	70+11	3	140+21		
42-4-1010	Failed to Drive as Required on (Divided/Controlled-Access) Highway	TIA	152	70+11	3	140+21		
42-4-1010	Vehicle Crossed Roadway Dividing (Space/Median/Barrier) in an Unlawful Manner	TIA	227	70+11	3	140+21		
35-46-105	Knowingly Permitted Livestock on Public Highway	M	904	SUM	0			
18-3-208	Reckless Endangerment	M3	MKC	SUM	0			

Code	Description							
42-4-1401 (1)	Reckless Driving	MT2	140	SUM	8	SUM	771	SUM
42-4-1402 (2)(a)	Careless Driving	MT2	141	150+17	4	300+33		
42-4-1402 (2)(b)	Careless Driving Caused Bodily Injury	MT1	139	SUM	4	SUM		
42-4-1402 (2)(c)	Careless Driving Caused Death	MT1	138	SUM	12	SUM	772	SUM
42-4-1403	Following Too Closely Behind Fire Apparatus	TIA	149	30+7	3	60+13		
42-4-1404	Drove Vehicle Over Fire Hose	TIB	150	15+7	0			
42-4-1703	Aiding and Abetting - To Wit: (Specify the Offense or Infraction)	VAR	998	SUM	0			
42-4-109.5	Operated Low-Speed Electric Vehicle Where Prohibited	TIB	961	SUM	0		961	SUM
25-14-204	Violated Restrictions on Tobacco Use	PO2	TRV	SUM	0			

Interference

Code	Description							
18-3-206	Menacing: Placed Another Person in Fear of Imminent Serious Bodily Injury	M3	MKB	HB	RA			
18-3-206	Menacing: Placed Another Person in Fear of Imminent Serious Bodily Injury by Use of a Deadly Weapon	F5	FKH	NIBR	RA			
18-4-509 (2)	Defaced (Public/Private) Property	M2	961	HB	RA			
18-5-102 (3)	Presented Forged Document to Police Officer	F5	999	NIBR	RA			
18-5-902	Identity Theft	F4	FTA	NIBR	RA			
18-5-903	Criminal Possession of a Financial Device	F5	FTB	NIBR	RA			
18-5-905	Possession of Identity Theft Tools	F5	FTC	NIBR	RA			
18-5-113	Criminal Impersonation	F6	FDJ	NIBR	RA			
18-8-111 (1)	Made False Report to Authorities	M3	MND	HB	RA			
18-8-112 (1)	Impersonating a Peace Officer	F6	F9A	SUM	RA			
18-9-107 (1)(a)	Obstructed (Highway/Street/Sidewalk)	M3	MNS	HB	RA			
18-9-114	Hindering Transportation	M2	MNX	HB	RA			

STATUTE 2011	CHARGE	CLS	Comm. Code	Fine + S.C.	PT	Safety Zone Fine	Commercial Vehicle Code	Commercial Vehicle Fine
	Interference (Continued)							
18-9-116	Throwing Missiles at Vehicles	PO1	PDG	HB	0			
18-9-116 (2)	Throwing Missiles at Bicycles	M2	918	SUM	0			
18-9-117	Unlawful Conduct on Public Property (Fires/Prohibited Activities by Lawful Order)	M3	MNZ	HB	0			
33-15-106	Built Fire Where Prohibited (Only Use if Fire is on Division of Parks Land)	M3	MPG	SUM	0			
42-4-611	Misuse of Authorized Distress Flag	M	970	SUM	0			
42-4-107	Disregarded (Lawful Order/Direction) of Police Officer Directing Traffic	MT2	900	SUM	3			
42-4-1716 (2)	Failed to Obey Summons to Appear in Court	MT2	903	SUM	0			
42-13-105	Released Vehicle Held by Colorado State Patrol Officer Without Authorization	M3	908	SUM	0			
18-13-128 (1)	Illegally Assisted a Person to (Enter/Remain in/ Travel Through) the (U.S./Colorado)	F3	HSA	SUM	0			
18-3-501 (1)(a)	(Sold/Bartered/Leased) an Adult Person in a Human Trafficking Transaction	F3	HSA	SUM	0			
18-3-501 (1)(b)	Received an Adult Person in a Human Trafficking Transaction	F3	HT1	SUM	0			
18-3-501 (3)	Participated in Human Trafficking Involving an Adult Illegally in the U.S.	F2	HT2	SUM	0			
18-3-502 (1)(a)	(Sold/Bartered/Leased) a Child in a Human Trafficking Transaction	F3	HTA	SUM	0			
18-3-502 (1)(a)	Received a Child in a Human Trafficking Transaction	F3	HTB	SUM	0			
18-3-503	Coercion of Involuntary Servitude	F6	HTC	SUM	0			

42-4-1105 (8)(a)	Removed Immobilization Device Prior to End of Order	MT2		SUM	5		
42-4-1105 (8)(b)	Removed Immobilization Device Prior to Payment of Fees	MT2		SUM	5		
Lane Usage							
42-4-806	Drove Vehicle Through or Within Pedestrian Safety Zone	TIA	145	70+11	3	140+21	
42-4-1007 (1)(a)	Changed Lanes When Unsafe	TIA	221	100+11	3	200+21	773
42-4-1007 (1)(a)	Failed to Drive in Single Lane (Weaving)	TIA	223	100+11	3	200+21	
42-4-1007 (1)(b)	Drove Vehicle in Center Lane When (Unnecessary/Prohibited)	TIA	224	100+11	3	200+21	
42-4-1007 (1)(c)	Failed to Drive in Designated Lane	TIA	225	100+11	3	200+21	
42-4-1007 (1)(d)	Changed Lanes Where Prohibited by Official Traffic Control Device	TIA	300	100+11	4	200+21	
42-4-1011	(Illegal Use Of/Obstructed) a Runaway Vehicle Ramp	TIA	231	200+33	3	400+65	
42-4-1012 (3)(a)	Drove Unauthorized Vehicle In High Occupancy Lane	TIA	232	65+1	0		
42-4-1012 (3)(b)	Drove Unauthorized Vehicle in High Occupancy Lane Three or More Times	TIA	232	125+1	0		
42-4-1013 (1)	Drove Vehicle in Passing Lane When Prohibited (Posted 65 MPH or more roadway)	TIA	204	100+1	3	200+1	
Lights / Reflectors							
42-4-204 (1)	Failed to Display Lamps When Required	TIA	611	15+7	2		
42-4-202	Operated Vehicle With Defective/Missing Headlamps	TIA	609	35+11	1		
42-4-205 (1)	Motor Vehicle Not Equipped With Head Lamps as Required	TIB	613	15+7	0		100+11

STATUTE 2011	CHARGE	CLS	Comm. Code	Fine + S.C.	PT	Safety Zone Fine	Commercial Vehicle Code	Commercial Vehicle Fine
	Lights / Reflectors (Continued)							
42-4-205 (2)	Motorcycle Not Equipped With Head Lamp as Required	TIB	614	15+7	0			
42-4-205 (3)	Height of Headlamp Failed to Meet Requirements	TIB	612	15+7	0			
42-4-206 (1)	Vehicle Not Equipped With Tail Lamps as Required	TIB	615	15+7	0			
42-4-206 (2)	Height of Tail Lamp Failed to Meet Requirements	TIB	618	15+7	0			
42-4-206 (3)	Vehicle Had (No/Defective) License Plate Lamps	TIB	619	15+7	0			
42-4-206 (4)	Vehicle Failed to Have Reflector as Required	TIB	617	15+7	0			
42-4-206 (5)	1958 or Newer Vehicle Failed to Have Two Reflectors as Required	TIB	617	15+7	0			
42-4-206 (6)	Height of Reflector Failed to Meet Requirements	TIB	616	15+7	0			
42-4-207	Vehicle Not Equipped With (Clearance/Side Marker) (Lamps/Reflectors) as Required	TIB	620	15+7	0			
42-4-208	Vehicle Had (Defective/No) Stop Light(s)	TIB	623	15+7	0			
42-4-208	Vehicle Not Equipped With Turn Signals as Required	TIB	624	15+7	0			
42-4-211	(Farm Tractor/Farm Equipment/Implement of Husbandry/Animal-Drawn Vehicle) Not Equipped With (Lamps/Reflectors) as Required	TIB	627	15+7	0			
42-4-212	(Spot Lamps/Fog Lamps/Auxiliary Passing Lamps/Auxiliary Driving Lamps) Failed to Meet Requirements	TIB	544	15+7	0			
42-4-212	Improper Use of (Spot Lamps/Fog Lamps/ Auxiliary Passing Lamps/Driving Lamps)	TIB	628	15+7	0			

42-4-213 (4)	(Unauthorized/Improper) Use of Green Light on (Motor/emergency) Vehicle	TIA	539	15+7	0
42-4-214	Lamps on Service Vehicle (Failed to Meet Requirements/Not Yellow)	TIB	645	15+7	0
42-4-214	Failed to Display Lamps on Service Vehicle as Required	TIB	645	15+7	0
42-4-215	Signal (Lamps/Devices) Failed to Meet Requirements	TIB	629	15+7	0
42-4-215	Vehicle Did Not Have Turn Signals as Required	TIB	630	15+7	0
42-4-216	Vehicle Had No Upper-Lower Beam (Switch/Indicator)	TIB	631	15+7	0
42-4-217 (1)	Improper Headlight Distribution	TIA	633	15+7	0
42-4-217 (1)(a)	Failed to Dim Lights When Approaching an Oncoming Vehicle	TIA	632	15+7	2
42-4-217 (1)(b)	Failed to Dim Lights When Following Another Vehicle	TIA	632	15+7	2
42-4-218	Single-Beam Head Lamps Failed to Meet Requirements	TIB	634	15+7	0
42-4-219	Displayed More Than Four Lamps When Prohibited	TIB	635	15+7	0
42-4-220 (3)(a)	Motor Vehicle had High Intensity Light Improperly Directed	TIB	999	15+7	0
42-4-220 (4)	(Had for Sale/Sold/Offered for Sale) Lighting Equipment (Altered from Original Design/Not Approved by the Dept of Revenue)	TIB	999	15+7	0
42-4-220 (5)	(Had for Sale/Sold/Offered for Sale) Lamp or Device Without Name Under Which Approval was Granted by Dept of Revenue	TIB	999	15+7	0
42-4-220 (6)	(Used/Attached/Operated) an Unapproved Lamp or Lighting Device Upon a Motor Vehicle	TIB	643	15+7	0

STATUTE 2011	CHARGE	CLS	Comm. Code	Fine + S.C.	PT	Safety Zone Fine	Commercial Vehicle Code	Commercial Vehicle Fine
Lights / Reflectors (Continued)								
42-4-222 (1)	Improper Auxiliary (Signal Lamps/Audible Signal) on (Volunteer Firefighter Vehicle/Volunteer Ambulance Attendant)	TIB	638	15+7	0			
42-4-222 (1)	Misuse of Auxiliary (Signal Lamps/Audible Signal) by (Volunteer Firefighter/Volunteer Ambulance Attendant)	TIB	644	15+7	0			
42-4-231	Drove on Highway With Park Lights When Headlights Required	TIB	642	15+7	0			
Low-Power Scooters								
42-2-103	Drove Low-Power Scooter Without Valid Driver's License	TIB	081	15+7	0			
42-4-109 (1)	Low-Power Scooter Rider Failed to Obey Provisions of Article 4 (State Violation, i.e., Failed to Signal, or Speeding)	TIB	924	15+12	0	30+13		
42-4-109 (2) thru (6)	Rode Low-Power Scooter in an Improper Manner (Specify the Violation)	TIB	925	15+12	0	30+13		
42-4-109 (11)	Low-Power Scooter Failed to Use Bicycle Path When Directed By Official Signs	TIB	926	15+12	0	30+13		
42-3-311 (1)	Low-Power Scooter (Not Registered/Registration Decal Not Affixed)	TIB	056	15+7	0			
42-4-220	Low-Power Scooter Did Not Have (Lamp/Reflector/ Audible Signal/Brake) as Required	TIB	931	15+7	0			
42-4-224	Unlawful Use of (Siren/Whistle) upon a Low-Power Scooter	TIB	551	15+7	0			
42-4-220	Motor-Driven Cycle Not Equipped With Head Lamp as Required	TIB	931	15+7	0			

42-4-232 (1)	Low-Power Scooter (Operator/Passenger) Had No Protective Eye Wear as Required	TIA	161	15+7	0	
42-4-109 (6.5)	Low-Power Scooter (Operator/Passenger) Under 18 Not Wearing an Approved Protective Helmet on Highway (Primary)	TIA	170	100+31	3	200+46
42-4-232 (3)	Low-Power Scooter Not Equipped With Passenger Footrests	TIA	161	15+7	0	
Motorcycles						
42-4-232 (1)	Motorcycle (Operator/Passenger) Had No Protective Eye Wear as Required	TIA	161	15+7	0	
42-4-1502 (4.5)(a)	Motorcycle (Operator/Passenger) Under 18 Not Wearing an Approved Protective Helmet (Primary)	TIA	170	100+31	3	200+46
42-4-232 (3)	Motorcycle Not Equipped With Passenger Footrests	TIA	161	15+7	0	
42-4-1502	Improper Riding on Motorcycle: (State Violation)	TIA	157	35+7	3	70+13
42-4-1503	Illegal Operation of Motorcycle on Lane Roads	TIA	226	35+7	3	70+13
42-4-1504	Person on Motorcycle Clung to Another Vehicle	TIA	158	35+7	3	70+13
Obscured Vision / Interference With Driver						
42-4-201 (1)	Number of Persons in Front Seat of Vehicle Obstructed Vision	TIA	450	35+11	0	
42-4-201 (1)	Number of Persons in Front Seat of Vehicle Interfered With Driver	TIA	451	35+11	0	
42-4-201 (2)	Driver of Vehicle Allowed Passenger to Ride in an Unsafe Manner	TIA	457	35+11	0	
42-4-201 (3)	Television Visible to Vehicle Operator	TIA	465	35+11	0	
42-4-201 (4)	Driver's Vision Obstructed Through Required Glass	TIA	452	35+11	0	
42-4-201 (5)	Passenger in Vehicle (Interfered With/Obstructed Vision of) Driver	TIA	453	35+11	0	

STATUTE 2011	CHARGE	CLS	Comm. Code	Fine + S.C.	PT	Safety Zone Fine	Commercial Vehicle Code	Commercial Vehicle Fine
	Obscured Vision / Interference With Driver (Continued)							
42-4-201 (5)	Driver of Vehicle Allowed Passenger to Interfere With Driving	TIA	454	35+11	0			
42-4-201 (6)	Person (Hung On/Attached Himself) to the Outside of Vehicle	TIA	456	35+11	0			
42-4-201 (6)	Driver Permitted Person to (Hang On/Attach Himself) to the Outside of Vehicle	TIA	457	35+11	0			
42-4-227 (1)	Material on (Windshield/Front Side Windows) Presented (Nontransparent/Metallic/Mirrored Appearance *(Note: Metallic/Mirrored Applies to Any Window)*	TIB	466	50+17	0			
42-4-227 (3)(b)	Person (Installed/Covered/Treated) (Windows/Windshield) with Material that Does Not Meet Requirements	M	466	SUM	0			
42-4-239 (5)(a)	Person <18 Used Telephone While Operating a M.V.	TIA	587	50+7	1			
42-4-239 (5)(b)	Person <18 Used Telephone While Operating a M.V. (Subsequent Violation)	TIA	588	100+7	1			
42-4-239 (5)(a)	Person 18 and Over Engaged in Text Messaging While Operating a Motor Vehicle	TIA	585	50+7	1			
42-4-239 (5)(b)	Person 18 and Over Engaged in Text Messaging While Operating a Motor Vehicle (Subsequent Viol.)	TIA	586	100+7	1			
42-4-504 (5)	Projecting Load on Vehicle Obstructed Driver's Vision	TIB	462	75+26	0			
42-4-1411	Drove Vehicle While Wearing Earphones	TIB	467	15+7	0			
42-4-226 (2)	Load Obstructed View to Rear – No Mirrors	TIB	554	15+7	0			

	Oversize / Overwidth / Overlength / Overweight / Projecting Load				
42-4-502	Width of (Vehicle/Load) Exceeded 8 Foot 6 Inches	TIB	510	75+25	0	510	75+25
42-4-502 (2)(a)	Load of Loose Hay Exceeded 12 Ft. Width	TIB	513	75+25	0	513	75+25
42-4-502 (2)(b)	Load of Small Rectangular Hay Bales on a Single Vehicle Exceeded (10 Foot 6 Inches in Width)	TIB	513	75+25	0	513	75+25
42-4-502	Width of Bus Exceeded 8 Feet 6 Inches	TIB	511	75+25	0	511	75+25
42-4-503	Load Projected Beyond Fender of Left Side of Passenger Vehicle	TIB	515	15+7	0	515	15+7
42-4-503	Load Projected More Than 6 Inches on Right Side of Passenger Vehicle	TIB	516	15+7	0	516	15+7
42-4-504 (6)	Rear Projection of Load Exceeded 10 Feet	TIB	529	75+25	0	529	75+25
42-4-504 (5)	Load Projected Beyond Grill Assembly or Front Wheels	TIB	517	75+25	0	517	75+25
42-4-504 (1)	Height of Vehicle Exceeded 13 Feet	TIB	518	75+25	0	518	75+25
42-4-504 (1)	Height of Vehicle Exceeded 14 Feet 6 Inches on Designated Highway	TIB	519	75+25	0	519	75+25
42-4-504 (2)	Single Vehicle Exceeded 45 Feet in Length	TIB	520	75+25	0	520	75+25
42-4-504 (3)	Bus Exceeded 60 Feet in Length	TIB	520	75+25	0	520	75+25
42-4-504 (4)	Combination of Vehicles Exceeded (Four Units/ 70 Feet in Length)	TIB	521	75+25	0	521	75+25
42-4-504 (4.5)	(Saddle Mount Combination/Laden Truck Tractor Semitrailer Combination /Auto or Boat Transporter) Exceeded (Four Units/75 Feet)	TIB	521	75+25	0	521	75+25
42-4-505	Operated Longer Vehicle Combination Where Prohibited	TIB	521	75+25	0	521	75+25
42-4-507	(Wheel/Axle) Loads Exceeded Maximum Lawful Limit (Specify) (See List Pg. 28)	MT2	522	List	0	522	List

STATUTE 2011	CHARGE	CLS	Comm. Code	Fine + S.C.	PT	Safety Zone Fine	Commercial Vehicle Code	Commercial Vehicle Fine
	Oversize / Overwidth / Overlength / Overweight / Projecting Load (Continued)							
42-4-508	Gross Weight of Vehicle Exceeded Maximum Lawful Limit (Specify) (See List Pg. 28)	MT2	523	List	0		523	List
42-4-106 (3)	Vehicle Exceeded Posted Weight Limitation (Specify Posted and Actual Weights)	TIB	530	35+11	0		530	35+11
42-4-509 (3)	(Refused/Failed) to Stop for Weighing (Load/Vehicle)	MT2	525	50+17	0		525	50+17
42-4-510	Exceeded Maximum Permitted Weight on (Axle/Gross) Weight Authorized by Transport Permit (See List Pg. 28)	MT2	527	List	0		527	List
42-4-510	Failed to Have Escort Vehicle When Required By Oversize/Overweight Permit	MT2	527	250+ 93.50	0		527	250+ 93.50
42-4-510	Failed to Reduce Speed When Required by Oversize/Overweight Weight Permit	MT2	527	250+ 93.50	0		527	250+ 93.50
42-4-510 (12)(a)	Operated Vehicle in Violation of Overwidth/Overlength Permit (For weight violations see page 28)	MT2	527	35+11	0		527	35+11
42-4-510 (12)(b)	Owner Moved Manufactured Home Without a Paid Ad Valorem Tax Certificate and a Transportable Manufactured Home Permit	PO2	531	SUM	0		531	SUM
42-4-510 (12)(b)	Owner Moved Manufactured Home Without a Paid Ad Valorem Tax Certificate and a Transportable Manufactured Home Permit 2 or More Times	M3	531	SUM	0		531	SUM
42-4-510	(Failed to Obtain/Violation of) Super Load Permit	MT1	532	SUM	0		532	SUM

Parking Violations

42-4-210	Failed to Display Required Lights When Parked	TIB	350	15+7	0
42-4-1201	Improper Starting From Parked Position	TIA	144	30+7	3
42-4-1202	(Stopped/Parked/Left Standing) Vehicle on Paved Portion of Highway	TIB	350	30+7	0
42-4-1204	Improper (Stopping/Standing/Parking) - Specify the Violation	TIB	350	15+7	0
42-4-1204	Improper Moving of Parked Vehicle	TIB	354	15+7	0
42-4-1205 (1)	Parked Vehicle More Than 12 Inches From Curb	TIB	350	15+7	0
42-4-1205 (1)	Failed to Park as Close as Practical to Edge of Shoulder	TIB	350	15+7	0
42-4-1205 (2)	Parked Vehicle (on Wrong Side of/in Wrong Direction on) Roadway	TIB	350	15+7	0
42-4-1206	Failed to (Lock Ignition of/Remove Key From) Parked Vehicle	TIB	350	15+7	0
42-4-1206	Parked Vehicle Without Setting Brakes	TIB	350	15+7	0
42-4-1206	Parked Vehicle on Grade Without Turning Wheels to Side of Curb	TIB	350	15+7	0
42-4-1207	(Opened Door/Left Door Open) Into Lane of Traffic (When Not Safe/and Interfered With Traffic)	TIB	916	15+7	0
42-4-1208 (5)	Improper Use of Designated Disabled Parking When Not Disabled (1st Offense)	TIB	362	350+33	0
42-4-1208 (5)	Improper Use of Designated Disabled Parking When Not Disabled (2nd Offense)	TIB	362	600+33	0
42-4-1208 (5)	Improper Use of Designated Disabled Parking When Not Disabled (3rd/Subsequent Offense)	M	365	SUM	0
42-4-1208 (7)	Improper Use of Disability (License Plate/ Placard) To Receive Disability Privileges (1st Offense)	M	366	SUM	0

STATUTE 2011	CHARGE	CLS	Comm. Code	Fine + S.C.	PT	Safety Zone Fine	Commercial Vehicle Code	Commercial Vehicle Fine
Parking Violations (Continued)								
42-4-1208 (7)	Improper Use of Disability (License Plate/Placard) To Receive Disability Privileges (2nd Offense)	M	366	SUM	0			
42-4-1208 (7)	Improper Use of Disability (License Plate/Placard) To Receive Disability Privileges (3rd/Subsequent Offense)	M	366	SUM	0			
42-4-1208 (11)(a)	Illegal (Use/Creation) of Disabled (License Plate/Placard)	M	367	SUM	0			
42-4-1208 (11)(b)	Illegal (Use/Creation) of Disabled (License Plate/Placard) for Remuneration	M	367	SUM	0			
42-4-1208 (15)(a)	Misuse of Time Limited Disabled Parking	TIB	368	150+33	0			
42-4-1208 (16)(a)	Improper Commercial Use of Disability (License Plate/Placard)	TIB	369	150+33	0			
Passing								
42-4-802 (4)	Passed Vehicle Stopped for Pedestrian in (Marked/Unmarked) Crosswalk	TIA	203	30+7	3	60+13		
42-4-1002	Failed to Yield One-Half of the Roadway to Oncoming Vehicle	TIA	190	100+11	4	200+21		
42-4-1003 (1)(a)	Passed on Left in Unsafe Manner	TIA	192	100+11	4	200+21		
42-4-1003 (1)(b)	Driver Failed to Give Way When Overtaken	TIA	193	100+11	3	200+21		
42-4-1004	Passed on Right When (Not Permitted/Not Safe)	TIA	194	100+11	4	200+21		
42-4-1005 (1)	Passed on Left When Not Clear to Traffic	TIA	195	100+11	4	200+21		
42-4-1005 (1)	Passed Without Giving Oncoming Traffic Sufficient Clearance	TIA	201	100+11	4	200+21		
42-4-1005 (2)(a)	Passed on (Hill/Curve) When View Obstructed	TIA	197	100+11	4	200+21		

42-4-1005 (2)(b)	Passed When (Crossing/Within 100 Ft. of) (Intersection/Railroad Crossing)	TIA	196	100+11	4	200+21	
42-4-1005 (2)(c)	Passed Within 100 Ft. of (Bridge/Tunnel/Viaduct) When View Obstructed	TIA	200	100+11	4	200+21	
42-4-1005 (3)	Passed on Left When Prohibited By (Signs/Markings)	TIA	199	100+11	4	200+21	
42-4-1007 (1)(b)	(Attempted to Pass/Passed) on Shoulder of Right Hand Traffic Lane	TIA	222	100+11	4	200+21	
	Pedestrian / Animal Rider Violations						
42-4-808	Pedestrian Failed to Yield Right-of-Way to Disabled Person	TIA	999	70+11	0	140+21	
18-13-107 (1)	Non-disabled Person Used (White Cane/Blazed Orange Leash for Dog)	PO1	PMC	HB	RA		
42-4-604	Pedestrian (Disregarded/Failed to Obey) Traffic Control Signal	TIA	400	100+11	0	220+21	
42-4-801	Pedestrian Disregarded Traffic Control Device	TIB	401	15+7	0	30+13	
42-4-802 (3)	Pedestrian Suddenly (Walked/Ran/Rode Bicycle) Into Path of Vehicle	TIA	411	15+7	0	30+13	
42-4-803	Pedestrian Failed to Yield Right-of-Way to Vehicle	TIB	402	15+7	0	30+13	
42-4-803	Pedestrian Failed to Cross Roadway as Required	TIB	407	15+7	0	30+13	
42-4-805 (1)	(Pedestrian/Animal Rider) Failed to (Walk/Ride) (Along/Upon) Roadway as Required	TIB	408	15+7	0	30+13	
42-4-805 (2)	Pedestrian Solicited Rides in Roadway	TIB	404	15+7	0	30+13	
42-4-805 (3)	Pedestrian on Highway Under the Influence of (Alcohol/Controlled Substance)	TIB	803	15+7	0	30+13	
42-4-805 (4)	Animal Rider on Highway Under the Influence of (Alcohol/Controlled Substance)	TIB	802	15+7	0	30+13	

STATUTE 2011	CHARGE	CLS	Comm. Code	Fine + S.C.	PT	Safety Zone Fine	Commercial Vehicle Code	Commercial Vehicle Fine
Pedestrian / Animal Rider Violations (Continued)								
42-4-805 (7)	Vehicle (Endangered/Impeded) Traffic to Pick Up Pedestrian	TIB	160	15+7	0	30+13		
42-4-805 (8)	(Pedestrian/Animal Rider) Failed to Yield to Emergency Vehicle	TIB	410	15+7	0	30+13		
42-4-109 (8)	(Rode/Lead) Animal on Wrong Side of Highway	TIB	408	15+12	0	30+13		
42-4-109 (12)	(Parent/Guardian) Knowingly Permitted Child to Violate Section 42-4-109	TIB	901	15+12	0	30+13		
Recreational Vehicles / Areas / Services								
42-4-109 (9)	Used (Skis/Sled/Skates/Coaster/Toy Vehicle/etc.) on Highway	TIB	901	15+12	0	30+13		
42-4-109 (12)	(Parent/Guardian) Knowingly permitted Child to Violate Section 42-4-109	TIB	901	15+12	0	30+13		
42-4-1408	Operated Motor Vehicle in Recreation Area or District Where Prohibited	TIB	159	15+7	0			
33-14-102 (1)(a)	Failed to (Register/Comply With Registration Requirements Relating to) Snowmobile	PO2	MPA	SUM	0			
33-14-104 (5)	Failed to Display Valid Registration (Decal/Number) on Snowmobile	PO2	MPJ	SUM	0			
33-14-104 (6)	Displayed Unauthorized Number on Snowmobile/ Failed to (Carry/Provide) Registration Certificate	PO2	MPJ	SUM	0			
33-14-105	Failed to (Surrender Registration for/Re-register) Snowmobile as Required	PO2	MPK	SUM	0			
33-14-105 (3)	Failed to Notify Division of Wildlife of (Theft/ Destruction/Removal From State) of Snowmobile	PO2	MPK	SUM	0			

33-14-109 (1)	Minor Under Age 10 Operated Snowmobile (unless supervised or on family land)	PO2	PPS	SUM	0	
33-14-109 (2)	Minor Under Age 16 Operated Snowmobile Without (Supervision/Safety Certificate) Note: Does not apply on family land	PO2	PPS	SUM	0	
33-14-110	Snowmobile Operation on Roadway	PO2	MPL	SUM	0	
33-14-111 (1)	Operated Snowmobile on Right-of-Way of Interstate Highway	PO2	PPA	SUM	0	
33-14-111 (2)	Operated Snowmobile on Highway in an Unlawful Manner	PO2	PPA	SUM	0	
33-14-112	Operated Snowmobile on Railroad Right-of-Way (Except when crossing at intersection)	PO2	PPB	SUM	0	
33-14-113	Operated Snowmobile on Private Property Without Permission	PO2	PPC	SUM	0	
33-14-114	Snowmobile Operated on Highway Did Not Have Required Equipment	PO2	PPD	SUM	0	
33-14-115 (1)	Failed to Notify Police of Snowmobile Accident	PO2	MPB	SUM	0	
33-14-115 (3)	Failed to Report Accident to Division of Wildlife	PO2	MPB	SUM	0	
33-14-116 (1)	Careless Operation of a Snowmobile	PO2	PPE	SUM	0	
33-14-116 (2)	Reckless Operation of a Snowmobile	M	MPC	SUM	0	
33-14-116 (3)	Operated Snowmobile Under the Influence of (Alcohol/Controlled Substance)	M	MPC	SUM	RA	
33-14-116 (4)	Permitted Unlawful Operation of Snowmobile	PO2	PPE	SUM	0	
33-14-117 (1)(a)	Hunted Wildlife From Snowmobile	PO2	PPF	SUM	0	
33-14-117 (1)(c)	(Harassed/Drove) Wildlife With Snowmobile (Except to protect crops or property)	PO2	PPF	SUM	0	
33-14-117 (1)(b)	Unlawfully Carried Weapon on Snowmobile	PO2	907	SUM	0	
33-14.5-102	Failed to (Register/Comply With Registration Requirements Relating to Off-Highway Vehicle)	PO2	MPD	SUM	0	

STATUTE 2011	CHARGE	CLS	Comm. Code	Fine + S.C.	PT	Safety Zone Fine	Commercial Vehicle Code	Commercial Vehicle Fine
Recreational Vehicles / Areas / Services (Continued)								
33-14.5-108	Operated Off-Highway Vehicle on Roadway of Streets and Highways Where Prohibited	PO2	MPE	SUM	0			
Registration / Title								
42-3-103 (1)	Failed to Obtain Registration Within 60 Days of Purchase of Vehicle	TIB	030	50+17	0			
42-3-103 (4)(a)	Failed to Obtain Valid Colorado Registration Within 30 Days After Becoming a Resident	M	031	SUM	0			
42-6-140	Failed to Obtain Colorado Title Within 30 Days after Becoming Resident	M	044	SUM	0			
42-3-113 (6)	No Registration Card in Vehicle	TIB	032	15+7	0			
42-3-113 (7)	Failed to Notify Authorities within 30 Days of Change of Name or Address	TIB	050	15+7	0			
42-3-202 (1)	Vehicle Had No Number Plates Attached	TIB	035	15+7	0			
42-3-202 (1)	Vehicle Had Only One Number Plate Attached	TIB	037	15+7	0			
42-3-202 (1)(b)	Vehicle Validation Tab/Sticker Improperly Attached	TIB	036	15+7	0			
42-3-202 (2)(a)	Number Plate(s) Improperly Attached	TIB	036	15+7	0			
42-3-202 (2)(a)	Vehicle Number Plates Not Clearly (Legible/Visible)	TIB	036	15+7	0			
42-3-233 (4)	Improper Display of Livery License Plates	TIB	024	75+25	0			
42-3-116 (7)(c)	Misuse of Demonstration Plates on Special Mobile Machinery	MT2	058	50+17	3			
42-3-202 (2)(b)	Number Plate Obstructed by (Distorted/Colored/Smoked/Tinted/Scratched/Dirty) Device	TIA	049	100+33	3			

42-3-114	Displayed Expired Number Plates (See List Pg. 28)	TIB	038	List	0		
42-3-203 (3)(a)	Displayed Expired Temporary Permit (See List Pg. 28)	TIB	039	List	0		
42-3-116 (2)	(Manufacturer/Transporter/Dealer) Failed to Display Number Plate as Required	TIB	030	50+17	0		
42-3-116 (4)(a)	(Failed to Display/Misused) Depot Tag	TIB	030	50+17	0		
42-3-304 (2)	Operated Vehicle in Excess of Declared Vehicle Weight	TIB	040	50+17	0		
42-3-304 (8)(a)	Transporter Misused In-transit Plate	TIB	043	50+17	0		
42-3-304 (7)(b)	Transporter Failed to Keep Written Record of Vehicles Transported	TIB	999	50+17	0		
42-3-304 (8)(b)	Improper Use of Manufacturer Plate	TIB	043	50+17	0		
42-3-305 (4)(a)	Used Farm Truck in Commercial Operation	TIB	040	50+17	0		
42-3-121 (1)(a)	Failed to Display Valid Registration	TIB	040	75+25	0		
42-3-121 (1)(a)	(Operated/Permitted Use of) Unregistered Vehicle	TIB	041	75+25	0		
42-3-121 (1)(b)	(Displayed/Possessed/Offered For Sale) (Fictitious/Cancelled/Revoked/Suspended/Altered/Stolen) (Title/Number Plate/Validation Tab or Sticker)	MT2	042	SUM	0		
42-3-121 (1)(c)	(Lent/Permitted Unauthorized Use of) (Title/Registration Card/Number Plate)	TIB	042	35+11	0		
42-3-121 (1)(d)	Failed to Surrender (Title/Registration Card/Number Plate) as Required	MT2	042	SUM	0		
42-3-121 (1)(e)	(Made False Statement/Gave Fictitious Name or Address) on Registration Application	MT2	042	SUM	0		
42-3-121 (1)(f)	Permitted/Used(Noncommercial/Recreational) Vehicle to Transport (Cargo/Passengers) for (Hire/Commercial Purposes)	TIB	040	75+25	0		

STATUTE 2011	CHARGE	CLS	Comm. Code	Fine + S.C.	PT	Safety Zone Fine	Commercial Vehicle Code	Commercial Vehicle Fine
Registration / Title (Continued)								
42-3-122 (1)	Committed Perjury on a Motor Vehicle Registration Application	PO1	999	SUM	0			
42-3-126 (1)	Failed to Notify Authorities Within 30 Days of Change of Vehicle Primary Color	TIB	050	15+7	0			
42-6-139 (2)	(Registered/Titled) Vehicle in County Other than County of Residence	M	046	SUM	0			
42-4-1409 (7)	Failed to Sign Affirmation of Insurance	TI	955	15+7	0			
42-3-204 (2)(a)(III)(d)(III)	Failed to Return Revoked Disability (License Plate/Placard)	TIB	364	15+5	0			
42-3-236 (6)	Failed to (Return/Display) Taxicab License Plates as Required * Effective January 1, 2012 - All taxicab vehicles must obtain the license plate between January 1, 2012 and December 31, 2012 *	TIB	025	75+25	0			
Right-of-Way (Vehicle / Pedestrian)								
42-4-604	Failed to Yield Right-of-Way on Right Turn After Stop at Red Light	TIA	370	100+11	3	200+21		
42-4-701	Failed to Yield Right-of-Way as Required at Uncontrolled Intersection	TIA	371	70+11	3	140+21		
42-4-703 (4)	Failed to Yield at Yield Intersection	TIA	372	70+11	3	140+21		
42-4-703 (3)	Failed to Yield Right-of-Way When Proceeding From Stop Sign	TIA	373	70+11	3	140+21		
42-4-704	Failed to Yield Right-of-Way Upon Entering Highway (Use when vehicle enters from any place other than a roadway)	TIA	374	70+11	3	140+21		
42-4-705 (1)	Failed to Yield Right-of-Way to Emergency Vehicle	TIA	375	70+17	4	140+33		

42-4-1402	Careless Driving: Failed to Yield Right-of-Way to a Stationary (Emergency/Tow Carrier) Vehicle - 42-4-705 (2)	MT2	141	150+17	4	300+33
42-4-1402	Careless Driving: Failed to Yield Right-of-Way to a (Stationary/Slow Moving) (Maintenance/ Repair/Construction) Vehicle - 42-4-705 (2.5)	MT2	141	150+17	4	300+33
42-4-1402	Careless Driving: Failed to Yield Right-of-Way to a Stationary Vehicle Where Tires are Being Equipped With Chains - 42-4-705 (2.6)	MT2	141	150+17	4	300+33
42-4-711 (2)	Failed to Yield Right-of-Way to Ascending Vehicle on Narrow Mountain Highway	TIA	146	100+11	3	220+21
42-4-710 (1)	Failed to Yield Right-of-Way to Pedestrian Upon Emerging From (Alley/Driveway/Building)	TIA	378	70+11	4	140+21
42-4-710 (2)	Failed to Yield Right-of-Way to Pedestrian Upon Entering (Alley/Driveway/Building)	TIA	378	70+11	4	140+21
42-4-712 (1)	Failed to Yield Right-of-Way to Authorized (Vehicle/Pedestrian) in Highway Work Area	TIA	382	70+11	3	140+21
42-4-712 (2)	Failed to Yield Right-of-Way to Authorized Service Vehicle Displaying Flashing Yellow Light	TIA	382	70+11	3	140+21
42-4-802 (1)	Failed to Yield Right-of-Way to Pedestrian in Crosswalk	TIA	376	30+7	4	60+13
42-4-802 (5)	Failed to Yield Right-of-Way to Pedestrian at Steady Walk Signal	TIA	377	30+7	4	60+13
42-4-807	Driver Failed to Exercise Due Care for Pedestrian	TIA	381	70+11	4	140+21
42-4-808	Driver Failed to Yield Right-of-Way to Disabled Person	TIA	380	70+11	6	140+21

STATUTE 2011	CHARGE	CLS	Comm. Code	Fine + S.C.	PT	Safety Zone Fine	Commercial Vehicle Code	Commercial Vehicle Fine
Safety Belt / Restraints									
42-2-105.5 (4)	Operator Under Age 18 Driving With More Passengers Than Seat Belts	TIA	468	65+11	2			
42-2-105.5 (3)	Operator Under 18 (Not Wearing Seat Belt/ Allowed Occupants Without Seat Belts/Child Restraint Systems) *THIS CHARGE IS NON-ARRESTABLE*	TIA	580	SUM	2			
42-4-236 (2)(a)(I)	Failed to (Provide/Properly Use) An Approved Child Restraint System in Rear Seat of Vehicle (4 – 7 Years of Age) (Primary Offense)	TIB	574	65+17	0			
42-4-236 (2)(a)(II)	Failed to (Provide/Properly Use) Rear Facing Child Restraint System in Rear Seat of Vehicle (Less Than 1 Year Old and Less Than 20 lbs) (Primary)	TIB	574	65+17	0			
42-4-236 (2)(a)(III)	Failed to (Provide/Properly Use) (Forward/Rear) Facing Child Restraint System (1 - 3 Years of Age/ More Than 20 lbs but Less Than 40 lbs) (Primary)	TIB	574	65+17	0			
42-4-236 (2)(b)	Failed to (Provide/Properly Use) Seatbelt/Child Restraint 8-15 Years of Age (Secondary Offense)	TIB	574	65+17	0			
42-4-237 (2)	Drove Vehicle When Safety Belt Not in Use	TIB	575	65+7	0			
42-4-237 (2)	Drove Vehicle When Front Seat Passenger Not Secured By Safety Belt	TIB	960	65+7	0			
School Bus									
42-4-707 (1)	(School Bus/Commercial) Driver (Failed to Stop/ Used Improper Gear) at Railroad Crossing When Required	TIA	317	70+11	4		317	70+11

Code	Description	Type						
42-4-1901	Operated School Bus on Mountainous Terrain With Passengers in (Front Row Seats/Seats Next to Emergency Exit) When School Bus Not Equipped With Supplementary Brake Retarders	TI	999	35+11	0		999	35+11
42-4-1903 (1)	Failed to Stop for Stopped School Bus Displaying Flashing Red Lights	MT2	420	SUM	6			
42-4-1903 (6)(b)	Failed to Stop for Stopped School Bus Displaying Flashing Red Lights Two or More Times Within Five Years	MT1	420	SUM	6			
42-4-1903 (2)	School Bus Driver Failed to Actuate Visual Signals as Required	TI	422	SUM	2			
42-4-1903 (5)	School Bus Driver Failed to Stop as Required	TI	421	SUM	3			
Signaling								
42-4-903	(Failed to Signal as Required/Gave Improper Signal) for (Turn/Stop/Sudden Decrease in Speed)	TIA	433	70+11	2	140+21		
42-4-903	Improper Use of Flashing Turn Signal	TIA	433	70+11	2	140+21		
42-4-608 (1)	Failed to Use Turn Signals	TIA	436	70+7	2	140+13		
42-4-609	Gave Improper Hand Signal	TIA	437	15+7	2	30+13		
Speed								
42-4-1101 (1)	Speeding (1-4 MPH Over Prima Facie Limit)	TIA	020	30+22	0			
42-4-1101 (1)	Speeding (5-9 MPH Over Prima Facie Limit)	TIA	004	70+26	1			
42-4-1101 (1)	Speeding (10-14 MPH Over Prima Facie Limit) [Commercial Vehicle Only]	TIA			4	270+48	015	135+32
42-4-1101 (1)	Speeding (15-19 MPH Over Prima Facie Limit) [Commercial Vehicle Only]	TIA			4	270+48	770	135+32
42-4-1101 (1)	Speeding (10-19 MPH Over Prima Facie Limit)	TIA	005	135+32	4			
42-4-1101 (1)	Speeding (20-24 MPH Over Prima Facie Limit)	TIA	006	200+48	6		769	200+48
42-4-1101 (1)	Speeding (25-39 MPH Over Prima Facie Limit)	MT2	006	SUM	6		769	SUM
42-4-1101 (1)	Speeding (40 MPH Over Prima Facie Limit)	MT2	016	SUM	12		769	SUM

STATUTE 2011	CHARGE	CLS	Comm. Code	Fine + S.C.	PT	Safety Zone Fine	Commercial Vehicle Code	Commercial Vehicle Fine
	Speed (Continued)							
42-4-1101 (1)	Speeding (1-4 MPH Over Posted Limit in Construction/School Zone)	TIA	020		0	60+28		
42-4-1101 (1)	Speeding (5-9 MPH Over Posted Limit in Construction/School Zone)	TIA	004		1	140+36		
42-4-1101 (1)	Speeding (10-19 MPH Over Posted Limit in Construction/School Zone)	TIA	005		4	270+48		
42-4-1101 (1)	Speeding (20-24 MPH Over Posted Limit in *Construction Zone Only*)	TIA	006		6	540+80	769	540+80
42-4-1101 (1)	Speeding (20-24 MPH Over Posted Limit in *School Zone Only*)	TIA	006		6	400+80	769	400+80
42-4-1101 (1)	Speeding (25-39 MPH Over Posted Limit in Construction/School Zone)	MT2	006		6	SUM	769	SUM
42-4-1101 (1)	Speeding (40 MPH or more Over Posted Limit in Construction/School Zone)	MT2	006		12	SUM	769	SUM
42-4-1101 (8)(b)	Speeding (1-4 MPH Over the Maximum 75 MPH Limit)	TAI	020	30+22	0			
42-4-1101 (8)(b)	Speeding (5-9 MPH Over the Maximum 75 MPH Limit)	TAI	004	70+26	1			
42-4-1101 (8)(b)	Speeding (10-14 MPH Over the Maximum 75 MPH Limit) [Commercial Vehicle Only]	TIA			4	270+48	015	135+32
42-4-1101 (8)(b)	Speeding (15-19 MPH Over the Maximum 75 MPH Limit) [Commercial Vehicle Only]	TIA			4	270+48	770	135+32
42-4-1101 (8)(b)	Speeding (10-19 MPH Over the Maximum 75 MPH Limit)	TAI	005	135+32	4			
42-4-1101 (8)(b)	Speeding (20-24 MPH Over the Maximum 75 MPH Limit)	TAI	006	200+48	6			

| 42-4-1101 (8)(b) | Speeding (25-39 MPH Over the Maximum 75 MPH Limit) | MT2 | 006 | SUM | 6 | |

REFERENCE SECTION ONLY: The following are considered Prima Facie speeds except when a special hazard exists:

- 20 MPH on narrow, winding mountain highways
- 25 MPH in any business district
- 30 MPH in any residential district
- 40 MPH on open mountain highways
- 45 MPH for all vehicles, single rear axle, in excess of 20,000 lbs, transporting trash where a higher speed is posted and the vehicle is operating under the exemption provided in 42-4-507 (3)
- 55 MPH on other open highways not on the Interstate system and are not surfaced, four-lane Freeways or expressways
- 65 MPH on surfaced four-lane highways of the Interstate system or are freeways or expressways

42-4-1101 (8)(g)	Low Powered Scooter Exceeded Max. Speed of 40 MPH (1-4 MPH Over)	TIA	021	50+22	0	100+44
42-4-1101 (8)(g)	Low Powered Scooter Exceeded Max. Speed of 40 MPH (5-9 MPH Over)	TIA	022	75+26	2	150+52
42-4-1101 (8)(g)	Low Powered Scooter Exceeded Max. Speed of 40 MPH (10-19 MPH Over)	TIA	023	100+32	4	200+64
42-4-1101 (3)	Exceeded Safe Speed for Conditions (Indicate actual speed/safe speed)	TIA	007	100+26	3	220+41
42-4-1103 (1)	Impeded Normal Flow of Traffic	TIA	008	50+22	3	100+33
42-4-1104 (1)	Exceeded Posted Safe Speed on Elevated Structure	TIA	009	30+22	3	100+33
42-4-1106	Violated Left Lane Minimum Speed on I-70 Corridor (Posted 6% Grade)	TIA	019	100+32	3	
42-4-1105 (1)(a)	Engaged in Speed Contest	MT1	001	SUM	12	
42-4-1105 (2)(a)	Engaged in Exhibition of Speed	MT2	017	SUM	5	
42-4-1105 (3)(a)	(Aided in/Facilitated) a Speed Contest	MT2	010	SUM	12	
42-4-1105 (3)(a)	(Aided in/Facilitated) an Exhibition of Speed	MT2	018	SUM	5	
42-4-1105 (3)	Obstructed Highway Incident to a Speed Contest	MT2	010	SUM	12	

STATUTE 2011	CHARGE	CLS	Comm. Code	Fine + S.C.	PT	Safety Zone Fine	Commercial Vehicle Code	Commercial Vehicle Fine
Speed (Continued)								
42-4-1413	(Eluded/Attempted to Elude) a Police Officer	MT2	011	SUM	12			
18-9-116.5	Vehicular Eluding Created a Substantial Risk of Bodily Injury by Operating a Vehicle in a Reckless Manner	F5	012	NIBR	12			
18-9-116.5	Vehicular Eluding Resulted in Bodily Injury to Another Person	F4	013	NIBR	RA			
18-9-116.5	Vehicular Eluding Resulted in Death to Another Person	F3	014	NIBR	RA			
Spilling Loads / Damaging Highway / Littering								
18-4-511 (4)	Littering	PO2	PMF	HB	0			
18-4-511 (6)	Littering from Motor Vehicle	PO2	PMF	HB	0			
42-4-512	Damaged (Highway/Highway Structure)	TIA	495	75+25	0			
42-4-1406 (1)(a)	(Left/Deposited/Threw) Foreign Matter on Highway	TIB	490	35+11	0	70+21		
42-4-1406 (1)(b)	(Left/Deposited/Threw) Burning Material from a Motor Vehicle	M2	491	SUM	0	SUM		
42-4-1406 (2)	Failed to Remove (Lighted/Burning) Matter (Left/Deposited/Thrown) on Highway	TIB	491	35+11	0	70+21		
42-4-1406 (3)	Removed Wrecked or Damaged Vehicle From Highway Without Removing Injurious Substance From Highway	TIB	999	35+11	0	70+21		
42-4-1406 (4)	Excavated on Highway Without Authorization	TIB	492	35+11	0	70+21		
42-4-1406 (4)	Constructed on Highway Without Authorization	TIB	493	35+11	0	70+21		
42-4-1406 (5)(b)(II)	(Left/Deposited/Threw) Human Waste Container on Highway	M2	488	SUM	0	SUM		

Statute	Description							
42-4-1407(I)	Spilled Load on Highway/Failed to Cover Load/No Flaps When Required	TIB	494	35+11	0	70+21	494	35+11
42-4-1407 (2.4)(a)	Vehicle Transporting Trash or Recyclables Failed to (Cover/Properly Secure) Load on Highway	TIB	494	35+11	0	70+21		
42-4-1407 (3)(b)	Spilled Load From Car/Pick-Up Truck on Highway	TIA	498	100+31	3	200+61		
42-4-1407 (3)(c)	Spilled Load from Car/Pick-Up Truck on Highway Causing Bodily Injury	MT2	499	SUM	3	SUM		
18-4-511 (1)	(Left/Deposited/Threw) Litter On (Public/Private/Water)	PO2	PMF	HB	0			
18-9-107	Obstructed (Highway/Street/Sidewalk)	M3	MNS	HB	0			
43-5-301	Obstructed Highway	M	497	SUM	0			
43-5-303	Allowed Water to (Flow/Fall/Sprinkle) on Highway to Cause a Hazard to Vehicular Traffic	M	497	SUM	0			
43-1-417	(Erected/Used/Maintained) Unlawful Highway Advertising Device	M	MN2	SUM	0			
42-4-1407.5	Splash Guards Required	TIB	579	35+11	0			
Theft								
18-4-401 (1)(a)/(d)	Theft (Refer to Statute for wording) Value Less Than $500 / Value $500 to Less Than $1,000 / Value $1,000 to Less than $20,000 / Value More than $20,000	M2 / M1 / F4 / F3	MTA / MTA / FTA / FTA	SUM / SUM / NIBR / NIBR	RA			
18-4-401 (5)	Theft From Another Person by Force	F5	FTA	NIBR	RA			
18-4-402 (3)	Theft of Rental Property (Auto) Less Than $500	M2	MTB	SUM	RA			
18-4-402 (3.5)	Theft of Rental Property (Auto)($500 But Less Than $1,000)	M1	MTB	NIBR	RA			
18-4-402 (4)	Theft of Rental Property (Auto) $1,000 but less than $20,000	F5	FTB	NIBR	RA			

STATUTE 2011	CHARGE	CLS	Comm. Code	Fine + S.C.	PT	Safety Zone Fine	Commercial Vehicle Code	Commercial Vehicle Fine
Theft (Continued)								
18-4-402 (5)	Theft of Rental Property (Auto) $20,000 or more	F3	FTB	NIBR	RA			
18-4-410 (3)	Theft by Receiving (Auto) Less Than $500	M2	MTD	SUM	RA			
18-4-410 (3.5)	Theft by Receiving (Auto) $500 but less than $1,000	M1	MTD	SUM	RA			
18-4-410 (4)	Theft by Receiving (Auto) $1,000 But Less Than $20,000	F4	FTC	NIBR	RA			
18-4-410 (5)	Theft by Receiving (Auto) $20,000 or More	F3	FTC	NIBR	RA			
18-4-410 (6)	Theft by Receiving/Selling/Disposing of Goods (Value $1000 or More)	F3	FTC	NIBR	RA			
18-4-418 (2)(a)	Knowingly Failed to Pay for Fuel ($100 or Less)	M3	MTD	SUM	RA			
18-4-418 (2)(b)	Knowingly Failed to Pay for Fuel (More Than $100 but Less Than $500)	M2	MTD	SUM	RA			
Towing								
42-4-1405	Person Rode in Trailer	TIB	156	15+7	0	30+13		
42-4-506 (2)	Failed to Use White Flag on Tow (Chain/Cable/Rope)	TIB	471	15+7	0			
42-4-506 (3)	Failed to Use Safety Chain or Cable on Towed Vehicle	TIB	472	15+7	0			
42-4-506 (1)	Unlawful Drawbar	TIB	473	15+7	0			
42-4-1008 (2)	Unlawful Following by Vehicle Drawing Another Vehicle (Following too Closely)	TIA	165	100+ 11	4	200+21		
42-4-241 (1)	Unlawful (Use/Removal) of Tow Truck Signage	M3	MTS	SUM	0			

Traffic Controls

42-4-106 (6)	Disobeyed Sign Closing Highway for (Construction/Event)	TIB	999	35+11	0	
42-4-603	(Failed to Observe/Disregarded) Traffic Control Device	TIA	300	100+11	4	200+21
42-4-604	Failed to Obey Lane-Use Control Signal	TIA	220	100+11	4	200+21
42-4-604	Failed to Obey Traffic Control Signal	TIA	304	100+11	4	200+21
42-4-604	Failed to Stop for Traffic Control Signal at Place Required	TIA	305	100+11	4	200+21
42-4-605	Failed to Obey Flashing (Red/Yellow) Signal Light as Required	TIA	310	70+11	4	140+21
42-4-606	Displayed Unauthorized (Sign/Signal/Marking/Device)	TIA	311	15+7	0	30+13
42-4-607 (1)(a)	(Attempted to/Removed/Altered/Defaced/Knocked Down/Injured) Traffic Control (Sign/Device)	TIB	314	50+17	0	100+33
42-4-607 (1)(b)	Unlawfully (Possessed/Sold) Electronic Device Designed to Affect a Traffic Control Device	TIB	324	50+17	0	100+33
42-4-607 (2)(a)	Interfered With Traffic Control Device By Using Electronic Device	TIA	312	100+33	3	200+65
42-4-607 (2)(b)	Use of Device to Change Traffic Signal Caused Bodily Injury	MT1	323	SUM	3	SUM
42-4-612	Failed to Proceed (With Caution/as Required) at Inoperative or Malfunctioning Control Signal	TIA	320	70+11	4	140+21
42-4-703 (3)	(Disregarded/Failed to Stop as Required at) Stop Sign at Through Highway	TIA	319	70+11	4	140+21
42-4-706	Disregarded (Railroad Signal/Crossing Gate/Barricade/Flagman)	TIA	315	70+11	4	
42-4-706 (1)	Disregarded Stop Sign at Railroad Crossing	TIA	315	70+11	4	

STATUTE 2011	CHARGE	CLS	Comm. Code	Fine + S.C.	PT	Safety Zone Fine	Commercial Vehicle Code	Commercial Vehicle Fine
Traffic Controls (Continued)								
42-4-707	(School Bus/Commercial Vehicle) Failed to Stop at Railroad Crossing When Required	TIA	317	70+11	4			
42-4-708	Unlawful Moving of Heavy Equipment Across Railroad Grade Crossing	TIB	318	35+11	0			
42-4-712 (3)	Disregarded (Instructions/Signals) of Authorized Flag-Person in Highway Work Area	TIA	914	70+11	3	140+21		
42-4-806	Drove Vehicle Through Safety Zone	TIA	145	70+11	3	140+21		
42-4-613	Failed to Pay (Toll/Fee/Rate) Established by Regional Transportation Authority	TIA	966	35+11	3			
Turns								
42-4-603	Made Turn Where Prohibited by Traffic Control Device	TIA	300	100+11	4	200+21		
42-4-604	Made (Right/Left) Turn on Red Light Where Prohibited by Sign	TIA	271	100+11	4	200+21		
42-4-702	Failed to Yield Right-of-Way When Turning Left in Front of Approaching Traffic	TIA	278	70+11	3	140+21		
42-4-901 (1)(a)	Made Right Turn From Wrong (Position/Lane)	TIA	274	70+11	3	140+21		
42-4-901 (1)(b)	Made Left Turn From Wrong (Position/Lane)	TIA	273	70+11	3	140+21		
42-4-901 (1)(c)	Made Improper Left Turn at Multi-turn Intersection	TIA	280	70+11	3	140+21		
42-4-901 (2)	Failed to Turn as Required by Traffic Control Device	TIA	276	70+11	3	140+21		
42-4-901 (2)	Failed to Turn From Turn-Only Lane	TIA	276	70+11	3	140+21		
42-4-902 (1)	Made U-Turn on Hill or Curve	TIA	270	70+11	3	140+21		

42-4-902 (2)	Made Unsafe U-Turn at Intersection	TIA		270	70+11		3	140+21
42-4-902 (3)	Made U-Turn Where Prohibited	TIA		270	70+11		3	140+21
42-4-1010 (1)	(Improper Turn/Turned Where Prohibited) Across Median of Divided Highway	TIA		279	70+11		3	140+21
	Wrong Way / Wrong Side							
42-4-1001	Failed to Drive Vehicle (on Right Side of Road/ in Right-Hand Lane) as Required	TIA		250	70+11		4	140+21
42-4-1001 (1)(b)	Failed to Yield Right-of-Way When Forced to Drive on Left Side of Road	TIA		251	70+11		4	140+21
42-4-1002	Failed to Yield One-Half of the Roadway to Oncoming Vehicle	TIA		190	100+11		4	200+21
42-4-1006 (1)	Drove Vehicle Wrong Way on One-Way Roadway	TIA		254	70+11		3	140+21
42-4-1006 (2)	Drove Vehicle Wrong Way Around Rotary Island	TIA		256	70+11		3	140+21
42-4-1010 (1)	Drove Vehicle on Wrong Side of Divided Highway	TIA		253	70+11		4	140+21

Presumptive Penalty and Enforcement Guide

Registration Violations Fine Schedule (CRS 42-3-114)		
Number of days beyond renewal period that registration has been expired	Penalty	Surcharge
1 to 29 days	$35.00	$8.00
30 to 59 days	$50.00	$12.00
60 days and over	$75.00	$18.00

Penalty Chart for Weight in Excess of Weight Authorized by Special Permit (42-4-510)			
Excess weight (Pounds)	Penalty 42-4-510	Penalty 42-4-510 (1)(A)(II)	Surcharge
1 - 2,500	$ 50.00	$ 100.00	$ 47.00
2,501 - 5,000	$ 100.00	$ 200.00	$ 97.00
5,001 - 7,500	$ 200.00	$ 400.00	$ 193.00
7,501 - 10,000	$ 400.00	$ 800.00	$ 385.00
Over 10,000	$150.00 for each 1,000 pounds additional overweight plus $400.00	$300.00 for each 1,000 pounds additional overweight plus $800.00	$145.00 for each 1,000 pounds additional overweight plus $297.00

PCC CODES (CSP Use Only)	
Animal Caused	AC1
REDDI/Road Rage	RED
Computer Flag	CPR
Bolo's	BOL
Agency Assist	AOA
Motorist Assist	MA1
Abandoned Vehicle	AV1
Vehicle 2 in Crash	VH2
Pedestrian	PED
Suspicious Vehicle	SV1
Medical Caused	MED

PATROL CODES (CSP Use Only)	
Routine Patrolling	P
RADAR	R
VASCAR	V
LIDAR	L
Aircraft	F
Accident	A
Accident Under $1,000	B
Safety Check	S
Sobriety Checkpoint	C
Traffic Complaint	T

Presumptive Penalty and Enforcement Guide

PRESUMPTIVE PENALTIES

Felony Offenses (F) – Defined in CRS 18-1.3-401						
	Presumptive Ranges					
Class	Min	Max	Mandatory Parole	Crimes w/ extra-ordinary risk of harm	3rd Habitual conviction	4th Habitual conviction
1	No Fine Life	No Fine Death	None	N/A	No Parole (40 years)	4 Times the Max
2	$5,000 and/or 8 yrs	$1 Million and/or 24 yrs	5 yrs	N/A		
3	$3,000 and/or 4 yrs	$750,000 and/or 12 yrs	5 yrs	Max = 16 yrs		
4	$2,000 and/or 2 yrs	$500,000 and/or 6 yrs	3 yrs	Max = 8 yrs		
5	$1,000 and/or 1 yr	$100,000 and/or 3 yrs	2 yrs	Max = 4 yrs		
6	$1,000 and/or 1 yr	$100,000 and/or 1.5 yrs	1 yr	Max = 2 yrs		
Not Specified In Statute	None	$100,000 and/or 5 yrs	2 yrs			

PRESUMPTIVE PENALTIES
(continued)

Misdemeanor Offenses (M) – Defined in CRS 18-1.3-501			
	Presumptive Ranges		
Class	Min	Max	Crimes w/ Extraordinary Risk of Harm
1	6 mo $500 + CS+SC	18 mo $5,000 + CS+SC	Max = 2 yrs
2	3 mo $250 + CS+SC	12 mo $1,000 + CS+SC	
3	$50	6 mo $750 + CS+SC	

Petty Offenses (PO) – Defined in CRS 18-1.3-503		
	Presumptive Ranges	
Class	Min	Max
1	None	6 mo $500
2	Specified by Section Defining Offense	

Misdemeanor Traffic Offenses (MT)		
	Presumptive Ranges	
Class	Min	Max
1	10 days $300 + SC+CS	1 yr $1,000 + SC+CS
2	10 days $150 + SC+CS	90 days $300 + CS+CS

SC = Surcharge
CS = Community Service

Traffic Infractions (TI)		
	Presumptive Ranges	
Class	Min	Max
A	$15 + SC	$100 + SC
B	$15 + SC	$100 + SC

No Points May Be Assessed for Class B Traffic Infractions

Presumptive Penalty and Enforcement Guide

SAFETY ZONE DEFINITIONS
(Fines Doubled)

Highway Maintenance, Repair, Construction Zone	C.R.S. 42-4-614 Safety Zone Fines may be used when: • Maintenance, repair or construction zones are be occurring will occur within 4 hours. • They shall be designated with signs notifying an increase in fines at the beginning and end zones,
School Safety Zone	C.R.S. 42-4-615 Safety Zone Fines may be used when: • Appropriate signs indicate penalties and surcharges will be doubled. • The placement of the signs and traffic control devices shall designate when the area is a school safety zone. • Does not apply when fines are doubled by a zone designated for construction, repair or maintenance.

Wildlife Crossing Zone	C.R.S. 42-4-615 Safety Zone Fines may be used when:
	• The zone begins at an erected sign designating a wildlife crossing zone.
	• The zone ends:
	  ○ At a sign designating the end of the zone or,
	  ○ The distance indicated on the initial sign or,
	  ○ 1/2 mile beyond the initial designated beginning.
	• Signs may designate times of day and periods of the calendar year when the zone is in effect.
	• Does not apply when:
	  ○ Fines are already doubled by Construction or School Zones or,
	  ○ The initial sign does not state that fines are increased or,
	  ○ The violation is committed during a time that the area is not deemed a wildlife crossing zone.

Drug Schedule Reference Guide

Schedule I
Defined as a substance that has <u>no currently accepted medical use</u> and has a high potential for abuse. For a complete list see 18-18-203

Drug Name	Street Name/Other Names
Synthetic Opiates:	
• Acetylcodone	Acetydihydrocodeine
• Benzethidine	
• Difenoxin	Lyspafen
• Dimenoxadol	
• Hydroxpethidine	
• Methylfentanyl	White China
• Morpheridine	
• Phenomorphan	
Opium Derivatives:	
• Benzylmorphine	
• Dihydromorphine	
• Heroin	Dope, Junk, Smack, H
• Nicocodeine	
• Normorphine	
Hallucinogenic Substances:	
• Bufotenine	Bufo toad venom
• 2,5-dimethoxy-4-methylamphetamine	DOM, STP (Serenity, Tranquility, and Peace)
• Methlyenedioxyamphetamine	MDA
• Methylenedioxymethamphetamine (MDMA)	Ecstasy, E, X, XTC, Rolls, Beans, Adam
• Mescaline	Peyote, Buttons; Mescalito
• Psilocybin / Psilocyn	Shrooms, Magic Mushrooms, Sacred Mushrooms
• d-lysergic acid diethylamide (LSD)	Acid, L, Tabs, Blotter, Doses, Trips
• N,N-Dimethylamphetamine	DMT, Dimitri
• 4-bromo-2,5-dimethoxyphenethylamine (2C-B)	Nexus, Bees
• San Pedro Cactus	Also Peyote
• Ibogaine (Iboga plant)	
• Morning glory	Heavenly Blue, Tlilitzin, Badoh Negro
CNS Depressants:	
• Methaqualone	Quaaludes, Ludes
CNS Stimulants:	
• Cathinone	Khat, Quat
• Methcathinone	
Misc:	
• Gammahydroxybutyrate (Date Rape Drug)	GHB

Drug Schedule Reference Guide

Schedule II
Defined as a substance that has <u>an accepted medical use</u> and has a high potential for abuse. For a complete list see 18-18-204

Drug Name	Street/Prescription Name
Most Synthetic Opiates:	
• Dihydrocodeine	Didrate
• Fentanyl	Sublimaze
• Methadone	Dolophine
• Meperidine	Demerol
• Sufentanil	Sufenta
• Raw, powdered, granular opium, opium poppy or opium straw etc.	Joy Plant, Pen Yan, Paregoric
• Codeine	
• Hydrocodone	
• Hydromorphone	Dilaudid
• Meperidine	Demerol
• Morphine	MS Contin, Roxanol, Duramorph
• Oxycodone	Percodan, Percocet
• Oxymorphone	Oxycontin
• Thebaine	
Coca Leaves or Derivatives:	
• Cocaine	Coke, Crack, Blow, Snow, Nose Candy
CNS Depressants:	
• Amobarbital	Tuinal
• Pentobarbital	Nembutal
• Secobarbital	Barbs, Barbies, Downers, Blues, Nembies, Seccies
CNS Stimulants:	
• Amphetamine	Dexedrine, Biphetamine
• Methamphetamine	Meth, Speed, Crystal, Glass, Crank, Tweak, Yaba, Desoxyn
• Methylphenidate	Daytrana, Ritalin
Precursor to Amphetamine and Methamphetamine and Phencyclidine:	
• Phenyacetone	
• methyl ketone	
• Piperdine	
• Morpholine	
• Benzyl	

Drug Schedule Reference Guide

Schedule III
Defined as a substance that has <u>an accepted medical use</u> and potential for less abuse than schedule I or II. For a complete list see 18-18-205

Drug Name   **Street/Prescription Name**

Any substance that contains any derivative of Barbituric acid:
- Chorhexadol   Mecoral
- Lysergic acid (LSD Precursor)
- Sulfonmethane

Muscle Relaxers/Non Narcotic Pain Relief:
- Cyclobenzaprine   Flexeril
- Carisoprodol   Soma
- Tramadol   Ultram

CNS Depressants: (Mixed with one or more substances or in suppository form)
- Amobarbital
- Secobarbital
- Pentobarbital

Example CNS Stimulants:
- Chlorphentermine   Pre-Sate, Lucofen, Apsedon, Desopimon
- Clortermine   Voranil

Misc:
- Tiletamine or Zolazepam or their salts   Telazol
- Nalorphine
- Anabolic Steroids   Sinesex, Stenediol
- Dronabinol (Synthetic THC)   Marinol
- Ketamine   Ketaset, Special K, K

Schedule IV
Defined as a substance that has <u>an accepted medical use</u> and a low potential for abuse. For a complete list see 18-18-206

Drug Name   **Street/Prescription Name**

Example Narcotic Drugs:
- Propoxyphene   Darvon
- Butorphanol   Stadol

Example CNS Depressants:
- Alprazolam   Xanax
- Barbital
- Chloral Hydrate
- Clonazepam   Klonipin
- Diazepam   Valium
- Lorazepam   Ativan
- Meprobamate   Milltown

Drug Schedule Reference Guide

• Midazolam	Versed
• Phenobarbital	Luminal
• Temazepam	Restoril

Example CNS Stimulants:
- Cathine (Constituent of the Khat plant)

• Mazindol	Sanorex
• Phentermine	Fastin

Misc:

• Modafinil	Provigil
• Pentazocine	Talwin
• Sibutramine	Meridia
• Butorphanol	Stadol
• Zolpidem	Ambien

Schedule V
Defined as a substance that has <u>an accepted medical use</u> and a less potential for abuse then schedule IV. For a complete list see 18-18-207

Drug Name	Street/Prescription Name

Example Narcotic Drugs (Limited Quantities):

• Cough syrup that contains not more than 200 milligrams of codeine per 100 milliliters	Cosanyl, Robitussin A-C, Cheracol, Pediacof

Misc:
1) Pyrovalerone (Stimulant mostly prescribed overseas)

Note: The Drug Enforcement Administration schedules marijuana and marijuana concentrate (Hash or hash oil) as a schedule I controlled substance. Marijuana does not appear in the Colorado schedule and is listed separately under title 18.

NIBRS System Codes

National Incident Based Reporting System (NIBRS) Codes

Type Of Weapon/Force Involved			
11	Firearm (Type not stated)	50	Poison
12	Handgun	60	Explosives
13	Rifle	65	Fire/Incendiary
14	Shotgun	70	Narcotic/drugs
15	Other Firearm	85	Asphyxiation
20	Knife/Cutting Instrument	90	Other
30	Blunt Object	95	Unknown
35	Motor Vehicle	99	None
40	Personal Weapons		

Location of Offense			
01	Air/Bus Terminal	14	Hotel/Motel/etc
02	Bank/Savings and Loan	15	Jail/Prison
03	Bar/Night Club	16	Lake/Waterway
04	Church/Synagogue/Temple	17	Liquor Store
05	Commercial Office Building	18	Parking Lot/Garage
06	Construction Site	19	Rental/Storage Facility
07	Convenience Store	20	Residence/Home
08	Department/Discount Store	21	Restaurant
09	Drug Store/Dr. Office/Hospital	22	School/College
10	Field/Woods	23	Service/Gas Station
11	Government/Public Building	24	Specialty Store (TV,Fur, etc)
12	Grocery/Supermarket	25	Other/Unknown
13	Highway/Roadway/Alley		

Suspected Drug Codes			
A	Crack Cocaine	J	PCP
B	Cocaine (all other)	K	Other Hallucinogens
C	Hashish	L	Amphetamine/Methamphetamine
D	Heroin	M	Other Stimulants
E	Marijuana	N	Barbiturates
F	Morphine	O	Other Depressants
G	Opium	P	Other Drugs (Tranquilizers/Valium/etc)
H	Other Narcotics (Codeine/Demerol, Percodan)	U	Unknown
I	LSD	X	More than 3 drug types

NIBRS System Codes

National Incident Based Reporting System (NIBRS) Codes

Measurement Codes

GM	Gram		ML	Milliliter
KG	Kilogram		LT	Liter
OZ	Ounce(s)		FO	Fluid Ounce(s)
LB	Pound(s)		GL	Gallon
DU	Dosage Unit		NP	Number of Plants

Property Description Codes

01	Aircraft		22	Non-negotiable Instrument
02	Alcohol		23	Office-type Equipment
03	Automobiles		24	Other Motor Vehicles
04	Bicycle		25	Purses/Handbags/Wallets
05	Buses		26	Radios/TVs/VCRs
06	Clothes/Furs		27	Recordings/Audiovisual
07	Computer Hardware/Software		28	Recreational Vehicles
08	Consumable Goods		29	Structures: Single Occupancy Dwellings
09	Credit/Debit Cards		30	Structures: Other Dwellings
10	Drugs/Narcotics		31	Structures: Other Commercial Business
11	Drug/Narcotic Equipment		32	Structures: Industrial/Manufacturing
12	Farm Equipment		33	Structures: Public/Community
13	Firearms		34	Structures: Storage
14	Gambling Equipment		35	Structures: Other
15	Heavy Construction/Industrial Equipment		36	Tools: Power/Hand
16	Household Goods		37	Trucks
17	Jewelry/Precious Metals		38	Vehicle Parts/Accessories
18	Livestock		39	Watercraft
19	Merchandise		77	Other
20	Money		88	Pending Inventory
21	Negotiable Instruments			